FINANCIAL
ACCOUNTING
A · N · D
REPORTING

FINANCIAL
ACCOUNTING
A · N · D
REPORTING

MARK E. HASKINS
University of Virginia

KENNETH R. FERRIS
Thunderbird, American Graduate School of International Management

ROBERT J. SACK
University of Virginia

BRANDT R. ALLEN
University of Virginia

IRWIN

Homewood, IL 60430
Boston, MA 02116

Sponsoring editor: Jeff Shelstad
Developmental editor: Carolyn Nowak
Developmental editor, supplements: Nancy Lanum
Marketing manager: John E. Biernat
Project editor: Karen Murphy
Production manager: Diane Palmer
Art coordinator: Mark Malloy
Compositor: The Clarinda Co.
Typeface: 10/12 Times Roman
Printer: R. R. Donnelley & Sons Company

Library of Congress Cataloging-in-Publication Data

Financial accounting and reporting / Mark E. Haskins . . . [et al.].
    p.   cm.
  Includes index.
  ISBN 0-256-08782-2
  1. Financial statements. 2. Corporations—Accounting.
  I. Haskins, Mark E.
  HF5681.B2F456 1993
  657′.3—dc20   91–45035

Printed in the United States of America
1 2 3 4 5 6 7 8 9 0 DOC 9 8 7 6 5 4 3 2

To our students, who have sought to know more
and in doing so have challenged us to find
better ways to teach.

ABOUT THE AUTHORS

Mark E. Haskins Mr. Haskins is an associate professor of Business Administration at the Darden Graduate School of Business Administration at the University of Virginia. He received his Bachelor of Business Administration from the University of Cincinnati and his Master of Business Administration from Ohio University. He received his Doctor of Philosophy in Accounting from Pennsylvania State University.

Mr. Haskins has worked as an auditor for the international accounting firm Arthur Young & Co. He is also a private consultant, primarily for small business, and has provided executive education programs for IBM, U.S. Navy, INTELSAT, Liquid Carbonic, and the U.S. Postal Service.

He has published articles in numerous practitioner and academic business journals and makes numerous presentations each year on the use of the case method in accounting courses. Mr. Haskins is coauthor of another Irwin text titled *Corporate Financial Reporting: Text and Cases,* by Brownlee, Ferris & Haskins. His current research interests focus on the role of a corporate control environment in fostering reliable financial reporting and on the cultural factors influencing differences in international financial reporting.

Kenneth R. Ferris Kenneth R. Ferris is a Distinguished Professor of World Business at the American Graduate School of International Management (Glendale, Arizona). He received a B.B.A. and an M.B.A. from George Washington University, and earned an M.A. and a Ph.D. from Ohio State University. He previously served on the faculties of Northwestern University and Southern Methodist University, and has taught at numerous academic institutions in Australia, Japan, and New Zealand. Professor Ferris is the author of *Financial Accounting* and *Corporate Reporting: A Casebook,* and also a co-author of *Corporate Financial Reporting* by Brownlee, Ferris, and Haskins, both published by Irwin.

Robert J. Sack Mr. Sack is a Professor of Business Administration at the Darden School, the University of Virginia. He joined the Darden School after three years as the Chief Accountant of the SEC's Enforcement Division and 25 years in public practice as a partner of Touche Ross & Co. In his role with the SEC, Mr. Sack supervised the work of the staff accountants within the Enforcement Division, advised the Division staff on accounting and auditing matters, and played a major role in the direction of the Division's financial fraud program. With Touche Ross, Mr. Sack held a number of positions, including that of National Director of Accounting and Auditing Practice, and Director of Professional Standards for Touche Ross International. A graduate of Miami University (Ohio), Mr. Sack is an alumnus member of Miami's Business Advisory Council.

Mr. Sack is a much sought-after lecturer on issues of ethics in accounting. He has served on the consulting panel for the "Integrated Guidance on Internal Control" project and was a member of the Advisory Board of the National Commission on Financial Fraud.

He is serving a third year on the AAA Task Force on Professionalism and Ethics, and recently completed a three-year term as Managing Co-Editor of *Accounting Horizons*.

Brandt R. Allen   Brandt R. Allen is the James C. Wheat Professor of Business Administration and Associate Dean for Executive Education at the Darden Graduate Business School, University of Virginia. Before joining the Virginia faculty in 1970, he was a professor at the Harvard Business School and before that a research engineer with the Boeing Company.

He is a well known author, consultant, and lecturer in both the United States and Europe on the subject of information systems management. His current research focus is on how companies formulate and implement information systems strategy. He is a member of the Conference Board's Council of Information Management Executives. Professor Allen holds a B.S. in mathematics, an M.B.A. from the University of Washington and a doctorate from Harvard University in control and information systems.

PREFACE

STATEMENT OF PURPOSE

In a past issue of the *Saturday Review,* an article titled "18,000,000 Books Nobody Reads" cited corporate annual reports as very low in interest, clarity, and understandability. This text's primary objective is, to a large extent, to confront this problem by developing future business leaders' financial-statement literacy and to do so in a way that is firmly grounded in the issues of modern business concerns. The literacy objective incorporates the abilities to (1) understand the nature of business transactions, (2) identify relevant economic events for reporting, (3) determine the most appropriate financial measures for those events, and (4) analyze the effects of those events in firm performance and financial condition. To this end, an underlying theme of the text is that accounting is not divorced from the world it describes or from the behaviors it measures and influences.

Philosophically, we believe that an introductory accounting text, whether used at the undergraduate or MBA level, does not need to explore every nuance of accounting practice and thought. Rather, the most important and predominant contemporary and classical accounting conventions are our foci. In this regard, the goal is to expose and discuss the underlying rationales of those practices and evaluate their effectiveness in providing useful information for decision making. Foremost among the practices investigated are those that purport to portray corporate financial position, operating results, cash flows, manager performance, and financial strength.

Even though the rule orientation of accounting practice cannot be ignored, both the classroom and the boardroom are appropriate places for questioning and debating those rules and conventions. Such scrutiny is crucial because it is important for students to develop an understanding of the management choices that must be made regarding what information to report, how best to report it, when to do so, and where controls are needed to assure reliable and relevant reporting. A critical aspect of these choices, dealt with in this text, is a concern for (1) the characteristics of information that make it most useful for decision making; (2) the characteristics of decision makers that also influence the usefulness of information; and (3) the subsequent behavior of managers, subordinates, and external constituencies that can be expected as a result of implementing certain reporting choices.

There are two reasons for our management/user approach. First, it allows us to deal comprehensively with a complex topic. Second, it helps the student retain a focus on concepts and ideas, rather than on procedures. This approach requires considerable discipline on the part of the student, to mentally delegate his or her time to an understanding of business issues and a mastery of the basic financial reporting concepts without becoming too preoccupied with accounting mechanics. Thus, this text is designed primarily for those courses and student groups where the focus is on a balance between the understanding and use of accounting information and its preparation. Provided with a backdrop of contemporary management and financial concerns, students will see that accounting is a significant part of the world it purports to portray, and that it is not an end in itself. On the contrary, students are provided the perspective that accounting information is a critical instrument in presenting a corporation's financial picture to important external constituencies. The raising of issues and concerns springing from this orientation facilitates a focus on substance and also frames the student's learning because they have the comfort of a more familiar general business context for thinking about the accounting issue at hand.

KEY FEATURES

Real world based. The authors view accounting as an integral part of corporate decision making and financial analysis. Thus, accounting is not an end but a means to achieving relevant and reliable insights about business conditions, results, and opportunities. The book repeatedly grounds the discussion of accounting issues and methods in contexts of management decision making, financial analysis, management judgments and estimates, behavioral consequences, and/or the political arena, whichever context is most germane. Such an approach poses accounting as a vital, dynamic phenomenon rather than a sterile, procedural set of mechanics. To this end, the text contains *over 50* excerpts from recent annual reports that serve to highlight the realities of the issue at hand and to exemplify the fact that the financial reporting issues presented are pertinent to the day-to-day information concerns faced by real-world managers, lenders, investors, and financial-statement users in general.

Holistic business approach. The book's managerial orientation frequently leverages the discussion of a particular topic via linkages with strategic and other functional area concerns typically encountered by managers. For example, receivables issues involve credit and collection policies in addition to the accounting issues. Inventory topics include the operations concerns of such things as JIT and standard costing.

Opportunities for student involvement. The end-of-chapter materials provide opportunities for a well-rounded student experience. Discussion questions provide issues for thought and debate where "solutions" are well reasoned, integrated views as opposed to looking up the chapter paragraph that provides the answer. Problems are structured to provide ample opportunities for polishing one's procedural skills as well as for developing a feel for the differences in results when different methods, assumptions, and/or judgments are invoked. The cases provide real-world settings for exploring the usefulness of accounting information to decision makers who have different perspectives and purposes, come from different environments, and value different outcomes.

Group work and communication skills. Many of the cases lend themselves to group assignments and/or classroom presentation and write-up. Instructors are presented with materials that provide lots of degrees of freedom in this regard.

Ethics and international. *Haskins and Sack* have been actively engaged in the development and teaching of ethics materials and courses. Such a perspective is imbedded throughout the text. *Haskins and Ferris* teach international financial reporting courses and provide a chapter on that topic that has also benefitted from the many years of international work experience of *Sack and Allen*.

Improved course materials. *Haskins, Sack, and Allen* have a combined total of over 35 years of teaching experience at the University of Virginia's Darden Graduate Business School, a school consistently ranked in the top ten worldwide in MBA and executive education. Early drafts of the book have been classroom tested at the Darden School for the past three years. The book has also benefitted greatly from the many years of undergraduate and graduate teaching experience that *Ferris* brings to the team.

Key terms. The language involved in financial reporting encompasses many new terms. Each time a new key term is used in the text, it appears in bold type. In addition, a listing of key terms appears at the end of each chapter and an extensive glossary appears at the end of the text.

Appendices. In order to provide instructors a number of degrees of freedom regarding the depth with which to explore a topic, many chapters contain appendices that provide opportunities for exploring a particular topic in a more detailed manner. It is important to note, however, that a comprehensive, powerful course can be constructed without having to use the appendices.

ORGANIZATION

This text consists of four major parts and is organized not unlike other texts in its basic sequencing. Do not, however, conclude that it is just like other texts. As has already been pointed out, the orientation taken toward topics, the emphasis placed on certain facets of the topics, and the integration with a larger context that make this text distinctive.

Part I. These introductory chapters provide the background for the entire text. In particular, the first chapter's presentation of the PepsiCo annual report sets the financial reporting agenda and "creates the need to know." During its discussion, students realize that accounting quickly transcends the necessary but mundane concerns of a green-eye-shaded bookkeeper to encompass those of key managers interested in knowing, among other things, what has been achieved, identifying what remains to be done, monitoring and motivating people better, and efficiently, effectively, and inexpensively raising capital from external sources.

Using generally familiar business contexts, a variety of basic skills are then developed in the remaining Part I chapters. Paramount among the skills developed are (1) the double-entry method of recording transactions; (2) preparation of basic balance sheets and statements of income and owners' equity; (3) familiarity with the language of accounting; and (4) an understanding of some of the fundamental concepts of accounting (e.g., accrual vs. cash, matching, historical costs, materiality) and of the process by which accounting standards are set.

The objectives of these three chapters is for students to become comfortable defining a users' information needs, report the most pertinent information in the most useful way, interpret the story reflected by the information, identify the key assumptions underlying the information being reported, and consider the alternative interpretations that would arise with certain changes in some of the key assumptions. Establishing such a dialectical process at a text's outset is important because students must continually consider such an array of issues in order to appreciate and understand the evolutionary nature of contemporary accounting practice.

Part II. The three chapters in this section of the text introduce in more detail the three basic financial statements—the balance sheet, income statement, and statement of cash flows. All three chapters draw heavily on the concepts, language, and concerns raised in Part I. Moreover, all three chapters integrate the PepsiCo annual report presented in Chapter 1 into their discussions as well as utilizing other corporate annual report examples.

An explicit premise running through these three chapters is that management has a great deal of influence over the results presented. That is, the financial statements are discussed in such a way as to highlight the fact that they are a part of management's thinking as they make decisions throughout the years. We believe such an orientation not only is valid, but also ascribes a great deal of vitality to the statements because they are not merely a sterile codification process of numerous transactions whose total implications and results are not known until year-end.

The purpose of dealing so intensely with these financial statements at this point in the text is that subsequent chapter topics can then be discussed and debated as to their impact on the three financial statements. Such an objective parallels the manager concerns raised in the chapters and poses very effective learning opportunities for students' recognition of both the key accounting *and* managerial concerns.

Part III. The chapters in this part are centered on the theme of measuring, reporting, interpreting, and using financial information pertaining to assets, liabilities, and owners' equity. It is in these chapters that students really begin to see clearly and powerfully that accounting simply describes events and circumstances, and those descriptions are a joint product of certain official guidelines, and, more importantly, of the assumptions, actions, and judgments of managers. These chapters consider the financial reporting issues surrounding some of the daily and strategic concerns of managing assets, liabilities, and owners' equity. Moreover, they explore the tension between reporting the ''most favorable'' versus the ''most realistic'' picture.

As an example, the text and some of the end-of-chapter materials pertaining to marketable equity securities bring to light the issues of (1) distinguishing the relative merits of reporting historical costs versus current market values, and (2) dealing with the prescriptive nature of FASB rules. Both issues underlie much of financial reporting. In particular, the first issue is often viewed by the uninformed as a shortcoming of financial reporting. We believe students should be sensitive to the pros and cons of reporting costs *and* current values and should be able to identify situations where one or the other may be more appropriate. In regard to the second issue, students become acutely aware of the volatility that is possible in reported earnings if how things are to be reported is simply left to the discretion of management. They thus realize a need for constraining the discretion available to managers in reporting their companies' financial position and results of operations. This is not to say that the need for management judgments and the consequences of such decisions become less important; on the contrary, a thorough knowledge of official guidelines (constraints) is merely an important prerequisite to identifying viable reporting options, structuring business transactions compatibly with the most desirable ways of reporting them, and factoring into one's decisions the information needs of their interested constituencies.

Besides grounding an accounting issue in the context of a business decision or a users' information needs, the chapters also leverage students' understanding of other topics to help in their learning of particular financial reporting topics that may be new to them. For example, anticipating the potentially overwhelming nature of the bonds, leases, and pension topics, the text builds on a thread common to all three topics and familiar to most business students at this point in their education—the present value of a stream of future cash flows. As each of these three topics is introduced via this touchstone, the awesomeness of dealing with the technical aspects of their financial reporting requirements fades. In fact, for most students, the literacy threshold for these three topics, which at the outset seemed unachievably distant, becomes reachable with the use of the present value perspective building block already familiar and mastered by most.

Part IV. This final section of the book provides students with some classical financial analysis tools and then challenges them to use those tools in conjunction with what they have learned about financial reporting to create a corporate "story" based on a company's annual report. The desire is for students to bring together financial reporting disclosures, managerial concerns, and user perspectives in such a way as to be able to fully flesh out (1) a corporate picture of financial strengths/weaknesses, and (2) an awareness of the extent to which reported results could have been different if other legitimate judgments, estimates, and methods had been invoked. In this same vein, students are introduced to the notion of "quality of earnings" and provided an orientation to some ways of thinking about the quality of a company's earnings.

The final chapter provides a brief overview of the financial reporting environment and practices in two other countries—Japan and the United Kingdom. This chapter contains recent annual reports from Toyota and British Petroleum. We view this chapter as integral to a first course in financial reporting because it provides one more opportunity for students to digest the details of an annual report and to then articulate (1) their understanding of the company, (2) the key accounting conventions used, and (3) how those conventions might have been different for that particular company and how they do differ, if at all, from U.S.-based practices. Pedagogically, stark contrasts in settings (i.e., foreign versus U.S.) are used to highlight the financial reporting concerns that transcend borders and those that do not. The PepsiCo annual report can also be revisited to provide a basis for review and compare/contrast with the Toyota and BP reports. Such an end for the text provides a valuable opportunity for students to consolidate much of what has been learned, to experience a real sense of accomplishment, and to broaden their perspective to the international world of financial reporting.

SUPPLEMENTAL MATERIALS

An *Instructor's Manual* is available to accompany the text. The manual provides "solutions" and suggestions for class discussion. In addition, the manual provides several possible course outlines with pertinent assignments. Finally, for those instructors interested in using the end-of-chapter cases, a discussion of our view of the case method is presented.

Two other supplements are available. Some instructors may find the companion *Test Bank* a useful resource. For a number of courses, instructors may find added leverage for student learning is possible through the suggestion that students utilize the companion *Study Guide*.

ACKNOWLEDGMENTS

We gratefully acknowledge the helpful criticisms and constructive suggestions of the following individuals who reviewed the manuscript at various stages of its development:

Professor Paul K. Chaney
Vanderbilt University

Professor Marshall K. Pitman
University of Texas/San Antonio

Professor Roger H. Chope
University of Oregon

Professor Joseph H. Bylinski
University of North Carolina

Professor Richard G. File
University of Nebraska

Professor Dennis Murray
University of Colorado

Professor Albert A. Schepanski
University of Iowa

Professor Janet I. Kimbrell
Oklahoma State University

Professor Philip M. J. Reckers
Arizona State University

Professor Robert Knechel
University of Florida/Gainesville

Professor Peter Wilson
Duke University

It is also important that we acknowledge the special contributions of Professor Philip M. J. Reckers (Arizona State University), study guide author, Professor Guy Owings (Pittsburg State University), test bank author, and Professor Michael Clair (College of San Mateo), the end-of-chapter materials checker.

We would also like to thank Marcia Floyd, Alice Doster, and Debbie Ehrenworth for their conscientious efforts in helping us prepare the various manuscripts involved. Finally, we thank Carolyn Nowak, Jeff Shelstad, and Lew Gossage of Richard D. Irwin, Inc. for their support in the conceptualization and preparation of this product.

Mark E. Haskins
Kenneth R. Ferris
Robert J. Sack
Brandt R. Allen

NOTE TO THE STUDENT:

This text was created to provide you with a high-quality educational resource. As a publisher specializing in college texts for business and economics, our goal is to provide you with learning materials that will serve you well in your college studies and throughout your career.

The educational process involves learning, retention, and the application of concepts and principles. You can accelerate your learning efforts by utilizing the features found in this text:

New concepts and terms are located after the summary at the end of each chapter. The new concepts and terms are referenced with appropriate page numbers.

Demonstration problem with solution. Several chapters contain a demonstration problem that will list a real-life situation and ask you to solve a problem associated with the material.

Issues for discussion foster a conceptual approach. Many are laid out in point/counterpoint structure and will incorporate ethics. Located at the end of the chapter, Issues for Discussion employ several concepts at a time and expose you to the integration of several topics in a problem material environment.

Cases. Each chapter incorporates several case problems designed to suit the individual chapter material.

Key Terms all appear in bold face color type. A listing of key terms will appear at the end of each chapter. A glossary of key terms appears at the end of the text.

In addition to the learning features presented in the text, you may wish to consider using the *Study Guide*. The *Study Guide,* prepared by Philip M. J. Reckers of Arizona State University, is designed to help you better your performance in the course. This supplement highlights key points in the text and provides you with assistance in mastering basic concepts. For each chapter, the guide includes the main focus and objectives, review of key ideas, true/false, multiple choice, and matching questions. Check your local bookstore or ask the manager to place an order for you today.

We at Irwin sincerely hope that this text will assist you reaching your goals both now and in the future.

CONTENTS IN BRIEF

CONTENTS

―――――――― PART ――――――――
II

Using and Understanding the Basic Financial
Statements 139

CHAPTER
4

The Balance Sheet 140

CHAPTER
5

The Income Statement 192

CHAPTER
6

The Statement of Cash Flows 243

──────────── PART ────────────
III

Measuring and Reporting Assets and Equities
Using Generally Accepted Accounting
Principles 295

C H A P T E R
7

Trade Receivables and Marketable
Securities 296

C H A P T E R
8

Inventories and the Cost of Goods Sold 340

──────

C H A P T E R
9

Noncurrent Intercorporate Investments 381

──────

CHAPTER
10

Noncurrent Assets: Fixed Assets, Intangible Assets, and Natural Resources 433

CHAPTER
11

Accounting for Liabilities: Basic Concepts, Current Liabilities, and Interest-Bearing Debt 480

C H A P T E R
15

Financial Reporting in Foreign Countries 673

PART I

Overview of Accounting and Financial Statements

CHAPTER 1

An Introduction to Business Activities and the Role of Accounting as the Language of Business

Accounting is a language used by businesspeople to communicate the financial health of their enterprise. Like any language, accounting adheres to certain conventions and concepts which users of financial statements must understand to appreciate the story conveyed by a company's use of this language. The primary objective of this book is to help you understand those concepts and conventions, and consequently become literate and conversant in the language of accounting.

ACCOUNTING AS A LANGUAGE

Businesspeople use accounting to communicate with interested stakeholders both inside and outside a company. Within a company, for example, managers use accounting to communicate the organization's results to those senior managers who have oversight responsibility and to those line managers who have day-to-day operational responsibilities. This internal accounting communication serves two principal purposes. First, it describes the effectiveness with which the various levels of management exercise their stewardship of the company's resources. That stewardship analysis is important to both the company and its managers. Those responsible for overseeing the company want to know whether management deserves increased operating autonomy or requires more intense, critical scrutiny. More directly, incentive compensation schemes are often based on the stewardship results included in internal management reports—should operating management be rewarded or reprimanded for this period's reported results? Second, accounting reports assist management in making decisions that influence the enterprise's future operations. These decisions often focus on such questions as whether the company should increase its investment in plant and equipment or should sell its assets to minimize its losses. Should the company try to raise the price on its products, or should it try to reduce the cost of producing its products? Should the company's limited resources (for example, advertising funds or research and development funds) be allocated to Product A or Product B? To answer these questions, and others, managers need relevant, reliable, and timely accounting information.

Businesspeople must also communicate financial results to individuals outside the company. For example, managers need to communicate with current or potential investors; with creditors, customers, and suppliers; with labor unions, consumer unions, and other sociopolitical groups; and with state, local, and federal government agencies, such as the Internal Revenue Service. Again, accounting is the language by which these communications are made possible.

These various outside constituencies use accounting reports to evaluate the stewardship of top-level management and to make decisions about the company. These decisions often focus on such questions as whether investors should buy shares of stock in the company or invest their resources in some other company. Should creditors extend loans to the company, or should an existing loan be called? If an investor decides to invest or a creditor decides to extend a loan, what price is appropriate for the stock, and what interest rate should be charged on the loan? How does the risk of an investment in this particular company compare with the risks involved in other available investment alternatives? Other interested parties have similar "investment" decisions to make. For example, should labor negotiators push for increased employee benefits or agree to wage and salary reductions? Accounting information serves a critical role in the deliberations of all of these external parties.

No language created by humanity has ever been able to claim perfect communication effectiveness. Although accounting has wide acceptance as *the* financial communication media, everyone who is involved with it acknowledges its limitations. In the following chapters, we will focus on the ways accounting is used in the business world, and we will also identify the areas in which accounting conventions remain inadequate. The notion of accounting as a language to be used as a communication vehicle and the importance of the issues that that language endeavors to address raise important questions for managers whether they are responsible for the company as a whole or merely a segment of a larger entity. Every manager has the obligation to do the most effective job possible communicating the results of his or her business responsibility so that the most advantageous decisions can be made. To make that communication effective, managers must know how to make the best use of the available accounting conventions and, when necessary, develop supplemental communications. It will be obvious that managers often have a vested interest in the decisions that will be made regarding their company. That vested interest has the potential to be a conflict of interest. All managers have an ethical obligation to use accounting in such a way as to describe objectively and fairly the results of their enterprises—regardless of the effect that communication may have on their personal well-being.

FINANCIAL VERSUS MANAGERIAL ACCOUNTING

For intracompany communications, managers can, and usually do, establish accounting rules and conventions to use solely in the company's *internal* reporting system. As a consequence, the reports produced by the internal reporting system can be tailored to the specific informational needs of a variety of different managers. For example, a production manager might need accounting information about the number and cost of units in production, and a sales manager might need information focusing on the selling price and quantities available for sale. Thus, the internal reporting system may produce a diverse set of accounting reports, each prepared to satisfy a particular informational need of its internal user. The rules and conventions that guide the internal reporting system can be designed by the managers themselves to suit their specific informational needs. This internal reporting system is commonly called **managerial accounting.**

Although internal accounting reports may vary between companies, *external* accounting reports are more standardized. Because a wide and varied audience reads external accounting reports, it is obviously more efficient if all reporting companies follow a somewhat uniform approach in preparing their external financial reports. Although some unique "dialects" are used in highly specialized industries, by and large, external financial reporting adheres to a common body of communication practices mutually accepted and established by the financial community. The rules and conventions that guide the public communication of financial results are referred to as **generally accepted accounting principles** or GAAP, and the process is commonly called **financial accounting.**

The most prevalent form of external accounting communication is referred to as the **financial statements** included in the quarterly and annual reports distributed to a company's external constituencies. All companies that have publicly traded debt or equity securities must issue financial statements prepared in accordance with GAAP. We say that financial statements "must" be prepared in accordance with GAAP because the requirement is both legal and pragmatic. The financial community has come to expect GAAP-based statements as the standard form of financial communication and is generally unwilling to invest the time and effort to understand a unique accounting language proposed by any one company. The requirement is also a legal one—the courts have determined that companies with publicly traded securities must issue GAAP-based financial statements in order to comply with the financial statement-filing requirements of the federal securities laws.

The **Securities and Exchange Commission** (SEC) was established by the U.S. Congress to administer the laws that regulate the marketplace for publicly traded securities. The SEC has the responsibility to oversee the activities of the securities markets and has the authority to regulate broker-dealers, stock exchanges, and the financial disclosure system required of companies that have securities in the hands of the public. As part of that mandate, the SEC has the statutory authority to establish the "form and content" of the financial statements that public companies must provide to their securityholders. For a number of reasons, the SEC has used that authority sparingly. The SEC has chosen to mandate general business disclosures (description of business risks and opportunities, details of management compensation plans, etc.) but has, by and large, delegated to the private sector the establishment of specific accounting standards.

In response to that delegation by the SEC, the financial community established the **Financial Accounting Standards Board** (FASB) in 1973. The Board has seven full-time members and more than 100 research and support people. The Board's activities are funded by voluntary contributions from the largest CPA firms, major corporations, the securities industry, and other members of the financial community. Board members are selected for their expertise in financial accounting and reporting without regard to their previous affiliations. Board members are to be independent in their deliberations and so they must sever all business ties when they accept an appointment to the FASB.

The accounting standards promulgated by the FASB are accepted by the SEC and the courts as meeting GAAP requirements for reports of companies with publicly traded securities. The **American Institute of Certified Public Accountants** (AICPA) has also resolved that the standards promulgated by the Board are to represent GAAP for the general purpose, publicly distributed financial statements of privately held companies as well. We will have more to say about the process of setting accounting standards and the organizations involved in Chapter 2.

The principal focus of this text is financial accounting and the generally accepted accounting principles established by the FASB. It should be noted, however, that most companies maintain multiple reporting systems—an internal system for management communications and an external system for communication with outside constituencies. And, since some outside constituencies may have special interests (and the power to demand special responses), a company may actually maintain multiple external reporting systems. For example, a company may use a GAAP reporting system for its shareholders and bankers, a separate system following the Internal Revenue Service Code for its income tax filings, and a third system to present financial information required by applicable regulatory agencies, such as the Office of Thrift Supervision (for savings and loan institutions) or the Federal Energy Regulatory Commission (for public utilities).

The internationalization of our economy has added another dimension to the accounting communications required of most companies. If, for example, a company has debt or equity securities traded on the public exchanges of other countries, it will probably be required to prepare financial reports according to the GAAP and tax rules of those countries as well. Each major country has developed its own approach to creating financial accounting standards. As a consequence, although there is some uniformity, significant differences in these standards also exist worldwide. Participants in the international markets, however, have become impatient with those reporting differences and argue that they create impediments to the flow of capital between countries, and the capital market regulators (e.g., the SEC in the United States) in the leading countries have mandated that these reporting differences be reconciled. In 1990, a major effort to harmonize international accounting standards was under way; that program is discussed in Chapter 15.

Before we leave this introduction to GAAP, one final observation is in order: GAAP-based accounting is not so categorical and as rule oriented as it might seem on the surface. It is true that some basic conventions and rules have been established through common usage or pronouncement and must be accepted as they are; however, as with any language, the application of GAAP provides for a surprising amount of latitude in the preparation of financial statements. That flexibility arises as a result of three factors. First, for some transactions, widely diverse accounting approaches had become entrenched as alternative GAAP long before the SEC or the FASB was established, and so those equally acceptable alternative approaches remain in the "language." Second, the financial community continues to develop creative new business transactions, and until new standards are established—the standard-setting process can take a long time—diverse accounting approaches to those creative transactions will become accepted in practice. And, third, business transactions are complex and unique, and very often managers face a real challenge as they try to apply a broadly written, generalized financial reporting standard to their particular business events. This flexibility in GAAP is sometimes frustrating to students because it means that there may be more than one acceptable answer to a question. But that flexibility is important to the workings of the system. It provides an exciting challenge for managers to make the best use of the potential power of the accounting language in communicating the essence of the business they have created.

THE FINANCIAL REPORTING PROCESS— AN OVERVIEW

In spite of the very important role that GAAP play in the accounting communication process, GAAP alone report nothing—they are simply the *medium* by which a company's financial activities can be measured and reported to the various interested constituencies. Exhibit 1.1 provides a diagram illustrating the process of preparing a company's financial statements. The process of preparing the financial statements really flows through the center of the diagram, subject to the control of management and the influence of the independent auditor. We can see from this illustration that financial statements are nothing

EXHIBIT 1.1

Overview of the Accounting Communication Process

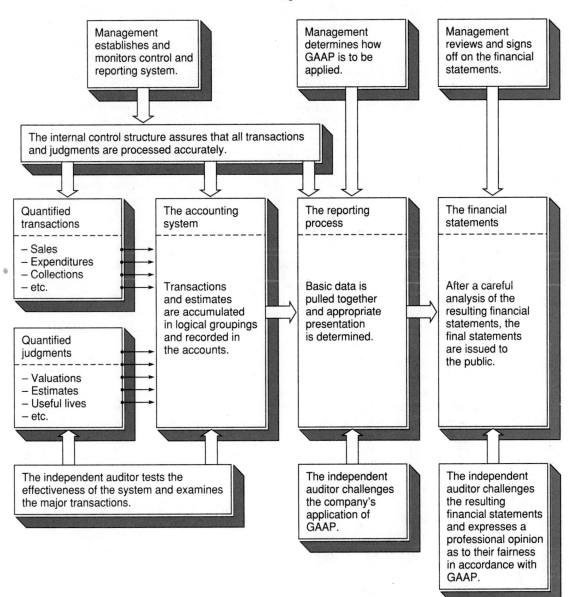

more than the summary of all of a company's business transactions and a wide variety of financial judgments made by management. Those transactions and judgments are subject to a company's **internal control structure,** which assures that all transactions and all necessary judgments have been recognized and that they are classified and correctly described in the company's records. A company's accounting system sorts all of the transactions and judgments into similar or related groupings and then aggregates that input so that the summarized financial statements can be prepared. Moving through the center of the diagram, the summary of that data and its presentation in the financial statements follows the requirements of GAAP.

As suggested by the top portion of the diagram, the design and maintenance of an internal control structure and the preparation of financial statements are the direct responsibility of corporate management. Corporate management is responsible for maintaining a system of internal control that ensures that all transactions are recognized, that all judgments are made, and that the raw data are summarized and presented fairly. Management establishes the system and has internal auditors and other systems checks to monitor its performance. At the culmination of the process, management evaluates the resulting financial statements to be sure that the end result makes good business sense.

The challenge in the review of the resulting financial statements centers on whether or not the statements reflect the reality of the business as management, at all levels, understands it to be. The responsibility for the review begins with financial management, but it also includes operating management, the top management of the entity, and, in all likelihood, the company's board of directors. Many corporate financial statements are accompanied by a report from top management and the board of directors, which acknowledges its responsibilities for the fairness of the financial statements, and which asserts its discharge of those responsibilities.

Although corporate management is responsible for preparing the financial statements and ensuring their overall fairness, the independent external auditor is responsible for testing the underlying accounting data and expressing an opinion as to the fairness of the resulting financial statements. As we noted earlier, for a number of reasons, management might have a vested interest in the financial picture that the statements portray, and because of the potential for a serious conflict of interest, the financial community has determined that it is useful to have an independent opinion as to the fairness of those statements. Almost every company, therefore, engages an **independent auditor** to review its financial statements for fairness and consistency with GAAP.

An auditor's examination of a set of financial statements (typically referred to as an **audit**) is conducted according to a set of professional standards referred to as **generally accepted auditing standards** (GAAS). Those standards require the auditor to test the way the system processes routine transactions, to consider the appropriateness of the accounting methods used in individually material transactions, and to evaluate the application of GAAP in the company's financial statements. Because an audit relies on test samples of the company's transactions and financial statement accounts, an auditor is typically not held responsible for immaterial errors in the financial statements or for small frauds. But most courts have said that an auditor is responsible for finding material misstatements, whether they result from accounting errors or from management fraud.

Based on their examination, independent auditors issue a report presenting an opinion as to the fairness of the financial statements prepared by management. We will review the content of that report in more detail when we look at the PepsiCo financial statements in the next section of this chapter. The most important element of the auditor's report is the **auditor's opinion.** If all goes well, the auditor expresses the opinion that the financial statements do present fairly the company's financial condition and results of operations in accordance with generally accepted accounting principles. Obviously, the financial community expects to see such a positive opinion (sometimes referred to as a *"clean" opinion*) in every company's financial statements. Occasionally, an auditor finds it necessary to issue an opinion indicating that the financial statements *do not* fairly present the company's financial condition and results of operations in accordance with GAAP for one reason or another. However, the power of the public's expectations is typically so great that most managers work diligently to avoid a financial reporting dispute with their independent auditors.

PEPSICO, INC.—AN ILLUSTRATION

Presented at the end of this chapter is the Financial Review section of the 1990 annual report of a company with whose products you are quite familiar—PepsiCo, Inc. The typical corporate annual report contains more than the basic financial statements and the related text. In some cases, portions of the annual report may be used as a means to advertise the various products of a company. In other cases, portions of the annual report may be used as a public relations effort, highlighting particular social or financial accomplishments of the company. Most companies devote considerable effort to the annual report, and it serves a multitude of purposes. Most of the information in corporate annual reports is interesting, telling us something about the company and its management and providing a context within which we can evaluate the company's financial health and prospects. Our focus throughout this text will be on the financial information contained in the annual report.

To focus our discussion and to illustrate the rules and conventions used in accounting, we will often refer to examples from actual financial statements. As a central example, we have elected to use the financial report of PepsiCo, Inc. Consider, for the moment, the contents of PepsiCo's accounting report. The first section, "Business Segments," reveals that PepsiCo operates internationally in three distinct lines of business: soft drinks, snack foods, and restaurants. PepsiCo's various product lines are sufficiently diverse and popular that it would be surprising if you had not come into contact with at least one of its products. PepsiCo's product lines include the following well-recognized tradenames:

Soft Drink Segment	Snack Food Segment	Restaurant Segment
■ Pepsi-Cola ■ Mountain Dew ■ Slice ■ 7-Up (International)	■ Frito-Lay (including Doritos, Ruffles, Lay's, Fritos, Cheetos, and Tostitos)	■ Pizza Hut ■ Taco Bell ■ Kentucky Fried Chicken

The financial data included in this first section (e.g., net sales, operating profits, capital spending) are presented on a business segment basis (i.e., soft drink, snack food, and restaurant). With that information, the interested reader can readily determine which line (or lines) of business was most (least) profitable for the company, and which business segment contributed most (least) to the overall financial health of the entire company. For 1990, PepsiCo's soft drink segment produced the largest net sales ($6.523 billion), while its snack food segment produced the largest operating profits ($934.4 million).

The next seven sections of the Financial Review present the basic financial statements for PepsiCo, as well as management's analysis of those statements. The basic financial statements presented in this report include:

- consolidated statement of income
- consolidated balance sheet
- consolidated statement of cash flows
- consolidated statement of shareholders' equity

The word *consolidated* preceding each of the statements refers to the fact that the reported financial results relate not only to PepsiCo, Inc., but also to all of its wholly owned or majority-owned (i.e., more than 50 percent of the voting shares) subsidiaries as well as certain joint ventures controlled by PepsiCo.

Following the financial statements are the "Notes to the Consolidated Financial Statements." These explanatory **footnotes** expand on the presentation in the basic financial statements. The basic statements are usually summarized to a significant degree, and a company often concludes that readers will need more detail to understand fully the reported results. For example, on page 23, PepsiCo provides details of its $5.6 billion in long-term debt (see "Long-term Debt"). Further, the basic statements are all expressed in concrete numbers, but a company may have a number of transactions in process that are not yet precisely measurable. For example, on page 26, PepsiCo explains in the "Contingencies" footnote that it has directly and indirectly guaranteed obligations aggregating $97 million. The company obviously hopes that it will not be called upon to make good on any of those guarantees, and until a future event happens to force the company to act on its guarantees, the exact dollar amount that it will have to expend cannot be determined. Because the future cost of fulfilling those guarantees cannot be currently measured with any degree of precision, they are not reflected in the basic financial statements, and the company's exposure is simply footnoted for the reader's information.

Finally, since GAAP often provide for a number of acceptable approaches to deal with a particular financial reporting issue, the footnotes can be used to describe the policy selected when the choice from those alternatives is important to a company's financial presentation and to a reader's understanding of the company's financial health. For example, on page 21, PepsiCo describes the accounting policy it has followed for research and development expenses (see the "Summary of Significant Accounting Policies" footnote), among other things. PepsiCo explains that the company's pretax net income for 1990 was reduced by $101 million because its policy is to charge all research and development expenses to income when they are incurred. The reader is entitled to know that the company follows that policy rather than a policy of deferring those costs and charging them to expense in future years when the related products are brought to market. The reader is also entitled to know how much that policy affected the current period's income statement, and PepsiCo provides that information.

Corporate management has an obligation to make a full and fair disclosure of a company's financial affairs, and management uses the basic financial statements, supplemented with footnotes, to discharge that responsibility.

Following the footnotes are two credibility-ensuring documents: the statement of "Management's Responsibility for Financial Statements" and the "Report of KMPG Peat Marwick Independent Public Accountant." The "Statement of Management's Responsibility for Financial Statements" is a public acknowledgment of this responsibility by PepsiCo's management; it is an assertion that the company's system of internal control is adequate and offers a pledge by top management that the presented data are fair, free from bias, and reliable.

The "Report of KMPG Peat Marwick Independent Public Accountants" follows the standard, three-paragraph approach that the AICPA recommends and that the financial community has come to expect. The first paragraph of the report is a statement of the scope of the audit examination and a brief statement differentiating management's responsibilities for the financial statements from those of the independent auditor. The second paragraph states whether or not the audit was performed in accordance with generally accepted auditing standards. It also briefly explains what an audit entails and emphasizes the auditor's role in investigating possible material misstatements of the financial statements. The third paragraph is a statement of opinion as to whether the company's financial condition and results of operations have been reported "fairly, in all material respects … in conformity with generally accepted accounting principles." The opinion expressed by PepsiCo's independent public accountant, KPMG Peat Marwick, is the standard "clean" or **unqualified opinion.**

Finally, to permit the financial statement user to conduct a trend analysis of the company's financial results over a number of years or quarters, the "Selected Financial Data" section presents selected accounting data for an 11-year period; the "Quarterly Financial Data" section presents quarterly financial data for the prior eight quarters.

Overall, the annual accounting report contains an enormous quantity of financial information about a company and its operations. Quarterly accounting reports are usually far less detailed than annual reports, but they play an important role in the financial reporting system because they provide timely information about the trends of a company's business. We suggest that you take a few moments to familiarize yourself with the general content of the annual financial report of PepsiCo, Inc., presented in the following pages.

PEPSICO, INC. 1990 FINANCIAL REVIEW

Business Segments

This information constitutes a Note to the Consolidated Financial Statements. (tabular dollars in millions)

PepsiCo operates on a worldwide basis within three industry segments: soft drinks, snack foods and restaurants. Management's discussion and analysis of PepsiCo's industry segments is presented in the text beginning on pages 13, 21 and 29 under the caption "Management's Analysis."

The soft drinks segment primarily manufactures concentrates and markets Pepsi-Cola, Mountain Dew, Slice and their allied brands worldwide and 7UP internationally, and operates soft drink bottling businesses principally in the United States. The soft drinks segment data reflect a number of acquisitions of franchised bottlers, the largest of which were the domestic bottling businesses of General Cinema Corporation and Grand Metropolitan Incorporated acquired in 1989 and 1988, respectively.

The snack foods segment primarily manufactures and markets snack chips. The snack foods segment data reflect the 1989 acquisitions of Smiths Crisps Limited and Walkers Crisps Holdings Limited (the U.K. operations), which manufacture and market snack chips in the United Kingdom.

The restaurants segment data include the operations of Pizza Hut, Taco Bell and Kentucky Fried Chicken (KFC) and reflect the acquisitions of several franchised domestic and international restaurant operators, which were not significant in the aggregate. Restaurant net sales include net sales by company-owned restaurants, initial franchise fees, royalty and rental payments from restaurants operated by franchisees, gains on sales of restaurant businesses and net sales to franchisees by PFS, PepsiCo's restaurant distribution operation.

All acquisitions were accounted for under the purchase method and, accordingly, the results of the acquired businesses are included from their respective dates of acquisition. (See Note to Consolidated Financial Statements on page 43.) The acquisition of the U.K. operations had a significant impact on PepsiCo's international operations, as reflected in the international data presented.

Net corporate expenses consist primarily of interest expense, interest income and other corporate items that are not allocated to the business segments. Beginning in 1990, no interest income was allocated to the segments. The portion of interest income previously allocated consisted principally of interest income on certain international short-term investments and on domestic capital sublease receivables. This change provides more meaningful comparisons, as movements in balances of the investments and sublease receivables due to any future changes in corporate controlled investing/financing strategies could distort the rate of operating profit growth of the related business segment. Further, a current review of industry reporting practices supports the exclusion of interest income of this nature from segment operating profits. To improve comparability, segment operating profits for 1989 and 1988 have been restated to reclassify interest income of $36.5 million and $22.8 million, respectively, to Interest and Other Corporate Expenses, Net. Also, segment identifiable assets for 1989 and 1988 have been restated to reclassify the combined related international portfolios and domestic capital sublease receivables of $124.8 million and $157.6 million, respectively, to Corporate Assets.

PepsiCo has invested in a number of joint ventures in which it exercises significant influence, but not control. Equity in net income of these affiliates, which is also included in net corporate expenses, was $2.0 million, $13.4 million and $15.8 million in 1990, 1989 and 1988, respectively. The decline in 1990 reflects a $15.9 million unusual charge to reduce the carrying value of a Pizza Hut international joint venture investment. The investments in affiliates and related equity in net income are not material to the industry segment data.

Corporate identifiable assets consist principally of offshore short-term investments and investments in affiliates. PepsiCo's investments in affiliates totaled $1.1 billion, $676 million and $500 million at year-end 1990, 1989 and 1988, respectively. At year-end 1990, the largest of these investments consisted of $327 million in a Mexican cookie business acquired in late 1990. Other joint venture investments included $204 million in a domestic franchised bottler, $119 million in the KFC Japan joint venture and $78 million in a Canadian snack food operation.

In determining geographic area data, the results of PepsiCo's centralized soft drink concentrate manufacturing facilities in Puerto Rico and Ireland have been allocated based upon actual concentrate sales to the respective geographic areas. Certain centralized international administrative expenses in each of the three industry segments have been allocated based upon sales volumes or number of restaurants in the respective geographic areas.

1990 and 1989 consisted of 52 weeks, while 1988 consisted of 53 weeks.

Net Sales
($ In Millions)

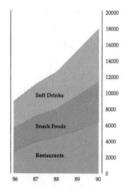

Segment Operating Profits
($ In Millions)

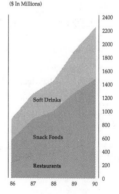

PEPSICO, INC. 1990 FINANCIAL REVIEW

Industry Segments:	Net Sales			Operating Profits[a]			Identifiable Assets[b]		
	1990	1989	1988	1990	1989	1988	1990	1989	1988
Soft Drinks: Domestic	$ 5,034.5	$ 4,623.3	$ 3,667.0	$ 673.8	$ 577.6	$ 405.7			
International	1,488.5	1,153.4	971.2	93.8	98.6	49.6			
	6,523.0	5,776.7	4,638.2	767.6	676.2	455.3	$ 6,465.2	$ 6,198.1	$3,994.1
Snack Foods: Domestic	3,471.5	3,211.3	2,933.3	732.3	667.8	587.0			
International	1,582.5	1,003.7	581.0	202.1	137.4	45.2			
	5,054.0	4,215.0	3,514.3	934.4	805.2	632.2	3,892.4	3,310.0	1,608.0
Restaurants: Domestic	5,540.9	4,684.8	3,950.3	447.2	356.5	298.4			
International	684.8	565.9	430.4	75.2	57.8	41.9			
	6,225.7	5,250.7	4,380.7	522.4	414.3	340.3	3,448.9	3,070.6	3,061.0
Total: Domestic	14,046.9	12,519.4	10,550.6	1,853.3	1,601.9	1,291.1			
International	3,755.8	2,723.0	1,982.6	371.1	293.8	136.7			
	$17,802.7	$15,242.4	$12,533.2	$2,224.4	$1,895.7	$1,427.8	$13,806.5	$12,578.7	$8,663.1

Geographic Areas:[a],[b]									
United States	$14,046.9	$12,519.4	$10,550.6	$1,853.3	$1,601.9	$1,291.1	$ 9,980.7	$ 9,593.4	$ 7,208.9
Europe	1,344.7	771.7	415.5	108.5	53.8	12.6	2,255.2	1,767.2	174.4
Canada and Mexico	1,089.2	899.0	726.3	164.2	117.1	52.5	689.5	409.5	324.4
Other	1,321.9	1,052.3	840.8	98.4	122.9	71.6	881.1	808.6	955.4
							13,806.5	12,578.7	8,663.1
Corporate Assets							3,336.9	2,548.0	2,472.2
Total	$17,802.7	$15,242.4	$12,533.2	2,224.4	1,895.7	1,427.8	$17,143.4	$15,126.7	$11,135.3
Interest and Other Corporate Expenses, Net[a]				(557.0)	(545.2)	(300.6)			
Income from Continuing Operations Before Income Taxes				$1,667.4	$1,350.5	$1,127.2			

	Capital Spending			Depreciation and Amortization Expense		
	1990	1989	1988	1990	1989	1988
Soft Drinks	$ 334.1	$ 267.8	$ 198.4	$338.1	$306.3	$195.7
Snack Foods	381.6	257.9	172.6	232.5	189.3	156.8
Restaurants	460.6	424.6	344.2	306.5	269.9	271.3
Corporate	21.9	9.2	14.9	6.9	6.5	5.5
	$1,198.2	$ 959.5	$ 730.1	$884.0	$772.0	$629.3

Results by Restaurant Chain:	Net Sales			Operating Profits[a]		
Pizza Hut	$2,949.9	$2,453.5	$2,014.2	$245.9	$205.5	$149.7
Taco Bell	1,745.5	1,465.9	1,157.3	149.6	109.4	75.7
KFC	1,530.3	1,331.3	1,209.2	126.9	99.4	114.9
	$6,225.7	$5,250.7	$4,380.7	$522.4	$414.3	$340.3

(a) **Unusual Items:** Results for the years presented were affected by several unusual credits and charges, the impacts of which were a net credit of $35.2 million ($4.2 charge after-tax or $0.01 per share) in 1990, a net credit of $4.4 million ($1.8 after-tax) in 1989 and a net charge of $23.9 million ($16.3 after-tax or $0.02 per share) in 1988. The unusual items were as follows:

Soft Drinks: 1990 included a $10.5 million in charges for receivables exposures related to highly leveraged domestic retail customers. 1989 included a $32.5 million credit resulting from a decision to retain a bottling operation in Japan previously held for sale and a $12.3 million reorganization charge to decentralize international operations. 1988 included a $14.5 million reorganization charge to decentralize domestic operations and a $9.4 million loss resulting from the sale of a Spanish winery.

Snack Foods: 1990 included $10.6 million in charges for receivables exposures related to highly leveraged domestic retail customers. 1989 included a $6.6 million reorganization charge to decentralize

domestic operations and a $4.3 million credit resulting from a decision to retain a domestic cookie production facility previously held for sale.

Restaurants: 1990 included a $17.0 million domestic and a $0.6 million international charge for closures of certain underperforming restaurants as follows: $9.0 million at Pizza Hut, $4.0 million at Taco Bell and $4.6 million at KFC. 1990 also included an $8.0 million charge to consolidate domestic Pizza Hut field operations and a $2.4 million charge to relocate international Pizza Hut headquarters. 1989 included reorganization charges of $8.0 million at KFC and $5.5 million at Taco Bell to consolidate domestic field operations.

Corporate: 1990 included a $118.2 million gain from an initial public stock offering by PepsiCo's KFC joint venture in Japan, an $18.0 million charge for accelerated contributions to the PepsiCo Foundation and a $15.9 million charge to reduce the carrying value of a Pizza Hut international joint venture investment.

(b) The identifiable assets at year-end 1988 were not restated for certain previously consolidated KFC international joint ventures reported under the equity method since 1989.

Consolidated Statement of Income

(in millions except per share amounts)
PepsiCo, Inc. and Subsidiaries
Fifty-two weeks ended December 29, 1990 and December 30, 1989 and fifty-three weeks ended December 31, 1988

	1990	1989	1988
Net Sales	**$17,802.7**	$15,242.4	$12,533.2
Costs and Expenses			
Cost of sales	**8,609.9**	7,467.7	5,957.4
Selling, administrative and other expenses	**6,948.1**	5,841.4	5,154.3
Amortization of goodwill and other intangibles	**189.1**	150.4	72.3
Gain on joint venture stock offering	**(118.2)**	–	–
Interest expense	**688.5**	609.6	344.2
Interest income	**(182.1)**	(177.2)	(122.2)
	16,135.3	13,891.9	11,406.0
Income from Continuing Operations Before Income Taxes	**1,667.4**	1,350.5	1,127.2
Provision for Income Taxes	**576.8**	449.1	365.0
Income from Continuing Operations	**1,090.6**	901.4	762.2
Discontinued Operation Charge (net of income tax benefit of $0.3)	**(13.7)**	–	–
Net Income	**$ 1,076.9**	$ 901.4	$ 762.2
Income (Charge) Per Share			
Continuing operations	**$ 1.37**	$ 1.13	$ 0.97
Discontinued operation	**(0.02)**	–	–
Net Income Per Share	**$ 1.35**	$ 1.13	$ 0.97
Average shares outstanding used to calculate income (charge) per share	**798.7**	796.0	790.4

See accompanying Notes to Consolidated Financial Statements.

**Allocation Of
1990 Net Sales**

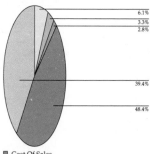

6.1%
3.3%
2.8%
39.4%
48.4%

■ Cost Of Sales
□ Selling, Administrative
   and Other Expenses
■ Net Interest Expense
□ Income Taxes
□ Income from Continuing Operations

PEPSICO, INC. 1990 FINANCIAL RE·VIEW

Management's Analysis—Results of Operations

PepsiCo's three industry segments operate in highly competitive domestic and international markets that are impacted by local economic factors including inflation, changing commodity prices and wage legislation, as well as worldwide recessionary cycles. PepsiCo has mitigated these influences by enhancing the appeal and value of its products through brand promotion, improved quality and prudent pricing actions and by containing costs through increased manufacturing and distribution efficiencies. The extent to which these and other strategies continue to be successful will substantially affect future growth rates of the businesses.

Results for the periods presented reflected acquisitions of several franchised soft drink bottling operations, the largest of which was the domestic bottling business of General Cinema Corporation acquired in March 1989, as well as the July 1989 acquisition of the Smiths and Walkers snack chip businesses in the United Kingdom (the U.K. operations). Results also reflected the 1989 reconsolida-tion of a bottling operation in Japan previously held for sale and the sale of certain domestic bottling operations in late 1988. Accord-ingly, the discussions below are supplemented, where significant, with comparisons excluding the estimated first year impact of the above operations (collectively "the Acquisitions"). Comparisons excluding the first year impact of the Acquisitions are determined by excluding from reported current year amounts the results of the Acquisitions for the corresponding periods that such operations were not reflected in reported prior year amounts. Comparisons of 1989 and 1988 results were also affected by one more week in the 1988 reporting period.

Net Sales, Costs and Expenses
Net sales rose 17% in 1990 and 22% in 1989. Excluding the first year impact of the Acquisitions, net sales increased 14% in both 1990 and 1989. The growth in both years was driven by volume gains in all three industry segments as well as additional restaurant units. International net sales represented 21%, 18% and 16% of consoli-dated net sales in 1990, 1989 and 1988, respectively, primarily reflecting the U.K. operations and strong growth in existing businesses. The trend of an increasing international component of net sales and operating profits is expected to continue. Manage-ment's Analysis of the results of each industry segment is presented in the text beginning on pages 13, 21 and 29.

Cost of sales as a percentage of net sales was 48.4%, 49.0% and 47.5% in 1990, 1989 and 1988, respectively. The 1990 decrease principally reflected higher pricing and lower ingredients costs in domestic soft drinks and snack foods. The 1989 increase principally reflected lower menu prices at Taco Bell and the acquisitions of businesses with lower gross margins.

Selling, administrative and other expenses rose 19% in 1990 and 13% in 1989. Unusual charges in 1990 (see Note to Consolidated Financial Statements on page 35) added one and one-half points to the 1990 growth rate of these expenses. The 1990 and 1989 growth reflected higher sales volumes, increased promotional expenses, additional restaurant units and the additional operating expenses of the Acquisitions.

The increase in amortization of goodwill and other intangibles principally reflects the significant 1989 acquisitions. A portion of the amortization expense is deductible for U.S. income tax purposes, and the after-tax expense amounts per share were $0.20, $0.16 and $0.08 in 1990, 1989 and 1988, respectively.

The joint venture stock offering gain of $118.2 million ($53.0 after-tax or $0.07 per share) relates to the August 1990 initial public offering (IPO) to Japanese investors of shares of PepsiCo's Kentucky Fried Chicken joint venture in Japan (KFC-J). (See Note to Consolidated Financial Statements on page 44.)

Interest expense rose 13% in 1990 compared to 77% in 1989. The increases reflected higher average domestic borrowings to finance the Acquisitions, and a decline in average interest rates in 1990 compared to an increase in 1989. Interest income rose 3% in 1990 compared to 45% in 1989, reflecting higher average balances of offshore short-term investment portfolios in both years and the change in interest rate trends.

Income from Continuing Operations Before Income Taxes
Income from continuing operations before income taxes rose 23% in 1990 compared to 20% in 1989. Excluding the first year impact of the Acquisitions (with related financing costs), the increases were 28% and 35% in 1990 and 1989, respectively. The growth in both years reflected double-digit operating profit advances in all three industry segments driven by volume gains as well as additional restaurants units. International operating profits represented 17%, 15% and 10% of combined segment operating profits in 1990, 1989 and 1988, respectively, with the increases primarily reflecting strong volume growth and the U.K. operations.

Provision for Income Taxes
The effective tax rates on income from continuing operations were 34.6%, 33.3% and 32.4% in 1990, 1989 and 1988, respectively. The effective tax rate for 1990 would have been 33.0% excluding the KFC-J IPO gain, which had an effective tax rate of 55.2%. This rate reflected the lower U.S. tax basis of PepsiCo's investment in KFC-J compared to its book value, which includes nondeductible good-will. The 1989 increase was primarily due to the growth in nondeductible amortization of goodwill and other intangibles. PepsiCo expects that its effective tax rate will increase in 1991 due to a number of factors including a disproportionate increase in earnings in high tax jurisdictions, as well as the absence of certain foreign tax loss carryforwards.

As the Financial Accounting Standards Board (the FASB) contin-ues to review and evaluate possible amendments to recently issued rules for accounting for income taxes, including a further exten-sion of the adoption date, PepsiCo is unable to predict the final FASB requirements and therefore cannot reasonably estimate the effects of adoption.

Income Per Share from Continuing Operations
Income per share from continuing operations rose 21% to $1.37 in 1990 compared to a 17% increase in 1989 to $1.13. First year dilution per share related to the Acquisitions was an estimated $0.04 in 1990 and $0.15 in 1989. Reported dilution represents the after-tax results of acquisitions, including amortization of goodwill and other intangibles and estimated financing costs, through the first year subsequent to the acquisition dates.

The 1990 and 1989 growth rates in income per share from continuing operations were not significantly affected by the net impact of the KFC-J IPO gain, other unusual items in all three years and one more week in the 1988 reporting period.

P E P S I C O , I N C .   1 9 9 0   F I N A N C I A L   R E V I E W

Consolidated Balance Sheet

(in millions except per share amount)
PepsiCo, Inc. and Subsidiaries
December 29, 1990 and December 30, 1989

	1990	1989
ASSETS		
Current Assets		
Cash and cash equivalents	$ 170.8	$ 76.2
Short-term investments, at cost which approximates market	1,644.9	1,457.7
	1,815.7	1,533.9
Notes and accounts receivable, less allowance: $90.8 in 1990 and $57.7 in 1989	1,414.7	1,239.7
Inventories	585.8	546.1
Prepaid expenses and other current assets	265.2	231.1
Total Current Assets	4,081.4	3,550.8
Investments in Affiliates and Other Assets	1,505.9	970.8
Property, Plant and Equipment, net	5,710.9	5,130.2
Goodwill and Other Intangibles, net	5,845.2	5,474.9
Total Assets	$17,143.4	$15,126.7
LIABILITIES AND SHAREHOLDERS' EQUITY		
Current Liabilities		
Short-term borrowings	$ 1,626.5	$ 866.3
Accounts payable	1,116.3	1,054.5
Income taxes payable	443.7	313.7
Other current liabilities	1,584.0	1,457.3
Total Current Liabilities	4,770.5	3,691.8
Long-term Debt	5,600.1	5,777.1
Nonrecourse Obligation	299.5	299.4
Other Liabilities and Deferred Credits	626.3	610.4
Deferred Income Taxes	942.8	856.9
Shareholders' Equity		
Capital stock, par value 1⅔¢ per share: authorized 1,800.0 shares, issued 863.1 shares	14.4	14.4
Capital in excess of par value	365.0	323.9
Retained earnings	4,753.0	3,978.4
Currency translation adjustment	383.2	66.2
	5,515.6	4,382.9
Less: Treasury stock, at cost: 74.7 shares in 1990, 72.0 shares in 1989	(611.4)	(491.8)
Total Shareholders' Equity	4,904.2	3,891.1
Total Liabilities and Shareholders' Equity	$17,143.4	$15,126.7

See accompanying Notes to Consolidated Financial Statements.

Management's Analysis–Financial Condition

PepsiCo's principal objective is to increase the value of its share-holders' investment through integrated operating, investing and financing strategies that maximize cash returns on investments and optimize the cost of capital. The cost of capital is a weighting of cost of debt and cost of equity, with the latter representing a measure of expected return to investors in PepsiCo's stock. PepsiCo estimates its current cost of capital to be approximately 11%. PepsiCo's strong financial condition provides continued access to capital markets throughout the world.

Assets

Total assets increased $2.0 billion or 13% over 1989. This increase reflected purchases of property, plant and equipment (PP&E), equity investments in international snack foods operations, acquisitions of franchisees in soft drinks and restaurants and normal growth of the businesses.

Substantially all of PepsiCo's short-term investments consist of high-grade marketable securities portfolios held offshore. The majority of the investments represent portfolios in Puerto Rico, reflecting the strong operating cash flows of centralized soft drink manufacturing facilities that operate there under a tax incentive. These funds may be remitted to the United States for a nominal local tax under the conditions provided by a tax incentive grant that expires in 2006. (See Note to Consolidated Financial Statements on page 46.) PepsiCo continually reassesses its alternatives to redeploy these and other offshore portfolios, considering other investment opportunities, tax consequences and overall financing strategies.

Investments in affiliates and other assets increased $535 million in 1990. This growth included a $327 million equity investment in a cookie business in Mexico and a $78 million net change in other joint venture activity.

PepsiCo's purchases of PP&E totaled $1.2 billion and $960 million in 1990 and 1989, respectively, led in both years by the restaurants segment. Spending increases in 1990 reflected manufacturing capacity and productivity enhancement projects in international snack foods, investments in high growth markets of international soft drinks and new unit development at Taco Bell and Pizza Hut.

Goodwill and other intangibles increased $370 million in 1990, principally reflecting the translation impact of a weaker U.S. dollar on the goodwill and other intangibles arising from the 1989 acquisition of the U.K. operations, as well as the value of franchise rights reacquired in the acquisitions of franchisees.

Liabilities

Total liabilities rose $1.0 billion or 9% over 1989, reflecting $583 million of increased debt to partially fund PP&E purchases, acquisitions and other investments. The increase also reflected normal growth and liabilities of acquired operations.

PepsiCo's available credit facilities with lending institutions, which exist largely to support the issuances of short-term borrowings, were $3.5 billion at year-end 1990.

In December 1990, the FASB issued Statement of Financial Accounting Standards No. 106 (SFAS 106), "Employers' Accounting for Postretirement Benefits Other Than Pensions," which requires the recognition of postretirement benefit expenses on an accrual basis. PepsiCo has not yet determined the impact of adoption of SFAS 106. PepsiCo expects to implement SFAS 106 by its required adoption date in 1993.

Financial Leverage

In managing its capital structure, PepsiCo utilizes financial leverage to optimize the overall cost of capital, considering the favorable tax treatment of debt, while maintaining operating and financial flexibility.

PepsiCo measures leverage on a net basis, which takes into account its large offshore short-term investment portfolios. These portfolios are managed as part of PepsiCo's overall financing strategy and are not required to support day-to-day operations. Therefore, PepsiCo believes its net debt position, which reflects the pro forma remittance of the portfolios, net of related taxes, as a reduction of total debt (excluding the nonrecourse obligation) is the most meaningful historical cost measure of financial leverage used in the business. PepsiCo's ratio of net debt to net capital employed (defined as net debt, other liabilities and deferred credits, deferred income taxes and shareholders' equity) was 47%, 51% and 37% at year-end 1990, 1989 and 1988, respectively. The decline in the 1990 ratio reflected net capital growth that exceeded the growth in net debt. The increase in 1989 over 1988 reflects the additional debt required to finance the 1989 acquisitions.

PepsiCo also measures financial leverage on a market value basis. Management believes that market leverage (defined as net debt as a percent of net debt plus the market value of equity, based on the stock price at the end of the reporting period) better measures PepsiCo's financial leverage from the perspective of investors in its securities, as it reflects how much of the current value of PepsiCo is financed with debt. Unlike historical cost measures, the market value of equity is based primarily on the expected future cash flows that will both support debt and provide returns to shareholders. The market net debt ratio was 22%, 24% and 20% at year-end 1990, 1989 and 1988, respectively. PepsiCo has established a target range for its market net debt ratio of 20-25%. PepsiCo believes that it can safely exceed this range on a short-term basis to take advantage of strategic acquisition opportunities.

Because of its strong cash generating capability, PepsiCo believes that its current leverage level does not significantly affect its overall cost of debt or reduce its flexibility to invest in the business.

PepsiCo's negative operating working capital position, which principally reflects the cash sales nature of its restaurant operations, is an interest-free source of capital. Operating working capital, which excludes short-term investments and short-term borrowings, was a negative $708 million and $732 million at year-end 1990 and 1989, respectively.

Shareholders' Equity

The currency translation adjustment increased to $383 million at year-end 1990 compared to $66 million at year-end 1989. The change was almost entirely due to the impact of the weaker U.S. dollar on the translation of financial statements of the U.K. operations.

Return on average shareholders' equity primarily represents a combination of operating performance and the effect of financial leverage. Based on income from continuing operations, PepsiCo's return on average shareholders' equity was 24.8% in 1990 compared to 25.6% in 1989. The decrease reflected growth in average shareholders' equity that exceeded the growth in income, primarily because of the change in the currency translation adjustment.

PEPSICO, INC. 1990 FINANCIAL REVIEW

Consolidated Statement of Cash Flows

PepsiCo, Inc. and Subsidiaries
Fifty-two weeks ended December 29, 1990 and December 30, 1989 and fifty-three weeks ended December 31, 1988
(in millions)

	1990	1989	1988
Cash Flows from Continuing Operations:			
Income from continuing operations	$ 1,090.6	$ 901.4	$ 762.2
Adjustments to reconcile income from continuing operations to net cash generated by continuing operations:			
Gain on joint venture stock offering	(118.2)	–	–
Depreciation and amortization	884.0	772.0	629.3
Deferred income taxes	106.1	71.2	20.1
Other noncash charges and credits–net	120.3	128.4	213.4
Changes in operating working capital, excluding effect of acquisitions and sales of businesses:			
Notes and accounts receivable	(124.8)	(149.9)	(50.1)
Inventories	(20.9)	(50.1)	13.8
Prepaid expenses and other current assets	(61.6)	6.5	37.8
Accounts payable	25.4	134.9	138.2
Income taxes payable	136.3	80.9	55.1
Other current liabilities	72.8	(9.4)	74.7
Net change in operating working capital	27.2	12.9	269.5
Net Cash Generated by Continuing Operations	2,110.0	1,885.9	1,894.5
Cash Flows from Investing Activities:			
Acquisitions and investments in affiliates	(630.6)	(3,296.6)	(1,415.5)
Purchases of property, plant and equipment	(1,180.1)	(943.8)	(725.8)
Proceeds from joint venture stock offering	129.6	–	–
Proceeds from sales of property, plant and equipment	45.3	69.7	67.4
Proceeds from sales of businesses	–	–	283.2
Net sales (purchases) of short-term investments	(181.8)	12.3	(201.7)
Other, net	(119.7)	(97.9)	(58.7)
Net Cash Used for Investing Activities	(1,937.3)	(4,256.3)	(2,051.1)
Cash Flows from Financing Activities:			
Proceeds from issuances of long-term debt	777.3	71.7	475.3
Payments of long-term debt	(298.0)	(405.4)	(190.0)
Net proceeds from (payments of) short-term borrowings	(86.2)	2,925.5	231.3
Cash dividends paid	(293.9)	(241.9)	(199.0)
Purchases of treasury stock	(147.7)	–	(71.8)
Other, net	(28.6)	(28.9)	(24.4)
Net Cash Generated by (Used for) Financing Activities	(77.1)	2,321.0	221.4
Effect of Exchange Rate Changes on Cash and Cash Equivalents	(1.0)	(17.1)	(1.4)
Net Increase (Decrease) in Cash and Cash Equivalents	94.6	(66.5)	63.4
Cash and Cash Equivalents–Beginning of Year	76.2	142.7	79.3
Cash and Cash Equivalents–End of Year	$ 170.8	$ 76.2	$ 142.7
Supplemental Cash Flow Information:			
Cash Flow Data			
Interest paid	$ 656.9	$ 591.1	$ 286.5
Income taxes paid	$ 375.0	$ 239.7	$ 234.7
Schedule of Noncash Investing and Financing Activities			
Issuance of treasury stock and debt for acquisitions	$ 105.1	$ 103.9	$ 328.2
Liabilities assumed/disposed of in connection with acquisitions/sales of businesses	$ 231.8	$ 446.8	$ 300.0
Issuance of treasury stock for compensation awards and conversion of debentures	$ 13.5	$ 9.3	$ 26.4
Additions of capital leases	$ 18.1	$ 15.7	$ 4.3

See accompanying Notes to Consolidated Financial Statements.

PEPSICO, INC. 1990 FINANCIAL REVIEW

Management's Analysis–Cash Flows

Cash flow activity in 1990 reflected strong cash flows from continuing operations of $2.1 billion and net proceeds from issuances of debt of $393 million. Major funding needs included purchases of property, plant and equipment (PP&E) of $1.2 billion, acquisitions and investments in affiliates of $631 million and dividends of $294 million.

Net Cash Generated by Continuing Operations

One of PepsiCo's most significant financial strengths is its internal cash generation capability. In fact, in 1990 each industry segment generated cash from operations sufficient to fund its PP&E purchases, acquisitions and affiliate investments, with cash flows from domestic businesses funding international uses of cash. As the chart below illustrates, in each of the past three years, net cash generated by continuing operations has been well in excess of amounts required to fund purchases of PP&E and dividend payments. This excess cash flow has been decreasing over the last three years due principally to major PP&E investment programs that will continue into 1991. Excess cash flow is expected to decline in 1991 but resume growth in the following years.

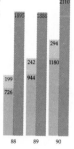

Net Cash Generated by Continuing Operations vs. Purchases of PP&E and Dividends Paid
($ In Millions)

2110
1895 1886
294
242 1180
199 944
726

88   89   90

■ Net Cash Generated
■ PP&E Purchases
■ Dividends Paid

Net cash generated by continuing operations in 1990 increased $224 million or 12% over 1989, while 1989 was about even with 1988. The joint venture stock offering gain relates to the initial public offering of a KFC joint venture in Japan. (See Note to Consolidated Financial Statements on page 44.) The comparisons of 1990 to 1989 changes in the individual components of operating working capital are affected by numerous increases and decreases in various accounts, none of which had a significant impact on cash generated by continuing operations. The 1989 decrease in cash flows provided by operating working capital principally reflected additional investment required to support sales growth in the comparatively more working capital intensive bottling and snack foods businesses acquired. The increase of $112 million and $143 million in depreciation and amortization noncash charges in 1990 and 1989, respectively, reflected growth in PP&E as well as the amortization of goodwill and other intangibles and depreciation expense associated with acquisitions.

Investing Activities

PepsiCo's investing activities over the past three years reflected strategic spending in all three industry segments through acquisitions, investments in affiliates and purchases of PP&E. Acquisitions and investments in affiliates for cash totaled $631 million in 1990 and included an equity investment in a cookie business in Mexico, several domestic and Canadian franchised soft drink bottlers and several franchised restaurant operators. PepsiCo continues to seek opportunities to strengthen its position in its domestic and international industry segments through strategic acquisitions. Purchases of PP&E are expected to increase from $1.2 billion in 1990 to approximately $1.5 billion in 1991. About 40% of that amount is targeted for the restaurants segment, with the balance evenly divided between the soft drinks and snack foods segments. The planned PP&E spending reflects restaurant unit expansion, and increased capacity for worldwide soft drinks bottling and snack foods manufacturing operations. The net purchases of short-term investments in 1990 reflected growth in the Puerto Rico and other offshore portfolios due to cash flows generated by worldwide soft drink concentrate and international snack foods operations. The net sales of short-term investments in 1989 reflected the $331 million liquidation of certain offshore portfolios to finance a portion of the purchase price of the U.K. operations.

Financing Activities

Financing activities decreased $2.4 billion from 1989 reflecting lower acquisition-related borrowing in 1990. The 1989 acquisitions were initially funded primarily through short-term borrowings. Long-term refinancing of these borrowings has been integrated into PepsiCo's overall financing strategies and activities.

In September 1990 PepsiCo filed a shelf registration statement with the Securities and Exchange Commission covering potential debt issuances of $1.5 billion. Debt issuances under this shelf registration, all occurring after year-end, totaled $1.0 billion through February 1991, with terms of one to three years. PepsiCo intends to file a shelf registration in the near future covering potential debt issuances of $2.5 billion. Debt issuances under these shelf registrations are intended principally to refinance existing short-term borrowings.

Cash dividends declared were a record $302 million in 1990 and $253 million in 1989. PepsiCo targets a dividend payout of approximately one-third of the prior year's earnings, thus retaining sufficient earnings to enhance productive capability and provide financial resources for growth opportunities.

Share repurchase decisions are evaluated considering the target capital structure and other investment opportunities. In 1990, PepsiCo repurchased 6,310,100 shares at a cost of $148 million. The number of shares repurchased approximates shares issued in conjunction with 1990 acquisitions as well as shares expected to be issued in conjunction with the probable acquisition of the franchised domestic KFC operations of Collins Foods International, Inc. in 1991. Including these repurchases, 14.4 million shares have been purchased under the 45 million share repurchase authority granted by PepsiCo's Board of Directors in 1987.

PEPSICO, INC. 1990 FINANCIAL REVIEW

Consolidated Statement of Shareholders' Equity

(shares in thousands, dollars in millions, except per share amounts)
PepsiCo, Inc. and Subsidiaries
Fifty-two weeks ended December 29, 1990 and December 30, 1989 and fifty-three weeks ended December 31, 1988

| | Capital Stock | | | | Capital in Excess of Par Value | Retained Earnings | Currency Translation Adjustment | Total |
| | Issued | | Treasury | | | | | |
	Shares	Amount	Shares	Amount				
Shareholders' Equity, December 26, 1987	863,083	$14.4	(81,844)	$(553.6)	$280.9	$2,776.7	$ (9.8)	$2,508.6
1988 Net income						762.2		762.2
Cash dividends declared (per share-$0.27)........................						(209.2)		(209.2)
Shares reissued to Employee Stock Ownership Plan....................			365	2.5	1.6			4.1
Payment of compensation awards and exercise of stock options			972	6.6	0.5			7.1
Conversion of debentures			3,047	20.7	(2.6)			18.1
Translation adjustments							33.8	33.8
Purchase of treasury stock			(6,198)	(71.8)				(71.8)
Shares issued in connection with acquisitions			9,009	85.9	22.2			108.1
Shareholders' Equity, December 31, 1988	863,083	$14.4	(74,649)	$(509.7)	$302.6	$3,329.7	$ 24.0	$3,161.0
1989 Net income						901.4		901.4
Cash dividends declared (per share-$0.32)........................						(252.7)		(252.7)
Payment of compensation awards and exercise of stock options			901	6.2	2.6			8.8
Conversion of debentures			456	3.1	0.8			3.9
Translation adjustments							42.2	42.2
Shares issued in connection with an acquisition........................			1,266	8.6	17.9			26.5
Shareholders' Equity, December 30, 1989	863,083	$14.4	(72,026)	$(491.8)	$323.9	$3,978.4	$ 66.2	$3,891.1
1990 Net income						1,076.9		1,076.9
Cash dividends declared (per share-$0.38)........................						(302.3)		(302.3)
Shares reissued to Employee Stock Ownership Plan....................			8	0.1	0.2			0.3
Payment of compensation awards and exercise of stock options			1,072	7.8	9.1			16.9
Conversion of debentures			549	3.9	1.7			5.6
Translation adjustments							317.0	317.0
Purchase of treasury stock			(6,310)	(147.7)				(147.7)
Shares issued in connection with acquisitions			2,013	16.3	30.1			46.4
Shareholders' Equity, December 29, 1990 .	**863,083**	**$14.4**	**(74,694)**	**$(611.4)**	**$365.0**	**$4,753.0**	**$383.2**	**$4,904.2**

Certain amounts above have been restated to reflect the 1990 three-for-one stock split.
See accompanying Notes to Consolidated Financial Statements.

PEPSICO, INC. 1990 FINANCIAL REVIEW

Notes to Consolidated Financial Statements

(tabular dollars in millions except per share amounts)

Summary of Significant Accounting Policies

Principles of Consolidation. The financial statements reflect the consolidated accounts of PepsiCo, Inc. and its wholly-owned subsidiaries. All significant intercompany accounts and transactions have been eliminated. Investments in affiliates in which PepsiCo exercises significant influence but not control are accounted for by the equity method, and the equity in net income is included in the Consolidated Statement of Income under the caption "Selling, administrative and other expenses." Certain reclassifications were made to 1989 and 1988 amounts to conform with the 1990 presentation.

Stock Split. On July 26, 1990, PepsiCo's Board of Directors authorized a three-for-one stock split of PepsiCo's Capital Stock effective for shareholders of record at the close of business on August 10, 1990. The number of authorized shares was also increased from 600 million to 1.8 billion. The Consolidated Financial Statements for 1990, as well as all other share data in this report, reflect this stock split and the increase in authorized shares. Prior year amounts also have been restated for the stock split. The par value remained 1⅔ cents per share, with capital in excess of par value reduced by the total par value of the additional shares.

Goodwill and Other Intangibles. Goodwill and other intangibles arose from the allocation of purchase prices of businesses acquired, with the largest portion representing the value of Pepsi-Cola franchise rights reacquired in the acquisitions of franchised domestic soft drink bottling operations. Goodwill and other intangibles are amortized on a straight-line basis over appropriate periods generally ranging from 20 to 40 years. Accumulated amortization was $548 million and $359 million at year-end 1990 and 1989, respectively.

Marketing Costs. Marketing costs are included in the Consolidated Statement of Income under the caption "Selling, administrative and other expenses." Costs of materials in inventory and prepayments are deferred, and certain promotional discounts are expensed as incurred. All other costs of advertising and other marketing and promotional programs are charged to expense ratably over the year in which incurred, generally in relation to sales.

Classification of Restaurant Operating Expenses. Operating expenses incurred at the restaurant unit level consist primarily of food and related packaging costs, labor associated with food preparation and customer service, and overhead expenses. For purposes of the Consolidated Statement of Income, food and packaging costs as well as all labor-related expenses are classified as "Cost of sales," and all other unit level expenses are classified as "Selling, administrative and other expenses."

Cash Equivalents. Cash equivalents are comprised of funds temporarily invested (with original maturities not exceeding three months) as part of PepsiCo's management of day-to-day operating cash receipts and disbursements. All other investment portfolios, primarily held offshore, are classified as short-term investments.

Net Income Per Share. Net income per share is computed by dividing net income by the weighted average number of shares and share equivalents outstanding during each year.

Research and Development Expenses. Research and development expenses, which are expensed as incurred, were $101 million, $91 million and $84 million in 1990, 1989 and 1988, respectively.

Acquisitions and Investments in Affiliates

During 1990 PepsiCo completed several acquisitions and affiliate investments in all three industry segments aggregating $736 million, comprised of $631 million in cash, $59 million in notes and $46 million in PepsiCo Capital Stock. The activity included acquisitions of a 54% equity interest in a Mexican cookie business, franchised soft drink bottlers in Canada and franchised domestic restaurant operators.

During 1989 PepsiCo completed a number of acquisitions with purchase prices aggregating $3.4 billion, principally for cash. The acquisitions included the franchised domestic soft drink bottling operations of General Cinema Corporation (GC Beverage), acquired on March 23, 1989 for $1.77 billion, and Smiths Crisps Limited and Walkers Crisps Holdings Limited (the U.K. operations), two snack chips companies in the United Kingdom, acquired on July 1, 1989 for $1.34 billion. The remaining activity consisted primarily of acquisitions of franchised domestic soft drink bottlers and restaurant operators.

Acquisition and affiliate investment activity in 1988 aggregated $1.8 billion, principally comprised of over $1.4 billion in cash, $220 million in notes and $108 million in PepsiCo Capital Stock. The majority of these acquisitions were franchised domestic soft drink bottlers, the largest of which were the bottling operations of Grand Metropolitan Incorporated acquired on August 4, 1988 for $705 million in cash. On December 31, 1987 PepsiCo also acquired a 20% equity interest in Pepsi-Cola General Bottlers, Inc. (the remaining equity of which is owned by Whitman Corporation), contributing $177 million in cash and certain previously consolidated bottling operations with an aggregate carrying value of $17 million.

The acquisitions have been accounted for by the purchase method; accordingly, their results are included in the Consolidated Financial Statements from their respective dates of acquisition.

The following table presents the unaudited pro forma combined results of PepsiCo and the 1989 acquisitions of GC Beverage and the U.K. operations as if they had occurred at the beginning of 1989 and 1988, and a substantial majority of the 1988 acquisitions as if they had occurred at the beginning of 1988. The aggregate impact of acquisitions in 1990 and all other acquisitions for 1989 and 1988 was not material to PepsiCo's net sales, income or income per share; accordingly, no related pro forma information is provided. The pro forma information does not necessarily represent what the actual consolidated results would have been for these periods and is not intended to be indicative of future results.

	1989	1988
Net sales	$15,620.2	$13,930.9
Net income	$ 859.3	$ 649.3
Per share	$ 1.08	$ 0.82

PEPSICO, INC. 1990 FINANCIAL REVIEW

Business Segments
Information regarding industry segments and geographic areas of operations is provided on pages 34 and 35.

Joint Venture Stock Offering
PepsiCo's Kentucky Fried Chicken joint venture in Japan (KFC-J) completed an initial public offering (IPO) to Japanese investors on August 21, 1990. KFC-J is a joint venture whose principal shareholders are Mitsubishi Corporation and PepsiCo. The IPO consisted of 6.5 million shares of stock in KFC-J. Each principal shareholder sold 2.25 million shares and an additional two million new shares were sold by KFC-J. As a result of these transactions, each principal shareholder's interest declined from 48.7% to 30.5%.

PepsiCo's sale of 2.25 million shares generated pretax cash proceeds of $129.6 million. The resulting one-time gain from the IPO of $118.2 million ($53.0 after-tax or $0.07 per share) is comprised of a $94.3 million gain ($42.3 after-tax) from PepsiCo's sale of the 2.25 million shares and a $23.9 million ($10.7 after-tax) noncash equity gain from the sale of the two million new shares by KFC-J.

Discontinued Operation Charge
The discontinued operation charge of $14.0 million ($13.7 after-tax or $0.02 per share) represents additional amounts provided in 1990 for various pending lawsuits and claims relating to a business sold in a prior year. Substantially all of the charge is a capital loss for which PepsiCo derives no current tax benefit.

Inventories
Inventories are valued at the lower of cost (computed on the average, first-in, first-out or last-in, first-out methods) or net realizable value. Inventories computed on the last-in, first-out (LIFO) method comprised 54% and 56% of inventories at year-end 1990 and 1989, respectively.

	1990	1989
Raw materials, supplies and in-process ..	$315.4	$295.1
Finished goods	285.3	266.5
Total (approximates current cost)	600.7	561.6
Excess of current cost over LIFO cost	(14.9)	(15.5)
	$585.8	$546.1

Property, Plant and Equipment
Property, plant and equipment are stated at cost. Depreciation is calculated principally on a straight-line basis over the estimated useful lives of the assets. Depreciation and amortization expense in 1990, 1989 and 1988 was $686 million, $610 million and $547 million, respectively.

	1990	1989
Land	$ 785.4	$ 702.0
Buildings and improvements	3,173.7	2,815.6
Capital leases, primarily buildings	265.4	241.9
Machinery and equipment	4,753.2	4,058.9
	8,977.7	7,818.4
Accumulated depreciation and amortization	(3,266.8)	(2,688.2)
	$5,710.9	$5,130.2

Leases
PepsiCo has noncancelable commitments under both capital and operating leases, primarily for restaurant units. Certain of these units have been subleased to restaurant franchisees. Lease commitments on capital and operating leases expire at various dates through 2032.

Future minimum lease commitments and sublease receivables under noncancelable leases are as follows:

	Commitments		Sublease Receivables	
			Direct	
	Capital	Operating	Financing	Operating
1991	$ 39.2	$ 179.2	$11.5	$ 8.2
1992	35.1	160.9	10.9	7.8
1993	32.3	144.3	9.2	7.4
1994	30.6	130.4	9.0	6.9
1995	28.2	122.1	6.7	6.2
Later years .	175.3	582.8	22.1	29.1
	$340.7	$1,319.7	$69.4	$65.6

At year-end 1990 the present value of minimum lease payments for capital leases was $194 million, after deducting $1 million for estimated executory costs (taxes, maintenance and insurance) and $146 million representing imputed interest. The present value of minimum receivables under direct financing subleases was $46 million after deducting $23 million of unearned interest income.

Rental expense and income were as follows:

	Rental	
	Expense	Income
1990	$272.7	$10.5
1989	236.9	14.2
1988	219.7	13.2

Included in the above amounts were contingent rental expense of $21.4 million, $20.8 million and $16.8 million and contingent rental income of $4.9 million, $4.5 million and $4.6 million in 1990, 1989 and 1988, respectively. Contingent rentals are based on sales by restaurants in excess of levels stipulated in the lease agreements.

PEPSICO, INC. 1990 FINANCIAL REVIEW

Short-term Borrowings and Long-term Debt	**1990**	1989
Short-term Borrowings		
Commercial paper (7.9% and 8.7% weighted average interest rate at year-end 1990 and 1989, respectively)	**$3,168.8**	$3,081.8
Current maturities of long-term debt issuances	**1,085.0**	316.8
Notes	**624.8**	594.8
Other borrowings	**247.9**	422.9
Amount reclassified to long-term debt **(A)**	**(3,500.0)**	(3,550.0)
	$1,626.5	$ 866.3
Long-term Debt		
Short-term borrowings, reclassified **(A)**	**$3,500.0**	$3,550.0
Notes due 1991 through 1998 (7.9% weighted average interest rate at year-end 1990 and 1989) **(B)**	**1,513.7**	871.1
Zero coupon notes, $1.1 billion due 1991-2012 (14.0% semi-annual weighted average yield to maturity at year-end 1990 and 1989)	**348.1**	308.7
Swiss franc perpetual Foreign Interest Payment bonds **(C)**	**209.9**	209.1
European Currency Units 7⅝% and 7⅜% notes due 1990 and 1992 **(D)**	**135.2**	239.3
Pound sterling 9⅛% notes due 1993 **(D)**	**115.5**	96.8
Swiss franc 5¼% bearer bonds due 1995 **(D)**	**104.7**	86.9
Australian dollar notes due 1990 (13.3% weighted average interest rate at year-end 1989)	**–**	81.5
Italian lire 10½% notes due 1991 **(D)**	**88.8**	79.0
Canadian dollar 8¾% notes due 1991 **(B)**	**64.6**	64.6
Capital lease obligations (See Note on page 44.)	**193.8**	179.3
Other, due 1991-2020 (8.9% and 9.0% weighted average interest rate at year-end 1990 and 1989, respectively)	**410.8**	327.6
	6,685.1	6,093.9
Less current maturities of long-term debt issuances	**(1,085.0)**	(316.8)
Total long-term debt	**$5,600.1**	$5,777.1

Long-term debt is carried net of any related discount or premium and unamortized debt issuance costs. The debt agreements include various restrictions, none of which is presently significant to PepsiCo.

The annual maturities of long-term debt through 1995, excluding capital lease obligations and the reclassified short-term borrowings, are: 1991-$1.1 billion; 1992-$531 million; 1993-$474 million; 1994-$120 million and 1995-$134 million.

(A) At year-end 1990 $3.5 billion of short-term borrowings were classified as long-term, reflecting PepsiCo's intent and ability to refinance these borrowings on a long-term basis, through either long-term debt issuances or rollover of existing short-term borrowings. At year-end 1990 and 1989, PepsiCo had revolving credit agreements aggregating $3.5 billion and $3.6 billion, respectively, with the current agreements covering potential borrowings through 1994 and 1995. These available credit facilities provide the ability to refinance short-term borrowings.

(B) PepsiCo has entered into interest rate swap agreements to effectively convert $679 million of fixed interest rate debt issuances to variable rate debt with a weighted average interest rate of 7.8% at year-end 1990. The differential to be paid or received on interest rate swaps is accrued as interest rates change and is charged or credited to interest expense over the life of the agreements. Due to the frequency of interest payments and receipts, PepsiCo's credit risk related to interest rate swaps is not significant.

(C) The coupon rate of the Swiss franc 400 million perpetual Foreign Interest Payment bonds issued in 1986 is 7½% through 1996. The interest payments are made in U.S. dollars at a fixed contractual exchange rate. The bonds have no stated maturity date. At the end of each 10-year period after the issuance of the bonds, PepsiCo and the bondholders each have the right to cause redemption of the bonds. If not redeemed, the coupon rate will be adjusted based on the prevailing yield of 10-year U.S. Treasury Securities. The principal of the bonds is denominated in Swiss francs. PepsiCo can and intends to limit the ultimate redemption amount to the U.S. dollar proceeds at issuance, which is the basis of the carrying value in both years.

(D) PepsiCo has entered into currency exchange agreements to hedge its foreign currency exposure on these issues of non-U.S. dollar denominated debt. At year-end 1990, the agreements effectively established U.S. dollar liabilities of $49 million with a weighted average fixed interest rate of 9.9% and $294 million with a weighted average variable interest rate of 7.5%. The carrying values of these agreements, which are based on current exchange rates, aggregated $101 million in receivables at year-end 1990. Changes in these values resulting from exchange rate movements are offset by the changes in the carrying values of the underlying foreign currency denominated obligations, which are also based on current exchange rates.

The counterparties to PepsiCo's interest rate swaps and currency exchange agreements discussed above consist of a diversified group of financial institutions. PepsiCo is exposed to credit risk to the extent of nonperformance by these counterparties; however, PepsiCo regularly monitors its positions and the credit ratings of these counterparties and considers the risk of default to be remote.

PEPSICO, INC. 1990 FINANCIAL REVIEW

Nonrecourse Obligation

In 1987 PepsiCo entered into an agreement related to a non-recourse obligation (the Obligation) under which it received net proceeds of $299 million. The Obligation and related interest are payable solely from future royalty payments from certain independent domestic franchisees of one of PepsiCo's restaurant chains for a period not to exceed 10 years. The Obligation carries a variable interest rate (8.4% as of December 29, 1990) based upon a commercial paper rate. Under the terms of the agreement, principal repayments during the first five years can be readvanced; as it is PepsiCo's intent to elect this provision, the entire Obligation is considered noncurrent. Principal repayments, net of amounts readvanced, are estimated to be $244 million over the next five years.

Income Taxes

Provision for income taxes on income from continuing operations:

		1990	1989	1988
Current–	Federal	$301.5	$221.7	$235.2
	Foreign	126.6	89.5	52.8
	State	62.3	38.0	40.6
		490.4	349.2	328.6
Deferred–	Federal	66.0	95.7	37.4
	Foreign	12.5	1.2	1.7
	State	7.9	3.0	(2.7)
		86.4	99.9	36.4
		$576.8	$449.1	$365.0

The deferred income tax provision, which results from differences in the timing of recognition of revenue and expense for financial reporting and tax purposes, included amounts related to depreciation of property, plant and equipment of $34.5 million, $36.3 million and $44.0 million and amortization of intangibles of $46.0 million, $47.3 million and $15.6 million in 1990, 1989 and 1988, respectively.

U.S. and foreign income from continuing operations before income taxes:

	1990	1989	1988
U.S.	$ 915.5	$ 843.4	$ 773.4
Foreign	751.9	507.1	353.8
	$1,667.4	$1,350.5	$1,127.2

Consistent with the allocation of income for tax purposes, approximately 50% of the income arising from the sale of soft drink concentrates manufactured in Puerto Rico is included in Foreign in the above table. Under the terms of a Puerto Rico tax incentive grant that was amended in 1989 and expires in 2006, the allocated soft drink concentrate manufacturing profits and all investment earnings in Puerto Rico were taxed at rates of approximately 7% and 4% in 1990 and 1989, respectively, with a nominal tax provided in 1988. The 7% Puerto Rico tax is applicable through 2006.

PepsiCo's soft drink concentrate manufacturing profits in Ireland were exempt from income tax through mid-1989 when a 10% tax, applicable through 2010, became effective.

Deferred taxes were not provided on unremitted earnings of foreign subsidiaries that are intended to be indefinitely reinvested. These unremitted earnings aggregated approximately $605 million at year-end 1990, exclusive of amounts that if remitted in the future would result in little or no tax under current tax laws and the amended Puerto Rico tax incentive grant.

Reconciliation of the U.S. federal statutory tax rate to PepsiCo's effective tax rate on income from continuing operations:

	1990	1989	1988
U.S. federal statutory tax rate	34.0%	34.0%	34.0%
State income tax net of federal tax benefit	1.9	2.0	2.2
Earnings in jurisdictions taxed at lower rates (principally Puerto Rico and Ireland)	(3.9)	(3.9)	(3.7)
Nondeductible amortization of goodwill and other intangibles	1.6	2.0	1.4
Tax basis difference related to joint venture stock offering	1.6	–	–
Other, net	(0.6)	(0.8)	(1.5)
Effective tax rate	34.6%	33.3%	32.4%

Deferred income taxes reflected in the Consolidated Balance Sheet under the caption "Deferred Income Taxes" included amounts related to timing differences of $741.9 million and $635.9 million and Safe Harbor leases of $200.9 million and $221.0 million in 1990 and 1989, respectively. Prepaid income taxes of $11.6 million in 1990 are reflected under the Consolidated Balance Sheet caption "Prepaid expenses and other current assets." Current deferred income taxes of $8.2 million in 1989 are reflected under the Consolidated Balance Sheet caption "Other current liabilities."

In 1981 and 1982 PepsiCo invested in Safe Harbor leases (the Leases). These transactions, which do not impact the provision for income taxes, decrease income taxes payable over the initial years of the Leases and increase them over the later years. The deferred federal income taxes payable related to the Leases are based on the current U.S. federal statutory tax rate. Taxes payable related to the Leases are estimated to be $40 million over the next five years.

In December 1989 the Financial Accounting Standards Board (the FASB) amended Statement No. 96 on Accounting for Income Taxes to extend the required adoption date to 1992. As the FASB continues to review and evaluate possible amendments, including a further extension of the adoption date, PepsiCo is unable to predict the final FASB requirements and therefore cannot reasonably estimate the effects of adoption.

PEPSICO, INC. 1990 FINANCIAL REVIEW

Retirement Plans

PepsiCo has noncontributory defined benefit pension plans covering substantially all full-time domestic employees as well as contributory and noncontributory defined benefit pension plans covering certain international employees. Benefits generally are based on years of service and compensation or stated amounts for each year of service. PepsiCo funds the domestic plans in amounts not less than minimum statutory funding requirements nor more than the maximum amount that can be deducted for federal income tax purposes. International plans are funded in amounts sufficient to comply with local statutory requirements. The plans' assets consist principally of equity securities, government and corporate debt securities and other fixed income obligations. Capital Stock of PepsiCo accounted for approximately 18.1% and 16.8% of the total market value of the plans' assets at year-end 1990 and 1989, respectively.

In 1989, PepsiCo acquired Smiths Crisps Limited and Walkers Crisps Holdings Limited, two snack chips companies in the United Kingdom (the U.K. operations). The U.K. operations' employees were covered by various plans, including multiemployer plans. Pension expense and the required disclosures under SFAS 87 were not determinable until completion in late 1990 of a preliminary allocation of the assets of those plans, the transfer of relevant employees to separate plans and the appropriate actuarial valuations. Accordingly, the 1990 information presented below includes both the domestic plans and the U.K. operations' plans, while the 1989 and 1988 information includes only the domestic plans.

Other international plans are not significant in the aggregate and therefore are not included in the disclosures below. None of these other international plans was significantly over or underfunded at year-end 1990.

The net pension expense (credit) for company-sponsored plans (the Plans) included the following components:

	1990	1989	1988
Service cost of benefits earned.............	$48.1	$ 32.0	$ 24.8
Interest cost on projected benefit obligations	63.3	47.1	40.0
Return on the Plans' assets:			
Actual	(27.0)	(154.6)	(86.1)
Deferred gain (loss) ...	(55.9)	89.9	23.5
	(82.9)	(64.7)	(62.6)
Amortization of net transition gain	(19.0)	(19.0)	(19.0)
Pension expense (credit) .	$ 9.5	$ (4.6)	$(16.8)

For certain Plans accumulated benefits exceeded the assets, but the related amounts were not significant. Reconciliations of the funded status of the Plans to the prepaid pension liability included in the Consolidated Balance Sheet are as follows:

	1990	1989
Actuarial present value of benefit obligations:		
Vested benefits....................	$(549.9)	$(449.0)
Nonvested benefits	(90.8)	(75.0)
Accumulated benefit obligation	(640.7)	(524.0)
Effect of projected compensation increases	(101.9)	(92.1)
Projected benefit obligation	(742.6)	(616.1)
Plan assets at fair value	985.7	869.8
Plan assets in excess of projected benefit obligation.....................	243.1	253.7
Unrecognized prior service cost	42.4	26.2
Unrecognized net gain	(84.6)	(104.0)
Unrecognized net transition gain	(148.1)	(167.1)
Prepaid pension liability	$ 52.8	$ 8.8
Included in:		
"Investments in Affiliates and Other Assets"	$ 85.3	$ 31.2
"Other current liabilities"	(17.0)	(14.3)
"Other Liabilities and Deferred Credits"	(15.5)	(8.1)
	$ 52.8	$ 8.8

The assumptions used in computing the information above were as follows:

	1990	1989	1988
Discount rate-pension expense (credit)	9.1%	10.1%	10.0%
Expected long-term rate of return on plan assets	10.2%	10.0%	10.0%
Discount rate-projected benefit obligation	9.5%	9.0%	10.1%
Future compensation growth rate	5.0%-7.0%	5.0%-7.0%	5.0%-7.0%

The 1990 discount rates and rate of return represent weighted averages, reflecting the combined assumptions for domestic and the U.K. operations' plans in 1990.

Full-time domestic employees not covered by the Plans generally are covered by multiemployer plans as part of collective-bargaining agreements. Pension expense for these multiemployer plans was not significant in the aggregate.

PepsiCo provides health care and life insurance benefits to certain retired nonunion employees, the costs of which are expensed as incurred. In December 1990, the FASB issued Statement of Financial Accounting Standards No. 106 (SFAS 106), "Employers' Accounting for Postretirement Benefits Other Than Pensions," which requires the recognition of postretirement benefit expenses on an accrual basis. PepsiCo has not yet determined the impact of accounting for these costs on an accrual basis; however, the 1990 expense for health care claims incurred and life insurance premiums paid was $20.4 million. PepsiCo expects to implement SFAS 106 by its required adoption date in 1993.

PEPSICO, INC. 1990 FINANCIAL REVIEW

Employee Incentive Plans

In 1989 PepsiCo established the PepsiCo SharePower Stock Option Plan. Under this plan, which was approved by the Board of Directors, all employees who meet eligibility requirements may be granted stock options. Executive officers, part-time and short-service employees principally comprise the non-eligible group. Executive officers may be granted similar benefits under the 1987 Long-Term Incentive Plan. A stock option represents the right, exercisable in the future, to purchase one share of PepsiCo Capital Stock at the fair market value on the date of the grant. The number of options granted is based on a percentage of the employee's annual earnings. The grants may be made annually, have a term of 10 years from the grant date and generally become exercisable ratably over the five years after the grant date. SharePower options were granted to approximately 91,000 and 77,000 employees in 1990 and 1989, respectively.

The shareholder-approved 1987 Long-Term Incentive Plan (the Plan), effective January 1, 1988, provides long-term incentives to key employees through stock options, performance shares, stock appreciation rights (SARs) and incentive stock units (Units). The Plan authorizes up to a maximum of 54 million shares of PepsiCo Capital Stock to be purchased or paid pursuant to grants by the Compensation Committee of the Board of Directors (the Committee), which is composed of outside directors. There were 34 million and 43 million shares available for future grants at year-end 1990 and 1989, respectively. Payment of awards other than stock options is made in cash and/or PepsiCo Capital Stock as determined by the Committee.

Under the Plan, a stock option is exercisable for a specified period generally falling between 1 and 15 years from the date of grant. A performance share, equivalent to one share of PepsiCo Capital Stock, generally vests and is payable four years after the date of grant, contingent upon attainment of prescribed performance criteria. Employees may receive partial performance share awards if they become eligible for new or increased awards subsequent to a grant. A stock option is granted with each performance share. Beginning with the 1988 award, a specified number of additional stock options are granted in lieu of a performance share. These additional stock options may be converted to a performance share at the employee's election within 60 days from the date of grant.

SARs, available to certain senior management employees holding stock options, may be granted in the year the related options become exercisable. They allow the employees to surrender an option for an amount equal to the appreciation between the option exercise price and the fair market value of PepsiCo Capital Stock on the date the SAR is exercised. SARs expire no later than the expiration date of the related options. The maximum number of stock options that can be surrendered for SARs is 30% of outstanding options that have been exercisable for more than one year. During 1990, 147,570 SARs were granted. SARs outstanding at year-end 1990 and 1989 were 272,568 and 168,954, respectively.

Under the Plan, eligible middle management employees were granted Units, and beginning in 1989, stock options are granted in lieu of the Units. A Unit is equivalent in value to the fair market value of one share of PepsiCo Capital Stock at specified dates over a six-year vesting period from the date of grant. Units outstanding at year-end 1990 and 1989 were 585,149 and 671,902, respectively.

The combined estimated costs of performance shares, SARs and Units, expensed over the applicable vesting periods of the awards, were $13 million, $25 million and $16 million in 1990, 1989 and 1988, respectively.

Award activity for 1990 and 1989 was as follows:

	SharePower Plan	Long-Term Incentive Plan	
	Stock Options	Stock Options	Performance Shares
		(000's)	
Outstanding at December 31, 1988.	–	17,480	2,918
Granted.	10,742	2,109	15
Exercised/Paid	–	(614)	–
Surrendered for performance shares . .	–	(49)	16
Surrendered for SARs. . .	–	(29)	
Cancelled.	(697)	(572)	(147)
Outstanding at December 30, 1989.	10,045	18,325	2,802
Granted.	8,808	12,179	–
Exercised/Paid	(37)	(868)	(2,346)
Surrendered for performance shares . .	–	(1,228)	409
Surrendered for SARs. . .	–	(44)	–
Cancelled.	(1,589)	(1,490)	(69)
Outstanding at December 29, 1990.	17,227	26,874	796
Exercisable at December 29, 1990.	1,840	4,139	

Option prices per share:

	SharePower	Long-Term Incentive
Exercised during 1990	$17.58	$4.11 to $20.00
Exercised during 1989	–	$4.11 to $ 8.75
Outstanding at year-end 1990	$17.58 to $25.96	$4.11 to $26.44

The above Long-Term Incentive Plan activity includes grants to middle management employees of 1,070,436 and 850,785 stock options in 1990 and 1989, respectively, 692,880 of which were exercisable at year-end 1990.

Contingencies

PepsiCo is subject to various claims and legal contingencies. While the ultimate liability that could result from these matters cannot be determined presently, management believes such liability will not have a material adverse affect on PepsiCo's business or financial condition.

At year-end 1990 PepsiCo was contingently liable under direct and indirect guarantees aggregating $97 million. The guarantees are primarily issued to support financial arrangements of certain restaurant and soft drink bottling franchisees and PepsiCo joint ventures. PepsiCo manages the risk associated with these guarantees by performing appropriate credit reviews in addition to retaining certain rights as a franchisor or joint venture partner.

PEPSICO, INC. 1990 FINANCIAL REVIEW

Management's Responsibility for Financial Statements

To Our Shareholders:

Management is responsible for the preparation, integrity and objectivity of the consolidated financial statements and related notes. To meet these responsibilities, we maintain a system of internal control, supported by formal policies and procedures, which include an active Code of Conduct program intended to ensure key employees adhere to the highest standards of personal and professional integrity. PepsiCo's internal audit function monitors and reports on the adequacy of and compliance with our internal controls, policies and procedures. Although no cost effective internal control system will preclude all errors and irregularities, we believe the established system of internal control provides reasonable assurance that assets are safeguarded, transactions are recorded in accordance with our policies and the financial information is reliable.

The consolidated financial statements have been prepared in conformity with generally accepted accounting principles applied on a consistent basis, and include amounts based upon our estimates and judgments, as required. The consolidated financial statements have been audited by our independent auditors, who have expressed their opinions with respect to the fairness of the statements. Their audits included a review of the system of internal control and tests of transactions to the extent they considered necessary to render their opinions.

The Audit Committee of the Board of Directors is composed solely of outside directors. The Audit Committee meets periodi-

cally with our independent auditors, PepsiCo internal auditors and management to review accounting, auditing, internal control and financial reporting matters. Both our independent auditors and internal auditors have free access to the Audit Committee.

Wayne Calloway

Wayne Calloway
Chairman of the Board and Chief Executive Officer

Robert H. Dettmer

Robert G. Dettmer
Executive Vice President and Chief Financial Officer

Robert L. Carleton

Robert L. Carleton
Senior Vice President and Controller

Report of KPMG Peat Marwick Independent Auditors

Board of Directors and Shareholders
PepsiCo, Inc.

We have audited the accompanying consolidated balance sheet of PepsiCo, Inc. and subsidiaries as of December 29, 1990, and the related consolidated statements of income, shareholders' equity, and cash flows for the year then ended, appearing on pages 34, 35, 36, 38, 40, 42 through 48. These financial statements are the responsibility of PepsiCo, Inc.'s management. Our responsibility is to express an opinion on these financial statements based on our audit. The consolidated financial statements of PepsiCo, Inc. and subsidiaries as of December 30, 1989 and for each of the years in the two-year period ended December 30, 1989 were audited by other auditors whose report, dated February 6, 1990, expressed an unqualified opinion on those statements.

We conducted our audit in accordance with generally accepted auditing standards. Those standards require that we plan and perform the audit to obtain reasonable assurance about whether the financial statements are free of material misstatement. An audit includes examining, on a test basis, evidence supporting the

amounts and disclosures in the financial statements. An audit also includes assessing the accounting principles used and significant estimates made by management, as well as evaluating the overall financial statement presentation. We believe that our audit provides a reasonable basis for our opinion.

In our opinion, the financial statements referred to above present fairly, in all material respects, the consolidated financial position of PepsiCo, Inc. and subsidiaries at December 29, 1990, and the results of its operations and its cash flows for the year then ended in conformity with generally accepted accounting principles.

KPMG Peat Marwick

New York, New York
February 5, 1991

PEPSICO, INC. 1990 FINANCIAL REVIEW

Selected Financial Data

(in millions except per share, shareholder and employee amounts, unaudited) PepsiCo, Inc. and Subsidiaries	Compounded 10-Year 1980-90	Compounded 5-Year 1985-90	Annual 1-Year 1989-90	1990	1989
Summary of Operations					
Net sales	13.6%	18.6%	16.8%	$17,802.7	$15,242.4
Cost of sales and operating expenses				15,628.9	13,459.5 (c)
Interest expense				688.5	609.6
Interest income				(182.1)	(177.2)
				16,135.3	13,891.9
Income from continuing operations before income taxes	14.4%	19.5%	23.5%	1,667.4	1,350.5
Provision for income taxes				576.8	449.1
Income from continuing operations	16.6%	20.7%	21.0%	$ 1,090.6	$ 901.4
Net income	15.2%	14.6%	19.5%	$ 1,076.9	$ 901.4
Income per share from continuing operations	16.8%	21.9%	21.2%	$ 1.37	$ 1.13 (c)
Net income per share	15.5%	15.7%	19.5%	$ 1.35	$ 1.13
Cash dividends declared per share	10.6%	14.5%	19.7%	$ 0.383	$ 0.320
Average shares and equivalents outstanding				798.7	796.0
Cash Flow Data(e)					
Net cash generated by continuing operations	16.5%	20.9%	11.9%	$ 2,110.0	$ 1,885.9
Acquisitions and investments in affiliates for cash				$ 630.6	$ 3,296.6
Purchases of property, plant and equipment for cash	10.2%	8.9%	25.0%	$ 1,180.1	$ 943.8
Cash dividends paid	10.2%	12.8%	21.5%	$ 293.9	$ 241.9
Year-End Position					
Total assets	17.9%	23.8%	13.3%	$17,143.4	$15,126.7
Total debt (f)	23.8%	38.0%	8.4%	$ 7,526.1	$ 6,942.8
Shareholders' equity				$ 4,904.2	$ 3,891.1
Per share	13.0%	21.7%	26.4%	$ 6.22	$ 4.92
Market price per share	24.5%	26.7%	20.5%	$ 25¾	$ 21⅜
Shares outstanding				788.4	791.1
Employees	10.7%	15.5%	15.8%	308,000	266,000
Shareholders of record				107,000	95,000
Statistics					
Return on average shareholders' equity(g)				24.8%	25.6%
Return on net sales(g)				6.1%	5.9%
Historical cost net debt ratio(h)				47%	51%
Market net debt ratio(i)				22%	24%

All share and per share amounts have been restated to reflect the 1990 three-for-one stock split described in the Note to Consolidated Financial Statements on page 43.

(a) PepsiCo adopted the Financial Accounting Standard (SFAS) No. 87 on Employers' Accounting for Pensions. Prior years are not restated for SFAS 87.

(b) PepsiCo adopted the Financial Accounting Standard (SFAS) No. 52 on Foreign Currency Translation. Prior years are not restated for SFAS 52.

(c) In 1984 a $156.0 charge ($62.0 after-tax or $0.07 per share) was recorded related to a program to sell several company-owned international bottling operations. In 1985 a $25.9 credit ($14.9 after-tax or $0.02 per share) was recorded to reflect better than anticipated results from the program. In 1989, an additional $32.5 credit ($21.5 after-tax or $0.03 per share) was recorded related to a decision to retain a bottling operation in Japan previously held for sale.

(d) Included a $79.4 charge ($79.4 after-tax or $0.09 per share) related to a reduction in net assets of certain international bottling operations.

(e) PepsiCo adopted the Financial Accounting Standard (SFAS) No. 95 on Reporting of Cash Flows in 1988. Years prior to 1986 are not restated for SFAS 95. Cash flows from other investing and financing activities, which are not presented, are an integral part of total cash flow activity.

(f) Total debt includes short-term borrowings, long-term debt and the nonrecourse obligation. (See Notes to Consolidated Financial Statements on pages 45 and 46.)

(g) The return on average shareholders' equity and return on net sales are calculated using income from continuing operations.

(h) The historical cost net debt ratio represents total debt (excluding the nonrecourse obligation) reduced by the pro forma remittance of offshore investment portfolios, as a percent of capital employed (net debt, other liabilities and deferred credits, deferred income taxes and shareholders' equity).

(i) The market net debt ratio represents net debt (see Note h) as a percent of net debt plus the market value of equity, based on the year-end stock price.

PEPSICO, INC. 1990 FINANCIAL REVIEW

1988	1987[a]	1986	1985	1984	1983	1982[b]	1981	1980
$12,533.2	$11,018.1	$9,017.1	$7,584.5	$7,058.6	$6,568.6	$6,232.4	$5,873.3	$4,955.9
11,184.0	9,890.5	8,187.9	6,802.4[c]	6,479.3[c]	5,995.7	5,684.7[d]	5,278.8	4,435.7
344.2	294.6	261.4	195.2	204.9	175.0	163.5	147.7	112.7
(122.2)	(112.6)	(122.7)	(96.4)	(86.1)	(53.6)	(49.1)	(35.8)	(27.1)
11,406.0	10,072.5	8,326.6	6,901.2	6,598.1	6,117.1	5,799.1	5,390.7	4,521.3
1,127.2	945.6	690.5	683.3	460.5	451.5	433.3	482.6	434.6
365.0	340.5	226.7	256.7	180.5	169.5	229.7	213.7	200.3
$ 762.2	$ 605.1	$ 463.8	$ 426.6	$ 280.0	$ 282.0	$ 203.6	$ 268.9	$ 234.3
$ 762.2	$ 594.8	$ 457.8	$ 543.7	$ 212.5	$ 284.1	$ 224.3	$ 297.5	$ 260.7
$ 0.97	$ 0.77	$ 0.59	$ 0.51[c]	$ 0.33[c]	$ 0.33	$ 0.24[d]	$ 0.32	$ 0.29
$ 0.97	$ 0.76	$ 0.58	$ 0.65	$ 0.25	$ 0.33	$ 0.27	$ 0.36	$ 0.32
$ 0.267	$ 0.223	$ 0.209	$ 0.195	$ 0.185	$ 0.180	$ 0.176	$ 0.158	$ 0.140
790.4	789.3	786.5	842.1	862.4	859.3	854.1	837.5	820.5
$ 1,894.5	$ 1,334.5	$1,212.2	$ 817.3	$ 981.5	$ 670.2	$ 661.5	$ 515.0	$ 458.3
$ 1,415.5	$ 371.5	$1,679.9	$ 160.0	$ –	$ –	$ 130.3	$ –	$ –
$ 725.8	$ 770.5	$ 858.5	$ 770.3	$ 555.8	$ 503.4	$ 447.4	$ 414.4	$ 447.4
$ 199.0	$ 172.0	$ 160.4	$ 161.1	$ 154.6	$ 151.3	$ 142.5	$ 126.2	$ 111.2
$11,135.3	$ 9,022.7	$8,027.1	$5,889.3	$4,876.9	$4,446.3	$4,052.2	$3,960.2	$3,309.7
$ 4,107.0	$ 3,225.0	$2,865.3	$1,506.1	$ 948.9	$1,073.9	$1,033.5	$1,214.0	$ 888.6
$ 3,161.0	$ 2,508.6	$2,059.1	$1,837.7	$1,853.4	$1,794.2	$1,650.5	$1,556.3	$1,509.7
$ 4.01	$ 3.21	$ 2.64	$ 2.33	$ 2.19	$ 2.13	$ 1.96	$ 1.89	$ 1.84
$ 13⅛	$ 11¼	$ 8¾	$ 7⅞	$ 4⅝	$ 4¼	$ 3¾	$ 4⅛	$ 2⅞
788.4	781.2	781.0	789.4	845.2	842.0	840.4	824.4	821.5
235,000	225,000	214,000	150,000	150,000	154,000	133,000	120,000	111,000
94,000	92,000	87,000	72,000	62,000	60,000	48,000	49,000	51,000
26.9%	26.5%	23.8%	23.1%	15.4%	16.4%	12.7%	17.5%	16.2%
6.1%	5.5%	5.1%	5.6%	3.9%	4.3%	3.3%	4.6%	4.7%
37%	35%	40%	24%	11%	23%	30%	38%	32%
20%	18%	23%	12%	7%	16%	20%	23%	23%

Net Sales
($ In Millions)

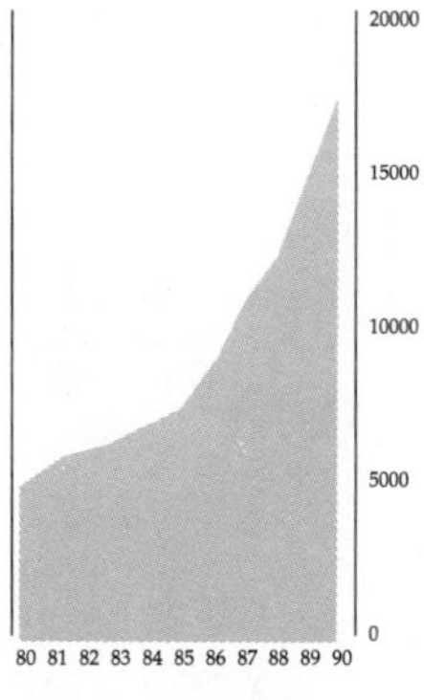

Income Per Share From Continuing Operations
($ In Millions)

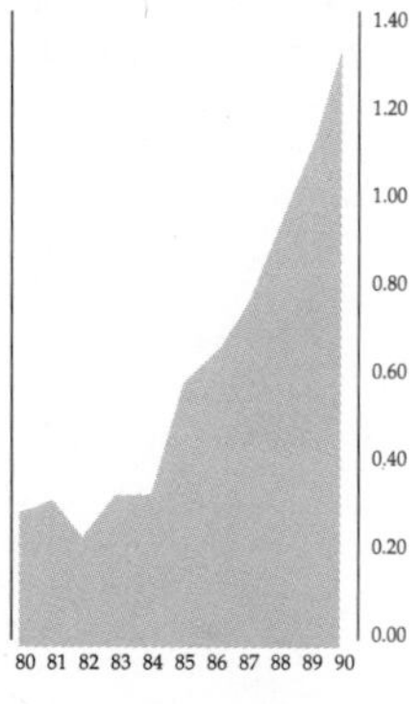

PEPSICO, INC. 1990 FINANCIAL REVIEW

Quarterly Financial Data

(in millions except per share amounts, unaudited)

	First Quarter (12 Weeks)		Second Quarter (12 Weeks)		Third Quarter (12 Weeks)		Fourth Quarter (16 Weeks)		Full Year (52 Weeks)	
	1990	1989	1990	1989	1990	1989	1990	1989	1990	1989
Net sales..........................	$3,677.7	2,958.3	4,204.7	3,592.7	4,475.7	3,901.6	5,444.6	4,789.8	17,802.7	15,242.4
Gross profit........................	$1,874.7	1,529.7	2,200.7	1,854.8	2,307.8	1,976.1	2,809.6	2,414.1	9,192.8	7,774.7
Income from continuing operations before income taxes..............	$ 275.6	252.1	438.9(a)	396.5(b)	566.0(c)	406.2	386.9(d)	295.7(e)	1,667.4	1,350.5
Provision for income taxes............	$ 93.7	87.0	146.4	131.6	215.7	136.9	121.0	93.6	576.8	449.1
Income from continuing operations....	$ 181.9	165.1	292.5	264.9	350.3	269.3	265.9	202.1	1,090.6	901.4
Discontinued operation charge........	$ –	–	–	–	(13.7)	–	–	–	(13.7)	–
Net income	$ 181.9	165.1	292.5	264.9	336.6	269.3	265.9	202.1	1,076.9	901.4
Income (charge) per share:										
Continuing operations............	$ 0.23	0.21	0.36	0.33	0.44(c)	0.34	0.34	0.25	1.37	1.13
Discontinued operation............	$ –	–	–	–	(0.02)	–	–	–	(0.02)	–
Net income per share................	$ 0.23	0.21	0.36(a)	0.33(b)	0.42	0.34	0.34(d)	0.25(e)	1.35	1.13

NOTE: The per share amounts have been restated to reflect the three-for-one stock split described in the Note to Consolidated Financial Statements on page 43.

(a) Included a $9.1 unusual charge ($5.5 after-tax or $0.01 per share) to write-off receivables due to a major domestic retail customer filing for bankruptcy.

(b) Included a $22.2 net unusual credit ($15.0 after-tax or $0.02 per share) consisting of a $32.5 credit resulting from a decision to retain a bottling operation in Japan previously held for sale, partially offset by an $8.0 reorganization charge to consolidate domestic field operations of KFC and a $2.3 net charge in domestic snack foods.

(c) Included a $70.6 net unusual credit ($23.8 after-tax or $0.03 per share) consisting of a $118.2 credit from an initial public stock offering by PepsiCo's KFC joint venture in Japan, partially offset by an $18.0 charge for accelerated contributions to the PepsiCo Foundation, a $17.6 charge for the intended closures of certain underperforming restaurants and a $12.0 charge for potentially uncollectible receivables from highly leveraged domestic retail customers.

(d) Included a $26.3 unusual charge ($22.5 after-tax or $0.03 per share) consisting of a $15.9 charge to reduce the carrying value of an international Pizza Hut joint venture investment, an $8.0 charge to consolidate domestic Pizza Hut field operations and a $2.4 charge to relocate international Pizza Hut headquarters.

(e) Included a $17.8 unusual charge ($13.2 after-tax or $0.02 per share) consisting of a $12.3 reorganization charge to decentralize international soft drinks operations and a $5.5 reorganization charge to consolidate domestic field operations of Taco Bell.

Stock Performance

PepsiCo was formed through the 1965 merger of Pepsi-Cola Company and Frito-Lay, Inc. A $1,000 investment in our stock made in 1965 was worth approximately $38,000 on December 29, 1990, assuming the reinvestment of dividends. Past performance is not necessarily indicative of future returns on investments in PepsiCo Capital Stock.

As the chart at the far right illustrates, the return on PepsiCo Capital Stock compares favorably with the performance of the Standard & Poor's 400 over the past five years.

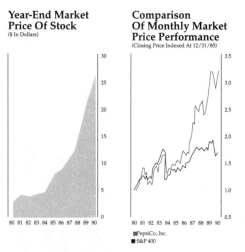

Year-End Market Price Of Stock
($ In Dollars)

Comparison Of Monthly Market Price Performance
(Closing Price Indexed At 12/31/85)

■ PepsiCo, Inc.
■ S&P 400

PEPSICO, INC. 1990 FINANCIAL REVIEW

Capital Stock Information

Stock Trading Symbol

PEP

Stock Exchange Listings

New York, Midwest, Basel,
Geneva, Zurich, Amsterdam, Tokyo

At year-end 1990 there were approximately 107,000 shareholders of record.

Dividend Policy

Cash dividends are declared quarterly. Quarterly cash dividends have been paid since PepsiCo was formed in 1965, and dividends have increased for 19 consecutive years.

Consistent with PepsiCo's current payout target of approximately one-third of the prior year's income from continuing operations, the 1990 dividend payout ratio was 34% of 1989 earnings.

Dividends Declared Per Share (in cents)*

Quarter	1990	1989
1	8⅓	7
2	10	8⅓
3	10	8⅓
4	10	8⅓
Total	38⅓	32

Dividend Reinvestment Plan

Shareholders may increase their investment in our stock by enrolling in PepsiCo's Dividend Reinvestment Plan. A brochure explaining this convenient plan, for which PepsiCo pays all fees, is available from our transfer agent:

Manufacturers Hanover Trust Company
450 West 33rd Street
New York, New York 10001

Stock Prices*

The high, low and closing prices for a share of PepsiCo Capital Stock on the New York Stock Exchange, as reported by The Dow Jones News/Retrieval Service, for each fiscal quarter of 1990 and 1989 were as follows (in dollars):

1990	High	Low	Close
Fourth Quarter	27⅞	21	25¾
Third Quarter	27⅞	21¾	25¼
Second Quarter	25½	20⅝	24⅝
First Quarter	21½	18	20½

1989			
Fourth Quarter	22	18	21⅜
Third Quarter	20¾	17	18¾
Second Quarter	18⅜	14¼	17¼
First Quarter	14¾	12⅝	14½

*Dividend and stock price information reflect the 1990 three-for-one stock split.

Shareholder Information

Financial Information

Security analysts and representatives of financial institutions are invited to contact:

Margaret D. Moore
Vice President, Investor Relations
Telephone: (914) 253-3035

Shareholder Inquiries

Questions concerning your dividend reinvestment account, dividend payments or address changes should be addressed to PepsiCo's transfer agent:

Manufacturers Hanover Trust Company
Security Holder Relations
P.O. Box 24935, Church Street Station
New York, New York 10249
Telephone: (212) 613-7147

Please mention PepsiCo, your name as printed on your stock certificate, your social security number, and include your address and telephone number in all correspondence.

Shareholders' Meeting

The Annual Meeting of Shareholders will be held at PepsiCo World Headquarters on Anderson Hill Road, Purchase, New York, at 10 a.m. (EDT), Wednesday, May 1, 1991. Proxies for the meeting will be solicited by an independent proxy solicitor. This Annual Report is not part of the proxy solicitation.

If you need additional assistance or information, or would like to receive free of charge a copy of PepsiCo's Form 10-K and 10-Q reports filed with the Securities and Exchange Commission, contact:

**Manager of Shareholder Relations
PepsiCo, Inc.
Purchase, New York 10577
Telephone: (914) 253-3055**

PepsiCo's Annual Report contains many of the valuable trademarks owned and used by PepsiCo and its subsidiaries and affiliates in the United States and internationally to distinguish products and services of outstanding quality.

SUMMARY

Accounting is the language of business. Accounting reports are used to convey information about the financial health and performance of companies to various external constituencies such as creditors, lenders, shareholders, public interest groups, employees, and various governmental agencies.

The focus of this text is on financial accounting and the generally accepted accounting principles used in preparing quarterly and annual accounting reports. Our goal is to help you become financial statement literate and to be conversant in the language of accounting.

NEW CONCEPTS AND TERMS

Accounting (p. 2)
American Institute of Certified Public
   Accountants (p. 5)
Audit (p. 8)
Auditor's opinion (p. 9)
Financial accounting (p. 4)
Financial Accounting Standards Board (p. 5)
Financial statements (p. 4)
Footnotes (p. 10)
Generally accepted accounting principles
   (p. 4)

Generally accepted auditing standards (p. 8)
Independent auditor (p. 8)
Internal control structure (p. 8)
Managerial accounting (p. 4)
Securities and Exchange Commission (p. 5)
Stewardship (p. 3)
Unqualified opinion (p. 11)

ISSUES FOR DISCUSSION

D1.1 Identify five different users of accounting information and discuss briefly the kinds of decisions they must make and the kinds of accounting information they should have in making those decisions.

Assume that the PepsiCo, Inc., financial statements are typical of the statements provided by U.S. companies to their public stockholders. Do those statements meet the information needs you outlined above? To the extent that they do not, why might that be so? Where might your user go to find the information needed?

D1.2 Assume that you are the chief accounting officer of a major manufacturing company. Identify and describe five principal differences that might exist between your company's managerial accounting reports and its financial accounting reports. Why might those differences exist?

D1.3 Assume that you are a member of Congress and that it is the early 1930s. The Depression is a very painful reality for everyone. The financial reporting systems in our country have been allocated part of the blame for the financial collapse, and new answers are being sought for old questions. A number of different voices are arguing their positions. Some believe that we ought to have a government-mandated financial reporting system to which every company that wants to sell stock to the public must adhere. Others who believe that the marketplace will reward those companies that provide useful information and will penalize those that do not argue that we should have no standardized financial reporting requirement. They argue that each company should be allowed to devise its own report to shareholders. In the middle ground are those who argue for some standardization of financial reports disseminated to the public but at the same time insist that the standardized format be developed by private sector initiative.

a. Outline the advantages and disadvantages of each of the above three alternatives from the standpoint of the financial community as a whole.

b. Assume that each of the three alternatives is offered in legislation. Which alternative would you vote for, and why?

D1.4 In your own words, explain what is meant by an internal control structure. You may find it helpful to couch your explanation in the context of a hypothetical company, for example, a rapidly growing manufacturer of electronic components.

D1.5 Chapter 1 describes the role of the Financial Accounting Standards Board and suggests that Board members ought to be experienced professionals but also must be independent of their former employers. Why would you think those two requirements might be important?

D1.6 Senator Paul Tsongas, a 1992 presidential candidate, suggested that we change the rules that now require all publicly held companies to issue quarterly reports. He suggests that we follow the practice of some other countries and require only semiannual reports. Outline the advantages and disadvantages of that proposal from as many different perspectives as you think might be relevant.

D1.7 Based on your reading of the report of PepsiCo management and the report from the independent auditor on page 27, describe in your own words the responsibilities of management and of the auditors for the preparation of the PepsiCo financial statements. How are they similar? How are they different? That division of responsibilities has evolved over time. Why might it have evolved as it did?

D1.8 In footnote 1, PepsiCo describes its policies with regard to marketing costs. What other approach could management have taken with regard to those costs? How might PepsiCo's financial statements have been different if an alternative approach had been adopted?

D1.9 Based on your reading of the PepsiCo financial statements, identify five measures of performance that you believe to be important and explain why you selected those five. Also identify five measures of PepsiCo performance that you believe might be important to a decision to buy PepsiCo shares but are not available to you from these financial statements. Why might those measures not be reported in a public financial statement?

D1.10 Assume that you will have dinner tomorrow night with an old college friend who is now a successful CPA. Based on your reading of the PepsiCo financial statements, identify the 10 most important questions about accounting and the financial reporting process that you would like to pose to your friend. (Try to make those questions as complete as possible. At the conclusion of this course, you ought to go back and see how many of those questions you can answer for yourself.)

The Basic Financial Statements and Generally Accepted Accounting Principles

---

Chapter Outline

- The Basic Financial Statements: An
  Introduction
  Balance Sheet
  Income Statement
  Statement of Owners' Equity
  Statement of Cash Flows

- Some Fundamental Questions in Accounting
- The Standard-Setting Process
- The Basic Financial Statements Illustrated:
  PepsiCo, Inc.
- Summary

This chapter introduces the four basic financial statements and poses (and answers) some fundamental questions that all preparers of financial statements must address. Those basic statements are required by generally accepted accounting principles (GAAP). In addition, GAAP outline how those statements are to be prepared. In effect, GAAP provide the answers to the questions we pose here. This chapter also describes how those governing principles came to be.

THE BASIC FINANCIAL STATEMENTS:
AN INTRODUCTION

Under generally accepted accounting principles, companies report their financial activities using four basic financial statements:

- The **balance sheet,** also referred to as the **statement of financial position,** presents in summary form the assets a company owned, the liabilities the company owed to its lenders and suppliers, and the funds that the owners of the company have invested or left in the company to provide for its operating needs, as of a specific date.

- The **income statement,** also referred to as the **statement of earnings** or operations, summarizes those transactions that produced revenue for a company as a result of selling products or services and those transactions that resulted in expenses for the company during a given period. The difference between the aggregate revenues and aggregate expenses is the net income (or loss) for the company.

- The **statement of owners' equity** summarizes the major transactions that affected the owners' investment in a company, including the company's net income (or loss) and the amount of those earnings that were distributed to the owners during a given period.

- The **statement of cash flows** summarizes the sources of a company's cash funds available for use during a given period and the uses that the company made of those funds.

Under GAAP, all companies are required to provide a balance sheet, an income statement, and a statement of cash flows as part of their annual report. A statement of owners' equity is also frequently provided, although that information may also be presented as part of a company's financial statement footnotes rather than as a separate financial statement. Together, these statements form the nucleus of most accounting reports. We will briefly overview the contents and purpose of each statement now and will consider each one in detail in subsequent chapters.

Balance Sheet

The purpose of the balance sheet is to present, as of a particular point in time, the various resources available for use by a company and the sources from which the company funded the acquisition of those resources. These resources are generally referred to as its **assets,** and the sources of those resources are either its **liabilities** or its **equity.** As you might surmise, equity is a source of funding provided by its owners. Liabilities, on the other hand, are the sources of funding provided by a company's creditors. Hence:

- **Assets** are tangible or intangible resources, which can be measured in dollars, are owned or controlled by a company, and are expected to provide future economic benefit to the company.

- **Liabilities** refer to the dollar measures of the company's obligations to repay money loaned to it, to pay for goods or services it has received, or to fulfill its warranty obligations.

■ **Owners' equity** refers to the dollar measures of the owners' investment in a company, which may be either in the form of direct investment through the purchase of shares of stock or indirectly through the retention of some of the company's earnings that would otherwise be paid out to the owners.

The relationship between the assets (A), liabilities (L), and owners' equity (OE) of a company represents the foundation of accounting. This fundamental relationship may be expressed as:

$$A = L + OE.$$

In words, the assets of a company always equal the sum of its liabilities and its owners' equity. Stated alternatively, every resource has a source. Not only does this relationship represent the cornerstone of accounting, but also it is the basis for the balance sheet. The balance sheet is like a snapshot presenting the assets of a company juxtaposed against its liabilities and owners' equity as of a particular moment. In effect, it presents a picture of the resources available to a company today for its future operations and the sources the company used to obtain those resources.

Pictorially, the balance sheet looks like this:

	Liabilities
Assets	
	Owners' equity

Note that the right and left sides of this box must always be equal. The composition or relative proportions of the right side, however, will vary depending on the way in which a company obtains its assets.

Income Statement

Although the balance sheet presents the status of a company's assets, liabilities, and owners' equity *as of* a particular point in time, the income statement presents the results of a series of income-generating transactions *over* a period of time. The income statement reports the revenues earned and the expenses incurred by the company during a given period of operations:

■ **Revenues** are the actual or expected cash inflows arising from a company's sales of products or services. Revenues produce increases in both the owners' equity and the assets of a company.

■ **Expenses** are the costs a company incurred in its efforts to generate revenues. Expenses result in a decrease in owners' equity and a reduction in assets (i.e., the cost to produce the goods sold) and/or an increase in a liability (e.g., wages owed to employees who performed the service provided to the customer).

■ **Net income** (or loss) is the excess (or insufficiency) of revenues over expenses; it represents a summary measure of the overall performance of a company for a given period. Net income is associated with an increase in net assets and owners' equity, whereas a net loss is associated with a decrease in net assets and owners' equity.

The relationship between the revenues (R), expenses (E), and net income (NI) of a company may be expressed as

$$R - E = NI,$$

and this expression forms the basis of the income statement.

Statement of Owners' Equity

The owners' investment in a company may take several forms: direct investment through the purchase of shares of stock or indirect investment through the retention of some (or all) of the company's earnings for a period. Thus, the statement of owners' equity measures the change in the owners' investment in a company over a period of time:

■ **Capital stock** represents the proceeds a company received from the sale of stock to its shareholders. Sales of stock *between* shareholders do not impact the company's financial statements because those transactions have no effect on the company.

■ **Dividends** are the earnings of a company that are paid out to the owners. In a corporation, the owners are not automatically entitled to receive a distribution of the company's earnings, which are paid out to shareholders only when the board of directors believes it will be safe (for the company) to do so. Because shareholders are not entitled to dividends, the payment of dividends is not considered to be an expense to the company. They are understood to be nothing more than a distribution of earnings, and the accounting for dividends follows that understanding.

■ **Retained earnings** are a company's earnings that are retained in the enterprise for future corporate use. The retention of earnings is, by definition, associated with an increase in the owners' investment in the company.

Note that retained earnings are aggregated in one account. This account represents the accumulation of all net income earned by a company since its beginning, less the dividends paid out by the company over that same time period. The net of all of those incomes and dividends is the balance in the Retained Earnings account. Continuing our algebraic expressions, the Retained Earnings account can be expressed as:

$$NI \text{ (for all periods)} - D \text{ (for all periods)} = RE \text{ (at the end of this period).}$$

It will be apparent that capital stock is the *contributed* capital of a company and that retained earnings refer to the *earned* capital; that is, retained earnings are the capital that the company earned for itself and that the board of directors has retained for the company's future use. Thus, the relationship between retained earnings, owners' equity, and the owners' investment in the shares of stock (CS) as of the balance sheet date for a company may be expressed as:

$$OE = CS + RE.$$

Substituting the more complex, equivalent expression for RE, which we detailed above, demonstrates the relationship between the income statement and the statement of owners' equity:

OE (to date) = CS (to date) + NI (for all periods) − D (for all periods).

We can also use these expressions to demonstrate the relationship between the income statement, the statement of owners' equity, and the balance sheet, as follows:

A (to date) = L (to date) + CS (to date) + NI (for all periods) − D (for all periods).

Looking at the relationship between the balance sheet, the income statement, and the statement of owners' equity in a different way, we might try to diagram it as in Exhibit 2.1.

E X H I B I T 2 . 1

Diagrammatic Relationship of the Balance Sheet, the Income Statement, and the Statement of Owners' Equity

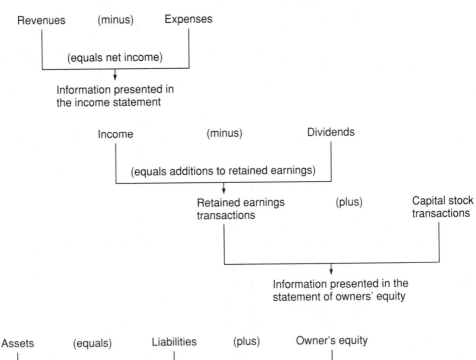

Returning to the pictorial depiction of the balance sheet presented earlier in this chapter, the relationship between the income statement with the beginning-of-year balance sheet and the end-of-year balance sheet can be shown as in Exhibit 2.2.

Exhibits 2.1 and 2.2 show how the net income for a period flows into the end-of-period retained earnings balance. Please note that the addition to retained earnings for the period also results in some combination of increases in assets and/or decreases in liabilities. That has to be so because the basic accounting equation (i.e., A = L + OE) requires the balance sheet to be in balance. The net addition to retained earnings for the year is, in fact, an aggregation of a variety of transactions during the period, which have affected a variety of balance sheet accounts. In addition, the balance sheet has been further affected by a variety of other, nonincome transactions. Only in the simplest companies would the increase in retained earnings be directly traced to an increase in a specific asset account. Thus, in summary, investors can see whether their investment has increased (or decreased) over the year (or period) by comparing the equity section of the balance sheet

EXHIBIT 2.2

Diagrammatic Relationship of the Income Statement and Balance Sheet

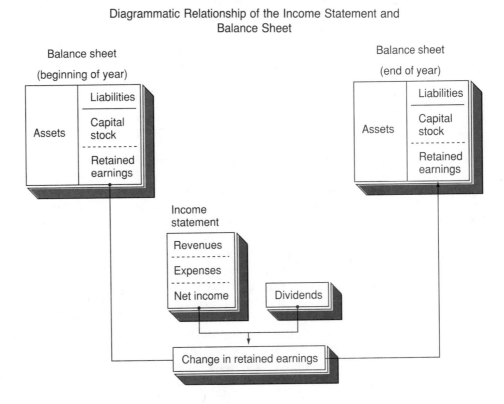

from one point in time to the next. The income statement shows in detail how the operations of the company contributed to that increase (or decrease).

Statement of Cash Flows

The purpose of the statement of cash flows is to explain the change in cash occurring between two successive accounting periods. The cash flows of a company may be conveniently segmented into three principal categories of interest to financial statement users: cash flows from operations, from investing, and from financing.

Cash flows from operations refers to the net cash flows resulting from the company's principal business operations. In essence, the operating cash flow measures the net income of the company on a cash basis. **Cash flows from investing** refers to making and collecting loans, acquiring and disposing of another company's debt or equity instruments, and buying and selling long-lived assets (e.g., buildings and equipment). Finally, **cash flows from financing** refers to the activities of a company to obtain funds from existing and new shareholders, provide them a return *on* and a return *of* their investment, and borrow and repay amounts borrowed. In total, the statement of cash flows essentially summarizes all of the changes occurring in the cash account as it appears on the balance sheet.

Integrating the statement of cash flows into our pictorial depiction of financial reporting yields Exhibit 2.3.

It is worth saying again: The change in cash for the year is not the same as the change in retained earnings because those two numbers are the net aggregations of a great variety of transactions that affect many other balance sheet accounts, in addition to their impact on cash or retained earnings.

SOME FUNDAMENTAL QUESTIONS IN ACCOUNTING

The discussion in the preceding portions of this chapter has attempted to explain the basis of accounting and the interrelationships of the basic financial statements. In addition, although some of these descriptions were intentionally abstract, the process of actually preparing financial statements to communicate the activities of a particular company to the various interested constituencies is never an abstract exercise. Preparing financial statements requires a real person to find specific answers to specific questions. These questions and the answers that have become generally accepted form the backbone of our present set of generally accepted accounting principles. It will be useful at this stage of our inquiry to consider those questions and the answers that are outlined for us in GAAP.

To pursue these questions and their answers, let us create a context. As you think through the following discussion, assume that you have formed a new company to borrow some money to buy an apartment building. Let us assume that you have invested $20,000 of your own money in the company, that the company borrowed $80,000 from a bank, and that the company then paid $100,000 to buy an existing apartment building. The company's business will be to collect rent from the tenants, pay for maintenance and

EXHIBIT 2.3

Diagrammatic Relationship of the Basic Financial Statements

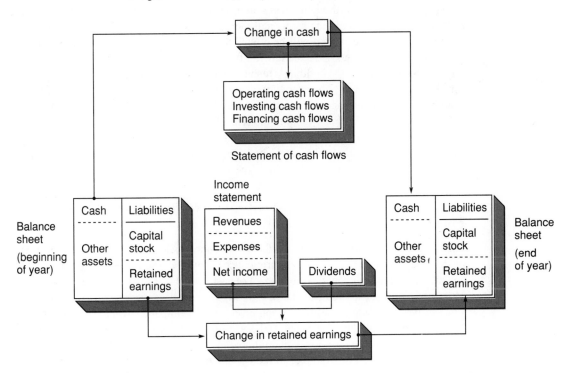

utilities, pay the principal and interest on the debt, and pay you any profits that may result from the company's operations. As you periodically prepare financial statements to report the status of the company and its success or failure, you will be forced to address the following questions:

What Is the Entity Whose Operations Are to Be Covered by This Report?

You could elect to prepare financial statements that reported all of your personal assets and activities, which would of course include the real estate venture you just created; alternatively, you could prepare statements that reflected only the assets and the activities of the real estate company by itself. To make that decision you might ask, "What information does the expected reader of these statements need to know? What information does the reader of these statements have a right to know?" For example, if the bank is entitled to look at only the real estate business to satisfy the $80,000 loan, the financial statements you prepare for it should cover only the business' activities. However, if the bank has the right to look at the real estate business *and* your personal activities to satisfy the bank loan, it might ask for combined financial statements that cover the business' activities, as well as your own personal activities.

Along that line of thought, you might also argue that the company's financial statements should include the assets and the activities of your building's tenants—after all, their financial well-being will be crucial to your success and to the bank's ability to collect on its loan. However, although you fully control your corporation, neither you nor your company controls the building's tenants. Their assets are not available to you, except for the rent they owe. That same thinking directs GAAP. Under GAAP, financial statements include or encompass only the activities of a particular entity and any other entities that it controls. For example, the typical published corporate financial statements include the legal parent company and all of the subsidiary companies it controls, but the statements do not include the activities of its diverse stockholders or its suppliers or customers. This convention is known as the **entity concept.**

What Measurement Basis Should Be Used in Preparing These Financial Statements?

The simplest measurement basis for the preparation of financial statements is the **cash basis.** The cash basis involves measuring success by the amount of cash on hand at the end of a period as compared to the amount of cash on hand at the beginning of the period. More cash is good; less cash is bad.

Cash-basis accounting is used by some very small companies when there is very little difference between the long-range and short-range views of the business. Cash-basis accounting focuses on cash today and ignores the future cash-generating potential of any other form of asset. For example, in the hypothetical case we are using as our model, a balance sheet prepared on a cash basis of accounting would show no assets (or liabilities) for your company after its purchase of the building; in addition, the income statement would show a loss of $20,000 because of the cash downpayment. The cash basis of accounting ignores the fact that the building your company owns has a value—a value based on its potential to generate additional cash flows in the future. The cash basis of accounting is concerned with only the current cash effect and ignores the possibility of *future* cash effects. Cash-basis accounting, for example, ignores the fact that your company purchased the building because you expected it to earn more cash (in the future) than you initially paid for it and that the building retains that future cash-generating ability. Cash-basis accounting is not considered to be GAAP.

This is not to imply, however, that cash flow information is not useful. It would be very useful to the readers of your company's financial statements to know that all of the company's cash was used for the down payment on the building and that the company would have to borrow funds to meet an immediate emergency. Cash flow information is important to financial statement readers who want a near-term perspective on a company. The financial community has indicated that it wants cash flow information for its near-term decisions, but there has also been a demand for more sophisticated measures of financial status and of operating results.

At the other extreme, you could prepare the financial statements for your real estate business on a **fair value basis.** Under fair value accounting, assets and liabilities are included on a balance sheet at the value of their expected future cash flows, which is, of course, their current market value. If it is not immediately apparent to you why the market value of an asset should be the present value of its future cash flows, stop a minute and think about the thought process you might follow in a decision to purchase 100 shares of PepsiCo stock. You would most likely make an estimate of the dividends you would receive in the future and the increase in share price that might develop during the period you expect to hold the stock. You would then reduce those expected future cash flows back to today's value, using a discount rate equal to the percentage of return you expect on a common stock such as PepsiCo. If the expected future cash flows, discounted at the rate of return you demand, are more than the current market price of the PepsiCo stock, you would buy the stock; alternatively, if the present value of those expected cash flows is less than the current price of the PepsiCo stock, you would (should) look for another investment. That same process describes almost every asset purchase (and sale) decision—including your decision to have your company buy an apartment building for $100,000.

Under fair value accounting, the building you purchased in our example would, at the outset, be valued at $100,000 (presumably you paid fair value for your purchase). If its market value increased to $110,000 by the end of the next accounting period, the balance sheet would reflect that new value, and the $10,000 gain would be included with all of the company's other transactions in the determination of the business' profit for the period. Under this basis, owners' equity is simply the difference between the aggregate fair value of the assets and of the debt. Similarly, income (or loss) is simply the difference in the owners' equity at the beginning and at the end of an accounting period. The fair value method has intuitive appeal—it is logical to see the equity of the company as the net fair value of all of its assets and liabilities. However, it is difficult to implement because it is often difficult to obtain fair and accurate valuations of assets and liabilities. Fair value accounting is not yet accepted under GAAP.

GAAP require a middle ground, the **accrual method** of accounting. Accrual accounting assumes that assets *will* generate future cash flows, but because the future is uncertain, a conservative assumption is made that those future cash flows *will be no more* than the assets' original cost. No value in excess of the assets' cost is ever recognized. This convention is called the historical **cost concept.** However, sometimes we know just enough about the future to be worried. If we know enough about the future to be concerned about whether the assets will generate enough cash flow to cover their cost, the values are reduced to the lower, expected future cash flow. Financial people reduce this idea to a shorthand expression, "Assets are carried at the lower of cost or market." This pragmatic modification of the historic cost concept illustrates another accounting axiom: "Never anticipate gains but always anticipate losses."

Accrual accounting is more sophisticated than cash-basis accounting because it understands that your expenditure to buy the building was made with the reasonable expectation that you would realize a future cash flow benefit from your purchase. But the accrual method is more practical than the fair value method because it ignores "what if" value changes. In fact, under accrual accounting, assets are valued at their *future* cash flows only when the amounts of those future flows are validated by a transaction with a third party. Going back to our model, the building you purchased would continue to be carried at its historical cost of $100,000 even though a number of qualified appraisers assured you that it *could* be sold for $110,000. Only when the building is sold to a third party—when that third party takes on the risks of ownership—will that increase in value be recognized in your company's financial statements.

Accrual accounting also recognizes the reality of credit in the business world. It measures the cash consequences of a promise given or received when the promise is exchanged, not when the cash actually changes hands. If you sell the building for $110,000 and a third party buys it, promising to pay $110,000 12 months from today, your company would record that promise as an asset (referred to as a *receivable*) at the expected cash flow of $110,000. Similarly, you would remove the building from your balance sheet because it is no longer yours. The liability to the bank remains because you can't pay off the bank loan with a promise—you have to wait until the buyer actually gives you the cash before you can pay off the debt. The difference between the asset value ($110,000) and the debt ($80,000) is the owners' equity. The difference between that equity balance ($30,000) at the end of the period and the equity balance at the beginning ($20,000) is the company's income for the year.

Should Your Company's Financial Statements Forecast the Future or Should They Report on the Past?

Most people who read a financial report are interested in the company's future and are only passively interested in its past. Investors and lenders are interested to know what management did with the assets entrusted to its care during the last year, but, more importantly, they want to know whether their investment in the company will bear fruit in the future. With that reader interest in mind, some companies—especially relatively new ones—have prepared financial statements on a prospective basis, outlining the financial results they *expect* to have in the next several years. All projections are by definition uncertain, and most companies have been reluctant to expose themselves to the criticism that would inevitably follow a missed projection. Although prospective-oriented financial statements have a logical appeal, they have not been widely used and are not considered part of GAAP.

GAAP financial statements report a company's historical results based on real transactions with third parties. Some have described this focus on the past as the **transaction concept.** Under our present financial system, companies publicly report their historical results and usually keep private their expectations about the future. Individual financial statement readers use that historical information and factor in their own feelings about the future to make their personal estimates of the company's future results. In effect, the historic financial statements become the basis for individual projections of the company's future results. Some people will make that extrapolation more successfully than others—some people are more successful investors than others.

How Should the Company's Ongoing Operations Be Allocated over Time to Prepare Reports for a Specific Period?

Measuring a company's success would be simple if we had only to summarize its operations at the end of its life. The owner's original cash investment would have been fully exploited and converted back to cash. Success would be determined by whether there was more cash at the end than there was at the start. Your company purchased the building because you thought it would produce future cash flows for you. If we could wait 30 years until you were ready to retire, we might accumulate all of the company's cash receipts, including rentals and the proceeds from the final sale of the property; in addition, we would accumulate all of the company's disbursements, including payments for maintenance and the bank loan. If the receipts exceeded the disbursements by more than $20,000 (your original investment), you could say that the company was successful. It will be obvious that neither you nor the bank will want to wait 30 years to determine whether the venture was successful. And, consequently, GAAP attempt to deal with the problem of measuring results in those intervening years through a convention known as the **periodic measurement concept.**

Under GAAP, individual business transactions are assessed to determine whether the actions involved impact the current measurement period, a future measurement period, or a series of future periods. Then all of the financial effects of a transaction are accumulated, matched, and recorded in the appropriate measurement period. In a manufacturing example, if a company manufactured goods in June and sold them in September, the financial statements would recognize the revenue from the sale, the prior costs to make the items sold, and an estimate of the future cost of possible warranty work on the merchandise—all in the measurement of income for the month of September.

But let us return to our real estate example. Assume that a tenant signed a three-year lease on a suite in your building and that the lease is cancelable with 60 days' notice. The leasing agent who found the tenant for you earned a $15,000 commission, payable immediately. GAAP require you to recognize the rent income monthly, as the lease runs its course. Thus, the rental income is allocated to the periods when it is earned, a convention known as the **allocation concept.** But what should the company do about the commission paid? GAAP allow you to treat that payment as an asset when paid and then require you to allocate it as an expense over the periods when the rent is received. The logic behind this is that the rent would not have been received without that payment to the agent; thus, GAAP require that the rental income be matched with the cost of earning that income, a convention known as the **matching concept.** It is also true that the largest asset involved in earning the rent is the building itself. Under GAAP, *all* costs involved in earning revenue must be matched against that revenue, including the cost of long-lived assets like buildings. GAAP require you to allocate the $100,000 cost of the building over its expected revenue-earning life of, say, 30 years—another illustration of the allocation concept. Allocation and matching are important requisites to the notion of measuring company results period by period.

How Conservative (Aggressive) Should I Be When Making the Estimates Required by These Financial Statements?

As you read the preceding discussion, you may have asked what would happen if the building has a longer (or shorter) life than 30 years. If it actually has a life of 50 years, you will have allocated too much of the building's cost to the early years and as result will have reported too little net income in those years. You also may have wondered what would happen if the tenant occupying your suite on a three-year lease moved after the first year. In that case, you would have allocated too little commission expense to that first year, and income would have been overstated. Estimates are involved in almost every allocation decision that managers make as they prepare GAAP-based financial statements. Because no one (especially investors and lenders) likes unpleasant surprises, most managers adopt a conservative posture as they make those estimates. The logic is that it is better to be conservative about the future so that surprises, if any, are good surprises. This convention is known as the **conservatism concept.**

It should be apparent from the real estate example we discussed above that the application of conservatism can create a conflict between future and current results: Protecting against unpleasant future surprises may distort current results. Consider the following example from the retailing world. An expenditure for employee training that precedes the opening of a new store could justifiably be accounted for as an asset when the expenditure is made and then allocated to expense over some future period after the store is open and generating sales. In effect, those training costs would be matched with the revenues they are expected to generate. An alternative, more conservative view would be to treat those training expenditures as expenses immediately when they are incurred. That posture could be justified by arguing that future sales from the store are uncertain and until they are realized, the benefits expected from the training are unrealized as well. The store manager must make that allocation decision—future period versus current period expense—based on the likelihood that future sales will be sufficient to recover the training expenditures. This decision requires careful, informed judgment and a sense of balance: An ultraconservative policy may result in an unrealistically bleak financial picture for the current period, whereas an ultraliberal policy may result in an unrealistically positive picture for the current period, followed by disproportionately high expenses in future periods.

Do All Assets of My Company Still Have the Potential to Earn Cash Equal to Their Carrying Value Today?

GAAP provide for the fact that allocation estimates will sometimes prove to be wrong and that expenditures that you treated as assets in one period are occasionally seen subsequently as having no future cash-earning benefit. When that happens, GAAP require that the remaining asset value be charged off as an expense in the period when that discovery is made. (This is another application of the shorthand expression we referred to earlier—assets are carried at the **lower-of-cost-or-market value.**) Well-managed companies have programs in place to challenge periodically the carrying value of all of their assets to make sure that any declines in estimates of future benefits are recognized as soon as they become apparent. (Incidentally, GAAP does not permit companies to go back and restate prior years' financial statements for incorrect estimates. If hindsight shows that you were too conservative or too liberal, the effect of the adjustment required is to be recognized only in the financial statements for the period when you realize that your estimate was faulty.)

May I (Must I) Change My Estimates or My Accounting Principles?

Companies occasionally find that their assets continue to have value, that the future period of benefit is now seen to be different, and that they must change their accounting estimates. Suppose that after 10 years your company decided that the useful economic life of its building was really 50 years rather than 30 years. No accounting would be required at that time because you would simply spread the remaining cost over the remaining (now 40) years. If you concluded that the building life was really only 20 years instead of 30 years, the remaining cost would be allocated over the remaining 10 years. The financial community assumes that financial statements are prepared consistently from one period to the next so that a series of income statements covering a period of years fairly reports the trend in income. The fundamental estimates are not changed year to year but only when required by the facts. If significant estimates are changed, GAAP require that a footnote be included in the financial statements to explain the change and the dollar effect of the change on the future years' income statements.

For many types of economic transactions, a number of alternative GAAP accounting methods are available to record a transaction, each producing a very different accounting result. When alternative reporting approaches exist, GAAP simply require that a company disclose in the footnotes accompanying its financial reports the accounting method that has been selected. Should circumstances change, warranting the use of a different accounting principle, the effect of the change on reported income must be disclosed in the footnotes to permit financial statement users to compare current period results with results from the prior period, which were determined using the old accounting method— reflecting the **consistency concept.**

How Much Detail Must I (May I) Include in These Financial Statements?

The ideal accounting report includes all material (i.e., significant) information but excludes all trivial or irrelevant details. The financial community (and the courts) have said that financial statements must include all "material information." *Material information* has been defined as information that might influence the decisions of a reasonable person. Managers must ask themselves whether details about their company's financial status would influence the decisions of a potential investor; if so, the information must be included in the basic financial statements themselves or in the related footnotes.

It follows from that understanding about the content of the financial statements themselves that management will, when making accounting estimate decisions, focus its attention principally on those items that might have a material effect on the accounting reports. Clearly, careful judgments are required in preparing a set of financial statements, and the responsible manager will exercise that judgment thinking all the while about the potential readers of the financial statements: investors, creditors, and the public. This convention is known as the **materiality concept.**

THE STANDARD-SETTING PROCESS

As noted in Chapter 1, the financial statements of a company are often distributed to a diverse set of external constituencies: shareholders, creditors, lenders, employees, and public interest groups. Over time, the financial community has come to agree on a set of answers to the questions posed above (and many more) for those general purpose financial statements, with the objective that the statements would meet most of the information needs of most of the members of that community. The generalized answers to the questions that arise in preparing financial statements are referred to as *generally accepted accounting principles*. The phrase "generally accepted" suggests that the principles emerge from practice as a consensus and that interpretation is partly true. Today, however, financial transactions are complex and the need for timely information from companies is acute. The financial community has decided that it would be inappropriate to wait for a consensus to emerge about a new accounting question and has agreed therefore that the consensus should be led by an authorized standard-setting body. The following discussion explains more fully how that consensus, or GAAP, comes to be.

At the turn of the century, the financial community was relatively small. When local businesses borrowed strictly from local banks, personal reputations were more important than financial status in the granting of a loan. Stocks and bonds were investment vehicles only for a small, wealthy, well-acquainted group. To the extent that investments were made outside that group, they were based on personal recommendations of investment bankers. Because communication between creditor and borrower, or between investor and investee, could be direct and personal, financial reporting tended to be tailored and unique, even informal. That informal financial reporting system served the community well for a number of years, but as the community itself grew and became more diverse, the need for a more rigorous reporting system became apparent.

The need for more formal regulation of the form and content of financial reporting became dramatically apparent with the stock market crash of 1929. The widespread impact of the crash made it clear that a reporting system that relied on personal contact was no longer appropriate. Because the *public* was now seen to be affected by the country's financial system, and more particularly by the financial reporting system, Congress passed the Securities Acts of 1933 and 1934 and created the Securities and Exchange Commission (SEC).

The SEC has the responsibility to regulate the various stock exchanges, the broker-dealers who buy and sell on those exchanges, and mutual funds. The Commission also has the authority to establish the "form and content" of the financial disclosures to be required of publicly held companies. Under the Commission's rules, any company that sells stocks or bonds to the public must prepare a financial disclosure package (referred to as a **prospectus**) to give potential investors the information they need to decide whether to buy a company's securities. Every company that has sold securities to the public in the past must prepare an annual disclosure package (referred to as **Form 10-K**) and quarterly reports (referred to as **Form 10-Q**). Those annual and quarterly reports are designed to help existing investors decide whether they want to retain their investment or to sell and to help potential investors decide whether they want to buy a given company's securities.

Although the SEC has the statutory authority to establish the requirements for corporate reporting, it has chosen to exercise its authority very sparingly. The Commission has established some requirements for disclosure of basic business information, but almost from the beginning, it elected to delegate the development of accounting standards to the private sector. There are probably a number of reasons for that delegation policy. First, the original SEC commissioners concluded that the best accounting rules for the nation's complex financial community would be developed by practitioners with field experience rather than by government employees. Second, the commissioners also concluded that the financial community was more likely to follow rules that it had established for itself than rules that had been set by outsiders, especially a governmental agency. Finally, it became apparent to the Commission that enormous pressure was likely to be brought to bear on whoever was responsible for accounting standards. The SEC chose to stand behind the private sector and prod it on rather than face the pressure groups directly.

At the Commission's prodding, the major certified public accounting (CPA) firms, under the auspices of the American Institute of Certified Public Accountants, began the process of establishing written, standardized, generally accepted accounting principles in 1936. Until 1959, that effort was staffed by senior executives of the leading CPA firms. They were enormously productive at the start, but eventually their deliberations on matters of principle bogged down in debates over firm preference. Apparently, it was difficult for such strongly motivated, visible people to compromise ardently held firm positions. To focus those deliberations on the issues, a new standard-setting body was established in 1959 and staffed with technical experts from each of the large CPA firms. This group, the Accounting Principles Board (APB), was again effective in its early years but was overwhelmed by the ''go-go'' financial years of the late 1960s. Some people argued that the APB became too technical, too restrictive, and not sufficiently practical. Others argued that the APB had been too willing to compromise in the interest of producing timely new standards. In any event, the criticism from the community became so strong that the APB lost its standard-setting effectiveness. It was abolished in 1973 and the Financial Accounting Standards Board (FASB) was created to take its place.

With the recognition that the prior standards-setting efforts, relying as they did on the major CPA firms, suffered from at least an appearance of narrow focus, the FASB was designed to appeal to the financial community as a whole. The Board is funded by voluntary contributions from four different accounting organizations, The Securities Industry Association, The Financial Analysts Association, and several large corporations. Board members are selected on the basis of their general reputation in the field without regard to their prior affiliation.

The Board's procedures require extensive due process. It solicits community advice as it considers its agenda. When a new issue is added to the Board's agenda, the staff researches the issue and prepares a discussion memorandum that outlines all of the important points of view that have been expressed. The Board solicits written comments in response to its discussion memorandums and very often holds public hearings. Based on community input and the Board's own deliberations, an exposure draft of a new statement is prepared and circulated for additional comments. After considering public responses to the exposure draft, the Board makes final refinements and issues a **statement of financial accounting standards.**

The pronouncements of the Board have considerable authority. The SEC considers them to be GAAP for purposes of complying with U.S. securities laws, and CPA firms consider the Board's statements to be GAAP when they evaluate the fairness of general purpose financial statements, whether those statements are prepared to be filed with the SEC or to be used by private companies outside the SEC's jurisdiction.

The Board was quite successful in its early years, and in its 17-year history has issued more than 100 statements, as well as a wide variety of interpretative releases. In more recent years, the Board has been subject to increased criticism. Some members of the business community argue that the Board had become too concerned with technical accounting questions and that the cost of complying with the FASB's statements exceeds the benefits to the financial community. That critical assessment is partly true. But it is also true that several of the Board's statements have forced companies to recognize liabilities that were not previously reflected in their financial statements. Part of the criticism of the Board is the reaction one might expect whenever more rigorous standards are imposed. Time will tell whether the financial community will continue to support a self-regulated standard-setting process or whether the SEC will be forced to assume that responsibility.

In addition to the pronouncements of the FASB and its predecessors, GAAP are also established by prevailing accounting practice. In the past, as much as 75 percent of GAAP may have been unwritten precedent. Today, as a result of the aggressive work of the FASB, the reverse is true and probably less than 25 percent of GAAP are based solely on informal, unwritten precedent. However, since business is a dynamic process with new financial transactions always being created, it is unlikely that this 75/25 relationship will change. No standard-setting agency could ever hope to keep up with the rapid evolution of finance and accounting. When no formal accounting pronouncements exist, new GAAP will be inferred from practices developed by accounting practitioners drawing on the fundamental concepts that have historically formed the basis for all GAAP.

THE BASIC FINANCIAL STATEMENTS ILLUSTRATED: PEPSICO, INC.

In its 1990 annual report, PepsiCo presented four basic financial statements:

- consolidated statement of income
- consolidated balance sheet
- consolidated statement of cash flows
- consolidated statement of shareholders' equity

The "Consolidated Statement of Income" (see Chapter 1) reveals that in 1990 PepsiCo earned net income of $1,076.9 million on net sales of $17,802.7 million. To generate that $17,802.7 million in sales, PepsiCo consumed more than $16,135.3 million in resources and incurred $576.8 million in income taxes.[1]

Note that PepsiCo effectively discloses two broad categories of deduction against revenues: cost and expenses, and the provision for income taxes. The first category represents the costs and expenses to conduct the company's operations, and the second is, of course, the income taxes for which the company is liable. Income taxes are usually reported as a separate line-item expense because many financial statement users believe that **income before taxes** is an important measure of a company's performance. It measures management's success in pricing its products and controlling the costs of conducting its operations. **Net income,** on the other hand, is an aftertax measure of a company's performance and reflects the difference between *all* revenues and *all* costs and expenses (including PepsiCo's one-time charge of $13.7 million in 1990 for pending lawsuits and claims relating to a business sold in a prior period). **Net income** is the increase in the owners' equity for the period attributable to the operations of the company.

Finally, note that PepsiCo's statement of income also reports the company's **net income on a per share basis.** This measure has become an important indicator of a firm's performance in the financial community because it represents a standardized measure (by the number of common shares of stock outstanding) and hence facilitates comparisons between companies, as well as within the same company across time. PepsiCo's net income per share reveals a steady increase from $0.97 per share in 1988, to $1.13 per share in 1989, to $1.35 per share in 1990.

Now consider PepsiCo's "Consolidated Balance Sheet." This statement reveals that, as of year-end 1990, PepsiCo had total assets and total equities of $17,143.4 million. Note that the company segmented its assets and equities into a number of different categories:

Assets	Equities
Current assets	Current liabilities
Investments in affiliates and other assets	Long-term debt
Property, plant, and equipment	Nonrecourse obligation
Goodwill and other intangibles	Other liabilities and deferred credits
	Deferred income taxes
	Shareholders' equity

Although it is premature to try to explain all of these categories, several observations are noteworthy. First, PepsiCo has effectively categorized its assets in two ways: (1) total assets are divided into current and noncurrent categories, and (2) within the noncurrent asset category, the assets are classified by their principal characteristic. **Current assets** are those assets whose consumption is anticipated within the next year (or the company's operating cycle if longer than a year), whereas **noncurrent assets** are long-lived assets

---

[1]Although PepsiCo, Inc., reported income taxes of $576.8 million (excluding the tax benefit of $0.3 million associated with the loss on discontinued operations), the company actually paid significantly less than that because a portion of the reported tax expense was deferred until future periods. The topic of deferred income taxes is discussed in Chapter 12.

whose consumption or use will occur over many years. Within the noncurrent asset category, there are three principal asset groupings: investments, tangible assets (i.e., property, plant, and equipment, which have a physical presence), and intangible assets (i.e., goodwill, which has no physical presence).

Second, PepsiCo has similarly classified its liabilities in two ways: (1) total liabilities are divided into current and noncurrent categories and (2) within the noncurrent category, the liabilities are classified by their principal characteristic. Current liabilities refer to obligations that will be satisfied or paid within the next year, whereas noncurrent liabilities will be satisfied or paid sometime in the future beyond the next year. The noncurrent liabilities category has four subcategories: (1) long-term debt, (2) unsecured or nonrecourse debt, (3) miscellaneous debt, and (4) deferred taxes.

Turning now to PepsiCo's "Consolidated Statement of Shareholders' Equity," note that it has five principal equity accounts: Capital Stock Issued, Capital Stock Held in Treasury, Capital in Excess of Par Value, Retained Earnings, and Currency Translation Adjustment. The Capital Stock account represents the proceeds from sales of the company's stock directly to its shareholders. For legal purposes, these shares carry a **par value** of $0.0167 per share, and when the company sells a share for an amount in excess of the par value, this excess amount is recorded in the Capital in Excess of Par Value account. Thus, the sum of the Capital Stock (at par value) account and the Capital in Excess of Par Value account represents the total funds of the owners directly invested in the company by stock purchase.

The Retained Earnings account is, as we described earlier, the aggregate of all of PepsiCo's earnings less the aggregate of all of the dividends paid to company shareholders. In essence, the retained earnings are funds that rightly belong to the stockholders but that have been indirectly reinvested in the company's operations.

Occasionally, a company may find it advantageous to repurchase some of its capital shares. When this occurs, the cost of the repurchased shares are classified as treasury stock, and this amount is subtracted from the total owners' equity. PepsiCo uses the Currency Translation Adjustment account to reflect changes in the currency rates between the U.S. dollar and the currency of the foreign countries in which it conducts its operations. Such exchange rate fluctuations cause the U.S. dollar–equivalent value of PepsiCo's overseas assets (e.g., those in the United Kingdom) to fluctuate from year to year. These fluctuations are summarized in the Currency Translation Adjustment account.

Finally, consider PepsiCo's "Consolidated Statement of Cash Flows." This statement reveals that in 1990 PepsiCo added $94.6 million to its cash (and cash equivalents) balance as follows (in millions):

Net Cash Generated by Continuing Operations	$ 2,110.0
Net Cash Used for Investing Activities	(1,937.3)
Net Cash Generated by (Used for) Financing Activities	(77.1)
Effect of Exchange Rate Changes on Cash and Cash Equivalents	(1.0)
Net Increase (Decrease) in Cash and Cash Equivalents	$ 94.6

In the following chapters, we will explain in greater detail the meaning of each of these accounts, and we will learn how such statements can be prepared and analyzed.

SUMMARY

Under GAAP, companies are required to report their financial activities using the basic financial statements: the balance sheet, the income statement, the statement of owners' equity, and the statement of cash flows. Although management is responsible for the preparation of the basic statements, it is required to use the methods approved or established by the FASB and endorsed by the SEC. In general, the overall criterion used to decide what information should be included in the accounting reports is the overall fairness of the financial picture presented to statement users.

NEW CONCEPTS AND TERMS

Accrual method (p. 43)

Allocation concept (p. 45)

Assets (p. 35)

Balance sheet (p. 35)

Capital stock (p. 37)

Cash basis (p. 42)

Conservatism concept (p. 46)

Consistency concept (p. 47)

Cost concept (p. 43)

Current assets (p. 51)

Current liabilities (p. 52)

Dividends (p. 37)

Entity concept (p. 42)

Equity (p. 35)

Expenses (p. 36)

Fair value basis (p. 43)

Income statement (p. 35)

Intangible assets (p. 52)

Investments (p. 52)

Liabilities (p. 35)

Lower-of-cost-or-market value (p. 46)

Matching concept (p. 45)

Materiality concept (p. 48)

Net income (loss) (p. 37)

Noncurrent assets (p. 51)

Noncurrent liabilities (p. 52)

Owners' equity (p. 36)

Periodic measurement concept (p. 45)

Prospectus (p. 49)

Retained earnings (p. 37)

Revenues (p. 36)

Statement of cash flows (p. 35)

Statement of earnings (p. 35)

Statement of financial position (p. 35)

Statement of owners' equity (p. 35)

Tangible assets (p. 52)

Transaction concept (p. 44)

Treasury stock (p. 52)

ISSUES FOR DISCUSSION

D2.1 Distinguish between cost and value, and explain how these two ideas are used in preparing financial statements intended for use in the annual report to shareholders.

D2.2 Companies frequently say that their employees are their most important assets. Where do those assets appear on published balance sheets? Why should that be so?

D2.3 You are the sole owner of a company whose accounting records reflect an equity of $275,000. Assuming that you are ready to retire, would you agree to sell your business for $275,000? Why or why not? If you decide to accept an offer of more than $275,000, what value would you think the purchasor would use in his or her subsequent financial reports for the net assets purchased from you? Why? Assume that you rejected a firm offer of more than $275,000 and decided to wait for a better offer. What value should you use in your subsequent financial statements? Why?

D2.4 Consider yourself a prospective investor. Explain briefly how you might use the three basic financial statements (the balance sheet, the income statement, and the statement of cash flows) in your investment decision. What different insights would you expect those three different statements to provide for your investment decision?

D2.5 In 1990, PepsiCo reported net income for the year of $1,076.9 million (as reported in the statement of net income) and a net increase in cash and cash equivalent of $94.6 million (as reported in the statement of cash flows). What do those two numbers mean to you as a potential investor in PepsiCo?

D2.6 We say that the accounting equation forces the right side of the balance sheet always to be in balance with the left side, or that every resource has a source. A company's earnings for the year, retained for use in the business, represent a source. Where might that source have been invested? Where would we find the equivalent of that source on the left-hand side of the balance sheet?

D2.7 A number of sources of funds are available to a company, and those different sources are compensated in different ways. A supplier might sell steel to the company on a credit basis, asking for payment in full by 90 days. A bank would be willing to lend money to the company for periods of 90 days for any number of years. A shareholder, thinking that the shares can always be sold to someone else if need be, is willing to invest funds in the company. Where do these sources appear in the balance sheet? Where does the compensation required by the sources for the uses of their funds appear in the income statement?

D2.8 A college friend has been quite successful with a computer software company she began shortly after graduation. The company now needs more money for expansion, and your friend is about to sell stock to a select group of investors. She has been preparing financial statements for her company for her own use but will now have to prepare financial reports for outsiders. Explain for your friend the advantages and disadvantages of adopting aggressive accounting policies or conservative accounting policies. Give as many examples as you can, together with your overall explanation.

D2.9 You are the president of a small computer company that led the market in the introduction of a low-priced lap-top computer. With a manufacturing cost of $1,500 and a retail price of $3,000, the company did quite well. In the last several years, the major companies in the industry have surpassed your original product by introducing a few technical refinements. You are now ready to introduce Version 2 of your product, which will be a dramatic leap over the competition. However, you still have about 5,000 units of the earlier model. Your salespeople tell you that you have only two alternatives. The salespeople are confident that the units can be sold to college students at a discounted price of $500 each. Alternatively, it may be possible to sell those units at full retail price in some of the less developed countries. How (and why) should this choice be reflected in your company's financial statements?

D2.10 Since you won $100,000 in the state lottery, you have been besieged with proposals to invest your gains. Most recently, Harry Schultz, president of Schultz Corporation, has suggested that you invest $50,000 in the common stock of his company's manufacturing subsidiary. He has shown you the financial statements of the subsidiary and they look promising. On the balance sheet, you see that the assets are mostly raw material inventory and production equipment. The liabilities are quite small and consist mostly of ordinary trade payables to creditors. The income statements show a steady growth in sales and a very satisfactory return. You understand that Schultz

Corporation as a whole has not been doing well recently because of price-cutting competition. The president assures you that the manufacturing side of the business is quite healthy and urges your investment.

Would you buy an equity interest in the manufacturing subsidiary? Why or why not? If you are uncertain about making the investment at this time, outline the additional information you would like to have before making that investment, and explain why that information might be important to you.

PROBLEMS

P2.1 Using the accounting equation. Applying the basic accounting equation to the Northfield Corporation at two successive year-ends yields the following results:

Year end	Assets	=	Liabilities	+	Equity
1990	$40,000	=	$30,000	+	$10,000
1991	$35,000	=	$20,000	+	$15,000

Required:

Assuming that no dividends were declared and that no additional capital was invested by the owners, what amount would Northfield have reported as its net income or loss for the 1991 year? Please explain your answer in the context of the facts here.

P2.2 Accounting concepts. Think about each of the situations described below in the context of the preceding discussion, "Some Fundamental Questions in Accounting" (pages 40–48):

a. Disneyland in Anaheim, California, sells coupon books of 20-, 30-, and 40-ride tickets that can be used anytime that the park is open. During January 1991, the amusement park sold $14 million worth of these coupon books. The proceeds were recorded initially as a liability, not as revenue.

b. Disneyland reports on its balance sheet the Anaheim, California, property on which the amusement park is located at its purchase price in 1955.

c. Sky Rider, Inc., specializes in the design and construction of roller coaster rides for amusement parks around the world. Each custom ride takes about two and one-half years to design and build, and the firm typically works on only three or four rides at a time. Nevertheless, the company publishes an annual report with a full income statement detailing its revenues and expenses for each year.

d. Taco Bell, a division of PepsiCo, Inc., owns numerous "taco ranches." The costs to develop each ranch are deferred and reported on the balance sheet as an asset, to be written off over the estimated commercially productive lives of the "taco trees."

e. Mac Donald purchased 800 shares of capital stock in PepsiCo, Inc., in January 1989 for $28 per share on the advice of his stockbroker, Ham Berger. Mac then sold one-half of the purchased shares at $33 per share in August of that same year. PepsiCo's annual report, however, reveals that 863,083,000 shares have been outstanding, and that there have been no changes in that number for the last three years. The average book value of the outstanding shares has been $13.50 per share.

Required:

For each of the above situations, describe the accounting concept or principle which applies, as the basis for the accounting followed.

P2.3 PepsiCo and the accounting equation. Think about the PepsiCo financial statements we studied in Chapter 1. Assume that the company entered into the transactions listed below.

Required:

Using the three-part box described in this Chapter,

| Assets | Liabilities |
| | Owners' equity |

describe in your own words how the following six transactions might affect PepsiCo's financial statements:

 a. the sale of common stock to a group of investors for $1 million.
 b. the sale of a new issue of bonds to investors in the amount of $5 million.
 c. use of the proceeds of the stock sale and the bond sale to retire a $6 million bank debt.
 d. the purchase of $100,000 worth of sausage for the production of pizza, paid in cash as demanded by the sausage maker.
 e. the purchase of $250,000 worth of cans and bottles for bottling Pepsi, to be paid for within 30 days.
 f. results for the month of January indicating the aggregate net income from all the units of $25 million.

P2.4 Projections from historic financials. Pepsico does not publish earnings projections, but they do provide historical detailed segment information, multi-year income statements, and cash flow statements, and they also provide text commentary (i.e., "Management's Analysis"). Study Pepsico's business segment data, its income statement, its cash flow statement, and the related management commentaries, and prepare the following:

Required:

 a. Based solely on the data in the statements and the related commentaries, what would *you* project Pepsico's 1991 net income to be? Explain the factors which influenced your judgment.

 b. Identify five pieces of information you would like to have, that make your projection more reliable. Where would you go to get that information? Do you think you could convince the FASB of the importance of that information, so that it would be provided to public stockholders in future financial statements? Why or why not?

P2.5 Accrual versus cash basis accounting. Meredith, Miller and Associates, Inc., is a management consulting group which was organized for business on August 1, 1991. Greg Meredith and Kate Miller each contributed $20,000 cash for shares of capital stock in the new company. The firm also borrowed $15,000 from a local bank on September 1, 1991; the loan was to be paid in full on August 30, 1992, with interest at the rate of 12 percent annually.

The new company rented office space on September 1, paying two months' rent in advance. The regular monthly rental fees of $600 per month were to be made on the first day of each month beginning on November 1. The company purchased a word-processing system and a fax machine in early August at a total cost of $3,600 cash. The owners estimated that the useful life of the office equipment was three years.

For the five months ended December 31, 1991, the company had rendered $31,000 in consulting services. Of this amount, $19,000 had been collected by year-end. Other costs incurred and paid in cash by year-end included:

Utilities	$ 550
Part-time typist/secretary	6,000
Miscellaneous office supplies	325

Unpaid bills at year-end included a telephone bill for $75 and wages for the typist-secretary of $600.

Required:

You have been retained by the firm of Meredith, Miller and Associates, Inc., to prepare a set of accounting statements as of December 31, 1991. Using the above information, prepare a balance sheet, an income statement using the accrual basis of accounting, an income statement using the cash basis of accounting, and a statement of cash flows. On the basis of your findings, be prepared to comment on the performance of the company during its first five months of operations.

P2.6 Accounting data attributes. As a part of its effort to develop a conceptual basis for accounting, the FASB prepared the following chart. The Board felt that its rule-making program would proceed on a more solid foundation if it could outline conceptually the most important qualities that accounting data should have: it was understood that proposed accounting standards would then be judged against these qualities, to see if the new standard would produce accounting information that would achieve these qualities at an acceptable cost. This chart has become a benchmark for the Board and other accounting thinkers (see p. 58).

Required:

For each quality identified by the FASB, describe in your own words what that quality means, and how it might be manifested in a set of accounting data.

P2.7 Focusing on the users of accounting information. Look again at the chart in P2.6. When the FASB outlined that Hierarchy of Accounting Qualities, they had in mind a general purpose use of the resulting accounting data. But, of course, there are many users of accounting information, including current stockholders, future stockholders, creditors, employees, etc. Each user group will have different uses for accounting data, and so different attributes of accounting will be more or less important to each.

Required:

Identify three different user groups that might have an interest in accounting data, and prepare a single-page paper on each, discussing which of the accounting qualities outlined in the chart in P2.6 might be most important to them, and why.

Financial Accounting Standards Board Conceptual Framework
A Hierarchy of Account Qualities

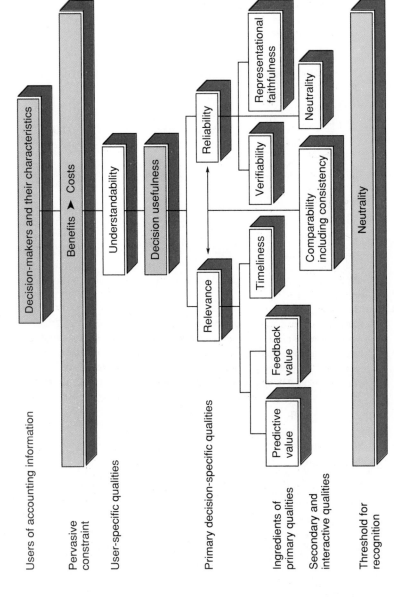

Users of accounting information

Decision-makers and their characteristics

Pervasive
constraint

Benefits ▶ Costs

User-specific qualities

Understandability

Decision usefulness

Primary decision-specific qualities

Relevance

Reliability

Predictive
value

Feedback
value

Timeliness

Verifiability

Representational
faithfulness

Neutrality

Comparability
including consistency

Ingredients of
primary qualities

Secondary and
interactive qualities

Threshold for
recognition

Neutrality

Source: FASB, *Statement of Financial Accounting Concepts No. 2*

P2.8 Annual report information. The following list identifies a number of items which might tell you something about a company. Study this list from the standpoint of a potential investor.
(1) Brief history of business
(2) Financial statements for last five years (audited if possible)
    (a) Balance sheets
    (b) Profit and loss and surplus statements
(3) Evaluation of labor relations and terms of union contracts
(4) Description, age, and general evaluation of plants, manufacturing equipment, warehouses, branches, and delivery equipment, owned or leased
(5) Trend of sales of each of principal products for five years
(6) Description of corporate structure
(7) Number of employees
(8) Explanation of unusual items on financial statements
(9) List of officers and directors, their affiliations and background
(10) Principal competitors—comparative share of market
(11) Stock distribution, number of stockholders, principal holders
(12) Description of marketing and distribution methods, areas
(13) Details of debt
(14) Status of income tax audit and liability
(15) Percentage ownership of stock available for acquisition
(16) Description and cost of fringe benefits (insurance, medical, pensions)
(17) Details of unrecorded and contingent liabilities
(18) Description of any option, incentive, or profit sharing plans
(19) Organization, functions of principal executives, ages
(20) Description of principal customers—share of business
(21) Projection of sales and earnings over next five years
(22) Willingness of management to continue in business
(23) Terms of principal contracts and leases
(24) Extent of export sales
(25) Major capital expenditures presently authorized
(26) Status of litigation and any other claims or suits against the compnay
(27) Extent of advertising
(28) Estimate of major capital expenditures required over next five years
(29) Copies of annual reports to shareholders
(30) Copy of charter and bylaws
(31) Cost of capital
(32) Social responsibility activities
(33) Major subsidiaries and affiliates

Required:

Prepare a brief paper identifying the top 10 items from the list that you would want to be able to study and review. Why did you select those items? Which would you expect to find in the company's annual report to stockholders?

P2.9 Prolific FASB. Since its inception in the early 70s, the FASB had issued 106 Financial Accounting Statements (FAS) as of June 1, 1991, as well as numerous interpretations and concepts releases. Listed below are the titles of the 106 FASs. Study the list from the standpoint of a user of financial statements, from the standpoint of a corporate executive, or from the standpoint of a preparer of financial statements.

FASB Statements (FAS)

No.	Title
1	Disclosure of Foreign Currency Translation Information
2	Accounting for Research and Development Costs
3	Reporting Accounting Changes in Interim Financial Statements (an amendment of APB Opinion No. 28)
4	Reporting Gains and Losses from Extinguishment of Debt (an amendment of APB Opinion No. 30)
5	Accounting for Contingencies
6	Classification of Short-Term Obligations Expected to Be Refinanced (an amendment of ARB No. 43, Chapter 3A)
7	Accounting and Reporting by Development Stage Enterprises
8	Accounting for the Translation of Foreign Currency Transactions and Foreign Currency Financial Statements
9	Accounting for Income Taxes—Oil and Gas Producing Companies (an amendment of APB Opinions No. 11 and 23)
10	Extension of "Grandfather" Provisions for Business Combinations (an amendment of APB Opinion No. 16)
11	Accounting for Contingencies—Transition Method (an amendment of FASB Statement No. 5)
12	Accounting for Certain Marketable Securities
13	Accounting for Leases
14	Financial Reporting for Segments of a Business Enterprise
15	Accounting by Debtors and Creditors for Troubled Debt Restructurings
16	Prior Period Adjustments
17	Accounting for Leases—Initial Direct Costs (an amendment of FASB Statement No. 13)
18	Financial Reporting for Segments of a Business Enterprise—Interim Financial Statements (an amendment of FASB Statement No. 14)
19	Financial Accounting and Reporting by Oil and Gas Producing Companies
20	Accounting for Forward Exchange Contracts (an amendment of FASB Statement No. 8)
21	Suspension of the Reporting of Earnings per Share and Segment Information by Nonpublic Enterprises (an amendment of APB Opinion No. 15 and FASB Statement No. 14)
22	Changes in the Provisions of Lease Agreements Resulting from Refundings of Tax-Exempt Debt (an amendment of FASB Statement No. 13)
23	Inception of the Lease (an amendment of FASB Statement No. 13)
24	Reporting Segment Information in Financial Statements That Are Presented in Another Enterprise's Financial Report (an amendment of FASB Statement No. 14)
25	Suspension of Certain Accounting Requirements for Oil and Gas Producing Companies (an amendment of FASB Statement No. 19)
26	Profit Recognition on Sales-Type Leases of Real Estate (an amendment of FASB Statement No. 13)
27	Classification of Renewals or Extensions of Existing Sales-Type or Direct Financing Leases (an amendment of FASB Statement No. 13)
28	Accounting for Sales with Leasebacks (an amendment of FASB Statement No. 13)
29	Determining Contingent Rentals (an amendment of FASB Statement No. 13)
30	Disclosure of Information about Major Customers (an amendment of FASB Statement No. 14)
31	Accounting for Tax Benefits Related to U.K. Tax Legislation Concerning Stock Relief
32	Specialized Accounting and Reporting Principles and Practices in AICPA Statements of Position and Guides on Accounting and Auditing Matters (an amendment of APB Opinion No. 20)
33	Financial Reporting and Changing Prices
34	Capitalization of Interest Cost
35	Accounting and Reporting by Defined Benefit Pension Plans
36	Disclosure of Pension Information (an amendment of APB Opinion No. 8)
37	Balance Sheet Classification of Deferred Income Taxes (an amendment of APB Opinion No. 11)
38	Accounting for Preacquisition Contingencies of Purchased Enterprises (an amendment of APB Opinion No. 16)
39	Financial Reporting and Changing Prices: Specialized Assets—Mining and Oil and Gas (a supplement to FASB Statement No. 33)
40	Financial Reporting and Changing Prices: Specialized Assets—Timberlands and Growing Timber (a supplement to FASB Statement No. 33)

FASB Statements (FAS)

No.	Title
41	Financial Reporting and Changing Prices: Specialized Assets—Income-Producing Real Estate (a supplement to FASB Statement No. 33)
42	Determining Materiality for Capitalization of Interest Cost (an amendment of FASB Statement No. 34)
43	Accounting for Compensated Absences
44	Accounting for Intangible Assets of Motor Carriers (an amendment of Chapter 5 of ARB 43 and an interpretation of APB Opinions 17 and 30)
45	Accounting for Franchise Fee Revenue
46	Financial Reporting and Changing Prices: Motion Picture Films (a supplement to FASB Statement No. 33)
47	Disclosure of Long-Term Obligations
48	Revenue Recognition When Right of Return Exists
49	Accounting for Product Financing Arrangements
50	Financial Reporting in the Record and Music Industry
51	Financial Reporting by Cable Television Companies
52	Foreign Currency Translation
53	Financial Reporting by Producers and Distributors of Motion Picture Films
54	Financial Reporting and Changing Prices: Investment Companies (an amendment of FASB Statement No. 33)
55	Determining whether a Convertible Security Is a Common Stock Equivalent (an amendment of APB Opinion No. 15)
56	Designation of AICPA Guide and Statement of Position (SOP) 81-1 on Contractor Accounting and SOP 81-2 concerning Hospital-Related Organizations as Preferable for Purposes of Applying APB Opinion 20 (an amendment of FASB Statement No. 32)
57	Related Party Disclosures
58	Capitalization of Interest Cost in Financial Statements That Include Investments Accounted for by the Equity Method (an amendment of FASB Statement No. 34)
59	Deferral of the Effective Date of Certain Accounting Requirements for Pension Plans of State and Local Governmental Units (an amendment of FASB Statement No. 35)
60	Accounting and Reporting by Insurance Enterprises
61	Accounting for Title Plant
62	Capitalization of Interest Cost in Situations Involving Certain Tax-Exempt Borrowings and Certain Gifts and Grants (an amendment of FASB Statement No. 34)
63	Financial Reporting by Broadcasters
64	Extinguishments of Debt Made to Satisfy Sinking-Fund Requirements (an amendment of FASB Statement No. 4)
65	Accounting for Certain Mortgage Banking Activities
66	Accounting for Sales of Real Estate
67	Accounting for Costs and Initial Rental Operations of Real Estate Projects
68	Research and Development Arrangements
69	Disclosures about Oil and Gas Producing Activities (an amendment of FASB Statements No. 19, 25, 33, and 39)
70	Financial Reporting and Changing Prices: Foreign Currency Translation (an amendment of FASB Statement No. 33)
71	Accounting for the Effects of Certain Types of Regulation
72	Accounting for Certain Acquisitions of Banking or Thrift Institutions (an amendment of APB Opinion No. 17, an interpretation of APB Opinions 16 and 17, and an amendment of FASB Interpretation No. 9)
73	Reporting a Change in Accounting for Railroad Track Structures (an amendment of APB Opinion No. 20)
74	Accounting for Special Termination Benefits Paid to Employees
75	Deferral of the Effective Date of Certain Accounting Requirements for Pension Plans of State and Local Governmental Units (an amendment of FASB Statement No. 35)
76	Extinguishment of Debt (an amendment of APB Opinion No. 26)
77	Reporting by Transferors for Transfers of Receivables with Recourse
78	Classification of Obligations That Are Callable by the Creditor (an amendment of ARB No. 43, Chapter 3A)

FASB Statements (FAS)

No.	Title
79	Elimination of Certain Disclosures for Business Combinations by Nonpublic Enterprises (an amendment of APB Opinion No. 16)
80	Accounting for Futures Contracts
81	Disclosure of Postretirement Health Care and Life Insurance Benefits
82	Financial Reporting and Changing Prices: Elimination of Certain Disclosures (an amendment of FASB Statement No. 33)
83	Designation of AICPA Guides and Statement of Position on Accounting by Brokers and Dealers in Securities, by Employee Benefit Plans, and by Banks as Preferable for Purposes of Applying APB Opinion 20 (an amendment of FASB Statement No. 32 and APB Opinion No. 30 and a rescission of FASB Interpretation No. 10)
84	Induced Conversions of Convertible Debt (an amendment of APB Opinion No. 26)
85	Yield Test for Determining whether a Convertible Security Is a Common Stock Equivalent (an amendment of APB Opinion No. 15)
86	Accounting for the Costs of Computer Software to Be Sold, Leased, or Otherwise Marketed
87	Employers' Accounting for Pensions
88	Employers' Accounting for Settlements and Curtailments of Defined Benefit Pension Plans and for Termination Benefits
89	Financial Reporting and Changing Prices
90	Regulated Enterprises—Accounting for Abandonments and Disallowances of Plant Costs (an amendment of FASB Statement No. 71)
91	Accounting for Nonrefundable Fees and Costs Associated with Originating or Acquiring Loans and Initial Direct Costs of Leases (an amendment of FASB Statements No. 13, 60, and 65 and a rescission of FASB Statement No. 17)
92	Regulated Enterprises—Accounting for Phase-in Plans (an amendment of FASB Statement No. 71)
93	Recognition of Depreciation by Not-for-Profit Organizations
94	Consolidation of All Majority-Owned Subsidiaries (an amendment of ARB No. 51, with related amendments of APB Opinion No. 18 and ARB No. 43, Chapter 12)
95	Statement of Cash Flows
96	Accounting for Income Taxes
97	Accounting and Reporting by Insurance Enterprises for Certain Long-Duration Contracts and for Realized Gains and Losses from the Sale of Investments
98	Accounting for Leases: • Sale-Leaseback Transactions Involving Real Estate • Sales-Type Leases of Real Estate • Definition of the Lease Term • Initial Direct Costs of Direct Financing Leases (an amendment of FASB Statements No. 13, 66, and 91 and a rescission of FASB Statement No. 26 and Technical Bulletin No. 79-11)
99	Deferral of the Effective Date of Recognition of Depreciation by Not-for-Profit Organizations (an amendment of FASB Statement No. 93)
100	Accounting for Income Taxes—Deferral of the Effective Date of FASB Statement No. 96 (an amendment of FASB Statement No. 96)
101	Regulated Enterprises—Accounting for the Discontinuation of Application of FASB Statement No. 71
102	Statement of Cash Flows—Exemption of Certain Enterprises and Classification of Cash Flows from Certain Securities Acquired for Resale (an amendment of FASB Statement No. 95)
103	Accounting for Income Taxes—Deferral of the Effective Date of FASB Statement No. 96 (an amendment of FASB Statement No. 96)
104	Statement of Cash Flows—Net Reporting of Certain Cash Receipts and Cash Payments and Classification of Cash Flows from Hedging Transactions (an amendment of FASB Statement No. 95)
105	Disclosure of Information about Financial Instruments with Off-Balance-Sheet Risk and Financial Instruments with Concentrations of Credit Risk
106	Employers' Accounting for Postretirement Benefits Other Than Pensions

Required:

Prepare a one-page essay discussing the attributes of the above list, from either the perspective of a user or a preparer. (Hint: you might look for patterns of certain types, general vs. specific statements, numbers of revisions, etc.)

P2.10 Accounting politics. Consider the following statements that have been made about accounting and accounting standards:

"The numbers that accountants report have, or at least are widely thought to have, a *significant* impact on *economic behavior*. Accounting rules therefore affect human behavior. Hence, the process by which they are made is said to be political. It is then only a short step to the assertion that such rules are properly to be made in the political arena, by counting heads and deciding accounting issues by some voting mechanism."[1]

"The process of setting accounting standards can be described as democratic because like all rule-making bodies the Board's right to make rules depends ultimately on the consent of the ruled."[2]

"The [FASB's] objective must be responsive to many more considerations than accounting theory or our notions of economically useful data. . . . Corporate reporting standards should result in data that are useful for economic decisions *provided that the standard is consistent with the national macro economic objectives and the economic programs designed to reach these goals.*"[3]

"Information cannot be neutral—it cannot therefore be reliable—if it is selected or presented for the purpose of producing some chosen effect on human behavior. It is this quality of neutrality which makes a map reliable; and the essential nature of accounting, I believe, is cartographic. Accounting is financial mapmaking."[4]

"Some [would say that] the financial phenomena which accountants must report are not independent of the reporting methods selected."[5]

Required:

Prepare a one-page essay explaining your views on the debate described in the above quotes. Your analysis should consider the implications of both sides of the argument, both for the external users of financial statements and for the preparers of that data.

P2.11 The cost today of future benefits. The CEO of JJ Corp., JoAnn Jones, was visibly upset. The regular monday morning meeting of the Executive Committee had gone reasonably well (sales were up, costs were under control), but it had come to a very disturbing conclusion. The Chief Financial Officer had offered some concluding comments describing a new ruling from some organization called the Financial Accounting Standards Board, which threatened to wipe out the Company's net worth. The JJ Corp. contract with the union required, among other things, that the company pay the Blue Cross/Blue Shield bills for retirees and their spouses. In the past, those

---

[1,4,5]Solomans, D., "The Politicization of Accounting," *The Journal of Accountancy* (November 1978), pp. 65–72.

[2]*The Structure of Establishing Financial Accounting Standards* (Stanford, Conn: FAF, April 1977), p. 19.

[3]David M. Hawkins, "Financial Accounting, the Standards Board and Economic Development," one of the 1973–74 Emanuel Saxe Distinguished Lectures in Accounting, published by the Bernard M. Baruch College, City University of New York, April 1975. pp. 7–8.

insurance premiums had been charged to expense in the period when they were paid: that accounting process was simple and straightforward, although the expenses had gone up dramatically in recent years. Under this new accounting rule, JJ Corp. would be required to estimate, as the employees worked, how much the insurance premiums would be after they retired. A pro rata portion of that future payment was to be allocated as an expense to the periods when the employees were working. The current charge for that future payment was sure to depress current net income materially. Worse, the new rule required the company to record a liability now, for the payments to be due to those employees currently retired. To record that liability, the company would have to record a reduction in shareholder's equity. The preliminary estimate of that liability was greater than the company's net worth, as of the most recent year-end.

Jones had been concerned about the impact of the rising cost of health insurance, and had joined with other executives in the state to "do something about health care costs." This move from the FASB was not what she had in mind, however. She argued with her CFO, saying, "How can we possibly estimate what those future premiums might be? How can we predict how many employees will stay with us until retirement, or how long they will live after retirement? And health care costs cannot stay this high—we *will* find a way to reduce them. If we base our estimates of future payments on the premiums we are paying today, we will seriously over-charge current earnings. It may be that the company will be forced to drop health insurance coverage as a benefit. Then what will we do with those accrued charges?"

Required:

Based on the discussion above and your reading of Chapter 2, prepare a two-page commentary on this issue, arguing in your own words Jones' point of view, and then the probable basis of the FASB requirement. State your own conclusion, making sure that it is well justified.

P2.12 Regulation without representation. After an extended discussion between Jones and her CFO regarding the requirements of the FASB's new accounting statement, "Other Post-Employment Benefits" (the initial phase of that discussion was outlined in Problem 2.11 above), Jones finally accepted the idea that the new statement was GAAP, and was a fact of life. The impact of that statement on her company's financial statements made her angry, nonetheless. She said that she was putting her health care cost campaign on the back burner, and that she resolved to do something about the accounting profession instead. She asked how it was possible that the FASB could make such an important ruling without some check on its authority. She made some reference to the Boston Tea Party. She asked the company's attorney and the CFO to look into the authority and the standing of the FASB. A little later they reported back to her, explaining that the Securities Laws had given statutory authority for accounting rule-making to the Securities and Exchange Commission, which had delegated that authority to the FASB. They explained the Board's independent status, and its funding basis. Jones immediately picked up her dictaphone and composed a letter to her congressperson, arguing that accounting was too important to be left to the accountants, and demanding that the SEC take back its rule-making position. She explained to her associates that she was sure that the business community would have a stronger voice in accounting matters if they could speak through their congressional representatives, and through them to the SEC.

Required:

Prepare a one-page memorandum for Jones, explaining why she should not send that letter. You may also suggest some other courses of action for her, as long as you can develop strong logic for your alternatives.

P2.13 Current value reporting. The managers of Property Developments, Inc., were concerned about the depressed price at which the company's stock was trading. It had not gotten much above the $5 range, suggesting that Wall Street thought the company was worth about $5,000,000. The company's net worth, according to the most recent financial statements, was about $4,500,000, but everyone knew that the historic cost financial statements seriously understated the value of the company's portfolio of shopping plazas and apartment complexes. It was suggested that the market price of the stock might go up if the value of the company's properties was better understood by a wider audience. PDI management discussed together the pros and cons of preparing and publishing current value financial statements for the company. Eventually they agreed that the potential benefit was worth the cost, and the discussion turned to implementation of the idea. An interesting and heated argument ensued as to the definition of "current value" as the term might be used in connection with the preparation of current value financial statements.

The Operations Manager argued that the properties should be valued at 8 times their cash flow, inasmuch as that is the way the company looked at properties they were considering buying.

The Construction Manager argued that the current value of the properties was the current cost of replacing them, given the inflation that had swept through the construction industry.

The Chief Financial Officer argued that the properties ought to be valued at the price obtained in the sale of comparable properties, inasmuch as that is the way a potential raider would look at the individual properties in a campaign to liquidate the company.

Required:

Assume that the company is going to prepare current value basis financial statements as a supplement to its GAAP-based, historic cost statements; how should the current values be determined—On the basis of some multiple of current cash flow? On the basis of replacement cost? On the basis of comparable properties' sale prices? Present the rationale for your position.

P2.14 Fortunate Corporation finally finds a buyer. Fortunate Corporation had been through very difficult times. Its principle product had been left behind in a consumer style shift, and the company had been forced to get along by manufacturing and selling accessory products. New management had come in and had resolved to reduce excess capacity (and operating costs) to maintain the viability of at least some aspects of the company. They put the company's original facility, old Plant #1, on the market, but there were very few inquiries from potential buyers. Then one day, close to the end of the fiscal year, the realtor called to tell them disturbing news: the State Highway Department had announced plans to build a bypass around town, and were planning to route the new road right through the center of old Plant #1. The plant and its land was on the books at $10,000,000. Based on the realtor's advice, the company was asking $11,500,000 in its current campaign to dispose of the property; the attorney was able to get a firm commitment from the state, that it would buy the property from the company, paying $12,000,000 three years from today, in accordance with "eminent domain" procedures.

Required:

Discuss the application of the notion of "lower of cost or market" in this situation. How should this situation be reflected in the company's current year's financial statements? Why?

P2.15 Applications of materiality concept. Consider the application of the idea of materiality in each of the following situations. Assume that for the year ended December 31, 1991, the company has total assets of $10,000,000 and net worth of $3,000,000. Assume that sales were

$10,000,000 two years ago, $11,000,000 last year, and $12,000,000 this year, and that net income was $400,000 two years ago, $550,000 last year, and $650,000 this year.

a. Research and development had never been a major expense for the company, but had been growing about 5 percent a year. In 1991, it had grown to $500,000. The company had always disclosed in a footnote the amount of R&D expense it had incurred each year, but had never included it as a separate line item in the income statement. R&D expenses had always been included in the line item "General and Administrative Expenses."

b. The company's subsidiary in Australia had a fire in its accounting department in mid-December, and will not be able to get its financial reports into the home office in accordance with the original schedule for the preparation of the annual report to stockholders. Waiting until the data can be reconstructed and delivered to the home office will mean postponing the usual shareholder meeting for at least a month. In its report to the home office for the eleven months ended November 30, 1991, the subsidiary reported assets of $1,000,000; total equity of $300,000, and earnings-to-date of $25,000.

c. Each year the company counted all of the products-in-inventory on hand at all of its locations, priced out those inventory count sheets, and adjusted the balance sheet inventory amount to equal the values indicated by the price quantity count sheets. That process had been completed in early January and the inventory account had been adjusted up to $3,000,000. The rest of the work required to pull together the financial statements was almost done, and that was good because the final statements had been promised to the bank early next week. Unfortunately, the inventory control manager called to report an error in the inventory pricing process. It seems that the computer program used to price the count sheets had slipped a decimal point: a product which should have had a value of $5 had been priced at $50. As a result the total inventory was overvalued by $250,000. That error overstated inventory by 8.3 percent, total assets by 2.5 percent, and after-tax income for the year by 19 percent.

d. The financial statements were completed and delivered to the bank and mailed to the shareholders. The manager of the Tuscon plant called to say that an accounting employee had disappeared yesterday, and that when people had checked around they found that $10,000 in cash was gone from the plant vault. The employee had been responsible for the plant's payroll and vendor payment system. The plant had processed about $4,000,000 in payroll and $7,000,000 in vendor purchases last year.

Required:

For each of the situations outlined above, explain what you think the company ought to do, giving particular consideraton to the concept of materiality. How should the notion of materiality impact the decisions suggested by the above situations?

P2.16 Consolidating the entire entity. The following exhibit presents the balance sheet of General Motors Corporation on a fully consolidated basis, including all of the accounts of General Motors Acceptance Corporation. The next exhibit presents General Motors treating GMAC as though it was an investment. (Note that the shareholders' equity is the same in both presentations. You should also know that GMAC's total assets are $105 billion, its liabilities are $97 billion, and its shareholders' equity is $8 billion. GM owns 100 percent of GMAC and so its $8 billion investment in GMAC is included in the line "Equity in Net Assets of Unconsolidated Affiliates" in the second exhibit.)

General Motors
Consolidated Balance Sheet
For the Years Ended December 31, 1989 and 1990
(Dollars in Millions Except per Share Amounts)

	December 31,	
	1990	1989
Assets		
Cash and cash equivalents	$ 3,688.5	$ 5,625.4
Other marketable securities	4,132.9	4,587.9
Total cash and marketable securities(Note 11)	7,821.4	10,213.3
Finance receivables—net (Note 12)	90,116.2	92,354.6
Accounts and notes receivable (less allowances)	5,731.3	5,447.4
Inventories (less allowances) (Note 1)	9,331.3	7,991.7
Contracts in process (less advances and progress payments of		
$2,353.1 and $2,630.7) (Note 1)	2,348.8	2,073.3
Net equipment on operating leases (less accumulated depreciation		
of $2,692.6 and $3,065.9)	5,882.0	5,131.1
Prepaid expenses and deferred charges	4,751.6	3,914.7
Other investments and miscellaneous assets (less allowances)	7,252.5	5,050.2
Property (Note 1)		
Real estate, plants, and equipment—at cost (Note 14)	67,219.4	63,390.7
Less accumulated depreciation (Note 14)	38,280.8	34,849.7
Net real estate, plants, and equipment	28,938.6	28,541.0
Special tools—at cost (less amortization)	7,206.4	5,453.5
Total property	36,145.0	33,994.5
Intangible assets—at cost (less amortization) (Notes 1 and 6)	10,856.4	7,126.3
Total Assets	$ 180,236.5	$ 173,297.1
Liabilities and Stockholders' Equity		
Liabilities		
Accounts payable (principally trade)	$ 8,824.4	$ 7,707.8
Notes and loans payable (Note 15)	95,633.5	93,424.8
United States, foreign, and other income taxes (Note 9)	3,959.6	5,671.4
Other liabilities (Note 16)	38,255.2	28,456.7
Deferred credits (including investment tax credits—		
$723.0 and $915.4)	1,410.1	1,403.9
Total Liabilities	148,082.8	136,664.6
Stocks Subject to Repurchase (Notes 1 and 17)	2,106.3	1,650.0
Stockholders' Equity (Notes 3,4,5 and 17)		
Preferred stocks ($5.00 series, $153.0; $3.75 series, $81.4)	234.4	234.4
Preference stocks (E $0.10 series, $1.0; H $0.10 series,		
$1.0 in 1989)	1.0	2.0
Common stocks		
$1-2/3 par value (issued, 605,592,356 and 605,683,572 shares)	1,009.3	1,009.5
Class E (issued, 100,220,967 and 48,830,764 shares)	10.0	4.9
Class H (issued, 34,450,398 and 35,162,664 shares)	3.5	3.5
Capital surplus (principally additional paid-in capital)	2,208.2	2,614.0
Net income retained for use in the business	27,148.6	31,230.7
Subtotal	30,615.0	35,099.0
Minimum pension liability adjustment (Note 6)	(1,004.7)	—
Accumulated foreign currency translation and other adjustments	437.1	(116.5)
Total Stockholders' Equity	30,047.4	34,982.5
Total Liabilities and Stockholders' Equity	$ 180,236.5	$ 173,297.1

Reference should be made to the Notes to Financial Statements.

General Motors Operations with GMAC on an Equity Basis
Consolidated Balance Sheet
For the Years Ended December 31, 1989 and 1990
(Dollars in Millions)

	December 31,	
	1990	1989
Assets		
Current Assets		
Cash and cash equivalents	$ 3,491.3	$ 5,455.7
Other marketable securities	1,115.2	1,615.0
Total cash and marketable securities	4,606.5	7,070.7
Accounts and notes receivable		
Trade	16,691.1	18,037.4
Nonconsolidated affiliates	2,998.0	3,758.8
Inventories	9,331.3	7,991.7
Contracts in process	2,348.8	2,073.3
Prepaid expenses and deferred income taxes	3,968.0	2,374.4
Total Current Assets	39,943.7	41,306.3
Equity in Net Assets of Nonconsolidated Affiliates	9,752.2	9,000.1
Other Investments and Miscellaneous Assets	6,692.7	5,761.8
Property	36,034.7	33,895.2
Intangible Assets	10,355.5	6,801.7
Total Assets	$102,778.8	$96,765.1
Liabilities and Stockholders' Equity		
Current Liabilities		
Accounts payable	$ 8,188.8	$ 7,659.2
Loans payable	3,117.8	2,301.7
Income taxes payable	1,148.5	706.4
Accrued liabilities	15,851.5	13,409.2
Stocks subject to repurchase	822.0	—
Total Current Liabilities	29,128.6	24,076.5
Long-Term Debt	4,614.5	4,254.7
Payable to GMAC*	12,918.0	14,460.5
Capitalized Leases	309.3	311.0
Other Liabilities	23,027.6	15,584.3
Deferred Credits	1,449.1	1,445.6
Stocks Subject to Repurchase	1,284.3	1,650.0
Stockholders' Equity	30,047.4	34,982.5
Total Liabilities and Stockholders' Equity	$102,778.8	$96,765.1

*For marketing and financial reasons, GM has assumed part of the dealer inventory financing previously provided by GMAC. To help support these receivables, General Motors entered into a financing agreement with GMAC through 1996, which provides that GMAC will extend loans to GM up to a maximum of $17 billion which bear interest at floating market rates. GMAC services these receivables for General Motors for a fee. This financing agreement ensures that GMAC's ongoing funding activities continue, and returns to GMAC the approximate amount of interest and fees it would have earned had it retained the dealer inventory financing business. At December 31, 1990, $12,718.0 million of such loans were outstanding at a rate of 10.0%, compared with $14,328.0 million at a rate of 10.5% a year earlier. Interest and fees paid by GM to GMAC totaled $1,233.7 million in 1990, $1,469.2 million in 1989, and $1,042.5 million in 1988.

Required:

Both exhibits present the Balance Sheet of General Motors, but they rely on different underlying assumptions. Which presentation seems best to you, and why?

P2.17 Articulated financial statements. Under GAAP, the net earnings for the year less the dividends accrued must be equal to the change in net assets from the end of last year to the end of the current year. Some have suggested that balance sheets ought to be prepared on a current value basis, so as to present a better measure of the shareholders' equity. That idea has been difficult to sell to the financial community because it implies that the income statement would reflect year-to-year changes in value, and those value-driven fluctuations would make it appear that management was not in control of the company. To deal with that concern, it has been suggested that the balance sheet be prepared on a current-cost basis and that the income statements ought to be prepared on a historic cost basis. In effect, those commentators are willing to do away with the idea that the balance sheet and the income statement are inextricably linked — that they need not be articulated.

Required:

Prepare two short memos, each addressed to the president of Property Developments, Inc. (P 2.13 above). One memo should argue that the company's balance sheet and income statement could be prepared on different bases, and that they do not need to "articulate." The other memo should argue that the statements should be prepared on the same basis and that it is important to preserve the GAAP requirement of articulation.

P2.18 Standards for the MD&A. The Securities and Exchange Commission requires (among other things) that companies provide full financial statements to their shareholders every year, and a text presentation called "Management Discussion and Analysis" (the MD&A). The financial statements must be prepared in accordance with GAAP, but there are no standards for the preparation of the MD&A. The SEC's rules for the MD&A simply require management to explain the changes in results from one year to the next, comment on the company's liquidity, and highlight any factor which might make the current statements an inappropriate basis for predicting future trends for the company. Compliance with this requirement has been uneven; some companies have presented quite detailed analytical comparisons of results between years, and some have confined their presentations to simple statements explaining, for instance, that unit sales are up while unit prices have declined. There has been some debate as to whether the SEC (or the FASB) should set more specific standards for the MD&A presentations: more specific standards would obviously enhance the comparability of information between companies, but more specific standards could inhibit the presentations of what is essentially very qualitative information.

Required:

Visit your school's library, and select three annual reports from three different companies in the same industry. Read the president's letter and make your own analysis of the companies' results, as reflected in the financial statements. With that general background, study the MD&A presentation in those reports. Based on your assessment of the quality of those MD&A presentations, prepare a one-page letter addressed to the Securities and Exchange Commission, arguing for either a greater specificity in the MD&A requirements, or for continued flexibility in the rules. Your letter should flow logically from the results of your study of the three examples.

CASES

C2.1 An Accounting Game: The Sheepherders (Part One).* In the high mountains of Chatele, two sheepherders, Deyonne and Batonne, sit arguing their relative positions in life—an argument which has been going on for years. Deyonne says that he has 400 sheep, while Batonne has only 360 sheep. Therefore, Deyonne is much better off. Batonne, on the other hand, argues that he has 30 acres of land while Deyonne has only 20 acres; then too, Deyonne's land was inherited while Batonne had given 35 sheep for 20 acres of land 10 years ago. This year he gave 40 sheep for 10 additional acres of land. Batonne also makes the observation that of Deyonne's sheep 35 belong to another man, and he merely keeps them.

Deyonne counters that he has a large one-room cabin that he built himself. He claims that he has been offered three acres of land for the cabin. Besides these things, he has a plow, which was a gift from a friend and is worth a couple of goats, two carts which were given him in trade for a poor acre of land, and an ox which he had acquired for five sheep.

Batonne goes on to say that his wife has orders for five coats to be made of homespun wool, and that she will receive 25 goats for them. His wife has 10 goats already, three of which have been received in exchange for one sheep just last year. She has an ox which she acquired in a trade for three sheep. She also has one cart which cost her two sheep. Batonne's two-room cabin, even though smaller in dimension than Deyonne's, should bring him two choice acres of land in a trade. Deyonne is reminded by Batonne that he owes Tyrone three sheep for bringing up his lunch each day last year.

Required:

In your opinion, who is wealthier—Deyonne or Batonne?

C2.2 An Accounting Game: The Sheepherders (Part Two).† A year has elapsed since you solved Part One of the Sheepherders Game. After studying your solution to Part One, Deyonne and Batonne grudgingly accepted your opinion as to their relative wealths at the end of last year. The passage of time has not diminished their penchant for argument, however. Now they're arguing about who had the largest income for the year just ended.

Deyonne points out that the number of sheep which he personally owns at year-end exceeds his personal holdings at the beginning of the year by 80, whereas Batonne's increase was only 20. Batonne replies that his increase would have been 60 had he not traded 40 sheep during the year for 10 acres of additional land. Besides, Batonne points out that he exchanged 18 sheep during the year for food and clothing items, whereas Deyonne exchanged only seven for such purposes. The food and clothing has been pretty much used up by the end of the year.

Batonne is happy because his wife made five coats during the year (fulfilling the orders she had at the beginning of the year) and received 25 goats for them. She managed to obtain orders for another five coats (again for 25 goats)—orders on which she has not yet begun to work. Deyonne points out that he took to making his own lunches this year; therefore, he does not owe Tyrone

---

*M. Carlson and J. W. Higgins, "A Games Approach to Introducing Accounting," *Accounting Education: Problems and Prospects* (Sarasota, Fla.: American Accounting Association, 1974).

†M. Carlson and J. W. Higgins, "A Games Approach to Introducing Accounting," *Accounting Education: Problems and Prospects* (Sarasota, Fla.: American Accounting Association, 1974).

anything now. Deyonne was very unhappy one day last year when he discovered that his ox had died of a mysterious illness. Both men are thankful, however, that none of the other animals died or was lost.

Except for the matters reported above, each man's holdings at the end of the current year are the same as his holdings at the end of last year.

Required:

How would you, as an outside observer to this argument, define "income?" Given your definition, whose income—Deyonne's or Batonne's—was greater for the past year?

C2.3 Accrual versus cash basis accounting. Apex Machine Tool found itself with an exciting opportunity. A valued customer ordered a special tool and said that it would pay $10,000 a year in rent, over a 10-year period, for the use of the tool. Apex ran some numbers and estimated that the tool could be built for $60,000 ($25,000 in material, $10,000 in design cost, and $15,000 in labor and other factory costs), although it was clear that fabrication of the tool would take the better part of a year to complete.

On November 1, 1990, Apex's board of directors approved the project. During the next two months, all of the engineering was completed; during January 1991, the steel was ordered and received; the fabrication was completed during the rest of 1991; the tool was delivered to the customer in December 1991. To finance the purchase of the steel and pay for the cost of the engineering and fabrication, Apex borrowed $60,000 using the rental agreement from the customer as collateral. The bank insisted that the principle on the loan ($60,000) be repaid in equal annual installments of $10,000 beginning December 31, 1992. The bank also insisted on annual interest payments, due December 31 each year, at 10 percent of the average amount of the loan outstanding during the year.

The customer is very happy with the tool but has said that it does not expect to have any use for it after the 10-year rental period. Apex plans to take the tool back at the end of the rental period and is sure that it will be good for many more years of useful service. At this time, however, Apex has no other customers in mind for the tool.

Required:

a. Create a time line for the 12 years beginning 1990 (as illustrated below) and indicate in words where—in which period—the events described above will fall for both a cash basis and an accrual basis.

Cash basis
Accrual basis |————1990————|————1991————|————1992————|

b. Put a label on each of those events, on each side of the line; for example, using the cash basis of accounting, what is the nature of the steel purchase in the early part of 1991? What is the nature of that purchase, using the cash basis of accounting?

c. Create two sets of income statements for this project, for each of the years 1990, 1991, 1992, 1997, and 2001. One set of statements should use the cash basis of accounting and one set should use the accrual basis.

d. Describe in your own words how the management of Apex might have applied the matching concept and the allocation concept to the above situation, and how its judgments might have been effected by the notion of conservatism.

The Accounting Process

Chapter Outline

I n Chapter 2, we considered the basic financial statements and the fundamental accounting concepts that are followed in preparing those statements. This chapter discusses and illustrates the accounting process by which an enterprise records the financial results of its business transactions and then reports those financial results in its basic financial statements.

ACCOUNTING INFORMATION SYSTEMS

As noted in Chapter 1, the purpose of accounting is to measure the financial impact of economic events and transactions as they affect an enterprise and to communicate those financial results to various accounting information users. Thus, the basic processes of accounting involve *measuring, recording, reporting,* and *analyzing* financial information.

In this chapter, we will touch briefly on the process of measuring, reporting, and analyzing. We will have more to say about measuring assets and liabilities in subsequent chapters as we discuss accounting for individual assets and liabilities, and we will have more to say about reporting and analyzing specifically in the next two chapters and again in the individual asset and liability chapters. The principal focus of this chapter, however, is on the recording process. We have elected to devote considerable attention to the recording process in this early chapter because that process provides the foundation for much of the remaining, more sophisticated accounting discussion. The user of accounting information need not know all the details of the mechanics of accounting record-keeping; but to interpret accounting information effectively, the user must have a good understanding of the basic process itself.

Measuring

A wide variety of information about an enterprise might be useful to investors and other third parties. However, accounting systems measure, record, and report only those events and transactions that can be objectively measured. For example, it may be quite significant that the president of a company resigned or that a new president has been hired, and a press release describing those events may be given quite wide distribution. However, because the economic consequences of this type of qualitative event are very difficult to measure objectively, it will neither be recorded in the accounting records of the company nor reported in the company's financial statements. The cost of any severance pay due the resigned president *can* be measured objectively and thus *will* be recorded as an obligation in the company's accounts and reflected in its financial statements.

Measurement questions are frequently difficult. Although most economic events and transactions (e.g., sales of merchandise for cash, purchases of equipment, payment of salaries) can be measured relatively easily, the more complex events and transactions (e.g., sales on credit terms, expenditures for research and development, the purchase of another business), present more serious measurement problems, as we will see in later chapters.

Imagine the spectrum of possible transactions on a continuum that looks like this:

Impact is apparent and measurable.	Impact is likely and estimable.	Impact is uncertain and unmeasurable.

Accounting attempts to deal with all of those events and transactions that are, at best, objectively measurable and at least reasonably estimable. For example, at the far left side of the spectrum, the purchase of merchandise is recorded quite routinely at the amount to be paid to a vendor. In the middle of the spectrum, a product recall is probably recognized in the financial statements, assuming that the cost of the recall can be estimated with a reasonable degree of certainty. Other events and transactions, the financial effects of which cannot be reasonably foreseen or quantified, must be communicated to those third parties who have an interest in the company through other communication techniques. As an example of an event at the far right side of the spectrum, think about a company that is ready to bring a potentially dramatic new product to market; the event will almost certainly be described in press reports and in the president's letter in the annual report to stockholders. But because the financial success of the new product is not known and because its impact cannot be measured until the market reacts, the event of the new product launch is not recognized in the financial statements. As you can imagine, management depends on its accounting systems to deal with the events and transactions on the left-hand side of the continuum and spends more of its time attempting to estimate fairly the effects of those transactions in the middle and to communicate thoroughly the effects of those transactions on the right.

Recording

Accounts and the double-entry system. The accounting system of any enterprise is effectively an **information system.** That is, it is a system in which financial information about economic events and transactions is evaluated, processed, and then reported to various information users (e.g., managers and other interested third parties). Like all information systems, an accounting system contains files in which the basic data can be stored for future use or processing. In accounting systems, these files are known as **accounts.**

Thus, when a business transaction occurs, the dollar effects of the transaction are measured, and those measured effects are recorded and stored in the appropriate accounts. Each account represents an asset, a liability, or a component of owners' equity. In theory, a company could maintain only three accounts: an asset account, a liability account, and an owners' equity account. Most companies, however, have many more accounts; the number of accounts needed depends on the complexity of the business and the amount of detail to be presented in the accounting reports. For example, a company may maintain one account labeled "Cash" and accumulate in that account all of the financial effects of events and transactions that impact its cash. On the other hand, many companies maintain individual accounts for different kinds of property and equipment—a separate account for trucks, another for tools, and a third for the factory building. Again, the number of accounts maintained depends on the complexity of the business and on the amount of detail that is to be presented in the basic financial statements.

In manual accounting systems, the accounts are known as **T-accounts,** principally because their format depicts a large "T." The vertical trunk of the "T" effectively divides the account into two sides, a left side and a right side. One side is used to accumulate the effects of those transactions that increase the account balance; the other side is used to accumulate the effects of those transactions that decrease the account balance. As we shall see in a later discussion, whether the right side or the left side is used to accumulate increases or decreases depends on the nature of the account. The **balance** in the account at any time is simply the difference between the total of the increases and the total of the decreases.

Computer-based accounting systems also depend on the concept of accounts. The fundamentals of the recording process are the same whether the system is manual or computer based. The dollar value of each measurable event or transaction is ascribed to the particular accounts affected; the processing system aggregates all those transactions that affect particular accounts and then holds that aggregation ready for subsequent processing. When the processing for a period is complete, the balances in the accounts are determined, and those balances are displayed in a financial report. In a computerized system, the accounts no longer have a left-hand side and a right-hand side, and the increases and decreases are simply entered into the account chronologically. The accounts still act as the repository for the aggregation of transactions, however, and still produce a *balance,* which is the aggregate of all of that account's transactions.

It may be helpful to visualize an account as a discrete place where the financial effects of economic events and transactions are accumulated. For example, a simple hypothetical asset account might appear as follows under a manual system and a computerized system:

Manual Accounting System			Computerized Accounting System	
Asset Account			**Asset Account**	
Beginning balance	10,000		Beginning balance	10,000
	1,000	$ 500	Entry	1,000
	2,000	1,500	Entry	(500)
	3,000	2,000	Entry	2,000
Ending balance	12,000		Entry	(1,500)
			Entry	(2,000)
			Entry	3,000
			Ending balance	12,000

The individual accounts, of course, mean nothing. Only when a company's transactions are recorded or entered in the accounts do they begin to have information value.

Let us turn our attention for a moment to the process of entering data into the accounts. Recall that we previously observed that every *resource* has a *source* and that the purpose of the balance sheet is to present an enterprise's resources (assets) and the sources that the enterprise drew on to obtain those resources (liabilities and owners' equity). The fundamental accounting equation, Assets = Liabilities + Owners' equity, requires that the total sources and resources always be in balance. To maintain that balance, every recordable business transaction must have two aspects. Some transactions result in an increase in an asset and in a liability; some result in the reverse. Some result in an increase in an asset and an increase in owners' equity; some result in the reverse. Some result in an increase in one asset and a decrease in another asset, and some result in an increase in a liability and a decrease in owners' equity.

Consider, for example, a retailer's purchase of merchandise inventory for cash. In this instance, one asset (inventory) of the company increased, while another asset (cash) decreased. If the retailer purchased the inventory on credit, an asset (inventory) increases as does a liability (accounts payable to suppliers). When the enterprise pays its supplier for the inventory, its liabilities (accounts payable) decrease as do its assets (cash). *All* of the many transactions of even the most complex company are expressed in exactly the same way—an increase or a decrease in one account must, of necessity, result in an equal change in another account. Regardless of the transaction, the basic accounting equation must always remain in balance.

In accounting, the two aspects of a transaction are recognized simultaneously by recording a data entry in the affected accounts. The two aspects of a transaction are recorded at the same time so that the accounting equation, A = L + OE, always remains in balance. This method of simultaneously recording the dual economic effects of a business transaction is called the **double-entry record-keeping system.** Although other record-keeping systems exist (i.e., single entry and triple entry), the double-entry system is preferred throughout the world business community.

Accounts represent the repositories (i.e., the physical place) where the financial effects of a company's economic events and transactions are accumulated; **entries** represent the dollar expression of those events—that is, the physical input to those accounts. As management thinks through the accounting impact of any business transaction, it usually visualizes the transaction in the form of an entry—which accounts are affected, which accounts are increased, and which decreased. It is almost always easy to visualize one half of an entry, but sometimes the other half of the entry is more problematic. For example, paying a $10,000 bill for advertising clearly reduces cash, but what should the other side of the entry be? Should another asset, perhaps Customer Awareness be increased? Or, should Owners' Equity be decreased because the advertising is simply a business expense? As you confront accounting questions, you will find it helpful to think through the two sides of each entry in this way. Remember that the accounting equation (again, A = L + OE) must remain in balance. That discipline is the principal advantage of the double-entry system.

Thinking through a debit and a credit. As we noted earlier, manual systems use accounts that are physically divided into a left-hand side and a right-hand side. For reasons that are now lost in time, the left-hand side of those accounts is referred to as the *debit side* and the right-hand side is referred to as the *credit side.* The words *debit* and *credit* are, unfortunately, used in a variety of ways in the business world, as with credit memo or debit memo. When they are used in an accounting record-keeping context, **debit** and **credit** are simply shorthand ways to refer to the part of an accounting entry that affects the left-hand (debit) side of an account and the right-hand (credit) side of an account, respectively. (Incidentally, when those terms are written, the shorthand is often carried further—debit is usually abbreviated ''dr.'' and credit is usually abbreviated ''cr.'')

The use of the debit and credit terms gained wide acceptance during the period when manual accounting systems were in place. They continue to be widely used in accounting discussions today—even in these days of computerized systems when accounts do not have a right- or left-hand side but are simply a collection of electronic impulses. Some additional background on the use of these words and some expansion on the way the words are used in the electronic age may be helpful.

Custom has determined that, at least in the United States, balance sheets are prepared with assets on the left-hand side of the balance sheet and the liabilities and owners' equity on the right-hand side. From that convention, it followed that an increase to an asset account was entered on the left-hand side of the asset T-account, whereas increases in liabilities and owners' equity were entered on the right-hand side of the T-accounts. From that custom, it followed further that an increase to an asset was a debit entry (entered on the left), whereas a decrease to an asset was a credit entry (entered on the right). Of course, an increase to a liability or an owners' equity account was a credit entry, and decreases to liabilities and owners' equity accounts were debit entries. Finally, because revenues and expenses accrued to the benefit of the owners, an increase in a revenue account was always a credit entry, but an increase to an expense was always a debit entry. The logic of this system of maintaining accounts—that is, the use of debits and credits—can be more readily seen in the following illustration:

Account Title

Left	Right
Debt	Credit

The balance sheet accounts can be depicted as follows:

Assets		=	**Liabilities**		+	**Owners' Equity**	
Dr.	Cr.		Dr.	Cr.		Dr.	Cr.
(+)	(−)		(−)	(+)		(−)	(+)

Income statement accounts can be depicted in this way:

Revenues		−	**Expenses**		=	**Net Income**	
Dr.	Cr.		Dr.	Cr.		Dr.	Cr.
(−)	(+)		(+)	(−)		(−)	(+)
						(Loss)	(income)

The words *debit* and *credit* continue to be used in the same way even in companies in which the accounting system is computerized—the debit entry means an increase in an asset or a decrease in a liability or owners' equity account, and so forth. The day may come when an increase in an asset account is referred to simply as an *increase* and a decrease in a liability account is referred to simply as a *decrease*. Until that day comes, however, it is easier for accountants and businesspeople to adapt to existing conventions and refer to those entries as *debits* and *credits*.

Let us sum up and try to encapsulate the ideas that we have been discussing. We have said that every accounting transaction must affect at least two accounts and that the debit side of the transaction must always equal the credit side. We have also stated that accountants and businesspeople analyze a transaction by considering which accounts are affected, in what amounts, and the various debit and credit entries that are required. Finally, the steps involved in developing an entry to reflect a business transaction can be summarized as follows:

1. Is the transaction (or event) complete and is its effect objectively measurable?
2. What kind of account (e.g., asset, liability, or owners' equity) is affected? What specific accounts are affected?
3. Are the affected accounts increased or decreased, and by how much?
4. What are the debit (left-hand) and credit (right-hand) effects of the transaction according to the rules of double-entry accounting for entering data in the accounts?

When that thinking process is complete, the transaction can be reduced to a written entry so that the information can be processed by the accounting system. A typical entry format looks like this:

```
Debit (Dr.)   Account Name . . . . . . . . . . . . . . .  Amount
        Credit (Cr.)   Account Name . . . . . . . . . . . . . . . . .    Amount
```

Most accounting information systems require a standardized format for their accounting entries to ensure that the system processes all entries properly. Throughout the remainder of this text, we will follow these widely accepted recording rules:

1. The left-hand (debit) portion of an entry will be presented first.
2. The right-hand (credit) portion will be indented to the right of the left-hand portion.
3. The Dr. and Cr. designations will be included, as will the increase (inc.) and decrease (dec.) designation.
4. The full name of the affected account will be used, as will the account classification—asset (A), liability (L), owners' equity (OE), revenue (R), or expense (E).

As we work through the illustrations in this chapter, it may be useful to approach the analysis of each transaction using the same four-step approach that management thinks through for each transaction:

1. Is the transaction (or event) complete and is the effect objectively measurable?
2. What kind of account (e.g., asset, liability, or owners' equity) is affected? What specific accounts are affected?
3. Are the affected accounts increased or decreased by the transaction and by how much?
4. What are the debit (left-hand) and credit (right-hand) effects of the transaction according to the rules of double-entry accounting for entering data in the accounts?

To illustrate this analytical approach, consider the earlier example in which a retailer purchased merchandise inventory on credit for, say, $30,000. Your responses to the above four questions might appear as follows:

Question	Answer
1. Status of the transaction:	Complete and measurable.
2. Accounts affected:	Asset—Merchandise Inventory (A).
	Liability—Accounts Payable (L).
3. Amounts involved:	Merchandise Inventory increased by $30,000.
	Accounts Payable increased by $30,000.
4. Left-hand/right-hand effects:	Enter $30,000 on left side of Merchandise Inventory account (a debit) and $30,000 on right side of Accounts Payable account (a credit).

Reduced to entry format, this transaction (and the answers to the four questions) can be summarized as follows:

	Left-side	Right-side
Dr. Merchandise Inventory (A)	(inc.) 30,000	
Cr. Accounts Payable (L)		(inc.) 30,000

As a second illustration, consider a transaction involving the payment of $30,000 by the retailer for the merchandise previously purchased. Following the four steps outlined earlier, we depict this transaction below:

Dr. Accounts Payable (L).	(dec.) 30,000	
Cr. Cash (A)		(dec.) 30,000

These two transactions would be reflected in the retailer's T-accounts as follows:

Cash (A)		Inventory (A)	
Beginning bal. XXX		Beginning bal. XXX	
	30,000	30,000	

Accounts Payable (L)	
	Beginning bal. XXX
30,000	30,000

Pictorially, these transactions affect the accounting equation as follows:

■ The purchase of inventory:

Assets	Liabilities
Inventory	Accounts Payable
+ 30,000	+ 30,000
	Owners' equity

■ The payment of the invoice for previously purchased merchandise:

	Liabilities
Assets	Accounts Payable
Cash	− 30,000
− 30,000	
	Owners' equity

The size of the two halves of the box (depicting the balance sheet) may increase or decrease as transactions are recorded, but the two sides must always remain in balance. Before continuing, think about other transactions that might affect the company and visualize how they would affect the parts of the box.

Processing and Preparing the Financial Statements

After a series of business transactions have been stated as entries for the accounting information system, those entries are then aggregated by account. This aggregation process is called posting, in that the individual entries are posted to the affected accounts, which are contained in the general ledger.

The processes of analyzing business transactions, recording the financial effects as entries in the accounting system, and then posting the data to the ledger T-accounts continues on a day-to-day basis in most companies. At some regular interval (weekly, monthly, quarterly, or annually), the net effect of the individual transactions posted to each account (i.e., the balance) is determined, and the account balances are drawn together into a set of accounting reports. To produce the accounting reports, a number of end-of-period information processing activities must be undertaken, principally to ensure that the accounting information is reliable.

In addition to the entries that have been developed on an ongoing day-to-day basis, some adjusting entries may be required as of the end of the period. Company management frequently uses the end of the period as a stimulus to challenge objectively its financial position and ask some of the fundamental questions we discussed in Chapter 2. For example, you will remember that we said that a fundamental question had to do with the allocation of the effects of a company's operations over time. More specifically, a chief financial officer might ask whether the product development expenses that have been accumulated in an expense account should be treated as an expense this year or as an asset and allocated over the expected life of the new product. Another question raised in Chapter 2 asked whether all of the company's assets were likely to produce future cash flows in excess of their carrying values. More specifically, management might ask about the value of inventory reflected in the inventory account. It might ask the operations and marketing people to challenge whether there might be a product obsolescence problem or a lower-of-cost-or-market problem that requires a reduction in the carrying value of the inventory. And, following up on another question posed in Chapter 2, management might challenge its perception of the lawsuit recently filed against the company. Although an aggressive, defensive posture may be appropriate for the courtroom, management must ask for a conservative estimate of the cost of that suit and then consider whether that estimate of loss needs to be recognized in the accounts and in the financial statements. Depending on the answers to such introspective questions, additional entries may be required to adjust the balances in the accounts before the accounting process can be brought to a close for the period.

Another end-of-period activity is the preparation of a **trial balance.** The trial balance is a list of the account balances from the general ledger. The trial balance has two uses: (1) it provides an opportunity to examine the aggregated results of the individual entries to see whether the resulting balances make sense as compared to what management expected them to be and (2) it provides an opportunity to see whether the sum of the accounts with ending debit balances equals the sum of the accounts with ending credit balances. If that review of the trial balance identifies any errors or omissions, they are corrected with further adjusting entries. Depending on the extent of those final corrections, an adjusted trial balance may be prepared to prove that the system is now ready to produce the financial statements. Although the trial balance does not provide any guarantee that the information in each account is accurate, it does verify that the overall recording and posting processes have been completed in a numerically consistent fashion.

Finally, after all necessary and appropriate adjustments to the accounts have been made, the income statement for the company can be prepared. Procedurally, after the income statement is prepared, a series of entries is made to transfer information pertaining to the period's operations (as contained in the revenue and expense accounts) to the cumulative Retained Earnings account in the balance sheet. These entries are called **closing entries** because they close, or set equal to zero, all of the income statement accounts. In addition to closing out the income statement accounts, closing entries are also used to close the Dividend Declared account by transferring its balance to retained earnings. The accounts that are closed at the end of an accounting period are referred to as **temporary accounts.**

The closing entry process is an important phase in the functioning of an accounting system. Not only does it provide the necessary link between the income statement, the balance sheet, and the statement of owners' equity, but also it serves an important information maintenance role. That is, the income statement measures the performance of the enterprise for a given period of time. As such, the income statement accounts should contain only information pertaining to the current accounting period. By setting the income statement account balances equal to zero at the end of each period, the closing entry process ensures that no operations-related data from a previous accounting period are carried forward into a succeeding operating period.

After the closing process is complete, the balance sheet, the statement of owners' equity, and the statement of cash flows may be prepared. To prepare the statements, management uses the basic data from the trial balance (the balances of each of the individual accounts) and presents that data in a way that most meaningfully communicates the company's results. During the preparation of the financial statements, some accounts can be aggregated, but other balances may have to be disaggregated and very significant transactions may have to be reported separately. In addition, the reporting process goes

---

EXHIBIT 3.1

The Accounting Cycle

Phase	Information Activity	Time Frame
1. Measuring and recording	Analyze economic transactions. State transactions in accounting language with entries. Post entries to ledger accounts.	During the accounting period
2. Processing: Summarizing, verifying, and aggregating	Prepare trial balance. Prepare adjusting data entries. Prepare closing entries	End of period
3. Reporting	Prepare financial statements.	End of period

---

beyond the presentation of the account balances—management may decide that for a full and fair presentation of the company's results, supplemental footnotes are required. In the end, management must satisfy itself that the resulting financial presentation is fair and in accordance with GAAP. This entire process is called the **accounting cycle** and is depicted in Exhibit 3.1.

THE ACCOUNTING PROCESS ILLUSTRATED: BLUE RIDGE HARDWARE CO.

To illustrate the accounting process and the preparation of the basic financial statements, we will trace the business activities of a hypothetical company, Blue Ridge Hardware Co., from its first transaction through the end of its first year of operations. This illustration assumes a manual accounting system because it is easier to see the development of the entries and the flow of those entries through the accounts into the final financial statements using the paper trail of a manual system.

First Year of Operations

In the following pages, the basic business transactions that a small retailer might encounter during its first year of operations are presented. The illustration outlines the entries required as a result of those transactions. Finally, the accounting process is completed with the preparation of a trial balance and the formal financial statements. For simplicity in this illustration, all similar transactions that occurred throughout the year have been grouped and only the yearly totals are recorded. For example, transaction no. 5 in the following illustration reflects the total merchandise purchased by the business on account throughout the entire year. On the company's books, however, each purchase of merchandise inventory made throughout the year would have been recorded separately and chronologically.

Transaction no. 1. On April 1, 1990, two friends formed the Blue Ridge Hardware Co. and filed for a corporate charter from the state. Each invested $5,000 cash in the new company and received 5,000 shares of stock for the investment. For the company's records, the following entry is required:

```
Dr.  Cash (A) . . . . . . . . . . . . . . . . . . (inc.) 10,000
     Cr.  Capital Stock (OE) . . . . . . . . . . . . . . . .     (inc.) 10,000
```

GAAP say that a company may not generate income as a result of transactions with its owners. This receipt of cash increases equity but not retained earnings. It impacts the balance sheet but not the income statement.

Transaction no. 2. Also on April 1, 1990, a three-year lease was signed for the building in which the hardware store is located. The lease called for a monthly rental of $300 and was cancelable by either the lessor or the lessee (Blue Ridge Hardware) with at least 60 days' advance notice.

No entry is needed. This business transaction does not affect the financial resources or obligations of Blue Ridge Hardware. Even though the business signed the lease, the contract is an **executory agreement** that will be consummated over time. Because the business uses the building, the monthly lease payments are recorded (see transaction no. 11). However, on the day that this particular lease is signed, no assets or liabilities of the hardware store are affected, and hence no amounts need to be entered into the accounts.

Transaction no. 3. A total of $7,500 was borrowed from a local bank on April 1, 1990. Repayment is to be made over a five-year period, and interest at 12 percent per year is due annually on March 31 on the unpaid balance:

```
Dr.  Cash (A) . . . . . . . . . . . . . . . . . . (inc.) 7,500
     Cr.  Bank Loan Payable (L) . . . . . . . . . . . . . . .     (inc.) 7,500
```

This receipt of cash is not a revenue item because it must be paid back sometime in the future. Note that the loan carries with it an obligation to pay interest on the borrowed funds. That commitment is not recorded when the loan proceeds are received because (like the lease payments in transaction no. 2) interest accrues over time and is recorded only as time elapses—usually at the end of each accounting period during the adjusting entry process.

Transaction no. 4. During the month of April, store equipment was purchased for $10,000 cash:

```
Dr.  Store Equipment (A) . . . . . . . . . . . . (inc.) 10,000
     Cr.  Cash (A) . . . . . . . . . . . . . . . . . . . . .     (dec.) 10,000
```

Transaction no. 5. During the year, merchandise inventory in the amount of $57,400 was purchased on credit. Payment was usually due within 30 days of the purchase date:

```
Dr.  Merchandise Inventory (A) . . . . . . . . . (inc.) 57,400
     Cr.  Accounts Payable (L) . . . . . . . . . . . . . . .     (inc.) 57,400
```

The purchase of equipment in transaction no. 4 is simply an exchange of one asset for another. Similarly, the purchase of inventory in transaction no. 5 is also treated as the acquisition of an asset even though the various suppliers have not yet been paid. The inventory purchase transaction recognizes the payment promise that Blue Ridge Hardware made when it ordered and received the merchandise. The fulfillment of that promise to pay is recognized as a separate, subsequent transaction (e.g., see transaction no. 10). The equipment and the inventory are both considered to be assets because they both have continuing value and because both will help the store produce future cash flows from future operations. Because the expense associated with these cash payments will benefit future operations and because we want to match that expense with the related benefit, we treat the expenditures as assets today and charge them to expense in future transactions (e.g., see transactions no. 8 and 15).

Transaction no. 6. During the year, cash sales amounted to $29,800:

```
Dr.  Cash (A)  . . . . . . . . . . . . . . . . . . .  (inc.) 29,800
     Cr.  Sales Revenue (R)  . . . . . . . . . . . . . . . . .        (inc.) 29,800
```

Transaction no. 7. During the year, credit sales amounted to $44,700:

```
Dr.  Accounts Receivable (A)  . . . . . . . . . . .  (inc.) 44,700
     Cr.  Sales Revenue (R)  . . . . . . . . . . . . . . . . .        (inc.) 44,700
```

These two types of sale (i.e., transactions no. 6 and no. 7) can be considered as revenues for the company because they result from consummated transactions with third-party customers and because they represent completion of the seller's earnings process. The company has no obligation to return any amount of these sums and has no obligation to do any further work for the third-party customers. Note that the credit sales are treated as revenues just as though they had been collected in cash. The collection of those receivables is treated as a separate transaction affecting only the balance sheet (e.g., see transaction no. 9).

Transaction no. 8. The cost of merchandise sold during the year totaled $44,700:

```
Dr.  Cost of Merchandise Sold (E) . . . . . . . .  (inc.) 44,700
     Cr.  Merchandise Inventory (A) . . . . . . . . . . . . .        (dec.) 44,700
```

This entry matches the cost of the merchandise sold with the revenue generated by its sale. The amount of the original purchase price of the merchandise that is to be allocated to the sale transaction is typically the subject of considerable study and analysis by financial managers and will be covered in detail in later chapters of this book.

Transaction no. 9. Collections of cash from accounts receivable totaled $40,500:

```
Dr.  Cash (A) . . . . . . . . . . . . . . . . . . .  (inc.) 40,500
     Cr.  Accounts Receivable (A) . . . . . . . . . . . . . .        (dec.) 40,500
```

Transaction no. 10. Payments for merchandise inventory previously purchased on credit amounted to $53,600:

```
Dr.  Accounts Payable (L)  . . . . . . . . . . . .  (dec.) 53,600
     Cr.  Cash (A) . . . . . . . . . . . . . . . . . . . . . .        (dec.) 53,600
```

Transactions no. 9 and 10 are examples of transactions that affect only the balance sheet—they represent an exchange of one asset for another or a settlement of a liability using an asset. The revenue or expense aspect of these transactions was recognized earlier because of the recognize-all-promises nature of accrual accounting.

Transaction no. 11. Cash paid for building rent for the year totaled $3,600:

```
Dr.  Rent Expense (E) . . . . . . . . . . . . . (inc.) 3,600
     Cr.  Cash (A) . . . . . . . . . . . . . . . . . . . . . .    (dec.) 3,600
```

Transaction no. 12. Cash wages paid to employees totaled $14,600. As of March 31, 1991, wages earned by employees but not yet paid were $700:

```
Dr.  Wage Expense (E) . . . . . . . . . . . (inc.) 15,300
     Cr.  Cash (A) . . . . . . . . . . . . . . . . . . . . . .   (dec.) 14,600
     Cr.  Wages Payable (L) . . . . . . . . . . . . . . . . .   (inc.)    700
```

Transaction no. 13. Cash paid for utilities amounted to $450. Blue Ridge Hardware estimated that when the March bills were all processed, the company would owe an additional $200 as of March 31, 1991:

```
Dr.  Utilities Expense (E) . . . . . . . . . . . . . . . (inc.) 650
     Cr.  Cash (A) . . . . . . . . . . . . . . . . . . . . . .   (dec.) 450
     Cr.  Utilities Payable (L) . . . . . . . . . . . . . . . .   (inc.) 200
```

Transaction no. 14. On March 31, 1991, the interest on the bank loan for the first year was paid:

```
Dr.  Interest Expense (E) . . . . . . . . . . . . . . . (inc.) 900
     Cr.  Cash (A) . . . . . . . . . . . . . . . . . . . . . .   (dec.) 900
```

Transactions no. 13, 14, and 15 recognize the various operating expenses for the store for the current period. These transactions are charged to expenses—that is, they are *not* added to an asset—because they create no measurable future value for the company and therefore require no allocation to a future period and because they assisted in generating the company's revenues for the period and should therefore be matched with those revenues.

Transaction no. 15. At year-end, the owners estimated that the store equipment had a 10-year life and that one year had passed. Hence, an adjusting entry was made to allocate $1,000 of the original cost (see transaction no. 4) of the equipment to expense in this first period:

```
Dr.  Depreciation Expense (E) . . . . . . . . . . . (inc.) 1,000
     Cr.  Accumulated Depreciation (CA) . . . . . . . . . . .   (inc.) 1,000
```

Some portion of the original cost of the store equipment was used to produce the revenues earned in this period. Under GAAP, the cost of long-lived assets must be allocated to specific accounting periods—the usual way to accomplish this allocation is to estimate the useful life of the asset and to charge a pro rata portion of the cost of that asset to expense each elapsed year. This process of allocation is called **depreciation.**

At times it will be useful to know the original cost of a company's plant and equipment. Therefore, rather than reduce the asset account directly, the annual depreciation allocation is credited to a **contra asset** (CA) account called *Accumulated Depreciation*. This contra account is reported on the balance sheet as a deduction from the store equipment account, thereby not only preserving the original cost of the equipment but also reporting its net *undepreciated cost*. The undepreciated cost is often referred to as its **book value**.

Transaction no. 16. Estimated federal and state income taxes paid during the year amounted to $600. At fiscal year-end, an additional $2,300 in taxes were due on the income actually earned during the year:

```
Dr.  Income Tax Expense (E) . . . . . . . . . . . (inc.) 2,900
     Cr.  Cash (A) . . . . . . . . . . . . . . . . . . . . . . .   (dec.)   600
     Cr.  Income Taxes Payable (L) . . . . . . . . . . . . . .   (inc.) 2,300
```

Transaction no. 17. Cash dividends of $2,000 were declared and paid:

```
Dr.  Dividends Declared (COE) . . . . . . . . . . (inc.) 2,000
     Cr.  Cash (A) . . . . . . . . . . . . . . . . . . . . . . .   (dec.) 2,000
```

Repeating an earlier observation, **dividends** are not considered to be an expense of the business but are understood to be distributions of profits to owners. As such, a dividend declaration affects only the balance sheet—a distribution of the income that is added to retained earnings for the year. The Dividends Declared account is a subaccount of the owners' equity section, and when the accounts for the year are closed, it is closed to the Retained Earnings account as a partial offset to the earnings for the year.

We can now derive the individual account balances for Blue Ridge Hardware as of March 31, 1991. First, we establish a separate account for each specific asset, liability, owners' equity, revenue, and expense account. Together, these accounts form the **chart of accounts** for Blue Ridge Hardware. Since April 1, 1990, was the first day of operations, the beginning balance in each account is $0. Second, we record (i.e., post) each entry in the appropriate ledger account and then determine the fiscal year-end balance of each account. The resulting preclosing account balances are shown in Exhibit 3.2.

To verify that the company's accounts are in balance, we can prepare a trial balance using the ledger account balances in Exhibit 3.2. As Exhibit 3.3 reveals, the trial balance for Blue Ridge Hardware is in balance, suggesting that an equivalent amount of debits and credits were posted to the accounts. Note, however, that a balanced trial balance does not ensure the accuracy of the data in the particular accounts.

The next step in the accounting process involves preparing the income statement, which is followed by preparing the closing entries for the temporary accounts and a balance sheet, a statement of owners' equity, and a statement of cash flows. These final steps in the accounting cycle are illustrated sequentially in Exhibit 3.4 through Exhibit 3.8. Visualize the management of Blue Ridge Hardware as they study the account balances in the trial balance, as they think about the kinds of transactions summarized in each account, and as they decide how the accounts should be displayed in the financial statements. On one level, the process is relatively easy: the temporary accounts—which include the revenue and expense accounts—appear on the income statement, and the

EXHIBIT 3.2

Blue Ridge Hardware Co.
Ledger Accounts
For the Fiscal Year Ended March 31, 1991

Balance Sheet Accounts:

Assets = **Liabilities** + **Owner's Equity**

Assets

Cash

4-1-90	0		
(1)	10,000	(4)	10,000
(3)	7,500	(10)	53,600
(6)	29,800	(11)	3,600
(9)	40,500	(12)	14,600
		(13)	450
		(14)	900
		(16)	600
		(17)	2,000
	87,800		85,750
3-31-91	2,050		

Accounts Receivable

4-1-90	0	(9)	40,500
(7)	44,700		
	44,700		40,500
3-31-91	4,200		

Merchandise Inventory

4-1-90	0	(8)	44,700
(5)	57,400		
3-31-90	12,700		

Store Equipment

4-1-90	10,000	
(4)	10,000	
3-31-90	10,000	

Accumulated Depreciation Store Equipment

		4-1-90	0
		(15)	1,000
		3-31-91	1,000

Liabilities

Accounts payable

(10)	53,600	4-1-90	0
		(5)	57,400
		3-31-91	3,800

Wages Payable

		4-1-90	0
		(12)	700
		3-31-91	700

Income Taxes Payable

		4-1-90	0
		(16)	2,300
		3-31-91	2,300

Utilities Payable

		4-1-90	0
		(13)	200
		3-31-91	200

Bank Loan Payable

		4-1-90	0
		(3)	7,500
		3-31-91	7,500

Owner's Equity

Capital Stock

		4-1-90	0
		(1)	10,000
		3-31-91	10,000

Retained Earnings

		4-1-90	0

Dividends Declared

4-1-90	0	
(17)	2,000	
3-31-91	2,000	

Income Statement Accounts:

Sales Revenue

4-1-90	0		
(6)	29,800		
(7)	44,700		
	74,500		

Cost of Merchandise Sold

4-1-90	0		
(8)	44,700		
	44,700		

Wage Expense

4-1-90	0		
(12)	15,300		
	15,300		

Income Tax Expense

4-1-90	0		
(16)	2,900		
	2,900		

Interest Expense

4-1-90	0		
(14)	900		
	900		

Rent Expense

4-1-90	0		
(11)	3,600		
	3,600		

Utilities Expense

4-1-90	0		
(13)	650		
	650		

Depreciation Expense

4-1-90	0		
(15)	1,000		
	1,000		

EXHIBIT 3.3

Blue Ridge Hardware Co.
Trial Balance as of
March 31, 1991

Account Title	Debit Balance	Credit Balance
Cash	$ 2,050	
Accounts Receivable	4,200	
Merchandise Inventory	12,700	
Store Equipment	10,000	
Accumulated Depreciation		$ 1,000
Accounts Payable		3,800
Wages Payable		700
Utilities Payable		200
Income Taxes Payable		2,300
Bank Loan Payable		7,500
Capital Stock		10,000
Retained Earnings		0
Dividends Declared	2,000	
Sales		74,500
Cost of Merchandise Sold	44,700	
Rent Expense	3,600	
Wage Expense	15,300	
Utilities Expense	650	
Income Tax Expense	2,900	
Interest Expense	900	
Depreciation Expense	1,000	
Total	$100,000	$100,000

EXHIBIT 3.4

Blue Ridge Hardware Co.
Income Statement
For the Year Ended March 31, 1991

Net revenues		$74,500
Less: Cost of merchandise sold		(44,700)
Gross margin		29,800
Less: Operating expenses		
Rent expense	$ 3,600	
Wage expense	15,300	
Utilities expense	650	
Depreciation expense	1,000	
		(20,550)
Income from operations		9,250
Less: Interest expense		(900)
Income before taxes		8,350
Less: Federal and state income taxes		(2,900)
Net income		$5,450
Net income per share (10,000 shares outstanding)		$0.545

EXHIBIT 3.5

Blue Ridge Hardware Co.
Closing Entries as of
March 31, 1991

To close the revenue accounts:				
Dr. Sales Revenue (R)	(dec.)	$74,500		
Cr. Retained Earnings (OE)			(inc.)	$74,500
To close the expense accounts:				
Dr. Retained Earnings (OE)	(dec.)	$69,050		
Cr. Cost of Merchandise Sold (E)			(dec.)	$44,700
Cr. Rent Expense (E)			(dec.)	3,600
Cr. Wage Expense (E)			(dec.)	15,300
Cr. Utilities Expense (E)			(dec.)	650
Cr. Interest Expense (E)			(dec.)	900
Cr. Depreciation Expense (E)			(dec.)	1,000
Cr. Income Tax Expense (E)			(dec.)	2,900
To close the Dividends Declared account:				
Dr. Retained Earnings (OE)	(dec.)	$ 2,000		
Cr. Dividends Declared (COE)			(dec.)	$2,000

EXHIBIT 3.6

Blue Ridge Hardware Co
Balance Sheet
As of March 31, 1991

Assets		Equities	
Current assets:		Current liabilities:	
Cash	$ 2,050	Accounts payable	$ 3,800
Accounts receivable	4,200	Wages payable	700
Merchandise inventory	12,700	Utilities payable	200
Total current assets	$18,950	Income tax payable	2,300
		Total current liabilities	$ 7,000
Noncurrent assets:		Noncurrent liabilities:	
Store equipment	10,000	Bank loan payable	7,500
Less:		Total liabilities	$14,500
Accumulated depreciation	(1,000)		
Total noncurrent assets	$ 9,000	Owners' equity:	
		Capital stock	10,000
Total assets	$27,950	Retained earnings	3,450
		Total liabilities and owners' equity	$27,950

EXHIBIT 3.7

Blue Ridge Hardware Co.
Statement of Owners' Equity
As of March 31, 1991

	Capital Stock		
	Shares	Dollars	Retained Earnings
At April 1, 1990	0	0	0
Stock sales	10,000	$10,000	
Net income for the year			$5,450
Dividends declared			(2,000)
At March 31, 1991	10,000	$10,000	$3,450

EXHIBIT 3.8

Blue Ridge Hardware Co.
Statement of Cash Flows
For the Year Ended March 31, 1991

Operating activities:	
Net income	$5,450
Add: Depreciation on store equipment	1,000
	$6,450
Adjustments for:	
Accounts receivable	(4,200)
Merchandise inventory	(12,700)
Accounts payable	3,800
Wages payable	700
Utilities payable	200
Income tax payable	2,300
Cash flow from operating activities	$(3,450)
Investing activities	
Purchase of store equipment	$(10,000)
Cash flow from investing activities	$(10,000)
Financing activities	
Cash dividends paid	$(2,000)
Proceeds from bank loan	7,500
Sale of capital stock	10,000
Cash flow from financing activities	$15,500
Increase in cash	$2,050
Cash, beginning of year	0
Cash, end of year	$2,050

permanent accounts—which include the assets, liabilities, and owners' equity accounts—appear on the balance sheet. The temporary accounts are called *temporary* because they are used during only one accounting period and then start over again the following year to measure the results of operations for that new year. Permanent accounts are called *permanent* because the balances carry forward from one year to the next.

On a different level, the process of preparing financial statements from a trial balance is more difficult. Management must decide which accounts can be combined, which should be presented as separate line items on the statements, and which accounts must be analyzed (i.e., broken down into more detail). The objective of this process is to be sure that the financial statements include enough information to present a fair picture of the company without obscuring the reality with too much detail.

To put you in the mind of the Blue Ridge Hardware owners, study the trial balance and the ledger accounts (Exhibits 3.2 and 3.3) and see how those data were pulled into the resulting financial statements in Exhibits 3.4, 3.6, and 3.8. To take the process further and ensure that you understand the closing entry process and the linkage between net income and retained earnings, we suggest that you post the journal entries from Exhibit 3.5 to the ledger accounts in Exhibit 3.2. After this posting, all temporary accounts should have a zero ending balance, and the net income of Blue Ridge Hardware will have been transferred to Retained Earnings.

Analysis of Blue Ridge Hardware Co.

Now that the accounting process is complete and the financial reports of Blue Ridge Hardware prepared, let us briefly consider what these reports reveal about the enterprise. First, Exhibit 3.4, the income statement, indicates that for the year ended March 31, 1991, Blue Ridge Hardware earned net income of $5,450 on net revenues of $74,500. Since most companies have more expenses than can be justified by the volume of sales during their initial building years, they often lose money during their first year (or years) of operations; hence, it is encouraging that Blue Ridge Hardware achieved a positive net income—its sales volume exceeded its cost of operations. Exhibit 3.7 reveals that, on the basis of these earnings, the enterprise also declared and paid a dividend in the amount of $2,000. And, since the full amount of net income for the period was not distributed as a dividend, the owners' investment in the enterprise grew by $3,450. Several important points here merit restatement. First, dividends are not reported as an expense of the business on the income statement but instead are a distribution of the company's income to its stockholders. Second, to the extent that the income for the period is not distributed as dividends, it has the same effect as if the owners had invested that amount of new funds in the enterprise.

With respect to the financial condition of the enterprise, Exhibit 3.6, the balance sheet, reveals that at year end, Blue Ridge Hardware has the following:

- Total assets (and total equities) of $27,950.
- Total liabilities of $14,500.
- Owners' equity of $13,450.

The owners' equity, or the company's **net worth,** is that value that would remain *if* all assets could be converted to cash at their balance sheet values and then used to satisfy all existing liabilities. The liquidation of a company, however, is a rare event, and it is also unlikely that the cash liquidation values of the assets would exactly equal their book value. Consequently, an alternative description of owner's equity or net worth is to say that it is the **net book value** of all assets minus the book value of all liabilities.

The balance sheet also reveals that Blue Ridge Hardware has current assets totaling $18,950, which exceeds not only its total current liabilities of $7,000 but also the sum of current and noncurrent liabilities (i.e., $14,500). This indicates that the enterprise is relatively secure in terms of its ability to pay off its outstanding obligations. Finally, Exhibit 3.8, the statement of cash flows, reveals that the enterprise generated a net cash inflow from financing activities in the amount of $15,500 and spent $10,000 in cash on investing activities. An additional $3,450 was spent in support of the company's operations, leaving a net cash balance of $2,050 at year end. To ensure the continued success of the enterprise, it is important for Blue Ridge Hardware to become a net positive generator of cash flows from operations. Clearly, the company will become viable only if the cash flows from operating activities become positive.

SUMMARY

The purpose of this chapter has been to discuss and illustrate the accounting process used in preparing accounting reports. This process involves several distinct activities: analyzing business transactions to assess their financial effect on the assets, liabilities, and equities of an enterprise, recording this analysis in various data files, verifying the accuracy of the recording process, and, finally, preparing and analyzing the financial statements.

Although it is important for you to understand how accounting reports are prepared and how the accounting system operates, our principal goal is to ensure that you understand fully how accounting reports communicate and what they reveal about the operations and financial condition of the enterprise. Thus, in the chapters that follow, we focus our attention not on the process of financial statement preparation but on analyzing important business transactions for the purpose of accounting and of understanding what information the accounting statements convey.

NEW CONCEPTS AND TERMS

Accounts p. 75)

Accounting cycle (p. 83)

Accounting information system (p. 75)

Adjusting entries (p. 81)

Balance (p. 75)

Book value (p. 87)

Chart of accounts (p. 87)

Closing entries (p. 82)

Contra account (p. 87)

Credit (p. 77)

Debit (p. 77)

Depreciation (p. 86)

Dividends (p. 87)

Double-entry record-keeping system (p. 77)

Entries (p. 77)

Executory agreement (p. 84)

General ledger (p. 81)

Net book value (p. 94)

Net worth (p. 94)

Permanent accounts (p. 93)

Posting (p. 81)

T-accounts (p. 75)

Temporary account (p. 82)

Trial balance (p. 82)

ISSUES FOR DISCUSSION

D3.1 Describe at least five events that a company is likely to experience that would not be measured, recorded, and reported in the company's financial statements.

D3.2 A number of accounting educators have likened the accounting process of recording transactions to that of the typical filing system found in most offices. Explain the parallels as you see them.

D3.3 Visualize the millions of transactions that a Fortune 500 company would engage in throughout a year with a variety of other parties, for differing dollar amounts, and for different purposes. Identify some of the ways in which errors might enter the accounting cycle and suggest mechanisms that might minimize the likelihood of those errors occurring and/or going undetected.

D3.4 What purposes are served by the preparation of a trial balance, balance sheet, and income statement? How frequently should they be prepared?

D3.5 The accounting cycle described in this chapter is a standard approach employed by most companies, who will then often modify it to better suit their needs. Discuss some of the unique circumstances of particular companies that would possibly lead to slight modifications and/or customizations of the accounting cycle.

D3.6 The income statements prepared by Atlantic Coast Manufacturing Company detail the company's results of operations for the year ended December 31, 1991. Some of the line items from that income statement appear below. For each of those items, describe in your own words what the source of the numbers might have been.

a. Sales—$500,000

b. Payroll Expense—$250,000

c. Bad Debt Expense—$25,000

d. Computer Depreciation—$30,000

e. Selling Expense—$75,000

D3.7 Atlantic Coast Manufacturing maintains cash in a box at the reception desk and in the plant for buying stamps and paying for other small expenses; each box usually contains $250. The company maintains three different bank accounts with a local bank. One is its general corporate account with an average balance of $1 million, another is the factory payroll account with an average balance of $250,000, and the third is the executive payroll account with an average balance of $50,000. The company usually has between $100,000 and $200,000 of excess cash invested in U.S. Treasury bills. Atlantic has total assets of $10 million and a net worth of $4 million.

How many general ledger accounts should the company maintain to collect the transactions affecting its cash and its cash-equivalent items? How many line items should the company present on its balance sheet to describe its cash and cash-equivalent items? Please explain the reasoning behind your answers.

D3.8 Describe each of the following in your own words. Explain how each enters into recording and processing financial data and in preparing and presenting financial statements.

a. Permanent and temporary accounts

b. Adjusting entries and closing entries

c. The trial balance

D3.9 As you worked through the accounting process illustrated by the Blue Ridge Hardware example, you learned something about the accounting process and you enhanced further your understanding of accounting concepts. That understanding will be developed further in subsequent chapters, but it will be useful to articulate your developing understanding as it grows. In that context, describe the following in your own words:

a. The difference between an asset and an expense

b. The impact of accrual accounting on the measurement of operating results

c. The notion of depreciation

D3.10 You are the president of a small paint manufacturer located in the Pacific Northwest. Your paint products are sold throughout a three-state area. Because the economy has been flat, your business has been hurt. Nonetheless, sales for 1991 were about $25 million and net income was about $3 million. It is now February 1992, and as you begin to draw together the data you need for your company's 1991 report to shareholders, the production people bring you distressing news. It appears that one lot of paint that was shipped late last year is defective. If it is applied when the weather is at all humid, the paint blisters and peels very badly. They have already notified the distributors and begun a recall, but it appears that some of that batch has gotten into the retail distribution network and in fact has been sold to contractors and homeowners. Production people estimate the cost of recalling the entire lot at $300,000. However, if anyone has actually used the paint on a job site, the paint will have to be scraped off carefully and thoroughly. There obviously is no way to know how much of the paint might have been sold to end users and how much of it might have been applied on specific jobs.

How should this event be reflected in the company's financial statements?

PROBLEMS

P3.1 Statement preparation. Using the following information taken from the trial balance for Purdue Corporation for 1992, prepare an income statement, a balance sheet, and a statement of stockholder's equity for the Purdue Corporation as of December 31, 1992.

Accounts Payable: $22,200   Accounts Receivable: $25,300
Advertising: $3,500   Capital Stock: $50,000
Cash: $1,100   Cost of Goods Sold: $228,000
Dividends Paid: $7,500   Gross Sales: $300,000
Income Tax Expense: $10,000   Income Tax Payable: $4,000
Interest Expense: $1,200   Land: $32,600

Building (net): $25,000
Depreciation Expense: $800
Notes Payable: $4,000
Office Salaries: $25,000
Office Supplies Used: $1,500
Salaries Payable: $800

Merchandise Inventory: $32,000
Long-Term Debt: $15,000
Notes Receivable: $4,800
Office Supplies Inventory: $700
Retained Earnings: 1/1/92: $18,000
Sales Returns and Allowances: $15,000

P3.2 Transaction analysis. Indicate the effect (increase or decrease) of each of the following events on a company's assets, liabilities, and owners' equity:

a. Selling capital stock

b. Signing a three-year lease on a building

c. Paying three months' rent in advance

d. Purchasing supplies for cash

e. Purchasing equipment on account

f. Purchasing merchandise on account

g. Obtaining a six-month bank loan

h. Selling merchandise for cash in excess of its cost

i. Selling merchandise on account in excess of its cost

j. Paying an account payable

k. Paying property taxes

P3.3 Transaction analysis. Indicate the effect of each of the following transactions on the accounts listed below by placing a plus (+) or a minus (−) in the appropriate columns.

	Assets			Liabilities		Owners' Equity	
Transactions	Cash	Accounts Receivable	Supplies	Accounts Payable	Notes Payable	Capital Stock	Retained Earnings
a. Sold additional shares of capital stock.							
b. Borrowed money from a local bank and signed a note.							
c. Purchased supplies for cash.							

		Assets		Liabilities		Owners' Equity	
Transactions	Cash	Accounts Receivable	Supplies	Accounts Payable	Notes Payable	Capital Stock	Retained Earnings
d. Rendered services and collected cash for those services.							
e. Rendered services to customers who agreed to pay for those services within 30 days.							
f. Purchased supplies on account.							
g. Paid salary expense.							
h. Paid office rent.							
i. Collected cash from customers for whom services were previously performed.							
j. Paid interest on the loan.							
k. Used supplies in connection with performing services.							
l. Repaid part of the bank loan principal.							
m. Paid cash dividends to stockholders.							

P3.4 Transaction analysis and T-accounts. The following are *selected* accounts and account balances of the TAP Company on June 30, 1991:

	Balance
Account:	Debit (Credit)
Cash	$ 125,230
Accounts Receivable	230,520
Office Equipment	358,600
Accumulated Depreciation	(105,400)
Notes Payable	(34,000)
Accounts Payable	(35,000)
Sales Revenue	(478,720)
Sales Discounts	24,000
Gain on Sale of Office Equipment	(4,000)
Inventory	219,340
Purchase Discounts	(2,220)
Cost of Sales	287,232

In addition, the TAP Company entered into the following transactions during the month of July 1991:

July 6   Sold for $7,000 some office equipment that had originally cost $20,000; accumulated depreciation taken to date on the equipment totaled $15,000.

July 7   Sales transactions in the amount of $20,000 were completed, on account, with terms of 2/10, net 30.

July 10   Purchased $10,000 worth of merchandise inventory for cash.

July 15   Purchased a new word processing system costing $40,000, paying $15,000 down and signing a 90-day note, with interest at 10 percent for the balance.

July 16   Received payment of $19,600 for the July 7 sales transactions.

July 19   Completed sales transactions for cash in the amount of $42,000.

July 20   Purchased $26,000 worth of merchandise inventory on account with terms of 2/10, net 30.

July 22   Returned $2,000 worth of defective merchandise from the July 20 purchase for a credit to TAP's account.

July 27   Paid the remaining balance of July 20 purchase less an appropriate discount.

Required:

Analyze and record the above transactions in journal entry form and then determine the July 31 account balances using T-accounts.

P3.5 Account analysis. Up-n-Down Corporation has published annual financial statements since it first sold stock to a group of nonfamily-member investors. The company's balance sheets at December 31, 1990 and 1991, were as follows:

	December 31,	
	1990	**1991**
Cash	$ 222	$ 17
Accounts Receivable	7,523	8,003
Less: Allowance for Doubtful Accounts	−116	−170*
Inventories	6,745	5,848
Prepaid Insurance	805	632*
Deferred catalog costs	1,519	2,483*
Land and buildings	4,344	4,344*
Equipment	2,858	3,268*
Less: Accumulated depreciation	−1,682	−2,457*
Total assets	$ 22,218	$ 21,968
Accounts payable	$ 8,022	$ 6,801
Bank borowings	7,445	6,925*
Salaries payable	453	585
Taxes payable	1,111	1,298
Capital stock	3,110	3,110*
Retained earnings	2,077	3,249*
Total liabilities and equity	$ 22,218	$ 21,968

Required:

For each of the accounts starred above, describe the transactions that might have accounted for the changes in the balances between the two years. Your descriptions should indicate whether the entry used to record the transaction(s) increased or decreased the account and what other accounts might have been affected by the other side of the entry.

P3.6 Account Analysis. The T-account below depicts a number of transactions that increased and decreased the cash account of Holcum, Inc., during 1991.

Cash (A)

1-1-91	Balance	-0-	(E)	Pd. for store eq.		10,000
(A)	From capital stock	10,000	(F)	Cash sales returned		500
(B)	Bank loan payable	9,000	(G)	Pd. mdse. suppliers		53,600
(C)	Cash sales	30,300	(H)	Paid rent		3,600
(D)	Collections of receiv.	40,500	(I)	Paid employees		14,600
			(J)	Paid for utilities		450
			(K)	Pd. est. income tax		600
			(L)	Pd. other expenses		500
			(M)	Pd. on bank loan—On principal $1,500, interest $450		1,950
			(N)	Paid dividends		1,500
12-31-91	Balance	2,500				

Required:

For each of the identified entries (A through N), prepare a one- or two-sentence explanation of the event which caused the transaction. Be sure that your explanation describes the other account which would have been affected by the entry.

P3.7 Resources and sources. Resourceful Products Incorporated includes the following asset accounts in its balance sheet.

a. Cash

b. Land

c. Merchandise inventory

d. Accounts receivable

e. Delivery truck

f. Factory building

g. Investments

Required:

Thinking about the basic accounting equation, where every resource has a source, list the most likely source or sources for each of the resources identified above.

P3.8 Events and the affected accounts. Consider the following events which were part of the activities of the Springtime Sales Company during 1991:

a. Sales of merchandise on account

b. Purchase of merchandise on account

c. Purchase of a delivery truck, with a 10 percent downpayment

d. Sale of common stock for cash

e. Purchase of a Certificate of Deposit with a bank transfer

f. Purchase of a three-year insurance policy for cash

g. Amortization of one year's coverage of the insurance policy

h. Payment of wages to hourly employees

i. Payment of a dividend to shareholders.

Required:

For each of the above events, describe the nature of the accounts which would be affected (asset, liability, equity, etc.) and, in the context of the basic accounting equation, explain the rationale for your answer.

P3.9 Event Analysis. The accounting records of the Floyd Corporation include the following entries:

(a)	Accounts Receivable	70,400	
	Revenue		70,400
(b)	Cash	78,960	
	Accounts Receivable		78,960
(c)	Operating Expenses	720	
	Supplies on Hand		720
(d)	Equipment	2,720	
	Cash		2,720
(e)	Accounts Payable (trade)	2,560	
	Cash		2,560
(f)	Notes Payable	20,000	
	Interest Expense	160	
	Cash		20,160
(g)	Dividends	12,800	
	Cash		12,800

Required:

For each entry, prepare a one-sentence description of the underlying event.

P3.10 Event Analysis. The accounting records of the Cecil, Inc., include the following entries:

(a)	Rent Expense	4,500	
	Prepaid Rent		4,500
(b)	Unearned Passenger Revenue	27,000	
	Passenger Revenue		27,000
(c)	Salaries Expense	4,950	
	Salaries Payable		4,950
(d)	Repairs and Maintenance Expense	7,800	
	Accounts Payable		7,800
(e)	Repairs and Maintenance Expense	5,550	
	Spare Parts on Hand		5,550
(f)	Accounts Receivable	3,800	
	Office Equipment		3,800
(g)	Land	24,500	
	Cash		2,450
	Notes Payable		22,050
(h)	Cash	6,900	
	Accounts Receivable		6,900
(i)	Cash	12,000	
	Capital Stock		12,000

Required:

For each entry, prepare a one-sentence description of the underlying event.

P3.11 Account balances. The Detail Corporation Inc. maintains a complex accounting system bacause management likes to have a fully detailed financial statement package every month, covering all phases of the company's operations, for their evaluation and planning meetings. Some of the accounts the company maintains are:

a. Cash in Bank—Knoxville Plant

b. Allowance for Doubtful Accounts—Southeast Region

c. Raw Material Inventory—Knoxville Plant

d. Forklift Trucks—Knoxville Plant

e. Accumulated Depreciation—Forklift Trucks/Knoxville

f. Flour Sales—Southeast Region

g. Doubtful Account Expense—Southeast Region

h. Interest Expense—Tennessee Bank Loan

Required:

a. For each of the above accounts, indicate whether the account balance would normally be on the left-hand side or the right-hand side. Provide a single sentence explaining why, in concept, the balance might normally be on that side.

b. For each of the above accounts, describe the nature of the entries which might affect the accounts; as part of that description, provide one illustrative entry affecting the right-hand side of the account and one affecting the left-hand side of the account.

P3.12 More complex events and the affected accounts. Consider the following series of events which were part of the activities of the OnTime Manufacturing Company during the year 1991:

a. On June 30, 1991, the Treasurer called the company's banker and asked her to buy a Treasury bill, debiting the company's account. The bill cost $100,000 and carried an interest rate of 10 percent, the interest to be paid at maturity. At December 31, 1991, the company still had the investment.

b. On March 31, 1991, the company bought a lift truck to help move material around in the factory. The truck cost $25,000, but the dealer agreed to finance $20,000 of the purchase price. The company signed a five-year note for $20,000, at 10 percent interest, with interest payable quarterly and principle payable in five equal annual installments.

c. To prepare for a substantial expansion, the company sold $10,000,000 of 10-year, 8 percent bonds on October 1, 1991. An investment banker helped put together the offering document, and an attorney researched the legal aspects of the offering. The total of the professional fees paid to these two firms was $75,000. The bonds require semiannual interest payments, and require that the principle be paid in full at maturity.

d. The company owned a piece of land next to its main plant, which they intended to use for the expansion discussed in point c, above. During December 1991, the company paid an engineering company $50,000 to make soil tests on the land, and paid an architect $50,000 for a preliminary drawing of the anticipated new plant expansion. By the time December 31, 1991, had come, however, the economy had softened substantially, and there was now considerable question as to whether the market was really ready to buy more of the company's products. It was decided to put the expansion plans on the back burner for at least a year.

For each of the above events, describe the nature of the accounts that would be affected (asset, liability, equity, etc.) at the date of the event and as of December 31, 1991, and, in the context of the basic accounting equation, explain the rationale for your answer.

P3.13 Still more unusual events.

a. The 1990 annual report from Scott Paper Company includes the following footnote:

> **Business Improvement Program** In 1990, the Company recorded a charge before
> income taxes of $175.9 million most of which is recorded in other costs and expenses
> from operations principally for the estimated effect of the planned sale during 1991 of
> nonstrategic businesses and assets and the elimination of redundancies. The planned
> divestments include most of the Company's foodservice business; its specialty papers
> business including its paper mill in Westbrook, Maine, and a converting facility in
> Belgium; and its bulk nonwovens business with manufacturing facilities in the United
> States and Germany. The estimate also includes provisions for the expected operating
> results of these businesses prior to the disposal dates and an allocation of interest expense
> based on the net assets being sold.
>
> These planned divestments are part of a business improvement program which also
> includes substantially reducing capital spending, lowering working capital levels, and
> intensifying cost-reduction efforts.

Required:

How would this business improvement program have been recognized in the company's accounts
in 1990? In what ways was the business program not reflected in the 1990 accounts? What entries
might have been made, and what accounts would have been affected? Explain the rationale the
company might have used to support its combination of accounting and disclosure.

b. Hercules Incorporated describes its exposure for environmental problems with the following
footnote in its 1990 annual report (000 omitted):

> **(d) Environmental:** Hercules has been identified as a potentially responsible party by
> various federal and state authorities for cleanup at numerous waste disposal sites, the most
> significant being Jacksonville, Arkansas, with possible claims of $30,000-$40,000. Due to
> the number of parties involved (at most sites), the multiplicity of possible solutions, the
> evolving technology, and the years of remedial activity required, the company is unable
> to assess and quantify the extent of its responsibility at the majority of sites involved.
> However, provision has been made for future remediation costs of $13,400 (including
> $10,000 associated with the sale of a business) during 1990 and $7,550 during 1989 for
> sites at which an estimated future minimum liability has been determined. Management
> believes, based upon opinion of company counsel, that any ultimate liability over the
> amount accrued will not materially affect the consolidated financial position of the
> company.

Required:

How would this environmental exposure have been recognized in the company's accounts in 1990?
In what ways was the environmental exposure not reflected in the 1990 accounts? What entries
might have been made, and what accounts would have been affected? Explain the rationale the
company might have used to support its combination of accounting and disclosure.

P3.14 Aggregation and disaggregation. The annual report to shareholders published by United Foods for the year ended February 28, 1991, includes a balance sheet as shown in Exhibit I (just the asset side) and footnotes, two of which are shown in Exhibit II.

Required:

a. Why might the company have presented its inventory and its other assets as single line items on the balance sheet, and then provided the detail of those accounts in the footnotes? Could the company have expanded the line items in the balance sheet to include the details from the footnotes? What factors might the company have considered in making the decision they did?

b. (i) What accounts would have been affected when the inventory of raw materials was recognized? (ii) What accounts would have been affected when the inventory of growing crops was recognized? (iii) Prepare the entry the company made when it recognized the insurance claim.

E X H I B I T   I

United Foods
Balance Sheets
For the Years Ended February 28, 1990 and 1991

	February 28,	
	1991	1990
Assets		
Current:		
Cash and cash equivalents	$ 1,367,000	$ 1,103,000
Accounts and notes receivable, less allowance of	16,320,000	15,108,000
$212,000 and $286,000 for possible losses (Note 4)		
Inventories (Notes 1 and 4)	54,363,000	40,159,000
Prepaid expenses and miscellaneous (Note 2)	3,047,000	2,536,000
Total current assets	75,097,000	58,906,000
Property and equipment (notes 4 and 9)		
Land and land improvements	8,185,000	6,693,000
Buildings and leasehold improvements	19,177,000	18,755,000
Machinery, equipment, and improvements	63,929,000	57,902,000
	91,291,000	83,350,000
Less accumulated depreciation and amortization	(37,102,000)	(32,480,000)
Net property and equipment	54,189,000	50,870,000
Other assets (note 3)	10,887,000	2,164,000
	$140,173,000	$111,940,000

EXHIBIT II

United Foods

Note 1. Inventories

Inventories are summarized as follows:

	February 28,	
	1991	**1990**
Finished products	$39,589,000	$33,806,000
Cotton held for resale	1,949,000	—
Raw materials	7,771,000	2,437,000
Growing crops	1,692,000	1,608,000
Work-in-process	864,000	831,000
Merchandise and supplies	2,498,000	1,477,000
Inventories	$54,363,000	$40,159,000

Substantially all finished product and raw material inventories of the company's frozen vegetable division are valued at cost (last-in, first-out), not in excess of market. If current costs had been used, inventories would have been approximately $5,000,000, $5,000,000, and $6,000,000 higher than reported at February 28, 1991, 1990, and 1989, respectively, and the net income would have decreased approximately $33,000 or $.00 per share for fiscal 1991 and $800,000 or $.06 per share for fiscal 1990, and the net loss would have decreased approximately $200,000 or $.02 per share for fiscal 1989.

Note 3. Other Assets

Other assets consist of the following:

	February 28,	
	1991	**1990**
Insurance claim receivable	$ 6,630,000	$ —
Deposits with plan trustees	1,447,000	1,160,000
Loan receivable from cotton pickery	1,432,000	—
Miscellaneous	1,378,000	1,004,000
Other assets	$10,887,000	$2,164,000

The insurance claim arose from a May 1990 fire that destroyed a portion of one of the company's California food processing facilities. The insurance coverage is based on replacement cost, and the amount of the claim is based on payments received and insurance company representatives' estimates of the replacement costs of the property destroyed. The company recorded an estimated gain on the insurance claim of $6,440,000 in fiscal 1991. The claim may be increased when actual costs for the replacement property are finalized. Replacement of the destroyed facility will defer income taxes on this gain.

P3.15 Industry specific accounts. The following account titles were selected from 1990 annual reports published by various major companies:

a. "Amortization of Special Tools"

b. "Dealer Deposits"

c. "Accrued Marketing"

d. "Timber and Timberlands, Net of Timber Depletion"

e. "Leasehold Costs, Improvements, Store Fixtures, and Equipment"

f. "Exploration Expense"

g. "Charge for Discontinuing Automatic Blanket Operations"

h. "Operating Revenues:
Local Service
Interstate Access
Intrastate Access
Toll
Other"

Required:

For each of the above account titles, indicate whether the account is a balance sheet account or an income statement account. And for each caption describe the kinds of event(s) which might be reflected in the account.

P3.16 Transaction analysis: The Bash Company. The Bash Company, a Charlottesville, Virginia, retailer, was formed on July 1, 1990. During the month of July, the corporation experienced *11* different business transactions. At the end of the month, Bash prepared the following trial balance:

Bash Company
Trial Balance
July 31, 1990

Account	Debit (Left)	Credit (Right)
Cash	103,000	
Accounts Receivable	6,500	
Allowance for Doubtful Accounts		600
Inventory	10,000	
Equipment (net of $500 depreciation taken to date)	119,500	
Accounts Payable		50,000
Loan Payable (10 annual payments)		120,000
Interest Payable		1,000
Salaries Payable		8,000
Capital Stock		50,000
Retained Earnings		?
	239,000	?

Transaction Number	Accounts Affected	Dollar Effect	
		Debit (Left)	Credit (Right)
1			
2			
3			
4			
—5			
6			
7			
8			
9			
10			
11			

Required:

Based on the data contained in the trial balance: *a.* Fill in the two empty boxes with the appropriate amounts. *b.* Use the preceding chart to prepare the accounting entries for the *11* transactions that occurred during July. The transactions may be recorded in any order.

Note the following:

1. All sales were on account.
2. All asset purchases were on credit, and no payments were made against these liabilities during the month.
3. No cash was paid for any of the expenses incurred during the month.
4. Because of an unexpected occurrence, one account receivable (totaling $500) was written off during the month.

P3.17 Transaction analysis: Denver Wholesale Sporting Goods, Inc.   Below is a partial list of business events entered into by Denver Wholesale Sporting Goods, Inc., during the first fiscal quarter of 1990. Determine how each event, as of the date it occurred, would be recognized, if at all, in the 1990 financial statements. If the event should not be recognized, write NOT RECOGNIZED. If the event should be recognized now for financial-reporting purposes, indicate how (e.g., + or −) and by what dollar amount each of the following financial statement components would be affected (if there is no change in a particular column, leave that space blank): Cash Flow, Net Current Assets (current assets minus current liabilities), Total Assets, Net Assets (total assets minus total liabilities), and Net Income.

M = Million
(Enter + or − and dollar amount or NOT RECOGNIZED)

		Cash Flow	Net Current Assets	Total Assets	Net Assets	Net Income
O.	Sold capital stock for $3M.	+3M	+3M	+3M	+3M	
a.	Purchased $8M of merchandise on account.					
b.	Sold merchandise for $5M cash (entry for sales only).					
c.	Recognized $4M cost of merchandise just sold (entry for cost only).					

		Cash Flow	Net Current Assets	Total Assets	Net Assets	Net Income
		M = Million (Enter + or − and dollar amount or NOT RECOGNIZED)				
d.	Borrowed $4M cash, issuing a 90-day, 10% note.	_____	_____	_____	_____	_____
e.	Paid $4M loan (d. above) plus $.1M interest (for 90 days).	_____	_____	_____	_____	_____
f.	Received an order for $3M of merchandise to be shipped next quarter.	_____	_____	_____	_____	_____
g.	Collected a $.5M account receivable.	_____	_____	_____	_____	_____
h.	Bought equipment for $1M cash.	_____	_____	_____	_____	_____
i.	Signed a year's rental agreement for office space for $.1M a month.	_____	_____	_____	_____	_____
j.	Sold for $.4M cash a long-term stock investment that had cost $.5M (in prior years, the investment's market value fluctuated between $.6M and $.7M).	_____	_____	_____	_____	_____
k.	Paid cash dividends of $.2M.	_____	_____	_____	_____	_____
l.	The company has been told that its warehouse and material-handling equipment shown at $10M net would cost $15M if replaced today.	_____	_____	_____	_____	_____

| | **M = Million** | | | | |
| | **(Enter + or − and dollar amount or NOT RECOGNIZED)** | | | | |
	Cash Flow	Net Current Assets	Total Assets	Net Assets	Net Income
m. Paid a $.3M account payable.	_____	_____	_____	_____	_____
n. Recognized $.4M annual depreciation on equipment.	_____	_____	_____	_____	_____
o. Bought a $6M machine, paying $2M in cash and signing a 10-year note for the balance.	_____	_____	_____	_____	_____
p. The board of directors authorized $10M for capital expenditures to be made next year.	_____	_____	_____	_____	_____
q. Received notice of a lawsuit against the company for $1M.	_____	_____	_____	_____	_____
r. Sold a machine that had a book value of $1.5M for $2.0M cash.	_____	_____	_____	_____	_____
s. Discovered that, because of obsolescence, inventory that cost $.8M was estimated to have a net realizable value of only $.5M.	_____	_____	_____	_____	_____
t. An account receivable of $.2M from a sale made during 1989 was determined to be uncollectible.	_____	_____	_____	_____	_____

P3.18 Transaction analysis: Computer Corner, Inc. In the fall of 1990, Gary Reed inherited $100,000. He promptly quit his job, and he and his wife Connie decided to take $75,000 of the inheritance and start their own business. In January 1991, the Reeds opened Computer Corner, Inc., a small retail computer store. At the end of 1991, the trial balance of Computer Corner, Inc. appeared as follows:

Computer Corner, Inc.
Trial Balance
December 31, 1991

Account	Balance Left-Hand	Balance Right-Hand
Cash	23,700	
Accounts Receivable	39,300	
Allowance for Uncollectible Accounts		4,000
Inventory	65,000	
Prepaid Rent	4,000	
Property and Equipment (Net)	22,500	
Accounts Payable		25,000
Salaries Payable		3,500
Interest Payable		3,000
Loan Payable		30,000
Common Stock		75,000
Retained Earnings		14,000
	154,500	154,500

The following information pertains to the business during its first year of operation:

1. Signed a five-year lease in January that stipulated a monthly rent of $4,000.

2. Borrowed $30,000 in January from a local bank. The term of the loan was five years and the interest rate was 10 percent.

3. Cash sales for the year totaled $200,000. Credit sales for the year totaled $180,000.

4. One account receivable in the amount of $500 was written off in November as uncollectible.

5. Inventory purchased during the year totaled $280,000. All inventory purchases were on an accounts payable basis.

6. Purchases of property and equipment for the year totaled $25,000 and were paid in cash.

7. Operating expenses for the year included the following:

Supplies	$ 3,500
Utilities	3,000
Insurance	2,000
Salaries	70,000
Advertising	6,500
	$85,000

Included in the Salaries figure was $50,000 attributable to Gary and Connie Reed.

8. The Reeds withdrew $8,000 during the year that was not salary related.

Required:

Based on the information presented above in items 1–8 and in the December 31, 1991, trial balance, prepare the journal entries to record the activities of Computer Corner, Inc., for 1991, *including* the initial investment by the owners. Your entries do not need to be recorded in any particular sequence.

P3.19 Transaction analysis—The Eastside Bank and Trust Co. The trial balances for the Eastside Bank and Trust Co., as of June 30, 1991, and July 31, 1991, were as follows (000 omitted):

At June 30,				At July 31	
Debit (left)	Credit (right)			Debit (left)	Credit (right)
1,200		Cash on hand		1,040	
3,000		Short-term investments		3,000	
300		Interest receivable		325	
20,000		Mortgage loans		19,800	
	2,000	Allowance for credit losses			2,000
8,000		Bank equipment		8,200	
	2,000	Accumulated depreciation on bank equipment			2,045
5,000		Long-term investments		5,000	
	15,000	Deposits			15,675
	12,000	8%, 10-year bonds, dated 1/31/91			12,000
	480	Interest payable			80
	500	Accrued dividends			-0-
	3,020	Retained earnings			3,020
	2,500	Capital stock			2,500
	-0-	Dividend income			50
	-0-	Interest income			225
	-0-	Interest expense		155	
	-0-	Bad debts expense		-0-	
	-0-	Rent expense		10	
	-0-	Payroll expense		15	
	-0-	Other expense		50	

The bank follows the practice of charging a borrower's mortgage with the interest due each month, and crediting a depositor's account with the interest paid each month. The short-term investment portfolio consists of municipal bonds, which pay interest at different dates during the year, mostly during the spring and fall months. The long-term investments consist of common stocks, which pay dividends whenever they are declared, usually in the month following a quarter-end.

Required:

Prepare the entries which would have been required to recognize the bank's activities in July, up to the point as reflected in the above trial balance. There will be 14 entries: these 14 entries treat all similar transactions as having been summarized in one transaction, so that, for example, interest on all mortgages should be recognized in one entry.

P3.20 Preparation of financial statements—The Eastside Bank and Trust Co. Assume the following additional facts about the Eastside Bank and Trust Company, discussed in P3.19:

a. Assume that the market value of the short-term investments (municipal bonds) is about equal to the cost.

b. Assume that the market value of the long-term investments (common stocks) is $4,750, well below the recorded cost, and that the drop is consistent with the dramatic drop in the overall market on July 29, after it was reported that there were new, unsettling developments in foreign affairs.

c. Assume that most of the mortgages are fixed term mortgages and that they carry an average interest rate of 12 percent.

d. Assume that in early July, a large, out-of-town bank announced that it was opening a branch office down the street from Eastside's office and that it was going to offer 6.5 percent on its deposits, as long as they were left on deposit for at least one year. Eastside has only been paying 6 percent on its deposits.

e. Assume that the economy in Eastside's community had been reasonably healthy, but that one of the major industries in town has announced that it has lost a defense contract; that contract loss could translate into a 4 percent jump in the area's unemployment rate.

f. Assume that Eastside's normal income tax rate is 40 percent.

Required:

a. Using the data from the trial balances in P3.19 and the information from the above assumptions, make any adjusting entries you think might be required for the Bank's accounts as of July 31, 1991; prepare the closing entries for the Bank, as of the end of July; and prepare the bank's July financial statements.

b. Based on those financial statements and the understanding about the bank's operations you have gained as a result of your preparation of those statements, outline and briefly discuss the five most important recommendations you would present to the bank's executive committee when they meet next week to review the financial statements for July, and to consider plans for the second half of 1991.

CASES

C3.1 Transaction analysis: Garland Creations, Inc.* Sandy Lawson had been determined to own her own company after completing her MBA. As an accomplished seamstress, she had always had a little business on the side making clothes for friends and specialty stores. The success of the Cabbage Patch dolls convinced her that there was money in stuffed toys. She decided that there was an unexploited niche for a family of animals, each having its own personality.

She took the savings of $7,044 that she had accumulated over the years and, with $263 worth of materials, set out to realize her dreams. Her family were very supportive and lent her $6,000 on a short-term note. She used $3,000 of this to purchase the specialized sewing equipment that she needed to make the animals.

From her years in the clothing business, she managed to find a supplier willing to let her have 90 days credit and invested in an additional $7,364 of materials on 90-day credit terms. Her own car was on its last legs so she purchased a good secondhand pickup truck for $6,600 that she financed through a bank with a $1,600 deposit. One of the family had an unused garage where she could set

*This case was prepared by Michael F. van Breda. Copyright 1988 by Michael F. van Breda.

up her equipment. Installation of the equipment cost her $1,053. A year's insurance to cover the equipment cost an additional $1,000. A variety of different supplies necessary to get her operations off the ground absorbed another $963.

By the end of the first six months, she had made a substantial payment to her supplier, leaving a balance owed of $3,726 in the account. Sales had gone well and brought in a very welcome and reassuring inflow of cash totaling $12,325. She attributed these sales partly to the advertisement that she had run in a trade magazine that had cost her $2,442.

Although she had not been able to repay her family or the bank any of the capital that they had lent her, she had paid the family $360 in interest. Wages had totaled $10,697.

While everyone else headed off for New Year's Eve parties, Sandy Lawson sat down at her desk to determine how well her business had done in the first six months of its life. She had worked extremely hard making stuffed toy animals and was proud of the different personalities that she had been able to create. They surrounded her on all sides as she pored over the numbers.

The results, as she figured them, were very pleasing to her. They appear below.

Garland Creations
Income Statement
For Six Months Ended December 31, 1989

Revenue		$12,325
Opening Inventory	$ 263	
Purchases	7,364	
Wages	10,697	
Prepaid Expenses	2,053	
Supplies	963	
Total	21,340	
Less: Closing Inventory	16,005	
Cost of Goods Sold		5,335
Gross Margin		6,990
Advertising Expenses		2,442
Interest Expense		360
Net Income		$ 4,118

Garland Creations
Balance Sheet
As of December 31, 1989

Cash	$ 616
Inventory	16,005
Current Assets	$16,621
Equipment	3,000
Truck	6,600
Total assets	$26,221
Accounts Payable	$ 3,726
Notes Payable	6,000
Current Liabilities	$ 9,726
Bank Loan	5,000
Capital	7,307
Retained Earnings	4,188
Total Equities	$26,221

Required:

a. Using the description of events in the case and the financial statements provided, replicate the journal entries and the T-accounts Sandy prepared to record the first six months of her business.

b. Where you believe it appropriate, adjust her accounting to better reflect the events. Revise her statements accordingly.

c. Comment on how well the business has done.

C3.2 Overview of the accounting cycle: Photovoltaics, Inc.* Photovoltaics, Inc., is a Texas-based manufacturer and distributor of photovoltaic solar energy units. The company was founded in 1990 by Arthur Manelas and Harry Linn. Manelas, formerly a research scientist with NASA, had been operating a small photovoltaic manufacturing company in Massachusetts when Linn, a marketing consultant to industry and himself an owner of a solar energy company in Oregon, proposed the joint venture.

The founders planned to take advantage of a major shift in consumer attitudes from fossil fuel energy production to cleaner, cheaper energy generation using wind, water, or sun. The joint venture would merge Linn's marketing experience and access to capital with Manelas' prior manufacturing knowledge and government patent on the photovoltaic unit.

The development of photovoltaic technology had begun in 1954 when scientists at the Bell Laboratories found that crystals of silicon could turn sunlight into electricity. The scientists observed that an electric current was produced when photons, or light energy, would strike silicon

---

*This case was prepared by Kenneth R. Ferris. Copyright 1990 by Kenneth R. Ferris.

atoms, thereby causing electrons to be released. The first application of this technology involved the U.S. space program; NASA used photovoltaic solar cells to power the Vanguard I satellite in 1958.

Today, photovoltaic cells are used to power buoys in shipping channels, transmitters on mountain tops, and communication equipment on offshore drilling platforms. In remote locations in Indonesia, Africa, and Australia, where electrical service neither exists nor is cost justified, photovoltaic arrays are used to generate electricity to power such life-sustaining equipment as water pumps and medical refrigerators storing vaccines.

Compared with power generated from such traditional sources as hydroelectric-, coal-, or oil-fueled plants, early photovoltaic arrays were prohibitively expensive (e.g., $2,000 per peak watt). Recent technological advances, however, made the cells so efficient and economical (i.e., $1.85 per peak watt) that they were now competitive with existing alternative energy sources. Elmer B. Kaelin, president of the Potomac Edison Company, warned utility executives that the day was quickly approaching when ''homeowners will have every incentive to install solar collectors and pull the plug on the electric company.''

Convinced that excellent market opportunities for the solar arrays existed, Linn began preparing a prospectus that could be used to help raise capital to significantly expand Manelas' current operations. The two founders had located a manufacturing facility in Lowell, Massachusetts, that would cost approximately $8 million to acquire and equip with updated production equipment. Based on his prior experience, Linn knew that prospective investors would expect to see the following:

- A statement of financial position classifying the company's assets and equities as they would appear at the preproduction stage
- A pro forma earnings statement for the first year of operations
- A pro forma balance sheet as it would appear at the end of the first year of operations
- A pro forma cash flow statement for the first year of operations

In anticipation of preparing these reports, Linn collected the following information and arrived at the following projections:

Data related to preproduction transactions

1. Ten million shares of common stock (par value $1) were authorized for sale by the charter of incorporation. Manelas received 500,000 shares in exchange for rights to the photovoltaic patent, and Linn received an equal number of shares after capitalizing the firm with $500,000 in personal funds.

2. Incorporation and attorney's fees amounted to $27,000.

3. The $8 million purchase price of the manufacturing facility and equipment was to be allocated as follows: building—$4.5 million, land—$750,000, and equipment—$2.75 million. In addition, raw materials and partially completed solar units had been purchased on credit from Manelas' original manufacturing company at a cost of $1.3 million. A note, secured by the inventory itself and accruing interest at a rate of 10 percent per annum on the unpaid balance, was issued to Manelas.

Projected data

4. Sales of common stock to independent investors and venture capitalists would total 2.5 million shares. A selling price of $3.25 per share was set and transaction costs of 1.5 percent of the stock proceeds were projected.

5. Revenues from the sale of solar arrays for the first year were projected to be $480,000, with one fifth of this amount estimated to be uncollected by year-end. The company had decided to follow a particularly rigid credit policy until operations were well established; hence, no provision for bad debts would be established because no uncollectible accounts were anticipated.

6. Cash purchases of raw materials were estimated at $70,000; the cost of units sold was projected at $215,000.

7. Insurance on the building, equipment, and inventory was expected to cost $2,700 per year.

8. Labor costs were estimated at $72,000; selling and administrative costs were projected at 2 percent of gross sales.

9. The useful life of the acquired assets were estimated as follows:

Building:	20 years
Equipment:	10 years

Linn decided to write the patent off over its legal life of 17 years and the organizational costs (i.e., incorporation and attorney fees) over 5 years.

10. Salaries to Linn and Manelas were set at $20,000 each for the first year.

11. No principal repayments would be made on the 10 percent notes issued to Manelas during the first year of operations.

12. Income taxes would be calculated as follows:

Income Level	Tax Rate
$0–50,000	15%
50,001–75,000	25
75,001–100,000	34
100,001–335,000	39
335,001–above	34

The company would be required to pay 80 percent of its taxes by year end.

13. Fifty percent of net income after taxes would be distributed to investors as dividends.

Required:

a. Consider the informational needs of a developing company. Design an efficient accounting system for Photovoltaics, Inc. What accounts would be needed?

b. Prepare the three accounting statements needed for the prospectus.

c. As a prospective investor in the company, what factors would you look for in the accounting statements to help you decide whether or not to invest in the venture?

C3.3 Accounting Cycle: Skyler Pharmacy*

From its beginning in 1976 through February 28, 1990, Skyler Pharmacy operated as a single proprietorship with Mr. Bennett Skyler as owner. On March 1, 1990, the business was incorporated as Skyler Pharmacy, Inc., and the business

---

*This case is based on Jameson's Pharmacy (K), prepared by Billy T. O'Brien under the supervision of Almand R. Coleman, Professor of Business Administraton. Names and figures have been disguised. All rights reserved by the University of Virginia Graduate School of Business Administration Sponsors.

changed its fiscal year from the calendar year to the 12 months ended February 28th. For federal income tax purposes, the corporation qualified as a Sub-Chapter S small business corporation, whose income, whether distributed or not, was taxed directly to the individual stockholder(s).

When Mr. Skyler began the store in 1976, he planned to emphasize his prescription service and to sell prescription and standard drug items only. The character of the store he planned permitted the use of modest quarters (627 square feet store area). The original quarters leased in 1976 were still being used in 1992 despite a sizable increase in sales volume. The increase in annual sales volume and the large proportion of sales represented by prescriptions are indicated in the following tabulation:

Year	Total Sales	Prescription Sales	Number of Prescriptions
1976 (10 mos.)	$ 33,963	$12,592	10,491
1977	56,549	23,456	18,888
1978	67,631	27,147	20,742
1979	72,661	29,936	21,985
1980	77,315	34,186	22,697
1981	83,371	38,950	22,410
1982	86,186	42,156	23,656
1983	78,994	37,519	20,223
1984	83,220	44,716	20,349
1985	95,268	58,006	22,955
1986	104,782	67,037	24,399
1987	120,614	74,715	25,782
1988	123,174	77,620	25,078
1989	129,507	85,328	27,586
12 mos. ended 2/28/91	129,334	84,009	26,570
12 mos. ended 2/28/92	126,715	85,681	26,699

In 1991–92, the store's employees were:

Mr. Bennett Skyler, Manager and Pharmacist
Mr. Samuel R. Rison, Pharmacist (resigned during year)
Mr. Heartwell B. James, Pharmacist (replaced Mr. Rison)
Ms. Irene Gowen, Store Clerk
Ms. Lois West, Store Clerk
Ms. Eva Mae Boulware, Store Clerk
Mr. John Randolph Hart, Delivery Man and Janitor

Because his employees used exceptional tact and courtesy in dealing with customers, Mr. Skyler maintained a salary scale above the "going rate" in the community. The store was not operated at nights or on Sundays. Mr. Skyler, however, utilized a telephone call service which enabled customers to reach either him or his other pharmacist at all hours for emergency prescription needs.

Credit and Collection

Mr. Skyler commented on his receivable problems as follows:

"Aside from prescriptions, I spend more of my time on credit and collections than on anything else. That and getting my accounting records to balance take up a good part of my time. In this community we have monthly payrolls for the most part. This means that I have to wait at least a month to collect for my charge sales, so I have a pretty heavy investment in receivables. But I've gotten a number of good accounts from other stores who have found it necessary to reduce their receivables investment.

"My credit procedure is fairly informal. I know the people of this community, so when customers ask for credit, I either know or can find out pretty quickly what their credit reputation is. If they don't meet my requirements, I sell to them for cash only. Of course, I make some mistakes in extending credit. My mistakes are usually 'slow pay' customers who are able to pay me but pay somebody else instead. Occasionally a 'slow pay' customer turns into a 'no pay' one, and I have to write the account off, but I don't have many like this.

"The way I bill, at the end of each month, I always have at least one month's sales in my month-end receivables. At the end of February I sent out bills for $15,720, of which $6,928 represented February sales being billed for the first time. Before we send out the bills, Miss West puts on my desk the ledger sheets of 'slow pay' customers, and I go over these to see which ones seem to be so because of unusual circumstances I know about. For the others on the list, I indicate the ones to receive one of my special collection letters. One of the letters I use reads as follows:

> We are sorry that we must again remind you of your account, now past due, as shown on the enclosed photostatic copy of your ledger sheet.
>
> This merchandise was charged to you with the understanding that we would receive payment within 30 days—it has been much longer.
>
> We cannot afford to give terms longer than this because our employees are paid twice a month, and our purchases are on a strict 30-day basis.
>
> Our credit standing is important to us, just as yours is to you. We can't settle our accounts unless you pay us—and so it is all down the line. This business of paying bills is simply a 'round robin' affair, and each of us is dependent on the other fellow.
>
> So, please send us a check before you lay this letter aside. We really can use the money, and will appreciate your cooperation.
>
> Sincerely yours,
>
> SKYLER PHARMACY
> Bennett Skyler'

"From time to time I've wondered how far I should go in extending credit, whether I'm being too tight, and what it would mean if I took on more marginal customers."

Record Keeping

Mr. Skyler attempted to maintain his record keeping at a minimum:

1. *He deposited all receipts in the bank each day, and made all disbursements by check.* He established a "change fund" of $225 which was kept in the cash register at all times. Since he deposited the exact amount of his daily receipts in the bank (on the following morning), he made the bank become a sort of second bookkeeper and proof for him with respect to cash receipts and cash disbursements.

2. *He eliminated the usual merchandise purchases journal and accounts payable account.* After the end of each month when he received statements from his suppliers and other creditors, he held his Check Disbursement record open, drew checks to the suppliers and others for the discounted

amounts of their bills, and entered the checks in the check disbursement record in the month when the purchases were made or expenses incurred. He held the checks he drew in this fashion until their respective discount dates when he mailed them to the suppliers.

3. *He had one of his store clerks keep the customers' charge accounts and send out monthly statements.* Each morning the clerk spent about an hour at the bookkeeping machine, posting to the customers' ledger accounts and monthly statements the charge sales tickets and "received on account" tickets for the previous day.

Mr. Skyler's primary records were: *(a)* his cash register, *(b)* his Sales and Cash Receipts record, and *(c)* his Check Disbursement record.

Mr. Skyler's Sales and Cash Receipts record was a record of the store's daily totals for:

(1) Cash Sales (including excise taxes)

(2) Charge Sales (including excise taxes)

(3) Bank Deposits

(4) Cash Received on Account

(5) Excise Taxes Collected (memo record)

To obtain daily totals for these five items, Mr. Skyler utilized his daily cash register tape (giving totals for cash sales, cash received on account, and excise taxes collected), together with *(a)* tickets for Charge Sales to be charged to individual customers' accounts and *(b)* tickets for cash "Received on Account" showing the individual customers' accounts to be posted. He made an adding machine run of the Charge Sales tickets to get the day's total to be entered in the Sales and Cash Receipts record. He proved:

(1) The total of each day's "Received on Account" tickets against his cash register total.

(2) The total of the bank deposit (made the following morning) against the sum of the day's totals for cash sales and cash received on account.

He entered the day's total for the five items in the five columns of his Sales and Cash Receipts record which he totaled for each month. At the end of the year, he summarized the monthly figures.

Mr. Skyler's Check Disbursement record was a chronological record of disbursements by check as recorded from check stubs. This record showed the date, check number, and payee, and entry of the amount of the check in columns for:

(1) Merchandise Paid For

(2) Salaries and Wages

(3) Other Store Expenses

(4) Other Payments

He totaled these columns monthly, and at the end of the year summarized the monthly figures. Mr. Skyler made it a practice to take every discount available to him, so the amounts in the Merchandise-Paid-For column represented the discounted amounts. As a matter of personal interest, Mr. Skyler maintained a memo record of the discounts he took each month, and for the year as a whole.

Mr. Skyler kept the Sales and Cash Receipts and Check Disbursements records himself, for the information it afforded him. At the end of each year, he supplied the year's totals and other information to a local certified public accountant as a basis for the preparation of the corporation's income tax return.

In March 1992, the following information was available with respect to the corporation's fiscal year ended February 28, 1992:

1. *Balance Sheet as of beginning of fiscal year, March 1, 1991:*

   Assets

Cash in Store (change fund)	$ 225
Cash in Bank	11,964
Trade Receivables	14,852
Merchandise Inventory	15,884
Store Equipment and Other Fixed Assets (Net)	2,346
Organization Costs	236
	$ 45,507

   Liabilities

Accounts Payable	$ 4,614
Accrued Taxes	1,059
Bonus Payable to S. R. Rison	2,274
Capital Stock	34,000
Retained Earnings	3,560
	$ 45,507

2. *Twelve Months' Summary of Sales and Cash Receipts record:*

Cash Sales (including $78 excise tax)	$ 46,697
Charge Sales (including $118 excise tax)	80,018
Bank Deposits	125,462
Cash Received on Account from Customers	78,765

3. *Twelve Months' Summary of Check Disbursement record:*

Merchandise paid for (net of $2,049 discounts)	$ 69,738
Salaries and Wages (including $11,750 for B. Skyler)	33,697
Other Store Expenses	12,184
	$115,619
Other Payments	30,609
Total Check Disbursements	$146,228

4. *Analysis of ''Other Payments'':*

Payments on accounts payable outstanding at 2/28/91		$ 4,614
Payments on accrued taxes outstanding at 2/28/91		1,059
Payment on bonus payable (S. R. Rison) outstanding at 2/28/91		2,274
Donations to United Fund, T.B. Association, Chamber of Commerce*		125
Excise Tax Paid		196
Refunds to customers for sales returned		100
Capital items:		
Freeyer	$ 1,300	
Stamp Machine	121	
Store Sign	490	
Leasehold Improvements	537	
Office Chair	58	2,506

Paid to B. Skyler:		
Advance to B. Skyler	$ 7,972	
Dividend on capital stock	11,763	19,735
Total (as per #3 above)		$30,609

*Mr. Skyler continued, in the corporation's records, his former practice of keeping donations separately recorded from other store expenses. The local C.P.A. considered these donations as other store expenses of the corporation.

5. *Unrecorded Borrowing from Bank:*

On February 9, 1992, Mr. Skyler had arranged for a $5,000, 5 percent 60-day loan from the bank. The interest of $42 was deducted from the proceeds and the Pharmacy's account was credited with $4,958 on February 9, 1992. An entry needs to be made to record this transaction with care being taken to allocate the $42 interest, one third to Retained Earnings and two thirds to Prepaid Interest.

6. *A reconciliation of the bank account at February 28, 1992, showed as follows:*

Balance as per bank statement 2/28/92	$ 3,211
Add: Deposits of 2/26, 2/27, and 2/28 receipts in transit to bank	846
	$ 4,057
Deduct: Outstanding checks	7,897
Adjusted overdraft per books 2/28/92	$(3,840)

The difference between the "adjusted overdraft per books" of $(3,840), shown above, and the balance of $(3,844) shown by the Pharmacy's records was $4. It was decided that it would not be worthwhile to try to trace down this difference, so an adjustment of $4 is to be made to the bank balance and Other Store Expenses.

Included among the "outstanding checks" were 43 checks totaling $7,347 which had actually been drawn after February 28, 1992, and which had been entered in the February Check Disbursement record which had been held "open."

These checks had been drawn for merchandise purchased in February and for other store expenses incurred in February. An entry is to be made to restore the total of these checks, $7,347, to Cash in Bank and to Accounts Payable at February 28, 1992.

7. *Mr. Skyler "Summary of Trade Receivables from Customers" showed as follows:*

Total amount of customers' accounts at March 1, 1991	$14,852
Charge sales during year	80,018
	$94,870
Received on account during year	78,765
Total amount of customers' accounts unpaid at February 28, 1992	$16,105

Note: The total of the balances of individual customer's statements mailed at February 28, 1992, was $15,720. The difference of $385 represented accounts determined to be worthless and written off.

8. Mr. Skyler and his employees listed and counted the merchandise stock on hand at February 28, 1992. Those items of merchandise which had become obsolete were shown at no value or at a nominal value, while all currently salable items were valued at the price which the store had paid for them. The inventory sheets were then totaled. The total inventory for the prescription department was $8,661 and for other merchandise in the store, $7,672. The final figure for the entire inventory at February 28, 1992, was therefore $16,333.

Mr. Skyler observed that through experience, and as a result of keeping his own records, he had a "feel" for how much inventory he had on hand at any one time. He noted that the $16,333 physical inventory figure was pretty close to his preliminary estimate of $16,000 for stock on hand at February 28, 1992.

9. The local C.P.A. prepared a depreciation schedule for the fiscal year ended February 28, 1992, as follows:

Kind of Property	Date Bought	Original Cost	Cost Remaining @ 3/1/91	Depr. Life	Year's Depr.
Blower, etc.	1977	$ 164	$ 14	15	$ 11
Typewriter and cabinet	1979	315	15*	10	–0–
Cash register	1980	390	25*	10	–0–
Ledger tray	1980	47	5*	10	–0–
Safe	1981	363	187	20	18
Pricing machine	1985	197	86	10	20
Air conditioners	1986	780	177	7	111
Stenorette	1986	246	16	5	49
Various office equipment	1987	866	529	10	87
Copier	1988	342	251	10	34
1980 Truck (salvage $100)	1989	1,722	1,041	5	323
		$5,432	$2,346		$653

Additions during 1991–92:

Stamp machine	1991	121	—	10	6
Freeyer	1991	1,300	—	5	130
Office chair	1991	58	—	10	3
Leasehold improvements	1991	537	—	6	45
Store sign	1991	490	—	10	25
		$7,938	$2,346		$862

Add: Cost of additions during 1991–92	2,506
	$4,852
Deduct: Depreciation for year	862
Cost remaining at 2/28/92	$3,990

*Estimated salvage value

An entry should be made for depreciation for the year.

10. The local C.P.A. noted also:

   a. That employer social security taxes for January and February 1992, in the amount of $194, had been incurred and needed to be shown as a liability at 2/28/92.

   b. That, similarly, the corporation had incurred state income taxes in the amount of $432 for the fiscal year ended 2/28/92.

   He thought it would be all right to combine these two items into one total, and so make only one entry.

11. The local C.P.A. observed that, for income tax purposes, the corporation had elected to amortize organization costs of $295 over a 60-month period. An entry for $59 amortization should be made.

12. Mr. Skyler had entered into profit-sharing arrangements with both Mr. Rison and Mr. James, the terms of which provided for an annual bonus based upon the corporation's net profit before bonus but after providing for their regular salaries and for a salary of $11,750 to Mr. Skyler. These salaries are included in the $33,697 total for Salaries and Wages (#3 above). On the basis of the information developed by him, the local C.P.A. determined the bonuses to be $367 for Mr. Rison and $612 for Mr. James, no part of which had been paid at 2/28/92.

Required:

a. Prepare accounting entries for 1992 events in usual form:

   (1) In analyzing transactions for the information contained in Items 2, 3, and 4, it is suggested you break it up as follows:

   (a) One entry, designated *A*, for cash sales.
   (b) Another entry, designated *B*, for charge sales.
   (c) Another entry, designated *C*, for collections on customer accounts.
   (d) One entry, *D*, for merchandise paid for, for salaries and wages, and for other store expenses.
   (e) Another entry, *E*, for "other payments" (Item 4).

   (2) Make entries, designated *F, G, H*, etc., as and if appropriate, for the remainder of the information given.

b. Enter your entries in the T-accounts on pp. 126–127.

c. Prepare a Trial Balance.

d. Prepare a Combined Statement of Income and Retained Earnings by filling in blanks appropriately on the form attached (page 127).

e. Prepare a Comparative Balance Sheet by filling in blanks on form attached (page 128).

f. Prepare a simple statement of cash receipts and disbursements for 1991–92 by filling in blanks appropriately below:

Beginning Balance	$
ADD: Cash Receipts	
	$
DEDUCT: Cash Disbursements	
Ending Balance	$

g. How would you explain to the inquisitive Mr. Skyler:

   (1) Why "Cash Receipts" above are not the same as "Sales" income on the income statement?

   (2) Why "Cash Disbursements" above are not the same as "Cost of Goods Sold" and "Expenses" on the income statement?

Cash on hand—Change fund (asset)

3/1/91 Balance	225	

Cash in bank (asset)

3/1/91 Balance	11,964	

Trade receivables (asset)

3/1/91 Balance	14,852	

Merchandise inventory (asset)

3/1/91 Balance	15,884	

Store equipment and other fixed assets (asset)

3/1/91 Balance	2,346	

Prepaid interest (asset)

3/1/91 Balance	−0−	

Organization costs (asset)

3/1/91 Balance	236	

Advances to B. Skyler (asset)

3/1/91 Balance	−0−	

Notes payable—bank (liability)

Accounts payable (liability)

	3/1/91 Balance	4,614

Accrued taxes (liability)

	3/1/91 Balance	1,059

Bonus payable—S. R. Rison (liability)

	3/1/91 Balance	2,274

Bonus payable—H. B. James (liability)

Capital stock (owners equity)

3/1/91 Balance	34,000

Retained earnings (owners equity)

3/1/91 Balance	3,560

Skyler Pharmacy, Inc. (K)
Combined Statement of Income and Retained Earnings
For Fiscal Year Ended February 28, 1992

	Amount
Sales (less discounts, returns, and allowances)	$_____
Cost of Goods Sold:	
Inventory—Beginning of Year. . . . . $_____	
Add Merchandise Purchases . . . . _____	
$_____	
Deduct Inventory—End of Year . . . . _____	
Total Cost of Goods Sold	_____
Gross Margin.	$_____
Expenses:	
Proprietor's Salary . . . . $_____	
Employees' Compensation . . . . _____	
Depreciation . . . . _____	
Debts Charged Off. . . . . _____	
All Other Store Expenses. . . . . _____	
Total Expenses.	_____
Net Profit for Year	$_____
Retained Earnings Balance, 3/1/91	_____
	$_____
Deduct Dividends	_____
Retained Earnings, 2/28/92	$_____

Skyler Pharmacy, Inc. (K)
Comparative Balance Sheets
February 28, 1992 and March 1, 1991

	2/28/92	3/1/91	Increase (Decrease)
Assets			
Cash in Store and in Bank	$_____	$12,189	$_____
Trade Receivables	_____	14,852	_____
Merchandise Inventory	_____	15,884	_____
Store Equipment and Other Fixed Assets (Net)	_____	2,346	_____
Prepaid Interest	_____	–0–	_____
Organization Costs	_____	236	_____
Advances to B. Skyler	_____	–0–	_____
Total Assets	$_____	$45,507	$_____
Liabilities and Owners' Equity			
Notes Payable—Bank	$_____	$ –0–	$_____
Accounts Payable	_____	4,614	_____
Accrued Taxes	_____	1,059	_____
Bonus Payable—S. R. Rison	_____	2,274	_____
Bonus Payable—H. B. James	_____	–0–	_____
Capital Stock	_____	34,000	_____
Retained Earnings	_____	3,560	_____
Total Liabilities and Owners' Equity	$_____	$45,507	$_____

C3.4 Projected Financial Statements: The Law Brothers.*

In the summer of 1959, John and Harry Law were considering a proposal by Tom Johnson that the three men form a new corporation for the packing and distribution of oysters.

Background

In 1939, John Law, graduate of an eastern graduate business school, and Harry Law, law school graduate, bought a farm on the Rappahannock River in Virginia and operated it as a partnership. They retained as manager Tom Johnson, who had served in the same capacity for the previous owner.

Two years later, in 1941, they decided to go into the oyster planting business and accordingly purchased a lease on approximately 200 acres of planting grounds in the river along the farm's shore line.[1] They also had a 42-foot oyster boat built for "dredging" and made Mr. Johnson boat captain and manager of the planting operations.

Mr. Johnson managed both businesses until 1954 when he retired as manager of the farm. To augment his income from the planting operation, he purchased a truck, hired a driver, and began

---

[1]The Commonwealth of Virginia authorized 20-year leases on private planting grounds. These leases were salable and renewable.

*Case prepared by H. Lee Boatwright, Jr., 1960, under the supervision of Almand R. Coleman, Professor of Business Administration. Case revised in 1966.

All rights reserved by the Sponsors of the Graduate School of Business Administration, University of Virginia. Names, places, and figures have been disguised.

distributing oysters from several packing houses in the area to hotels, restaurants, and food stores around the state.

Thus by 1959, all three men had eighteen years of experience in planting oysters and a good understanding of the packing operation through association with it. Since 1954, Mr. Johnson had also developed contacts with a number of distribution outlets.

The Planting Operation

Oysters in the Rappahannock River were rarely known to "strike" (reproduce) but they did grow large and fat. On the other hand, in the lower James River they struck annually but did not grow to a sufficient size for harvesting. It was the practice, therefore, for the Rappahannock planters to buy the young "seed oysters" from the lower James River and plant them in the Rappahannock, where they were allowed to mature.

The seed oysters were planted in the fall and left for three years before they were harvested. During this time the death rate was high. For example, seed oysters ran about 1,000 to 1,200 per bushel, while mature oysters averaged from 250 to 300 per bushel. The harvest, however, was usually on a one-for-one basis; that is, one bushel recovered for one bushel planted. Thus about three fourths of the oysters died during the three-year period.

Sometimes unusual factors such as blight, fungus attacks, and weather conditions caused even higher losses. In 1955, Hurricane Hazel destroyed about 70 percent of the oyster crop in the Rappahannock River, because the heavy rainfall brought too much fresh water and silting into the oyster growing areas.

Two further risks which had been of concern to those in the oyster business were the possible increases (1) in river pollution by industrial plants and city sewage operations, and (2) in silting caused by clearing and cultivating the lands along the river banks.

The mature oysters were harvested from September through March by "dredging."[2] They were usually thin in the early fall after the warm summer months, but grew fatter during the winter. The demand for oysters, however, began in late August and early September, notwithstanding their poorer condition then.

Operation of the Public Rocks

The Commonwealth of Virginia maintained public oyster grounds for the many local water men who made their living oystering in the winter and crabbing or fishing in the summer. The "tongers," as these men were called, had small boats and brought up the oysters by hand with tongs, since no dredging was permitted on the public rocks. A good tonger could generally get about ten to twelve bushels on a favorable day, but during bad weather, when the river was rough, they could not go out at all because of the small size of their boats. The public rocks were open only from October 1 to March 31.

The tongers usually sold their catch to local packing houses, but at times when the demand was high, they sold some oysters to "buy boats" which came out in the river from packers who wanted to fill out their capacity. These buy boats generally offered a slightly better price than the tongers could get from the local packers.

---

[2]A "dredge" is a very large rake trailing a net which catches the oysters as they are raked off the bottom. The dredge is dragged along the oyster bed until the net is full, then winched in and dumped on deck.

The Packing Operation

The packing house bought oysters from both private planters and tongers as needed to fill capacity or meet customer orders. Generally the house bought that amount on one day which it expected to pack the next. The price fluctuated considerably with the supply and demand.

Two different methods of purchase were used. The tonger was paid by the bushel when he unloaded his catch. The price per bushel had ranged in 1957 and 1958 from $2.75 to $3.75. For the private planters, on the other hand, "buying them on the meats" was most common. The planter was paid by the gallon according to how much his oysters shucked out. Here, of course, a great deal depended on how fat the oysters were, but over the course of a season one bushel would generally average out about 5½ pints of "meat." The price paid to the planter was the going price for bulk oysters at the plant site ($4.50 to $5.50 per gallon in the preceding two years) less the labor cost of shucking ($1.00 per gallon) and a charge (20¢ per bushel) for overhead and handling. The packer made his profit on the increase from blowing (which will be explained below) and the value of the shells.[3] Exhibit I shows a sample calculation of "buying on the meats."

The oysters were carried from the large bins in which they were stored into the shucking room where they were shucked (opened) by hand. The shuckers were paid strictly on piece-rate, one dollar per gallon, and could open on the average about twelve gallons per day.

The shuckers also performed the grading function. Oysters were sold in two sizes, selects and standards. Selects were large oysters and measured about 250 per gallon. All of the smaller oysters were classified as standards. In the fall, when the oysters were thin, there were more standards than selects, but during the winter there were more selects, so that over the course of a season they averaged out about even.

After being shucked, the oysters went to the blowing room where they were put into large vats of fresh water for washing. Air was blown in from the bottom to agitate and wash the oysters. Since during this operation the oysters took on some water and air, they actually increased in size. For example, five gallons before blowing produced about six afterwards.

E X H I B I T   I

THE LAW BROTHERS
Sample Calculation of Buying on the Meats

Purchase	176 bushels		
Production (5½ pts./bu.)	121 gallons		
Payment due planters:			
Gross ($5.00/gal.)			$605.00
Less:			
Wages paid to shuckers ($1.00/gal.)		$121.00	
Overhead and handling charge ($.20/bu.)		35.20	156.20
Net to planter			$448.80

---

[3]One bushel of oysters produced a bushel of shells which could be sold for 13¢ per bushel.

Next the oysters were packed in cans and put on ice until they were sold. The packer usually had regular customers who picked up the oysters at the plant on the same or following day. Because the produce was perishable,[4] the packing house tried to process only enough to meet a known demand. For this reason the inventory rarely exceeded one day's "shell stock" and one day's packed oysters.[5] Customers paid their bills fairly promptly, so that accounts receivable averaged about seven days' sales.

Some packers had their own trucks for distribution to wholesalers, restaurants, hotels, and independent grocers who required delivery.

In 1957 and 1958, the packers' selling price had fluctuated between $4.50 and $5.50 for standards and $5.50 and $6.50 for selects.

See Exhibit II for further information on the oyster industry.

The Proposal

In the spring of 1959, Johnson came to the Law brothers with a proposal that they start a packing business. He had done much of the preliminary planning since he intended to go into the venture anyway, but he wanted them in to ensure a supply of oysters. He offered to put up one half or one third of the capital required in order to get the business underway.

Johnson had already selected a plant site which was well-located in a protected cove with plenty of water for the boats to come in very close to the bank. This meant that not only did the site have an advantage over many houses that were located in unprotected areas and thus could not unload oysters in bad weather, but that it was not necessary to build a long and expensive unloading dock. There was also an advantage in handling efficiency since the oysters could be unloaded very near the storage bins. The two and a half acres of land would cost $1,420, and Johnson estimated that improvements, including the dock, would run about $1,500.

In the next few months, Johnson and the Laws visited other packing houses to determine the size of the building, the layout, and the equipment required. The packers with whom they talked were somewhat discouraging, saying that business had not been good in recent years. John Law commented on this, "Yes, they were discouraging, but we saw that they were all driving Buicks, so we didn't pay too much attention to it."

The three men decided that a plant providing room for 25 shuckers would be the most efficient, because there would be a minimum of indirect labor. With 25 shuckers or less, only one man would be needed to distribute oysters in the shucking room and only one to run the blowing and packing operations. Harry Law observed, "We found that the oyster house, to be most economical, had to be built for 25 shuckers or multiples of 25."

The second reason for choosing this size was that the Laws' oyster grounds would provide about 20,000 bushels of the estimated practical capacity of 35,000 bushels per season. If the plant were larger, they would have to rely more heavily on the tongers to fill out capacity. On this subject, Harry Law commented, "We don't want to get too large, because we want to use our oysters when we can't get rock oysters."

---

[4]Oysters would stay fresh about a week to ten days if properly iced.

[5]Some of the large packers froze oysters for year-round distribution, and for such an operation a much larger investment in inventory and equipment was required. A small local packer had also experimented unsuccessfully with freezing oysters.

E X H I B I T I I

THE LAW BROTHERS
Additional Technical Note on Oyster Industry Consisting of:
(1) News Articles in the Richmond Times-Dispatch about the Time of the Case and
(2) Additional Information on Packing Cans and Oyster Shells

Richmond Times-Dispatch
January 18, 1960, Issue

RAPPAHANNOCK OYSTERS ACCLAIMED FOR QUALITY
by Christine Hall

Urbanna, January 17

"'The Rappahannock accounts for about one third of Virginia's total oyster production, which in turn is one half of the United States' total.' Ryland said.

"'Until a few years ago,' he added, 'Virginia contributed only about a third of the total. But Delaware, New Jersey, and New York oyster grounds have suffered a 90 percent loss in their annual crop.'

"Oyster harvesting is big business. With a total production of approximately 10,500,000 gallons—or 75 million pounds—the United States supplies five-eighths of all market oysters produced in the world.

"The two methods permitted for harvesting oysters from the Rappahannock River are known as patent tonging and shaft tonging. The use of patent tongs, a mechanical grappling device operated by a motor, is restricted to the lower river in water depths of 20 to 30 feet.

First Three Months

"Virginia law allows the use of patent tongs only during the first three months of each oyster season—October through December—on the Rappahannock, but in Chesapeake Bay the legal period is extended through February.

"Shaft tonging begins with the opening of oyster season on the public grounds or 'Rock,' October 1, and continues until the season closes at the end of April.

"Oystermen operate shaft, or hand tongs, from open boats. The shafts or handles range in length from 24 to 32 feet, and are attached to long-toothed, pincer-line tongs hinged together. With this device the oysters are

located on the bottom and brought to the surface, where they are dumped on the culling board in the boat.

"Most boat crews consist of two tongers and a third man who culls the catch by throwing back all oysters under the legal size of three inches in length. A few watermen prefer to work alone, tonging and culling their catch in turn.*

Public and Private Grounds

"Virginia's annual oyster harvest is taken from both public and private grounds. The public rock is maintained by the Commission of Fisheries at state expense for the benefit of the public. A $3.50 license, an oyster boat, and know-how are the only items required to get into the business of tonging oysters from public grounds, which contain some 300,000 acres of the state's river and bay bottoms.

"Private grounds, which account for an additional 125,000 acres, are leased from the state by the planters at a present annual rate of $1 per acre in the rivers, and 50 cents an acre in Chesapeake and part of Mobjack Bay, Ryland explained.

"Ryland and 55 other inspectors patrol the public oyster grounds in 16 police boats to enforce the state's oystering laws."

March 14, 1960, Issue
MIDDLESEX OYSTERMEN HARD HIT BY WEATHER
by Christine Hall

Urbanna, March 13

"Bad weather has cost Middlesex County oystermen an estimated $350,000 in lost income in the past two weeks.

"The estimate was furnished by J. W. Ferguson, the largest seafood packer in this area. He said, 'I normally buy about 4,200 bushels of oysters a week, but since March 1, I have only been able to buy 275 bushels—200 week before last and only 75 bushels last week.'

---

*The requirement that tongers throw back "all oysters under the legal size of three inches in length" accounts for the fact that oysters bought from tongers will usually be "cleaner" than those

acquired from planters. This accounts for the difference between the price per bushel paid tongers and the "net" per bushel paid to the planter in "buying them on the meats."

E X H I B I T   I I

(continued)

"Ferguson, who owns two of approximately 35 oyster packing houses on the Rappahannock River, estimated that he buys 12 percent of the 8,500 bushels of oysters tonged daily from the river's public oyster grounds.

"Boats and oystermen on both sides of the river have been kept ashore for nearly three weeks by the extreme cold, high winds, ice and snow. The limited number of boats that ventured into the river on calm days were soon forced back to shore by the cold. 'You just can't hold onto an icicle but so long, and that is what the tongs would be after a few dips into the water,' Ferguson said.

"The lack of activity on the public rocks has thrown at least 600 people out of work temporarily. The tongers were being paid $3.50 per bushel for the oysters.

"Seafood packing houses in the area have been forced to either close down or resort to dredging from their private oyster grounds. Mechanically operated dredge boats are not hampered by cold weather unless the creeks are completely locked in by ice.

" 'We have been operating our packing houses with oysters dredged from our private beds,' Ferguson said. 'Our main problem, however, has been the heavy snow preventing our employees from getting to work.' The Ferguson Seafood Packing Company employs 94 people—60 of them oyster shuckers.

"Oystermen and packers alike are looking forward to the return of normal operations, possibly this week, because the seafood business is Middlesex County's biggest industry."

October 1, 1960, Issue
OYSTER SEASON OPENS TODAY

Urbanna, September 30

"Despite the rumors of high oyster mortalities in the Rappahannock River, oyster boats from Tangier Island, Mathews, and Gloucester began arriving in Middlesex County creeks Friday in preparation for the opening of the season Saturday.

"The Rappahannock's most productive grounds, a 40-mile stretch which extends along the entire shoreline length of Middlesex County, is the working area for some 1,000 boats. This area produces one-third of Virginia's oysters. A normal day's catch from the Rappahannock, in a good season, is approximately 15,000 bushels.

"Oyster buyers and packers were uncertain Friday just what they would pay per bushel for the Saturday catch. Estimates ranged from $3.50 to $4.25. B. B. Newman, an Urbanna buyer, said the first day would be more or less a guess. 'We really won't know what to pay until after a load has been bought, shucked out, and the condition of the oysters determined,' he said.

"Thirty to thirty-five buy boats operate on the river, some coming from as far away as the Eastern Shore and Maryland. These large boats buy oysters from the smaller tonight boats and deliver to the packing houses.

"Speculation as to the condition of the oysters that will be tonged Saturday was the topic of conversation along the waterfront Friday. . . ."

"Regardless of the reports that oysters will be scarce this season, oystermen by the hundred will be out on the Rappahannock when day breaks Saturday morning. 'We will wait and see for ourselves,' is the consensus of the watermen."

October 23, 1960, Issue
TO PLANT OR NOT TO PLANT?—OYSTER THREAT FACED WITH MIXED EMOTIONS

Urbanna, October 22

" 'The next generation won't even remember it,' one oysterman said here this week.

"Said another: 'We can work, we can sell, and we can be sure we are in the market this winter at least.' Then he added, 'as for next winter and the future . . .' He shrugged and spread his hands.

"Oystermen all along the Rappahannock and elsewhere in Virginia face a deadly threat to their livelihood. It is the mysterious MSX that has been blamed for destroying Delaware's oyster industry and heavily damaging Maryland's.

"The oyster killer was discovered in Virginia last year, and already it has caused widespread mortalities—up to 80 percent in some state waters. Last week a marine scientist said evidence of the deadly micro-organism has been found in the Rappahannock River and the valuable seed beds in the James River.

Trace Noted

"In both places, only a trace of MSX was noted. The scientists cautioned against alarm. They noted that although it is fatal to oysters, the tiny organism has no effect on humans.

"Fat and tasty Rappahannock River oysters are famous throughout the world. Almost all taken from the

EXHIBIT II

(continued)

river are produced in a 40-mile stretch of the river extending from the mouth at Chesapeake Bay.

"The annual catch from this area represents about one third of the total oyster production in Virginia. Watermen working the beds in the river tong approximately 15,000 bushels of oysters from the Rappahannock each day of the oyster season. The entire economy of the area is tied in with the oyster industry and an oyster killer would seriously affect the income of a large number of workers.

Certain Beds Favored

"Tiny oysters—or spats—are born and grow initially at their best in certain beds, as in the lower James. But later, the small oyster—the seed—is transplanted and thrives in other beds. The Rappahannock is usually a highly favorable environment.

"Oysters require three years to mature. Those planted this year will be tonged and sold in 1963, if they are still alive.

"There's the gamble. The oysterman now is faced with the decision of whether it is worth the risk to plant for a crop he may not harvest.

"Last March, two Norfolk oyster firms—the two largest in Virginia—stopped buying and planting seed oysters.

"And while many Rappahannock River watermen are optimistic about the future of the oyster industry, some have followed the Norfolk firm's example.

"J. W. Ferguson of Remlik, an oysterman who also operates one of the largest packing firms on the Rappahannock, said, 'I'm being cautious this year. I've only planted about 4,000 bushels of seed so far this year.' In a normal year, Ferguson said he plants about 50,000 bushels.

"Ferguson said he felt the quantity of seed oysters planted by Virginia oystermen this season will depend to a large extent on prices demanded for seed by James River tongers.

"Under the present risk, 60 cents a bushel is the top price which planters can afford to pay, he said.

"This is almost bottom price. The tongers want $1 or more per bushel, and the James River Tongers Association is considering asking the Virginia Commission of Fisheries to relax the law prohibiting the sale of seed oysters outside the state in order to boost the seed market price.

"The Rappahannock oyster planters argue that the tongers should bear some of the risk, too. R. H. Woodward of Middlesex County, president of the Virginia Oyster Planters Association, said 'I think most planters will agree that 60 cents is the top price which can be paid for seed under present conditions.'

"Woodward said he felt that most planters would agree to a suggested plan of paying the tongers 40 cents a bushel and putting an additional 60 cents per bushel into a bank fund. If the planter made a profit from the seed, the extra 60 cents would be paid to the tongers, said Woodward, and if the seed died, the extra money would help the planter cover his loss.

"Ferguson said he believes firmly that the oyster industry will survive the MSX crisis.

"'The next generation won't ever remember this thing we call MSX,' he said. 'And my guess is that oysters will soon build an immunity to it and which will make it run out long before we begin to run out of oysters.'

"Other Rappahannock River oystermen also continue planting.

"'We'll just take the chance on MSX,' said F. S. Garret, Jr., of Bowlers Wharf in Essex County, one of the river's largest planters. 'We can't say we were not warned, but in this business you have to keep re-planting or get out.'"

Answers to Specific Questions on Cans and Shells (as of the time of the case)

I. Do the oyster houses buy enough cans for a season at one clip, or do they buy little by little through the season?

   Packers do not generally order enough cans for a season but do give the supplier an estimate of the need. In some cases the cans have to be lithographed to show the brand and in all instances the packer's number has to appear on the lid. For this reason the packer must keep the supplier informed well in advance of his needs. The majority would not have adequate storage place for a season's supply.

II. Will a bushel of shells bring 13 cents? Are the shells a salable item, or are they hard to move?

   Shells are readily salable on the shellpile at some 12–14 cents per bushel, the variance in the price being largely dependent upon where the purchaser proposes to use them. The majority of the shells are purchased by the state and are put on the public oyster bottom, that is to say, bottom within the Baylor survey. It costs the planter an additional 6 cents per bushel to load and plant the shells so that the cost to the planter on the bottom is approximately 20 cents per bushel, These are planted for the purpose of making available material on which the spat can catch, thereby creating the strike.

A local contractor estimated that the building would cost about $18,000. The equipment required would run about $4,000.

Consideration was given to taking over Johnson's trucking business to provide some initial customers. If so, the company would pay Johnson $3,100 for his truck and hire his driver to make deliveries and serve as a general handyman around the plant.

Next, the three estimated the operating costs and expenses which would be incurred, based on their experience and the information they had been able to gather. They knew that cans would cost 25¢ per gallon but had to estimate the other expenses for such things as electricity, telephone, gas and oil, etc. These, they thought, would run about $150 per week for the seven-month, thirty-week season.[6]

The salaries, to be paid only during the season, would be as follows:

Manager (Johnson)	$80.00 per week
Truck driver	$80.00 per week
Blowing room operator	$60.00 per week
Oyster carrier	$50.00 per week

The Laws made no provision for paying themselves salaries, although they thought that each would have to put in at least one day per week at the plant on business matters, plus some time on day-to-day operating decisions.

Finally, the Law brothers and Johnson discussed how they would set up and finance the business if it looked like a good venture. They decided that if they went into the venture they would incorporate and elect to be taxed as a partnership under sub-chapter S of the Internal Revenue Code. Harry Law pointed out: "We would incorporate for two reasons: limited liability and divisibility in the case of death."[7] Since they would draw virtually all of the earnings out of the business, the tax election would avoid double taxation on the profits.

To finance the business they intended to borrow as much as possible from the local bank. John Law said, "We're pretty sure we can get a ten-year mortgage on the fixed assets[8] for about 50 percent of their value. We would have to put up the rest."

Other Considerations

In speaking of his views on the proposal, Harry Law said that he had been thinking for a number of years that such a move would be advantageous. "We will be paid the same amount for our shell stock and anything the packing business makes will be just gravy. John and I have discussed the matter from time to time, but neither of us has wanted to take the supervision job nor, up to now, had we found anyone we felt we could rely on to do a good job for us. The manager's job requires a lot of knowledge of the business, long hours, and the ability to deal effectively with the tongers, shuckers, and buyers. Without Johnson's interest, we probably would not now be seriously considering the plan."

---

[6]As was customary, they would also have to operate a small store for the shuckers who bought their lunches at the plant. This store would carry bread, canned meats, beans, cigarettes, candy, etc., but the Laws did not expect it to have a substantial effect on profit.

[7]All three men were in their fifties.

[8]Except the truck.

John Law said he had two main thoughts on the matter. "Since he (Johnson) has been here for twenty years, I would be doubly interested in any business proposition which would help him as well as us. He has done a splendid job operating our boat and managing the planting and harvesting of our oysters. We would be willing to assume new business risks with Johnson that we wouldn't assume with others because of our past successful relationship. We hope we can work out something with him. We don't want him to go in with someone else.

"Secondly, since there is no exact market for shell stock (a bushel of shell stock is inexact because it shucks out differently and therefore brings a different price), the one way that buyer and seller can know best what they are doing is to sell 'em on the meats. To do this, each jag (boatload) has to be separated. Then you are dependent on your shucking house to be honest with you. Also, a shucker who shucks on a piece rate basis might push aside the small oysters. There is less pressure on the shucking house to be efficient in keeping jags separated and in preventing the shuckers from passing over the small ones when it is buying on the meats.

"When you sell this way, you are subject to such errors. By selling to ourselves, I feel we could eliminate some of these errors.

"Another thing. Seafood prices change rather rapidly according to supply and demand. There is no quoted price in the paper or anything. When an Indian summer comes along, the price of a gallon may drop 50 cents or a dollar.[9] As a planter you don't keep up with the market as well. I think sometimes the shucking houses don't reflect a rising market in their buying prices as quickly as they do when prices are off. At any rate I think we can eliminate this uncertainty."

There were some deterrent factors which the Laws considered. The most important of these was the serious blight which had hit the Delaware Bay area, cutting production there in half from 1957 to 1958. There were indications that the 1959 crop in the Delaware Bay would be almost completely destroyed. This blight had not as yet been found in the Chesapeake Bay growing areas, but it had made its appearance on the ocean side of the Eastern Shore. There was a possibility that if the blight got into the Chesapeake, the whole industry would be out of business indefinitely.

Secondly, a branch of the AFL-CIO had been attempting to organize the menhaden fishing industry in the area. Indications were that attempts would be made to organize the shuckers also. The latter had not had a raise in pay for seven or eight years in spite of the large increase in retail prices over the same period.

Lastly, the Laws knew that competition in the area for the public rock catch would be strong, particularly when the demand was high.

Required:

1. Let us suppose the two Law brothers forecast that the minimum volume the business would handle in the first year would be the 20M bushels from themselves plus 5M bushels from tongers. Does this seem a reasonable assumption? Let's suppose further that they projected transactions as follows (Do these seem reasonable? If you think any are questionable, note and supply alternative):

---

[9]Unseasonably warm weather brought a marked decrease in the demand for oysters.

		Prior to 10/1/59	10/1/59 to 4/15/60, incl.
Stockholders pay in cash for capital stock	(A)	26,500	—
Receive cash from bank for $12,500 6% 10-year mortgage .	(B)	12,500	—
Pay cash for property, plant, and equipment	(C)	30,000	—
Pay cash for oysters bought from John and Harry Law:			
4M bu. @ $2.75, ...	(D)	11,000	
and 16M @ $2.75		—	(N) 44,000
Pay cash for oysters bought from tongers: 5M bu. @ $3.25 .		—	(O) 16,250
Pay shuckers @ $1 per gallon:			
3,700 bu. @ 70% equals 2,590 gals.	(E)	2,590	
16,300 bu. @ 70% equals 11,410 gals.		—	(P) 15,160
5,000 bu. @ 75% equals 3,750 gals.			
Pay salaries @ $270 a week	(F)	1,080	(Q) 7,020
Pay for cans @ 25¢, 8M and 13.3M, respectively	(G)	2,000	(R) 3,325
Pay for elec., tel., gas & oil, etc.	(H)	600	(S) 3,900
Sell oysters @ $5.50 average price:			
In Sept., 2,590 gals. @ 120% = 3,108 gals. less 308			
unsold at Sept. 30	(I)	15,400	
After Sept., 15,160 @ 120% = 18,192 gals. plus 308			
unsold at Sept. 30		—	(T) 101,750
Cost of oysters sold:			
2,800 gals @ 4.357	(J)	12,200	—
18,500 gals.		—	(U) 82,125
Receive on account	(K)	9,400	(V) 107,750
Shell pile developed: 3,700 @ 13¢	(L)	481	
21,300 @ 13¢		—	(W) 2,769
Sell shells for cash		—	(X) 3,250
Pay semi-annual installment on mortgage			
(12,500 ÷ 14.87747486 = 840.20)			
Interest $375, on principal, $465		—	(Y) 840
Recognize depreciation on buildings and equipment	(M)	150	(Z) 900
Pay dividends to stockholders		—	—

2. Pick out of the transactions above those which involve receiving or paying cash, and prepare a projected statement of cash receipts and disbursements with three columns:

> 1st column—Head "Prior to 10/1/59"
> 2nd column—Head "10/1/59 to 4/15/60"
> 3rd column—Head "Total"

What conclusions can you draw from this statement?

3. Prepare an "analysis of transactions" for transactions *A* through *M* occurring in period "Prior to 10/1/59." (Note: Enter all costs of oysters, shucking, and cans in Inventories account.)

4. Enter the transactions into T-accounts:

> Cash on Hand and in Bank (18 lines)
> Accounts Receivable (6 lines)
> Inventories of Oysters in Shells, Shucked Oysters,
>   Canned Oysters, Cans, and Oyster Shells (14 lines)
> Property, Plant, and Equipment (5 lines)
> Mortgage Payable (2 lines)
> Capital Stock (2 lines)
> Retained Earnings (14 lines)

5. Determine the balance of each T-account.

6. Enter transactions *N* through *Z*, for period 10/1/59 to 4/15/60, directly into T-accounts.

7. Prepare a trial balance of the T-accounts as of 4/15/60.

8. Prepare projected income statement for the period from beginning business through April 15, 1960.

9. What does the projected income statement show that the projected cash receipts and disbursements statement does not? And *vice versa?*

10. Let's suppose now that the two Law brothers forecast that the business might buy 10M more bushels from tongers in the first year. How much would revenue change? How much would expenses change? How much net profit?

11. Should the two Law brothers go into the venture? What risks would they be taking? What problems are they likely to have?

PART II

Using and Understanding the Basic Financial Statements

CHAPTER 4

The Balance Sheet

Chapter Outline

As defined in Chapter 2, the **balance sheet,** or statement of financial position, is an accounting report that summarizes the assets a company owned, the liabilities it owed, and the owners' investment—their original investment and that share of prior years' earnings that have been left with the company. The balance sheet may be thought of as a photograph of the financial status and condition of a company. The balance sheet, like a photograph, depicts the assets and the equities of a company *as of* a particular date. To appreciate fully the photograph's color, texture, and tone—that is, to understand the complete image in that picture—the financial statement user must understand the specific elements that compose the balance sheet and how these elements are related. That understanding is the focus of this chapter.

140

THE ELEMENTS OF THE BALANCE SHEET

The principal elements of a company's balance sheet are its assets, liabilities, and owners' equity. To provide a context for the discussion of these elements, we will refer to Exhibit 4.1, which presents PepsiCo's consolidated statement of financial condition for 1990 with comparative data for 1989. This statement details the year-end balances for each of PepsiCo's principal asset accounts, as well as the principal creditor and owner claims on those assets.

We have said that a balance sheet presents a picture of a company's financial status at a given point in time. Theoretically, a balance sheet could be prepared as of any day of the year. Most companies monitor individual elements of their balance sheet on a daily or weekly basis, but normally the complete financial picture is taken only as of a month-end, a quarter-end, or a year-end. Most companies use a calendar year for their accounting reports, but they are not required to do so. In fact, it is often more logical to use a different 12-month period, referred to as a **fiscal year,** ending after a business peak. Many retail companies, for example, use a fiscal year that ends in February or March because December and January are significant trade periods. As an example, Circuit City Stores, Inc., the largest consumer electronics retail chain in the United States, uses a fiscal year ending on the last day of February. Obviously, fiscal year companies define the end of the quarter consistently with their notion of a "year." PepsiCo divides its fiscal year into 13 four-week periods, and so, of course, every so often the company must have a 53-week year.

Assets

A company's assets are the resources that it owns or controls, and that it expects to provide future economic benefit to the company. Assets are the company's resources that, in turn, can be deployed to generate a profit for the company. Exhibit 4.1 reveals that PepsiCo had more than $17,143.4 million in assets as of December 29, 1990, placing it 23rd in the Fortune 500 asset rankings. The following are PepsiCo's four principal asset categories:

- Current Assets.
- Investments in Affiliates and Other Assets.
- Property, Plant, and Equipment, net.
- Goodwill and Other Intangibles, net.

PepsiCo's **current assets** (see Exhibit 4.1) include the assets that the company expects to sell or consume as part of its operations during the next year. These assets include cash and cash equivalents, short-term investments, accounts and notes receivable, inventories, and prepaid expenses (and any miscellaneous current assets). The order of presentation of the current assets is intended to inform the reader of the relative liquidity of the assets. Thus, the most liquid current asset is cash, whereas the least liquid is the prepaid expenses. This presentation format of most-to-least liquid is also followed for the asset category as a whole. Thus, the most liquid assets (i.e., current assets) are listed first with the least liquid assets (i.e., the intangible assets) listed last.

EXHIBIT 4.1

PepsiCo, Inc.

Consolidated Balance Sheet

(in millions except per share amount)
PepsiCo, Inc. and Subsidiaries
December 29, 1990 and December 30, 1989

	1990	1989
ASSETS		
Current Assets		
Cash and cash equivalents	$ 170.8	$ 76.2
Short-term investments, at cost which approximates market	1,644.9	1,457.7
	1,815.7	1,533.9
Notes and accounts receivable, less allowance: $90.8 in 1990 and $57.7 in 1989	1,414.7	1,239.7
Inventories	585.8	546.1
Prepaid expenses and other current assets	265.2	231.1
Total Current Assets	4,081.4	3,550.8
Investments in Affiliates and Other Assets	1,505.9	970.8
Property, Plant and Equipment, net	5,710.9	5,130.2
Goodwill and Other Intangibles, net	5,845.2	5,474.9
Total Assets	$17,143.4	$15,126.7
LIABILITIES AND SHAREHOLDERS' EQUITY		
Current Liabilities		
Short-term borrowings	$ 1,626.5	$ 866.3
Accounts payable	1,116.3	1,054.5
Income taxes payable	443.7	313.7
Other current liabilities	1,584.0	1,457.3
Total Current Liabilities	4,770.5	3,691.8
Long-term Debt	5,600.1	5,777.1
Nonrecourse Obligation	299.5	299.4
Other Liabilities and Deferred Credits	626.3	610.4
Deferred Income Taxes	942.8	856.9
Shareholders' Equity		
Capital stock, par value 1⅔¢ per share: authorized 1,800.0 shares, issued 863.1 shares	14.4	14.4
Capital in excess of par value	365.0	323.9
Retained earnings	4,753.0	3,978.4
Currency translation adjustment	383.2	66.2
	5,515.6	4,382.9
Less: Treasury stock, at cost: 74.7 shares in 1990, 72.0 shares in 1989	(611.4)	(491.8)
Total Shareholders' Equity	4,904.2	3,891.1
Total Liabilities and Shareholders' Equity	$17,143.4	$15,126.7

See accompanying Notes to Consolidated Financial Statements.

The item **cash and cash equivalents** refers to funds held in corporate bank accounts, cash on hand at various company locations, and cash invested in short-term financial instruments, such as certificates of deposit. **Short-term investments,** on the other hand, are temporary, highly marketable investments that PepsiCo has in stocks and/or bonds of other companies, such as IBM or AT&T. When a company has a temporary surplus of cash on hand, it may invest these funds in short-term investments to maximize the return on those funds until they are again needed for operations. Because these short-term investments are readily converted to cash, they are frequently aggregated with cash and cash equivalents and called the **liquid assets** of a company. (PepsiCo subtotals its liquid assets—$1,815.7 million in 1990—but does not label them as such.) These liquid assets include cash and other assets that can be readily converted to cash.

The item **accounts and notes receivable** represents the amounts owed to PepsiCo by its customers who purchased the company's products on credit but had not, as of year-end, paid for those purchases. Accounts receivable are also frequently called **trade receivables** and usually represent sales whose payments are expected in 30, 60, or 90 days after the customer has received the goods and been billed for them. Notes receivables, on the other hand, represent credit sales whose payments are usually not expected within 90 days and because of the large amount of money involved, the amount owed is formally stated in a contractual agreement to pay (i.e., a "note"). Under GAAP, sales involving accounts or notes receivable are recognized as revenues earned that period following the **accrual method;** that is, the sale is recorded because the selling company has completed its part of the sale transaction and expects to be paid. The asset received in exchange for the goods delivered is a promise to be paid, and thus a receivable is recorded by the selling company. In accounting entry form, the application of this concept can be illustrated as follows:

```
Dr.  Accounts Receivable (A) . . . . . . . . . .  (inc.) $10,000
     Cr.  Sales (R)  . . . . . . . . . . . . . . . . . . . .        (inc.) $10,000
```

At the time of sale, the receivables are recorded at the cash equivalency that PepsiCo expects to receive from the credit sale. When companies make an individual sale on credit, they fully expect to collect the cash. Realistically, however, management also knows that some part of the total receivables yet to be collected will prove to be uncollectible. Therefore, an amount reflecting this estimated uncollectible portion, called the **allowance for uncollectible accounts,** is recorded as a contra asset and deducted from the receivable balance reported on the balance sheet. Because management knows that the uncollectible accounts estimate pertains to credit sales already recorded as revenue, the **matching concept** requires that the current period's operating results include an estimate of the cost of that loss, called the **Bad Debts Expense.** Together, these two important concepts can be illustrated with the following single entry:

```
Dr.  Bad Debts Expense (E) . . . . . . . . . . .  (inc.) $2,000
     Cr.  Allowance for Uncollectible Accounts (CA)  . . . . . . .     (inc.) $2,000
```

Looking at the current asset section of PepsiCo's balance sheet, we can see how the effects of these concepts are disclosed on the balance sheet:

	1990	1989
Current Assets		
Cash and cash equivalents	$ 170.8	$ 76.2
Short-term investments, at cost		
which approximates market	1,644.9	1,457.7
	1,815.7	1,533.9
Notes and accounts receivable, less		
allowance: $90.8 in 1990 and		
$57.7 in 1989	1,414.7	1,239.7
Inventories	585.8	546.1
Prepaid expenses and other current assets	265.2	231.1
Total Current Assets	$4,081.4	$3,550.8

Note that the allowance account is netted against the outstanding balance of notes and accounts receivable—a common financial disclosure practice.

The item **inventories** refers to the aggregate cost of the salable merchandise owned by PepsiCo that is available to meet customer demands. PepsiCo's footnotes reveal that the Inventory account includes amounts for raw materials (e.g., sugar), supplies (e.g., cartons), materials in process (e.g., cola syrup in mixing vats), as well as finished goods (e.g., Pepsi concentrate in barrels ready to ship to bottlers). Inventory is recorded on the company's books at its cost, the price paid to suppliers plus any additional costs incurred to date to convert the inventory materials or supplies into a final salable condition. The difference between the aggregate cost of the finished goods available for sale and the expected sales price represents PepsiCo's potential profit, which under GAAP is not recorded in the financial statements until the merchandise has actually been sold.

The final item in the current assets section of the balance sheet is **prepaid expenses.** These assets involve expenditures for the prepayment of such items as rent, insurance, or taxes. Some contractual arrangements (e.g., rent and insurance) often require payment in advance; in other arrangements, prepayments may earn certain price discounts from suppliers and therefore simply make good business sense. In either case, prepaid expenses represent past cash outflows for which the company expects to receive some future benefit. Following the **allocation concept,** which we discussed in Chapter 2, that prepayment will be removed from the asset account and charged to an expense account over time as the future benefits are realized.

Although a portion of PepsiCo's assets are clearly identified as *current,* by inference the remaining assets are considered *noncurrent.* Because of the delineation between current and noncurrent assets (and liabilities), PepsiCo's balance sheet can be said to be a **classified balance sheet.** That delineation, however, is not required in all cases, and when no delineation of current and noncurrent assets (or liabilities) exists, the balance sheet is considered to be an **unclassified balance sheet.** The decision to present a classified balance sheet or an unclassified balance sheet is usually tied to the company's **operating cycle.** If the company's operating cycle—that is, the period of time between beginning production of a product and collecting the proceeds from the sale of a finished product—is less than one year, a classified balance sheet is prepared. An unclassified balance sheet is often used by companies whose operating cycle is longer than one year (e.g., a winery, a timber company, a real estate development company).

Noncurrent assets are a company's long-lived resources whose consumption or use will take place over more than one accounting period. These assets are frequently segmented into tangible and intangible assets. **Tangible assets,** like property, plant, and equipment, possess identifiable physical characteristics, whereas **intangible assets,** like goodwill, do not. Nonetheless, both tangible and intangible assets possess revenue-producing characteristics that make them valuable to a company over future periods.

Among PepsiCo's noncurrent assets are investments and other assets; property, plant, and equipment; and goodwill and other intangibles. From Exhibit 4.1, these noncurrent assets are disclosed as follows:

	1990	1989
Investments in Affiliates and Other Assets	$1,505.9	$ 970.8
Property, Plant, and Equipment, net	5,710.9	5,130.2
Goodwill and Other Intangibles, net	5,845.2	5,474.9

Long-term investments involve investments in other companies' stocks or bonds that will be maintained for longer than just the coming year, and other assets represent an aggregation of miscellaneous assets that are, individually, immaterial in amount. **Property, plant, and equipment,** on the other hand, are those long-lived, tangible assets necessary to conduct a company's basic business operations. For a company such as PepsiCo, this category includes its manufacturing equipment and facilities, storage equipment, and vehicles. These assets are often called the **fixed assets** of a company. Like inventory, a company's fixed assets are an integral part of its basic operations, but they differ from inventory in two important respects. First, property, plant, and equipment are not owned for the purpose of being sold to customers. Second, these assets are expected to benefit PepsiCo's operations for many years. Because of the extended productive life of these assets, the company's cost of property, plant, and equipment is expensed over the assets' expected useful lives rather than totally in the year of acquisition.

The process of allocating a fixed asset's cost over various years is called **depreciation** and is based on the **allocation concept** discussed in Chapter 2. When an asset is depreciated, a portion of its original cost is charged to expense, and the other side of the entry increases a contra asset account. As you will remember from the discussion of Blue Ridge Hardware in Chapter 3, many financial statement users want to know the original cost of plant and equipment; hence, the annual depreciation charge is not deducted from the asset account directly but rather is accumulated in a contra asset account. The contra asset account is presented on the asset side of the balance sheet but usually carries a credit balance.

The expense account is called **Depreciation Expense;** the contra asset is called **Accumulated Depreciation.** The actual accounting entry appears as follows:

```
Dr.  Depreciation Expense (E) . . . . . . . . . (inc.) $30,000
     Cr.  Accumulated Depreciation (CA). . . . . . . . . . .      (inc.) $30,000
```

The balance in the Accumulated Depreciation contra asset account, as reported on the balance sheet, includes not only the current period's charge to expense but also that portion of the asset's cost that has been allocated (i.e., expensed) in prior accounting periods. The Accumulated Depreciation account balance is deducted from the Property, Plant, and Equipment account balance in reporting the net fixed assets in the balance sheet. The original cost of an asset less the balance in the Accumulated Depreciation account is called the **net book value** or carrying value of the asset. A review of PepsiCo's footnotes reveals that the acquisition cost of its property, plant, and equipment was $8,977.7 million as of December 29, 1990, and the accumulated depreciation as of that date was $3,266.8 million. Only the net book value of these assets (i.e., $5,710.9 million) is included in the company's total assets.

We will have more to say about the accounting for property, plant, and equipment and about the process of depreciation in Chapter 10. At this point, however, it is perhaps helpful to emphasize that accounting depreciation is intended *only* as a process to allocate prior cash expenditures to future periods. From an economic standpoint, plant and equipment lose *and* gain value over time as a result of a wide variety of factors. As we noted in our discussion of the historic **cost concept** in chapter 2, GAAP accounting is based on original costs and thus does not deal with day-to-day, year-to-year changes in *market values*. Hence, the financial statements do not reflect the impact that economic effects such as new technologies or increased market demand might have on the values of a company's plant and equipment. Again, depreciation is simply the process of allocating the original cost of an asset over the future periods expected to benefit from that earlier investment.

The final noncurrent asset account is **Goodwill and Other Intangibles.** In the context of accounting, *goodwill* does *not* refer to a company's favorable or positive consumer image or to the costs PepsiCo incurred for constructive environmental or societal projects. Instead, goodwill indicates that PepsiCo previously acquired one or more companies for a purchase price in excess of the *fair market value* of the acquired company's net assets (i.e., its total assets minus total liabilities). Thinking about PepsiCo's acquisition program, we can see how the company might have purchased a substantial amount of goodwill by paying a premium for its acquisition of the well-established, successful Kentucky Fried Chicken and Pizza Hut franchises. The phrase **Other Intangibles** refers to the cost of miscellaneous identifiable intangible assets, such as franchise rights, trade names, or trademarks, which PepsiCo has acquired or developed. Like property, plant, and equipment, the cost of goodwill and other intangible assets is normally allocated over the expected useful life of these assets. The process of allocating the cost of an intangible asset over its useful life is called amortization.

Liabilities

As defined in Chapter 2, the liabilities of a company are the dollar measures of its obligations to repay money loaned to it, to pay for goods or services it has received, or to fulfill commitments it has made. In essence, a company's liabilities represent claims on its assets. As with assets, it is convenient to aggregate liabilities into current and noncurrent categories, which delineate the expected repayment period for the liability. Thus, a **current liability** is an obligation due during the next operating cycle or the next year, whichever is longer. A **noncurrent liability** is one that will be paid at some future point in time beyond the next operating cycle or year.

PepsiCo's balance sheet shows that the company has five principal liability categories:

- Current Liabilities
- Long-Term Debt
- Nonrecourse Obligation
- Other Liabilities and Deferred Credits
- Deferred Income Taxes

Within the **Current Liabilities** category, PepsiCo discloses four different accounts: Short-term Borrowings, Accounts Payable, Income Taxes Payable, and Other Current Liabilities. The basis for the sequencing of these accounts is not as clear-cut as it is on the asset side of the balance sheet. The sequencing within the current liability section and on the entire right-hand side (i.e., the equity side) of the balance sheet is primarily intended to reflect the priority standing of the various creditors (i.e., short-term borrowings are listed before accounts payable). That priority ranking, however, is tempered by the expected order of repayment of the various current liabilities (i.e., current liabilities followed by long-term debt, accounts payable followed by taxes payable). The disclosure of these accounts (see Exhibit 4.1) on PepsiCo's balance sheet appears as follows:

	1990	1989
Current Liabilities		
Short-term borrowings	$1,626.5	$ 866.3
Accounts payable	1,116.3	1,054.5
Income taxes payable	443.7	313.7
Other current liabilities	1,584.0	1,457.3
Total Current Liabilities	**$4,770.5**	**$3,691.8**

Short-term borrowings may refer to either short-term bank borrowings, current maturities of long-term debt, or trade notes payable. **Trade notes** represent amounts owed to suppliers for goods or services purchased on credit. Short-term bank (or other financial institution) borrowings refer to cash loans that are usually due in 90 to 180 days. **Current maturities of long-term debt,** on the other hand, represent the portion of long-term bank or other borrowings that are due to be paid within the next operating cycle or year. As an example, the principal portion of a 20-year mortgage that is due to be paid in the next 12 months is classified in the current liabilities section of the balance sheet.

Like trade notes payable, **accounts payable** or **trade payables** represent the amounts owed to various suppliers for goods and services purchased on credit but not yet paid. The common business practice of giving a purchaser 30 days to pay results in an account receivable for the seller/supplier and an account payable for the buyer/user. The item **income taxes payable** represents PepsiCo's estimate of the income taxes that will be owed to federal, state, local, and foreign authorities when the tax returns for the period are completed sometime in 1991. Under accrual accounting, the balance sheet must reflect all obligations owed as of the date of the statement, even if the exact amounts due are not immediately determinable. Thus, the preparation of the 1990 balance sheet may require that some liabilities, such as the 1990 deferred income taxes, be estimated. Finally, **Other current liabilities** represent those miscellaneous obligations of the company, which individually are immaterial in amount and thus are aggregated. Examples of this might include various accrued expenses such as wages owed for work done or utilities payable for electricity already used.

PepsiCo's noncurrent liabilities fall into four principal categories: long-term debt, nonrecourse obligation, other liabilities and deferred credits, and deferred income taxes. According to PepsiCo's footnotes, the **long-term debt** includes amounts borrowed from financial institutions, various bonds sold in the United States and in other countries, certain types of long-term lease obligations, and certain short-term borrowings reclassified as long term. A **bond** is a financial instrument carrying a specified rate of interest (the **coupon rate**) and a specified repayment date (the **maturity date**), which is normally sold to investors as a way to raise funds for a company. PepsiCo's footnotes reveal that the company has sold bonds denominated in U.S. dollars, Swiss francs, Australian dollars, British pounds, Italian lire, and Canadian dollars. The lease obligations refer to noncancelable lease arrangements involving the use of various leased assets, such as Pizza Hut or Taco Bell restaurants and equipment. The short-term borrowings reclassified as long term reflect PepsiCo's intent (and ability) to refinance these borrowings on a long-term basis, either by the issuance of new long-term debt or by a "rollover" of the existing short-term borrowing (usually through a revolving credit agreement). From Exhibit 4.1, these noncurrent obligations are disclosed as follows:

	1990	1989
Long-term Debt	$5,600.1	$5,777.1
Nonrecourse Obligation	299.5	299.4
Other Liabilities and Deferred Credits	626.3	610.4
Deferred Income Taxes	942.8	856.9

PepsiCo's liability, **nonrecourse obligation,** demonstrates an interesting technique for raising cash. As described in the footnote entitled "Nonrecourse Obligation" (page 24), the company borrowed $299 million in 1987 from investors, and, rather than pledging trucks or other tangible assets as collateral for that borrowing, PepsiCo gave investors the right to receive future royalty payments from certain of its domestic franchised operations. PepsiCo received cash from the investors, promised to pay back the borrowings, and assured the investors that if the repayments were not forthcoming from the company in the normal course of business, the investors would have first call on the cash to be received from its franchise operations. The liability is referred to as *nonrecourse* because in a worst-case situation, with PepsiCo in financial difficulty, the investors could not look to any other PepsiCo assets except the future cash stream from the designated franchise operations for repayment.

Other liabilities and deferred credits is an aggregation of miscellaneous long-term liabilities and various accounts having a credit balance. Finally, **Deferred Income Taxes** refers to U.S. and foreign income taxes that are not currently being paid but will be paid at some future date. The topic of deferred income taxes is covered in detail in Chapter 12.

Owners' Equity

Owners' equity refers to the owners' or shareholders' investment in a company. As noted in Chapter 2, the shareholders' investment usually takes two primary forms: the shareholders' purchase of shares of stock from the company and the company's retention of a portion of its earnings.

When a company sells shares of stock, the proceeds are reflected in the **Capital Stock** account. The securities laws of some states permit companies to sell **no-par value stock,** and companies incorporated in those states may include the entire proceeds from a stock sale in a single account designated simply as *Capital Stock* or **Common Stock.** However, most states in the United States require that a company's capital stock carry a **par value** or **stated value.** The par or stated value of a stock is the *legal value* of a single share of stock and is, in theory, the portion of shareholders' equity that may not legally be paid out as a dividend. That distinction is only theoretical, however, because the par or stated value is established (and can be changed by) the board of directors. Normally, there is no relationship between par value and the fair market value of a stock. For example, although PepsiCo issued capital stock with a par value of $0.0167, its shares traded on the New York Stock Exchange during 1990 in the range of $18 to $28.

From Exhibit 4.1, PepsiCo's owners' equity section on the balance sheet appears as follows:

	1990	1989
Shareholders' Equity		
Capital stock, par value 1 2/3 ¢ per		
share: authorized 1,800.0 shares,		
issued 863.1 shares	14.4	14.4
Capital in excess of par value	365.0	323.9
Retained earnings	4,753.0	3,978.4
Currency translation adjustment	383.2	66.2
	5,515.6	4,382.9
Less: Treasury stock, at cost: 74.7		
shares in 1990, 72.0 shares in 1989	(611.4)	(491.8)
Total Shareholders' Equity	**$4,904.2**	**$3,891.1**

Because most companies intentionally set a relatively low par or stated value, shares of stock are normally sold at a price in excess of their par or stated value. When this occurs, the excess is reflected in the **Paid-in Capital in Excess of Par (or Stated) Value** account. Thus, the combination of the par value and Capital in Excess of Par Value accounts represents the total contributed capital of a company.

It is instructive to pause here and put this discussion of shareholder's capital in perspective. The distinction between the par value of a stock and the total proceeds received on the sale of the stock is important only for some very narrow legal purposes and is of no consequence to company's management. In fact, some companies organized in "par value" states have decided to ignore the distinction in preparing their financial statements and simply present a combined total for capital stock. That aggregate common stock amount represents the amount that the shareholders have paid the company for the stock purchased directly from the company. The discussion of the **entity concept** in

Chapter 2 pointed out that the financial statements reflect only the transactions of the entity, not the transactions of the owners on their own behalf. Therefore, the financial statements reflect purchases of shares by the shareholders directly from the company as well as sales of shares back to the company. However, the company's financial statements do *not* reflect purchases and sales of shares between shareholders and other outsiders.

A company's **charter of incorporation** specifies, among other things, the maximum number of shares of capital stock that can be issued; these are often referred to as the **authorized shares.** When authorized shares are sold to investors, they become **issued shares.** In the United States, companies may repurchase some of their issued shares and retire them or hold them as **treasury stock. Outstanding shares** represent the company's issued shares less any shares held in the treasury. Treasury stock is usually repurchased with the intent to reissue it at some future date, perhaps to the company's employees or to facilitate a merger with another company. Because treasury stock is no longer on the open market but is expected to be reissued, it is accounted for as a contra shareholders' equity account.

Remember that capital stock is recorded at the price that the purchasing shareholders paid when they bought the stock directly from the company. Logically, treasury stock is also recorded at the price that the company paid when it reacquired the shares on the open market. Because stock markets tend to fluctuate in response to many factors, there is almost always a difference between the original issue price and the price at which treasury shares are repurchased. Because the GAAP accounting model does not reflect changes in the value of a company's stock from year to year, a company's repurchase of any significant number of shares can result in an anomalous presentation of its owners' equity. For example, note that as of December 29, 1990, PepsiCo held $611.4 million in treasury stock, which exceeds the total proceeds that it received from the original sale of the stock (i.e., $379.4 million) by $232 million. A number of companies purchased substantial amounts of their own stock during major restructurings in the 1980s, and, as a result, their aggregate owners' equity is a nominal balance or even a negative number. It is worth repeating that owners' equity, or net worth, is the difference between the company's assets stated at their book values and the company's liabilities stated at their book values. Owners' equity would be a measure of the fair value of a company *only* if the book value of the assets and the liabilities were also equal to their market values — a coincidence that rarely happens, and so the owners' equity number must be understood to be no more (or less) than a balancing number that forces a company to discipline its accounting process and maintain the $A = L + OE$ equation.

The second principal form of shareholders' equity is the *earned capital* or **retained earnings.** The retained earnings of a company represent the historical, cumulative portion of net income that has been retained in the company to support on-going operations and has not been paid out to shareholders as dividends. PepsiCo's financial statements reveal that of the $1,076.9 million in net income earned in 1990, 28 percent, or $302.3 million, was paid as dividends to capital stock shareholders, leaving $774.6 million as an addition to retained earnings.

Finally, PepsiCo, like many large companies, conducts a significant portion of its operations in foreign countries. The "Business Segments" section of PepsiCo's financial statements (see Chapter 1) reveals that in 1990, foreign operations generated approximately 17 percent of the company's operating profits. Many of these operations are conducted by wholly owned foreign subsidiary corporations. To prepare the *consolidated* financial statements presented in PepsiCo's annual reports, the financial results of these foreign subsidiaries must be combined with the results of the domestic (i.e., U.S.) operations.

As you are probably aware, many factors work to cause fluctuations in the relative exchange rate of the U.S. dollar with foreign currencies, making it difficult to combine the financial data of foreign subsidiaries with those of domestic subsidiaries. Much of the effect of foreign currency exchange rate fluctuation is captured in the current income statement, but special financial reporting issues (to be discussed in Chapter 9) arise involving assets and liabilities acquired in periods prior to the current period. In essence, PepsiCo's foreign assets and liabilities held in 1989 were consolidated at the exchange rate that existed in 1989; yet in 1990, those assets and liabilities must be consolidated at 1990's exchange rate. To capture the effect of any exchange rate fluctuations between the two periods, a separate shareholders' equity account, the **Currency Translation Adjustment** account, is used. In 1990, PepsiCo's Currency Translation Adjustment account increased by $317 million, reflecting a substantial decline in the value of the U.S. dollar relative to the various foreign currencies in countries where PepsiCo maintains operations.

CONCEPTS AND CONVENTIONS UNDERLYING THE BALANCE SHEET

The measurement and valuation of the various asset and equity accounts on the balance sheet reflect a diverse set of GAAP concepts subject to a variety of management estimates, judgments, and preferences. In Chapters 7–13, we will discuss these issues at length; however, for the moment, let us simply overview the core set of concepts and conventions.

An Overall Balance Sheet Focus

As noted in Chapter 2, the fundamental measurement system used to prepare the balance sheet is the accrual method. Under the accrual method, the financial effects of a transaction are recognized when it occurs without regard to the timing of its cash effects. Thus, the amounts due from customers for product sales that have not yet been paid for (i.e., accounts and notes receivable) may be recognized as assets. In addition, the amounts owed for purchases of inventories or other assets (i.e., accounts and notes payable) may be reported as liabilities on the balance sheet. Thus, whether or not cash has been received or paid is irrelevant. Assets are recognized on the balance sheet when a company takes possession of or receives title to an asset, and liabilities are recorded when it has incurred an obligation.

Assets

As noted earlier in this chapter as we discussed PepsiCo's various asset accounts, the initial value assigned to each asset on the balance sheet is its acquisition cost, which is assumed to be the fair market value at the time of acquisition. For accounting purposes, *acquisition cost* is defined to encompass more than just the invoice price of an asset. All costs incurred in bringing an asset to its intended, usable condition are considered to be part of its cost. Thus, transportation costs or legal fees associated with acquiring an asset are a part of its cost in addition to the purchase price.

The value of most assets, however, fluctuates over time. In some cases, as with land, the value may increase, whereas with other assets, such as a car, the value will probably fall. Under the historical *cost concept,* however, the original acquisition cost of an asset is preserved on the balance sheet. There are a number of reasons for this rigidly observed convention. Most importantly, original cost values represent objective evidence as to the value of an asset at least at one point in time. Experience has demonstrated that it is often quite difficult (and expensive) to obtain similarly objective, reliable measures at points in time after the original purchase date. An estimated market value established by management for its own company's assets often proves to be optimistic—and is, of course, subject to manipulation. In the United States, corporate management has generally been reluctant to estimate market values for assets in part because those estimates have so often proven to be wrong and the management involved has lost credibility. Interestingly, users have also been reluctant to give much credence to estimated values and so there has been no market demand for that information. As a result, GAAP-based financial statements in the United States recognize value changes only when they are validated by a sale in an arm's length transaction to a third party.

That fear of estimated values is a fact in the United States but is not necessarily present in other countries. In many other countries (especially Australia, Canada, and the United Kingdom), periodically appraising the fixed assets of a company and reflecting those appraised values in the company's balance sheet is perfectly acceptable. That asset write-up process has the advantage of quantifying, for the reader of the financial statements, the effect of changes in value on a company. For example, the write-up of assets logically results in an increase in owners' equity; that increase in asset value and that increase in owners' equity could mitigate the anomaly that results when a company buys back its own stock at an aggregate amount greater than the original proceeds received when it was issued. Also, the depreciation of those appraised values increases the company's operating costs and provides a clearer measure of the company's ability to increase its own sales prices in concert with changes in the purchasing value of the local currency. Because those value changes are not reflected in the financial statements of U.S. companies, statement users must (and usually do) make their own adjustments, mentally, as they consider the meaning of those historical cost-based numbers.

What is true for increases in an asset's value, however, is not the case if the value of an asset declines over time. In such a case, the diminishment in value should be recognized in the financial statements in one of several ways. Consider, for example, the current assets. Because current assets are considered to be available for use in current operations and for the repayment of current liabilities, an attempt is made to value these assets at their *net realizable value*. Thus, as we see in the case of PepsiCo, when a portion of the outstanding accounts or notes receivables is *not* expected to be collected, an estimate of the uncollectible amount is created and is deducted from the gross receivable balance. As a consequence, only the net realizable value (i.e., the net collectible value) of the receivables is included in the total current asset balance.

Similarly, if the market value of a short-term investment has fallen below the investment's original cost, the value of the investment should be reduced (i.e., written down) to the lower market value using a convention called the **lower-of-cost-or-market** method. Under this method, an *Allowance for Decline in Value of Short-term Investments*—a contra account—is created and deducted from the original cost of the investment, thereby reflecting only the net realizable value of the investment in the current asset total. As might be expected, inventories are also valued using the lower-of-cost-or-market convention. Inventory cost is usually substantially less than its normal sales price, but occasionally product obsolescence or physical damage reduces the net realizable value of inventory below its carrying cost. Companies typically make periodic analyses of their inventories and when cost/market problems appear, that decline in value is recognized as an expense during the period when the decline occurs. An entry for that write-down might look like this:

```
Dr.  Cost of Obsolete Inventory (E) . . . . . . . (inc.) $10,000
     Cr.  Allowance for Obsolete Inventory (CA). . . . . . . .     (inc.) $10,000
```

In the case of noncurrent assets, the downward revaluation process may occur in several forms. In general, if the value of any asset becomes permanently impaired, such that the future revenue-producing capacity of the asset is materially diminished, the value of the asset should be written down. If, for example, PepsiCo held stock in another company for speculative investment purposes and the value of the stock fell permanently, perhaps because the company lost a major lawsuit involving its principal business activity, PepsiCo's balance sheet valuation of the investment would be written down. That write-down will be recorded as a contra asset account on the balance sheet, the *Allowance for Decline in Value of Long-Term Investment,* and as a loss in the current period's income statement.

The value of some assets, however, declines over time due to their use in operations. Property, plant, and equipment, for example, are consumed (or used up) in the process of producing goods and services for sale by a company. This kind of value diminishment is recognized under the **matching concept.** Each period a portion of the original cost of property, plant, and equipment is removed from the balance sheet and assigned to the income statement as depreciation expense. Although this allocation process is designed to reflect the consumption of property, plant, and equipment due to operations, it does not necessarily ensure that the balance sheet value of these assets will be equivalent to their current market value. Indeed, other market factors may cause the value of property, plant, and equipment to be greater than, or less than, its reported net book value. As noted above, if a decrement in value due to other than normal wear and tear is judged to be permanent, the value of the asset should be written down. In no case, however, would an appreciation in value be recognized unless and until the asset is sold.

To summarize, then, assets are initially recorded at their acquisition cost. When such values decline due to market externalities or to internal use, the asset values are reduced. When such values increase, with few exceptions (see chapters 7 and 9), no recognition is given in the financial statements. Thus, it may be said that asset values are rarely overstated but may indeed be understated relative to their current fair market value.

Liabilities

The valuation of liabilities on the balance sheet is substantially less complex than the valuation of assets. Theoretically, *all* liabilities are valued at the **present value** of the future cash outflows (or other equivalent asset flows) required to satisfy the obligation. The present value of a liability is determined by **discounting** the required future cash outflows using a given rate of interest called the *discount rate* (see Chapter 11). In a word, the discounting process recognizes the time value of money and the fact that a dollar due tomorrow is less costly than a dollar due today. For example, $1,000 due one year from today discounted at 8 percent has a present value of only $925.93.

Although present value is the fundamental valuation approach used for all liabilities, as a practical matter it is rarely used to value short-term liabilities. By definition, short-term liabilities are expected to be satisfied or paid off in the coming year, and there is little difference between the *maturity value* of a short-term liability and its present value. Thus, current liabilities are normally reported on the balance sheet at their maturity value or the amount of cash (or other equivalent assets) required to satisfy the obligation at its maturity or due date. Long-term liabilities are also usually stated at their present values because they carry an (unrecorded) interest obligation. So long as the required interest on an obligation is equal to the market rate of interest on the date when the debt is incurred, the debt can be considered to be stated at its present value. The present value of a liability is determined only once—when the obligation is initially incurred. Unlike assets, liabilities are never revalued on the balance sheet to reflect changes in their underlying market values.

Owners' Equity

Although the valuation of assets and liabilities may be defined or explained with reference to specific valuation concepts or methods, the valuation of shareholder or owners' equity is generally not. The valuation of owners' equity on the balance sheet is not an independent process but is the residual valuation that results from subtracting the liabilities from the assets. Capital stock is valued at the amount of assets received in exchange for the stock; treasury stock is valued at its acquisition cost. However, the reported value of retained earnings—the residual earnings after dividends have been paid—depends on the revenues and expenses reflected in the income statement. As you learned from your work in Chapter 3, every revenue and expense decision impacts an asset or a liability and so the residual of those asset-liability/revenue-expense accounting decisions comes to rest in retained earnings.

ANALYZING FINANCIAL STATEMENTS

As we observed in Chapter 1, accounting is a language, a communication device, and therefore not an end in itself. Thus, the presentation of accounting information in a stylized format such as the balance sheet is merely the beginning of the communication process. The recipient of the balance sheet and the other basic financial statements must then use the presented financial data to draw inferences and conclusions about the financial status of a company. Hence, we now focus on the question of how to analyze, evaluate, and interpret balance sheet data.

The analysis of the balance sheet, and of the basic financial statements in general, can occur at various levels of sophistication. At the most fundamental level, an analyst or other financial statement user can review and identify the absolute level of various important account balances. For example, it may be important to note the absolute level of cash on hand. If the level of cash on hand is sufficient to meet a company's most urgent needs (i.e., to pay employee salaries and replenish sold inventory), it is unlikely that the company will need to borrow money in the current period to support operations.

In most cases, however, merely identifying the absolute level of various account balances does not provide sufficient information to analyze fully a company's financial position. The absolute level of inventory on hand, for example, informs us only that a company does have some inventory on hand to begin operations in the next period; the absolute level does not tell us, however, whether the available inventory will be sufficient to sustain sales or whether the company will need to purchase or manufacture additional units and, if so, how soon.

To address these more sophisticated questions, it is often useful to construct **ratios** of various related account balances. For example, to assess the adequacy of existing inventory levels, it might be instructive to compare the level of inventory on hand to the level of cost of goods sold in the prior period. This ratio would then indicate whether the existing inventory was sufficient to cover expected sales, assuming that they are approximately equivalent to the prior period sales.

Ratio analysis is frequently used to gain a more complete understanding of a company's financial stature and condition. Ratios may be investigated both within a given accounting period and across a number of accounting periods. When ratios (or absolute balances) are compared across time periods, particular trends in a company's financial condition or operations may be identified. Not surprisingly, this type of across-period analysis is called **trend analysis.** To facilitate the analysis of financial trends, most companies provide accounting data for at least the current period and the prior period. Moreover, some companies, such as PepsiCo, provide summary financial data for as many as 10 years in the annual report. Later in this chapter, we will consider some ratio trend data for PepsiCo.

Trend analysis is also often aided by the use of **common-size financial statements,** in which all amounts are expressed as a percentage of some base financial statement item. For example, a common-size balance sheet might express all asset accounts as a percentage of total assets and all equity accounts as a percentage of total equities. Trend analysis of common-size statements permits the analyst to determine, for example, how the relative composition of total assets or total equities is changing over time.

In addition to comparing a company's performance from one year to the next, it is also instructive to compare the financial results of a given company with those of other companies within the same industry or with industry averages. For example, by comparing the financial results of PepsiCo with those of other soft drink and/or restaurant companies, an investor may be able to identify which firm presents the best investment opportunity within the industry. Similarly, Standard and Poor's and Moody's investor services, among others, provide industry data to permit comparisons of one company against the average of all companies within a given industry. Use of such data may enable an investor to determine whether a company is outperforming or underperforming the average for that industry. Later in this chapter we will compare PepsiCo's balance sheet information to that of the overall beverage industry and to a variety of industry averages.

Perhaps the most advanced level of financial analysis involves predicting the future financial performance of a company. Most companies prepare *projections* or **pro forma financial statements** based on assumptions about the future for their own internal planning purposes, but very few companies issue those financial statements publicly. The policy of publishing historic financial statements rather than projections is based on two factors. First, actual results almost always turn out differently than the original projections, and few executives have been willing to subject their credibility to the inevitable criticism when actual results are different than the projections. The second factor is economic; if the results are materially different from the forecast, someone is sure to sue. Even if the projections were prepared in good faith, the company and its management will be forced to devote significant efforts to defend the projections.

Nonetheless, investments should always be made on the basis of expectations about the future, not on the results of the past. Under our present financial structure, companies do not publish projections, but independent *financial analysts* do. They prepare and analyze their own pro forma financial statements for publicly traded companies based on published history and carefully developed assumptions about the company's future environment. Building on that history and assumptions about the future, financial analysts develop pro forma financial statements and then commit themselves to estimates of the analyzed company's future earnings. We will return to this topic in chapters 5 and 6, where the preparation of pro forma cash flow and income statements will be illustrated.

ANALYZING THE BALANCE SHEET

Ratio analysis is typically utilized to gain an understanding of a company's liquidity, solvency, profitability, and asset management effectiveness. **Liquidity** refers to the likelihood or ability of a company to satisfy its short-term obligations; **solvency** refers to a company's ability to satisfy its long-term obligations. **Profitability,** on the other hand, refers to a company's overall income-generating ability, and **asset management effectiveness** refers to the ability of a company's managers to utilize its assets effectively to produce a return for the company's creditors and owners.

Most profitability ratios are based on income statement accounts; consequently, this topic will be deferred until Chapter 5. The balance sheet, however, is a good source of information regarding a company's liquidity, solvency, and asset management effectiveness. We now turn to some widely accepted indicators of these financial characteristics.

Liquidity

Liquidity is frequently evaluated on the basis of four indicators: (1) the level of cash on hand, (2) the quick ratio, (3) the level of working capital, and (4) the current ratio.

The level of cash (and cash equivalents) on hand is a precise indication of the level of highly liquid resources available for a company's debt repayment or other operating needs. Cash on hand is very measurable and therefore quite certain, but it is also a very conservative measure of liquidity. Only in the most extreme circumstances would a company have to pay all of its bills using only its cash on hand. Hence, a more realistic measure of liquidity is the **quick ratio,** which is calculated as follows:

$$\text{Quick ratio} = \frac{\text{Cash} + \text{Marketable securities} + \text{Accounts receivable}}{\text{Current liabilities}}.$$

The quick ratio examines only the liability coverage provided by the **quick assets,** those highly liquid current assets such as cash, cash equivalents, short-term investments, and receivables. Accounts and notes receivables are considered to be quick assets because they can usually be sold to a factor. A **factor** is a financial institution or a financial corporation that buys receivables from other companies at a discount (i.e., at a price less than the amount to be collected) and earns a profit when the receivables are collected.

A somewhat more general indicator of liquidity that is broader in scope is the level of working capital. Working capital is measured as current assets minus current liabilities. Thus **working capital** is a measure of the net current assets that would be available to support a company's continuing operations *if* all of its current assets could be converted to cash at their balance sheet values and the proceeds used to satisfy its current liabilities. The equation is as follows:

$$\text{Working capital} = \text{Current assets} - \text{Current liabilities}.$$

A ratio based on the concept of working capital is the **current ratio,** which is calculated by dividing current assets by current liabilities:

$$\text{Current ratio} = \frac{\text{Current assets}}{\text{Current liabilities}}.$$

Both working capital and the current ratio are "coverage" indicators; the former indicates the extent to which current assets cover current liabilities in an *absolute* sense, and the latter indicates the extent of coverage in a *relative* sense. A high current ratio (i.e., a substantial amount of working capital) indicates good liquidity, suggesting that a company's currently maturing obligations are likely to be paid on time. A ratio that is too high, however, may suggest an unproductive use of resources because the current assets might be used more effectively by converting them to cash and purchasing, for example, high-yield stocks or bonds.

To illustrate these liquidity measures, let us consider PepsiCo's balance sheet for 1990 (see Exhibit 4.1). This balance sheet reveals that, as of December 29, 1990, PepsiCo had cash and cash equivalents of $170.8 million on hand, working capital of $(689.1) million, a current ratio of 0.86:1, and a quick ratio of 0.68:1. The current and quick ratios reveal that for every dollar of current liabilities, PepsiCo held $0.86 of current assets and $0.68 of quick assets.

EXHIBIT 4.2

Financial Ratios for 1990 for Selected Industries
and for The Coca-Cola Company and PepsiCo, Inc.

Panel A: Industry Data

Industry	Current Ratio	Quick Ratio	Total Debt to Total Assets	Long-Term Debt to Owners' Equity	Times Interest Earned	Inventory Turnover	Receivable Turnover
Air transportation	1.1:1	0.8:1	69 percent	0.96:1	0.9 times	16.9 times	5.2 times
Beverages	2.7:1	1.3:1	40 percent	0.66:1	4.3 times	8.4 times	16.8 times
Chemicals	1.7:1	1.0:1	48 percent	0.41:1	5.1 times	2.9 times	2.9 times
Retail	3.7:1	1.3:1	41 percent	0.26:1	1.7 times	2.1 times	9.2 times
Steel	1.8:1	1.0:1	56 percent	0.48:1	3.4 times	9.3 times	8.2 times

Panel B: Coca-Cola and PepsiCo

Coca-Cola	0.96:1	0.56:1	59 percent	0.29:1	9.7 times	4.8 times	12.2 times
PepsiCo	0.86:1	0.68:1	71 percent	1.14:1	10.2 times	15.2 times	13.4 times

Source: Dun & Bradstreet's *Industry Norms & Key Business Ratios.*

To determine whether these measures indicate high, low, or average liquidity, one can compare them to existing industry averages, to those of a competitor (see Exhibit 4.2), and to the results of prior years. Since PepsiCo's balance sheet contains comparative data for 1989, a trend analysis can be easily undertaken.

	1990	1989
Cash and cash equivalents	$170.8 million	$76.2 million
Working capital	(689.1) million	(141.0) million
Current ratio	0.86:1	0.96:1
Quick ratio	0.68:1	0.75:1

A comparison indicates that PepsiCo's liquidity in 1990 deteriorated somewhat from that in 1989. Although the level of cash and cash equivalents increased by more than $94 million, the level of working capital declined by more than $548 million. The decline in working capital is also depicted in the decline in both the current and quick ratios. PepsiCo's liquidity position appears to be quite comparable to Coca-Cola's liquidity in 1990 (see Exhibit 4.2). Although PepsiCo's current ratio was slightly below that of Coca-Cola (0.86 versus 0.96, respectively), its quick ratio was somewhat higher (0.68 versus 0.56, respectively).

Solvency

Solvency refers to a company's long-term debt repayment ability and is frequently evaluated on the basis of three indicators: (1) the total debt-to-total assets ratio, (2) the long-term debt-to-equity ratio, and (3) the times-interest-earned ratio. The first two ratios measure the relative *amount* of long-term debt outstanding; the third ratio is a *coverage* ratio of the extent to which current debt interest charges are being covered by current earnings.

The concept of solvency and the thrust of these debt-level ratios suggest a negative connotation, as though debt is to be avoided and reduced whenever possible. Debt is not always bad; in fact, it is sometimes healthy. A more positive way to describe a company's debt level is to say that the stockholders' equity is **leveraged;** in effect, a leveraged company supplements its owners' funds with funds from other sources to "lever up" the return to the owners. Before we explore these debt-level ratios, it is appropriate to consider debt at a conceptual level.

The level of debt a company carries—its leverage—is a strategic decision, and that decision is based on the degree of certainty associated with its future cash flows. If the future cash flows are relatively predictable, the company may be able to borrow funds with bank loans or bond issuances at relatively low rates of interest. If a company can borrow money at an after-tax cost that is lower than the cost of its equity funds, that borrowing enables the company to increase its return to its owners. (It may very well be possible to use borrowed funds less expensively than equity funds because interest expense is tax deductible whereas dividends are not.) For example, assume that a company is considering a plant expansion project that is expected to cost $1 million and is expected to earn $100,000 after taxes. If the company is now earning a 10 percent return for its stockholders, that expansion project will not make the company (or its stockholders) any better off. But if the company can borrow 80 percent of those funds at an after-tax cost of 8 percent, the return on the shareholders' investment in this project will grow to 18 percent, as follows:

	Project Funded with Equity Funds	Project Funded with Borrowed Funds
Cost	$1,000,000	$1,000,000
Borrowed funds	0	800,000
Stockholder funds invested	1,000,000	200,000
Expected return	100,000	100,000
Interest cost		64,000
Net return to stockholders	100,000	36,000
Rate of return	10%	18%

Leverage is powerful, but it has the power to hurt as well as help. If the project in our example is not as successful as was planned and earns only $50,000 a year, the company will lose money on the $200,000 investment of equity funds. The decision to lever up or lever down is, perhaps, the ultimate expression of management balance. Too much leverage cheats the stockholders of their maximum return. PepsiCo explains its strategy with these words:

> In managing its capital structure, PepsiCo utilizes financial leverage to optimize the overall cost of capital, considering the favorable tax treatment of debt, while maintaining operating and financial flexibility.

The ratios that follow describe a company's debt exposure, but they should be looked at from two perspectives. Creditors obviously want to maximize their protection, but stockholders look for the best balance of debt and equity to ensure the highest return at the least level of risk.

The **total debt-to-total-asset ratio** is a measure of the extent to which a company's assets are financed by creditors and is calculated as follows:

$$\text{Total debt-to-total assets ratio} = \frac{\text{Total debt}}{\text{Total assets}} .$$

In general, the lower the ratio, the more solvent a company is thought to be. The higher the ratio, the less solvent and the more leveraged a company is considered to be.

The reciprocal of that equation is leverage generally expressed as a whole number:

$$\text{Leverage} = \frac{\text{Total assets}}{\text{Total equity}} .$$

The lower the leverage number is, the more the company has used equity to finance its assets and the lower its exposure to downturns in its business. The higher the number is, the more the company is relying on its creditors for financing, and the more benefits the shareholders derive from those borrowed funds—and the more exposed they are to the risks of the company's business.

The **long-term debt-to-equity ratio** measures the relative composition of a company's long-term capital structure, or **capitalization,** and is calculated as:

$$\text{Long-term debt-to-equity ratio} = \frac{\text{Long-term debt}}{\text{Owners' equity}} .$$

PepsiCo reports a variation of this ratio in its annual report:

$$\text{Total debt-to-total capital employed} = \frac{\text{Total long-term debt}[1]}{\text{Total long-term debt + Shareholders' equity}} .$$

In general, the lower this ratio, the higher the proportion of long-term financing provided by the owners and the more solvent a company is thought to be. Alternatively, the higher this ratio, the more leveraged a company is and the less solvent it is thought to be. In general, creditors like a lower debt-to-equity ratio (or *total debt-to-total capital employed ratio*) because they have a prior claim on a company's assets and prefer to have a larger equity cushion beneath them.

A final index of a company's ability to manage its long-term debt is given by the **times-interest-earned ratio,** also known as the *interest coverage ratio:*

$$\text{Times-interest-earned ratio} = \frac{\text{Net income before income tax + Interest expense}}{\text{Interest expense}} .$$

Note that this ratio is calculated using pretax net income since interest is a tax-deductible expense; hence, the numerator is a measure of a company's pretax, pre-interest income. This ratio measures the extent to which a company's earnings during a period cover its interest payments for the same period. In general, the higher the ratio the better, although

---

[1]Total debt excludes PepsiCo's nonrecourse obligation and is reduced by a pro forma amount from its offshore short-term portfolios.

a high ratio may indicate either high pretax profits or low debt levels. In either case, a high ratio is generally associated with greater solvency and the ability to add new borrowings (i.e., increased leverage) in the future. A very low ratio may indicate that the company may be missing an opportunity to generate positive marginal returns by not sufficiently leveraging its assets. The times-interest-earned ratio is an income statement–based indicator of solvency.

To illustrate these solvency ratios, consider again information drawn from PepsiCo's 1990 financial statements:

	1990	1989
Total debt-to-total assets ratio	71.4%	74.2%
Long-term debt-to-equity ratio	1.14:1	1.48:1
Times-interest-earned ratio	10.2 times	8.6 times

As compared to that in 1989, PepsiCo's solvency in 1990 improved somewhat. The percentage of assets financed by external borrowings declined from 74.2 percent to 71.4 percent, and the ratio of long-term debt to equity declined from 1.48 times to 1.14 times. (Stated alternatively, the level of long-term debt as a percentage of equity declined from 148 percent to 114 percent.) The times-interest-earned ratio improved from 8.6 times to 10.2 times. As compared to Coca-Cola (see Exhibit 4.2), PepsiCo's times-interest-earned ratio is marginally better (i.e., 10.2 times versus 9.7 times), although its long-term debt-to-equity ratio is substantially below that of Coke (i.e., 1.14 versus 0.29). This latter result reflects PepsiCo's increased borrowings associated with its recent acquisitions, and Coca-Cola's decision to decentralize its bottling operations–related debt to its 49 percent–owned subsidiary, Coca-Cola Enterprises, Inc.

Asset Management

Asset management refers to how efficiently a company utilizes its assets. A company with superior asset management usually experiences superior earnings and profitability relative to competitors within its industry. Asset management effectiveness is usually investigated with respect to a company's inventory, receivables, and noncurrent assets. Five such indicators are (1) the inventory turnover ratio, (2) the number of days of inventory on hand, (3) the accounts receivable turnover ratio, (4) the average receivable collection period, and (5) the noncurrent asset turnover ratio.

The quality of a company's inventory management is often revealed by the inventory turnover ratio and the number of days of inventory on hand. The **inventory turnover ratio** measures the number of times that the average level of inventory on hand was sold, or turned, during an accounting period and is calculated as follows:

$$\text{Inventory turnover ratio} = \frac{\text{Cost of goods sold for the period}}{\text{Average inventory held during the period}}.$$

In general, the higher the inventory turnover ratio, the more profitable a company is and the more effective the inventory management is thought to be. A high turnover rate also helps to reduce the potential of loss due to product obsolescence or deterioration. If the turnover ratio is too high, however, it may indicate that the company is losing sales opportunities because inventory levels are inadequate. Unfortunately, there is no ideal turnover rate, and to judge the effectiveness of inventory management, it is important to compare this ratio to that of prior periods, to industry averages, or to competitor ratios (see Exhibit 4.2).

An instructive derivative of the inventory turnover ratio is the **number of days' inventory-on-hand ratio.** This ratio highlights whether inventory levels are appropriate for the current level of sales volume and is calculated as follows:

$$\text{Number of days' inventory on hand} = \frac{365 \text{ days}}{\text{Inventory turnover ratio}}.$$

This indicator measures the average number of days required to liquidate the existing stock of inventory based on current sales volume. A high number of days' inventory-on-hand ratio usually reflects an excessive quantity of inventory on hand, suggesting that current production should be curtailed. Alternatively, a very low number of days' inventory-on-hand ratio may also be problematic, indicating an inadequate quantity of inventory on hand and the potential for lost sales or customer complaints. Like the inventory turnover ratio, the number of days' inventory-on-hand ratio has no ideal number.

The quality of receivable management is usually evaluated in the context of the accounts (notes) receivable turnover ratio and the average receivable collection period. The **receivable turnover ratio** is a measure of the rate at which a company's accounts and notes receivable are converted to cash. In general, a high ratio indicates excellent receivables management. A low ratio, on the other hand, may indicate serious problems in the sales-receivables-collection cycle. The ratio is calculated as follows:

$$\text{Receivable turnover ratio} = \frac{\text{Net credit sales (for the period)}}{\text{Average receivable balance (for the period)}}.$$

A derivative of the receivable turnover ratio is the **average receivable collection period,** which measures the average number of days that a receivable is outstanding before the amount is collected. This ratio provides a good indication of the quality of the cash collection policies a company followed relative to the credit terms granted and is calculated as

$$\text{Average receivable collection period} = \frac{365 \text{ days}}{\text{Receivable turnover ratio}}.$$

A low collection period (in days) not only indicates effective asset management but also provides evidence as to the liquidity of a company's accounts and notes receivable.

These ratios are abstractions, but the impact of the underlying numbers is quite real. It is generally understood that inventory carrying costs are annually at least 20 percent of the value of the inventory. These carrying costs include the cost of the funds invested, the cost of storage and insurance, and the cost of spoilage, which occurs simply because the inventory is on hand. Management must trade off that inventory carrying cost against its need for customer service as it evaluates its inventory turn statistics. The trade-off may not have to be all that painful, however: One major manufacturer found that it was carrying 10 different variations of the same part, each minutely different from the other, because these parts were used on 10 different finished products. The company found that it was able to maintain its customer service levels *and* reduce its inventory levels by redesigning the basic part so that it could be used on all of the finished products, regardless of their variation.

Similarly, accounts receivable have a real cost to the seller, including the cost of the funds invested, the service costs, and the cost of bad debt losses. Typically, bank credit card companies charge the merchant 4 percent of the amount of a charge sale to cover its credit operations costs and provide some measure of profit. Again, management must weigh the cost of its own credit operations against the profit potential of the sale, which might be lost should the customer go somewhere with easier credit policies.

A final indicator of the quality or effectiveness of a company's asset management is given by the **noncurrent asset turnover ratio.** Unlike the previous four ratios that focus on the current assets, this ratio examines a company's utilization of its long-term revenue-producing assets. The ratio is calculated as

$$\text{Noncurrent asset turnover ratio} = \frac{\text{Net sales (for the period)}}{\text{Average noncurrent asset balance}}.$$

In general, the higher the ratio the better. A high turnover ratio indicates that management is effective in generating revenues from the noncurrent assets that it has at its disposal. A high turnover rate can also be problematic, however, if the reason for the high turnover is the liquidation of the company's noncurrent assets. Similarly, a decreasing ratio may not necessarily indicate poor noncurrent asset utilization if the decline is a result of an increased investment in noncurrent assets.

To illustrate the asset management ratios, consider again PepsiCo's 1990 financial statements:

	1990	1989
Inventory turnover ratio	15.2 times	15.1 times
Number of days' inventory on hand	24.0 days	24.1 days
Receivable turnover ratio	13.4 times	13.7 times
Average receivable collection period	27.2 days	26.6 days
Noncurrent asset turnover ratio	3.3 times	3.2 times

PepsiCo's asset management position in 1989 and 1990 compares very favorably. Although the inventory turnover ratio and the number of days' inventory on hand have improved somewhat, the receivable turnover ratio and average receivable collection period have deteriorated slightly; the noncurrent asset turnover ratio improved marginally. As compared to Coca-Cola (see Exhibit 4.2), PepsiCo's inventory turnover occurs 15.2 times per year versus only 4.8 times for Coca-Cola, and its receivable turnover is 13.4 times versus 12.2 times for Coca-Cola. Both of these turnover ratios indicate PepsiCo's superior asset management.

SUMMARY

The balance sheet is one of the basic financial statements prepared to communicate a company's financial status and condition. The balance sheet summarizes the assets a company owned, the liabilities it owed, and the accumulated funds that its owners have invested in or left with the company to cover its operating needs.

The balance sheet may be used to investigate a company's liquidity, solvency, leverage, and asset management effectiveness. By itself, the balance sheet reveals very little about the profitability of a company's operations. Hence, development of a complete understanding of a company's financial health requires considerations beyond the balance sheet, such as an analysis of the income statement, which is the focus of the following chapter.

NEW CONCEPTS AND TERMS

Accounts payable (p. 147)

Accounts and notes receivable (p. 143)

Accumulated depreciation (p. 145)

Allowance for uncollectible accounts
  (p. 143)

Amortization (p. 146)

Asset management effectiveness (p. 156)

Authorized shares (p. 150)

Average receivable collection period
  (p. 162)

Bad debts expense (p. 143)

Bond (p. 148)

Cash and cash equivalents (p. 143)

Charter of incorporation (p. 150)

Classified balance sheet (p. 144)

Common-size financial statements (p. 155)

Common stock (p. 149)

Coupon rate (p. 148)

Current maturities of long-term debt
  (p. 147)

Current ratio (p. 157)

Deferred income taxes (p. 148)

Discounting (p. 154)

Factor (p. 157)

Fiscal year (p. 141)

Goodwill (p. 146)

Inventory (p. 144)

Inventory turnover ratio (p. 161)

Issued shares (p. 150)

Leverage (p. 159)

Liquid assets (p. 143)

Liquidity (p. 156)

Long-term debt (p. 148)

Long-term debt-to-equity ratio (p. 160)

Long-term investments (p. 145)

Matching concept (p. 143)

Maturity date (p. 148)

No-par value stock (p. 149)

Noncurrent asset turnover ratio (p. 163)

Nonrecourse obligation (p. 148)

Notes payable (p. 147)

Number of days' inventory-on-hand ratio
  (p. 162)

Operating cycle (p. 144)

Other assets (p. 145)

Outstanding shares (p. 150)

Paid-in capital in excess of par (stated)
  value (p. 149)

Par value (p. 149)

Prepaid expenses (p. 144)

Present value (p. 154)

Profitability (p. 156)

Pro forma financial statements (p. 156)

Property, plant, and equipment (p. 145)

Quick assets (p. 157)

Quick ratio (p. 157)

Ratio (p. 155)

Receivable turnover ratio (p. 162)

Short-term investments (p. 143)

Solvency (p. 156)

Stated value (p. 149)

Times-interest-earned ratio (p. 160)

Total debt-to-total asset ratio (p. 160)

Total debt-to-total capital employed ratio
  (p. 160)

Trade notes (p. 147)

Trade payables (p. 147)

Trade receivables (p. 143)

Trend analysis (p. 155)

Unclassified balance sheet (p. 144)

Working capital (p. 157)

ISSUES FOR DISCUSSION

D4.1 Most companies present a classified balance sheet, that is, they divide both assets and liabilities into long-term and short-term items. Banks do not do that, but instead present an unclassified balance sheet that makes no distinction between current and long-term items. See the following asset presentation from Synovus Financial Corporation. Why might an unclassified balance sheet be appropriate for a bank?

Consolidated Statements of Condition
Synovus Financial Corp.
(In thousands)

	December 31	
	1989	**1988**
Assets:		
Cash and due from banks, including cash deposits at the Federal Reserve in order to meet reserve requirements of $24,356 and $15,869 for 1989 and 1988, respectively	$ 162,425	$ 137,212
Short-term, interest earning deposits with banks	6,237	3,613
Federal funds sold	77,795	46,717
Investment securities (approximate market value of $438,623 and $341,795 for 1989 and 1988, respectively) (note 2)	435,348	347,916
Loans (note 3)	1,615,345	1,341,892
Less:		
Unearned income	(22,471)	(19,912)
Reserve for possible loan losses (note 3)	(26,628)	(21,372)
Loans, net	1,566,246	1,300,608
Premises and equipment (note 5)	75,319	61,098
Other assets	87,045	59,777
Total assets	$2,410,415	$1,956,941

D4.2 The current liability section of most balance sheets includes an item called *current payments on long-term debt*. If that item represents payments due on long-term debt, why is it included in current liabilities? Does the current asset section of those balance sheets include an item called *current depreciation on long-term assets?* Why or why not?

D4.3 The current assets and liabilities from The Mead Corporation's 1990 balance sheet are as follows (all dollar amounts in millions):

December 31	1990	1989
Current assets:		
Cash and cash equivalents	$ 21.1	$ 21.1
Accounts receivable, less allowance for doubtful accounts of $24.0 in 1990 and $25.6 in 1989	528.9	536.1
Inventories (Note B)	394.6	381.0
Prepaid expenses	37.4	42.4
Total current assets	$982.0	$980.6

December 31	1990	1989
Current liabilities:		
Accounts payable:		
Trade	$261.4	$290.1
Affiliated companies	28.1	64.7
Outstanding checks	102.6	57.7
Accrued wages	83.3	84.1
Taxes, other than income	52.8	50.1
Other current liabilities	152.7	132.7
Current maturities of long-term debt	12.7	12.6
Total current liabilities	$693.2	$692.0

How would you explain the fact that the company has a current liability titled, "Outstanding Checks"? How might that fact affect your perceptions of the company's liquidity? How would it affect the company's current ratio? Its Working capital? Its Quick ratio?

D4.4 Monsanto describes its credit standing with the following words (from the Management Discussion and Analysis segment reviewing the Balance Sheet).

Monsanto Maintains Strong Financial Position

Monsanto's financial position remained strong in 1990, as evidenced by Monsanto's current "A" or better debt rating. Financial resources were adequate to support existing businesses and to fund new business opportunities.

   Working capital at year-end 1990 was at the same level as that of the prior year-end. Receivables increased primarily as a result of higher fourth quarter 1990 sales versus the prior year's fourth quarter sales. The increase in current liabilities principally related to the Agricultural Products restructuring and increased short-term debt. . . .

   Total short- and long-term debt at year-end 1990 was $258 million higher than that of the prior year-end. The additional long-term debt was used principally for capacity expansions. To maintain adequate financial flexibility and access to debt markets worldwide, Monsanto management intends to maintain an "A" debt rating. Important factors in establishing that rating are the ratio of total debt to total capitalization, which was 35 percent, and the interest coverage ratio, which was 4.8 in 1990. . . .

   Monsanto uses financial markets around the world for its financing needs and has available various short- and medium-term bank credit facilities, which are discussed in the notes to financial statements. These credit facilities provide the financing flexibility to take advantage of investment opportunities that may arise and to satisfy future funding requirements.

In your own words, describe Monsanto's interest in maintaining its "A" rating. Why might they be interested in that rating? What would you expect the company to do to preserve that rating?

D4.5 The balance sheet presents a picture of a company's assets, liabilities, and equities as of a point in time. In general, the balance sheet reports items at their historical cost. Consider the typical line items reported in a balance sheet. As the manager of the company publishing the balance sheet, which items would you prefer to report at current market values? As a potential investor in the company, which ones would you like to have information on, regarding their market values? Discuss how the demand for market value information may or may not be consistent with the reporting notions of relevance and reliability.

D4.6 The value of ratio analysis depends to a great extent on one's ability to interpret the ratios in the context of a company's particular environment. In this regard, discuss how the quick and current ratios for companies in the following industries may or may not differ.

- Defense contractor
- Distillery
- Hotel chain
- Sports franchise

D4.7 The 1980s and the start of the 1990s have been periods of major changes in the way companies are organized and financed. Elaborate on how corporate balance sheets would be impacted by such phenomena as corporate acquisitions, junk bonds, downsizing, outsourcing of production/assembly, and just-in-time inventory techniques.

D4.8 Consider the PepsiCo balance sheet presented at the end of Chapter 1. Identify all the line items in that balance sheet that you believe are based on certain subjective judgments and/or estimates of PepsiCo management. What is the nature of each of those subjective decisions? Identify several such areas of judgment and discuss whether the judgmental discretion now allowed should be reduced via additional standard setting.

D4.9 In PepsiCo's "Selected Financial Data" section of its annual report, presented in Chapter 1, it is reported that the 1990 historical cost net debt ratio is 47 percent and its market net debt ratio is 22 percent. Fully explain and interpret these two items.

D4.10 Consider the following phrases, which express important balance sheet ideas:

a. Realizable value—Present value
b. Fixed assets—Intangible assets
c. Liabilities—Owners' equity

Prepare a commentary on each of the above pairings, explaining how they are alike and how they are different—in the context of a company's balance sheet.

D4.11 Consider the following asset account titles, taken from different companies' 1990 published financial statments. In addition to describing the account, these account titles also express important balance sheet ideas.

a. Contracts in Process
b. Construction in Process
c. Debt Issuance Costs

Prepare a commentary on each of the above titles, covering the following points: *(i)* why the item in question is considered to be an asset, *(ii)* what kinds of costs might have been added to the account to achieve the current balance, and *(iii)* when and how the cost of the asset will be allocated to future operations.

D4.12 Consider the following typical business items:

a. A ten-ton, bulk-material, over-the-road truck
b. A million-dollar, ninety-day note payable
c. One thousand shares of common stock
d. Computer software designed to control inventory quantities

How might these items be classified in different companies' balance sheets? Each item can be classified at least two different ways, and several could be classified more than two ways, depending on the company involved and the surrounding circumstances.

PROBLEMS

P4.1 Account identification. Identify each of the following accounts as either assets, liabilities, or owners' equity:

a. Accounts Payable

b. Prepaid Insurance A

c. Cash

d. Capital Stock

e. Supplies Inventory

f. Rent Payable

g. Land and Building

h. Advance Deposit by Customer L

i. Loan Payable

j. Accounts Receivable

k. Retained Earnings

l. Warranty Liability

m. Marketable Securities A

n. Receivables from Employees A

P4.2 Comparisons of asset mix. Different companies will have different assets for their use, largely because of the characteristics of their industry but also because of the maturity of the individual company and other company-specific factors. Individual companies will fund those assets with different sources as well, depending on the cost and availability of capital to the industry, and to the specific company.

Required:

a. Select five different companies—three in the same industry and two in completely different industries—and for each company determine the percentage of assets represented by cash and cash equivalents, receivables, inventory, plant and equipment, and long-term investments and other assets. Comment on the similarities and the differences you may have noticed.

b. Calculate the current ratio for each of the five companies you selected. Compare the ratios for each of the companies, and explain what the ratio tells you about that company and about the group of companies in your sample.

P4.3 Current and non-current assets and liabilities. Consider the following account titles from 1990 balance sheets:

a. Accrued Wages

b. Inventories

c. Machinery and Equipment

d. Investment in Affiliates

e. Deferred Income Taxes

f. Other Liabilities

g. Treasury Stock

h. Senior Subordinated Debentures

i. Accumulated Depreciation

j. Prepaid Expenses

k. Obligation under Capital Lease

l. Goodwill

m. Convertible Class A Preferred Stock

Required:

Identify each account title as either a current asset or a currrent liability, or a non-current asset or a non-current liability. Where there is a question in your mind about any item, make an assumption, and explain your assumption and your classification.

P4.4 Financial Analysis. Collins Cutlery has a current ratio, based on its June 30, 1991, balance sheet, of 2:1. During the following six months, the following independent events took place.

1. Sold warehouse for cash.
2. Declared a cash dividend on common stock.
3. Sold merchandise on account (at a profit).
4. Retired mortgage notes which would have matured in 1999.
5. Paid cash for a patent.
6. Temporarily invested cash in government bonds.
7. Purchased inventory for cash.
8. Wrote off an account recievable as uncollectible.
9. Paid the cash dividend on common stock.
10. Purchased a computer and gave a two-year promissory note.
11. Collected accounts receivable.
12. Borrowed from bank on a 120-day promissory note.

Required:

For each of the above events, indicate the effect of that event on Collins' working capital and current ratio, and its ratio of total debt to equity. Make whatever assumptions you believe necessary to complete this exercise.

P4.5 Balance sheet preparation. Presented below in alphabetical order are the balance sheet accounts of the Grow Company as of December 31, 1991:

Accounts payable	$ 2,480	Capital stock, $1 par	$25,000
Accounts receivable	2,150	Discount on bonds payable	500
Accumulated depreciation—buildings	5,300	Equipment	20,000
Accumulated depreciation—equipment	3,510	Income taxes payable	2,500
Allowance for uncollectible accounts	300	Inventory—raw material	1,800
Bonds payable (due 2010)	8,000	Inventory—finished goods	4,200
Buildings	15,000	Land	13,000
Cash	3,200	Marketable securities (short-term)	1,500
		Paid-in capital in excess of par value	15,000
		Patent	10,000
		Retained earnings	?
		Trademark	10,000
		Wages Payable	750

Required:

Prepare the December 31, 1991, balance sheet of the Grow Company.

P4.6 Balance sheet accounts: assets. The Dow Jones Company presents the following items in the asset side of its balance sheet. Explain why the items with asterisks might be considered assets for Dow Jones. Comment on the source of the numbers attributed to those assets.

Dow Jones & Company, Inc.
Consolidated Balance Sheets
December 31, 1989 and 1988
(in thousands)

	1989	1988
Assets		
Current assets:		
Cash and cash equivalents	$ 46,197	$ 60,791
Accounts receivable—trade, net of allowance for		
doubtful accounts of $14,151 in 1989 and $13,221 in 1988	160,843	138,964
Newsprint inventory (Notes 1 & 5)*	18,439	21,026
Deferred income taxes (Notes 1 & 7)*	9,483	
Other current assets	33,805	44,703
Total current assets	268,767	265,484
Investments in Associated Companies at equity (Note 4)*	71,896	83,414
Other investments (Notes 3 & 6)	82,736	103,205
Plant and property, at cost:		
Land	21,661	21,661
Buildings and improvements	306,387	269,688
Equipment	1,000,679	889,218
Construction in progress*	41,498	44,053
	1,370,225	1,224,620
Less, allowance for depreciation (Note 1)	652,468	539,528
	717,757	685,092
Excess of cost over net assets of businesses		
acquired, less accumulated amortization of		
$82,236 in 1989 and $54,880 in 1988 (Notes 1 & 2)*	1,510,120	963,939
Other assets	37,060	10,647
Total assets	$2,688,336	$2,111,781

P4.7 Balance sheet accounts: liabilities. Contel Corporation lists the following items in the current liabilities section of the balance sheet. Explain what these items are and why they have to be recorded by Contel as a liability. Why are they current liabilities? Comment on the source of the numbers attributed to those liabilities.

**Contel Corporation
Balance Sheet
As of December 31
(in thousands)**

	1987	1986
Liabilities and Stockholders' Equity		
Current liabilities:		
Current maturities of long-term obligations and preferred stock redemptions	$ 194,419	$ 93,640
Interim borrowings	173,073	26,279
Accounts payable	478,579	404,029
Accrued taxes	67,088	166,929
Accrued interest	33,345	35,520
Accrued benefits	53,178	74,444
Advance billings and customer deposits	63,294	77,058
Other	169,429	100,972
	$1,232,405	$978,871

P4.8 Short-term and long-term debt. Snap-On Tools Corporation includes a footnote in its 1990 Annual Report, describing its debt situation as follows:

At December 29, 1990, the Company had bank lines of credit totaling $101.3 million available for short-term borrowing, including support of commercial paper issuance. Of this amount, $100 million required compensating balances of 2 percent. Notes payable to banks totaled $11.5 million as of December 29, 1990, and $6.0 million as of December 30, 1989. Commercial notes payable totaled $65.0 million as of December 29, 1990, and $31.0 million as of December 30, 1989. There were no short-term borrowings during 1988.

Maximum short-term borrowings outstanding at the end of any month in 1990 and 1989 were $77.0 million and $37.0 million, respectively. The average outstanding borrowings were $56.7 million in 1990 and $16.6 million in 1989. The weighted average daily interest rates for 1990 and 1989 were 8.1 percent and 9.3 percent, respectively. The weighted average interest rates on outstanding borrowings at December 29, 1990, and December 30, 1989, were 8.1 percent and 8.7 percent, respectively.

Interest payments approximated $7.3 million and $3.8 million for 1990 and 1989, respectively. For 1988, interest expense approximated interest payments.

The Company's annual maturities on its long-term debt due in the next five years are $.4 million for years 1991 through 1994 and $.2 million for 1995.

The Company's long-term debt consisted of the following for fiscal years ended (amounts in thousands):

	1990	1989
6.6% revenue bonds payable in varying annual installments through 2009	**$6,400**	$6,500
Other	**1,300**	1,625
	7,700	8,125
Less: Current maturities	**(425)**	(425)
Total long-term debt	**$7,275**	$7,700

Required:

a. What amounts will Snap-On Tools report in its December 29, 1990, Balance Sheet, as its short-term and long-term debt balances?

b. In your own words, what other interesting information did you gather from the footnote? Why might the management of Snap-On Tools have decided to make that information available to us?

P4.9 Working with ratios. At lunch one day in the First National Bank's executive dining room, you notice a co-worker lunching by himself and studying a set of financial statements. He seems frustrated and is talking to himself. You hear him say, as he picks up his briefcase and leaves, "I do not understand what is going on with this borrower—none of this makes any sense to me." You start to follow him out, when you notice that he has left a scratch sheet behind covered with figures and notes. The bulk of his scratching appear to be a set of ratios. The scratch sheet is as follows and the stock holdings are as they were:

ROE	22%	19%
Working capital	20,000	5,000
Current ratio	1.25	1.07
Quick ratio	0.5	0.5
Trade receivables, days' sales outstanding	73.00	81.11
Inventory turnover	1.25	1.69
Interest coverage	3.75	4.17
Long-term debt to equity	0.8	0.6
% dividends to equity	22%	19%

Required:

Identify five important things that may have been going on with this borrower this year, which might explain the ratios developed by your frustrated friend.

P4.10 Balance sheets in the United States and abroad. In the United States, GAAP require companies to present their balance sheets in descending order of liquidity; for example, the asset side begins with cash and concludes with intangible assets. In many other countries, the balance sheets focus on the productivity of the assets, and so they begin with property, plant, and equipment, add net current assets, deduct long-term liabilities and end with owners' equity. As an illustration of that different perspective, the following exhibit presents the balance sheet of an English music and film rental company, Thorne EMI. The next exhibit presents the balance sheet of Time Warner, a United States publishing and entertainment company.

Required:

Prepare a one-page paper outlining the results of your review of the exhibits. Your paper should explain which presentation might be preferred by which type of financial statement user, and why. You should express your own preference and justify your position logically. Based on your knowledge of U.S. business history and your thinking about the thrust of the U.S. approach to balance sheet presentation, comment on why that presentation might have evolved here.

Thorne EMI
Balance Sheet
(at March 31)

	Notes	1991 £m	1990 £m
Fixed assets			
Music publishing copyrights	9	**269.7**	216.8
Tangible fixed assets	10	**1,192.0**	1,126.3
Investments	11	**119.6**	109.6
Net assets of retail financing subsidiaries		**—**	19.2
		1,581.3	1,471.9
Current assets			
Stocks	12	**354.0**	363.5
Debtors	13	**816.4**	693.7
Investments: cash equivalents	14	**48.9**	45.3
Cash at bank and in hand	14	**95.5**	83.6
		1,314.8	1,186.1
Creditors: amounts falling due within one year			
Borrowings	14	**(185.1)**	(125.6)
Other creditors	15	**(1,200.3)**	(1,137.9)
		(1,385.4)	(1,263.5)
Net current liabilities		**(70.6)**	(77.4)
Total assets less current liabilities		**1,510.7**	1,394.5
Creditors: amounts falling due after more than one year			
Borrowings	14	**(353.5)**	(319.4)
Other creditors	16	**(47.3)**	(16.2)
		(400.8)	(335.6)
Provisions for liabilities and charges			
Deferred taxation	17	**(36.6)**	(36.2)
Other provisions	18	**(175.7)**	(146.6)
		(212.3)	(182.8)
		897.6	876.1
Capital and reserves			
Called-up share capital	19	**77.5**	96.6
Share premium account	19	**159.8**	55.6
Other reserves	20	**627.2**	646.1
Goodwill	20	**(710.6)**	(653.6)
Profit and loss reserve	20	**503.5**	498.6
		657.4	643.3
Shareholders' funds			
Minority interests	21	**240.2**	232.8
		897.6	876.1

Time Warner
Balance Sheet
(at December 31, in millions of dollars)

	1990	1989
Assets		
Current assets:		
Cash and equivalents	$ 172	$ 234
Receivables, less allowances for doubtful receivables and returns of $761 and $766	2,071	2,005
Inventories	1,239	1,006
Other current assets	464	589
Total current assets	3,946	3,834
Receivables due after one year	552	435
Noncurrent inventories	1,759	1,876
Investments	1,874	1,455
Land and buildings	776	701
Cable television equipment	2,585	2,362
Furniture, fixtures, and other equipment	1,180	975
	4,541	4,038
Less accumulated depreciation and amortization	(1,415)	(1,094)
Property, plant, and equipment, net	3,126	2,944
Excess of cost over net assets acquired	9,073	9,044
Cable television franchises	3,097	3,281
Music copyrights, record catalogues, and other assets	1,910	1,922
Total assets	**$25,337**	**$24,791**
Liabilities and Shareholders' Equity		
Current liabilities:		
Accounts payable and accrued expenses	$3,601	$3,137
Debt due within one year	31	54
Accrued income taxes	19	79
Total current liabilities	3,651	3,270
Long-term debt	11,184	10,838
Deferred income taxes	2,637	2,546
Unearned portion of paid subscriptions	521	449
Other liabilities	1,030	932
Shareholders' equity:		
Preferred stock, $1 par value, 250 million shares authorized, 117.9 and 111.7 million shares issued, $5.954 and $5.584 billion liquidation preference	118	112
Common stock, $1 par value, 750 million shares authorized, 70.4 million shares issued	70	70
Paid in capital	6,919	6,537
Retained earnings	499	1,299
Treasury stock, at cost, 12.9 million common shares and .7 million preferred shares in 1990, and 13 million common shares in 1989	(1,292)	(1,262)
Total shareholders' equity	6,314	6,756
Total liabilities and shareholders' equity	**$25,337**	**$24,791**

P4.11 Assets at cost or at current value. Pacific Dunlop is an Australian manufacturer of latex products, clothes, and electrical equipment. The company follows normal Australian accounting for its plant and equipment, providing regular revaluations by independent appraisers, and by the company officers. The results of that accounting are detailed in the following footnote from the 1990 financial statements. (The Australian-GAAP based balance sheet reports total property, plant, and equipment of $1,008,197.)

Property, Plant, and Equipment

		Consolidated	
		1990 ($000)	1989 ($000)
(a) Freehold land	Independent valuations 31/12/1988	82,874	91,383
	Officers' valuations 31/12/1988	608	804
	At cost	15,498	16,537
		98,980	108,724
(b) Freehold buildings	Independent valuations 31/12/1988	110,452	116,660
	Officers' valuations 31/12/1988	964	992
	At cost	54,011	52,282
		165,427	169,934
	Less provision for depreciation	16,535	12,005
		148,892	157,929
(c) Leasehold land and buildings	Independent valuations 31/12/1988	9,661	12,381
	Officers' valuations 31/12/1988	1,107	1,192
	At cost	17,685	9,963
		28,453	23,536
	Less provision for amortisation	4,484	3,445
		23,969	20,091
(d) Plant and equipment	Independent valuations 1965–1985		77
	Officers' valuations 1970–1983	4,915	4,915
	Deemed value 1962	47	990
	At cost	959,018	902,218
		963,980	908,200
	Less provision for depreciation	427,430	375,464
		536,550	532,736
(e) Leased plant and equipment	At cost	89,664	45,863
	Less provision for amortisation	14,776	14,072
		74,888	31,791
(f) Buildings and plant under construction	At cost	124,918	83,489
		1,008,197	934,760

Required:

Comment on the Australian accounting policy, as exemplified in the Pacific Dunlop footnote. Should the accounting profession in the U.S. permit a similar policy for fixed assets? What would the advantages and disadvantages be for such a policy for U.S. companies? For their financial statement presentation? For their internal management? For their public policy position?

P4.12 Foreign currency adjustments. Monsanto, Procter & Gamble, Seagrams, and Snap-On Tools all made the same general statement in their footnotes regarding their policies for the translation of financial statements of subsidiaries which conduct business in currencies other than the U.S. dollar. Monsanto's statement is typical: "Most of Monsanto's ex-U.S. entities' financial statements are translated into U.S. dollars using current exchange rates. Unrealized currency adjustments in the Statement of Consolidated Financial Position are accumulated in shareholders' equity."

The accumulated currency adjustment accounts in shareholders' equity for the four companies, at year end 1990 and 1989, were as follows (in millions of dollars):

	Balance in the Account	
	1990	**1989**
Monsanto	188	24
Procter & Gamble	44	(63)
Snap-On Tools	(152)	(103)
Seagrams	(13)	(158)

Required:

Assume that the underlying balance sheets of the companies' non-U.S. subsidiaries have not changed significantly. Explain what has happened to cause the changes in the accumulated currency adjustments in each case.

P4.13 Leverage. A condensed balance sheet and a condensed income statement for the Lever-Up Corporation for 1991 are as follows:

Condensed Balance Sheet (000 omitted)		Condensed Income Statement (000 omitted)	
	12/31/91		**12/31/91**
Current assets	4,500	Sales	25,000
Fixed assets (net)	9,000	Cost of sales	16,250
Goodwill	2,500	Administrative and	6,200
Total assets	$16,000	selling expenses	
		Interest expense	640
Current liabilities	3,000	Pre-tax income	2,010
8% bonds payable	8,000	Income tax	804
Total equity	5,000		
Liabilities and equity	$16,000	Net income	$ 1,206

Lever-Up's sales have been as high as $30,000,000 and as low as $20,000,000 during the last five years, but its interest cover (profit before taxes and interest) has always been in excess of 4.5 during all of those years. The company has maintained an open line of credit with its bank, which would allow it to borrow up to $5,000,000 for a five-year term, at 10 percent.

Required:

a. Using the above exhibits as a base, prepare at least four different sets of pro forma financial statements to demonstrate the effect of an increase in leverage on the company's ROE. Two of your pro forma presentations should assume the same sales and operating expenses, but different levels of borrowing. As the debt is increased, reduce the level of borrowing. The other pro forma presentations should assume an increase in debt, and increased and decreased levels of sales (assume that cost of sales vary in proportion with sales and that other expenses are fixed).

b. Prepare a one-page letter addressed to the Chairman of the Board of Lever-Up, outlining some of the things she might think about as the Board of Directors considers a change in the company's debt/equity structure.

P4.14 Treasury stock. The H. J. Heinz Company has 287,400,000 common shares outstanding and that has been the case for the last several years. The company reported that it had 59,900 shares of its convertible preferred stock outstanding and that it has 33,881,804 shares in its treasury at May 2, 1990, and that it had 30,437,230 shares in its treasury at May 3, 1989. The shareholders' equity balance sheet accounts for the company were (thousands of dollars):

	1990	1989
Convertible Preferred Stock	599	757
Common Stock	71,850	71,850
Additional Capital	152,158	109,665
Retained Earnings	2,560,780	2,263,829
Translation Adjustments	(73,910)	(89,205)
Total outstanding stock	2,711,447	2,356,896
Treasury shares	(777,548)	(579,658)

Required:

Calculate the per-share values of the Preferred Stock, the Common Stock, the total outstanding stock, and the treasury shares, for each year. Why are some values the same each year? Why are some different? Why should there be a difference in the per-share value of the outstanding stock and the treasury stock?

P4.15 3M versus Philip Morris Companies, Inc. Philip Morris is a global consumer products company, manufacturing and marketing tobacco (e.g., Marlboro), food (e.g., Kraft) and beer (e.g., Miller) brands around the world. 3M is a global leader, not only in consumer markets (e.g., Scotch tape) but also in industrial, commercial, and health care markets. Their balance sheets are presented in the following exhibits.

Required:

Calculate all pertinent ratios as well as common-size balance sheets for both companies. Note the key differences and similarities. Comment on the relative positions of each one, year-to-year and to each other, from the perspective of a potential investor in the companies' common stock.

Philip Morris Companies, Inc.
Consolidated Balance Sheets
(in millions of dollars)

	1990	1989
Assets		
Consumer products		
Cash and cash equivalents	$ 146	$ 118
Receivables, net	4,101	2,956
Inventories:		
Leaf tobacco	2,458	2,202
Other raw materials	1,934	1,521
Finished product	2,761	2,028
	7,153	5,751
Other current assets	967	555
Total current assets	12,367	9,380
Property, plant, and equipment, at cost:		
Land and land improvements	664	611
Buildings and building equipment	4,004	3,554
Machinery and equipment	8,480	7,305
Construction in progress	1,133	887
	14,281	12,357
Less accumulated depreciation	4,677	3,900
	9,604	8,457
Goodwill and other intangible assets		
(less accumulated amortization of $1,178 and $745)	19,037	15,682
Other assets	1,675	1,569
Total consumer products assets	42,683	35,088
Financial services and real estate		
Finance assets, net	3,220	2,845
Real estate held for development and sale	418	383
Other assets	248	212
Total financial services and real estate assets	3,886	3,440
Total assets	$46,569	$38,528

Philip Morris Companies, Inc.
Consolidated Balance Sheets
(in millions of dollars)
continued

	1990	1989
Liabilities		
Consumer products		
Short-term borrowings	$ 1,034	$ 489
Current portion of long-term debt	863	752
Accounts payable	2,462	1,917
Accrued liabilities:		
Taxes, except income taxes	851	596
Employment costs	832	805
Other	3,553	2,876
Income taxes	1,366	1,190
Dividends payable	399	318
Total current liabilities	11,360	8,943
Long-term debt	15,285	13,646
Deferred income taxes	1,316	897
Other liabilities	3,499	2,622
Total consumer products liabilities	31,460	26,108
Financial services and real estate		
Short-term borrowings	724	633
Long-term debt	836	905
Deferred income taxes	1,382	1,111
Other liabiities	220	200
Total financial services and real estate liabilities	3,162	2,849
Total liabilities	34,622	28,957
Contingencies (Note 13)		
Stockholders' Equity		
Common stock, par value $1.00 per share (935,320,439 shares issued)	935	935
Earnings reinvested in the business	10,960	9,079
Currency translation adjustments	561	143
	12,456	10,157
Less cost of treasury stock (9,101,348 and 6,790,848 shares)	509	586
Total stockholders' equity	11,947	9,571
Total liabilities and stockholders' equity	$46,569	$38,528

Minnesota Mining and Manufacturing Company and Subsidiaries
As of December 31, 1990 and 1989
(dollars in millions)

	1990	1989
Assets		
Current Assets		
Cash and cash equivalents	$ 294	$ 413
Other securities	297	339
Accounts receivable—net	2,367	2,075
Inventories	2,355	2,120
Other current assets	416	349
Total current assets	5,729	5,296
Investments	471	342
Property, Plant, and Equipment—net	4,389	3,707
Other assets	490	396
Total	$11,079	$9,741
Liabilities and Stockholders' Equity		
Current Liabilities		
Accounts payable	$ 811	$ 689
Payroll	377	332
Income taxes	342	305
Short-term debt	736	455
Other current liabilities	1,073	905
Total current liabilities	3,339	2,686
Deferred Income Taxes	160	200
Other Liabilities	710	592
Long-Term Debt	760	885
Stockholders' Equity—net	6,110	5,378
Shares outstanding—1990: 219,833,403; 1989: 222,663,756		
Total	$11,079	$9,741

P4.16 Mobil versus Amoco. Mobil Corporation and Amoco Corporation are two of the world's leading oil exploration and production companies. The exhibits contain three-year comparative balance sheets for both companies.

Required:

Calculate all pertinent ratios as well as common-size balance sheets, and then comment on the relative positions of each company. Based on just this balance sheet analysis, which company do you believe to be in the strongest financial position? Does it appear that they have similar attitudes toward leverage and liquidity? Why might their approach be the same? Why not? Why might they have taken the approach to liquidity and leverage that they did?

Amoco Corporation
Consolidated Statement of Financial Position
At December 31, in millions of dollars

	1990	1989	1988
Assets			
Current assets			
Cash	268	231	233
Marketable securities	2,131	949	294
Accounts and notes receivable (net)	4,226	3,606	3,341
Inventories			
Crude oil and petroleum products	361	379	385
Chemical products	412	379	364
Other products and merchandise	43	47	39
Materials and supplies	317	307	277
Prepaid expenses and income taxes	458	530	460
	8,216	6,428	5,393
Investments and other assets			
Investments and related advances	483	503	725
Long-term receivables and other assets	804	852	706
	1,287	1,355	1,431
Properties			
At cost	43,818	42,430	41,509
Less—Accumulated depreciation, depletion, etc.	21,112	19,783	18,414
Net	22,706	22,647	23,095
Total assets	32,209	30,430	29,919
Liabilities and shareholders' equity			
Current liabilities			
Current installments of long-term obligations	215	257	225
Short-term obligations	492	483	444
Accounts payable	3,697	3,114	2,909
Accrued liabilities	1,216	1,162	984
Taxes payable (including income taxes)	1,179	872	906
	6,799	5,888	5,468
Long-term debt			
United States dollars	4,946	5,326	5,512
Foreign currencies	66	68	247
	5,012	5,394	5,759
Capitalized lease obligations	237	264	290
Deferred credits and other non-current liabilities			
Income taxes	4,716	4,394	4,342
Other	1,363	793	712
Minority interest in subsidiary companies	14	13	6
Shareholders' equity			
Common stock	2,138	2,178	2,208
Earnings retained and invested in the business	11,925	11,536	11,172
Foreign currency translation adjustment	5	(30)	(38)
	14,068	13,684	13,342
Less—Common stock held in treasury—at cost	—	—	—
Total shareholders' equity	14,068	13,684	13,342
Total liabilities and shareholders' equity	32,209	30,430	29,919

Mobil Corporation
Balance Sheet
At December 31, in (millions)

	1988	1989	1990
Assets			
Current assets			
Cash and cash equivalents	$ 889	$ 1,485	$ 1,138
Accounts and notes receivable	5,113	5,706	7,134
Inventories			
Crude oil and petroleum products	3,270	2,993	3,064
Chemical products	389	381	434
Other, including materials and supplies	822	824	805
Total inventories	4,481	4,198	4,303
Prepaid expenses and other current assets	695	531	656
Total current assets	11,178	11,920	13,231
Investments and long-term receivables	2,939	2,787	3,054
Properties, plants, and equipment, at cost	43,493	44,575	47,568
Less accumulated depreciation, depletion,			
and amortization	19,645	21,129	23,087
Net properties, plants, and equipment	23,848	23,446	24,481
Deferred charges and other assets	855	927	899
Total assets	$38,820	$39,080	$41,665
Liabilities and Shareholders' Equity			
Current liabilities			
Short-term debt	$ 902	$ 1,645	$ 3,016
Accounts payable and accrued liabilities	6,043	6,156	7,132
Income, excise, state gasoline, and other taxes payable .	2,379	2,495	2,755
Deferred income taxes	931	920	750
Total current liabilities	10,255	11,216	13,653
Long-term debt	6,498	5,317	4,298
Reserves for employee benefits	514	707	768
Deferred credits and other noncurrent obligations	1,448	1,173	1,197
Accrued restoration and removal costs	526	595	665
Deferred income taxes	3,848	3,751	3,947
Minority interest in subsidiary companies	45	47	65
Shareholders' equity	15,686	16,274	17,072
Total Liabilities and Shareholders' Equity	$38,820	$39,080	$41,665

P4.17 Spring's Industries, Inc. The following exhibit includes some excerpts from Spring's Industries, Inc.'s "Selected Financial Data" section of their 1990 annual report. Spring's manufactures and markets home furnishings, finished fabrics, and industrial textiles. Some of their major brand names are Springmaid, Bali, and Ultima.

Required:

Review the data and comment on the financial condition of Spring's over the 10-year period presented. In particular: *(a)* What is Spring's average accounts receivable collection period and days' sales in inventory? *(b)* Asset turnover? *(c)* Long-term debt-to-equity ratios? *(d)* Total debt-to-assets ratio? What do those ratios indicate to you, as a potential investor? Finally, what might explain the fluctuating current ratio?

Spring's Industries, Inc.
Selected Financial Data

	1990	1989	1988	1987	1986	1985	1984	1983	1982	1981
Class A stock price range:										
High	39½	45¼	38¾	38¼	28 1/16	23	20⅛	22⅜	20⅛	13 3/16
Low	16⅞	30½	27	20¾	20½	15⅝	15¼	17 3/16	10	8½
Capital Expenditures and Depreciation *(in millions)*:										
Capital expenditures	$117.8	$108.3	77.1	$69.9	57.0	$37.4	50.9	$67.1	39.9	$37.1
Depreciation	72.6	67.5	62.1	57.8	55.6	37.6	31.9	27.6	23.5	21.5
Shareholders and Employees:										
Approximate number of shareholders	3,400	3,500	3,700	3,400	3,300	3,400	3,500	3,500	3,800	4,500
Average number of employees	23,200	24,100	23,400	23,100	23,500	17,000	16,800	18,000	19,400	20,200
Statistical Data:										
Income to net sales	(0.4)%	3.4%	2.9%	3.4%	2.2%	1.3%	3.8%	4.1%	4.3%	4.4%
Net income (loss) to average shareholders' equity	(1.2)%	11.6%	10.2%	11.5%	7.3%	3.0%	8.4%	9.2%	11.3%	11.4%
Operation return on assets employed (e)	7.7%	11.2%	12.0%	12.3%	8.8%	4.4%	9.7%	10.7%	12.5%	16.4%
Inventory turnover (f)	5.6	5.8	6.2	5.8	5.0	5.7	5.8	5.8	5.1	5.4
Accounts receivable turnover (g)	6.2	6.4	6.4	6.5	6.3	6.2	6.2	6.3	6.2	6.3
Net sales divided by average assets (h)	1.6	1.7	1.7	1.6	1.5	1.5	1.5	1.5	1.6	1.9
Current ratio	2.5	2.4	2.7	3.0	3.3	3.1	4.8	4.4	5.2	3.9
Selected Balance Sheet Data *(in millions)*:										
Working capital	$356.5	$354.9	$389.8	$428.1	$402.2	$381.1	$279.8	$270.5	$283.7	$255.9
Property:										
Cost	1,087.9	978.0	872.5	803.6	749.3	710.3	561.7	536.1	484.9	452.2
Accumulated depreciation	(563.7)	(503.0)	(448.0)	(410.5)	(366.0)	(324.6)	(311.2)	(296.9)	(285.7)	(267.2)
Net	524.2	475.0	424.5	393.1	383.3	385.7	250.5	239.2	199.2	185.0
Total assets	1,201.1	1,188.4	1,118.3	1,083.7	1,010.4	1,013.1	615.0	602.2	561.1	543.3
Long-term debt	260.4	227.5	238.5	256.8	271.0	308.1	39.1	46.4	50.4	54.4
Shareholders' equity	560.9	585.1	541.6	505.0	464.6	442.2	441.2	419.0	395.8	364.7

(e) Pretax income before restructuring costs and interest expense divided by average of month-end total assets used in continuing operations.
(f) Cost of goods sold divided by average of month-end inventories.
(g) Net sales divided by average of month-end receivables.
(h) Net sales divided by average of month-end total assets used in continuing operations.

Note: Selected financial data includes M. Lowenstein Corporation, Uniglass, and Carey-McFall from their dates of acquisition in November 1985, February 1988, and March 1989, respectively.

CASES

C4.1 Analyzing the balance sheet: United Foods. The comparative balance sheets of United Foods, as of February 28, 1991 and 1990, are presented below. Perform a ratio analysis on the company and comment on its solvency, its liquidity, and its return on assets. What advice would you have for United Foods management? (Note that the company earned $5.8 million in 1991 on sales of $170 million. The company's gross margin was $38.2 million. Note also that in 1991, the item Other Assets includes an insurance claim receivable for $6.6 million, which is the estimated replacement cost of a processing plant destroyed in a fire. Filing and recording that claim resulted in an after-tax gain of $4.0 million, which is included in net income for 1991.)

UNITED FOODS
Comparative Balance Sheet
As of February 28, 1991 and 1990

	February 28	
	1991	**1990**
Assets		
Cash and cash equivalents	$ 1,367,000	$ 1,103,000
Accounts and notes receivable, less allowance of		
$212,000 and $286,000 for possible losses (Note 4) . .	16,320,000	15,108,000
Inventories (Notes 1 and 4)	54,363,000	40,159,000
Prepaid expenses and miscellaneous (Note 2)	3,047,000	2,536,000
Total current assets	75,097,000	58,906,000
Property and equipment (Notes 4 and 9):		
Land and land improvements	8,185,000	6,693,000
Buildings and leasehold improvements	19,177,000	18,755,000
Machinery, equipment, and improvements	63,929,000	57,902,000
	91,291,000	83,350,000
Less accumulated depreciation and amortization . . .	(37,102,000)	(32,480,000)
Net property and equipment	54,189,000	50,870,000
Other Assets (Note 3)	10,887,000	2,164,000
	$140,173,000	$111,940,000

UNITED FOODS
Comparative Balance Sheet
As of February 28, 1991 and 1990
(continued)

	February 28	
	1991	**1990**
Liabilities and Stockholders' Equity		
Current liabilities:		
Accounts payable	$ 12,715,000	$ 6,996,000
Accruals:		
Compensation and related taxes.	3,533,000	2,744,000
Pension contributions (Note 10)	876,000	1,455,000
Income taxes (Note 7)	128,000	853,000
Workers compensation insurance	1,074,000	870,000
Miscellaneous	1,263,000	1,730,000
Current maturities of long-term debt (Note 4)	1,034,000	881,000
Total current liabilities	20,623,000	15,529,000
Long-term debt, less current maturities (Note 4)	60,199,000	43,186,000
Deferred income taxes (Note 7)	2,934,000	
Total liabilities	83,756,000	58,715,000
Commitments and contingencies (Notes 3, 9, 10 and 11)		
Stockholders' equity (Notes 5 and 6):		
Preferred stock, $1 par—shares authorized, 10,000,000 .		
Common stock, Class A, $1 par—shares authorized,		
25,000,000; issued 7,642,650 and 7,635,732	7,643,000	7,636,000
Common stock, Class B, $1 par—shares authorized,		
10,000,000; issued 7,102,987 and 7,109, 905	7,103,000	7,110,000
Additional paid-in capital	8,720,000	8,901,000
Retained earnings (Note 4)	38,335,000	35,269,000
	61,801,000	58,916,000
Treasury stock, at cost, 1,890,004 and 1,991,004 shares .	(5,384,000)	(5,691,000)
Total stockholders' equity	56,417,000	53,225,000
	$140,173,000	$111,940,000

C4.2 Analyzing the balance sheet: Tyson Foods, Inc. The comparative balance sheets of Tyson Foods at September 30, 1990 and 1989, are presented below. Perform a ratio analysis on the company and comment on its liquidity, solvency, and return on assets. Compare the results of your work on the Tyson balance sheet with the results of your work on the United Foods balance sheet and comment on the circumstances of the two companies and their apparent strategies. (Note that Tyson earned $120 million in 1990 on sales of $3,825 million. Gross margin was $748.5 million.)

	1990	1989
Assets		
Current assets:		
Cash and cash equivalents	$ 16,943	$ 56,490
Accounts receivable	90,839	247,979
Inventories	472,264	408,663
Other current assets	5,812	6,124
Net assets held for sale		30,396
Total current assets	585,858	749,652
Property, plant, and equipment, at cost:		
Land	36,945	24,492
Buildings and leasehold improvements	480,691	435,075
Machinery and equipment	876,555	796,166
Land improvements and other	54,057	55,238
Buildings and equipment under construction	50,020	44,291
	1,498,268	1,355,262
Less: Accumulated depreciation	427,152	334,506
Net property, plant, and equipment	1,071,116	1,020,756
Excess of investments over net assets acquired	784,209	745,778
Investments and other assets	59,879	69,894
Total assets	$2,501,062	$2,586,080
Liabilities and Shareholders' Equity		
Current liabilities:		
Current portion of long-term debt	$ 70,058	$ 55,048
Trade accounts payable	203,915	212,001
Accrued salaries and wages	118,947	98,020
Federal and state income taxes payable	8,489	16,714
Accrued interest payable	17,029	6,618
Other current liabilities	64,723	75,747
Current deferred income taxes		5,564
Total current liabilities	483,161	469,712
Long-term debt	950,407	1,319,385
Deferred income taxes	404,506	349,263
Shareholders' equity:		
Common stock ($.10 par value):		
Class A—Authorized 60,000,000 shares; issued 34,734,131 shares in 1990 and 31,574,473 shares in 1989	3,473	3,157
Class B—Authorized 40,000,000 shares; issued 34,241,259 shares in 1990 and 34,244,499 shares in 1989	3,424	3,425
Capital in excess of par value	171,021	75,306
Retained earnings	500,268	382,661
	678,186	464,549
Treasury stock—668,587 shares in 1990 and 1,162,986 shares in 1989, at cost	9,343	10,041
Unamortized deferred compensation	5,855	6,788
Total shareholders' equity	662,988	447,720
Total liabilities and shareholders' equity	$2,501,062	$2,586,080

C4.3 Balance sheets tell a story. Presented below are six 1989 balance sheets. The balance sheet amounts are expressed as percentages of total assets in order to reflect relative amounts for each account. Each balance sheet represents a different company from a different industry. The industries and companies represented are:

Commercial Bank (Sovran Financial Corp.)
Supermarket Chain (Albertson's Inc.)
Advertising Agency (Interpublic Group)
Discount Store Chain (Wal-Mart Stores, Inc.)
Electric Utility (Pacific Gas & Electric Co.)
Chemical Co. (Dow Chemical Co.)

Match the industry with the appropriate column based on your understanding of some of the financial implications of operating in that industry. The identifications often require two or more distinguishing features.

	Year Ended					
	(1) 12/31	(2) 2/2	(3) 12/31	(4) 12/31	(5) 11/31	(6) 12/31
Assets						
Cash and equivalents	11.3	5.1	.3	.5	.2	5.1
Accounts receivable	65.5	2.7	6.9	12.4	2.0	66.0
Inventory	—	27.2	3.1	12.8	52.7	—
Other current assets	—	2.2	3.9	7.4	2.2	7.7
Total current assets	76.8	37.2	14.2	33.1	57.1	78.8
Net plant and equipment	2.2	60.3	74.8	34.5	41.9	7.6
Other assets	21.0	2.5	11.0	32.4	1.0	13.6
Total assets	100%	100%	100%	100%	100%	100%
Liabilities						
Notes payable	15.9	.7	2.9	10.3	.6	3.1
Accounts payable	73.5	23.6	3.8	10.3	21.9	56.3
Accrued taxes	—	1.5	.1	1.2	1.9	2.4
Other current liabilities	.6	4.9	4.3	7.5	8.1	7.7
Total current liabilities	90.0	30.7	11.1	29.3	32.5	69.5
Long-term debt	1.9	11.1	36.6	17.4	18.8	2.1
Other liabilities	1.7	7.9	12.0	7.9	1.4	6.5
Total liabilities	93.6	49.7	59.7	54.6	52.7	78.1
Equity						
Preferred stock	—	—	5.4	—	—	—
Common stock and surplus	1.6	6.5	24.7	12.6	3.6	8.6
Retained earnings	4.8	43.8	10.2	41.5	43.7	18.1
Treasury stock	—	—	—	(8.7)	—	(3.8)
Total equity	6.4	50.3	40.3	45.4	47.3	22.9
Total liabilities and equity	100%	100%	100%	100%	100%	100%

C4.4 Balance sheet reviews. Reproduced following are three balance sheets from companies in very different industries. After a careful reading of each, hypothesize as to what industries are represented. Be prepared to explain your choice by highlighting specific attributes of each balance sheet.

	Dollars in millions	
	1990	1989
Assets		
Cash and due from banks	$ 2,222	$ 2,344
Interest-bearing deposits with banks	1,696	3,518
Federal funds sold and securities purchased under resale agreements	1,410	2,464
Trading account assets	3,211	2,975
Investment securities *(market value $8,559 and $6,555)*	8,556	6,546
Loans	40,554	39,001
Reserve for possible credit losses	(2,139)	(2,677)
Premises and equipment	880	808
Customers' liability on acceptances	1,178	970
Accrued interest receivable	710	895
Other assets	3,252	3,635
Total assets	$61,530	$60,479
Liabilities		
Demand deposits in domestic offices	$ 6,367	$ 6,653
Time deposits in domestic offices	18,049	18,498
Deposits in foreign offices	15,780	16,483
Total deposits	40,196	41,994
Federal funds purchased and securities sold under repurchase agreements	7,203	4,813
Long-term debt	2,531	3,400
Other borrowings	3,866	3,526
Acceptances outstanding	1,187	982
Accrued taxes and other expenses	1,019	1,084
Other liabilities	2,100	1,299
Total liabilities	58,102	57,098
Shareholders' Equity		
Nonredeemable preferred stock	579	479
Common stock *(outstanding 73,161,618 and 69,935,708 shares)*	73	70
Surplus	2,171	2,089
Undivided profits	605	743
Total shareholders' equity	3,428	3,381
Total liabilities and shareholders' equity	$61,530	$60,479

	(thousands)	
	1990	**1989**
Assets		
Electric utility plant		
Production	$1,382,758	$1,388,061
Transmission	325,310	318,758
Distribution	542,840	518,208
General	147,321	133,443
Construction work in progress	30,218	23,748
	2,428,447	**2,382,218**
Less—Accumulated depreciation	741,856	674,678
	1,686,591	1,707,540
Current Assets		
Cash and temporary cash investments	661	628
Accounts receivable	32,974	33,762
Materials and supplies, at average cost	22,319	3,408
Fuel inventory, at average cost	97,530	108,349
Prepayments and other	14,195	15,612
	167,679	161,759
Deferred charges and other assets	15,419	10,801
	$1,869,689	**$1,880,100**
Capitalization and Liabilities		
Capitalization		
Common stock, $18 par value, authorized 7,600,000 shares, issued and outstanding 7,536,640 shares	$ 135,660	$ 135,660
Paid-in capital	245,000	245,000
Retained earnings	260,894	259,509
Total common stock equity	**641,554**	**640,169**
Preferred stock		
Not subject to mandatory redemption	14,358	14,309
Subject to mandatory redemption	36,422	36,095
Long-term debt	576,095	595,988
Total capitalization	**1,268,429**	**1,286,561**
Current liabilities		
Long-term debt due within twelve months	2,769	2,564
Advances from affiliates	14,320	13,584
Accounts payable	22,658	45,012
Customer deposits	12,605	12,513
Accrued taxes	24,990	15,675
Accrued interest	19,083	19,217
Other	19,617	17,569
	116,042	126,134
Deferred credits		
Income taxes	361,141	357,367
Investment tax credits	102,295	107,229
Other	21,782	2,809
	485,218	**467,405**
	$1,869,689	**$1,880,100**

	(in thousands)	
	1990	1989
Assets		
Current Assets		
Cash and cash equivalents *(Note F)*	$ 2,008,983	$ 1,655,264
Accounts receivable, net of allowance of $87,632 and $74,345	3,206,765	2,965,408
Inventories *(Note A)*		
Raw materials	352,976	360,135
Work-in-process	479,472	570,064
Finished goods	705,810	707,802
Total inventories	1,538,258	1,638,001
Prepaid expenses	345,797	255,195
Net deferred federal and foreign income tax charges	521,809	381,140
Total Current Assets	7,621,612	6,895,008
Property, Plant, and Equipment, at Cost *(Note A)*		
Land	352,296	300,540
Buildings	1,712,204	1,599,673
Leasehold improvements	569,885	530,773
Machinery and equipment	4,392,609	3,817,587
Total property, plant, and equipment, at cost	7,026,994	6,248,573
Less accumulated depreciation	3,158,902	2,602,677
Net property, plant, and equipment	3,868,092	3,645,896
Other assets, net *(Note G)*	165,117	126,875
Total Assets	$11,654,821	$10,667,779
Liabilities and Stockholders' Equity		
Bank loans and current portion of long-term debt *(Note H)*	$ 12,538	$ 29,755
Accounts payable	660,819	553,818
Federal, foreign and state income taxes	453,997	445,977
Salaries, wages and related items	472,153	300,393
Deferred revenues and customer advances *(Note A)*	903,038	833,831
Other current liabilities *(Note M)*	787,224	230,265
Total Current Liabilities	3,289,769	2,394,039
Net deferred federal and foreign income tax credits	33,137	102,048
Long-term debt *(Note H)*	150,001	136,019
Total Liabilities	3,472,907	2,632,106
Stockholders' Equity *(Notes I and J)*		
Common stock, $1.00 par value; authorized 450,000,000 shares; issued 130,008,231 shares	130,008	130,008
Additional paid-in capital	2,565,487	2,469,711
Retained earnings	6,257,199	6,366,418
Treasury stock at cost; 7,453,501 shares and 8,471,655 shares	(770,780)	(930,464)
Total Stockholders' Equity	8,181,914	8,035,673
Total Liabilities and Stockholders' Equity	$11,654,821	$10,667,779

The Income Statement

A s defined in Chapter 2, the **income statement,** or statement of earnings, summarizes transactions that produce **revenue** for a company as a result of selling a product or service and transactions that result in **expenses** for the company. By summarizing revenues and expenses, the income statement presents a picture of the overall profitability of a company's operations.

Some argue that the income statement is the most important of the standard accounting statements because net income (or, colloquially,

"the bottom line") is the basis for so many financial decisions. Management is rewarded or punished in large part depending on whether actual income is or is not equal to planned income. Stock prices rise or fall in large part because the company reports net income higher or lower than the market's expectations. And, because of the frequently immediate reaction to its announcement, net income for the year is often taken to be the essence of that year's business activity.

EXHIBIT 5.1

Did a Shearson Unit Pad Its Profits?

Shearson Lehman Hutton's Boston Co. unit said it was investigating accounting transactions that may have overstated aftertax earnings by as much as $15 million in the first three quarters of 1988. President James von Germeten and two other senior executives have taken paid leaves of absence, apparently at least for the length of the inquiry.

Representatives wouldn't comment on the focus of the review, and von Germeten couldn't be reached. But outsiders and some Shearson executives speculated that von Germeten, under pressure to produce earnings, may have inflated revenues and improperly deferred expenses at a Boston Co. unit. The company, which has grown rapidly since Shearson acquired it in 1981, is expected to earn $150 million before taxes this year—accounting for a large chunk of Shearson's profits.

Source: *Business Week* (January 9, 1989)

Because of the importance of net income, management is often under great pressure as it anticipates the preparation of the income statement for its company. Unfortunately, the normal, healthy pressure for results is sometimes translated into pressure for *reported* results, as the article in Exhibit 5.1 from the January 9, 1989, issue of *Business Week* demonstrates.

Perhaps because the evaluation of both companies and managements depends largely on the basis of reported net income has the measurement of income under generally accepted accounting principles (GAAP) been so rigorously defined. Recorded net income does not attempt to measure changes in values of the assets owned by a company, nor does it measure the company's qualitative accomplishments during the year. An accounting system could be designed to capture and report some or all of that type of information. However, faced with a trade-off between the reliability and relevance of presented information, the financial community (including company managements) has determined that a more reliable measure of income is more important than a broader, perhaps more relevant measure of income.

Financial analysts, for example, have said that they would prefer to have companies quantify only those activities that can be reasonably measured and provide supplementary information about all other activities, such as the value inherent in new products or in the appreciation of a company's assets. Analysts believe that they can evaluate those qualitative developments more objectively on their own.

Most managements have supported a narrow definition of "income" because they prefer to be measured by a more concrete, more predictable measure of performance. For example, asset appreciation is excluded from the income statement in part because it is so hard to measure, in part because it fluctuates and suggests that a company's results are unstable, and in part because it is so completely out of management's control.

Fundamentally, management and analysts know that a living, functioning company is too complex to be represented simply by a single measure of performance. PepsiCo, for example, accomplished much more in 1990 than simply earning $1.35 per share. Thorough financial analysis requires considering all of the numbers in the income statement and asking about their relationships. What is the trend of net income? Does it appear that sales prices are keeping pace with cost increases or are they falling behind? To what degree was income depressed this year as a result of resolving a long-standing problem, and therefore clearing the way for increased income in the future? The users of financial statements should also look beyond the income statement and ask about the company's cash flows and the strength of its balance sheet. Finally, to develop a complete picture of a company's results, financial statement users should go beyond the statements and investigate nonfinancial factors, including such things as a company's market share, customer loyalty, and new product development. A wise management provides footnotes and other textual commentaries describing the events of the year and encourages financial statement users to use the income statement only as a starting point for analysis.

Having said all of that, the financial community is occasionally too impatient to study a company in depth and, when pressed for immediate decisions, looks for short cuts. Net income and earnings per share are the most commonly used shorthand measures of performance, and the income statement maintains its foremost position as *the* vehicle to report a company's financial results. The objective of this chapter is to help you understand the components of the income statement, how it is prepared, and how it can be used.

THE ELEMENTS OF THE INCOME STATEMENT

Terminology and Concepts

When first introduced to the income statement, people often think it strange that such an important topic should be encumbered by so many apparently overlapping and confusing terms. Perhaps the terminology problem can be traced to the attention given to the measurement of income—many people have looked at the subject from diverse viewpoints, and their different perspectives seem to have spawned many different words to express slightly different ideas. But perhaps it is simpler than that—perhaps the terminology problem is just a reflection of the inherent complexity of the subject. In any event, the words used are sometimes difficult. Because the topic is so important, it is useful to focus initially on the terminology used in connection with the income statement and to establish a common frame of reference for our subsequent discussions.

Revenues. The senior concept in the income statement, the term **revenues** refers to a company's actual (or promised) cash inflows resulting from a completed sale of the company's products or the satisfactory delivery of its services. To help you distinguish between a company's revenues and its *cash receipts,* consider the following:

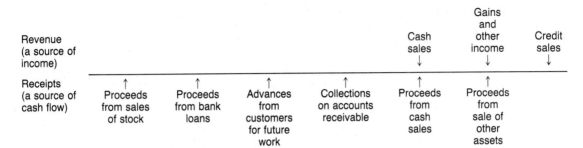

Revenue (a source of income)					Cash sales ↓	Gains and other income ↓	Credit sales ↓
Receipts (a source of cash flow)	↑ Proceeds from sales of stock	↑ Proceeds from bank loans	↑ Advances from customers for future work	↑ Collections on accounts receivable	↑ Proceeds from cash sales	↑ Proceeds from sale of other assets	

Cash inflows from the sale of stock or from borrowed money are not revenues but are financing transactions because the entity has continuing responsibilities to the providers of those funds. Cash deposits from a customer in advance of the delivery of a product or service are not revenues, nor will they be recognized as such until the "seller" completes its part of the bargain. In sum, revenues are those cash inflows (or expected cash inflows) that the company has earned and to which it is entitled to retain without qualification. Revenues are part of a company's income stream under accrual accounting. Some revenues also involve the receipt of cash, but others do not. Cash receipts, on the other hand, enter into the determination of a company's cash flows, which is the subject of Chapter 6.

Sales. A legal term, **sales** suggests that the title to property has passed from a seller to a buyer. Most legal sales transactions qualify as revenue, but the accounting world is more interested in the substance of a transaction than in its legal form. Not all legal sales qualify as revenues for accounting purposes, however, as we shall see.

Gains and losses. A **gain** is the net revenue a company earned as a result of a business transaction that is not a normal sales of products or delivery of services. For example, a company that sells an excess piece of land that it had purchased earlier for possible expansion will recognize a gain in its income statement to the extent that the sales price of the land is more than the original cost. Conversely, if the sales price is less than the land's cost, the company will recognize a **loss**.

Income. A generic term, **income** usually means revenue from sources other than product sales or from gain-producing transactions, such as interest income or rent income.

Expenses. This term encompasses all actual or expected cash outflows, or allocations from prior years' cash outflows, which cannot be justified as an addition to an asset account or a reduction in a liability. To help you distinguish between **expenses** and *cash expenditures,* consider the following chart:

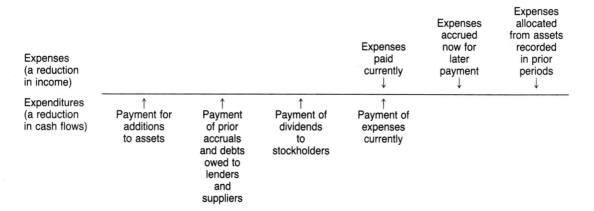

As we said in Chapter 3, an accounting entry to record an expenditure must have two sides—the credit side is, of course, a reduction in cash, but whether the debit side is an increase in an expense or an increase in an asset (or a reduction in a liability) depends on a careful analysis of the reason for the expenditure. Principal payments on debt are not expenses because they are simply the repayment of funds provided earlier by a lender. Similarly, expenditures for the reacquisition of some of the company's stock, or dividends paid to the shareholders, are not expenses because they are transactions with the owners. (Remember from our work with Blue Ridge Hardware in Chapter 3 that interest is an expense and, therefore, a deduction from revenues in determining net income, but dividends are not an expense and instead are considered to be a distribution of net income to the shareholders.) An expenditure that creates a future value for the company may be considered an asset. If no measurable value results from an expenditure, it will be treated as an expense. Most often, an asset created in one year will become an expense in a future year—as with the annual allocation to expense that we call *depreciation.*

Cost. An awkward word, **cost** is best understood when used in conjunction with an explanatory adjective such as material cost, product cost, transportation cost, and so forth. *Cost* is often a synonym for an actual or an expected expenditure, either an expense or an expenditure. You will hear businesspeople refer to the cost of a new machine, meaning the expenditure required for the asset. Or they will talk about the cost of a transaction, meaning the commission and delivery expenses incurred in connection with making a sale. The ambiguity of the term actually carries over to the traditional terminology used in preparing the income statement. For example, the biggest deduction from revenue in the measurement of net income is referred to as the **cost of goods sold,** which is the total cost of the products removed from inventory and delivered to customers as a result of sales. On the other hand, the other deductions from revenue on the income statement are **selling expenses** and **general and administrative expenses,** which are expenditures that were necessary for the operations of the business during the year.

Net income. The final financial result of all of an entity's operations for the year, net income is the difference between total revenues (including product and service revenues, net gains from other transactions, and interest and other income) and the total of the cost of goods sold and operating expenses. The phrases *net income* and *net earnings* are often used interchangeably, and the income statement itself is often referred to as the *earnings statement*. There are a number of intermediate designations on the income statement, such as **income from operations, income before extraordinary items,** and **income before taxes.** Consider again the basic accounting equation we studied in Chapter 2:

$$A = L + OE .$$

Remember that we said that all changes in owners' equity between one year and the next are reported as either transactions with stockholders or as net income and that all net income items would be presented in the income statement. Conceptually, then,

$$\text{Last year } A = L + (CS + \overline{RE})$$
$$\searrow - = \text{This year's income.}$$
$$\text{This year } A = L + (CS + \overline{RE})$$

Net income is the difference between revenues and expenses for the year, but it can also be seen as that part of the change in owners' equity from one year to the next that can be attributed to transactions with third parties—parties other than the owners.

Profit or loss. This is occasionally a synonym for income. Most often **profit** (or **loss**) is used to describe the income (or loss) effect of an *individual* transaction.

Unfortunately, some of these words are used casually in practice and are often used interchangeably. To understand what meaning is intended, it is important to consider the context in which a word is used and to focus on its meaning in that context.

Revenue and Revenue Recognition

Income statements always begin with revenue—sales, rent, services, or interest, depending on the nature of the business. Decisions about revenue recognition are among the most important accounting decisions a manager must make. For a simple transaction, for example, a retail sale of merchandise for cash, it is easy to determine which period's income statement should benefit—the revenue is recognized in the period when the merchandise and the cash are exchanged. For more complex transactions, such as the sale of a partially completed building in exchange for cash and a long-term note receivable, it is much more difficult to know whether a sale has really occurred and to decide when the revenue should be recognized. Should the sale be included in the income statement in (1) the period in which the parties agreed to the transaction, (2) the period the building is completed, or (3) the period the note is finally paid off in cash? Take a moment and think about when revenue should be recognized in the sale of a life insurance policy, the construction of a submarine for the Navy, or the provision of legal services.

To make those **revenue recognition** decisions—that is, to decide whether a company is entitled to recognize revenue from a transaction in the current period—management must answer three important questions.

Has the buyer accepted substantially all of the risk associated with the product sold (or service provided)? A seller almost always retains some risk related to an item sold as the result of its customer service policies, which provide for product return or repair under warranty. To qualify for revenue recognition at the time of an exchange, however, the transaction must burden the seller with only ordinary business risks that can be estimated with a reasonable degree of certainty. Almost every consumer product company recognizes revenue when its products are delivered to the customer, and such companies simultaneously recognize an expense and a liability for the estimated warranty services that may be required. If those future expenses cannot be estimated with reasonable accuracy—because, for example, it is a very new product and there is not sufficient experience to suggest what the rate of warranty repair will be—the sale itself should not be recorded but should be treated as deferred revenue. In such a case, the revenue would be deferred until the ultimate results from the transaction can be estimated more precisely.

Have we earned the right to the proceeds from this sale because we have completed our share of the transaction? The seller of a software package such as Lotus 1-2-3 can answer that question affirmatively when the disks and the manuals are delivered to the customer—in that case the delivery completes the earnings process because Lotus need do nothing more to the product to satisfy the customer. On the other hand, the producer of custom-designed software cannot answer that question affirmatively until the software has been programmed, debugged, and tested successfully on the customer's hardware. Only when all of that has been done can the seller say that the earnings process is complete for that transaction, and only then can the sale be recognized in the seller's income statement. In some very predictable long-term contract situations, the seller may be able to say that the earnings process is complete in phases and, as each phase is completed, recognize a pro rata share of the total expected revenue on the contract and the total expected cost of fulfilling that contract. This accounting convention is referred to as **percentage of completion** accounting (see Chapter 14 for further discussion). Aside from that unique exception, however, sale transactions can be recorded as revenue only when management can objectively affirm that the company's earnings process has been completed.

Can we estimate the collectibility of proceeds from this sale with a reasonable degree of certainty? Under accrual accounting, a seller makes no distinction between cash sales and credit sales on the assumption that collectibility of any resulting receivable is reasonably assured and that any credit loss can be estimated and recorded coincident with recognizing the revenue. However, when the terms of a transaction or the financial status of a buyer raise serious questions about the collectibility of the receivable resulting from the sale, recognition of the revenue should be deferred until that credit question is resolved. In some questionable collectibility situations, the seller may be entitled to recognize revenue on an installment basis; that is, the seller will recognize a pro rata portion of the total expected revenue and a pro rata portion of the total expected cost of the sale as the cash payments are received. The question of collectibility is similar to the

EXHIBIT 5.2

General Motors
Footnote Disclosure: Revenue Recognition Policy

Sales are generally recorded by the Corporation when products are shipped to independent dealers. Provisions for normal dealer sales incentives and returns and allowances are made at the time of sale. Costs related to special sales incentive programs are recognized as sales deductions when these incentive programs are announced.

Certain sales under long-term contracts, primarily in the defense business, are recorded using the percentage of completion (cost-to-cost) method of accounting. Under this method, sales are recorded equivalent to costs incurred plus a portion of the profit expected to be realized on the contract, determined based on the ratio of costs incurred to estimated total costs at completion. Profits expected to be realized on contracts are based on the Corporation's estimates of total sales value and cost at completion. These estimates are reviewed and revised periodically throughout the lives of the contracts, and adjustments to profits resulting from such revisions are recorded in the accounting period in which the revisions are made. Estimated losses on contracts are recorded in the period in which they are identified.

Excerpted from the footnotes to General Motors' annual report.

first question regarding risk passage—management must be able to estimate reasonably the amount of loss the company will incur as the result of a possible bad debt. If that loss cannot be reasonably estimated based on experience, the recognition of the revenue must be deferred until that uncertainty is resolved.

Most companies' sales transactions are straightforward, and the financial statement user can assume that the preceding three questions were asked and answered in a routine fashion. However, when a company's business is complex, the footnotes to the financial statements will describe the revenue recognition policies being followed. For example, in General Motors' annual report, the company explains that it records a sale when it ships a car to an independent dealer rather than when the car is sold to the ultimate buyer. GM evidently follows that practice because it is confident that the dealer has assumed all substantive risk at the time of shipment. General Motors' description of its revenue recognition policy is presented in a footnote, which is reproduced in Exhibit 5.2.

Occasionally, a management group feels pressured to produce increasing net income numbers—the pressure may be from higher-level management or shareholders who want (expect) the company to perform well—and someone in the group will provide an inadequate or incorrect answer to one of the revenue recognition questions. Unless one of the other members of the group protests, the company's income will be misstated. That misstatement may keep income high for a period and forestall a day of reckoning in the market place, but an incorrect answer to a revenue recognition question almost always becomes public, and the human and corporate cost to correct those misstatements is usually very great. Three cases involving misstatement are illustrated in Panel A of Exhibit 5.3. You will note that in several cases, more than one revenue recognition question was asked, and more than one wrong answer was given.

EXHIBIT 5.3

Panel A—Revenue Recognition Questions and Answers

Case 1

A manufacturer of designer jeans maintained a policy to sell only to customers whose accounts receivable were current (i.e., only the most recent month's purchases were unpaid). However, at the end of a quarter when sales were below budget, an order came in from a major customer whose account was 90 days past due. At the direction of the CEO, the company recorded the sale in the period when the order was received but held the delivery, setting the jeans aside in the warehouse. The customer was told that the merchandise would be shipped when the account receivable was paid up to a current status. That transaction did *not* qualify for revenue recognition in the period when the order was received because by the manufacturer's own policies, there was a question as to the collectibility of the receivable. Because of its refusal to ship the merchandise, the manufacturer retained all risk on the goods "sold." (Who bore the risk, for example, of a fire in the warehouse or of a dramatic change in styles?) Revenue could have been recognized in the period when the customer's account status was acceptable and when the product was shipped to the customer.

Case 2

A manufacturer of computer equipment maintained a policy to recognize revenue when its products were shipped, pursuant to a valid customer order. So long as the products were on the leading edge of technology, the policy was appropriate because shipment by the manufacturer was the equivalent of customer acceptance. However, there came a time when the competition caught up with the company's products, and customers frequently accepted shipment *subject to* testing against a competing product in their own installations. (Had the customer accepted all risk for the equipment?) The company didn't always win those competitions, and many of its shipments were returned. When the business circumstances changed, the company's revenue recognition policies should have changed to recognize revenue only in the period when it had formal customer acceptance in hand. Only then could the company be sure that risk had passed on the "sales" and that collectibility could be estimated with any reasonable degree of certainty.

Case 3

An operator of a computer service bureau also ran a school in which students from disadvantaged neighborhoods were trained on word processors and other computer equipment. The teaching was provided by computer-driven programmed instruction, and the students worked on their programs in labs under the direction of proctors. The tuition was paid periodically by government grants as the students completed phases of the program. The company recognized all of the revenue from the course (less a provision for dropouts) as soon as a student signed up for the course. (Had the company essentially completed its portion of the transaction?) Revenue should *not*, however, have been recognized "up front" when the students signed up because to complete the earnings process and to ensure their estimates of drop-outs, the company had to coach the students through the training and encourage their completion of the course work. Revenue should have been recognized only in the periods when the students completed phases of their course work, and the company completed that phase of its "earnings process."

Expenses and Expense Recognition

In preparing the income statement, questions concerning the recognition of both revenue and expenses must be addressed. Although the challenges to revenue recognition may be the most dramatic questions posed to management in connection with the preparation of the income statement, measurement of net income is also affected by costs and expenses. And, in fact, management must address similar questions regarding the recognition of expenses.

EXHIBIT 5.3

(continued)

Panel B—Expense Recognition Questions and Answers

Case 1

A manufacturer of high-tech products was faced with increasing competition and was forced to produce new models of its products before all of the engineering was complete. To meet production schedules, it was necessary to do significant handwork on each unit, which was very expensive. It was decided to send that handwork to a subcontractor because of its cheaper labor rate. Apparently arguing that a failure in tool design caused the production problem and required the handwork, management had the subcontractor bill the handwork as tooling. The manufacturer accounted for those tooling charges as long-term assets and depreciated them against income over five years. (Did the handwork have the potential to earn future cash flows?) The subcontractor agreed to the mislabeled billings because the job was important to their own income. Clearly, the handwork added no new value to the manufacturer and should have been accounted for as part of the current period's cost of sales. The fraud was uncovered when an employee of the subcontractor finally "blew the whistle" on the mislabeled billings.

Case 2

A cable TV company was experiencing much greater growth than it had anticipated. Management was concerned that the growth could not be sustained and so decided to "park" some of its current income for future years. To do so, it set up reserves and charged current operations with expenses for possible inventory obsolescence. (Were all costs and expenses associated with the current year's revenues appropriately recognized?) In later years, the growth did begin to slow down and eventually slowed disastrously. Rather than recognizing the effect of that slowdown in the income statement, management drew down on some of those reserves, crediting current income with a reversal of the prior years' expenses. Those machinations only postponed the inevitable, however, and the company eventually entered bankruptcy. The shareholders sued management because they were misled on the up side and on the down side of the company's business cycle. The shareholders argued that they wanted to know the naked facts about the company's earnings, period by period, and that they had been misled by managements' "smoothed" results.

Case 3

A bank had substantial loans outstanding to oil and gas producers at a time when oil prices collapsed. Looking at the collateral behind its loans, the bank realized that under current conditions, the collectibility of those loans was very questionable. Management delayed making any addition to the bank's loan-loss reserve (and taking a current period charge to bad debts expense) because it had some studies suggesting that oil prices would eventually recover. (Were the bank's judgments and estimates sufficiently conservative?) Oil prices did not recover sufficiently, however, and the bank's major borrowers eventually collapsed. When that occurred, the bank had to make a major addition to its loan-loss reserve. The shareholders sued, arguing that management knew about the probability of the loan-loss problem much earlier and had it accounted for the probable losses conservatively, the shareholders would have had a fairer picture of the bank's operations much sooner.

Have we included in our income statement all of the costs and expenses associated with the benefits we realized during the year? In an accrual accounting system, management's first obligation is to match expenses with benefits in the accounting period in which the benefits are realized. Some benefits are transaction based—the obvious example being sales to customers. In the case of sales, the **matching principle** requires that all costs and expenses connected with the sale be recognized in the same accounting period as the related revenue. Those costs and expenses to be matched against sales include some prior period costs that have been deferred as inventory until the period in which the product is sold. Those costs include the actual current period costs to make the sale, including commissions and freight, as well as certain future costs, such as the estimated cost of warranty work and estimated losses due to bad debts. Some benefits also flow to the company with the passage of time. For example, interest expense is an expense of the current period because the company has had the use of the borrowed funds for the period. Or an insurance premium paid in advance to cover three years of insurance is recorded originally as an asset; that asset is then allocated to insurance expense, one-third in each of the covered years. The application of the matching principle requires some thought—management must look carefully at the benefits realized during the year and then think carefully about all the past, current, and future expenses that might be connected with those benefits.

As we prepared these financial statements, have our judgments and estimates been appropriately conservative? The decision as to whether an expenditure is an expense of the current year or whether it is an asset and is to be allocated to expense in future years is sometimes a difficult judgment. Some managers argue that an expenditure has a clear benefit and should therefore be allocated to future years. Others argue that the benefit is tenuous and the expense should therefore be recognized immediately. For example, some argue logically that an advertising campaign is sure to build product awareness and customer loyalty. Because those benefits will produce future sales, it might be argued that some portion of those advertising expenditures should be treated as an asset and deferred into future periods so that they can be matched against the future sales the campaign generates. However, because those future benefits are uncertain (and because they are very difficult to measure), the principle of conservatism forces companies to recognize those expenditures as expenses in the period they are incurred.

In practice, management is often tempted to be optimistic. After all, an entrepreneur who has devoted three years to developing a new product must believe strongly in that product to have devoted so much time to it. It naturally follows that the entrepreneur is confident of success and therefore wants to match the costs of that product development with the expected future sales. Determining whether an entity has been appropriately conservative requires an extraordinary amount of objectivity from a responsible management group. It is also possible, however, to be too conservative. An overly conservative approach to the asset/expense decision results in an unduly pessimistic income statement for the current period and an unrealistically profitable picture in subsequent years. As in all key management decisions, the answer is balance: management must balance its application of the matching principle, which requires the deferral of some expenditures until future periods, with its application of the conservatism principle, which stipulates that the only surprises that should arise in future years should be good surprises.

Do all of our assets still have the potential to earn future cash flows equal to their current costs? Have we recorded as liabilities all of the future expenditures we are likely to have to make? In addition to our challenge of the income statement, we ought to challenge the balance sheet as well. GAAP require that an impairment of an asset and the recognition of a liability be recorded—and a charge to expense be recorded as well—when it is probable that an asset impairment/liability incurrence has occurred and when the amount of the expense can be estimated reasonably. In this context, "probable" is understood to mean that a future event confirming the impairment/incurrence is likely to occur.

Some expenses are probable because they are a natural consequence of a company's activities. For example, it is probable that a company that sells a consumer product with a warranty will incur some warranty expense, and so an estimate of that expense is recorded in the period in which the sales are recorded. Other expenses are probable because of forces outside the company and so are recorded in the period that the outside events become probable. For example, a fashion goods manufacturer knows that its inventory is subject to obsolescence and so analyzes the inventory periodically and records an adjustment to the carrying value of its unsold products when they become unfashionable and difficult to sell.

Some expenses become probable over time as the asset impairment becomes more serious or the threat of a liability becomes more tangible. For example, when a company is sued, its attorneys are not likely to be able to estimate the probability of losing the suit or the possible cost of such a loss. As time goes on, however, they form a clearer picture of the litigation and have a better estimate of winning or losing. At an intermediate stage in the litigation, they may develop an opinion as to the probability of losing the suit, but they still may be a long way from being able to estimate the cost of such a loss. Thus, the company may be required to include a footnote to its financial statements warning of the possibility of such a loss, but the expected future liability is not recognized in the balance sheet, nor is the expense recognized in the income statement. Eventually, a time will come when a settlement is under discussion or when a judgment has been reached and the dollar cost of that lawsuit loss can be reasonably estimated. At that time, the liability and the expense connected with that lawsuit are recorded in the financial statements.

As you have thought about the three revenue recognition questions and the three expense recognition questions, you have perhaps realized that the critical issues have to do with *timing*. Because the income statement presents the results of operations for a given period of time, all of the critical questions having to do with the preparation of the income statement are timing issues—when, in which period, should an event be recognized? For example, an expenditure for a new roof can be added to the cost of a building and depreciated over the building's remaining life or it can be charged to maintenance expense all at once at the time of the expenditure. Intellectually, we might debate the nature of the expenditure—whether the new roof is an addition to the building or whether it is simple maintenance—but the practical effect of that debate would be a focus on the timing of the impact of that expenditure on net income. Because an income statement measures results over one period of time, and because income statements for a period of years measure trends of income, the timing of revenue recognition and expense recognition are critical. Management must make those decisions as objectively as possible to produce the fairest measure of results of operation for the period.

To help you review your understanding of expenses and expense recognition, return to Exhibit 5.3 and consider the three cases in panel B. Note the expense questions asked and how they were answered.

REPORTING THE RESULTS OF OPERATIONS: PEPSICO, INC.

Traditionally, income statements are prepared with revenues listed first, followed by various categories of expense deductions, to arrive at a "bottom line," or net income. Income statements may be condensed for brevity, as in the case of PepsiCo, Inc. (see Exhibit 5.4), or expanded for detail, providing many useful subtotals.[1] For example, one important subtotal is the **gross margin** or **gross profit,** calculated as net sales minus the cost of sales or services. Another subtotal is **income from continuing operations,** which measures the profitability of a company's principal line of business activity.

Recurring and Nonrecurring Items

The results of a company's operations are frequently broken down into *recurring* and *nonrecurring* categories. Recurring (or continuing) results are those that can reasonably be expected to reoccur in future periods and are usually summarized as income from continuing operations. In the minds of many financial analysts, the income from recurring or continuing operations is the most important indicator of a company's performance because of its value in predicting future earnings performance. Nonrecurring income (or losses), on the other hand, refers to events or transactions that are *not* expected to recur in future periods. This category includes **unusual** and **extraordinary items** (such as loss due to fire or natural phenomena), as well as **discontinued operations.** In 1990, for example, PepsiCo reported a $13.7 million discontinued operations charge (net of related income tax benefits of $0.3 million) for expected future lawsuits and claims relating to a business sold in 1989. GAAP define (and provide explicit accounting treatment for) extraordinary items and discontinued operations. "Unusual" events are defined by financial statement users themselves, based on their reading of the footnotes, "Management's Discussion and Analysis," and other company news releases.

Discontinued Operations

When a company decides to divest itself of a division, a subsidiary, or other business segment (so long as it is a separate, major line of business), all of the final period's sales and expenses related to that segment should be netted together and reported in a single line on the next income statement with the designation **net income from discontinued operations.** That line item, for the period when the divestiture decision is made, also includes an estimate of the loss to be incurred on the sale of the division or segment (it would not include an estimated gain, of course). All prior periods' income statements presented for comparative purposes should be restated to place the results of that to-be-sold-segment in the discontinued operations line.

---

[1]Published income statements are almost always comparative, with the results for the current year and at least one, often two, prior years presented. The presentations are consistent, even if classifications in prior years have to be adjusted to conform to the current year's format.

EXHIBIT 5.4

PepsiCo, Inc.
Consolidated Statement of Income

Consolidated Statement of Income

(in millions except per share amounts)
PepsiCo, Inc. and Subsidiaries
Fifty-two weeks ended December 29, 1990 and December 30, 1989 and fifty-three weeks ended December 31, 1988

	1990	1989	1988
Net Sales	**$17,802.7**	$15,242.4	$12,533.2
Costs and Expenses			
Cost of sales	**8,609.9**	7,467.7	5,957.4
Selling, administrative and other expenses	**6,948.1**	5,841.4	5,154.3
Amortization of goodwill and other intangibles	**189.1**	150.4	72.3
Gain on joint venture stock offering	**(118.2)**	–	–
Interest expense	**688.5**	609.6	344.2
Interest income	**(182.1)**	(177.2)	(122.2)
	16,135.3	13,891.9	11,406.0
Income from Continuing Operations Before Income Taxes	**1,667.4**	1,350.5	1,127.2
Provision for Income Taxes	**576.8**	449.1	365.0
Income from Continuing Operations	**1,090.6**	901.4	762.2
Discontinued Operation Charge (net of income **tax benefit of $0.3)**	**(13.7)**	–	–
Net Income	**$ 1,076.9**	$ 901.4	$ 762.2
Income (Charge) Per Share			
Continuing operations.	**$ 1.37**	$ 1.13	$ 0.97
Discontinued operation	**(0.02)**	–	–
Net Income Per Share	**$ 1.35**	$ 1.13	$ 0.97
Average shares outstanding used to calculate income (charge) per share	**798.7**	796.0	790.4

See accompanying Notes to Consolidated Financial Statements.

For example, in 1987 PepsiCo sold a retail bakery operation, recognizing a $15.9 million before-tax loss and a $9.0 million after-tax loss. The results of the operations of the subsidiary, through the date of sale, were included in PepsiCo's consolidated income statement under the caption "Loss from discontinued operations."

Extraordinary Items

Because of the importance attached to the figure referred to as *net income*, only one figure in the income statement is so designated, and *all* items of revenue and expense are included in the determination of that amount. Certain events are so unusual and significant that they are called *extraordinary* and hence warrant separate identification on the income statement. When extraordinary items are reported on the income statement, an intermediate subtotal is designated *income before extraordinary items*. To guard against the liberal use of the extraordinary item presentation, GAAP define an extraordinary item as being both *unusual* (possessing a high degree of abnormality and clearly unrelated to the normal business of the entity) and *infrequent* (not reasonably expected to reoccur in the near future). As might be expected, extraordinary item presentation in published financial statements is rare.

As an example, the Squibb Corporation concluded that events in the Middle East had seriously impaired its business investment there and so recorded an extraordinary write-off in its 1986 income statement. The company was evidently satisfied that the combination of problems in that area met the criteria—unusual and infrequent—to qualify as extraordinary. Squibb Corporation's 1986 income statement and footnote disclosure of the extraordinary item are presented in Exhibit 5.5.

Changes in Accounting Policies

The **consistency concept** discussed in Chapter 2 requires consistent application of the same accounting methods from one year's financial statements to the next to facilitate yearly comparisons of financial results. Consistency is a goal, however, not a categorical requirement. As the economic conditions that a company faces change, sometimes changing the accounting methods and policies it has used to depict its operations is also beneficial. In some instances, accounting policy changes may also be mandated by the Financial Accounting Standards Board (FASB) or the Securities and Exchange Commission (SEC).

When a company implements an accounting policy change, the current period's income statement is prepared using that new policy as if it had been adopted on the first day of the period. In addition, the effect of that change on the beginning balance sheet accounts is included in the current year's income statement as a separate line item designated as the "cumulative effect of a change in accounting principle."

For example, during fiscal year 1988, Centex Corporation adopted SFAS No. 96 on "Accounting for Income Taxes." Centex's income statement for the year ended March 31, 1988, discloses the cumulative effect of the adoption of SFAS No. 96, which positively impacted the company's net income by $50.1 million. Exhibit 5.6 presents Centex's footnote disclosure relating to this accounting policy change.

Earnings per Share

Because the *absolute level* of net income is often difficult to compare between periods and among different companies (largely because the level of revenue-producing assets differs over time and between companies), it is accepted practice for companies to report a standardized measure of their performance. Under GAAP, net income is divided by the number of shares of a company's capital stock, and the resulting standardized measure of performance is called **earnings per share.**

Unfortunately, the rules followed in calculating earnings per share (EPS) are quite complex, and an in-depth discussion of those rules will be deferred until Chapter 14. For the moment, however, it is sufficient to understand only that **primary earnings per share** results from dividing the weighted average number of common shares outstanding during the year (together with outstanding options and warrants) into the net income for the year,

EXHIBIT 5.5

Squibb Corporation and Subsidiaries
Statement of Consolidated Income
Years Ended December 31, 1986 and 1985
(in thousands except per share figures)

	1986	1985*
Net sales	$1,784,629	$1,403,794
Costs and expenses:		
Cost of sales	566,049	476,899
Marketing and administrative	621,600	465,109
Research and development	163,045	139,887
Other (income) expenses, net	23,366	(14,674)
	1,374,060	1,067,221
Profit from operations	410,569	336,573
General corporate income (expenses):		
Interest income	48,035	40,315
Interest expense	(45,195)	(35,231)
Other, net	(35,702)	(18,210)
	(32,862)	(13,126)
Income before taxes on income	377,707	323,447
Provision for taxes on income	114,068	105,797
Income from continuing businesses	263,639	217,650
Income from discontinued businesses		
(net of taxes)	13,095	8,949
Gain on disposal of discontinued		
business (net of taxes)	187,571	—
Income before extraordinary item	464,305	226,599
Extraordinary item	(68,014)	—
Net income	$ 396,291	$ 226,599
Per share:		
Income from continuing businesses	$ 4.90	$ 4.03
Income from discontinued businesses	0.24	0.17
Gain on disposal of discontinued		
businesses	3.49	—
Income before extraordinary item	8.63	4.20
Extraordinary item	(1.26)	—
Net income	$ 7.37	$ 4.20

*Restated to reflect discontinued businesses.
See accompanying notes to consolidated financial statements.

Extraordinary Item

During 1986, the Corporation determined that its operations in certain countries were adversely affected because of an escalating war, social upheaval, the weakening economies of the oil producing nations and growing political instability. In addition, many of these governments imposed severe restrictions on pharmaceu-

EXHIBIT 5.5 continued

**Squibb Corporation and Subsidiaries
Statement of Consolidated Income
Years Ended December 31, 1986 and 1985
(in thousands except per share figures)**

tical price increases, including price freezes, prohibited the sale of certain pharmaceutical products and placed increasingly stringent controls on additional investments and the ability to obtain foreign exchange for remittances.

The Corporation identified certain assets and operations, where because of the above, it was probable that their carrying values would not be realized.

Accordingly, the Corporation wrote off such assets and operations to reflect their permanent impairment and recorded an extraordinary loss of $68,014,000 (with no tax benefit), or $1.16 a per share. Future results related to such assets or operations will be recognized based on actual cash flows.

which is available to the common shareholders (that is, the net income for the year reduced by any dividend payable to preferred shareholders). Companies that have preferred stock or debt that is convertible into common stock may also have to provide a second earnings per share measure—**fully diluted earnings per share**—to show how the possible conversion of those securities might affect the EPS calculation.

At the end of each quarter and the end of each year, publicly held companies release earnings information for the period, in total, and on a per share basis. Those quarterly reports are summarized in the financial press and then are used on an ongoing basis in calculating various stock market indicators, such as the price/earnings multiple (or P/E ratio) reported in the daily stock price tables. **Price/earnings multiples** are frequently used as a shorthand test of a company's stock price. An analyst might say, for example: "With a P/E multiple of 12, in an industry where the average multiple is 15, Company X's common stock appears to be a good buy." In addition, some analysts forecast a

EXHIBIT 5.6

**Centex Corporation
Footnote Disclosure: Accounting Policy Change**

Income Taxes

During fiscal 1988, the company adopted SFAS No. 96, "Accounting for Income Taxes," which, among other things, requires companies to currently recognize the effect of changes in statutory tax rates on temporary differences for which deferred income taxes were previously provided. Accordingly, the company recognized a gain in fiscal 1988 of $50.1 million as the cumulative effect of this change in accounting for income taxes, representing the reduction in the deferred tax liability at April 1, 1987, resulting from the statutory decrease in corporate tax rates from 46 percent to 34

percent. Prior to adoption of SFAS No. 96, the provision for income tax was based on transactions included in the determination of pretax accounting income with appropriate provisions for deferred income taxes based on the statutory rates in effect at the time the temporary differences arose. Under SFAS No. 96, deferred tax liabilities and related expense accounts will be adjusted each year for changes in statutory tax rates. The effect of this change in accounting principles for the year ended March 31, 1988, was not significant.

company's earnings for the forthcoming year and, using the current P/E multiple, then forecast next year's expected stock price.

During 1990, for example, PepsiCo's common stock traded on the New York Stock Exchange at a P/E multiple of 20. If earnings per share had been 1.90, what price might PepsiCo's stock have traded at? (Answer: $38).

ANALYZING THE INCOME STATEMENT

The principal focus of the income statement is the current operations of a company, and thus the overall **profitability** of those operations. An analysis of profitability may occur in two ways. First, the absolute level of revenues, gross margin, or net income, for example, can be investigated over time (i.e., a trend analysis). Second, a series of profitability ratios can be calculated.

As noted in Chapter 4, trend analysis is frequently aided by the use of common-size financial statements. A common-size income statement expresses all statement items as a percentage of gross revenues (see Exhibit 5.7).

Two widely used profitability ratios are the rate of return on total assets and the rate of return on owners' equity. The **return on total assets** (ROA) measures a company's overall performance or effectiveness in using its available resources to generate income. The ROA is also sometimes called the *return on investment* (ROI) and is calculated as

$$\text{Return on assets} = \frac{\text{Net income after tax}}{\text{Average total assets}}.$$

Because net income is generated throughout an accounting period, it would be inappropriate to measure the ROA using either the total assets at the beginning or the end of the period. Both total asset figures represent only a single point in time and may be skewed (either high or low). Hence, in an effort to obtain an assessment of the level of assets available throughout the entire accounting period, an average of the total assets is used in the ROA denominator.

Technically, ROA should be computed using average "operating assets" and "operating" income. In most but not all situations, the operating numbers are the same as the totals reported in the financial statements. For example, in the PepsiCo case for 1990, we should base our calculation of ROA using income before discontinued operations, and we should remove from the average assets any asset measures attributable to those discontinued operations that might still be included in the beginning and ending asset balances. We do not have the data to adjust PepsiCo's asset balances, so we leave the effect of the discontinued operations in the income measure *and* in the asset measure. When making an ROA calculation and comparing one company's results against another, or one year's results against an array of prior years, it is important to be sure that the income and asset measures are determined consistently.

In general, the higher the ROA, the more profitable a company is thought to be. Since there is no ideal measure of ROA, it is important to compare the ROA to that of prior periods, to other competitor companies, and to industry averages.

The **return on owners' equity** (ROE) also measures a company's performance in using its assets to generate income; however, unlike the ROA, this measure relates a company's profitability only to the resources provided by its owners. The ROE is calculated as follows[2]:

$$\text{Return on equity} = \frac{\text{Net income after tax}}{\text{Average owners' equity}}.$$

In general, the higher the ROE, the more profitable a company is thought to be.

Another useful set of profitability indicators is called the *profit margin ratios*. These ratios measure the relative profitability of a company's revenues. For example, the **gross profit margin ratio** is computed as:

$$\text{Gross profit margin} = \frac{(\text{Revenues} - \text{Cost of goods sold})}{\text{Net sales}}.$$

The gross profit margin ratio indicates the percentage of each dollar of revenue that is realized as gross profit after deducting the cost of goods or services sold. It represents the profit available to cover a company's other operating expenses, such as selling and administrative expenses, interest, and taxes. It provides an indicator of a company's pricing policies.

The most popular margin ratio is the *net profit margin ratio* or, as it is frequently referred to, the **return on sales** (ROS):

$$\text{Return on sales} = \frac{\text{Net Income after tax}}{\text{Net sales}}.$$

The ROS indicates the percentage of each dollar of sales revenue that is earned as net income and that may be retained in the company to support future operations or that may be paid to shareholders in the form of a dividend. Again, it is an indicator of a company's pricing policies and practices as well as its ability to control its ongoing expenses.

It is instructive to note that ROS is one of the component ratios that form the ROA ratio:

$$\text{Return on assets} = \text{ROS} \times \text{Asset turnover ratio}.$$

$$= \frac{\text{Net income after tax}}{\text{Net sales}} \times \frac{\text{Net sales}}{\text{Average total assets}}.$$

$$= \frac{\text{Net income after tax}}{\text{Average total assets}}.$$

---

[2]If a company has both common and preferred stock outstanding, the ROE is usually calculated only for the common stock, as follows:

$$\text{Return on common equity} = \frac{(\text{Net income after tax} - \text{Preferred stock dividends})}{\text{Average common shareholders' equity}}.$$

The common shareholders' equity includes the following accounts: Common Stock at Par (or Stated) Value, Paid-in Capital in Excess of Par (or Stated) Value, Retained Earnings, and Treasury Stock.

The asset turnover ratio is a measure of the effectiveness of a company's utilization of available resources to generate sales; it was discussed in Chapter 4.

It is noteworthy that the three profitability indicators, ROA, ROE, and ROS, are closely linked to the financial characteristic of **leverage,** as discussed in Chapter 4. So long as the cost of additional debt does not exceed the return generated from the borrowed assets, each of the profitability indicators should be enhanced. However, as increasing amounts of debt are assumed by a company, these profitability ratios, particularly the ROE, are threatened. We will have more to say about this in Chapter 11.

Using PepsiCo's consolidated statement of income (see Exhibit 5.4), we can calculate these profitability ratios, and they are as follows:

	1990	**1989**
Return on assets	6.7%	6.9%
Return on equity	24.5%	25.6%
Gross profit margin	51.6%	51.0%
Return on sales	6.0%	5.9%

As compared to 1989, PepsiCo's profitability in 1990 remained relatively stable. Although the return on assets and return on sales were down slightly (probably reflecting PepsiCo's significant growth by acquisition), the gross profit margin and the return on sales were up marginally. As compared to Coca-Cola in 1990, which achieved a gross profit margin of 59.0 percent and a return on sales of 13.5 percent, PepsiCo's results in that year were competitive, although not nearly so strong.

Risk and Pro Forma Financial Statements

The analysis of profitability is not an end in itself but is often undertaken as part of a broader assessment of the relative riskiness of a company. In the case of a lending institution evaluating the desirability of lending funds to a company, the principal focus is on default risk, whereas in the case of an investment or brokerage house evaluating the desirability of investing funds in a company, the principal focus is on operational risk.

Default risk refers to the probability that a company will be unable to meet its short-term or long-term obligations. The liquidity and solvency ratios discussed in Chapter 4 provide a good assessment of the probability of default risk.[3] **Operational risk,** on the other hand, refers to the probability that a company will experience unforeseen or unexpected events or factors that consequently will reduce or impair its revenue and earnings streams (and implicitly its cash flow stream). These factors or events may be economy wide (e.g., general inflation, recession, or high interest rates), industry wide (e.g., increased competition, changes in technology, or raw material/labor constraints), or firm specific (e.g., labor disputes, equipment failure, or product safety considerations).

---

[3]It is important to note that the liquidity and solvency ratios are not independent of the profitability ratios. Indeed, high volatility in current profitability, combined with low liquidity and solvency, may suggest a high degree of default risk.

Assessing the operational riskiness of a company involves, in part, developing an understanding of a company's marketplace, its competition, its sensitivity to inflation and interest rate changes, and its ability to respond to new opportunities. By analyzing the resiliency of past operations to prior economic changes, it is possible to formulate assessments as to how well (or poorly) current and future operations might respond to future economic changes and opportunities.

The ability to assess operational (and default) risk is tied in part to the ability to generate insightful pro forma financial statements. As discussed in Chapter 4, **pro forma financial statements** are projected or forecasted financial statements. These forecasts are crucial to lending and investment decisions, for example, because the repayment of debt and the payment of future dividends depend substantially on a company's future profitability.

To illustrate the development of a pro forma income statement, we return to our example of the Blue Ridge Hardware Co. In Chapter 3, we used the transactions of the Blue Ridge Hardware Co. as a basis to prepare financial statements after one year of operations (see Exhibits 3.4, 3.6, and 3.8). The income statement of Blue Ridge Hardware as of March 31, 1991, is reproduced in Exhibit 5.7.

As a starting point for preparing a pro forma income statement, it is useful to understand the relationship between the various income statement accounts. One way to do this is to prepare a common-size income statement. Exhibit 5.7 presents such a

EXHIBIT 5.7

Blue Ridge Hardware Co.
Income Statement
For the Year Ended March 31, 1991

		Income Statement	Common-Size Statement
Net revenues		$ 74,500	100%
Less: Cost of merchandise sold		(44,700)	60.0
Gross margin		29,800	
Less: Operating expenses			
Rent expense	$ 3,600		4.8
Wage expense	15,300		20.5
Utilities expense	650		0.9
Depreciation expense	1,000		1.3
		(20,550)	
Income from operations		9,250	
Less: Interest expense		(900)	1.2
Income before taxes		8,350	
Less: Federal and state			
income taxes		(2,900)	3.9
Net income		$ 5,450	7.3

statement for Blue Ridge Hardware for the first year of operations. If multiple periods of data are available, it is best to prepare common-size statements for several periods to determine whether the percentage relationships vary significantly between periods or at various levels of activity.

Since a common-size income statement relates all other account balances to the revenue figure, the most important projection is that of revenues. For illustrative purposes, let us assume that Blue Ridge Hardware is considering an advertising campaign as a means to generate additional future sales. On the basis of discussions with a local advertising agency, Blue Ridge anticipates an expenditure of $2,000 for print advertising to produce a 15 percent growth in sales.

To service the expected increase in customer demand, an additional investment in inventories will be required. However, the cost of merchandise is not expected to increase linearly with sales because volume purchase discounts will be available to lower the overall cost. Thus, the cost of merchandise sold is projected to decline to 57 percent of revenues from the 1991 level of 60 percent. All other outlays for operating expenses are expected to remain fixed in amount since no new employees or store operating hours will be required to handle the expected growth in sales. Further, income taxes are anticipated to remain at 35 percent of pretax income (i.e., $2,900/$8,350).

EXHIBIT 5.8

Blue Ridge Hardware Co.
Pro Forma Income Statement*
For the Year Ended March 31, 1992

Net revenues		$85,675
Less: Cost of merchandise sold		(48,835)
Gross margin		$36,840
Less: Operating expenses		
Rent expense	$ 3,600	
Wage expense	15,300	
Utilities expense	650	
Depreciation expense	1,000	
Advertising expense	2,000	
		(22,550)
Income from operations		14,290
Less: Interest expense		(720)
Income before taxes		13,570
Less: Federal and state income taxes		(4,750)
Net income		$ 8,820

*Assumptions
1. Revenues will increase by 15 percent in response to an advertising campaign costing $2,000.
2. Because of volume purchase discounts, the cost of merchandise sold as a percentage of revenues will decline by 3 percent.
3. All other operating expenses will remain fixed.
4. Income taxes will average 35 percent of pretax income.

Using these assumptions, it is possible to prepare a pro forma income statement for 1992 to assess the relative impact of the advertising campaign on Blue Ridge Hardware's profitability. Exhibit 5.8 presents a pro forma income statement for the year ended March 31, 1992, which reveals that net income after tax is projected to grow to $8,820, or an increase of $3,370. Thus, if our assumptions are reasonable, it is clear that the profitability of the company is substantially enhanced by the advertising campaign investment. Since advertising may help develop long-term customers, the effects may also have a carryover effect beyond 1992.

Just as the preparation of a pro forma income statement was used to evaluate the desirability of undertaking an advertising campaign, pro forma statements may also be used to evaluate the desirability of lending money to Blue Ridge Hardware or of investing in it. In Chapter 6, we will see how the pro forma income statement of Blue Ridge Hardware can be used to construct a pro forma statement of cash flows and a pro forma balance sheet.

SUMMARY

The income statement summarizes transactions that produce revenue for a company as a result of selling a product or service and transactions that result in expenses. It measures the overall profitability of operations and reports the profitability in a number of ways: gross margin, income from continuing operations, net income, and earnings per share.

The measurement of profitability is guided by a number of revenue and expense recognition conventions, principally the accrual concept, the allocation concept, and the matching concept. Evaluating the profitability of operations may be accomplished through a trend analysis of net income or through the calculation of various profitability ratios such as the ROA, ROE, or ROS. It is important to consider pro forma income statements, which can be prepared using reasonable and realistic assumptions of future period activities.

NEW CONCEPTS AND TERMS

Default risk (p. 211)
Discontinued operations (p. 204)
Earnings per share (p. 208)
Extraordinary item (p. 204)
Fully diluted earnings per share (p. 208)
Gain (p. 195)
Gross margin (p. 204)
Gross profit (p. 204)
Gross profit margin ratio (p. 210)
Income from continuing operations (p. 204)
Net income before extraordinary items
     (p. 197)

Net income from discontinued operations
  (p. 204)
Operational risk (p. 211)
Percentage of completion (p. 198)
Primary earnings per share (p. 208)
Price/earnings multiples (p. 208)
Return on owners' equity (p. 209)
Return on sales (p. 210)
Return on total assets (p. 209)
Sales (p. 195)
Unusual item (p. 204)

ISSUES FOR DISCUSSION

D5.1 Two accountants, arguing an income statement presentation issue, summarize the debate with these points:

Point: The income statement should report *only* the results of transactions directly related to the current period's operations of a company.

Counter-point: The income statement should report *all* transactions affecting the owners' interest in a company, except those involving dividends and capital stock.

Evaluate these two perspectives—which one do you agree with, and why? Which of the following transactions do you feel should (or should not) be reported in a company's current income statement:

1. A gain on the sale of a subsidiary.
2. An unexpected loss due to a fire in the company warehouse.
3. The damages award received as settlement of a lawsuit.
4. A correction to the company's income statement from two years before.
5. Winning the grand prize of $40 million in the New York state lottery—the CEO purchased the ticket using company funds.

D5.2 It has frequently been noted that financial reporting can either adopt a balance sheet focus or an income statement focus, but that it is impossible to do both. The gist of such a statement is that if accounting focuses on the measurement of assets and liabilities, revenues and expenses become a function of how assets and liabilities are reported. Said another way, the basic equation must balance (A = L + OE) and if two of the three factors (A and L) are prescribed, the third (OE) is whatever it takes to balance the equation. On the other hand, if the measurement of revenues and expenses is accounting's foremost concern (OE), then the assets and liabilities reported on a balance sheet are determined by those revenue and expense measurements.

Comment on the juxtaposition of these two views.

D5.3 H.J. Heinz includes the following paragraph in its accounting policies footnote. Comment on each of the statements here (you may ignore the sentence that describes the tax policy) from the standpoint of a Heinz plant manager. What factors would the manager consider in the application of these policies, and how might those considerations affect the Heinz income statement?

> *Property, Plant and Equipment:* Land, buildings and equipment are recorded at cost. For financial reporting purposes, depreciation is provided on the straight-line method over the estimated useful lives of the assets. Accelerated depreciation methods are generally used for income tax purposes. Expenditures for new facilities and improvements which substantially extend the capacity or useful life of an asset are capitalized. Ordinary repairs and maintenance are expensed as incurred. When property is retired or otherwise disposed, the cost and related depreciation are removed from the accounts and any related gains or losses are included in income.

D5.4 Flowers Industries bakes and distributes bread and other bakery products throughout the South. In 1986, the company began a program of selling its distribution routes to its salespeople in an effort to give those people an increased stake in the business and provide them with an incentive to develop the territory more fully. Flowers includes the following footnote in its financial statements for 1988. Do you agree with Flowers' policy? Why or why not?

Long-Term Notes Receivable and Deferred Income

The Company has sold a portion of its routes to independent distributors. The income from these sales is recognized as the cash payments are received.

The amounts due under the notes receivable from the distributors of $21,595,000 and $14,448,000 have also been included in deferred income at July 2, 1988 and June 27, 1987, respectively. At July 2, 1988 and June 27, 1987, $20,112,000 and $13,476,000, respectively, are included in other long-term assets.

D5.5 General Motors' income statement for 1990 included a special charge of $3.3 billion, which it described as a special provision for scheduled plant closings and other restructurings. The charge is described in Note 7, as follows:

NOTE 7. Special Provision for Scheduled Plant Closings and Other Restructurings

In 1990, a special restructuring charge of $3,314.0 million was included in the results of operations to provide for the closing of four previously idled U.S. assembly plants, as well as provide for other North American manufacturing and warehouse operations which will be consolidated or cease operating over the next three years. As a result, consolidated net loss was increased by $2,087.8 million or $3.47 per share of $1-2/3 par value common stock.

A similar provision was made in 1986 in the amount of $1,287.6 million for costs associated with scheduled plant closings in the U.S. and other restructurings of foreign operations that were reasonably estimable at the time.

During 1990, 1989, and 1988, a net of $1,731.7 million, $148.1 million, and $218.6 million, respectively, was charged against these reserves.

Discuss the appropriateness of charging the 1990 income with this expense. Is it an appropriate charge against 1990, as opposed to 1991 or 1992? Why or why not? Why should it not be reallocated back to 1989 or prior years?

D5.6 The Boston Celtics Limited Partnership presents the following footnote in their annual report:

Revenue and Expense Recognition: Revenues and expenses are recognized when revenues and the related costs are earned or incurred. Ticket sales and television and radio broadcasting fees generally are recorded as revenues at the time the game to which such proceeds relate is played. Team expenses, principally player and coaches' salaries, related fringe benefits and insurance, and game and playoff expenses, principally National Basketball Association attendance assessments, arena rentals and travel, are recorded as expense on the same basis. Accordingly, advance ticket sales and advance payments on television and radio broadcasting contracts and payments for team and game expenses not earned or incurred are recorded as deferred game revenues and deferred game expenses, respectively, and amortized ratably as regular season games are played. General and administrative and selling and promotional expenses are charged to operations as incurred.

Comment on the reasoning underlying such policies.

D5.7 Grumman Corp. produces jet fighters for the U.S. Navy, and has other defense department contracts for production and research projects. The company describes its revenue recognition policies in the following footnote:

Revenue recognition

Sales under fixed-price production contracts are recorded at the time of delivery. Sales, including fees earned, under cost-reimbursement and research, development, test, and evaluation contracts are recorded as costs are incurred.

Certain contracts contain cost and/or performance incentives. Such incentives are included in sales at the time actual performance can be related to the target and the earned amount can be reasonably determined. Accordingly, earnings recorded in one period may include adjustments related to sales recorded in a prior period. Losses on contracts are recorded when they become known.

Comment on the reasoning underlying those policies.

D5.8 Immediately following PepsiCo's income statement presented in the 1990 Annual Report is a report titled "Management Analysis—Results of Operations" (see page 15 in Chapter 1). In that analysis a number of improvements in performance are cited, as the company compares 1990, 1989, and 1988. Interpret these improvements from the standpoint of a prospective investor. Do you believe the improvements noted in net sales, expenses, income before taxes, and provisions for taxes represent operating improvement and efficiencies as a result of outside circumstances, the impact of one-time events, or the result of creative accounting? Come to a conclusion on the individual factors cited by the company, and come to a conclusion regarding the improved operating results overall. Explain your conclusions.

D5.9 Goodyear Tire and Rubber Company has reported "unusual items" in its income statements in each of the last three years. The Income statement form the 1990 annual report to stockholders is as follows. Also presented is the company's footnote which explains those unusual items.

	Year Ended December 31,		
(Dollars in millions, except per share)	1990	1989	1988
Net Sales	$11,272.5	$10,869.3	$10,810.4
Other Income	180.6	216.1	217.6
	11,453.1	11,085.4	11,028.0
Cost and Expenses:			
Cost of goods sold	8,805.1	8,234.7	8,291.7
Selling, administrative and general expense	1,999.6	1,863.7	1,745.1
Interest expense	328.2	255.3	231.8
Unusual items	103.6	109.7	78.8
Other expenses	74.5	44.6	37.0
Foreign currency exchange	72.1	87.9	87.6
Minority interest in net income of subsidiaries	14.1	18.6	19.2
	11,397.2	10,614.5	10,490.5
Income before Income Taxes and Extraordinary Item	55.9	470.9	537.5
United States and Foreign Taxes on Income	94.2	281.5	187.4
Income (loss) before Extraordinary Item	(38.3)	189.4	350.1
Extraordinary Item—Tax Benefit of Loss Carryovers	—	17.4	—
Net Income (loss)	$ (38.3)	$ 206.8	$ 350.1

Comment on the designation of these items as "unusual" items, qualifying for separate identification in the income statement. Why are they not unusual items? Why are they not a normal part of the flow of transactions, which are included in "costs and expenses"?

Notes to Financial Statements
The Goodyear Tire & Rubber Company and Subsidiaries
(in millions)

	1990	1989	1988
Unusual Items			
A summary of the pretax unusual charges follows:			
Restructuring	$ 66.4	$ 18.4	$27.9
Plant closure and sale of facilities	15.0	43.0	—
Discontinued segment—			
Environmental cleanup costs	22.2	—	—
Sale of assets	—	48.3	—
Pension settlement/asset reversion	—	—	50.9
	$103.6	$109.7	$78.8

1990

The restructuring of United States tire operations during the second quarter resulted in a charge of $20.0 million ($12.2 million after tax) from the reduction of personnel in various sales, distribution and other operations and other associated costs. The Company also incurred restructuring charges of $46.4 million ($38.2 million after tax) during the third quarter. The costs resulted from: a realignment of European tire marketing, distribution and production operations, which will eliminate approximately 1,180 jobs by mid-1992; the phaseout of medium and heavy truck tire production at the Valleyfield, Quebec, Canada, plant; and the rationalization of certain tire and related production operations in Canada and Argentina.

The decision to close the New Bedford, Massachusetts, roofing systems plant resulted in a charge of $15.0 million ($9.2 million after tax) during the second quarter for personnel reduction and other plant closure costs.

The Company recorded a charge of $22.2 million ($13.5 million after tax) during the third quarter for environmental cleanup costs associated with a business segment discontinued in 1986.

1989

The Company accrued expenses of $18.4 million ($10.9 million after tax) for the reduction of bias-ply truck tire capacity at the Gadsden, Alabama, plant and from the realignment of the Canadian operations.

The Company sold its South African tire and general products manufacturing subsidiary for $41.0 million. A loss of $43.0 million ($52.0 million after tax) was recorded in the second quarter, the majority of which was due to the recognition of the decreased value of the Company's assets in South Africa arising from the devaluation of the South African Rand during the past several years.

The Company's oil transportation subsidiary, All American Pipeline Company, sold about 435 miles of unused 30-inch pipe for $70.0 million in the second quarter. A loss of $48.3 million ($43.0 million after tax) was recorded on the sale.

1988

The Company, in an effort to reduce operating expenses, consolidated tasks and eliminated duplicate job responsibilities at a cost of $27.9 million ($17.1 million after tax) in the fourth quarter.

The Company settled its pension liability for the principal domestic salary plan for all benefits accrued to June 30, 1988, through the purchase of annuity contracts from major insurance companies during the fourth quarter. A loss of $10.9 million was recorded. In a related transaction excess assets of $400.0 million before taxes were reverted to the Company. Excise tax of $40.0 million was incurred on the asset reversion making the total charge to Unusual Items $50.9 million. The combined effect of these transactions, together with the reversal of deferred tax recorded on the 1986 pension settlement, resulted in an after tax charge of $9.7 million in 1988. Proceeds to the Company amounted to $210.0 million after deducting excise tax and federal and state income taxes. For further information regarding the tax effects on the transaction, see the note to the financial statements entitled Income Taxes.

D5.10 Pick up a current copy of *The Wall Street Journal* and refer to the page which gives you the statistics on the stocks which make up the Dow Jones Industrial Average. Pick two very different companies from that group of 30 and look up their stock trading data for that day from the table "New York Stock Exchange Composite Transactions." Explain why those two companies might have different price/earnings ratios. (You should review the annual reports to stockholders for your two companies, and you may have to review other business periodicals to get a fuller understanding of the factors affecting the companies.)

PROBLEMS

P5.1 Income statement preparation. On July 1, 1992, Tom and Sam Parks formed a window-washing business. The following information pertains to their first month's operations:

Total cash received	$2,400
Cash paid out:	
Purchased supplies	90
Purchased used truck	800
Paid employees	550
Paid July rent for office space	150

Although the Parks brothers expected most of their work to come from single engagements, they did enter into two contracts early in July. The first contract, with Budget Shoe Store, specified that Tom and Sam were to wash Shoe Store's windows at a rate of $40 per month for a period of one year. In partial return for that favorable price, Budget Shoe Store paid the Parks brothers six-months' cash in advance at the time of the contract. The second contract was with Economy Drugs. This contract was also for a one-year period and called for Tom and Sam to wash the drugstore's windows at a rate of $50 per month to be paid on the 10th of the month after the services are performed. The $50 payment for July services was subsequently received on August 10. There were no supplies on hand as of July 1 and supplies on hand at July 31 had cost $40. The brothers' truck was estimated to have a useful life of 2.5 years.

Required:

Prepare an income statement for the Parks brothers for the month of July.

P5.2 Transaction analysis: Cash versus accrual basis. The Midlands Corporation began the year with $10,000 cash, some other assets, some vendor payables, and $8,000 in owners' equity. During this current year, Midlands entered into a number of transactions, including the following:

Transaction	Income Statement		Cash Balance	
x. Purchased land for $5,000 cash.	No Effect	_____	Decrease	5,000
a. Paid salaries of $700.	_____	_____	_____	_____
b. Purchased a $23,000 machine, giving a $23,000 note with an interest rate of 12%.	_____	_____	_____	_____
c. Paid dividends of $2,500.	_____	_____	_____	_____
d. Paid rent of $600.	_____	_____	_____	_____
e. Sold additional capital stock for $8,000 cash.	_____	_____	_____	_____
f. Used $300 worth of supplies previously purchased.	_____	_____	_____	_____

Transaction	Income Statement		Cash Balance	
g. Recorded depreciation expense of $200.	_____	_____	_____	_____
h. Collected a $75 account receivable.	_____	_____	_____	_____

Required:

Determine the effect of each of the preceding transactions on a company's income statement and its cash balance. Under the column headed Income Statement, indicate whether the transaction results in a revenue or an expense and the dollar amount involved. Under the Cash Balance column, indicate whether the cash balance would increase or decrease and indicate the dollar amount involved. If a transaction has no effect on the income statement or the cash balance, indicate this in the appropriate column.

P5.3 Sales returns. In December 1990, Barton Industries, Inc., disclosed that it would restate its results for the third quarter because a sale it had booked was returned during the fourth quarter. According to a news release by the maker of oil field equipment, the restatement would reduce its third-quarter revenues from $8.1 million to $7.1 million, and its net income from $1.0 million to $400,000.

Required:

Determine the accounting entries required for the third quarter restatement. Ignore any income taxes.

P5.4 Income measurement. At the beginning of 1991, M. Carlson, the owner and operator of a large agricultural concern, had no inventories on hand. During 1991, however, his company produced 80,000 bushels of corn, 100,000 bushels of soybeans, and 160,000 bushels of barley. Upon completion of the harvest, Carlson sold one-half of each of his crops at the following prices: corn, $4.50 per bushel; soybeans, $3.25 per bushel; and barley, $2 per bushel. At year-end, the remaining half of Carlson's crop was unsold.

To operate the company, Carlson incurred costs during 1991 of $370,000, including $100,000 in depreciation on his buildings and equipment. Moreover, Carlson estimates that his selling and delivery costs on the crops average $0.42 per bushel; these costs are included in his total operating costs given above. Finally, the commodities price quotations reported in *The Wall Street Journal* at year-end revealed that the current market price per bushel for each of the crops was as follows: corn, $5 per bushel; soybeans, $3.47 per bushel; and barley, $2.20 per bushel.

Presented following is the balance sheet for M. Carlson, Inc., as of January 1, 1991:

M. Carlson, Inc.
Balance sheet
As of January 1, 1991

Assets			Liabilities and Equity	
Cash		$ 75,000	Liabilities	$ -0-
Land		300,000	Owners' equity:	
Buildings and equipment	$750,000		Capital stock	550,000
			Retained earnings	225,000
Less: Accumulated				
depreciation	(350,000)	400,000		
Total assets		$775,000	Total equities	$775,000

Required:

Prepare an income statement and balance sheet for the company as of December 31, 1991. Prepare a list of the accounting policy decisions that you made in arriving at these statements.

P5.5 Income statement concepts. Consider these juxtapositions, each of which suggest some important income statement ideas:

(a) Gain versus income

(b) Loss versus expense

(c) Realized versus recognized

(d) Deferred versus prepaid

Required:

Prepare a commentary on each of the above juxtapositions, explaining how the contrasted items are alike and how they are different, and how each of them might be considered in the presentation of the income statement.

P5.6 More income statement concepts. Consider the following juxtapositions, each of which suggest some important income statement decisions:

(a) Asset versus expense

(b) Earned versus unearned

(c) Current period charge versus future period charge

(d) Current period charge versus prior period charge

(e) Operating items versus extraordinary items

Required:

Prepare a commentary on each of the above juxtapositions, explaining how the contrasted items are alike and how they are different, and the factors which might require them to be treated differently—in the context of the income statement.

P5.7 Asset or expense.   The King Corporation reported net income of $5,000,000 in 1990, and it appears that 1991 will be much the same. During 1991 the company made the following expenditures:

1. $125,000 was spent to resurface the employee parking lot. That resurfacing has to be done every five years or so.

2. $250,000 was spent to upgrade the air cleaning system in the paint department. The system as it was had worked satisfactorily, but the U.S. Department of Labor had recently promulgated new rules (effective three years from today) which would have required the changes the company made voluntarily.

3. $450,000 was paid to an architect for the design of a new research center. The center was the dream of the prior CEO, but has now been shelved because the new officers are more cautious about the future.

4. $300,000 has been spent this year on the development of a new computer-based order entry system. The idea behind the new system is that salespeople in the field will be able to enter orders into the system directly, electronically, so that they can be shipped the very next day. Everyone hopes that the new system will enhance customer service and help stop a sales slide. The system appears to be on track, but another $200,000 will have to be spent before it can be demonstrated that it will work as planned.

5. The company's Texas plant was shut down for about three months this year because of the slow economy. The company struggled to find a way to keep their employees busy, so they could keep as many of them as possible. The employees agreed to accept half pay, and the company found maintenance work and training for them. At the end of the period, about 85 percent of the work force was still on the roll, and when the company went back to work, production resumed without a hitch. The maintenance work done by the employees in this time cost about $500,000; the training time cost the company another $400,000.

Required:

Prepare a one-paragraph memo discussing each of the above expenditures, discussing whether the other side of the entry should be an addition to an asset or an expense charge. Explain your position.

P5.8 Revenue recognition.   Consider the following unique company situations:

1. The American Health Club sells lifetime memberships, costing $1,200, which allow the member unlimited use of any of the company's 100 facilities around the country. The initiation fee may be paid in 24 monthly installments, with a 1 percent interest charge on the unpaid balance.

2. Universal Motors has always offered a limited, 24-month warranty program on its cars, but to counter the incredible competition in the industry, the company has come to the conclusion that they must do something more. With that in mind, they have developed a new program: for a $500 payment at the time of purchase, the customer can buy a five-year warranty which will cover replacement of almost all parts and labor. The purchased warranty expires at the end of five years or when the customer sells the car, whichever occurs first.

3. Community Promotions Corporation sells coupon books which give the holder a 10 percent discount (up to $10) from any of the 25 participating merchants. The buyer of the coupon book pays $50 for the book, but obviously can realize up to $250 in benefits. Community Promotions convinces the merchants to participate in the program at no cost, arguing that they will build traffic and have the opportunity for repeat businesses from the coupon book holders.

4. Household Furnishings Emporium sells appliances and furniture with installment contracts. Those contracts usually carry interest rates of 16 percent or more. When the company has accumulated $200,000 of contracts with a year or more to go, they sell the contracts to a finance company on a non-recourse basis. The company continues to service the contracts and is paid a service fee which is based on the cash they collect and turn over to the finance company. If a contract goes bad, Household turns it over to a collection agency and has no further responsibility for it. In January the company sold contracts with a face value of $250,000 and received $275,000 in cash.

5. Neighborhood News Inc. prints and distributes a weekly newspaper throughout the county. Local merchants order a certain number of the papers each week, and pay for them on delivery. The company always takes back any unsold papers, however, and gives the merchant credit.

Required:

For each of the above situations, prepare a short paper describing the revenue recognition policy the company ought to follow, and explaining the basis for your recommendation.

P5.9 Income statement classification. Net income for The Multi Corporation, for the year ended December 31, 1991, is $10,000,000. There is some debate, however, about the presentation of the income statement, and the classification of certain events which could be considered material to that net income. In thinking about these items, it will be important to know that Multi manufactures and distributes a line of automobile aftermarket accessories, which are sold through Sears and other major retail outlets. The events which follow all occurred, or were recognized during the year.

1. A fire destroyed a warehouse in New Jersey. The loss was $2,500,000, half of which was covered by insurance.

2. The company completed a defense contract which produced a $1,250,000 profit. The contract used excess capacity in the plant, and the gross margin went directly to the bottom line. The company hopes to bid on similar contracts, but is not sure that there will be a repeat opportunity.

3. An order of seat covers for an East-Coast auto parts chain was found to be defective and was returned and scrapped. The loss on the order was $250,000, and the company gave the customer an additional discount of $500,000 on future orders in the hopes of protecting the relationship.

4. The company spent $1,000,000 on the development of a catalog, which is to be used to sell parts by direct mail. The catalog probably has a useful life of 24 months. In the first three months of the mail order operations, sales exceeded expectations substantially.

5. To insure its source of merchandise, the company has made investments in several Pacific Rim supplier companies. An opportunity came to sell one of those investments at a substantial gain. The company agreed to the sale, received $4,000,000 in cash, realized a $2,000,000 gain, and invested the entire proceeds in a new supplier just beginning business in Mexico.

6. A loan to a manufacturer of car radios was written off this year. In fact, it had been clear for some time that the $1,500,000 note was worthless, but the radio maker was part of a complex of companies, some of whom were important to Multi. Multi's CEO had elected to keep a low profile with regard to the radio maker and had refused to press for payments of principle or interest, for fear of alienating the other companies in the group. But now, other sources had been found so that the complex was less significant as a supplier, and Multi forced the hand of the radio maker, pushing it into bankruptcy.

Required:

Prepare a paragraph discussing each event, describing how the item should be treated in Multi's income statement for 1991. Should the item be classified as unusual, extraordinary, or ordinary. Should the item be carried forward into next year (as an asset) or carried back to last year (as a prior period adjustment)? Be sure to explain the rationale for your decision.

P5.10 Quarterly income statements. Li'l Tyke sells toys in its own stores throughout the Midwest. It is a very seasonal business, with about 80 percent of sales coming in the period November 15 to December 31. Unfortunately, to have a presence in the market for those peak times, the store must remain open all year around. The company struggles to present a reasonable picture of its operations during the early part of the year, and it worries particularly about the requirement to present quarterly reports to its stockholders. The president has come up with several ideas to deal with this problem in 1992, and he asked you to consider these suggestions:

1. Everyone agrees that the company sells its toys at a higher markup during its peak season, but no one knows for sure how much the difference might be. The real margin for the year isn't known until the year-end inventory is counted and the real cost of sales is determined. The president proposes to use the last year's actual gross margin percentage to determine the gross margin for each of the first three quarters. He will determine an actual gross margin for 1992 after the year-end inventory, and will use that number to prepare the income statement for the year as a whole. That 1992 gross margin will also be used to develop the gross margins for the first three quarters of 1993.

2. Most of the company's advertising is spread evenly over the period September 1 through December 15. The president has negotiated with the advertising agency to allow the company to pay for those advertisements during the month of December. He proposes to expense the advertising expense 20 percent in the third quarter and 80 percent in the fourth quarter—which is approximately proportionate to the way sales are realized during that six-month period.

3. The president has also negotiated with the landlords of most of the store locations to allow the company to pay the rent in a lump sum total in the month of December. He proposes to expense the rent over the year on a pro rata basis, following the expected sales pattern.

Required:

Prepare a brief paragraph discussing each of the president's proposals for the Li'l Tyke's quarterly income statements. Do you agree with his plans? Why or why not?

P5.11 Balance sheet and income statement ratios. Business analysts often talk about the "DuPont Ratio" (so named because it was developed by financial analysts in the DuPont Corporation many years ago), and by that they mean this interconnection of balance sheet and income statement ratios ("leverage" is assets over equity):

$$\text{Return on sales} \times \text{Asset turnover} = \text{Return on assets} \times \text{Leverage}$$
$$= \text{Return on equity.}$$

Let us make some assumptions about two different companies, and state those assumptions in terms of their most important balance sheet and income statement ratios:

Suppose Co. X's financial results depict

$$2\% \text{ (ROS)} \times 3.4 \text{ (Asset turnover)} = 7\% \text{ (ROA)} \times 3 \text{ (Leverage)}$$
$$= 21\% \text{ (ROE)}.$$

whereas Co. Y's financials show,

$$7\% \text{ (ROS)} \times 1.5 \text{ (Asset turnover)} = 10.5\% \text{ (ROA)} \times 2 \text{ (Leverage)}$$
$$= 21\% \text{ (ROE)}.$$

Required:

a. Which company would you rather manage? Why?

b. Which company would you rather invest in? Why?

P5.12 Working with income statement ratios. At lunch one day in the executive dining room of the Crest Investment Company, you notice a co-worker lunching by herself, and studying a set of financial statements. She seems frustrated and is talking to herself. You hear her say as she picks up her brief case and leaves, "I do not understand what is going on with this company—none of this makes any sense to me." You start to follow her out when you notice that she has left a scratch sheet behind covered with figures; in fact, they appear to be a set of ratios, as follows:

	L/Y	T/Y
AVG PRICE	$ 5.10	$ 4.80
ROS	8.23%	6.23%
SALES INCREASE	18.30%	−2.00%
GROSS MARGIN	37.50%	35.00%
R&D/SALES	8.17%	6.67%
G&A/SALES	10.62%	12.50%
EFF TAX RATE	40.00%	42.50%
ASSET TURN	0.95	1.08
ROA	8.68%	5.75%
ROE	20.98%	13.84%

Required:

Identify five important things that may have been going on with this company this year which may explain the ratios developed by your frustrated friend.

P5.13 Pro forma income statements. The Quandary Corporation is at a crossroads and must decide whether to expand a new product line or allow its mainline business to work toward liquidation. Income statements for the last three years are as follows:

The Quandary Corporation
Income Statements

	2 Years Ago	Last Year	This Year	Next Year	2 Years Out
Sales of old product	$10,000	$8,000	$7,000		
Cost of sales—old product	6,000	5,000	4,550		
Marketing costs—old product	1,500	1,280	1,225		
Depreciation—old product	500	450	400		
Interest—old product	200	180	150		
Contribution—old product	1,800	1,090	675		
Sales—new product	1,000	3,000	4,000		
Cost of sales—new product	750	2,175	2,800		
Marketing costs—new product	200	600	800		
Depreciation—new product	100	110	150		
Interest—new product	50	55	75		
Contribution—new product	(100)	60	175		
Corporate expenses	450	475	500		
Income before taxes	1,250	675	350		
Income taxes	500	270	140		
Net income	$ 750	$ 405	210		
Net assets employed—old prod.	5,000	4,800	4,600		
Net assets employed—new prod.	1,000	1,100	1,500		
Owners' equity	3,600	3,800	3,900		

Required:

Prepare two sets of pro forma income statements for 1992 and 1993, one set assuming that $10,000,000 is invested in an expansion of the new product line, and one set assuming that the new product line is abandoned. Prepare a memo for the president of Quandary, commenting on the pro forma statements. Your memo should explain the assumptions you made in the preparation of the pro forma statements, and should interpret those statements to help the CEO decide what to do about the new product line.

P5.14 Revenue recognition. At the beginning of 1990, John Cornell decided to quit his current job as construction supervisor for Walsh, Inc., a construction company headquartered in Chicago, Illinois, and formed his own company. When he resigned, he had a written contract to build a custom home in Evanston, Illinois, at a price of $400,000. The full price was payable in cash when the house was completed and available for occupancy.

By year-end 1990, Cornell's new company, Distinctive Homes, Inc., had spent $50,000 for labor, $107,740 for materials, and $3,800 in miscellaneous expenses in connection with construction of the home. Cornell estimated that the project was 70 percent complete at year-end. In addition, construction materials on hand at year-end cost $2,600.

During the year, Distinctive Homes, Inc., had also purchased a small run-down house for $95,000, spent $32,000 fixing it up, and then sold it on November 1, 1990, for $175,000. The buyer paid

$25,000 down and signed a note for the remainder of the balance due. The note called for interest payments only, at a rate of 12 percent per year, with a balloon payment for the outstanding balance at the end of 1992.

John's wife, Karen, was employed to keep the accounting records for Distinctive Homes, Inc., and on December 31, she prepared the following statement:

Distinctive Homes, Inc.
Where We Stand at Year-end

Assets		Debts and Capital	
Cash	$ 21,000	Accounts payable	$ 44,600
Material on hand	2,600	Owner's investment	242,540
House renovation contract	150,000	Sale of renovated house	175,000
Construction in progress	161,540		
Cost of renovated house	127,000		
Total assets	$462,140	Total debts and capital	$462,140

After reviewing the statement, John and Karen got into a discussion concerning the level of income the company earned during the year. John argued that the entire profit on the sale of the renovated home, along with 70 percent of the expected profit from the construction contract, had been earned. Karen, on the other hand, maintained that the profit on the renovation should be recognized only to the extent of the cash actually collected and that no profit should be recognized on the new home construction until it was completed and available for occupancy.

After discussing the problem at length, John and Karen agreed that there were four possible alternative approaches to measuring the company's income:

1. Report the entire amount of renovation income and a proportionate amount of construction contract income.

2. Report the entire amount of renovation income but none of the construction contract income.

3. Report the renovation income in proportion to the amount of cash received and the construction contract income in proportion to the amount of work completed.

4. Report the renovation income in proportion to the amount of cash received but none of the construction contract income.

Required:

Prepare the balance sheets and income statements that would result under each of the above four approaches. Which set of statements do you believe best reflects the results of Distinctive Homes, Inc., for 1990?

P5.15 Revenue recognition. Supercolider, Inc., is an independent research and development laboratory that undertakes contractual research for a variety of corporate and governmental clients. Occasionally, scientists at the laboratory undertake independent research, which, if successful (i.e., results in new products, designs, or technology), is then marketed by the company.

In January 1988, scientists at Supercolider began work on a number of minor research projects involving high-speed atom smashing. During 1988, costs incurred in these efforts amounted to $363,000. In May 1989, promising results emerged and were reported to the U.S. Department of Energy. Development costs incurred in 1989 through the end of May totaled $204,000.

At this point, Supercolider tried to secure a government contract to support the remainder of the research effort. The Department of Energy (DOE) was reluctant, however, to commit substantial sums until further tests had been completed. Nonetheless, to ensure that it retained the "first right of refusal," the DOE gave Supercolider a "seed grant" of $50,000 to help support the continuation of the studies; this grant carried a stipulation that the DOE would retain the right to acquire the results, patents, and copyrights from the research any time on or before December 31, 1990, for $2,400,000.

Further testing proved favorable, although additional development costs incurred in 1989 amounted to $325,000 and to $210,000 in 1990. On December 28, 1990, the DOE exercised its right and agreed to purchase the results, patents, and copyrights from the research. As previously agreed, the DOE paid Supercolider $300,000 immediately, with the remainder of the contract price payable in seven equal annual installments beginning on December 31, 1991, through December 31, 1997. On March 1, 1991, Supercolider delivered all scientific and legal documents, test results, and samples to the DOE offices in Washington, D.C.

Required:

Evaluate the facts of this case and determine when Supercolider, Inc., should recognize the various revenue streams associated with its work on this project. Also determine when Supercolider should recognize the various developmental costs. Be prepared to substantiate your position.

P5.16 Profitability Analysis. Digital Equipment Corporation presented its income statements in its 1990 annual report, as follows *(in thousands except per share data):* (The companion balance sheet for Digital was presented in P4).

	1990	1989	1988
Revenues *(Notes A and C)*			
Product sales	$ 8,145,491	$ 8,190,308	$ 7,541,241
Service and other revenues	4,797,032	4,551,648	3,934,205
Total operating revenues	12,942,523	12,741,956	11,475,446
Costs and Expenses *(Notes A, D and I)*			
Cost of product sales	3,825,897	3,468,307	3,042,172
Service expense and cost of other revenues	2,968,529	2,773,563	2,426,176
Research and engineering expenses	1,614,423	1,525,129	1,306,543
Selling, general and administrative expenses	3,971,059	3,638,868	3,065,555
Restructuring charges *(Note M)*	550,000	—	—
Operating income	12,615	1,336,089	1,635,000
Interest income	142,015	124,021	143,665
Interest expense	30,641	39,435	37,820
Income before income taxes	123,989	1,420,675	1,740,845
Provision for income taxes *(Notes A and E)*	49,596	348,065	435,212
Net income	$ 74,393	$ 1,072,610	$ 1,305,633
Net Income per Share *(Note B)*	$ .59	$ 8.45	$ 9.90
Weighted average shares outstanding *(Note B)*	125,222	127,008	131,923

Required:

Calculate all the profitabiity ratios for each of the three years presented. Perform other financial analysis you deem necessary in order to understand the financial health of Digital. Prepare a short commentary, summarizing the results of your work.

P5.17 Financial Analysis in the United States and in Japan. Following are the income statements from the 1990 annual reports of Kansai Electric Power Co., Inc. (serving Osaka, Japan) and Commonwealth Edison Company (serving Chicago, Illinois, USA).

Required:

Perform a financial analysis regarding the profitability of both companies and determine which of the two appear to be more successful in generating profits. Also, comment on the terminology used and the presentation employed in the two income statements.

The Kansai Electric Power Company, Incorporated
Statements of Income
Years ended March 31, 1991 and 1990

	Millions of Yen	
	1991	**1990**
Operating Revenues	¥2,245,007	¥2,075,296
Operating Expenses:		
Fuel	441,571	329,163
Purchased power	163,859	142,075
Maintenance	293,379	306,472
Depreciation	323,681	308,419
Taxes other than income taxes	140,383	132,957
Other	535,972	500,204
	1,898,845	1,719,290
Operating Income	346,162	356,006
Other (Income) Expenses:		
Interest expense	239,393	215,427
Exchange loss	—	14,369
Other, net	(2,953)	(1,722)
	236,440	228,074
Income before Provision for Reserve		
for Fluctuations in Water Level and Income Taxes	109,722	127,932
Provision for Reserve for Fluctuations in Water Level	1,668	6,525
Income before Income Taxes	108,054	121,407
Income Taxes (Note 8)	51,771	65,009
Net Income	¥ 56,283	¥ 56,398
	Yen	
Per Share of Common Stock:		
Net income—		
Primary	¥58	¥58
Assuming full dilution	¥57	¥56
Cash dividends applicable to period	¥50	¥49

Commonwealth Edison Company and Subsidiary Companies
Statements of Consolidated Income
(thousands except per share data)

		1990	1989	1988
Electric Operating Revenues (Notes 2 and 3):	Operating revenues	$5,798,350	$5,782,850	$5,613,338
	Provisions for revenue refunds	(536,364)	(31,800)	—
		$5,261,986	**$5,751,050**	**$5,613,338**
Electric Operating Expenses and Taxes:	Fuel (Notes 1, 3 and 10)	$978,775	$951,350	$991,244
	Purchased and interchanged power—net	(27,209)	(44,836)	17,358
	Deferred (under)/overrecovered energy costs—net (Notes 1 and 3)	8,415	(19,059)	(89,350)
	Operation	1,160,166	1,120,941	1,072,218
	Maintenance	489,463	435,664	434,402
	Depreciation (Note 1)	878,938	865,427	837,170
	Recovery of deferred plant costs	1,659	1,659	34,060
	Taxes (except income) (Note 14)	661,432	665,072	641,475
	Income taxes (Notes 1 and 13)—			
	Current—Federal	150,917	263,879	115,493
	—State	28,773	49,684	38,479
	Deferred—Federal—net	19,456	162,088	220,873
	—State—net	17,299	38,445	47,144
	Investment tax credits deferred—net (Notes 1 and 13)	(28,386)	83,529)	9,582
		$4,339,698	**$4,406,785**	**$4,370,148**
Electric Operating Income		**$ 922,288**	**$1,344,265**	**$1,243,190**
Other income and Deductions:	Interest on long-term debt	$ (648,603)	(620,589)	$ (648,871)
	Interest on notes payable	(577)	(7,685)	(8,607)
	Allowance for funds used during construction (Note 1)—			
	Borrowed funds	13,840	17,898	39,726
	Equity funds	22,526	24,856	94,970
	Current income taxes applicable to nonoperating activities (Notes 1 and 13)	(5,932)	2,445	17,669
	Disallowed Byron Unit 1 plant costs (Note 3)	(133,661)	(52,808)	—
	Income tax effect of disallowed Byron Unit 1 plant costs (Note 3)	(1,288)	5,570	(439)
	Miscellaneous—net	(40,302)	(20,269)	(117)
		$ (793,997)	**$ (650,582)**	**$ (506,669)**
Net income		**$ 128,291**	**$ 693,683**	**$ 737,521**
Provision for dividends on preferred and preference stocks		82,495	95,180	102,245
Net income on common stock		**$ 45,796**	**$ 598,503**	**$ 635,276**
Average number of common shares outstanding		212,032	211,647	211,233
Earnings per common share		**$0.22**	**$2.83**	**$3.01**
Cash dividends declared per common share		**$3.00**	**$3.00**	**$3.00**

P5.18 Financial Analysis. Circuit City Stores, Inc. is a premier retail outlet for consumer electronics and major appliances in the United States. Presented below are five years of selected earnings and balance sheet data (Years Ended February 28 or 29).

	1990	1989	1988	1987	1986
Consolidated Summary of Earnings					
(Amounts in thousands except per share data)					
Net sales and operating revenues	$2,096,588	$1,721,497	$1,350,425	$1,010,692	$705,490
Cost of sales, buying and warehousing	1,477,502	1,219,570	961,345	720,187	505,691
Gross profit	619,086	501,927	389,080	290,505	199,799
Selling, general and administrative expenses	482,229	379,045	291,489	213,816	157,521
Interest expense	8,757	8,382	8,391	5,189	2,257
Total expense	490,986	387,427	299,880	219,005	159,778
Earnings before income taxes	128,100	114,500	89,200	71,500	40,021
Provision for income taxes	50,000	45,025	38,800	36,200	18,000
Net earnings	$ 78,100	$ 69,475	$ 50,400	$ 35,300	$ 22,021
Net earnings per common share:					
Primary and fully diluted	$ 1.70	$ 1.52	$ 1.12	$ .79	$ .50
Number of common shares outstanding at year end	45,860	45,234	44,802	44,380	43,780
Average common shares outstanding— primary	46,068	45,542	44,850	44,500	44,260
Consolidated Summary Balance Sheets					
(Amounts in thousands)					
Current assets	$ 442,208	$ 366,893	$ 265,364	$ 195,482	$135,939
Property and equipment, net	250,006	206,052	155,246	147,213	83,331
Deferred income taxes	6,460	3,023	354	—	1,637
Other assets	14,981	11,513	12,277	18,922	23,029
Total assets	$ 713,655	$ 587,481	$ 433,241	$ 361,617	$243,936
Current liabilities	$ 222,243	$ 192,150	$ 116,218	$ 98,162	$ 82,285
Long-term debt	93,882	94,674	96,676	101,149	40,005
Deferred income taxes	—	—	—	1,392	—
Deferred revenue, deferred credits and other liabilities	38,244	27,040	18,934	11,643	9,874
Total liabilities	354,369	313,864	231,828	212,346	132,164
Stockholders' equity	359,286	273,617	201,413	149,271	111,772
Total liabilities and stockholders' equity	$ 713,655	$ 587,481	$ 433,241	$ 361,617	$243,936

	1990	1989	1988	1987	1986
Other Data					
Book value per share of common stock	$ 7.83	$ 6.05	$ 4.50	$ 3.37	$ 2.54
Cash dividends per share paid on common stock	$ .075	$ .055	$ .0375	$ .029	$ .024
Return on average stockholders' equity	24.6%	29.1%	28.7%	27.3%	22.0%
Funded debt to equity ratio	.26 to 1	.35 to 1	.48 to 1	.68 to 1	.36 to 1
Number of employees at year end	13,092	10,481	7,219	5,922	4,554
Number of retail units at year end	149	122	105	87	69

Required:

Calculate all pertinent ratios. Prepare common size financial statements. Explain the first four lines in the "other data" section. Overall, how has Circuit City Stores, Inc. been doing?

P5.19 Fortune 500 statistics. Presented below are selected return on sales (ROS), return on assets (ROA), return on equity (ROE), and sales per employee statistics for 1990 and 1989 Fortune 500 industry groupings.

Selected 1990 (top line) and 1989 Fortune 500 Industrials
Industry Medians

	ROS (%)	ROA (%)	ROE (%)	Sales/ Employees
Pharmaceuticals	14	13	26	$147,553
	13	14	25	$142,807
Petroleum refining	4	5	14	613,084
	3	4	10	537,026
Transportation equipment	3	4	9	120,859
	3	3	11	109,539
Mining, crude-oil products	9	4	15	375,204
	10	4	13	314,563
Apparel	3	4	13	64,869
	4	7	20	58,232
Computers and office equipment	6	6	12	132,407
	6	6	13	122,684
Chemicals	6	6	14	212,381
	6	6	13	205,813
Food	3	6	17	223,584
	3	5	15	211,323
Building materials	2	2	11	167,294
	2	3	4	155,000
Aerospace	3	5	13	132,100
	3	4	12	121,002
Electronics	3	4	13	111,478
	4	5	14	101,190

	ROS (%)	ROA (%)		ROE (%)	Sales/ Employees
Beverages	8	7		16	202,030
	8	7		23	194,426
Industrial and farm equipment	3	4		11	125,570
	4	4		12	112,091
Metals	4	4		11	185,079
	5	6		18	195,750
Motor vehicles and parts	2	2		7	130,265
	3	2		10	117,941
Scientific and photographic equipment	5	6		12	118,232
	5	7		13	112,718
Textiles	0	0		3	89,391
	2	3		10	80,901
Soaps and cosmetics	6	9		19	146,885
	4	8		19	209,117
500 Industrials median	4	5		13	154,064
	5	6		15	146,887

Required:

(This exercise assumes that you know something about the industries identified in the groupings. If you do not have a mental picture of the typical financial structure of the companies in the industry, some review of individual company financial statements may be in order.)

a. Identify the most significant differences in the ROS, ROA, and ROE performance of the industry groups, and explain why those extremes might occur.

b. Identify the most significant differences in results between 1990 and 1989, and explain what might have caused those differences.

c. How would you interpret the Fortune 500 industrial median statistics? Do you think they represent a historical low, high, or are we at an average period in our industrial history? Explain your opinion.

P5.20 Presenting segment information. All public companies include in their annual reports a footnote presenting information about the results of operations of the segments of their companies. The following exhibits are the segment footnotes from Capital Cities/ABC, Brown-Foreman Corporation, and Teledyne. Also, note that PepsiCo presented its segment information as a part of its Management Discussion and Analysis (see Chapter 1). All four companies adhere to the GAAP pronouncement for the presentation of segment data, but each presentation is somewhat unique.

Brown-Foreman Corporation

6. Business Segment Information

The company's operations have been classified into two business segments: wine and spirits and consumer durables. The wine and spirits segment includes the production, importing, and marketing of wines and distilled spirits. The consumer durables segment primarily includes the manfuacture and sale of china, crystal, and luggage. The "other" category principally involves the production and sale of jewelry and candles. The company has disposed of these businesses.

Summarized financial information by business segment for 1990, 1989, and 1988 is as follows *(in thousands):*

	1990	1989	1988
Net sales:			
Wine and Spirits	$ 974,846	$1,002,112	$1,002,770
Consumer Durables	317,716	284,967	248,134
Other	—	—	103,694
	$1,292,562	$1,287,079	$1,354,598
Operating income:			
Wine and Spirits	$ 204,484	$ 178,710	$ 158,134
Consumer Durables	39,430	47,519	39,788
Other	—	—	8,776
Corporate	(18,970)	(17,749)	(15,014)
	$ 224,944	$ 208,480	$ 191,684
Total assets:			
Wine and Spirits	$ 504,094	$ 524,943	$ 520,492
Consumer Durables	395,639	372,535	348,497
Corporate	121,251	105,794	63,295
	$1,020,984	$1,003,272	$ 932,284
Depreciation and amortization:			
Wine and Spirits	$ 19,250	$ 17,614	$ 16,973
Consumer Durables	14,406	13,158	11,914
Other	—	—	2,990
Corporate	175	102	81
	$ 33,831	$ 30,874	$ 31,958
Capital expenditures:			
Wine and Spirits	$ 27,051	$ 22,293	$ 15,907
Consumer Durables	22,365	15,341	8,430

	1990	1989	1988
Other	—	—	907
Corporate	651	317	275
	$ 50,067	$ 37,951	$ 25,519

Classes of products which contributed 10% or more to consolidated net sales:

	1990	1989	1988
American Spirits	$ 437,554	$ 398,782	$ 372,373
Imported Spirits	224,084	253,389	265,949
Wines and Specialties	313,208	349,941	364,448
	$ 974,846	$1,002,112	$1,002,770

There were no significant intersegment sales or transfers during 1990, 1989, and 1988. Operating income by business segment excludes interest income, interest expense, and net unallocated corporate expenses. Corporate assets consist principally of cash and cash equivalents, certain corporate receivables, and other assets.

Foreign assets and revenues, and export sales each represents less than 10% of the company's total. No material amounts of the company's sales are dependent upon a single customer.

7. Stockholders' Equity

Changes in consolidated stockholders' equity during the three years ended April 30, 1990, are shown in the accompanying Consolidated Statement of Retained Earnings and in the following table *(in thousands):*

	Capital in Excess of Par Value of Common Stock	Treasury Stock
Balance, April 30, 1987	$89,747	$(118,780)
Acquisition of treasury stock (Class A, 625,849 shares; Class B, 3,487,800 shares)	—	(198,455)

	Capital in Excess of Par Value of Common Stock	Treasury Stock
Treasury stock issued in connection with employee benefit plans (Class B, 567 shares)	14	10
Balance, April 30, 1988	$89,761	$(317,225)
Acquisition of treasury stock (Class A, 35 shares; Class B, 261 shares)	—	(16)

	Capital in Excess of Par Value of Common Stock	Treasury Stock
Balance, April 30, 1989 and 1990	$89,761	$(317,241)

The company acquired as treasury stock 625,849 shares of Class A and 3,487,800 shares of Class B common stock that were tendered to the company at $48 per share during 1988.

Adjustments from foreign currency financial statement translations during the three years ended April 30, 1990, were not material.

Capital Cities/ABC

8. Segment Data

The Company's business operations are classified into two segments: Broadcasting and Publishing. Broadcasting operations include the ABC Television Network and eight television stations, the ABC Radio Networks and 21 radio stations, and cable television programming services. The Publishing segment includes newspapers, shopping guides, various specialized business and consumer periodicals and books, research services, and database publishing. There are no material product transfers between segments of the Company, and virtually all of the Company's business is conducted within the United States. The segment data is as follows (000's omitted):

	1990	1989	1988	1987	1986
Broadcasting					
Net revenues	$4,283,633	$3,899,989	$3,749,557	$3,433,749	$3,153,619
Direct operating costs	3,331,316	2,943,321	2,904,668	2,680,582	2,554,932
Depreciation	75,088	74,333	76,303	73,730	78,952
Amortization of intangible assets	46,772	46,186	46,415	46,527	45,200
Total operating costs	3,453,176	3,063,840	3,027,386	2,800,839	2,679,084
Income from operations	$ 830,457	$ 836,149	$ 722,171	$ 632,910	$ 474,535
Assets at year-end	$4,250,540	$4,177,132	$3,927,891	$4,018,775	$4,186,650
Capital expenditures	105,475	173,078	138,043	102,425	104,278
Publishing					
Net revenues	$1,101,969	$1,057,405	$1,023,896	$1,006,597	$ 970,755
Direct operating costs	934,022	891,542	858,102	822,123	778,201
Depreciation	18,363	17,971	18,361	18,878	15,353
Amortization of intangible assets	17,213	17,448	17,713	18,879	18,202
Total operating costs	969,598	926,961	894,176	859,880	811,756
Income from operations	$ 132,371	$ 130,444	$ 129,720	$ 146,717	$ 158,999
Assets at year-end	$ 916,346	$ 899,499	$ 898,608	$ 908,193	$ 920,896
Capital expenditures	14,450	13,015	15,085	13,114	48,589

	1990	1989	1988	1987	1986
Consolidated					
Net revenues	$5,385,602	$4,957,394	$4,773,453	$4,440,346	$4,124,374
Income from operations	$ 962,828	$ 966,593	$ 851,891	$ 779,627	$ 633,534
General corporate expense	(39,613)	(44,081)	(35,862)	(33,637)	(30,856)
Operating income	923,215	922,512	816,029	745,990	602,678
Interest expense	(168,859)	(174,417)	(182,362)	(190,806)	(185,511)
Interest and other income	83,424	103,032	53,609	8,794	5,576
Income before income taxes	$ 837,780	$ 851,127	$ 687,276	$ 563,978	$ 422,743
Assets employed by segments	$5,166,886	$5,076,631	$4,826,499	$4,926,968	$5,107,546
Cash investments and other corporate assets	1,529,301	1,282,876	1,262,372	451,404	83,870
Total assets at year-end	$6,696,187	$6,359,507	$6,088,871	$5,378,372	$5,191,416

Teledyne Corporation

Note 9. Business Segments

Teledyne is a diversified corporation comprised of companies which manufacture a wide variety of products. The Company's major business segments include aviation and electronics, specialty metals, industrial and consumer.

Companies in the aviation and electronics segment produce aircraft and turbine engines, airframe structures, unmanned air vehicles, target drone systems, and equipment and subsystems for spacecraft and avionics. Other activities in this segment include the manufacture of military electronic equipment, aircraft-monitoring and control systems, semiconductors, relays and other related products and systems. Products in the specialty metals segment include zirconium, titanium, high temperature nickel based alloys, high-speed and tool steels, tungsten and molybdenum. Other operations in this segment consist of processing, casting, rolling and forging metals. The industrial segment is comprised of companies that manufacture a large range of air and water cooled, gasoline and diesel fueled engines, machine tools, dies and consumable tooling. The consumer segment manufactures oral hygiene products, shower massages, water and air purification systems, swimming pool and spa heaters and provides other products and services.

Information on the Company's business segments for the years ended December 31, 1991, 1990 and 1989 was as follows (in millions):

	1991	1990	1989
Sales:			
Aviation and electronics	**$1,339.2**	$1,471.4	$1,465.7
Specialty metals	**770.3**	853.7	922.7
Industrial	**763.6**	796.1	809.4
Consumer	**333.7**	324.6	333.4
	$3,206.8	$3,445.8	$3,531.2

Sales of operations which the Company plans to sell or close were $514.8 million for the year ended December 31, 1991, of which $368.8 million was in the industrial segment. Teledyne Monarch Rubber ceased operations in 1991 and accounted for approximately $55 million in 1991, $120 million in 1990 and $135 million in 1989 of industrial segment sales. Certain operations in the specialty metals segment were closed in 1990 with sales of approximately $55 million in 1990 and $90 million in 1989.

The Company's backlog of confirmed orders was approximately $1.9 billion at December 31, 1991, and $2.2 billion at December 31, 1990. Backlog of the aviation and electronics segment was $1.3 billion at December 31, 1991, and $1.6 billion at December 31, 1990.

The Company's sales to the U.S. government were $1.1 billion in 1991, and $1.2 billion in 1990 and 1989, including direct sales as prime contractor and indirect sales as subcontractor. Most of these sales were in the aviation and electronics segment. Sales by operations in the United States to customers in other countries were $535.6 million in 1991, $447.4 million in 1990, and

$445.0 million in 1989. Sales between business segments, which were not material, generally were priced at prevailing market prices.

Income (Loss) of Operations before Income Taxes:	1991	1990	1989
Aviation and electronics	$(18.3)	$ 44.5	$ 92.1
Specialty metals	45.8	92.0	123.1
Industrial	28.3	48.4	78.0
Consumer	19.4	38.7	35.0
Operating profit	75.2	223.6	328.2
Corporate expenses	56.1	76.7	53.1
Interest expense	61.9	68.4	69.6
Other income	(11.0)	(17.9)	(26.2)
	$(31.8)	$ 96.4	$231.7

Operating profit in 1991 included a restructuring charge of $107.6 million. The restructuring charge was $38.6 million in the aviation and electronics segment, $20.4 million in the specialty metals segment, $39.3 million in the industrial segment, and $9.3 million in the consumer segment.

Results of operations before tax for the aviation and electronics segment included provisions for losses from the performance of development and initial production fixed-price contracts of approximately $55 million in 1991 and $90 million in 1990. Operating profit in 1990 for the industrial segment and the specialty metals segment was adversely affected by estimated losses on disposal of certain unprofitable operating companies. In addition, strikes at certain engine manufacturing locations in both the industrial segment and the aviation and electronics segment adversely affected 1990 results. Corporate expenses for 1990 included the effect of strengthening aircraft product liability reserves.

	1991	1990	1989
Depreciation and Amortization:			
Aviation and electronics	$ 23.2	$ 29.5	$ 37.5
Specialty metals	28.5	27.1	24.1
Industrial	18.2	19.5	20.0
Consumer	6.5	6.8	7.3
Corporate	7.7	7.7	8.9
	$ 84.1	$ 90.6	$ 97.8
Identifiable Assets:			
Aviation and electronics	$ 365.8	$ 404.2	$ 405.5
Specialty metals	316.0	323.7	312.7
Industrial	267.2	294.3	272.2
Consumer	108.9	103.5	91.9
Corporate	661.5	550.6	505.1
	1,719.4	1,676.3	1,587.4
Net assets of discontinued insurance operations	—	—	1,880.8
	$ 1,719.4	$ 1,676.3	$ 3,468.2
Capital Expenditures:			
Aviation and electronics	$ 16.8	$ 19.7	$ 28.3
Specialty metals	42.2	49.4	52.3
Industrial	19.9	26.7	34.0
Consumer	8.0	10.9	21.2
Corporate	10.7	6.4	8.8
	$ 97.6	$ 113.1	$ 144.6

Required:

For all four companies, complete a ratio analysis on the segments reported, and prepare a separate commentary on the results of your analysis for each company. Prepare a fifth commentary, comparing and contrasting the four segment presentations and highlighting important differences between them. Which presentation did you prefer? Why?

CASES

C5.1 **The cost of ill-gotten sales: RJR Nabisco.** On September 21, 1989, RJR Nabisco announced that it would end the practice of *trade loading* in its domestic cigarette distribution business. According to a news release in *The Wall Street Journal,* the discontinuation of this merchandising practice would cause RJR, acquired by Kohlberg, Kravis Roberts in late 1988 in a

$25 billion leveraged buyout, to forgo $340 million in operating income in the last six months of 1989. *The Wall Street Journal* release reported that the practice was discontinued ''to curb excess inventories.''

Trade loading refers to a marketing practice in which manufacturers attempt to induce wholesale customers (known as *trade*) to purchase more inventory than they can currently sell. According to RJR officials, trade loading is a common practice in many industries, such as the food and beverage industry, and has been shown to be a highly effective marketing tool. For example, in spite of declining cigarette sales in the United States, RJR officials reported that trade loading had resulted in excess wholesaler purchases of more than 18.5 billion cigarettes as of January 1989, or approximately a six weeks' supply.

Trade loading typically involves *push* and/or *pull* price promotions. A push promotion, for example, involves a price discount from the manufacturer to the wholesaler, whereas a pull promotion involves a price discount (also financed by the manufacturer) from the wholesaler to the retailer. In the case of RJR, the timing of trade loading promotions was synchronized with industry pricing patterns. Beginning in 1983, tobacco manufacturers effectively institutionalized the practice of price increases (only) in June and December. Wholesalers typically responded to the anticipated price increases by purchasing large quantities of inventories just prior to the quarter ending June and December so that the inventory could be resold to retailers at the new, higher prices.

As a way to induce similar inventory purchases in the quarters ending in March and September, RJR and other tobacco producers instituted the push/pull price promotions. Thus, significant selling and shipping could be anticipated by tobacco producers at the end of each quarter.

In spite of the costs associated with maintaining and warehousing the excess inventory, wholesaler-distributors became heavily dependent on trade loading. According to *Fortune* magazine, ''Many would be breakeven operations or money losers if they did not get a quarterly surge from the load.'' Wholesaler-distributors also benefit, however, from the tobacco industry's generous product return policy: cigarettes that manufacturers regard as too stale to sell (i.e., those that are six months old) are eligible for a full return. In spite of this generous return policy, however, distributors frequently sold stale cigarettes because of their higher profit margin, a practice that concerned many manufacturers worried about product quality and customer satisfaction.

Required:

Evaluate the practice of trade loading. What are the costs and benefits of this practice? What are the implications of trade loading for the quality of reported earnings and assets? Why would RJR Nabisco stop this practice?

C5.2 Revenue recognition under long-term contracts: Buildmore Construction Company. In June 1988, Buildmore Construction Company (BCC) was employed by the city of Houston, Texas, to assist in constructing its new World Trade Center complex. BCC was to construct the superstructure of a multistory office building as part of the city's downtown redevelopment. The construction agreement called for work to begin no later than August 1988 and required the company to construct the concrete frame for the complex.

Under the terms of the three-year contract, BCC was to receive a total of $10 million in cash payments from the city of Houston, to be paid as follows: 25 percent when the project is 30 percent complete, 25 percent when the project is 60 percent complete, and the remaining 50 percent when the project has been fully completed (including all necessary building approvals). The contract, which was of a fixed price variety and hence did not provide for cost overrun recoupment, required that completion estimates be certified by an independent engineering consultant *before* any cash progress payments would be made.

In preparing its bid, BCC had estimated that the total cost to complete the project would be $8.3 million, assuming no cost overruns. Hence, under optimal conditions, the company anticipated a profit of approximately $1.7 million.

During the first year of the contract, BCC incurred actual costs of $2.49 million, and on June 30, 1989, the engineering consulting firm of C. Likert & Associates determined that the project had attained a 30 percent completion level. In the following year, BCC incurred actual costs of $3.1 million. As of June 30, 1990, the firm of C. Likert & Associates determined that the project had attained at least a 60 percent completion level. In their report to the City Authority, however, the consulting engineers noted that BCC might be facing a potential cost overrun situation. In response to this observation, the directors of BCC noted that they had anticipated that a number of economies of scale would arise during the final phases of construction and thereby offset any prior cost overruns.

By May 1991, BCC had completed the remainder of the project. Actual costs incurred during the year to June 30, 1991, amounted to $3.11 million. The firm received a certification for the fully completed work.

Accounting Decision

Prior to issuing the 1989 annual report, the controller's office of BCC determined that the proceeds from the World Trade Center contract would be accounted for using the *completed contract* method. Under this approach, the recognition of income is postponed until essentially all work on the contract has been completed. This method previously had been utilized by the company to account for construction contract income, and it appeared to be a prudent alternative, given the possibility of some cost overrun during the life of the current contract.

Under the completed contract approach, revenues (and thus expenses) are recognized on completion or substantial completion of a contract. In general, a contract is regarded as substantially complete if the remaining costs to complete the project are insignificant in amount. Funds expended under the contract are accounted for in an asset account, Construction in Progress, while progress payments received during the construction phase are accounted for in a deferred or unearned revenue account. Although income is not recognized until completion of the contract, any expected losses should be recognized immediately when identified.

In the process of reaching the decision to use the completed contract method, the controller's office of the Buildmore Construction Company had reviewed *Accounting Research Bulletin No. 45*, "Long-Term Construction Type Contracts." This pronouncement identifies the *percentage of completion* method as the preferred method to account for long-term construction contract income, at least when the estimated costs to complete a contract and the extent of construction progress can be reasonably estimated. Under this method, revenues are recognized in proportion to the amount of construction actually completed in a given period.

Required:

a. Assuming that BCC had no other sources of revenues or expenses, determine the level of profits to be reported for the years ended June 30, 1989, 1990, and 1991, utilizing the following revenue recognition methods:
   1. Percentage of completion.
   2. Completed contract.
   3. Cash basis. (Note: Assume that the City Authority remits cash payments on the same day as work completion certification.)

b. Which set of results (from part *a*) best reflects the economic performance of the company over the period 1989–1991? What criteria did you apply in the foregoing assessment?

c. What are the advantages and disadvantages of each of the methods from part *a*?

C5.3 Revenue and Expense Recognition: Emergetel. Emergetel manufactures and sells two-way radio equipment used by police and fire departments and similar agencies. Unit sales have held steady over the last several years, but sales prices have been declining because of international competition. Earnings have been depressed and so has the company's stock price.

California has become the company's most difficult sales territory. Because of the reduction in state and local tax rates in California, agencies responsible for purchasing radio equipment have sought to reduce costs and have turned to less expensive equipment from off-shore suppliers. But even more frustrating, Emergetel's remaining California customers have become very demanding, insisting on top performance in very difficult circumstances—in intense urban environments and in rugged, hilly terrain. The Emergetel maintenance staff serving the California area is always the busiest of any in the company.

Harry Smith was assigned sales responsibility for the California territory in late 1985, just after the company lost a bid for a comprehensive new radio system in San Diego. That was a traumatic loss for the company, because San Diego had used Emergetel equipment since 1952. The loss of an established customer hurt in three ways: the company lost the sales of the new equipment to be installed; it lost the service revenue on the ongoing maintenance; but perhaps most important, the company lost the opportunity to provide replacement and expansion equipment. Once a customer accepted a major new radio system, it was likely to stay with that supplier for ongoing enhancements. Over the life of a customer relationship, Emergetel estimated that the maintenance and add-on business was worth 10 times the original order.

Smith had worked the state tirelessly, although he had few sales to show for his effort. In late 1990, he came home with a *big* winner. He convinced the State Highway Patrol, the police departments from Los Angeles and the Bay Area, and the State Game and Wildlife Agency to go together and purchase a single radio system from Emergetel that would tie all four agencies' communication systems together. To satisfy the demands of each of those powerful agencies, Smith had promised spectacular performance. To meet the exacting specifications, Emergetel would be forced to redesign its basic equipment and create a "California Special Radio." The engineers estimated that the redesign and tooling involved would take three months and cost $8,000,000. The basic contract totaled $30,000,000. At that price, Emergetel would lose $2,000,000 after covering its direct costs, the design and tooling costs, and an appropriate share of fixed costs. Even so, the long-term potential of the contract was enormous and Smith was awarded a bonus of $1,000,000, payable in three annual installments, beginning December 31, 1991.

The agencies also signed a combined five-year maintenance contract with Emergetel, providing for a fixed payment of $1,000,000 a quarter beginning March 31, 1992. Based on experience with similar systems, and factoring in the California environment, Emergetel estimated that there would be a 40 percent margin on that business.

The contracts were signed December 30, 1990. Prototype radios were to be delivered for testing by the agencies on March 31, 1991. The operational equipment was to be delivered in three equal stages: July 1991, September 1991, and November 1991. Everything was to be operational by December 30, 1991. The California Agencies agreed to pay $6,000,000 on December 30, 1990, and four additional installments of $6,000,000 at the end of each quarter during 1991.

Required:

(Assume that Emergetel uses a calendar year-end for financial reporting purposes and prepares public financial statements every quarter.)

1. How much of the expected $2,000,000 loss on the basic contract should be recognized in Emergetel's quarterly income statement(s) for the period(s):

   a. When the contract is signed $_____
   b. When the radios are delivered $_____
   c. During the term of the maintenance contract $_____
   d. When replacement or expansion radios are sold to the agencies $_____
   e. Other $_____

   Explain the rationale for your answer.

2. How much of the $8,000,000 spent for redesign and tooling on the "California Special Radio" should be recognized in Emergetel's quarterly income statement(s) for the period(s):

   a. When the contract is signed $_____
   b. When the radios are delivered $_____
   c. During the term of the maintenance contract $_____
   d. When replacement or expansion radios are sold to the agencies $_____
   e. Other $_____

   Explain the rationale for your answer.

3. How much of Smith's $1,000,000 bonus should be recognized in Emergetel's quarterly income statement(s) for the period(s):

   a. When the contract is signed $_____
   b. When the radios are delivered $_____
   c. During the term of the maintenance contract $_____
   d. When replacement or expansion radios are sold to the agencies $_____
   e. Other $_____

   Explain the rationale for your answer.

C5.4 Revenue and Expense Recognition: Entertainment Arts, Inc.   Entertainment Arts, Inc (EAI) develops videotapes using animation (much like standard cartoons) and moving clay models (like the dancing raisins). The videos were prominent parts of cable TV fare during after-school hours. They had proven to be very popular with the 8–12-year-old market, and many of the featured characters were well known to the members of that age group. Each video cost about $150,000 to make, but because the target audience group was constantly being replenished, it could be shown an infinite number of times. As each video was made, its cost was added to an asset account: the cost was amortized over 10 years to reflect the possibility that changed styles would ultimately make the video obsolete. At the time of this case, EAI had 92 films in its asset pool, with an average age of 3.5 years and an aggregate unamortized cost of $11,000,000.

The company received a proposal for a license on EAI characters from an agent who represented a number of manufacturers of children's products. Three companies asked for an exclusive right to use EAI characters in their markets for a three-year period, and each proposed to pay EAI a 1 percent royalty on any of its products' sales where the product used an EAI character in its design. The agent asked EAI for a commission of $75,000 as compensation for bringing all of the parties together. EAI asked for details, and the agent explained the three companies' plans as follows:

	Planned Annual Sales of EAI Related Products
Lunch box manufacturer	$1,500,000
Clothing manufacturer	3,500,000
Toy manufacturer	5,000,000

EAI argued that it would be giving something up by singing this agreement, and that it wanted more for its sacrifice than the 1 percent royalty proposed. So, EAI countered with this proposal:

	Minimum Annual Royalty Payable	1% Royalty on Annual Sales Over
Lunch box manufacturer	$10,000	$1,000,000
Clothing manufacturer	25,000	2,500,000
Toy manufacturer	40,000	4,000,000

After some further negotiating, a three-year contract was signed: the manufacturers agreed on the guaranteed minimum royalty but insisted that the annual minimum payments would be paid at the end of each year, at the same time the obligation for any additional royalty was due. And, as a concession to complete the deal, the agent agreed to reduce her commission to $60,000.

1. What should EAI's Revenue Recognition Policies be for this license agreement? Please explain all the considerations which entered into your policy proposal.

2. What should EAI's accounting policy be with regard to the aggregate unamortized cost of the videos ($11,000,000) as a result of this transaction? Please explain.

3. What should EAI's accounting policy be with regard to the $60,000 commission paid? Please explain.

CHAPTER 6

The Statement of Cash Flows

Chapter Outline

- The Statement of Cash Flows
  A Historical Perspective
  The Importance of Cash Flows
- The Elements of the Statement of Cash Flows
  Statement Format
  Preparing a Statement of Cash Flows

- Analyzing Cash Flows
  Cash Flow Ratios
  Pro Forma Cash Flows
- Summary
- Appendix: A Generalized Method of
  Forecasting Cash Flows from Operations

For many years, the principal focus of all financial statement users—creditors, investors, and managers alike—was the accrual-based financial statements, namely the balance sheet and the income statement. These two statements were thought to be not only *necessary* but also *sufficient* to present a complete picture of the financial condition and operations of a company. In recent decades, however, financial statement user preference has shifted from a purely accrual-based information orientation to one that includes *both* accrual and cash flow information. In recognition of these changing consumer preferences, the FASB in 1987 adopted SFAS No. 95, "Statement of Cash Flows," which specifies the format for a statement of cash flows that is now required in all published financial statements. The purpose of this chapter is to help students to gain an understanding of the information conveyed by the statement of cash flows and to learn how the statement is prepared and how it can be used and analyzed.

THE STATEMENT OF CASH FLOWS

A Historical Perspective

A noted authority on financial reporting once observed:

> For more than 500 years, until the 1930s, the central focus of financial reporting throughout the world was cash flow and solvency. So I find it somewhat amazing that for the past 50 years, which includes the entire lifespan of the Securities and Exchange Commission and the period of greatest development of external reporting in the United States, the financial community has been obsessed with the income statement and its all-important bottom-line figures—net income and earnings per share.[1]

To help you understand the irony suggested by this observation, the following presents a brief historical perspective of the U.S. financial community. Until the 1920s, the investing public in the United States made relatively few stock investments, and when such stock investments were made, they were typically based on personal contacts and conversations between the investee and the officers of the investor company. In fact, the most common type of financing involved debt between a lending institution and a borrower. Consequently, the principal use of financial statements was to enable creditors to evaluate lending opportunities and to justify the loans that were made; stock investors made relatively little use of such information. Hence, it stands to reason that the financial reporting characteristic of that era focused on liquidity and credit-related information rather than on earnings and investment-related information.

With the advent of a broader public market for stock investments in the late 1920s, the focus of financial statement interest shifted to income and earnings per share. As the level of stock investing increased, the financial community became increasingly interested in earnings and other accrual-based measures. This shift in focus was logical, even if excessive, in that the net income reported by a company *is* a better predictor of future earnings than is cash flow.[2]

Only after a number of spectacular bankruptcies by companies that had reported positive earnings streams did this earnings fixation begin to subside, with the pendulum swinging back toward a more balanced view. Although some may argue that cash is king in financial markets today, it is safe to say that an intelligent reader of financial statements looks at *both* the earnings picture and the cash flow picture.

The need for information to supplement the accrual-based income statement was first addressed in 1971 when the predecessor to the FASB, the Accounting Principles Board, required the inclusion of a statement of changes in financial position (SCFP) in published financial statements. At that time, businesses were generally given the option of denominating the SCFP in terms of cash or working capital. Virtually all publicly held companies chose the seemingly more sophisticated working capital format for this statement.

---

[1]B.S. Thomas, ''The Perils of Ignoring Cash Flow,'' *Directors & Boards*, Fall 1983, pp. 9–10.

[2]The interested reader is referred to Chapter 3 of *The Modern Theory of Financial Reporting* by L. Brown (Homewood, Ill.: BPI/Irwin, 1987).

The purpose of the SCFP was to explain how a company had funded its activities during the year, with *funds* defined as working capital. However, it did not take long for financial statement users to become disenchanted with the working capital approach to the SCFP because although working capital had a conceptual meaning (i.e., current assets minus current liabilities), it did not fully indicate the level of resources available for such normal operating functions as paying for purchases or investments.

This trend of increasing dissatisfaction with the SCFP was, in part, the result of a progressively more widespread call from the investing community for information pertaining to a business enterprise's cash flows. At about this same time, the FASB was also looking into the issue of cash flows. The Board's study, begun in 1981, culminated with the issuance of SFAS No. 95, "Statement of Cash Flows," in November 1987.

SFAS No. 95 requires businesses to include a statement of cash flows when issuing published financial statements. The FASB believes that this requirement will help readers and users of financial statements assess the following:

1. A business's ability to generate future cash flows.
2. Its ability to meet obligations and pay dividends.
3. The effectiveness with which its management has fulfilled its cash-stewardship function.

In short, the required cash flow information is intended to aid in determining the amount, timing, and uncertainty of *future* cash flows.

The Importance of Cash Flows

Cash flows represent the most fundamental and prevalent economic events engaged in by businesses. In fact, talk to just about any small business owner, entrepreneur, banker, or chief financial officer and he or she will tell you that the "bottom line" of the income statement has little to do with staying solvent. It is cash planning—specifically, understanding the sources and uses of current and future cash flows—that often makes the difference between corporate success and failure.

Businesses that manage cash effectively benefit in numerous ways. For example, they benefit by having lower financing costs. By accurately forecasting the amount and timing of cash flows, managers minimize their need to borrow, thus lessening their company's interest expense. In addition, improving the amount of cash generated from operations decreases the need to solicit external financing, thus preserving proportionate shareholder value and unused debt capacity.

Cash is also important to external users of financial statements. Stockholder and creditor interests are seldom settled by means other than cash. Therefore, cash flow information is very useful in enabling these users to assess a company's ability to (1) generate future positive cash flows from operations, (2) meet its maturing obligations, and (3) pay dividends.

Concerning this point, accrual accounting often masks a company's underlying cash flows. Under the accrual basis of accounting, revenues are recognized at the time of sale, not when cash is received. Thus, credit sales increase net income but not current cash inflows. The accrual basis of preparing an income statement also reports such noncash expenses as depreciation, amortization, and accrued warranty estimates, which reduce net income and further widen the gulf between it and cash flows. From a balance sheet perspective, when a business enters into a loan agreement, the loan is reflected as an increase in loans payable. As the loan is repaid, cash outflows increase and the loan's payable balance decreases. At no time, however, does any record of the cash outflow for the loan repayment appear in the income statement; only the interest expense appears there. For reasons such as this, a business can easily find itself with an income statement that portrays an attractive net income number but without sufficient cash for tomorrow's tax bill, payroll, dividend, or loan payment. To ensure that such payments can be made, and that operations continue in an orderly manner, managers must manage both the timing and amount of cash flows.

THE ELEMENTS OF THE STATEMENT OF CASH FLOWS

The primary objective of the statement of cash flows (SCF) is to explain the change in cash and cash equivalents occurring during a given reporting period. Recall from Chapter 2 that this relationship can be portrayed as in Exhibit 6.1.

For purposes of the SCF, *cash* includes currency on hand and demand deposits and **cash equivalents,** which are short-term, liquid investments (e.g., U.S. Treasury bills) that are both readily convertible to cash and so close to maturity as to be essentially risk free. Companies must disclose which items are considered to be cash equivalents in their financial statements. Government securities of terms longer than three months, debt securities of terms longer than three months, and equity securities are not considered to be cash equivalents.

Statement Format

The SCF should clearly classify cash flows into three principal areas of activity: operating, investing, and financing. **Investing activities** primarily affect the noncurrent asset accounts and include such transactions as making and collecting loans, acquiring and disposing of other entities' debt instruments or equity investments, and buying and selling property, plant, equipment, and other long-lived productive assets. Cash flows from **financing activities** are the results of transactions generally affecting the noncurrent liability and stockholders' equity accounts and include such transactions as obtaining resources from owners and providing them a return *on* and a return *of* their investment and borrowing and repaying amounts borrowed. Finally, **operating activities** primarily affect the income statement and working capital accounts—in essence, the cash flows from sales of goods or services and cash payments for acquisition of the inputs used to provide the goods or services sold (e.g., raw materials and labor). One helpful way to ascertain the appropriate categorization of a given business transaction is to think about the person

EXHIBIT 6.1

The Relationship between the Statement of Cash Flows and
Consecutive Balance Sheets

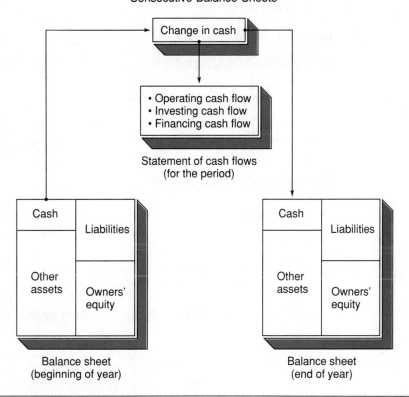

who might be making the decision to engage in the transaction: operations people generally make the *operating* decisions, the finance department is likely to be making the *investment* decisions, and the treasurer's office typically makes the *financing* decisions.

Operating activities. In regard to the operating activities section of the SCF, two presentation methods are permissible: the direct method and the indirect method (see Exhibit 6.2). The **direct method** presents major classes of cash receipts and payments. The direct method involves reporting, at a minimum, the **cash flows from operating activities** as the difference between the receipts and payments pertaining to the following separately reported items:

- Cash collected from clients and customers.
- Dividends and interest received.
- Other receipts of operating cash, if any, such as insurance and lawsuit settlements and refunds from suppliers.

E X H I B I T 6 . 2

The Statement of Cash Flows: Direct versus Indirect Methods

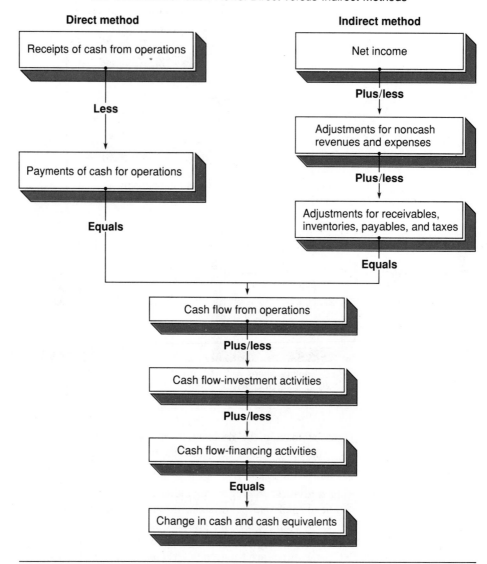

- Cash payments for wages and other goods and services received.
- Interest paid.
- Taxes paid.
- Other operating cash payments, if any, such as charitable contributions.
- Refunds to customers and lawsuit settlements.

The distinctive feature of the **indirect method** of presenting the SCF is that it reconciles a company's accrual net income with its cash flows from operations. Beginning with net income (see Exhibit 6.3), the reconciliation process converts net income to its cash-basis equivalent by (1) adding back the noncash expenses (e.g., deferred income taxes, depreciation, and amortization expense) deducted that period in deriving net income and subtracting the noncash revenues (e.g., undistributed earnings of affiliates) included in the period's net income, and (2) subtracting any gains and adding back any losses incurred on various transactions (e.g., the sale of a noncurrent asset or the early retirement of long-term debt) that will be reported in the investing and financing sections of the SCF. The first type of adjustment is designed to eliminate any noncash items that are included in net income under the accrual basis of accounting, whereas the second type of adjustment is designed to avoid the double counting of certain cash flows. For example, if a long-term investment recorded on the books at $100,000 is sold for $120,000, the entire cash inflow of $120,000 should be reported on the SCF as an investing activity. To avoid double counting the $20,000 cash inflow representing the gain on the sale, the $20,000 gain included in accrual net income is subtracted from net income in deriving cash flow from operations in the SCF.

To complete the conversion of the accrual net income figure to the cash flows from operations figure under the indirect method, a final set of adjustments involving the operations-related current asset and current liability accounts is needed. Consider, for example, the fact that the sales figure in PepsiCo's income statement (most of which represents credit sales) is equal to this period's cash inflows from sales activities *only if* the year-end accounts receivable balance remains unchanged as compared to the receivable balance at the beginning of the period. This situation is reflected in Scenario 1 of Panel A in Exhibit 6.4. If, during the year, PepsiCo collected less than it billed its customers for credit sales, thereby creating an increase in the ending accounts receivable balance, the net income figure in the SCF needs to be reduced by the increase in receivables in order to approximate the period's true cash inflows from sales. Scenario 2 in Panel A of Exhibit 6.4 depicts this situation, as does PepsiCo's SCF for 1990, 1989, and 1988. Finally, a reduction in the ending receivable balance as compared to the beginning balance indicates that more cash had been collected than is reflected in the current period's sales figure. Thus, the amount of the reduction in the receivable balance should be added to the net income figure on the SCF in order to reflect this higher cash inflow. See, for example, Scenario 3 in Panel A of Exhibit 6.4.

This final set of adjustments needed to derive the cash flow from operations may involve more accounts than the Accounts Receivable account. Consider for example, the case of inventory. Every period, service businesses accumulate billable time, merchandisers make new purchases, and manufacturers produce additional items. If reported inventory amounts have increased beyond the beginning of period balance (i.e., purchases have exceeded sales of inventory), an increased outflow of cash has occurred. Thus, the net increase in inventory must be subtracted from the accrual-based net income to reflect accurately the total cash spent or invested in inventory. On the other hand, if the reported ending inventory amounts have declined relative to their beginning balances, the net decline represents a part of the cost of goods sold that is deducted in the income statement but for which no cash was expended this period. This means that the amount of the net

EXHIBIT 6.3

Consolidated Statement of Cash Flows

PepsiCo, Inc. and Subsidiaries
Fifty-two weeks ended December 29, 1990 and December 30, 1989 and fifty-three weeks ended December 31, 1988
(in millions)

	1990	1989	1988
Cash Flows from Continuing Operations:			
Income from continuing operations	$ 1,090.6	$ 901.4	$ 762.2
Adjustments to reconcile income from continuing operations to net cash generated by continuing operations:			
Gain on joint venture stock offering	(118.2)	–	–
Depreciation and amortization	884.0	772.0	629.3
Deferred income taxes	106.1	71.2	20.1
Other noncash charges and credits–net	120.3	128.4	213.4
Changes in operating working capital, excluding effect of acquisitions and sales of businesses:			
Notes and accounts receivable	(124.8)	(149.9)	(50.1)
Inventories	(20.9)	(50.1)	13.8
Prepaid expenses and other current assets	(61.6)	6.5	37.8
Accounts payable	25.4	134.9	138.2
Income taxes payable	136.3	80.9	55.1
Other current liabilities	72.8	(9.4)	74.7
Net change in operating working capital	27.2	12.9	269.5
Net Cash Generated by Continuing Operations	2,110.0	1,885.9	1,894.5
Cash Flows from Investing Activities:			
Acquisitions and investments in affiliates	(630.6)	(3,296.6)	(1,415.5)
Purchases of property, plant and equipment	(1,180.1)	(943.8)	(725.8)
Proceeds from joint venture stock offering	129.6	–	–
Proceeds from sales of property, plant and equipment	45.3	69.7	67.4
Proceeds from sales of businesses	–	–	283.2
Net sales (purchases) of short-term investments	(181.8)	12.3	(201.7)
Other, net	(119.7)	(97.9)	(58.7)
Net Cash Used for Investing Activities	(1,937.3)	(4,256.3)	(2,051.1)
Cash Flows from Financing Activities:			
Proceeds from issuances of long-term debt	777.3	71.7	475.3
Payments of long-term debt	(298.0)	(405.4)	(190.0)
Net proceeds from (payments of) short-term borrowings	(86.2)	2,925.5	231.3
Cash dividends paid	(293.9)	(241.9)	(199.0)
Purchases of treasury stock	(147.7)	–	(71.8)
Other, net	(28.6)	(28.9)	(24.4)
Net Cash Generated by (Used for) Financing Activities	(77.1)	2,321.0	221.4
Effect of Exchange Rate Changes on Cash and Cash Equivalents	(1.0)	(17.1)	(1.4)
Net Increase (Decrease) in Cash and Cash Equivalents	94.6	(66.5)	63.4
Cash and Cash Equivalents–Beginning of Year	76.2	142.7	79.3
Cash and Cash Equivalents–End of Year	$ 170.8	$ 76.2	$ 142.7
Supplemental Cash Flow Information:			
Cash Flow Data			
Interest paid	$ 656.9	$ 591.1	$ 286.5
Income taxes paid	$ 375.0	$ 239.7	$ 234.7
Schedule of Noncash Investing and Financing Activities			
Issuance of treasury stock and debt for acquisitions	$ 105.1	$ 103.9	$ 328.2
Liabilities assumed/disposed of in connection with acquisitions/sales of businesses	$ 231.8	$ 446.8	$ 300.0
Issuance of treasury stock for compensation awards and conversion of debentures	$ 13.5	$ 9.3	$ 26.4
Additions of capital leases	$ 18.1	$ 15.7	$ 4.3

See accompanying Notes to Consolidated Financial Statements.

E X H I B I T   6 . 4

**Three Scenarios for Changes in
Accounts Receivable and Accrued Wages Payable
and Their SCF Reporting**

Panel A: Accounts Receivable

Scenario	Accounts Receivable 12/31/92	Credit Sales included in 1993 Net Income	1993 Cash Collections	Accounts Receivable 12/31/93	1993 SCF Net Income Adjustment Related to a Change in Accounts Receivable
1	$10,000	$100,000	$100,000	$10,000	–0–
2	10,000	100,000	95,000	15,000	($5,000)
3	10,000	100,000	102,000	8,000	2,000

Panel B: Accrued Wages Payable

Scenario	Accrued Wages Payable 12/31/92	Wage Expense Deducted in 1993 Net Income	1993 Cash Outflow for Wages	Accrued Wages Payable 12/31/93	1993 SCF Net Income Adjustment related to a Change in Accrued Wages Payable
1	$ 4,000	$ 40,000	$ 40,000	$ 4,000	–0–
2	4,000	40,000	37,000	7,000	$3,000
3	4,000	40,000	43,500	500	(3,500)

decline must be added back to the accrual-based net income number to accurately reflect the actual cash outflows for inventory. In this regard, Exhibit 6.3 depicts PepsiCo's adjustment to reduce accrual net income in 1990 and 1989 for an increase in inventories in deriving cash flow from operations, whereas in 1988 just the opposite is shown.

Similar analyses apply to the accounts payable and to the accrued expenses payable that are a function of purchasing materials, supplies, and labor used in conducting a firm's operations. For example, an increase in accrued expenses payable (e.g., accrued wages payable) in effect represents a form of cash inflow because the business has not yet expended cash for some of the expenses currently deducted in the income statement (see Panel B in Exhibit 6.4). Alternatively, a decrease in accrued expenses payable in effect signifies an additional cash outflow for expenses booked on the current and/or prior income statement, thus necessitating a reduction in the cash-based net income estimate on the SCF in order to bring it into line with this period's actual cash outflows for expensed items.

It is important to understand fully these current asset and current liability adjustments. One way to facilitate one's understanding of the need for these adjustments is to focus on the more intuitively obvious accounts as was done for accounts receivable and accrued wages payable in Exhibit 6.4. Once you become familiar with how the adjustments to these accounts relate to the SCF, the remaining working capital accounts can be viewed as extensions of the same logic but applied to different balance sheet accounts. Another means to achieve a greater level of understanding of these adjustments is actually to prepare an SCF—an opportunity for which is presented in a subsequent section of this chapter.

It is worth noting that accounts pertaining to the current portion of long-term debt and notes payable are more appropriately considered financing activities than operating activities and are therefore excluded from the conversion of net income to cash flows. Thus, the sum of net income plus all of the adjustments described above (as necessitated by the indirect method of preparing an SCF) results in the amount of cash generated internally by a company, or its *cash flows from operations*. Most companies (like PepsiCo) prefer the indirect method of presenting the SCF over the direct method because it provides a link to the income statement and balance sheet, and it is generally less costly to prepare. The FASB, on the other hand, prefers the direct method because it presents a company's major types of cash receipts and payments. As shown in Exhibit 6.2, the cash flows from operations are the same regardless of which method is used. Moreover, if the direct method is used, a reconciliation of net income to cash flow from operations must be presented in a separate schedule.

Cash flows from operations is arguably the most important cash flow indicator for users of financial statements because it demonstrates the ability of a company's operations to generate cash for its stockholders, creditors, or future investment. It informs the financial statement reader whether the business is a net provider or a net user of cash in its core internal operations. If the operations of a business use more cash than they provide, cash must then be provided by liquidating investments, seeking further external financing, or decreasing the company's reserves of cash and cash equivalents. If, on the other hand, the operating activities provide cash, such as the case for PepsiCo, this additional cash will be available to invest in the business, to repay prior financing, to pay dividends, or merely to increase the cash reserves of the company. In 1990, PepsiCo's continuing operations generated a whopping $2.1 billion in cash flows, which was available to finance a variety of firm-related activities.

Investing activities. The next section of the SCF, as shown in PepsiCo's SCF (Exhibit 6.3), reports cash flows from investing activities. This section presents the uses and provisions of cash from investments, with the term *investment* used quite broadly. This section details the amounts a company has invested in its own business, equity investments in other firms, and dispositions and purchases of other assets. From Exhibit 6.3, we can see that in 1990 PepsiCo invested more than $630 million in new acquisitions and investments; more than $1.18 billion in purchases of property, plant, and equipment; and more than $181 million in purchases of short-term investments. PepsiCo's 1990 SCF also reveals that the company sold $129.6 million in stock from a joint venture and received $45.3 million from the sale of property, plant, and equipment. Overall in 1990, PepsiCo's investing activities involved net cash outflows of $1,937.3 million.

Financing activities. The final section of an SCF is the cash flow from financing activities. This section details the changes in the capital structure of a company and payments made to provide a return to investors on (and of) their investments in the firm. If cash flows from operations are positive, the company may wish to reduce its debt load, pay dividends, or buy back some of its outstanding shares. These choices must be considered in light of the firm's capital expenditure needs. If, on the other hand, the cash flows from operations are negative, or if they are positive but investing activities used more cash than operations provided (e.g., as for PepsiCo in 1988 and 1989 as revealed in Exhibit 6.3), a firm might want to reconsider paying cash dividends; it could be argued that paying dividends under these circumstances involves a partial liquidation of the firm.

Noncash investing and financing activities. Businesses sometimes engage in noncash investing and financing activities. For example, the conversion of debt into owners' equity does not involve any cash inflows or outflows, nor does the acquisition of a piece of equipment financed entirely by the seller. Such noncash activities are either reported in a supplement to the SCF, as in Exhibit 6.3 for PepsiCo, or are disclosed elsewhere in the financial statements. Exhibit 6.3 reveals, for example, that PepsiCo issued $105.1 million in treasury stock and debt as part of the consideration given for various acquisitions of new companies it made during 1990.

Preparing a Statement of Cash Flows

With the preceding discussion in mind, the best way to gain a full understanding of the SCF is to prepare one. The following simplified example is designed to illustrate the preparation of an indirect method SCF, produced from the comparative income statements (Exhibit 6.5) and balance sheets (Exhibit 6.6) of the Oakencroft Cabinet Company.

In preparing Oakencroft's SCF, it is useful to recall the basic accounting equation regarding assets, liabilities, and owners' equity:

$$A = L + OE. \tag{1a}$$

Moreover, it is useful to note that the change in total assets from one period to the next must equal the sum of the changes in liability and owners' equity accounts over that same period. Thus, Equation (1a) can be restated as

$$\Delta A = \Delta L + \Delta OE \tag{1b}$$

where Δ is interpreted as "the change in." Remember also that assets and liabilities are both composed of current (C) and noncurrent (NC) portions, so Equation (1b) can be restated as

$$\Delta CA + \Delta NCA = \Delta CL + \Delta NCL + \Delta OE. \tag{2a}$$

A further breakdown of current assets into their components of cash, accounts receivable, inventories, and prepaid expenses permits a restatement of Equation (2a) as

$$\Delta \text{Cash} + \Delta AR + \Delta \text{Inv} + \Delta \text{Ppd Exp} + \Delta NCA = \Delta CL + \Delta NCL + \Delta OE. \tag{2b}$$

Rearranging this equation to isolate the change in cash, we see that

$$\Delta \text{ Cash} = \underbrace{\Delta \text{ CL} - \Delta \text{ AR} - \Delta \text{ Inv} - \Delta \text{ Ppd Exp}}_{\text{Operating activities}} - \underbrace{\Delta \text{ NCA}}_{\substack{\text{Investing} \\ \text{activities}}} + \underbrace{\Delta \text{ NCL} + \Delta \text{ OE}}_{\substack{\text{Financing} \\ \text{activities}}}. \quad (3)$$

The dynamics of the statement of cash flows can easily be discerned from this alternative presentation of the accounting equation. For example, if a current liability such as accrued wages payable is increased, the effect is an increase in cash (or a positive cash flow)—in essence, a form of spontaneous financing. If, on the other hand, there is an increase in a current asset account such as Inventory or Prepaid Expenses, cash decreases.

As noted earlier, the starting point for preparing an SCF using the indirect method is the accrual net income for the period. From such a starting point, the net income number must be adjusted for the noncash revenues and expenses that are present in the income statement—primarily depreciation, amortization, deferred taxes,[3] and the undistributed earnings of affiliate companies.[4] The 1992 Oakencroft income statement (see Exhibit 6.5) reveals, for example, that $9,033 was deducted as depreciation expense. Because depreciation of property, plant, and equipment requires no cash outlay, the $9,033 must be added back to net income in deriving an estimate of the cash flows from operations. Oakencroft's income statement reveals no other noncash revenues or expenses with the exception of deferred income taxes. From the balance sheet and the income statement footnote, in 1992 there was a decrease in the Deferred Taxes Liability account with a commensurate reduction in the total tax expense amount. The overall effect of this change represents an additional cash outlay this period for income taxes owed from an earlier accounting period; that is, the tax expense for this additional amount was recorded in an earlier accounting period but was not paid until this period. Thus, the decrease in deferred tax liabilities in 1992 represents a decrease in operating cash flows this period that was not revealed in the 1992 income statement where only $18,383 was deducted as tax expense. Remembering the relationships from Equation (3), we recognize that this decrease in a liability should, therefore, be subtracted from net income in the operating activities section.

As pointed out earlier, the objective of the SCF is to explain the change in cash and cash equivalents by reporting all of the changes in the noncash accounts. In a sense, this is like trying to define a word without using the word in the definition. In effect, the SCF provides a definition of the change in cash by examining all of the other balance sheet

---

[3]In the United States, a company may prepare its income tax return using different accounting principles than it uses to prepare its financial statements. To the extent that the amount of tax that would be due if the financial statement basis had been used is different from the taxes shown on the tax return, that difference is recorded as *deferred taxes*. Therefore, deferred taxes are different from taxes payable because the deferred taxes become a liability only at some future and uncertain time. Deferred taxes represent a form of interest-free borrowing by the company and are a reconciling item between earnings and cash flow. Taxes currently payable represent the amount of taxes shown on the current tax return, less any prepayments. This topic is discussed in Chapter 12.

[4]In certain circumstances, a company may include in its own income statement the income of another company that it controls. Those earnings are recognized as they are reported by the other company on the theory that the controlling company could cause those earnings to be remitted to it at any time. Obviously, to the extent that the earnings are not remitted to the parent company in cash, those earnings are an adjustment to accrual earnings to arrive at the operating cash flow. This topic is discussed in Chapter 9.

EXHIBIT 6.5

Oakencroft Cabinet Company
Income Statement
(in thousands of dollars)

	For the Year Ended	
	December 31, 1992	December 31, 1991
Net sales	$419,991	$341,656
Costs and expenses:		
Cost of sales	(280,746)	(228,681)
Depreciation	(9,033)	(6,843)
Selling, general, and administrative	(85,469)	(65,610)
	(375,248)	(301,134)
Income from operations	44,743	40,522
Interest expense	(1,877)	(1,570)
Other income	2,081	2,807
Earnings before taxes	44,947	41,759
Federal income taxes*	(18,383)	(17,606)
State income taxes	(1,900)	(1,143)
Net income	24,664	23,010
Retained earnings, beginning of year	138,273	121,476
Less: Cash dividends	(6,920)	(6,213)
Retained earnings, end of year	$156,017	$138,273

*Federal income tax expense included the following:

	1992	1991
Current amount	$18,603	$17,456
Deferred amount	(220)	
Total	$18,383	$17,606

account changes. Thus, the next step in our efforts to develop Oakencroft's SCF (see Exhibit 6.7) is to focus on the adjustments to net income associated with changes in the current asset and current liability operations-related accounts.

From the balance sheet data in Exhibit 6.6, note that accounts receivable increased $10,010 from 1991 to 1992. This means that the company billed its customers for more than it collected from them, which represents sales for which collections have not yet been received. The amount is thus shown as a reduction to net income in the pursuit of converting an accrual-based net income amount to an operating cash flow estimate. With similar logic, the balance sheet data also reveal that accounts payable (along with wages payable and accrued liabilities) increased, indicating that the company was billed for more expenses than it paid; hence, this amount is like a provision of cash and is therefore shown as a positive cash flow. The sum of these items (i.e., net income *plus/minus* the noncash revenues and expenses *plus/minus* the changes in working capital accounts) equals the cash flow from operating activities of $29,672.

EXHIBIT 6.6

Oakencroft Cabinet Company
Balance Sheet
(in thousands)

As of

	December 31, 1992	December 31, 1991	Increase/ Decrease in Account Balance
Assets			
Cash	$ 1,393	$ 2,419	$(1,026)
Short-term Treasury bills	21,172	13,305	7,867
Receivables, less allowances of $3,118 in 1992 and $2,814 in 1991	113,834	103,824	10,010
Inventories:			
Raw materials	19,541	15,305	
Work in process	17,143	14,771	
Finished goods	8,791	5,157	
	45,475	35,233	10,242
Other current assets	5,037	3,229	1,808
Total current assets	$186,911	$158,010	
Property, plant, and equipment:			
Land	3,586	2,842	
Buildings and fixtures	53,082	44,082	
Machinery and equipment	66,978	51,041	
	123,646	97,971	25,675
Less: Accumulated depreciation	50,115	41,082	(9,033)
	73,531	56,889	16,642
Other assets	9,445	18,095	(8,650)
Total assets	$269,887	$232,994	$36,893

The investment section of the SCF shows changes in the balance sheet for investments in property, plant, equipment (PP&E), in equity securities from other companies, and in other assets. Note that the balance sheet data indicate that PP&E increased by $25,675. The change in the accumulated depreciation account of $9,033 equals this period's depreciation expense, which has already been placed as an adjusting item in the operating section of Oakencroft's SCF. In the absence of any sales of PP&E during the year, the $25,675 figure equals the cost of purchases of PP&E made this year.

It is often helpful to construct a T-account for the PP&E accounts to facilitate these calculations. In this example, the T-accounts are very straightforward:

EXHIBIT 6.6

(continued)

	As of		
	December 31, 1992	December 31, 1991	Increase/ Decrease in Account Balance
Liabilities			
Notes payable	$ 6,099	$ 3,682	$ 2,417
Current portion of long-term debt	979	1,717	(738)
Accounts payable	20,134	11,033	9,101
Wages payable	15,941	13,144	2,797
Accrued liabilities	10,014	7,478	2,536
Accrued taxes	18,409	14,588	3,821
Total current liabilities	71,576	51,642	
Long-term debt	23,270	24,463	(1,193)
Deferred taxes	9,697	9,917	(220)
Total liabilities	$104,543	$ 86,022	
Stockholders Equity			
Common stock	$ 10,714	$ 10,443	271
Retained earnings	156,017	138,273	17,744
	166,731	148,716	
Less: Treasury shares	(1,387)	(1,744)	357
Total stockholders' equity	$165,344	$146,972	
Total liabilities and stockholders' equity	$269,887	$232,994	$36,893

Property, Plant, and Equipment		**Accumulated Depreciation**	
1/1/92 97,971		1/1/92 41,082	
Purchases 25,675		This year's expense 9,033	
12/31/92 123,046		12/31/92 50,115	

If, however, the financial statements had informed readers that PP&E originally costing $10,000 had been sold for $8,000 and the 1992 depreciation expense was $12,033, the reconstruction of the T-accounts would reveal the following:

Property, Plant, and Equipment				Accumulated Depreciation		
1/1/92	97,971				1/1/92	41,082
		Cost of PP&E sold	10,000	Accumulated depreciation on PP&E sold 3,000	This year's expense	12,033
PP&E purchases	35,675					
12/31/92	123,646				12/31/92	50,115

Thus, in this hypothetical scenario, it is possible to identify purchases of PP&E totaling $35,675. In addition, it is also possible to determine that $3,000 of depreciation expense had been accumulated over the years for the particular PP&E item sold. In sum, then, the transaction to record the sale would have been as follows:

```
Dr.  Cash (A) . . . . . . . . . . . . . . . . . . . . . . . .   8,000
Dr.  Accumulated Depreciation (CA) . . . . . . . . . . . .   3,000
     Cr.  Property, Plant, and Equipment (A) . . . . . . . . . . . . .        10,000
     Cr.  Gain on sale of Property, Plant, and Equipment (G) . . . . . .         1,000
```

Under this scenario, the SCF would report a $1,000 subtracting adjustment to net income in the operations section and a line item of $8,000 for "proceeds of PP&E sale" in the investing section, as well as another line item of $35,675 for purchases of PP&E. Since we were not informed of any PP&E sales, we must assume the base case in which purchases of PP&E cost $25,675 and depreciation expense was $9,033.

The final section of the SCF, financing activities, shows the net changes in cash flows as a result of payments and proceeds from loans, stock sales and stock repurchases, dividends paid to shareholders, and other financing transactions. Note the increase in short-term notes payable of $2,417. This amount is a provision of cash for the company and is shown as a positive cash flow. In determining the payments on long-term debt ($1,931), both the amounts currently due and those that are noncurrent should be considered. Cash dividends paid to stockholders always represent a use of cash and thus are shown as a negative cash flow.

As a vehicle to verify that the entire change in the retained earnings balance has been accounted for in the SCF, it is useful to reconstruct the changes in this account balance using a T-account. In the Retained Earnings T-account portrayed following, note that the net income and dividend figures, both of which now appear in the SCF, fully explain the change in Oakencroft's Retained Earnings account for the period:

Retained Earnings

	1/1/92	138,273
1992 dividends 6,920	1992 net income	24,664
	12/31/92	156,017

The format for reporting these results is shown in Exhibit 6.7. The sum of the three separate sections represents the increase (or decrease) in cash and cash equivalents for the period. When added to the beginning balance of cash and cash equivalents, the resulting sum should equal the ending cash and cash-equivalent balance on the latest balance sheet.

EXHIBIT 6.7

Oakencroft Cabinet Company
Statement of Cash Flows
(in thousands)

	For the year ended December 31, 1992
Operating activities	
Net income	$24,664
Add: Depreciation and amortization	9,033
Other noncash expenses	–0–
Less: Noncash revenues	–0–
Adjustment for deferred taxes	(220)
Receivables, decrease (increase)	(10,010)
Inventories, decrease, (increase)	(10,242)
Payables, increase, (decrease)	14,434
Taxes, increase (decrease)	3,821
Other	(1,808)
	(5,008)
Cash flow from operating activities	$29,672
Investing activities	
Purchases of Property, plant and equipment	(25,675)
Other	8,650
Cash flow from investing activities	($17,025)
Financing activities	
Proceeds from short-term notes payable	2,417
Payments on long-term loans	(1,931)
Sale of stock	271
Reissue of treasury stock	357
Cash dividends paid to stockholders	(6,920)
Cash flow from financing activities	($ 5,806)
Increase (decrease) in cash and cash equivalents	$ 6,841
Cash and cash equivalents, beginning of year	$15,724
Cash and cash equivalents, end of year	$22,565

If all of the balance sheet changes reflected in Exhibit 6.6 have been included in the SCF, it should balance to the actual change in the cash and cash-equivalent balance (i.e. $6,841 for Oakencroft), and the SCF is then complete.

ANALYZING CASH FLOWS

By using the basic relationships depicted in Equation (3), the statement of cash flows itself, and cash flow ratio analysis, financial statement users can increase their understanding of an enterprise and answer questions such as these:

- What is the relationship between cash flows and earnings?
- How are dividends being financed?
- How is debt repayment to be achieved?
- Does the company require outside financing?
- How are the cash flows from operations being used?
- Is management's financial policy reflected in the cash flows?

In Chapters 4 and 5, we saw that financial ratio analysis could be applied to income statement and balance sheet accounts to reveal various insights about a company. Traditional ratio analysis, and even the income statement itself, however, will not provide insights regarding issues such as the timing of cash flows or the effects of operations on liquidity. To obtain this kind of information it is necessary to analyze the information presented in the statement of cash flows.

Cash Flow Ratios

Some useful cash flow ratios are presented in this section. The list is not comprehensive but should indicate the relative merit of analyzing the SCF by developing applicable ratios. Each ratio is discussed in light of the PepsiCo information presented in Exhibit 6.3. Individually, each ratio gives limited information as of a single point in time, but taken over a period of years and examined in conjunction with other ratios, the cash flow ratios can reveal trends that provide insights about the company and its industry.

Operating funds ratio. Calculated as net income divided by cash flows from operations, the operating funds ratio can be used to indicate the portion of operating cash flows provided by net income. Depreciation methods and the management of current asset and current liability accounts are the principal factors highlighted by this ratio because they are the principal adjustments to net income used in calculating the cash flows from operations. This ratio for PepsiCo in 1990 was 0.52, indicating that the cash flows from operations were greater than net income and that, on average, there were sizable positive adjustments to accrual net income. Given the capital-intensive nature of PepsiCo's business, there was a large depreciation and amortization expense component (i.e., $884 million) to the income adjustments made to arrive at the cash flows from operations. Moreover, given the consistent, positive track record of PepsiCo's management, one would expect only minor fluctuations in the operations-related current asset or current liability accounts, with only a modest (and most probably positive) impact on cash flows.

Normal operating conditions are likely to yield ratios in the 0.25 to 1.0 range, but not all healthy companies have such ratios and not all ratios in that range are necessarily good. Different management objectives and different industries tend to be characterized by different "normal" ratio ranges. For example, very high growth periods can result in ratios consistently greater than 1.0 because of the normal increases in receivables and inventories that characterize rapid growth. For example, Josten's, Inc., achieved a 21 percent growth in sales during 1989, and its operating funds ratio for that year was 1.14.

As with all ratios, one must be careful to examine the underlying events reflected by such ratios. A troubled company also may have especially high levels of receivables and inventory giving rise to a high operating fund ratio. For example, the Grumman Corporation reported a decline in 1989 sales but an operating funds ratio of 1.4, reflecting a decline in its cash flow from operations due to a sizable investment in unsold inventory.

Investment ratio. Calculated as capital expenditures divided by depreciation plus sales of assets, the **investment ratio** reveals the relative level of investment in capital assets and whether a company's productive asset base is expanding or shrinking. The ratio provides some insight regarding management's plans for the future and its analysis of the future economy. In 1990, this ratio for PepsiCo was 1.61. The fact that this ratio exceeds 1.0 indicates that PepsiCo's management increased the company's relative investment in property, plant, and equipment during the period. Ratio amounts less than 1.0 usually indicate a situation in which the management is, in effect, "harvesting" past investments in capital assets or is not investing in property, plant, and equipment at the same (or faster) rate than these productive assets are being consumed. For example, in the late 1980s, the Grumman Corporation was forced into a period of retrenchment, as revealed by its 1989 investment ratio of 0.58.

Cash flow adequacy ratio. The **cash flow adequacy ratio** is calculated as the cash flows from operations divided by long-term capital expenditures plus dividends and long-term debt repayment. This ratio helps reveal whether or not a business is providing sufficient funds through operations to match expenditures for its current capital structure and future asset base. In 1990, PepsiCo's cash flow adequacy ratio was 0.88, which indicates that insufficient cash was being generated from operations to provide for the firm's expanded level of long-term investments, dividends, and debt repayment. In general, the closer this ratio is to zero, the greater is a company's dependency on creditors and owners for additional financing to execute plant and equipment expansion programs; the reverse is also true. Because expenditures for these types of items tend to vary from year to year, ratios less than 1.0 are not cause for alarm unless they are consistently below 1.0 for a number of accounting periods. In this regard, Grumman Corporation had a negative cash flow adequacy ratio in 1987, a 0.05 ratio in 1988, and 0.20 in 1989. Clearly, Grumman's ratio trend is in the appropriate direction, but the ratios have been so low that it must be concluded that Grumman's management faces a significant challenge to financially service its creditors and shareholders as well as its equipment replacement needs.

Cash sources percentages. This ratio (i.e., individual cash flow sources divided by the total sources of cash) for each specific source of cash indicates the degree to which a company provides cash from operations, by external borrowing or other means. The 1990 PepsiCo cash flow statement shown in Exhibit 6.3 reveals that the total sources of cash (i.e., all of the positive cash flow entries) equaled $3,387.7 million. Individual ratios for each source can be calculated to show the relative importance of a particular activity to the cash flows of the company. For example, 22.9 percent of PepsiCo's cash inflows were provided by long-term borrowings ($777.3 ÷ $3,387.7), while 1.3 percent was generated by sales of property, plant, and equipment ($45.3 ÷ $3,387.7). Such percentages indicate PepsiCo's high need for short-term funds, suggesting that cash-flow management is primarily a timing issue for PepsiCo, rather than an inability to generate internally adequate levels of cash flows. Moreover, the 1.3 percent indicates a very low dependence on fixed asset liquidations for cash infusions. It is interesting to note that for 1989, the Grumman Corporation had a long-term borrowing-to-total cash inflows ratio that closely approximated PepsiCo's short-term borrowing-to-total cash inflows ratio. These ratios reflect Grumman's relative inability to generate cash flows internally and, consequently, the company's dependency on external sources of cash flows to operate.

Dividend payout ratio. Dividends are among the main concerns of a company's stockholders and, consequently, the amount of cash dividends paid divided by available cash flows from operations is an important indicator for this group of investors. The percentage of cash flow paid to investors is an indication of management's commitment to a company's dividend policy as well as high-return projects available to the company for investment. PepsiCo's dividend payout ratio in 1990 was 13.9 percent, a level that is not unusual for healthy companies. A ratio greater than 100 percent is definitely cause for further investigation because it indicates that the company is paying dividends with funds not provided by the normal operations of the business. Moreover, as this ratio approaches 100 percent, concern should increase as to the ability of a company to maintain such dividend levels in that the proportion of internally generated cash needed to service those dividends is likewise approaching 100 percent. This clearly indicates that less internally generated cash will be available to cover other demands. For example, in 1989, Grumman Corporation's dividend payout ratio was 78 percent, indicating a relatively small amount of internally generated cash available to support the continuing operations of the company's businesses.

Many companies and industries use meaningful cash flow ratios that differ from those noted here. Thus, students are encouraged to consider ratios that are applicable to each industry or situation that they encounter.

Pro Forma Cash Flows

Just as it is instructive to examine various ratios based on the actual reported cash flow components, it is also useful to investigate a company's *expected* cash flows. In Chapter 5, we demonstrated that through the use of reasonable and realistic assumptions, it is possible to prepare forecasted or pro forma financial statements. And, just as it is instructive to consider a pro forma income statement, it is useful to examine a pro forma statement of cash flows to anticipate the amount, sources, and uses of subsequent periods' available cash resources.

Using the pro forma income statement for Blue Ridge Hardware Co. (Exhibit 5.8 from Chapter 5) as a starting point, we can develop a pro forma statement of cash flows. To do so, however, requires several additional assumptions that might include the following:

1. The ending balance in accounts receivable increases by 10 percent of the growth in revenues (i.e., $0.10 \times \$11,175$).
2. The ending inventory increases by 5 percent of the existing value of goods currently on hand (i.e., $0.05 \times \$12,700$).
3. The ending balance of accounts payable increases by $200.
4. Since no new employees need to be hired and since operating hours are not extended, the ending balances in wages and utilities payable remain unchanged.
5. Income taxes are paid quarterly; hence, at year-end, only the last quarter's taxes remain unpaid (i.e., $0.25 \times \$2,900$).
6. Since all of the equipment and fixtures are new, no asset purchases or replacements are required until 1993.
7. As required by the loan agreement, one fifth of the outstanding bank loan is repaid (i.e., $0.20 \times \$7,500$).
8. Cash dividends remain at $2,000.

Using these assumptions, along with the Blue Ridge Hardware pro forma income statement from Chapter 5, we can prepare a pro forma statement of cash flows for Blue Ridge Hardware. As revealed in Exhibit 6.8, the cash flows from operating activities are projected to be $6,692 for the year ended March 31, 1992. After paying the cash dividends and the partial loan repayment, the cash balance is projected to increase by $3,192. Such a favorable increase may be viewed by interested parties as a healthy cushion of cash inflows over cash outflows, thus providing a relative amount of comfort regarding the company's ability to generate adequate cash resources in the coming year. (Those students interested in reviewing a slightly different approach to cash flow forecasting are referred to the appendix at the end of this chapter.)

By incorporating the assumptions used in the preparation of the pro forma income statement and the statement of cash flows, it is also possible to prepare a pro forma balance sheet for Blue Ridge Hardware Co. Exhibit 6.9 reveals that if our assumptions hold true, the level of total assets and equities will reach $31,895 by March 31, 1992.

EXHIBIT 6.8

Blue Ridge Hardware Co.
Pro Forma Statement of Cash Flows
For the Year Ended March 31, 1992

Operating activities	
Net income	$ 8,820
Add: Depreciation on store equipment	1,000
Adjustments for working capital needs:	
Increase in accounts receivable	(1,118)
Increase in merchandise inventory	(635)
Increase in accounts payable	200
Increase in wages payable	–0–
Increase in utilities payable	–0–
Decrease in income tax payable	(1,575)
Cash flow from operating activities	$ 6,692
Investing activities	$ –0–
Financing activities	
Cash dividends paid	(2,000)
Partial repayment of bank loan	(1,500)
	$(3,500)
Increase in cash	$ 3,192
Cash, beginning of year	2,050
Cash, end of year	$ 5,242

EXHIBIT 6.9

Blue Ridge Hardware Co.
Pro Forma Balance Sheet
As of March 31, 1992

Assets		Equities	
Currents assets:		**Current liabilities:**	
Cash	$ 5,242	Accounts payable	$ 4,000
Accounts receivable	5,318	Wages payable	700
Merchandise inventory	13,335	Utilities payable	200
Total current assets	$23,895	Income tax payable	725
		Total current liabilities	$ 5,625
Noncurrent assets:			
Store equipment	10,000	**Noncurrent liabilities**	
Less: Accumulated depreciation	(2,000)	Bank loan payable	6,000
Total noncurrent assets	$ 8,000	Total liabilities	$11,625
		Owners' equity:	
		Capital stock	10,000
		Retained earnings	10,276
		Total liabilities and	
Total assets	$31,895	owners' equity	$31,895

SUMMARY

Informed observers and businesspeople realize that the "bottom line" (i.e., net income) has little to do with staying solvent and, hence, staying in business. Cash planning—specifically, the ability to understand the sources and uses of current and future cash flows—often makes the difference between business success and failure. Firms with excellent products, new equipment, and creative marketing efforts have gone out of business because they mistook earnings profitability for cash solvency.

A balance sheet, an income statement, and a statement of cash flows together provide managers, creditors, and investors alike with important information that is useful in developing a complete understanding of a company's financial status and health. Moreover, as we observed with regard to the balance sheet and income statement, it is possible to construct various ratios from the statement of cash flows that provide insights beyond the absolute level of cash provided or used. It would be quite misleading to suggest that information regarding cash flows is superior to that of earnings in providing a clear and true picture of a company's financial health. *Both* are important; but it is also worth noting the thoughts of one financial writer:

> Though my bottom line is black, I am flat upon my back,
> My cash flows out and customers pay slow.
> The growth of my receivables is almost unbelievable;
> The result is certain—unremitting woe!
> And I hear the banker utter an ominous low mutter,
> "Watch cash flow."[5]

Herbert S. Bailey, Jr., with
apologies to Edgar Allan Poe's
"The Raven"

NEW CONCEPTS AND TERMS

Cash equivalents (p. 246)
Cash flow adequacy ratio (p. 261)
Cash flows from operating activities (p. 247)
Direct method (p. 247)
Dividend payout ratio (p. 262)
Financing activities (p. 246)

Indirect method (p. 249)
Investing activities (p. 246)
Investment ratio (p. 261)
Noncash investing and financing activities (p. 253)
Operating activities (p. 246)
Operating funds ratio (p. 260)

---

[5]R. Green, "Are More Chryslers in the Offing?" *Forbes,* February 2, 1981, p. 69.

A Generalized Method of Forecasting Cash Flows from Operations

Managers and other users of financial statements are often interested in (1) ascertaining the sensitivity of a company's cash flows to varying economic factors and (2) estimating future cash flows from operations. Assume that you are such a user and you are again focusing on the Oakencroft Cabinet Company whose 1991 and 1992 balance sheets and 1992 income statement are presented in Exhibits 6.5 and 6.6. Assume that the company's projected 1993 sales figure is $540,000,000 and that the 1992 financial relationships will be the same in 1993. The task you are faced with is to forecast cash flows from operations and determine the effect on cash flow from operations due to (1) a possible sales decline of 15 percent from 1992, (2) a negative 3 percent net profit margin, and (3) a 50 percent increase in the relationship between the accounts payables and accruals amount versus the sales figure.

To forecast the cash flow from operations and to assess its sensitivity to various account balance changes, it is first necessary to develop a model of the underlying relationships. It is important to recall that the cash flows from operations figure is a function of net income, noncash expenses and noncash revenues, and the changes in the current asset and current liability accounts related to the company's operating activities. These latter items generally pertain to such items as accounts receivable and accounts payable. One model of these relationships is given by the following:

Forecasted cash flow from operations =

$$\left(\frac{NI}{S_c} + \frac{Depn}{S_c}\right)S_p + \frac{L}{S_c}(S_p - S_c) - \frac{A}{S_c}(S_p - S_c)$$

where

$\dfrac{NI}{S_c}$ = Current net income as a percent of current net sales

$\dfrac{\text{Depn}}{S_c}$ = Current depreciation expense as a percent of current net sales

$\dfrac{L}{S_c}$ = Liabilities that increase or decrease proportionately with sales, as a percent of current net sales

$\dfrac{A}{S_c}$ = Assets that increase or decrease proportionately with sales, as a percent of current net sales

S_c = Current year's net sales figure

S_p = Projected yearly sales figure

Using the above equation, the following summarization of Oakencroft's 1992 financial statement relationships, and the fact that 1992 depreciation expense was $9,033,000 yields the following estimate of the cash flows from operations:

1992 Relationships

Assets:		Percentage of Sales
Receivables	$133,834,000	27.1
Inventories	45,475,000	10.8
		37.9

Liabilities:		
Payables	$ 36,075,000	8.6
Accruals	28,423,000	6.8
		15.4

1993 Forecasted Cash Flows from Operations:

(0.059 + 0.022) 540,000,000 + 0.154 (540,000,000 − 419,991,000) − 0.379 (540,000,000 − 419,991,000) = 43,740,000 + 18,481,386 − 45,483,411 = $16,737,975

Thus, 1993 forecasted cash flows from operations represent a net of $16,737,975, based on the assumed relationships. Clearly, this is a sizable amount, yet it is also considerably lower than the actual 1992 cash flows from operations of $29,672,000 (i.e., see Exhibit 6.7).

To see how sensitive this projection is to changes in the various assumptions, a sensitivity analysis can be undertaken. Remember that the 1992 relationships between the various financial statements remain constant *except for* the one change in assumption being focused on in the sensitivity analysis:

Sales Decline of 15 Percent:

Forecasted sales = $372,000,000 (15% less than 1992 sales) .

Hence,

0.081(372) + 0.154(372 − 419.9) − 0.379(372 − 419.9) = 30.13 − 7.38 + 18.15
= Revised forecasted cash flow from operations = $40,900,000.

This revised cash flow projection is a function of declining inventories and receivables (at 37.9 percent rate), which with profits and depreciation become a "source" of cash while declining payables and accruals (at a 15.4 percent rate) become a "use" of cash.

Negative 3 Percent Net Profit Margin:

$$(-0.03 + 0.022)540 + 0.154(540 - 419.9) - 0.379(540 - 419.9) = -4.32 + 18.5$$
$$- 45.52 = \text{Revised forecasted cash flow from operations} = (\$31,340,000).$$

In this scenario, the net loss and the increase in receivables and inventories become a "use" of cash.

A 50 Percent Increase in the Accounts Payable Plus Accruals-to-Sales Ratio:

1992 Liabilities-to-sales ratio = 0.154; the 50 percent increase = 0.231.

Hence,

$$0.081(540) + 0.213(540 - 419.9) - 0.379(540 - 419.9) = 43.74 + 27.74 - 45.52$$
$$= \text{Revised forecasted cash flow from operations} = \$25,960,000.$$

When assets are supported to a greater extent by payables and accruals than before, the $(L/S_c - A/S_c)$ ratio becomes smaller, which means fewer are needed in the way of other sources of cash. This means that the more external funds support sales-sensitive assets (i.e., large $(L/S_c - A/S_c)$ ratio), the more external funds will be needed or reduced when these assets increase or decrease.

These simple examples and the basic approach to forecasting the cash flow from operations provide a simple but useful means for analysts, creditors, investors, and managers to assess more fully the amount and timing of a company's future cash flows.

ISSUES FOR DISCUSSION

D6.1 The statement of cash flows is a required basic financial statement.

a. What are the objectives of the statement of cash flows?

b. Identify two types of transactions that would be disclosed in a separate schedule with the statement of cash flows because they do not affect cash during the reporting period.

c. What effect, if any, would each of the following items have on the statement of cash flows assuming the *direct* method presentation is used to present cash flows from operations?
(1). Accounts receivable—trade.
(2). Inventory.
(3). Depreciation.
(4). Deferred tax liability from interperiod allocation.
(5). Issuance of long-term debt in payment for a building.
(6). Payoff of a current portion of long-term debt.
(7). Sale of a fixed asset resulting in a loss.

D6.2 A company acquired a building, paying a portion of the purchase price in cash and issuing a mortgage note payable to the seller for the balance.

a. In a statement of cash flows, what amount is included in investing activities for the above transaction?

b. In a statement of cash flows, what amount is included in financing activities for the above transaction?

D6.3 Prior to SFAS No. 95 requiring a statement of cash flows, companies had the option to report their changes in financial condition on a cash flow or working capital basis. In 1972, fewer than 5 percent of publicly filed reports were on a cash flow basis whereas just prior to the issuance of SFAS No. 95, 70 percent had been. Discuss why this shift to a cash flow focus may have occurred and whether you see merit in such a shift.

D6.4 Which subgroup(s) of financial statement readers is (are) likely to be most interested in the statement of cash flows and why?

D6.5 Discuss in general the distinctions between accrual-based accounting and cash-based accounting.

D6.6 Why do you think the FASB chose to segregate the statement of cash flows into operating, financing, and investing activity sections? Identify other categorizations that they might have considered or that you believe would have had merit.

D6.7 One of the most frequent reasons for the failure of new businesses is poor cash flow management. Explain.

D6.8 Discuss the pros and cons of evaluating division managers on a ''net cash provided by operations'' basis.

D6.9 If you could receive only one cash flow figure from a company, what figure would you request? Why?

D6.10 Discuss the direct and indirect methods of presenting net cash flows from operating activities. Which do you find most useful? Why?

PROBLEMS

P6.1 Account analysis. If you were given a company's year-end balance sheets and annual income statements, together with a record of dividends declared for a series of years and were asked to prepare cash flow statements for the company, what additional information concerning retained earnings, income taxes, investments in subsidiary and affiliated companies, and property, plant, and equipment (net) would you like to have? What would you do if you could not get such additional information?

P6.2 Statement of cash flows (indirect method). Presented below is a variety of items involving cash flows taken from the financial records of Phoenix Equipment Company for the period ended December 31, 1991:

Net income	$370,000
Payment of dividends	50,000
Fifteen-year debentures, issued at face value	200,000
Depreciation	46,000
Amortization	12,000
Beginning cash balance	23,000
Equipment purchased	80,000
Building purchased	140,000
Accounts receivable decreased	2,000
Accounts payable decreased	4,000
Inventories increased	7,000

Required:

Using the above facts, prepare a statement of cash flows using the indirect method.

P6.3 Classification of cash flow items. Identify whether each of the following is properly classified as an operating, investing, or financing activity in a statement of cash flows. Explain your rationale.

a. Receipts from sales of property, plant, and equipment and other productive assets.

b. Interest payments to lenders and other creditors.

c. Proceeds from issuing equity instruments.

d. Payments to acquire debt instruments of other entities (other than cash equivalents).

P6.4 Cash flows from operations. The following information is available from Sand Corporation's accounting records for the year ended December 31, 1991:

Cash received from customers	$770,000
Rent received	15,000
Cash paid to suppliers and employees	410,000
Taxes paid	130,000
Cash dividends paid	30,000

Required:

Determine the cash flow provided by operations for 1991.

P6.5 and P6.6 Calculating cash flows. Problems P6.5 and P6.6 are based on the following information:

King City Corporation has estimated its business activity for December 1991. Selected data from these estimated amounts are as follows:

Sales	$330,000
Gross profit (based on sales)	30%
Increase in trade accounts receivable during month	$ 11,500
Change in accounts payable during month	–0–
Increase in inventory during month	$ 6,000

Variable selling, general, and administrative expenses (S,G,&A) include a charge for uncollectible accounts of 1 percent of sales. Accounts receivable write-offs were $4,000. Total S,G,&A is $35,500 per month plus 15 percent of sales. Depreciation expense of $20,000 per month is included in fixed S,G,&A.

P6.5. On the basis of the above data, what is the cash *inflow* from operating activities for December?

P6.6. On the basis of the above data, what is the cash *outflow* from operating activities for December?

P6.7 Account analysis.

1. A company's accounts receivable decreased from the beginning to the end of the year. In the company's statement of cash flows (operating activities shown using the direct method), the cash collected from customers would be:

   a. Sales revenues plus accounts receivable at the beginning of the year.

   b. Sales revenues plus the decrease in accounts receivable from the beginning to the end of the year.

   c. Sales revenues less the decrease in accounts receivable from the beginning to the end of the year.

   d. The same as sales revenues.

2. In a statement of cash flows (operating activities shown using the indirect method), a decrease in prepaid expenses should be:

   a. Reported as an inflow and outflow of cash.

   b. Reported as an outflow of cash.

   c. Deducted from net income.

   d. Added to net income.

3. In a statement of cash flows in which the operating activities section is prepared under the indirect method, a gain on the sale of an investment should be presented as a (an):

   a. Addition to net income.

   b. Deduction from net income.

   c. Inflow and outflow of cash.

   d. Outflow of cash.

4. A company's wages payable increased from the beginning to the end of the year. In the company's statement of cash flows in which the operating activities section is prepared under the direct method, the cash paid for wages would be:

   a. Salary expense plus wages payable at the beginning of the year.

   b. Salary expense plus the increase in wages payable from the beginning to the end of the year.

   c. The same as salary expense.

   d. Salary expense less the increase in wages payable from the beginning to the end of the year.

5. A loss on the sale of machinery in the ordinary course of business should be presented in a statement of cash flows (using the indirect method for cash flows from operations) as a (an):

   a. Deduction from net income.

   b. Inflow and outflow of cash.

   c. Addition to net income.

   d. Outflow of cash.

6. In a statement of cash flows using the indirect method for operating activities, an increase in inventories should be presented as a (an):

   a. Deduction from net income.

   b. Inflow and outflow of cash.

   c. Addition to net income.

   d. Outflow of cash.

7. Deferred income tax expense resulting from temporary differences related to depreciation of plant assets should be presented in a statement of cash flows based on the indirect method for reporting cash flow from operations as a (an):

   a. Noncash financing and investing activity reported in a separate schedule.

   b. Financing activity.

   c. Addition to net income.

   d. Deduction from net income.

8. The amortization of bond premium on long-term debt should be presented in a statement of cash flows, using the indirect method for cash flow from operating activities, as a (an):

   a. Financing activity.

   b. Deduction from net income.

   c. Addition to net income.

   d. Investing activity.

P6.8, P6.9, and P6.10 Statement of cash flows. Problems P6.8, P6.9, and P6.10 are based on the following:

Canterbury Corporations' balance sheet as of December 31, 1992 and 1991, and information relating to 1992 activities are presented on page 273.

	December 31,	
	1992	**1991**
Assets		
Cash	$ 130,000	$ 100,000
Short-term investments	300,000	—
Accounts receivable (net)	610,000	410,000
Inventory	580,000	600,000
Long-term investments	300,000	400,000
Plant assets	1,700,000	1,000,000
Accumulated depreciation	(450,000)	(450,000)
Goodwill	90,000	100,000
Total assets	$3,260,000	$1,160,000
Liabilities and Stockholders' Equity		
Accounts payable and accrued		
liabilities	$ 925,000	$ 720,000
Short-term debt	225,000	—
Common stock, $10 par value	800,000	700,000
Additional paid-in-capital	370,000	250,000
Retained earnings	940,000	490,000
Total liabilities and		
stockholders' equity	$3,260,000	$2,160,000

Information relating to 1992 activities
- Net income was $690,000.
- Cash dividends of $240,000 were declared and paid.
- Equipment costing $400,000 and having a carrying amount of $150,000 was sold for $150,000.
- A long-term investment was sold for $135,000. There were no other transactions affecting long-term investments in 1992.
- 10,000 shares of common stock were issued for $22 a share.
- Short-term investments consist of Treasury bills maturing on June 30,1993.

P6.8. Calculate Canterbury's 1991 net cash provided by operating activities.

P6.9. Calculate Canterbury's 1991 net cash used in investing activities.

P6.10. Calculate Canterbury's 1991 net cash provided by financing activities.

P6.11 and P6.12 Cash flow from investing and financing. Problems P6.11 and P6.12 are based on the following:

Montvue Corporations' transactions for the year ended December 31, 1992, included the following:

- Acquired 50 percent of the common stock of Melvin Corp. for $325,000 cash, which was borrowed from a bank.
- Issued 5,000 shares of its preferred stock for land having a fair value of $500,000.
- Issued 500 of its 11 percent debenture bonds, due in 1997, for $590,000 cash.
- Purchased a patent for $375,000 cash.
- Paid $250,000 on a bank loan.
- Sold investment securities for $1,095,000.
- Had a net increase in customer deposits of $210,000.

P6.11. Determine Montvue's net cash provided by investing activities for 1992.

P6.12. Determine Montvue's net cash provided by financing activities for 1992.

P6.13, P6.14, P6.15, and P6.16 Account analysis. Problems P6.13, P6.14, P6.15, and P6.16 relate to data to be reported in the statement of cash flows of Wigton Hardware Shops, Inc., based on the following information:

WIGTON HARDWARE SHOPS, INC.
Balance sheets

	December 31	
	1992	1991
Assets		
Current assets:		
Cash	$ 250,000	$ 150,000
Accounts receivable—net	940,000	680,000
Merchandise inventory	560,000	320,000
Prepaid expenses	150,000	100,000
Total current assets	1,900,000	1,250,000
Long-term investments	80,000	—
Land, buildings, and fixtures	1,130,000	600,000
Less: Accumulated depreciation	110,000	50,000
	1,020,000	550,000
Total assets	$3,000,000	$1,800,000
Equities		
Current liabilities:		
Accounts payable	$ 500,000	$ 410,000
Accrued expenses	170,000	160,000
Dividends payable	70,000	—
Total current liabilities	740,000	570,000
Note payable—due 1997	500,000	—
Stockholders' equity:		
Common stock	1,200,000	900,000
Retained earnings	560,000	330,000
	1,760,000	1,230,000
Total liabilities and stockholders' equity	$3,000,000	$1,800,000

WIGTON HARDWARE SHOPS, INC.
Income Statements

	Year ended December 31,	
	1992	1991
Net credit sales	$7,400,000	$5,000,000
Cost of goods sold	6,000,000	4,200,000
Gross profit	1,400,000	800,000
Expenses (including income taxes)	1,000,000	520,000
Net income	$ 400,000	$ 280,000

Additional information available included the following:

- All accounts receivable and accounts payable related to trade merchandise. Accounts payable are recorded net and always are paid to take all of the discount allowed. The allowance for doubtful accounts at the end of 1992 was the same as at the end of 1991; no receivables were written off against the allowance during 1992.
- The proceeds from the note payable were used to finance a new store building. Capital stock was sold to provide additional working capital.

P6.13. Determine Wigton's cash collected during 1992 from accounts receivable.

P6.14. Determine Wigton's cash payments during 1992 on accounts payable to suppliers.

P6.15. Determine Wigton's net cash provided by financing activities for 1992.

P6.16. Determine Wigton's net cash used in investing activities during 1992.

P6.17 Cash flow analysis. Monsanto Company makes and markets high-value chemical and agricultural products, pharmaceuticals, low-calorie sweeteners, industrial process equipment, man-made fibers, plastics, and electronic materials. Monsanto's cash flow statements for a recent three-year period are presented below. Net sales for 19X2, 19X1, and 19X0 were $7,639, $6,879, and $6,747 million, respectively.

MONSANTO COMPANY
Statement of Consolidated Cash Flow
(in millions)

	19X2	19X1	19X0
Operating activities:			
Net income (loss)	$ 436	$ 433	$ (98)
Add: Income tax expense (benefit)	237	203	(170)
Deduct: Extraordinary gain			(30)
Income (loss) before income taxes and extraordinary gain	637	636	(298)
Income tax payments	(229)	(221)	(273)
Items that did not use (provide) cash:			
Depreciation and amortization	679	780	599
Restructuring expense (income)	(32)	(158)	949
Other	37	(9)	(39)
Working-capital changes that provided (used) cash:			
Accounts receivable	(172)	117	2
Inventories	(22)	(2)	(54)
Accounts payable and accrued liabilities	13	(173)	—
Other	(19)	80	41
Nonoperating gains from asset disposals (before tax)	(26)	(90)	(392)
Cash provided by operations	902	960	535
Investing activities:			
Property, plant, and equipment purchases	(505)	(520)	(645)
Acquisition payments for Searle, net of cash acquired of $216			(2,538)
Acquisition and investment payments (other than Searle)	(59)	(29)	(78)
Investment and property disposal proceeds	75	503	1,469
Cash used in investing activities	(489)	(46)	(1,792)
Financing activities:			
Net change in short-term financing	150	33	(108)
Long-term debt proceeds	26	675	415
Long-term debt repayments	(122)	(1,139)	(555)
Searle acquisition financing proceeds			2,754
Short-term debt repayments (Searle acquisition)		(348)	(1,154)
Treasury stock purchases	(339)		(91)
Dividend payments	(212)	(199)	(188)
Other financing activities	33	45	18
Cash (used in) provided by financing activities	(464)	(933)	1,091
Decrease in cash and cash equivalents*	$ (51)	$ (19)	$ (166)

*Includes cash, time deposits, certificates of deposit, and short-term securities.

Required:

a. Historically, one of Monsanto's strong points has been its ability to provide significant cash flow from operations. Although operating income improved in 19X2, cash provided by operations declined. Briefly explain how this happened.

b. Cumulatively, over this three-year period, has Monsanto
   (1). Experienced a net increase or decrease in inventories? How do you know?
   (2). Been able to increase the level of cash provided by operations as a percentage of *total gross cash inflows?* If so, is this increase a sign of good management? Why? If not, is this a sign of bad management? Why?

c. Explain how depreciation and amortization can be the single largest source of cash in 19X2 and 19X1.

d. What might account for the fact that in 19X1, accounts receivable "provided" cash, whereas in 19X2 it "used" cash?

e. As of December 31, 19X2, Monsanto's ending retained earnings balance was $3,282 million. What was Monsanto's December 31, 19X1, retained earnings balance?

P6.18 Statement of cash flows (indirect method). Presented below are the balance sheet accounts of Carbide Cutters, Inc., as of December 31, 1991 and 1990.

	1991	**1990**
Assets		
Cash	$ 371,000	$ 207,000
Marketable equity securities, at cost	250,000	350,000
Allowance to reduce marketable equity securites to market	(10,000)	(25,000)
Accounts receivable, net	650,000	615,000
Inventories	810,000	890,000
Investments in Power Tool Corp., at equity	320,000	290,000
Property, plant, and equipment	1,145,000	1,070,000
Accumulated depreciation	(345,000)	(280,000)
Patent, net	109,000	118,000
Total assets	$3,300,000	$3,235,000
Liabilities and Stockholders' Equity		
Accounts payable and accrued liabilities	$ 745,000	$ 860,000
Note payable, long-term	700,000	1,000,000
Deferred income taxes	190,000	190,000
Common stock, $10 par value	850,000	650,000
Additional paid-in capital	230,000	170,000
Retained earnings	585,000	365,000
Total liabilities and stockholders' equity	$3,300,000	$3,235,000

Additional Information:

■ On January 2, 1992, Carbide Cutters sold equipment costing $55,000, with a carrying amount of $38,000, for $28,000 cash.

■ On March 31, 1992, Carbide Cutters sold one of its marketable equity security holdings for $119,000 cash. There were no other transactions involving marketable equity securities.

■ On April 5, 1992, Carbide Cutters issued 20,000 shares of its common stock for cash at $13 per share.

■ On July 1, 1992, Carbide Cutters purchased equipment for $130,000 cash.

Carbide Cutters' net income for 1992 is $315,000. Carbide Cutters paid a cash dividend of $95,000 on October 26, 1992.

■ Carbide Cutters acquired a 20 percent interest in Power Tool Corp.'s common stock during 1989. There was no goodwill attributable to the investment, which is appropriately accounted for by the equity method. Power Tool reported net income of $150,000 for the year ended December 31, 1992. No dividend was paid on Power Tool's common stock during 1992.

Required:

Prepare a statement of cash flows for Carbide Cutters, Inc., for the year ended December 31, 1992, using the indirect method.

P6.19 Account reconstruction.

a. Presented below is the consolidated statement of cash flows from Guman Corporation's 19X2 annual report. Also presented is the company's consolidated balance sheet as of December 31, 19X2. In the empty column provided in Guman's consolidated balance sheet, please reconstruct the company's December 31, 19X1, balance sheet.

b. Explain the following:

(1). In 19X0, Guman paid $37,691 thousand of cash dividends to its shareholders when earnings were only $35,650 thousand, a difference of $2,041 thousand; yet the cash balance went down only $1,612 thousand. Why? How can a company pay dividends in excess of earnings?

(2). How can a company have more depreciation and amortization than net income?

(3). (i). Over the three-year period, 19X0–X2, was Guman in a strong or weak cash flow condition? Please explain.

(ii). Please explain the most significant items that affected Guman's cash flow during this period.

Guman Corporation and Subsidiaries
Consolidated Statement of Cash Flow
($ in thousands)

Sales	$3,506,348	$3,591,308	$3,325,062

	Year Ended December 31,		
	19X2	**19X1**	**19X0**
Cash flows from operating activities			
Net income	$ 67,264	$ 86,465	$ 35,650
Items affecting cash from operations:			
Depreciation and amortization	112,402	113,854	103,593
Decrease/(increase) in:			
Accounts receivable and marketable securities (Note 1).	80,929	(207,912)	15,076
Inventories..	(166,290)	(97,195)	(189,024)
Prepaid expenses..	(13,110)	8,739	(21,274)
Increase/(decrease) in:			
Accounts payable, wages and employee benefits (Note 2).	6,158	73,978	9,912
Income taxes payable	12,470	31,800	(43,141)
Deferred income taxes..	(17,900)	(13,200)	(41,560)
Other—Current liabilities	(33,814)	12,346	40,196
	(19,155)	(77,590)	(126,222)
Net cash provided/(required) by operating activities	48,109	8,875	(90,572)
Cash flows from investing activities:			
Capital expenditures...	(65,725)	(118,119)	(177,700)
Proceeds from sale of capital assets	1,457	10,097	4,928
Net cash used in investing activities.....................................	(64,268)	(108,022)	(172,722)
Cash flows from financing activities:			
Increase/(decrease) in short-term debt	(18,000)	(30,549)	35,528
Proceeds from long-term debt..	200,000	184,889	281,105
Repayment of long-term debt...	(131,054)	(31,081)	(22,408)
Redemption of preferred stock...	(2,525)	(2,502)	(2,375)
Common stock issued	5,526	5,726	7,573
Dividends paid	(37,288)	(37,436)	(37,691)
Net cash provided by financing activities	16,659	89,047	261,732
Net increase/(decrease) in cash for the period	500	(10,100)	(1,612)
Cash—January 1, ...	19,264	29,364	30,976
Cash—December 31,..	$ 19,764	$ 19,264	$ 29,364
Note 1: Accounts receivable and marketable securities			
Note 1: Marketable securities	($ 11,464)		
Accounts receivable	92,393		
	$ 80,929		
Note 2: Accounts payable, wages, and employee benefits			
Accounts payable...	($ 12,681)		
Wages and employee benefits	18,839		
	$ 6,158		

Guman Corporation and Subsidiaries
Consolidated Balance Sheet
($ in thousands)

	December 31	
	19X2	**19X1**
Assets		
Current assets		
Cash	$ 19,764	
Marketable securities (at cost, approximating market)	42,095	
Accounts receivable	709,560	
Inventories, less progress payments	1,028,924	
Prepaid expenses	48,187	
Total current assets	1,848,530	
Property, plant, and equipment, less accumulated depreciation	539,207	
Noncurrent assets		
Long-term receivables	44,016	
Investments	87,194	
Other	72,115	
	203,325	
Total	$2,591,062	
Liabilities and Shareholders' Equity		
Current liabilities		
Short-term debt	$ 102,789	
Accounts payable	263,857	
Wages and employee benefits payable	96,491	
Income taxes	154,700	
Advances and deposits	21,943	
Other current liabilities	119,796	
Total current liabilities	759,576	
Long-term debt	846,423	
Deferred income taxes	46,069	
Other liabilities	83,762	
Preferred stock	37,561	
Common stock—$1.00 par value, authorized 80,000,000 shares; outstanding 32,966,991 and 32,720,816 shares (net of treasury stock)	296,056	
Retained earnings	521,615	
Total	$2,591,062	

CASES

C6.1 Cash flow statement preparation: FHAC Corporation. It was early 1991, and Ed Garrett was sitting at his desk staring at a set of financial statements. The financial statements (see following pages) were those of FHAC Corporation. They represented the raw materials for Garrett's first assignment as a credit analyst for Metroplex National Bank.

Garrett's immediate supervisor, Katherine Miller, had received the FHAC statements as part of a loan application package. Because FHAC was a privately held company, the statements did not have to conform to existing SEC disclosure requirements, and since the statements were unaudited, they did not fully conform to existing FASB requirements. The only significant omission from

SEC/FASB standards that Miller had noticed was the absence of a cash flow statement. Rather than ask the new customer to provide one, she decided to ask Garrett to derive one from the existing financial data.

Required:

Prepare a statement of cash flows for FHAC for fiscal year 1990. On the basis of this statement and the other available statements, prepare an evaluation of the creditworthiness of FHAC assuming that the company is interested in (1) a short-term loan of $15 million for working capital purposes and (2) a $75 million five-year loan for capital asset purchases.

FHAC Corporation
Balance Sheet
(in thousands)

	As of December 31	
	1990	1989
Assets		
Current assets		
Cash	$ 14,696	$ 16,390
Receivables:		
Trade	20,378	10,808
Other	324	866
Inventories	15,967	3,843
Prepaid expenses	197	2,414
Total current assets	51,562	34,321
Noncurrent assets:		
Property, plant, and equipment (at cost)	258,908	152,145
Less: Accumulated depreciation	(34,224)	(11,516)
Total noncurrent assets	224,684	140,629
Deferred charges and other assets	2,041	1,666
Total assets	$278,287	$176,616
Liabilities and Shareholders' Equity		
Current liabilities		
Accounts payable	$ 20,160	$ 16,710
Accrued expenses payable	2,901	1,077
Income taxes payable	203	–0–
Current maturities on long-term debt	6,826	5,301
Total current liabilities	30,090	23,088
Long-term liabilities		
Convertible subordinated debentures	10,056	10,061
Notes payable	123,949	79,900
Deferred income taxes	44,730	20,464
Total long-term liabilities	178,735	110,425
Shareholders' equity		
Capital stock	1,380	912
Additional paid-in capital	19,949	16,552
Retained earnings	48,133	25,639
Total shareholders' equity	69,462	43,103
Total liabilities and shareholders' equity	$278,287	$176,616

FHAC Corporation
Statement of Income
(in thousands)

	As of December 31	
	1990	**1989**
Net revenue	$122,733	$60,095
Less: Costs and expenses		
Cost of operations	28,250	13,818
General and administrative	5,777	2,541
Interest	9,901	5,389
Depreciation and amortization	22,708	7,118
	66,636	28,866
Net income before income taxes	56,097	31,229
Provision for income taxes:		
Current	203	
Deferred	24,266	12,804
Total	24,469	12,804
Net income after income taxes	$ 31,628	$18,425
Dividends paid	9,134	4,268
Transferred to retained earnings	$ 22,494	$14,157

C6.2 Cash flow statement preparation and interpretation: Compton Computing Systems (A)[6]. Phillip Brantly, chief financial officer of Compton Computing Systems, sat in his office and considered the company's financial performance for 1987. He had reason to be pleased because just about every measure of financial performance had shown strong improvement for the first three quarters of 1987 and he had no reason to suspect that the last quarter would be any different. However, as he prepared for the final presentation of the 1988 budget to the board of directors, scheduled for December 11, he was uneasy about the economy and how it might affect Compton's financing and capital investment plans for next year. He knew that the board would have detailed discussions of alternative levels of expenditures and contingency financing plans for 1988. Thus, in the two weeks remaining before the meeting, he would need to complete his 1987 projected end-of-year financial statements. Using these statements as a base, he would then be able to determine whether sufficient funds from operations were being generated to portend a favorable cash flow in general through early 1988 and whether the company should proceed with the capital expenditures scheduled for early 1988.

The Company

Compton Computing Systems, headquartered in San Francisco, California, designed, manufactured, and serviced electronic products and systems for measurement and computation applications for general industry use. In addition to a full line of computers and computer-related hardware, Compton also produced and sold an impressive array of electronic test equipment, component parts, and medical test products. Compton's basic business purpose was to provide the capabilities and support needed to help customers worldwide improve their personal and business effectiveness.

---

[6]This case was prepared by Mark E. Haskins and John B. Bristow. Copyright 1988 by the Darden Graduate School Foundation, Charlottesville, Virginia.

The company was founded in 1958 to manufacture electronic measurement devices. It had started research into computers almost at founding and had marketed computers and computer systems since the early 1960s. Emphasis on quality and reliability allowed the company to grow rapidly. An increased need for capital forced the company to go public in 1962, and earnings had been sufficient to pay dividends to stockholders consecutively since 1965.

Through three quarters of 1987, financial performance had been strong. Orders were up 16 percent with net revenue up 25 percent. The fourth quarter, not yet complete, was one of great interest to Brantly. The United States and world economies, after four years of expansion, were having a modest growth year. In October, however, tremendous volatility hit the stock market with the Dow Jones Industrial Average dropping more than 500 points in one day and trading volume in excess of half a billion shares. Immediate predictions of economic slowdown and recession spread. Many companies began to rethink their outlook for 1988.

Compton's budget for capital expenditures for 1988 had recently been revised and was now predicated on an immediate slowdown in demand for computers and computer systems domestically and worldwide. In addition, several contingency cost-reduction plans had been readied for implementation if and when revenues started declining. All in all, Brantly believed the company was positioned to withstand a recessionary year.

Preparation for the December Meeting

The 1988 budgetary process at Compton Computing Systems, begun in May 1987, was now complete except for the final approval of the board of directors. What concerned Brantly most was that, through November, indications pointed to a near-record quarter for orders. In fact, Compton's backlog of orders was increasing. National and international economic indicators also showed a strong business environment. The predicted downturn was not yet occurring. A retrenchment at the wrong time in the business cycle would be very costly to the company. Therefore, Brantly intended to go before the board prepared to discuss several alternative capital spending levels. This presentation would require 1988 pro forma financial statements for each of the economic scenarios and comparison with 1987's financial performance. Because actual 1987 financial statements would be unavailable prior to the end of the year, he would have to project those as well.

Brantly had spent most of the day gathering the information he needed to complete the 1987 financial statement projections and had now completed the balance sheets and income statements (presented below). All that remained was to complete the statement of cash flows (SCF) for 1987 by applying the indirect method to his recently completed income statement and comparative balance sheet. He knew from the data he had collected that, in 1987 and 1986, principal payments on the long-term debt had been $49 and $42 million, respectively. He also knew that the company had not disposed of any property or equipment in 1986 but in 1987 had disposed of a building originally costing $18 million, whose book value at the time of the sale was $10 million, for $10 million cash. After reviewing the 1986 SCF, he decided to complete this part of his task before leaving for home that evening.

Required:

Prepare a statement of cash flows for Compton Computing Systems for 1987.

Compton Computing Systems (A)
Consolidated Income Statements
(millions of dollars)

	For the Year Ended December 31		
	Projected 1987	Actual 1986	Actual 1985
Net revenue:			
Equipment	$6,315	$5,622	$5,267
Services	1,775	1,480	1,238
	8,090	7,102	6,505
Cost and expenses:			
Cost of equipment sold	2,723	2,479	2,423
Cost of services	1,062	874	743
Research and development	901	824	685
Marketing and selling	1,612	1,397	1,181
Administration and general	830	748	715
	7,128	6,322	5,747
Earnings before taxes	962	780	758
Provisions for taxes	318	264	269
Net earnings	$ 644	$ 516	$ 489
Notes on financial statements:			
Depreciation	$ 342	$ 321	$ 299

Compton Computing Systems (A)
Consolidated Balance Sheets
(millions of dollars)

	As of December 31		
	Projected 1987	Actual 1986	Actual 1985
Assets			
Cash and cash equivalents	$2,645	$1,372	$1,020
Accounts receivable	1,561	1,344	1,249
Inventories:			
Finished goods	480	427	401
Parts and assemblies	637	554	592
Other current assets	167	117	80
Total current assets	5,490	3,814	3,342
Property, plant, and equipment:			
Land	275	243	230
Buildings and improvements	2,081	1,891	1,653
Equipment	1,761	1,557	1,400
	4,117	3,691	3,283
Less: Accumulated depreciation	1,789	1,455	1,134
	2,328	2,236	2,149
Other assets	315	237	189
Total assets	$8,133	$6,287	$5,680
Liabilities			
Notes payable	$ 240	$ 229	$ 235
Accounts payable	364	285	268
Accrued wages and benefits	488	395	397
Accrued taxes	229	164	111
Deferred revenues	150	117	100
Other current liabilities	331	230	179
Total current liabilities	1,802	1,420	1,290
Long-term debt	827	110	102
Other liabilities	134	134	92
Deferred taxes	348	249	214
Total liabilities	3,111	1,913	1,698
Stockholders' Equity			
Preferred stock, $1 par	–0–	–0–	–0–
Common stock and paid-in capital in excess of $1 par (less Treasury stock of $68 in 1987 and 1986)	776	712	780
Retained earnings	4,246	3,662	3,202
Total stockholders' equity	5,022	$4,374	$3,982
Total liabilities and stockholders' equity	$8,133	$6,287	$5,680

Compton Computing Systems (A)
Statement of Cash Flows
For the Year Ended December 31, 1986
(numbers in parentheses indicate reductions in cash; millions of dollars)

Operations:

Net income	$ 516
Depreciation and amortization	321
Adjustment for deferred revenue	17
Adjustment for deferred taxes	35
	889
Adjustments for:	
Increase in receivables	(95)
Decrease in inventories	12
Increase in accounts payable and other accruals	15
Increase in accrued taxes	53
Increase in other current assets	(37)
Increase in other current liabilities	51
	(1)
Cash flow—operations	888
Investing:	
Payments for additions to property, plant, and equipment	(408)
Increase in other assets	(48)
Cash flow—investing	(456)
Financing:	
Payments on notes payable	(6)
Proceeds from long-term debt	50
Payments on long-term debt	(42)
Increases in other liabilities	42
Repurchase of stock	(68)
Cash dividends paid	(56)
Cash flow—financing	(80)
Increase (decrease) in cash	352
Cash and equivalents—January 1	1,020
Cash and equivalents—December 31	$1,372

C6.3 Cash flow statement preparation and industry comparison: Compton Computing Systems (B)[7]

Elizabeth Oakes, an outside director of Compton Computing Systems, sat watching the fog roll in over the Golden Gate Bridge from her office near the Embarcadero. A very familiar sight to her, the fog signaled evening and the close of another day. She had less than a week until the special board meeting at Compton's headquarters.

During the last meeting of the board of directors on December 11, Oakes had listened with great interest to CFO Phillip Brantly present information on the cash flow and cash position of Compton Computing Systems. There had been much debate regarding different economic scenarios and the appropriate management response to the uncertain economy. The meeting had ended with a number

---

[7]This case was prepared by Mark E. Haskins and John B. Bristow. Copyright 1988 by the Darden Graduate School Foundation, Charlottesville, Virginia.

of questions unanswered, so the board had agreed to meet three weeks later—January 4—to approve the final 1988 budget for the company. Prior to that meeting, Oakes wanted to review information on other companies, both inside and outside the computing industry to form an opinion on how Compton Computing Systems could respond to the changing economic environment. Her position as senior partner of Oakes, Glass, & Abernathy, a nationally known investment management firm, gave her ready access to financial information on a number of businesses with which to compare Compton. Her intention was to determine what other manufacturing companies had been doing recently regarding capital expenditures and the ways in which those expenditures were being financed. Her staff had provided the names of several suitable companies, and from that list she had chosen two to review that evening.

Background on Compton Computing Systems is found in Case 6.2.

Preparation for the January 4 Meeting

A trusted member of Oakes' staff had strongly recommended that she study the financial data on Reliant Information Technologies Corporation, a sizable computer manufacturer competing directly in many of the same markets as Compton. Reliant Information Technologies designed, manufactured, and sold general-purpose computer systems and provided peripheral equipment, software, communications systems, and related products and services, including training and maintenance. Reliant Information Technologies marketed its systems to end users by its own sales force and a variety of third-party sales channels. Since its inception in 1968, it had installed more than 226,000 computer systems worldwide.

Oakes saw that Reliant Information Technologies had not been profitable in 1986. She was interested to determine how the loss would affect Reliant Information Technologies' cash flow from operations and whether the loss might have affected its 1987 capital expenditures relative to those for 1986. Reliant Information Technologies also had just embarked on a cost-reduction and restructuring program similar to the plan for Compton presented by Brantly at the last board meeting. As a part of this restructuring, Reliant Information Technologies had disposed of equipment with a net book value of $3.669 million. The cash purchase price in that amount had been collected in the third quarter of fiscal 1987. Oakes also learned that new long-term loans in the amount of $17.812 million had been subscribed during fiscal 1987.

The other company Oakes chose to study was Adolph Coors. Adolph Coors Company was a leading American brewer. In its 115-year history, Coors had become an increasingly diversified corporation, however, with operations in brewing, ceramics, aluminum, transportation, energy, food products, packaging, and biotechnology. Its ongoing success was based on an uncompromising commitment to quality, dedicated management, technological superiority, and talented employees.

Oakes chose Coors for review because it was a diversified, well-managed company that, like Compton, had limited stock distribution. While not nearly as closely held as Coors (the Coors family controlled the Coors voting stock), Compton did have several substantial blocks of stock controlled by a few stockholders. Oakes wondered how this situation might affect dividend distributions, capital expenditures, and cash flows. Coors was also conservative regarding its use of debt financing. Compton had a low but increasing, long-term debt-to-equity ratio, and she wondered whether a company could effectively provide cash for expansion without use of significant debt. During 1987 Coors had not assumed any new long-term debt and, according to company sources, did not expect to in 1988. Coors did receive $25.692 million in cash for selling plant assets with a net book value of that amount.

Oakes, Glass, & Abernathy's files had contained information on both Reliant Information Technologies and Coors, but because the 1987 annual statements for both companies had not yet been released, her staff had projected fourth-quarter financials in order to give Oakes annual 1987 financial statements. Before her were the 1986 and 1987 income statements and balance sheets for Reliant Information Technologies and the company's statement of cash flows for 1987, which she had completed. The Coors 1986 and 1987 income statements and balance sheets were also on her desk. She knew that, after completing a statement of cash flows for Coors, she would need to analyze thoroughly the information she had gathered.

Required:

a. Review the financial statements provided on Compton (from Case 6.2), Reliant Information Technologies, and Coors. Construct a statement of cash flows for Coors. While concentrating on the cash flow statements for the three companies, compare and contrast the companies and discuss the differences and similarities apparent from the financial statements concerning management's cash policies and debt policies, and make generalizations regarding the respective industries.

b. With Reliant Information Technologies having a loss for 1987, why was its cash flow from operations positive? What were the largest *uses* of cash from its statement of cash flows?

c. Why did Coors have a decrease in cash in 1987 when the income statement showed a positive net income?

d. How was Coors financing increases in investments?

e. What are the similarities and differences in the statements of cash flow of the three companies?

f. Were indications of managements' policies and abilities discernible from the financial statements?

g. Which company was the best prepared to meet a recessionary market? A growing market? Why? What financial information led you to these conclusions?

h. What assumptions and associated limitations arise when comparing and contrasting the Reliant Information Technologies and Coors statements of cash flow with the SCF for Compton?

i. What insights into the operations of a company might be gained by using the direct method SCF that are not readily apparent using the indirect method for SCF?

Reliant Information Technologies Corporation
Consolidated Income Statements
(in thousands)

	For the Year Ended December 31	
	Projected 1987	Actual 1986
Revenue:		
Equipment	$ 859,455	$ 868,269
Services	414,893	399,690
	1,274,348	1,267,959
Cost and expenses:		
Cost of revenues	608,810	639,574
Depreciation	107,727	92,657
Research and development	159,410	143,076
Marketing expenses	405,005	360,962
Other administrative expenses	53,800	11,000
	1,334,752	1,247,269
Income (loss) from operations	(60,404)	20,690
Other income	2,491	13,175
Interest expense	46,194	30,467
Income before income taxes and equity in net loss of unconsolidated affiliate	(104,107)	3,398
Income tax benefit (provision)	6,987	(945)
Net income before equity in net loss of unconsolidated affiliate	(97,120)	2,453
Equity in net loss of unconsolidated affiliate	(15,189)	(23,433)
Writedown of investment in unconsolidated affiliate	(14,769)	–0–
Net income (loss)	($ 127,078)	($ 20,980)

Reliant Information Technologies Corporation
Consolidated Balance Sheets
(in thousands)

	As of December 31	
	Projected 1987	Actual 1986
Assets		
Cash and cash equivalents	$ 136,676	$ 271,537
Marketable equity securities	–0–	30,126
Receivables, less allowance of $25,904 in 1987 and $21,744 in 1986	274,925	260,498
Inventories	189,538	237,585
Other current assets	34,858	23,350
Total current assets	635,997	823,096
Notes receivable	19,481	23,236
Property, plant, and equipment, net	398,944	367,422
Other assets including investments in affiliates	21,062	51,020
Total assets	$1,075,484	$1,264,774
Liabilities and Stockholders' Equity		
Notes payable	$ 38,740	$ 33,451
Accounts payable	103,441	75,536
Other current liabilities	245,369	210,935
Total current liabilities	387,550	319,922
Long-term debt	79,990	240,734
Deferred service revenue	13,378	14,144
Total liabilities	480,918	574,800
Stockholders' equity:		
Common stock	302,639	268,182
Retained earnings	279,749	406,827
Cumulative foreign currency translation adjustment	12,178	14,965
Total stockholders' equity	594,566	689,974
Total liabilities and stockholders' equity	$1,075,484	$1,264,774

Reliant Information Technologies Corporation
Projected Statement of Cash Flows
For the Year Ended December 31, 1987
(numbers in parentheses indicate reductions in cash; thousands of dollars)

Operations:	
Net income	($127,078)
Depreciation	107,727
Other noncash expenses	29,958
Adjustment for deferred taxes	(766)
	9,841
Adjustments for:	
Increase in receivables	(14,427)
Decrease in inventories	48,047
Increase in accounts payable	27,905
Increase in other current assets	(11,508)
Increase in other current liabilities	34,434
	$ 84,451
Cash flow—operations	$ 94,292
Investing:	
Payments for additions to property, plant, and equipment	($142,918)
Proceeds from sale of property, plant, and equipment	3,669
Net sales of marketable equity securities	30,126
Decrease in notes receivable	3,755
Cash flow—investments	($105,368)
Financing:	
Proceeds from notes payable	$ 5,289
Payments on long-term debt	(178,556)
Proceeds from long-term debt	17,812
Proceeds from sale of stock	34,457
Dividends	–0–
Cash flow—financing	($120,998)
Effect of exchange rate changes in cash	(2,787)
Increase (decrease) in cash	(134,861)
Cash and equivalents—January 1	271,537
Cash and equivalents—December 31	$136,676

Adolph Coors Company
Consolidated Income Statement
(in thousands)

	For the Years Ended	
	Projected December 27, 1987	Actual December 28, 1986
Sales	$1,503,805	$1,464,881
Less: Beer excise taxes	153,066	149,951
	1,350,739	1,314,930
Cost and expenses:		
Costs of goods sold	778,943	754,217
Marketing, general and administrative	362,293	336,528
Research and development	21,682	23,443
	1,162,918	1,114,188
Operating income	187,821	200,742
Other (income) expense:		
Interest income	(10,582)	(13,214)
Interest expense	2,604	3,219
Depreciation expense	99,240	91,968
Miscellaneous, net	10,511	8,376
Income before taxes	86,048	110,393
Taxes	37,900	51,000
Net income	$ 48,148	$ 59,393

Adolph Coors Company
Consolidated Balance Sheet
(thousands of dollars)

	Projected as of December 27, 1987	Actual as of December 28, 1986
Assets		
Cash and cash equivalents	$ 113,434	$ 150,464
Accounts and notes receivable	109,208	99,560
Inventories:		
Finished goods	17,254	18,464
In process	32,881	31,037
Raw materials	64,357	68,409
Packaging materials	40,208	38,632
	154,700	156,542
Prepaid expenses and other current assets	66,591	61,255
Tax prepayments	7,703	5,216
Total current assets	451,656	473,037
Properties, at cost, less accumulated depreciation	975,781	901,172
Excess of cost over net assets of businesses acquired, less accumulated amortization	3,356	3,538
Other assets	25,700	18,175
Total assets	$1,456,493	$1,395,922
Liabilities and Stockholders' Equity		
Accounts payable	$ 85,627	$ 75,203
Accrued salaries and benefits	39,132	43,772
Taxes, other than income	26,542	27,840
Income tax liability	9,418	10,759
Other accrued expenses	48,531	43,168
Total current liabilities	209,250	200,742
Accumulated deferred taxes	189,056	181,137
Other liabilities	26,376	17,903
Total liabilities	424,682	399,782
Stockholders' equity:		
Class A common, voting, $1 par	1,260	1,260
Class B common, nonvoting, no par.	39,773	34,578
Retained earnings	1,013,865	983,943
	1,054,898	1,019,781
Less: Class B treasury shares, 10,863,376 in 1987 and 11,123,876 in 1986	23,087	23,641
Total stockholders' equity	1,031,811	966,140
Total liabilities and stockholders' equity	$1,456,493	$1,395,922

Measuring and Reporting Assets and Equities Using Generally Accepted Accounting Principles

CHAPTER 7

Trade Receivables and Marketable Securities

Chapter Outline

- Trade Receivables
    Net Realizable Value and Uncollectible
    Accounts
    Comprehensive Illustration: Accounting for
    Receivables
    Trade Receivable Disclosures
    Factoring and Pledging
    Notes Receivable
    Analyzing Trade Receivables

- Marketable Securities
    Temporary Value Declines
    Permanent Value Declines
    Sales
    Transfers
    Marketable Debt Securities
    Analyzing Marketable Securities
- Summary

I n the previous chapters, we introduced some of the fundamental concepts involved in preparing the three basic financial statements. In a sense, the preceding chapters attempted to demystify the process of constructing a set of financial statements. It is important, however, not to lose sight of the fact that many challenges are inherent in the desire to report on the financial condition and results of operations for a variety of companies engaged in diverse and different activities, with varied histories, and run by managers with different ideas of how best to achieve certain results, all to the satisfaction of absentee owners who have their own agendas. In light of such circumstances, if the formulation of generally accepted accounting principles seems an imposing task, it is. We must remember that the overall objective of financial reporting is to provide useful information to decision makers. Such an objective necessitates a closer look at the various components making up those three basic financial statements so that you, the user of financial statement information, will be able to comprehend the financial story those statements tell.

Consider the fact that the assets reported on a company's balance sheet may be used in a variety of capacities to benefit the company. For example, one asset, cash, may be used to buy inventories or pay employee salaries. Inventories, another asset, may be sold to produce revenues and, hence, new cash inflows. Machinery and equipment may be used to produce new inventory units to sell to customers. Thus, each asset category on the balance sheet effectively serves one or more specialized functions within a company.

In this chapter, we focus on the accounting for and valuing of trade receivables and marketable securities. Although these two *current assets* differ as to their origin, they have some similar attributes. Both, for example, are *liquid assets;* they can be readily converted into cash. Both are subject to valuation adjustments for financial reporting purposes—accounts receivable are reported at their **net realizable value** (i.e., the amount of cash flows expected to be realized when they are liquidated), and marketable securities are reported at the **lower-of-cost-or-market value.**

Our objective in this chapter is to learn how these current assets arise, how they are accounted for, how they can be managed and utilized effectively, and how they may be analyzed. We begin with a consideration of trade receivables.

TRADE RECEIVABLES

In Chapter 6, we noted that managing **accounts** or **trade receivables** is an important component of the larger concern of managing a company's cash and cash flows. For most businesses, the extension of credit to customers is a normal part of generating sales. Credit sales, however, do not provide immediate cash inflows; indeed, they actually create some uncertainty regarding the timing and amount of expected future cash inflows. Consequently, prior to making a credit sale, management must weigh the cost of the anticipated benefit of increased sales by extending credit to customers who would normally not be willing to purchase goods on a strictly cash basis against the cost associated with the possible uncollectibility of a customer's promised payments of cash.

The accounting entry to record the receipt of a promise to be paid that is generated by a $1,000 credit sale of merchandise is:

```
Dr. Accounts Receivable (A) . . . . . . . . . 1,000
    Cr. Sales (R)  . . . . . . . . . . . . . .         1,000
```

Notice that in this transaction, even though cash is not received, the revenue is still considered to have been earned because the earnings process is assumed to be complete, and is therefore recognized in the accounting period when the sale is made. When cash is collected on the account receivable generated by this credit sale, the following transaction is recorded:

```
Dr. Cash (A) . . . . . . . . . . . . . . . . 1,000
    Cr. Accounts Receivable (A) . . . . . . . . .         1,000
```

Notice that this cash-collection event does not affect the company's profitability in the period in which the event is recorded, nor does it change the level of total assets as of the recording date. The cash-collection event is merely an exchange of one asset for another, and the accounting entry reflects that fact.

Conventional accounting practice is to use the account title Accounts Receivable or Trade Receivable only for those receivables arising from normal, recurring credit sales. From a manager's perspective, this practice permits the identification of amounts still to be collected from customers who have already received the goods purchased. If the balance to be collected increases during a period when credit sales are relatively stable, a manager is readily able to monitor such a change and, by investigation, to determine whether the increase is due to the collection department's ineffective job or due to more lenient credit terms having been offered to customers. Receivables generated by other events, for example by a cash advance to an employee, should not be commingled with the unremitted credit-sales balances still reflected in the Accounts Receivable account. Separate accounts should be created for these other types of receivables to preserve the ease with which this monitoring may be done.

The primary reason that a company extends credit to customers is to increase sales. From a customer's point of view, credit purchases are preferable to cash purchases, in part because they are convenient and in part because they allow the customer to retain the use of its cash for an additional period of time. From the seller's point of view, there is clearly a delay in obtaining the cash associated with having made a credit sale versus having made a cash sale. The managerial issue for the seller is whether the increase in sales as a result of offering the credit terms more than offsets the cost of granting credit.

A number of costs are associated with extending credit to customers. There is, for example, the "time value of money"; that is, one dollar received tomorrow is not worth as much as one dollar received today. Thus, future receipts from customers implicitly reflect the cost of doing without those funds for, in many cases, a significant amount of time (e.g., 30 to 60 days). In addition, regardless of the care managers take to investigate the creditworthiness of customers, some accounts receivable inevitably prove to be uncollectible. This cost of making sales on a credit basis must be weighed against the benefits of such a sale. Because of these two costs of extending credit to customers, managers often offer discounts to credit customers to accelerate cash payments (i.e., to induce credit customers to pay prior to the end of the normal credit period) and to increase the probability of actually being paid (i.e., to reduce the probability that credit customers will use their limited cash for other seemingly higher priority purposes).

To see the relative attractiveness of offering discounts to credit customers, consider the typical credit term of 2/10, net/30. Translated, this term means that if a customer pays for a credit purchase within 10 days of being invoiced, the amount due is 2 percent less than the invoice amount. If, on the other hand, payment is not remitted within the 10-day discount period, full payment is expected within 30 days. Thus, the key issue is whether the 2 percent discount will be seen as a sufficient inducement for a customer to pay 20 days early. In this case, the answer should be an emphatic "yes" in that the 2 percent savings, when annualized, is equivalent to an opportunity cost of 36 percent annually (i.e., 365/20 × 0.02). Thus, a credit customer would be well advised to borrow money from a bank, even at the usurious rate of 30 percent annually, to take advantage of a 2 percent discount offered by a seller.

Net Realizable Value and Uncollectible Accounts

From a financial reporting perspective, accounts receivable are to be reported in the balance sheet at their net realizable value (i.e., net collectible amount). The use of net realizable value as a valuation basis for trade receivables stems from the fact that receivables are a current asset and that it is assumed that financial statement users will compare the level of current assets with the level of current liabilities to assess a company's *liquidity,* or short-term default risk. Hence, to ensure that statement users obtain an accurate assessment of liquidity, the current assets (excepting prepaid expenses) are valued at (or an approximation of) their net realizable or cash collectible amount.

One additional financial reporting concern evolves from the *matching principle.* As mentioned earlier, one of the costs of selling goods on a credit basis is the cost involved in the likely event that not all customers will pay what is owed. Indeed, the experience of virtually all companies indicates that some customers will not pay what they owe, that their accounts will be uncollectible. In view of this reality, the matching principle dictates that an expense for the cost of doing credit business be recorded in the period in which the benefit (i.e., the sales revenue) from doing credit business is recorded. Of course, if at the time of a credit sale, management knew which specific customer would not pay, the credit sale would not be made. Such a situation leads to the realization that in order to achieve the matching principle and report receivables at their net collectible amount, an *estimate* of their net realizable value that is consistent with prior experience involving customer defaults must be made. In reporting this estimated net realizable amount, the gross amount of the receivables account is reduced by establishing a contra asset account for an estimated **allowance for uncollectible accounts.** To establish an appropriate allowance amount, managers may use one of two estimation approaches, both a historically based percentage: (1) a percentage of each period's credit sales or (2) a percentage of the year-end balance in accounts receivable. It is worth repeating that neither of these approaches identifies *specific* uncollectible accounts, but rather *estimates* dollar amounts of possible uncollectible accounts.

The particular method to estimate the dollar value of uncollectible accounts that relies on a **percentage of credit sales** assumes that a certain proportion of a period's credit sales' will never be collected. For example, if credit sales for the year are $1 million and if 3 percent, the historic average of credit sales never collected, is estimated to be the amount that will prove to be uncollectible, the following transaction is recorded at period-end:

```
Dr.  Bad Debt Expense (E)  . . . . . . . . . . . . . . . . .  30,000
     Cr.  Allowance for Uncollectible Accounts (CA) . . . . . . . . . . .      30,000
```

Notice the income statement emphasis implicit in this method of estimating the net realizable value of accounts receivables. The $30,000 bad debt expense amount recorded this period is derived from a calculation based on the same period's credit sales and is thus a direct matching of expenses to related revenues. It is also important to note that a contra asset account is used for the allowance account. The reason for this is that specific customer accounts have not yet been identified as uncollectible and that the Accounts Receivable account, which is an aggregation of *specific* customer receivables, cannot be reduced directly. Thus, the desired goal of reporting receivables in the balance sheet at their net realizable value is achieved by creating a contra asset account that is netted against gross accounts receivable for financial reporting purposes. For example, PepsiCo's consolidated balance sheet reveals the following presentation for accounts (and notes) receivable:

	(in millions)	
	1990	**1989**
Notes and accounts receivables, less allowance: $90.8 in 1990 and $57.7 in 1989	$1,414.7	$1,239.7

The contra asset account serves to reduce the gross receivables amount reported in the balance sheet to an estimated net collectible amount. This contra asset account balance represents, as of a specific point in time, an amount believed to indicate the amount of outstanding customer accounts that will never be collected. Subsequently, if evidence is obtained regarding a *specific* customer account that will not be collected (e.g., a customer goes bankrupt), the receivables account can be directly reduced along with a similar reduction in the contra asset account (in essence, a portion of the contra asset account's estimated balance is no longer needed). In summary, under the percentage-of-credit-sales method to estimate uncollectible accounts, the balance in the Allowance for Uncollectible Accounts is increased each period by an amount based on a percentage of credit sales (this amount is also the period's bad debt expense to be recorded under this method) and decreased by the dollar amount of *specific* accounts deemed uncollectible and therefore written off.

A second and perhaps more intuitively appealing implementation of the allowance method requires an **aging of the outstanding end-of-period accounts receivable.** A large part of a given period's credit sales has already been collected by period-end; therefore, this approach focuses only on those accounts yet to be collected. Under the aging method, outstanding accounts receivable are grouped according to the number of days they are past due. Typical "age" categories for the accounts receivable are current, 1–30 days overdue, 31–60 days overdue, 61–90 days overdue, and more than 90 days overdue. It is normally the case that as receivables become increasingly overdue, a larger percentage of them will prove to be uncollectible. Thus, for each of the increasingly overdue categories, a larger percentage estimate is applied to the respective receivables balance in determining an aggregate estimate of period-end uncollectible receivables.

The aging approach focuses on determining a targeted figure for the period-end balance in the allowance for uncollectible accounts. The difference between the targeted ending allowance for the Uncollectible Accounts balance and its existing balance is the *adjustment to be made to* the contra asset account and is the amount recorded as that period's bad debt expense. The transaction recorded under this method is substantially the same as that shown in the percentage-of-credit-sales example, but the amounts are likely to differ.

Note that under either allowance method, *specific* uncollectible accounts receivable were not identified at the time of recording the bad debt expense and adjusting the net realizable value amount of the receivables. When a specific account receivable is finally identified as uncollectible, it is removed from the books. Under either of the allowance methods, adjusting the books to reflect this writing-off of a specific account merely involves reducing the balance in the contra asset Allowance for Uncollectible Accounts and the balance in the Accounts Receivable asset account. Such entry has no income statement effect, nor does it affect either the total assets or the total current assets, or the net realizable value of accounts receivable reported in the balance sheet. The income statement and balance sheet effects were anticipated and recognized at the time management recorded the *estimate* of the uncollectible accounts using either the percentage-of-credit-sales approach or the aging of outstanding receivables approach.

Under either of the allowance methods, if a specific account that has previously been removed from the books (i.e., written off) subsequently turns out to be collectible, the prior entry made to reduce the receivable account and the contra asset account is simply reversed in the amount that is now considered to be collectible. This transaction increases the balance in both the Accounts Receivable account and the Allowance for Uncollectible Accounts account by the amount now deemed to be collectible.

Comprehensive Illustration: Accounting for Receivables

As a comprehensive example of the financial reporting issues for accounts receivables posed so far, consider the following information pertaining to United Department Stores, Inc. (UDS), for the fiscal year ending January 31, 1992. All amounts are in millions of dollars.

1. For the year, UDS had net sales of $10,512, of which $3,951 were credit sales.
2. The beginning Accounts Receivable balance as of February 1, 1991, was $1,623.5. The beginning balance in the Allowance for Uncollectible Accounts was $36.5.
3. Collections during the year were $3,953.
4. During the year, specific accounts receivable totaling $34.2 were deemed to be uncollectible and were written off (i.e., removed from the Accounts Receivable account).
5. Receivables totaling $2.0 that had been previously written off were subsequently deemed to be collectible.
6. As of January 31, 1992, the following aging schedule was prepared for UDS's accounts receivable:

	Amount
Uncollected billings on account:	
Current	$ 62.8
1 to 30 days past due	1,025.2
31 to 60 days past due	356.9
61 to 90 days past due	129.7
Longer than 90 days past due	14.7
Total accounts receivable outstanding	$1,589.3

7. In the judgment of UDS's management and based on past experiences of account collections, the following amounts were anticipated to be uncollectible:

1/4 of 1% of all current accounts:	0.0025 × 62.8	=	$ 0.16
1/2 of 1% of all accounts 1–30 days past due:	0.005 × 1,025.2	=	5.13
2.5% of all accounts 31–60 days past due:	0.025 × 356.9	=	8.92
10% of all accounts 61–90 days past due:	0.10 × 129.7	=	12.97
50% of all accounts more than 90 days old:	0.50 × 14.7	=	7.35
			$34.53

During the year, UDS would have recorded, in total, the following amounts reflecting its sales activity:

```
Dr.  Cash (A) . . . . . . . . . . . . . . . . . . . . . . . .  6,561
Dr.  Accounts Receivable (A) . . . . . . . . . . . . . . . .  3,951
     Cr.  Sales (R)  . . . . . . . . . . . . . . . . . . . .         10,512
```

In addition to the above sales entry, an entry would need to be made to adjust the Inventory and Cost of Goods Sold accounts (see Chapter 3).

During the year, collections of the accounts receivable would be recorded as follows:

```
Dr.  Cash (A) . . . . . . . . . . . . . . . . . . . . . . . .  3,953
     Cr.  Accounts Receivable (A)  . . . . . . . . . . . . . .        3,953
```

Next, the transactions recorded during the year to report accounts that were written off, as well as to reestablish the accounts previously written off that were later deemed to be collectible, should be recorded in this way:

```
Dr.  Allowance for Uncollectible Accounts (CA) . . . . . . . . . .  34.2
     Cr.  Accounts Receivable (A) . . . . . . . . . . . . . . . . .        34.2
Dr.  Accounts Receivable (A) . . . . . . . . . . . . . . . . . .  2.0
     Cr.  Allowance for Uncollectible Accounts (CA) . . . . . . . . .        2.0
```

At year-end, management must determine the net realizable value of the outstanding accounts receivable. In this case, UDS uses the aging method; thus, the *ending balance* in the Allowance for Uncollectible Accounts represents what management believes to be the receivables' net realizable value. Using the balances in the aging schedule and the percentage estimates given by management, we determine that the ending balance in the contra asset allowance account should be $34.53. Because the balance in the contra asset account after the previous two transactions were recorded is $4.3, the provision made for uncollectible accounts during this period must be $30.23. In essence, the $30.23 (a plug figure) is the amount required to balance the contra asset allowance account to the targeted ending balance. It is also the amount of the bad debt expense to appear on the current period's income statement. The transaction to record this would be as follows:

Dr. Bad Debt Expense (E) 30.23
       Cr. Allowance for Uncollectible Accounts (CA) 30.23

A reconstruction of the contra asset allowance T-account is helpful in following the flow of these transactions:

Allowance for Uncollectible Accounts

Accounts written-off	34.2	Beginning balance (2/1/91)	36.5
		Restoration of previously written-off accounts	2.0
		Subtotal	4.3
		1992 bad debt expense	30.23
		Targeted ending balance (1/31/92)	34.53

If UDS had used the percentage-of-credit-sales method instead of the aging method, the recorded transactions would remain the same except for the last one involving the Bad Debt Expense account. Assuming that the percentage-of-credit-sales rate used by management was 1 percent, the estimate for uncollectible accounts would be $39.5 ($3,951 credit sales $\times$ 0.01). Recall that under the percentage-of-credit-sales approach, this amount is *not* the targeted ending balance for the allowance account but is the amount by which the allowance account is increased. Thus, in this case, the year-end balance in the allowance account is $43.8 (i.e., $39.5 + $4.3). Take a moment to verify this amount.

It must be noted that a company that uses the percentage-of-credit-sales method must also carefully evaluate the resulting year-end balance in the allowance account. If that balance continues to increase from period to period, it suggests that the percentage of sales factor applied in prior periods is too high and does not reflect the company's real uncollectible accounts experience. If, on the other hand, that balance becomes negative (i.e., a debit balance), the percentage-of-credit-sales factor used to estimate uncollectibles has been too low. In either event, management may decide to adjust the percentage factor to a rate more likely to result in increases to the allowance account that, over time, are similar to the amounts subsequently removed from the contra asset account as *specific* receivables are deemed to be uncollectible.

This latter statement is true for both allowance methods. This is so because under either allowance method, managers actually anticipate that some portion of a company's promises to be paid will be broken. Consistent with the matching principle, the allowance methods attempt to match the cost of granting credit (i.e., the bad debt expense) to the period in which the benefit (i.e., the credit sale) was recorded. Thus, the increases and decreases to the contra asset allowance account indicate differences between the timing of recording an estimate as an anticipated uncollectible and the actual default of a specific account. Consequently, if the percentage factors used to estimate the future uncollectibles reflect the actual level of uncollectible accounts over a number of periods, the balance in the allowance account should achieve a steady state.

E X H I B I T   7 . 1

Illustration of Two Allowance Methods
for Estimating Uncollectible Accounts

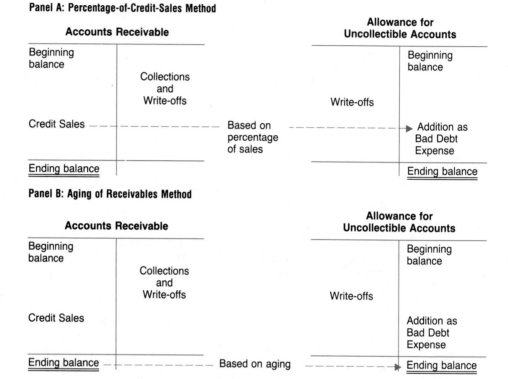

Panel A: Percentage-of-Credit-Sales Method

Accounts Receivable

**Allowance for
Uncollectible Accounts**

Panel B: Aging of Receivables Method

Accounts Receivable

**Allowance for
Uncollectible Accounts**

It may be helpful to visualize the operations of the two allowance methods as presented in Exhibit 7.1. Notice that with the percentage-of-credit-sales method, the allowance account is adjusted *by* the calculated amount, whereas with the aging method, the allowance account is adjusted *to* a targeted, calculated amount.

There is one additional means to account for bad debts. The **direct write-off method** is not acceptable for publicly issued financial statements but is in fact the only acceptable method for tax purposes. Only when evidence is available by which management determines that a *specific* customer's account is not likely to be collected is a bad debt expense recorded and the Accounts Receivable account balance reduced to the net amount expected to be collected. Under this method, no allowance account is created, nor is there any attempt to record the bad debt expense amount in the period when the credit sale was made. The entry would be as follows:

        Dr. Bad Debt Expense (E) 500
             Cr. Accounts Receivable (A)   500

E X H I B I T   7 . 2

PepsiCo, Inc.
Current Assets
(in millions)

	December 29, 1990	December 30, 1989
Current assets:		
Cash and cash equivalents,		
at cost (approximates market)	$1,816	$1,534
Trade accounts receivable, less		
allowances of $91 in 1990		
and $58 in 1989	1,415	1,240
Inventories	586	546
Prepaid expenses and other		
assets	265	231
Total current assets	$4,082	$3,551

From a managerial perspective, deciding to write off an account receivable, whether under one of the allowance methods or under the direct write-off method, can be problematic. Managers typically require convincing evidence that a specific account is indeed uncollectible before they delete it from their records. Indirect evidence such as a customer's declaration of bankruptcy or more direct evidence such as correspondence from the customer disputing the amount owed is generally considered to be sufficient evidence to warrant reducing the Accounts Receivable account. In spite of such evidence and despite recording the account write-off, management should continue to attempt to collect any outstanding amount.

Trade Receivable Disclosures

As mentioned earlier, trade receivables appear in the balance sheet in the current assets section and are reported at their net realizable value. Most annual reports present the Trade Receivables account balance *net* of the Allowance for Uncollectible Accounts, either with the balance in the allowance account disclosed beside it or subtracted in the column of reported amounts. Exhibit 7.2, which presents the current asset section of PepsiCo's 1990 balance sheet, illustrates this typical method of receivable presentation.

Note that the reader learns from the balance sheet of the amount that PepsiCo management expects ultimately to collect ($1,415 million), as well as the amount of gross accounts receivable not expected to be collected ($91 million). The sum of these two figures is the amount of gross accounts receivable not yet collected as of year-end 1990.

Exhibit 7.3 illustrates another acceptable format for reporting accounts receivable. The balance sheet of Springs Industries presents only the net realizable value of receivables; the footnotes disclose the balance in the Allowance for Doubtful Accounts account. Such an approach is acceptable, although less common than the approach chosen by PepsiCo.

EXHIBIT 7.3

Springs Industries Inc.
Current Assets and Receivables Disclosure
(in thousands)

	December 29, 1990	December 30, 1989
Current assets:		
Cash and cash equivalents	$ 4,734	$ 6,216
Accounts receivable	304,397	313,620
Inventories	239,790	265,123
Other	38,936	21,634
Total current assets	$587,857	$606,593

Note 1. Summary of Significant Accounting Policies:

Accounts Receivable: Springs has a diverse customer base within a variety of industries. The Company performs ongoing credit evaluations of its customers' financial condition and, generally, requires no collateral from its customers.

The allowance for doubtful accounts was approximately $7,631,000 and $7,669,000 in 1990 and 1989, respectively, which management believes is adequate to provide for normal credit losses, as well as losses for customers which have filed for protection under the bankruptcy laws.

Factoring and Pledging

Most companies consider the management of accounts receivable (i.e., the efforts undertaken to make sure that payments are promptly received) a normal part of their day-to-day operations. However, if a company decides that it does not want to expend the resources necessary to manage the accounts or finds itself short of cash, the company may *factor* its accounts receivable. **Factoring** is a process by which a company can convert its receivables into cash by selling them at face value less a service charge for processing the transaction and for the time value of money. Typically, the service charge for factoring receivables is very expensive, from 15 percent to as much as 50 percent or more. How much will be paid to a factor (usually a financial institution) is largely a function of whether the receivables are sold **with** or **without recourse. With recourse** means that the factor can return a receivable to the company and collect from the company if the receivable turns out to be unpaid as of a certain date. **Without recourse** means that the factor assumes the risk of any losses on collection. In either case, the customer owing the money may or may not be notified that a factor is the ultimate recipient of its payment.

The following disclosures regarding factored receivables appeared as a footnote to the financial statements in the annual reports of Hallwood Group, Inc., and Beckman Instruments, Inc.:

Hallwood Group, Inc.

During the fiscal year ended July 31, 1990, the Company's textile products subsidiary, Brookwood Companies Incorporated ("Brookwood"), maintained factoring agreements which provided that all receivables resulting from credit sales (excluding the United States Government) shall be sold to the factor, without recourse, subject to a 7/10% commission and the factor's prior approval. Brookwood paid interest on factor advances at its bank's prime rate plus 1 1/2% in 1990 and 2% in 1989 (11 1/2% at July 31, 1990). At July 31, 1990, the factors had advanced $5,842,000 against such factored receivables.

Beckman Instrument, Inc.
During 1990, the Company received proceeds of $47.1 million from factoring trade receivables. The Company is contingently liable for the possible uncollected portion of the factored receivables, if any, which was $9.4 million at December 31, 1990.

These footnotes disclose the extent to which each company has factored its receivables and something of the terms (limited recourse) of those sales. The Beckman footnote also discloses the remaining uncollected receivables under its agreement, an amount for which Beckman is liable to the extent that the accounts ultimately prove to be uncollectible.

Another way a firm can use accounts receivables to expedite its cash inflows is to *pledge* them as collateral for a short-term bank loan that may not have been obtainable without the pledge. In **pledging,** a company normally retains title to the accounts receivable but pledges that it will use the proceeds from collection of the receivables to repay the loan.

The following disclosure regarding pledged accounts appeared as a footnote to the financial statements presented in the 1988 annual report to stockholders of NEC Corporation:

The following are pledged as security for bank loans and long-term debt at March 31, 1988:

Description	In Millions of Yen	In Thousands of U.S. Dollars
Current notes and accounts receivable	9,139	73,702
Marketable securities (noncurrent)	3,171	25,573
Investment securities—other	628	5,065
Long-term receivables, trade	33,268	268,290
Property, plant, and equipment (net book value)	127,186	1,025,694

Notice from the footnote that NEC management has used (pledged) current notes and accounts receivable as well as long-term trade receivables as collateral for their borrowings.

Notes Receivable

Businesses sometimes accept promissory notes from customers in exchange for services or merchandise sold on credit or in place of an outstanding account receivable that a customer is unable to pay according to the original credit terms. A *promissory note* is a legal document that is signed by the customer (*the maker*) promising to pay to the company (*the payee*) a dollar amount (*the principal*) plus interest. The note may become due in total on a stated maturity date or in segments on several dates, at which time(s) the payee receives from the maker the stipulated amount(s) plus any accrued interest.

A promissory note, or note receivable, might be arranged by a seller if a customer is a high credit risk or needs a longer time than usual to pay. Companies often convert overdue accounts receivable to notes receivable so that the amount in question, the new payment date, and an interest charge for the extended payment time may all be formally and specifically stated and agreed to by the customer. Notes receivable classified as current assets are carried in the financial statements at net realizable value, or alternatively, face value, less any allowance for uncollectible accounts. The evaluation process for possible uncollectible notes is exactly the same as for accounts receivable. If, on the other hand, the notes receivables are more properly classified as noncurrent, they should be reported at the present value of the expected future cash flows. Later chapters will have more to say about such noncurrent accounts, their valuation, and the concept of present value.

Because promissory notes receivable are negotiable instruments, businesses sometimes sell or pledge notes receivable to a bank (or any other type of factor) to obtain cash prior to the due date of the note. Such transactions are similar to factoring and pledging accounts receivable in that the payee receives the face value of the note less some fee or discount.

Analyzing Trade Receivables

The level of investment a company might have in receivables at any particular time is affected by many conditions: seasonal, cyclical, or growth changes in sales; the market the company serves; the company's credit and collection policies; and inflation.

The investment in receivables is closely related to the volume of sales for the period immediately preceding a given balance sheet date. If sales during that period were low, either because of seasonal or cyclical changes or declining markets, the accounts receivable balance should, all else being equal, be lower than in periods when credit sales were high.

The market a company serves also has a bearing on its receivables balance. In some markets, business cannot be conducted without using credit. Other markets, by custom, require longer or shorter credit terms than usual to facilitate commerce. For example, Wendy's Corporation requires prompt payment of a percentage of weekly sales from its franchisees, which primarily conduct business with customers on a cash basis. In the recent past, the average receivable collection period for Wendy's, Inc., was about six days. In contrast, many of the credit sales of Northrup Corporation are to the U.S. government, which relies on numerous administrative reviews prior to authorizing payment to its suppliers. Thus, it is not surprising that Northrup's financial statements reveal collection periods from the various segments of its government contracts (representing about 90 percent of Northrup's sales) ranging from 60 days to more than two years.

A company's credit policy is an important competitive weapon. By allowing more and more potential credit customers to qualify for credit sales, a company's revenues and accounts receivable balances are likely to increase. At the same time, however, the carrying costs and potential losses from uncollectible accounts may also increase. Periods of high interest rates and periods of uncertain business conditions obviously raise the cost of carrying receivables. Thus, a company must weigh the costs of additional sales (increased interest expense and bad debts) against the benefits (increased revenues and increased cash inflows).

Inflation is another factor to be considered in managing a company's investment in receivables. During periods of inflation, the purchasing power of the dollar diminishes. Consequently, future collections of receivables represent collections of cheaper dollars. The lost purchasing power of those cheaper dollars is a cost of making credit sales.

Many procedures can be used to evaluate the quality of a company's accounts receivable management. Most methods deal with ratio analysis, and the most common index is the **average receivable collection period.** As discussed in Chapter 4, the average collection period is computed as

$$\text{Average receivable collection period} = \frac{\text{Average accounts receivable balance}}{\text{Total net credit sales/365 days}}.$$

The receivable collection period gives a rough measure of the length of time that a company's accounts receivable have been outstanding.[1] A comparison of this measure with a company's credit terms, with the measure for other firms in the same industry, and with the figures for prior periods indicates a company's efficiency in collecting receivables and its trends in credit management.

Other receivable-related ratios may also be of interest to managers, creditors, and investors; these may include (1) the ratio of accounts receivable that are written off divided by credit sales or by total receivables and (2) the ratio of credit sales to total sales, which reveals how dependent a company is on credit sales. Ratios involving the written-off accounts receivable reveal how correct management has been in determining those customers to which to grant credit, as well as management's effectiveness in collecting those credit sales. In a similar vein, the aging schedule is a good indicator of the quality of the accounts receivables at a particular point in time. (Such information is usually not available to the public but it is useful to management.) Frequent preparation of an aging schedule may be crucial to the timely management of credit.

Managers must use such analytical tools to manage their investment in accounts receivable throughout the credit cycle. This cycle, starting with the approval of a credit sale and ending with the receipt of cash, is important to a company's continuing operations. Inattention to the details involved throughout the cycle often results in incurring an opportunity cost because of cash being needlessly tied up in accounts receivable and, in the worst case, may cause a firm to be critically short of cash.

MARKETABLE SECURITIES

As we have just seen, the management of accounts receivable involves managerial attention to the collection of the promises to pay that a company has received from its customers. In contrast, the management of marketable securities principally involves the managerial concern of how best to invest a company's surplus cash until such funds are needed to support its regular operations.

---

[1]There are different ways to make this calculation. For example, rather than using the average accounts receivable balance, the year-end balance could be used. Another way would be to use credit sales for the fourth quarter divided by 91 days, divided into the year-end balance in accounts receivable.

EXHIBIT 7.4

**Financial Reporting of Current
Marketable Equity Securities**

For each security held, is market value less than cost (or adjusted cost)? — No → Include the security in the aggregate portfolio of short-term securities

↓ Yes

Is this a temporary market decline? — Yes → Include the security in the aggregate portfolio of short-term securities

↓ No

Market value for this security becomes the newly established cost basis and the loss is applied to current income.

Is market value of portfolio below cost? — No → Make sure allowance account has a zero balance

— Yes → Adjust the allowance account, reflecting the change in current income

The term **marketable securities** refers to the investment of surplus cash resources in the securities (e.g., stocks and bonds) of other corporate entities. A readily accessible market for these securities makes them highly liquid investments. In addition, as with the net realizable value considerations associated with accounts receivables, the accounting for these highly liquid investments involves the application of the *conservatism concept* through the use of the **lower-of-cost-or-market method.** As we consider the specific issues involved, the principal focus will be on equity (stock) investments, which management intends to hold for less than a year, thus rendering them in the current asset category for balance sheet presentation purposes.

Prior to 1975, publicly held companies reported their short-term investments in marketable equity securities on a variety of bases. Some companies used historical cost, some used market price, some used the lower of cost or market, and some applied more than one of these approaches to different categories of securities. During 1973 and 1974, many securities experienced a significant drop in market price. Consequently, for many of the corporations reporting their investments in marketable equity securities at cost, the reported balance sheet amounts were in excess of current market values. For other corporations for which the reported amounts had been reduced to reflect market declines, the partial recovery in the stock market during 1975 resulted in the securities being reported in the balance sheet at amounts that were below original cost and below current market value.

EXHIBIT 7.5

Bowne & Co., Inc.
Marketable Securities Disclosures

ty securities, notes
mpany intends to
d as current mar-
re held pri-
ds and carried

at the lower of cost or market. Realized and unrealized gains and losses were immaterial in each. Realized gains and losses are determined on a specific identification basis.

he reporting of investments in marketable *equity* securities, the FASB
Financial Accounting Standards No. 12, "Accounting for Certain
s" (SFAS No. 12).[2] Because SFAS No. 12 is complex in its original
, this chapter provides a simplified explanation of when and how to apply it. Exhibit 7.4 includes a series of pertinent issues and questions to be considered in the application of SFAS No. 12. We will consider this exhibit at length in the following sections as we investigate the financial reporting requirements and related management judgments for short-term investments in marketable equity securities.

Before discussing Exhibit 7.4, note that we are considering only short-term investments in marketable equity securities. The criterion for classifying a security as current versus noncurrent is the length of time management *intends* to continue holding it (see, for example, the Bowne & Co., Inc., disclosure in Exhibit 7.5). As a general rule, if a security is to be held less than a year, it is classified as a current investment and thus a current asset. If management's intent is to hold a particular equity security for a period exceeding one year, the financial reporting requirements resulting from that long-term intention differ. These requirements are discussed in Chapter 9.

Temporary Value Declines

The initial step in accounting for current investments in marketable equity securities, as the diagram in Exhibit 7.4 indicates, is to compare the current fair market value of each separate equity security with its recorded cost. If the fair market value is less than its cost, management must determine whether that decline is permanent or temporary, an important determination that affects the way in which the decline is handled.

Temporary declines in value are viewed as short-term fluctuations that are anticipated to reverse themselves in the short term (e.g., a general decline in the stock market). For example, if 500 shares of BFH, Inc., stock were purchased in September 1992 at a price of $100 per share and if at year-end the shares were trading at $86 per share, assuming no permanent impairment of the stock's value, the decline in share price would be considered temporary. If, on the other hand, BFH, Inc., had recently been found guilty

---

[2]SFAS No. 12 does not apply to not-for-profit organizations, mutual life insurance companies, or employee benefit plans, nor does it apply to investments in marketable debt securities.

of violating the U.S. antitrust laws or if one of its leading revenue-producing products had been found to be environmentally hazardous, the decline in stock price might reasonably be judged to be permanent.

If management decides that a market decline in the value of an individual security that it holds as a short-term investment is indeed temporary, that security need not be accounted for further on an individual basis and is aggregated with (1) other current marketable equity securities also exhibiting temporary declines and (2) those current marketable equity securities whose market values are in excess of their cost. Then, if the market value of this portfolio of *aggregated securities* is lower than its *aggregated cost,* an accounting entry must be made to reflect this overall decline in portfolio value. This portfolio-wide application of the lower-of-cost-or-market valuation method is accomplished by creating a contra asset account, or *valuation allowance,* and reducing current earnings by recording an **unrealized loss.**

Recall from an earlier chapter that a **loss** represents a reduction in the value of an asset held by a company, whereas a **gain** represents an increase in an asset value. Neither losses nor gains relate to the principal business activity of a company, although both must be reported on the income statement. Hence, losses should not be confused with expenses, nor gains with revenues. It is also important to note that this portfolio loss is unrealized. That is to say, the loss does exist today; it has not been consumated through a sale at which time the loss would become realized. The fact that the loss is unrealized, however, does not preempt the need to recognize it in the accounts.

Consider, for example, the portfolio of current marketable equity securities in Exhibit 7.6. In this example, the aggregate market value of the current portfolio at the end of Year 1 is $71,000 as compared with an aggregate recorded cost of $75,000. Assuming that management judges the decline in the value of securities 2 and 3 to be temporary, the following transaction would be recorded at the end of Year 1:

```
Dr.  Unrealized Loss (L) . . . . . . . . . . . . . . . . . . . . . . . . . . . 4,000
    Cr.  Allowance for Market Decline in Current Marketable Equity Portfolio (CA) .    4,000
```

E X H I B I T 7 . 6

**Hypothetical Investment Portfolio
of Current Marketable Equity Securities**

	At the End of Year 1			At the End of Year 2		
	Recorded Cost	**Market**	**Gain (Loss)**	**Recorded Cost**	**Market**	**Gain (Loss)**
Security 1	$20,000	$22,000	$ 2,000	$20,000	$23,000	$ 3,000
Security 2	30,000	25,000	(5,000)	30,000	27,000	(3,000)
Security 3	25,000	24,000	(1,000)	25,000	24,000	(1,000)
Total	$75,000	$71,000	$(4,000)	$75,000	$74,000	$(1,000)

The rationale for decreasing this period's net income, and, hence, owners' equity in this way (i.e., recording an unrealized loss on the income statement) is that management expects to hold a current equity security for less than one year. Therefore, it is assumed that a portfolio market decline below cost, even if temporary, is unlikely to reverse itself before the securities in the portfolio are sold. The accounting convention of conservatism therefore leads to the practice of recognizing the loss immediately, even though it has not yet been realized via an actual sale of securities.

Applying the same process to the portfolio at the end of Year 2, we find that the aggregate value of the portfolio is only $1,000 below its original cost. The valuation allowance, however, has a $4,000 credit balance carried over from Year 1, so the valuation allowance account must be adjusted to reflect the $3,000 recovery. The entry at the end of Year 2 would be this:

```
Dr.  Allowance for Market Decline in Current Marketable Equity Portfolio (CA)  .  3,000
     Cr.  Unrealized Gain (G) . . . . . . . . . . . . . . . . . . . . . . . . . .        3,000
```

This adjustment leaves a $1,000 balance in the contra asset account, which represents the difference between the portfolio's current aggregate market value ($74,000) and its aggregate cost (still $75,000).

But what if the aggregate market value of the portfolio is *higher* than its aggregate cost? Imagine, for instance, that the market value of the current marketable equity securities portfolio in Exhibit 7.6 at the end of Year 2 is $77,000 (i.e., $2,000 in excess of its cost). It is important to remember that the lower-of-cost-or-market method of valuing investments precludes those investments from being reported on the balance sheet at an amount higher than their original cost (in this example, $75,000). In such a case, any existing balance in the valuation allowance account must be brought to zero; to do this, the entry noted above would be for $4,000 instead of $3,000.

A subtle but important point to note at this juncture is that even though the SFAS No. 12 application of the lower-of-cost-or-market guidelines precludes reporting a current *portfolio* of marketable equity securities at a value above recorded cost, it does not preclude the implicit reporting of an *individual* security at a value above its recorded cost. Indeed, the application of lower of cost or market on a portfolio-wide basis provides for netting individual security market gains and losses in determining the target balance to be reported in the contra asset valuation allowance account. Such a netting of gains and losses is quite consistent with the portfolio theory of managing investments in marketable equity securities. That is, one way investors can diversify their investment risk is to hold a portfolio of investments in a variety of companies—the classic notion of "don't put all your eggs in one basket." If only market declines were considered in reporting for marketable equity securities, the Year 1 targeted allowance account balance of $4,000 in Exhibit 7.6 would have been $2,000 more, or $6,000. In effect, under the portfolio approach to lower of cost or market, the $2,000 **unrealized gain** on Security 1 is implicitly being recognized. Thus, SFAS No. 12 cannot be construed as a strict application of the lower-of-cost-or-market valuation method but as a modified application. Given the readily available and objective sources for determining the market value of these securities (e.g., stock exchange quotes), this slight modification is not viewed as a significant violation of the conservatism principle. In fact, given the overriding concern

EXHIBIT 7.7

Hughes Supply, Inc.
Current Marketable Securities Disclosures
(in thousands)

	1987	1986
Current Assets:		
Cash and short-term investments....................	$ 6,613	$ 1,601
Accounts receivable, less allowance for losses of $1,106 and $1,322..........	48,505	44,009
Refundable income taxes...	88	438
Deferred income taxes.......	408	—
Inventories..........................	64,490	53,613
Prepaid expenses..............	3,423	2,627
Total current assets............	$123,527	$102,288

Notes to Consolidated Financial Statements
Note 1 (In Part): Summary of Significant Accounting Policies:
Short-Term Investments:
Marketable equity securities are carried at the lower of cost or market and other investments are carried at cost, which approximates market.

Note 3: Short-Term Investments
Consolidated short-term investments consist of the following (in thousands):

	January 30, 1987	January 31, 1986
Money market funds, at cost.......................	$2,582	$ —
Repurchase agreements, at cost...........	1,217	680
Marketable equity securities, at lower of cost or market	2,403	275
	$6,202	$955

Marketable equity securities are stated at market in 1987 (cost was $2,483,000), and at cost in 1986 (market was $312,000). At January 30, 1987, gross unrealized gains and losses were approximately $65,000 and $145,000, respectively. Net realized gains included in income were $100,000 in fiscal 1987 (none in fiscal 1986 and 1985). Net unrealized losses included in income were $80,000 in fiscal 1987 (none in fiscal 1986 and 1985). The aggregate unrealized loss in the marketable equity securities portfolio has substantially reversed through March 16, 1987.

of providing useful information to financial statement users, the modification of the lower-of-cost-or-market method for these short-term investments is both necessary and desirable.

The disclosure for Hughes Supply, Inc., in Exhibit 7.7 illustrates some of the issues discussed thus far. Notice that the 1987 difference between market value and cost was $80,000. This difference was used to reduce the balance sheet amount from the original cost figure of $2,483,000 to $2,403,000, the lower market amount. The $80,000 is also reconcilable as the difference between the current marketable equity security portfolio gross unrealized gains of $65,000 and its gross unrealized losses of $145,000.

Permanent Value Declines

What happens if management deems the decline in value of a particular short-term marketable equity security to be permanent? (Notice that we are speaking of an *individual* security, not an entire portfolio.) Such a decline perhaps results from events—disap-

disappearing markets, adverse governmental legislation, litigation, or other similar, fundamental changes—that damage the long-term earnings potential of the company that issued the security.

Accounting for a permanent decline is quite straightforward. Since the decline in value for a given security is not expected to recover—that is, is thought to be permanent—a loss is recognized immediately even though the security has not yet been sold. For example, assume that management decides that the $3,000 decline in Year 2 for Security 2 in Exhibit 7.6 is a permanent decline. To recognize this loss, an entry is required to reduce directly the carrying value of the security (i.e., no contra asset account is used) and to record the loss:

Dr. Realized Loss (L) 3,000
     Cr. Marketable Equity Security No. 2 (A)   3,000

After a particular security is written down because of a permanent decline, it can never be written up above this newly established adjusted cost basis. For this example, the recorded "cost" of Security 2 is now $27,000, the figure that will be used for comparison with future years' market values. The new (adjusted) aggregate cost of the current portfolio is now $72,000, and the aggregate market value for the current portfolio at the end of Year 2 is $74,000. Thus, the portfolio market value is $2,000 above its adjusted cost. Therefore, an entry in Year 2 to adjust the contra asset allowance account established in Year 1 is necessary. The allowance account for current marketable equity securities currently has a credit balance of $4,000 from the Year 1 adjustment, and this balance must be reduced to zero to recognize the appreciation in the portfolio's aggregate market value (after adjusting for the permanent decline in value of Security 2). The entry would be as follows:

Dr. Allowance for Market Decline of Current Marketable Equity Portfolio (CA) . 4,000
    Cr. Unrealized Gain (G)   4,000

For a moment consider the managerial task of deciding whether a particular security's decline in value is permanent or temporary. In the absence of unambiguous evidence, management may prefer to identify a decline as temporary rather than permanent because permanent declines are immediately (and adversely) reflected in both the income statement, via a recorded loss, and the balance account, via an account write-down. As noted above, a temporary decline in value in one security may be offset by a temporary gain in value in another, thereby avoiding both an income statement and a balance sheet adjustment. Moreover, the label *temporary* conveys the optimistic impression that a future recovery is possible. Thus, there are a number of considerations that, in the absence of definitive evidence, might cause management to be biased toward the "temporary" designation for individual security declines in value. Indeed, these very concerns were at issue in the Fleet/Norstar Co. case reported in Exhibit 7.8.

E X H I B I T   7 . 8

Temporary versus Permanent
Declines in Marketable Equity Security Portfolio

SEC Limits Use
of 'Temporary'
Loss Principle

By Ken Rankin

WASHINGTON—The Securities and Exchange Commission issued a sharp warning against the use of accounting maneuvers which mask the magnitude of investment loss triggered by the recession.

The warning came on the heels of a fresh SEC enforcement action against Fleet/Norstar, a Providence, R.I.–based financial group charged with using questionable accounting procedures which effectively concealed a near–$25 million decline in the value of the firm's investments.

"This proceeding should be a timely reminder to all public companies that generally accepted accounting principles require that all unrealized losses in investment securities portfolios must be recognized currently, except where any such decline in the market value of securities is 'temporary,' " said SEC Chairman Richard C. Breeden.

Compliance with this GAAP standard "requires disciplined analysis and objective evidence to support carrying a marketable equity security at an amount exceeding its trading market price," he said.

In the case of Fleet/Norstar, company officials had attempted to portray the sharp market value decline of the firm's portfolio as only "temporary," but SEC concluded that it was unlikely that the company would ever fully recover its investments.

The commission's order was prompted by Fleet's accounting for investments in marketable equity securities of various bank holding companies in New England.

According to SEC, the company carried these securities on its balance sheet at an aggregate cost basis

(i.e. the "historical purchase price") which was some $74 million more than their current aggregate market value.

Because of the depressed economic conditions in the New England region, some of the securities in Fleet's portfolio were trading at less than 20 percent of their original cost. Although the prospects for recovering Fleet's original investment in this stock was "unfavorable," the company nevertheless characterized the declines in market value of these securities as "only temporary," SEC said.

In addition to failing to recognize "other than temporary" declines in its portfolio value, SEC charged the company with ignoring GAAP requirements for recognizing such investment losses.

Moreover, Fleet's "internal accounting controls were insufficient to provide reasonable assurances that the information pertinent to the proper accounting" for its investments was adequately considered, the agency said.

In signing the consent order, Fleet was not required to admit any wrongdoing but did agree to refrain from such violations of the SEC Act in the future.

The company also restated its 1990 financial statements to reduce the carrying value of its investment portflio and recognize multi-million-dollar losses on certain securities. As a result, Fleet's net loss for last year ballooned from $48.9 million to $73.7 million.

Furthermore, SEC announced that the company implemented additional internal control procedures to ensure its compliance with both Federal securities law and with GAAP.

Source: Accounting Today, September 9, 1991.

Sales

At some point in time, a company's investment manager will decide to sell a security held in its portfolio. Such an event is likely to result in the realization of either a gain or loss that should be recognized (i.e., recorded) at the time of sale. If we assume that in Year 3 Security 3 is sold for $27,000, the entry to record that event is:

```
Dr.  Cash (A) . . . . . . . . . . . . . . . . . . . . . . . . .  27,000
      Cr.  Current Marketable Equity Security (A) . . . . . . . . . . . .  25,000
      Cr.  Gain on Sale of Security 3 . . . . . . . . . . . . . . . .   2,000
```

Notice that there is no attempt to ascertain that part of the valuation allowance account applicable to Security 3. Any adjustment to the allowance account will be made at the end of Year 3 when the portfolio's aggregate market value and cost are again compared and the allowance adjusted accordingly. Such comparison will simply no longer involve Security 3. If Security 3 were sold for $20,000 instead of $27,000, the preceeding entry would record a $5,000 loss on the sale.

Transfers

Securities that were once considered current may be reclassified as noncurrent if management's intent for holding them changes. If a security is reclassified as noncurrent, it is transferred to the noncurrent portfolio of marketable equity securities at its lower-of-cost-or-market value, determined at the date of transfer. If a group of securities changes classification, those securities are transferred individually rather than aggregately. Thus, if the market value of an individual security is below its cost, the security is transferred at its current market value, which becomes its new cost basis, and a loss is recognized as of the date of transfer. Whether the decline is temporary or permanent does not matter. In such a case, the relevant fact is that its market value is less than its original cost, so a loss must be recognized when the security changes status from current to noncurrent.

As an example, suppose that management decides that it will hold a security for several years rather than several months because there seems to be some real price appreciation potential and no immediate need for the cash. In such a case, the security will be reclassified as a noncurrent security. If the market value at the date of reclassification is $90,000 and its original cost was $100,000, a $10,000 loss would have to be recorded to reflect the lower market value figure. The entry to reflect this would be:

```
Dr.  Loss on Transfer of Marketable Equity Security (L)  . . . .  10,000
Dr.  Noncurrent Marketable Equity Security (A) . . . . . . . .  90,000
    Cr.  Current Marketable Equity Security (A)  . . . . . . . . . . . 100,000
```

The disclosure of Golden Nugget, Inc., in Exhibit 7.9 describes this very phenomenon. The note, in particular, identifies a $215,000 loss recorded as the result of transferring a number of securities from their current to noncurrent portfolios in 1990 whereas in 1989, a much larger loss on transfer of $3,560,000 was recorded.

Marketable Debt Securities

SFAS No. 12 does not apply to marketable debt securities such as bonds. The financial reporting guidelines for marketable debt securities are, however, relatively straightforward and are consistent with many of SFAS No. 12's marketable equity security reporting guidelines.

Regardless of their balance sheet classification, debt securities are normally recorded at cost. The current versus noncurrent classification of debt securities is usually determined by the maturity date of the debt security. If a bond is scheduled to mature

---

EXHIBIT 7.9

Golden Nugget, Inc.
Transfer of Marketable Securities

Marketable securities are carried at the lower of aggregate cost or market value. Marketable securities transferred from current assets to noncurrent assets are recorded at the lower of cost or market value on the date of transfer.

At December 31, the Company's marketable securities portfolio included high-yield securities issued by certain U.S. corporations as follows:

Net realized gains (losses) on the sale of marketable securities are included in the "Interest and other income" caption in the accompanying Consolidated Statements of Operations as follows: 1990—$(3,812,000); 1989—$16,375,000; 1988—$4,797,000. Also included in "Interest and other income" is a credit for a reduction in the valuation allowance of $2,321,000 in 1990 and a charge for the recognition of a valuation allowance of $5,307,000 in 1989. There were no valuation allowances recorded during 1988.

Subsequent to December 31, 1990, the Company liquidated its marketable securities investment portfolio

and recorded a realized loss of $476,000 and a credit for the elimination of the unrealized loss of $2,986,000 at December 31, 1990.

During 1990 and 1989, the Company reclassified certain high-yield securities with a cost of $220,000 and $19,978,000, respectively, from marketable securities to noncurrent investments, which are included in the "Other assets—Other, net" caption in the accompanying Consolidated Balance Sheets. The reclassifications were based on management's intent to hold these securities for the foreseeable future due to the impairment of liquidity for these securities. In connection with the reclassifications, the Company recorded losses of $215,000 and $3,560,000 during 1990 and 1989, respectively, to adjust the cost of the securities to their respective market values on the date of transfer.

In the first quarter of 1989, the Company realized gains on sales of marketable securities of $24,429,000 which were partially offset by unrealized losses of $4,152,000.

---

within the next year, it is usually considered to be a current security, and vice versa. The only exception to this practice is management's intention to sell a bond within the coming year.

Consistent with the general concern for conservatism, investments in marketable debt securities may be written down to a lower market value if *both* of the following conditions are met:

1. The decline in market value is substantial.
2. The decline in market value did not result from a temporary condition.

If management judges *both* of these criteria to be applicable to a particular debt security, market value should become that debt security's new cost basis, and a loss is recorded in that period's income statement. After a debt security is written down, it can never be written up above its newly established cost, even if the market value recovers. It is also important to realize that a debt security's cost and market value are compared *individually,* not in the aggregate.

As an example, assume that XYZ company holds a bond, classified as a current asset, that was originally purchased for $1,000. This bond's current market value is $600, and management believes that the $400 decline is substantial and permanent. Thus, an entry must be made to recognize this lower market value; the entry is as follows:

    Dr. Realized Loss on Current Debt Security (L) 400
        Cr. Current Debt Security (A)   400

The reported amount of the debt security is now $600, and it can never be written up above this newly established cost.

Analyzing Marketable Securities

The analysis of marketable securities, like that of accounts receivable, principally relates to the liquidity of a company. Because marketable securities are highly liquid, they constitute an important source of immediate cash inflows, thereby alleviating a company's need to borrow in the short term or to factor receivables. Thus, the larger a company's investment in marketable securities, the larger its available cash reserves at its disposal.

As noted above, marketable equity securities are valued at their recorded cost or at their net realizable value as a consequence of the application of the lower-of-cost-or-market method on a portfolio basis. Although this valuation approach ensures that the liquidity value of a portfolio is not overstated, it does not prevent the true liquidity value from being understated. That is, the net realizable value of a company's portfolio of equity securities may actually be quite a bit greater than is reported in the company's balance sheet. Unfortunately, it is unlikely that a financial statement user will be able to assess the magnitude, or even the existence, of such an understatement because under current SEC disclosure regulations, a company's specific equity holdings need not be disclosed unless and until the level of ownership interest in another company equals or exceeds 5 percent of that company's outstanding shares.

Another analytical concern relates to the valuation of marketable debt securities. Since these debt investments are valued at their cost basis, it is quite possible that the short-term realizable value of such investments is less than (or more than) their reported cost. And, as a consequence, the liquidity of a company may be over/understated. This problem may be particularly acute when a company has a substantial investment in marketable debt securities or when the investment is in high risk, so-called junk bonds. Recognizing the price sensitivity of debt investments in general and junk bonds in particular, the FASB is developing new reporting guidelines that would require financial institutions, and ultimately all companies, to value such investments at their market value if lower than cost.

SUMMARY

Trade receivables and marketable securities are two key current assets. Although not considered to be cash equivalents, they are nonetheless both readily convertible into cash.

Trade receivables are evidence of a company's revenue-production function. Although high receivable balances are not risky in and of themselves, the risk of noncollection of cash is inherent in all "promises to pay" and thus should be closely monitored.

Marketable securities represent the temporary investment of excess cash into corporate securities. These investments must be highly liquid to permit their easy conversion into cash when needed to support a company's operations. In Chapter 9, we will discuss accounting for intercorporate investments when the purpose of the investment is premised in the long-run income objectives of the company.

NEW CONCEPTS AND TERMS

Aging of receivables (p. 300)

Allowance for market decline in current marketable equity portfolio (p. 312)

Direct write-off method (p. 304)

Factoring (p. 306)

Marketable securities (p. 310)

Net realizable value (p. 297)

Percentage of credit sales (p. 299)

Pledging (p. 307)

Unrealized gain (p. 313)

Unrealized loss (p. 312)

With (without) recourse (p. 306)

ISSUES FOR DISCUSSION

D7.1 How might a product manager test the reasonableness of a company's bad debt expense and its allowance for uncollectible accounts?

D7.2 What are the deficiencies of the direct write-off method for determining a company's periodic bad debt expense?

D7.3 What are the two basic allowance methods used to estimate a company's periodic bad debt expense, and what is the theoretical justification for each?

D7.4 Distinguish between trade and nontrade receivables. Is this a useful distinction for financial reporting purposes? Explain.

D7.5 A local florist follows the policy of billing customers at the end of each month. During the past six months, sales have remained steady but the company's accounts receivable balance has increased substantially. What steps might the owner consider taking to reduce the store's accounts receivable balance?

D7.6 Discuss the significance of the net realizable value concept as it applies to receivables.

D7.7 Once a company writes off a specific account receivable, would you expect its collections effort to cease? Explain.

D7.8 Recreate the pro and con debate that most likely took place prior to the enactment of SFAS No. 12. Focus specifically on the question of retaining a strict historical cost perspective versus a lower-of-cost-or-market perspective for marketable equity securities.

D7.9 Applying the lower-of-cost-or-market rule to investments in long-term marketable equity securities may result in the creation of a contra owners' equity account. One of the primary purposes served by such an account is to smooth reported net income. Discuss the pros and cons of such an objective and of such a technique for achieving that objective.

D7.10 Peruse the five latest issues of *The Wall Street Journal,* identifying two or three companies having a 52-week low in their stock prices and report on whether such a decline in price is or is not permanent. What issues did you focus on in making the judgment as to the permanent or temporary nature of the low?

D7.11 Might the desire for reporting a certain level of earnings have any bearing on whether certain investments in marketable equity securities are classified as current versus noncurrent? Explain.

D7.12 SFAS No. 12 details a lower-of-cost-or-market criterion for investments in marketable equity securities. In the approach to implementing SFAS No. 12, some securities actually are being "reported" at market values that are in excess of their cost. Explain.

PROBLEMS

P7.1 Estimating bad debts expense. The trial balance of Aha Company at the end of its 1992 fiscal year included the following account balances:

Account	Debit	Credit
Accounts Receivable	$48,900	
Trade Notes Receivable	12,500	
Marketable Securities	15,000	
Allowance for Bad Debts	2,500	
Sales		$500,000

The company has *not yet* recorded any bad debt expense for 1992.

Required:

Determine the amount of bad debt expense to be recognized by Aha Company for 1992 assuming the following independent situations:

a. Experience shows that 90 percent of all sales are credit sales and that an average of 1 percent of credit sales prove to be uncollectible.

b. An analysis of the aging of trade receivables indicates that probable uncollectible accounts at year-end amount to $1,500.

c. Company policy is to maintain a balance sheet provision for bad debts equal to 3 percent of outstanding trade receivables.

P7.2 Accounting for bad debts. The following data were associated with the trade receivables and bad debts of CPL, Inc., during 1992:

1. The opening balance in the Allowance for Doubtful Accounts was $710,000 at January 1, 1992.

2. During 1992, the company realized that specific trade receivable accounts totaling $820,000 had actually gone bad and had been written off.

3. A trade receivable of $50,000 was paid during 1992. This account had previously been written off as a bad debt in 1991.

4. The financial officer decided that the Allowance for Doubtful Accounts would need a balance of $920,000 at the end of 1992.

Required:

a. Prepare journal entries to show how these events would be recognized in an accounting system using:

(1). The allowance method for bad debts.

(2). The direct write-off method for bad debts.

b. Discuss the advantages and disadvantages of each method with respect to the following accounting conventions:

(1). Matching

(2). Conservatism.

P7.3 Valuing long-term receivables. Ken's Sub Shoppe, Inc., is a franchiser that offers for sale an exclusive franchise agreement for $30,000. Under the terms of the agreement, the franchisee will receive a variety of services associated with the construction of a Ken's Sub Shoppe, access to various product supply services, and continuing management advice and assistance once the retail unit is up and running. The contract calls for cash payments of $10,000 per year for three years.

Required:

How should Ken's Sub Shoppe, Inc., account for the sale of a franchise contract?

P7.4 Aging accounts receivables. The following data were taken from the accounts receivable records of Cavalier Products Company as of December 31, 1991:

Receivable Age Classification	Receivable Balances Outstanding	Probability of Noncollection
0–10 days	$100,000	0.5%
11–30 days	60,000	1.0
31–60 days	50,000	2.5
61–90 days	40,000	4.0
91–120 days	30,000	6.5
Over 120 days	5,000	10.0

A prior credit balance of $1,000 existed in the Allowance for Uncollectible Accounts account.

Required:

Determine the amount of bad debt expense to be recorded at year-end 1991 by Cavalier Products Company.

P7.5 Ratio analysis. Presented below are summary financial data for Coca-Cola Enterprises, Inc., and PepsiCo, Inc.

	1989	1988
Net sales (in millions):		
Coca-Cola Enterprises, Inc.	$ 3,882	$ 3,875
PepsiCo, Inc.	15,242	12,533
Net trade receivables (in millions):		
Coca-Cola Enterprises, Inc.	297	294
PepsiCo, Inc.	1,240	979

Required:

Using the above data, calculate the accounts receivable turnover and average number of days' receivable collection period for each company. What is your evaluation of each company's credit management policy?

P7.6 Factoring and pledging receivables. Feed and Seed Stores, Inc., was experiencing a temporary shortage of cash related to unusually high seasonal sales. To alleviate the shortage, the CFO of the company proposed that some of the company's accounts receivables be sold. A factor based in New York offered to buy up to $1 million of the company's receivables on a nonrecourse basis at a fee of 16 percent of the amount factored.

As an alternative, the CEO of the company proposed borrowing an equivalent amount from the Citizens and Southern Bank, using the outstanding receivables as collateral for the loan. Under the terms of the borrowing agreement, Feed and Seed would receive 80 percent of the value of all receivables assigned to the bank and would be charged a 2 percent service fee based on the actual dollar amount of cash received and 12 percent annual interest on the outstanding loan. The CEO estimated that the loan effectively would be repaid within 60 days.

Required:

Evaluate the two alternatives. Which one is better from the company's perspective? How would you account for each transaction?

P7.7 Allowance account analysis. From inception of operations to December 31, 1991, Harris Corporation provided for uncollectible accounts receivable under the allowance for uncollectible accounts method with increases to the allowance account being made *monthly* at 2 percent of credit sales. Harris' usual credit term is net 30 days.

The balance in the Allowance for Doubtful Accounts was $130,000 at January 1, 1991. During 1991, credit sales totaled $9,000,000, monthly estimates for doubtful accounts were made at 2 percent of credit sales, $90,000 of bad debts were written off, and recoveries of accounts previously written off amounted to $15,000. Harris installed a computer facility in November 1991 and an aging of accounts receivable was prepared for the first time as of December 31, 1991. A summary of the aging is as follows:

Classification by Month of Sale	Aged Accounts Receivable as of December 31, 1991	Estimated Percentage Uncollectible
November–December 1991	$1,140,000	2%
July–October	600,000	10
January–June	400,000	25
Prior to January 1, 1991	120,000	75
Total receivable December 31, 1991	$2,260,000	

Based on an item-by-item review of the collectibility of the accounts in the "Prior to January 1, 1991" aging category, receivables totaling $60,000 were written off on December 31, 1991 (these were included in the $120,000 and represent write-offs in addition to the $90,000 previously written off). In addition, effective with the year ended December 31, 1991, Harris adopted a new accounting method for estimating the allowance for doubtful accounts, choosing to report the amount indicated by the year-end aging analysis of accounts receivable.

Required:

a. We know that the January 1, 1991, balance in the allowance account was $130,000. Reconstruct all of the 1991 accounting transactions affecting the allowance account.

b. What is the December 31, 1991, allowance account balance?

P7.8 Accounting for marketable securities. Philpott Mining invests its excess idle cash in marketable equity securities. The following portfolio of stocks as of December 31, 1991, were all purchased in 1991.

	As of December 31, 1991	
	Cost	Market Value
Current portfolio		
Nella Co.	$40,000	$36,000
Zen, Inc.	33,000	34,000
Aldon Co.	19,000	18,500
	$92,000	$88,500
Noncurrent portfolio		
Leslie, Inc.	$18,000	$16,500
Diane Properties, Inc.	19,000	18,800
Stillfied Co.	12,000	13,000
	$49,000	$48,300

During 1992, all Zen, Inc., shares were sold. In addition, all Diane Properties, Inc., shares were transferred to the current portfolio at a time when their market value equaled $17,000. As of December 31, 1992, the total market value of the current portfolio, now comprising Nella, Aldon, and Diane Properties, was $75,000. The remaining securities, composing the noncurrent portfolio, had a total market value of $29,200 as of December 31, 1992.

Required:

a. Prepare all necessary *1991* transactions pertaining to Philpott Mining's marketable equity security investments. You may ignore the purchase transaction.

b. Prepare all necessary *1992* transactions pertaining to Philpott Mining's marketable equity security investments. You may ignore the sales transaction.

c. As of December 31, 1993, the current portfolio had an aggregate market value of $78,000. Assuming that there had been no partial sales of any shares of these stocks during 1993, what year-end book entry (if any) is required on December 31, 1993.

P7.9 Lower of cost or market. Presented below is the marketable securities footnote taken from Exxon Corporation's 19X1 annual report:

	19X1	19X0
Current assets:		
Marketable securities	$620,000,000	$908,000,000

Marketable securities are stated at the lower of cost or market.

Marketable securities at year-end 19X0 were carried at cost, which was $1 million less than their fair market value. At year-end 19X1, marketable securities were carried at their fair market value, which was $5 million below cost.

Required:

What lower-of-cost-or-market book entry did Exxon record at

a. Year-end 19X0?

b. Year-end 19X1?

P7.10 Analyzing marketable securities. Presented below are the marketable security footnote disclosures contained in Scope Industries 19X1 annual report.

Notes to Consolidated Financial Statements

Note 1 (In Part): Summary of Significant Accounting Policies

Marketable Securities:

The current and noncurrent portfolios of marketable securities are each stated at the lower of aggregate cost or market at the balance sheet date and consist of common and preferred stocks and notes. Dividend and interest income are accrued as earned.

Unrealized losses on current marketable securities are charged to income. Unrealized losses on noncurrent marketable securities are recorded directly in a separate shareowners' equity account. Realized gains or losses are determined on the specific identification method and are reflected in income.

Note 2: Marketable Securities

In fiscal year 19X1, the Company transferred its current holdings in various banks' common stocks to noncurrent marketable securities. A $932,908 unrealized loss resulting from the transfer was charged against income.

Required:

a. How are the current versus noncurrent marketable securities classifications determined?

b. In Note 1, Scope Industries uses the terms *realized* and *unrealized*. Briefly discuss what is meant by each of these terms.

c. What was the entry (if any) that may have been made as a result of the Note 2 information? Assume that the cost carried in the current asset accounts for the transferred securities was $3 million. If there is no entry, explain why.

P7.11 Accounting for receivables. Suppose that Tentex Company had the following balances in certain of its accounts on December 31, 1992 (in thousands of dollars):

Trade receivables	$350.0	(debit balance)
Allowance for estimated uncollectible accounts	10.2	(credit balance)

and that transactions during 1993 were (in thousands of dollars)

1. Sales on account	$1,585.0
2. Collections on account—$1,549.4 less cash discounts of $27.4	1,522.0
3. Sales returns (from credit sales)	8.5
4. Accounts written off as uncollectible	5.4
5. Accounts previously written off now determined to be collectible	0.7
6. Provision for uncollectible accounts (based on percent of credit sales)	8.0

Required:

Prepare entries for the 1993 transactions. At what figure will Tentex show:

a. Net sales in its 1993 income statement?

b. Net trade receivables in its balance sheet of December 31, 1993?

P7.12 Accounting for receivables. Moss Products, Inc., was formed in 1982. Sales have increased on the average of 5 percent per year during its first 10 years of existence, with total sales for 1992 amounting to $350,000. Since incorporation, Moss Products has used the allowance method to account for bad debts. The company's fiscal year is the calendar year.

On January 1, 1992, the company's Allowance for Uncollectible Accounts had a *right-hand* balance of $4,000. During 1992, accounts totaling $3,300 were written off as uncollectible.

Required:

a. What does the January 1, 1992, credit balance of $4,000 in the Allowance for Uncollectible Accounts represent?

b. Since Moss Products wrote off $3,300 in uncollectible accounts during 1992, was the prior year's bad debts estimate overstated?

c. Prepare the entries to record

(1). The $3,300 write-off during 1992.

(2). Moss Products' 1992 bad debts expense assuming these two independent situations: (i) experience indicates that 1 percent of total annual sales prove uncollectible and (ii) an aging of the December 31, 1992, accounts receivable indicates that potential uncollectible accounts at year-end total $4,500.

P7.13 Credit policy review. The president, sales manager, and credit manager of Hacket Corporation were discussing the company's present credit policy and possible changes. The sales manager argued that potential sales were being lost to the competition because of Hacket Corporation's tight restrictions on granting credit to consumers. He stated that if credit were extended to a new class of customer, this year's credit sales of $2,500,000 could be increased by at least 20 percent next year with only a corresponding increase in uncollectible accounts of $10,000 over this year's figure of $37,500. With a gross margin on sales of 25 percent, the sales manager continued, the company would certainly come out ahead.

The credit manager, however, believed that a better alternative to easier credit terms would be to accept consumer credit cards like VISA or MasterCard for charge sales. The credit manager said that he had been reading on this topic and he believed this alternative offered the chance to increase sales by 40 percent. The credit card finance charges to Hacket Corporation would amount to 4 percent of the additional sales.

At this point, the president interrupted by saying that he wasn't at all sure that increasing credit sales of any kind was a good thing. In fact, he thought that the $37,500 figure was altogether too high. He wondered whether or not the company should discontinue offering sales on account.

Required:

a. Determine whether Hacket Corporation would be better off under the sales manager's proposal or the credit manager's proposal.

b. Address the president's suggestion that all credit sales be abolished.

P7.14 Lower of cost or market. The chief financial officer of Plow and Mantel Co. recently heard about a proposed new accounting rule related to investments in marketable equity securities. The proposal is that *all* marketable equity securities be presented at market value on the balance sheet and the changes that occur in market value be reflected in income in the current period. The CFO cannot argue with the point that market value on the balance sheet is more informative, but she sees no reason why changes in market value should be reflected in income of the current year.

The controller of Plow and Mantel Company also has misgivings about the possible new rule and has recommended the following alternatives:

1. Recognize realized gains and losses from changes in market value in income and report unrealized gains and losses in a special balance sheet account on the equity side of the balance sheet.

2. Report realized and unrealized gains and losses from market value changes in a statement separate from the income statement or as direct charges and credits to a stockholders' equity account.

3. Recognize gains and losses from changes in market value in income based on long-term yield; for example, use the past performance of the enterprise over several years (a 10-year period has been suggested) to determine an average annual rate of yield because of an increase in value.

To the CFO of Plow and Mantel Company, these recommendations seemed very reasonable.

Required:

a. Discuss the pros and cons of the proposed new rule. Is it preferable to the lower-of-cost-or-market rule now in effect? Why or why not?

b. Evaluate the controller's alternatives.

P7.15 Accounting for marketable securities. Geisler Company has followed the practice of reporting its investments in current marketable equity securities at the lower of cost or market. At December 13, 1991, its account Investment in Current Marketable Equity Securities had a balance of $50,000, and the Allowance for Decline in Market Value of Current Marketable Equity Securities account had a balance of $3,000. Analysis disclosed that on December 31, 1990, the facts relating to the securities were as follows:

	Cost	Market	Allowance Required
Carraway Company	$21,000	$19,000	$2,000
Dunstan Company	12,000	9,000	3,000
Wilcox Company	19,500	20,400	–0–
	$52,500	$48,400	$5,000

During 1991, Dunstan Company stock was sold for $9,100; the difference between the $9,100 and the "new adjusted basis" of $9,000 was recorded as a gain on sale of securities. The market price of the remaining stocks on December 31, 1991, were Carraway Company, $19,900; Wilcox Company, $20,800.

Required:

a. Did Geisler Company properly apply this rule on December 31, 1990? Explain.

b. Did Geisler Company properly account for the sale of Dunstan Company stock? Explain.

c. Are there any additional entries necessary for Geisler Company at December 31, 1991, to reflect the facts on the balance sheet and income statement in accordance with generally accepted accounting principles? Explain.

P7.16 Accounting for marketable securities. Brownlee Bearings Company has the following securities in its short-term portfolio of marketable equity securities on December 31, 1991:

	Cost	Market
2,000 shares of Miller Motors, common	$ 68,500	$ 60,250
10,000 shares of Erving, Inc., common	257,500	257,500
1,000 shares of Magic Ltd., preferred	52,500	56,000
	$378,500	$373,750

All of the securities were purchased in 1991.

In 1992, Brownlee Bearings completed the following securities transactions:

March 1. Sold 2,000 shares of Miller Motors, common, at $30 per share less fees of $1,500.

April 1. Bought 1,000 shares of American Steel, common, at $45 per share plus fees of $1,000.

August 1. Transferred Magic Ltd., preferred, from the short-term portfolio to the long-term portfolio when the stock was selling at $50 per share.

Brownlee Bearings Company portfolio of marketable equity securities appeared as follows on December 31, 1992:

	Cost	Market
10,000 shares of Erving, Inc., common	$257,500	$291,000
1,000 shares of American Steel, common	46,100	41,000
	$303,600	$332,000

Required:

Prepare the accounting entries for Brownlee Bearings Company for

a. The 1991 adjusting entry.

b. The sale of Miller Motors stock.

c. The purchase of American Steel stock.

d. The transfer of Magic Ltd. stock from the short-term to the long-term portfolio.

e. The 1992 adjusting entry.

P7.17 Accounting for reclassified securities. Hires, Inc., purchased marketable equity securities at a cost of $350,000 on March 1, 1991. When the securities were purchased, the company intended to hold the investment for more than one year. Therefore, the investment was classified as a noncurrent asset in the company's balance sheet for the year-ended December 31, 1991, and stated at its then market value of $300,000.

On September 30, 1992, when the investment had a market value of $310,000, management reclassified the investment as a current asset because the company intended to sell the securities within the next 12 months. The market value of the investment was $325,000 on December 31, 1992.

Required:

a. At what amount should the investment be reported on September 30, 1992, after the decision to reclassify it as a current asset?

b. How would the investment in the marketable equity securities be reported in the financial statements of Hires, Inc., as of December 31, 1992, so that the company's financial position and operations for the year 1992 would reflect and report properly the reclassification of the investment from a noncurrent asset to a current asset?

P7.18 Bad debt policy review. The controller for Franklin Corporation provides you, the credit manager, with the following list of accounts receivable written off in the current year.

Date	Customer	Amount
March 31	Smith & Robertson, Inc.	$6,400
June 30	Lanahan Associates	3,700
September 30	Cheryl's Dress Shop	5,120
December 31	Frank Corporation	5,800

Franklin Corporation follows the policy of recording bad debt expense as accounts are written off. The controller maintains that this procedure is appropriate for financial statement purposes because the Internal Revenue Service will not accept other methods for recognizing bad debts.

All of Franklin Corporation's sales are on a 30-day credit basis. Sales for the current year total $1,800,000, and analysis has indicated that bad debt losses historically approximate 1.5 percent of sales.

Required:

a. Do you agree or disagree with Franklin Corporation's policy concerning recognition of bad debt expense? Why or why not?

b. If Franklin were to use the percent of credit sales allowance method for recording bad debt expense, net income for the current year would change by how much?

P7.19 Accounting for receivables. The preliminary trial balance for Rotch Consulting Company shows the following balances:

	Dr.	Cr.
Accounts Receivable	$74,800	
Allowance for Doubtful Accounts	2,080	
Sales		$379,000
Sales Returns and Allowances	2,800	

Required:

Using the data above, prepare the accounting entries to record each of the following independent cases:

a. The company wants to maintain the Allowance for Doubtful Accounts at 2 percent of gross accounts receivable.

b. To obtain additional cash, Rotch factors $18,000 of accounts receivable with Dallas Credit Corp. The finance charge is 10 percent of the amount factored.

c. To obtain a one-year loan of $55,000, Rotch assigns $64,000 of accounts receivable to Ace Accounts. The finance charge is 6 percent of the loan; the cash is received and the accounts are turned over to Ace.

P7.20 Financial statement disclosure: marketable securities.

a. Tub Factory Corporation invested its excess cash in temporary investments during 1991. As of December 31, 1991, the portfolio of short-term marketable equity securities consisted of the following common stocks:

Security	Quantity	Per Share Cost	Per Share Market
Holden, Inc.	1,000 shares	$14	$19
Coates Corp.	3,000 shares	27	21
Carey Marine	2,000 shares	36	31

What descriptions and amounts should be reported in Tub Factory's December 31, 1991, balance sheet relative to temporary investments?

b. On December 31, 1992, Tub Factory's portfolio of short-term marketable equity securities consisted of the following common stocks:

| | | Per Share | |
Security	Quantity	Cost	Market
Holden, Inc.	1,000 shares	$14	$21
Holden, Inc.	2,000 shares	20	21
Lakeshore Company	1,000 shares	17	14
Carey Marine	2,000 shares	36	20

During 1992, Tub Factory sold 3,000 shares of Coates Corp. at a loss of $10,000 and purchased 2,000 more shares of Holden, Inc., and 1,000 shares of Lakeshore Company.

(1). What descriptions and amounts should be reported in Tub Factory's December 31, 1992, balance sheet?

(2). What descriptions and amounts should be reported to reflect the data in Tub Factory's 1992 income statement?

c. On December 31, 1993, Tub Factory's portfolio of short-term marketable equity securities consisted of the following common stocks:

| | | Per Share | |
Security	Quantity	Cost	Market
Carey Marine	2,000 shares	$36	$47
Lakeshore Company	500 shares	17	15

During 1993, Tub Factory sold 3,000 shares of Holden, Inc., at a gain of $12,000 and 500 shares of Lakeshore Company at a loss of $2,300.

(1). What descriptions and amounts should be reported in Tub Factory's December 31, 1993, balance sheet?

(2). What descriptions and amounts should be reported to reflect the above in Tub Factory's 1993 income statement?

d. Assuming that comparative financial statements for 1992 and 1993 are presented, draft the footnote necessary for full disclosure of Tub Factory's transactions and position in marketable equity securities.

P7.21 Accounting for receivables. Holt Company has significant amounts of trade accounts receivable outstanding at any given time. Holt uses an allowance method to estimate bad debt expense instead of the direct write-off method. During the year, some specific accounts were written off as uncollectible, and some that were previously written off as uncollectible were collected.

Besides trade accounts receivable, Holt also has some interest-bearing notes receivable for which the face amount plus interest, at the current market rate of interest, is due at maturity. The notes were received on August 1, 1990, and are due on July 31, 1992.

Required:

a. How should Holt Company account for the collection of the accounts previously written off as uncollectible?

b. How should Holt Company report the effects of the interest-bearing notes receivable on its December 31, 1991, balance sheet and its income statement for the year ended December 31, 1991? Why?

P7.22 Estimating bad debts. Bolt Company's allowance for doubtful accounts had a credit balance of $10,000 at December 31, 1991. On a monthly basis during the year, for quick and ready reference purposes, Bolt accrues bad debt expense at 4 percent of credit sales. During 1992, Bolt's credit sales amounted to $1,500,000, and uncollectible accounts totaling $44,000 were judged to be hopelessly uncollectible and thus were written off. The year-end aging of accounts receivable indicated that a $40,000 allowance for doubtful accounts was desirable at December 31, 1992.

Required:

What should Bolt's 1992 bad debt expense be? Explain.

P7.23 Accounting for receivables. Longhorn Company had the following information relating to its accounts receivable at December 31, 1991, and for the year ended December 31, 1992:

Accounts receivable at 12/31/91	$1,000,000
Allowance for doubtful accounts at 12/31/91	60,000
Credit sales for 1992	5,300,000
Collections from customers for 1992	4,650,000
Accounts written off 9/30/92	70,000
Estimated uncollectible receivables per treasurer's aging of receivables at 12/31/92	110,000

Required:

a. At December 31, 1992, Longhorn's allowance for doubtful accounts should be how much?

b. At December 31, 1992, Longhorn's gross accounts receivable balance should be how much?

CASES

C7.1 Accounting for bad debts: Omni Products Division. The following two scenarios should be analyzed independently.

Scenario A: The period-end analysis model. The manager of Omni Products Division, Harry Smith, was quite satisfied with all of his section leaders and had developed a high level of trust in their day-to-day decisions. Still, he insisted that he be involved in the critical, long-range judgments. For example, his accounting and control section was efficient and largely trouble free. However, he carefully monitored the sensitive areas, including the status of collections on accounts receivable, the follow-up on slow-pay customers, and the reasonableness of the on-going provision for estimated bad debt losses.

Smith's monitoring effort was complicated by the fact that Omni's average sale was less than $1,000 and that the division carried more than 10,000 open customer accounts. He found it difficult to put his hands around the situation because of the amount of detail in the file. To help him monitor the receivables–collections–bad debt situation, he had engaged a consultant some years ago to establish a statistical sampling system. Under the system, the Omni computer section produced a special report each quarter that analyzed the accounts receivable balances based on the dates of the unpaid invoices. This aging report was useful to Smith, helping him identify trends in the status of the receivables.

One of Smith's accounting people tracked a sample of accounts from each aging category and determined which of those sampled accounts were ultimately uncollectible. Based on a simple formula developed by the consultant, the clerk used those findings to calculate a factor for each aging category that would predict what proportion of those accounts would ultimately be uncollectible. The accounting clerk tested the results of the current studies against the numbers developed by the original study and always found that the original numbers were quite valid:

For Every Dollar in the Aging Category	Amount that Will Prove to Be Uncollectible
Current (0–30 days)	$0.00
1 month past due (30–60 days)	0.005
2 months past due (60–90 days)	0.05
3–4 months past due (90–150 days)	0.20
5–6 months past due (150–210 days)	0.50

Smith trusted the system and always had the accounting people adjust the period-end allowance for possible bad debts to the amount indicated by the quarterly aging report—the category totals multiplied by the above factors. In the interim months, he had his people record an estimated provision for possible bad debts, but the quarterly financial statements that were sent to the home office always included a revised provision for possible bad debt losses that was simply a forced number from the updated allowance account.

At March 31, 1992, the allowance account was adjusted to $2,658,000, the amount indicated by the aging-analysis process at that date. During the months of April, May, and June, accounts totaling $1,942,000 were turned over to the attorneys and written off. During April and May, Smith had his accounting people provide $500,000 a month for possible bad debt losses. The aging of the accounts at June 30, 1992, showed the following:

	(000)
Current	$158,000
1 month past due	43,200
2 months past due	8,240
3–4 months past due	3,650
5–6 months past due	1,840
Total Accounts Receivable balance at June 30, 1992	$214,930

Required:

Determine the amount of the provision for bad debt losses for the month of June 1992.

Scenario B: The percent-of-credit-sales model. The manager of Omni Products Division, Harry Smith, was quite satisfied with all of his section leaders and had developed a high level of trust in their day-to-day decisions. Still, he insisted that he be involved in the critical, long-range judgments For example, his accounting and control section was efficient and largely trouble free. However, he carefully monitored the sensitive areas, including the status of collections on accounts receivable, the follow-up on slow-pay customers, and the reasonableness of the on-going provision for estimated bad debt losses.

Smith's monitoring effort was complicated by the fact that Omni's average sale was less than $1,000 and that the division carried more than 10,000 open customer accounts. He found it difficult to put his hands around the situation because of the amount of detail in the file. To help him monitor the receivables–collections–bad debt situation, he had engaged a consultant some years ago to establish a statistical sampling system. Following the system, a clerk randomly selected a small number of credit sales each week and followed them through to their conclusion—either collection in cash after varying periods or a write-off because of the buyer's inability to pay. The system was easy to operate, and Smith had been assured that the results of the sample would give a very accurate reflection of the results to be expected from total credit sales. However, because the system required the clerk to follow each sampled credit sale to its conclusion, the results were not always available as quickly as Smith would have liked.

Over the past several years, the results of the system had tracked Smith's expectations, given the state of the economy in each period. The results of the study showed:

Report Dated	For the Year Ended	Average Period until Collection	Percentage of Sales Ultimately Written-off
July 5, 1988	December 31, 1987	14.2 weeks	5.5
July 8, 1989	December 31, 1988	12.4 weeks	4.8
July 7, 1990	December 31, 1989	10.5 weeks	4.6
June 28, 1991	December 31, 1990	9.3 weeks	4.5

Based on the trend through the July 1990 report, Smith had instructed his accounting people to provide for estimated losses from bad debts for the year ending December 31, 1990, at 4.6 percent of sales, and during the first half of 1991, the division had provided for possible bad debt losses using that 4.6 percent factor. When the June 1991 report came out, Smith was delighted. He had his accounting people reduce the provision for estimated bad debt losses to 4.5 percent of sales, effective with the July 1991 monthly financial statement. They continued with that estimate through the rest of 1991 and through the first six months of 1992. However, as the 1991 spring season wore on, Smith became anxious about the continued use of that low estimate because his customers were experiencing tighter times and the number of days' sales in the receivables balance was growing, suggesting that the trend of the late 80s was reversing.

The allowance for possible bad debts had a balance of $2,152,000 at December 31, 1991, and through the first six months of 1992, a provision of $3,803,040 had been added to the allowance based on six-month sales of $84,512,000. During that same period of time, accounts totaling $4,203,000 had been turned over to the attorneys for collection and written off. When the results of the statistical study for the year ended December 31, 1991, was completed on July 15, 1992, it confirmed Smith's fears. It showed that credit sales made during the year ended December 31, 1991, took 11.2 weeks to turn cash and that 4.7 percent of those sales were never collected but were written off. He called a meeting to review this situation with his sales and credit people. He got the sense that the ship had not been run as tightly as he would have liked, and he resolved to understand how that had happened. His immediate concern was the package of financial statements he was to send to the home office the next day for the month of June and the six months ended June 30, 1991. After consulting with his staff, he resolved to add to the allowance for possible bad debts. He instructed his accounting people to increase the six-month provision for possible losses from bad debts to 4.75 percent of sales, taking the effect of the new rate of provision as a special charge against operations for June.

Required:

Calculate the revised allowance balance as of June 30, 1992.

C7.2 Accounting for marketable securities: FHAC Corporation.

During 1990, FHAC Corporation invested $25 million of working capital in short-term equity securities. At year-end, the portfolio carried the following market values:

Securities	Cost Basis	Current Market Value
AT&T, common stock	$12,000,000	$ 8,000,000
General Motors, Class E common stock	8,000,000	10,000,000
Georgia Pacific, preferred stock	5,000,000	5,000,000
Total	$25,000,000	$23,000,000

In early February 1991, FHAC decided to liquidate its position in General Motors because the company needed cash for seasonal inventory purchases; the market value of the stock was $10.4 million at the time of the sale. On March 31, 1991, FHAC's remaining portfolio carried the following market values:

Securities	Cost Basis	Current Market Value
AT&T, common stock	$12,000,000	$ 8,200,000
Georgia Pacific, preferred stock	5,000,000	4,500,000
Total	$17,000,000	$12,700,000

By year-end 1991, the aggregate market value of FHAC's portfolio was $18.6 million; no securities were sold or added to the portfolio during the remainder of the year.

Required:

Evaluate the facts of this case and determine the income statement effects of the transactions involving FHAC's portfolio of marketable securities. Also identify the cash flow effects of the transactions.

C7.3 Accounting for marketable securities: Malibu Enterprises[3].

Pete Compton, the controller of Malibu Enterprises, was preparing the company's financial statements for the year ended December 31, 1986. Over the past several years, Malibu Enterprises had been successfully marketing leisure-time products in California. In 1985, for the first time, the business had produced excess cash, which Compton invested in financial securities. Malibu's investment portfolio as of December 31, 1985, is detailed below.

For the most part, Malibu's stock investments had not advanced with the 1985 bull market. Their performance was fairly lackluster, but the decision had been made to hold them in the belief that at some point they would climb with the rest of the market. The stock market, however, slowed near the end of 1986, and the growth of some of the stocks in Malibu's portfolio also slowed—in some cases, even reversed.

---

[3]This case was prepared by Mark E. Haskins. Copyright 1987 by the Darden Graduate Business School Foundation, Charlottesville, Virginia.

Looking at the securities' 1986 year-end market values (shown below) Compton was particularly concerned about the Vicorp Restaurants stock. Vicorp's price had declined sharply during 1986, and the current market value was below Malibu's original purchase price. Compton called his broker, Jeff Holliday, to find out what was happening.

"Well, Pete, the story at Vicorp is not that good. Its fiscal year, which ended last October, reflected a substantial loss, and the common stock dividend was suspended in August. The acquisition of Sambo's Restaurants is requiring more cash than anticipated and is taking more time to become profitable than planned. These delays will probably continue into next year, so I do not foresee a rapid turnaround."

"Okay, Jeff, thanks for the information. By the way, did you check the maturity dates on those bonds for me?"

"I sure did. None of your bonds are scheduled to mature this coming year. While I've got you on the line, Pete, I'd like to double-check those trigger prices that you wanted me to sell some of your stocks at: Diebold at 48, FPL Group at 35, Humana at 36, and Service Corp. at 39. Do you still want these in effect?"

"Sure do."

"Great. Let me know when you want to sell any of the others."

Malibu Enterprises
Investment Portfolio
December 31, 1985

	Shares	Original Cost	Market Value
Equities			
Current:			
Diebold, Inc.	700	$ 29,400	$ 28,788
FPL Group	750	20,625	21,094
Humana	750	20,438	23,344
Service Corp. International	800	23,500	25,400
Thousand Trails	1,000	17,750	9,000
		$111,713	$107,626
Noncurrent:			
General Motors	400	$ 31,850	$ 28,750
IBM	200	27,175	31,100
Martin Marietta	500	24,375	25,500
Mattel, Inc.	1,500	23,625	17,813
A. H. Robins	1,000	17,000	11,125
Vicorp Restaurants	1,000	24,625	18,000
		$148,650	$132,288
Bonds			
Ford Motor Company		21,925	$ 21,575
Union Carbide		21,725	21,150
Xerox		20,425	20,650
		$ 64,075	$ 63,375

Source: *Barron's.*

Malibu Enterprises
Investment Portfolio Market Values
December 31, 1987

Security	Market Value
Equities	
Diebold, Inc.	$ 32,113
FPL Group	24,000
General Motors	26,850
Humana	15,188
IBM	24,400
Martin Marietta	25,375
Mattel, Inc.	12,188
Service Corp. International	28,400
A. H. Robins	8,000
Thousand Trails	2,875
Vicorp Restaurants	11,000
	$210,389
Bonds	
Ford Motor Company	$ 20,900
Union Carbide	21,750
Xerox	21,300
	$ 63,950

Source: *Barron's.*

"Well, my attitude toward the Martin Marietta and Mattel investments has changed. I'm not pleased with the way Martin Marietta's recent round of contract bidding has gone, nor am I comfortable any longer with the uncertainties posed by the toy industry. If you have any hot tips, let me know."

"O.K. Anything else?"

"Nope. It's been good talking to you again. Thanks for your time, Jeff."

Compton hung up the phone and contemplated the information Holliday had given him. He also decided it was time to study the reports he had seen in the business press (see next page). Compton knew that his auditor wanted to see the financial statements at the end of the week, so he was determined to finish his books today.

Required:

How should Malibu's marketable securities be reported in the year-end balance sheet and income statement?

Malibu Enterprises
Information Pertinent to the A. H. Robins Investment

The management for Thousand Trails, Inc., announced today that the company had a $50.4 million loss for 1986. The company's 1986 revenue was $113.4 million, down 35 percent from 1985. Its troubles were further compounded when its auditors said that they would issue a qualified opinion of the financial statements, due within the next 30 days, unless the company and its lenders agreed to restructure its debt. Thousand Trails management responded that it had already started to negotiate with its lenders. The company's total outstanding debt is $185.6 million, and its shareholders' equity is $28.5 million. James E. Claus, vice president of finance, said that he could not disclose the specific details of the restructuring discussions. He said "The company will survive long-term."

At one point, Thousand Trails was considered a rising star by Wall Street analysts, primarily because of the company's earnings growth. Thousand Trails, however, records the full price of its memberships (currently $7,500) as revenue, even though members pay only 40 percent of the fee, on average, as an initial downpayment. Earnings peaked in 1984 at $19.1 million, and the stock price also peaked at 29 1/2. Even with its record earnings, Thousand Trails used $52 million more cash than it generated in 1984. To provide itself with additional funds, the company obtained more debt and sold its receivables. In 1985, the company earned $1.8 million from revenues of $173.7 million. Thousand Trails lost members before payments were made in full, so it had to write off $11 million in paper revenues that had been prematurely booked. In 1986, the company had to write off $5.6 million for this same reason.

In trading yesterday, Thousand Trails closed at $3.25, down 31.25 cents.

Source: Forbes, July 14, 1986.

Malibu Enterprises
Information Pertinent to the A. H. Robins Investment

Robins' Reorganization Plan Specifies Added Debt of $1.35 Billion, Asset Sales
By Sonia Steptoe
Staff Reporter of The Wall Street Journal

A. H. Robins Co.'s proposed $1.85 billion bankruptcy-law reorganization plan would saddle the company with enormous debt and leave it in a weakened financial position for the next five years.

But officials of the 121-year-old, family-owned company apparently regard such a predicament as a necessary price to pay for remaining independent.

Some creditors' lawyers in the case, however, continue to regard the Robins proposal as unacceptable and plan to oppose it. They say hearings and arguments over the plan are likely to consume several months. "It's going to be a long summer," said one attorney.
Negative Net Worth
According to court documents filed Friday, the Richmond, Va.–based health products maker would assume $1.35 billion in additional debt and liabilities, bringing its total liabilities to $2.88 billion. The plan also would leave Robins with a negative net worth over the next five years of between $368 million and $1.37 billion. Net worth is assets minus liabilities. Robins also said in the papers that it would take a $1.42 billion charge against earnings in 1987 to cover its Dalkon Shield–related liabilities under the plan. The charge would result in a projected $1.42 billion net loss for the year.

In 1986, Robins earned $82 million, or $3.38 a share, on sales of $790 million.

In addition, Robins would sell almost $400 million in assets to fund the plan and pay as much as $73 million in fees to its investment bankers and lenders. Robins also wouldn't pay its quarterly dividend of 19 cents a share for the next five years. The company hasn't paid a dividend since 1984.

"(Robins) will be highly (leveraged) and management will have to be careful," said a source close to the company. "But they will be able to continue operating the business."
Trust Fund for Claims
Robins sought protection from creditors under Chapter 11 of the federal Bankruptcy Code in August 1985 because of mounting suits and claims related to its Dalkon Shield intrauterine contraceptive device.

Its proposed reorganization plan would establish a $1.75 billion trust to settle the 320,000 Shield-related claims and $100 million to pay other creditors. Initial

Malibu Enterprises
Information Pertinent to the A. H. Robins Investment

funding for the trust would include a $75 million cash payment from Robins and a five-year, $1.68 billion letter of credit from a group of banks. A court hearing on the plan is set for July 21.

The financial disclosure statement accompanying the company's reorganization plan discloses an expensive, tangled web of debt financing. Robins says Manufacturers Hanover Trust Co. and Chemical Bank would be co-agents for the credit letter, guaranteeing $500 million each. The remaining $675 million would come from a banking syndicate that hasn't been formed.

Robins said it would fund the letter of credit with proceeds of an $800 million offering of high-yield, high-risk debt. Commonly referred to as junk bonds, the debt would have an average interest rate of 11.5% and an average life of between 10 and 12 years, Robins said.

Selling Certain Assets

Additional funding would come from the company's future cash flow, a $100 million bank credit line and selling certain assets and subsidiaries.

The revolving credit line, which would be in addition to the letter of credit, also would be provided by Manufacturers Hanover, one of Robins's largest unsecured creditors. The filing doesn't say which assets or product lines Robins contemplates selling.

Robins also said it might have to sell more assets, or seek alternative debt financing in the future, depending

on "actual operating performance, market conditions and other factors."

The plan still must be approved by the judge presiding over the bankruptcy-law case, the company's creditors and the Dalkon Shield claimants. One issue that is ripe for debate is whether the Robins proposal serves the interests of the creditors and claimants. Under bankruptcy-law rules, the company must show that its plan gives claimants and creditors as much as they would get if the company were liquidated.

Robins and its investment advisers contend that a sale would yield between $1.29 billion and $1.43 billion, or only 63% to 68% of the amount available under its plan, for paying Shield claimants and unsecured creditors.

But other parties in the case dispute that analysis. They point out that two bidders, New York-based American Home Products Corp. and Fort Washington, Pa.–based Rorer Group Inc., offered to pay more than $2 billion for Robins. One lawyer commented: "How can they claim that when the company already has commanded between $2.3 billion and $2.5 billion (from prospective purchasers)?"

Like the Robins plan, the American Home and Rorer proposals contemplated a $1.75 billion trust fund and full payment to the other Robins creditors. But claimants' lawyers said the cash-backed trusts involved fewer risks for their clients than the Robins plan.

Source: *The Wall Street Journal,* May 4, 1987.

CHAPTER 8

Inventories and the Cost of Goods Sold

Visualize the items that are on the shelves of the Richfood Supermarket. Visualize the millions of gallons of oil in various stages of refinement at Exxon sites around the world. Visualize a General Motors factory with various types of cars in various stages of completion. Such images are the images of these companies' inventories—their stock in trade, composed of the goods purchased and/or manufactured to sell to their customers. On the balance sheet, inventories are regarded as current assets because

they are expected to be sold and to benefit a business during the next operating cycle. The inventory items sold during a period, and therefore no longer on hand at period-end, are matched against that period's sales revenue and recorded in the income statement as the cost of goods sold. It must be quickly pointed out that in determining the amount to report for the cost of goods sold, however, management is accorded considerable leeway, and the alternative inventory accounting methods available can significantly affect both the balance sheet (i.e., the reported cost of ending inventory) and the income statement (i.e., the reported cost of goods sold attributable to that period).

How does PepsiCo, Exxon, General Motors, or Richfoods account for its vast and varied inventories? The focus of this chapter is the accounting and valuation issues involving inventories and the cost of goods sold. The inventory accounting method chosen by management depends on the nature of the industry, certain tax considerations, and a variety of other factors discussed below. The informed reader is advised to consider both the balance sheet and the income statement effects during the following discussion.

SOME BASIC RELATIONSHIPS: THE COST OF INVENTORY

For all companies, the principal accounting concept involved in valuing inventories is that all goods available for sale during a period must, at year-end, either have been sold or remain in ending inventory. For a *merchandising* business like K mart, which simply buys goods and sells them as is, this relationship is depicted in Panel A of Exhibit 8.1, and in the following equations:

$$\text{Beginning inventory} + \text{Net purchases} = \text{Cost of goods available for sale.} \quad (1)$$

$$\text{Cost of goods available for sale} - \text{Cost of goods sold} = \text{Ending inventory.} \quad (2)$$

In accounting for a *manufacturing* company's inventory, such as that of General Motors, which transforms raw materials into a final product, the same basic principle applies, although the process is a bit more complicated and involves a larger number of costs. Manufactured inventories are usually composed of three categories: **raw materials** (RM), which includes materials and purchased parts awaiting assembly or manufacture; **work in process** (WIP), which includes partially completed products still in the factory; and **finished goods** (FG), which includes fully assembled or manufactured goods available for sale. Each of these three physical categories of inventory must be represented in the accounting process.

Raw Materials

Accounting for the raw materials component of a manufacturer's inventory is similar to accounting for inventory transactions of a merchandising company. The beginning inventory *plus* purchases *equals* the raw materials available for use. These raw materials available for use remain either unused at year-end (and thus in the inventory of unused raw materials at the end of the accounting period) or have been placed in production. This relationship is shown in the following equations:

$$\text{Beginning RM inventory} + \text{Net purchases of RM} = \text{Cost of} \\ \text{RM available for use.} \quad (3)$$

$$\text{Cost of RM available for use} - \text{Ending RM inventory} = \text{Cost of RM used.} \quad (4)$$

E X H I B I T   8 . 1

Status of Inventory Items at Year-End

Panel A: Merchandising companies

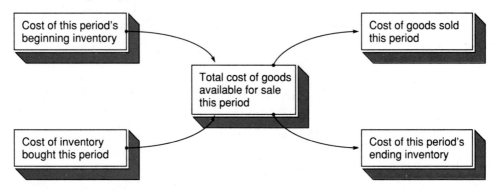

Panel B: Manufacturing companies

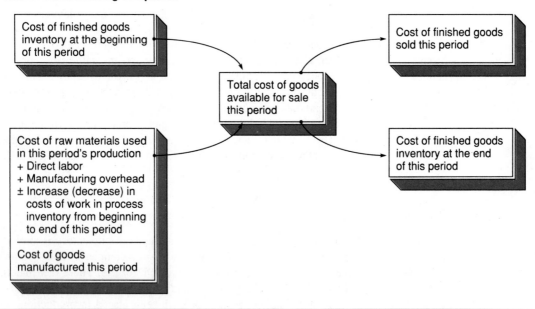

Work in Process

During the work in process phase of production, the cost of **direct labor** (i.e., the labor expended to convert raw materials to finished goods) and all *manufacturing overhead* costs must be assigned to the products being produced. Thus, beginning work in process inventory *plus* the cost of raw materials used during the period *plus* direct labor costs incurred during the period *plus* manufacturing overhead for the period *less* ending work in process inventory *equals* the cost of goods manufactured during the period. These relationships are shown in the following equations:

$$\text{Beginning WIP inventory} + \text{Cost of RM used} + \text{Direct labor cost} + \text{Manufacturing overhead costs} = \text{Total manufacturing costs.} \qquad (5)$$

$$\text{Total manufacturing costs} - \text{Ending WIP inventory} = \text{Cost of goods manufactured.} \qquad (6)$$

A word about the need and method to assign manufacturing overhead costs to work in process inventories is warranted. **Manufacturing overhead** is a phrase commonly used to describe all factory-related costs, other than raw materials and direct labor, involved in the production of a completed product: electricity, maintenance, supervision, depreciation of machines, and so on. Factory costs are considered to be **product costs,** and thus need to be assigned to the cost of inventory rather than expensed on the income statement as incurred. The nonfactory-related costs of a manufacturer, such as selling expenses, are called **period costs** and are treated as expenses in the income statement in the period when they are incurred.

As an example, visualize a mattress manufacturing company that uses four raw materials in its production process: fabric, padding, lumber, and springs. To make one mattress, the production supervisor requisitions from the warehouse the appropriate quantity of each raw material (see Panel A, Exhibit 8.2). Once in the factory, the fabric and padding are used by workers to make the outer surface of the mattress. Other workers use the lumber to make the mattress frame. Additional labor is required to mount the springs on the frame and then to cover it with the padded outer surface. The cost of labor incurred in performing these tasks is as much a part of the final cost of a completed mattress as the actual materials in it and thus must be added to the inventory account. Manufacturing overhead costs related to these production operations are also incurred. These costs are for items such as equipment maintenance, cleaning supplies, and power, as well as the cost of insurance, taxes, and depreciation pertaining to the factory. A share of these overhead costs must be added to the primary product costs (i.e., raw materials and direct labor) to have a complete cost for a particular manufactured mattress (see Panel B, Exhibit 8.2) because they are a necessary part of the production process and, consequently, represent part of the total cost of the final product.

Notice in Exhibit 8.2 that the accounting process for manufactured inventories parallels the actual production process. When raw materials sit in a warehouse, their cost sits in the Raw Materials Inventory account. As raw materials and labor start being introduced into the manufacturing process, a Work in Process Inventory account accumulates such costs for the goods in various stages of partial production. Finally, when production is

---

E X H I B I T   8 . 2

An Illustration of a Manufacturing Process
and Associated Manufacturing Costs

Panel A: Manufactuuring Process for One Queen-Sized Mattress

Beginnning Warehouse Supply of Raw Materials	Supervisor's Requisition	Production/ Assembly Process	Finished Goods Produced
1,000 yds. fabric	10 yds. ⟶	Covering	
1,000 yds. padding	10 yds. ⟶		One mattress
1,000 board ft. lumber	60 bd. ft. ⟶	Frame	
1,000 springs	40 ⟶	Springs	

Panel B: Inventory Accounts for Queen-Sized Mattress
Paralleling Panel A's Production

Beginnning Inventory Account of Raw Materials	Additions to Work in Process Inventory Account		Additions to Finished Goods Inventory Account
$3,000 fabric ⟶	10 yds @ $3/yd. ⟶	$ 30	
$2,000 padding ⟶	10 yds. @ $2/yd. ⟶	$ 20	
$ 500 lumber ⟶	60 bd ft. @ $.50/bd ft. ⟶	$ 30	
$ 800 springs ⟶	40 springs @ $.80/spring ⟶	$ 32	
	Direct labor:		
	Covering (1 hr. @ $25/hr.)	$ 25	
	Frame (1 hr. @ $20/hr.)	$ 20	
	Assembly (1 hr.@ $10/hr.)	$ 10	$195
	Manufacturing overhead*		
	Indirect labor	$ 5	
	Supplies	$ 4	
	Utilities	$ 1	
	Depreciation	$ 15	
	Other	$ 3	
		$195	

*The manufacturing overhead amounts are allocations from accumulated indirect cost pools based on some predetermined, estimated relationship (e.g., for every direct labor hour, $5 of depreciation is assigned to the cost of a single mattress). The raw materials and direct labor costs are determined by the actual quantity of materials and labor used in making the one mattress.

---

completed on an item, it is physically transferred to a finished goods warehouse or storeroom and the costs accumulated for that finished item are likewise transferred from the Work in Process Inventory account to the Finished Goods Inventory account.

It is worth noting that a problem arises when a company no longer manufactures only a single product. When it manufactures multiple products, it becomes necessary to determine just how much of the manufacturing overhead costs (e.g., factory depreciation, equipment maintenance, and supervisors' wages) should be included in the cost of Model A versus Model B. We can readily agree that each of two manufactured models contains a certain quantity of raw material and labor (e.g., 40 springs for the deluxe queen mattress versus 15 for a crib-size mattress) and that it took 5 hours of labor to assemble one queen-size mattress but only 2 hours of labor to assemble the crib-size mattress. However, no comparable objective assessments are possible for costs such as the factory building's depreciation, equipment maintenance, or supervisors' wages. Similarly, other manufacturing overhead costs such as inspection, warehousing, power, and so on, are not easily quantifiable ingredients of each separate finished model.

The fact that there is no objectively measurable means to determine the manufacturing overhead costs assignable to each of two models produced does not, however, preclude the need to allocate those costs to the final cost of models A and B for balance sheet reporting purposes. Ideally, the costs not *directly* attributable to inventory units but necessary for their production should be assigned to the finished products by astute managers on a basis reflecting the demands by the various products on those manufacturing resources. For example, manufacturing overhead costs are often allocated to products on the basis of direct labor hours required to produce the product, the machine hours required to produce it, production floor space devoted to the product, the number of production order changes required, or some other measurable allocation basis.

As a simple example of the allocation of factory overhead costs, assume that such costs are expected to total $1 million for the year. Assume further that the number of direct labor hours devoted to each of the two final products has been chosen as the allocation base and that the estimated total number of direct labor hours to produce the volume of products needed to fulfill projected sales is 40,000. These estimates result in an allocation scheme whereby, for every one hour of direct labor incurred in making a particular product, $25 of these manufacturing overhead costs are to be assigned to each finished product ($1 million ÷ 40,000 hours = $25/hour).

The issue of allocating manufacturing overhead costs to various product lines has received increasing attention from corporate managers as the direct material and direct labor cost components of manufactured products have been reduced through various overt cost-cutting measures. At the same time, the use of robotics and other technological innovations in production processes have helped to increase the relative share of overhead costs associated with manufactured products. In spite of the many systematic overhead allocation schemes devised over the years, in the final scheme, they are *all* arbitrary to some degree. Consequently, no single best, theoretically defensible method to allocate manufacturing overhead costs exists. Therefore, even though manufacturing overhead cost allocations are necessary to value a company's ending inventories in the balance sheet, managers must use caution when making strategic operating decisions based, at least in part, on allocated cost information. Given such a situation, it is not surprising that managers are continually searching for more accurate and informative allocation schemes to achieve a better matching of expenses to revenues and thus better measures of performance over time.

Finished Goods

At the end of the manufacturing phase, all costs associated with a completed product are transferred to the Finished Goods Inventory. Accounting for finished goods in a manufacturing firm is again very much like that for a merchandising company. The cost of beginning finished goods (FG) inventory *plus* the cost of goods manufactured (those costs transferred from work in process) *equals* the period's cost of goods available for sale. As of the end of a period, these costs must be attributed to either ending finished goods inventory (unsold goods) or to cost of goods sold. Hence, as depicted in Panel B of Exhibit 8.1, the following relationships exist:

$$\text{Beginning FG inventory + Cost of goods manufactured = Cost of goods available for sale.} \qquad (7)$$

$$\text{Cost of goods available for sale} - \text{Cost of goods sold = Ending FG inventory.} \quad (8)$$

ACCOUNTING FOR INVENTORY COSTS

So far we have not mentioned the *physical* movement of inventory through a business. Clearly, purchased goods come into a company's facilities, and sold goods leave the premises. The following are pertinent questions that arise when a product is sold: Was that a sale of an item purchased or manufactured yesterday or last month? Does the answer to this question matter?

For a moment, visualize a business that makes and sells a large volume of a single model of chair. All during the year, the company incurs various costs to produce the chairs and to sell the finished product. Assume that you and another customer both arrive at the company's showroom simultaneously. You happen to walk in the west entrance, and the other customer walks in the east entrance. The showroom is full of identical chairs, and both of you select the first chair that you see. Unknown to either of you, the chair you selected was manufactured six months ago, and the one that the other customer chose was manufactured yesterday. Are the actual costs of manufacturing incurred by the company for your chair different than those of the other customer's chair? They *probably* are because of material cost increases or a few more minutes of labor devoted to one or the other of them. Does that fact result in the other customer paying a different price for the chair than you pay? *Probably not.* If the different costs do not result in different sales prices, there is no real need for the company even to bother keeping track of the fact that the other customer bought a chair from yesterday's production and you bought one from a prior month's production. But the company does have to record a reduction in the costs accumulated in the Finished Goods Inventory account and assign them to the Cost of Goods Sold account as a result of its sales to both of you.

Several acceptable methods are used to determine what inventory costs to identify with a particular sale. These cost-flow methods are discussed shortly, and examples of each are presented later. It first must be noted, however, that the *accounting* cost-flow method chosen by management to assign inventory costs to the cost of goods sold need *not* match the actual *physical* flow of inventory items into and out of a company's warehouse or showroom. As satisfying as it may be to know that inventory item no. 59, produced on June 11, 1991, was the item actually sold on August 20, 1991, and its particular cost is the cost deducted from inventory and added to the cost of goods sold, there are other considerations, providing more valued benefits, that diminish the importance of such a strict matching of actual inventory with actual items sold. These other considerations are discussed in the following sections.

Specific Identification Method

This cost-flow method is usually reserved for high-value, easily distinguishable items such as cars and jewelry and does require individual accounting for each inventory item. Under this approach, the costs associated with an inventory item are "attached" to it and remain in the inventory account as long as the specific item is on hand. The **specific identification method** is the only cost-flow approach that results in the costs flowing from the balance sheet (i.e., ending inventory) to the income statement (i.e., cost of goods sold) in a sequence exactly matching the product's physical flow from storeroom to customer.

Exhibit 8.3 is the inventory method footnote from the financial statements of Ryan Homes, Inc., a regional builder of residential dwellings in the mid-Atlantic and southeastern United States. It describes the company's use of the specific identification method and how a company's inventory cost-flow method might be presented in the financial statements. The decision by Ryan Homes to adopt this method appears quite reasonable—the company builds distinctive and expensive homes, which are generally sold one at a time.

The main disadvantage to the specific identification method is that its use is impractical for some types of businesses (e.g., mass merchandisers and mass manufacturers of homogeneous products) because of the very detailed inventory system required to track each item or each lot of goods purchased or manufactured. On the other hand, the matching of cost of goods sold to the sales revenue of the period perfectly matches the physical flow of specific inventory items, consequently achieving a perfect income statement matching of revenue generated from the item sold and its actual cost.

Average Cost Method

The **average cost method** accounts for inventory costs in a manner that is especially useful when it is impossible (or at least impractical) to attempt to identify specifically the particular units of inventory sold, typically because large volumes of many types of similar products are sold. This is the case for such companies as food wholesalers, supermarkets, and retailers in general, and the Quaker Oats Company in particular.

E X H I B I T   8 . 3

Ryan Homes, Inc.
Inventory Method Disclosure: Specific Identification

Inventories

Inventories are stated at the lower of cost or market value.

Cost of lots, completed and uncompleted housing units, and land in process of development represent the accumulated actual cost thereof. Field construction supervision salaries and related direct overhead expenses are included in inventory costs. Selling, general and administrative costs are expensed as incurred. Upon settlement, the cost of the units is expensed on a specific identification basis.

Exhibit 8.8, presented later in this chapter, notes that Quaker Oats Company uses the average cost method for about 27 percent of its ending inventory. With the advent of cost-effective electronic product label scanners, retailers' ability to track the physical flow of products, and thus their costs, has greatly improved. Whether managers of companies using such tracking devices will consequently abandon the simple average cost method has yet to be determined.

The average cost method is based on the *assumption* that the costs of the items sold and therefore charged against revenue should be the average unit cost of all the items available for sale during the period. The average cost of a particular inventory item (e.g., Quaker Oats' instant oatmeal cartons) is determined simply by dividing the sum of the different unit costs incurred for the instant oatmeal cartons available for sale during the year by the number of different unit costs represented in that quantity of carton. The resulting unit cost is used to compute both the balance sheet ending inventory cost and the income statement cost of goods sold. The advantages of this approach are that it is very easy to compute and it is very objective in its determination of profits for the period. The disadvantage is that the cost attributed to a single item is not, in reality, a cost that has ever been paid for the item (i.e., it is an average).

A variation of the average cost method is the **weighted-average cost method.** Under this method, the calculation of the cost of ending inventory (and cost of goods sold) is accomplished as under the average cost method except that each cost is weighted by the number of inventory units available at that cost. The weighted-average cost method is generally believed to be preferable to the average cost method because it takes into consideration the relative quantity of goods purchased at a given unit cost. Thus, if 100 units of inventory were purchased at $10 each and 1,000 at $14 each, the average cost method produces an average unit cost of only $12 (i.e., ($10 + $14) ÷ 2), which does not reflect the substantial difference in quantities purchased at the two costs. The weighted-average cost per unit, however, would be $13.64 (i.e., [(100 × $10) + (1,000 × $14)] ÷ 1,100 units), emphasizing the large volume of purchases at the higher cost of $14. The advantages and disadvantages of this method are the same as those for the average cost method.

First-in, First-out (FIFO)

The **first-in, first-out** cost-flow method accounts for inventory under the *assumption* that the first product physically purchased or manufactured is the first product physically sold. Remember that the actual physical flow of inventory does not need to be on a FIFO basis in order for a company to elect to account for it on a FIFO basis. Thus, under the FIFO method, the costs assigned to the Cost of Goods Sold account for the products sold during the period are not the most recent costs paid, but they do represent an actual cost incurred for the item albeit at some point in the past. In times of rapid inflation, the cost of goods sold under FIFO is likely to be low relative to a product's current replacement cost and current selling price and will result in higher net income and thus higher income taxes payable vis-à-vis other inventory cost-flow methods. On the other hand, ending inventory account balances will approximate the product's current replacement cost, especially if inventory turnover is frequent (i.e., if the inventory items are on hand for only a short

EXHIBIT 8.4

Tyson Foods, Inc.
Inventory Method Disclosure: FIFO

Inventories, valued at the lower of cost (first-in, first-out)
or market, consist of the following:

	(In Thousands)	
	1990	1989
Dressed and further- processed products	**$225,819**	$ 73,049
Live poultry and hogs	**154,894**	153,676
Hatchery eggs and feed	**36,874**	36,719
Supplies	**54,677**	45,219
	$472,264	$408,663

period of time). Exhibit 8.4 presents the inventory footnote disclosure of Tyson Foods, Inc., that indicates the company's use of the FIFO method, a choice that is intuitively appealing given the perishable nature of the product that this company sells.

Last-in, First-out (LIFO)

The **last-in, first-out** cost-flow method accounts for inventory under the *assumption* that the last product physically purchased or manufactured is the first one physically sold. Following the reasoning of the FIFO method, this approach means that under LIFO, the cost of the products sold closely approximates the current replacement cost of the product (i.e., the most recent costs incurred in acquiring the item).

For company management, LIFO has advantages and disadvantages just the opposite of those of FIFO. Whereas FIFO presents ending inventory in the balance sheet at an approximation of current **replacement cost** (i.e., the most recent cost incurred in acquiring the item), the LIFO method states the inventory balance at a mixture of costs incurred in the distant past. In times of high inflation (deflation), the reported ending balance of the inventory account under LIFO can be significantly lower (higher) than under FIFO. On the other hand, FIFO does not report cost of goods sold at the most recent costs; the LIFO method approximates current replacement cost as the cost reported in the income statement for each product sold (except, as will be discussed later, when the quantity of inventory sold during the period exceeds the quantity acquired during the period). Exhibit 8.5 presents the inventory footnote disclosure from the annual report of the General Motors Corporation, which describes that company's predominant use of the LIFO method.

The General Motors disclosures in Panel A of Exhibit 8.5 reveal a rich and useful set of inventory-related insights. For example, not all of the company's inventories are accounted for using the LIFO method. Indeed, the inventories of GM Hughes Electronics and overseas subsidiaries are not accounted for on a LIFO basis but on either FIFO or

EXHIBIT 8.5

General Motors Corporation
Inventory Method Disclosure: LIFO

Panel A

Inventories

Inventories are stated generally at cost, which is not in excess of market. The cost of substantially all domestic inventories other than the inventories of GM Hughes Electronics Corporation (GMHE) is determined by the last-in, first-out (LIFO) method. If the first-in, first-out (FIFO) method of inventory valuation had been used for inventories valued at LIFO cost, such inventories would have been $2,598.8 million higher at December 31, 1990 and $2,445.4 million higher at December 31, 1989. The cost of inventories outside the United States and of GMHE is determined generally by FIFO or average cost methods.

	(Millions)	
Major classes of inventory	**1990**	**1989**
Productive material, work in process, and supplies	$4,098.0	$3,816.9
Finished product, service parts, etc.	5,233.3	4,174.8
Total	$9,331.3	$7,991.7

Panel B

As a result of decreases in U.S. inventories, certain inventory quantities carried at lower LIFO costs prevailing in prior years, as compared with the costs of current purchases, were liquidated in 1989 and 1988. These inventory adjustments favorably affected income before income taxes by approximately $244.8 million in 1989 and $20.5 million in 1988.

average cost. Moreover, the FIFO cost basis of the inventories that are accounted for on a LIFO basis is presented; the cost that would have been reported for ending inventory if the FIFO method had been used would have been $2,598.8 million higher than the 1990 reported LIFO cost. Since this difference pertains to a balance sheet account (inventory) and since we learned earlier that A = L + OE, this difference also represents the *cumulative* decrease in pretax earnings (a part of OE) through 1990 that General Motors has experienced as a consequence of being on the LIFO method instead of the FIFO method. In other words, if inventories would have been higher by this amount, cost of goods sold would have been lower, resulting in $2,598.8 million higher pretax profits under the FIFO method. The decrease in pretax earnings for just 1990 is the difference between the 1990 cumulative inventory valuation differential and the 1989 cumulative inventory valuation differential, $2,598.8 million less $2,445.4 million, or $153.4 million. Given a 34 percent income tax rate for the company in 1990, taxes were $52.2 million less in 1990 than they would have been using a FIFO valuation for those inventory items accounted for under the LIFO method. Thus, in 1990 alone, more than $52 million in cash was saved on income taxes by using the LIFO method. Indeed, such tax consequences are a major motivation for companies to adopt the LIFO method.

The PepsiCo annual report (see Chapter 1) presents the same type of information in its inventory footnote as shown for GM in Panel A of Exhibit 8.5, albeit arrayed somewhat differently. A majority (54 percent in 1990) of PepsiCo's inventory is accounted for using LIFO. PepsiCo's footnotes indicate that total inventory cost is $585.8 million for 1990 and that it would have been $600.7 million if LIFO had not been used for any of the items. This figure of $600.7 million approximates current costs (i.e., the amount that would be the result of using a FIFO or average cost method). The $14.9 million excess of current cost over LIFO cost parallels the $2,598.8 million noted in the GM disclosures.

A Numerical Illustration

To assist you in understanding the calculations necessary to derive the cost of ending inventory to be presented in the balance sheet and the cost of goods sold for the income statement, we now consider a numerical illustration.

Assume that FHAS Company begins the year with 100 units of an item in inventory and makes the following additions to inventory:

	Quantity	Cost	Total Cost
Beginning inventory:	100 units	@ $1.00	$100.00
Purchase no. 1	110 units	@ $1.10	121.00
Purchase no. 2	120 units	@ $1.25	150.00
Purchase no. 3	115 units	@ $1.50	172.50
Goods available for sale	445		$543.50

Assume further that the company sells 300 units for $2 cash per unit and has 145 units left in inventory at year-end. Reported ending inventory and cost of goods sold under the FIFO, LIFO, and weighted-average cost methods would be as follows:

FIFO

Sales (300 units at $2 per unit)			$600.00
Cost of goods available for sale		$543.50	
Less: Cost of goods sold			
100 units at $1.00	$100.00		
110 units at $1.10	121.00		
90 units at $1.25	112.50		
Cost of goods sold		(333.50)	(333.50)
Ending inventory (145 units)			
(115 units at $1.50 + 30 units at $1.25)		$210.00	
Gross Profit			$266.50

Weighted-Average Cost

Sales (300 units at $2 per unit)		$600.00
Cost of goods available for sale	$543.50	
Less: Cost of goods sold		
300 units at $1.2213*	(366.39)	(366.39)
Ending inventory		
(145 units at $1.2213)	$117.11	
Gross profit		$233.61

*$543.50/445 units = $1.2213.

LIFO

Sales (300 units at $2 per unit)			$600.00
Cost of goods available for sale		$543.50	
Less: Cost of goods sold			
115 units at $1.50	$172.50		
120 units at $1.25	150.00		
65 units at $1.10	71.50		
Cost of goods sold		(394.00)	(394.00)
Ending inventory (145 units)			
(100 units at $1.00 + 45 units at $1.10)		$149.50	
Gross profit			$206.00

As these examples indicate, in times of rising costs, the cost of goods sold is highest using LIFO and lowest using FIFO, with the weighted-average cost method falling between them. The valuation of the units remaining in inventory is highest using FIFO and lowest using LIFO, again with weighted-average cost falling between the two. These characteristics are important when managers are contemplating what picture of their company to portray in the year-end financial statements.

An important part of inventory accounting under the LIFO method is the notion of **inventory layers** and **inventory-layer liquidation.** During a given period, if the inventory purchased or manufactured exceeds the quantities sold, the result is the addition of a ''layer'' (increment) to the ending inventory balance. Such was the case in the simple numerical example just presented—45 units were added during the period to the beginning inventory level of 100 units. This type of phenomenon is depicted in the 19×2 column in Exhibit 8.6. This 19×2 layer is distinct from the 19×1 layer preceding it in that it reflects an addition of units to ending inventory that will be reported at 19×2 costs. The 19×1 layer, on the other hand, will be costed at 19×1 costs. Together, the sum of the two layers' costs will be reported as the cost of inventory in the 19×2 balance sheet.

In Exhibit 8.6, the 19×2 ending inventory consists of 450 units, composed of a layer of 200 units from 19×1 and a layer of 250 units from 19×2. Both of these LIFO layers will be maintained in inventory through subsequent periods until a net *decrease* in inventory takes place because of sales exceeding inventory additions. When this occurs, the prior period's inventory layers are sequentially liquidated. For example, 19×3 witnessed a reduction of the 19×2 layer in the amount of 100 units. The liquidation of a LIFO layer results in the inventory costs of a prior period being used to determine the current period's cost of goods sold deducted from the current period's revenue. Assuming

EXHIBIT 8.6

LIFO Layering
(all amounts are units of inventory)

	19×1	19×2	19×3	19×4
Beginning inventory	0	200	450	350
Purchases	1,000	1,550	900	1,100
Sales	(800)	(1,300)	(1,000)	(1,050)
Ending inventory	200	450	350	400

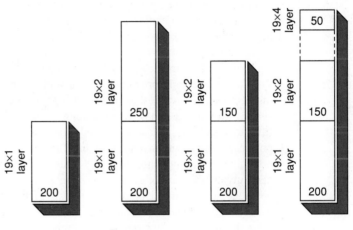

Base year
(year of LIFO adoption)

annual cost increases, the matching of these old (perhaps as much as three or four years) costs with current revenues will result in higher profits than if only current period costs had been used in figuring the current period's cost of goods sold. Note that in Panel B of Exhibit 8.5, General Motors' LIFO-valued inventories for certain products were reduced in 1989, and net income before taxes was increased by $244.8 million. Such a boost to 1989 earnings was certainly anticipated and orchestrated by GM management as opposed to its being merely "a pleasant surprise." Indeed, many companies are reducing inventory quantities on hand through outsourcing of production and/or just-in-time production techniques. Lowering inventory levels is often motivated by a desire to reduce the annual carrying costs associated with storing, handling, and insuring large quantities of goods, as well as a desire to garner the capital tied up in goods on hand and to minimize potentially large losses associated with obsolescence.

A prior year's layer, once liquidated, will never be reestablished in subsequent periods. This is true in Exhibit 8.6 for 19x4—a gap exists in the 19x2 layer for that part of the layer liquidated in 19x3, which will never be reestablished.

Inventory Systems: Periodic versus Perpetual

Determining how much of the goods available for sale during a period are still on hand and how much should be charged against income for the period is obviously critical to measuring a company's performance during a period. In addition to the cost-flow method decision, management must also adopt either a perpetual inventory system or a periodic inventory system to record ending inventory costs and cost of goods sold. Under a **periodic system,** the quantity of inventory on hand at any given time must be determined by physically counting the inventory items (usually once a year). The physical count, costed at an appropriate cost (i.e., LIFO, FIFO, or average), determines the balance sheet's ending inventory cost. The cost of goods sold for the period can then be determined from the basic relationship of beginning inventory *plus* purchases *minus* the costs attributable to ending inventory quantities. (A periodic system was assumed in the numerical examples above.)

When using a **perpetual system,** management maintains and regularly updates (often daily or, with computer assistance, continuously) an extensive inventory record-keeping system that is able to provide current inventory and cost of goods sold information on a moment's notice (rather than only after a physical count of items on hand). The perpetual system provides a continuous updating of both the Cost of Goods Sold and Ending Inventory account balances. Sound business practice suggests doing an occasional physical count of the inventory on hand to verify the accuracy of a perpetual system.

A final issue involving inventory systems, but which will not be discussed at length here, involves the use of *standard product costs* rather than actual costs. Standard product costs are the estimated or projected costs of producing a product. Standard costs are widely used by managers for internal reporting and control purposes, and some companies carry this use over to external financial reporting. Inventory may be costed using standard cost estimates as long as the standard cost of the inventory is not materially different from actual costs. Regardless of whether or not management decides to use standard costs, decisions are still necessary regarding whether to use a periodic system or a perpetual system and what cost-flow method to adopt.

LOWER OF COST OR MARKET

As has been discussed to this point, the basis of accounting for inventories is historical cost (whether actual or standard), defined as the consideration given up to acquire an asset, including the costs incurred to bring a good to a salable condition. These costs include, but are not limited to, transportation (inbound and/or outbound, depending on the circumstances), handling fees, labor costs, and overhead costs. Costs resulting from the marketing and selling activities of a company, even those directly related to a particular product, are normally not included as part of inventory costs.

A departure from the historical cost basis in reporting inventories is necessary when the "market value" of the ending inventory falls below its "cost" (as determined under one of the cost-flow methods). This can occur any time during the normal course of operations because of spoilage, obsolescence, or falling market prices for the goods. For example, consider a computer leasing company. Large quantities of computers have recently been technologically superseded by a newer generation of computers and are not likely to be able to maintain their previous marketability—thus, these computers decline in market value. This decline in market value should be recognized as an expense of the period in which the reduction in value takes place and the Inventory account balance should be adjusted to the lower value. Most companies maintain inventory control systems to help them monitor changing market values and inventory obsolescence.

Certain guidelines pertain to the determination of an inventory's current market value. Because there is no New York Stock Exchange equivalent for all the various items composing different businesses' investments in inventories, specifying a market value can be quite subjective, and thus the need for guidelines exists. To avoid gross manipulations of the lower-of-cost-or-market concept, the accounting profession has defined *market value* as the *replacement cost* of an item. Replacement cost is the cost that a company would incur today to reproduce or reacquire a similar item. Information pertaining to replacement cost is usually compiled from vendor catalogs, engineering estimates, and/or appraisals. Replacement cost is assumed to be the market value, subject to lower and upper boundaries, that should be compared to the recorded historical cost in determining whether a lower-of-cost-or-market adjustment is needed.

The upper boundary (or *ceiling*) has been defined by accounting standard setters as the net realizable value (NRV) of the inventory, that is, the company's selling price of the item less the costs of completing its production and of selling it. The lower boundary (or *floor*) for setting the market value is net realizable value less a normal profit margin. Both boundaries are generalized attempts to keep market value within a reasonable range given the nature of a particular company's inventory and its selling market. As long as replacement cost lies between these two values, it is considered to be a fair approximation of market value. If replacement cost is below the lower boundary, the lower boundary amount is used as the best approximation of market value. Similar considerations apply to the upper boundary. Once a market value is ascertained, inventories should be reported at the lower of their historical cost or market value.

If, for example, a write-down of $1,000 of the inventory's cost is required because its market value has fallen below cost, the following journal entry is made:

Dr. Cost of Goods Sold (E) 1,000
        Cr. Allowance for Decline in the Value of Inventory (CA)   1,000

Note that the decline in the inventory value is added to the cost of goods sold on the income statement, and an allowance account (a contra asset account) is reported on the balance sheet as a deduction from the inventory account. In fact, the allowance account is rarely seen on the balance sheet; most often it is netted out against the balance in the inventory account. Some companies avoid the use of an allowance by crediting the amount of the inventory reduction directly against the inventory account. In either case, once inventory values have been written down, they cannot be written back up even if the value of the inventory recovers its previously lost value. Exhibit 8.7 summarizes these lower-of-cost-or-market considerations.

E X H I B I T   8 . 7

Lower of Cost or Market for Inventory

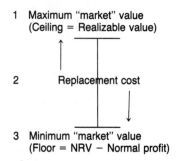

1   Maximum "market" value
    (Ceiling = Realizable value)

2   Replacement cost

3   Minimum "market" value
    (Floor = NRV − Normal profit)

Cost lower than market (chosen from 1, 2, or 3)?

If yes	If no
No inventory adjustment	Adjust inventory to "market"

FINANCIAL STATEMENT DISCLOSURE

In general, the requirements for financial statement disclosure for inventories include the following:

1. A description of the accounting principles a company used in determining reported inventory costs.
2. Reference to any accounting principles or methods of accounting peculiar to the industry in which a company operates.
3. Major categories of inventories.

Exhibit 8.8 presents the inventory disclosure from the annual report of the Quaker Oats Company. Notice that the disclosure reveals the costs attributable to three categories of inventory: finished goods, grains and materials, and supplies. Quaker Oats would not be expected to have a large work in process inventory category given the relatively short production time for its products. What amounts the company does have are probably included in the grains and materials category. Also note that the disclosures make explicit mention of the lower-of-cost-or-market valuation issue and that the LIFO method is utilized for the largest percentage of inventory items. With regard to LIFO, the disclosures reveal what the value of the LIFO-accounted inventories would have been if LIFO had not been used.

To maintain interperiod comparability, financial statement readers may assume the consistent application of cost-flow methods from period to period. If, however, a change

EXHIBIT 8.8

Quaker Oats Company
Inventory Disclosure
(in millions)

	June 30		
	1991	**1990**	**1989**
Inventories:			
Finished goods	$309.1	$324.1	$326.0
Grain and Materials	86.7	110.7	114.1
Supplies	26.5	39.1	39.0
Total inventories	$422.3	$473.9	$479.1

Inventories. Inventories are valued at the lower of cost or market, using various cost methods, and include the cost of raw materials, labor and overhead. The percentage of year-end inventories valued using each of the methods is as follows:

	June 30		
	1991	**1990**	**1989**
Last-in, first-out (LIFO)	**61%**	62%	63%
Average quarterly cost	**27%**	27%	22%
First-in, first-out (FIFO)	**12%**	11%	15%

If the LIFO method of valuing certain inventories were not used, total inventories would have been $18.9 million, $27.9 million, and $31 million higher than reported at June 30, 1991, 1990, and 1989, respectively.

in inventory accounting method is adopted (e.g., from FIFO to LIFO), company management is required to disclose the nature of the change and its effect on net income, including, whenever possible, a restatement of prior years' financial statements as if the new method had been in effect during those prior years. The disclosures by Kaiser Aluminum and Richfood Holding, Inc. (a grocery chain holding company) regarding their changes in inventory accounting methods are presented in Exhibit 8.9.

Note that in April 1990, Richfood Holding changed from FIFO to LIFO for virtually all of its inventory. For the year subsequent to that change, net income was $640 million less than it would have been had the company remained with FIFO. Such an impact highlights the rising cost nature of this business and points to the fact that ending inventory at April 1991, under the newly adopted LIFO method, is lower than if it had continued to be reported at more recent costs as the FIFO method would have done. Indeed, the note points to a $1,024 million difference in ending inventory figures. The note also highlights the fact that prior years' financial statements cannot be restated as if they too had been prepared using the LIFO method. Such a restatement is simply not possible because ending inventory would have to be converted to the "oldest" costs, and it would be purely arbitrary to assume any base prior year start point other than this year—the year of making the change.

EXHIBIT 8.9

Financial Statement Disclosures:
Inventory Method Changes

Panel A: Richfood Holding, Inc., Change to LIFO

1. Inventories

The Company values its inventory at the lower of cost or market. Effective April 29, 1990, the Company changed its method of determining cost from the first-in, first-out (FIFO) method to the last-in, first-out (LIFO) method for approximately 91% of its inventories. Remaining inventories are stated at the lower of cost or market using the FIFO method (see note 3).

3. Inventories
As a result of the change to the LIFO inventory valuation method for the fiscal year ended April 27, 1991 (see note 1), net earnings decreased by $640, or $.06 per share. There is no cumulative effect for this change on prior years since the ending inventory as previously reported at April 28, 1990, is the beginning inventory for LIFO purposes. Accordingly, pro forma results of operations for the prior years had LIFO been followed are not determinable. The current replacement cost of LIFO inventories exceeded reported cost by $1,024 at April 27, 1991. The Company believes that the use of the LIFO method better matches current costs of goods sold with current revenues from inventory sales.

Panel B: Kaiser Aluminum & Chemical Corp., Change to FIFO

Millions of dollars, except share amounts

4. Inventories
In 1985 the corporation changed its method of valuing its domestic aluminum raw materials, including primary aluminum, and certain industrial and specialty chemicals to the first-in, first-out (FIFO) method from the last-in, first-out (LIFO) method. The corporation is in the process of completing a refinancing of its bank debt and the financial position of the corporation is of increasing interest to investors and others who extend credit to the corporation. The FIFO method of inventory valuation is a better measure to reflect the current value of such inventories and the financial position of the corporation. In addition, under the current economic environment of low inflation and the corporation's decreasing inventories and production costs, the FIFO method results in a better matching of costs and revenues as compared to the LIFO method.

The FIFO method of accounting has been applied retroactively, and prior-year financial statements have been restated. This change increased inventory value by $190.7 and retained earnings by $104.1 at December 31, 1985, and increased the net loss by $9.1 ($.21 per share) because the effect of a FIFO cost write-down in 1985 exceeded the effect of liquidating a LIFO layer with higher unit costs than the current FIFO costs. The change increased the 1984 net loss by $43.5 ($.99 per share) because a FIFO cost write-down was required by a market price decline in 1984. The 1983 net loss was reduced by $24.7 ($.57 per share) because the FIFO inventory value increase of $82.6 exceeded the $57.9 benefit from the 1983 LIFO liquidation.

Operating supplies inventories were $72.4 and $76.5 at December 31, 1985 and 1984. Finished goods, work in process, and raw materials have been combined because they are sold at various stages of processing.

On the other hand, Kaiser discloses its change in 1985 from LIFO to FIFO and notes that a retroactive restatement is possible. Such a restatement actually results in the previously reported 1984 loss being increased by $43.5 million and the 1983 loss being reduced by $24.7 million. If additional prior years were reported in Kaiser's 1985 annual report, they too would be restated because for any previous year-end date, it is possible to determine what ending inventory costs would have been under FIFO. They would simply be those closest to that point in time. Notice that Kaiser and Richfood both claim that the change in method is prompted by a belief that a better matching of expenses and revenues is achieved by the current method.

ANALYZING INVENTORIES

Analyzing a company's investment in inventories typically focuses on two questions: Is the investment in inventory likely to produce an adequate return to the company? Is the level of investment in inventory appropriate for anticipated future sales?

With respect to the first question, a widely used financial indicator is the **gross profit margin ratio:**

$$\text{Gross profit margin ratio} = \frac{\text{Gross profit margin}}{\text{Net sales}}.$$

This ratio indicates the percentage of each sales dollar that is available to cover a company's period expenses and to provide a return to its owners *after* the cost of goods sold has been deducted. Clearly, the higher this ratio, the more profitable a company's sales of inventory will be. For 1990, PepsiCo's gross profit margin ratio is 0.52 [($17,802.7 − $8,609.9) ÷ $17,802.7], which is moderately high when compared to 0.45 for Philip Morris or 0.23 for General Motors in 1990. A low ratio may indicate several concerns: (1) the company is underpricing its products or (2) when a product is competitively priced, the cost to manufacture it is too high, perhaps due to inefficiencies in the manufacturing process or in the purchase of raw materials or to the payment of excessively high wages to production employees. The gross profit margin ratio is important to managers because it allows them to determine whether the root of low earnings is attributable to the company's period costs or to its product costs. Likewise, this ratio is important to investors and creditors by enabling them to identify well-managed companies.

With respect to the second question above, two financial ratios are often reviewed: (1) the inventory turnover ratio and (2) the average days inventory on hand. As discussed in Chapter 4, the **inventory turnover ratio** measures the number of times that the average level (or dollar investment) in inventory was sold, or "turned," during a given accounting period:

$$\text{Inventory turnover ratio} = \frac{\text{Cost of goods sold for the period}}{\text{Average inventory held during the period}}.$$

In general, the higher the inventory turnover ratio, the better. A high turnover ratio such as PepsiCo's 15.2 ($8,609.9 ÷ 565.9) signals a reduced potential for losses attributable to product obsolescence, which in the case of PepsiCo indicates that it is probably incurring minimal costs to maintain an investment in inventory, and, simply given the nature of PepsiCo business, a high ratio is to be expected. GM's inventory turnover ratio is 11. Does this make sense given GM's business? Excessively high turnover ratios, however, may be problematic if the cause is an insufficient investment in inventory. For example, when a company fails to maintain an adequate supply of inventory to meet its customers' needs, it may create order backlogs and customer dissatisfaction, not to mention the possibility of lost sales. On the other hand, a low ratio not warranted by the nature of the company's business, may indicate excessive inventory that may not be salable.

The **average number of days' inventory on hand** ratio indicates the average number of days of inventory supplies on hand to meet customer needs, based on recent sales data:

$$\text{Average number of days' inventory on hand} = \frac{365 \text{ days}}{\text{Inventory turnover ratio}}.$$

The 1990 average number of days' inventory on hand for PepsiCo was 24 days (365 ÷ 15.2), and 33 days for GM. This ratio is important because it reveals whether there is an adequate quantity of inventory on hand or whether there is an excessive quantity; the latter indicates the need to slow or halt production. For both GM and PepsiCo, these figures appear about right—neither too high to cause worries of slow moving products nor too low to cause worries of not being able to meet customer orders. Unfortunately, there is no ideal target for the average number of days' inventory on hand or for the inventory turnover ratio. In fact, these indicators vary substantially among industries and often within the same industry. As a general rule, potential investors, lenders, and managers are well advised to compare these indicators for a given company against the leading firm in that industry.

In conclusion, it is important to note that all of the above financial indicators are closely tied to the specific inventory cost-flow assumption utilized by a company. Thus, during a period of rising costs, it would be quite reasonable to expect that a FIFO-accounted

E X H I B I T   8 . 1 0

Inventory Ratio Analysis with and
without LIFO Effects

	PepsiCo		General Motors	
	With LIFO	**Without LIFO**	**With LIFO**	**Without LIFO**
Gross profit margin ratio	0.52	0.52[h]	0.23	0.23[h]
Inventory turnover ratio	15.2	14.8[k]	11.1	8.6[k]
Average number of days' inventory on hand	24	25	33	42

company would have a higher gross profit margin ratio but lower inventory turnover ratio than would a LIFO-accounted company. In addition, for cross-company comparisons in which the companies use different cost-flow assumptions, the ending inventory and current period earnings amounts should be adjusted for the LIFO company so that it may be compared more appropriately to the FIFO company. Such adjustments would parallel those described earlier for General Motors (Exhibit 8.5). A comparison of these three ratios with and without LIFO is presented in Exhibit 8.10. Note that a significant difference in GM's inventory turnover ratio occurs when the effects of LIFO are deleted from ending inventory and cost of sales. As higher costs are left in inventory and lower costs are assigned to cost of sales (as is the case for adjusting GM to FIFO), inventory turnover does not appear as good. Thus, as seen here, inventory-related financial indicators should be investigated with an eye toward determining the likely impact of the inventory accounting method on the ratios themselves.

SUMMARY

For most nonservice companies, inventories represent a significant current asset. For merchandising companies, inventories may represent the largest single asset category.

Inventories (and cost of goods sold) are usually valued using one of several common cost-flow methods: FIFO, LIFO, or average cost. In addition, the ending inventory must always be evaluated relative to its market (or replacement) value to ensure that the value reported on the balance sheet is not overstated and approximates its net realizable value.

The effective management and utilization of inventory is a hallmark of a well-run company. Thus, analyzing the nature of and investment in inventories is important to investors, creditors, and managers. In addition to reviewing the financial statement disclosure relating to inventories, the financial statement user would be wise to calculate such asset management ratios as the inventory turnover ratio and the average number of days' inventory on hand ratio. These ratios are useful indicators of the quality of a given company's inventory management.

NEW CONCEPTS AND TERMS

Allowance for decline in value of inventory (p. 355)
Average cost method (p. 347)
Direct labor costs (p. 343)
Finished goods inventory (p. 341)
First-in, first-out (p. 348)
Gross profit margin ratio (p. 359)
Inventory layer (p. 352)
Inventory-layer liquidation (p. 352)
Last-in, first-out (p. 349)

Manufacturing overhead (p. 343)
Period cost (p. 343)
Periodic inventory system (p. 354)
Perpetual inventory system (p. 354)
Product cost (p. 343)
Raw materials inventory (p. 341)
Replacement cost (p. 349)
Specific identification method (p. 347)
Weighted-average cost method (p. 348)
Work in process inventory (p. 341)

ISSUES FOR DISCUSSION

D8.1 For each of the companies listed below, state whether you think that the company would have more dollar value in raw materials, work in process, or finished goods inventory. Explain your reasons.

a. Printing plant.

b. Paper manufacturing company.

c. Specialty machine shop.

d. Toy company.

e. Tire manufacturer.

D8.2 Which of the companies listed below would you expect to have the highest inventory turnover ratio? The lowest inventory turnover ratio? Why?

a. Supermarket.

b. Department store.

c. Automobile manufacturer.

d. Jewelry store.

D8.3 In general, what criteria should be used to determine which costs should be included in inventory?

D8.4 In general, why is the lower-of-cost-or-market rule used to report inventory?

D8.5 During periods of rising prices, a perpetual inventory system would result in the same dollar amount of ending inventory as a periodic inventory system under which inventory cost flow methods? Explain your answer.

D8.6 Identify and discuss three or four factors contributing to the particular investment in inventory that a company might have.

D8.7 The original cost of an inventory item is above its replacement cost. The replacement cost is above its net realizable value. Under the lower-of-cost-or-market method, the inventory item should be reported at what amount? Explain.

D8.8 A company records inventory at the gross invoice price. Theoretically, how should warehousing costs and cash discounts available affect the costs in inventory? Explain.

D8.9 Theoretically, how should insurance on raw materials while in transit and cash discounts taken on purchased raw materials affect the costs to be included in a manufacturer's inventory?

D8.10 The original cost of an inventory item is above its replacement cost and its net realizable value. The replacement cost is below its net realizable value less the normal profit margin. As a result, under the lower-of-cost-or-market method, the inventory item should be reported at the net realizable value less the normal profit margin. Explain the rationale for this practice.

PROBLEMS

P8.1 Calculating inventory values.   The following information was taken from the accounting records of Read-for-Knowledge, Inc., a national supplier of comic books to retail outlets throughout North America:

	Batman versus the Scum of New York City	King Kong Meets Ronald Reagan
Inventory, January 1	1,500,000 copies at $0.10	1,000,000 copies at $0.30
Purchases: May 12	600,000 copies at 0.15	1,000,000 copies at 0.20
Aug. 20	600,000 copies at 0.20	500,000 copies at 0.15
Sales: March 3	1,200,000 copies at 0.25	900,000 copies at 0.35
July 8	300,000 copies at 0.30	300,000 copies at 0.35
September 21	900,000 copies at 0.25	200,000 copies at 0.35
Replacement cost: December 31	0.15	0.25

Required:

Using the above information, calculate the following:

a. The cost of goods sold for each product for the year assuming that the FIFO method is used in a *perpetual* inventory system.

b. The value of the ending inventory for each product assuming that the LIFO method is used in a *periodic* inventory system.

c. The value of ending inventory for each product assuming that the FIFO method is used in a *periodic* inventory system.

P8.2 Cost-flow identification.   Listed below are three methods of inventory costing, each of which is identified by a letter. Indicate the method that is referred to in the following descriptive statements. If none of the methods listed below apply to a statement, then so indicate.

a.   LIFO

b.   FIFO

c.   Weighted average

x.   None of the above

_____ 1. Cost of goods sold is highest in a period of steadily rising prices.

_____ 2. The ending inventory is priced at the cost of the most recently acquired goods.

_____ 3. Requires that records be maintained at both cost and selling price for goods placed in stock.

———— 4. Most appropriately matches current costs with current revenues.

———— 5. Would yield greatest tax savings in a period of inflation.

———— 6. Produces highest ending inventory figure after a period of steadily falling prices.

P8.3 Calculating inventory values. The following data were taken from the records of The Bakery for the year 1992:

Beginning inventory:	100 lbs. at $10	$1,000
Purchases:	100 lbs. at $12	1,200
	50 lbs. at $10	500
	200 lbs. at $14	2,800
	300 lbs. at $13	3,900
	50 lbs. at $12	600
		$9,000

Sales were $8,000 (500 lbs. at $16.00 per lb.) and operating expenses were $1,500.

Compute each of the following under LIFO, FIFO, and the lower-of-cost-or-market methods. Assume that the year-end market price is $12 per pound.

a. Cost of goods sold.

b. Ending inventory.

c. Income before taxes.

P8.4 Evaluating inventory errors. The following errors were made by Gunnison Corporation during 1992. Indicate the effect of each of these errors on the financial statements for 1992 and 1993 by completing the chart provided below. Use the following codes for your answers: O = overstated, U = understated, and N = no effect. (Gunnison Corporation uses the periodic inventory system.)

Error 1. The company failed to record a $500 sale on account at the end of 1992. The merchandise had been shipped and was not included in the ending inventory. The sale was recorded in 1993 when cash was collected from the customer.

Error 2. The company failed to record a $700 purchase on account at the end of 1992 and also failed to indicate the goods purchased in the ending inventory. The purchase was recorded in 1993 when payment was made to the creditor.

Error 3. The company failed to make an entry for a $200 purchase on account at the end of 1992, although it included this merchandise in the inventory count. The purchase was recorded when payment was made to the creditor in 1993.

Error 4. The company failed to count goods costing $400 in the physical count of goods at the end of 1992.

		Total Revenue	Total Expense	Net Income	Total Assets	Total Liabilities	Total Owners' Equity
1992	Error 1						
	Error 2						
	Error 3						
	Error 4						
1993	Error 1						
	Error 2						
	Error 3						
	Error 4						

P8.5 Inventory value calculation. Use the following information to answer parts *a* through *e:*

Raw materials inventory—June 1	$ 75
Raw materials purchased during June	650
Raw materials inventory—June 30	40
Other manufacturing costs—variable	150
Other manufacturing costs—nonvariable	220
Direct labor	400
Work in process—June 1	60
Work in process—June 30	25
Finished goods inventory—June 1	90
Finished goods inventory—June 30	150
Gross margin	125
Selling and administrative expenses—variable	10
Selling and administrative expenses—nonvariable	25

Required:

Calculate the following:

a. The cost of materials used for June.

b. Without influencing your answer to part *a*, assume that the cost of materials used to be $660 during June. Use this figure for the remainder of this question. This will eliminate carry-through errors. What was the cost of goods manufactured for June?

c. Without influencing your answer to part *b*, assume that the cost of goods manufactured for June was $1,500. What was the cost of goods sold for June?

d. Without influencing your answer to part *c*, assume that the cost of goods sold for June was $1,400. What was the sales revenue for June?

e. What were the earnings for June?

P8.6 Calculating cost of goods sold. The following information is available concerning the Halsey Manufacturing Corporation:

```
Beginning inventories:
  Raw materials . . . . . . . . . . . . . . . . . . . . . . . . . . . . . .    $ 10,000
  Goods in process . . . . . . . . . . . . . . . . . . . . . . . . . . . .       4,500
Ending inventories:
  Raw materials . . . . . . . . . . . . . . . . . . . . . . . . . . . . . .      15,000
  Goods in process  . . . . . . . . . . . . . . . . . . . . . . . . . . .        6,000
Raw materials used  . . . . . . . . . . . . . . . . . . . . . . . . . . .       70,000
Direct labor . . . . . . . . . . . . . . . . . . . . . . . . . . . . . . .      50,000
Total manufacturing costs . . . . . . . . . . . . . . . . . . . . . . . .      152,000
Cost of goods available for sale  . . . . . . . . . . . . . . . . . . . .      155,000
Cost of goods sold . . . . . . . . . . . . . . . . . . . . . . . . . . . .     148,000
Gross profit  . . . . . . . . . . . . . . . . . . . . . . . . . . . . . . .    127,000
Income  . . . . . . . . . . . . . . . . . . . . . . . . . . . . . . . . . .    102,000
```

Required:

Compute the following:

a. Raw materials purchased.

b. Raw materials available for use.

c. Manufacturing overhead.

d. Cost of goods manufactured.

e. Sales revenue.

f. Finished goods inventory, beginning.

g. Finished goods inventory, ending.

h. Operating expenses.

P8.7 LIFO vs. FIFO. DFW, Inc., began business on January 1, 1986, after taking over the business of Dallas–Ft. Worth Partnership. Partnership had been a manufacturer of custom souvenir products. At the time of the takeover, Partnership had on hand 7,500 Dallas Cowboy souvenir pennants valued at $1.35 each.

DFW, Inc., operated as a wholesale manufacturer from 1986 through 1991, selling its customer-designed pennants to various retail stores and distributors throughout the Texas area. During that period, the cost to produce and handle the pennants rose steadily and by the end of 1990, the cost had increased to $3 per pennant.

During 1991, however, the price spiral finally broke. A general recession throughout the United States had caused a drop in the cost of labor (unemployment in Texas had exceeded 7 percent) and in the cost of many raw materials. By mid-1991, the cost to produce a pennant had fallen to approximately $1.35.

Required:

Assume that DFW, Inc., ended 1991 with 5,000 pennants on hand and that the manufacturer regularly maintained a base stock of at least 5,000 pennants at all times. Based on these facts, indicate whether each of the following statements is true or false, and explain your reasoning.

a. Both LIFO and FIFO would produce exactly the same total reported profit for the period 1986–1991.

b. LIFO would show a higher profit for 1991.

c. FIFO would show a higher profit for 1986.

d. The inventory of pennants on the balance sheet at year-end 1988 would be valued higher if LIFO were used.

e. The inventory of pennants on the balance sheet at year-end 1991 would be $6,750 under both LIFO and FIFO.

f. LIFO would show a lower profit than FIFO for each of the years 1986 through 1990.

P8.8 LIFO company versus FIFO company.   Presented below are the financial statements of two companies that are identical in every respect except the method of valuing their inventories. The method of valuing inventory is LIFO for LIFO Company and FIFO for FIFO Company.

Comparative Income Statements

	FIFO Company	LIFO Company
Sales	$20,000,000	$20,000,000
Less: Cost of sales	9,200,000	11,280,000
Gross profit	$10,800,000	$ 8,720,000
Less: Operating expenses	5,000,000	5,000,000
Net income	$ 5,800,000	$ 3,720,000

Comparative Balance Sheets

	FIFO Company	LIFO Company
Assets		
Cash	$ 3,000,000	$ 3,000,000
Receivables	6,000,000	6,000,000
Inventory	3,800,000	1,720,000
Total current assets	$12,800,000	$10,720,000
Total noncurrent (net)	20,000,000	20,000,000
Total assets	$32,800,000	$30,720,000
Equities		
Current liabilities	$ 4,200,000	$ 4,200,000
Noncurrent liabilities	9,000,000	9,000,000
Total liabilities	$13,200,000	$13,200,000
Total owners' equity	19,600,000	17,520,000
Total equities	$32,800,000	$30,720,000

Required:

Using the two sets of financial statements, calculate the following ratios or financial indicators for each firm.

a. Current ratio.
b. Inventory turnover ratio.
c. Average days' inventory on hand.
d. Return on total assets.
e. Total debt to total assets.
f. Long-term debt to owners' equity.
g. Gross margin ratio.
h. Return on sales.
i. Return on equity.
j. Earnings per share (assume 2 million shares outstanding).

Based on the above ratios in part *a–j,* which company represents the following:

k. The best investment opportunity?
l. The best acquisition opportunity?
m. The best lending opportunity?

P8.9 Ratio analysis. Presented below are summary financial data for Coca-Cola Enterprises, Inc., and PepsiCo, Inc.

	1989	1988
Cost of goods sold (in millions):		
Coca-Cola Enterprises, Inc.	$2,313	$2,268
PepsiCo, Inc.	7,468	5,957
Year-end inventory (in millions):		
Coca-Cola Enterprises, Inc.	128	125
PepsiCo, Inc.	546	442

Required:

Using the above data, calculate the inventory turnover and the average number of days' inventory on hand for 1989 for each company. What is your evaluation of each company's inventory management policy?

P8.10 Lower of cost or market. Joan Sack was the proprietor of a bookstore in Charlottesville, Virginia. In 1991, she decided to relocate her store to a new shopping mall and to expand her inventory as well. To finance the new facility and the increased inventory, she decided to approach the Wachovia Bank for a loan.

In preparation for a meeting with her accountant to prepare the financial statements that she knew the bank would require as part of her loan application, she collected the following information about her book inventory for the prior three years:

	Cost	Replacement Cost
December 31, 1988	$100,000	$100,000
December 31, 1989	130,000	110,000
December 31, 1990	150,000	140,000

Joan also carried a very small collection of videotapes of movies based on books sold in the store. Because of the limited number of tapes on hand, she made a detailed analysis of her inventory.

	Videotape				
	1	**2**	**3**	**4**	**5**
Cost	$5.00	$5.00	$5.00	$ 5.00	$5.00
Net realizable value	5.10	5.50	4.80	4.20	4.70
Net realizable value less the normal store profit	4.80	5.30	4.70	4.00	4.60
Replacement cost	5.30	5.20	4.60	4.10	4.80
Number on hand	5	4	8	10	8

She realized that carrying the videotapes had not been very profitable and decided that if the loan were approved, she would discontinue selling them.

Required:

Based on the above information, determine the value of Joan's book inventory at the end of each year. Also, what value should she assign to her videotape inventory?

P8.11 Estimating inventory values. Kahn Sporting Goods Shops' accounting records indicated the following information:

$$\begin{array}{ll}
\text{Inventory, 1/1/91} & \$ \quad 400,000 \\
\text{Purchases during 1991} & 2,500,000 \\
\text{Sales during 1991} & 3,400,000
\end{array}$$

A physical inventory taken on December 31, 1991, resulted in an ending inventory of $325,000. Kahn's gross profit on sales has remained constant at 25 percent in recent years. Kahn suspects some inventory may have been taken by a new employee.

Required:

At December 31, 1991, what is the estimated cost of missing inventory?

P8.12 Estimating destroyed inventory. Weiss Company sells its merchandise at a gross profit of 30 percent. The following figures are among those pertaining to Weiss' operations for the six months ended June 30, 1991:

$$\begin{array}{ll}
\text{Sales} & \$ 220,000 \\
\text{Beginning inventory} & 48,000 \\
\text{Purchases} & 130,000
\end{array}$$

Required:

On June 30, 1991, all of Weiss' inventory was destroyed by fire. What is the estimated cost of this destroyed inventory?

P8.13 Calculating cost of goods sold. The following information was taken from Omaha Company's accounting records for the year ended December 31, 1991:

$$\begin{array}{ll}
\text{Decrease in raw materials inventory} & \$ \ 13,000 \\
\text{Increase in finished goods inventory} & 35,000 \\
\text{Raw materials purchased} & 330,000 \\
\text{Direct labor payroll} & 200,000 \\
\text{Factory overhead} & 320,000 \\
\text{Freight out} & 35,000
\end{array}$$

There was no work in process inventory at the beginning or end of the year.

Required:

Calculate Omaha's 1991 cost of goods sold.

P8.14 Inventory valuation. Powell, Inc., purchased a significant amount of raw materials inventory for a new product that it is manufacturing. Powell purchased insurance on these raw materials while they were in transit from the supplier.

Powell applies the lower-of-cost-or-market method to these raw material inventory items. The replacement cost of the raw materials is above the net realizable value and both are below the original cost.

Powell uses the average cost inventory method for these raw materials. In the last two years, each purchase has been at a lower price than the previous purchase, and the ending inventory quantity for each period has been higher than the beginning inventory quantity for that period.

Required:

a. What is the theoretically preferable method that Powell should use to account for the insurance costs on the raw materials while they were in transit from the supplier? Why?

b. (1) At which amount should Powell's raw materials inventory be reported on the balance sheet? Why?

   (2) In general, why is the lower-of-cost-or-market method used to report inventory?

c. What would have been the effect on ending inventory and cost of goods sold had Powell used the LIFO inventory method instead of the average cost inventory method for the raw materials? Why?

P8.15 Inventory decisions. Oliver Company sells chemical compounds made from fasbium and uses LIFO inventory. The inventory on January 1, 1990, consisted of 3,000 lbs. costed at $45 per pound. Purchases and ending inventories in the subsequent years were as follows:

Year	Average Purchase Price per Pound during Year	Cost of Units Purchased	December 31 Inventory
1990	50	$384,000	3,600 lbs.
1991	51	352,000	2,600 lbs.
1992	52	448,000	4,000 lbs.

Because of temporary scarcities, fasbium is expected to cost $62 per pound in 1993. Sales for 1993 are expected to require 7,000 pounds of fasbium. The purchasing agent suggests that the inventory be allowed to decrease to 600 pounds by the end of 19x3 and be replenished to 4,000 pounds in early 1994. The controller argues that such a policy is foolish. She argues that if inventories are allowed to decrease, the company will pay a very large amount in income taxes (at its current income tax rate of 40 percent). She suggests that the company maintain a 1993 year-end inventory of 4,000 pounds.

Required:

a. Calculate the cost of goods sold and the dollar value of ending inventory for 1993, assuming (1) the purchasing agent's advice is followed and (2) the controller's advice is followed.

	Purchasing Agent	**Controller**
Cost of goods sold	$_____	$_____
Ending inventory	$_____	$_____

b. Calculate the tax savings for 1993 if the advice of the controller is followed rather than that of the purchasing agent.

c. If you were making the decision, what other information might you consider in choosing whose advice to follow? (Please list.)

P8.16 Inventory disclosures. Presented below is the inventory footnote taken from a recent Merck & Co., Inc., annual report. When necessary, assume a 40 percent corporate income tax rate.

Merck & Co., Inc. and Subsidiaries
Notes to Financial Statements

Substantially all domestic inventories are valued using the last-in, first-out method (LIFO). Remaining inventories are valued at the lower of first-in, first-out (FIFO) cost or market.

(in millions)

Inventories at December 31 consisted of:	19x1	19x0
Finished goods	$359.6	$299.5
Raw materials and work in process	343.0	335.1
Supplies	46.4	41.5
Total (approximate current cost)	749.0	676.1
Reduction to LIFO cost	89.4	96.3
	$659.6	$579.8

Inventories valued at LIFO composed approximately 46 percent and 42 percent of inventories at December 31, 19x1 and 19x0, respectively.

Required:

a. What dollar amount for inventories appears in Merck's December 31, 19x1, balance sheet?

b. If Merck had used current costs for ending inventory valuation rather than those generated by LIFO:

  (1). What dollar amount would have appeared for inventories in its December 31, 19x1, balance sheet?

  (2). To what extent would its December 31, 19x1, retained earnings balance be different? Higher or lower?

  (3). To what extent would its 19x1 net income be different? Higher or lower?

P8.17 Inventory disclosures. The 19x2 Reynolds Metals annual report contained the following footnote description of its accounting policies with respect to inventories:

Note A—Significant Accounting Policies

Inventories

Inventories are stated at the lower of cost or market. Cost of inventories of approximately $283 million in 19x2 and $321 million in 19x1 is determined by the last-in, first-out method (LIFO). Remaining inventories of approximately $422 million in 19x2 and $385 million in 19x1 are determined by the average or first-in, first-out (FIFO) methods. If the FIFO method was applied to LIFO inventories, the amount for inventories would increase by approximately $576 million at December 31, 19x2 and $498 million at December 31, 19x1. As a result of LIFO, costs and expenses increased by $78 million in 19x2 and $29 million in 19x1 and decreased by $60 million in 19x0. Included in the total LIFO effect are liquidations of prior year inventories of $26 million in 19x0.

Since certain inventories of the Company may be sold at various stages of processing, no practical distinction can be made between finished products, in-process products, and other materials, and therefore inventories are presented as a single classification.

Required:

a. What would the balance sheet inventory amounts have been in 19x2 and 19x1 if *all* inventories had been reported on a FIFO basis?

b. Please explain the significance of using LIFO for some inventories and FIFO for others. Why do you think Reynolds Metals does this?

c. Explain what happened to Reynolds' inventories in 19x0.

d. Suppose Reynolds had always used FIFO for all inventories and assume the company's 19x2 income tax rate was 34 percent. What difference would it have made in its 19x2 income statement? The balance sheet as of December 31, 19x2? The 19x2 cash flow statement?

P8.18 Calculating net sales. Harbor Company's usual sales terms are net 30 days, FOB shipping point. Sales, net of returns and allowances, totaled $2,600,000 for the year ended December 31, 1991, before year-end adjustments. Additional data are as follows:

- On December 27, 1991, Harbor authorized a customer to return, for full credit, goods shipped and billed at $40,000 on December 15, 1991. The returned goods were received by Harbor on January 4, 1992, and a $40,000 credit memo was issued and recorded on the same date.

- Goods with an invoice amount of $75,000 were billed and recorded on January 3, 1992. The goods were shipped on December 30, 1991.

- Goods with an invoice amount of $90,000 were billed and recorded on December 30, 1991. The goods were shipped on January 3, 1992.

Required:

Harbor's adjusted net sales for 1991 should be reported at what amount?

P8.19 Lower of cost or market. Dewey Distribution Company has determined its December 31, 1991, inventory on a FIFO basis at $201,000. Information pertaining to that inventory follows:

Estimated selling price	$210,000
Estimated cost of disposal	15,000
Normal profit margin	33,000
Current replacement cost	175,000

Dewey records losses that result from applying the lower-of-cost-or-market method.

Required:

At December 31, 1991, calculate the loss that Dewey should recognize.

P8.20 Inventory method comparisons. Fawcett Company was formed on January 2, 1991, to sell a single product. Over a two-year period, Fawcett's acquisition costs have increased steadily. Physical quantities held in inventory were equal to three months' sales at December 31, 1991, and zero at December 31, 1992. Assuming the periodic inventory system, the inventory cost method that reports the highest amount for each of the following is:

	Inventory December 31, 1991	Cost of Sales 1992
a.	LIFO	LIFO
b.	LIFO	FIFO
c.	FIFO	FIFO
d.	FIFO	LIFO

Explain your answer.

CASES

C8.1 Inventory cost flows: Paragon Electronics, Inc.[1]   One of the first tasks Greg Lemond was assigned on his recent appointment as assistant controller of Paragon Electronics, Inc., involved a review of Paragon's accounting for inventories. One of the specific requests made by Maria Sells, the controller, had been for Lemond to investigate the financial results of two different cost-flow methods: LIFO and weighted average. Paragon uses the periodic FIFO cost-flow method. Lemond contemplated what might be the most informative means to make the appropriate comparisons.

Paragon Electronics, Inc., was a small electronics firm that specialized in the design and production of state-of-the-art electronic systems for advanced Department of Defense projects. Under one particular new project, Paragon had a contract to supply a "package" of subassemblies that were used by a much larger prime contractor (Aero, Inc.) in the production of a new guidance system. Aero, Inc., made all but a select few of the subassemblies used to build the completed guidance system. For those that it did not make, it had chosen a single-source supplier, Paragon, in order to minimize contracting and administrative costs. Paragon manufactured all of the subassemblies contracted to it by Aero, Inc., except the pulsed integrated gyro accelerometer (PIGA). Paragon had found that it would be possible to purchase the PIGA subassemblies from an outside source at a price roughly equivalent to what Paragon's production costs would be. The option of purchasing the

---

[1]This material was prepared by Mark E. Haskins of the Darden School of Business Administration, with the assistance of Monty Parker. Copyright 1986 by the Darden Graduate School Foundation, Charlottesville, Virginia.

PIGAs allowed Paragon to (1) meet its component "package" contract with Aero, Inc., and (2) pursue other contract opportunities using the facilities that would otherwise have been used for PIGA production.

Lemond decided to use the PIGA inventory for his LIFO, FIFO, and weighted-average inventory method comparisons because, as a distinct component not produced internally, he would not have to be concerned with such issues as cost allocations, transfer prices, and so on. He recalled that under the Aero, Inc., contract, Paragon was to supply 500 PIGAs over a six-year period at a price of $950 per unit. Due to production constraints and demands from other programs, Paragon's sole-source supplier would commit to provide only 100 PIGAs a year over a five-year period. The PIGAs would be purchased at the beginning of the year. The unit costs for the PIGAs would increase the first two years due to the market's limited supply but then would decline as competitive sources came on line. Applicable freight and handling costs were included in the purchase price. Relevant selling and general and administrative expenses were expected to be $6,000 a year through 1990 and $2,000 in 1991. For analytical purposes, all purchases and sales between Paragon and its suppliers and customer could be assumed to be on a cash basis.

Lemond noted all of this information and developed a form (see below) to analyze the PIGA pro forma inventories under the three different cost-flow assumptions. After completing the three relevant versions of this form, Lemond planned to analyze the impact of each of the three methods on each year's balance sheet (see the December 31, 1985, balance sheet), income statement, and cash flow (assuming a 46 percent income tax rate, the same inventory method was used for book and tax purposes, and all taxes are paid currently).

Required:

Perform the analysis Lemond intends to do.

Paragon Electronics, Inc.
LIFO

Year Total	PIGA Purchases by Paragon Units	PIGA Purchases by Paragon Unit Cost	Units Sold to Aero, Inc.	Ending Inventory Units	Unit Cost	Total	Units	Cost of Goods Sold Unit Cost
1986	100	$700	80					
1987	100	800	110					
1988	100	850	92					
1989	100	750	104					
1990	100	650	94					
1991	–0–	N/A	20					

Paragon Electronics, Inc.
(continued)

Year Total	PIGA Purchases by Paragon Units	Unit Cost	Units Sold to Aero, Inc.	Ending Inventory Units	Unit Cost	Total	Units	Cost of Goods Sold Unit Cost
				FIFO				
1986	100	$700	80					
1987	100	800	110					
1988	100	850	92					
1989	100	750	104					
1990	100	650	94					
1991	–0–	N/A	20					
				Weighted Average				
1986	100	$700	80					
1987	100	800	110					
1988	100	850	92					
1989	100	750	104					
1990	100	650	94					
1991	–0–	N/A	20					

Paragon Electronics, Inc.
Balance Sheet
For the Year Ending December 31, 1985

Assets		Liabilities & Owners' Equity	
		Liabilities	
Cash	$ 500,000	Account payable	$ 300,000
Accounts receivable	140,000	Accrued expenses	100,000
Inventory	700,000	Current liabilities	400,000
Current assets	$1,340,000	Bonds payable	200,000
		Total liabilities	$ 600,000
Property, plant,		**Owners' Equity**	
and equipment	2,000,000	Retained earnings	$1,140,000
		Common stock	1,600,000
Total assets	$3,340,000	Total equity	$2,740,000
		Total liabilities	
		and owners' equity	$3,340,000

C8.2 LIFO valuation—Champion Spark Plug Company, 1980.[2] Champion Spark Plug Company was principally involved in manufacturing, distributing, and marketing spark plugs, windshield wipers, and other automotive components. Through various subsidiaries, however, Champion was also engaged in manufacturing coating-application equipment, health-care equipment, and cold-drawn steel. Champion made more than 850 types of spark plugs, diesel-starting glow plugs, and related items for a wide array of power-driven devices. Consider the following excerpts from Champion's 1980 annual report:

	(in millions)		
	1980	**1979**	**1978**
Net earnings	$ 36.9	$ 56.9	$ 55.3
Inventory	$261.4	$240.8	$227.1

In 1979, the company adopted the last-in, first-out (LIFO) method of determining costs for substantially all of its U.S. inventories. In prior years, inventory values had been principally computed under the lower of cost or market, first-in, first-out (FIFO) method. The effect of the change on the operating results for 1979 was to reduce net earnings by $5.8 million, or $0.15 per share.

Inventory balances at December 31, 1980 and 1979, would have been $26.8 million and $10.7 million higher, respectively, if U.S. inventory costs had continued to be determined principally under FIFO rather than LIFO. Net earnings on a primarily FIFO method basis would have been $45.6 million, or $1.19 per share, compared to $62.7 million, or $1.64 per share, in 1979.

During 1980, certain inventory balances declined below the levels at the beginning of the year resulting in a smaller increase in the LIFO reserve than would have occurred if these inventory

---

[2]Case prepared by Mark E. Haskins. Copyright 1990 by the Darden Graduate School Foundation, Charlottesville, Virginia.

levels had not declined. Net earnings in 1980 would have been $1.3 million ($0.03 per share) lower had the LIFO reserve addition not been affected by reduced inventories.

It was not practical to determine prior year effects of retroactive LIFO application.

Required:

Using the financial information provided, identify the unknowns in the table below. Assume that the effective tax rate for Champion during 1979 and 1980 was 46 percent. (Because the rate was actually a fraction less than 46 percent, any minor "unexplained" differences can be attributed to rounding errors.)

		1980	1979	1978
a.	Inventories on LIFO basis	$___	$___	NA
b.	Inventories on FIFO basis	$___	$___	$___
c.	Cumulative decrease in pretax earnings resulting from switch to LIFO	$___	$___	NA
d.	Single-year decrease in pretax earnings resulting from switch to LIFO	$___	NA	NA
e.	Single-year decrease in after-tax earnings resulting from switch to LIFO	$___	NA	NA

NA = Not available.

1987

For 1987, Champion's inventory disclosures in the annual report provided the following information:

	(in millions)	
	1987	**1986**
Net earnings	$ 19.1	$ (17.2)
Inventory	$189.9	$174.6

Total inventory costs determined by the LIFO method were $94.3 million at December 31, 1987, and $94.9 million at December 31, 1986. LIFO inventories were $30.9 million and $29.0 million less than estimated current costs at December 31, 1987 and 1986, respectively.

During 1987, 1986, and 1985, certain inventory reductions resulted in liquidations of LIFO inventory quantities. The effect of the reductions was to increase 1987 net earnings by $.5 million, decrease the 1986 net loss by $.2 million, and decrease 1985 net earnings by $.3 million.

In 1986, the company refined its classification of certain costs used in the valuation of domestic inventories. Such reclassifications resulted in a more uniform approach to the valuation of inventories by all domestic operations. The effect of these classification changes was to increase 1986 cost of goods sold by approximately $4.9 million.

Required:

f. What is Champion describing when it talks about "liquidations of LIFO inventory quantities?"
g. Were the reported LIFO inventory dollar balances affected by these liquidations at the end of each of these three years? If so, by what amount? If not, why not? (Note that in 1987 Champion's income tax rate changed from 46 percent to 40 percent.)

C8.3 LIFO valuation—Boyd Enterprises.[3] Boyd Enterprises is a manufacturer of parts used mainly in facsimile equipment and other small office machines. For many years, the company manufactured these parts in several states across the United States. Early in 1989, however, one of the company's principal customers announced its intention to buy machines completely ready for assembly from Japan. The news forced Boyd to close its Texas plant and dispose of its inventories at that location.

The company's 1989 annual report, which appeared early in 1990, disclosed that the closure of the Texas facility had precipitated a dramatic deterioration in its business accompanied by a significant liquidation of its inventories. The notes to the financial statements made the following facts about its inventories available to shareholders.

Note 1—Summary of Significant Accounting Policies
Inventories are stated at the lower-of-cost-or-market value. Cost of inventories is determined by the last-in, first-out method (LIFO) which is less than current cost by $87,609 and $55,952 at December 28, 1988, and December 30, 1989, respectively.

During 1989, inventory quantities were reduced resulting in a liquidation of LIFO inventory quantities carried at lower costs prevailing in prior years as compared with the 1989 cost of production. As a result, income before taxes was increased by $62,310, equivalent to $2.10 per share after applicable income taxes, of which $26,190 before tax, equivalent to $0.88 per share after applicable income taxes, was reflected in cost of product sold and the balance was included as a reduction of the shutdown/disposal provision (see Note 6).

Note 6—Shutdown Disposal Provision
In the third quarter of 1989, a provision was recorded for the closing of the Texas facilities which are to be sold or otherwise disposed of. The after-tax provision of $55,595 is equivalent to $2.93 per common share and covers estimated losses on the disposition of property, plant, and equipment, and inventories and employee severance and other costs. Net sales of products from these facilities included in consolidated sales totaled $92,465 in 1987, $121,012 in 1988, and $147,554 in 1989.

The note regarding quarterly results told a similar story.

Note 12—Quarterly Results (Unaudited)
During the third and fourth quarters of 1989, inventory quantities were reduced, resulting in a liquidation of LIFO inventory quantities carried at lower costs prevailing in prior years as compared with the cost of 1989 production. As a result, income before taxes was increased by $62,310, equivalent to $2.10 per share after applicable income taxes, of which $36,120 before taxes, equivalent to $1.22 per share after applicable income taxes, was included as a reduction of the shutdown/disposal provision with the balance reflected in cost of goods sold.

---

[3]This case was prepared by Kenneth R. Ferris and Michael F. van Breda. Copyright 1990 by Michael F. van Breda and Kenneth R. Ferris.

Examination of its situation revealed that, in 1986, Boyd had moved from keeping its inventory on a first-in, first-out, (FIFO) basis to a LIFO basis. A note to the financial statements at the time described the change.

Note 2—Change in Inventory Valuation Method

In 1986, the company adopted the last-in, first-out (LIFO) method of determining costs for substantially all of its U.S. inventories. In prior years, inventory values were principally computed under the lower of cost or market, first-in, first-out (FIFO) method.

The effect of the change on the operating results for 1986 was to reduce net earnings after tax by $4,714, or 25 cents per share. The inventory balance at December 31, 1986, would have been $7,365 higher if inventory costs had continued to be determined principally under FIFO, rather than LIFO.

It was not practical to determine prior year effects of retroactive LIFO application.

The income statements for the years 1986 through 1989, along with the inventory shown in the balance sheet for each year, appear below. Details of the units purchased each year are also presented.

Boyd Enterprises
Selected Financial Data

	1986	1987	1988	1989
Revenue	$1,058,422	$1,236,091	$1,421,526	$1,277,107
Cost of sales	797,232	958,210	1,085,134	971,550
Gross margin	261,190	277,881	336,392	305,557
Selling and administration	192,775	207,332	209,884	212,567
Loss on write-off (net)	–0–	–0–	–0–	55,595
Income tax	24,629	25,398	45,543	33,476
Net income	43,785	45,151	80,965	3,919
Inventory (per ending balance sheet)	$ 147,304	$ 208,948	$ 232,006	$ 111,904

Required:

Using the 1986 footnote, explain the change in the inventory valuation from FIFO to LIFO. What are the costs and benefits of such an accounting change? Compute the LIFO reserve for each year and show how the company arrived at the effect of $62,310 for the liquidation of LIFO inventory in 1989. Assume an effective tax rate of 36 percent.

Boyd Enterprises
Inventory Summary

	Units	Unit Cost
Opening inventory	60,000	$2.00
Purchases in 1986	103,652	2.00
	293,920	2.10
Sales in 1986	383,920	
Purchases in 1987	282,220	2.20
	153,450	2.60
Sales in 1987	407,650	
Purchases in 1988	193,210	2.70
	202,250	2.90
Sales in 1988	386,920	
Purchases in 1989	196,320	2.90
	82,000	3.00
Sales in 1989	332,580	

CHAPTER 9

Noncurrent Intercorporate Investments

Chapter Outline

I n today's complex business community, it is quite common to find companies investing in each other. These intercorporate investments may involve both debt and equity securities and may be for either short or long duration. In Chapter 7, we considered the accounting associated with temporary intercorporate investments. The focus of this chapter is on long-term intercorporate investments.

Long-term intercorporate investments may be undertaken for a variety of reasons, for example to gain control of a major customer, to provide capital to a struggling supplier, or simply to provide additional sources of income for the investor-company. As a way to organize our discussion of the accounting issues surrounding long-term intercorporate investments, we will focus on the extent of ownership implied by the investment. When a company (the investor) owns a relatively small proportion of the outstanding voting stock of another company (the investee), the investment is most commonly accounted for using the **lower-of-cost-or-market method.** When the investor-company owns sufficient voting stock in the investee to be able to *influence* the activities of the investee, the **equity method** will most likely be used. When an investor owns sufficient voting stock to *control* the activities of the investee-company, the financial results of the two companies must be reported on a **consolidated basis.** There are a number of different ways to acquire the stock of another company and, in recognition of that fact, two different approaches have evolved to account for the acquisition of all (or nearly all) of another company's stock—the **purchase method** and the **pooling-of-interests method.** In this chapter, we focus on the accounting and analytical issues associated with the lower-of-cost-or-market method, the equity method, and consolidation accounting. The consolidation section is divided further to deal with the accounting and business implications of the use of the pooling-of-interests and the purchase methods in the acquisition of another company.

PASSIVE INTERCORPORATE INVESTMENTS

The Lower-of-Cost-or-Market Method

When an investor company acquires bonds or preferred stock issued by another company, those investments are, by definition, **passive investments** in that they give the investor no authority or control over the investee's activities. Similarly, when a company acquires a relatively small portion of the voting common stock issued by another company, that investment also is considered passive so long as the investor has no intent to influence or control the investee's business activities. As a general rule, when an investment involves less than 20 percent of the outstanding voting shares of a company, it is assumed that the investor-company is unable to influence significantly the activities of the investee-company. All long-term passive investments, whether passive because of their terms or because of the extent of the investor's ownership, are understood to be investments solely for the purpose of income and are therefore treated in much the same way as short-term investments. As you will recall from Chapter 7, the lower-of-cost-or-market method (LCM) is stipulated for such investments under *Statement of Financial Accounting Standards No. 12.*

Temporary Value Declines

The initial step in valuing a portfolio of noncurrent investments is to compare the current market value of each *separate* security with its recorded cost. If the market value of a security is less than its cost, management must determine whether the decline is permanent or temporary. Permanent declines must always be recognized in the financial statements, as we will discuss later. Temporary declines in long-term investments involving bonds (or redeemable preferred stock) need not, however, be recognized in the financial statements because management is entitled to assume that those securities will

EXHIBIT 9.1

Flowchart of SFAS No. 12:
Valuation of Noncurrent Marketable Equity Securities
Using the Lower-of-Cost-or-Market Method

On a security-by-security basis, is market value less than cost (or adjusted cost)?

No

Yes

Is this a temporary market decline?

Yes

Is market value of aggregate noncurrent portfolio below cost?

No

Make sure allowance account has a zero balance.

Yes

Adjust the contra-asset allowance account, reflecting the change in the contra-owners' equity allowance account.

No

Market value becomes newly established cost basis and loss is applied to current income *as if* realized.

ultimately be redeemed at their maturity value. Equity securities (common stocks and ordinary preferred stocks), which by definition are not redeemable, present more difficult problems. They are the focus of Exhibit 9.1 and the remainder of this discussion. The flow chart in Exhibit 9.1 presents the questions to be considered in the application of SFAS No. 12 to noncurrent equity investments.

Under SFAS No. 12, temporary declines are considered to be short-term market fluctuations that can reasonably be expected to reverse themselves. If management determines that a decline in the value of an individual security (or group of securities) is temporary, it is then necessary to consider the portfolio of noncurrent securities only in the aggregate. If the market value of that aggregate portfolio is lower than its aggregate cost, an accounting entry is necessary to reflect this decline in value.

Consider, for example, the hypothetical portfolio of noncurrent securities depicted in Exhibit 9.2. At the end of Year 1, the portfolio's market value is $5,000 below its original cost. Thus, an accounting entry must be made to reflect this lower aggregate market value:

Dr.   Unrealized Decline in Noncurrent Equity Portfolio (COE) . . . . . Inc. 5,000
    Cr.   Allowance for Decline in Noncurrent Equity Portfolio (CA) . . . .   Inc. 5,000

E X H I B I T   9 . 2

Hypothetical Portfolio of Noncurrent
Equity Securities

| | At the End of Year 1 | | | At the End of Year 2 | | |
	Cost	Market	Over (Under)	Cost	Market	Over (Under)
Security 1	$50,000	$47,000	$(3,000)	$50,000	$47,000	$ (3,000)
Security 2	45,000	43,000	(2,000)	45,000	35,000	(10,000)
Totals	$95,000	$90,000	$(5,000)	$95,000	$82,000	$(13,000)

In contrast to the accounting treatment followed for a current portfolio of securities, the "unrealized decline" in portfolio value is not treated as an income statement loss but as a contra owners' equity (COE) account. Since management expects to hold the noncurrent securities for more than one year, an assumption is made that the temporary decline is likely to reverse itself by the time the securities are sold in the future. Following that logic, the temporary decline in value in any one year is *not* charged against current earnings but is accumulated in a contra owners' equity account. It is assumed that these year-to-year temporary declines and recoveries will eventually net to zero.

If the portfolio of noncurrent securities recovers its lost value in the future, a reversal of the above entry will be recorded to the extent of the portfolio recovery, but in no circumstances can the portfolio be written up above its original cost basis of $95,000.

Exhibit 9.3 presents excerpts from the footnotes to the financial statements of Borg-Warner Corporation, which illustrate the financial disclosures associated with these issues.

Permanent Value Declines

If, on the other hand, management concludes that the decline in value of a particular security is permanent, a loss is recognized immediately even though the security has not yet been sold. For example, if management decides that the $10,000 decline of Security 2 in Exhibit 9.2, as of the end of Year 2 is a permanent decline, the entry to record the loss would appear as follows:

    Dr. Realized Loss on Noncurrent Security (Loss) . . Inc. 10,000
         Cr. Noncurrent Security 2 (A) . . . .   Dec. 10,000

After a security is written down because of a permanent decline, it can never be written up above this newly established adjusted cost. For this example, Security 2's adjusted cost is now $35,000, and this figure will be used for comparison with future years' market values. The new aggregate (adjusted) cost of the noncurrent portfolio is now $85,000 ($50,000 + $35,000). Since the aggregate market value of the portfolio at the end of Year 2 is $82,000, the allowance account should carry a balance of only $3,000. However, the

EXHIBIT 9.3

Borg-Warner Corporation and Consolidated Subsidiaries
Financial Statement Disclosures: Noncurrent Marketable Securities
(in millions)

	December 31	
	1986	**1985**
Shareholders' equity:		
Capital stock:		
Preferred stock, liquidation preference $2.3 million in 1986 and $2.9 million in 1985	.1	.2
Common stock, 91,824,968 shares issued in 1986 and 1985	229.6	229.6
Capital in excess of par value	147.6	151.5
Retained earnings	1,398.7	1,461.5
Currency translation adjustment	(54.4)	(85.0)
Investment valuation allowance	(39.2)	—
	1,682.4	1,757.8
Less treasury common stock, at cost	157.6	105.3
Total shareholders' equity	1,524.8	1,652.5

Beginning in 1986, Borg-Warner's investment in Hughes Tool Company was accounted for on the cost method as a long-term marketable security. Accordingly, its carrying value of $91 million at December 31, 1986, based upon quoted market prices, is net of an unrealized loss of $39.2 million that is recorded as a valuation reserve in shareholders' equity.

balance in the allowance account, which was carried over from Year 1, is $5,000. Thus, an adjustment of $2,000 to the allowance account is necessary:

Dr. Allowance for Decline in Noncurrent Equity Portfolio (CA) . . . Dec. 2,000
    Cr. Unrealized Decline in Noncurrent Equity Portfolio (COE) . . . .   Dec. 2,000

Note that the adjustment has no income statement effect but is fully reflected in the balance sheet accounts. Of course, there is no cash flow effect either.

The drafters of SFAS No. 12 recognized that they had created a temptation for corporate management with the provision that allows a temporary decline in the value of a noncurrent portfolio to be an adjustment to owners' equity rather than a charge against current income. They were concerned that some managers would be tempted to reclassify a below-market security from its current classification to noncurrent just to avoid recognizing that market-value loss in a company's income statement. To guard against that temptation, SFAS No. 12 also includes a provision that requires *any* transfer of a security from current to noncurrent (or vice versa) to be made at the security's then current market price. Thus, unavoidably, any shortfall in value must be recognized in income in the period of transfer. That market price at the date of transfer then becomes the new "cost" basis for the security.

ACTIVE INTERCORPORATE INVESTMENTS

When an investor company acquires a sufficiently large voting interest to influence or control the business activities of an investee company, the investment is considered to be an active investment. Typically, investments involving ownership interests of 20 to 50 percent are evidence of **significant influence,** whereas investments involving more than 50 percent of a company's voting stock represent **control** situations.

The Equity Method

When an investor's ownership of an investee's voting stock is of such a size that the investor is able to influence the way the investee conducts its business (e.g., to pressure the investee to make a larger dividend payout), the investor is required to adopt the equity method of accounting. Under the **equity method,** the investor records its initial investment at the cost it paid to acquire the stock. Then, on an ongoing basis, the investor adds to its income its pro rata share of the investee's income (or subtracts its pro rata share of the investee's losses). For example, assume that an investor owns 30 percent of the voting shares of Investee Corporation (e.g., 30,000 shares of 100,000 shares outstanding) and that the investee's net earnings for 1992 were $360,000; the investor's entry to record its share of that income is as follows:

Dr. Investment in Investee Corporation (A) . . . . Inc. 108,000
     Cr. Equity in Earnings of Investee Corporation (Income) . . . .   Inc. 108,000

Notice that the income recognized by the investor is added to the original cost of the investment. When an investee pays a dividend, the investor treats that cash receipt as a liquidation of part of its investment. Assuming that the investee pays a dividend of $3 a share, the accounting entry by the investor follows:

Dr. Cash (A) . . . . Inc. 90,000
     Cr. Investment in Investee Corporation (A) . . . .   Dec. 90,000

In effect, the equity method puts the investor/investee relationship on an accrual basis so that the investor recognizes income from the investment when it is earned rather than when it is paid out in cash.

An assumption of the above example is that Investee Corporation had income for the year. The same accounting is required if the investee incurs a loss; the investor is obligated to recognize its pro rata share of the investee's loss, reducing its income and its investment in the investee. This proration explains, at least in part, the rationale for equity accounting: There was a concern that a company could sell off a controlling share of the part of its business that was losing money and, under the lower-of-cost-or-market method, avoid the recognition of those losses. The provisions of equity accounting (which are detailed in Accounting Principles Board [APB] Opinion No. 18) created a middle ground between a fully controlled investment and a nominal passive investment. In that middle ground, an investor is required to recognized its pro rata share of its investee's net income or its investee's net losses.

Under APB Opinion No. 18, the equity method must be used when an investor has the ability to exercise significant influence over an investee. Evidence of "ability to influence" includes, for example, the ability to elect individuals to an investee's board of directors or to force dividend increases. The guidelines also suggest that ownership of more than 20 percent of an investee's outstanding voting stock is presumptive evidence of the ability to influence. Very few companies have justified the equity method for an investment without a 20 percent holding of voting stock, and, conversely, very few companies have been able to avoid the equity method if they own more than 20 percent of an investee's voting stock. Note that an investor may not select the cost method or the equity method; the use of one method over another is mandatory, based on voting-stock ownership, unless evidence to the contrary exists.

Under the equity method of accounting, an investor's investment account (i.e., its investment in the investee) equals its original cost, plus its share of the investee's earnings since the date of acquisition, less any dividends received. Note that the investor's original cost may be more (or less) than its pro rata share of the investee's net book value. Under equity accounting, any such excess (or deficiency) is amortized against (to) income in a like manner to goodwill over a period of years.

As reflected in Exhibit 9.4, the investment account balance is reported as a single line item on the investor's balance sheet. Similarly, the investor's share of an investee's earnings for a period is reported as a single line item on the investor's income statement. Note that the income recognized is the investor's share of the investee's reported net earnings without regard to whether those earnings were distributed in cash.

Disclosure. Exhibit 9.4 presents the financial disclosures of the equity method for the Occidental Petroleum Company. These disclosures reveal that Occidental's share of its affiliated companies' sales was $714 million in 1990, and Occidental's share of the earnings generated by those sales appears on Occidentals' income statement. The difference between Occidental's "investment," shown as one line on its balance sheet, and its share of the affiliates' equity is the net of advances to and from those affiliated companies. In other words, Occidental has investments in its affiliated companies that can be considered relatively permanent. In addition to those investments, Occidental has made long-term loans to (or borrowed from) its affiliates; it distinguishes between the advances and the investments because it expects the advances to be repaid at a specified future date. However, for presentation in its balance sheet, the company combines its investments in, and its advances to, those affiliates to show the amounts at risk in those businesses.

Consolidation Accounting

When an investor owns enough of an investee's voting stock to be in a position to control the investee, rather than simply exert "significant influence" over it, the investor must include all of the investee's assets and liabilities, and revenue and expenses in its financial statements as though it owned those assets and liabilities and incurred those revenues and expenses directly. The investor continues to account for its investment in the investee

EXHIBIT 9.4

**Occidental Petroleum Company
Equity Method Disclosures**

	December 31	
Balance Sheet:	**1990**	**1989**
Current assets:		
Cash and cash equivalents (Note 1)	$ 285	$ 209
Marketable securities, at cost that approximates market (Note 1)	79	94
	364	303
Receivables—		
Trade, net of reserves of $29 in 1990 and $31 in 1989	2,395	2,061
Joint ventures, partnerships and other	369	240
Inventories (Notes 1 and 5)	1,123	1,102
Prepaid expenses and other	200	268
Total current assets	4,451	3,974
Long-term receivables, net	146	265
Investments in and advances to, net of advances from, affiliates (Notes 1 and 15)	609	777
Property, plant, and equipment, at cost (Notes 1, 2, 3, 7, and 8):		
Oil and gas operations	8,057	8,202
Natural gas transmission operations	5,698	5,885
Chemical operations	5,196	5,195
Agribusiness operations	921	805
Coal operations	1,129	1,417
Corporate and other	202	207
	21,203	21,711
Less accumulated depreciation, depletion, and amortization	(7,316)	(6,726)
	13,887	14,985
Other assets (Note 1)	650	740
	$19,743	$20,741

Income Statement:	**1990**	**1989**	**1988**
Revenues:			
Net sales and operating revenues—			
Oil and gas operations	$ 3,727	$ 2,804	$ 2,798
Natural gas transmission operations	2,310	2,489	2,456
Chemical operations	5,040	5,163	4,617
Agribusiness operations	10,187	9,131	9,068
Coal operations	672	656	658
Interdivisional sales elimination	(242)	(175)	(180)
	21,694	20,068	19,417
Interest, dividends and other income	253	186	276
Gains dispositions of assets, net (Note 3)	88	81	14
Gain on issurance of common stock of subsidiaries (Note 3)	—	—	176
Equity in net income of affiliates	25	29	50
	22,060	20,364	19,933

Costs and other deductions

Cost of sales	18,149	16,364	15,782
Selling, general, and administrative and other operating expenses	1,195	1,358	1,456
Depreciation, depletion, and amortization of assets	1,051	1,031	990
Restructuring and other charges (Note 2)	2,169	—	—
Exploration expense	130	144	148
Interest and debt expense, net	960	966	940
Minority interests in net income of subsidiaries and partnerships	29	26	43
	23,683	19,889	19,359
Income (loss) before taxes and extraordinary gain (loss)	(1,623)	475	574
Provision for domestic and foreign income and other taxes (Notes 1 and 11)	65	219	261
Income (loss) before extraordinary gain (loss)	(1,688)	256	313
Extraordinary gain (loss) (Note 4)	(7)	29	(11)
Net income, (loss)	$ (1,695)	$ 285	$ 302
Earnings (loss) applicable to common stock	$ (1,702)	$ 278	$ 295
Earnings (loss) per common share:			
Income (loss) before extraordinary gain (loss)	$ (5.80)	$ .92	$ 1.26
Extraordinary gain (loss)	(.02)	.11	(.05)
Earnings (loss) per common share (Note 1)	$ (5.82)	$ 1.03	$ 1.21

From the footnotes:

Investments in affiliates are accounted for under the equity method. Occidental's investments in affiliated companies, which are 50 percent or less owned, consist primarily of joint-interest pipelines and a 48 percent investment in the common stock of Canadian Occidental Petroleum Ltd. (CanadianOxy). Occidental has a 50 percent interest in Island Creek of China Coal Ltd., which had approximately a 50 percent interest in a surface coal mine joint venture in China. As part of the restructuring program, Occidental has decided to exit this business. The operations of other affiliated companies, which primarily are 50 percent owned, are in oil and gas, natural gas transmission, chemicals and coal. Affiliates paid dividends of $63 million to Occidental in 1990. Cumulative undistributed earnings

since acquisition, in the amount of $106 million, of 50-percent-or-less-owned affiliates have been accounted for by Occidental under the equity method. The aggregate market value of the investment in CanadianOxy, based on the quoted market price for CanadianOxy common shares, was $397 million at December 31, 1990, compared with an aggregate book value of $321 million. Occidental and its subsidiaries received transportation charges of $48 million and purchased $2 million worth of natural gas from certain equity method pipeline ventures during the year ended December 31, 1990. The following table presents Occidental's proportional interest in the summarized financial information of its affiliates (in millions):

Year Ended December 31.

	1990	1989	1988
Revenues	$714	$672	$654
Costs and expenses	689	643	604
Net income	$ 25	$ 29	$ 50

under the equity method for its *internal* records, but because the investee is a controlled company (rather than simply an "influenced" one), it is no longer appropriate for the investee to report its investment in its balance sheet as a single line item, nor does it report income from the investment as a single item in its income statement. Instead, when the investor reports to its shareholders, it replaces those single investment asset and investment income numbers with all the details they represent (i.e., the investor includes in its consolidated financial statements all the assets, liabilities, revenues, and expenses it controls by virtue of its ownership of the investee).

For example, consider the following set of balance sheets, which assumes that Investor Corporation paid $550 in cash for 100 percent of the outstanding stock of Investee Corporation on January 1, 1991:

Investor Corporation
Balance Sheets
At January 1, 1991

	Preinvestment	Adjustments	Postinvestment
Cash	$1,550	(550)	$1,000
Accounts receivable	1,500		1,500
Inventory	1,800		1,800
Net property, plant, and equipment	2,200		2,200
Investment in Investee Corporation		550	550
Total assets	$7,050	-0-	$7,050
Accounts payable	$ 900		$ 900
Long-term debt	3,500		3,500
Owners' equity	2,650		2,650
Total liabilities and owners' equity	$7,050	-0-	$7,050

Note that immediately following the investment, the aggregate value of the corporation's total assets is unchanged—only the mix of those assets is changed.

If Investor Corporation desires to prepare a consolidated balance sheet, as would be required of a publicly held corporation, it is a simple matter to replace the Investment in Investee Corporation account with Investee's assets and liabilities. In the following consolidated balance sheet, we assume that the total owners' equity of Investee Corporation was $550 on January 1, 1991[1]:

---

[1]An investor may acquire all of the stock of an investee from the investee corporation's stockholders, and thereby own the investee's net assets by virtue of its ownership of the outstanding stock. Alternatively, the investor may elect to buy the investee's net assets directly from the investee corporation, leaving the investee's corporate "shell" in the hands of its previous owners. The accounting for such a purchase of net assets is exactly the same as with any other asset acquisition, which is the subject of Chapter 10. The unique accounting described in this chapter applies to those cases in which the investor acquires an investee by purchasing its outstanding stock.

Investor Corporation
Balance Sheets
At January 1, 1991

	Investor	Investee	Adjustments	Consolidated Investor
Cash	$1,000	$ 500		$1,500
Accounts receivable	1,500	800		2,300
Inventory	1,800	600		2,400
Net property, plant, and equipment	2,200	1,200		3,400
Investment in Investee Corporation	550		(550)	
Total assets	$7,050	$3,100	(550)	$9,600
Accounts payable	$ 900	$ 300		$1,200
Long-term debt	3,500	2,250		5,750
Owners' equity	2,650	550	(550)	2,650
Total liabilities and owners' equity	$7,050	$3,100	(550)	$9,600

Note that the consolidated financial statements that are sent to Investor Corporation's shareholders include all of its assets and liabilities, as well as the assets and liabilities of Investee Corporation. The process of combining those two financial statements (the "consolidation") substitutes Investee's assets and liabilities (in effect, its owners' equity or net assets) for Investor's investment account. That process can also be described in the following formula:

$$\text{Investor's aggregate investment} = \text{Investee's total net worth} = \text{Investee's individual assets} - \text{Investee's individual liabilities}$$

The three factors in the above equation are equal, and so consolidation accounting simply substitutes Investee's individual assets and its individual liabilities for the aggregate Investor's investment.

After a year's operations, the consolidation of the two companies' income statements would appear as follows:

Investor Corporation
Income Statement
Year Ended December 31, 1991

	Investor	Investee	Adjustments	Consolidated Investor
Sales	$5,000	$2,000		$7,000
Cost of goods sold	(2,000)	(1,100)		(3,100)
Expenses	(2,500)	(600)		(3,100)
Income from investment in Investee Corporation	300		(300)	
Net income	$ 800	$ 300	(300)	$ 800

Note that in the preparation of the consolidated income statement, Investor's single line item "Income from investment in Investee Corporation" is expanded to reflect all the sales and expenses it controls by virtue of that investment.

Most often, the investor and the investee continue to maintain their own accounting records as though they were stand-alone, unaffiliated entities. The investor accounts for its investment in the investee for its *internal* purposes using the equity method, recording its share of the investee's income as investment income and recording an addition to its investment account. (Note that the investee increases its retained earnings as a result of its income for the year and at the same time increases its assets—receivables, inventory, and so on. As a result of that income, the investor increases its retained earnings account and at the same time increases its investment account.)

However, because the investor's ownership interest is 100 percent, the only *external* financial statements that will be prepared reflect a full consolidation of the two parties (i.e., combining investor and investee). The preparation of those consolidated balance sheets, income statements, and cash flow statements occurs only when a financial report is prepared for distribution to the directors, stockholders, or other external users of the financial statements. The "adjustments" illustrated here exist only on work sheets (or on a floppy disk) as part of the process of putting the two companies' records together for the consolidated financial statement presentation.

This example is grossly oversimplified because Investor owns all the stock of Investee and because the cost of Investor's investment is exactly equal to Investee's net assets. We will demonstrate more realistic examples in the following section when we consider the method of acquisition of these investments. Before we move on, however, you should study these simplified illustrations and be sure that you understand the basic concepts of consolidation accounting: Consolidated financial statements combine two (or more) companies' activities as though they conducted business as one entity. Consolidated financial statements substitute full details of the investee's assets and liabilities for the investor's single investment number, and the full details of the investee's operations for the investor's single investment income number. Finally, note that net income reported in the consolidated income statement is the same as for Investor—only the details are different.

Generally accepted accounting principles require that the investor present consolidated financial statements when it has the ability to control the activities of an investee. An investor's ability to elect a majority of the members of an investee's board of directors is presumed to be evidence of such control. Accounting guidelines also suggest that ownership of more than 50 percent of the outstanding voting stock is presumptive evidence of the ability to control. That quantitative measure is followed almost without exception in practice. Few companies are able to justify the preparation of consolidated financial statements with their investees without ownership of more than 50 percent of an investee's outstanding stock. Few companies are able to avoid such a consolidation when they own more than 50 percent of an investee's outstanding stock.[2]

---

[2]Until 1989, a company that owned a finance company (e.g., General Motors and its wholly owned finance subsidiary, General Motors Acceptance Corporation) could avoid consolidation of that entity's assets and liabilities by arguing that the finance company was a disparate business and that combining the finance company's activities with other operations would result in a confusing financial statement. Most wholly owned finance companies were reported on the equity method. As of January 1, 1988, however, that practice is no longer acceptable. SFAS No. 94 requires the consolidation of all controlled entities, regardless of the nature of the businesses.

In summary, a company's accounting for an investment in the voting common stock of another company follows this chart:

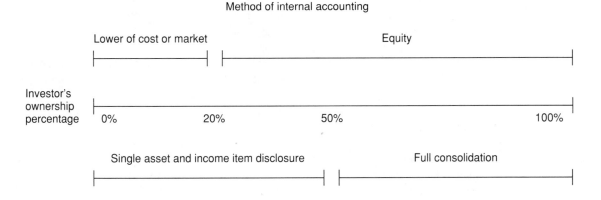

These three approaches (i.e., lower of cost or market with single line item presentation, equity method accounting with single line item presentation, and equity method accounting with full consolidation) are not alternatives—selection of one is required by the particular circumstances faced by an investor. The approach to be used is almost always dictated by the degree of ownership of an investor in an investee.

POOLING-OF-INTERESTS VERSUS PURCHASE METHOD OF ACCOUNTING

The consolidation process is relatively straightforward so long as the price paid by the investor (its investment) is exactly equal to the investee's net book value. That fortuitous situation could occur in real life, but it would be extremely rare. It could more easily exist when the investor began the investee from scratch. In that case, the investor's investment would, of course, always be equal to the investee's net worth simply because of the workings of the equity method.

When one company acquires an existing, operating company, the price it pays is influenced by many factors in addition to the investee's net book value. For example, Investor Corporation may offer to exchange one of its shares for each of Investee Corporation shares owned by the Investee Corporation shareholders. That offer would consider Investee Corporation's prospects for the future, the current fair value of its assets, as well as its GAAP-based book value. If Investor Corporation's shares are trading at $2 and there are 1,000 shares of Investee Corporation's stock outstanding, the total consideration in this transaction has the value of $2,000. Investor Corporation could have very good reasons for making that offer even though Investee Corporation's book value is only $550. However, if Investee Corporation shareholders feel strongly about the future of their company, they might refuse the share-for-share, $2,000 offer, and ask for more consideration. To complete the deal, Investor Corporation may have to agree to exchange 1.5 of its shares for the Investee Corporation shares outstanding, increasing the value of the consideration in the transaction to $3,000.

In theory, Investor Corporation's accounting for this transaction ought to recognize the fair value of the consideration given in the exchange—whether the consideration is in cash, bonds, notes, warrants, or shares of its own stock. That consideration given is, in theory, the new cost of the net assets acquired. In this model, the cost of Investor Corporation's investment is $3,000, even though Investee Corporation's net book value—stated at its historic cost—is only $550. The difference between that new cost—for the investor—and the old cost—for the investee—complicates the consolidation of the two companies' financial statements. As a result of that problem, financial people created two quite different approaches to the accounting for the acquisition of an operating company.

Accounting for the Initial Investment in an Investee

An investor's original (initial) investment can be recorded in two ways. As with the acquisition of most other assets, the acquisition of stock in another company is *usually* recorded at the fair value of the consideration given in the transaction, and that fair value is understood to be the *cost* of the asset acquired. When the original investment is recorded by the investor at its cost, it is (logically) referred to as a **purchase,** and the accounting for such purchase transactions will be discussed in a later section of this chapter. The following section deals with the **pooling-of-interests** method, which is a unique exception to the normal rule of accounting for acquisitions at their *cost*. Under the pooling-of-interests method, the initial investment is recorded by an investor at the investee's book value.

Acquiring an Investment in Another Company: The Pooling-of-Interests Method

When an investor company acquires substantially all of the outstanding voting stock of an investee company, giving its own voting stock in exchange, it may be possible to record the acquisition under the pooling-of-interests method of accounting. The criteria under the **pooling-of-interests method** are exacting: the investor must acquire substantially all (i.e., at least 90 percent) of the investee's stock; the consideration must all be in stock; the stock exchanged must be voting common stock for voting common; and the exchange must be accomplished within strict time limits. In theory, the accounting is not elective: if a transaction meets the criteria, the pooling-of-interests method must be used; if not, the purchase method applies. Because the specific rules of the pooling method are quite detailed, it is often difficult for an investor who prefers to use it to make sure that all criteria have been satisfied. Conversely, a company that has decided that it does not want its acquisition of an investee to be accounted for using the pooling method can easily cause one of the criteria to be violated, which automatically converts the acquisition into a purchase.

The theory supporting the pooling-of-interests method of accounting rests on the understanding that there has been a complete, pro rata merging of the existing equity interests in two companies. (Remember that the criteria for the pooling method require that the acquisition method involve an exchange of voting stock for voting stock.) Based on that presumption, the pooling-of-interests method assumes that the two companies have been together *since the beginnings of their businesses,* just as though the investor had created the investee from scratch. As a consequence of that assumption, the stock issued by an investor to acquire an investee and the resulting asset (the investment) are both recorded at the book value of the investee's net assets, *without* regard to the market value of the shares issued in the exchange—or the market value of the investee's net assets.

For instance, consider again the investment by Investor Corporation in Investee Corporation, which we first considered on page 390. In that case, we assumed that the acquisition took place on January 1, 1991, and that Investor paid cash exactly equal to Investee's net assets. Let us now assume instead that Investor issued 1,000 shares of its voting stock, which has a market value of $2 a share, in exchange for Investee's net assets. With that assumption, under the pooling method, the following entry would be recorded on Investor's books:

```
Cr.  Investment in Investee Corporation (A). . . . . . . . .  Inc. 550
       Cr.  Common Stock (OE) . . . . . . . . . . . . . . . . . . .      Inc. 550
```

Investor Corporation's pre- and postinvestment balance sheets would appear as follows:

Investor Corporation
Balance Sheets
At January 1, 1991

	Preinvestment	Adjustments	Postinvestment
Cash	$1,550		$1,550
Accounts receivable	1,500		1,500
Inventory	1,800		1,800
Net property, plant, and equipment	2,200		2,200
Investment in Investee Corporation		550	550
Total assets	$7,050	550	$7,600
Accounts payable	$ 900		$ 900
Long-term debt	3,500		3,500
Owners' equity	2,650	550	3,200
Total liabilities and owners' equity	$7,050	550	$7,600

Note that Investor Corporation's investment and the stock that it gave up in the exchange are recorded at the net worth of Investee Corporation as determined by Investee's historical cost balance sheet. The implicit value of the stock given up as consideration (i.e., $2,000) is not recognized in Investor's financial statements.

After the date of the acquisition, Investor recognizes Investee's earnings according to the equity method (an increase in its investment account and an increase in its net earnings) and treats any dividends received as an increase in cash and a decrease in its investment. At any time, therefore, Investor's investment account is exactly equal to Investee's owners' equity—its net assets. Thus, when consolidated financial statements are prepared for release to the public, the two companies' assets and liabilities, and revenues and expenditures are simply combined. The pooling-of-interests method of accounting forces Investor's investment to equal Investee's net worth (and, of course, the aggregate of the assets less the liabilities) because a pro rata sharing of the equity relationship is a tenet of the method itself. Because Investee's net worth is equal to its assets less its liabilities and because the Investor's investment is always equal to the Investee's net worth, preparation of consolidated financial statements for pooled entities is quite simple. Investor's investment account and Investee's equity are eliminated, and the remaining assets and liabilities are added together. Investee's individual assets and liabilities take the place of Investor's investment account.

The following balance sheet and income statement illustrate the application of pooling accounting under the assumption that the acquisition took place on January 1, 1991, in an exchange of voting common stock. Note that the numbers are very much the same as in the first set of consolidated statements, except that Investor's Equity account is increased by $550 to reflect its issuance of stock in the acquisition, and its Cash account is restored to $1,550 because the earlier statements assumed that the acquisition had been a cash transaction.

Investor Corporation
Balance Sheets
At January 1, 1991

	Investor	Investee	Adjustments	Consolidated Investor
Cash	$1,550	$ 500		$ 2,050
Accounts receivable	1,500	800		2,300
Inventory	1,800	600		2,400
Net property, plant, and equipment	2,200	1,200		3,400
Investment in Investee Corporation	550		(550)	
Total assets	$7,600	$3,100	(550)	$10,150
Accounts payable	$ 900	$ 300		$ 1,200
Long-term debt	3,500	2,250		5,750
Owners' equity	3,200	550	(550)	3,200
Total liabilities and owners' equity	$7,600	$3,100	(550)	$10,150

Investor Corporation
Income Statement
Year Ended December 31, 1991

	Investor	Investee	Adjustments	Consolidated Investor
Sales	$5,000	$2,000		$7,000
Cost of goods sold	(2,000)	(1,100)		(3,100)
Expenses	(2,500)	(600)		(3,100)
Income from investment	300		(300)	
Net income	$ 800	$ 300	(300)	$ 800

Because the underlying theory assumes that the two companies have always been together, any financial statements presented after the pooling-of-interests must be restated to present the companies *as if* they had always been consolidated, even for those financial statements of the periods prior to the acquisition. Financial statements for periods *prior* to the acquisition issued *after* the acquisition will be restated to reflect the acquisition but also will include a footnote detailing the historical results of operations as they were originally reported. It is important, however, to stress that in the basic statements (i.e., the balance sheets, income statements, and statements of cash flow) for all years shown are presented as if the companies had always been together.

Note that the consolidated owners' equity is equal to the sum of the two companies' equity balances before the transaction; that result is inevitable under the pooling-of-interests method because the shares issued in the acquisition are valued at an amount equal to the aggregate equity of the investee company. That is so without regard to the market value of the shares issued or the par (legal) value of the shares issued. The "adjustment" entry in the preceding illustration eliminates the value of the Investee's equity to avoid double counting. The value of Investee's equity is reflected in the shares issued by Investor, and that is the value carried over to the equity section of the consolidated balance sheet.

You will note in these examples that we have shown only one number for owners' equity and have made no distinction between the par value of the stock, the paid-in-capital-in-excess of par value, or even retained earnings. Those distinctions are important primarily for legal reasons. After a pooling of interests, the accountants and attorneys make the necessary adjustments to the two companies' equity accounts to meet the requirements of the state laws of incorporation. If it is at all possible, they try to make the adjustments in such a way that the consolidated retained earnings is the sum of the two companies' retained earnings prior to the combination. That adjustment is, of course, consistent with the notion that the two companies have always been one company, but on a more practical level, it also may give the combined entity more flexibility in paying dividends.

To illustrate the always-one-entity theory, consider this presentation by Alltel Corp. regarding its acquisition of Systematics, Inc., on May 31, 1990:

On May 31, 1990, the Company completed its merger with Systematics, Inc. ("Systematics"). In connection with the merger, 1.325 shares of the Company's common stock were exchanged for each share of Systematics common stock outstanding, resulting in the issuance of approximately 14.7 million common shares.

The merger was accounted for as a pooling of interests and, accordingly, the accompanying financial statements have been restated to include the accounts and results of operations of Systematics for all periods prior to the merger. The restatement increased retained earnings at January 1, 1988, from that previously reported by $53,569,000. Revenues, net income and earnings per share of the separate companies for the years ended December 31, 1990, 1989, and 1988 were as follows:

	Thousands, except per share data		
	1990	**1989**	**1988**
Revenues and sales:			
ALLTEL	$1,318,979	$1,266,684	$1,068,480
Systematics	254,806	223,959	196,929
Combined	$1,573,785	$1,450,643	$1,265,409
Net income:			
ALLTEL	$ 171,084	$ 153,921	$ 125,039
Systematics	21,715	20,794	17,823
Combined	$ 192,799	$ 174,715	$ 142,862
Earnings per share:			
ALLTEL	$2.54	$2.32	$1.94
Systematics	$1.48	$1.39	$1.20
Combined	$2.35	$2.13	$1.79

Because this transaction was a pooling, Alltel restated its 1989 and 1988 financial statements for presentation in the 1990 annual report to stockholders and reported results of operations as reflected in the "combined" lines in the footnote. Note also that Alltel restated its retained earnings as of January 1, 1988 (the first day of the period covered by the financial statements) to include Systematic's retained earnings at that date.

The pooling-of-interests method of accounting can be attractive when an investor's earnings are relatively flat but the earnings trend of the investee is rising. In that case, the effect of the pooling is to show a more attractive earnings trend for the combined entity. Other advantages of the pooling-of-interests method of accounting will become apparent after we examine the alternative—the purchase method.

Acquiring the Stock of Another Company: The Purchase Method

Any acquisition of one company's stock by another that does not qualify under the pooling-of-interests criteria *must* be accounted for under the purchase method. Under the **purchase method,** an investment in another company is recorded at the cash-equivalent cost of the consideration given up. For instance, let us assume that to acquire the Investee

Corporation's investment, Investor Corporation gave 1,000 shares of its own stock with a fair value of $2 a share. The entry to record that acquisition using purchase accounting would be this:

```
Dr.  Investment in Investee Corporation (A) . . . . . . . Inc. 2,000
     Cr.  Common Stock (OE) . . . . . . . . . . . . . . . . . .          Inc. 2,000
```

That entry seems more logical than the entry we recorded using the pooling-of-interests method because it reflects the true economic value in the exchange rather than the investee's historic net worth. However, recording that value on the books of the investor could complicate our subsequent consolidation. When we combine the two companies' financial statements, we want to be able to offset Investee's net assets (i.e., its owners' equity) against Investor's investment. To be able to do that, we must adjust Investee's accounting records.

The purchase method of accounting makes the logical assumption that an investor receives something of equal value for the consideration it gives up, even if the assets acquired are not all immediately visible. The purchase method requires that an investor determine fair values for all of the investee's *identifiable* assets and liabilities. The investor's investment is then compared with the aggregate net fair value of the investee's identifiable assets and liabilities; if any excess purchase price remains, that excess is recorded as an intangible asset (referred to as *goodwill* or *purchase price in excess of net assets acquired*). After this revaluation, the investee's net assets (i.e., the fair value of the identifiable assets plus the goodwill less the fair value of its liabilities) will equal the investor's purchase price. Note that the goodwill is recorded as an asset by the investor and must be amortized against the combined company's future net income—that amortization period may not exceed 40 years.

For example, assume that in the earlier example, Investor gave its stock with a value of $2,000 to acquire all of the outstanding stock of Investee. Remember that the investor made this entry in its records:

```
Dr.  Investment in Investee Corporation (A) . . . . . . . Inc. 2,000
     Cr.  Owners' Equity (OE) . . . . . . . . . . . . . . . . . .          Inc. 2,000
```

Also assume that the fair values of all the identifiable assets and liabilities of Investee Corporation were equal to their book values except for property, plant, and equipment which had been appraised at $2,500. Because Investor controls Investee completely, Investor can order Investee to revalue its assets and liabilities. In effect, Investor tells Investee to ignore its historic cost valuations and asks it to recognize the current market values at the time of Investor's acquisition, which is, naturally, Investor's cost. This process is referred to as *push-down accounting*. In our model, Investee would make the following entry to recognize Investor's acquisition cost:

```
Property, Plant, and Equipment (A) . . . . . . . . . . . Inc. 1,300
Goodwill (A) . . . . . . . . . . . . . . . . . . . . . . Inc.   150
     Owners' Equity . . . . . . . . . . . . . . . . . . . . . .          Inc. 1,450
```

Investee's records now reflect Investor's purchase price as follows:

Investee Corporation
Balance Sheet

	Before the Acquisition	Purchase Adjustments	After the Acquisition
Cash	$ 500		$ 500
Accounts receivable	800		800
Inventory	600		600
Net property, plant, and equipment	1,200	1,300	2,500
Goodwill		150	150
Total assets	$3,100	1,450	$4,550
Accounts payable	$ 300		$ 300
Long-term debt	2,250		2,250
Owners' equity	550	1,450	2,000
Total liabilities and owners' equity	$3,100	1,450	$4,550

Treating this acquisition as a purchase, the consolidated balance sheet would appear as follows:

Investor Corporation
Balance Sheet
As of January 1, 1991

	Investor	Investee*	Adjustments†	Consolidated Investor
Cash	$1,550	$ 500		$ 2,050
Accounts receivable	1,500	800		2,300
Inventory	1,800	600		2,400
Net property, plant, and equipment	2,200	2,500		4,700
Investment in Investee Corporation	2,000		(2,000)	
Goodwill		150		150
Total assets	$9,050	$4,550	(2,000)	$11,600
Accounts payable	$ 900	$ 300		$ 1,200
Long-term debt	3,500	2,250		5,750
Owners' equity	4,650	2,000	(2,000)	$ 4,650
Total liabilities and owners' equity	$9,050	$4,550	(2,000)	$11,600

*Restated to reflect appraisal of property, plant, and equipment at $2,500 and the goodwill apparent in the acquisition.

†Some companies allow the investee to retain its historic cost for its own records and record the adjustments required for purchase accounting only during consolidation. Other companies follow the approach here and restate the investee's assets and liabilities at their fair values as of the date of the purchase (the balancing increase is to the investee's owners' equity accounts). Some companies insist on push-down accounting so that the managers of the investee entity can see how the investor is measuring their effort; after all, after the acquisition, the investee management is responsible for earning a return on a larger net asset base. Some companies make the management of the investee responsible for earning a return on the new values of the identifiable assets but not on the goodwill.

The income statement at the end of Year 1 will look very much like the earlier example, except, of course, that Investee's income will be less because the company's operations must now absorb the additional depreciation on the new cost of the property, plant, and equipment and the amortization of the goodwill. Of course, the investment income recognized by Investor will also be reduced.

Investor Corporation
Income Statement
Year Ended December 31, 1991

	Investor	Investee	Adjustments	Consolidated Investor
Sales	$ 5,000	$ 2,000		$ 7,000
Cost of goods sold	(2,000)	(1,100)		(3,100)
Expenses	(2,000)	(400)		(2,400)
Depreciation	(500)	(300)		(800)
Income from investment	200		(200)	
Net income	$ 700	$ 200	(200)	$ 700

The purchase method of accounting is quite logical because it records the net assets acquired at their fair value (as well as the consideration given up at its fair value). Some managers, however, object to purchase accounting because it combines the assets of the investee company at their fair value with the assets of the investor company, which are still stated at their historic cost. Some managers also object to the inclusion of an intangible asset labeled *goodwill* on their balance sheet. They apparently believe that readers of the statements discount the value of any such asset, and thus they prefer the pooling-of-interests method because it presents a "cleaner" balance sheet. Finally, on a more pragmatic note, some managers object to the purchase method because the higher asset values, including the newly recognized goodwill, result in increased amortization and depreciation expenses, which depress future earnings.

Another point to note is that a purchase transaction is presumed to have taken place on the day the transaction is consummated. Thus, the subsequent financial statements for an investor reflect the activities of the investee *only* from the date of the purchase. The consolidated owners' equity section is that of only the investor; the consolidated retained earnings is the retained earnings of the investor plus (minus) any investee earnings (loss) since the acquisition. The prior financial statements are not restated, although a footnote to the statements outlines what the investor's results of operations would have been if the two companies had been combined in prior years. For example, one of the largest business combinations was the purchase of RCA by General Electric Co. Consider the annual report presentation by GE describing its acquisition of RCA in Exhibit 9.5. General Electric's income statement in the 1986 annual report (which includes the operations of RCA only after June 1986) reported earnings per share of $2.73 in 1986 and $2.50 in

General Electric Company
Footnote Disclosure: RCA Acquisition

2 RCA acquisition and related matters

On June 9, 1986, GE acquired RCA Corporation and its subsidiaries (RCA) in a transaction for which the total consideration to former RCA shareholders was $6,406 million in cash. RCA businesses included the manufacture and sale of a wide range of electronic products and related research and services for consumer, commercial, military and space applications; the National Broadcasting Company's (NBC) radio and television stations and network broadcasting services; and domestic and international message and data communications services.

The acquisiton was accounted for as a purchase, and the operating results of RCA have been consolidated with those of GE since June 1, 1986. The purchase price ($6,426 million, including $20 million of related costs) has been allocated to the assets and liabilities of RCA based on appraisal and evaluation studies completed during 1987. The excess of purchase price over the estimate of fair values of net assets acquired (goodwill) was $3.7 billion, which is being amortized on a straight-line basis over 40 years.

Unaudited pro forma consolidated results of operations for the years 1986 and 1985, assuming RCA had been acquired at the beginning of each period, are shown below.

Pro Forma Consolidated Operations
(dollar amounts in millions; per-share amounts in dollars)

	1986	1985
Sales	$38,997	$37,258
Net earnings	2,471	2,143
Net earnings per share	2.71	2.36

These pro forma operating results were prepared in 1986 based on estimates and assumptions including purchase price allocation. Final purchase price allocation would not have changed the pro forma results significantly. Such pro forma results are not necessarily indicative of the consolidated results which would have been reported if the RCA acquisition had actually occurred at the beginning of each respective period presented or which may be reported in the future.

1985. A comparison of those GAAP/purchase accounting numbers with the pro forma earnings per share results from the footnote (which describes what the results would have been had the purchase taken place on the first day of 1985) suggests that the interest cost related to the transaction, the extra depreciation on the appraised values of the RCA assets, and the amortization of the goodwill were more than the earnings of RCA during those periods.

A more current illustration is BellSouth's acquisition of Mobile Communications Corporation of America as detailed in Exhibit 9.6. MCCA's net book value, according to its balance sheet at December 31, 1988, was $196 million. As you might expect, Bell-South reported a substantial increase in intangible assets in its 1989 balance sheet as a consequence of the acquisition.

Special Consolidation Problems

Minority positions. Occasionally, an investor is unable to acquire all of the outstanding voting stock of an investee, and a *minority shareholder position* remains outstanding. So long as the investor owns more than 50 percent of the investee's outstanding voting stock,

EXHIBIT 9.6

BellSouth, Inc.
Footnote Disclosure: MCCA Acquisition

In April 1989, BellSouth acquired Mobile Communications Corporation of America ("MCCA"), a national cellular telephone and paging company, for approximately $710 million in BellSouth common stock. The acquisition has been accounted for as a purchase and, accordingly, the acquired assets and liabilities have been recorded at their estimated fair values at the date of acquisition. MCCA's results of operations are included in BellSouth's consolidated statements of income beginning May 1, 1989.

The following unaudited pro forma financial information shows the results of operations for the periods ended December 31, 1989 and 1988 as if the acquisition had occurred at the beginning of each respective period:

	For the Years Ended December 31,	
	1989	**1988**
Total operating revenues	**$14,028.7**	$13,692.5
Income before extraordinary item and cumulative effect of change in method of accounting	**$ 1,683.6**	$ 1,631.7
Net income	**$ 1,729.7**	$ 1,631.7
Earnings per share: Income before extraordinary item and cumulative effect of change in method of accounting	**$ 3.52**	$ 3.44
Earnings per share	**$ 3.62**	$ 3.44

The pro forma results are not necessarily indicative of what would have occurred had the acquisition actually been made on January 1 of the periods presented or of future operations of the combined companies. The pro forma results include the effects of the preliminary purchase accounting adjustments. The pro forma information includes the accelerated amortization of the value attributed to the subscriber base over six years and the amortization of the value attributed to the remaining licenses and other intangibles on a straight-line basis over 40 years.

the purchase method of accounting and full consolidation are required. The minority shareholders' ownership of the investee's net worth is carried into the consolidated financial statements just above the investor's owners' equity and just below its long-term debt. (For ratio purposes, it is either considered part of long-term debt or ignored.) In a published income statement, the earnings of the investee company attributable to the minority shareholders' interest are reported just after income after taxes, just before the net earnings line.

For example, returning to our initial illustration in which Investor Corporation paid cash to acquire the stock of Investee Corporation and for which the fair value of Investee's assets were equal to their cost, assume now that Investor paid only $440 in cash and acquired only 80 percent of the outstanding voting stock of Investee. This transaction would be accounted for as a purchase because it was a cash transaction and because Investor did not acquire *all* of the stock of Investee. The balance sheet at January 1, 1991, would therefore appear as follows:

Investor Corporation
Balance Sheet
At January 1, 1991

	Investor	Investee	Adjustments	Consolidated Investor
Cash	$1,110	$ 500		$1,610
Accounts receivable	1,500	800		2,300
Inventory	1,800	600		2,400
Net property, plant, and equipment	2,200	1,200		3,400
Investment in investee corporation	440		(440)	
Total assets	$7,050	$3,100	(400)	$9,710
Accounts payable	$ 900	$ 300		$1,200
Long-term debt	3,500	2,250		5,750
Minority interest			110	110
Owners' equity	2,650	550	(550)	2,650
Total liabilities and owners' equity	$7,050	$3,100	(440)	$9,710

The practical effect of consolidation accounting for those situations in which an investor owns less than 100 percent of the investee is to turn the minority shareholders of the investee into quasi creditors of the consolidated entity.

Intercompany transactions. When an investor has an interest in an investee of more than 50 percent and the two companies do business with each other, those intercompany transactions must be eliminated at the time the investor's consolidated financial statements are prepared. For example, intercompany receivables and payables, and intercompany sales and expenses must be offset. When one company sells to the other and some of those intercompany sales remain in the consolidated entity's inventory at the balance sheet date, any profit on those sales must be eliminated in proportion to the investor's ownership share.

Taxation Issues

Under current U.S. tax laws, when one company owns less than 20 percent of another, up to 70 percent of the dividends that an investor receives from an investee are excludable from the investor's taxable income. When an investor company owns between 20 and 80 percent of an investee company, up to 80 percent of any dividends received may be excluded. The theory behind this tax break is that an investee has already paid tax on its own income and the shareholders of the investor will have to pay tax on that income again when it is ultimately distributed to them. The U.S. Congress concluded that to tax that income a third time, as it passed through the investor's hands, was unnecessary and inappropriate.

Further, the equity method is not allowable for tax purposes. Except for consolidation situations, which are described below, an equity method investor reports income from an investee on its tax returns only as it receives dividends. When the investor owns between 20 and 50 percent of the investee and uses the equity method for its financial statements, it accrues the income tax expense it expects to pay on its income from the investee as it recognizes its share of that income. That tax due is not immediately payable (it won't be until the dividend is received in cash), but the accrual is recorded as a tax expense when the income is recorded and set up as a deferred tax liability.

Tax regulations permit investor companies to file consolidated tax returns that combine the activities of its investee companies so long as the investor owns 80 or more percent of the investee's voting stock. In those situations, the combined companies pay only one level of tax on their combined income.

When the investor owns more than 50 percent of an investee's voting stock but less than 80 percent, it uses the full consolidation method for its financial statements and recognizes in its consolidated income statements its share of the investee's income. The investor's tax return, however, reflects income from the investment only as it is received as a dividend, in cash. The investor should provide for the taxes on the income that it has recognized in the equity method and that it will have to pay when that investee income is received. Note that the preceding sentence said ''should provide'' rather than ''must provide.'' Accounting rules permit a company to argue against any such provision on the theory that, because it can *control* the investee, it can determine when and how that income will be distributed; thus, it can force the income to be distributed in a tax-free manner.

An investor and an investee who come together in a stock exchange can elect to use the pooling-of-interests method of accounting for tax purposes (referred to as a *tax-free reorganization*) whether or not the transaction is a pooling for financial statement purposes. In those situations, the tax characteristics of the investee carry over into the new combined entity. It may be attractive for companies to arrange such a situation when an investee has tax attributes (i.e., prior operating losses or high tax-basis assets, for instance) that are particularly attractive. That tax-pooling election also may be attractive to the former shareholders of the investee: Their tax basis in the investee stock they gave up carries over to the basis of the investor stock they receive in exchange, and they pay no tax until they decide to sell their new investor stock.

Most acquisitions are treated as purchases for tax purposes, and when they are, the consolidated corporation is entitled to depreciation on the adjusted cost basis of the investee's *identifiable* assets, as incorporated in the consolidated financial statements. (As you might expect, when a transaction is accounted for under the purchase method for tax purposes, the shareholders of the investee company must pay tax at the time of the exchange, based on the difference between their cost basis in the investee stock and the fair value of the consideration they receive.) Tax regulations permit an investor to take a deduction for depreciation or amortization on the new basis of all identifiable assets acquired in a taxable acquisition, except for goodwill. The amortization of goodwill, required by GAAP, is not a deductible expense for tax purposes.

Other Management Considerations

During the 1960s and 1970s, conglomerates were popular with Wall Street on the theory that a diverse company could protect a shareholder in the same way as a diverse portfolio might (i.e., via risk diversification). Companies in cyclical industries sought investees in countercyclical businesses to balance their aggregate income stream. However, some conglomerates became so complex that it became difficult to evaluate how their assets were employed or what the sources of their revenues were. Accounting standard setters have attempted to deal with that problem by insisting that consolidated companies report supplemental, summarized line-of-business information. (See, for example, Chapter 1, which presents line-of-business information for PepsiCo, Inc.)

Even with the availability of line-of-business information, conglomerate companies have fallen out of favor with the investment community, in part because market analysts have become specialized by industry and no single analyst can follow a company as complex as, say, General Electric. Moreover, the more attractive components of a conglomerate were often ignored by the market, causing the stock price of such companies to languish. Given those problems, there has been a move to deconglomerate. Coca-Cola Company, for example, pulled together a large proportion of its bottlers into one investee company and then sold 51 percent of the voting stock in that company to the public. The financial statements of Coca-Cola report its share of the bottling business as a single line on its balance sheet and on its income statement. The bottling company has a higher leverage and a higher level of fixed assets than does the primary Coca-Cola business. The deconsolidation of the bottling business removed that debt and those fixed assets from the consolidated Coca-Cola financial statements.

The following footnote from Coca-Cola's 1986 annual report describes that transaction:

> On September 12, 1986, the Company transferred the operating assets of substantially all previously owned and recently acquired bottling companies in the United States to Coca-Cola Enterprises Inc. (Enterprises), a wholly owned subsidiary. In connection with these transactions, Enterprises assumed approximately $233 million of debt incurred by the Company in conjunction with certain of the acquisitions. In addition, in September 1986, Enterprises acquired the Coca-Cola bottling companies controlled by John T. Lupton and his family and the soft drink bottling operations of BCI Holdings Corporation (the successor to The Beatrice Companies, Inc.) and the remaining interest in The Detroit Bottling Company, Inc. for an aggregate cost of approximately $2.25 billion; these acquisitions were funded with borrowings under a credit agreement entered into by Enterprises with a syndicate of banks. The Company is not a party to the credit agreement and has not guaranteed any of the borrowings thereunder.
>
> On November 21, 1986, Enterprises sold 71.4 million shares of its unissued common stock for net proceeds of approximately $1.12 billion. This transaction reduced the Company's ownership interest to 49 percent and resulted in a pretax gain of $375 million. Consistent with its reduced ownership interest, the Company has commenced reporting its

investment in Enterprises under the equity method of accounting. The consolidated financial statements have been restated to reflect Enterprises under the equity method of accounting for all periods presented. The restatement had no effect on shareholders' equity, income from continuing operations, net income or related per share amounts.

The application of the purchase method of accounting can create significant new values for an investee in the consolidated financial statements of an investor. Those new values must be allocated against future income as depreciation or amortization of goodwill. In theory, the investor's cost "pushed down" to the investee should be spread over the assets in the same way for tax purposes as they are for financial reporting purposes because the judgments required for the asset revaluations should be the same. However, for tax purposes, there is pressure to associate the new "costs" with depreciable assets rather than goodwill to obtain tax deductions for that expense. From a financial statement perspective, there is pressure to associate that "acquisition cost" with goodwill because goodwill can be amortized over a period as long as 40 years—typically a much longer period than the depreciable life used for property, plant, and equipment. Financial managers gather as much evidence as they can about the values of the assets acquired in the purchase so that their judgments are well supported. They also carefully balance the pressures that call for allocating that acquisition cost to short-lived depreciable assets or to goodwill.

SUMMARY

In today's complex business community, it is quite common to find that companies invest in each other. These long-term intercorporate investments are undertaken for a variety of reasons, for example to gain control over a major competitor or supplier, to diversify business risk, and to produce additional income and cash flows.

The financial reporting of these investments is largely dictated by the extent of the investor's stockholdings in the investee. When a relatively small (i.e., less than 20 percent of the outstanding shares) amount of stock is owned, the investor most commonly reports its investment using the lower-of-cost-or-market method. When the size of the investment is sufficient to influence the operating activities of the investee (i.e., usually 20 to 50 percent stockholding), the equity method is most likely to be used. Finally, when an investor gains control of an investee (i.e., its stockholding exceeds 50 percent of the outstanding shares), the financial results of the two companies must be reported on a consolidated basis. Such investments may be accounted for using the purchase method or, under certain circumstances, the pooling-of-interests method.

NEW CONCEPTS AND TERMS

Cumulative Translation Adjustment account (p. 409)
Current rate method (p. 409)
Economic exposure (p. 409)
Equity method (p. 386)
Foreign exchange risk (p. 409)
Functional currency (p. 409)

Passive investment (p. 382)
Pooling-of-interests method (p. 394)
Purchase method (p. 399)
Significant influence (p. 386)
Transaction exposure (p. 409)
Translation exposure (p. 409)

APPENDIX 9

Accounting for Foreign Operations

There appears to be a fairly well-established pattern of evolution for most business enterprises: After successfully establishing a local market, the enterprise then seeks out other new markets. Thus, it is not at all surprising to find that most mature, successful U.S. companies have expanded their area of operations beyond the borders of the United States. When a company does establish operations outside the United States, a question arises as to how best to financially portray those foreign operations.

Essentially, there are two choices. First, the company may prepare financial statements for its foreign operations (i.e., subsidiary, affiliate, or division) using the generally accepted accounting principles of the host foreign country, expressing those statements in the currency (e.g., dollar in Canada, yen in Japan, or peso in Mexico) of the host country. Second, the company may prepare financial statements for its foreign operations using U.S. GAAP and translating the value of those foreign operations into U.S. dollars.

Because of the diversity in GAAP among countries, the FASB has determined that the second option is the most informative one for U.S. analysts, creditors, and investors; thus, it is required for companies issuing publicly traded securities on U.S. exchanges. Consequently, in this appendix, we focus on how such companies translate their foreign operations into U.S. equivalents and how that information can be used to understand the foreign activities of a company. In Chapter 15, we consider the topic of GAAP in foreign countries, focusing specifically on the accounting practices followed by companies in Japan and the United Kingdom to illustrate the diversity of accounting practice between countries.

Foreign Exchange Risk

In prior chapters, we discussed the various types of *risk* that companies face as part of their normal business operations. The two principal types of risk are operating risk and default risk. When a company maintains foreign operations, however, it is also subject to a third type of risk—**foreign exchange risk.** This type of risk occurs because the exchange rates between the U.S. dollar and foreign currencies are rarely stable, creating value changes in international operations.

Foreign exchange risk is usually thought to result from three elements: translation exposure, transaction exposure, and economic exposure. **Translation exposure** occurs as a result of the need to translate (or convert) the financial statements of a foreign division or subsidiary into U.S. dollars in order to prepare consolidated financial statements for the entire company. This type of exposure is solely the result of the *consolidation process* and, consequently, is sometimes referred to as *accounting exposure.* **Transaction exposure** occurs during the normal course of international business transactions when a lag occurs between the date on which a contract is signed or goods delivered and the date of payment. This type of exposure has real cash flow consequences if the exchange rate changes between the date the transaction occurs and the date the currency exchange occurs. **Economic exposure** is a prospective concept focusing on the impact of exchange rate fluctuations on the future operations of a foreign division or subsidiary. Since the value of a foreign subsidiary is equal to the present value of its future cash flows in U.S. dollar equivalents, a change in the exchange rate alters the value of the subsidiary's operations.

Translation of Foreign Operations

In an effort to standardize the accounting for foreign operations, the FASB adopted SFAS No. 52, "Foreign Currency Translation," in 1981. This accounting standard stipulates that the translation of foreign operations should be undertaken using a "functional currency" approach. A company's (or subsidiary's) **functional currency** is defined to be the currency of the primary economic environment in which it operates. Thus, a subsidiary that does business exclusively or principally in Japan has a functional currency of the yen.

Under SFAS No. 52, the foreign subsidiary's accounts should be determined (or redetermined, as the case may be) using U.S. GAAP and initially reported in terms of its functional currency. The foreign subsidiary's financial statements thus prepared are then *translated* into U.S. dollars using the **current rate method.** Under this approach, the subsidiary's income statement is converted into U.S. dollars using the average exchange rate for the period, and its balance sheet is converted at the exchange rate existing on the date of the translation (e.g., December 31).

Gains and losses due to translation (or accounting) exposure are accumulated into an owners' equity account, the **Cumulative Translation Adjustment account,** and have no effect on current income. Gains and losses due to transaction exposure are reported as a separate line item on the company's income statement.

Exhibit 9A–1 illustrates the translation process for FHAS, Inc. Note that since the exchange rate of the U.S. dollar declined relative to the Australian dollar (or alternatively, the Australian dollar increased in value relative to the U.S. dollar), the value of FHAS's Australian subsidiary's net assets and operations increased over the 1990 fiscal year. As a consequence, the prior accumulation in the Translation Adjustment account, represent-

EXHIBIT 9A – 1

FHAS, INC.
Translation of Foreign Financial Statements

FHAS, Inc., is a U.S. corporation with a foreign subsidiary operating principally in Australia. The foreign subsidiary, hereafter called Pty. Limited, was founded in 1980 and had a cumulative translation adjustment of $(10,780) as of January 1, 1990. The exchange rates between the Australian and U.S. dollars in 1990 were as follows:

January 1:	.74	($1 Aus. = $.75 U.S.)
December 31:	.78	($1 Aus. = $.78 U.S.)
Average:	.76	

Pty. Limited
Statement of Income
December 31, 1990

	Australian Dollars (Functional Currency)	Exchange Rate	U.S. Dollars
Sales	$1,148,000	.76	$872,480
Costs and expenses:			
Cost of sales	$ 588,000	.76	$446,880
Depreciation	56,700	.76	43,092
General and administrative	101,500	.76	77,140
Interest	35,000	.76	26,600
	$ 781,200		$593,712
Net income before taxes	366,800		278,768
Income taxes	186,200	.76	141,512
Net income	$ 180,600		$137,256

ing an exchange loss, was eliminated, ultimately ending the period in a gain position. This gain remains unreported until the Australian subsidiary is sold or its operations discontinued.

The translation process illustrated in Exhibit 9A–1 was accomplished using a few basic conventions:

1. Assets and liabilities on the balance sheet are translated at the end-of-period exchange rate.
2. Owners' equity (in this case, common stock and retained earnings) is translated at the exchange rate in effect when the account balance was created.
3. The income statement is translated at the average exchange rate for the period.
4. Dividends are translated at the actual exchange rate at the time of payment.

E X H I B I T   9 A – 1

(continued)

**Pty. Limited
Balance Sheet**

	Beginning-of-Year			End-of-Year		
	Australia $	Exchange Rate	United States $	Australia $	Exchange Rate	United States $
Assets						
Cash	$ 28,000	.75	$ 21,000	$ 63,000	.78	$ 49,140
Accounts receivable	84,000	.75	63,000	103,600	.78	80,808
Inventory	98,000	.75	73,500	140,000	.78	109,200
Property, plant, and equipment (net)	476,700	.75	357,525	462,000	.78	360,360
Total assets	$686,700		$515,025	$768,600		$599,508
Liabilities						
Accounts payable	$ 84,700	.75	63,525	56,000	.78	43,680
Long-term debt	350,000	.75	262,500	280,000	.78	218,400
Total liabilities	$434,700		$326,025	$336,000		$262,080
Stockholders' equity:						
Common stock	$ 42,000	H*	$ 25,830	$ 42,000	H*	$ 25,830
Retained earnings	210,000	H*	173,950	390,600		311,206
Cumulative translation adjustment	—		(10,780)	—		392
Total Equity	$252,000		$189,000	$432,600		$337,428
Total liabilities and equity	$686,700		$515,025	$768,600		$599,508

Reconciliation of ending balance in retained earnings:

	U.S. dollars
Retained earnings, 1/1/1990	$173,950
Net income (restated)	137,256
Retained earnings, 12/31/1990	$311,206

Reconciliation of Cumulative Translation Adjustment account:

Balance, 1/1/1990	$(10,780)
Adjustment for beginning net assets, with increase in exchange rate from $.75 to $.78: $252,000 × $.03	7,560
Adjustment for net income, with increase in exchange rate from average of $.76 to $.78: $180,600 × $.02	3,612
Balance, 12/31/1990	$ 392

*Refers to the historic exchange rate in effect when the account balance was created.

Take a moment to review the income statement and balance sheet in Exhibit 9A–1 and consider the reconciliation of the ending balance in the Retained Earnings and Cumulative Translation Adjustment accounts.

As a consequence of the translation process, financial statement users are able to view, in a single set of financial statements, all of a company's operations—both foreign and domestic—using a consistent set of accounting methods (i.e., U.S. GAAP). Thus, the process of determining whether a company's overall performance has increased (or (declined) is made easier. Note that the process of translating the various accounts of a foreign subsidiary into their U.S. dollar equivalents is a necessary step *preceding* the consolidation of those accounts with the U.S. parent. Once the translation process is complete, the consolidation process as described in Chapter 9 can be undertaken.

ISSUES FOR DISCUSSION

D9.1 What accounting basis should be used for long-term investments in marketable common and preferred stocks of other companies? Should those investments be maintained at cost, market value, or some other value? Why? How should fluctuations in the current market value of long term investments affect the income statement of the investing company? Why? Are long-term investments in marketable bonds of other companies valued in the same manner as long-term investments in marketable equity securities (common and preferred stocks)? Why are they treated the same or differently?

D9.2 Explain in your own words the equity method of accounting for investments in voting common stock. Why is it called the *equity method?* When should it be used?

D9.3 What factors must management consider as they deliberate between the use of the cost method and the equity method?

D9.4 The equity method is occasionally referred to as a "one-line" consolidation. What does that expression mean to you? Is it a fair description of equity accounting?

D9.5 ABC Company was tired of being number two and so it acquired all of the outstanding stock of DEF Company, nearly doubling its sales volume. The next weekend, three promising young managers employed by ABC were discussing the recent acquisition while playing a not-so-quick round of golf. John Russell was ruminating on the accounting and reporting implications of the acquisition and off-handedly referred to it as a *purchase*. Debbie Tepper interrupted him and said that he must never use the word *purchase* again in that context. She argued that the transaction ought to be treated as a pooling because it would be so much easier to explain. At this point, Chris Ruiz spoke up and reminded his two companions that they were having enough trouble with their golf game without worrying about less-important matters such as business combinations. Ruiz then stated that their argument was senseless anyway because in the long-term, there was no real difference between these two accounting methods. Comment on Ruiz' statement. Include both balance sheet and income statement considerations in your discussion.

D9.6 World Wide, Inc., had just completed its acquisition of Local Manufacturing, and the acquisition team was now assessing their prize. The purchase price had been $25,000,000. Local had paid off all of its liabilities prior to the acquisition. The fair value of Local's receivables and inventory seemed to be about the same as the book value, at $8,000,000. The $5,000,000 net book value in equipment and trucks was also approximately equal to fair value. The appraisers were having a hard time coming up with a fair value for local's plant and land, however. One appraiser came in with a value of $5,000,000 for the building and $2,000,000 for the land. Another appraiser came in with values of $6,000,000 for the building and $4,000,000 for the land. Assume that World Wide management pushed the appraisers to reconcile their differences but without success: The variation in the appraisal numbers remained.

As the chief executive officer of World Wide, outline the factors you would consider in making your decision about the appropriate values for Local's plant and land.

D9.7 Financial accounting standards are continually being refined and improved. Perhaps the time has come to revise the accounting standards for marketable equity securities. These assets, by definition, have readily determinable values. Large portfolios can and are valued easily by computer on a daily basis. Would it be better for companies to carry their long-term equitable securities at market values? Should gains and losses resulting from changes in market prices be recorded in income or recorded in an equity account until realized? Argue both sides of this issue and then take a position.

D9.8 The pooling-of-interests method is based on the understanding that two companies of roughly equal size come together to form a new entity; it makes less sense to think of a pooling as a large firm acquiring a smaller one. At what point should pooling be unacceptable due to a relative difference in size between the two firms? Be specific! For example, should it be three times assets, four times revenues?

D9.9 Accounting standards in some countries refuse to acknowledge the notion of purchased goodwill being an asset. If purchased goodwill is not an asset, what should be done with the difference which exists when the purchase price of an acquisition exceeds any fair values that could be assigned to the net assets acquired? Of all the alternative treatments of purchased goodwill that you can identify, what is the best solution?

D9.10 The previous question gives rise to the following question: Why is purchased goodwill not like inventory, property, and equipment? Aren't they all "costs waiting to be expensed"?

PROBLEMS

P9.1 Accounting for intercorporate investments: the equity method. In January 1989, Contran Corp. acquired a 40 percent ownership interest in the National Lock Company, paying $3.5 million. During the year, National Lock declared (and paid) its usual dividends totaling $240,000. Following a year-end audit by its independent auditors, National Lock released its 1989 earnings report, which showed earnings of $850,000 for the year.

Bill Montgomery, controller for Contran, considered this information and how it should be reflected in Contran's 1989 financial statements. With some concern, he also noted that, as of December 31, 1989, Contran's original investment was now worth only $3.25 million—according to National Lock's quoted share prices in the over-the-counter market. He was confident, however, that the market price decline was only temporary, and he expected a full recovery in 1990.

Required:

How should Contran value its investment in National Lock at year-end 1989? Assume that National reported a *loss* of $300,000 for 1989. How would Contran's valuation of National Lock change?

P9.2 Applying the lower-of-cost-or-market method. As of December 31, 1990, Kelsey Corporation held the following long-term investments in marketable securities, all of which represent less than 10 percent of the outstanding stock of the individual companies:

Investment	Cost	Market	Lower of Cost or Market
Common stock of Company A	$ 50,000	$ 75,000	$ 50,000
Preferred stock of Company A	30,000	25,000	25,000
Common stock of Company B	80,000	60,000	60,000
Common stock of Company C	100,000	95,000	95,000
	$260,000	$255,000	$230,000

Required:

At what amount should Kelsey Corporation's long-term investments be shown on its December 31, 1990, balance sheet? Why? Prepare any entry(ies) required.

P9.3 Applying the lower-of-cost-or-market method (continued). During the year ended December 31, 1991, the chief financial officer of Kelsey Corporation (the subject of problem P9.2) became discouraged about the prospects for Company B. The market value of the investment dropped to $45,000, and it was decided to put the investment in Company B up for sale. At December 31, 1991, the investment was transferred to the Current Investment account, and Kelsey's broker was instructed to sell the investment whenever its value came back above $50,000.

The market value of the remaining long-term investments were as follows at December 31, 1991:

Common Stock of Company A	$82,500
Preferred Stock of Company A	28,000
Common Stock of Company C	98,000

Required:

At what amount should Kelsey Corporation's long-term investments be shown on its December 31, 1991, balance sheet? Why? Prepare any entry(ies) required.

P9.4 Applying the equity method. On January 5, 1990, Westover Corporation purchased 30 percent of the outstanding common stock of Graydon Corporation at a total cost of $600,000. During 1990, Graydon Corporation declared and paid quarterly dividends totaling $120,000. For its fiscal year ended December 31, 1990, Graydon Corporation reported net income of $290,000. On December 31, 1990, the market value of Westover Corporation's investment in the common stock of Graydon Corporation was $675,000.

Required:

a. Prepare the entries required for Westover Corporation with respect to its investment in Graydon Corporation for the 1990 fiscal year.

b. At what amount should Westover Corporation's investment in Graydon Corporation be shown on Westover's December 31, 1990, balance sheet? What effect will all of this have on Westover's income statement for 1990?

c. Answer parts *a.* and *b.* assuming this new set of facts: (1) only 10 percent of Graydon Corporation's outstanding common stock was purchased on January 5, 1990; (2) the cost was $200,000; and (3) the December 31, 1990, market value of the investment was $225,000.

P9.5 Accounts affected by purchase accounting. On July 1, 1990, Hager Corporation purchased all of the outstanding shares of Laws Corporation at a total cost of $520 million. Payment consisted of 13 million shares of $1 par value common stock of Hager Corporation having a market value of $40 per share. As of June 30, 1990, the book value and fair market value of Laws Corporation's net assets are shown below:

**Laws Corporation
Balance Sheet Values
(in millions)**

	Book Values (6/30/90)	Fair Market Values (6/30/90)
Assets		
Inventory	$ 31.7	$ 34.1
Other current assets	72.9	72.9
Land	6.3	17.1
Property, plant, and equipment (net)	39.6	63.6
Trademarks and patents	7.9	96.7
	$158.4	$284.4
Liabilities and Stockholders' Equity		
Current liabilities	$ 31.6	$ 31.6
Long-term debt	4.8	4.8
	36.4	36.4
Common Stock ($1 par)	10.9	
Additional paid-in capital	12.3	
Retained earnings	98.8	
	122.0	
	$158.4	

Required:

Assuming that Laws Corporation is to become a wholly owned subsidiary of Hager Corporation, identify the accounts on the consolidated balance sheet of Laws Corporation that will be affected by the acquisition on July 1, 1990, and specify the amounts by which each of these accounts will be affected assuming the following:

a. The purchase method is used.
b. The pooling-of-interests method is used.

P9.6 Application of purchase accounting. The statements of financial position of Company P and Company Q and the fair value of Company Q's assets at December 31, 1990, were as follows (in thousands of dollars):

	Historic Costs		Company Q Fair Value
	Company P	**Company Q**	
Assets:			
Cash	$1,100	$ 50	$ 50
Trade receivables	500	225	225
Inventories	1,000	125	175
Property, plant, and equipment (net)	2,500	250	450
	5,100	650	900
Deduct liabilities	750	100	100
Net assets	4,350	550	800
Stockholders' equity:			
Capital stock (No par)	3,000	200	
Retained earnings	1,350	350	
	$4,350	$550	

Memo: Market value per share at 12/31/90 was $200 for Company P's stock and $400 for Company Q's.

Required:

The management of Company P was considering several approaches to the acquisition of Company Q.

Approach 1. If, as of December 31, 1990, Company P negotiated to purchase the assets and assumed the liabilities of Company Q for $800,000 cash:

a. What entry(ies) would Company P make? Company Q?
b. How would the statements of financial position look for Company P and Company Q after these entries had been made?
c. What entry(ies) would Company P and Company Q make and how would the financial statements look afterward if the purchase price was $900,000 in cash?

Approach 2. If, as of December 31, 1990, Company P negotiated to purchase all of Company Q's assets and assumed all of Company Q's liabilities, as above, but instead of cash payment, the purchase price was 4,000 shares of Company P stock:

d. What entry(ies) would Company P make? Company Q?
e. How would the statements of financial position look for Company P and Company Q after these entries were made?
f. What entry(ies) should Company P and Company Q make and how would the financial statements look afterward if the purchase price were paid to Company Q by issuance of 4,500 shares of Company P's stock?

Approach 3. If, as of December 31, 1990, Company P negotiated to purchase from the stockholders of Company Q their shares for $400 cash per share (Company Q was to become a subsidiary of Company P.):

g. What entry(ies) would Company P make? Company Q?

h. How would the consolidated statement of financial position for Companies P and Q look at December 31, 1990?

i. What entry(ies) would Company P and Company Q make and how would the consolidated statement of financial position look afterward if the price paid for each Company Q share was $450?

Approach 4. If, as of December 31, 1990, Company P negotiated with the stockholders of Company Q to issue 4,000 shares of its voting common stock in exchange for 2,000 shares of Company Q's stock. Company Q was to become a subsidiary of Company P:

j. What entry(ies) would Company P make? Company Q?

k. How would the consolidated statement of financial position of Company P and Company Q look at December 31, 1990?

l. What entry(ies) would Company P and Company Q make and how would the consolidated statement of financial position look afterward if Company P were to exchange 4,500 shares of its stock for all of the 2,000 shares of Company Q?

P9.7 Contrasting the equity method and lower-of-cost-or-market method. The balance sheet of DAE Corporation at December 31, 1990, shows a long-term investment in the common stock of Wallace Corporation of $350,000. The investment was purchased by DAE in January 1987. The following information pertaining to Wallace Corporation is available:

Year	Income or (Loss)	Dividends Paid
1987	($ 30,000)	–0–
1988	120,000	$50,000
1989	150,000	60,000
1990	200,000	80,000

Required:

a. Assuming that DAE Corporation's investment represents a 10 percent interest in Wallace, determine how much DAE paid for Wallace's stock in January 1987.

b. Assuming that DAE Corporation's investment represents a 25 percent interest in Wallace Corporation, determine how much DAE paid for Wallace's stock in January 1987.

P9.8 Contrasting pooling-of-interests and purchase accounting. Preacquisition balance sheets of Al and Syd corporations are shown below:

	Preacquisition Balance Sheets (in thousands)	
	Al Corporation	Syd Corporation
Assets		
Cash	$ 8,000	$ 2,500
Marketable securities	5,000	3,500
Accounts receivable (net)	7,500	5,000
Inventories (LIFO)	19,000	9,500
Fixed assets (net)	38,000	23,000
Other assets	4,500	1,500
Total assets	$82,000	$45,000
Liabilities and stockholder's equity		
Accounts payable	$ 9,500	$ 7,500
Other current liabilities	4,000	3,000
Bonds payable	11,000	
Other long-term debt	7,500	12,500
Common stock ($10 par)	12,000	
Common stock ($5 par)		6,000
Capital in excess of par	7,000	2,000
Retained earnings	31,000	14,000
Total liabilities and stockholders' equity	$82,000	$45,000

Subsequent to a six-month period of intense negotiating, Al Corporation agreed to purchase all of the outstanding common stock of Syd Corporation at a price of $29.4 million. In arriving at this price, Al Corporation placed the following fair market values on Syd Corporation's assets:

Asset	Fair Market Value (thousands)
Cash	$ 2,500
Marketable securities	4,500
Accounts receivable (net)	3,500
Inventories	13,000
Fixed assets (net)	28,000
Other assets	0
Total	$51,500

According to the terms of the agreement, Al Corporation was to issue one share of its common stock in exchange for each share of Syd Corporation's outstanding common stock. Subsequent to the exchange of common stock, Syd Corporation was to become a wholly owned subsidiary of Al Corporation. The current market price of Al Corporation's common stock was $24.50 per share.

Required:

Al Corporation expects to be able to account for its acquisition of Syd Corporation using the pooling-of-interests method. There is, however, some question about a possible violation of one of the numerous pooling criteria. You have been asked by Al Corporation's management to prepare a consolidated balance sheet to reflect the acquisition of Syd Corporation under both the pooling-of-interests and the purchase methods of accounting.

P9.9 Application of the pooling-of-interests method of accounting. On November 9, 1990, Shea & Shea Corporation merged with Garbo Associates by an exchange of one share of Shea & Shea for one share of Garbo. Shea & Shea issued 1,891,678 of its shares and accounted for the transaction using the pooling-of-interests rather than the purchase method. In accounting for the issue of 1,891,678 shares, Shea & Shea increased its no-par common stock account $3,300,000.

Garbo's net assets on November 9, 1990, can be approximated:

Capital stock (1,891,678 shares)		$ 3.3 million
Retained earnings at 12/31/89	$25.5	
Net income 1/1/90 to 11/9/90 (313 days)		
313/365 of $6.2	$5.3	
Less dividends	2.1 3.2	
		$28.7 million
Garbo's estimated owners' equity (net assets)		$32.0 million

For purposes of the questions to follow, assume that the market value of Shea & Shea stock at November 9, 1990, was $50 a share, or a total of $94.6 million for the 1,891,678 shares issued in the exchange.

Required:

a. What entry did Shea & Shea make to record the acquisition of Garbo? Why?

b. What difference(s) would it have made if Shea & Shea had treated the transaction under the purchase rather than the pooling-of-interests method?

c. If you had been a Garbo stockholder, are there any reasons that you would have preferred receiving one share of Shea & Shea stock for each Garbo share you owned rather than $50 in cash?

d. If you were a part of Shea & Shea's management, are there any reasons you would have preferred treating the share-for-share exchange under the pooling-of-interests method rather than under the purchase method?

P9.10 Application of consolidation accounting. Joann Jones was the plant manager of World Wide Incorporated's California assembly plant. She was pulling together the material for the company's year-end reporting package to send to World Wide's home office. Her systems people gave her the following statistical detail for the year:

	Actual Invoice Cost		
Supplier	Beginning Inventory	Purchases	Ending Inventory
Worldwide subsidiaries:			
Arizona	$25,000	$175,000	$20,000
Northeast	15,000	125,000	18,000
Southwest	12,000	250,000	10,000
Outside contractors:			
National	14,000	85,000	12,000
Amalgamated	8,000	62,000	6,500

World Wide's home office told Jones that the Arizona plant had experienced a 25 percent profit rate during the last several years, Northwest had experienced a 20 percent rate, and Southwest had experienced a 15 percent rate.

Required:

Calculate for Jones the value of her plant's ending inventory and material segment of the cost of goods sold for the year.

P9.11 Analyzing Acquisition Data. The pertinent information concerning Bausch & Lomb was extracted from the company's annual report for 1989. Presented below is an excerpt from the president's letter describing the first full year of the company's new oral care division. Also presented are excerpts from the footnotes describing the company's acquisition of Dental Research Corporation in 1988. It is also important to know that Bausch & Lomb reported the following results for the three years ended December 31, 1989:

	1989	1988	1987
Net earnings (000)	$114,367	$97,886	$85,340
Earnings per share	$ 3.78	$ 3.27	$ 2.81

Required:

Based on this information, answer the following questions:

a. How much did Bausch & Lomb pay to acquire Dental Research? What did it get for its money? What does the figure $119,000 represent? As a member of management, how might you feel about that figure? As a former stockholder of Dental research? As a stockholder of Bausch & Lomb?

b. What do the earnings numbers below tell you? If you had an opportunity to interview the management of Bausch & Lomb, what questions might you ask about the performance of the company?

c. How would Bausch & Lomb's results have been different if the company had used the pooling-of-interests method to account for the acquisition?

Bausch & Lomb
Excerpts from President's Letter to Shareholders

In our new oral care business, sales of *Interplak* instruments are very effective against dental plaque, and their clinically documented performance has led to a high rate of recommendation by dental professionals.

Another step in developing a full line of oral care products was taken in 1989 with the successful introduction of the *Interprobe* periodontal exam and

charting system used to diagnose and monitor gum disease. In 1990 the oral care line will be expanded further by the addition of an *Interplak* brand of toothpaste specially formulated for use with the *Interplak* device. The year will also see *Interplak* products marketed extensively in Europe and the Far East for the first time.

Baush & Lomb
Excerpts from Footnotes: Dental Research Corp.

During the fourth quarter of 1988, the company acquired all shares of Dental Research Corporation for $133,000,000 in cash and promissory notes and established the company's oral care division. The division manufactures and markets the patented *Interplak* line of devices used by consumers for the removal of dental plaque. The acquisition has been accounted for as a purchase and, accordingly, the net assets and results of operations of Dental Research Corporation have been included in the company's consolidated financial statements commencing on November 1, 1988. The total acquisition cost exceeded the fair value of the net assets acquired by approximately $119,000,000, and this amount is being amortized over a forty-year period on a straight-line basis.

The following unaudited pro forma summary combines the consolidated results of operations of the company and Dental Research Corporation as if the acquisition had occurred at the beginning of the 1988

and 1987 fiscal years, after giving effect to certain adjustments, including the amortization of goodwill, increased interest expense on the acquisition debt and related income tax effects. This pro forma summary does not necessarily reflect the results of operations as they would have been if the company and Dental Research Corporation had constituted a single entity during such periods.

	Fiscal Years	
	1988	**1987**
	(Unaudited)	
Net sales	$1,032,128*	$870,710
Net earnings	96,580	78,466
Net earnings per common share	3.23	2.58

*Dollar amounts in thousands except per share data

CASES

C9.1 Consolidated vs. unconsolidated reporting: UFS Corporation. ''Why me?'' thought Connie Likert. ''My first day on the job at the bank and instead of getting a company with a nice single set of financial statements, I get five separate sets of statements that supposedly fit together.''

Likert had just started as a new credit analyst for the First National Bank of Bruceton Mills, having just completed an MBA degree with a major in finance at the local university. From the loan officer responsible for this client, Likert learned the following information about each of the four companies associated with UFS Corporation and about UFS Corporation itself.

UFS Corporation. UFS Corporation is a manufacturing company whose principal products are microwave ovens, refrigerators, and conventional ovens. The company has had a long history (more than 50 years) of selling high-quality, high-priced home appliances; however, recent reductions in the price of competitor products forced UFS to consider ways to provide assistance to its customers to help them buy its products. As a consequence, UFS started its own finance subsidiary, the UFS Acceptance Corporation, to assist customers in financing their purchases.

UFS Corporation is also associated with three other companies. It holds an 80 percent interest in Scrub-All, a company that makes automatic dishwashers. UFS purchased this interest in Scrub-All because the company's product line complemented its own items, and the products were of a quality that UFS would have had difficulty duplicating. Further, to ensure a steady supply of chrome parts for its appliances, UFS obtained a 10 percent interest in the common stock of Acme Chrome Company. Well over 50 percent of Acme's sales were attributed to purchases by UFS and Scrub-All. Further, to compete in the low-end market for various appliances, UFS Corporation formed a joint venture with Whirlwind Products Co. to produce such appliances.

UFS Acceptance Corporation. Created nearly five years ago, UFS Acceptance Corporation is a wholly owned subsidiary that purchases consumer notes from its parent, UFS Corporation. UFS Acceptance borrows funds from several banking institutions on a medium- and long-term basis, and uses the margins between the short-term interest rates on the consumer notes and the rates on its medium- and long-term liabilities to cover its overhead costs. The parent company guarantees all of the borrowings of UFS Acceptance Corporation.

Scrub-All Company. With an ownership interest of 80 percent of the common stock of Scrub-All, UFS Corporation controls the tactical and strategic policies of Scrub-All Company through an interlocking board of directors. Scrub-All, like UFS, sold its consumer notes to UFS Acceptance Corporation. The family that originally started Scrub-All still holds a 20 percent ownership interest in the common stock of the company.

Acme Chrome Company. To guarantee a steady supply of chrome parts and a quality cadre of people who could work with the engineers of UFS in the design of new parts, UFS purchased a 10 percent interest in Acme Chrome Company. Over the years, a strong relationship had developed between UFS and Acme. For example, Acme schedules the production runs of its other customers around the production needs of UFS and Scrub-All.

Spotless Appliance Company. Both UFS Corporation and Whirlwind Products Company (an otherwise unrelated company) contributed half of the funds necessary to start Spotless Appliance Company. Spotless Appliance Company makes low-end priced appliance models that are sold under the Spotless trade name or are labeled with various department store names. The board of directors of Spotless Appliance Company consists of an equal number of members voted in by each of UFS Corporation and Whirlwind Products Company and three members from outside either of the respective companies. Any debt of Spotless is guaranteed by both UFS Corporation and Whirlwind Products Company.

Kirk Tennant, the loan officer responsible for UFS, provided Likert with the financial statements of the five companies (presented on the following pages) and asked her to answer some basic credit review questions concerning an expansion loan application that had been received from UFS management. Before Likert could complete the credit review, she identified the following questions that needed to be answered so that she could understand the relationship between the various companies.

Required:

a. Why are the investments in Acme Chrome and Spotless Appliance Companies shown on the UFS Corporation balance sheet while the investments in Scrub-All and UFS Acceptance Corporation are omitted?

b. What is meant by the carrying value "at equity" for the investment in Spotless Appliance Company?

c. Why is the investment in Acme Chrome Company shown "at cost"?

d. Explain the Goodwill account. What other name is sometimes used instead of *goodwill* and to what company is this account related?

e. What is meant by "minority interest" and to what company is this account related? Is this a liability or an equity account?

f. What are UFS Corporation's current ratio, debt-to-equity ratio, and debt-to-asset ratio? Are these ratios at an acceptable level?

g. How would the balance sheet of UFS Corporation appear if Spotless Appliance Company were consolidated? Would you recommend consolidation for Spotless?

h. How would the ratios calculated in part *f* differ after the consolidation of Spotless Appliance? Can an argument be made for consolidating Acme Chrome Company?

i. How would the balance sheet of the parent company appear without including any of the consolidated subsidiaries? Which balance sheet would you use to make this credit decision?

UFS CORPORATION
Consolidated Statement of Financial Position
December 31, 1990

Assets

Current assets	$ 37,500,000
Notes receivable	58,000,000
Investment in stock of Spotless Appliance at equity (50%)	1,750,000
Investment in stock of Acme Chrome Company (10%) at cost	5,600,000
Other assets	101,500,000
Goodwill	3,200,000
Total assets	$207,550,000

Liabilities and Stockholders' Equity

Current liabilities	$ 31,500,000
Long-term liabilities	102,100,000
Minority interest	7,500,000
Common stock	15,000,000
Retained earnings	51,450,000
Total liabilities and stockholders' equity	$207,550,000

UFS ACCEPTANCE CORPORATION
Statement of Financial Position
December 31, 1990

Assets

Current assets	$ 8,000,000
Notes receivable	58,000,000
Other assets	6,500,000
Total assets	$72,500,000

Liabilities and Stockholders' Equity

Current liabilities*	$ 5,000,000
Long-term debt	47,100,000
Common stock ($1 par)	10,000,000
Retained earnings	10,400,000
Total liabilities and equities	$72,500,000

---

*$3,000,000 of the current liabilities is a promissory note to UFS Corporation. UFS Corporation accounts for this as a long-term receivable in other assets.

SCRUB-ALL COMPANY
Statement of Financial Position
December 31, 1990

Assets

Current assets	$16,400,000
Other assets	52,600,000
Total assets	$69,000,000

Liabilities and Stockholders' Equity

Current liabilities	$13,350,000
Long-term liabilities	18,150,000
Common stock	12,000,000
Retained earnings	25,500,000
Total liabilities and stockholders' equity	$69,000,000

ACME CHROME COMPANY
Statement of Financial Position
December 31, 1990

Assets

Current assets	$14,750,000
Other assets	36,250,000
Total assets	$51,000,000

Liabilities and Stockholders' Equity

Current liabilities	$ 5,000,000
Long-term liabilities	15,000,000
Capital stock	18,750,000
Retained earnings	12,250,000
Total liabilities and stockholders' equity	$51,000,000

SPOTLESS APPLIANCE COMPANY
Statement of Financial Position
December 31, 1990

Assets

Current assets	$ 8,500,000
Other assets	16,000,000
Total assets	$24,500,000

Liabilities and Stockholders' Equity

Current liabilities	$ 3,000,000
Long-term debt	18,000,000
Common stock ($1 par)	6,000,000
Retained earnings	(2,500,000)
Total liabilities and equities	$24,500,000

C9.2 Purchase vs. Pooling: The Steady Growth Saga. Steady Growth, Inc. (SGI), began business in 1974, as part of an effort to popularize natural foods, a subject that was of passionate interest to its founders. The founding group was part counterculture and part agricultural engineer. It successfully developed a line of alternative, organic fertilizers and pesticides. Sales grew modestly but steadily and by 1981 had reached $25 million a year. SGI produced 30 different items all sold under the Steady Growth trade name. Organic farmers marketed their products explaining that they used only Steady Growth products; natural food stores specifically advertised products as "grown the Steady Growth way." To provide funds for its own growth and to share the benefits of the business, SGI sold stock in 1982 to the natural food wholesale and retail community. The founding group retained about 60 percent of the stock, but the publicly held shares traded occasionally on the Pacific Coast Exchange at prices that approximated SGI's book value per share, about $20.

In early 1989, the press was full of stories about chemical contamination of the apple and other fruit crops. Overnight, the general public became interested in organically grown produce and SGI found itself swamped with orders. As the spring planting season began, SGI's inventory was completely sold out and production capacity for the year was committed by orders taken in March. SGI management looked at its order books and decided that the company might be ready finally to move into the really "big time." They worked with a team of financial advisers and developed a plan for a management-led leveraged buy-out. They arranged to borrow the requisite funds and proposed a cash repurchase of all the stock in the hands of the public at $30 a share.

But SGI was not the only company to notice the public interest in natural foods. Enormous, Inc., a large food chain, notified SGI's board of directors that it would be interested in acquiring the company. Later SGI's board received a similar proposal from an international chemical concern. A spirited bidding war ensued. After several weeks of intense negotiations, SGI's board agreed to recommend to the shareholders that they tender their stock to Enormous in a share-for-share exchange. Enormous' shares were actively traded, and on the day of the announcement, the market price of its stock was $40 a share.

The exchange was completed on September 30, 1989, and SGI became a wholly owned subsidiary of Enormous. Some of the founders of SGI took their new-found wealth and left to pursue other interests. Some stayed on, in part because of the salary promised by Enormous and in part because they still believed in the need to promote the cause of natural foods. Enormous sent in a team of transitional managers to help get SGI into the mainstream. As part of their initial review, the Enormous team members determined that the book value of SGI's assets and liabilities equaled their market values, with a few exceptions: SGI's land had appreciated to a current market value of $4,500,000 and the equipment (which had all been handmade) had a current value of $6,000,000. On the other hand, SGI had been rather lenient with its credit policies, and the Enormous staff determined that an additional doubtful account allowance of $500,000 was required. The transitional team also noted that SGI had paid $1,250,000 for a 15 percent interest in a fruit drink business, which was now worth only $1,000,000. SGI had been committed to the fruit drink company, but as part of the planning for the leveraged buyout, management had decided to sell the investment and had transferred the asset to the current category. Finally, SGI's original funding had been in the form of a government-subsidized loan, which had carried a 5 percent interest rate. Because of the low interest rate, the present value of the loan was now only $17,500,000.

The trade name Steady Growth was registered to SGI and was now an Enormous asset. Unfortunately, none of the industry experts on the transitional team were able to put a market value on that asset.

Required:

a. Using the preacquisition historical data presented below, prepare consolidated balance sheets for Enormous as of September 30, 1989, giving effect to the acquisition of SGI. Prepare one balance sheet assuming that the purchase method was used in the acquisition and one assuming the pooling-of-interests method was used.

b. What consolidated earnings will Enormous report in its interim report for the nine months ended September 30, 1989?
   (1). Under the purchase method?
   (2). Under the pooling-of-interests method?

c. When will the extra $500,000 allowance for doubtful accounts appear as a provision in an income statement under the pooling-of-interests method? Under the purchase method?

d. At what amount did you record SGI's appreciated land? At what amount did you record Enormous' appreciated long-term investments? Did you treat them the same? If not, why not?

e. At what amount did you record the stock issued to the SGI shareholders? Did you record the stock issued at the same amount for both the purchase and pooling-of-interests methods? If so, why? If not, what happened to the difference?

f. Outline the pros and cons that might be presented in arguments for or against the pooling-of-interests and purchase methods of accounting in this situation.

ENORMOUS, INC.
Preconsolidated Balance sheet
September 30, 1989
(millions)

	Preacquisition Historical Data	
	Enormous	**SGI**
Current assets		
Cash	$ 31.0	$ 2.0
Accounts receivable	15.0	4.5
Inventories	31.0	0.5
Investments		1.0
Total current assets	77.0	8.0
Fixed assets (net of accumulated depreciation)		
Machinery and equipment	25.0	5.0
Buildings	112.0	18.0
Trucks	54.0	0.5
Land	19.0	2.5
Net Fixed Assets	210.0	26.0
Investments (market value $12)	8.0	
Goodwill	2.0	
Total assets	$297.0	$34.0
Current liabilities		
Accounts payable	$ 25.0	$ 6.0
Accrued expenses	12.0	3.5
Total current liabilities	37.0	9.5
Mortgages and loans payable	165.0	18.0
Owners' equity		
Common Stock		
Retained Earnings		
Total Owners' Equity	95.0	6.5
Total liabilities and equity	$297.0	$34.0
Earnings, 1/1/89 to 9/30/89	$3.02	$2.78
Shares outstanding	1,250,000	40,625
Market price per share of common stock	$40	$20

C9.3 Analyzing consolidated statements: Sony Corporation. On the following pages are the consolidated balance sheets of the Sony Corporation's 1990 annual report. Footnote 1 of this annual report included the following:

Basis of consolidation and accounting for investments in affiliated companies

The consolidated financial statements include the accounts of the parent company and, with minor exceptions, those of its majority-owned subsidiary companies. All significant intercompany transactions and accounts are eliminated. Investments in 20% to 50% owned companies are stated, with minor exceptions, at cost plus equity in undistributed earnings; consolidated net income includes the company's equity in current earnings of such companies, after elimination of unrealized intercompany profits.

The excess of the cost over the underlying net equity of investments in consolidated subsidiaries and affiliated companies accounted for on an equity basis is allocated to identifiable assets based on fair market value at the date of acquisition. The unassigned residual value, which is recognized as goodwill, is amortized on a straight-line basis principally over a 40-year period, with the exception of minor amounts which are charged to income in the year of acquisition.

Footnote 2 was as follows:

2. U.S. dollar amounts

U.S. dollar amounts are included solely for convenience. These translations should not be construed as representations that the yen amounts actually represent, or have been or could be converted into, U.S. dollars. As the amounts shown in U.S. dollars are for convenience only, the rate of ¥ 157 = U.S. $1, the approximate current rate at March 30, 1990, has been used for the purpose of presentation of the U.S. dollar amounts in the accompanying financial statements.

Footnote 3 included the following paragraphs pertaining to acquisitions:

3. Acquisitions

On January 5, 1988, the company acquired from CBS Inc. all of the outstanding common stock of CBS Records Inc. and its affiliates, which are operating primarily in the record business, for approximately U.S. $2 billion in cash. The purchase agreement provides for an additional payment in the form of a dividend to CBS Inc. from the acquired company based on its net worth at the acquisition date. The amount of the additional payment is still subject to the determination of net worth.

In November 1989, the company acquired all of the outstanding shares of common stock of Columbia Pictures Entertainment, Inc. (CPE) and The Guber-Peters Entertainment Company (GPEC), which are operating primarily in the film business, for approximately U.S. $3.4 billion and U.S. $0.2 billion, respectively.

All of the acquisitions were accounted for as purchases and the company's consolidated financial statements include operating results of the acquired companies for the periods from the dates of acquisition. The excess of the purchase price over the net assets acquired has been allocated to identifiable assets such as inventories, land, property, plant and equipment and intangible assets (primarily artist contracts and music catalogues), based upon the estimated fair value of such assets. The excess of the acquisition costs over the amounts preliminarily assigned to identifiable assets less liabilities assumed is recognized as goodwill.

Property, plant and equipment and various intangible assets, after the above allocations, are depreciated or amortized based on estimated useful lives. In the case of artist contracts and music catalogues, the amounts are amortized on a straight-line basis principally over 16 years and 21 years, respectively. Goodwill is being amortized on a straight-line basis principally over a 40-year period.

Required:

Part 1.

  a. Sony acquired CBS Records in 1988 and Columbia Pictures in 1989. Where, if at all, do these investments appear on the balance sheets of Sony Corporation presented on pages 430 and 431?
  b. Footnote 1 refers to investments carried "at cost plus equity in undistributed earnings." What does this mean? What are some reasons why an investment such as this might *decline* in its carrying value?
  c. Footnote 1 also says that "consolidated net income includes the company's equity in current earnings of such companies, after elimination of unrealized intercompany profits."
  (1). What is meant by "unrealized intercompany profits"?
  (2). Why are unrealized intercompany profits eliminated?

Part 2 We now concern ourselves with Sony's acquisition of Columbia Pictures. In November 1989, Sony acquired all of the common stock of Columbia Pictures for ¥ 534 billion (U.S. $3.4 billion) cash. You may assume that Sony did *not* revalue any of Columbia's assets or liabilities when it brought Columbia onto its (Sony's) books.

The condensed March 31, 1990, balance sheet for Sony is given in Column 1; whereas Column 2 presents Columbia Pictures' balance sheet just prior to acquisition (converted into yen). Of course, there could be differences in Sony's balance sheet between the date of acquisition of Columbia, November 1989, and the published March 31, 1990, financial statements, but we will ignore them. We assume that Column 1 depicts Sony's consolidated balance sheet immediately *after* the acquisition of Columbia.

(All figures in billions of yen.)

	(1) Sony and Columbia Consolidated	(2) Columbia Pictures
Current assets	2,197	126
Film inventories (total)	173	173
Property, and investments (net)	1,037	125
Goodwill and other assets	963	125
Total assets	4,370	549
Total liabilities	2,923	392
Minority interests	17	—
Net assets	1,430	157
Common stock	698	173
Retained earnings	695	(16)
Other	37	—
Total equity	1,430	157

d. Using the summary information presented above, prepare a balance sheet for the Sony Corporation as it would have appeared *before* the acquisition of Columbia.

e. Prepare a consolidated balance sheet for the Sony Corporation and its Columbia Pictures' subsidiary subsequent to the acquisition assuming Sony had acquired Columbia by issuing 66.75 million common shares (market value ¥ 534 billion) and had accounted for the acquisition under the pooling-of-interests method.

Sony Corporation and Consolidated Subsidiaries
Consolidated Balance Sheets

	Millions of yen		Thousands of U.S. dollars (Note 2)
	March 31		March 31,
	1989	1990	1990
Assets			
Current assets:			
Cash and cash equivalents (Note 4)......................................	¥ 297,889	¥ 451,668	$ 2,876,866
Time deposits (note 9)..	33,665	182,533	1,162,631
Marketable securities (Note 7)...................................	91,115	54,784	348,943
Notes and accounts receivable, trade (Note 6)......................	432,692	696,950	4,439,172
Allowance for doubtful accounts and sales returns................	(32,957)	(46,560)	(296,561)
Inventories (Note 5)	483,648	692,966	4,413,796
Income tax prepayments	51,408	57,637	367,115
Prepaid expenses and other current assets..........................	76,338	111,555	710,541
Total current assets...	1,433,798	2,201,533	14,022,503
Noncurrent inventories—film (Notes 5 and 14)	—	168,788	1,075,083
Investments and advances..			
Affiliated companies (Note 6)	16,015	14,834	94,484
Officers and employees	2,445	2,315	14,745
Security investments and other (Note 7).............................	94,975	151,213	963,140
	113,435	168,362	1,072,369
Property, plant, and equipment (Notes 9 and 14):			
Land...	86,964	114,002	726,127
Buildings...	267,351	415,835	2,648,631
Machinery and equipment	726,564	908,646	5,787,554
Construction in progress..	24,611	90,693	577,663
	1,105,490	1,529,176	9,739,975
Less—Accumulated depreciation..	560,714	661,048	4,210,497
	544,776	868,128	5,529,476
Other assets (Notes 3 and 8):			
Intangibles..	141,779	168,748	1,074,828
Goodwill	59,168	629,401	4,008,923
Other	71,819	165,125	1,051,752
	272,766	963,274	6,135,503
	¥2,364,775	¥4,370,085	$27,834,936

	Millions of yen		Thousands of U.S. dollars (Note 2)
	March 31		March 31,
	1989	1990	1990
Liabilities and Stockholders' Equity			
Current liabilities:			
Short-term borrowings (Note 9)................................	¥ 224,637	¥ 757,017	$ 4,821,764
Current portion of long-term debt (Notes 9 and 14)...............	12,797	76,715	488,631
Notes and accounts payable, trade (Note 6)	468,784	580,932	3,700,204
Notes payable, construction	21,323	27,375	174,363
Dividends payable..	6,461	8,770	55,860
Accrued income and other taxes.....................................	84,752	112,664	717,605
Other accounts payable and accrued liabilities......................	266,568	432,418	2,754,254
Total current liabilities..	1,085,322	1,995,891	12,712,681
Long-term liabilities:			
Long-term debt (Notes 9 and 14).....................................	220,790	645,969	4,114,452
Accrued pension and severance costs (Note 10)	61,319	70,949	451,904
Deferred income taxes..	36,928	46,493	296,134
Other long-term liabilities...	33,699	163,846	1,043,605
	352,736	927,257	5,906,095
Minority interest in consolidated subsidiary companies.............	14,901	16,879	107,510
Stockholders' equity (Note 12):			
Common stock, ¥50 par value—			
Authorized—920,000,000 shares			
Issued: 1989—282,602,923 shares	114,641		
1990—331,928,730 shares		278,038	1,770,943
Additional paid-in capital...	232,050	419,417	2,671,446
Legal reserve	10,535	13,566	86,408
Retained earnings appropriated for special allowances..........	16,313	20,547	130,872
Retained earnings..	600,184	674,962	4,299,121
Cumulative translation adjustment	(61,907)	23,528	149,860
	911,816	1,430,058	9,108,650
Commitments and contingent liabilities (Note 15)			
	¥2,364,775	¥4,370,085	$27,834,936

The accompanying notes are an integral part of these statements.

C9.4 Purchase vs. pooling: Alliance Corporation. Subsequent to an unsuccessful hostile takeover attempt, Alliance Corporation entered into friendly negotiations for the acquisition of Felker Corporation. Following a two-month period of discussions, Alliance Corporation agreed to purchase all of the outstanding common stock of Felker Corporation at a price of $36 million. In arriving at this price, Alliance Corporation placed the following fair market values on Felker Corporation's assets at the time of acquisition:

Felker's Assets	Fair Market Values ($ thousands)
Cash	$ 1,300
Marketable securities	1,800
Accounts receivable (net)	1,900
Inventories	10,700
Fixed assets (net)	21,400
Patents	5,500
Other assets	–0–
Goodwill	–0–
Total	$42,600

According to the terms of the agreement, Alliance Corporation was to issue *two* shares of its common stock in exchange for each share of Felker Corporation's outstanding common stock. Subsequent to the acquisition, Felker was to become a wholly owned subsidiary of Alliance. The market price of Alliance Corporation's common stock at the time of the acquisition was $45 per share.

Required:

Alliance Corporation expects to be able to account for its acquisition of Felker Corporation using the pooling-of-interests method. The resulting consolidated balance sheet under this method follows. Also shown is Felker Corporation's preacquisition balance sheet. Using these two balance sheets and the information provided above, prepare the preacquisition balance sheet for Alliance Corporation and the consolidated balance sheet, assuming the acquisition is accounted for using the purchase method.

	Preacquisition Balance Sheets ($ thousands)		Consolidated Balance Sheets ($ thousands)	
	Alliance Corp.	Felker Corp.	Purchase Method	Pooling-of-Interests Method
Assets				
Cash	————	$ 1,300	————	$ 4,800
Marketable securities	————	1,500	————	3,900
Accounts receivable (net)	————	2,100	————	7,300
Inventories	————	11,800	————	35,500
Fixed assets (net)	————	18,600	————	60,000
Patents	————	1,700	————	5,700
Other assets	————	500	————	2,800
Goodwill	————	1,500	————	1,500
Total	$————	$39,000	$————	$121,500
Liabilities and Stockholders' Equity				
Accounts payable	————	$ 2,700	————	$ 11,200
Other current liabilities	————	1,400	————	4,400
Long-term debt	————	8,000	————	28,000
Common stock (no par)	————	1,400	————	20,100
Retained earnings	————	25,500	————	57,800
Total	$————	$39,000	$————	$121,500

CHAPTER 10

Noncurrent Assets: Fixed Assets, Intangible Assets, and Natural Resources

N oncurrent assets represent the principal long-term revenue-producing assets of most companies. In the case of a manufacturing company, the fixed assets (or property, plant, and equipment) are used to manufacture the products that are ultimately sold to customers. In the case of a computer software development company, a copyright on a computer software package provides the company with the monopolistic right to the earnings stream associated with the sale of the package. In the case of an oil and gas company, the oil and gas properties or leaseholds the company owns provide it with access to new salable reserves.

The focus of this chapter is on the analysis and financial reporting issues pertaining to these three types of noncurrent assets. Two important financial reporting questions characterize the financial management of these assets: What cost should be assigned to the asset (i.e., capitalized to the balance sheet)? How should the asset's cost systematically be expensed (i.e., matched) against the revenues produced by the asset?

FIXED ASSETS AND DEPRECIATION

Fixed assets are long-lived tangible assets acquired with the intention of deriving a benefit from their *use* in a business rather than from their resale. Fixed assets include such *property, plant, and equipment* (PP&E) as buildings; land used or held as factory and office locations (not depreciable); land improvements such as landscaping, parking lots, and so on; machinery and equipment; office furniture and fixtures; and vehicles.

The primary financial reporting issues associated with fixed assets that must be addressed by managers are the following:

1. Determining the cost to be recorded in the balance sheet at the time of acquisition (i.e., the capitalization issue).
2. Determining the annual income statement depreciation expense to be reported (i.e., the allocation issue). In this regard, decisions must be made regarding the preferred depreciation method, the estimated useful life of the asset, and its estimated salvage value.
3. Distinguishing between those fixed asset-related expenditures made subsequent to the initial acquisition (e.g., repairs and improvements) that should be expensed when incurred and those that should be capitalized (i.e., added to the asset's reported balance sheet value) and subsequently depreciated over future periods.
4. Accounting for the sale or other disposition of an asset.

Determining Original Cost: The Capitalization Issue

Fixed assets are initially reported in the balance sheet at their original cost (i.e., the outlay of cash or cash equivalents at the date of purchase). Generally, the original acquisition cost of a fixed asset includes *all* costs incurred in getting the asset ready for its intended use. For example, surveying costs incurred in obtaining title to a tract of land are a part of the land's acquisition cost. If a tract of land has a building on it that is not needed by the purchaser, the cost of razing the building is also a part of the purchaser's cost of the land. In addition, when a company contracts with another party to construct a new building, all costs incurred up to the time the building is turned over to the company are part of its acquisition cost. Such costs are likely to include architect's fees, payments to the contractor, and interest on the funds borrowed to complete the construction of the property. In the case of machinery and equipment, original cost includes purchase price, freight in, and the cost of initial installation. An example regarding these items is presented in Exhibit 10.1.

As an incentive to purchase a particular piece of equipment, sellers often offer discounts to potential purchasers. When a cash discount is received on the purchase of equipment (or any other asset, for that matter), the equipment's cost should be reported net of the discount. Another means to attract potential buyers involves various

EXHIBIT 10.1

Determining the Cost of an Asset

Omar Corporation paid $200,000 for a tract of land that had an old gas station on it. The gas station was razed at a cost of $10,000, and a new warehouse was constructed at a cost of $250,000. In addition, several other costs were incurred:

Legal fees (for the purchase of the land)	$ 5,000
Architect's fees	22,000
Interest on construction loan	18,000

Omar Corporation should record two assets as follows:

Dr. Land (A) $215,000
 Cr. Cash (A) $215,000

(The value of the land is determined as follows: $200,000 + $10,000 + $5,000 = $215,000.)

Dr Building (A) $290,000
 Cr. Cash (A) $290,000

(The value of the building is determined as follows: $250,000 + $22,000 + $18,000 = $290,000.)
  It is important to distinguish between the land and the building because only the building will be depreciated. The land will not be depreciated but will continue to be reported at its original cost until it is sold.

seller-sponsored financing plans. For example, a buyer's recorded cost when fixed assets are sold on an installment payment basis is not the sum of the total payments to be made but is the present value of the installment obligation (i.e., today's cash-equivalent purchase price) as of the date of purchase. Present value will be discussed in Chapter 11. Fixed assets also may be acquired by issuing a company's capital stock. In this case, the cash-equivalent value of the issued stock as of the date of the transaction should be used to measure the cost of acquiring the assets. Sometimes an old asset is traded in on a new one (e.g., a used truck for a new one). In such an arrangement, the cash-equivalent value of the old asset plus the cash paid for the new one becomes the acquisition cost of the new asset to be reported on the balance sheet.

   It is important to note that a popular means by which corporate managers may obtain property is to lease it under a long-term, noncancelable lease. If the lease meets certain criteria, generally accepted accounting principles stipulate the recording of a leasehold right as an asset and a lease obligation as a liability. Under these circumstances, the leased asset would be depreciated in the same way as any other fixed asset owned by the company, except that the depreciation period may be limited by the lease term. A more detailed description of lease accounting is provided in Chapter 12.

Depreciation: The Allocation Issue

The purpose of recording depreciation is to reflect the "using up" of the productive capacity of a company's PP&E and to match this cost of doing business with the revenues that the PP&E helped generate. The process of recording depreciation is nothing more than allocating the depreciable cost (i.e., recorded cost less estimated salvage value) of a company's PP&E to the accounting periods during which the PP&E is used. Depreciating PP&E is, however, not intended to establish a market valuation process for the PP&E. (A word of caution: Sometimes the business use of the term *property, plant, and equipment* is meant to include the land owned by a company on which its plant, offices, loading terminals, and so forth are built. In such circumstances, even though the gross dollar amount reported for PP&E on the balance sheet may include the cost of land, such costs are *not* depreciable. In such circumstances, land is not viewed as being "used up" and therefore is not depreciated.)

The periodic amount of PP&E cost allocated to the income statement is called *depreciation expense* and serves to reduce the net income of the period. In determining a given period's depreciation expense, corporate financial managers must assess the useful lives and salvage values of the PP&E items, as well as select a rational and systematic method to allocate the costs of the PP&E items over their respective estimated useful lives. These three management decisions (i.e., useful life, salvage value, and depreciation method) involve considerable discretion and judgment and may frequently have a significant financial effect on a company's reported earnings. Each of these decisions is discussed at length in the following sections.

Throughout the ensuing discussion, it is important to remember that it is possible that a PP&E item that has been fully depreciated in the accounting records may still be an integral part of a company's operations and/or may be sold to another company at a significant price. It is also important to note that book value does not approximate an asset's fair market value, nor is it intended to.

Useful life. In estimating the useful lives of various PP&E components, managers must consider the manner in which the assets are expected to be used and maintained. Generally, useful lives are established based on the assumption that normal repairs and maintenance will be made to keep the assets in good operating condition. In situations in which maintenance programs deviate from what is considered normal, estimated useful lives should be adjusted accordingly.

The two primary factors that managers should consider when estimating the useful lives of their PP&E are physical life and technological life. **Physical life** refers to the length of time an asset can reasonably be expected to last before it physically wears out. When physical life is influenced more by the passage of time than by use (e.g., for a building) or when it is difficult to assess the level of usage, useful life is usually expressed in terms of years. When physical life is influenced more by use (e.g., for a machine or a vehicle) than by the passage of time, useful life is often expressed in terms of expected output (e.g., units produced or miles driven).

For a great many PP&E items, the concept of technological life has a greater relevance to managers in estimating useful life than does physical life. **Technological life** refers to the length of time an asset can reasonably be expected to generate economic benefits before it becomes obsolete. Two types of obsolescence must be considered: product obsolescence and process obsolescence. **Product obsolescence** pertains to the market lives of the products that are produced by the PP&E. For example, auto manufacturers normally depreciate tooling costs over two or three years because of the product obsolescence brought about by frequent model changes even though the physical life of the tooling equipment may be many more years. **Process obsolescence** pertains to the PP&E item itself becoming obsolete because of subsequent technological improvements. For example, the useful lives of computer equipment have generally been set with the expectation that process obsolescence would occur prior to the time the equipment was physically worn out.

It is important to note that this discussion of estimating useful lives of PP&E pertains solely to financial reporting. As discussed in a later section of this chapter, the Internal Revenue Service (IRS) specifies its own useful life rules for federal income tax purposes.

Depreciation methods. For financial reporting purposes, corporate management has a choice of several generally accepted methods for allocating the depreciable cost of PP&E over an asset's estimated useful life. The common element among these alternatives is that they each result in a rational, systematic process of cost allocation.

1. **The straight-line method**—When the straight-line method is used, the annual depreciation expense is determined by dividing the *depreciable* cost of an asset by its estimated life. The *depreciable cost* is the original cost less the estimated salvage value; hence,

   Annual depreciation expense $= (1/n)$ [Cost $-$ Salvage value]

   where n $=$ estimated life in years.

   For example, consider an asset with an original cost of $10,000, an estimated salvage value of $400 (and thus a depreciable cost of $9,600) and an estimated useful life of five years. Under straight-line depreciation, the depreciable cost of $9,600 is divided by 5 to give an annual depreciation figure of $1,920 for each of the five years of the asset's estimated useful life.

2. **Double-declining-balance method**—This method requires the calculation of the straight-line percentage rate (i.e., $1/n$), which is then doubled, and applied each year to the PP&E's decreasing *net book value* (i.e., recorded cost less depreciation taken to date). The amount of depreciation taken to date for a particular asset is often referred to as the asset's **accumulated depreciation.** Salvage value is ignored in determining net book value, but the recording of depreciation expense should stop when the asset's net book value equals its salvage value. Hence,

   Annual depreciation expense $= (2/n)$ Net book value.

   Consider again an asset with an original cost of $10,000, salvage value of $400, and an estimated life of five years. The straight-line percentage rate is 20 percent (i.e., 1/5 years) and the double-declining-balance rate is 40 percent (i.e., 2/5). Thus, under the declining-balance method, depreciation is 40 percent of $10,000, or $4,000 for the first year; 40 percent of $6,000 (i.e., $10,000 less $4,000), or $2,400, for the second year; 40 percent of $3,600 (i.e., $10,000 less $6,400), or $1,440, for the third year, and so on. When the accumulated depreciation recorded for this asset reaches $9,600, its depreciation expensing stops.

3. **Sum-of-the-years' digits method**—Just as the double-declining-balance method results in the recording of larger depreciation expense amounts in the early years of an asset's life (referred to as an *acceleration of depreciation*), so also does the sum-of-the-years' digits (SYD) method.

Under this method, declining fractions are applied to the asset's *depreciable cost*. The denominator of the fraction is the sum of the digits of the years of useful life (i.e., SYD = $n(n+1)/2$). The numerator is the number of years of useful life remaining, including the present year. The only rationale behind the mechanics of the SYD method is that it is systematic and results in higher depreciation expense amounts earlier in an asset's life than under the straight-line method.

Consider again an asset costing $10,000 with an estimated salvage value of $400, a depreciable cost of $9,600, and an estimated life of five years. The sum of the years' digits (1,2,3,4, and 5) is 15. Hence, depreciation expense for the first year is 5/15ths of $9,600, or $3,200; for the second year, it is 4/15ths of $9,600, or $2,560; for the third year it is 3/15ths of $9,600, or $1,920, and so on.

4. Physical-unit methods.

    a. Machine-hour method—The number of hours a machine is to be used during its useful life is often a better basis for determining depreciation expense than the mere passage of time. Under the machine-hour method, depreciation expense is determined according to the number of hours the asset is actually used during an accounting period relative to the total number of hours it can ultimately be used (i.e., the usage or productivity rate):

Annual depreciation expense =
$$\frac{\text{Actual machine hours used in this period}}{\text{Total estimated machine hours}} \times [\text{Cost} - \text{Salvage value}].$$

Referring again to the asset with a cost of $10,000, an estimated salvage of $400, and a depreciable cost of $9,600, its estimated lifetime hours are 19,200, and the hours actually used during the first year are 1,800. The depreciable cost of $9,600 divided by the total hours of 19,200 yields $.50 to be allocated to each hour of use. Depreciation expense for the first year on this machine is therefore $900 (1,800 times $.50 per hour of use).

    b. Units-of-production method—This method is conceptually similar to the machine-hour method except that an estimate is made of the number of units to be produced by a machine during its useful life. Depreciation expense for a period is then determined according to the number of units actually produced during the period relative to the estimated lifetime potential of the machine.

       Again using the example of an asset with a cost of $10,000 and an estimated salvage value of $400, assume that its projected units of production are 48,000. The asset's depreciable cost of $9,600 divided by 48,000 units yields $.20 depreciation expense per unit produced. Thus, if in its first year of use, 5,000 units are produced, the depreciation expense for that year is $1,000.

The double-declining-balance and sum-of-the-years' digits methods are generally referred to as accelerated methods of depreciation. The phenomenon captured by accelerated depreciation methods is that more depreciation expense is recorded in the early years of an asset's life as compared to the amount that would be recorded under the straight-line method. Two reasons frequently given for using accelerated methods are (1) that the asset is more useful in its earlier years because it is more efficient and less subject to obsolescence then and (2) that repairs and maintenance complement the accelerated depreciation over the useful life of the asset because repair and maintenance expenses are normally greater in later years. This latter notion may be more clearly understood through the following graphic representation:

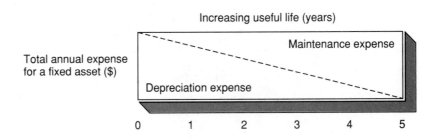

Exhibit 10.2 summarizes the results of the five depreciation method examples. Note the variability across the different methods for any given year. In spite of this variability, however, the *total* depreciation expense reported over the life of an asset must be the same under each of the methods. Thus, it can be seen that the financial reporting of depreciation is fundamentally a decision concerning the *timing* as to when an asset's cost is systematically allocated to the income statement in the form of depreciation expense to reflect the cost of using the asset.

The accounting entry to record the annual depreciation expense on an asset appears as follows:

Dr. Depreciation Expense (E) $4,000	
Cr. Accumulated Depreciation (CA)	$4,000

Note that the cost basis of the asset is preserved in the PP&E account because the credit entry is to a contra asset account. Using this approach, the balance sheet will reveal not only the original cost basis of the asset but also its total depreciation taken to date and its remaining undepreciated cost. From this information, it is also possible to make rough estimates of the age of a company's assets—the larger the net book value (i.e., cost minus accumulated depreciation) relative to the original cost of the PP&E, the newer (on average) are the company's assets.

Presented in Exhibit 10.3 are the financial statement disclosures of three companies pertaining to their choices of asset lives and depreciation methods. In reviewing those examples, consider the impact of the different lives and methods on the companies' reported depreciation expense and depreciable fixed assets. In particular, note that for machinery and equipment, Snap-On-Tools Corporation generally uses shorter estimated lives than Kmart Corporation and uses mostly accelerated depreciation methods rather than the straight-line method. Clearly, Snap-On-Tools Corporation records a larger depreciation expense deduction sooner than Kmart, all other things being equal. Also note that Ace Hardware Corp., which has somewhat different asset lives than the other two companies, uses a variety of depreciation methods and has five categories of PP&E

E X H I B I T 1 0 . 2

Comparison of Depreciation methods*

	Depreciation Method				
Year	Straight-Line	Double-Declining Balance	Sum-of-the Years' Digits	Machine Hours	Units-of-Production
1	$1,920	$4,000	$3,200	$ 900	$1,000
2	1,920	2,400	2,560	2,700	3,200
3	1,920	1,440	1,920	2,050	2,200
4	1,920	880	1,280	2,050	1,800
5	1,920	880	640	1,900	1,400
	$9,600	$9,600	$9,600	$9,600	$9,600

*Assumptions: A machine with an original cost of $10,000 is estimated to have a useful life of five years and an estimated salvage value of $400; the machine is assumed to be operated for the following number of hours, producing the following number of units:

Year	Hours Operated	Units Produced
1	1,800	5,000
2	5,400	16,000
3	4,100	11,000
4	4,100	9,000
5	3,800	7,000
	19,200	48,000

versus four and three for Snap-On-Tools and Kmart, respectively. Such variations between companies highlight some of the latitude left to management as they decide how "best" to depreciate their assets.

Capitalizing depreciation. The depreciation allocated to each accounting period may be charged, in part, against net income as a period expense (as has already been discussed) and, in part, to work-in-process inventory as manufacturing overhead (see Chapter 7). To the extent that the depreciation costs are incurred "under the factory roof" (i.e., are a part of the costs of manufacturing a product), management should capitalize them as a product cost by increasing the Work-in-Process Inventory account instead of recording depreciation expense on the income statement. If added to Work-in-Process Inventory, the depreciation will become a deduction in the income statement only when the finished goods with which it is associated are sold and an accounting entry for the cost of goods sold is made.

Changes in Depreciation Accounting Policy

During the course of depreciating either a particular asset or an entire array of fixed assets, corporate financial managers may decide to modify or adjust their initial estimates and decisions underlying the calculation of depreciation. For example, a change in the

EXHIBIT 10.3

Selected Depreciation-Method and Asset-Life Disclosures

Panel A—Snap-on-Tools Corporation

Property and equipment

Land, buildings, machinery and equipment are carried at original cost. Depreciation and amortization are provided for primarily by using accelerated depreciation methods on all property acquired prior to December 31, 1989. For financial statement purposes, the Company adopted the straight-line depreciation method for all property acquired after December 30, 1989. The Company believes the new method will more accurately reflect its financial results by better matching costs of new property over the useful lives of these assets. In addition, the new method more closely conforms with that prevalent in the industry. The effect of the change was not material to the 1990 financial results.

The estimated service lives of property and equipment are as follows:

Buildings and improvements	5 to 45 years
Machinery and equipment	3 to 15 years
Furniture and fixtures	3 to 15 years
Transportation vehicles	2 to 5 years

Panel B—Ace Hardware Corp.

Depreciation expense is computed on both straight-line and accelerated methods based on estimated useful lives as follows:

	Useful Life (Years)	Principal Depreciation method
Buildings and improvements	10–40	Straight line
Warehouse equipment	5–10	Sum of years
Office equipment	3–10	Various
Manufacturing equipment	3–20	Straight line
Transportation equipment	3–7	Straight line

Panel C—Kmart Corporation

Depreciation: The company computes depreciation on owned property principally on the straight-line method for financial statement purposes and on accelerated methods for income tax purposes. Most store properties are leased and improvements are amortized over the term of the lease but not more than 25 years. Other annual rates used in computing depreciation for financial statement purposes are 2% to 4% for buildings, 10% to 14% for store fixtures, and 5 % to 33% for other fixtures and equipment.

depreciation method from the double-declining-balance method to the straight-line method might be undertaken because other similar companies are predominantly using the straight-line method. In this case, the decision to change depreciation methods is probably motivated by management's desire to appear to be using the industry-preferred method, as well as a desire to improve the firm's within-industry comparative financial standing. When such a change in accounting method is made, its cumulative effect is recorded on a net of taxes basis in the current financial statements, and all subsequent financial statements reflect the use of the new method.

To illustrate such a change, consider again the data presented in Exhibit 10.2. Assume, for example, that in Year 3 a change from the double-declining-balance method (DDB) to the straight-line method is to be made. Through the end of Year 2, depreciation totaling $6,400 has been taken under the DDB method, whereas if the straight-line method had been used, only $3,840 in depreciation deductions would have been recorded. Thus, at the beginning of Year 3, an entry to restate the depreciation account balances would be needed as follows:

```
Dr.  Accumulated Depreciation (CA). . . . . . . . . . . . . . $2,560*
    Cr.  Cumulative Effect of Change in Accounting Method . . . . . .        $2,560
```

*($6,400 − $3,840 = $2,560)

The account Cumulative Effect of Change in Accounting Method is reported on the company's Year 3 income statement and thus will increase the period's net income. Because of the unusual nature of this account, it is separately and prominently disclosed on the income statement if material in amount. In addition to the above entry to reflect the change in depreciation method, the regular Year 3 depreciation expense under the new method also needs to be recorded:

```
Dr.  Depreciation Expense (E). . . . . . . . . . . . . . . . $1,920
    Cr.  Accumulated Depreciation (CA)  . . . . . . . . . . . . .        $1,920
```

Another depreciation-related change often made by corporate financial managers involves the estimated useful life of an asset or a group of assets. This type of change involves a change in the *estimate* rather than in the *method* and is usually dealt with on a prospective, or future, basis. For example, if in Year 3 management decided that the expected useful life of an asset being depreciated was really eight years instead of five, no accounting entry would be required to restate the previous depreciation deductions. Instead, all future depreciation deductions would be based on an estimated life of eight, not five years. Thus, an estimate change such as this does not affect prior published financial statements but only future reported results.

When accounting method or estimate changes are undertaken by management, the effect of the change on the current financial statements must be described in the company's footnotes. Exhibit 10.4 presents such footnote disclosures made by two very prominent corporations—AT&T and General Motors. Note in Panel A that AT&T changed three things—depreciation method, estimated useful lives, and estimated salvage value. All three changes were effective beginning in 1989 and had the combined effect of decreasing 1989 net income by almost $400 million. AT&T mentions that the portion of this decrease attributable to the cumulative effect of just the change in depreciation method is not material and thus not reported separately in the note or in the income statement. On the other hand, the financial effect of General Motors' change is to increase pretax earnings by more than $1.2 billion. The change made by GM, however, did not involve a change in depreciation method but *only* in estimated useful lives, and even though material, it is thus not required to be shown separately in the income statement. It is important to note that although GM's pretax earnings increased substantially due to this accounting change, there was *no* increase in the company's operating cash flows, nor was there any increase in the operating efficiency of the company (the same can be said for AT&T).

Some Misconceptions about Depreciation

A number of common misconceptions exist concerning depreciation accounting. One misconception states that for financial reporting purposes, depreciation expense reflects the decline in the market value of the depreciable asset; in other words, original cost less accumulated depreciation should approximate an asset's current fair market value.

EXHIBIT 10.4

Changes in Depreciation Methods and Estimates

Panel A—AT&T

Accounting Change
Effective January 1, 1989 for certain network equipment, AT&T changed its method of depreciation from straight-line to sum-of-the-years' digits, shortened the estimated depreciable lives and decreased the estimated net salvage. These changes were implemented to better match revenues and expenses because of rapid technological changes occurring in response to customer requirements and competition. The new depreciation method was applied retroactively to all digital circuit, digital operator services and radio equipment and was applied to digital electronic switching equipment placed into service after December 31, 1988. Other network equipment, principally lightguide cable and central office buildings, continues to be depreciated on a straight-line basis. The changes in estimates of depreciable lives and net salvage were made

prospectively. The effect of these changes on 1989 results was to decrease net income by approximately $393 million or $.36 per share. The cumulative prior years' effect of the change in depreciation method was not material.

Panel B—General Motors

Depreciation and Amortization
In the third quarter of 1987, the Corporation revised the estimated service lives of its plants and equipment and special tools retroactive to January 1, 1987. These revisions, which were based on 1987 studies of actual useful lives and periods of use, recognized current estimates of service lives of the assets and had the effect of reducing 1987 depreciation and amortization charges by $1,236.6 million or $1.28 per share of $1-2/3 par value common stock (post-split).

The recording of depreciation is a process of cost allocation, not of valuation. Accordingly, depreciation expense is not intended to equal the change in asset market value or to indicate the market value of the unallocated cost of assets at the end of any period.

A second depreciation myth is that the purpose of depreciation is to provide for the replacement of assets at the end of their useful lives.

The costs allocated to depreciation expense are costs *already incurred* without reference to the costs to be incurred when, and if, an asset is replaced. Moreover, the recording of depreciation does not assume that assets are to be replaced at the end of their useful lives by similar assets.

Another misconception is that depreciation provides cash.

As discussed in Chapter 6, the statement of cash flows usually lists net income first among the sources of operating cash flows. To adjust this figure to a cash-based net income approximation, depreciation is added back. The sum of net income plus depreciation and other similar items is then labeled *cash flow from operations*. As a consequence of this separate listing of depreciation in the statement of cash flows, some financial statement readers have been led to the false conclusion that depreciation provides cash. This is *not* so! Depreciation is a noncash expense that is recognized under the accrual basis of accounting but in no way constitutes a cash inflow. Depreciation does, however, reduce the taxable net income amount reported on a company's tax return and thus lowers the amount of taxes to be paid. So, to the extent that depreciation reduces the cash outflow for taxes otherwise due, it can be thought of as having an indirect cash flow benefit.

Tax Depreciation

In 1986, Congress passed the Tax Reform Act of 1986—the second time in 5 years and the fourth time in 25 years that the tax rules concerning depreciable assets had undergone major revision.[1] Each successive piece of legislation sought to restrict the diversity of depreciation practices employed by different corporate managers for similar assets (e.g., to standardize the estimated useful life of similar assets) and reflected a particular fiscal policy of the U.S. government at the time of passage (e.g., the use of shorter estimated asset lives was an attempt to stimulate increased corporate investment in capital assets). Under rules put in place by the 1986 Tax Reform Act, the **Modified Accelerated Cost Recovery System** (MACRS) is the only accelerated depreciation method acceptable for tax purposes; straight-line, machine-hours, and units-of-production methods are also still acceptable nonaccelerated methods.

MACRS defines eight classifications of fixed asset lives and uses the term *cost recovery* in place of the term depreciation:

MACRS Classification	Asset Description
3-year property	Race horses and some special-use tools
5-year property	Autos, trucks, R&D equipment, certain technological equipment, computers, office machinery
7-year property	Office furniture, railroad track and rolling stock, some agricultural structures, and other unclassified property
10-year property	Vessels, barges, and tugs
15-year property	Communications equipment and water-treatment facilities
20-year property	Some real property, sewage-treatment facilities, and general-use agricultural buildings
27.5-year residential real property	Residential real property
31.5-year nonresidential real property	Most building and plant facilities

Under MACRS, the cost of 3-year, 5-year, 7-year, and 10-year property may be recovered using the double-declining-balance method over 3, 5, 7, and 10 years, respectively. The cost of 15-year and 20-year property may be recovered using the 150 percent-declining-balance method over 15 and 20 years; the costs of 27.5-year and 31.5-year property are to be recovered using only the straight-line method. When using MACRS, estimated salvage value is **not** considered.

---

[1]For assets put in service before 1962, IRS *Bulletin F* rules apply. For assets placed in service after 1962 and before 1971, managers may choose general depreciation rules or the Class Life System (CLS). After 1971 but before 1981, the taxpayer may choose from the Asset Depreciation Range (ADR) System or the general depreciation rules. In 1981, the Economic Recovery Tax Act of 1981 inaugurated the use of the Accelerated Cost Recovery System (ACRS), which applies to all assets placed in service between 1981 and 1986. Assets placed in service after 1986 are subject to MACRS.

Under MACRS, the cost of 3-year, 5-year, 7-year, and 10-year property may be recovered using the double-declining-balance method over 3, 5, 7, and 10 years, respectively. The cost of 15-year and 20-year property may be recovered using the 150 percent-declining-balance method over 15 and 20 years; the costs of 27.5-year and 31.5-year property are to be recovered using only the straight-line method. When using MACRS, estimated salvage value is **not** considered.

For tax purposes, all asset classes except the 27.5-year and 31.5-year classes must also conform to the **half-year convention.** An asset is said to have been put in service or disposed of at the mid-point of the year regardless of the date actually placed in service or disposed of, thereby allowing one half of a year's depreciation in the year in which the asset was placed in service and one-half year's depreciation in the year in which the asset is disposed of. Moreover, for those classes of assets using one of the declining-balance methods, a switch to the straight-line method is permitted at the time during an asset's life when the prospective annual straight-line depreciation amounts, recalculated using the net book value and remaining life as of that instant, exceeds that year's declining-balance method amount.

For new and used assets placed into service after December 31, 1986, the current tax law requires the use of MACRS as the only accelerated method. Companies must continue to use previously adopted tax depreciation methods on all fixed assets put into service prior to 1987. Those methods might include ACRS, sum-of-the-years' digits, various declining-balance methods, or other methods previously acceptable to the IRS.

Financial reporting and tax depreciation. The depreciation expense that a company records for external financial reporting is usually not the same amount as is reported on its income tax return. This may occur for a variety of legitimate reasons. For example, a company may choose to use the straight-line method of depreciation for its external financial statements but the MACRS method (as required by the IRS) for its income tax return.

For external financial statements, corporate financial managers typically adopt depreciation methods that result in a total depreciation expense for the year that indicates the cost of utilizing their fixed assets for the period while also striving to maximize reported net income. For tax-return purposes, management should use the method permitted by the IRS that gives them the greatest tax savings. As a result, many corporate managers choose accelerated methods of depreciation and IRS lives for income tax-return purposes but the straight-line method and longer estimated useful lives for financial reporting purposes. In such cases, the income tax actually owed (per the tax return) is not the same amount as the income tax due on the income reported in the published annual report. In general, the tax liability (per the tax return), tax expense (per the accounting records), and related difference are recorded in an accounting entry such as the following:

```
Dr.  Income Tax Expense (E) . . . . . . . . . . . . . . . . . . $120
     Cr.  Income Taxes Payable (L) . . . . . . . . . . . . . . . . .          $100
     Cr.  Deferred Income Taxes (L) . . . . . . . . . . . . . . . .            20
```

A detailed discussion of the Deferred Income Taxes account noted in the above entry is left until Chapter 12. For now, it is important only to recognize the need for such an account in order to reconcile the difference between the tax expense and the tax liability

<u>E X H I B I T   1 0 . 5</u>

PACIFIC GAS & ELECTRIC CO
Financial Reporting versus Tax-Return Depreciation

Depreciation

For financial reporting purposes, depreciation of plant in service is computed using a straight-line remaining life method. For federal income tax purposes, the most liberal depreciation methods allowed by the Internal Revenue Code generally are used.

Exhibit 10.5 presents the depreciation disclosures of the Pacific Gas & Electric Company (PG&E) that highlight the differences in financial reporting and tax-return depreciation. To illustrate the effect of such differences, we assume that PG&E purchased a piece of production equipment costing $100,000 that is classified under MACRS as five-year property. Assume further that PG&E's chief financial officer has decided to use straight-line depreciation for financial reporting purposes and estimates that the equipment will be used for eight years and have a salvage value of $20,000 at the end of the eighth year. If the corporation uses a half-year convention for both tax and financial reporting purposes, the depreciation schedules for both tax and financial reporting purposes will be as follows:

Year	MACRS Tax-Return Depreciation Expense	Financial Reporting Depreciation Expense
1	$ 20,000	$ 5,000
2	32,000	10,000
3	19,200	10,000
4	11,520	10,000
5	11,520*	10,000
6	5,760	10,000
7	0	10,000
8	0	10,000
9	0	5,000
Total	$100,000	$80,000

*Beginning in Year 5, the straight-line method over the asset's remaining years (1.5) provides a depreciation amount greater than that from the continued use of the double-declining-balance method; thus, Year 5's allowable depreciation switches to a straight-line amount.

In Year 1, PG&E will show depreciation expense of $5,000 in its income statement but will deduct $20,000 in its tax return for cost recovery under MACRS. This procedure will cause income on the company's tax return to be $15,000 less than its accounting income and, at a 34 percent tax rate, will defer $5,100 in taxes to subsequent years. In its income statement, PG&E will show its tax expense based on its income statement profit and, as a result, will recognize a deferred tax liability of $5,100 in its balance sheet.

Two additional aspects of this example are important to note. First, capital-investment decisions involving net present value and internal rate of return techniques employing the cash flows resulting from depreciation-generated tax savings should be based on tax-return depreciation deductions, not those reported for financial reporting purposes (these topics are usually part of a managerial finance course). Second, as noted earlier, MACRS ignores the salvage value of an asset, and this permits greater tax-return depreciation deductions over the life of an asset than would otherwise be taken in the published income statement. On the other hand, the IRS has reduced the amount of flexibility available to a company when preparing its tax return by eliminating those decisions relating to the length of an asset's life, the expected salvage value, and effectively, the method of depreciation.

Repairs, Maintenance, and Betterments

Costs incurred for the purpose of maintaining the existing service level of PP&E are classified as *repairs and maintenance* and should be treated by managers as expenses of the period in which they are incurred. Costs incurred to improve an asset beyond its original service potential are viewed as betterments and should be capitalized rather than expensed in the period incurred. Capitalizing betterments increases an asset's book value because their costs are added to the asset's original recorded cost. The capitalized cost is subsequently expensed over future periods as an additional component of depreciation. The first part of Phelps Dodge Corporation's PP&E footnote (see Panel B, Exhibit 10.7) makes this same distinction.

Distinguishing between an ordinary repair or maintenance expenditure and an asset betterment expenditure is difficult in many instances. For both financial accounting and income tax purposes (in this area, financial reporting and tax treatment are the same), management's rationale for a particular expenditure and the nature of the asset alteration itself are important factors in determining whether the expenditure is properly recorded as a repair/maintenance expense item or as a betterment item. For example, replacing a roof on a production plant after 2 years is probably a repair item to be expensed, whereas replacing a roof after 20 years is probably best treated as a betterment item to be capitalized on the balance sheet. Similarly, servicing the engines of a fleet of trucks every 5,000 miles represents a normal maintenance expense, but rebuilding the engines after 100,000 miles of use represents a betterment expenditure because the life of the asset has been extended.

The reporting of these asset-related expenditures should attempt to reflect the intended purpose of the expenditure. For financial reporting purposes, managers generally argue for capitalizing such expenditures in order to keep current reported profits as high as possible (by reducing the current level of deductions against net income). For tax purposes, however, the greatest benefit is achieved by expensing as many of these PP&E-related expenditures in the current period as is permitted. Once again, this situation presents another instance about which there may be disagreements between corporate management and the IRS as to what constitutes a repair/maintenance and what constitutes a betterment. It does stand to reason, however, that the logic applied to a particular expenditure would lead to a single classification that should be used for both tax and financial reporting purposes.

Accounting for the Sale or Disposition of an Asset

When a PP&E item is sold or otherwise disposed of, both the original cost and the associated accumulated depreciation must be removed from the books. If the proceeds from the disposal exceed the asset's net book value (i.e., original cost less accumulated depreciation), a gain is recognized. If the proceeds are less than the net book value, a loss is recognized. For example, if a machine with an original cost of $90,000 and accumulated depreciation of $70,000 is sold for $30,000 cash, the entry to record the sale is as follows:

Dr.	Cash (A)	$30,000	
Dr.	Accumulated Depreciation (CA)	70,000	
	Cr. Machine (A)		$90,000
	Cr. Gain on Sale (G)		10,000

The $10,000 gain on sale appears in the income statement covering the period in which the sale was made. Consistent with the reporting of gains from the sale of inventory, the gain on the sale of PP&E is reported in the period in which the sales event takes place rather than in the period in which the asset's market value appreciated above its net book value. This latter possibility, as discussed in Chapter 7, is the approach followed for current marketable equity securities. The principal difference between these two approaches relates to the degree of objectivity present when trying to assess when the appreciation in asset value occurred. In the absence of a market mechanism, like the stock market, to establish appreciated value objectively, GAAP relies on the occurrence of an actual sale transaction as a signal to record value appreciation (i.e., a gain on sale).

In contrast to a gain on the sale of inventory, which is considered to be operations related, the gain (or loss) on the sale of PP&E is considered to be a nonoperating event because it is assumed that the company is not in the business of selling its PP&E. Thus, in the statement of cash flows (Chapter 6) and in the income statement (Chapter 5), PP&E sales are reported but not as part of continuing operations. Exhibit 10.6 depicts the fact that Northrup Corporation reported gains and losses from sales of PP&E as a separate line item in its income statement and statement of cash flows. Moreover, in order to report the total proceeds from such sales, which would include amounts recognized as gains, Northrup's operating cash flows section shows an adjustment for the gains and losses, and the total proceeds are then shown in the investing activities section.

Financial Statement Presentation and Disclosure

In the balance sheet, PP&E are shown in the noncurrent asset section. Land is reported at its original cost, whereas buildings, machinery, vehicles, and equipment are shown at original cost less the portion of that cost previously allocated as depreciation.

The annual expense for depreciation may or may not be shown in the body of the income statement. If it is not reported separately in the income statement, the amount expensed may be found in the notes to financial statements or as a line item in the statement of cash flows. The notes to the financial statements include substantial

EXHIBIT 10.6

NORTHRUP CORPORATION
Income Statement
(in millions)

Year ended December 31	1990	1989	1988
Net sales	$5,489.8	$5,248.4	$5,797.1
Cost of sales:			
Operating costs	4,747.7	4,691.9	5,257.6
Administrative and general expenses	450.5	533.2	514.3
Operating margin	291.6	23.3	25.2
Other income(deductions):			
Gain(loss) on disposals of property, plant and equipment	103.0	(8.6)	.6
Interest income	2.8	2.0	2.2
Other, net	10.0	(4.5)	16.6
Interest expense	(94.9)	(123.7)	(98.5)
Income(loss) before income taxes and cumulative effect of accounting change	312.5	(111.5)	(53.9)
Federal and foreign income taxes(benefit)	102.1	(31.0)	(23.0)
Income(loss) before cumulative effect of accounting change	210.4	(80.5)	(30.9)
Cumulative effect on prior years of change in accounting for income taxes			135.1
Net income(loss)	$ 210.4	(80.5)	$ 104.2
Weighted average common shares outstanding	47.0	47.0	47.0
Earnings(loss) per share before cumulative effect of accounting change	$ 4.48	$ (1.71)	$ (.65)
Cumulative effect on prior years of change in accounting for income taxes, per share			2.87
Earnings(loss) per share	$ 4.48	$ (1.71)	$ 2.22

continued

information regarding a company's fixed assets, depreciation policies, and related expenditures. Complete examples of the required financial statement disclosures for PP&E are presented in Exhibit 10.7.

Managerial Issues

The property, plant, and equipment purchase decision is one of the most important decisions a manager makes because of the size of the investment and the long-term nature of the asset and related financing. A number of financial considerations that parallel some of this chapter's earlier discussions are involved in such purchase decisions. If the decision to buy a piece of equipment is determined, in part, on the asset's estimated net present value or internal rate of return (two very common capital budgeting techniques), then the asset's estimated useful life, periodic tax depreciation amount, salvage value, initial cost, and gains or losses on disposal of the assets being replaced are important

E X H I B I T   1 0 . 6

(continued)

Partial Consolidated Statement of Cash Flows
(in millions)

Year ended December 31	1990	1989	1988
Reconciliation of Net Income(Loss) to Net Cash			
Provided by (Used in) Operating Activities			
Net income(loss)	$ 210.4	$ (80.5)	$ 104.2
Adjustments to reconcile net income(loss) to net			
cash provided(used):			
Depreciation and amortization	186.6	220.6	240.8
Common stock issued to employees	3.7	5.1	4.8
Amortization of restricted award shares	1.3	4.9	3.4
Loss(gain) on disposals of property,			
plant and equipment	(103.0)	8.6	(.6)
Non-cash pension cost(income)	(53.3)	7.3	2.7
Amortization of deferred gain on sale/leaseback	(2.3)		
Loss(gain) on sale of subsidiaries and affiliates		6.8	(12.7)
Gain on sale of direct financing leases		(12.9)	
Undistributed income of affiliates			(4.3)
Decrease(increase) in			
Accounts receivable	(1,085.4)	(1,209.0)	(1,034.4)
Inventoried costs	49.7	(85.9)	(5.1)
Prepaid expenses	.4	(4.3)	5.0
Refundable income taxes	8.1	1.2	(9.3)
Increase(decrease) in			
Progress payments	1,204.2	1,137.5	790.4
Accounts payable and accruals	(211.2)	54.2	64.0
Provisions for contract losses	(41.0)	59.9	145.6
Deferred income taxes	93.3	(34.0)	(176.8)
Income taxes payable	6.2	.8	(20.5)
Other non-cash transactions	(1.6)	(1.7)	(.2)
Net cash provided by (used in) operating activities	$ 266.1	$ 78.6	$ 97.0
Investing Activities			
Additions to property, plant and equipment	(121.2)	(186.8)	(254.2)
Proceeds from sale of property, plant and equipment	252.1	14.3	12.0
Proceeds from sale of subsidiaries and affiliates		1.1	67.3
Proceeds from sale of direct financing leases		21.9	
Dividends from affiliate, net of investments	.1		20.7
Other investing activities	(2.3)	4.8	6.2
Net cash provided by (used in) investing activities	128.7	(144.7)	(148.0)

factors to be considered. These factors are important because they influence the amount and timing of the cash flows generated by the particular asset under consideration and, thus, are an integral part in calculating the asset's net present value.

Some observers of corporate financial reporting have sarcastically observed that corporate accounting departments have become the best performing profit centers for many companies—a comment that reflects the bottom-line impact attributable to the various financial reporting alternatives available under GAAP. Recall from Chapter 8, for example, the discussion of how net income could be significantly influenced by

EXHIBIT 10.7

Fixed Asset Disclosure Excerpts

Panel A—Stone Container Corp.

Property, Plant, Equipment and Depreciation:
Property, plant and equipment is stated at cost.
Expenditures for maintenance and repairs are charged
to income as incurred. Additions, improvements and
major replacements are capitalized. The cost and
accumulated depreciation related to assets sold or
retired are removed from the accounts and any gain or
loss is credited or charged to income.

For financial reporting purposes, depreciation is
provided on the straight-line method over the estimated
useful lives of depreciable assets, or over the duration of
the leases for capitalized leases, based on the following
annual rates:

Type of Asset	Rates
Machinery and equipment.	5% to 33%
Buildings and leasehold improvements . .	2% to 7%
Land improvements	4% to 7%

Effective January 1, 1990, the Company changed its
estimates of the useful lives of certain machinery and
equipment at its paper mills. Mill asset depreciation lives
that previously averaged 16 years were increased to an
average of 20 years, while mill asset depreciation lives
that previously averaged 10–12 years were increased to
an average of 14–16 years. These changes were made
to better reflect the estimated periods during which such
assets will remain in service. The change had the effect
of reducing depreciation expense by $39.8 million and
increasing net income by $20.2 million, or $.34 per
common share, in 1990.

Panel B—Phelps Dodge Corp.

PROPERTY, PLANT AND EQUIPMENT. Property, plant and
equipment are carried at cost. Cost of significant assets
includes capitalized interest incurred during the
construction and development period. Expenditures for
replacements and betterments are capitalized;
maintenance and repair expenditures are charged to
operations as incurred.

The principal depreciation methods used are the units
of production method for mining, smelting and refining
operations and, for other operations, the straight-line
method based upon the estimated lives of specific
classes or groups of depreciable assets. Upon disposal
of assets depreciated on a group basis, cost less
salvage is charged to accumulated depreciation.

Values for mining properties represent mainly
acquisition costs or pre-1932 engineering valuations.
Depletion of mines is computed on the basis of an
overall unit rate applied to the pounds of principal
products sold from mine production.

Mine exploration costs and development costs to
maintain production of operating mines are charged to
operations as incurred. Mine development expenditures
at new mines and major development expenditures at
operating mines which are expected to benefit future
production are capitalized and amortized on the units of
production method over the estimated commercially
recoverable minerals.

management's choice of LIFO versus FIFO for purposes of valuing ending inventory and
the cost of goods sold. A similar concern exists with regard to fixed assets: Management's
choice of depreciation method, expected useful life, and anticipated salvage value can
have a material, direct effect on the company's bottom line. Recall our earlier example
involving General Motors, which increased 1988 net income by more than $1 billion
through discretionary PP&E accounting policy decisions. Although managers do have this
flexibility available to them under GAAP, changes in accounting methods and estimates
must be documented in the published financial statements. Such changes should be
infrequent to avoid the appearance of overt earnings management.

Other, less critical management concerns include reducing the clerical costs associated
with the accounting for fixed assets. In this regard, most companies, as a matter of policy,
set a lower limit (e.g., $500) for capitalizing assets. The purchase of any item costing less
than this amount is expensed. This policy reduces the number of items that must be

depreciated on a periodic basis even though many of those assets expensed will be used for more than one year. Because of the immateriality of these small dollar items, they do not affect the overall accuracy of the financial statements.

Another clerical-saving policy involves depreciating assets for a half-year in the year of acquisition and in the final year of its planned life rather than using the actual fractional parts of the year. Many companies adopt a half-year depreciation convention for the year of acquisition. Under this convention, capitalized property is depreciated on a six-month basis for the first year regardless of when it was acquired. A similar convention is normally adopted for the year of disposition if the asset is not fully depreciated at the time of disposition. Fortunately, the IRS recognizes the validity of this convention.

Time and money also can be saved by using similar policies for both accounting and tax purposes when possible. Adopting the same depreciation method for general accounting as that used for tax purposes, for example, minimizes the amount of work required to maintain two sets of records. Managers still must ensure, however, that fixed asset costs are allocated for accounting purposes in a rational and systematic manner. Managers also should be concerned with preserving cash flows to the company through well-planned tax depreciation policies.

INTANGIBLE ASSETS

Accounting for assets such as inventories and property, plant, and equipment seems relatively straightforward because these items are tangible in nature and their revenue-producing potential as assets is readily apparent. In contrast, the accounting for an intangible asset may not be so readily apparent because such assets do not physically produce goods or services. The term **intangible asset** refers to "certain long-lived legal rights and competitive advantages developed or acquired by a business enterprise"[2] exemplified by such items as patents, trademarks, and franchises. In the following section, we will focus on such questions as: What cost figure should be assigned to a trademark on the balance sheet? Should a trademark be depreciated? If so, what is its useful life?

In fact, the financial reporting for most intangible assets is similar to that for fixed tangible assets such as property, plant, and equipment. At the date of acquisition, an intangible asset's cost must be determined and recorded at the fair market value of (1) the consideration given up or (2) the item acquired, whichever is more clearly determinable. When payment is noncash, every effort should be made to determine the market value of the noncash payment. If that is not possible, then the corporate financial manager should attempt to determine the market value of the intangible asset received. The consideration given (or the value of the asset received) becomes the basis for recording the asset—in effect, its recorded cost.

Consider, for example, the purchase of a franchise agreement for a combination of cash and capital stock. At the time of the purchase, the capital stock has a market value of

---

[2]*1988 GAAP Guide* (New York: Harcourt Brace Jovanovich, 1987), p. 21.02.

$250,000; hence, the accounting entry to record the acquisition of the franchise appears as follows:

```
Dr.  Franchise (A) . . . . . . . . . . . . . . . . . . . $300,000
     Cr.  Cash (A)  . . . . . . . . . . . . . . . . . . . . . .       $ 50,000
     Cr.  Capital Stock (OE) . . . . . . . . . . . . . . . . .         250,000
```

Over its useful economic life, the intangible asset's recorded cost must be allocated to the periods benefited. GAAP assumes that the economic utility (i.e., the useful potential) of an intangible asset declines (is used up) over its life, and therefore the total cost should be systematically allocated as a period expense against the income of the company. This process, which is similar to the depreciation of fixed assets, is referred to as **amortization**. The period of time over which the recording of amortization takes place depends on the estimated economic life of the asset and varies from case to case. Generally accepted accounting principles provide the following insights:

> The recorded costs of intangible assets should be amortized by systematic charges to income over the periods estimated to be benefited. . . . The cost of each type of intangible should be amortized on the basis of the estimated life of that specific asset. . . . The period of amortization should not, however, exceed 40 years.[3]

Amortization of an intangible asset normally relies on the straight-line method over the estimated economic life of the asset unless an alternative method can be shown to comply more closely with the "using up" of the asset. By convention, amortization expense usually results in a direct reduction to the intangible asset account rather than an increase to a contra asset allowance account as is done for depreciation charges related to property, plant, and equipment. In the previous franchise example, if the contractual term of the franchise agreement was 10 years, the accounting entry to record each year's amortization expense is as follows:

```
Dr.  Franchise Amortization Expense (E) . . . . . . . . . . $30,000
     Cr.  Franchise (A) . . . . . . . . . . . . . . . . . . . . .         $30,000
```

As with any asset, when intangible assets are disposed of, sold, or exchanged, they must be removed from the accounts, and any gain or loss recorded at that time. Continuing with the previous example, assume that after eight years the franchise is sold for a cash payment of $80,000. The entry appears as follows:

```
Dr.  Cash (A) . . . . . . . . . . . . . . . . . . . . . . $80,000
     Cr.  Franchise (A) . . . . . . . . . . . . . . . . . . . . .       $60,000
     Cr.  Gain on Sale of Franchise (G)  . . . . . . . . . . . . .        20,000
```

A Taxonomy for Intangible Assets

Intangible assets may differ from one another in several key ways. Depending on these key dimensions, the accounting for the intangible asset under consideration may differ from that described above for the franchise example.

---

[3]Accounting Principles Board, *Opinion No. 17 "Intangible Assets"* (APB, 1970), par. 9.

From a financial reporting perspective, managers must consider three key character-istics of intangibles. The first characteristic is *identifiability and separability:* Can the intangible asset be considered separately and distinctly from the other assets of the company? The usual test for separate identity is to determine whether the asset can be sold individually (e.g., a patent) or is so intertwined with the company that it cannot be separated (e.g., customer goodwill). The second issue pertains to the *manner of acquisition:* Was the intangible asset developed internally (e.g., a proprietary manufac-turing process) or was it purchased externally (e.g., a franchise or an exclusive license)? A final issue pertains to the expected *period of benefit:* What is the economic life of the intangible asset? For some intangible assets, such as patents and franchises, the maximum economic life is legally or contractually determined. For others, such as trademarks, the economic life is not easily determined because of the potential for continual legal renewals and extensions. Moreover, the useful life of an intangible asset, like a trademark or patent, may be affected by product or process obsolescence, competitors' actions, and changes in technology. The only guidelines available to managers in choosing an appropriate useful life is that the period selected should not be longer than the intangible's legal life, if it has one, and it cannot exceed 40 years in any case.

Exhibit 10.8 presents a useful summary of these dimensions with a taxonomy for a variety of intangible assets that distinguishes between those that are specifically identifiable and separable and those that are not and between those assets developed internally and those acquired externally.

Accounting Guidelines

Internally developed intangibles. The costs associated with internally developed intangible assets that are not specifically identifiable and separable are expensed against income in the period incurred. Stated in the language of current financial reporting standards, costs ". . . inherent in a continuing business and related to the enterprise as a whole—such as [customer] goodwill—should be deducted from income when incurred."[4] On the other hand, those internally incurred costs associated with identifiable and separable intangible assets are expensed unless they are incurred under contract to an outside party. A classic example are those R&D expenses incurred under a contractual agreement for the benefit of another entity. These expenses should be capitalized as an inventory-type item (i.e., one held for sale) as opposed to a depreciable asset (i.e., one held for internal production).

On the other hand, consider the issue of in-house research and development costs. Prior to 1975, accounting convention was to capitalize R&D expenses, based on the observation that such expenses were investments in the products and operations of the future and were thus a cost of bringing those future assets to a usable condition. However, because of practical realities (i.e., less than 1 in 10 new product ideas ever go to market and the ability to predict which one will be successful is highly uncertain), capitalizing R & D expenditures seldom achieved the ultimate matching of revenues and expenses it sought to achieve.

---

[4]Accounting Principles Board, *Opinion No. 17.*

EXHIBIT 10.8

Classification Framework for Intangible Assets

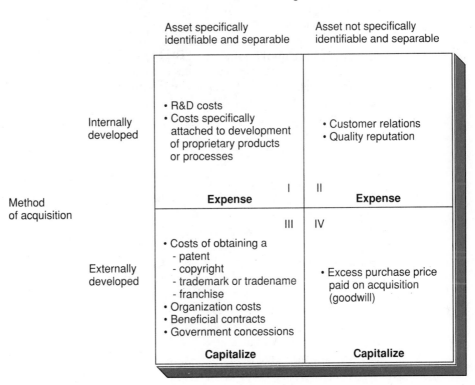

A recent case in point highlights the nontrivial issue of accounting for R & D expenditures. During the 1980s, Burroughs Wellcome spent and expensed more than $80 million on R & D that ultimately led to the AIDS drug AZT. As the R & D was being incurred, management did not know whether the outcome would result in an effective, marketable AIDS drug. All expenditures therefore were expensed, as were another $700 million of R & D on other diseases that produced nothing of significance. On the day that the Food and Drug Agency approved AZT, it became a valuable asset that was not and could not be reported on the balance sheet. In setting the retail price for AZT, however, Wellcome managers asked this question: What is the cost of the product? Various stakeholders in the pricing decision argued for quite different points of view—some argued that only the $80 million specifically associated with the AZT product development should be considered; others argued that AZT pricing had to be sufficient to recover the entire R & D budget of $780 million. Still others argued that the price should be merely the cost involved in manufacturing the drug. This debate illustrates the divergent views that exist as to whether R & D should be considered part of a product's cost, and, if so, whether only direct R & D costs or both direct and indirect costs be considered. Financial reporting practice does not help management in this case because it requires the conservative "solution" of treating R & D expenditures as a period cost rather than a product cost. In so doing, GAAP emphasizes objectivity over subjectivity, conservatism over optimism, and results in a decoupling of accounting policy from strategic management decisions.

Externally developed intangibles. The consideration paid to external parties for control of specifically identifiable and separable intangible assets (Exhibit 10.8, Quadrant III) should be capitalized and systematically amortized over the economic life of the asset (but not to exceed 40 years). Examples include government concessions (e.g., licenses to develop a country's resources), beneficial contracts for goods or services below market rates, and trademarks.

Patents, for example, are exclusive legal rights to products registered with the United States Patent Office; they recognize the holder's right to use, manufacture, dispose of, and control in every way the patented product or process without hindrance from others. Patents have a legal life of 17 years, but their economic life may be much shorter because of technological obsolescence. Similarly, *copyrights* are legal rights of protection given to the creators of published materials. Copyright law has recently been changed so that copyrights now extend protection for the life of the creator plus 50 years, or if the copyright is held by a corporation (deemed to have an indeterminate life), 75 years from the date of first publication. *Franchises* are the rights granted by one company to another to use a specific designation in their business; use can be limited in term by contract or be renewable indefinitely to create essentially an indeterminate life. If a franchise is renewable indefinitely, it should be amortized over a period not to exceed 40 years. PepsiCo's largest intangible asset noted in its footnote is for its franchises. *Trademarks* are federally registered claims of ownership to names, symbols, slogans, or other devices providing distinctive identity of a product. Although they have no legally limited life, trademarks often have limited economic life. If an estimate of the economic life can be made, it should be used as the term for amortization of the asset. If no estimate of economic life can be made, the asset should be amortized over a period not to exceed 40 years. As noted in Exhibit 10.8 (Quadrant III), the costs of obtaining a patent, copyright, franchise, or trademark should be capitalized as intangible assets. It is important to note that the costs of producing an asset (e.g., a feature motion picture) should be reported as an asset separate from the costs incurred in obtaining the copyright on the film.

Exhibit 10.9 presents several corporate disclosures for intangible assets representing different approaches to amortization. Note in particular McDonnell Douglas' statement as to the variety of intangible assets reported in its balance sheet and to the fact that they are being amortized over 3 to 10 years. Rockwell International, on the other hand, chooses to amortize somewhat similar items over 5 to 20 years. Air Products' disclosure points out that internally incurred costs leading to a patent are expensed whereas externally incurred costs associated with acquisition of a patent are capitalized. Last, note how Polaroid Corp. reports the patents on all of its very valuable, highly lucrative proprietary products and processes—at $1. Since the bulk of such costs were internally incurred, and since the patent filing costs were probably immaterial relative to the asset's value, all such costs

EXHIBIT 10.9

Intangible Asset Disclosures

Panel A. Rockwell International Corp.
Intangible Assets
Intangible assets are summarized as follows (in millions):

September 30	1990	1989
Goodwill, less accumulated amortization (1990, $93.7; 1989, $72.2)	$ 598.3	$ 583.9
Patents, product technology and other intangibles, less accumulated amortization (1990, $404.2; 1989, $438.3)	429.5	510.7
Intangible pension asset (see note 16)	144.0	
Intangible assets	$1,171.8	$1,094.6

Goodwill represents the excess of the cost of purchased businesses over the fair value of their net assets at date of acquisition and generally is being amortized by the straight-line method over periods ranging from 15 to 40 years.

Patents, product technology and other intangibles relate principally to Allen-Bradley and are being amortized on a straight-line basis over their estimated useful lives, generally ranging from 5 to 20 years.

Panel B—McDonnell Douglas Corp.

Intangible Assets. Intangible assets consist of capitalized computer software and the unamortized balances of the excess of the cost of acquired companies (or significant interests therein) over the values assigned to net tangible assets. The latter amounts have been assigned to government programs, computer software, leaseholds, and goodwill. These intangibles are being amortized over three to ten years, except goodwill which has various periods up to 40 years.

Panel C—Polaroid Corp., 1990

Patents and Trademarks: Patents and trademarks are valued at $1.

Panel D—Air Products, Inc.

Patents. Expenses related to the development of patents are deducted from income as they occur. Patents acquired from other companies are recorded at their purchase price and charged to income over the remaining life of the patent.

---

were expensed. In order to draw the reader's attention to their patented propriety processes and products, however, Polaroid chooses to report them, albeit at the unique cost figure of $1.

Goodwill: Special considerations. As has already been mentioned, costs associated with internally created goodwill (e.g., public-service expenditures, employee development, charitable contributions, customer-service expenses, etc.) are not capitalized. They are expensed in the period in which they are incurred. As discussed in Chapter 9, the acquisition of another business, however, often creates the need to identify and record a goodwill intangible asset pertaining to the acquired company (Exhibit 10.8, Quadrant IV). Consider for a moment the fact that the only reason General Electric management was willing to pay in excess of $3.7 billion more for RCA Corporation than the fair market value of RCA's net assets was the customer loyalty, managerial talent, sound reputation, and so on, already built up by RCA (see Exhibit 10.10). Although RCA was never permitted to record an intangible asset for such goodwill-related factors, the external

E X H I B I T   1 0 . 1 0

General Electric Disclosure for RCA Acquisition

On June 9, 1986, GE acquired RCA Corporation and its subsidiaries (RCA) in a transaction for which the total consideration to former RCA shareholders was $6,406 million in cash. RCA businesses included the manufacture and sale of a wide range of electronic products and related research and services for consumer, commercial, military and space applications; the National Broadcasting Company's (NBC) radio and television stations and network broadcasting services; and domestic and international message and data communications services.

The acquisition was accounted for as a purchase, and the operating results of RCA have been consolidated with those of GE since June 1, 1986. The purchase price ($6,426 million, including $20 million of related costs) has been allocated to the assets and liabilities of RCA based on appraisal and evaluation studies completed during 1987. The excess of purchase price over the estimate for fair values of net assets acquired (goodwill) was $3.7 billion, which is being amortized on a straight-line basis over 40 years.

---

acquisition of RCA by General Electric was an event that justified General Electric's recording of RCA's goodwill. In essence, a marketplace valuation of that goodwill had been made and confirmed via the payment of a price for RCA in excess of RCA's net assets' appraised fair market value. This premium paid was recorded as goodwill on General Electric's books. Such goodwill is assumed to be of indeterminate life but, by convention, is amortized over a life not to exceed 40 years. *Amortization of goodwill is not permitted for tax purposes,* and this difference between IRS regulations and GAAP creates a permanent difference between tax and accounting records, with no related recognition of deferred taxes.

NATURAL RESOURCES

Natural resources include such assets as timber, oil, gas, iron ore, coal, and uranium. Like intangible assets, natural resources may be either internally or externally developed. When these assets are externally developed, they are reported on the balance sheet at their acquisition cost less any depletion taken subsequent to acquisition. Alternatively, when they are internally developed, several valuation approaches may be adopted.

The two principal valuation alternatives that exist for companies in the extractive industries are the full cost method and the successful efforts method. Under the **full cost method,** *all* costs associated with the exploration for and development of natural resources are capitalized to the natural resource accounts on the balance sheet. There is little disagreement over this method *except* when unsuccessful exploration activities are involved. Under the full cost method, the costs of unsuccessful exploration activities are also capitalized to the balance sheet under the philosophy that the development of new resource reserves is a speculative activity involving some inherent failure. In contrast, under the **successful efforts method,** only the costs associated with successful exploration and development activity are capitalized to the balance sheet accounts. The costs of any unsuccessful activity are expensed against net income.

Both the full cost and the successful efforts methods are generally accepted, and thus both are available for use by managers of natural resource companies in the extractive industries. In practice, however, only small resource companies tend to use the full cost method, whereas larger companies tend to prefer the successful efforts method (see panels A, B, and C, Exhibit 10.11), which is also the method of choice among most preparers of financial statements. Under both methods, however, the costs capitalized to the balance sheet are subject to certain constraints in a manner similar to the effect that the lower-of-cost-or-market method has on inventory. In the event that the current market value of a company's reserves of natural resources declines substantially, it may become necessary to write down the value of the capitalized balance sheet values. Thus, just as the lower-of-cost-or-market method prevents the overstatement of inventories and marketable securities, this "ceiling test" similarly constrains the value of natural resources on the balance sheet.

Natural resource companies not involved in the extractive industries, such as a timber company, usually capitalize all of their initial expenditures while expensing their on-going maintenance and development costs. Except in those cases involving forest fires, which destroy substantial portions of a company's timber reserves, the initial capitalized cost is carried on the balance sheet until the reserves are harvested (see Panel D, Exhibit 10.11).

Depletion

Depletion refers to the periodic expensing of the capitalized resource cost. Unlike depreciation, there is only one generally accepted depletion approach, the units-of-production method, which is conceptually similar to the units-of-production method of depreciation for machinery and equipment. First, an estimate is made of the number of units—barrels of oil, tons of coal, or board feet of timber—in an oil well, mine, or tract of timberland. Second, this estimate is divided into the original cost of acquiring the oil well, mine, or timber tract (less its estimated residual value) to determine the depletion per unit. For example, if the estimated number of tons of coal in a mine were 200,000 and the mine's original cost (less estimated residual value) was $820,000, the depletion rate per ton would be $4.10. If during the first year, 25,000 tons were taken out, the depletion expense for the year would be 25,000 times $4.10, or $102,500. The accounting entry follows:

```
Dr.  Depletion Expense (E) . . . . . . . . . . . . . . . $102,500
      Cr.  Allowance for Depletion (CA)  . . . . . . . . . . . . .        $102,500
```

The Allowance for Depletion account is conceptually similar to the Accumulated Depreciation account. The depletion approach described above is referred to as *cost depletion,* and it is generally used only for financial reporting purposes. Another method, known as *percentage depletion,* is permitted under U.S. tax provisions for certain depletable property such as minerals and other natural resources. This method is not permissible for financial reporting purposes because it is not an allocation approach based on the asset's cost basis. Under percentage depletion, the amount of depletion expense for a period is determined by taking a fixed percentage of the gross income from the property; however, the deduction may not exceed 50 percent of the taxable income from the

EXHIBIT 10.11

Natural Resource Disclosures

Panel A—Homestake Mining Co.

Exploration costs, including those incurred through partnerships and joint ventures, are charged to operations in the year incurred.

Preoperating and development costs relating to new mines and major programs at existing mines are capitalized. Ordinary mine development costs to maintain production and underground equipment acquisitions are charged to operations as incurred.

Depreciation, depletion and amortization of mining properties, mine development costs and major plant facilities are computed principally by the units-of-production method (based on estimated proven and probable ore reserves). Proven and probable ore reserves reflect estimated quantities of commercially recoverable reserves which the Company believes can be recovered in the future from known mineral deposits. Such estimates are based on current and projected costs and product prices.

Panel B—Amoco Corporation

Costs incurred in oil and gas producing activities— The corporation follows the successful efforts method of accounting. Costs of property acquisitions, successful exploratory wells, all development costs (including CO_2 and certain other injected materials in enhanced recovery projects), and support equipment and facilities are capitalized. Unsuccessful exploratory wells are expensed when determined to be non-productive. Production costs, overhead, and all exploration costs other than exploratory drilling are charged against income as incurred.

Depreciation, depletion, and amortization— Depletion of the cost of producing oil and gas properties, amortization of related intangible drilling and development costs, and depreciation of tangible lease and well equipment are computed on the units-of-production method.

The portion of costs of unproved oil and gas properties estimated to be non-productive is amortized over projected holding periods.

Panel C—Mobil Corp.

Oil and Gas Accounting Method

Mobil follows the "successful efforts" method of accounting prescribed by Financial Accounting Standard (FAS) 19, Financial Accounting and Reporting by Oil and Gas Producing Companies.

Exploration and Mineral Rights (Leases)

Direct acquisition costs of unproved mineral rights (leases) are capitalized and then amortized in the manner stated below. Payments made in lieu of drilling on nonproducing leaseholds are charged to expense currently.

Geological, Geophysical and Intangible Drilling Costs

Geological and geophysical costs are charged to expense as incurred. Intangible drilling costs of all development wells and of exploratory wells that result in additions to proved reserves are capitalized.

Depreciation, Depletion and Amortization

Annual charges to income for depreciation and the estimated cost for restoration and removal of major producing facilities are computed on a straight-line basis over the useful lives of the various classes of properties or, where appropriate for producing properties, on a unit-of-production basis by individual fields.

Costs of producing properties are generally accumulated by field. Depletion of these costs and amortization of capitalized intangible drilling costs are calculated on a unit-of-production basis.

Capitalized acquisition costs of significant unproved mineral rights and unamortized costs of significant developed properties are assessed periodically on a property-by-property basis to determine whether their values have been impaired; where impairment is indicated, a loss is recognized.

Capitalized acquisition costs of other unproved mineral rights are amortized over the expected holding period. When a mineral right is surrendered, any unamortized cost is charged to expense. When a property is determined to contain proved reserves, the mineral right then becomes subject to depletion on a unit-of-production basis.

Panel D—Stone Container Corp.

Timberlands

Timberlands are stated at cost less accumulated cost of timber harvested. The Company amortized its private fee timber costs over the total fibre that will be available during the estimated growth cycle. Cost of non-fee timber harvested is determined on the basis of timber removal rates and the estimated volume of recoverable timber. The Company capitalizes interest costs related to pre-merchantable timber.

property, computed without regard to the depletion deduction. Thus, the percentage depletion results from a specific provision in the tax laws and is not based on the cost of the natural resource.

For tax purposes, the accumulated percentage depletion can exceed the cost of the resource, whereas for accounting purposes, the accumulated cost depletion cannot exceed the original cost of the resource less its estimated residual value. The difference between the two depletion methods results in a permanent difference between tax accounting and financial accounting. As will be explained in Chapter 12, no deferred taxes are recognized for such permanent differences.

SUMMARY

Noncurrent assets are the principal long-term revenue-producing assets of most companies. Because of the significant dollar investment in these assets, the accounting methods adopted for them may have a material impact on both the balance sheet and the income statement of a company. Although the initial cash outflow to acquire these assets affects the statement of cash flows, the periodic amortization of intangibles, the depreciation of fixed assets, and the depletion of natural resources do not affect it; amortization, depreciation, and depletion expenses are added back to net income to adjust the accrual operating results for these noncash expenses to arrive at the cash flows from operations.

When evaluating the performance of a company or its management, it is important to consider how effectively the noncurrent assets were utilized. Such ratios as the asset turnover ratio and the return on noncurrent assets, as discussed in Chapter 4, are instructive indicators in this regard.

NEW CONCEPTS AND TERMS

Accelerated methods of depreciation (p. 438)
Accumulated depreciation (p. 437)
Allocation (p. 434)
Amortization (p. 453)
Capitalization (p. 434)
Depletion (p. 459)
Double-declining-balance method (p. 437)
Fixed assets (p. 434)
Full cost method (p. 458)
Half-year convention (p. 445)
Machine-hour method (p. 438)

Modified Accelerated Cost Recovery
    System (p. 444)
Physical life (p. 436)
Present value (p. 435)
Process obsolescence (p. 437)
Product obsolescence (p. 436)
Straight-line method (p. 437)
Successful efforts method (p. 459)
Sum-of-the-years' digits methods (p. 438)
Technological life (p. 436)
Units-of-production method (p. 438)

ISSUES FOR DISCUSSION

D10.1 Point: Research and development expenditures should be expensed when incurred.

Counter-point: Research and development expenditures should be capitalized until it is known whether or not a commercially viable product will result. If none results, then R&D should be expensed.

Required:

Evaluate the two viewpoints. Which one do you agree with, and why?

D10.2 Is the purpose of depreciation to provide for the replacement of a fixed asset once its useful life is over? If not, what is the purpose of depreciation?

D10.3 Is depreciation a source of cash? If not, why is depreciation added back to net income in the statement of cash flows?

D10.4 Is depreciation incurred "under the factory roof" treated as a period cost or as a product cost? Explain.

D10.5 What items should be included in determining the original cost of a new machine? Explain.

D10.6 Amos Company decides to build its own machine rather than to purchase a similar one from a machine manufacturer. Should the company capitalize the cost of its own laborers who work on building the machine? Explain.

D10.7 Once it has fully depreciated a fixed asset, can a company continue to use the asset? If so, can the company continue to record depreciation? If not, will net income be overstated?

D10.8 If a company originally estimates that a machine will last six years but after two years decides that the total useful life is more likely to be eight years, how should this change in estimate be treated for financial accounting and reporting purposes?

D10.9 When operations are discontinued at one of a company's plants and the property is offered for sale, should the plant be separately shown on the balance sheet while it is being held awaiting sale? Should the plant be shown at unallocated cost or at estimated selling price less cost to sell? Should it be shown as a current asset if the company plans to sell it within a year? Should the company continue recording periodic depreciation? Explain.

D10.10 How should a company account for normal repairs and maintenance for a building? For a replacement of the roof? For a general renovation of the building including air conditioning? Why?

D10.11 Digital Computer Company recently purchased a special machine that was made to the company's specifications. This machine has a physical life of 15 years at the proposed rate of production. The company's tax department reported that, for machines of this type, the Internal Revenue Service normally specifies 12 years as the period over which the machines are written off.

Required:

What factors should the company consider in estimating the useful life of this machine?

PROBLEMS

P10.1 Estimating depreciation and book value. Equipment costing $19,000, with a scrap value of $4,000, was purchased on January 1, 1990, by Yellow Creek Electrical Company. The estimated useful life of the equipment was five years or 75,000 units of production. Units produced were 12,000 in 1990 and 16,000 in 1991. Complete the following table.

Depreciation Method	Depreciation Expense		Book Value	
	1990	**1991**	**12/31/90**	**12/31/91**
Straight line				
Sum-of-the-years' digits				
Double-declining balance				
Units of production				

P10.2 Income statement preparation. Randolph Mining Corporation paid $3,040,000 for a tract of land containing valuable ore and spent $280,000 in developing the property during 1990 preparatory to beginning mining activities on January 1, 1991. Company geologists estimated that the mineral deposit would produce 6 million tons of ore, and it is assumed that the land will have a residual value of $20,000 after the ore deposit is exhausted. It is expected that it will take 12 to 14 years to extract all of the ore.

A record of capital investment during the last half of 1990, exclusive of the development costs previously mentioned, is as follows:

Asset	Estimated Service Life	Cost
Mine buildings	30 years	$300,000
Railroad and hoisting equipment	20 years	600,000
Miscellaneous mine equipment	10 years	120,000

The building, railroad, and hoisting equipment cannot be economically removed from the mine location, but other miscellaneous equipment is readily movable and has alternative uses.

Operations during 1991 are summarized below:

Tons of ore mined and sold at $4 per ton	500,000
Mining labor and other operating costs (exclusive of depreciation and depletion)	$950,000
Selling and administrative expenses	$140,000

Required:

Prepare an income statement for 1991. (Ignore income taxes.)

P10.3 Accounting for the sale of an asset. On January 1, 1987, Home Construction Corporation purchased a number of pieces of new equipment, including a new dump truck. The truck cost $25,000 and was expected to last 10 years. Home always used double-declining-balance depreciation for its financial reports and for tax purposes, and its depreciation calculations assume no residual values. By December 1991, interest rates had risen to 11 percent and the construction business had begun to slow down. Home found itself with idle equipment on its hands. One of the employees who was laid off as a result of the slowdown asked to buy the truck for use in a landscaping business he planned to start. On December 30, 1991, the company agreed to sell him the truck in exchange for a $10,000 note. The note obligated the employee to make four annual payments of $2,500.

Required:

a. What entry(ies) should Home make regarding the truck for the year ended December 31, 1991?

b. What entry(ies) should Home make regarding the truck for the year ended December 31, 1991, if the transaction with the employee is not consummated until January 4, 1992?

P10.4 Capitalization and amortization policy decisions. Keeler Company purchased a new machine to use in its operations. The new machine was delivered by the supplier, installed by Keeler, and placed into operation. It was purchased under a long-term payment plan with interest to be charged at the current market rate. The estimated useful life of the new machine is 10 years, and its estimated salvage value is significant. Normal maintenance was performed to keep the new machine in usable condition.

Keeler also added a wing to its factory building in order to provide much needed manufacturing floor space. In addition, Keeler made significant leasehold improvements to office space used as corporate headquarters.

Required:

a. What costs *should* Keeler capitalize for the new machine? Without focusing on specific depreciation methods, how *should* the machine be depreciated?

b. How *should* Keeler account for the normal maintenance performed on the new machine? Why?

c. How *should* Keeler account for the wing added to the factory building? How *should* the added wing be reported on Keeler's financial statements?

d. How *should* Keeler account for the leasehold improvements made to its office space? How *should* the leasehold improvements be reported on Keeler's financial statements?

P10.5 Fixed asset accounting policy. At the beginning of the year, Constance Dado acquired a computer to be used in her company's operations. The computer was delivered by the supplier, installed by Dado Corporation personnel, and placed into operation. The estimated useful life of the computer is five years, and its estimated salvage value is significant.

During the year, Dado also sold one of her executive limos purchased in a prior year for cash.

Required:

a. What costs should Dado capitalize for the computer?

b. Without discussing specific depreciation methods, what is the objective of depreciation accounting?

c. What is the rationale for using accelerated depreciation methods?

d. How should Dado account for and report the disposal of the limo?

P10.6 Accounting for fixed assets. The plant asset and accumulated depreciation accounts of Marietta Corporation had the following balances at December 31, 1991:

	Cost Basis	Accumulated Depreciation
Land	$ 250,000	$ —
Land improvements	160,000	40,000
Building	1,500,000	350,000
Machinery and equipment	1,158,000	405,000
Automobiles	150,000	112,000

The financial reporting policies of Marietta Corporation pertaining to depreciation of fixed assets follow: land improvements—straight-line, 15 years; building—150 percent declining balance, 20 years; machinery and equipment—straight-line, 10 years; automobiles—150 percent declining balance; 3 years. Depreciation is computed to the nearest month. All salvage values are assumed to be zero.

The following transactions occurred during 1992:

- On January 2, 1992, machinery and equipment were purchased at a total invoice cost of $240,000, which included a $5,500 charge for freight. Installation costs of $17,000 were incurred.

- On March 31, 1992, a machine purchased for $68,000 on January 2, 1988, was sold for $46,500.

- On June 1, 1992, expenditures of $40,000 were made to repave parking lots at Marietta's plant location. Damage caused by severe winter weather necessitated the work.

- On November 1, 1992, Marietta acquired a tract of land with an existing building in exchange for 9,000 shares of Marietta's $20 par value common stock that had a market price of $39 per share on this date. Marietta paid legal fees and title insurance totaling $24,000. The last property tax bill indicated assessed values of $250,000 for land and $50,000 for building. Shortly after acquisition, the building was razed at a cost of $35,000 in anticipation of new building construction in 1993.

- On December 31, 1992, Marietta purchased a new automobile for $15,000 cash and trade-in of an automobile purchased for $18,000 on January 2, 1991. The new automobile has a cash value of $19,000.

Required:

a. Prepare a schedule analyzing the changes in each of the plant assets during 1992 with detailed supporting computations. *Disregard the related accumulated depreciation accounts.*

b. For each asset classification, prepare a schedule showing depreciation expense for the year ended December 31, 1992.

c. Prepare a schedule showing the gain or loss from each asset disposal that would be recognized in Marietta's income statement for the year ended December 31, 1992.

P10.7 Depreciation policy. USX Corporation provided the following footnote in a recent set of financial statements detailing its depreciation policies.

Property, plant, and equipment—Except for oil and gas producing properties, depreciation is generally computed on the straight-line method based upon the estimated lives of the assets. The Corporation's method of computing depreciation of steel assets modifies straight-line depreciation based on the level of production. The modification ranges from a minimum of 80% at a production level of 50% of capacity and below, to a maximum of 130% for a 100% production level. No modification is made at the 85% production level, considered the normal long-range level.

Depletion of the cost of mineral properties, other than oil and gas, is based on rates which are expected to amortize the cost over the estimated tonnage of minerals to be removed.

Depreciation and depletion of oil and gas producing properties are computed at rates applied to the units of production on the basis of proved oil and gas reserves as determined by the Corporation's geologists and engineers.

When a plant or major facility within a plant is sold or otherwise disposed of by the Corporation, any gain or loss is reflected in income. Proceeds from the sale of other facilities depreciated on a group basis are credited to the depreciation reserve. When facilities depreciated on an individual basis are sold, the difference between the selling price and the remaining undepreciated value is reflected in income.

Required:

a. In *your own words,* explain USX's depreciation policy for steel assets.

b. What rationale would support USX's depreciation policy?

P10.8 Repair and maintenance expense. During 1991, Steamboat Company made the following expenditures relating to plant machinery and equipment:

■ Renovation of a group of machines at a cost of $60,000 to secure greater efficiency in production over their remaining five-year useful lives. The project was completed on December 31, 1991.

■ Continuing, frequent, and low-cost repairs at a cost of $45,000.

■ A broken gear on a machine was replaced at a cost of $6,000.

Required:

What total amount should be charged to repairs and maintenance in 1991?

P10.9 Cost capitalization. On June 30, 1990, Belpre, Inc., completed the rearrangement of a group of factory machines to secure greater efficiency in production. Belpre estimated that benefits from the rearrangement would extend over the remaining five-year useful lives of the machines. The following costs were incurred:

Moving	$42,000
Reinstallation	$64,000
Actual maintenance (performed at this time for convenience)	$ 9,000

Required:

How much of the costs incurred should be capitalized on June 30, 1990?

P10.10 Estimating depletion expense. In January 1991, Craig Mining Corporation purchased a mineral mine for $4 million with removable ore estimated by geological surveys at 2,300,000 tons. The property has an estimated value of $400,000 after the ore has been extracted. Craig incurred $1 million of development costs preparing the property for the extraction of ore. During 1991, 270,000 tons were removed and 240,000 tons were sold.

Required:

For the year ended December 31, 1991, Craig should include what amount of depletion in its cost of goods sold? Explain.

P10.11 Estimating amortization expense. Curtis Company bought a trademark from Kent Corporation on January 1, 1991, for $122,000. An independent consultant retained by Curtis estimated that the remaining useful life is 50 years. Its unamortized cost on Kent's accounting records was $61,000. Curtis decided to write off the trademark over the maximum period allowed.

Required:

How much should be amortized for the year ended December 31, 1991? Explain.

P10.12 Accounting for intangible assets. Robertson, Inc., seemed to have a balance sheet full of intangible assets. During 1991, four additional decisions were required regarding various intangible asset-related expenditures. Each is presented below.

Required:

a. Which of the following legal fees should be capitalized?

	Legal Fees to Obtain a Franchise	Legal Fees to Successfully Defend a Trademark
(1).	No	No
(2).	No	Yes
(3).	Yes	Yes
(4).	Yes	No

b. Which of the following costs of goodwill should be capitalized and amortized over their estimated useful lives?

	Cost of Goodwill from a Business Combination Accounted for as a Purchase	Cost of Developing Goodwill Internally
(1).	No	No
(2).	No	Yes
(3).	Yes	Yes
(4).	Yes	No

c. Which of the following costs of goodwill should be capitalized and amortized?

	Developing Goodwill	Restoring Goodwill
(1).	Yes	Yes
(2).	Yes	No
(3).	No	No
(4).	No	Yes

d. Legal fees incurred by a company in defending its patent rights should be capitalized when the outcome of the litigation is:

	Successful	Unsuccessful
(1).	Yes	Yes
(2).	Yes	No
(3).	No	No
(4).	No	Yes

P10.13 Accounting for intangible assets. Belle Corporation incurred $140,000 of research and development costs to develop a product for which a patent was granted on January 2, 1986. Legal fees and other costs associated with registration of the patent totaled $40,000. On March 31, 1991, Belle paid $55,000 for legal fees in a successful defense of the patent.

Required:

How much should be capitalized for this patent through March 31, 1991? Explain.

P10.14 Estimating R&D. Rose Ltd. incurred the following costs during 1991:

Modification to the formulation of a chemical product	$155,000
Trouble-shooting in connection with breakdowns during commercial production	$ 50,000
Design of tools, jigs, molds, and dies involving new technology	$170,000
Seasonal or other periodic design changes to existing products	$165,000
Laboratory research aimed at discovery of new technology	$225,000

Required:

In its income statement for the year ended December 31, 1991, Rose Ltd. should report research and development expense of how much? Explain.

P10.15 Accounting for asset exchanges. On June 30, 1991, Clay, Inc., exchanged 3,000 shares of North Corp. $20 par value common stock for a patent owned by South Co. The North stock was acquired in 1989 at a cost of $40,000. At the exchange date, North common stock had a fair value of $35 per share, and the patent had a net carrying amount of $90,000 on South's books.

Required:

Clay should record the patent at what amount? Explain.

P10.16 Capitalization policy. In starting a new warehousing business, Hires Partnership purchased 10 acres of land to be used as the site for a new warehouse. A building on the property was sold and removed by the buyer so that construction on the warehouse could begin.

Required:

How should the proceeds from the sale of the building be treated?

P10.17 Accounting for asset exchanges. On September 1, 1991, Ruane, Inc., exchanged a delivery truck for a parcel of land. Ruane bought this truck in 1989 for $12,000. As of September 1, 1991, the truck had a book value of $7,500 and a fair market value of $5,000. Ruane gave $7,000 in cash in addition to the truck as part of this transaction. The previous owner of the land had listed the land for sale at $14,000.

Required:

At what amount should Ruane record the land?

P10.18 Accounting for fixed assets. Kraft, Inc., included the following footnote in one of its recent annual reports:

> Properties are stated at cost. Depreciation is determined on a straight-line basis over estimated useful lives. For certain machinery and equipment, depreciation is determined on a composite basis over estimated group lives. The estimated useful lives are principally 10 to 40 years for buildings and improvements and 2 to 25 years for machinery and equipment.

On routine disposals of depreciable assets accounted for on a composite basis, the gross book value less the proceeds or salvage value is charged to accumulated depreciation. On all other sales or retirements of property, plant, and equipment, gain or loss is recognized. Expenditures for maintenance and repairs are charged to expense.

Required:

a. What does Kraft mean when it refers to depreciation "being determined on a composite basis"? Why might management have chosen this approach?

b. Do gains/losses on routine disposals of depreciable assets accounted for on a composite basis affect current period income? Explain.

c. Do gains/losses on all other sales or retirements of property, plant, and equipment affect current period net income? Explain.

P10.19 Estimating book values. Kaiser Aluminum and Chemical Corporation provided the following footnote in one of its recent financial statements, regarding its property, plant, and equipment:

Property, Plant, and Equipment and Long-Term Leases

December 31	19x1	19x0
Land and improvements	$ 171.5	$ 157.8
Buildings	386.8	359.0
Machinery and equipment .	2,342.3	2,206.1
Construction in progress	52.9	62.7
Total property—at cost	2,953.5	2,785.6
(includes idle facilities: $215.8 in 19x1 and $215.9 in 19x0		
Accumulated depreciation (includes idle	1,467.7	1,253.9
facilities: $130.8 in 19x1 and $126.1 in 19x0)		
Property, plant, and equipment—net	$1,485.8	$1,531.7

The idle facilities shown above consist of the corporation's Chalmette, Louisiana, aluminum smelter which is temporarily closed because of high energy and other costs and the market conditions for primary aluminum. In addition, production of alumina at Alumina Partners of Jamaica (ALPART) was temporarily suspended in August 19x0 due to the continuing adverse economic conditions impacting the aluminum industry. ALPART, a 50%-owned partnership, has an alumina plant in Nain, Jamaica. At December 31, 19x1 and 19x0, investments and advances include $32.5 and $32.0 for ALPART, which is accounted for by the equity method. The corporation is obligated to pay $72.4 and $79.0 of ALPART's debt at December 31, 19x1 and 19x0, as discussed in Note 12.

Management believes that market conditions will improve and that operating costs of the idle facilities can be reduced sufficiently to permit economic operation of these facilities in the future. The corporation's policy is to continue normal depreciation for temporarily closed facilities.

Required:

a. What is the net book value (NBV) of Kaiser's idle facilities at 12/31/x1?

b. If, as of 12/31/x1, an independent appraiser determined that the fair market value of the idle facilities was $50 million less than Kaiser's NBV, should the NBV be adjusted? Why or why not?

c. If the appraisal were $50 million more than NBV, should it be adjusted? Why or why not?

d. Why is Kaiser depreciating its idle facilities?

e. What rationale would support a decision not to continue depreciating facilities?

P10.20 Capitalization policy. On January 2, 1991, Keystone Corporation replaced its conveyor line with a more efficient one. The following information was available on that date:

Purchase price of new conveyor	$50,000
Carrying amount of old conveyor	$ 5,000
Fair value of old conveyor	$ 2,000
Installation cost of new conveyor	$ 8,000

The old conveyor was sold for $2,000.

Required:

What amount should Keystone capitalize as the cost of the new conveyor?

P10.21 Accounting for fixed assets. Presented below are selected PP&E disclosures from a recent Manville Corporation annual report:

MANVILLE CORPORATION
Consolidated Balance Sheets
December 31, 19x2 and 19x1
(thousands of dollars)

Assets	19x2	19x1
Current assets		
Cash (including time deposits of $5,742 in 19x2, $14,621 in 19x1)	$ 9,309	$ 19,180
Marketable securities, at cost (approximates market)	276,061	240,094
Receivables (net of allowances of $8,026 in 19x2, $8,998 in 19x1)		
Trade	254,302	233,303
Other	30,939	44,343
Inventories (Notes 2b and 4)	164,398	140,886
Prepaid expenses	17,288	21,902
Total current assets	752,297	699,708
Property, plant, and equipment, at cost (Note 2c)		
Land and land improvements	93,395	97,202
Buildings	308,421	302,909
Machinery and equipment	1,120,733	1,056,009
	1,525,549	1,456,120
Less accumulated depreciation and depletion	512,590	471,868
	1,012,959	984,252
Timber and timberlands, less cost of timber harvested	391,886	395,004
Property, plant, and equipment, net	1,404,845	1,379,256
Other assets (principally long-term receivables)	181,002	174,298
	$2,338,144	$2,253,262

Note 2—Summary of Significant Accounting Policies
Property, Plant, and Equipment, and Depreciation

Gains and losses from the normal retirement or replacement of property, plant, and equipment are reflected in accumulated depreciation with no effect on current period earnings. Gains and losses arising from abnormal dispositions are included in operations currently.

Depreciation and amortization are computed using the straight-line method based on estimated useful lives of the related assets. Depletion of mineral properties is calculated using the unit-of-production method. Expenditures for replacements and betterments are capitalized, while maintenance and repairs are charged against operations as incurred. The Company is engaged in a reforestation program which was initiated in 1972. Currently, the Company uses a 30 year rotation cycle which will convert its natural forest to timber plantations over approximately the next eighteen years. Cost of timber harvested is based on the unit cost rates calculated using the total estimated yield of timber to be harvested during the conversion period and the unamortized timber costs.

MANVILLE CORPORATION
Schedule V—Property, Plant, and Equipment
for the Years Ended December 31
(thousands of dollars)

Classification	Balance at Beginning of Period	Additions at Cost	Retirements	Other Deductions (a)	Balance at End of Period
19x2					
Land, including mineral properties, and land improvements	$ 97,202	$ 3,342	$ 3,723	$ (426)	$ 96,395
Buildings	302,911	11,052	2,829	(2,713)	308,421
Machinery and equipment	1,056,007	100,674	26,101	(9,847)	1,120,733
	1,456,120	115,068	32,653	(12,986)	1,525,549
Timber and timberlands	395,004	6,701	22	(9,797)	391,886
	$1,851,124	$121,769	$ 32,675	$(22,783)	$1,917,435
19x1					
Land, including mineral properties, and land improvements	$ 108,002	$ 2,210	$ 12,590	$ (420)	$ 97,202
Buildings	331,802	6,718	32,462	(3,147)	302,911
Machinery and equipment	1,090,337	99,409	124,993	(8,746)	1,056,007
	1,530,141	108,337	170,045	(12,313)	1,456,120
Timber and timberlands	402,034	2,359	4	(9,385)	395,004
	$1,932,175	$110,696	$170,049	$(21,698)	$1,851,124

(continued)

Classification	Balance at Beginning of Period	Additions at Cost	Retirements	Other Deductions (a)	Balance at End of Period
19x0					
Land, including mineral properties, and land improvements	$ 119,174	$ 1,237	$ 10,724	$ (1,685)	$ 108,002
Buildings	363,308	2,861	26,905	(7,462)	331,802
Machinery and equipment	1,202,490	53,348	139,488	(26,013)	1,090,337
	1,684,972	57,446	177,117	(35,160)	1,530,141
Timber and timberlands	406,205	3,837	581	(7,427)	402,034
	$2,091,177	$ 61,283	$177,698	$(42,587)	$1,932,175

Note:
(a) Includes the current year translation of the company's foreign operations and amounts for the cost of timber harvested.

MANVILLE CORPORATION
Schedule VI—Accumulated Depreciation, Depletion and
Amortization of Property, Plant, and Equipment
for the Years Ended December 31
(thousands of dollars)

Classification	Balance at Beginning of Period	Additions Charge to Costs and Expenses	Retirements	Other Charges Add (Deduct)(a)	Balance at End of Period
19x2					
Mineral properties, and land improvements	$ 36,134	$ 2,624	$ 2,450	$ (115)	$ 36,193
Buildings	102,350	10,099	2,494	(859)	109,096
Machinery and equipment	333,384	56,852	20,370	(2,565)	367,301
	$471,868	$69,575	$ 25,314	$ (3,539)	$512,590
19x1					
Mineral properties, and land improvements	$ 43,494	$ 2,761	$ 10,090	$ (31)	$ 36,134
Buildings	120,315	10,503	27,774	(694)	102,350
Machinery and equipment	382,903	55,395	102,920	(1,994)	333,384
	$546,712	$68,659	$140,784	$ (2,719)	$471,868

(continued)

Classification	Balance at Beginning of Period	Additions Charge to Costs and Expenses	Retirements	Other Charges Add (Deduct)(a)	Balance at End of Period
19x0					
Mineral properties, and land improvements	$ 43,669	$ 3,435	$ 5,109	$ 1,499	$ 43,494
Buildings	113,225	11,535	14,067	9,622	120,315
Machinery and equipment	367,853	61,931	72,535	25,654	382,903
	$524,747	$76,901	$91,711	$36,775	$546,712

Note:
(a) Includes the current year translation of the Company's foreign operations and in 19X0 includes $48,120 permanent impairment provision in the carrying amount of assets related to the Company's open-pit mining operation at Asbestos, Quebec, Canada.

Required:

a. Explain the first two sentences in Manville's Note 2, Property, Plant, and Equipment, and Depreciation.

b. Prepare the transaction to reflect Manville's 19x2 building retirements.

c. Between 19x1 and 19x2, the balance in Manville's buildings account increased by $5,512. Yet 19x2 depreciation expense on the buildings was less than 19x1 building depreciation expense by $404. Explain how this could happen.

d. Why did Manville use the units-of-production method for mineral properties rather than the straight-line method?

e. If Manville spent $1,000 on betterments and $800 for maintenance, how would these transactions be recorded?

f. Explain why "timber and timberlands" are classified under property, plant, and equipment, not as inventory in the balance sheet.

g. According to Manville's Note 2, cost of timber harvested "is based on the unit cost rates calculated using the total estimated yield of timber to be harvested during the conversion period and the unamortized timber costs." Explain how this is accomplished.

P10.22 Analyzing income statement data. The top part of a recent Pioneer income statement is as follows:

	(In thousands, except per share amounts)		
	19X2	19X1	19X0
Net sales	$874,871	$839,878	$884,726
Operating costs and expenses:			
Cost of goods sold	$399,464	$416,640	$426,768
Research and development	54,484	49,866	45,618
Selling	195,046	185,206	189,598
General and administrative	79,507	70,786	55,781
Restructuring and early retirement	—	—	12,913
Provision for plant closings	4,176	1,912	5,643
Loss on discontinued business (Note 3)	27,269	—	—
	$759,946	$724,410	$736,321
Operating income	$114,925	$115,468	$148,405

The top part of Pioneer's most recent cash flow statement is as follows:

	(in thousands)		
	19X2	19X1	19X0
Cash flows from operating activities			
Net income	$ 65,128	$ 53,939	$ 73,753
Noncash expenses included in net income:			
Depreciation	46,890	44,709	36,648
Amortization	3,023	2,924	3,055
Loss on disposal of property and equipment	7,044	4,962	6,919
Other	1,698	2,625	6,028
Foreign currency exchange losses	3,737	4,362	4,196
Change in assets and liabilities net of effects from purchase of subsidiaries:			
(Increase) in receivables	(17,343)	(16,995)	(36,272)
(Increase) decrease in inventories	41,427	22,655	(21,915)
Increase (decrease) in accounts payable and accrued expenses	26,614	(718)	22,281
Increase (decrease) in income taxes payable	11,102	(31,639)	4,137
Other prepaids, deferrals and accruals, net	(4,151)	10,153	(6,881)
Net cash provided by operating activities	$185,169	$ 96,977	$ 91,949
Cash flows from investing activities			
Purchase of property and equipment	$ (67,841)	$(72,768)	$(93,576)
Proceeds from sale of property and equipment	7,362	4,434	5,477
Purchase of subsidiaries, net of cash and cash equivalents acquired	(6,159)	—	(7,271)
Other	(4,390)	132	(1,059)
Net cash (used in) investing activities	$ (71,028)	$(68,202)	$(96,429)

On the 19x2 and 19x1 balance sheets, Pioneer included the following:

	(in thousands)	
Assets	**19X2**	**19X1**
Property and equipment (Note 5)	$ 46,457	$ 43,638
Buildings...	237,298	214,368
Machinery and equipment..	290,558	262,930
Construction in progress	12,451	27,008
	$586,764	$547,944
Less accumulated depreciation..	201,285	170,781
	$385,479	$377,163

Required:

a. The cash flow statement shows $46.89 million for depreciation for 19x2, yet this figure does not seem to appear on the consolidated statements of income. Please explain.

b. This $46.89 million of depreciation does not seem to explain the change in the accumulated depreciation figures that exists between the 19x1 and 19x2 balance sheets. Please explain; use figures as necessary.

c. The purchase of property and equipment shown on the cash flow statement of $67,841 thousand in 19x2 does not agree with the change in the property, plant, and equipment figures between the 19x1 and 19x2 balance sheets. Please explain; use figures as necessary.

CASES

C10.1 Fixed assets and natural resources: Salem Coal Company. Near the end of 1988, Andrew and Michael Miller formed the Salem Coal Company. According to the charter of incorporation, the purpose of the new business was to "locate, develop, extract, and transport" coal reserves in the state of West Virginia. The company remained closely held until January 1990, at which time a small public offering of common shares was held. According to the prospectus, the funds raised through the public offering would be used to acquire coal reserves and removal and transportation equipment and to construct miscellaneous facilities for the administration of the company's coal operations.

Approximately $4 million was raised through the offering and was dispersed during 1990 as follows:

1. In February; the Salem Coal Company paid $2.35 million for a tract of land in Grant District (Preston County) containing estimated coal reserves of 3.5 million tons. Following extraction and reclamation, it was anticipated that the land would have a resale value of $280,000 for agricultural purposes. In addition, the purchase price included a $50,000 reclamation bond that would be refunded if the reclamation work met certain standards established by the West Virginia Department of Natural Resources.

2. The following equipment was purchased:

Quantity	Item	Estimated Useful Life	Per Unit Price
1	Bulldozer	15 years	$195,000
1	Earthmover with dragline and stripping bucket	10 years	425,000
3	Dump trucks	5 years	75,000

The scrap value of the equipment at retirement was anticipated to be nominal. Signed checks for the equipment were delivered to the vendors on March 1.

3. A storage facility was constructed on the site at a cost of $150,000. It was anticipated that it would not be economically feasible to remove the building from the land after coal operations had terminated. In addition, it was uncertain whether the facilities might have alternative uses to subsequent landowners. Construction was completed by mid-May.

During May and June 1990, the company spent an additional $200,000 to prepare the site for operations. Finally, by mid-June, extraction operations began. By the end of 1990, 700,000 tons of coal had been mined and sold to the Monongahela Power Company at an average price of $15 per delivered ton.

Operating expenses (exclusive of depreciation and depletion) and selling and administrative expenses incurred in connection with the mining operations totaled $550,000.

Required:

a. Before financial statements can be prepared for the year ended December 31, 1990, a number of accounting policy decisions must be made. Prepare a list of those policy decisions and describe what accounting methods you would adopt and why. Assume that these decisions are to be made for financial reporting purposes only.

b. On the basis of your policy selections in part *a,* prepare an income statement and a partial balance sheet as of December 31, 1990. Assume an average tax rate of 34 percent.

c. Assume that (1) coal producers are eligible for a 10 percent "statutory percentage depletion allowance" and (2) a firm may choose to deplete its natural resources for *tax purposes* using either a unit of production approach *or* the statutory percentage depletion approach. Which method should the Salem Coal Company use and why?

C10.2 Amortization policy: Blockbuster Entertainment Corp. In May of 1989, Lee J. Seidler, a senior managing director and accounting analyst for Bear, Stearns & Co., issued a report critical of the accounting policies followed by Blockbuster Entertainment Corporation, the largest video store chain in the United States. In essence, Seidler suggested that Blockbuster's stock price was overvalued because of various questionable accounting policies used by the company. A portion of Seidler's comments are reproduced (with permission) below:

Have You Ever Seen a 40 Year Old Video Store?

Some of Blockbuster's mergers have been accounted for as purchases, others as poolings of interests. Pooling is usually more attractive, but Blockbuster Video (BV) takes most of the sting out of purchase accounting.

In a merger treated as a purchase, the price paid is first allocated to the fair values of assets that can be kicked, picked up or painted. Any excess becomes goodwill, which Blockbuster labels "intangible assets relating to acquired businesses." APB Opinion No. 17 requires that goodwill be amortized to income over 40 years or less.

In the past, many companies automatically adopted 40 year amortization. Current practice, which is usually required by the SEC, is to relate the amortization period to the nature of the business acquired. Thus, in a typical hi-tech acquisition the SEC requires goodwill to be amortized over 5 to 7 years; in bank purchases, over 15 to 20 years.

Have you ever seen a 40 year old videotape store? Will you ever see one? It is difficult to support the notion that goodwill associated with a videotape store has a life of more than a few years. The 10-K notes:

Both the Company and a franchise-owner have relocated a number of Blockbuster Video Superstores during the three year period ended December 31, 1988.

Reiterating this point, eight (of 80) Company owned stores that appeared in the 1987 10-K are not in the 1988 list. The maximum term of the Company's franchise agreement is 25 years.

There is no "correct" amortization period for this goodwill. Our guess is that five years would be reasonable for videotape stores. More important, we suspect that if the SEC considers this item it will require BV to bring its amortization period into this range. Applying five year amortization to BV's goodwill, rather than 40, would reduce 1988 EPS by $.14.

Stretching Videotape Amortization Way Out

BV drastically slowed its amortization of "hit" videotapes at the start of 1988. The change raised 1988 EPS $.11, of a total of $.57. In 1989, we estimate the change will add another $.13 to EPS.

Analysis of the impacts of the change is complicated by BV's confusing disclosure. The 1988 Form 10-K describes 1987 amortization differently than 1987 amortization was described in the original 1987 10-K. Discussions with the Company clarified matters.

In 1987 BV amortized its rental videotapes of hits, which are 20% to 25% of total inventory, over nine months straight-line. At the start of 1988, it switched to 36 months accelerated. The financial statements do not disclose how accelerated the curve is, but the Company says it uses 150% of straight-line, computed on a monthly basis.

The resulting amortization is not very accelerated. The cost of hit tapes is amortized as follows:

First 12 months	40%
Second 12 months	30%
Third 12 months	30%

This is pretty close to straight line. In effect, BV quadrupled the life of hit tapes.

BV seemed to imply that the longer amortization was demanded by the SEC, a comment which we doubt and which did not appear in the 10-K describing the change. Note that nine months is not necessarily right nor 36 months wrong. The right period (and curve) is the one that approximates revenue flows. By that standard, this curve seems slow for hit tapes.

Even with the slower curve, BV's 1989 earnings will face much higher amortization expense. In 1988, amortization was $15.7 million, mainly caused by purchases of $15.6 million of tapes in

1987. In 1988, the Company purchased $53.6 million of tapes. We estimate that the 1989 amortization will total $38 million (excluding charges from merged companies). That increase in amortization will require a substantial increase in tape rental revenue to maintain earnings.

Bear Sterns' analyst Steve Eisenberg suggests the necessary growth may not be forthcoming. Videotape ''rental tape'' shipments for the total industry grew an average 57% annual rate in the 1984–1988 period. Eisenberg predicts only 8.2% annual growth in 1989–1993.

Blockbuster EPS Recalculated

Following the adjustments proposed by Seidler, Blockbuster's 1988 earnings per share would be restated as follows:

EPS, as originally reported	$0.57
Less: Adjustment for faster goodwill amortization	(0.14)
Adjustment for change in tape amortization	(0.11)
Restated EPS	$0.32

In response to Seidler's report, Blockbuster's shares plunged $3.375 a share to $30 1/8. On the following day, the share price fell another $3.875 a share to close at $26 1/4.

Required:

Evaluate Seidler's arguments with respect to the Blockbuster accounting policies. Do you agree with him and, if so, why? If not, why not? Assuming that the market received no other information, do you agree that the price of the Blockbuster stock should have fallen by $7.25 per share following Seidler's report?

C10.3 Depreciation policy: Freshman Products. Freshman Products specializes in injection-molded, plastic trim parts for the auto industry (dash board knobs, etc.), supplying the Big Three U.S. companies and the domestic plants of the Japanese companies. Because of Freshman's reputation for service, one of the Big Three automakers asked if the company would bid on a new part—the pinch welt, which finishes off the inside edge of the door frame. Each car has at least 15 feet of that trim (it's about an inch in diameter), and all manufacturers use the same basic product. Even in a modest year, the industry requires about 40,000 miles of the welt. There are several welt manufacturers who already service the market, but all are subsidiaries of much larger companies. Freshman management believes that they can be successful with this new product by applying their brand of customer attention and thereby set themselves apart from their competition.

The welt, however, is an extruded part, and Freshman has no experience with extruded plastics and has no extruding equipment. Two extruding machines would be required to handle the volumes required by the bid, and they are estimated to cost $250,000 each. Used machines are available at less cost, but the new equipment is more energy efficient. There is excess space in the plant for this project, but the floor would have to be strengthened if the heavy extrusion equipment were to be moved in. Cost of the floor reinforcement would be $50,000. Shipping the new machines to the Freshman plant was likely to be $25,000; installation would probably cost $50,000; lighting in the new machine area would have to be improved at a cost of $30,000.

Extruded parts, like injected parts, are produced by the basic machine working on a die. The tool and die makers estimated that the two welt dies required for the extrusion machines would cost about $50,000 each.

The company uses straight-line depreciation in its financial reports prepared for the banks. Management has estimated a 30-year life on the plant (now 15 years old) and has set a 6-year life for all equipment because the injection machines (which are the biggest component of that asset class) tend to wear out over that period due to completing 100 stamping cycles an hour. Dies are depreciated over three years, not because they wear out, but because the customer product cycle runs about that long. All equipment and dies are assumed to have a 10 percent salvage value.

For tax purposes, the building is depreciated on the same basis and uses the same life as in the financial statements. The equipment and the dies are depreciated on the double-declining-balance (DDB) method for taxes, using the same lives as for the financial statements.

The manufacturer of the extrusion equipment claims that it will last at least 10 years with normal maintenance—the extrusion process is evidently not as self-destructive as is the injection process. The pinch welt is a generic product, which has been unchanged for at least the last 12 years: the auto companies have redesigned interiors a number of times recently, but they have continued to use the same welt design as they did when the product was first introduced. Freshman has never used a die for its complete physical life and so does not know how long these new welt extrusion dies might last. The tool and die makers have said that their best guess would be about five years.

Required:

Part 1

a. What depreciable life would you use for:

    (1). The extrusion machines? Why?
    (2). The other costs to be incurred in connection with the acquisition of those machines? Why?
    (3). The dies to be used in the extrusion process? Why?

b. Would you recommend using the same depreciation lives and methods for the tax returns and for the financial statements? Please explain your answer.

Part 2

Without regard to the answers you gave to question part *a*, assume that the dies are depreciated on a straight-line method over *five* years for financial statement purposes and on a DDB method over *three* years for tax purposes. Calculate the depreciation expense for each of those five years, for book and for tax.

	Year 1	Year 2	Year 3	Year 4	Year 5
Depreciation expense per books	_____	_____	_____	_____	_____
Depreciation expense per tax return	_____	_____	_____	_____	_____

Part 3

c. Assuming that income before depreciation on the dies and before tax expense was $100,000 in each year, prepare the book entries to record the dies' depreciation expense *and* the tax expense for Year 1. (Assume a 34 percent tax rate.)

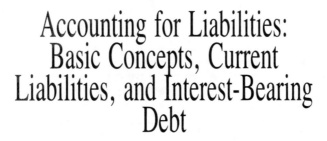

CHAPTER 11

Accounting for Liabilities: Basic Concepts, Current Liabilities, and Interest-Bearing Debt

Chapter Outline

- Conceptual Overview
- Current Liabilities: Payables and Accruals
- Loans, Bills, Notes, and Bonds
    Current Loans Payable

Bonds, Notes, and Loans: Long-term Debt
- Management Considerations
- Summary
- Appendix: The Time Value of Money

A s discussed in previous chapters, assets are the tangible and intangible resources owned or controlled by an entity. They represent the *uses* of cash and other funds of the firm. The *sources* of these funds are the entity's liabilities and owners' equity. Thus, when one looks at the assets on the balance sheet and wonders, "Where did the money for these assets come from?" the answer is that part came from the owners—the owners' equity—and the rest came from creditors—the liabilities. Creditors are any parties to which an entity owes money or other

consideration and may include lenders, suppliers, employees, or governmental agencies (such as the IRS). For many corporations, creditors are the largest source of funding. For example, as of December 31, 1990, more than 70% of PepsiCo's assets were funded by creditors.

Corporate liabilities present a number of accounting and valuation problems. Some liabilities are current and must be paid within a few days; others may extend 50 years or more. Some are for definite amounts that can be established from invoices, employment agreements, tax filings, and other documents; others, such as the provisions for anticipated warranty expenses, pensions, lawsuits, and deferred taxes, can only be estimated.

The purpose of this chapter is to consider the questions "What liabilities does a company have?" and "How should those liabilities be valued?" The three types of liabilities that present the most difficult valuation issues are saved for Chapter 12; these include leases,

pensions, and deferred income taxes. As we shall see in this chapter, in theory, *all* liabilities are to be reported at the present value of their related cash outflows. In reality, however, only some obligations are actually valued in this way. Students unfamiliar with the concept of present value, or the calculation of discounted cash flows, are urged to review the appendix to this chapter before proceeding.

CONCEPTUAL OVERVIEW

Every entity has a variety of obligations; only some of these are recognized in the financial statements as liabilities. Obligations are recognized as liabilities when they can be determined with reasonable precision, cannot be avoided, and are created by an event that has already occurred. Obligations that do *not* meet these three tests include, for example, a signed, binding contract to purchase certain products when the goods have not been received and a lawsuit for which damages have not yet been assessed.

As a general rule, short-term liabilities are recorded at their **face amount** (i.e., the amount printed on a bank note or an invoice), and long-term liabilities are recorded at their **present value** (i.e., the value *today* of receiving—or paying—a given sum of money). Although the conventional practice is to ignore present values on relatively short-term items such as accounts payable and accrued expenses payable (because the difference between the present value and face value of such a claim is usually insignificant), some current liabilities (e.g., the current portion of a mortgage payable) are nevertheless reported at their present values. Conversely, most long-term liabilities are carried at their present values, but a few are not, as shown in Exhibit 11.1.

CURRENT LIABILITIES: PAYABLES
AND ACCRUALS

Current liabilities are those obligations to be repaid during the next year or during the next operating cycle (if longer than a year in length). All other liabilities are noncurrent.

Accounts payable are the normally recurring obligations of a business for the purchase of materials, parts, fuel, and other items used in manufacturing or for purchases of merchandise to be resold, as in retailing. These liabilities are the easiest to value because an invoice or electronic transmission from the supplier provides the exchange price, and a receiving report from within the company indicates proper receipt of the item(s). The primary accounting policy issue a business entity faces here is whether to record the payable at its *gross* or *net* value.

If the merchandise purchased is for $10,000 and the payment terms are 2/10, net 30, the firm may pay the net amount ($9,800) within 10 days (i.e., net of the 2 percent discount), or it must pay the gross amount of $10,000 within 30 days. The transaction to

EXHIBIT 11.1

A Taxonomy of Liabilities

	Current liabilities	Noncurrent liabilities
Valued at face amounts	Accounts payable Accrued expenses Income taxes payable Dividends payable Unearned revenue Warranty obligations	Unearned revenue Warranty obligations

Valued at present value	Loans payable
	Current portion:
	   Notes payable
	   Bonds payable
	   Leases payable
		Loans payable
		Notes payable
		Bonds payable
		Leases payable
		Pension obligations

Shown at some other value	Deferred taxes	Deferred taxes Other liabilities

record the cash disbursement is relatively straightforward, but how should the company record the liability originally? Companies typically choose one accounting policy and follow it for all such purchases, even if they sometimes take the discount but do not at other times. If a company chooses to use the **gross method** (i.e. all purchases are initially recorded at the gross amount), when a discount is taken, the amount is recorded in the Purchase Discount account and appears on the income statement as miscellaneous revenue or as a reduction to the cost of sales. If, on the other hand, the **net method** is used (i.e. all purchases are initially recorded at the net amount), when a discount is missed because the entity did not pay on time, an expense entry to an account such as Purchase Discounts Lost or Interest Expense is generated. The latter is the most common policy in large firms. It is typically called the ''sore thumb'' choice because any discounts lost are highlighted.

Using the above example, the transactions would be recorded as follows:

Gross method

At the time of purchase:

```
Dr.  Inventory (A) . . . . . . . . . . . . . . . . . . . . . . $10,000
     Cr.  Accounts Payable (L) . . . . . . . . . . . . . . . . .          $10,000
```

If the discount is taken:

```
Dr.  Accounts Payable (L) . . . . . . . . . . . . . . . . $10,000
     Cr.  Cash (A) . . . . . . . . . . . . . . . . . . . . . . .           $9,800
     Cr.  Purchase Discounts (R) . . . . . . . . . . . . . . . .              200
```

If the discount is not taken, the liability is satisfied by a cash payment of $10,000.

Net method

At the time of purchase:

```
Dr.  Inventory (A)  . . . . . . . . . . . . . . . . . . . . . .  $9,800
     Cr.  Accounts Payable (L)  . . . . . . . . . . . . . . . . . . .         $9,800
```

If the discount is taken, as is assumed by this method, the liability is satisfied by a payment of $9,800. If the discount is not taken, the entry is:

```
Dr.  Accounts Payable (L) . . . . . . . . . . . . . . . . .  $9,800
Dr.  Purchase Discounts Lost (E)  . . . . . . . . . . . .      200
     Cr.  Cash (A)  . . . . . . . . . . . . . . . . . . . . . . . .         $10,000
```

Accrued Expenses Payable includes the obligations to employees for wages earned but not paid, the employer's portion of any salary or wage taxes due the government, and any amounts accrued for interest or rent expense. For example, if a company owes $15,000 for computer rental charges but payment is not due for another 10 days, the amount would be accrued by the following entry:

```
Dr.  Computer Rental (E)  . . . . . . . . . . . . . . . . .  $15,000
     Cr.  Accrued Expenses Payable (L)  . . . . . . . . . . . . .         $15,000
```

Payables and accruals, including current income taxes payable and dividends payable, are valued at their face amounts and are not discounted. The time and trouble to discount is generally not worth the effort for such a slight difference in value (and it would be needlessly confusing to many readers of financial statements). For example, the present value of the $15,000 of accrued computer rentals due in 10 days is $14,959.02, assuming a discount rate of 10 percent. The purist might argue that this amount should be recorded as the liability, with the difference of $40.98 recorded as interest expense. Fortunately, for both the readers of financial statements and the preparers, this practice is not followed unless the amounts are material.

Unearned revenue (or deferred income) is another current liability not usually reported at its present value; rather, it is shown at the amount received less whatever has been taken into income (i.e., earned) to date. For example, when an airline sells a ticket for $1,000 cash 30 days in advance of a scheduled flight, the transaction is recorded as:

```
Dr.  Cash (A)  . . . . . . . . . . . . . . . . . . . . . . . .  $1,000
     Cr.  Unearned Revenue (L) . . . . . . . . . . . . . . . . . .          $1,000
```

Since the service has not yet been rendered, the revenue has not been earned and thus cannot be recognized. When the passenger actually takes the flight and the airline receives the flight coupon, the transaction is recorded as:

```
Dr.  Unearned Revenue (L)  . . . . . . . . . . . . . . . . .  $1,000
     Cr.  Revenue (R)  . . . . . . . . . . . . . . . . . . . . . .          $1,000
```

Warranty obligations arise when a company sells a product and agrees to repair it and/or provide certain other services if the product fails. An automobile manufacturer, for example, may guarantee free repairs for four years or 60,000 miles, whichever comes first (it also may provide a loaner car while the repairs are being made). The accounting challenge for such obligations is one of *matching*. The sale is recorded when the buyer takes delivery of the car, but the repairs may not occur until some time far into the future. To match expenses with related revenues and avoid overstating income at the time of sale, the expected warranty costs associated with each car sale are estimated. These estimates are based on historical analysis, engineering assessments, and management judgment. At the time of sale or at the end of the sale's accounting period, an entry to record the expected warranty obligation is made:

```
Dr.  Warranty Expense (E)  . . . . . . . . . . . . . . . . . . $500
     Cr.  Estimated Warranty Obligation (L)  . . . . . . . . . . . . .        $500
```

When a cash payment is made by a dealer for warranty services provided to a customer, the following entry is made:

```
Dr.  Estimated Warranty Obligation (L)  . . . . . . . . . . . . $100
     Cr.  Cash (A)  . . . . . . . . . . . . . . . . . . . . . . . . . .        $100
```

Note that this accrual-oriented method to account for warranties has the effect of reflecting the *total* estimated warranty obligation and the *total* estimated warranty costs at the time of the sale. Hence, there will be no income statement impact in future periods for this particular car when warranty repairs are actually made. From time to time, adjustments are necessary to the estimating procedures to ensure that the total outstanding warranty obligation is a reasonable approximation of the total warranty costs yet to be incurred.

Exhibit 11.2, taken from PepsiCo's 1990 annual report, illustrates a typical format for reporting current liabilities. With the exception of short-term borrowings, each of the current liabilities is shown at its actual or face amount without considering its present value. PepsiCo's footnotes (see Chapter 1) provide further information about these current obligations, for example, the composition of the short-term borrowings and the income taxes due to federal, state, or foreign taxation authorities.

EXHIBIT 11.2

PEPSICO, INC. AND SUBSIDIARIES
Current Liability Section
As of December 29, 1990 and 1989
(in millions)

	1990	1989
Current liabilities:		
Short-term borrowings	$1,626.5	$ 866.3
Accounts payable	1,116.3	1,054.5
Income taxes payable	443.7	313.7
Other current liabilities	1,584.0	1,457.3
Total current liabilities	$4,770.5	$3,691.8

LOANS, BILLS, NOTES, AND BONDS

Loans and securities are two basic types of interest-bearing debt. *Loans* are monetary agreements between two parties. The parties negotiate and sign an agreement that sets forth the terms and conditions of the loan. Loans may be of a short duration or may extend for many years. Although almost anyone can borrow or lend money, commercial banks are typically the primary source of business loans for short and intermediate-term borrowing (i.e., up to five years). Life insurance companies, on the other hand, have been the traditional source of business loans with maturities of 10 or more years.

Debt in the form of *securities* includes bills, certificates, notes, and bonds. For these obligations, the borrower formalizes the terms and conditions of the loan in a document, which is then sold. The most common type of bill is a T-bill, or U.S. Treasury bill—a short-term U.S. government debt obligation. The most common type of certificate is the **certificate of deposit**, or CD—an obligation of a commercial bank. Notes and bonds are the most common form of intermediate and long-term debt securities issued by *corporations*. Bills, certificates, and, in some cases, notes, are short-term obligations with maturities of less than a year. The maturity period for notes is usually 1 to 10 years, and for bonds, usually more than 10 years.

Current Loans Payable

Loans, notes, certificates, bills, and other current interest-bearing debt (which will henceforth be called *current loans payable*) are recorded at their present value. For example, suppose a company borrows $100,000 for six months at 10 percent with interest payable monthly. Essentially, the company receives $100,000 upon signing the loan agreement and agrees to pay a total of $5,000 ($833.33 per month) in interest over six months and a lump sum of $100,000 in six months. Thus, the cash flows for this loan appear as follows:

		Cash flow at end of month						Total
	Now	**1**	**2**	**3**	**4**	**5**	**6**	
Loan proceeds	100,000							
Interest payments		(833)	(833)	(833)	(833)	(833)	(833)	(5,000)
Principal payment							(100,000)	(100,000)

This agreement calls for the company to repay $105,000 in total, but accounting practice for short-term loans (and long-term ones, for that matter) is to record them at their discounted or **present value.**[1] Thus, the entry to record the loan at its inception is:

```
Dr.  Cash (A) . . . . . . . . . . . . . . . . . . . . . .  $100,000
     Cr.  Loan Payable (L) . . . . . . . . . . . . . . . . . . . .          $100,000
```

---

[1] A financial calculator can be used to verify that the present value of the six monthly interest payments of $833, plus the principal payment of $100,000 in the sixth month, is indeed $100,000 when the interest rate is 10 percent (i.e., FV = −100,000, PMT = −833, N = 6, I = 0.833, 10%/12).

Each month an entry for the accrued interest is also necessary:

```
Dr.  Interest Expense (E) . . . . . . . . . . . . . . . . . . .  $833
    Cr.  Loan Interest Payable (L) . . . . . . . . . . . . . . . .          $833
```

A complication with some short-term loans is that they are often issued on a discounted basis, as if the interest were prepaid. For example, a company may agree to pay $100,000 in six months and receive only $95,000 now. Convention is to record this note at $100,000, with the difference going to a contra liability (CL) account. Thus, the transaction would be recorded as:

```
Dr.  Cash (A) . . . . . . . . . . . . . . . . . . . . .  $95,000
Dr.  Discount on Notes Payable (CL) . . . . . . . . . .    5,000
    Cr.  Notes Payable (L) . . . . . . . . . . . . . . . . . .          $100,000
```

Of course, this note is stated at its present value (i.e., $95,000), but the rate is not quite 10 percent (the effective rate is 10.53 percent). Each month an entry is made for the accrual of the prepaid interest:

```
Dr.  Interest Expense (E) . . . . . . . . . . . . . . . . . . .  $833
    Cr.  Discount on Notes Payable (CL) . . . . . . . . . . . . .          $833
```

After six months, the contra liability account will be zero, and the liability will reflect its maturity value of $100,000.

Sometimes a company may sign a note when it does not know the implicit interest rate; perhaps it knows only the actual payments to be made over time. (For example, the notes could be in exchange for a special, one-of-a-kind machine for which the buyer does not know the market value.) Conventional practice is to discount the payments at a rate that matches the risk characteristics of the note. For example, if the note is noncancelable, a low-risk debt rate such as the prime rate or the company's incremental borrowing rate may be used.

Bonds, Notes, and Loans: Long-Term Debt

The term **bond** refers to a variety of long-term obligations evidenced by a document that may be sold or traded. The entity issuing a bond is the borrower, and the buyer of those bonds is the lender. **Debentures,** for example, are general obligation bonds issued by a company. **Mortgage bonds** and **revenue bonds** are examples of bonds in which particular corporate assets are pledged as security for the debt.

Bond liabilities are recorded at their present value in a manner similar to that used for current loans payable. The present value of the combined interest and principal payments on a bond is the same as the principal outstanding on the bond when discounting is done at the effective interest rate on the bond. (If this concept is not clear, refer to the appendix for examples and an explanation.)

If bonds are issued or sold at their face amount, the accounting is straightforward. For example, assume that a company issues $50 million of 11 percent, 20-year debentures with annual interest payments. The entry to record the initial borrowing is:

```
Dr.  Cash (A) . . . . . . . . . . . . . . . . . $50,000,000
     Cr.  Bonds Payable (L) . . . . . . . . . . . . . . . .      $50,000,000
```

This entry assumes that the company sold the bonds itself, and thus incurred no transaction costs. In reality, most companies hire a bond underwriter to place or sell its debt securities and thus incur certain transaction fees when debt securities are sold.

When the annual interest payment is made, the following entry is recorded:

```
Dr.  Interest Expense (E) . . . . . . . . . . . . . $5,500,000
     Cr.  Cash (A) . . . . . . . . . . . . . . . . . . . . . .      $5,500,000
```

Assuming that the bonds are retired on the maturity date, we make the following entry:

```
Dr.  Bonds Payable (L) . . . . . . . . . . . . . $50,000,000
     Cr.  Cash (A) . . . . . . . . . . . . . . . . . . . . . .      $50,000,000
```

Like discounted notes, **bonds** present accounting problems because the amount printed on the face of a bond certificate may not be what the issuing company (the borrower) ultimately receives in cash, and from the buyers' perspective, it may not be what the purchaser (the lender) ultimately has to pay. Bonds often sell at a **premium** or **discount** when first issued because of interest rate changes in the bond market between the time the bonds are priced (and the certificates printed) and the time customers actually buy them. Most corporate bonds issued in the United States come to market at a slight discount because it is psychologically easier to sell a security at a discount than at a premium.

From the bond buyer's perspective, money is lent when the bonds are purchased. In exchange for cash the buyer receives a promise of a stream of cash flows (the annuity interest payments) over the life of the bond plus a terminal cash flow payment (the lump-sum principal repayment) at the **maturity date.** The value of these cash flows depends upon the interest rate, or **yield rate,** used to discount them. Interest (yield) rates change continually due to market forces such as world political conditions, the general health of the economy, inflation, and investor expectations, to name just a few.

For example, a $1,000, 20-year, 11 percent, annual interest payment bond may come to market when the yield rate for the class and risk of bond has just increased to 11 1/8 percent. Because of the rise in interest rates, the bond will actually sell for only $990.13, or a discount of $9.87.[2] Suppose an entire issue of these bonds with a face value of $50 million were sold in the market and brought the issuing firm $49,506,333. Note that 11 percent bonds pay $5.5 million per year in interest (the coupon amount), and $50 million (the **maturity value**) is to be repaid at the end of the 20th year. The present value of these payments at 11 percent is, of course, $50 million, whereas at 11 1/8 percent, the **effective rate,** the present value is only $49,506,333, which is the amount of cash that the bond-issuing company can expect to receive if the bonds are sold to yield 11 1/8 percent. The difference between the face amount of $50 million and the selling price of

---

[2]To verify this number using a financial calculator, the keying is FV = 1,000, PMT = 110 (i.e., 11% × $1,000), N = 20, I = 11.125 (i.e., 11 1/8%).

$49,506,333 is the *bond discount,* which must be amortized over the 20-year life of the debt. The following is the accounting challenge in a situation like this:

1. To show the bond liability at its present value, not its face amount.
2. To show the annual interest expense at the effective rate (11 1/8 percent), not the stated or **coupon rate** (11 percent).

The transaction to record the sale of bonds for this example is as follows:

```
Dr.  Cash (A) . . . . . . . . . . . . . . . . . .  $49,506,333
Dr.  Bond Discount (CL) . . . . . . . . . . . . .      493,667
     Cr.  Bonds Payable (L) . . . . . . . . . . . . . . . . .            $50,000,000
```

Thus, the bonds would be recorded initially on the balance sheet at $49,506.333, or at the present value at the time of issuance. At the end of each year, two transactions are required: one to record the interest paid on the bonds and the second to amortize the bond discount. Bond discounts (or premiums) are typically amortized over the life of a bond using the **effective interest method,** rather than straight-line amortization. To facilitate the preparation of the two transactions, the borrower usually prepares a bond amortization schedule similar to that in Exhibit 11.3. This schedule adjusts the actual interest expense, based on 11.125 percent on $49,506,333 in the first year, by amortizing the bond discount of $493,667. The key to Exhibit 11.3 is that the total yearly interest expense (column 2) is always 11 1/8 percent (the effective rate) of the outstanding net liability (column 5). Of course, the net liability is also equivalent to the present value of the future payments (cash interest to be paid plus the principal) at 11 1/8 percent.

Another way to think about this is that, in terms of face amounts, $50 million is being borrowed for 20 years on which $5.5 million per year (or $110 million in total) of interest will be paid in cash. In fact, however, only $49,506,333 is borrowed, although a full $50 million will be repaid in 20 years. The difference of $493,667 represents additional interest, and, thus, the total interest expense paid over the life of the debt is $110,493,667. By spreading the $493,667 over 20 years (as revealed in column 3 of Exhibit 11.3), the borrower's income statement shows an interest expense equal to 11.125 percent of the bond value as reported on the company's balance sheet (*not* 11 percent of $50 million).

The entries for Year 1 for this bond would be recorded as:

```
Dr.  Interest Expense (E) . . . . . . . . . . . . . .  $5,500,000
     Cr.  Cash (A) . . . . . . . . . . . . . . . . . . . . .           $5,500,000
```

and

```
Dr.  Interest Expense (E) . . . . . . . . . . . . . . . .  $7,580
     Cr.  Bond Discount (CL) . . . . . . . . . . . . . . . . . .          $7,580
```

The two separate entries can also be combined into one as follows:

```
Dr.  Interest Expense (E) . . . . . . . . . . . . . .  $5,507,580
     Cr.  Cash (A) . . . . . . . . . . . . . . . . . . . . .           $5,500,000
     Cr.  Bond Discount (CL) . . . . . . . . . . . . . . . . . .            7,580
```

EXHIBIT 11.3

Amortization of a Bond Discount

Year	(1) Coupon Interest (11.0%)	(2) Effective Interest (11.125%)	(3) Discount Amortization (2-1)	(4) Unamortized Discount (4-3)	(5) Present Value of Bond ($50,000,000-4)
				$493,667	$49,506,333
1	$5,500,000	$5,507,580	$7,580	$486,667	$49,513,913
2	5,500,000	5,508,423	8,423	477,664	49,522,336
3	5,500,000	5,509,360	9,360	477,664	49,522,336
4	5,500,000	5,510,401	10,401	457,904	49,542,096
5	5,500,000	5,511,558	11,558	446,345	49,553,655
6	5,500,000	5,512,844	12,844	433,501	49,566,499
7	5,500,000	5,514,273	14,273	419,228	49,580,722
8	5,500,000	5,515,861	15,861	403,367	49,596,663
9	5,500,000	5,517,625	17,625	385,742	49,614,258
10	5,500,000	5,519,586	19,586	366,156	49,633,844
11	5,500,000	5,521,765	21,765	344,391	49,655,604
12	5,500,000	5,524,187	24,187	320,204	49,679,796
13	5,500,000	5,526,877	26,877	293,327	49,706,673
14	5,500,000	5,529,867	29,867	263,459	49,736,541
15	5,500,000	5,533,190	33,190	230,269	49,769,731
16	5,500,000	5,536,883	36,883	193,387	49,806,631
17	5,500,000	5,540,986	40,986	152,401	49,847,599
18	5,500,000	5,545,545	45,545	106,855	49,893,145
19	5,500,000	5,550,612	50,612	56,243	49,943,757
20	5,500,000	5,556,243	56,243	-0-	50,000,000
Total	$110,000,000	$110,493,667	$493,667		

The income statement reflects total interest expense of $5,507,580 for Year 1. Note that this expense is exactly 11 1/8 percent of the outstanding bond liability (11 1/8 percent × 49,506,333 = $5,507,580).

For financial statement purposes, the details of each bond issue should be disclosed in the footnotes and should reveal the aggregate present value of all bond liabilities and the aggregate principal payments to be made for each over the next five years. Bond liabilities are shown in the balance sheet net of any premium or discount. On the balance sheet, the current principal obligation is classified as a current liability; the remainder is included under noncurrent liabilities. Thus, for the bonds under discussion here, at the end of Year 1, the balance sheet shows nothing related to these bonds under current liabilities (because no *principal* repayments are to be made in Year 2 and the accrued interest was paid in cash). The balance sheet reports $49,513,913 under noncurrent liabilities reflecting the *net* bond liability:

Bonds payable	$50,000,000
Less: Unamortized bond discount	486,087
Bonds payable (net)	$49,513,913

EXHIBIT 11.4

SUN MICROSYSTEMS, INC.
Long-Term Debt Disclosures.

2. Borrowing Arrangements. Borrowing arrangements consist of the following:

	June 30,	
(in thousands)	1991	1990
10.55% senior notes	$190,536	$190,258
6 3/8 % convertible subordinated debentures	117,013	115,584
10.18% mortgage loan	40,000	40,000
9.37% bank term loan	9,375	15,625
Other	1,404	4,417
	358,328	365,884
Less portion due within one year	6,893	6,977
Long-term debt	$351,435	$358,907

In September and December 1989, the Company signed agreements with a group of insurance companies and received $192 million from the sale of 10.55% senior notes due September 1996 and warrants to purchase 1,294,180 shares of Sun's common stock at $24.80 per share, after, and subject to further, anti-dilution adjustments. The warrants are currently exercisable and expire in September 1996. The notes are carried net of the fair value of the warrants, which is being amortized straight-line over the term of the notes. Interest on these notes is payable semi-annually beginning March 1990. Principal is payable in five equal installments beginning September 1992. Under the agreements, Sun is required to maintain various financial ratios and is restricted in its ability to pay cash

dividends. The Company was in compliance with all covenants at June 30, 1991.

The Company issued and sold $135 million of 6 3/8% convertible subordinated debentures in October 1989. The debentures are due October 15, 1999, and were sold at 84.9% of their face amount. They are carried net of original issue discount, which is being amortized by the interest method over the life of the issue. The effective annual yield to maturity is 8.67%. Interest is payable semi-annually beginning April 1990. Each debenture is convertible at the option of the holder into common stock at $25.00 per share and is redeemable at the option of Sun on or after November 2, 1992, at prices ranging from 92.5% of face value to 100% in 1998.

Exhibit 11.4 presents the footnote disclosure pertaining to long-term debt from the 1991 annual report for Sun Microsystems, Inc. Note that the 6 3/8 percent convertible subordinated debentures of 1999 are shown net of the amortized discount. Originally, these debentures must have sold for $114,615 thousand (84.9 percent of $135 million). Thus, the original issue discount was $20,385 ($135,000 − 114,615). By June 30, 1991, the discount had been amortized down to $17,987 thousand ($135,000 − 117,013).

The table in the footnote is particularly interesting because it shows that Sun has arranged its borrowings to minimize any near-term repayments of principal. Note that Sun's near-term principal repayments on more than $350 million of long-term borrowings are less than $7 million!

Although rare, bonds are also sometimes sold at a **premium.** It more difficult to sell securities at a premium for psychological reasons. Consequently, bond issuers usually err on the discount side when setting the interest rate to be printed on their bonds. When market interest rates are lower than a bond's coupon (stated) rate, however, a bond premium results. Conceptually, accounting for bond premiums is the reverse of accounting for bond discounts. Suppose, for example, that the $50 million in bonds actually sell for $50,501,800, resulting in an effective yield of only 10 7/8 percent.[3] The transaction for the issuer at the time of sale is:

Dr.	Cash (A)	$50,501,800
	Cr. Bonds Payable (L)	$50,000,000
	Cr. Bond Premium (L)	501,800

When the first interest payment is made at the end of Year 1, the two transactions necessary to record the interest payment and the amortization of the premium are as follows:

Dr.	Interest Expense (E)	$5,500,000
	Cr. Cash (A)	$5,500,000

and

Dr.	Bond Premium (L)	$7,928
	Cr. Interest Expense (E)	$7,928

These two separate entries can be combined into a single one as follows:

Dr.	Interest Expense (E)	$5,492,072
Dr.	Bond Premium (L)	7,928
	Cr. Cash (A)	$5,500,000

Note that the premium is amortized in a manner similar to that illustrated in Exhibit 11.3, except that the effect is to reduce the effective interest expense, not to raise it.

If a company chooses to retire its debt early (i.e., prior to its scheduled maturity date as printed on the bond certificate) by exercising call provisions or purchasing its debt securities in the open market, accounting practice requires that any gain or loss from the extinguishment of debt retirement be recognized in the current income statement as an extraordinary item.[4] For example, suppose that the $50 million in 11 percent bonds, sold at a premium, were retired after one year by repurchasing the bonds for an aggregate of $52 million. Since the book value of the bonds after one year is $50,493,872 ($50,501,800 − 7,928), the *seller* records a loss of $1,506,128:

Dr.	Loss on Early Retirement (Loss).	$ 1,506,128
Dr.	Bonds Payable (L).	50,000,000
Dr.	Bond Premium (L)	493,872
	Cr. Cash (A)	$52,000,000

---

[3]To determine the present value of these bonds using a financial calculator, the keying is FV = −50,000,000, PMT = −5,500,000, N = 20, I = 10.875.

[4]Early retirement of debt is a common occurrence. At first glance, it may seem inappropriate to treat the associated gains or losses as *extraordinary;* however, generally accepted accounting practice is to do just that to prevent corporations from attempting to ''manage earnings'' by retiring selected bonds as needed to raise or lower reported accounting income.

Purchasers of bonds sold at a premium or discount simply record the securities at their cost. They are carried at cost, and the premium or discount is amortized over the lifetime of the bonds.[5] For example, suppose that a company purchased the entire issue of $50 million in the above example at a cost of $49,506,333. (This could happen only if the underwriter received no commission and there were no other transaction fees or expenses.) At the end of the first year, the entry on the purchaser's books to record the receipt of interest income appears as follows:

Dr.	Cash (A)	$5,500,000
Dr.	Investment in Corporate Bonds (A)	7,580
Cr.	Interest Income (R)	$5,507,580

The result of this entry is that total interest income for the year is 11 1/8 percent of the bond asset. The cash received is only $5.5 million, or 11.11 percent of the bond asset, but the effective interest income becomes 11.125 percent once the bond discount is amortized.

As the business activities of American corporations become more global and as the nature of borrowing arrangements become more complex, the valuation of short- and long-term debt becomes ever more important. Accordingly, the footnote disclosures of these debts have become more extensive. PepsiCo, Inc., again provides an illuminating example. In Exhibit 11.5, parts of the footnote disclosure for short-term borrowings and long-term debt from the 1990 annual report describe PepsiCo's commercial paper, notes, bonds, and other long-term liabilities. Note that PepsiCo has debt denominated in Swiss francs, European currency units (ECU), British sterling, Italian lira, Australian dollars, Canadian dollars, and, of course, U.S. dollars.

The Swiss franc 400 million perpetual Foreign Interest Payment bonds are particularly interesting. Interest on these bonds is paid in U.S. dollars, whereas the principal is to be paid in Swiss francs. Apparently, PepsiCo has protected itself against foreign exchange loses through some type of hedging arrangement. Thus, the value of the bonds at the initial sale price in U.S. dollars is $209.9 million.

MANAGEMENT CONSIDERATIONS

In earlier chapters, we discussed the need to manage the components of working capital so as to minimize the amount of idle cash. We also observed that an important aspect of management's job was to balance

- The need to maintain an adequate working capital position (to be able to pay bills when they come due) against the cost of maintaining that liquid position.
- The need for inventory (to be able to fill orders promptly) against the cost of carrying that inventory.

---

[5]Bonds are not subject to the lower-of-cost-or-market guidelines established in SFAS No. 12 (see Chapter 7). If, however, there is a permanent impairment of a bond's market value, it should be written down accordingly.

EXHIBIT 11.5

PEPSICO, INC.
Footnote Disclosure for Short-Term
Borrowing and Long-Term Debt

	1990	1989
Short-term borrowings		
Commercial paper (7.9% and 8.7% weighted average interest rate at year-end 1990 and 1989, respectively) . . .	$ 3,168.8	$ 3,081.8
Current maturities of long-term debt issuances	1,085.0	316.8
Notes	624.8	594.8
Other borrowings	247.9	422.9
Amount reclassified to long-term debt **(A)**	(3,500.0)	(3,550.0)
	$ 1,626.5	$ 866.3
Long-term Debt		
Short-term borrowings, reclassified **(A)**	$ 3,500.0	$ 3,550.0
Notes due 1991 through 1998 (7.9% weighted average interest rate at year-end 1990 and 1989) **(B)**	1,513.7	871.1
Zero coupon notes, $1.1 billion due 1991–2012 (14.0% semi-annual weighted average yield to maturity at year-end 1990 and 1989).	348.1	308.7
Swiss franc perpetual Foreign Interest Payment bonds **(C)** .	209.9	209.1
European Currency Units 7.63% and 7.38% notes due 1990 and 1992 **(D)**.	135.2	239.3
Pound sterling 9.13% notes due 1993 **(D)**	115.5	96.8
Swiss franc 5.25% bearer bonds due 1995 **(D)**.	104.7	86.9
Austrailian dollar notes due 1990 (13.3% weighted average interest rate at year-end 1989).	—	81.5
Italian lire 10.5% notes due 1991 **(D)**	88.8	79.0
Canadian dollar 8.75% notes due 1991 **(B)**	64.6	64.6
Capital lease obligations (See Note on page 44.)	193.8	179.3
Other, due 1991–2020 (8.9% and 9.0% weighted average interest rate at year-end 1990 and 1989, respectively) . . .	410.8	327.6
	6,685.1	6,093.9
Less current maturities of long-term debt issuances	(1,085.0)	(316.8)
Total long-term debt	$ 5,600.1	$ 5,777.1

E X H I B I T   1 1 . 5

(continued)

Long-term debt is carried net of any related discount or premium and unamortized debt issuance costs. The debt agreements include various restrictions, none of which is presently significant to PepsiCo.

(A) At year-end 1990, $3.5 billion of short-term borrowings were classified as long-term, reflecting PepsiCo's intent and ability to refinance these borrowings on a long-term basis, through either long-term debt issuances or rollover of existing short-term borrowings. At year-end 1990 and 1989, PepsiCo had revolving credit agreements aggregating $3.5 billion and $3.6 billion, respectively, with the current agreements covering potential borrowings through 1994 and 1995. These available credit facilities provide the ability to refinance short-term borrowings.

(C) The coupon rate of the Swiss franc 400 million perpetual Foreign Interest Payment bonds issued in 1989 is 7.5% through 1996. The interest payments are made in U.S. dollars at a fixed contractual exchange rate. The bonds have no stated maturity date. At the end of each 10-year period after the issuance of the bonds, PepsiCo and the bondholders each have the right to cause redemption of the bonds. If not redeemed, the coupon rate will be adjusted based on the prevailing yield of 10-year U.S. Treasury Securities. The principal of the bonds is denominated is Swiss francs. PepsiCo can and intends to limit the ultimate redemption amount to the U.S. dollar proceeds at issuance, which is the basis of the carrying value in both years.

■ The need to extend credit (to be able to expand sales) against the cost of carrying those receivables.

This chapter's discussion of the liability side of the balance sheet has noted that the source of some of the costs involved in maintaining too liquid a position, namely tying up funds in cash, in inventory, or in receivables, could alternatively be used to reduce interest-carrying debt. To the extent that management can reduce the cost of that debt, it also reduces the cost of carrying working capital and thereby makes the balancing job easier and less critical.

Management can reduce some of the cost of carrying inventory by slowing down payments to suppliers. But suppliers are important stakeholders in the company, and an extended payment program is likely to cost the company in the long run. For example, suppliers may decide to cover their own costs of carrying a receivable due from a company by raising their prices. Or they may simply decide not to do business with the company at any price. Worse, an extended payout program may force the supplier into an illiquid position, or even cause bankruptcy, resulting in the loss of a critical resource for the company. Clearly, the management of payables requires delicate balancing.

The other liability accounts can be managed in a similar fashion to provide a certain amount of no-cost financing. Employees are occasionally content to defer their compensation because they can also defer their own personal taxes. Those deferred compensation plans can also fund the company's operations. The IRS allows the deferral of some income taxes, sometimes only from one year to the next, in other situations for the life of the company (e.g., when the company continues to add to its fixed asset base such that the tax effects of accelerated depreciation never does roll over—a topic discussed in the next chapter).

Liabilities need to be managed in much the same way as a company's assets to produce the greatest return on the shareholders' funds as is practical and consistent with the company's long-term goals and ethical values. Even the interest-bearing liabilities need to be managed for the benefit of shareholders. If a company earns 10 percent after tax on its assets, and shareholders expect a 20 percent return on their investment, it would appear to be foolish to borrow money for an expansion if borrowing costs are 12 percent. It would appear better to ask the shareholders for an additional infusion of capital. But interest on debt is tax deductible, whereas the dividends paid to stockholders are not. Therefore, the cost of a loan in this situation is really only 8 percent if we assume a 33 percent tax rate. With that perspective, borrowing makes sense because shareholders earn the extra 2 percent on the newly acquired assets *without* investing any more capital.

In theory, a company could borrow all of its funds and provide an infinite rate of return to its shareholders. It stands to reason, however, that no creditor would lend on that basis. Lenders require some equity protection for their risk, and as that protection decreases, their risk rises; and accordingly, they will charge more for their borrowings. Most managements today carefully manage their company's leverage ratio to operate with the least amount of shareholder capital, consistent with the most cost advantageous credit rating from their borrowers. Managing that relationship requires careful attention to the credit markets and to the attitudes of the company's credit suppliers.

SUMMARY

Liabilities are the short- and long-term obligations of a company, usually involving the repayment of cash. In this chapter, we learned that most current liabilities are valued at their face value, whereas most long-term liabilities are valued at their present value. The present value of a liability represents the amount of cash (or other assets) necessary to satisfy a liability *today*, as opposed to its maturity date in the future.

Understanding the extent of obligations that are present in a company is important. If a company has borrowed too much, it may face a high degree of *default risk* for nonpayment of its obligations. On the other hand, for most companies, borrowing some level of funds is usually advantageous so long as the company is able to produce a return on the borrowed funds that exceeds the cost of borrowing.

NEW CONCEPTS AND TERMS

Accrued expenses payable (p. 483)
Annuity (p. 499)
Bill (p. 485)
Bond (p. 486)
Certificate of deposit (p. 485)
Compound interest (p. 497)
Coupon rate (p. 488)
Debenture (p. 486)
Discount (p. 487)
Discounted value (p. 488)
Effective interest method (p. 488)
Effective rate (p. 487)
Face amount (p. 481)

Gross method (p. 482)
Maturity date (p. 487)
Maturity value (p. 487)
Mortgage bond (p. 486)
Net method (p. 482)
Note (p. 485)
Premium (p. 487)
Present value (p. 481)
Revenue bond (p. 486)
Time value of money (p. 496)
Unearned revenue (p. 483)
Warranty obligation (p. 483)
Yield rate (p. 487)

APPENDIX 11

The Time Value of Money

One of the most important and pervasive concepts in business is the **time value of money.** We take it for granted, for example, that when we deposit a sum of money in a bank or savings institution, we will receive *interest* on those deposited funds. In effect, the deposited funds have an income-producing feature—the time value of money. By allowing a bank or savings institution to use the funds, perhaps to loan them to someone else, we receive a fee (i.e., interest income).

Even when funds are not deposited in a financial institution, they are assumed to have a time value of money. For example, some automobile manufacturers advertise that a customer may buy their product, pay for the purchase over 48 months, but incur no interest charges. Realistically, it is improbable that any manufacturer is able to finance its customers' purchases over extended periods without charging some interest costs; in any case, such practice makes very little business sense. In most cases in which zero interest is advertised, the manufacturer has added an *implicit* cost of financing the purchase over time into the consumer's purchase price. When this occurs, the consumer is faced with an accounting dilemma, namely to determine the true cost of the item versus the implicit cost of paying for the purchase over 36, 48, or 60 months.

To illustrate, suppose that on December 31, 1991, Cavalier Company purchased a new delivery van from a local truck dealer, Keller Auto & Truck Company. According to the agreement between the two companies, Cavalier will pay Keller $20,000 on December 31, 1993—two years hence—and issues a noninterest-bearing note in that amount. On the basis of recent conversations with a loan officer at a bank, executives at Cavalier are aware that they could have borrowed the $20,000 for the two-year period at 10 percent interest. Thus, the accounting dilemma is to answer the following questions: What amount did Cavalier pay for the van? At what value should Cavalier's note be shown on the company's December 31, 1991, balance sheet?

Both questions can be answered by determining the cash equivalent value of the Cavalier note on December 31, 1991. Obviously, this figure is less than the $20,000 to be paid on December 31, 1993, because of the time value of money. If Cavalier had borrowed $1 from its banker at 10 percent, it would become $1.10 at the end of one year, and this $1.10 would become $1.21 at the end of a second year (if interest is compounded annually).[6] Thus, the problem is to determine the value of the Cavalier note *exclusive* of the time value of money. And, to accomplish this, we must look to present value concepts for help.

Present value refers to *today's* value of receiving (or paying) a given sum of money. For example, if we are able to deposit $1 in a bank today and interest is compounded annually at 10 percent, the value of our deposit will be $1.10 at the end of one year. The value to be received at the end of one year is known as the *future value*, and, computationally, is given by the following equation:

$$F_{n,i} = (1 + i)^n$$

where $F_{n,i}$ is the future (compounded) value of $1 at interest rate i for n periods. Thus,

$$F_{1,.10} = (1 + .10)^1 = 1.10.$$

To understand the concept of present value, it is a simple matter to consider merely the reverse (or inverse) of the concept of *future value*. For example, if we are to receive $1.10 in one year, and if interest is calculated at 10 percent annually, what is the value of that payment today? Using the equation for present value computations,

$$P_{n,i} = \frac{1}{(1 + i)^n}$$

we can readily determine that the present value of receiving $1 in one year at 10 percent interest is 0.90909. To determine the present value (PV) of receiving $1.10 in one year, it is a simple matter to multiply the two figures together:

$$PV = \$1.10 \ (0.09090) = \$1.$$

Thus, the present value of receiving $1.10 in one year at 10 percent interest is $1.

With these concepts in mind, we can now approach the problem of determining the cash equivalent value of the Cavalier note. The present value of Cavalier's $20,000 so-called noninterest-bearing two-year note should bear the same relationship to $20,000 as $1 does to $1.21. Hence,

$$\$PV/\$20,000 = \$1.00/\$1.21$$
$$\$PV = \$20,000 \times (\$1.00/\$1.21)$$
$$\$PV = \$20,000 \times 0.82645.$$

Thus, the present value factor for 10 percent compounded annually for two years is 0.82645. Therefore, $20,000 times 0.82645 is $16,529, the figure at which the note payable (and the van) should be shown on Cavalier's December 31, 1991, balance sheet.

To verify this figure, consider the perspective of Cavalier's banker. If the bank lent Cavalier the $16,529.00 on December 31, 1991, at 10 percent interest, the compounded amount owed one year later, at December 31, 1992, would become $18,181.90 ($16,529 × 1.10) and two years later, at December 31, 1993, would become $20,000 ($18,181.90

---

[6]The concept of compound interest is based on the assumption that interest earned on a savings deposit in the current period will be left on deposit so that in subsequent periods, interest will be earned not only on the original deposit but also on the interest on deposit from prior periods.

× 1.10). Thus, $16,529.00 at December 31, 1991, is equivalent, at 10 percent compounded annually, to $20,000 two years later. Stated alternatively, $16,529.00 is the present value of $20,000 in two years at 10 percent interest compounded annually.

Present Value Calculations and Inflation

The calculations just made illustrate the fact that, given a choice, one would prefer to have $1 today than $1 two years from now. As the figures revealed, at 10 percent interest, $1 today is really worth $1.10 in one year, not just $1.

Another reason to prefer $1 now compared with $1 two years from now is that, with inflation, the purchasing power of the dollar will decline. The present value techniques explained in this appendix are based on compound-interest factors and their reciprocal present value factors. These techniques do not perfectly account for inflation, but some acknowledgment of inflation effects may be made through the choice of interest factors. Although the choice of an interest factor is only a rough tool, more refined adjustments for inflation effects are beyond the scope of this appendix. Here the present value calculations deal with dollars with no discrimination as to possible differences in their purchasing power.[7]

Present Value Is the Reciprocal of Compound Interest

The calculations above also reveal that a present value factor for a specified rate and number of periods is the reciprocal of a **compound-interest** factor.[8] In the Cavalier Company example, the compound-interest factors, at 10 percent, are 1.10 for one year and 1.21 for two years, whereas the corresponding present-value factors are 0.90909 (1/1.10) for one year and 0.82645 (1/1.21) for two years.

Factors for determining the present value of a single future amount based on the equation $PV = 1/(1 + i)^n$ are given in Exhibit 11A–1. In the table, the present value factors for the specified rates and periods have been "rough-rounded" to two decimal places.[9] The "rough" factors shown in column 3 in footnote 9 closely match the factors

---

[7]In the Cavalier Company example, the company promised only to pay $20,000 on December 31, 1993, with no adjustment for the difference in purchasing power of the dollar that might occur between December 31, 1991, and December 31, 1993.

[8]The compound-interest factor, s, is determined as:

$$s = (1 + i)^n$$

where i is the interest rate and n is the number of periods. Compounding an amount is how savings accounts grow; that is, interest earned in Year 2 is based on the original investment and the amount of interest earned in Year 1.

[9] Because compound-interest factors and present value factors are reciprocals of each other, rough-rounded compound-interest factors may be derived by taking the reciprocal of the Exhibit 11A–1 factors. For example, rough compound-interest factors at a 10 percent rate would be:

(1) End of Year	(2) Exhibit 11A–1 Factor	(3) Reciprocal of Column 2
1	0.91	1.099
2	0.83	1.205
3	0.75	1.333
10	0.39	2.564

EXHIBIT 11A – 1

Present Value of $1 Received at End of Period Indicated
$$PV = 1/(1 + i)^n$$

End of Period	2%	4%	6%	8%	10%	12%	14%	16%	18%	20%	25%	30%
1	0.98	0.96	0.94	0.93	0.91	0.89	0.88	0.86	0.85	0.83	0.80	0.77
2	0.96	0.92	0.89	0.86	0.83	0.80	0.77	0.75	0.71	0.70	0.64	0.59
3	0.94	0.89	0.84	0.79	0.75	0.71	0.67	0.64	0.61	0.58	0.51	0.46
4	0.93	0.86	0.79	0.73	0.68	0.63	0.59	0.55	0.52	0.48	0.41	0.35
5	0.90	0.82	0.75	0.68	0.62	0.57	0.52	0.47	0.44	0.40	0.33	0.27
6	0.89	0.79	0.71	0.63	0.56	0.51	0.46	0.41	0.37	0.34	0.26	0.20
7	0.87	0.76	0.66	0.59	0.51	0.45	0.40	0.36	0.31	0.28	0.21	0.16
8	0.85	0.73	0.63	0.54	0.47	0.41	0.35	0.30	0.27	0.23	0.17	0.12
9	0.84	0.70	0.59	0.50	0.42	0.36	0.31	0.26	0.22	0.19	0.13	0.10
10	0.82	0.68	0.56	0.46	0.39	0.32	0.27	0.23	0.19	0.16	0.11	0.07
11	0.81	0.65	0.52	0.43	0.35	0.29	0.23	0.20	0.16	0.14	0.09	0.06
12	0.79	0.63	0.50	0.40	0.32	0.26	0.21	0.17	0.14	0.11	0.07	0.04
13	0.77	0.60	0.47	0.37	0.29	0.23	0.18	0.14	0.12	0.09	0.05	0.03
14	0.76	0.58	0.44	0.34	0.26	0.20	0.16	0.13	0.10	0.08	0.04	0.03
15	0.74	0.55	0.42	0.31	0.24	0.18	0.14	0.11	0.08	0.07	0.04	0.02
20	0.67	0.45	0.31	0.22	0.15	0.10	0.07	0.05	0.04	0.03	0.01	0.01
25	0.61	0.37	0.23	0.15	0.09	0.06	0.04	0.03	0.02	0.01	*	*
30	0.55	0.31	0.17	0.10	0.06	0.03	0.02	0.01	0.01	*	*	*
35	0.50	0.25	0.13	0.07	0.04	0.02	0.01	0.01	*	*	*	*
40	0.45	0.21	0.10	0.05	0.02	0.01	*	*	*	*	*	*

more precisely derived from the compound-amount formula $(1 + i)^n$, which produces the factors of 1.100, 1.210, 1.331, and 2.594. For many problems (when the future amount, the interest rate, or the number of periods are approximations), the use of the two-decimal factors in Exhibit 11A–1 should give answers as valid as the rough, raw data warrant. In the example of Cavalier Company, the 10 percent rate specified as the company's borrowing rate at December 31, 1991, is a rough approximation, and the precisely calculated $16,529 is perhaps no more valid than $16,600, approximated by the 0.83 factor in Exhibit 11A–1.

Present Value of an Annuity

The Cavalier Company illustration is an example of determining the present value of a future lump sum to be paid (or received). Now suppose that it is necessary to know the present value, at 8 percent annually, of $5,000 payable at the end of one year, another $5,000 payable at the end of two years, and another $5,000 payable at the end of three years. A uniform amount payable (or receivable) each period for a stated number of periods is called an **annuity.** To find the present value of an annuity of $5,000 for three years, compute the present value of each installment and then sum the three present value amounts:

End of Period	Present Value Factor (Exhibit 11A–1)	Present Value of $5,000 Payable
1	0.93	$ 4,650
2	0.86	4,300
3	0.79	3,950
	2.58	$12,900

A shorter way to figure the present value of such an annuity would be to go to an annuity present value table, which shows successive sums of present value factors, find the appropriate factor, and apply it to the constant annual annuity amount. Exhibit 11A–2 shows a factor of 2.58 for three years at 8 percent; this factor multiplied by the $5,000 annuity amount results in the present value figure of $12,900.

To verify this calculation, let us again assume the perspective of a lender. If a financial institution lent $12,900 repayable in three annual installments of $5,000 each, the debtor would record the receipt of $12,900 in cash and the associated liability for the same amount. At the end of each year, however, a $5,000 cash disbursement must be made to

EXHIBIT 11A – 2

Present Value of $1 Received at End of Period for N Periods

$$PV = 1/i[1 - 1/(1 + i)n]$$

End of Period	2%	4%	6%	8%	10%	12%	14%	16%	18%	20%	25%	30%
1	0.98	0.96	0.94	0.93	0.91	0.89	0.88	0.86	0.85	0.83	0.80	0.77
2	1.94	1.88	1.83	1.79	1.74	1.69	1.65	1.61	1.56	1.53	1.44	1.36
3	2.88	2.77	2.67	2.58	2.49	2.40	2.32	2.25	2.17	2.11	1.95	1.82
4	3.81	3.63	3.46	3.31	3.17	3.03	2.91	2.80	2.69	2.59	2.36	2.17
5	4.71	4.45	4.21	3.99	3.79	3.60	3.43	3.27	3.13	2.99	2.69	2.44
6	5.60	5.24	4.92	4.62	4.35	4.11	3.89	3.68	3.50	3.33	2.95	2.64
7	6.47	6.00	5.58	5.21	4.86	4.56	4.29	4.04	3.81	3.61	3.16	2.80
8	7.32	6.76	6.21	5.75	5.33	4.97	4.64	4.34	4.08	3.84	3.33	2.92
9	8.16	7.43	6.80	6.25	5.75	5.33	4.96	4.60	4.30	4.03	3.46	3.02
10	8.98	8.11	7.36	6.71	6.14	5.65	5.22	4.83	4.49	4.19	3.57	3.09
11	9.79	8.76	7.88	7.14	6.49	5.94	5.45	5.03	4.65	4.33	3.66	3.15
12	10.58	9.39	8.38	7.54	6.81	6.20	5.66	5.20	4.79	4.44	3.73	3.19
13	11.35	9.99	8.85	7.91	7.10	6.43	5.84	5.34	4.91	4.53	3.78	3.22
14	21.11	10.57	9.29	8.25	7.36	6.63	6.00	5.47	5.01	4.61	3.82	3.25
15	12.85	11.12	9.71	8.56	7.60	6.81	6.14	5.58	5.09	4.68	3.86	3.27
20	16.35	13.59	11.47	9.82	8.51	7.47	6.62	5.93	5.35	4.87	3.95	3.32
25	19.52	15.62	12.78	10.68	9.08	7.85	6.88	6.09	5.47	4.95	3.99	3.33
30	22.40	17.30	13.76	11.26	9.43	8.06	7.01	6.18	5.52	4.98	4.00	3.33
35	25.00	18.67	14.49	11.65	9.64	8.18	7.07	6.21	5.54	4.99	4.00	3.33
40	27.36	19.80	15.04	11.92	9.78	8.25	7.11	6.23	5.55	5.00	4.00	3.33

the bank, for a total outflow of $15,000 over the life of the loan. Clearly, each of the $5,000 payments contains amounts applicable to (1) the interest income required by the bank in exchange for forgoing the use of the $12,900 loaned to the debtor and (2) the repayment of the loan principal. The following table depicts the annual parts of each payment attributable to interest and principal:

		Portion of $5,000 Applied to	
		---	---
Year	Loan Principal at Beginning of Year	Interest at 8%	Principal Repayment
1	$12,900.00	$1,032.00	$ 3,968.00
2	8,932.00	714.56	4,285.44
3	4,646.56	371.72	4,628.28
		$2,118.28	$12,881.72*

*Not exact because of rounding.

Present value factors for uniform amounts payable at the end of each period, for a series of periods, are shown in Exhibit 11A–2 (rough-rounded to two decimal points) for specified rates and periods. Note that Exhibit 11A–2 presents merely the successive sums of the factors from Exhibit 11A–1.

An Illustration

Suppose that Cavalier Company wanted to raise $20 million by issuing bonds payable five years from the date of issue, with 10 percent interest payable annually. Suppose further that the net proceeds the company receives from the issuance of the bonds is $20 million. What liability should Cavalier report on its balance sheet?

The company will pay $30 million over the five-year period, but the present value, at 10 percent, is only $20 million:

Year	Interest (End of Year)	Principal at End of Year	Factor at 10% (Exhibit 11A–1)	Present Value Amount (Millions)*
1	$2.0	—	0.91	$ 1.82
2	2.0	—	0.83	1.66
3	2.0	—	0.75	1.50
4	2.0	—	0.68	1.36
5	2.0	—	0.62	1.24
		20.0	0.62	12.40
				$19.98

*A shorter way to do this problem would be to use an Exhibit 11A–2 factor: 3.79 (10 percent; 5 years) times $2 million annual interest cash outflows, which equals $7,580,000, and this plus $12,400,000, the present value of the single $20 million principal amount ($20 million times Exhibit 11A–1 factor of 0.62), gives $19,980.000.

Note that the present value of any interest-bearing obligation, discounted at its stated interest rate, is the same as the principal amount of the obligation. Stated alternatively, debt issued at a yield rate equal to its coupon rate will be sold at an amount equal to its face value.

Now suppose that two years after the above bonds were issued, an investor wished to buy $10,000 of the bonds at a price that would yield a 12 percent return. How much should the investor pay?

Graphically, the cash flows of such an investment involve an annuity stream of $1,000 in annual interest inflows (or 10 percent of $10,000) and a one-time principal receipt of $10,000. Using an effective interest rate of 12 percent, the investor should pay $9,500:

Cash Flows at End of Year			Exhibit 11A–1 Factors at 12%	Present Value Amount
1	2	3		
$1,000			0.89	$ 890.00
	$1,000		0.80	800.00
		$ 1,000	0.71	710.00
		10,000	0.71	7,100.00
				$9,500.00

Note that the appropriate present value interest factors were selected using the real (or effective) rate of interest (i.e., 12 percent) on the bonds, not the coupon or stated rate of interest (i.e., 10 percent). Even though the bonds carry a stated rate of 10 percent, the price at which the bonds may be bought (or sold) will fluctuate to enable the investor to earn a fair (market) rate of return.

ISSUES FOR DISCUSSION

D11.1 Compare and contrast the following transactions:

1. Tom Barry borrows $3,000 from his local bank, agreeing to repay a total of $3,600 in principal and interest over the coming year.

2. Dana Howard signs a noncancelable, nontransferable lease on an apartment for one year, agreeing to pay $3,600 in rent payments over the coming 12 months.

How would you account for each of these transactions?

D11.2 In 1981, American Airlines introduced its frequent flyer program, the Advantage Program, as a means to attract new and retain old customers. According to a study by Salomon Brothers, Inc., the potential revenue loss from the free tickets earned by the American Airlines passengers totaled $190 million by year-end 1988. How should American Airlines account for the unused (and unordered) tickets earned by its frequent flyer club members?

D11.3 What is the effect of purchase discounts on the manufactured costs of a product? What circumstances are possible in this situation? What is the impact of each on a product's cost?

D11.4 The following appeared in Centel Corporation's 1990 annual report:

In December 1989, an investor in The Argo Group, Inc. (TAGI) filed suit against a subsidiary of the company for damages from alleged breach of fiduciary duty and negligence related to the bankruptcy of a subsidiary of TAGI. The company cannot predict the ultimate outcome of this action but believes it will not have a material effect on the company's financial position. It this a liability? How should it be reported? Why?

D11.5 The following footnote appeared in the 1990 annual report of Bausch & Lomb, Inc.:

> The terms of a revolving credit and term loan agreement provide for a 364-day revolving credit line with a six-month term loan provision thereafter, under which the company may borrow up to $100,000,000. A commitment fee at a rate of .05% is charged on the unused portion. For any six-month period during the year the agreement includes a provision which allows the company to increase its borrowings up to an additional $150,000,000. A commitment fee of $62,500 per year is paid under this provision. The interest rate for total borrowings under the agreement is the prime rate or, at the company's option, a mutually acceptable market rate. At December 29, 1990, this revolving credit and term loan agreement supported $100,000,000 of unsecured promissory notes which have been classified as long-term debt. While the company intends to refinance these obligations, the level of the outstanding debt may fluctuate from time to time.

What business event has occurred? Bausch & Lomb's fiscal year ended December 29, 1990. What would you expect on its 1990 balance sheet and on the 1990 income statement related to this footnote?

D11.6 The Wall Street Journal of January 15, 1992, included an ad placed by BT Securities Corporation announcing a new issue. The details were:

> $150,000,000
> PLAYTEX Family Products Corporation
> 11 1/2% Senior Secured Notes Due 1997
> Price 99.50%

Explain what happened. What are the accounting issues?

D11.7 In accounting, a distinction is made between the concept of an *obligation* and a *liability*. Prepare a list of the different types of nonliability obligations that a company might have. What prevents each type from being a liability?

D11.8 What is the difference between *accounts payable* and *accrued expenses?* If an accrued item is not yet due, how can it be considered a liability?

D11.9 Consider the accounting for a deposit or prepayment. Why is this receipt of cash a liability? Does such an event leave the business better off or worse off than it was before?

D11.10 In the bond market in the United States (and in most other countries), bonds are traded freely. Bond prices, representing actual trades, are published in daily newspapers. Why not value bonds, notes, and other marketable liabilities at market for purposes of financial statement preparation? How would such a concept work? (What are the entries one would make each period?) Would this be better than using current GAAP?

PROBLEMS

P11.1 Bond valuation. MTF, Inc., was a manufacturer of electronic components for facsimile equipment. The company financed the expansion of its production facilities by issuing $10 million, 10-year bonds carrying a coupon rate of 8 percent, with interest payable annually on December 31.

The bonds had been issued on January 1, and at the time of the issuance, the market rate of interest on similar risk-rated instruments was 6 percent. Hence, the bonds were sold into the market at a price reflecting an effective yield of 6 percent.

Two years later, the market rate of interest on comparable debt instruments had climbed to a record high level of 12 percent. The CEO of MTF, Inc., realized that this might be an opportune time to repurchase the bonds, particularly since an unexpected surplus of cash made the outstanding debt no longer necessary.

	Present Value of $1 to Be Received at the End of Year n			Present Value of $1 to Be Received at the End of Each Year for n Years		
n	6%	8%	12%	6%	8%	12%
1	0.9434	0.9259	0.8930	0.9434	0.9259	0.8930
2	0.8900	0.8573	0.7970	1.8334	1.7833	1.6900
3	0.8396	0.7938	0.7120	2.6730	2.5771	2.4020
8	0.6274	0.5403	0.4040	6.2098	5.7466	4.9680
9	0.5919	0.5002	0.3610	6.8017	6.2469	5.3280
10	0.5584	0.4632	0.3220	7.3601	6.7101	5.6500

Required:

Using the present value data above, calculate the following:

a. The proceeds received by the company at initial issuance.

b. The interest expense to be reported in each of the two years that the bonds were outstanding.

c. The amount of cash needed to retire the debt after two years, assuming a yield rate of 12 percent.

d. Evaluate the merits of retiring the bonds early. Do you agree with the CEO?

P11.2 Accounting for zero-coupon debentures. In December 1990, Alza Corp. of Palo Alto, California, offered for sale $750 million of zero-coupon debentures. The bonds were offered for sale at $229.34 for each $1,000 face amount. Alza, a pharmaceutical products maker, expected to receive $166.4 million from the debt sale.

Required:

How would Alza Corp. account for the proceeds from the sale of bonds? Why would Alza want to sell zero-coupon bonds? Why would anyone buy them?

P11.3 Debt retirement. In March 1987, Continental Airlines sold $350 million of aircraft bonds. The bonds took their name from the fact that Continental had secured the debt with a pool of 53 airplanes and 55 engines, initially valued at $467 million.

By 1990, however, Continental was experiencing serious financial difficulties and lacked sufficient cash flows to continue operations. Consequently, with bondholder approval, Continental removed some of the planes from the pool and sold them to raise cash to support operations. After taking the airplanes from the asset pool, Continental was required (within a reasonable period of time) either to replenish the pool or to retire some of the bonds. Continental chose the latter option, and in late 1990, went into the market and repurchased $167 million (face value) of its aircraft bonds at a price of $.58 on the dollar.

Required:

a. Assuming that Continental initially issued the aircraft bonds at par value, how would the company account for the debt repurchase?

b. Was the decision to retire the debt a good one?

P11.4 Accounting for long-term bonds. On April 1, 1981, Nash Company sold to a group of underwriters $5,000,000 principal amount of its 8 percent bonds, the principal due 20 years from the date and interest due semiannually October first and April first, and received $5,200,000.

Required:

a. Why should the underwriters pay the company more than the face amount of the bonds?

b. What items concerning the bonds would appear on the company's balance sheet at December 31, 1990, and on its 1990 income statement, and at what amounts?

c. If the bonds are outstanding for the 20 years, as scheduled, what will be the net interest cost to the company for the 20 years? How much per year?

P11.5 Issuing bonds at a discount. On January 1, 1991, Jerry, Inc., issued $10,000,000 principal amount of its 14 percent bonds. The bonds were to be repaid at the end of 10 years, and interest was payable June 30 and December 31 of each year. Jerry, Inc., received $9,600,000 for the bonds.

Required:

a. Prepare an entry for the bonds at their issue date, January 1, 1991.

b. Prepare the entries relating to the bonds for June 30 and December 31, 1991.

c. Prepare an entry for the repayment of the bonds on December 31, 2000.

P11.6 Issuing bonds at a discount. On November 1, 1990, James Transfer Corporation issued $10,000,000 of 14 percent subordinated debentures due November 1, 2000. Interest is payable quarterly. Proceeds to the company were $9,760,000.

Required:

a. What entry(ies) would James Transfer make on its books on November 1, 1990, to record the issuance of the bonds?

b. How much cash will James Transfer pay the bondholders for interest during 1990?

c. How much bond interest expense will James Transfer show on its income statement for the fiscal year ended December 31, 1990?

d. How much bond interest payable will James Transfer show on its balance sheet as of December 31, 1990?

e. How much cash will James Transfer pay the bondholders on February 1, 1991?

f. What is the total amount of bond interest expense that James Transfer will report on its income statement over the life of the bond?

P11.7 Accounting for purchase discounts. Suppose two companies were similar except that the first, NetCo, usually takes all purchase discounts available from its vendors and thus records all purchases at net. The second company, GrossCo, does not usually take such discounts and, accordingly, records all purchases at invoice cost.

Required:

a. What entries would the two companies make if they purchase $10,000 of materials under the conditions of 2/10, net 30 (i.e., if you pay within 20 days, you may subtract 2 percent from the bill; otherwise, the bill is due in 30 days).

b. What entries would the two companies make on Day 9 if they both decided to take the discount?

c. What entries would the two companies make if they wait to pay the bill on Day 29?

d. What is the income statement impact of parts (b) and (c) on NetCo and GrossCo? What should these income statement items be called?

P11.8 Amortization of debt discount. In October 1989, Sun Microsystems, Inc., sold $135 million of 6 3/8 percent convertible subordinated debentures due October 15, 1999. They were sold at 84.9 percent of face value, an effective annual yield to maturity of 8.67 percent. Interest is to be paid semiannually beginning April 1990. As of June 30, 1991, the debentures were valued at $117,013 on Sun's balance sheet.

Required:

Assuming no early retirements or conversions, what will these debentures be valued at June 30, 1992?

P11.9 Accounting for zero-coupon debentures. Hallite Corporation issued $50 million face value of zero coupon debentures about January 1, 1983. The company realized $21 million. Suppose one half of the debentures was purchased by Holder Corporation, and that by December 31, 1991, interest rates for comparable risk, six-year notes was 7 percent.

Required:

a. What entries would the two companies make at the time of the sale?

b. What entries would the two companies make at the end of 1983?

c. At what values would these debentures be carried on the two companies' balance sheets at December 31, 1991?

d. At what price would you expect the Hallite Corporation zeros to trade at December 31, 1991?

e. Holder Corporation sold its Hallite zeros on January 2, 1992. What transactions did the two companies make then?

P11.10 Accounting for warranties. Signal Communications provides certain warranties for its products. As of January 1, 1991, the Provision for Estimated Warranty Costs account stood at $72,500. Warranty costs were estimated to be 0.5 percent of sales. Prepare entries related to warranties for the years 1991, 1992, and 1993 using the following:

	Sales (Millions)	Actual Warranty Costs
1991	$6.5	$53,200
1992	7.9	49,800
1993	5.8	61,100

Required:

a. What will appear on the income statements for each of these three years relating to warranties?

b. What will be the amount in the Provision for Estimated Warranty Costs account at December 31, 1993?

P11.11 Mortgages. A mortgage is a type of loan that is secured by property. Suppose a company acquired a building financed with a 20-year, 9 1/2 percent mortgage with level payments to be made monthly. An amount of $20 million was to be borrowed under this mortgage.

Required:

a. What would the payments be?

b. How would the mortgage appear in the company's balance sheet after the third year?

Suppose that after three years, the building is refinanced with a new 20-year mortgage; this time the rate is 8 percent. The amount of the new loan is to be the exact principal amount of the loan it replaces.

c. What difference would it make in the monthly payments?

d. What transactions would be made to repay the old loan and consummate the new one? Explain.

P11.12 Accounting for mortgages in the United Kingdom. Most home mortgages in the United Kingdom are of a variable-rate type. At the time the mortgage is issued, a monthly payment is determined by the bank or building society holding the mortgage. As interest rates change, the monthly payment typically remains constant (at least during the early years) while the principal is adjusted to account for the change in interest rates. The following is an example to see how this might work.

Suppose one had a 100,000 pound, 20-year mortgage established when interest rates were 10 percent. Monthly payments would be 965 pounds. Now suppose the following:

Month	Interest Rate Percentage
1	10
2	11
3	12
4	11
5	10
6	9

Required:

At the end of six months, what is the outstanding principal on this mortgage? How much interest has been paid?

P11.13 Analyzing debt securities. On January 16, 1992, Dayton-Hudson announced its intent to sell $200 million of debentures due January 15, 2012, with a coupon of 8.6 percent, priced at 99 7/8 percent.

Required:

What does this mean? (Explain the business event.) What will such an investment yield? (Assume the debentures paid interest semiannually.)

P11.14 Accounting for debt securities. In the Dayton-Hudson debentures described above (the $200 million at 8.6 percent of January 15, 2012), what would the yield be if the debentures sold for only $199 million? What entry would be made at the time of sale? What entry at December 31, 1992?

P11.15 Accounting for debt securities. Again with respect to the Dayton-Hudson debentures, interest rates had been falling rapidly in January 1992. Suppose that the 8.6 percent debentures due January 15, 2012, actually sold at a price yielding 8.495 percent.

Required:

How much would Dayton-Hudson receive? What accounting entry would be made when the bonds were sold? What entry would be made on December 31, 1992? On January 15, 1993?

CASES

C11.1 Bond valuation: R.J. Miller, Inc. R.J. Miller, Inc., is a real estate development company headquartered in Charleston, West Virginia. Since its inception in 1970, the company had been involved in the development of numerous shopping centers and apartment complexes in Virginia, West Virginia, and Maryland. In 1976, the company went public with an initial offering of 2.5 million shares of common stock. The public offering was quickly sold out at $10 per share. Over the next six years, the price of the common shares more than doubled.

Other than the initial public offering of stock, the company generated capital for its development projects primarily through the sale of limited partnership interests and bank borrowing. By 1979, however, interest rates had begun to climb sharply and, by 1980, the prime rate of interest (i.e., that rate charged by banks to their most preferred customers) had reached 20 percent. R.J. Miller, Inc., was not considered a preferred customer and consequently found itself facing the prospect of borrowing funds at nearly 22 percent.

To escape these high bank rates of interest, which substantially reduced profit margins, the firm decided to undertake a bond offering. On April 1, 1981, the company successfully completed the sale of 10-year, 15 percent coupon rate, first mortgage bonds having a maturity value of $40 million. The bonds required semiannual interest payments and were sold to yield 16 percent. They were callable at any time after April 1, 1986, at a price of $105 per bond, and were also convertible into R.J. Miller common stock ($1 par value) at any time after April 1, 1983, at a rate of 58.82 shares of common per $1,000 bond.

Over the next two years, interest rates fell by more than 50 percent. By April 1983, the prime rate of interest had fallen to 10½ percent. The stock market, in turn, had moved into a bullish trend with the Dow Jones Industrial Average breaking the 1,200 point barrier. In response to these market trends, the price of R.J. Miller common rose to $25 per share.

Required:

Use the charts below in calculating the following:

a. Determine the amount of the proceeds from the April 1, 1981, sale of bonds (ignore transaction costs). Illustrate the December 31, 1981, balance sheet disclosures related to the debt. (Use the effective interest method and use specific dollar amounts.)

b. Determine the amount of interest expense to be deducted during the year ended December 31, 1982. (*Note:* Use the effective interest method.)

c. Assume that bonds having a maturity value of $5 million are converted into common stock on April 1, 1983. Describe the balance sheet and income statement effects of the conversion. (Use specific dollar amounts.)

d. Assume that the market yield on the outstanding bonds is 12 percent per annum and that the price per share of common is $18.75. Assume also that on April 1, 1986, the firm decides to repurchase in the open market bonds having a maturity value of $20 million. Describe the balance sheet and income statement effects of this transaction. (Use specific dollar amounts.) Do you agree with this decision?

e. Assume that the company decides to force the conversion of the remaining outstanding bonds by calling the bonds as of December 31, 1988. Assume that on that date the company's common stock was trading at $28 per share. Show the journal entries needed to record (1) the calling of the bonds and (2) the conversion of the bonds. If you were a bondholder, what option would you take?

Present Value of $1

Period	6%	8%	12%	15%	16%
1	0.943	0.926	0.893	0.870	0.862
2	0.890	0.857	0.797	0.756	0.743
3	0.840	0.794	0.712	0.658	0.641
4	0.792	0.735	0.636	0.572	0.552
5	0.747	0.681	0.567	0.497	0.476
6	0.705	0.630	0.507	0.432	0.410
7	0.665	0.583	0.452	0.376	0.354
8	0.627	0.540	0.404	0.327	0.305
9	0.592	0.500	0.361	0.284	0.263
10	0.558	0.463	0.322	0.247	0.227
11	0.527	0.429	0.287	0.215	0.195
12	0.497	0.397	0.257	0.187	0.168
13	0.469	0.368	0.229	0.163	0.145
14	0.442	0.340	0.205	0.141	0.125
15	0.417	0.315	0.183	0.123	0.108
16	0.394	0.292	0.163	0.107	0.093
17	0.371	0.270	0.146	0.093	0.080
18	0.350	0.250	0.130	0.081	0.069
19	0.331	0.232	0.116	0.070	0.060
20	0.312	0.215	0.104	0.061	0.051

Present Value of $1 Per Period

Period	6%	8%	12%	15%	16%
1	0.943	0.926	0.893	0.870	0.862
2	1.833	1.783	1.690	1.626	1.605
3	2.673	2.577	2.402	2.283	2.246
4	3.465	3.312	3.037	2.855	2.798
5	4.212	3.993	3.605	3.352	3.274
6	4.917	4.623	4.111	3.784	3.685
7	5.582	5.206	4.564	4.160	4.039
8	6.210	5.747	4.968	4.487	4.344
9	6.802	6.247	5.328	4.772	4.607
10	7.360	6.710	5.650	5.019	4.833
11	7.887	7.139	5.938	5.234	5.029
12	8.384	7.536	6.194	5.421	5.197
13	8.853	7.904	6.424	5.583	5.342
14	9.295	8.244	6.628	5.724	5.468
15	9.712	8.559	6.811	5.847	5.575
16	10.106	8.851	6.974	5.954	5.668
17	10.477	9.122	7.120	6.047	5.749
18	10.828	9.372	7.250	6.128	5.818
19	11.158	9.604	7.366	6.198	5.877
20	11.470	9.818	7.469	6.259	5.929

C11.2 Purchase discounts: Olympic Distributors. Olympic Distributors of Seattle, Washington, distributes general hardware items to more than a thousand retail customers in the Northwest. Olympic's management manages its cash flow carefully and almost always takes the purchase discounts offered by its suppliers. Recently, many manufacturers have reduced their discounts or have changed the terms and conditions. Occasionally, Olympic has lost discounts by choosing to pay later. Naomi Herring, Olympic's accounts payable supervisor, set out to bring some order to the process. The company has a long-standing revolving loan agreement with Rainier Bank whereby the effective interest rate is one point over prime; thus, Olympic is currently paying 9.5 percent on its short-term borrowing. In the past three years, that cost has been as high as 14 percent and as low as 8.5 percent.

Herring rummaged through the pile of invoices on her desk, noting the different purchase discounts, terms, and conditions given by various vendors. Most fell into one of three categories:

1. 1/10 days, net 30.

2. 2/10 days, net 30.

3. Net 30 days, 2% monthly finance charge on balances over 30 days.

Required:

a. Prepare a table for interest rates from 10 to 20 percent, indicating for each of the three types of conditions whether Olympic should take the discounts for prompt payment or not.

b. How would you explain to a new employee why the typical 2/10, net 30 terms and conditions are really a good deal for a company paying (or earning) 12 percent on its money?

C11.3 Accounting for warranty costs: NoHo Manufacturing Co. NoHo Manufacturing Company has been selling equipment for many years. It is well-known to consumers because of its excellent customer service reputation. NoHo sells three types of machines: A, B, and C. When you purchase equipment from NoHo, you receive a six-year warranty. Estimating the warranty costs that would be incurred in the future is a complex issue for NoHo. Accuracy is important.

At the beginning of 1983, NoHo set up a new expense pool for warranty costs. The exhibit below presents the estimated number of sales units in each of the company's product lines, and the estimated warranty expense for each year beginning in 1983. This number was calculated by multiplying the average estimated warranty cost per unit of $809 (see below for this calculation) by the total number of units sold. The actual warranty costs incurred are also reported. For example, the estimated warranty expense for 1983 was $1,781 million, or $809 × 2,201,000 sales units. Actual warranty costs incurred during 1983 for equipment sold during 1983 were $426 million. (Warranty costs actually incurred for sales in model years before 1983 were charged to the old warranty expense pool.)

The column titled End-of-Year (EOY) Accumulated Warranty Liability was calculated by subtracting the actual warranty costs from the pool. The EOY Accumulated Warranty Liability account increased each year. By 1991, it was $2.305 billion although the actual warranty cost

| | Units Sold (000s) | | | | | (000s) | |
	A	B	C	Total	Actual Warranty	Estimated Warranty	End-of-Year Accumulated Warranty
1983	237	1,147	817	2,201	426,098	1,780,609	1,354,511
1984	243	1,125	849	2,217	1,241,539	1,793,553	1,906,525
1985	255	1,077	882	2,214	1,591,220	1,791,126	2,106,431
1986	267	1,010	921	2,198	1,773,030	1,778,182	2,111,583
1987	276	991	961	2,228	1,797,337	1,802,452	2,116,698
1988	287	953	985	2,225	1,805,745	1,800,025	2,110,978
1989	318	943	1,037	2,298	1,794,114	1,859,082	2,175,946
1990	317	901	1,043	2,261	1,786,900	1,829,149	2,218,195
1991	334	874	1,077	2,285	1,761,788	1,848,565	2,304,972
				20,127	13,977,771	16,282,743	

Estimated Warranty Expense
($ Per Unit)

Warranty Year	A	B	C	AVG $
1	126	281	97	168
2	437	558	80	358
3	210	238	60	169
4	86	108	48	81
5	10	25	27	21
6	11	9	15	12
				809

Based on a study done during 1982,
reflecting proposed changes in future
model year products.

incurred that year was only $1,762 million. Thus, there was a great discrepancy between the actual and the predicted.

The following tables present the actual number of units sold in each category as well as the actual warranty costs associated with them.

Actual Number of Units Sold

	1983	1984	1985	1986	1987	1988	1989	1990	1991
Unit A	237	244	258	268	281	292	310	322	336
Unit B	1,147	1,105	1,088	1,042	1,008	987	964	924	885
Unit C	817	851	870	903	943	975	1,001	1,021	1,088

Actual Warranty costs per Unit A ($)

Warranty Year	1983	1984	1985	1986	1987	1988	1989	1990	1991	AVG $
1	127	130	134	135	136	134	134	138	141	134
2	436	440	433	444	442	443	442	440		441
3	218	221	230	221	224	219	217			221
4	78	79	83	76	69	67				75
5	12	6	4	−1	−8					3
6	9	4	7	8						7

Negative figures are adjustments to previous costs.

Unit A Actual Warranty Costs per Year

										Total Costs
1983	30,999									30,099
1984	103,332	31,600								134,932
1985	51,666	107,252	34,699							193,617
1986	18,486	53,780	113,015	36,258						221,539
1987	2,844	19,348	59,329	119,106	38,288					238,910
1988	2,133	1,352	21,319	59,422	124,227	39,096				247,548
1989		994	1,143	20,289	62,954	129,383	41,649			256,414
1990			1,880	(328)	19,316	64,073	136,895	44,300		266,136
1991				2,051	(960)	19,604	67,117	141,579	47,268	276,660

Actual Warranty Costs per Unit B ($)

Warranty Year	1983	1984	1985	1986	1987	1988	1989	1990	1991	AVG $
1	279	286	287	291	291	289	289	294	291	289
2	560	556	559	559	559	556	555	553		553
3	235	237	240	243	247	253	246			243
4	111	110	110	110	109	108				110
5	22	21	14	12	11					16
6	12	12	19	17						15

Unit B Actual Warranty Costs per year

										Total Costs
1983	320,013									320,013
1984	642,320	315,527								957,847
1985	269,545	613,966	312,449							1,195,960
1986	127,317	262,082	607,678	303,361						1,300,438
1987	25,234	121,129	260,883	581,954	293,248					1,282,548
1988	13,764	22,882	119,887	252,642	563,762	285,355				1,258,298
1989		13,342	15,291	114,486	249,453	549,084	278,714			1,220,360
1990			20,334	12,898	109,735	249,565	534,954	271,357		1,198,841
1991				17,297	10,885	106,961	237,236	511,136	257,642	1,141,158

Actual Warranty Costs per Unit C ($)

Warranty Year	1983	1984	1985	1986	1987	1988	1989	1990	1991	AVG $
1	93	94	95	102	101	93	101	103	110	99
2	84	77	80	81	85	84	81	79		81
3	65	63	62	70	72	78	78			70
4	43	39	37	44	40	39				40
5	25	23	22	17	22					22
6	17	9	7	13						12

Unit C Actual Warranty Costs per Year

										Total Costs
1983	75,981									75,981
1984	68,628	80,132								148,760
1985	53,105	65,965	82,572							201,643
1986	35,131	54,058	69,386	92,478						251,053
1987	20,425	33,104	53,732	73,232	95,386					275,879
1988	13,889	19,566	32,067	63,533	80,502	90,348				299,905
1989		7,872	18,723	39,802	67,733	81,922	101,284			317,341
1990			5,888	15,732	37,793	76,145	80,987	105,378		321,923
1991				12,046	20,702	37,915	78,586	80,269	114,207	343,727

Required:

Is the pool too high or too low? Explain with figures to prove your case. If the pool were to be adjusted, what accounting entry would be required? Please explain.

C11.4 Estimating warranty liabilities: General Motors. Roger Smith, the chairman of General Motors, kept his promise to drive the first automobile produced at the Saturn Automobile Subsidiary. In the new, integrated manufacturing and assembly facility at Spring Hill, Tennessee, the ceremony was a brief and quiet one since GM did not wish to associate its name with the new cars; Saturn was to be a new American automobile. After eight years of planning and a total cost of more than $3 billion, the new high-tech automobiles went on sale in November 1990. The new company was steering clear of its GM ownership as much as it could. There were no corporate GM officials at the introduction of the cars, nor was there any mention of GM in any Saturn advertising. By December 1, only 2,162 cars had been built, but the 1991 plan targeted a volume of 120,000 units. Saturn's goal in its first year was to attract 55 percent of its buyers from non-GM owners.

With a base price of $7,995, the Saturn was predicted to get 27 miles a gallon in the city and 37 on the highway. To overcome the reluctance of car buyers to try a brand-new model that had not been tested in the real world, Saturns were offered with a guarantee. Initial buyers of the 1991 cars, if not completely satisfied, could return them for a full refund within 30 days or 1,500 miles. The guarantee presented a real challenge to those who had to estimate the costs of its warranty.

The 2,400-acre site of the Saturn complex is one of the most vertically integrated parts production and vehicle assembly plants ever built at a single location by the U.S. automotive industry. The equipment for the casting plant, including the metal melting systems, casting production equipment, and robots, has been designed for simplicity of operation, reliability, and durability. The plant has a modified "skillet" system, or moving sidewalk, which substantially increases manufacturing quality while reducing worker fatigue. Unlike typical U.S. auto assembly operations, major components are on site at the six-building Saturn plant.

The automobiles produced in this complex are quite different from those of other complexes. Some 35 percent of the exterior and interior components are produced in plant at Spring Hill. They have stylish aerodynamic design facilitated by the freedom of plastics. GM management considers the operation in Spring Hill to be the last word in auto production with plastic. Fender and rear quarter panels are injection molded of polyphenylene ethernylon alloy; door outers are of a special grade of Dow Chemicals' Pulse polycarbonate ABS ally, and front and rear facias are of thermoplastic olefin elastomers. The vertical side panels are made of plastic to eliminate annoying parking lot dents and dings. The plastic molds can be switched quickly, making for fast styling changes. Steel is used for the horizontal panels—the hood, roof, and trunk lid.

All Saturns have aluminum engines. The sedan comes with a single overhead-cam engine, and the sport coupe with a twin-cam, multivalve engine. The sedan was expected to accelerate from 0 to 60 miles per hour in less than eight seconds—good for its class. The power train plant is Saturn's most high-tech operation. The engine block and heads, the crankshaft, and the differential housing are formed by a newly perfected method called *lost-foam casting*. Molten metal is poured into molds containing plastic foam patterns of the desired parts. The plastic vaporizes, producing more intricate parts with greater precision, which then needs less costly machining to meet exacting dimensions, which translates into 30 percent less spending on tools and machinery. Lost-foam casting has been around for years, but Saturn is the first to apply it to high-volume production of large components such as engine blocks.

In addition, Saturn machines and assembles both manual and automatic transmissions on the same line in any sequence, a first for an American manufacturer. Doing both on the same line allows an exact match to car production, with no inventory buildup and at a lower investment. GM had never tried it before. In the past, the engineers designing automatics and those designing manuals worked for different divisions. The power train also was designed for ease of manufacturing, which reduced the number of operations required. One supplier estimated that production costs on the power train lines should be 20 to 40 percent lower than those of conventional engine plants.

The steps to world-class manufacturing in the engineering context began with an understanding of the benefits of designing the product and the process together and the need for quickly getting product concepts to market. The emphasis was not on technological solutions but on how people integrated solutions. The conventional practice of dividing product development into separate tasks to be done sequentially was not followed. Instead, the organization used simultaneous engineering so that projects were shaped by teams. Represented on these teams were finance, marketing, product design, manufacturing, engineering, and material engineering departments.

As part of its assault on rivals Toyota and Honda, Saturn's materials management operation developed a strict approach to finding the right transportation partners for the just-in-time manufacturing plant. Saturn sought carriers that were willing to enter into a long-term relationship and that had a proven performance record, a quality program in place, and a commitment to continuous improvement. GM also developed a strategy to train its 3,000-person workforce at the Saturn plant. The strategy combined the theories of GM, Japanese carmakers, United Auto Workers (UAW) members, and other leading U.S. firms, such as Hewlett-Packard and IBM. The individualized training plan recognized each worker's knowledge base and learning speed. Saturn cars were to be built using the teamwork concept with teams of 7 to 15 employees. Saturn trainers adopted a needs-driven, competency-based approach: Team members learned at their own pace and advanced only after they mastered a required task. The average employee received 300–600 hours of training, including team concepts and leadership skills. Thirteen days of training per employee per year were written into the UAW contract.

Required:

How should GM go about estimating the warranty liabilities for its new and very different Saturn car?

Prepared from publicly available sources of information.

Leases, Pensions, and Deferred Income Taxes

I n the previous chapter, we considered the valuation processes for current and noncurrent liabilities in general. In this chapter, we consider three unique liabilities that frequently arise in the financial statements of publicly held companies: leases, pensions, and deferred income taxes. Both leases and pensions depend on present-value concepts for their measurement; deferred income taxes, on the other hand, do not. Our focus in this chapter is similar to that of Chapter 11; namely, we consider two questions: "Do these obligations exist?" "If so, how should they be valued on the financial statements?"

LEASES

Leasing of assets is a common activity for many corporations, governmental agencies, and not-for-profit entities. It is used by large organizations and small ones, by the financially strong as well as the weak. Some types of leases result in the reporting of both assets and liabilities on the balance sheet, but others do not.

Companies lease assets for many reasons. They use leases, for example, as a form of financing that permits a company to acquire an asset without the immediate cash consequences of purchasing it. Moreover, companies with weak credit ratings sometimes find borrowing money difficult. Thus, for these companies, leasing may be the only way that they can obtain the assets needed to carry on their business. Financially healthy companies, on the other hand, often lease simply because they have better alternatives for investing their cash. Sometimes the decision to lease an asset is driven by tax considerations. Finally, many companies lease assets because they find the ancilliary services provided by leasing companies to be attractive. Leasing specialists often become experts at purchasing, installing, and maintaining the assets that they lease. They frequently make it easy to upgrade an asset and thereby obtain access to the latest available technology. Moreover, these leasing specialists often tailor the lease payments to the particular cash flow circumstances of the lessee. Just about any kind of asset can be leased—computers, copy machines, vehicles, aircraft, naval vessels, buildings, and manufacturing equipment, to name just a few.

As one might expect, there are some drawbacks to leasing. The interest rate implicit in the lease payments is frequently somewhat higher than long-term borrowing rates. In addition, lessees often face restrictions as to how an asset can be used. For example, if a purchased computer becomes redundant or is no longer needed, it can be sold, whereas with a leased computer, the lessee may be unable to cancel the lease without incurring a costly penalty.

From an accounting perspective, there are only two types of leases. **Operating leases** are nothing more than short-term rental agreements. For example, a grocery store (the *lessee*) may lease a new delivery vehicle from an auto dealership (the *lessor*) for one year. Accounting for such a lease is simple: Each month, an entry is made for the lease expense, which is deducted from revenues in the income statement. No lease asset or lease liability appears on the balance sheet. Since the company has use of the asset without having to purchase it, this type of arrangement is often referred to as **off-balance sheet financing.**

Other leases are simply long-term purchase agreements structured as leases; essentially, they are installment purchases. The grocery store, for example, might sign a noncancelable agreement to lease a delivery vehicle for four years at amounts sufficient to cover the cost of the vehicle, interest, and administrative costs and with an option to purchase the vehicle for a nominal sum at the end of the lease period. The substance of this type of lease agreement is clear: the company has acquired an asset and has incurred a liability. Except for legal distinctions, it is equivalent to borrowing the money and buying the asset outright. Leases of this type are called **capital leases** and appear as both assets and liabilities on the lessee's balance sheet. The periodic lease payments are discounted (see appendix to Chapter 11) at either the interest rate implicit in the lease or the lessee's borrowing rate, whichever is lower, and this present value amount is used to value both the leased asset and the lease liability on the balance sheet.

For many years, executives, accountants, leasing companies, and the Internal Revenue Service have considered what lease arrangements constitute a capital lease and thus necessitate disclosure on the balance sheet. In general, capital leases are leases whose terms meet *any* one of the following four tests:

1. Ownership is transferred to the lessee by the end of the lease (the *ownership test*).
2. The lease contains an option to purchase the asset at a bargain price (the *alternative ownership test*).
3. The lease term is equal to 75 percent or more of the remaining estimated economic life of the asset (the *economic life test*).
4. The present value of the minimum lease payments (excluding any "executory" costs for insurance, maintenance, taxes, and the like) equals or exceeds 90 percent of the fair market value of the asset (the *value test*).

If none of these conditions are met, the lease agreement is considered to be an *operating lease*.[1]

Accounting for Capital Leases

Terminology is critical to any discussion of leases. There are capital-lease **assets** and capital-lease **liabilities** and, of course, lease interest **expense** for lessees and lease **revenues** for lessors. The agreement itself is called the lease. From a lessee's perspective, the accounting issues related to capital leases involve measuring the lease liability and asset, the cost of financing (interest expense), and the cost of the use of the asset (amortization expense). The related accounting issues for a lessor, the owner of the asset, pertain to the valuation of the lease asset and the amount of lease revenue.

The following example will be used in this chapter to illustrate lease accounting for a lessee.[2]

Suppose American Airlines decides to acquire the use of a new Boeing 747 valued at $125 million. Because of its current cash position, the airline does not want to purchase the aircraft outright at this time. Instead, it decides to approach several insurance companies that might be interested in purchasing the aircraft and then leasing it to them. Assume that the best terms available are from Prudential Insurance Co. for a 10-year, quarterly installment, level payment, full-payout lease, with a quarterly payment of

---

[1]Some leases clearly fall in the middle, but no one has created any "middle ground" accounting rules. Many computer leases fit this description in that they run for most of the technological life of an asset and are noncancelable, but the leasing company (the lessor) keeps the asset and the deal is structured so that the lessor will actually lose money unless it can release or sell the asset at a good price at the end of the initial lease term.

[2]The accounting for lessors is discussed in Appendix 12A, "Leases in Detail."

$5,250,000. Assume further that the airline's borrowing rate is 14 percent, that the lease transfers ownership to the airline after the last payment, and that the airline is to perform all maintenance and repairs and is responsible for insuring the aircraft.

From the lessee's point of view, the agreement should be considered a capital lease. It meets both the ownership and the valuation tests of the capital-lease decision rules. The interest rate implicit in the lease is 12 percent (3 percent per quarter), which can be derived by simple present value techniques.[3] Because the implicit rate is lower than the company's incremental borrowing rate (i.e., 14 percent), the lease payments are discounted at the 3 percent quarterly rate. The present value of the capital-lease liability and the capital-lease asset is $125 million; hence, American Airlines would record the lease signing as:

Dr. Leased Aircraft (A) $125,000,000
      Cr. Capital Lease (L) $125,000,000

The lease liability will be amortized using an interest amortization schedule similar to a mortgage payment table that separates the lease payments into two parts, principal repayment and interest expense. The interest amortization schedule for the American Airlines/Prudential lease is shown in Exhibit 12A–1 in Appendix 12A to this chapter. The following entry illustrates how the quarterly lease payment at the beginning of the second quarter would be recorded:

Dr. Capital Lease (L) $1,658,000
Dr. Interest Expense (E)   3,592,000
      Cr. Cash (A) $5,250,000

Note that the payment of $5.25 million is divided into principal repayment and interest payment. The lease asset also must be depreciated following the asset-depreciation policies that American Airlines uses for similar assets.

Assuming that American Airlines amortized the leased asset over 12 years (or 48 quarters), the quarterly amortization expense would be $2,604,167 (i.e., $125,000,000/ 48), and the accounting entry would be

Dr. Depreciation Expense (E) $2,604,167
      Cr. Accumulated Depreciation (CA) $2,604,167

Capitalized leases for buildings and equipment are ordinarily included with other property, plant, and equipment, net of the accumulated depreciation, in the balance sheet. In classified balance sheets, the next year's principal reduction is shown as a current liability, and the noncurrent liabilities section includes the capital-lease liabilities less any current portion.

As can be seen in Exhibit 12.1 (Panel A), AMR Corporation, the parent company of American Airlines, listed its flight equipment acquired with capital leases separately from its other fixed assets. The capital-lease liability appeared, in part, as a current liability and

---

[3]Using a financial calculator, this can be easily derived. Since lease payments are made at the beginning of a period, set the calculator to *begin*. (The default option on many popular financial calculators assumes that cash flows occur at the end of a period.) Then, enter PV = 125,00,000, I = 3, N = 40 to obtain PMT = −5,250,288 – or a quarterly payment of $5.25 million.

the remainder as noncurrent. Thus, as of December 31, 1990, AMR Corporation valued its equipment and property under capital leases at $1,295 million; the principal outstanding on these leases was $1,656.8 million ($59.1 million current and $1,597.7 long term). Note that the capital-lease liability exceeds the capital base asset, no doubt because the asset was amortized on a straight-line basis while the effective interest method is used to amortize the capital-lease liability. Footnote 4 (Panel B of Exhibit 12.1) includes additional details of these leases and also describes other flight equipment under operating leases.

In summary, at the inception of a capital lease, the present value of the future lease payments is the value assigned to the capital-lease liability (net of any executory costs). Lease payments are discounted at the lessee's incremental borrowing rate unless the rate implicit in a lease is at a lower rate; then the implicit rate is used. The capital-lease asset is also valued at the present value of the lease payments. From that moment, the two figures are rarely the same. Assets acquired under capital leases are amortized using the straight-line (or some accelerated) method as if the assets were owned. Capital-lease liabilities are amortized using the effective interest method as if they were bonds.

Financial Disclosures for Capital Leases

At a minimum, the footnotes to a lessee's financial statements must show the following information for all capital leases:

1. The gross (undiscounted) lease payments.
2. The gross lease payments for each of the next five years and the total lease commitment (reduced by imputed interest).
3. The minimum rentals to be received under noncancelable subleases.
4. The total contingent rentals this year (leases based on something other than the simple passage of time).

For example, Exhibit 12.2 contains the PepsiCo, Inc., 1990 annual report footnote pertaining to its leases. The gross amount of these capital leases, most of which are for restaurants, was $340.7 million. The present value of these lease obligations, $193.8 million, is included on the balance sheet as long-term debt; the rest is interest and executory costs. Most of PepsiCo's leases are of the operating type and do not appear as liabilities.

Lessors follow rules similar to those for lease capitalization so long as there are no uncertainties as to the amounts to be received or any question as to their collectibility. Lease assets and liabilities for lessors must be shown separately on the balance sheet, and there are substantial footnote disclosure requirements as well. The accounting followed by lessors is discussed in Appendix 12A, "Leases in Detail."

EXHIBIT 12.1

AMR CORPORATION
Lease Disclosures

	December 31,	
	1990	**1989**
Panel A		
Equipment and property (Notes 3 and 5)		
Flight equipment, at cost	6,234.0	5,971.0
Less accumulated depreciation	2,025.1	2,068.2
	4,208.9	3,902.8
Purchase deposits for flight equipment	1,385.9	946.4
	5,594.8	4,849.2
Other equipment and property, at cost	3,569.9	2,785.4
Less accumulated depreciation	1,312.1	1,057.5
	2,257.8	1,727.9
	7,852.6	6,577.1
Equipment and property under capital Leases (Note 4)		
Flight equipment	1,641.1	1,516.8
Other equipment and property	288.0	269.5
	1,929.1	1,786.3
Less accumulated amortization	634.1	543.8
	1,295.0	1,242.5
Liabilities and Stockholders' Equity		
Current Liabilities		
Accounts payable	$ 966.3	$ 929.3
Accrued salaries and wages	416.7	423.9
Other accrued liabilities (Note 9)	1,005.1	823.5
Air traffic liability	1,117.5	869.4
Short-term borrowings (Notes 5 and 12)	1,209.7	162.9
Current maturities of long-term debt	50.3	210.1
Current obligations under capital leases	59.1	60.0
Total current liabilities	4,824.7	3,479.1
Long-term debt, less current maturities (Notes 3, 5, 8 and 12)	1,674.2	808.9
Obligations under capital leases, less current obligations (Notes 3 and 4)	1,597.7	1,496.9

PENSIONS

Of all the obligations of a corporation (or a government), pensions probably present the most complex accounting issues. The size of the private U.S. pension system is enormous. Perhaps one half of the full-time U.S. work force is covered by private pension plans, with thousands of billions of dollars being managed by pension-fund administrators. One private pension fund, TIAA-CREF, had more than $100 billion of invested pension assets in 1990. Some major corporations today have more pensioners than employees! Almost everyone has a stake in the pension system: current employees and

EXHIBIT 12.1

(continued)

Panel B

4. LEASES

AMR's subsidiaries lease various types of equipment and property, including aircraft, passenger terminals, equipment and various other facilities.

The future minimum lease payments required under capital leases (together with the present value of net minimum lease payments) and future minimum lease payments required under operating leases that have an initial or remaining non-cancelable lease term in excess of one year as of December 31, 1990, were as follows (in millions):

Year ending December 31,	Capital Leases	Operating Leases
1991	$ 185.1	$ 580.5
1992	184.7	612.1
1993	181.3	598.2
1994	179.4	584.9
1995	190.2	565.0
1996 and subsequent	2,275.6	11,817.0
	3,196.3[a]	14,757.7[a][b]
Less minimum sublease rentals	—	143.6
		$14,614.1
Less amount representing interest	1,539.5	
Present value of net minimum Lease payments	$1,656.8[c]	

[a]Future minimum payments required under capital leases and operating leases include $451.1 million and $4.3 billion, respectively, guaranteed by AMR relating to special facility revenue bonds issued by municipalities. Minimum sublease rentals relative to capital leases are $26.0 million.
[b]American has 226 aircraft under operating lease. Other AMR subsidiaries operate 129 regional aircraft under operating leases. During 1990, 36 Boeing 727-100s, 20 Boeing 727-200s. 2 Boeing 747SPs and 6 Fairchild Metro IIIs which were previously owned were sold and leased back.
[c]Includes $140.5 million guaranteed by American.

The aircraft leases can generally be renewed at rates based on fair market value at the end of the lease term for one to five years. Most aircraft leases have purchase options at the end of the lease term at fair market value, but generally not to exceed a stated percentage of the defined lessor's cost of the aircraft. Of the aircraft American has under operating lease, 15 Boeing 767-300ERs and 25 Airbus A300-600Rs are cancelable upon 30-days' notice during the initial 10-year lease term. At the end of that term, the leases can be renewed for periods ranging from 10 to 12 years.

Rentals and landing fees for 1990, 1989 and 1988 include rent expense of $788.2 million, $621.9 million and $441.7 million, respectively.

EXHIBIT 12.2

PEPSICO, INC.
Lease Disclosures

Leases

PepsiCo has noncancelable commitments under both capital and operating leases, primarily for restaurant units. Certain of these units have been subleased to restaurant franchisees. Lease commitments on capital and operating leases expire at various dates through 2032. Future minimum lease commitments and sublease receivables under uncancelable leases are as follows:

| | Commitments | | Sublease Receivables | |
	Capital	Operating	Direct Financing	Operating
1991	$ 39.2	$ 179.2	$11.5	$ 8.2
1992	35.1	160.9	10.9	7.8
1993	32.3	144.3	9.2	7.4
1994	30.6	130.4	9.0	6.9
1995	28.2	122.1	6.7	6.2
Later years	175.3	582.8	22.1	29.1
	$340.7	$1,319.7	$69.4	$65.6

At year-end 1990 the present value of minimum lease payments for capital leases was $194 million, after (deducting $1 million for estimated executory costs taxes, maintenance and insurance) and $146 million representing imputed interest. The present value of minimum receivables under direct financing subleases was $46 million after deducting $23 million of unearned interest income.

Rental expense and income were as follows:

| | Rental | |
	Expense	Income
1990	$272.7	$10.5
1989	236.9	14.2
1988	219.7	13.2

Included in the above amounts were contingent rental expense of $21.4 million, $20.8 million and $16.8 million and contingent rental income of $4.9 million, $4.5 million and $4.6 million in 1990, 1989 and 1988, respectively. Contingent rentals are based on sales by restaurants in excess of levels stipulated in the lease agreements.

retirees, corporate executives, investment managers and advisers, unions, government officials, the IRS, accountants and actuaries, shareholders, lenders, and even the Financial Accounting Standards Board.

As one might expect, one must learn a unique vocabulary before understanding the subject of pensions. In simple terms, a **pension** is a promise to pay certain benefits to employees as specified in an agreement (the plan). The terms *contribution* and its derivatives appear frequently in any discussion of pensions. Unfortunately, *contribution* can refer either to the amounts paid into the plan or to the amounts paid out of the plan to the pensioner. In regard to payments to a plan, *contributory* pension plans are those to which employees may be required to contribute. *Noncontributory* plans are the most common; the employer makes all the payments to such plans. On the pay-out side, regardless of who makes the actual contributions, defined-contribution and defined-benefit plans are the two broad types of pension plans.

Defined-Contribution Plans

Under a **defined-contribution plan** an employer promises to pay a specific amount per month (or quarter or year) to an employee's union or to an independent pension-fund administrator on behalf of an employee. The retirement plans for college professors are a good example.

Many U.S. colleges and universities pay a set percentage of a professor's salary each month to TIAA-CREF, a pension organization founded just for this purpose. If the professor moves from one university to another, the new employer begins paying to TIAA-CREF (assuming that the new employer also uses TIAA-CREF for this purpose, and most universities do). TIAA-CREF invests the money and keeps track of the contributions made on behalf of each professor and the related earnings on those contributions. Upon retirement, the faculty member then begins receiving a monthly pension check based on his or her accumulated pension account balance. The college or university really has no pension liability to the professors beyond making those monthly payments. A professor's retirement benefits are purely a function of the total contributions he or she earn over the years from various employers, plus the earnings on those funds (and his or her retirement age, gender, and certain choices made as to payout options). Thus, the more contributions made and the better the earnings record of the invested contributions, the larger the professor's retirement income.

Accounting for defined-contribution pension funds is a simple task. Each month, the employer makes an entry to record the pension expense and the accrued pension liability. Within a few days or weeks, the liability is satisfied by a check written to the pension fund.

Defined-Benefit Plans

These types of plans are more common than defined-contribution plans and much more complex. As the name suggests, **defined-benefit plans** specify the *future* amount an employee will receive on retirement. The amount is usually a function of age, years of service, salary level; other factors may also affect the amount. Companies must estimate the *current* cost of these future pension benefits and record this cost as the pension expense for the year. The offsetting entry is a current pension liability. Ordinarily, the company then eliminates this pension liability by paying cash (called *funding*) to an independent, third-party trustee. The trustee invests these funds and pays the retirees when they become eligible. This process is illustrated in Exhibit 12.3.

Money Flow for Defined-Benefit Pension Plans

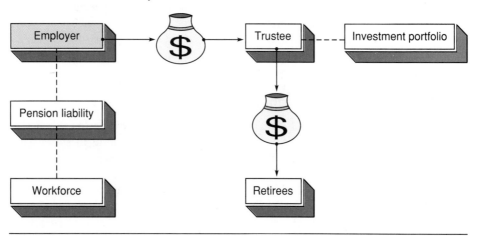

The assets of a pension fund appear on the books of the pension trust, not on the books of the employer. It is important to understand that the trustee is only the agent of the employer. *The employer's obligation remains even after it has made the payments to the trustee.* If the trustee makes poor investments and runs out of money, the employer is still obligated to pay the pensions for the committed retirement benefits.

Ideally, the trustee should have just enough funds to satisfy the terms of the pension agreement. Occasionally, however, a fund becomes overfunded and an employer may either stop contributing to the fund or may request that the trustee return the excess funds.

It is important to note that in the United States, corporations are *not* required to provide pensions to their employees. However, if they choose to do so, there are laws that prescribe how pensions are to be administered. The Employee Retirement Income and Security Act of 1974 **(ERISA)** is such a law. Tax regulations prescribe how much pension cost can be deducted for income tax purposes (usually it is the amount actually paid in cash by the company to the trustee). And, of course, generally accepted accounting practices specify how such costs are to be expensed, how liabilities are to be valued, and what supplemental information is to be disclosed in the footnotes.

Pension Expense

GAAP for defined-benefit pension plans require that the cost of pension benefits be recognized during the period in which those benefits are earned. For example, suppose that a particular pension plan promised an employee a monthly pension of 1.5 percent of her salary at retirement for each year of service to a company. Consequently, if the employee worked 30 years prior to retirement, she would receive a monthly pension equal to 45 percent of her monthly salary at retirement. Assuming that she worked from 1990 to 2020, she would begin receiving her pension payments in 2021. Clearly, however, some portion of the payments received in 2021 were earned in 1990. Consequently, the cost of that portion of her expected pension benefit, adjusted for various estimates, including the present value, must be recognized as **pension expense** in 1990.

A typical pension expense entry would appear as follows:

```
Dr.  Pension Expense (E) . . . . . . . . . . . . . . . .  $10,000
     Cr.  Accrued Pension Liability (L) . . . . . . . . . . . . . .        $10,000
```

The liability disappears when the year's pension expense is funded (i.e., when cash is paid to the pension trust):

```
Dr.  Accrued Pension Liability (L) . . . . . . . . . . . .  $10,000
     Cr.  Cash (A) . . . . . . . . . . . . . . . . . . . . . .        $10,000
```

If the pension liability is not funded, the accrued pension cost liability remains. If it is funded at an amount higher than the accrued pension liability, the account, Prepaid Pension Cost becomes an asset.

As you might expect, the accounting for defined-benefit pension plans requires considerable estimating: How many employees will qualify for pensions? How long will they work? How many will live to retirement age? What salaries will they be receiving? How long will they live while retired? How much will the trustee earn on the funds? What must the company pay now to satisfy all of its future obligations? Is the pension fund currently overfunded or underfunded? If underfunded, how should the company "catch up"?

For many years, defined-benefit pension plans were considered to be economic obligations but not accounting liabilities. It was argued that an employer did not legally have a liability to an employee *until* that employee actually reached retirement age—and then the only liability was to make one month's benefit payment! If the retiree lived another month, another month's benefit payment was due, and so on. How could pension promises made to employees with many years still to work be considered accounting liabilities when no one could know even what future salary levels would be?

In view of the history of this issue, today's accounting represents a compromise. Employers must record as expense the current cost of pension benefits earned by employees, but the estimates of the overall pension obligation is relegated to the footnotes and the emphasis is on the projected benefits at current salary levels. Only under a special circumstance, when the obligation significantly exceeds plan assets, is the pension obligation recorded as a balance sheet liability.

Financial Disclosures for Pensions

Because of the importance of pensions and the complexity presented by their accounting, GAAP require extensive footnote disclosure. Three items, pension expense, projected benefit obligation, and the plan assets at fair value, deserve special attention in these disclosures. We have already discussed the concept of pension expense. The **projected benefit obligation,** or PBO, is the present value of all pension benefits earned by employees as of a particular date. Of course, it must reflect expected mortality, future wage levels, and some of the other assumptions we have already mentioned. The term **plan assets at fair value** refers to the market value of the investment portfolio held by the pension trustee as of the balance sheet date.

Exhibit 12.4 illustrates these disclosure requirements. It is taken from the 1990 annual report of Betz Laboratories. The total pension expense (net pension cost) for 1990 was $4,482 thousand consisting of $3,800 thousand current service cost, $6,766 thousand interest cost on pension liabilities, and a $1,355 thousand loss for the year on investing the pension plan assets and certain adjustments. These calculations are explained more fully in Appendix 12B. Note that in 1989 and 1988, the trustees of Betz Laboratories earned money from investing the pension assets.

Footnote 3 also contains an explanation of the funded status of the plan. The PBO for Betz as of December 31, 1990, was $81,082 thousand; the market value of the plan assets at that date was only $78,238 thousand. The previous year, the circumstances were reversed; plan assets exceeded the PBO by a small amount. The other items listed in footnote 3 are explained in Appendix 12B.

Neither the PBO nor the plan assets appear on the balance sheet. GAAP for pensions are specified in SFAS No. 87, which requires the recording of a portion of the PBO as a pension liability on the balance sheet, but *only* when the PBO is "significantly underfunded." The test used to decide how much of the pension obligation should be recorded as a liability is based on a fourth figure, the **accumulated benefits obligation,** or ABO. The ABO is the present value of all pension benefits earned based on *current* salary levels. Thus, it is the same as the PBO but without the projection of future salary increases. Thus, a pension liability is recognized on the balance sheet only to the extent to which the ABO exceeds the plan assets:

> Accumulated plan benefits
> Less: Plan assets
> _____
> Minimum pension liability.

If this pension liability must be recognized, the entry reduces owners' equity unless the minimum liability arises because of changes in the plan that increase benefit levels and for certain other technical reasons. When this is the cause of the minimum liability, an asset account called the **Unfunded Pension Cost** is created. In summary, if a minimum pension liability arises as a consequence of an increase in pension benefits, the following entry is made:

```
Dr.  Unfunded Pension Cost (A) . . . . . . . . . . . . . . . . . . $XX
     Cr.  Pension Liability (L) . . . . . . . . . . . . . . . . . . . . . . .      $XX
```

But if a minimum pension liability results as a consequence of underfunding, the entry is as follows:

```
Dr.  Unfunded Pension Cost (COE). . . . . . . . . . . . . . . . $XX
     Cr.  Pension Liability (L) . . . . . . . . . . . . . . . . . . . . . . .      $XX
```

The test for the minimum pension liability is made each time financial statements are prepared.

E X H I B I T   1 2 . 4

BETZ LABORATORIES, INC.
Pension Disclosures

Note 3—Employee Retirement Plans

The Company has pension plans covering substantially all of its employees. In 1989, the Company adopted the provisions of Statement of Financial Accounting Standards (SFAS) No. 87, "Employers' Accounting for Pensions", in accounting for its foreign pension plans.

The effect of adopting was not material.

Net pension cost for the Company's defined benefit plans is comprised of the following elements (in thousands):

	1990	1989	1988
Service cost	$ 3,800	$ 3,260	$ 2,563
Interest cost	6,766	5,760	4,026
Return on plan assets	1,355	(12,334)	(4,417)
Amortization and deferral	(7,439)	6,493	(67)
Cost of foreign pension plans before adopting SFAS No. 87	—	—	503
Net pension plan	$ 4,482	$ 3,179	$ 2,608

The following table sets forth the funded status of the pension plans (in thousands):

	December 31	
	1990	1989
Actuarial present value of benefit obligations:		
Vested	$(58,091)	$(53,850)
Nonvested	(4,538)	(2,652)
Accumulated benefit obligation	(62,629)	(56,502)
Effect of projected future salary increases	(18,453)	(18,770)
Projected benefit obligation	(81,082)	(75,272)
Plan assets at fair value	78,238	76,244
Projected benefit obligation (in excess of) or less than plan assets	(2,844)	972
Unrecognized net gain	(6,154)	(11,121)
Unrecognized prior service cost	3,933	4,369
Unrecognized net obligation existing at transition	177	193
Adjustment required to recognize minimum liability	(546)	—
Net pension liability (included in retirement plan liabilities)	$ (5,434)	$ (5,587)

EXHIBIT 12.4

(continued)

Primary assumptions used in the actuarial computations were:

	December 31,	
	1990	**1989**
Discount rate	9.0%	8.5%
Rate of increase in future compensation levels	5.0%	5.0%
Long-term rate of return on plan assets	9.5%	9.5%

Benefits provided under the Company's defined benefit pension plans are primarily based on years of service and the employee's final average compensation. The Company's funding policy is to contribute an amount annually based upon actuarial and economic assumptions designed to achieve adequate funding of projected benefit obligations. Plan assets are principally invested in listed common stocks, bonds and common trust funds.

PepsiCo's footnote disclosure from its 1990 annual report is shown in Exhibit 12.5. It illustrates all of these points concerning the accounting for pensions. The company funds a number of defined-benefit plans. Total pension expense in 1990 was only $9.5 million because the return on the plan's assets and certain adjustments almost totally offset the present-value cost of the benefits earned by employees in 1990 and the interest cost on pension liability. The PBO for PepsiCo as of December 31, 1990, was $742.6 million, but the plan assets at that date were $985.7 million.

The last paragraph of this footnote is particularly interesting. During 1990, the FASB adopted SFAS No. 106, "Employer's Accounting for Postretirement Benefits Other Than Pensions," effective in 1993. The postretirement benefits of greatest concern are those related to health care. The impact of SFAS No. 106, when adopted, could be significant for many companies including PepsiCo.

DEFERRED INCOME TAXES

Income taxes represent one of the largest obligations arising from operations that a company must satisfy. Some of these taxes must be paid currently; others may be postponed for many years. This section focuses on those income taxes that, because of the particular provisions of the Internal Revenue Code, may be postponed until some future date.

Because of differences between GAAP and tax accounting, the amounts due to the taxation authorities for a given period are not necessarily the accounting income tax expense of that period. The accounting issue behind deferred taxes is one of matching: Income tax expense is the periodic cost associated with particular revenue and expense items recognized in that accounting period. This cost, however, is independent of when

EXHIBIT 12.5

PEPSICO, INC.
Pension Disclosures

Retirement Plans

PepsiCo has noncontributory defined benefit pension plans covering substantially all full-time domestic employees as well as contributory and noncontributory defined benefit pension plans covering certain international employees. Benefits generally are based on years of service and compensation or stated amounts for each year of service. PepsiCo funds the domestic plans in amounts not less than minimum statutory funding requirements nor more than the maximum amount that can be deducted for federal income tax purposes. International plans are funded in amounts sufficient to comply with local statutory requirements. The plans' assets consist principally of equity securities, government and corporate debt securities and other fixed income obligations. Capital Stock of PepsiCo accounted for approximately 18.1% and 16.8% of the total market value of the plans' assets at year-end 1990 and 1989, respectively.

In 1989, PepsiCo acquired Smiths Crisps Limited and Walkers Crisps Holdings Limited, two snack chips companies in the United Kingdom (the U.K. operations). The U.K. operations' employees were covered by various plans, including multiemployer plans. Pension expense and the required disclosures under SFAS 87 were not determinable until completion in late 1990 of a preliminary allocation of the assets of those plans, the transfer of relevant employees to separate plans and the appropriate actuarial valuations. Accordingly, the 1990 information presented below includes both the domestic plans and the U.K. operations' plans, while the 1989 and 1988 information includes only the domestic plans.

Other international plans are not significant in the aggregate and therefore are not included in the disclosures below. None of these other international plans was significantly over or underfunded at year-end 1990.

The net pension expense (credit) for company-sponsored plans (the Plans) included the following components:

	1990	1989	1988
Service cost of benefits earned..............	$ 48.1	$ 32.0	$ 24.8
Interest cost on projected benefit obligations	63.3	47.1	40.0
Return on the Plans' assets:			
Actual	(27.0)	(154.6)	(86.1)
Deferred gain (loss) ...	(55.9)	89.9	23.5
	(82.9)	(64.7)	(62.6)
Amortization of net transition gain	(19.0)	(19.0)	(19.0)
Pension expense (credit) .	$ 9.5	$ (4.6)	$(16.8)

For certain Plans accumulated benefits exceeded the assets, but the related amounts were not significant. Reconciliations of the funded status of the Plans to the prepaid pension liability included in the Consolidated Balance Sheet are as follows:

	1990	1989
Actuarial present value of benefit obligations:		
Vested benefits....................	$(549.9)	$(449.0)
Nonvested benefits	(90.8)	(75.0)
Accumulated benefit obligation	(640.7)	(524.0)
Effect of projected compensation increases	(101.9)	(92.1)
Projected benefit obligation	(742.6)	(616.1)
Plan assets at fair value	985.7	869.8
Plan assets in excess of projected benefit obligation......................	243.1	253.7
Unrecognized prior service cost	42.4	26.2
Unrecognized net gain	(84.6)	(104.0)
Unrecognized net transition gain	(148.1)	(167.1)
Prepaid pension liability	$ 52.8	$ 8.8
Included in:		
"Investments in Affiliates and Other Assets"	$ 85.3	$ 31.2
"Other current liabilities"	(17.0)	(14.3)
"Other Liabilities and Deferred Credits"	(15.5)	(8.1)
	$ 52.8	$ 8.8

The assumptions used in computing the information above were as follows:

	1990	1989	1988
Discount rate-pension expense (credit)	9.1%	10.1%	10.0%
Expected long-term rate of return on plan assets	10.2%	10.0%	10.0%
Discount rate-projected benefit obligation	9.5%	9.0%	10.1%
Future compensation growth rate	5.0%-7.0%	5.0%-7.0%	5.0%-7.0%

The 1990 discount rates and rate of return represent weighted averages, reflecting the combined assumptions for domestic and the U.K. operations' plans in 1990.

Full-time domestic employees not covered by the Plans generally are covered by multiemployer plans as part of collective-bargaining agreements. Pension expense for these multiemployer plans was not significant in the aggregate.

PepsiCo provides health care and life insurance benefits to certain retired nonunion employees, the costs of which are expensed as incurred. In December 1990, the FASB issued Statement of Financial Accounting Standards No. 106 (SFAS 106), "Employers' Accounting for Postretirement Benefits Other Than Pensions," which requires the recognition of postretirement benefit expenses on an accrual basis. PepsiCo has not yet determined the impact of accounting for these costs on an accrual basis; however, the 1990 expense for health care claims incurred and life insurance premiums paid was $20.4 million. PepsiCo expects to implement SFAS 106 by its required adoption date in 1993.

those particular revenue and expense items are recognized for tax purposes. If revenues and expenses are recorded in this year's income statement, the related income tax expense should also appear in this year's income statement *even* if the recognition of those revenues and expenses (and their associated income tax liability) can be deferred until some later date for tax purposes. This process is called **interperiod tax allocation;** it is really just another form of accrual accounting. It recognizes business events (in this case, the income tax expense) at some more appropriate moment than simply when the tax bill appears or must be paid in cash. Without interperiod tax accounting, a company's operating results can fluctuate wildly because of tax accounting conventions, even if the basic operations of the business are stable.

Almost all business events have the potential to be recognized at different times for tax purposes than for accounting purposes, but the most common accounting-tax differences leading to deferred income taxes are those listed in Exhibit 12.6. In the following illustration, we will use depreciation accounting to demonstrate the role of interperiod tax allocation.

An Illustration: Sample Company

Ideally, in published financial statements, the cost of an asset is assigned to various years in whatever manner best reflects the use of the asset over its lifetime. Tax accounting also expenses that same cost over the asset's life but often with different amounts being charged to different years. One often hears the expression that "companies keep two sets of books"; what this means is simply that tax rules are often different from GAAP. Moreover, companies have much different objectives when reporting income to the IRS than when reporting income to owners and potential shareholders. Thus, in the case of depreciation, although both tax and accounting statements reflect the same *total* depreciation expense over the life of an asset, the tax depreciation is typically accelerated or "front loaded" while the accounting depreciation is usually flat or straight line.

E X H I B I T 1 2 . 6

Common Business Events Associated with
Deferred income Taxes

Event	Prevalent Accounting Treatment	Prevalent Tax Treatment
■ Depreciation of long-term asset	■ Straight-line method	■ An accelerated method
■ Installment sales	■ Immediate recognition	■ Recognized when cash is received
■ Bad debt expense	■ Estimated and recognized in the period corresponding with the actual credit sale	■ Recognized when written off
■ Warranty expense	■ Estimated and recognized in the period of product sale	■ Recognized when paid

Imagine that a company purchases an asset costing $1,000, which, because of special tax incentives, can be depreciated over only two years (50 percent each year), and which, for accounting purposes, can be depreciated over four years (25 percent per year). For simplicity, assume that the company is subject to a 40 percent tax rate. The differences between the accounting depreciation and tax depreciation deductions are as follows:

	Year 1	Year 2	Year 3	Year 4
Accounting depreciation	$250	$250	$ 250	$ 250
Tax depreciation	500	500	–0–	–0–
Difference	(250)	(250)	250	250
Tax impact of difference at 40 percent	($100)	($100)	$ 100	$ 100

In essence, $250 *more* tax depreciation will be taken in years 1 and 2 and $250 *less* tax depreciation taken in years 3 and 4. Take a moment and consider the implications of these differences. The taxes actually due in years 1 and 2 will be $100 *lower;* in years 3 and 4, the actual taxes due will be $100 *higher* than will be reflected in the accounting income statements. In total, however, over the four-year period, the amount of taxes will be the same under either system. If this were the only accounting-tax difference that the company had, the accounting income tax expense in years 1 and 2 would simply be the taxes actually due plus $100. In years 3 and 4, this process would be reversed—the accounting income tax expense would be the taxes actually due minus $100.

In Exhibit 12.7, the effect of these accounting-tax differences, as well as the use of interperiod tax allocation to account for these differences, is illustrated. In this example, we assume that revenues for each period are $1,000 and that all other expenses other than depreciation total $400 per year. Note that the income tax liability (per the tax return) for each of the first two years would be only $40 and then would increase to $240 per year for the next two years. On the accounting income statement, the total income tax expense is adjusted to eliminate what would otherwise be a distortion caused by the special tax depreciation allowances. The additional $100 of income tax expense in years 1 and 2 increases the Deferred Tax Liability account. Note that this account builds up in years 1 and 2 and then reverses in years 3 and 4 when the total income tax liability is higher than the total income tax expense. Also note that the events that gave rise to this situation was the purchase of an asset and the decision to use different accounting and tax depreciation schedules.

The use of a deferred income tax account on the balance sheet eliminates the distortion that would otherwise occur if the current tax liability (per the tax return) were considered to be the income tax expense for the year. Deferred tax accounting makes the total income tax expense in the income statement conform to the accounting treatment used for depreciation in that statement.

The Deferred Income Tax account at the end of years 1, 2, and 3 is a liability in the sense that someday income taxes will be payable *in excess of what the accounting statements would otherwise suggest.* In simple terms, Sample Company temporarily avoided $100 of income tax payments in Year 1 because it used a more rapid method of depreciation for tax reporting than was used for accounting purposes. Someday that advantage will reverse; the fast depreciation write-offs will run out with straight-line

E X H I B I T   1 2 . 7

SAMPLE Company
Deferred Income Taxes

Income tax returns of Sample Corporation

	1	2	3	4	Total
Sales	$1,000	$1,000	$1,000	$1,000	
Depreciation	500	500			
All other expenses	400	400	400	400	
Taxable income	100	100	600	600	
Income tax @ 40%	40	40	240	240	560

On the balance sheets of Sample Corporation

	1	2	3	4
Deferred tax liability	$100	$200	$100	$0

Deferred tax liability

	0	Balance
	100	Year 1
	100	Balance
	100	Year 2
	200	Balance
Year 3 100		
	100	Balance
Year 4 100		
	0	Balance

Income statement of Sample Corporation

	1	2	3	4	Total
Sales	$1,000	$1,000	$1,000	$1,000	
Depreciation	250	250	250	250	
All other expenses	400	400	400	400	
Taxable Income	350	350	350	350	
Current income tax expense	40	40	240	240	
Deferred income tax expense	100	100	−100	−100	
Total income tax expense	140	140	140	140	560
Net income	210	210	210	210	

depreciation continuing on the accounting records. At that time, the tax return will reflect higher taxable income than the accounting statements, and the tax bills coming into the company will be far higher than what would be predicted from the figure for income before tax on the accounting income statement. Like a buffer, the Deferred Income Tax Liability Account is used to prevent such distortions. Expenses are credited to this account when temporary tax advantages lower taxable income, and when the differences reverse, the buffer is drawn down.

Temporary and Permanent Differences

Temporary differences. Interperiod tax allocation is used when tax returns and the accounting reports reflect temporary differences, as with depreciation. By definition, temporary differences always reverse themselves at some point: Tax depreciation may exceed accounting depreciation for a while for any particular asset, but eventually the reverse will occur and by the end of the life of the asset, the sum of the differences (positives and negatives) will always be zero. Accordingly, the deferred tax liability associated with this asset may increase for a few years on the balance sheet, but then it will decline and eventually become zero.

Even though the temporary difference that triggered the deferred tax liability (or asset if the account has a debit balance) will always reverse itself for any particular item having a temporary difference, it is possible for an account such as the Deferred Income Tax Liability to keep increasing *in total,* for example, if a business is growing and more assets are being acquired.

Permanent differences. Depreciation differences between tax and accounting statements illustrate a temporary difference because for any given asset, the total difference over time is zero. Permanent differences, on the other hand, arise when an item is included for accounting purposes but will never appear in the determination of taxable income (or vice versa). For example, interest on municipal bonds is a revenue item for accounting purposes but is not taxable—it represents a permanent difference in the income reported to the IRS versus the income reported to shareholders. Amortization of goodwill is another example—it is an accounting expense but is not tax deductible. Deferred taxes are never calculated for permanent differences; they are simply ignored in the interperiod tax allocation process.

Events that lead to temporary differences. Temporary accounting differences may arise as a result of four types of events:

1. Expenses (or losses) become tax deductible *before* being expensed for accounting purposes. The most frequent example of this is depreciation.
2. Revenues (or gains) become taxable *after* they are recognized in the accounting income statement. For example, certain types of installment sales are recognized as sales immediately but are treated as taxable income only as payments are received.
3. Expenses (or losses) become tax deductible *after* the recognition of the expense. This happens when a company provides warranties or guarantees on a product or service. Generally accepted accounting principles require such a company to

EXHIBIT 12.8

FORD MOTOR COMPANY
Deferred Income Tax Disclosures

Panel A	1990	1989
Assets:		
Automotive		
Cash and cash equivalents (Note 18)	$ 4,599.3	$ 4,045.3
Marketable securities, at cost and accrued interest (approximates market)	1,478.7	1,680.2
Total cash, cash equivalents and marketable securities	6,078.0	5,725.5
Receivables	3,537.0	4,703.4
Inventories (Note 1)	7,115.4	6,816.8
Other current assets (Note 5)	2,448.8	1,918.9
Net current receivable from Financial Services (Note 15)	319.5	344.6
Total current assets	19,498.7	19,509.2
Equity in net assets of affiliated companies (Notes 1 and 17)	2,180.0	4,178.5
Property, net (Note 6)	22,207.8	18,135.4
Other assets (Notes 1 and 2)	6,679.5	3,635.1
Net concurrent receivable from Financial Services (Note 15)	257.4	361.0
Total automotive assets	50,823.4	45,819.2
Liabilities and Stockholders' Equity		
Automotive		
Trade payables	$ 7,181.9	$ 7,486.8
Other payables	2,306.7	2,677.2
Accrued liabilities (Note 10)	8,370.2	6,794.7
Income taxes payable	155.8	684.9
Debt payable within one year (Note 11)	2,849.4	2,537.0
Total current liabilities	20,864.0	20,180.6
Long-term debt (Note 11)	4,552.9	1,137.0
Other liabilities (Note 10)	8,854.9	6,948.8
Deferred income taxes (Note 5)	1,515.7	1,876.9
Total automotive liabilities	35,787.5	30,143.3

estimate the expense and to record it when the revenue is recognized; tax rules permit warranty deductions only when the repairs or adjustments are actually made (essentially the cash basis).

4. Revenue (or gains) become taxable *before* being recognized as accounting income; rent collected in advance is such an item.

It should be noted that in the first two instances, accounting income exceeds taxable income, thus giving rise to a deferred tax liability; in the latter two examples, the reverse is true: There is a deferred tax asset that, in simple terms, is like a prepaid income tax. (To be precise, it is the income tax benefit of future deductions.) Many companies have both, perhaps a deferred tax liability because of different depreciation policies and a deferred tax asset because of the alternative treatment of warranty expenses.

EXHIBIT 12.8

(continued)

Panel B

Deferred income taxes result from timing differences in the recognition of revenues and expenses between financial statements and tax returns. The principal sources of these differences and the related effect of each on the company's provision for income taxes were as follows:

(in millions)	1990	1989	1988
Depreciation and amortization (excludes leasing transactions)	$ 78.8	$196.9	$ 139.0
Dealer and customer allowances and claims	(358.6)	(72.6)	(153.3)
Employee benefit plans	(65.1)	(77.0)	(116.5)
Leasing transactions	362.1	83.5	7.9
Alternative minimum tax	(391.4)	—	—

The Ford Motor Company provides an instructive example, presented in Exhibit 12.8. Note that in 1990, for example, the deferred tax expense for the Ford Motor Company due to accounting-tax depreciation differences *increased* the accounting income tax expense by $78.8 million and that dealer and customer allowances and claims, probably most of which are for warranty expense, *reduced* the accounting income tax expense by $358.6 million.

Accounting for Deferred Taxes

In 1992, the FASB adopted a new accounting standard for deferred taxes, SFAS No. 109. Under this opinion, which was discussed and debated at the Financial Accounting Standards Board for 10 years, companies must recognize the current and future tax consequences of events that have been recognized in either the financial statements or the tax returns. A deferred tax liability (or asset) must be recognized for all tax effects due to temporary differences. The key to SFAS No. 109 is that any temporary book-tax difference in the value of an asset or liability will result in taxable or tax deductible amounts in future periods. Such items must be valued using the marginal tax rates expected to apply to taxable income in future periods. Deferred tax assets, which may result from such book-tax difference, may need to be adjusted by a *valuation allowance* if it is "more likely than not" that some portion of the deferred tax asset will not be realized.

In the example of Sample Company (Exhibit 12.7), tax depreciation was figured on a two-year basis and accounting depreciation was taken over four years. Recall that the asset's original cost was $1,000; hence, the two depreciation schedules would be as follows:

	Tax Calculations		Accounting Calculations	
Year	Yearly Depreciation	End-of-year Undepreciated Cost	Yearly Depreciation	End-of-year Undepreciated Cost
1	$500	$ 500	$250	$ 750
2	500	–0–	250	500
3		–0–	250	250
4		–0–	250	–0–

At the end of Year 1, the balance sheet of Sample Company reflects an asset valued at $750:

Asset (at cost)	$1,000
Less: Accumulated depreciation	(250)
Asset (net)	$ 750

However, this asset has an undepreciated cost basis of $500 for tax purposes, and the difference between the two cost bases is $250. When the accounting basis temporarily differs from the tax basis for an asset (or a liability) like this, it means that income tax implications should be recognized.

In this case, at the end of Year 1, an additional tax liability will occur in the future because of the temporary accounting-tax difference. If tax rates are expected to remain at 40 percent, there will be a $100 additional tax liability (i.e., 0.40 × $250) in the future. Thus, the Deferred Tax Liability at the end of Year 1 should be $100, and the deferred tax expense amount to be recorded in Year 1 is also $100 (the beginning Deferred Tax Liability account was zero). The deferred taxes would be calculated as follows for the four years for the Sample Company:

	End of Year			
	1	2	3	4
Accounting asset NBV*	$750	$500	$250	$–0–
Tax asset NBV	500	–0–	–0–	–0–
Difference	$250	$500	$250	$–0–
Tax rate (during the year)	0.4	0.4	0.4	0.4
Deferred tax liability	$100	$200	$100	$–0–
Deferred tax expense	$100	$100	$(100)	$(100)

*(NBV = net book value.)

In reviewing the above figures, it is important to recall the purpose of deferred tax accounting: Deferred tax liabilities (and assets) measure the future tax expenditures (or benefits) that a company faces due only to the differences between tax accounting and financial statement accounting.

Using the above data for Sample Company, the asset's tax basis at the end of Year 1 is $250 below its accounting basis so that there should be a $100 deferred tax liability *associated with this asset* (i.e., 0.40 × $250). In the following year, the difference in the two cost bases is $500, so the deferred tax liability must be $200. To increase the liability requires an expense in Year 2 of $100; hence,

Years 1 and 2
Dr. Income Tax Expense (E) $100
    Cr. Deferred Taxes (L) $100

Years 3 and 4
Dr. Deferred Taxes (L) $100
    Cr. Income Tax Expense (E) $100

Note that at the end of Year 1, it was determined that the ending balance for deferred taxes should be $100. There was no beginning balance for deferred taxes, so the deferred tax expense is $100:

Deferred Tax Liability

	Beginning of Year 1 $ 0
	(Plug) Deferred tax expense 100
	End of Year 1 $100

In simple terms, each asset or liability that may reflect a temporary accounting-tax difference in carrying value is analyzed separately. The taxable or tax deductible amounts in future years are projected, and the deferred tax assets or liabilities are calculated each year at the incremental tax rate expected to apply to taxable income in future periods when the deferred tax assets and liabilities are realized. The deferred tax expense for each year is then the difference in the deferred tax liability or asset from the beginning of the year to the end of the year (i.e., a "plug"). In other words, the liability is calculated first and then the expense figure is derived to obtain the new balance for the deferred tax liability.

Deferred tax assets. The accounting for some items, such as warranties, is the reverse of that for depreciation. For example, the balance sheet may show a reserve for future warranty claim or some such liability. This represents a liability with an accounting-tax difference the other way: Expensing on the accounting statements has preceded its tax deduction. A **deferred tax asset** must be created to reflect this accounting-tax difference.

The following example illustrates how the accounting for warranties might lead to the creation of a deferred tax asset:

	At the End of Year		
	1	**2**	**3**
Accounting basis of warranty liability	$(500)	$(400)	$(200)
Tax basis of warranty liability	–0–	–0–	–0–
Difference	$(500)	$(400)	$(200)
Tax rate (during the year)	0.40	0.40	0.40
Deferred tax asset	$ 200	$ 160	$ 80
Deferred tax expense (benefit) for the year	$(200)	$ 40	$ 80

Suppose that during Year 1, an allowance for future warranty expense was established for the first time at $500. Since estimated warranty expenses cannot be deducted for tax purposes, at the end of Year 1 there is a liability with an accounting-tax difference, in this case $500. The deferred tax asset related to this liability is $200 (i.e., 0.40 × $500). The difference between the beginning and ending deferred tax assets is thus $200. As a consequence, a $200 deferred tax adjustment (or negative expense) exists. At the end of Year 2, the warranty is $400. Obviously, the actual warranty cost recognized on the tax return exceeded the warranty expense reflected in the accounting statements. Since this accounting-tax difference is $400, the deferred tax asset is $160 (i.e., 0.40 × $400). To reduce the deferred tax asset from its opening balance of $200, a deferred tax expense of $40 will be recorded. A similar situation occurs in Year 3.

Financial Disclosures for Deferred Taxes

The classification of deferred tax assets and liabilities in the balance sheet must reflect the classification of the liabilities or assets with which they are associated. Thus, deferred tax liabilities resulting from accounting-tax depreciation differences are always classified as noncurrent because the assets associated with it, fixed assets, are always classified as noncurrent. Although it is possible to have four deferred tax items in a balance sheet: current and noncurrent liabilities, and current and noncurrent assets, current deferred tax assets can be netted against current deferred tax liabilities; the same is true for noncurrent deferred tax assets and liabilities.

The footnotes must contain a reconciliation of the actual income tax expense to the tax provision at the statutory rate. Footnote 5 of Ford Motor's 1990 annual report (see Exhibit 12.9) illustrates this disclosure. This 1990 annual report was prepared early in 1991; Ford was anticipating changing its accounting for deferred taxes so as to conform to SFAS No. 96. This standard had been announced in 1987, but the mandatory adoption date had been extended three times. SFAS No. 109 superseded SFAS No. 96; adoption was mandatory for 1993 fiscal permitted. As a consequence of these attempts at a deferred tax standard, preparers of annual reports from 1987 to 1992 had a choice of standards:

Year	Standard for Deferred Taxes
1986	Opinion 11
1987	Opinion 11 or SFAS No. 96
1988	Opinion 11 or SFAS No. 96
1989	Opinion 11 or SFAS No. 96
1990	Opinion 11 or SFAS No. 96
1991	Opinion 11 or SFAS No. 96
1992	Opinion 11 or SFAS No. 96 or SFAS No. 109
1993	SFAS No. 109

Thus in 1992 companies could use the pre-1987 standard (Opinion 11), SFAS No. 96 or SFAS No. 109.

As the exhibit reveals, Ford had yet to adopt SFAS No. 96, so it continued to follow the old disclosure rules by which current deferred tax assets and liabilities were netted as were noncurrent deferred tax assets and liabilities. Also note that Ford's 1990 income tax expense of $530.4 million was very close to what it would have been at the statutory rate

EXHIBIT 12.9

FORD MOTOR COMPANY
Deferred Income Tax Disclosures

The FASB has issued Statement of Financial Accounting Standards No. 96, "Accounting for Income Taxes" ("SFAS No. 96"). Adoption of this standard is expected to be mandatory by first quarter 1993. When adopted, the standard will result in the restatement of the company's world-wide deferred tax balances to the statutory tax rates in effect at the time these balances are expected to be payable. Because many of these deferred taxes were recorded at higher tax rates in prior years, net income can be expected to increase in the year SFAS No. 96 is adopted, assuming no increase in statutory tax rates.

For the Automotive segment, deferred taxes are classified on the balance sheet between current and noncurrent with assets and liabilities netted for each classification. At December 31, 1990 and 1989, net deferred current tax assets of $1,339 million and $1,122 million, respectively, were included in other current assets and net deferred noncurrent tax liabilities of $1,516 million and $1,877 million, respectively, were included in deferred income taxes in the Automotive section of the consolidated balance sheet.

A reconciliation of the provision for income taxes compared with the amounts at the U.S. statutory tax rate is shown below:

(in millions)	1990	1989	1988
Tax provision at U.S. statutory rate of 34%	$ 541.2	$1,906.4	$2,786.2
Effect of:			
State and local income taxes	66.2	104.5	156.1
Foreign taxes over U.S. tax rate	114.7	183.9	183.2
Income not subject to tax or subject to tax at reduced rates	(124.6)	(137.6)	(38.6)
Other	(67.1)	55.2	(88.2)
Provision for income taxes	$ 530.4	$2,112.4	$2,998.7
Effective tax rate	33.3%	37.7%	36.6%

of 34 percent because income not subject to tax or subject to tax at lower rates offset the effect of state, local, and foreign income taxes.

Besides changing the classification of deferred tax assets and liabilities, SFAS No. 96 also mandated that deferred tax liabilities and assets be recorded at the tax rates expected to be in effect when the timing differences are realized and settled. As Ford Motor Company noted, historic tax rates had been used prior to SFAS No. 96 (and now SFAS No. 109). For a company such as Ford with substantial deferred tax liabilities computed on older and higher tax rates, the adoption of the new accounting opinion could result in a one-time increase in net income.

Exhibit 12.10 is taken from PepsiCo's 1990 annual report. One can see that for the period 1988 to 1990, PepsiCo deferred $222.7 million in income taxes, mostly U.S. taxes, or 16 percent of its total income tax expense of $1390.9 million. The timing differences leading to these deferrals were due to depreciation methods and amortization

EXHIBIT 12.10

PepsiCo, Inc.
Deferred Income Tax Disclosures

Income Taxes

Provision for income taxes on income from continuing operations:

	1990	1989	1988
Current– Federal	$301.5	$221.7	$235.2
Foreign	126.6	89.5	52.8
State	62.3	38.0	40.6
	490.4	349.2	328.6
Deferred–Federal	66.0	95.7	37.4
Foreign	12.5	1.2	1.7
State	7.9	3.0	(2.7)
	86.4	99.9	36.4
	$576.8	$449.1	$365.0

The deferred income tax provision, which results from differences in the timing of recognition of revenue and expense for financial reporting and tax purposes, included amounts related to depreciation of property, plant and equipment of $34.5 million, $36.3 million and $44.0 million and amortization of intangibles of $46.0 million, $47.3 million and $15.6 million in 1990, 1989 and 1988, respectively.

U.S. and foreign income from continuing operations before income taxes:

	1990	1989	1988
U.S....................	$ 915.5	$ 843.4	$ 773.4
Foreign	751.9	507.1	353.8
	$1,667.4	$1,350.5	$1,127.2

Consistent with the allocation of income for tax purposes, approximately 50% of the income arising from the sale of soft drink concentrates manufactured in Puerto Rico is included in Foreign in the above table. Under the terms of a Puerto Rico tax incentive grant that was amended in 1989 and expires in 2006, the allocated soft drink concentrate manufacturing profits and all investment earnings in Puerto Rico were taxed at rates of approximately 7% and 4% in 1990 and 1989, respectively, with a nominal tax provided in 1988. The 7% Puerto Rico tax is applicable through 2006.

PepsiCo's soft drink concentrate manufacturing profits in Ireland were exempt from income tax through mid-1989 when a 10% tax, applicable through 2010, became effective.

Deferred taxes were not provided on unremitted earnings of foreign subsidiaries that are intended to be indefinitely reinvested. These unremitted earnings aggregated approximately $605 million at year-end 1990, exclusive of amounts that if remitted in the future would result in little or no tax under current tax laws and the amended Puerto Rico tax incentive grant.

Reconciliation of the U.S. federal statutory tax rate to PepsiCo's effective tax rate on income from continuing operations:

	1990	1989	1988
U.S. federal statutory tax rate	34.0%	34.0%	34.0%
State income tax net of federal tax benefit	1.9	2.0	2.2
Earnings in jurisdictions taxed at lower rates (principally Puerto Rico and Ireland)	(3.9)	(3.9)	(3.7)
Nondeductible amortization of goodwill and other intangibles	1.6	2.0	1.4
Tax basis difference related to joint venture stock offering	1.6	–	–
Other, net........................	(0.6)	(0.8)	(1.5)
Effective tax rate	34.6%	33.3%	32.4%

Deferred income taxes reflected in the Consolidated Balance Sheet under the caption "Deferred Income Taxes" included amounts related to timing differences of $741.9 million and $635.9 million and Safe Harbor leases of $200.9 million and $221.0 million in 1990 and 1989, respectively. Prepaid income taxes of $11.6 million in 1990 are reflected under the Consolidated Balance Sheet caption "Prepaid expenses and other current assets." Current deferred income taxes of $8.2 million in 1989 are reflected under the Consolidated Balance Sheet caption "Other current liabilities."

In 1981 and 1982 PepsiCo invested in Safe Harbor leases (the Leases). These transactions, which do not impact the provision for income taxes, decrease income taxes payable over the initial years of the Leases and increase them over the later years. The deferred federal income taxes payable related to the Leases are based on the current U.S. federal statutory tax rate. Taxes payable related to the Leases are estimated to be $40 million over the next five years.

In December 1989 the Financial Accounting Standards Board (the FASB) amended Statement No. 96 on Accounting for Income Taxes to extend the required adoption date to 1992. As the FASB continues to review and evaluate possible amendments, including a further extension of the adoption date, PepsiCo is unable to predict the final FASB requirements and therefore cannot reasonably estimate the effects of adoption.

of intangibles, probably associated with leases. The favorable tax treatment on Puerto Rican earnings reduced the effective tax rate; state income taxes and the amortization of goodwill increased that rate. PepsiCo is another company that had delayed adopting SFAS No. 96. The last paragraph of their footnote disclosure almost anticipated a new opinion or a modification of SFAS No. 96.

SUMMARY

Leases, pensions, and deferred income taxes are significant obligations that present unique valuation issues. Capital leases are reported in the balance sheet at their present value; pension obligations are disclosed in the footnotes at their present value, and, under some circumstances, a portion of this obligation may appear on the balance sheet as a liability. Deferred income taxes, on the other hand, are not reported at their present value but are reported in the balance sheet.

Many types of leases exist, but only those that meet one or more of the four tests (i.e., ownership, alternative ownership, economic life, or value) are considered to be capital leases. Capital leases are recorded on the books of the lessee, as both an asset and a liability at their present value at the time the lease is signed. Lease assets are amortized in a manner similar to other depreciable assets as if the asset were owned. Lease liabilities, on the other hand, are amortized using the effective interest method as one would amortize a bond.

Pensions are important because of the sheer magnitude of the dollars involved. They are complex because of the variety of estimates one must make to value an entity's pension obligation. No matter how a pension is to be funded, whether by contributions from the employer, the employee, or both, the two basic types are defined-contribution and defined-benefit plans. The latter is more complex because accountants, actuaries, and management must estimate future benefits, employee mortality, and retirement ages, and the future earnings rate of pension assets. In situations in which the accumulated benefit obligation (or ABO) is less than the plan assets, a pension liability may be created reflecting this difference.

Differences between the accounting procedures adopted for tax purposes and for financial reporting purposes may result in deferred tax liabilities and/or assets and deferred tax expenses and/or benefits. Some items, such as goodwill amortization, result in permanent accounting-tax differences and are not subject to deferred tax accounting. Only temporary differences, such as those created by differences in depreciation, result in interperiod income tax allocations.

Three special appendices are included with this chapter. They are designed to further explain the accounting for leases, pensions, and deferred income taxes, and they contain additional examples of each.

NEW CONCEPTS AND TERMS

Accumulated benefits obligation (p. 528)

Capital lease (p. 518)

Deferred tax assets (p. 539)

Defined-benefit plan (p. 525)

Defined-contribution plan (p. 525)

ERISA (p. 526)

Interperiod tax allocation (p. 532)

Lease (p. 519)

Lessee (p. 519)

Lessor (p. 519)

Liability method (p. 537)

Off-balance sheet financing (p. 518)

Operating leases (p. 518)

Pension (p. 524)

Pension expense (p. 527)

Permanent differences (p. 535)

Plan assets at fair value (p. 528)

Projected benefit obligation (p. 527)

Temporary differences (p. 535)

Unfunded pension cost (p. 528)

Leases in Detail

Chapter 12 introduced the concepts of operating and capital leases and discussed the accounting for both types of leases from the lessee's perspective. Here we will explain more fully the calculations underlying the accounting for capitalized leases for both the lessee and the lessor. The accounting and required disclosures for capitalized leases for lessors, including the *direct-financing type* and *sales-type leases,* are also described.

We will continue to use the example of the Boeing airplane leased by American Airlines from Prudential Insurance Co. Recall that the present value of the lease was $125 million and that both the lease asset and the lease liability will be amortized, although on separate amortization schedules.

Amortization of the Lease Liability

Exhibit 12A–1 presents the lease amortization schedule for the American Airlines lease liability. Column 2 is the quarterly payment due at the beginning of each quarter, and columns 3 and 4 identify the interest expense portion and the principal reduction portion of this payment. Thus, the first quarter's payment is all principal reduction. After this payment, the principal is then $119,750,000.

The key to Exhibit 12A–1 is the way that the interest expense and principal recovery portions of the payment are separated. We know that the interest rate per quarter is 3 percent. Thus, for the second payment, the interest expense portion must be $0.03 \times$ $119,750,000$, or $3,592,000. Since the payment is always $5,250,000 per quarter for this lease, the remainder is the principal recovery, or $1,658,000 (i.e., $5,250,000 − 3,592,000). Since the principal balance is reduced by this amount, the ending principal balance for Quarter 2 is $118,092,000, or $119,750,000 − $1,658,000. Each quarter's

EXHIBIT 12A – 1

Lease Amortization Schedule:
Aircraft Financing Example
(in millions)

Qtr.	Payment	Interest Portion	Principal Reduction	Ending Principal
				$125.000
1	$ 5.250	$	$ 5.250	119.750
2	5.250	3.592	1.658	118.092
3	5.250	3.543	1.708	116.384
4	5.250	3.492	1.759	114.626
5	5.250	3.439	1.812	112.814
6	5.250	3.384	1.866	110.948
7	5.250	3.328	1.922	109.026
8	5.250	3.271	1.979	107.047
9	5.250	3.211	2.039	105.008
10	5.250	3.150	2.100	102.908
11	5.250	3.087	2.163	100.745
12	5.250	3.022	2.228	98.517
13	5.250	2.956	2.295	96.222
14	5.250	2.887	2.364	93.859
15	5.250	2.816	2.435	91.424
16	5.250	2.743	2.508	88.916
17	5.250	2.667	2.583	86.334
18	5.250	2.590	2.660	83.673
19	5.250	2.510	2.740	80.933
20	5.250	2.428	2.822	78.111
21	5.250	2.343	2.907	75.204
22	5.250	2.256	2.994	72.210
23	5.250	2.166	3.084	69.126
24	5.250	2.074	3.177	65.949
25	5.250	1.978	3.272	62.678
26	5.250	1.880	3.370	59.308
27	5.250	1.779	3.471	55.837
28	5.250	1.675	3.575	52.261
29	5.250	1.568	3.682	48.579
30	5.250	1.457	3.793	44.786
31	5.250	1.344	3.907	40.879
32	5.250	1.226	4.024	36.855
33	5.250	1.106	4.145	32.711
34	5.250	0.981	4.269	28.442
35	5.250	0.853	4.397	24.045
36	5.250	0.721	4.529	19.516
37	5.250	0.585	4.665	14.851
38	5.250	0.446	4.805	10.046
39	5.250	0.301	4.949	5.097
40	5.250	0.153	5.097	(0.000)
Totals	$210.012	$85.012	$125.000	

payment is separated in this manner. Note that the last payment's principal recovery is $5,097,000, just exactly the outstanding principal balance at the beginning of the last quarter.[4]

Note one more thing about Exhibit 12A–1: The total payments are $210,012,000, of which $85,012,000 is interest and the rest principal. Thus, in American's footnotes, the lease would be disclosed as follows:

Future minimum lease payments	$210,012,000
Less: Amount representing interest	85,012,000
Present value of minimum lease payments	$125,000,000

Amortization of the Lease Asset

In Chapter 12, we learned that the depreciation policies for capital-lease assets are the same as those that a lessee adopts for similar owned assets. If, however, American depreciates its other aircraft over 12 years on a straight-line approach, it has an interesting problem: What time frame should it use to amortize the leased asset when the lease runs for 10 years and the asset's normal depreciable life is 12 years?

Convention is to use the economic life of a leased asset if ownership is expected to transfer to the lessee and to use the lease lifetime only if the lease qualifies for capitalization because it meets the economic-life or valuation tests (but not one of the ownership tests). In the airline case, the asset-depreciation period should be 12 years or 48 quarters; hence, the leased asset will be depreciated at the rate of $10,416,667 per year (or $125 million divided by 12 years).

The interest rate used by a lessor in setting the terms of a lease is often not divulged by the lessor to the lessee. The lessor may have received discounts or other incentives from the original manufacturer and may wish to keep such arrangements confidential. If the market value of the asset is known, then, of course, the rate can be derived by simple present value analysis. If, however, the market value of the asset is unknown and the lessor's implicit interest rate is also unknown, then the lessee must use its own incremental borrowing rate as the discount rate.

Accounting for the Lessor

If a lease meets *any* of the four tests discussed in Chapter 12, the lessor treats the agreement as a capitalized lease if it meets two *additional* tests: (1) there is reasonable assurance that the lease payments will be received and (2) there are no other major uncertainties as to costs or revenues. The need for these two additional tests is obvious:

---

[4]One might ask why there is any interest portion at all in the last payment since the payment is made at the *beginning of the period*. The explanation is that annuities such as this lease with 40 payments, with payments made at the beginning of the period, are really liabilities that extend over only 39 periods. It is as if one borrowed $119,750,000 and repaid it at $5,250,000 per quarter for 39 quarters, with payments made at the end of the period—when the interest expense for that period had been accrued.

A lease asset (lease receivable) must not be recorded if collectibility is in doubt, and the amount of the receivable must be known at the inception of the lease for an accounting entry to be recorded. Assuming that a lease meets these criteria, it is then necessary for the lessor to determine whether the lease is a *direct-financing-type* or a *sales-type* capital lease. This decision rests on whether or not the asset's market value is the same as the lessor's cost of the asset.

In the case of the airplane lease, the insurance company enters into a typical *direct-financing lease* arrangement when, at the lease date, the airplane's cost to the lessor (Prudential Insurance Co.) is the same as its current market value. The insurance company first buys the airplane and carries it on its books as an asset. Later, when the lease is signed, the airplane asset will be replaced by a capital-lease asset (i.e., a receivable). As lease payments are received, the reported amount of the leased asset will decline according to the amortization schedule. The insurance company's profit on the transaction will come from the interest income associated with the lease payments (i.e., from financing the airline's purchase of the aircraft).

When Prudential purchases the airplane from Boeing, the recorded transaction is as follows:

```
Dr.  Aircraft (A) . . . . . . . . . . . . . . . . $125,000,000
    Cr.  Cash (A)  . . . . . . . . . . . . . . . . . . . .        $125,000,000
```

When the lease agreement is signed, the asset is removed from the insurance company's books and is replaced by two accounts: Minimum Lease Payment Receivable (the total undiscounted lease receivable) and Unearned Revenues (the future interest payments to be received). Referring to Exhibit 12A–1, note that the total payments are to be $210,012,000. In the leasing industry, this figure is called the *minimum lease payment receivable*. The $85,012,000 is the unearned revenue, and the $125 million is the present value of the future lease payments (it is also the market value of the asset). Clearly,

Minimum lease payment receivable =

Unearned revenue + Present value of lease payments.

Thus, the insurance company makes the following entry when the lease is signed:

```
Dr.  Minimum Lease Payment Receivable (A). . .  $210,012,000
    Cr.  Unearned Revenue (L)  . . . . . . . . . . . . . .       $ 85,012,000
    Cr.  Aircraft (A) . . . . . . . . . . . . . . . . . . .          125,000,000
```

Each quarter, Prudential will make entries to record the receipt of the lease payment and to recognize its portion of the revenue earned. For example, the second-quarter entries would be:

```
Dr.  Cash (A) . . . . . . . . . . . . . . . . . . . .  $5,025,000
    Cr.  Minimum Lease Payment Receivable (A). . . . . . . . .        $5,025,000
Dr.  Unearned Revenue (L) . . . . . . . . . . . . .  $3,592,000
    Cr.  Interest Revenue (R)  . . . . . . . . . . . . . . . .         $3,592,000
```

At 3 percent per quarter, the quarterly interest income is $3,592,000 (i.e., 0.03 × 119,750,000 = 3,592,000).

In contrast to the direct-financing lease example just described, when a manufacturing company makes a product and then leases it, it generates a *sales-type lease* (i.e. the asset's market value is not the same as the lessor's cost of the asset). The accounting issues become (1) how much profit the company should show on the sale of the product itself, as opposed to the interest revenue on the lease, and (2) when it should be shown.

Let us return to the American Airlines example and suppose that the Boeing Company, instead of a third-party insurance company, was to be the lessor at the same terms as those offered by Prudential. Suppose also that Boeing's cost of manufacturing the airplane was $100 million. When the lease is signed, Boeing makes an entry for this sales-type lease that recognizes a profit (or loss) on executing the lease (thus, the origin of the "sales-type" label). The following is the "sale" entry:

```
Dr.  Cost of Goods Sold (E) . . . . . . . . . . $100,000,000
Dr.  Minimum Lease Payment Receivable (A). . .  210,012,000
     Cr.  Sales (R) . . . . . . . . . . . . . . . . . . .      $125,000,000
     Cr.  Unearned Revenue (L) . . . . . . . . . . . . .         85,012,000
     Cr.  Inventory (A) . . . . . . . . . . . . . . . . . .      100,000,000
```

Under this type of lease, Boeing will make entries each quarter to record the receipt of the lease payment and to recognize the portion of the interest revenue earned as if it were a direct-financing lease. For example, these would be the second-quarter entries:

```
Dr.  Cash (A) . . . . . . . . . . . . . . . . . . . . . .  $5,025,000
     Cr.  Minimum Lease Payment Receivable (A). . . . . . . . .      $5,025,000
Dr.  Unearned Revenue (L) . . . . . . . . . . . . . .  3,592,000
     Cr.  Interest Revenue (R) . . . . . . . . . . . . . . . . .      $3,592,000
```

Disclosure for Lessors

Lessors with significant leasing activities have extensive disclosure requirements for both operating and capitalized leases. Ryder System, Inc., the largest truck-leasing and rental company in the world, is active as both a lessor and lessee. The lease footnote in its 1987 annual report (see Exhibit 12A–2) is typical of the disclosure required for both lessors and lessees.

From this exhibit, we can see that as a *lessor,* the value of the capitalized leases appearing in the balance sheet is $264,348,000 as of the end of 1987: $36,546,000 appears as part of current receivables; the rest is included in other assets. The difference between the lease asset ($264,348,000) and the total lease receivables ($366,123,000) is due to executory costs, unearned income (essentially the interest portion to be earned in the future), and "unguaranteed residuals," which are obligations of Ryder as lessor.

The figures at the bottom of the lease disclosure explain that as lessor, most of Ryder's leases are operating-type leases.

EXHIBIT 12A – 2

RYDER SYSTEM, INC.
Lease Disclosures

Operating Leases as Lessor. One of the company's major product lines is full-service leasing of commercial trucks, tractors and trailers. The standard full-service lease requires the company to furnish the customer a vehicle, together with all services, supplies and equipment necessary for its operation. These services include maintenance, parts, tires, licenses, taxes, a substitute vehicle if needed and, in most cases, fuel. The agreements provide for a fixed time charge plus a fixed per-mile charge and, in some instances, a provision for guaranteed mileage. A portion of these charges is usually adjusted in accordance with changes in the Consumer price Index. The company is also the lessor of aircraft and aircraft parts under operating lease agreements, which generally provide for fixed time charges.

Capital Leases as Lessor. The company leases additional commercial trucks, tractors, trailers and buses under agreements which are accounted for as direct financing leases. The provisions of these lease agreements are essentially the same as those described for operating leases, except for certain residual value guarantees. In addition, the company is the lessor of aircraft and aircraft parts under direct financing leases. These leases generally provide for fixed time charges with no residual value guarantees. The net investment in direct financing leases consists of:

In thousands	1987	1986
Minimum lease payments receivable	$ 366,123	305,843
Executory costs and unearned income	(132,643)	(111,041)
Unguaranteed residuals	30,868	25,360
Net investment in direct financing leases	264,348	220,162
Current portion included in receivables	(36,546)	(34,872)
Non-current portion included in other assets	$ 227,802	185,290

Capital Leases as Lessee. The company entered into certain vehicle lease arrangements accounted for as capitalized leases in the amounts of $49 million, $259 million and $204 million during 1987, 1986 and 1985, respectively. The leases provide to the various lessors the tax benefit of equipment ownership and provide for early termination as stipulated values. These leases are amortized over the effective economic lease term. At December 31, 1987 and 1986, the investment in capitalized lease equipment, net of accumulated amortization was $447 million and $478 million, respectively.

Lease Payments. Future mininum payments for all leases in effect at December 31, 1987, are as follows:

E X H I B I T   1 2 A – 2

(continued)

In thousands	Operating Leases as Lessor	Capital Leases as	
		Lessor	Lessee
1988	$ 652,237	62,225	$ 117,478
1989	510,264	62,484	112,275
1990	350,709	51,004	109,703
1991	208,766	52,627	108,539
1992	102,021	50,078	88,764
1992	60,274	87,705	73,934
Total	$1,884,271	366,123	610,693
Portion representing interest			(114,027)
Present value of minimum lease payments			$ 496,666

The above amounts related to the company as lessor are based upon the assumption that revenue earning equipment will remain on lease for the length of time specified by the respective lease agreements. Future minimum payments for operating leases include an estimate of the future fixed time and guaranteed mileage charges. This is not a projection of future fixed lease revenue; no effect has been given to renewals, new business, cancellations or future rate changes.

Pensions in Detail

This appendix presents some basic pension terminology and illustrates the calculations necessary to determine a company's pension expense. It explains the significance of the required footnote disclosures for defined-benefit plans and interprets an actual pension footnote. Finally, an example of pension accounting is presented.

Terminology

To understand the valuation of defined-benefit pension obligations and the disclosure of pension expense, and liability and asset information reflected in corporate annual reports, one must first learn the language of pension accounting. The following concepts and definitions are essential for a complete understanding of pension accounting.

Plan assets—the market value of the assets in a pension fund under the control of a trustee. These assets are owned by the pension fund or trust, a separate legal entity, and appear on the balance sheet of the trust, not of the employer-company.

Accumulated benefit obligation (ABO)—the present value of the projected payments a company must make in the future to satisfy the retirement benefits that have already been earned by employees and retirees. Discounting of the future cash outflow is done using an interest rate termed the *settlement rate,* an external market rate reflecting the return on high-quality, fixed-income investments. Projections are made using only *current* salary levels but with assumptions for mortality and so on. Conceptually, if a company were to terminate a pension agreement now and seek to settle whatever obligations it had to employees and retirees by making a single payment now to an external pension administrator, the ABO would be the amount it owed. Note that an employer can cancel a pension agreement, but it is obligated to pay benefits for the accumulated years of service each employee has earned until the agreement is canceled. Also note that, as each year passes, qualified employees "earn" another year of benefits.

Projected benefit obligation (PBO)—an obligation similar to the ABO except that it is based on projected or future salary levels. Consequently, the PBO is usually higher than the ABO. The PBO is the present value (using the settlement rate) of the pension benefits that have been earned to date by employees and retirees. It reflects expected mortality, expected salary increases, and expectations about employee turnover.

Expected rate—the expected long-term rate of return on a pension fund's assets. This rate is used to estimate what the trustee will earn on a fund's invested assets.

Vested benefits—*vested* means that an employee has met the minimum plan tenure requirements and is qualified to receive pension benefits. In most corporate pension plans, employees must work full-time for a defined period of time, say two years, before they become eligible for a pension. For example, suppose that two people joined a company at the same time and that one quit after two years and the other left after four years. If the company had a three-year vesting requirement, the first person would receive no pension. The second person would be eligible for a pension based on the four years of service. A company's PBO for all employees and retirees might be $130 million, but perhaps only $110 million for vested employees and retirees—those with more than the required years of service (i.e., the vesting period).

Funded status of the plan—the difference between the projected benefit obligation (PBO) and a plan's assets at market value.

Net gain or loss—the difference between the actual earnings of a plan for a year and the expected earnings (expected rate times beginning of the year value of the plan's assets). If the difference is included in pension expense, it is considered "recognized." If it is accumulated and amortized at some later date, it is termed *the accumulated, unrecognized net gain or loss*. Generally accepted accounting practice is to recognize the net gains or losses only when they exceed a threshold (i.e., 10 percent of the higher of the PBO or the plan assets).

Financial Accounting Standard 87 (SFAS No. 87)—the current GAAP for pensions.

Net obligation—the difference between the PBO and the plan assets at the time SFAS No. 87 was adopted. It is also called the *transition asset (or liability)*. It is amortized or recognized in the income statement on a straight-line basis over the expected working lives of the work force at the time SFAS No. 87 was adopted.

Accrued or prepaid pension cost—the cumulative total of the unfunded pension expense or, if funding has exceeded the cumulative expenses, the cumulative prepaid pension cost.

Service cost (or **current service cost** or **normal cost**)—the present value of the benefits earned in the current year by the existing employees in a plan. Perhaps the best way to conceptualize service cost is the following. As each year goes by, the employees should say to themselves, "I've just put in another year of service toward retirement. I'll get another X percent of my ending salary in each retirement check." The employer must predict just how many of those employees will survive to begin collecting their retirement and how long that retirement will last. The present value cost of this obligation, for just this year, is the *service cost*. Calculating the service cost requires projections of mortality and future salary levels. Discounting the future payments is done at the settlement rate.

Prior service cost—when a pension plan is first adopted, an employer often gives credit to the existing employees for their years of service prior to the adoption of the plan. For example, 63-year-old employees will suddenly be treated as if they had been in the plan since they were hired. They may get 35 or 40 years of service "with the stroke of a pen.'' The present value of this prior (or past) service is estimated by using projected salary levels, mortality, and the settlement rate. The same thing happens when a plan's benefit levels are increased and made retroactive.

Interest cost—for the year, the beginning of the year PBO times the settlement rate. Conceptually, interest cost is like saying ''At the beginning of this year, our total pension obligation (as measured by the PBO) on a discounted basis was $320 million. We are now at the end of the year, one year closer to the payouts. Hence, the value of the obligation has increased by a year's interest.''

Actual return on plan assets—the total actual earnings of the pension-fund assets for a year.

Actuarial gains and losses—a catchall category for the favorable and unfavorable adjustments arising from changes in expected mortality (and other actuarial) assumptions.

Additional minimum liability—an amount in addition to any current accrued or prepaid pension cost that may be required to be shown as a pension liability when a plan's assets are less than the ABO.

Accounting for Defined-Benefit Plans

Each year, actuaries and accountants project the number of an employer's present work force who will survive to retirement and the life expectancies for those projected retirees. Salary levels are projected, benefits calculated, and an expected pension payout schedule is prepared as of the end of each accounting period. This payout schedule is then discounted using a *settlement rate* to derive a *projected benefit obligation* (PBO). A similar calculation, the *accumulated benefit obligation* (ABO), is prepared using only current salary levels. Thus, there are two liability figures—one assuming current salary levels and one assuming salary progression. It is important to note that these ''liabilities'' do not necessarily appear in the employer's balance sheet; at this stage, they are simply calculations.

Under SFAS No. 87, the *pension expense* for a given year to be reported by an employer is the net of the following four items:

1. The *service cost* for the year (i.e., the present value cost of future benefits earned by employees for this year only).

2. *Plus* the *interest cost* on the PBO as of the beginning of the year, which is like the debt service cost on the total pension liability as of the beginning of the year.

3. *Less* the *actual return on plan assets* for the year (i.e., what the pension fund actually earned). In an ideal world, the pension fund's assets at the beginning of the year would equal only the PBO at the beginning of the year. During the year, the fund would earn only the year's interest cost on the PBO, so items 2 and 3 would offset one another.

4. *Plus/minus* four miscellaneous adjustments:
   (a) The difference between the actual return on plan assets and the expected return on plan assets for the year. The effect is to replace the actual return on plan assets with the *expected return on plan assets*. The differences between actual and

expected returns are accumulated and, if they exceed a threshold, are amortized over the expected working lifetime of the employees. This adjustment smooths the recognition of differences between the actual and expected earnings rate.

(b) Actuarial gains and losses are treated the same way.

(c) The difference between the PBO and the total fund assets at the time SFAS No. 87 was adopted is called the *net obligation* or *transition amount*. It too is amortized over the expected work force service life.

(d) If the plan is modified in later years and these modifications lead to prior service costs, this cost is also amortized.

The concept underlying this complex calculation of the yearly expense is based on the following logic: In a perfect world, a company's pension expense should be only its current pension service cost. This amount would be paid to the pension trust, which would add it to the fund's assets. Each year, the fund's invested assets would earn just what was expected. In such situation, the PBO (the present value of the total pension obligation) would always equal the fund's assets. The following exemplifies this "perfect world" situation:

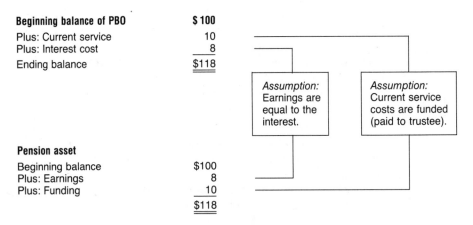

Beginning balance of PBO	**$ 100**
Plus: Current service	10
Plus: Interest cost	8
Ending balance	$118

Pension asset	
Beginning balance	$100
Plus: Earnings	8
Plus: Funding	10
	$118

Assumption: Earnings are equal to the interest.

Assumption: Current service costs are funded (paid to trustee).

In such a world, the pension assets would always be equal to the pension obligation. In the real world, however, many things are different:

- Actual earnings are rarely equal to expected earnings. The effect of SFAS No. 87 is to substitute the expected return for the actual return and then amortize the accumulated differences between the two over time if the cumulative amount gets "too big" (i.e., it smooths out the effects of stock and bond market swings).

- Sometimes management increases the benefits level. This has an immediate impact on the PBO (it increases it). The new obligation created by these plan modifications (i.e., prior service costs) is amortized over time—another smoothing activity.

- Sometimes the actuaries change their mortality tables or make similar changes to their assumptions. This can either immediately raise or lower the PBO. SFAS No. 87 smooths this by amortizing the actuarial gain or loss over time.

■ Finally, when SFAS No. 87 was first adopted, most companies had a PBO different from their fund assets. This difference, or "transition amount," is amortized over time.

The consequence of all of these smoothings and adjustments is to ensure that, for a company that funds its pension costs on a timely basis, the plan assets approximate the PBO over time without causing the annual pension expense to fluctuate widely.

Disclosure Requirements for Defined-Benefit Plans

Companies with defined-benefit pension programs must disclose the nature of their programs, types of benefits, funding policies, and actuarial methods. They must also disclose both the settlement rate and the expected earnings rate, the major elements of the actual pension expense, the ABO, and the PBO. The cumulative overfunded and underfunded status of different pension plans for a single employer cannot be netted together.

The 1990 footnote disclosure of PepsiCo, Inc., presented in Exhibit 12–5 (see page 531), is typical of footnotes under the disclosure requirements of SFAS No. 87. PepsiCo's pension expense for 1990 was only $7.5 million, comprising $48.1 million of service cost (i.e., the present value of benefits earned by employees during the year) and $63.3 million of interest cost on the PBO, offset by $27 million of actual earnings for the year on the plan's assets. Apparently, the plan trustee earned $55.9 less than expected on the fund's assets in 1987—no doubt because of the Gulf crises and resulting decline in stock market values:

Expected earnings	$82.9 million
Actual earnings	27.0
Expected − actual	55.9

The opposite situation must have occurred in 1989. That year the trustee's actual earnings exceeded the expected earnings by $84.9 million.

We can also see that the PepsiCo pension assets must have exceeded the PBO at the time it adopted SFAS No. 87 because the amortization of the transition amount, $17.9 million a year, reduced the overall pension expense. The unrecognized prior service cost adjustment was netted in the Deferred gain (loss) account.

Defined-Benefit Pension Liability on the Balance Sheet

Under certain circumstances, a pension liability other than the current accrued or prepaid pension cost amounts discussed earlier could appear on a company's balance sheet. SFAS No. 87 requires that, whenever total pension-fund assets are less than the ABO (i.e., the present value of the projected benefits *without* salary progression), a minimum liability is to be recognized in the employer's balance sheet even though the pension assets are under the control of and on the books of the pension plan.

Three situations are possible. When there is no current accrued or prepaid pension cost, the additional minimum liability is just the ABO minus the plan assets—*the unfunded ABO*. When there is a current *prepaid* pension cost, the additional liability is the unfunded ABO plus the prepaid pension cost. When there is a current accrued pension liability, the additional liability is the unfunded ABO less the accrued pension cost (except that when the unfunded liability is less than the accrued pension liability, there is no additional minimum liability).

For example, consider the following situation:

Accumulated benefit obligation (ABO)	$(3,500)
Provision for salary progression	(2,100)
Projected benefit obligation (PBO)	$(5,600)
Fair value of plan assets	3,000
Funded status of plan (underfunded)	$(2,600)
Unrecognized net gain or loss	400
Unrecognized net obligation	1,800
(Accrued) prepaid pension cost	$ (400)

The unfunded ABO is thus $500:

ABO	$(3,500)
Plan assets	3,000
	$ 500

The additional minimum liability is $100:

Unfunded ABO	$500
(Accrued) prepaid pension cost	(400)
	$100

The requirement to reflect this minimum liability on the employer's balance sheet was the result of a compromise by the FASB between the dictates of accounting theory and the realities of business practice. One might easily argue that when the pension assets are less than the *PBO*, the difference is an obligation of the employer that should be recognized just like any other liability. The compromise resulted in the FASB's decision that a liability need be recognized in the balance sheet only when the plan assets were less than the *ABO*.

In the above example, the difference between the ABO and the plan assets is $500, but the firm already has a $400 accrued pension liability. This portion of the liability has already been recognized and expensed but has not yet been funded. Hence, the additional, minimum liability to be shown on the balance sheet is $100.

Conditions leading to the recognition of a minimum liability usually arise when a new plan is adopted and benefits are granted for prior service. The "goodwill" created in the work force by the new plan is considered to be an intangible asset, and an entry would be made as follows:

Dr.	Unamortized Pension Cost (A)	$100
	Cr. Pension Liability (L)	$100

Each year, the previous year's minimum liability and related asset are removed from the books and a new liability and asset added if conditions indicate that an unfunded ABO exists. Some critics refer to this as a ''post-it'' entry that appears each year as a different figure as long as the fund's assets do not exceed the value of the ABO.

If the ABO exceeds the fund's assets *by an amount in excess of the unrecognized prior period costs and the unrecognized net obligation,* the excess amount is deducted from the recorded pension asset and is a contra equity. In other words, if the ABO exceeds the fund assets for reasons other than the cost of prior service, the plan is essentially underfunded, and it should appear as a liability without any offsetting asset. In the example just discussed, this would not be the case since the unrecognized net obligation or transition amount is $1,800.

Pension accounting is complex because pensions are complex. SFAS No. 87 introduced many new and potentially confusing concepts such as the PBO and ABO, the additional minimum liability, and the unrecognized net obligation. It may be some time before readers of financial statements become thoroughly familiar with this information, but its impact on reported net income and the statement of financial position is not likely to be significant for most large publicly traded corporations. The same cannot be said about a related issue—postretirement medical costs. These costs are predicted to rise rapidly in the next decade. Most corporations have provided no funding or reserves for such costs. A new accounting opinion (SFAS No. 106, effective for 1993 fiscal year) by the FASB could add significant liabilities to U.S. corporate balance sheets for these future obligations, and it could make the complexity of pensions pale in comparison.

A Complete Example

Exhibit 12B–1 reports the pension expense for a hypothetical company that adopted SFAS No. 87 in 1987; Exhibit 12B–2 illustrates the derivation of accrued or prepaid pension cost following the format used in most U.S. annual reports today. In this particular illustration, the company experiences five years when the expected returns exceed the actual returns on the invested plan assets. Then the reverse is true. In addition, the actuarial assumptions change in 1990 and 1993. In 1989, the plan is awarded to grant retroactive (prior service) benefits to employees. The effects of these events will be reflected in the pension assets and liability.

To begin, consider the first three lines of Exhibit 12B–2. The company's pension liability (PBO) at the beginning of 1987 was $400 larger than the pension assets of $3,000. Note that in this illustration, the pension liability rises steadily (in years such as 1989, it seems to jump considerably), and the plan assets lag behind for several years resulting in a sharp increase in the unfunded PBO. Beginning in 1993, however, the fund's assets increase dramatically. In spite of these large changes in assets, the PBO, and the funded status of the plan, the pension expense (Exhibit 12B–1) reflects only gradual changes, which is exactly what SFAS No. 87 attempts to achieve.

In following the calculations, perhaps the first thing that one should note is that at the time of adoption of SFAS No. 87, the difference between the PBO and the plan assets is the unrecognized net obligation (i.e., $400). This amount is amortized over 10 years (the projected average working lifetime of the present employees) and becomes a part of the

EXHIBIT 12B – 1

Calculation of Pension Expense

	1987	1988	1989	1990	1991	1992	1993	1994
Service cost	300	310	320	330	340	350	360	370
Interest cost	340	404	475	605	708	813	930	1,039
Actual return on plan assets	(240)	(267)	(201)	(214)	(567)	(847)	(1,103)	(1,114)
Net amortization (see below)	(20)	(17)	(141)	(193)	88	252	366	212
Pension expense	380	430	454	528	569	568	553	506
Explanation of net amortization:								
Amortization—unrecognized net (gain)/loss	–0–	–0–	–0–	–0–	2	–0–	–0–	–0–
Actual−expected earnings	(60)	(57)	(231)	(283)	(4)	162	276	122
Amortization−Unrecognized net obligation	40	40	40	40	40	40	40	40
Amortization−Unrecognized prior service cost	–0–	–0–	50	50	50	50	50	50
Net amortization	(20)	(17)	(141)	(193)	88	252	366	212

EXHIBIT 12B – 2

Reconciliation of (Accrued) Prepaid Pension Cost

	Begin				End of Year				
	1987	1987	1988	1989	1990	1991	1992	1993	1994
Projected benefit obligation	(3,400)	(4,040)	(4,754)	(6,049)	(7,084)	(8,133)	(9,296)	(10,386)	(11,794)
Fair value of assets	3,000	3,240	4,317	4,972	5,713	6,850	8,265	9,921	11,542
Funded status of plan	(400)	(800)	(437)	(1,078)	(1,371)	(1,283)	(1,031)	(464)	(253)
Unrecognized prior service Cost		–0–	–0–	450	400	350	300	250	200
Unrecognized net (gain) loss		60	117	348	731	733	571	94	(27)
Unrecognized net obligation	400	360	320	280	240	200	160	120	80
(Accrued) prepaid pension cost	–0–	(380)	–0–	–0–	–0–	–0–	–0–	–0–	–0–

E X H I B I T   1 2 B – 3

Calculation of Projected Benefit Obligation

	1987	1988	1989	1990	1991	1992	1993	1994
Projected benefit obligation– Beginning	(3,400)	(4,040)	(4,754)	(6,049)	(7,084)	(8,133)	(9,296)	(10,386)
Add: Service cost	(300)	(310)	(320)	(330)	(340)	(350)	(360)	(370)
Interest	(340)	(404)	(475)	(605)	(708)	(813)	(930)	(1,039)
New prior service cost	–0–	–0–	(500)	–0–	–0–	–0–	–0–	–0–
Acturial adjustment	–0–	–0–	–0–	(100)	–0–	–0–	200	–0–
Deduct: Pension benefits paid	–0–	–0–	–0–	–0–	–0–	–0–	–0–	–0–
Projected benefit obligation–end	(4,040)	(4,754)	(6,049)	(7,084)	(8,133)	(9,296)	(10,386)	(11,794)

pension expense for those years. If the company funds the expense each year by giving money to the pension trust, this will add to the assets and in 10 years close the gap between the assets and PBO if there were no other variances between what was expected and what actually happened.

One should next note Exhibit 12B–3, the calculation of the PBO. Each year, the PBO is increased by the current year's service cost and interest on the beginning of the year's PBO. The PBO is also increased when the terms of the pension plan are changed giving additional benefits to employees based on their past years of service. This benefit increase is called *prior service cost*. Note that this is assumed to occur in 1989. Actuarial adjustments also change the PBO as depicted in 1990 and 1993. The reader should note also what does not change the PBO: actual funding by the employer and earnings on the plan assets. The PBO is reduced as retirees begin receiving their benefits (i.e., when the projected payouts are actually made). To simplify matters, the assumption in this example is that there are as yet no retirees and their expected working life continues to be 10 years.

Exhibit 12B–4 illustrates the calculation of the plan assets. They are increased by company funding and the earnings on the fund. They decline when payouts are made to retirees.

E X H I B I T   1 2 B – 4

Calculation of Fair Value of Assets

	1987	1988	1989	1990	1991	1992	1993	1994
Fair value of assets—beginning	3,000	3,240	4,317	4,972	5,713	6,850	8,265	9,921
Add: Actual return on plan assets	240	267	201	214	567	847	1,103	1,114
Amount funded	–0–	810	454	528	569	568	553	506
Deduct: Pension benefits paid	–0–	–0–	–0–	–0–	–0–	–0–	–0–	–0–
Fair value of assets–end	3,240	4,317	4,972	5,713	6,850	8,265	9,921	11,542

Referring back to Exhibit 12B–1, the periodic pension expense is composed of service cost, interest on the PBO, actual return on the plan assets, and net amortization. (The actual derivation of service cost is not explained in this example.) Note that the interest cost is based on the beginning of the period PBO and the settlement rate, here assumed to be 10 percent. Pension expense is reduced by the actual earnings on the plan assets, or $240 in 1987.

The net amortization consists of four elements. The first is the amortization of the unrecognized net gain or loss. The logic of this adjustment is that over time most gains and losses (actual minus expected returns) should cancel one another. Only if the cumulative difference gets too large should one increase (or decrease) the level of expensing and funding. SFAS No. 87 chose the threshold of 10 percent. Hence, as long as the cumulative gain/loss on plan assets is less than 10 percent of the greater of the PBO or the plan assets, no amortization is necessary. If the net gain or loss exceeds this threshold, the amount in excess of 10 percent is amortized over the remaining working lifetime of the employees.

As explained in Exhibit 12B–5, only in 1992 does the cumulative deficit in expected earnings exceed the 10 percent level. The calculation of the unrecognized gain/loss is explained in Exhibit 12B–6. Note that it is decreased by amortization and increased (or

EXHIBIT 12B–5

Calculation of Amortization of Unrecognized Gain/Loss

	1987	1988	1989	1990	1991	1992	1993	1994
Unrecognized (gain)/loss–Beginning of year	–0–	60	117	348	731	733	571	94
10% of the greater of the PBO or fair value	340	404	475	605	708	813	930	1,039
Unrecognized (gain)/loss subject to amortization	–0–	–0–	–0–	–0–	22	–0–	–0–	–0–
Amortization of unrecognized (gain) loss	–0–	–0–	–0–	–0–	2	–0–	–0–	–0–

EXHIBIT 12B–6

Calculation of Unrecognized Gain (loss)

	1987	1988	1989	1990	1991	1992	1993	1994
Unrecognized (gain) loss–Beginning of year	–0–	60	117	348	731	733	571	94
Less: Amortization	–0–	–0–	–0–	–0–	2	–0–	–0–	–0–
Unrecognized (gain) loss–before adjustment	–0–	60	117	348	729	733	571	94
Add: Actuarial net (gain) loss	–0–	–0–	–0–	100	–0–	–0–	(200)	–0–
Net asset (gain) loss (actual–expected)	60	57	231	283	4	(162)	(276)	(122)
Unrecognized (gain)loss–end of year	60	117	348	731	733	571	94	(27)

E X H I B I T   1 2 B – 7

Calculation of Unrecognized Prior Service Cost

	1987	1988	1989	1990	1991	1992	1993	1994
Prior service cost–beginning of year		–0–	–0–	450	400	350	300	250
Add: New prior service cost	–0–	–0–	500	–0–	–0–	–0–	–0–	–0–
Less: Amortization of prior service cost	–0–	–0–	50	50	50	50	50	50
Prior service cost–end of year	–0–	–0–	450	400	350	300	250	200

decreased) by the difference between the expected and actual investment performance of the plan. Note also that it is affected by actuarial gains and losses. In this illustration, the actuarial changes in 1990 increased the unrecognized loss; in 1993, the change was a gain.

Returning to Exhibit 12B–1, note that the adjustment for the actual-expected earnings when combined with the actual return on plan assets results in the pension expense reflecting the expected return. Only if the accumulated actual-expected earnings is outside the 10 percent corridor does it affect pension expense. The two remaining items to be amortized have already been mentioned: the $400 unrecognized net obligation (on adoption of SFAS No. 87) and the prior service cost (calculated in Exhibit 12B–7).

A final word about this example. SFAS No. 87 requires a reconciliation of PBO and plan assets back to prepaid or accrued pension cost. If the pension expense is actually funded each year (as illustrated in all years except 1987), there should be no accrued as prepaid pension cost because the funded status of the plan should just be the sum of the following:

■ Unamortized net obligation (transition amount to SFAS No. 87).

■ Unamortized net gain or loss (cumulative actual-expected earnings).

■ Unamortized prior service cost (since inception of SFAS No. 87).

Deferred Income Taxes in Detail

The concept of *interperiod tax allocation* and the recognition of deferred tax liabilities and deferred tax assets were explained in Chapter 12. This explanation did not discuss one of the most important complications arising from deferred tax accounting: What happens when tax rates change? Furthermore, it did not discuss the important limits on recognizing deferred tax assets required by SFAS No. 109. These two items are explained in this appendix.

When Tax Rates Change

Chapter 12 explained the fundamentals of deferred tax accounting by using an illustration of the calculation of deferred tax expense and the associated deferred tax liability from Sample Company:

	End of Year			
	1	2	3	4
Accounting asset NBV	$750	$500	$ 250	$–0–
Tax asset NBV	500	–0–	–0–	–0–
Difference	$250	$500	$ 250	$–0–
Tax rate (during the year)	0.4	0.4	0.4	0.4
Deferred tax liability	$100	$100	$ 100	$–0–
Deferred tax expense	$100	$100	$(100)	$(100)

We will again refer to this example to explain what happens when income tax rates change.

SFAS No. 109 requires that when tax rates change, the changes are to be reflected in the accounting for deferred taxes when the legislation is enacted (i.e., signed by the president). This means that if, for example, the corporate income tax rates are increased in 1992, effective 1993, the effect of the change to the deferred tax liability and deferred tax assets is to be recorded in 1992. In the case of depreciation, the single largest cause of deferred taxes, this would mean higher deferred tax liabilities and, immediately, higher deferred tax expense.

Using this same example, if at the beginning of Year 3 the income tax rates were reduced to 30 percent, the changes (called *reversals*) in the accounting-tax differences at the new tax rate would yield a revised (and lower) deferred tax liability:

Year	Accounting-Tax Difference	Tax Rate	Deferred Tax Liability
3	$250	0.3	$ 75
4	250	0.3	75
	$500		$150

This change in the deferred tax liability and the related deferred tax benefit of $50 would be reflected in the first quarter of Year 3. At the end of Year 3, the deferred tax liability would be $75. The *net* deferred tax benefit for Year 3 is $125: $50 is the immediate benefit reflecting the effect of the lower income tax rate, and $75 reflects the Year 3 difference between accounting and tax depreciation—at the 30 percent rate.

The four-year summary table reflects exactly what will happen to Sample Company:

Accounting asset NBV	$750	$500	$250	$–0–
Tax asset NBV	500	–0–	–0–	–0–
Difference	$250	$500	$250	$–0–
Tax rate (during the year)	0.4	0.4	0.3	0.3
Deferred tax liability	$100	$200	$75	$–0–
Deferred tax expense (Benefit)	100	100	(125)	(75)

In years 3 and 4, the depreciation deductions on the tax return exceed the accounting depreciation expense. The deferred tax benefit adjusts for this difference, drawing down the balance in the deferred tax liability buffer. Year 3 also reflects the catch-up or adjustment to the deferred tax liability because of the changed tax rate. The impact of this catch-up is clearly seen in the revised income statements for Sample Company:

	Year 1	Year 2	Year 3	Year 4
Sales	$1,000	$1,000	$1,000	$1,000
Depreciation	250	250	250	250
All other expenses	400	400	400	400
Taxable income	350	350	350	350
Current income tax expense	40	40	180	180
Deferred income tax expense	100	100	−125	−75
Total income tax expense	140	140	55	105
Net income	210	210	295	245

The net income in Year 4 is higher than in years 1 and 2 because tax rates are lower. The Year 3 net income is even higher, by $50, because the tax rate was lowered before the deferred tax liability was reduced by the reversal of the accounting-tax depreciation charges. In effect, in years 1 and 2, a total of $500 of taxable income was deferred by Sample Corporation into year 3 and 4 when the tax rates were lower by 10 percent. This immediately saved $50 (0.10 × $500), which is reflected in Year 3, the year the tax rate changes were announced.

Deferred Tax Assets

No doubt the most controversial aspect of SFAS No. 109 is the valuation of deferred tax assets; in certain circumstances, the full amount of the deferred tax assets may *not* be included in the financial statements even though a company must include all deferred tax liabilities. For example, consider an event for which the expense deduction for tax purposes lagged behind the deduction for accounting purposes, as in the provision for warranty expenses. Diagrammatically,

> The provision for accounting warranty expenses (not for taxes)

leads to

> A temporary accounting-tax difference in warranty liability book values

that leads to

> A deferred tax asset and deferred income tax benefit

that leads to

> Lower tax expense and higher accounting net income

This is just the mirror image of the accelerated depreciation example but with the reverse effect: The income tax expense is shown at a lower amount than the current income taxes payable, and accounting net income is higher.

The logic may be consistent, but the FASB concluded that permitting deferred tax *benefits* due to accounting-tax differences on liabilities (such as warranty reserves) could violate the principal of conservatism, in that a company would have to assume that it would make profits in the future and therefore have to pay taxes and consequently actually have tax liabilities against which to offset its tax benefits. SFAS No. 109 prescribes that a *valuation allowance* be established if it is "more likely than not" that all or a portion of the deferred tax assets will not be realized. Such a valuation allowance is to be based upon management's judgment as to the likelihood of future taxable income. A firm with continuing losses and a real issue of "going concern" might need to establish a valuation allowance up to or equal to the amount of the deferred tax asset.

ISSUES FOR DISCUSSION

D12.1 **Point:** All leases should be capitalized on the balance sheet as liabilities.

Counter-point: Only capital leases should be treated as liabilities.

Evaluate the two viewpoints. Which one do you agree with, and why?

D12.2 The 1989 annual report of Gerber Products Company contained a footnote on retirement benefits, the majority of which is included in the exhibit below. Based on the information contained in it, answer the following pension-related questions:

a. Explain what is meant by a noncontributory defined-benefit plan with benefits based on employees' final average earnings.
b. What is the total amount of Gerber Products' pension expense shown in the company's 1989 income statement?
c. What is meant by
   (1). Vested benefit obligation?
   (2). Accumulated benefit obligation?
   (3). Projected benefit obligation?
d. Why is one of the components of the net periodic pension cost (credit) for the defined benefit plans the interest cost on the projected benefit obligation? How is the amount determined?
e. The actual return on plan assets has changed considerably from year to year from 1987 to 1989. Does this result in a very volatile annual pension expense figure for the defined benefit plans? Explain.
f. Are Gerber Products' defined benefit pension plans overfunded as of 1989? How do you know?

Gerber Products Co.

Note L—Retirement Benefits

The Company and its subsidiaries have a number of non-contributory defined benefits plans covering a majority of their employees. The benefits provided are generally based upon years of service and the employees' final average earnings (as defined). The Company's objective in funding these plans is to accumulate funds sufficient to provide for all accrued benefits and to maintain a relatively stable contribution level in the future.

The Company also sponsors defined contribution retirement plans covering a majority of its employees. Contributions are based on employees' earnings for non-contributory plans and on a percentage of employee contributions for contributory plans.

A summary of the composite of net periodic pension cost (credit) for the defined benefit plans and the total contribution charged to pension expense for the defined contribution plans follows:

(in thousands)	1989	1988	1987
Defined benefit plans:			
Service cost-benefits earning during the period	$ 4,878	$ 5,050	$ 4,510
Interest cost on projected benefit obligation	13,568	12,066	11,225
Actual return on plan assets	(24,299)	(11,750)	(26,821)
Net amortization and deferral	2,436	(8,272)	8,723
Net pension cost (credit) for defined benefit plans	(3,417)	(2,906)	(2,363)
Defined contribution plans	4,429	3,307	2,374
	$ 1,012	$ 401	$ 11

The amounts recognized in the consolidated statements of financial position at March 31 for the Company's defined benefit plans, all of which have plan assets in excess of their accumulated benefit obligations, are presented below:

(in thousands)	1989	1988
Actuarial present value of benefit obligations:		
Vested benefit obligation	$132,113	$114,444
Accumulated benefit obligation	$141,265	$122,146
Projected benefit obligation	$165,730	$147,100
Plan assets at fair value	239,183	212,642
Plan assets in excess of projected benefit obligation	73,453	65,542
Unrecognized net gain	(11,561)	(9,842)
Unrecognized transition asset net of amortization (deduct)	(30,336)	(30,590)
Prepaid pension costs	$ 31,556	$ 25,110

The expected long-term rate of return on plan assets, the weighted average discount rate and rate of increase in future compensation levels used in determining the actuarial present value of benefit obligations were 9.5%, 9% and 5%, respectively, in 1989 and 1988. The expected long-term rate of return on plan assets was 9.5% in 1987.

D12.3 Point: Deferred income taxes represent a liability.

Counter-point: Deferred income taxes represent owners' equity.

Evaluate the two viewpoints. Which one do you agree with, and why?

D12.4 Suppose you are the chief financial officer of a corporation and a director has some questions about your annual report. The director notes that accounts called *deferred tax* appear both on the asset and the liability sides of the balance sheet, and asks, "What are those things supposed to be?" How would you explain them to the director?

D12.5 Who benefits from a company-sponsored pension plan? When do those benefits happen? If there is a benefit, there is no doubt a cost somewhere. What are the costs of those benefits just identified? When are those costs paid?

D12.6 As an employee, would you prefer to receive a defined-benefit pension or a defined-contribution pension, assuming the pension benefits appeared to be about the same during that important first year of retirement?

D12.7 The 1990 annual report of Betz Laboratories contained the following footnote pertaining to income taxes. Explain what this footnote says (i.e., what was the income tax expense in those three years?). Why is that different from what the company says it paid? What caused the taxes to be deferred? Are there deferred tax assets or liabilities shown on the Betz balance sheets? Are these figures increasing or decreasing?

Note 2 – Provision for Income Taxes

The provision for income taxes consists of the following (in thousands):

1990	Currently Payable	Deferred	Total
Federal	$28,116	$ (388)	$27,728
State	4,494	(30)	4,464
Foreign	9,652	81	9,733
	$42,262	$ (337)	$41,925
1989			
Federal	$22,393	$ 714	$23,107
State	4,005	99	4,104
Foreign	7,519	330	7,849
	$33,917	$1,143	$35,060
1968			
Federal	$20,372	$ 192	$20,564
State	3,203	27	3,230
Foreign	6,495	129	6,624
	$30,070	$ 348	$30,418

Deferred taxes relate to the following timing differences (in thousands):

	1990	1989	1988
Depreciation	$ 1,039	$1,915	$ 1,536
Other items	(1,376)	(772)	(1,188)
	$ (337)	$1,143	$ 348

A reconciliation of the effective income tax rate with the applicable statutory federal income tax rate is as follows:

	1990	1989	1988
Federal tax rate	34.0%	34.0%	34.0%
State and local taxes, net of federal income taxes	2.4	3.1	2.5
Other items	2.6	1.5	2.1
Effective income tax rate	39.0%	38.6%	38.6%

The components of earnings before income taxes consist of the following (in thousands):

	1990	1989	1988
Domestic	$ 80,517	$68,979	$59,730
Foreign	26,882	21,941	19,073
	$107,399	$90,920	$78,803

The Company made income tax payments of $33,311,000, $31,361,000 and $30,889,000 for the years 1990, 1989 and 1988, respectively.

During 1987, the Financial Accounting Standards Board issued a final standard on accounting for income taxes which must be adopted in 1992. The Company expects the principal effect to be a reduction in its deferred tax liability.

D12.8 Explain the significance of vested versus nonvested pension benefits. Is a nonvested benefit a real obligation of a company? Does it meet the test of a liability? Present the arguments on both sides of this issue.

D12.9 The following information appeared in footnote 7 of Ingersoll-Rand's 1990 annual report:

How much debt appeared in the December 31, 1990, balance sheet? Explain.

Ingersoll-Rand, Inc.

Note 7—Long-term Debt and Credit Facilities

At December 31, long-term debt consisted of:

In thousands	1990	1989
8⅜% notes due 1994	$ 75,000	$ 75,000
8¼% notes due 1996	75,000	75,000
8.05% debentures due 1992–2004	69,100	69,100
4.75% notes due 1991	—	14,000
Other domestic and foreign loans and notes, at end-of-year average interest rates of 8.06% in 1990 and 8.32% in 1989, maturing in various amounts to 2013	46,063	46,816
	$265,163	$279,916

Debt retirements for the next five years are as follows: $21,212,000 in 1991, $9,974,000 in 1992, $16,618,000 in 1993, $87,950,000 in 1994 and $6,790,000 in 1995.

At December 31, 1990, the company had $395,000,000 in aggregate domestic lines of credit. These lines provide support for outstanding commercial paper of $104,750,000 at December 31, 1990. These lines also indirectly provide support for other financial instruments, such as letters of credit and comfort letters, as required in the normal course of business. Available foreign lines of credit were $461,190,000, of which $248,519,000 were unused at December 31, 1990. The company compensates banks for these lines. No major cash balances were subject to withdrawal restrictions. At December 31, 1990, the average rate of interest for

loans payable, excluding the current portion of long-term debt, was 11.3%.

At December 31, 1990 and 1989, the company had $109,250,000 and $87,000,000 respectively, of short-term debt and equivalent amounts of short-term investments, for which the company had a right of offset. Accordingly, the debt and investments have been eliminated from the December 31, 1990, and 1989 balance sheets.

Capitalized interest on construction and other capital projects amounted to $3,549,000, $4,136,000 and $3,810,000 in 1990, 1989 and 1988, respectively. Interest income, included in "Other income (expense)" was $13,926,000, $12,193,000 and $11,249,000 in 1990, 1989 and 1988, respectively

D12.10 National Medical Enterprises, Inc., included the following in its 1991 annual report:

Deferred income taxes are created by timing differences in the recognition of revenue and expense for tax and financial statement purposes. Deferred income tax expense is composed of the following:

(in millions)	1991	1990	1989
Depreciation and asset disposition differences	$ 11	$ 22	$ 23
Cash-basis accounting	(13)	(13)	(13)
Direct write-off method for doubtful accounts	(9)	(17)	(16)
Capitalized costs deducted as incurred for tax purposes	9	8	5
Other	(4)	6	(8)
Total deferred income tax expense (credit)	$ (6)	$ 6	$ (9)

Under the Tax Reform Act of 1986, all facilities using the cash-basis method of reporting for tax purposes were required to change to the accrual method effective fiscal year 1988. The difference between the accrual and cash basis as of that date is recognized for tax purposes over 10 years. Most of the cash-basis deferred tax liability at May 31, 1991 and 1990 is included in non-current deferred income taxes.

Explain each of the lines in this figure. What does the $11 million mean in 1991 for depreciation and asset disposition differences? What is the impact, if any, of these figures on the income, assets, owners' equity, and cash flow of the company?

D12.11 What entry would one use to establish a *valuation allowance* in conjunction with a deferred tax asset? What kind of acocunt is this asset? How would a person calculate the allowance?

PROBLEMS

P12.1 Accounting for leases: the lessee. SC Company leases an asset with a market value of $200,000 under conditions by which the company agrees to pay $47,479.28 each year for five years (assume annual payments at year-end). The agreement is noncancelable; five years is the expected economic life of the asset; there is no expected residual value to the asset. (Thus, the lease is to be capitalized.) The lease is executed on January 1, 1991.

Required:

a. What entry does the lessee make on January 1, 1991?
b. What entry does it make at the end of 1991 to record the cash payment of $47,479.28?
c. For 1991, what expenses will be reflected on the income statement with respect to the lease?
d. How will the lease asset and liability items appear on the books as of January 1, 1991? 1992? 1993? 1994? 1995? 1996?
e. How much of the lease liability will appear as a current item in the balance sheet as of December 31, 1991? How much of the leased asset will appear as a current item on that date?

P12.2 Accounting for leases: the lessor. SC Company leased the asset referred to in P12.1 from AC Company. The cost of the asset that AC Manufacturing Company leases to SC Company is $150,000. (This is a sales-type lease.)

Required:

a. What entry does the lessor make on January 1, 1991?

b. What entry does it make at the end of 1991 to record the cash received of $47,479.28? What other entry is required?

c. For the year 1991, what will be reflected on the income statement with respect to the lease?

d. What items will appear on the lessor's balance sheet as of December 31, 1991? 1992? 1993? 1994? 1995?

P12.3 Accounting for leases. Kenyon Auto Company owns land on which it can build a new showroom at a cost of $60,000. As an alternative, Kenyon can have Robbin Leasing Company build the showroom and Kenyon can lease it for $7,010 a year for 15 years, which is the estimated useful life of the building. Kenyon would pay all maintenance and insurance costs. The $7,010 a year will give Robbin an 8 percent return on its investment of $60,000. Lease payments would be made at the end of each year.

If Kenyon decides to lease the property, the following accounts will be used:

Leasehold Rights (A)
Lease Obligations (L)
Retained Earnings (OE) (Interest Expense)
Retained Earnings (OE) (Amortization of Leasehold Rights)

Required:

a. According to present GAAP, how should a lease of this type be classified and why?
   (1). By the lessee.
   (2). By the lessor.

b. If Kenyon decides to lease the showroom from Robbin, what entry(ies) will Kenyon make in its books on January 2, 1991, the date the lease would begin?

c. If Kenyon decides to lease the showroom from Robbin, what entry(ies) will Kenyon make on its books on December 31, 1991, the end of the lease year and the company's fiscal year?

P12.4 Deferred income taxes. The 1988 consolidated balance sheet of Wendy's International, Inc., contains an item listed in the liabilities and shareholders' equity section titled Deferred Income Taxes in the amount of $53,008,000. What does this number represent? If Wendy's had the opportunity either to increase or decrease the amount of this item, which would it prefer to do? Why?

Wendy's International, Inc.

5. Income Taxes

The provison for income taxes based on income (loss) before extraordinary gain for each year consisted of the following:

(In thousands)	1988	1987	1986
Current			
Federal................	$ 7.132	$(19.055)	$ 31.986
State and local.....	1.787	433	3.931
	8.919	(18.622)	35.917
Deferred:			
Federal................	6.141	3.591	(15.291)
State and local.....	256	(62)	(809)
	6.397	3.529	(16.100)
Income taxes (benefit)................	$15.316	$(15.093)	$ 19.817

The realignment program was substantially concluded in the fourth quarter of 1987, generating significantly greater tax benefits than previously anticipated. These additional benefits primarily related to the termination of operations of 22 restaurants in West Germany and amounted to $10.8 million, which was recorded in the fourth quarter of 1987.

The deferred tax provision for each year, resulting from differences in the timing of recognition of revenues and expenses for tax and financial reporting purposes, included the following:

In thousands	1988	1987	1986
Realignment..............	$ 3.360	$ 14.698	$(20.993)
Accelerated depreciation...........	6.914	10.392	12.390
Asset dispostions......	(1.394)	(11.485)	(5.800)
Reserves not currently deductible..................	(2.693)	(8.670)	(2.682)
Tax basis reporting ...	(943)	(1.223)	1.088
Other	1.153	(183)	(103)
	$ 6.397	$ 3.529	$(16.100)

A reconciliation of the statutory U.S. Federal income tax rate (34% in 1988, 40% in 1987, and 46% in 1986) to the company's effective tax rate based on income (loss) before extraordinary gain for each year is shown on page 573:

(In thousands)	1988	1987	19
Income taxes (benefit) at statutory rate	$ 14.895	$ (4.648)	$ 6.8
Effect of realignment............		(11.340)	11.3
Effect of foreign operations..........................	628	3.292	2.6
Effect of loss carrybacks........................	500	21	(5.3)
State and local taxes, net of federal benefit	1.348	222	1.5
Jobs and other tax credits...............................	(795)	(286)	(5)
Adjustment to previous liabilities.............................		(4.320)	2.9
Sale of subsidiaries	(2.381)	(1.360)	
Goodwill amortization	366	433	67
Other...................................	755	(107)	(3)
Income taxes (benefit) at effective rate	$ 15.316	$(15.093)	$ 19.8

The Financial Accounting Standards Board issued Statement No. 96 (SFAS No. 96)–"Accounting for Income Tax in 1987: Under this statement, the company will benefit by recording deferred tax liabilities as the new lower federal income tax rate, since these liabilities arose in years when higher rates were in effect. The company expects a significant nonrecurring benefit by the adoption of SFAS No. 96 when it is implemented in the first quarter of 1989.

P12.5 Deferred income taxes. The income tax footnote contained in the 1988 annual report for Wendy's International is presented in P12.4. Based on the information contained in it, answer the following questions:

a. How much income tax expense will Wendy's report in its income statement for 1988?
b. How much income tax for 1988 does Wendy's actually owe?
c. It appears that Wendy's deferred income taxes are caused by a variety of factors. Explain why depreciation is one of the causes and whether it was a benefit or a detriment to Wendy's in 1988. Identify one type of reserve that might be included in the category Reserves Not Currently Deductible.

P12.6 Deferred income taxes. Target Corporation is to begin its operations on January 1, 1990. Pro forma income statements for the new corporation are shown on p. 574. No provision has been made for deferred taxes. The only temporary book-tax differences are due to depreciation.

Required:

a. Use a 34 percent tax rate and complete the preparation of these pro forma statements.
b. What will Target show on its balance sheet each year (1990–1994) for deferred taxes?
c. Can you explain the company's calculation of current income tax expense in 1992?

Target Corporation
(millions)

	1990	1991	1992	1993	1994
Sales	$ 3,400	$ 3,604	$ 3,820	$ 4,049	$ 4,292
Less: COGS	1,598	12,712	1,834	12,964	2,103
Gross margin	1,802	1,892	1,987	2,085	2,189
Operating costs	633	681	729	777	826
Depreciation expense*	325	330	337	343	356
Income before tax	844	882	921	965	1,007
Current income tax	189	232	288	336	380
Deferred income tax					
Income tax expense	189	232	288	336	380
Net income	655	649	633	629	627
*Note the following:					
Book depreciation	325	330	337	343	356
Tax depreciation	612	528	411	320	245
Book value–assets	980	978	1,012	1,114	1,099
Tax value–assets	693	493	453	?	?

P12.7 Deferred income taxes. Suppose that Target Corporation were to revise its pro forma statements to include an accrual for estimated warranty expense (in addition to the effects of P12.6), but the recognition of these expenses would be delayed for tax purposes as follows:

	1990	1991	1992	1993	1994
Book warranty expense	112	132	137	128	119
Tax warranty expense	13	39	78	143	141

Required:

a. How would this affect the balance sheets? The income statements?
b. Would the balance sheets still balance?

P12.8 Changing income tax rates. What would happen to the pro forma statements in P12.7 if, in 1992, Congress overrode the president's veto and raised the corporate income tax rate to 38 percent effective in 1993?

P12.9 Estimating Pensions. Let us suppose that Barsack Corporation on January 1, 1991, adopted a pension plan providing for the retirement of its employees at age 65. The company will "fund" its pension costs each year on December 31 when it will deposit the required cash with the pension fund trustee.

For the purpose of simplifying calculations, let us suppose the following:

1. The company obligates itself to provide monthly payments to each employee who reaches age 65 while still employed.

2. The monthly payments will be made for a 10-year period—either to the employee (if he lives 10 years beyond age 65) or to his named beneficiary (for such portion of the 10-year period that the employee does not live).

3. The amount of the monthly payment will be $10 for each year of service—for example, for 15 years of service the payments will be $150 a month, or $1,800 a year.

4. The company had 600 employees at January 1, 1973, and these 600, all male (we are still supposing), worked all 1991 and were the same 600 employees the company had on December 31, 1991.

5. Data concerning the 600 employees *at December 31, 1991,* follow:
   a. 100 *40-year-old* employees had been with the company 16 years (15 years prior to January 1 1991).
   b. 500 *25-year-old* employees had joined the company just before January 1, 1991.

Let us suppose the standard ordinary table that shows, for 1,000 males at birth (that is, age 0), there would be living:

958 at age 25, *924* at age 40, *680* at age 65

Thus, for our purposes, we can say that for 100 living at age 40 on December 31, 1991, *73.6* (680/924 × 100) should be living at age 65. Let us say that 13.6 of this 73.6 would have left the company because of turnover (18.5 percent rate). You may assume, further, that the comparable turnover rate for the 25-year-olds over the next 40 years will be 25 percent (680/958 × 500 = *355*) living at December 31, 2031, of which 75 percent (*266*) would still be with the company.

Note: Please use a calculator in preparing your answers.

Required:

a. For the 100 employees age 40 at December 31, 1991, what is the present value, as of December 31, 2016, of the 10-year annuity of $108,000 a year ($120 × 15 years × 60 surviving employees)? (Calculate using monthly payments.)

   At a 4 percent rate? . . . . $_____

   At a 6 percent rate? . . . . $_____

b. What is the present value at December 31, 1991, and at January 1, 1991, of the above amounts:

   The 4 percent amount above at a 4 percent rate . . . . $_____

   The 6 percent amount above at a 6 percent rate . . . . $_____

c. What is the present value, as of *December 31, 2016,* and *December 31, 2031,* respectively, of the $120 for current service for 1991 to be provided for:

	At 4%	At 6%
(1) The survivors of the 100 employees aged 40 at December 31, 1991	_____	_____
(2) The survivors of the 500 employees aged 25 at December 31, 1991	_____	_____

d. What is the present value at *December 31, 1991,* of the amounts in part *c* above:

	At 4%	At 6%
(1) Employees aged 40 at December 31, 1991	_____	_____
(2) Employees aged 25 at December 31, 1991	_____	_____

e. As of January 1, 1991, how much cash would Newman Corporation have to pay the trustee to satisfy the pension obligation? At December 31, 1991? Explain.

P12.10 Pension Disclosures. The pension disclosures from CPC International's 1990 annual report are reproduced on pages 577–578.

Required:

a. What was the total pension expense appearing in CPC's income statement for 1990?
b. What do you consider to be the pension liability for CPC International as of the end of its 1990 year? Explain.
c. What are the total pension assets as of the end of the 1990 year? Do these assets exceed the total liability?
d. Reference is made in the footnote to a requirement that CPC recognize a "minimum liability" and, indeed, a line item, Employees' Pension, Indemnity, Retirement and Related Provisions, appears as a noncurrent liability for $158.8 million at year-end 1990 and for $123.4 million at year-end 1989. How does the footnote disclosure help to explain these figures? What else would you expect to find on the balance sheet related to these figures? Finally, how can CPC International argue that such a liability has no effect on either net income or cash flow?

CPC International

The following is a summary of the funded status of the Company's major domestic and foreign pension plans based on valuations as of September 30, 1990, and 1989:

$ Millions	Assets Exceed Accumulated Benefits	Accumulated Benefits Exceed Assets	Assets Exceed Accumulated Benefits	Accumulated Benefits Exceed Assets
Domestic plans				
Accumulated benefit obligation:				
Vested	$(312.7)	$ (49.7)	$(330.3)	$ (34.2)
Nonvested	(6.0)	(3.3)	(7.4)	(1.9)
Total	$(318.7)	$ (53.0)	$(337.7)	$ (36.1)
Projected benefit obligation	$(373.4)	$ (55.4)	$(398.9)	$ (36.1)
Plan assets at fair value	369.6	44.8	418.3	27.5
Projected benefit obligation (in excess of) less than plan assets	(3.8)	(10.6)	19.4	(8.6)
Unrecognized prior service costs	8.0	(1.4)	7.2	2.3
Unrecognized net loss (gain)	2.1	10.3	(33.4)	(1.4)
Unrecognized net obligation	16.7	1.2	21.7	1.6
Adjustment required to recognize minimum liability	—	(5.2)	—	(2.4)
(Accrued) prepaid pension cost at December 31	$ 23.0	$ (5.7)	$ 14.9	$ (8.5)
Foreign plans				
Accumulated benefit obligation:				
Vested	$ (98.7)	$(239.6)	$ (84.7)	$(196.4)
Nonvested	(10.8)	(13.9)	(9.2)	(11.4)
Total	$(109.5)	$(253.5)	$ (93.9)	$(207.8)
Projected benefit obligation	$(143.1)	$(282.6)	$(118.7)	$(231.4)
Plan assets at fair value	179.0	108.2	141.9	93.5
Projected benefit obligation (in excess of) less than plan assets	35.9	(174.4)	23.2	(137.9)
Unrecognized prior service costs	8.4	3.3	6.8	5.1
Unrecognized net loss (gain)	(27.8)	23.9	(16.1)	18.2
Unrecognized net obligation (asset)	(4.6)	21.7	(3.9)	20.8
Adjustment required to recognize minimum laibility	—	(32.8)	—	(26.7)
(Accrued) prepaid pension cost at December 31	$ 11.9	$(158.3)	$ 10.0	$(120.5)

Net periodic pension cost for 1990, 1989, and 1988 included the following components:

$ Millions	Domestic Plans			Foreign Plans		
	1990	1989	1988	1990	1989	1988
Cost of benefits earned during the year	$ 10.2	$ 7.7	$ 7.0	$ 12.9	$ 10.8	$ 9.8
Interest on projected benefit obligation	35.3	33.7	33.4	26.7	24.5	25.3
Actual return on plan assets	19.0	(87.1)	40.1	(16.3)	(12.8)	5.5
Net amortization and deferral	(54.5)	51.8	(73.8)	(.6)	(1.8)	(21.4)
Net periodic pension cost	$ 10.0	$ 6.1	$ 6.7	$ 22.7	$ 20.7	$ 19.2

The long-term rate of return on plan assets used in the determination of net periodic pension cost for 1990, 1989, and 1988 for the domestic plans was 11.0%, 10.1%, and 10.9%, respectively. For the foreign plans the rate was 8.2%, 8.1%, and 8.0% in 1990, 1989, and 1988, respectively. Weighted averages of actuarial assumptions used in the measurement of projected benefit obligation are as follows:

	Domestic Plans		Foreign Plans	
	1990	1989	1990	1989
Discount rates	9.0%	8.3%	7.8%	7.6%
Average annual increase in compensation	7.0%	6.6%	6.3%	6.3%

Beginning in 1989, the Company was required by FAS 87 "Employers' Accounting for Pensions" to recognize a "minimum liability" for pension plans when the accumulated benefit obligation of such plans exceeds plan assets and existing pension accruals. The recognition of this minimum liability has no effect on either net income or cash flow.

In addition, certain employees in the U.S. and in some foreign subsidiaries are covered by pension plans under which the Company's obligation to make contributions is defined as a percentage of the current salary of each employee covered by the plan. Benefits are based on the funds available in each employee's account from contributions, and from investment income on such contributions. The aggregate pension cost for these plans was $5.9 million in 1990, $10.9 million in 1989, and $9.1 million in 1988.

In addition to pension benefits, the Company provides certain health care and life insurance benefits for domestic retired employees. Substantially all of the Company's domestic employees become eligible for those benefits when they qualify for retirement. For 1990, 1989, and 1988, the costs of those benefits on a "pay-as-you-go" basis amounted to $6.8 million, $6.1 million, and $4.1 million, respectively, and were recognized as expense. Effective January 1, 1993, the Company will be required to recognize expense on an accrual basis as required by FAS 106 "Employers' Accounting for Postretirement Benefits Other Than Pensions." The impact of this change is unknown at this time. Outside the United States, payments made for Company-sponsored life insurance and post-retirement health care benefits are insignificant since, in most cases, government-provided benefits of this nature are adequate.

P12.11 Pension Disclosures. Again referring to the pension disclosures from the 1990 CPC International annual report in P12.10, reference is made in the last paragraph to the accounting for certain health care and life insurance benefits.

Required:

a. What is the difference between the "pay-as-you-go" and the accrual basis required by SFAS No. 106? Will this new treatment be better for the employees? For the shareholders?

b. If the accounting for these postretirement health care benefits is like that for pensions, and from working with the figures in the footnote, how large a liability for these items would you estimate CPC has?

P12.12 Deferred income taxes. Early in 1992, Strafford Corporation acquired a $100,000 asset that was to be depreciated on a straight-line basis for accounting purposes and on an accelerated basis for taxes according to the following schedules:

	Straight Line	Accelerated
1992	8,333	16,667
1993	16,666	27,778
1994	16,667	18,519
1995	16,667	12,347
1996	16,667	8,230
1997	16,667	8,230
1998	8,333	8,230
	100,000	100,000

Required:

Prepare a schedule illustrating the annual deferred tax entries for each year associated with this asset. Use a 34 percent tax rate. When will the deferred income tax liability begin to reverse?

CASES

C12.1 Lessee accounting: FHAC Corporation. FHAC Corporation was considering the purchase of a mini-supercomputer. Under a proposal from Convex Computer Co., FHAC could acquire the computer under a 10-year lease agreement. The lease proposal called for quarterly lease payments of $3,655.57 and carried an implicit interest rate of 8 percent. At the end of the lease agreement, FHAC would be entitled to purchase the computer for its expected residual value, currently estimated to be $10,000. Alternatively, FHAC could purchase the computer outright at a price of $115,000, inclusive of installation costs.

Required:

Evaluate the above proposals. Should FHAC lease or buy? How would each option (i.e., lease or buy) affect FHAC's financial statements?

C12.2 Lessee accounting: Sybra, Inc. Sybra, Inc., a newly incorporated research and development company, decided to lease additional laboratory space. The lease commenced on January 1, 1990, and was to extend through the 20-year period ending December 31, 2009. The annual rental rate on the new facility was $115,200 (exclusive of property taxes, maintenance, and insurance costs, which were also to be paid by Sybra). Because of the length of the lease and the generally poor rental market in Austin, Texas, Sybra had negotiated so that rent payments would be made only once a year on December 31.

The facility's original construction cost had been approximately $480,000, but its current market value was now in excess of $1 million. On the basis of conversations with the lessor, Sybra's chief financial officer determined that the lease payments included implicit interest at the rate of 10 percent per annum. Further, as of 1990, the facility was estimated to have a remaining useful life of 25 years. At the end of the initial 20-year-lease period, Sybra would have the option of renewing for another 10 years at a rate equal to one-half of the annual lease rate during the initial lease period.

Required:

a. What accounting treatment should be adopted for the above lease? Why?

b. Illustrate the balance sheet and income statement effects in 1990 for the lease agreement assuming that it is to be accounted for as (1) an operating lease and (2) a capital lease.

C12.3 Leases: Lion Metal Forming, Inc. On January 2, 1991, Lion Metal Forming, Inc., entered a lease for a new 50-ton hydraulic press costing $75,000 and having an estimated life of eight years. The management of Lion Metal believes the new press will be much more efficient than equipment presently in use and that it will allow Lion Metal to manufacture certain items that it previously had to subcontract out. The noncancelable term of the lease is seven years, at which time the press is returned to the lessor. The residual value is expected to be minimal. Rental payments of $16,433 are due at the *end* of each year. All executory costs are to be paid directly by Lion Metal, which depreciates its fixed assets on the straight-line basis. Its incremental borrowing rate is 15 percent.

Required:

a. Calculate the lessor's implicit interest rate in the lease.

b. Why does this lease qualify as a *capital lease* to Lion Metal for financial reporting purposes?

For questions c and d, assume the implicit rate is 12 percent.

c. Prepare the entry that Lion Metal should make to record the lease on January 2, 1991.

d. What amounts (properly labeled) related to the lease will appear in Lion Metal's:
   1. Balance sheet as of December 31, 1991.
   2. Income statement for the year ending December 31, 1991.

C12.4 Deferred income taxes: Jerris Corporation. Jerris Corporation was incorporated in late 1989 for the purpose of entering the quick-copy industry. At the beginning of 1990, it purchased copying equipment having a value of $60,000, an economic life of four years, and no anticipated salvage value. Lacking sufficient capital, Jerris' equipment purchase was financed by the manufacturer, who subsequently sold the note to Metroplex National Bank (MNB). Under the terms of the note, Jerris Corporation was required to submit periodic financial statements to MNB to ensure that the company was in compliance with the note's various covenants.

For purposes of the financial statements submitted to MNB, Jerris Corporation adopted the straight-line method of depreciation for the equipment; for Internal Revenue Service purposes, the company was required to use the Modified Accelerated Cost Recovery System (MACRS) with a three-year tax life.

At December 31, 1990, Jerris' accounting records revealed that the company had earned a pretax income of $14,000, *including* $1,000 of goodwill amortization. Mr. Jerris, the owner, decided that the company was likely to achieve that level of income for the next three years. In anticipation of preparing the financial statements for MNB and the tax return for the IRS, Jerris determined the following:

1. The current income tax rate was 30 percent and was expected to be 30 percent in 1991 and 40 percent thereafter.

2. Under the MACRS, a three-year asset would be depreciated at the following rates:

Year	Percentage
1	33.34
2	44.45
3	14.81
	7.40
	100.00

Required:

Assist Mr. Jerris in preparing the company's financial statements for MNB by determining the deferred income taxes for 1990 through 1993, assuming that he wants to apply the liability method of SFAS No. 96.

C12.5 Leases: Wendy's International, Inc. Presented below is the footnote pertaining to leases from the 1989 annual report of Wendy's International, Inc.

Wendy's International, Inc.–Leases

1. Leases

The company occupies land and buildings and uses equipment under terms of numerous lease agreements expiring on various dates through 2027. Terms of land only and land and building leases are generally for 20 to 25 years. Many of these leases provide for future rent escalations and renewal options. Certain leases require contingent rent determined as a percentage of sales, when annual sales exceed specified levels. Most leases also obligate the company to pay the costs of maintenance, insurance, and property taxes.

At each year-end, capital leases consisted of the following:

(In thousands)	1989	1988
Buildings	$ 53.703	$ 50.392
Accumulated amortization	(21.204)	(21.287)
	$ 32.499	$ 29.105

At December 31, 1989, future minimum lease payments for all leases, and the present value of the net minimum lease payments for capital leases, were as follows:

(In thousands)	Capital Leases	Operating leases
1990	$ 9.594	$ 21.415
1991	9.577	21.022
1992	9.420	20.909
1993	9.355	20.660
1994	9.019	19.155
Later years	48.505	143.402
Total minimum lease payments	95.470	$246.563
Amount representing interest ...	(43.927)	
Present value of net minimum lease payments	51.543	
Current portion	(3.139)	
	$ 48.404	

Rent expense for each year is included in company representing operating costs and amounted to:

(In thousands)	1989	1988	1987
Minimum rent on operating leases, net	$22.151	$21.901	$23.284
Coming Current expense	4.536	4.586	4.214
	$26.687	$26.487	$27.498

In connection with the franchising of certain restaurants the company has leased land, buildings, and equipment to the related franchise owners (see Note 7).

Most leases provide for monthly rentals based on a percentage of sales while others provide for fixed payments with contingent rent when sales exceed certain levels. Lease terms are approximately 10 to 20 years with one or more five-year renewal options. The franchise owners cut the cost of maintenance, insurance, and property taxes.

The company generally accounts for the building and equipment portions of the fixed payment leases as direct financing leases. The land portion of leases and leases with rents based on a percentage of sales are accounted for as operating leases.

At each year-end the net investment in financing lease receivables, included in other assets, consisted of the following:

Required:

a. According to the footnote, Wendy's is both a lessee and a lessor. From a cash flow perspective, does it appear that leasing activities will result in a net cash use or cash source for Wendy's in 1990? Explain (include specific dollar amounts where possible).

b. The footnote states that Wendy's occupies land and buildings and uses equipment under terms of numerous lease agreements. It also discloses that the company's leases are classified as either capital leases or operating leases.

(1). Explain the difference between a capital lease and an operating lease from a risk and reward of ownership perspective.

(2). It appears that building leases are treated as capital leases and that land and equipment leases are treated as operating leases. Of the four accounting criteria for capital leases, which *two* criteria were most likely met in regard to the building leases? Briefly explain your reasons.

c. How much interest expense relating to capital leases does Wendy's expect to incur in 1990?

d. How much rent expense did Wendy's show in its 1989 income statement?

e. What lease-related assets and liabilities, including dollar amounts, appeared in Wendy's December 31, 1989, balance sheet?

Current assets: Current liabilities:

Long-term assets: Long-term liabilities:

f. In calculating the present value of net minimum lease payments for capital leases, as a lessee, Wendy's deducted an amount representing interest. How would Wendy's go about deciding on the appropriate interest rate to use?

g. The footnote states that certain leases that entitle Wendy's to occupy buildings require the company to pay contingent rent, determined as a percentage of sales, when annual sales exceed specified levels. Give *two* reasons why Wendy's might want a "contingent rent" provision included in its leases.

(In thousands)	1989	1988
Total minimum lease receipts...	$ 39.566	$ 29.301
Estimated residual value	2.500	2.098
Amount representing unearned interest...................................	(19.278)	(16.237)
Current portion, included in accounts receivable	(466)	(177)
	$ 22.421	$ 14.985

Assess leased under operating leases are included in property and equipment, and amounted to $63.7 million in 1989 and $37.4 million in 1988.

At December 31, 1989, future minimum lease receipts were as follows:

(In thousands)	Financing Leases	Operating Leases
1990...............	$ 2.547	$ 2.164
1991...............	2.593	2.166
1992...............	2.626	2.162
1993...............	2.622	2.178
1994...............	2.690	2.162
Later years.....	26.488	21.722
	$39.566	$32.554

Rental income for each year is included in other
revenue and amounted to:

(In thousands)	1989	1988	1987
Minimum rental income, net.............................	$ 596	$ 520	$ 754
Contingent rental income.......................	2.882	1.923	1.122
	$3.478	$2.443	$1.876

C12.6 Leases: Nelson Leasing Company. In November 1991, Nelson Leasing Company requested an increase in its loan from Boston Trust Company. The operations of such a leasing company involve buying capital equipment (anything from computers to automobiles) and renting it to a user. The leasing company first finds a customer for the equipment. Then it negotiates with its bank for a loan with which to buy the equipment. The bank always requires an assignment of the lease payment, and it usually secures the loan further with a chattel mortgage on the equipment being leased. The lease contract is characteristically written in such a binding fashion that the lessee must make his or her lease payments for the equipment, whether or not it is used, unless the lessee goes into bankruptcy or resorts to similar legal proceedings.

The initial lease period might run for one to five years, occasionally longer, depending on the normal economic life of the equipment. The sum of the lease payments during the life of the lease normally exceeds by a small amount the total of (1) the price of the equipment, (2) its installation cost, and (3) the cost of interest on the leasing company's note. The leasing company makes its profit on renewals of the lease subsequent to its original term. Typically, the leasing company's note has a face amount equal to the total of the lease payments; this note is discounted at a rate that would give the leasing company sufficient cash to pay for and install the equipment.

When Nelson Leasing Company requested an increase in its loan, the company's most recent balance sheet was requested by the bank (see below). This balance sheet was taken to the loan committee meeting at which Nelson Leasing Company's request was discussed. The bank's senior vice president, Karla Walker, raised the following question: Should the bank lend money to a company that showed a deficit in working capital? Walker's experience had been primarily in the bank's trust department, but her present position required that she be aware of what was going on in the commercial loan department as well. To help understand Nelson's working capital position, it was explained that a loan due within one year was classified as a current liability on the leasing company's balance sheet; on the other hand, accounting practice forbade showing as a current asset the future leasing income, although it was almost certain to be received because of the financial standing of the lessees, and although it would be sufficient in amount to cover payments to the bank on the company's note.

Further, it was noted that each time the leasing company completes a series of transactions of borrowing from the bank and buying and leasing equipment, its stated working capital decreases.

Nelson Leasing Company
Balance Sheet as of Year Ending June 30, 1991
($ millions)

Asset

Cash and marketable securities	47
Notes receivable	
Accounts receivable (net)	
Inventory	
Total current assets	47
Deferred receivables	
Deferred charges and prepaid expenses	16
Equipment on lease (net)	175
Land and buildings	
Machinery and fixtures	
Total fixed assets	
Less: Depreciation	
Net fixed assets	
Other assets	4
Total	242

Equities

Notes payable–bank	
Notes payable–trade	
Due officers	6
Accounts payable–trade	23
Miscellaneous accruals	3
Taxes accrued and reserved	
Due bank–current	79
Portion (secured)	
Total liabilities–current	111
Due bank–deferred	120
Portion (secured)	
Total liabilities	231
Capital stock–preferred	
Capital stock–common	15
Earned surplus–deficit	(5)
Net worth (excluding intangibles)	10
Total	241
Total current assets	47
Total current liabilities	111
Working capital–Deficit	(64)
Current ratio	.42
NET sales	35
NET profit (loss)	(5)
Dividends or withdrawals	

For example, when Nelson Leasing Company bought a $1,000 machine and borrowed $1,000 from the bank, it added $1,000 to fixed assets, $330 to current liabilities, and $670 to long-term liabilities (for the second and third years of a three-year lease). Thus, stated working capital was lowered by $330, although the company was actually no worse off due to this transaction. This explanation satisfied Walker and, after further discussion, the loan request was granted.

Boston Trust Company
Alternative Balance Sheets
($ millions)

Assets	6/30/91 Alternative 1	6/30/91 Alternative 2
Cash and marketable securities	47	47
Notes receivable		
Accounts receivable (net)		
Inventory		
Lease income—current	79	
Total current assets	126	47
Deferred receivables—lease income	120	
Deferred chgs. and prepaid expenses	16	16
Equipment on lease (net)	175	175
Land and buildings		
Machinery and fixtures		
Total fixed assets		
Less depreciation		
Net fixed assets		
Other assets	4	4
Total	441	141
Equities		
Notes payable—bank		
Notes payable—trade		
Due officers	6	6
Accounts payable—trade	23	23
Misc. accruals	3	3
Taxes accrued and reserved		
Due bank—current (secured)	79	
Total current liabilities	111	32
Due bank—deferred (secured)	120	199
Contingent liability to bank		
Total liabilities	231	231
Deferred lease income	199	
Capital stock preferred		
Capital stock common		
Earned surplus	15	15
Capital surplus	(5)	(5)
Net worth (excl. intangibles)	10	10
Total	440	241
Total current assets	126	47
Total current liabilities	111	32
Working capital	15	15
Current ratio	1.13	1.47
Net sales	35	35
Net profit	(5)	(5)
Dividends and withdrawals		

Nevertheless, Philip Cannon, the officer in charge of this loan, wondered if it might not be possible to make future explanations of this type unnecessary by altering the way in which the bank records the leasing companies' balance sheets. Cannon asked Jan Du Bois, a member of the bank's credit department, to try to present a more accurate picture of the leasing company's real position via the balance sheet (generally the only statement used by the bank for credit analysis). Du Bois developed the two alternative balance sheets shown above.

Required:

What recommendation would you make to the bank?

Owners' Equity

A ccording to the basic accounting equation (i.e., A = L + OE), owners' equity is simply the difference between a company's assets and its liabilities. It is the amount that would be left over if the assets were liquidated at their book values and the liabilities were then paid off. Owners' equity is also sometimes referred to as the **net worth** or the net *book value* of a company. However, owners' equity can also be considered on its own terms—as one of the three elements of the accounting equation

—rather than only the residual of assets minus liabilities.

Owners' equity usually takes two principal forms: **contributed capital,** as represented by the capital stock of a company, and **retained capital,** as represented by the cumulative retained earnings of a company. For many companies, transactions involving the owners' equity accounts are simple and straightforward. In fact, some publicly held companies bypass the presentation of a formal statement of owners' equity and provide what little detail might be of interest to financial statement users as a part of a footnote or as part of the income statement. To a very large degree, the owners' equity accounts are of more interest to attorneys than to management or accountants because the attorneys are responsible for a company's legal status and because many of the transactions in the owners' equity accounts have to do with a company's legal life. However, the owners' equity accounts are always of interest to a company's shareholders because these accounts measure the shareholders' residual interest in the net assets of the company. For this reason, owners'

equity is also sometimes called *shareholder equity*.

In the first section of this chapter, we consider the various ways in which a company can be legally organized and explore some of the activities common to the corporate form of organization. In the second section, we examine some of the most common transactions affecting the owners' equity accounts, the accounting entries that are required, and the financial statement presentation that is conventionally followed. In the final section, we illustrate the typical owners' equity disclosures using data from PepsiCo's annual report.

THE FORM OF A BUSINESS ENTITY

Business entities can be organized in different ways, and the differences can be important. A business entity can be a proprietorship, a partnership, or a corporation, depending on the legal structure of the entity's ownership.

Many small businesses are organized as proprietorships or partnerships because both types are relatively simple and inexpensive to form. To establish a proprietorship, one simply obtains the required permits to do business from a local or state governmental agency. The same is true for a partnership except that, in addition, the partners typically execute a written contract among themselves detailing the terms of their financial arrangements. The desirability of having a written agreement is as great for a two-person partnership as it is for partnerships composed of hundreds of partners. Some of the items usually detailed in a partnership agreement include the amount of each partner's investment, the rights of partners to withdraw funds, the manner in which profits and losses are to be divided, and the procedure to be followed in admitting a new partner.

The Partnership

We can make some general statements about **partnerships** (and proprietorships) that flow in part from the legal characteristics accorded to partnerships and in part from the way businesspeople have applied these legal forms in practice:

- *Limited ownership:* As a practical matter, most partnerships have relatively few partners.
- *Owners as managers:* The partners frequently manage the business.
- *Mutual agency:* Each partner, acting within the scope of reasonable partnership activities, acts as an agent for the business entity, and any single partner may act on behalf of all the other partners.
- *Unlimited liability:* Ordinarily, each partner is personally liable for all of the debts of the partnership.

- *Division of profit and loss:* Partnership profits and losses may be divided in whatever manner the individual partners agree.

- *Withdrawal of resources:* Unless the partners agree otherwise, they may withdraw resources from the business in an amount equal to their total investment in the partnership any time they wish to do so.

- *Limited life:* Unless the partners agree otherwise, the death or withdrawal of a partner automatically dissolves a partnership.

- *Taxes:* The partnership itself is not subject to income tax. Income earned (or a loss incurred) by the partnership is taxable income for the partners, whether or not it is distributed. This requirement is sometimes an advantage (as in the early years of a real estate partnership when depreciation throws off large tax losses) and sometimes a disadvantage (as in the early years of a growing company that generates earnings but must retain the operating cash flow for reinvestment).

The Corporation

The creation of a corporation is a more complex, legal procedure than the creation of partnerships and proprietorships. The incorporators (the initial shareholders) must first apply to a state commission, requesting permission to form a corporation. When a state agency grants that permission, a new entity comes into being. The newly incorporated entity's **charter of incorporation** thereby creates a legal entity that can sell shares to stockholders, own property, borrow money and incur obligations, and sue and be sued, all in its own name independently of its owners.

Again, we can make some general statements about the operations of corporations, in part because of their legal characteristics and in part because of the way corporate life has evolved in practice:

- *Diverse ownership:* The owners of a corporation are called *stockholders,* and ownership in a corporation is evidenced by shares of capital stock. The number of stockholders a corporation may have is not limited. In most states, a corporation can be formed with as few as three stockholders. On the other hand, a corporation may be owned by a very large number of stockholders (General Motors' shares are owned by more than 925,000 investors) and the shares may be traded in a public market. The stock of a corporation may be held by individuals, mutual funds, or other corporations.

- *Separation of ownership and management:* The management of public corporations generally owns only a small percentage (or none) of the company's outstanding capital stock.

- *Limited liability:* As a separate legal entity, a corporation is responsible for its own debts. Stockholders are not personally liable for a corporation's debts, and the maximum financial loss that stockholders can incur is the amount of their investment in the corporation.

- *Withdrawal of resources:* Stockholders are entitled to withdraw resources from a corporation only in the form of dividends and only after the board of directors has authorized a dividend payment. Dividends are paid to all stockholders in proportion to their ownership of the corporation, unless otherwise provided in the stock agreement.

■ *Transferability of ownership:* Stockholders may buy and sell shares of capital stock in a corporation without interfering with the activities or the life of a corporation. Most of the millions of shares that are traded daily on the stock exchanges represent private transactions between independent buyers and sellers. The activities of the corporations themselves are unaffected by such transactions.

■ *Government regulation:* Although a corporation exists as a result of a charter granted by a state agency, no significant legal implications flow from the chartering process. For instance, no state charter requires any corporation to prepare financial statements or file annual reports with the state. A publicly held corporation—that is, one with more than 500 shareholders and more than $5 million in assets—is subject to the federal securities laws by virtue of the public distribution of its stock. It must register its stock with the Securities and Exchange Commission; and the SEC's regulations *do* impose significant legal obligations on the corporation, including the periodic public distribution of financial statements.

■ *Taxes:* As separate legal entities, corporations pay federal and state income taxes on their earnings. When any part of these earnings is subsequently distributed to stockholders in the form of dividends, the stockholders also pay income taxes on the amount of dividends received. This separation of entity and ownership provides the owners of a privately held corporation with an opportunity to plan their personal income. However, it also results in double taxation.[1]

A Glimpse of Corporate Life

Typically, individual stockholders have very little say in the management of the company they own. Small stockholders "vote with their feet," selling their stock if they conclude that the company is not going forward. Major stockholders can be more assertive and use their voting rights to elect a board of directors to represent them (and all stockholders). In most companies, the board of directors is responsible for the corporation's overall direction. The board of directors elects and oversees the corporate officers who are directly responsible for the day-to-day management of the corporation. The officers usually include a president, vice president, secretary, and treasurer.

The officers report periodically to the board of directors and at least once a year to the shareholders. The officers (management) usually present a business plan for the board's approval and request the board's advice and concurrence regarding major decisions. The board members, on the other hand, prepare employment agreements for the officers, and generally monitor their progress in moving the company forward according to the

---

[1]Under certain conditions specified by the Internal Revenue Code, corporations with no more than 35 shareholders may elect to be treated as a partnership for tax purposes and thus pay no corporate income tax. Instead, the owners of these companies, called *Subchapter S corporations,* pay personal income taxes on their respective share of the business' earnings regardless of whether the earnings are actually withdrawn (or not) from the business.

approved business plan. Board members and officers have significant legal obligations, as fiduciaries, to always work in the best interests of a company's stockholders.

Corporations typically hold an annual meeting of stockholders subsequent to the end of each fiscal year. A *fiscal year* is the 12-month period a corporation selects as its accounting year, and it may or may not be the calendar year. The annual meeting is held for purposes such as reviewing the past year's financial performance; discussing business, economic, and political issues of importance to the corporation; selecting an accounting firm to audit the corporation's financial statements; electing directors; and voting on any other business that requires stockholders' ratification. The board of directors also decides, depending on the corporation's earnings' history, expectations for the future, cash position and expected cash needs, and (last but not least) expectations of the stock market, how much of the corporation's earnings should be paid out to stockholders as dividends.

Even though corporate stock can be bought and sold without affecting the company, corporations must keep track of stockholder transactions to know who is entitled to receive dividends and who is entitled to vote at shareholder meetings. A small corporation can keep track of its stockholders relatively easily because it has few transactions involving the stock. For a large, publicly held company, however, keeping track of its stockholders is very difficult because its shares trade in large volumes every day on the public stock exchanges. In fact, many corporations engage the services of a transfer agent and registrar to record stockholder transactions, cancel old stock certificates, issue new ones, and maintain a current record of stockholder names and addresses and the number of shares each owns. Transfer agents and registrars are usually banks or trust companies.

Publicly held companies whose stock is registered with the SEC must publish quarterly and annual reports for use by stockholders and other interested parties. These reports generally include status reports on a company's progress, from both the chairperson of the board and the president, and financial statements for the period. The financial statements in the annual report are accompanied by a report from an independent accounting firm, stating the accountants' opinion as to whether the financial statements are presented fairly, in all material respects, in conformity with generally accepted accounting principles.

OWNERS' EQUITY TRANSACTIONS

The most common transactions affecting the owners' equity accounts include the recognition of revenue and expenses for the year (which net to net income), the payment of dividends, and the sale or repurchase of capital stock.

Sales of Stock

A corporation may sell stock to new stockholders or to its existing stockholders. Those stock sales are recorded in the owners' equity account at the net cash (or other consideration) that the company receives for the stock sold. The journal entry is straightforward:

```
Dr.  Cash (A) . . . . . . . . . . . . . . . . . . . . . . $50,000
    Cr.  Capital Stock, at Par Value (OE) . . . . . . . . . . . . .      $ 1,000
    Cr.  Paid-In-Capital in Excess of Par Value (OE) . . . . . . . .       49,000
```

Note that if the sale price of the stock exceeds the *par* (or *stated*) value of the purchased shares, the excess is recorded in the Paid-In-Capital in Excess of Par Value account. Thus, the sum of the Capital Stock account and the Paid-In-Capital in Excess of Par Value account represents the aggregate **contributed capital** of a company.

As noted in Chapter 4, par value is a legal value required by some state incorporation commissions. Originally, it was meant to be the minimum capital required to be contributed to, and maintained in, a company by the stockholders. That concept has eroded in practice, however, and today the concept of par value has very little practical significance. Nonetheless, most financial statements continue to distinguish between par value and paid-in capital in excess of par value.

Most often, stock is issued for cash and so the value of the capital received in the exchange is easy to determine. However, companies sometimes exchange their stock for other forms of assets, including the stock or bonds of another corporation. In these exchanges, the total capital received (and, in turn, the assets received) are valued at the market value of the stock issued or the asset received, whichever provides the most reliable measure of value. When shares of stock are actively traded, the per share market price from those trades is usually considered the most reliable measure of the value involved in a swap of stock for other forms of assets. When the stock is not actively traded, the transaction may have to be valued at the value of the asset exchanged. When the asset cannot be readily valued, the transaction may have to be valued at the contributor's (the asset owner's) cost.

Every corporation issues **common stock** as its basic, senior equity security. But it is also possible to raise capital by selling other equity securities with special terms. **Preferred stock,** for example, is an equity security with some of the characteristics of a bond. Preferred stocks usually carry a specific dividend rate, stated as an amount per share or as a percentage of its par value. A preferred stock is "preferred" in that its dividend requirements have a first claim on a company's earnings before any claims of the common shareholders. Thus, in the event that earnings are limited, the preferred shareholders must receive their full dividend before common shareholders receive any. Should a company be liquidated, the preferred stockholders are entitled to secure the par value of their shares before any distribution is made to the common stockholders.

A preferred stock may also be **cumulative;** that is, its dividend preferences accumulate year to year even if the company has not earned enough to pay the dividend in any one year.[2] Preferred stock may be **participating** in that it may share in a company's earnings in excess of its stated dividend requirements, along with the common stock. It may also be *convertible* into a stated number of common shares. It also may be *callable* in that a company may have the right to call the security for redemption, usually at a premium above the stated or par value of the stock.

Class B common stock usually has the same provisions as a company's regular common stock regarding liquidation and dividend rights, but it may have disproportionate (usually

---

[2]Unpaid accumulated dividends are called dividends in arrears, and although not representing a liability of a company until the dividends are declared, they must be disclosed in the footnotes to the financial statements.

lower) voting rights. For example, in some companies, the class B stock carries only one-tenth the voting power of a company's class A common stock. In many cases, the class B stock is traded publicly, but the class A stock can only be exchanged between members of the company's founding family. Class B stocks have become popular in recent years as a defense against hostile takeovers.

The accounting for preferred stock and class B common stock is straightforward, following the legal terms of the security. The footnotes to the financial statements detail any special provisions of these securities and describe any preference entitlement that might burden the common shares.

Retained Earnings Transactions: Net Income

As we saw in Chapter 3, revenue and expense-producing transactions affect many balance sheet accounts—cash, accounts receivable, inventory, fixed assets, liabilities—but ultimately, the effects of these transactions are recorded in the Retained Earnings account. It may be useful at this point to recall the relationship between the balance sheet and the income statement. As the chart (from Chapter 2) below depicts, these two statements are linked by the Retained Earnings account:

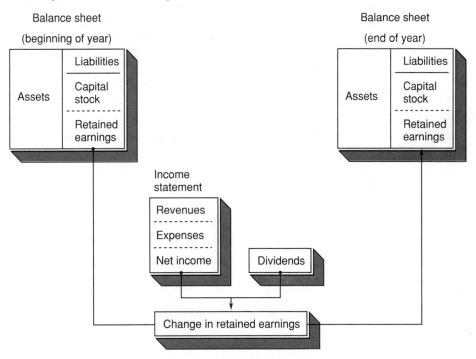

The net income for the period, less any dividends declared, is added to the Retained Earnings account on the balance sheet. This addition reflects the shareholders' increasing ownership interest in the net worth of the company.

Retained Earnings Transactions: Dividends

After net income, the second most common entry to the Retained Earnings account is the payment of dividends. We have said several times, but it is worth repeating—dividends are a distribution of a company's income to its shareholders but are not an expense of the business. The accounting entries to record a $5,000 cash dividend are as follows:

```
Dr.  Dividends Declared (COE) . . . . . . . . . . . . . $5,000
    Cr.  Dividends Payable (L) . . . . . . . . . . . . . . . .      $5,000
```

on the **date of declaration** by the board of directors and

```
Dr.  Dividends Payable (L) . . . . . . . . . . . . . . . . $5,000
    Cr.  Cash (A) . . . . . . . . . . . . . . . . . . . . . . .      $5,000
```

on the **date of payment.** To be entitled to receive a dividend, a shareholder must own the stock on the **date of record.** At the end of the accounting period, the Dividends Declared account is netted out against the retained earnings account (see Chapter 3).

Typically, dividends are paid in cash. Growth-oriented companies that have profitable places to invest their cash internally, however, may pay a **stock dividend** instead. The shareholders—who now own a few more shares than they did before the stock dividend—can then ride along with a company's expected growth, or they can liquidate part of their shareholdings by selling the stock dividend and converting it to cash. The accounting entry for a stock dividend is conceptually the same as for a cash dividend, except that the credit portion of the entry is an increase in common stock rather than a decrease in cash. The dollar value of the entry is measured by the fair market price of the stock issued at the date the dividend was declared:

```
Dr.  Stock Dividends Declared (OE). . . . . . . . . . . . . $5,000
    Cr.  Capital Stock, at Par Value (OE) . . . . . . . . . . . .     $  500
    Cr.  Paid-In-Capital in Excess of Par Value (OE) . . . . . . . . .     4,500
```

(This entry assumes that the fair market value of the shares issued was $5,000 and that the par value was $500.) As for a cash dividend, the Stock Dividend Declared account must be closed to Retained Earnings at the end of the accounting period and thus has the effect of transferring a portion of retained earnings to the capital stock accounts.

Stock Splits versus Stock Dividends

A company may "split" its stock for any number of reasons, but most often it is to reduce the market value of each share. The theory supporting a stock split is that investors will be more interested in a stock with a current market value of $25 than in one with a current market value of $100. Ordinarily, no journal entry is required for a stock split, although the number of shares outstanding increases and the par value (or stated value) of each share decreases proportionately. In a 2-for-1 stock split, for example, the number of shares outstanding doubles and the par value is halved, leaving the aggregate value of owners' equity unchanged. A **stock split** is, quite simply, a pro rata issuance of new shares to all existing shareholders.[3]

Sometimes a stock split is accounted for without changing a stock's par value. For example, on July 26, 1990, PepsiCo declared a 3-for-1 stock split. PepsiCo did not change the par value (i.e., $.0167) of its capital stock but transferred an amount equal to the total par value of the new shares from the Capital in Excess of Par Value account to the Capital Stock account.

The economic substance of a stock split is not very different from that of a stock dividend; however, the accounting implications are very different. Note that a stock dividend transfers some part of a company's retained earnings to the capital accounts whereas (usually) the accounting for a split simply reallocates the paid-in-capital over a larger number of shares. That theoretical accounting difference is perhaps justifiable when a split is large—2 for 1, or 4 for 1. That difference is less justifiable, however, with a smaller split. In fact, the American and New York Stock exchanges have adopted reporting rules that have become general practice. They have said that a stock split is any distribution of stock in *excess* of 25 percent of the previously outstanding shares, whereas a distribution of *less* than 25 percent is always considered a stock dividend. Thus, for example, under exchange rules, a stock distribution equal to 10 percent of the previously existing shares must be accounted for as a stock dividend even if it is legally described as a stock split. In that situation, the fair market value of the newly distributed shares is transferred from retained earnings to the capital accounts.

Treasury Stock Transactions

In the United States, companies may, at the discretion of management, buy back a proportion of their own outstanding stock. A company may, for example, repurchase its own stock because it has commitments for future issuances of stock to satisfy various stock options, stock warrants, or convertible securities (to be discussed shortly). Or a company may reacquire some of its own shares because it has excess cash and because the board of directors believes that the company's own stock represents the best investment opportunity for that cash. A company also may buy some of its outstanding shares because management believes that the current market price of the stock is too low, and it hopes to raise that price by reducing the supply of available shares.

If the reacquired shares are to be held and reissued sometime in the future, they are accounted for in a contra owners' equity account entitled **Treasury Stock.** The reacquired shares are usually recorded in the Treasury Stock account at the cost paid to repurchase the shares:

```
Dr.  Treasury Stock (COE) . . . . . . . . . . . . . . . . $15,000
     Cr.  Cash (A) . . . . . . . . . . . . . . . . . . . . . . . . .   $15,000
```

---

[3]A stock split may be either a *forward* split or a *reverse* split. A forward split increases the number of shares outstanding; a reverse split reduces the number of shares outstanding.

Note that a company's investment in its own stock is not considered to be an asset; instead, it is treated as a reduction in owners' equity.

When treasury stock is reissued as a result of a sale, or to satisfy stock options, warrants, or for the conversion of convertible bonds, the cost of the reissued shares is removed from the Treasury Stock account. If the proceeds related to that reissuance differ from the cost of the treasury shares issued, that difference is added to (or subtracted from) the Paid-In-Capital account. For example, suppose that Smith Company purchased 100 shares of its own stock at $12 a share in anticipation of the exercise of its $10 stock options by its employees. The entry to record that purchase is an increase in its Treasury Stock account (a contra owners' equity account) for $1,200 and a decrease in the Cash account of like amount. Assuming that options for 100 shares are exercised, the following accounting entry is made:

```
Dr.  Cash (A) . . . . . . . . . . . . . . . . . . . . . . . . $1,000
Dr.  Paid-In-Capital in Excess of Par Value (OE) . . . . . . . $  200
     Cr.  Treasury Stock (COE) . . . . . . . . . . . . . . . . . . .        $1,200
```

If a company reacquires its own shares with no intention of reissuing them, it formally, legally retires them. Instead of a debit entry to the Treasury Stock account, the company makes debit entries for the cost of the stock acquired to the Common Stock (at Par) account and the Paid-In-Capital account for any difference. If the spread between the par value and the per-share cost of the reacquired shares is more than the average per-share paid-in capital from prior issuances of stock, that excess may have to be charged against retained earnings.

Other Stock Transactions

Stock options. Many companies maintain **stock option plans** for their employees, and issuances of stock in satisfaction of those commitments are frequent owners' equity transactions. A stock option plan might work this way: Assume that Smith Company is on the verge of a new business cycle and that its board of directors concludes that management motivation will be a major factor in the company's success. At the present time, the company's stock is selling at $10 a share. The board might agree to grant options to key management people to purchase shares of the company's stock at $10 a share any time after five years from today, thereby creating a financial incentive for the executives.

Under most stock option plans, no accounting entry is necessary when such an option is granted. The entry to record the issuance of those shares when the employees exercise their options assumes that the transaction is simply a sale of stock at $10 a share—even if the stock price is $20 a share on the exercise date:

```
Dr.  Cash (A) . . . . . . . . . . . . . . . . . . . . . . . . $1,000
     Cr.  Common Stock, at Par Value (OE) . . . . . . . . . . . . .        $100
     Cr.  Paid-In-Capital in Excess of Par Value (OE) . . . . . . . . .        900
```

Stock option plans usually produce no tax deductions for a corporation; similarly, the employee has no taxable income as a result of the award of the option or the exercise of the option. The employee experiences a taxable gain when the stock is sold, and the gain is calculated based on the difference between the ultimate sale price of the stock and its option (purchase) price.

In recent years, a great variety of option plans has come into use, some of which do require the company to recognize an option expense over the option period and do require the employee to recognize taxable income. Companies establish one plan or another (sometimes combinations of plans) depending on the impact of the plans on their earnings and their tax position, and the needs of their employees.

warrants. A cash-short firm that is going through a difficult period may find that ble to sell new shares of stock at a price it believes is reasonable. In lieu of a stock mpany may sell **stock warrants,** which enable the holder to purchase shares of xed price at some time in the future. The proceeds from the sale of warrants added to the Paid-In-Capital in Excess of Par Value account:

Dr.   Cash (A) $5,000
     Cr.   Paid-In-Capital in Excess of Par Value. $5,000

When a warrant is exercised, the proceeds are added to the common stock account using the same theory as is followed for the exercise of stock options. Sometimes warrants for the purchase of common stock are issued in connection with the sale of a bond to make the bonds more attractive to potential purchasers. In those situations, some portion of the proceeds of the bond sale are allocated to the Paid-In-Capital in Excess of Par Value account, just as though the company had sold the bonds and the warrants separately.

Convertible securities. Many companies sell **convertible bonds** that enable the holder to exchange a bond for shares of common stock at a predetermined ratio (the conversion ratio). Convertible bonds are usually less expensive for the issuing corporation because they can be sold with a lower interest rate than would otherwise be required (i.e., because the conversion feature has value itself). Convertible bonds are attractive to the holder because they ensure a steady stream of interest income for a certain number of years, as well as the possibility of sharing in any potential appreciation of the common stock. The proceeds from the sale of a convertible bond increase the cash account and increase the bond account. If some of the bonds are subsequently converted, a pro rata share of the bond's carrying value is transferred from the Bond Payable account (a decrease) to the Common Stock and Paid-In Capital accounts (increases). Similar accounting is followed for convertible preferred stock.

Hybrid Transactions

Earlier we indicated that all transactions involving the owners' equity accounts that relate to stock issuances are reported in the statement of owners' equity and that all owners' equity transactions that involve revenue and expenses are reported in the income statement. For many years, the dividing line between the two types of transactions was clearly defined and stoutly defended. The accounting profession argued that it was important to include *all* income and expense items (and *only* those items) in the determination of income for the period. Recently, the line between income and equity transactions has become blurred. Today under GAAP, two nonstock events are reported in the statement of owners' equity, not in the income statement. The two nonstock items that may now be included in a statement of owners' equity are (1) the residual that results from translating the foreign currency value of assets and liabilities held outside the United States into U.S. dollars and (2) the residual that results from adjusting the carrying value of long-term investments to their current market value.

To describe the **currency translation adjustment,** it may be easiest if we use an example (see also the appendix to Chapter 9). Assume that a U.S.–based company has a subsidiary in Germany with receivables, inventory, equipment, and payables denominated in German marks. Obviously, adding together the company's dollar-stated accounts and its mark-stated accounts would not be appropriate. If the exchange rate stayed the same from one year to the next (e.g., 1 mark = \$.50 versus \$1 = 2 marks), it would be easy to convert the mark-stated accounts into their U.S.–dollar equivalents, and then to add those dollar-equivalent accounts to the U.S.–dollar-stated accounts.

Exchange rates do fluctuate, however, and sometimes they change dramatically. In previous years, the exchange rate between the U.S. dollar and the German mark has been 1 to 4, with a mark being equal to \$.25 U.S. Hence, a piece of equipment purchased for a company's German operations at that time might have cost 1 million marks and would therefore have had a U.S.–dollar cost of only \$250,000. Today, with an exchange rate of \$1 to 2 marks, the translated dollar cost for that piece of equipment would be \$500,000. Accountants and businesspeople have been concerned about the appropriate accounting for that extra \$250,000. No one wanted to include the apparent increase in asset value in the income statement because it did not seem to be a revenue item. In addition, the exchange rates might reverse in a subsequent period, and consequently companies would report fluctuations in earnings induced by the exchange markets rather than due to operations. Instead, it was agreed (in SFAS No. 52) that all such translation adjustments be included as a unique element of owners' equity until those assets or liabilities were liquidated, converted to U.S. dollars, and repatriated. Only after those non–U.S. assets (or liabilities) are realized in dollars will the resulting gain or loss be recognized in the income statement.

The second unique element of owners' equity is rare, but it builds on the same logic as the translation adjustment. A company that owns less than 20 percent of the stock of another company carries that investment at cost in its balance sheet. If the market price of that stock declines below its original cost, the holder should, following the lower-of-cost-or-market concept, recognize the loss currently by a write-down of the investment (see Chapter 9). But when such investments are made for long-term purposes, when the company has no plans to liquidate the investment in the foreseeable future, accounting practice does not require the market fluctuation loss to be recognized on the income statement currently. Under GAAP, any market adjustment related to an investment that is classified as a long-term investment is reported as a decrease in equity in the owners' equity statement but need not be included in the determination of its net income for that period.

OWNERS' EQUITY DISCLOSURES

To illustrate the typical annual report disclosures involving owners' equity, we again refer to the 1990 PepsiCo, Inc., annual report. Exhibit 13.1 presents the shareholders' equity section of the PepsiCo consolidated balance sheet. This exhibit presents summary

EXHIBIT 13.1

PEPSICO, INC.
Shareholders' Equity Section
As of December 29, 1990 and 1989
(in millions)

	1990	1989
Shareholders' Equity		
Capital stock, par value $.0167 per share:		
authorized 1,800 shares, issued		
863.1 shares	$ 14.4	$ 14.4
Capital in excess of par value	365.0	323.9
Retained earnings	4,753.0	3,978.4
Currency translation adjustment	383.2	66.2
Cost of treasury stock:		
74.7 shares in 1990		
72.0 shares in 1989	(611.4)	(491.8)
Total Shareholders' Equity	$4,904.2	$3,891.1

For the complete consolidated balance sheet, see the appendix to Chapter 1. 1989 data are restated to reflect a 3-for-1 stock dividend.

information concerning PepsiCo's shareholder equity accounts, whereas detailed information is presented in Exhibit 13.2, the *consolidated statement of shareholders' equity*. From these two exhibits, the following facts can be determined:

- PepsiCo has one class of capital stock—a $0.0167 par value, common stock. It is *authorized* to issue 1.8 billion shares, and as of December 29, 1990, 863.1 million shares had been *issued*. Only 788.4 million shares were *outstanding;* 74.7 million shares were held in treasury.

- The aggregate contributed capital at year-end was $379.4 million, whereas total shareholders' equity was $4,904.2 million.

- The aggregate cost of the 74.7 million shares held as treasury stock was $611.4 million. In 1990, 6.31 million shares were purchased at a cost of $147.7 million, and 3.64 million were reissued as follows:

Shares reissued	Purpose
8,000	Employee stock ownership plan
1,072,000	Exercise of stock options and compensation awards by employees
549,000	Conversion of debentures
2,013,000	Issued in connection with an acquisition

- Retained earnings at year-end 1990 amounted to $4,753.0 million. Net income of $1,076.9 million was added to the account, and cash dividends of $302.3 million deducted from it.

EXHIBIT 13.2

PEPSICO, Inc., and Subsidiaries
Consolidated Statement of Shareholders' Equity

Consolidated Statement of Shareholders' Equity

(shares in thousands, dollars in millions, except per share amounts)
PepsiCo, Inc. and Subsidiaries
Fifty-two weeks ended December 29, 1990 and December 30, 1989 and fifty-three weeks ended December 31, 1988

| | Capital Stock | | | | Capital in Excess of Par Value | Retained Earnings | Currency Translation Adjustment | Total |
| | Issued | | Treasury | | | | | |
	Shares	Amount	Shares	Amount				
Shareholders' Equity, December 26, 1987	863,083	$14.4	(81,844)	$(553.6)	$280.9	$2,776.7	$ (9.8)	$2,508.6
1988 Net income						762.2		762.2
Cash dividends declared (per share-$0.27)						(209.2)		(209.2)
Shares reissued to Employee Stock Ownership Plan			365	2.5	1.6			4.1
Payment of compensation awards and exercise of stock options			972	6.6	0.5			7.1
Conversion of debentures			3,047	20.7	(2.6)			18.1
Translation adjustments							33.8	33.8
Purchase of treasury stock			(6,198)	(71.8)				(71.8)
Shares issued in connection with acquisitions			9,009	85.9	22.2			108.1
Shareholders' Equity, December 31,1988	863,083	$14.4	(74,649)	$(509.7)	$302.6	$3,329.7	$ 24.0	$3,161.0
1989 Net income						901.4		901.4
Cash dividends declared (per share-$0.32)						(252.7)		(252.7)
Payment of compensation awards and exercise of stock options			901	6.2	2.6			8.8
Conversion of debentures			456	3.1	0.8			3.9
Translation adjustments							42.2	42.2
Shares issued in connection with an acquisition			1,266	8.6	17.9			26.5
Shareholders' Equity, December 30, 1989	863,083	$14.4	(72,026)	$(491.8)	$323.9	$3,978.4	$ 66.2	$3,891.1
1990 Net income						1,076.9		1,076.9
Cash dividends declared (per share-$0.38)						(302.3)		(302.3)
Shares reissued to Employee Stock Ownership Plan			8	0.1	0.2			0.3
Payment of compensation awards and exercise of stock options			1,072	7.8	9.1			16.9
Conversion of debentures			549	3.9	1.7			5.6
Translation adjustments							317.0	317.0
Purchase of treasury stock			(6,310)	(147.7)				(147.7)
Shares issued in connection with acquisitions			2,013	16.3	30.1			46.4
Shareholders' Equity, December 29,1990 .	863,083	$14.4	(74,694)	$(611.4)	$365.0	$4,753.0	$383.2	$4,904.2

Certain amounts above have been restated to reflect the 1990 three-for-one stock split.

EXHIBIT 13.3

PepsiCo, Inc.
Selected Footnote Disclosures:
Employee Incentive Plans

Employee Incentive Plans

In 1989 PepsiCo established the PepsiCo SharePower Stock Option Plan. Under this plan, which was approved by the Board of Directors, all employees who meet eligibility requirements may be granted stock options. Executive officers, part-time and short-service employees principally comprise the non-eligible group. Executive officers may be granted similar benefits under the 1987 Long-Term Incentive Plan. A stock option represents the right, exercisable in the future, to purchase one share of PepsiCo Capital Stock at the fair market value on the date of the grant. The number of options granted is based on a percentage of the employee's annual earnings. The grants may be made annually, have a term of 10 years from the grant date and generally become exercisable ratably over the five years after the grant date. SharePower options were granted to approximately 91,000 and 77,000 employees in 1990 and 1989, respectively.

The shareholder-approved 1987 Long-Term Incentive Plan (the Plan), effective January 1, 1988, provides long-term incentives to key employees through stock options, performance shares, stock appreciation rights (SARs) and incentive stock units (Units). The Plan authorizes up to a maximum of 54 million shares of PepsiCo Capital Stock to be purchased or paid pursuant to grants by the Compensation Committee of the Board of Directors (the Committee), which is composed of outside directors. There were 34 million and 43 million shares available for future grants at year-end 1990 and 1989, respectively. Payment of awards other than stock options is made in cash and/or PepsiCo Capital Stock as determined by the Committee.

Under the Plan, a stock option is exercisable for a specified period generally falling between 1 and 15 years from the date of grant. A performance share, equivalent to one share of PepsiCo Capital Stock, generally vests and is payable four years after the date of grant, contingent upon attainment of prescribed performance criteria. Employees may receive partial performance share awards if they become eligible for new or increased awards subsequent to a grant. A stock option is granted with each performance share. Beginning with the 1988 award, a specified number of additional stock options are granted in lieu of a performance share. These additional stock options may be converted to a performance share at the employee's election within 60 days from the date of grant.

SARs, available to certain senior management employees holding stock options, may be granted in the year the related options become exercisable. They allow the employees to surrender an option for an amount equal to the appreciation between the option exercise price and the fair market value of PepsiCo Capital Stock on the date the SAR is exercised. SARs expire no later than the expiration date of the related options. The maximum number of stock options that can be surrendered for SARs is 30% of outstanding options that have been exercisable for more than one year. During 1990, 147,570 SARs were granted. SARs outstanding at year-end 1990 and 1989 were 272,568 and 168,954, respectively.

Under the Plan, eligible middle management employees were granted Units, and beginning in 1989, stock options are granted in lieu of the Units. A Unit is equivalent in value to the fair market value of one share of PepsiCo Capital Stock at specified dates over a six-year vesting period from the date of grant. Units outstanding at year-end 1990 and 1989 were 585,149 and 671,902, respectively.

The combined estimated costs of performance shares, SARs and Units, expensed over the applicable vesting periods of the awards, were $13 million, $25 million and $16 million in 1990, 1989 and 1988, respectively.

Award activity for 1990 and 1989 was as follows:

	SharePower Plan	Long-Term Incentive Plan	
	Stock Options	Stock Options	Performance Shares
	(000's)		
Outstanding at December 31, 1988.	–	17,480	2,918
Granted.	10,742	2,109	15
Exercised/Paid	–	(614)	–
Surrendered for performance shares . .	–	(49)	16
Surrendered for SARs. . .	–	(29)	–
Cancelled.	(697)	(572)	(147)
Outstanding at December 30, 1989.	10,045	18,325	2,802
Granted.	8,808	12,179	–
Exercised/Paid	(37)	(868)	(2,346)
Surrendered for performance shares . .	–	(1,228)	409
Surrendered for SARs. . .	–	(44)	–
Cancelled.	(1,589)	(1,490)	(69)
Outstanding at December 29, 1990.	17,227	26,874	796
Exercisable at December 29, 1990.	1,840	4,139	

Option prices per share:

Exercised during 1990	$17.58	$4.11 to $20.00
Exercised during 1989	–	$4.11 to $ 8.75
Outstanding at year-end 1990	$17.58 to $25.96	$4.11 to $26.44

The above Long-Term Incentive Plan activity includes grants to middle management employees of 1,070,436 and 850,785 stock options in 1990 and 1989, respectively, 692,880 of which were exercisable at year-end 1990.

Contingencies

PepsiCo is subject to various claims and legal contingencies. While the ultimate liability that could result from these matters cannot be determined presently, management believes such liability will not have a material adverse affect on PepsiCo's business or financial condition.

At year-end 1990 PepsiCo was contingently liable under direct and indirect guarantees aggregating $97 million. The guarantees are primarily issued to support financial arrangements of certain restaurant and soft drink bottling franchisees and PepsiCo joint ventures. PepsiCo manages the risk associated with these guarantees by performing appropriate credit reviews in addition to retaining certain rights as a franchisor or joint venture partner.

■ The cumulative foreign currency translation account totaled $383.2 million at year-end—an increase of $317.0 million from the prior year, reflecting a substantial strengthening of foreign currencies relative to the U.S. dollar in those areas where PepsiCo maintains operations.

Because of the importance of employee stock option and stock compensation plans, the principal features of these plans are detailed in the footnotes to the financial statements. Exhibit 13.3 presents the footnote disclosure for PepsiCo's employee incentive plan.

SUMMARY

The owners' or shareholders' equity represents the residual value of a company, or its assets minus its liabilities. The transactions affecting the shareholder equity accounts are summarized in the statement of owners' equity. The principal owners' equity transactions include the sale of capital stock, the results of operations (i.e., the net income or net loss resulting from a company's principal business activity), the payment of dividends (either cash or stock), the exercise of stock options or warrants, the conversion of convertible preferred stock or debentures, and the purchase or reissuance of treasury stock. In addition to these transactions involving individuals or organizations outside the company, the statement of owners' equity also depicts two hybrid transactions: (1) the adjustment for foreign currency changes when consolidating the results of foreign operations and (2) the adjustment for valuation changes in the long-term investment portfolio.

The owners' equity of a company is also referred to as its *net worth* or *book value*. In many cases, the market value of a company, as defined by the market price of its capital stock, far exceeds the company's net worth or book value. Why this may be the case is the focus of Chapter 14.

NEW CONCEPTS AND TERMS

Charter of incorporation (p. 589)

Contributed capital (p. 587)

Convertible bonds (p. 597)

Cumulative preferred stock (p. 592)

Currency translation adjustment (p. 598)

Date of declaration (p. 594)

Date of payment (p. 594)

Date of record (p. 594)

Dividends in arrears (p. 592)

Participating preferred stock (p. 592)

Partnership (p. 588)

Preferred stock (p. 592)

Retained capital (p. 587)

Stock dividend (p. 594)

Stock option plans (p. 596)

Stock split (p. 595)

Stock warrant (p. 597)

Treasury stock (p. 595)

ISSUES FOR DISCUSSION

D13.1 Assume that you and two of your friends are about to form a business. Anticipating a meeting with your attorney, what factors should you consider in deciding between establishing a partnership or forming a corporation? Why might these factors be important to your planning?

D13.2 **Point:** Treasury stock should be accounted for as an asset; after all, a company's resources must be expended to repurchase the shares.

Counterpoint: Treasury stock should be accounted for as a contra owners' equity account in that the shares held in the treasury represent a reduction in the total shares outstanding.

Comment on the two viewpoints. Which one makes most sense to you, and why?

D13.3 Point: Investors who have agreed to buy shares in a growing company and who have signed notes for their stock subscriptions represent real stockholders, and their notes should be counted as assets and equity, even though they have not yet been paid in cash. That, after all, is what accrual accounting is all about.

Counterpoint: Stock subscriptions should not be recorded as assets because the funds are not available for the company's use until the notes are paid. We should treat notes receivables from stockholders differently than we treat notes from customers or creditors because the notes do not arise in the ordinary course of business. More importantly, the users of the financial statements are entitled to assume that shareholders' equity is really in place and is fully ready to absorb the deepest layer of business risk facing the company.

Comment on the two viewpoints. Which one makes the most sense to you, and why?

D13.4 What does the expression "vote with their feet" mean to you? Why should it be necessary for shareholders to vote with their feet? What message might management look for from such a voting process?

D13.5 Brown-Foreman Corporation has class A and class B common shares outstanding. Both the A and the B shares carry a par value of $.15, and both are paid the exact same dividend. The shares appear to be the same in every respect, except that the class A shares have a vote, whereas the class B shares do not. There are 12 million class A shares outstanding and 26.6 million class B shares outstanding. In the last quarter of 1990, the class A shares traded in a range between $75 and $57 1/2 a share; the class B shares traded in a range between $78 7/8 and $58 3/8 per share. Why would the company have these two classes of common stock outstanding? Would you expect the two classes to trade in the market at the same or at different prices? How would you interpret the price data in this case? What are the implications of that data for other companies that might be contemplating a two-class stock program?

D13.6 In 1988, the directors of Schuchardt Software Systems, Inc., declared a 2,000-for-1 stock split. SSS, Inc., a California-based publisher of business software, was organized in 1983 and each founding stockholder paid $5,000 per share. At that time, 84 individuals purchased stock in the company. Since then, the founding shareholders have sold a few shares between themselves at prices varying between $5,800 and $6,800 a share. The company is preparing itself for its initial offering of stock to the public.

Required:

a. Why would the directors decide on a 2,000-for-1 split?

b. Assume that the presplit par value of the company's stock was $100 per share. How could the company account for the stock split? (Provide an entry please.)

c. According to a company spokesperson, at the time of the stock split announcement, Schuchardt had not yet earned any income. Would this fact change your answer to part *b* above?

d. Assume that the company declared a 2,000 percent stock dividend instead of a stock split. How would you account for the stock dividend? (Provide an entry, please.)

D13.7 Georgia Pacific Corporation made the comment below in its 1990 annual report to shareholders:

Dividends and Share Repurchases In the past five years, we have distributed approximately $1.7 billion to our shareholders through a combination of dividends and stock repurchases.

Our policy is to pay dividends at a rate of approximately one-third of sustainable earnings, recognizing the cyclical nature of our business. Following four consecutive years with fourth-quarter dividend increases, we left our quarterly dividend unchanged in 1990.

We view the dividend payout in conjunction with our share repurchase program. Our board of directors authorized a share repurchase program that began in 1987 as a means of distributing excess cash to our shareholders and maintaining our ratio of debt to capital within a target range, currently set at 40 to 45 percent. In 1989, for example, cash provided by operations exceeded our capital expenditures and dividend payments by $729 million. Of this free cash flow, $468 million was used to repurchase 9.7 million shares of common stock. This brought total share repurchases since 1987 to 26.2 million at a cost of $1.1 billion.

In October 1989, we suspended our share repurchase program, anticipating the higher leverage that resulted from the Great Northern Nekoosa acquisition. Our board's authorization to repurchase shares remains in effect, however, and we expect to resume our share repurchase program after we reduce debt to an appropriate level.

Required:

a. Is the company justified in its position that dividends and share repurchases should be considered in the same way? Why or why not?

b. How are they the same and how are they different in their impact on the company?

c. How are they the same and how are they different in their impact on the shareholders?

D13.8 Quick Start, Inc., had a public offering of stock in 1985, and as a result, it had 250,000 common shares outstanding. Because of its need for cash, the company had never paid a dividend. Quick Start had been moderately successful, but it was subject to the seasonality that affected the automobile industry. Results for the last five years were as follows (in thousands):

Year	Net Income	Cash Flow from Operations
1985	$20,000	$32,000
1986	8,000	14,000
1987	12,000	15,000
1988	16,000	20,000
1989	19,000	22,000

The company has debt and lease commitments that require about $18,000,000 a year. Its capital expansion plans are now at a level at which they could be met by additional borrowing, and the company has open credit lines of $75,000,000 available. Retained earnings are $90,000,000. Because of pressure from the public stockholders, Quick Start's board of directors is considering making a dividend payment in 1990.

Required:

a. Outline all of the factors you might want the board to address as it considers the possibility of making a dividend payment. How much should the 1990 dividend be?

b. Suggest and justify a range of per share amounts that the board might consider.

PROBLEMS

P13.1 Stock issuances and dividend payments. CRS Corporation was incorporated on January 1, 1990, and issued the following stock, for cash:

1,000,000 shares of no-par common stock were authorized; 100,000 shares were issued on January 1, at $24 per share.

200,000 shares of $10 par value, 10 percent cumulative preferred stock were authorized, and 50,000 shares were issued on January 1, 1992, at $12 per share.

The year went relatively well. Net income was $525,000, and the board of directors declared dividends of $175,000.

Required:

Prepare the entries required to record the issuances of the shares of stock and the payment of the dividends.

P13.2 Issuing stock to the founders. Three entrepreneurs have come together to exploit an invention that one of them recently patented. The inventor has very little cash, but he is willing to put his patent into the venture. Similarly, the second entrepreneur has very little cash, but he has a manufacturing plant he can contribute to the venture. (The plant is presently vacant but can be used to manufacture the inventor's product. The plant was recently appraised as having a value of between $180,000 and $225,000.) The third entrepreneur has plenty of cash, and she is willing to put $200,000 into the new venture. They agree to form a corporation and that each will receive 2,000 shares of common stock for the contributions of cash, the building, and the patent.

Required:

Prepare the entries required to record the issuance of the stock. Explain your rationale for the entries you made and the numbers you used.

P13.3 Preferred stock characteristics. Beneficial Corporation has four issues of preferred stock outstanding in addition to its common stock. All of these issues are detailed in the following footnote. Describe in your own words the characteristics of each of these preferred stock issues.

Beneficial Corporation and Subsidiaries

10. Capital Stock

The number of shares of capital stock outstanding is as follows:

	December 31	
	1990	**1989**
5% Cumulative preferred— $50 par value. Authorized, 585,730	**407,718(a)**	407,718(a)
$5.50 Dividend cumulative convertible preferred— no par value–$20 stated value (each share convertible into 4.5 shares of common; maximum liquidation value. $3,252,900 and $3,476,800). Authorized, 1,164,077	**32,529**	34,768
$4.50 Dividend cumulative preferred–$100 par value. Authorized, 103,976	**103,976**	103,976
$4.30 Dividend cumulative preferred–no par value– $100 stated value. Authorized, 1,069,204	**836,585**	836,585
Common–$1 par value. Authorized, 60,000,000	**22,414,564(b)**	22,404,494(b)
After deducting treasury shares (a) 5% cumulative preferred (b) Common	**178,012** **4,822,088**	178,012 4,822,066

P13.4 Stock splits. In 1990, Monsanto Corporation declared a 2-for-1 stock split. The operational highlights from the first page of the company's 1990 annual report to stockholders states that the data have been adjusted for the effect of the split.

	1990	1989	1988
Net sales	$8,995	$8,681	$8,293
Net income	$ 546	$ 679	$ 591
Per share:			
Net income	$ 4.23	$ 5.01	$ 4.14
Dividends	1.88	1.65	1.475
Shareowners' equity	32.51	29.79	27.60
Depreciation and amortization	$ 739	$ 690	$ 703
Cash provided by operations	$1,104	$1,037	$1,304
Research and development expenses	$ 612	$ 598	$ 575
Return on shareowners' equity	13.6%	17.6%	15.4%
Percent of total debt to total capitalization	35%	33%	34%
Shareowners (year-end)	62,230	61,942	66,066
Shares outstanding (year-end, in millions)	126	132	138
Employees (year-end)	41,081	42,179	45,635

Required:

Which line items from the highlights would have been adjusted to give effect to the stock split, and what would the effect of the adjustment have been?

P13.5 Treasury stock transactions. Smith Company has sold stock to its employees and to outsiders at various times during its life, as follows:

1984	100,000 shares originally sold at par value for $100,000 in cash.
1984	10,000 shares issued to an employee as an inducement to sign an employment contract; no cash exchanged.
1985	25,000 shares sold to an independent investor for $50,000 in cash.
1986	100,000 shares sold to a group of 25 investors at $30 a share.
1987	A 2-for-1 stock split declared.
1988	500,000 shares sold in a public offering through Merrill Lynch at $25 a share.
1989	100,000 shares given to the top management as a bonus. The market price was then $20.

In 1990, the company purchased 50,000 shares on the open market at $12 a share.

Required:

a. Prepare the entry required to record the 50,000 share purchase, assuming the company plans to reissue the shares as a bonus to the employees at a future date.

b. Prepare the entry required to record the share purchase, assuming the company plans to retire the reacquired shares.

P13.6 Convertible preferred stock. In 1985, Clever Corp. raised $1,000,000 in capital by the sale of 10,000 shares of convertible preferred stock, par value $100. The preferred stock required an annual dividend of only $4 a share even though the prime rate at the time was 10 percent. Each share of preferred stock was convertible into five shares of Clever common stock, which had a market value of $10 at the time of the preferred stock issuance.

Required:

a. Prepare the entry to record the sale of the preferred stock. How would you propose to recognize the value of the conversion feature in the financial statements? Please provide the rationale for your answer.

b. Why would Clever want to issue convertible preferred instead of regular preferred or additional common stock?

c. Why would an investor buy the Clever convertible preferred when it pays only a $4 dividend?

P13.7 Convertible preferred, revisited. In 1991, all of the holders of Clever Corp. convertible preferred stock (discussed in P13.6) turned in their shares for conversion and were given five shares of common for each share of preferred.

Required:

a. Why would the holders of the preferred stock turn their shares in for redemption at this time?

b. What entry would Clever Corp. make at the time of the conversion?

P13.8 Stock options. Aggressive Corporation was doing very well with its new product line, and it seemed as though the company could double in size over the next three years. It was a tense time for the management people, however, and the good fortune brought its own questions. Do we have enough inventory to meet demand? Should we expand the plant to accommodate one more assembly line? If we encourage sales by granting extended credit terms, how will we pay our own bills? Nonetheless, management had worked very hard for a long time with very little reward and members were delighted to bask in the prospects of the future. The board of directors was pleased, too, and at the end of the year awarded the top five people stock options, which would enable each of them to buy 10,000 shares of the company's stock at $9, the current market price. It was indeed a happy new year.

Required:

a. Why might Aggressive's board of directors have believed it appropriate to issue the stock options to the top management people at this time at $9 a share?

b. How might you feel about the stock options if you were one of the top management people? Why? How might you feel if you were a nonmanagement shareholder in the company?

c. Prepare the entry required to recognize the issuance of the options at the issue date. Explain the reasons for your entry.

P13.9 Stock options exercised. Three years after Aggressive's board of directors issued the stock options to its top five employees (see P13.8) the company's sales had grown nearly three times and profits were up 250 percent. The stock market had recognized the company's success, and the shares regularly traded at $32. Three of the top five employees exercised their options in full, but the other two had not as yet done so.

Required:

a. Prepare the entry required to recognize the exercise of the options for 30,000 shares. Explain the rationale for your entry and then explain the source of your numbers.

b. What factors might have motivated the three management people to have exercised their stock options? What factors might have motivated the other two to hold on to the options, at least for the time being?

P13.10 Describing stock options. Seagram Company, Ltd., began a stock option program for its employees in 1989. The status of the program, as of the end of each of the last three years, is described in footnote 3 to the company's 1990 report to stockholders as follows:

Stock Option Activity	Twelve Months Ended January 31,		
	1991	**1990**	**1989**
Options outstanding at the beginning of the period	1,357,025	830,975	—
Granted	1,025,125	870,660	855,035
Average grant price	$77.75	$69.75	$54.37
Exercised	(191,950)	(291,285)	—
Average exercise price	$63.62	$54.37	—
Cancelled	(90,180)	(53,325)	(24,060)
Options outstanding at the end of the period	2,100,020	1,357,025	830,975
Average exercise price	$70.58	$64.00	$54.37
Exercisable	1,106,545	507,015	—
Shares reserved for options at the end of the period	2,416,745	3,351,690	4,169,025

Under the Company's employee stock option plan, options may be granted to purchase the Company's common shares at not less than the fair market value of the shares on the date of the grant. The options become exercisable commencing one year from the grant date and expire ten years after the grant.

Required:

In your own words, describe the events depicted by each of the line items in the table from the footnote. What do the numbers in the table mean? What might the sources of those numbers be?

P13.11 Accounting for stock warrants. Poorboy had been through difficult years, but management was hopeful that the recent financial restructuring and product reorganization would turn things around. The company needed cash to carry out its new strategy, but the banks had refused any further credit extension. The stock was trading at an all-time low, around $2.50 per share. (Interestingly, the par value of the company's common stock is also $2.50.) An investment adviser suggested that the company consider selling warrants. After some negotiation, the adviser helped the company sell 1,000,000 warrants, each good for the purchase of a share of common stock at $5 in eight years. The warrant sale raised $500,000.

Required:

a. Why might the market pay $500,000 for warrants to purchase Poorboy's stock at $5 a share eight years from now when the company has been through such difficult times and when that same market has concluded that the company's common stock is worth only $2.50?

b. Prepare the entry required to record the sale of the warrants. Explain the rationale for your entry and your numbers.

P13.12 Stock warrant redemptions. Five years after Poorboy's emotional reorganization (and its sale of warrants), things were finally looking up. Sales were growing, earnings were up very nicely, and cash flow was finally looking strong. The common stock was trading at about $10 a share. Management looked for a place to put the excess cash flow and decided to buy some of the company's stock back. An investment adviser suggested buying the warrants back because the same impact on the outstanding common stock could be had with a little less cash outflow. (The warrants were then trading at about $6.25.) Poorboy published an offer to buy and subsequently did purchase all of the outstanding warrants at $7.50 each.

Required:

a. Prepare the entry to record the purchase of the warrants, assuming they will be retired after acquisition.

b. Prepare the entries that would have been required had the company purchased $7,500,000 of common stock instead of the warrants and had all warrant holders tendered their warrants for conversion.

c. What do you think of the company's warrant buy back?

P13.13 Stock compensation programs. Footnotes 9 and 10 from the annual report to shareholders from the Snap-On Tools Corporation read as follows:

Incentive Stock Plans
Note 9:

Employees of the Company are entitled to participate in an employee stock purchase plan up to a maximum of 100 shares each year. The purchase price of the common stock is the lesser of the closing market quotation on the May 15 beginning, or the May 14 ending, of each plan year. The Board of Directors may terminate this plan at any time. For 1990, 1989 and 1988, shares issued under the employee stock purchase plan were 69,392, 80,487 and 90,448. At December 29, 1990, shares totaling 312,460 were reserved for issuance to employees under this plan, and the Company held contributions of approximately $1.8 million for the purchase of common stock which had a closing market quotation of $35.88 per share on May 15, 1990.

The Company has a stock option plan for directors, officers and key employees. Option shares unexercised, granted, exercised, surrendered and reserved for future grants during the three years ended December 29, 1990, were as follows:

Number of Shares for Fiscal Years

	1990	1989	1988
Beginning balance granted, but not exercised	**1,650,498**	960,098	1,252,792
Granted	**582,500**	864,850	—
Exercised	**(104,418)**	(160,270)	(286,894)
Surrendered	**(32,950)**	(14,180)	(5,800)
Ending balance granted, but not exercised	**2,095,630**	1,650,498	960,098
Shares reserved for future grants at year-end	**2,105,901**	2,655,451	1,506,121

On April 28, 1989, the Board of Directors reserved 2 million additional common shares for issuance under the 1986 Incentive Stock Program.

As of December 29, 1990, 243 persons held options for 704,822 shares at $20.56 which expire on January 10, 1996; 1,285 persons held options for 808,308 shares at $35.50 which expire on January 5, 1999; seven persons held options for 7,000 shares at $32.75 which expire on April 27, 2000; and 2,607 persons held options for 575,500 shares at $29.88 which expire on August 23, 2000. Since the option price equals the market value at the date granted, no amounts are charged to earnings upon their grant. As options are exercised, amounts received in excess of par value are credited to additional contributed capital.

Capital Stock
Note 10:

On October 26, 1990, the Board of Directors approved a Dealer Stock Purchase Plan for franchised dealers and reserved 200,000 shares of common stock for issuance under this plan. The date of the first offering under this plan is May 15, 1991, with an additional and separate offering on May 15, in each following year until the plan is terminated by the Company or all shares reserved under the plan have been purchased. The purchase price of the common stock is the lesser of the closing market price of the stock on the offering date of a plan year or the succeeding offering date.

On June 22, 1990, the Board of Directors approved the Dividend Reinvestment and Stock Purchase Plan and reserved 1 million shares of common stock for issuance under this plan. Under this plan, shareholders who elect to participate can invest all or a portion of their cash dividends and additional optional cash payments in shares of common stock of the Company based upon the market price of the stock on the dividend pay date or investment date in the case of additional optional cash payments.

On August 26, 1988, the Board of Directors authorized the Company to purchase up to 2 million shares of the Company's common stock through open market transactions. As of December 31, 1988, the Company had purchased and retired 1.1 million shares of common stock under this program at an average price of $35 per share. No additional shares were purchased during 1989 or 1990.

Required:

Comment on each of the following:

a. From the company's perspective, what is the purpose of each of these four stock plans?

b. How do the programs differ in terms of the impact on the participant and on the company?

c. What accounting is afforded each of the programs?

P13.14 Shareholders' equity on a per share basis. Hercules Incorporated presents selected financial data as the first page of its annual report to stockholders. You will note that it reports stockholders' equity per share as $41.35 as of December 31, 1990. In a later section of the report, the company presents the market prices of its stock for the past two years. That table reports that the stock closed at $31 5/8 on December 31, 1990.

	1990	1989	1988	1987	1986
For the year					
Net sales	$ 3,199.9	$ 3,091.7	$ 2,802.1	$ 2,693.0	$ 2,615.1
Profit (loss) from operations	190.1	(121.3)	129.7	176.9	185.4
Income (loss) before cumulative effect of					
changes in accounting principles	96.0	(96.4)	120.4	820.7	226.7
Net income (loss)	96.0	(81.3)	120.4	820.7	226.7
Dividends	105.0	103.6	92.9	98.5	93.8
Per share of common stock					
Earnings (loss) before cumulative effect					
of changes in accounting principles	2.04	(2.09)	2.55	14.74	4.02
Earnings (loss)	2.04	(1.76)	2.55	14.74	4.02
Dividends	2.24	2.24	2.00	1.84	1.72
Research and development	92.2	78.5	74.4	73.8	71.1
Depreciation	191.1	179.3	144.9	134.4	125.3
Capital expenditures	272.6	292.6	251.0	205.0	256.9
At year-end					
Working capital	692.0	615.6	949.2	1,299.0	660.1
Current ratio	1.8	1.7	2.8	3.6	2.6
Property, plant, and equipment—at cost	3,063.6	2,924.5	2,349.3	2,153.2	2,240.2
Total assets	3,699.6	3,653.2	3,325.3	3,492.1	2,914.3
Long-term debt	601.0	575.7	428.6	488.5	546.1
Stockholders' equity	1,942.0	1,897.2	2,044.5	2,189.9	1,703.2
per share	41.35	40.77	44.58	44.88	31.11
Common shares outstanding	47.0	46.5	45.9	48.8	54.8
Number of common stockholders	25,342	26,015	27,080	25,995	26,733
Number of employees	19,867	23,290	22,718	23,152	25,120

Required:

Explain why the stockholders' equity per share as reported in the selected financial data is not the same as the closing market price. What might cause the difference between the two numbers?

P13.15 Shareholder transactions. Value-Rite's 1989 annual report contained the following statement of consolidated changes in shareholder's investment:

| | Common Shares | | Capital Surplus | Retained Earnings |
	Number	Amount		
Balance 6/30/87	5,037,691	$1,679,230	$ 8,075,103	$50,591,554
(1) Employee stock options				
exercised	35,426	11,809	452,596	
(2) Conversion of 4.75%				
subordinated debentures . . .	84,418	28,139	1,916,861	
(3) Shares issued for stock				
split—Note G	2,571,251	857,084	(857,084)	
(4) Cash paid in lieu of fractional				
shares for stock split	(1,049)	(350)	(20,400)	
(5) Net income				15,386,046
(6) Cash dividends of $.75 1/3				
per share				(5,777,277)
Balance 6/30/88	7,727,737	2,575,912	9,567,076	60,200,373
(1) Employee stock options				
exercised	20,947	6,982	179,249	
(2) Conversion of 4.75%				
subordinated debentures . . .	237,670	79,224	3,762,776	
(5) Net income				18,549,662
(6) Cash dividends of $.92 per				
share				(7,341,486)
Balance 6/30/89	7,986,354	$2,662,118	$13,509,101	$71,408,349

Note G contained the following statement:

> On April 27, 1987, the board of directors declared a three-for-two stock split on the company's common shares, which was effected in form of a 50% stock dividend. The par value of the shares was transferred from capital surplus to the common shares account.

Required:

a. Is Value-Rite's common stock no par or par? Explain. If par, at what value?

b. Explain to a stockholder owning 100 shares of stock just what happened in transaction 3 (described in Note G) and how the stockholder will benefit from that transaction.

c. In your own words, explain the other transactions enumerated above, explaining the probable reason for the event and the probable source of the amounts used.

P13.16 Shareholders' transactions with treasury stock. Footnote 5 from the 1989 annual report of the H. J. Heinz Company follows:

(in thousands)	Cumulative Preferred Stock — Third, $1.70 First Series $10 par — Amount	Common Stock — Issued — Amount	Common Stock — Issued — Shares	Common Stock — In Treasury — Amount	Common Stock — In Treasury — Shares	Additional Capital — Amount
Balance April 30, 1986	$1,141	$ 71,850	143,700	$227,374	10,283	$ 85,882
Reacquired	—	—	—	236,165	5,471	—
Conversion of preferred into common stock	(171)	—	—	(1,295)	(77)	(1,124)
Stock options exercised	—	—	—	(10,430)	(619)	4,763
Reduction in par value of common stock	—	(35,925)	—	—	—	35,925
Other, net	—	—	—	166	3	—
Balance April 29, 1987	$ 970	$ 35,925	143,700	$451,980	15,061	$125,446
Reacquired	—	—	—	123,519	2,703	—
Conversion of preferred into common stock	(128)	—	—	(972)	(58)	(843)
Stock options exercised	—	—	—	(27,598)	(1,638)	11,013
Other, net	—	—	—	809	14	269
Balance April 27, 1988	$ 842	$ 35,925	143,700	$547,738	16,082	$135,885
Reacquired	—	—	—	97,508	2,056	—
Conversion of preferred into common stock	(85)	—	—	(693)	(38)	(608)
Conversion of subordinated debentures	—	—	—	(30,906)	(1,150)	3,784
Stock options exercised	—	—	—	(35,379)	(1,756)	6.293
Other, net	—	—	—	1,390	25	236
Balance May 3, 1989	$ 757	$ 35,925	143,700	$579,658	15,219	$145,590
Authorized Shares—May 3, 1989	76	—	600,000	—	—	—

Capital Stock: The preferred stock outstanding is convertible at a rate of one share of preferred stock into 4.5 shares of common stock. The company can redeem the stock at $25.50 per share.

In September 1986, the shareholders approved an increase to the authorized common stock of the company from 300,000,000 shares to 600,000,000 shares and to change the par value of the common stock from 50 cents per share to 25 cents per share.

On May 3, 1989, there were authorized, but unissued, 2,200,000 shares of third cumulative preferred stock for which the series had not been designated.

Required:

For each of the five transactions highlighted above,

a. Describe in your own words the underlying event, explaining in particular (i) the factor(s) that triggered the event and (ii) the probable source of the numbers used.

b. Prepare the probable entry(ies) that were required.

P13.17 Stock for debt exchange. In 1989, RJR Nabisco, Inc., was taken private by Kohlberg Kravis Roberts & Co. in a leveraged buyout. As part of the buy-out, RJR Nabisco issued large amounts of high-yield "junk bonds." For example, one part of the leveraged buyout involved the issuance of $2.86 billion of 17 percent bonds due in 2007.

Beginning in late 1990, KKR & Co. began efforts to reduce the level of debt carried on the books of RJR Nabisco. One such proposal involved the issuance of 82.8 million shares of RJR stock and $350 million of cash in exchange for $753 million (face value) of the 17 percent bonds.

Assume that the RJR Nabisco stock has a par value of $1; the stock, being privately held, has no readily determined market value; and the bonds are trading at their face value.

Required:

a. Why would the company make that exchange at this time?

b. What entry would the company make at the time of the exchange?

c. What entry would be made if the bonds were trading at $830 rather than $1,000 face value?

P13.18 Paying stock dividends. On November 21, 1963, the board of directors of Eastman Kodak Company declared a stock dividend of one share of common stock for each 20 shares outstanding, payable February 10, 1964, to holders of shares of common stock of record on January 3, 1964. In a message to stockholders, the company explained:

> The purpose of this stock dividend is to place in the hands of each shareholder tangible evidence of his share in the portion of the earnings of the Company which have been retained for use in the business and which are being capitalized by the stock dividend. . . . The receipt by you of this stock dividend does not increase your proportionate equity in the Company. However, a disposal of such dividend will reduce your equity in the Company by $4.7619. . . .
>   . . . $106 per share . . . is an approximation of the market value of the Company's Common Stock prior to the stock dividend declaration, [but] after taking into consideration the dilution resulting from the 5% stock dividend.

The par value per share of the company's common stock was $10, and 38,382,246 shares were outstanding prior to the declaration of the stock dividend. The company's retained earnings at September 8, 1963 (the end of its third quarter), was $397,727,028.

Required:

a. What entry should the company make for the stock dividend? When?

b. What was the approximate market value of the common stock prior to the declaration of the stock dividend?

P13.19 Convertible preferred stock. On August 16, 1990, *The Wall Street Journal* carried an advertisement concerning Baker Hughes. The following is from that advertisement: "Baker Hughes Incorporated has called for redemption of all its $3.50 Convertible Preferred Stock."

According to the advertisement, Baker Hughes had decided to exercise the redemption feature on its outstanding preferred stock and to redeem the stock at a price of $52.45 per share plus accrued dividends of $.16, for a total of $52.61, on August 31, 1990. The preferred stock also carried a conversion feature that would permit the owner to convert the preferred into 1.9608 shares of common stock (par value of $1). The market price of the common stock on August 13, 1990, was $32.625 per share. The advertisement emphasized that the conversion feature of the preferred stock expired on August 27, 1990.

Required:

a. Assume that Baker Hughes has 1 million shares of preferred stock outstanding, and that its par value is $5. How would the company account for (i) the redemption of all shares and (ii) the conversion of all shares.

b. If you held 100 shares of Baker Hughes preferred stock, which alternative (conversion or redemption) would you choose, and why?

c. If you were the CEO of Baker Hughes, which alternative would you prefer, and why?

P13.20 Translation of foreign financial statements. Graham International, Inc., is a subsidiary of a U.S.–based corporation, The Graham Group. Graham International is headquartered in Mexico City, Mexico, although it represents the parent company worldwide.

Presented below are Graham International's income statement for 1990, expressed in pesos, and its balance sheets as of December 31, 1989, and December 31, 1990, also expressed in pesos. The exchange rate between the Mexican peso and the U.S. dollar was as follows:

12/31/89	$.0004 (1 peso = $.0004 U.S.)
12/31/90	$.00036 (1 peso = $.00036 U.S.)
1990 average	$.00038

Graham International had been in existence since 1987 when it was capitalized with an investment of 3,000,000 pesos. At that time, the exchange rate was 1,800 pesos to the U.S. dollar. Since then, the company has earned (after taxes and dividends) 15,000,000 pesos, with a translation value of $7,500 U.S.

Required:

a. Prepare the translated (in U.S. dollar equivalents) financial statements of Graham International, Inc., at December 31, 1990.

b. Determine the balance (if any) required in the Translation adjustment account for the equity sector of The Graham Group's 1990 balance sheet.

GRAHAM INTERNATIONAL, INC.
Statement of Income
For the Year Ended December 31, 1990
(in thousands of pesos)

Sales	82,000
Less: Costs and expenses	
Costs of sales	42,000
Depreciation	4,050
Selling, general, and administrative expenses	7,250
Interest	2,500
	55,800
Net income before taxes	26,200
Less: Income taxes	13,300
Net income	12,900
Dividends paid to parent (12/31/90)	1,500

GRAHAM INTERNATIONAL, INC.
Balance Sheet
As of December 31
(in thousands of pesos)

	1989	1990
Assets:		
Cash	2,000	3,000
Accounts receivable	6,000	7,400
Inventory	7,000	10,000
Total current assets	15,000	20,400
Plant and equipment	39,000	42,000
Less: Accumulated depreciation	(4,950)	(9,000)
Net plant and equipment	34,050	33,000
Total assets	49,050	53,400
Equities:		
Liabilities		
Accounts payable	6,050	4,000
Long-term debt	25,000	20,000
Total	31,050	24,000
Owners' equity:		
Capital stock	3,000	3,000
Retained earnings	15,000	26,400
Total	18,000	29,400
Total equities	49,050	53,400

CASES

C13.1 Two Classes of Stock: World Wide, Inc. World Wide, Inc., had almost completed its acquisition program. It had acquired companies in the raw material segment of its industry, in the fabrication segment, and most recently in the distribution segment. Management bristled at the suggestion that the company was becoming a conglomerate; they preferred to think of it as a fully integrated company. Still, the company's stock price had languished, and some critics on Wall Street had begun to question its strategy. There was talk that the company would be worth more in parts than it was in total.

Lindsey Toma, the chief financial officer, was very concerned about activity in the company's stock. It appeared that someone was accumulating a block of stock, perhaps with the intention of instituting a raid. Toma suggested at a meeting of the World Wide Board that it adopt some defensive strategies. She said, "We have worked very hard to build this company, and we are close to realizing the potential of our plans. If we fail to act defensively now, some raider will be able to come in and reap the benefits of our work before the stock price rewards our long-time stockholders for their patience."

The company's attorney urged the board to look into the possibility of creating a two-class stock arrangement. He said he knew of a number of two-class situations, and he promised to find some good examples. Later that day, he sent all of the members of the board copies of pertinent portions of the 1989 annual report for Dow Jones & Company and a *Business Week* article that reported on a challenge to two-class stock plans.

The attorney's letter transmitting these two documents made two other points for perspective:

- The SEC had adapted some rules regarding two-stock plans, but those rules address only the most seriously disenfranchising plans. He said he was confident that his law firm could come up with a plan much like the Dow Jones Plan that would clear the SEC rule.
- The Dow Jones class B stock was originally issued in 1986 as a 50 percent stock dividend. He urged the board to authorize him to begin drafting such a plan for World Wide.

You have been a member of the board of World Wide for the last five years, and you have agreed with the acquisition program because you believe that the economies available to an integrated company will pay real benefits. However, you also have been concerned that the acquisitions have not come together as well as had been predicted, and you have become a little impatient with management's promises that the payoff is just around the corner.

Your academic training in economics has been a strong influence in your business life. You have been a passionate advocate for free market forces and have resisted the efforts of World Wide management to claim tariff protection from offshore competition.

Required:

Study the material in the exhibits and outline the advantages and disadvantages of adopting a two-class stock plan for World Wide. How will you vote if such a plan is eventually recommended to the Board by the attorney?

DOW JONES & CO.
1989 Annual Report Excerpts

Stockholders' Equity:		
Common stock, par value $1 per share; authorized 135,000,000 shares; issued 78,626,190 shares in 1989 and 77,961,638 shares in 1988	**78,626**	77,962
Class B common stock, convertible, par value $1 per share; authorized 25,000,000 shares; issued 23,554,831 shares in 1989 and 24,219,383 shares in 1988	**23,555**	24,219
	102,181	102,181
Additional paid-in capital	**150,031**	149,557
Retained earnings	**1,185,426**	940,989
	1,437,638	1,192,727
Less: Treasury stock at cost, 1,355,892 shares in 1989 and 1,345,560 shares in 1988	**32,437**	32,152
Total stockholders' equity	**1,405,201**	1,160,575
Total liabilities and stockholders' equity	**$2,688,336**	$2,111,781

NOTE 8. CAPITAL STOCK

The common stock and class B common stock have the same dividend and liquidation rights. The class B common stock has ten votes per share, free convertibility into common stock on a one-for-one basis and can be transferred in class B form only to members of a stockholder's family and certain others affiliated with a stockholder.

The SEC's Tough Call on
One Share, One Vote

From Business Week, December 29, 1987

Call it "junk stock." That's the label Roland M. Machold, the State of New Jersey's portfolio manager, has pinned on the rash of common stock being issued with limited voting rights—or none at all. "In the absence of a vote, you have to look at what a security is. It's nothing," says Machold, who also is co-chairman of the Council of Institutional Investors, a group of more than 40 public and private pension funds. With no leverage on companies to maintain returns, "It's worse than junk bonds," he adds.

Such objections were the focus of Securities & Exchange Commission hearings on Dec. 16-17 that examined the New York Stock Exchange's proposal to drop its one-share, one-vote rule in favor of one permitting multiple classes of common stock. But the argument transcends the issue of stock value and attendant voting rights. It's the focus of a controversy about who should control Corporate America.

MEDIA BLITZ. The debate comes as both large and small shareholders—not just gadflies— are showing greater interest in how companies operate, forcing disinvestment in South Africa or demanding compliance with environmental laws. "The old Wall Street rule— vote with your feet—is being replaced with a more activist role. I think that shareholders are just starting to recognize their responsibility to vote," notes Lawrence S. Speidell, trustee and portfolio manager for Batterymarch Financial Management in Boston, which always votes against multiclass stock proposals.

The SEC faces a tough decision. It is under pressure from a wide range of interests to turn thumbs down on the Big Board proposal. The opposition ranges from the Council of Institutional investors to Senator Howard Metzenbaum (D-Ohio) to ordinary shareholders.

Takeover artist T. Boone Pickens Jr. has mounted a media and mailing campaign against the proposal and formed a group called the United Shareholders' Assn. "You are witnessing the ultimate in takeovers," he says. He argues that abandoning one share, one vote lets management take over companies internally by concentrating voting power in the hands of friendly stockholders.

Even NYSE Chairman John J. Phelan Jr. appears uneasy about the proposal. While he thinks the Big

Board shouldn't dictate recapitalization decisions, he says: "I like my right to vote, whether I exercise it or not." But exchange officials feel they have little choice. Some of the best-known names on the Big Board, including General Motors Corp. and Dow Jones & Co., have adopted multiple classes of common stock and would have to be delisted if the rules aren't changed.

The NYSE has put a temporary hold on delisting for violations of the rule, and more companies may issue nonvoting stock for a variety of reasons. Moreover, without a rule change, NYSE companies could flee to the American Stock Exchange or the over-the-counter market, which allow dual classes.

American Stock Exchange chairman Arthur Levitt Jr. told commissioners he shares some of Phelan's concerns, even though he wants further easing of AMEX rules on dual-class listings. "Public shareholder voting is a key element of corporate accountability," he said as he pleaded for some shareholder safety standard. Commissioner Joseph A. Grundfest, remarking on the exchanges' dilemma, joked: "You're asking us to stop you before you kill again."

Despite the pervasive qualms, an unpublished SEC staff study of 65 cases of dual-class common stock could buttress agency approval of the rule change. "There is no evidence that the dual-class recapitalizations we have seen have been against shareholder interests," says Gregg A. Jarrell, the SEC's chief economist and co-author of the study.

The SEC study suggests that dual classes of stocks haven't been used often by widely held public companies. In 54 of the 65 companies, "insider holdings," usually with a family, accounted for an average of 50% of the outstanding stock before the recapitalization plan was announced. Share prices weren't hurt by the change, according to the study, though Jarrell wouldn't predict future price behavior. And proponents of the rule change argue that family-run companies should be able to use equity financing while retaining corporate control.

WHICH WAY? The commissioners' cautious questioning at the hearing makes it hard to tell which way they will go, though Chairman John S. R. Shad has in the past backed the idea of one share, one vote. An NYSE requirement that multiple listings be approved by a majority of current holders and independent directors may satisfy the commissioners. Or, worried that Congress may override an attempt to end the NYSE tradition, the SEC could revive efforts to encourage the exchanges to devise uniform voting standards. The commission may also O.K. the NYSE proposal on the ground that states have traditionally handled internal corporate-governance issues.

The commissioners' decision, which could come as early as March, will be a wrenching one—with broad consequences. Dual-class stock is perhaps the most violent of developments to date regarding shareholders' rights," says Robert A. G. Monks, president of Institutional Shareholder Services Inc., a Washington-based consulting group. "Once the shareholders have been disenfranchised by a company, there's no way to reverse it."

By Vicky Cahan, with Patricia Kranz, in Washington and Anthony Bianco in New York

---

C13.2 Performance-Oriented Stock: General Motors In 1984 and 1985, General Motors acquired Electronic Data Systems (EDS) and Hughes Aircraft Company (Hughes), giving cash and newly created shares of stock, GM-E and GM-H, respectively. The notes in the 1990 GM financial statements describe those transactions as follows:

Acquisitions and Intangible Assets

Effective December 31, 1985, the Corporation acquired Hughes Aircraft Company (Hughes) and its subsidiaries for $2.7 billion in cash and cash equivalents and 100 million shares of General Motors Class H common stock having an estimated total value of $2,561.9 million and which carried certain guarantees.

The acquisition of Hughes was accounted for as a purchase. The purchase price exceeded the net book value of Hughes by $4,244.7 million, which was assigned as follows: $500.0 million to patents and related technology, $125.0 million to the future economic benefits to the Corporation of the Hughes Long-Term Incentive Plan (LTIP), and $3,619.7 million to other intangible assets, including goodwill. The amounts assigned to the various intangible asset categories are being amortized on a straight-line basis: patents and related technology over 15 years, the future economic benefits of the Hughes LTIP over five years, and other intangible assets over 40 years. Amortization is applied directly to the asset accounts.

For the purpose of determining earnings per share and amounts available for dividends on common stocks, the amortization of intangible assets arising from the acquisition of Hughes is charged against earnings attributable to $1-2/3 par value common stock. The effect on the 1990, 1989, and 1988 earnings attributable to $1-2/3 par value common stock was a net credit (charge) of

$24.9 million, $17.8 million, and ($31.6) million, respectively, consisting of the amortization of the intangible assets arising from the acquisition, the profit on intercompany transactions, and the earnings of GMHE attributable to $1-2/3 par value common stock.

On October 18, 1984, the Corporation acquired Electronic Data Systems Corporation (EDS) and its subsidiaries for $2,501.9 million. The acquisition was consummated through an offer to exchange EDS common stock for either (a) $44 in cash or (b) $35.20 in cash plus two-tenths of a share of Class E common stock plus a nontransferable contingent promissory note issued by GM. This note is payable seven years after closing in an amount equal to .2 times the excess of $31.25 over the market price of the Class E common stock at the maturity date of the note. Contingent notes were issued in denominations termed "Note Factors," each of which represents five contingent notes. Holders were allowed to tender their notes for prepayment at discounted amounts beginning in October 1989. There are currently approximately 21.0 million contingent notes issued and outstanding. The maximum possible liability to the Corporation for such notes is approximately $654.7 million.

If the market price of Class E common stock at the maturity date of the notes were to equal the market price at December 31, 1990, $38.625 a share, no additional consideration for contingent notes outstanding at December 31, 1990 would be required.

The acquisition of EDS was accounted for as a purchase. The purchase price in excess of the net book value of EDS, $2,179.5 million, was assigned principally to existing customer contracts, $1,069.9 million, computer software programs developed by EDS, $646.2 million, and other intangible assets, including goodwill, $290.2 million. The cost assigned to these assets is being amortized on a straight-line basis over five years for computer software programs (fully amortized in 1989), about seven years for customer contracts, 10 years for goodwill, and varying periods for the remainder. Amortization is applied directly to the asset accounts.

For the purpose of determining earnings per share and amounts available for dividends on common stocks, the amortization of these assets is charged against earnings attributable to $1-2/3 par value common stock. The effect on the 1990, 1989, and 1988 earnings attributable to $1-2/3 par value common stock was a net charge of $111.3 million, $225.1 million, and $286.1 million, respectively, consisting of the amortization of the intangible and other assets arising from the acquisition less related income tax effects, the profit on intercompany transactions, and the earnings of EDS attributable to $1-2/3 par value common stock.

Both of those companies have been quite successful. GM management described the results of EDS and Hughes in the management discussion and analysis section of its 1990 annual report as follows:

Electronic Data Systems Corporation

Reflecting the continued strong growth of its non-GM business, Electronic Data Systems Corporation (EDS) achieved another record performance in 1990. Separate consolidated net income of EDS rose 14.2% to $496.9 million. Earnings per share attributable to Class E common stock were $2.08, up from $1.81 in 1989 and $1.57 in 1988, and are based on the Available Separate Consolidated Net Income of EDS (described in Note 10 to the Financial Statements).

EDS continues as the world leader in systems integration and communications services. Sales to sources outside GM and its affiliates rose 16.9% in 1990 to $2,787.5 million, reflecting EDS's continued success in obtaining new business as well as growth through acquisitions. Additionally, EDS continued to assist GM in a variety of automation projects being implemented in the Corporation's factories and offices.

EDS financial statements do not include the amortization of the $2,179.5 million initial cost to GM of EDS customer contracts, computer software programs, and other intangible assets, including goodwill, arising from the acquisition of EDS by GM in 1984. This cost, plus the $343.2 million cost of contingent notes purchased in 1986, less certain income tax benefits, was assigned principally to intangible assets, including goodwill, and is being amortized by GM over the estimated useful lives of the assets acquired. Such amortization was $205.7 million in 1990, $348.9 million in 1989, and $386.6 million in 1988.

For the purpose of determining earnings per share and amounts available for dividends on common stocks, such amortization is charged against earnings attributable to GM's $1-2/3 par value common stock. The effect of EDS operations on the earnings attributable to $1-2/3 par value common stock was a net charge of $111.3 million in 1990, $225.1 million in 1989, and $286.1 million in 1988, consisting of the previously described amortization less related income tax benefits, profit on intercompany transactions, and the earnings of EDS attributable to $1-2/3 par value common stock. The net charge does not reflect any estimate of the savings realized by GM from the installation of new computer systems within GM operations.

Summary Financial Data—EDS

(Dollars in millions except per share amounts)	Years Ended December 31,		
	1990	**1989**	**1988**
Revenues			
Systems and other contracts			
GM and affiliates	$3,234.2	$2,988.9	$2,837.0
Outside customers	2,787.5	2,384.6	1,907.6
Interest and other income	87.1	93.3	99.5
Total revenues	6,108.8	5,466.8	4,844.1
Costs and expenses	5,320.1	4,786.5	4,254.7
Income taxes	291.8	245.0	205.3
Separate consolidated net income	$ 496.9	$ 435.3	$ 384.1
Available separate consolidated net income*	$ 194.4	$ 171.0	$ 160.3
Average number of shares of Class E common stock outstanding (in millions)	93.5	94.5	101.8
Earnings attributable to Class E common stock on a per share basis	$ 2.08	$ 1.81	$ 1.57
Cash dividends per share of Class E common stock	$ 0.56	$ 0.48	$ 0.34

*Separate consolidated net income of EDS multiplied by a fraction, the numerator of which is the weighted average number of shares of Class E common stock outstanding during the period and the denominator of which is currently 239.3 million shares. The denominators during 1989 and 1988 were 238.7 million and 243.8 million shares, respectively. Available Separate Consolidated Net Income is determined quarterly.

GM Hughes Electronics Corporation

Earnings of GM Hughes Electronics Corporation (GMHE) declined 7.1% to $726.0 million, while revenues increased 3.2% to a record $11,723.1 million. Earnings per share attributable to Class H common stock were $1.82 in 1990, compared with $1.94 in 1989 and $2.01 in 1988, and are based on the Available Separate Consolidated Net Income of GMHE (described in Note 10 to the Financial Statements).

Earnings were down slightly as the result of reduced defense spending, lower motor vehicle production volumes, and a higher effective tax rate which were only partially offset by ongoing cost reduction efforts and increased electronic content in GM vehicles.

GMHE is the world leader in automotive and defense electronics and in commercial communications satellites. GMHE also provides direct support to GM through projects to automate the Corporation's factories and by supplying components and technologies for GM vehicles.

Both of GMHE's principal subsidiaries—Hughes Aircraft Company and Delco Electronics Corporation—achieved revenue increases in 1990. This improvement reflected growth in the commercial market for business communications networks and increasing demand for electronic components and systems in cars and trucks. In addition, these GMHE subsidiaries continued to pursue new business opportunities by entering into joint ventures and teaming arrangements with other companies. Included was the formation of a subsidiary, H E Microwave Corporation, to manufacture high technology electronics for both automotive and military applications.

For the purpose of determining earnings per share and amounts available for dividends on common stocks, the amortization of intangible assets arising from the acquisition of Hughes in 1985 is charged against earnings attributable to GM's $1-2/3 par value common stock. The effect of GMHE operations on the 1990, 1989, and 1988 earnings attributable to $1-2/3 par value common stock was a net credit (charge) of $24.9 million, $17.8 million, and ($31.6) million, respectively, consisting of amortization of the intangible assets, profit on intercompany transactions, and the earnings of GMHE attributable to $1-2/3 par value common stock. The net credit (charge) does not reflect any estimate of the savings and improvements in product development or plant operation resulting from the application of GMHE technology to GM's operations.

Summary Financial Data—GMHE

(Dollars in millions except per share amounts)	Years Ended December 31,		
	1990	1989	1988
Revenues			
Net sales			
Outside customers	$ 8,091.3	$ 7,647.7	$ 7,518.2
GM and affiliates	3,534.5	3,521.8	3,482.8
Other income—net	97.3	189.5	242.6
Total revenues	11,723.1	11,359.0	11,243.6
Costs and expenses	10,684.7	10,371.3	10,259.7
Income taxes	461.2	355.3	349.3
Income before cumulative effect of accounting change	577.2	632.4	634.6
Cumulative effect of accounting change	—	—	18.7*
Separate consolidated net income	577.2	632.4	653.3
Available separate consolidated net income			
Adjustments to exclude the effect of purchase accounting**	148.8	148.8	148.8
Earnings of GMHE, excluding purchase accounting adjustments	$ 726.0	$ 781.2	$ 802.1
Available separate consolidated net income*	$ 160.0	$ 188.1	$ 256.9
Average number of shares of Class H common stock outstanding (in millions)	88.1	95.7	127.9
Earnings attributable to class H common stock on a per share basis			
Before cumulative effect of accounting change	$1.82	$1.94	$1.96
Cumulative effect of accounting change	—	—	0.05
Net earnings attributable to Class H common stock	$1.82	$1.94	$2.01
Cash dividends per share of Class H common stock	$0.72	$0.72	$0.44

*Effective January 1, 1988, accounting procedures at Delco Electronics were changed to include in inventory certain manufacturing overhead costs previously charged directly to expense.

**Amortization of intangible assets arising from the acquisition of Hughes Aircraft Company.

***Earnings of GMHE, excluding purchase accounting adjustments, multiplied by a fraction, the numerator of which is the weighted average number of shares of Class H common stock outstanding during the period and the denominator of which is currently 399.7 million shares. The denominator during 1989 and 1988 was 400.0 million shares. Available Separate Consolidated Net Income is determined quarterly.

Footnote 10 from the GM 1990 annual report explains how the company computes earnings per share for its three classes of common stock:

Note 10: Earnings (Loss) per Share Attributable to and Dividends on Common Stocks

Earnings (Loss) per share attributable to common stocks have been determined based on the relative amounts available for the payment of dividends to holders of $1-2/3 par value, Class E, and Class H common stocks.

Prior to 1990, the effect on earnings per share of $1-2/3 par value common stock resulting from the assumed exercise of outstanding options, the delivery of stock awards, the assumed conversion of the preference shares discussed in Note 17, and the assumed exercise of the put options discussed in Note 1 was not material.

However, for 1990, the loss per share attributable to $1-2/3 par value common stock has been computed by dividing such loss by the average number of common and equivalent shares outstanding. The operations of the EDS and GMHE Incentive Plans and the assumed exercise of stock options do not have a material dilutive effect on earnings per share of Class E or Class H common stocks, respectively, at this time.

Dividends on the $1-2/3 par value common stock are declared out of the earnings of GM and its subsidiaries, excluding the Available Separate Consolidated Net Income of EDS and GMHE.

Dividends on the Class E and Class H common stocks are declared out of the Available Separate Consolidated Net Income of EDS and GMHE, respectively, earned since the acquisition by GM. The Available Separate Consolidated Net Income of EDS and GMHE is determined quarterly and is equal to the separate consolidated net income of EDS and GMHE, respectively, excluding the effects of purchase accounting adjustments arising at the time of acquisition, multiplied by a fraction, the numerator of which is the weighted average number of shares of Class E or Class H common stock outstanding during the period and the denominator of which is currently 239.3 million shares for Class E and 399.7 million shares for Class H. The denominators during 1989 and 1988 were 238.7 million and 243.8 million shares, respectively, for Class E and 400.0 million shares for Class H.

The denominators used in determining the Available Separate Consolidated Net Income of EDS and GMHE are adjusted as deemed appropriate by the Board of Directors to reflect subdivisions or combinations of the Class E and Class H common stocks and to reflect certain transfers of capital to or from EDS and GMHE. In this regard, the Board has generally caused the denominators to decrease as shares are purchased by EDS or GMHE, and to increase as such shares are used at EDS or GMHE expense for EDS or GMHE employee benefit plans or acquisitions.

Dividends may be paid on common stocks only when, as, and if declared by the Board of Directors in its sole discretion. The Board's policy with respect to $1-2/3 par value common stock is to distribute dividends based on the outlook and the indicated capital needs of the business. At the February 4, 1991 meeting of the Board, the quarterly dividend on the $1-2/3 par value common stock was reduced from $0.75 per share to $0.40 per share. This action was taken as a part of a comprehensive cost-cutting and cash-conservation program to strengthen GM's competitive position. The current policy of the Board with respect to the Class E and Class H common stocks is to pay cash dividends approximately equal to 30% and 35% of the Available Separate Consolidated Net Income of EDS and GMHE, respectively, for the prior year. At the February 4, 1991 Board meeting, the dividend on the Class E common stock was increased by 14% to a quarterly rate of $0.16 per share from a rate of $0.14 per share in 1990. The quarterly dividend on Class H common stock was continued at $0.18 per share.

GM's balance sheet and income statement from its 1990 annual report to stockholders are presented below. Read the above information and study the two GM financial statements.

Required:

a. How do the GM shareholders benefit from the results of EDS and Hughes? How do the holders of GM-E and GM-H shares benefit from the results of those two companies?

b. Why might GM have used these special shares in its acquisition program? What advantages did GM gain from the use of those special shares?

c. What operations and accounting problems might those shares have created for General Motors management? Outline your ideas for management of those problems.

GENERAL MOTORS
Statement of Consolidated Income

	Years Ended December 31,		
(Dollars in millions except per share amounts)	1990	1989	1988
Net sales and revenues (Note 1)			
Manufactured products	$107,477.0	$109,610.3	$107,815.2
Financial services	11,756.3	11,216.9	10,664.9
Computer systems services	2,787.5	2,384.6	1,907.6
Other income (Note 2)	2,684.3	3,720.1	3,253.9
Total net sales and revenues	124,705.1	126,931.9	123,641.6
Costs and expenses			
Cost of sales and other operating charges, exclusive of items listed below	96,155.7	93,817.9	92,506.0
Selling, general, and administrative expenses	10,030.9	9,447.9	8,735.8
Interest expense (Note 15)	8,771.7	8,757.2	7,232.9
Depreciation of real estate, plants, and equipment (Note 1)	5,104.1	5,157.8	5,047.0
Amortization of special tools (Note 1)	1,805.8	1,441.8	1,432.1
Amortization of intangible assets (Note 1)	451.7	568.6	601.9
Other deductions (Note 2)	1,288.3	1,342.4	1,351.0
Special provision for scheduled plant closings and other restructurings (Note 7)	3,314.0	—	—
Total costs and expenses	126,922.2	120,533.6	116,906.7
Income (loss) before income taxes	(2,217.1)	6,398.3	6,734.9
United States, foreign, and other income taxes (credit) (Note 9)	(231.4)	2,174.0	2,102.8
Income (loss) before cumulative effect of accounting change	(1,985.7)	4,224.3	4,632.1
Cumulative effect of accounting change (Note 1)	—	—	224.2
Net income (loss)	(1,985.7)	4,224.3	4,856.3
Dividends and accumulation of redemption value on preferred and preference stocks (Note 17)	38.2	34.2	26.0
Earnings (loss) on common stocks	($ 2,023.9)	$ 4,190.1	$ 4,830.3
Earnings (loss) attributable to common stocks			
$1-2/3 par value before cumulative effect of accounting change	($ 2,378.3)	$ 3,831.0	$ 4,195.0
Cumulative effect of accounting change	—	—	218.1
Net earnings (loss) attributable to $1-2/3 par value	($ 2,378.3)	$ 3,831.0	$ 4,413.1
Class E	$ 194.4	$ 171.0	$ 160.3
Class H before cumulative effect of accounting change	$ 160.0	$ 188.1	$ 250.8
Cumulative effect of accounting change	—	—	6.1
Net earnings attributable to Class H	$ 160.0	$ 188.1	$ 256.9
Average number of shares of common stocks outstanding (in millions)			
$1-2/3 par value	601.5	604.3	615.7
Class E	93.5	94.5	101.8
Class H	88.1	95.7	127.9
Earnings (Loss) Per Share Attributable to Common Stocks (Note 10)			
$1-2/3 par value before cumulative effect of accounting change	($4.09)	$6.33	$6.82
Cumulative effect of accounting change	—	—	0.35
Net earnings (loss) attributable to $1-2/3 par value	($4.09)	$6.33	$7.17
Class E	$2.08	$1.81	$1.57
Class H before cumulative effect of accounting change	$1.82	$1.94	$1.96
Cumulative effect of accounting change	—	—	0.05
Net earnings attributable to Class H	$1.82	$1.94	$2.01

Certain amounts for 1989 and 1988 have been reclassified to conform with 1990 classifications.

Reference should be made to the notes to financial statements.

General Motors
Consolidated Balance Sheet

	December 31,	
(Dollars in millions except per share amounts) Assets	1990	1989
Cash and cash equivalents	$ 3,688.5	$ 5,625.4
Other marketable securities	4,132.9	4,587.9
Total cash and marketable securities (Note 11)	7,821.4	10,213.3
Finance receivables—net (Note 12)	90,116.2	92,354.6
Accounts and notes receivable (less allowances)	5,731.3	5,447.4
Inventories (less allowances) (Note 1)	9,331.3	7,991.7
Contracts in process (less advances and progress payments of $2,353.1 and $2,630.7) (Note 1)	2,348.8	2,073.3
Net equipment on operating leases (less accumulated depreciation of $2,692.6 and $3,065.9)	5,882.0	5,131.1
Prepaid expenses and deferred charges	4,751.6	3,914.7
Other investments and miscellaneous assets (less allowances)	7,252.5	5,050.2
Property (Note 1)		
Real estate, plants, and equipment—at cost (Note 14)	67,219.4	63,390.7
Less accumulated depreciation (Note 14)	38,280.8	34,849.7
Net real estate, plants, and equipment	28,938.6	28,541.0
Special tools—at cost (less amortization)	7,206.4	5,453.5
Total property	36,145.0	33,994.5
Intangible assets—at cost (less amortization) (Notes 1 and 6)	10,856.4	7,126.3
Total assets	$180,236.5	$173,297.1

Liabilities and Stockholders' Equity

	1990	1989
Liabilities		
Accounts payable (principally trade)	$ 8,824.4	$ 7,707.8
Notes and loans payable (Note 15)	95,633.5	93,424.8
United States, foreign, and other income taxes (Note 9)	3,959.6	5,671.4
Other liabilities (Note 16)	38,255.2	28,456.7
Deferred credits (including investment tax credits—$723.0 and $915.4)	1,410.1	1,403.9
Total liabilities	148,082.8	136,664.6
Stocks subject to repurchase (Notes 1 and 17)	2,106.3	1,650.0
Stockholders' Equity (Notes 3, 4, 5, and 17)		
Preferred stocks ($5.00 series, $153.0; $3.75 series, $81.4)	234.4	234.4
Preference stocks (E $0.10 series, $1.0; H $0.10 series, $1.0 in 1989)	1.0	2.0
Common stocks		
$1-2/3 par value (issued, 605,592,356 and 605,683,572 shares)	1,009.3	1,009.5
Class E (issued, 100,220,967 and 48,830,764 shares)	10.0	4.9
Class H (issued, 34,450,398 and 35,162,664 shares)	3.5	3.5
Capital surplus (principally additional paid-in capital)	2,208.2	2,614.0
Net income retained for use in the business	27,148.6	31.230.7
Subtotal	30,615.0	35,099.0
Minimum pension liability adjustment (Note 6)	(1,004.7)	—
Accumulated foreign currency translation and other adjustments	437.1	(116.5)
Total stockholders' equity	30,047.4	34,982.5
Total liabilities and stockholders' equity	$180,236.5	$173,297.1

Reference should be made to the notes to financial statements.

C13.3 Trading Stock with Another Corporation: Colorado Mining Corporation

Colorado Mining Corporation owned the mineral rights to a silver claim in the northeast corner of the state. The mine itself had been inactive for some time, although the rights had been bought and sold several times in the last five years. CMC had purchased the rights most recently from a group of Denver attorneys, paying $50,000 in cash and giving two notes totaling $250,000. One note, for $100,000, bore interest at 10 percent and was due in 12 months; the other, for $150,000, carried a 5 percent interest rate and was due in five years.

Immediately on taking possession of the claim, CMC regraded the access roads and cleared the accumulated debris from the property. It hired a maintenance worker who began to pump water from the mine so that it could be worked. He brought out a few samples and had them processed and evaluated by an independent laboratory; the results showed that the samples contained good quality ore, although in small traces. The company also sent out a photographic team who took pictures of the activity, and the president managed to get a Denver newspaper to run a story on CMC's plans for reactivating the mine. The company spent about $15,000 on this start-up activity.

Latenight Entertainment, Inc., had once been a high-flying record and video producer, but its stars had fallen out of favor and the company was now inactive. In its glory days, the stock had an active following and had once traded as high as $12. There was no trading now, although there were still 150,000 shares outstanding, and there was a stockholder list with 350 names.

CMC purchased the stockholder list from a company called Corporate Brokers, Inc., and sent the Latenight shareholders a proposal whereby CMC would exchange its mining claim in exchange for 850,000 shares of Latenight stock. It also proposed that the name "Latenight Entertainment, Inc." be changed to Colorado Mining Corporation. In the offering document sent to the Latenight shareholders, CMC stated that the mine had the potential to produce $3,000,000 worth of silver in the next five years. On that basis, the offering document stated that the property was worth at least $1,000,000 and that the value of the Latenight shares would be worth $1 after the exchange was consummated. The exchange was approved by a majority of Latenight shareholders, and the transaction was completed as planned.

Required:

a. What accounting would be appropriate for *all* of the above acquisitions and exchanges in the affected companies' accounts? Please explain your proposed accounting.

b. Why would CMC want to enter into this exchange? What would you expect the next step in its plan to be? How might your accounting in part *a* help or frustrate that plan?

C13.4 Foreign Operations: Moon Computers, Inc.

Moon Computers manufactures IBM–compatible personal computers (PC) and computer-based workstations. The production takes place in various offshore and domestic locations. Final assembly takes place at the company's main plant in California, and that is where all customer shipments originate.

The sales price for the basic computer model to the company's distributors is $500. Occasionally, a large distributor negotiates a 10 percent discount as a result of a very large (250 units) order. Moon's full-absorption cost is about $375, and so there is not a great deal of negotiation room in the wholesale pricing.

In mid-1988, Shana Royo, the vice president of sales took a vacation in Italy, ostensibly to look at art but also to taste the wine. Royo met an Italian industrialist, however, and the conversation went from art to wine to computers. Royo came home with an order for 1,000 basic machines. The Italian customer wanted Moon's standard PC and opted to make the purchase using Moon's normal five-year lease. The customer pushed hard on prices, and Royo agreed to terms that would recover full-absorption manufacturing cost as well as cover the cost of money over the lease term.

An order of this size was exciting but awesome. The company was not in a position to finance such a large lease program with internal funds. After some investigation, the management team came up with this approach:

1. A new Swiss subsidiary was set up to handle the transaction. The new company would borrow 375,000 Swiss francs from a local Swiss bank with repayment terms that matched the expected cash flow from the Italian lease. The loan carried a 5 percent interest rate.

2. The Swiss subsidiary bought the computers from the U.S. parent for $375 each, using the proceeds of the bank loan. (For purposes of this discussion, we will assume that the conversion rate of the dollar and the franc was 1:1 at the time of the sale.)

3. The lease, payable in lira, carried an implicit interest rate of 10 percent. At that rate (and assuming a franc-to-lira exchange rate of 1:4), the present value of the lease was 500,000 francs.

All of this was accomplished just before the end of the 1988 year. As a result of this transaction, the U.S. parent recorded an all-cash, break-even sale to its subsidiary. The Swiss subsidiary treated the lease as a sales-type lease and recorded a profit on the transaction of 125,000 francs. The following is the subsidiary's income statement for the period ended December 31, 1988 (in Swiss francs):

Sales	500,000
Cost of sales	375,000
Swiss income tax	25,000
Net income	100,000

The following is from the Swiss subsidiary's balance sheet at December 31, 1988 (in Swiss francs):

Lease receivable	500,000
Loan payable	375,000
Taxes payable	25,000
Equity	100,000
Total liability and equity	500,000

The parent created an investment account, picking up the subsidiary's income as its initial investment.

Investment in Swiss Subsidiary (A).	100,000	
Retained Earnings (Subsidiary's Income) (OE)		100,000

When the consolidated income statement was prepared, the parent's one-line income from the subsidiary was replaced with the subsidiary's sale of $500,000, cost of $375,000, and tax expense of $25,000. (Technically, the subsidiary's cost of sales of $375,000 was eliminated against the parent's sale so that the consolidated income statement reflected the subsidiary's $500,000 sale and the parent's manufacturing cost of $375,000.) When the consolidated balance sheet was prepared, the $100,000 investment in the subsidiary was expanded to reflect the lease receivable, the bank debt, and the tax payable. (This plan assumes that payments are due on December 31 each year.)

The planned workout of this transaction looked like this:

	Swiss Bank Loan (sf)			Italian Lease (l)		
	Total Payment	Applied to		Total Payment	Applied to	
Year		Principal	Expense		Principal	Income
1989	87	68	19	528	328	200
1990	87	71	15	528	360	167
1991	87	75	12	528	396	131
1992	87	79	8	528	436	92
1993	87	82	5	528	480	48
		375			2,000	

We are now getting ready to prepare Moon's consolidated financial statements for the year ended December 31, 1990. Assume that the exchange rates stayed the same throughout 1989 but that during 1990, the lira weakened so that at the end of the year, it was 5 lira to the franc, and that the dollar weakened so that at the end of the year a franc was worth $1.20. Assume that the lease and loan payments were made on time each year at December 31. Assume that the Swiss taxes due each year were paid (or are due) in March of the following year.

Required:

a. Develop the balance sheet and income statement for the Swiss subsidiary for the year ended December 31, 1990, and prepare the entries required to record the activities of the Swiss subsidiary in the parent's books.

b. Explain how the Swiss subsidiary's assets, liabilities, and results of operations will be presented in the Moon consolidated financial statements for the year ended December 31, 1990. To do this, you may want to prepare the consolidation entry which distributes the parent's investment in the Swiss subsidiary, or you may want to prepare the Swiss subsidiary's translated balance sheet and income statement, which will be required for the preparation of the U.S. consolidated financial statements.

PART IV:

Using Accounting Data

CHAPTER 14

Analyzing and Understanding
Corporate Financial Reports

Chapter Outline

- Assessing the Quality of Reported Earnings
  and Financial Position
    - Return to Investors
- Financial Statement Analysis: An Illustration
    - Limitations of Ratio Analysis

- Horizontal and Vertical Analysis
- Accounting Information and Stock Prices
    - The Efficient Market Hypothesis
- Cash Flow Analysis Revisited
- Summary

I n the previous 13 chapters, we focused on developing an understanding of the principal elements of the basic financial statements. We considered what each account means individually and, in the aggregate, what the financial statements portray about a given company.

In this chapter, we attempt to broaden your understanding of accounting information and its uses by considering a number of advanced topics in the analysis of financial statements. To begin,

let us return to some of the basics of ratio analysis and consider several alternative viewpoints using PepsiCo's financial statements. Attention then will be turned to the alternative GAAP methods available for use in financial statements and how alternative GAAP impact ratio analysis and security prices. Finally, we return to the topic of evaluating a company's cash flows and developing pro forma statements from them.

ASSESSING THE QUALITY OF REPORTED EARNINGS AND FINANCIAL POSITION

Corporate financial reports are the primary means by which companies report their financial condition and performance to interested external parties. In the view of the FASB,

> Financial reporting should provide information that is useful to present and potential investors and creditors and other users in making rational investment, credit, and similar decisions.[1]

Implicit in these uses of financial reports are the concerns of users pertaining to a company's past performance, present condition, and future prospects. The first two of these are the primary focus of the financial statements, related footnotes, management discussion and analysis, and auditor's report. The latter is often the focus of management's letter to shareholders. Quite frankly, though, the assessment of future prospects is best served by users performing their own analysis of company performance and using supplementary third-party commentaries.

Many third-party sources of information about a company are readily available. To illustrate just one of these sources, Exhibit 14.1 presents the *Value Line* Investment Services financial evaluation of PepsiCo, Inc., as of February 22, 1991. Not only does this report present abbreviated financial statements and many basic ratios calculated for those statements, but also it presents a brief assessment of the strengths and weaknesses of PepsiCo's operations, as well as a prognosis for the future. For example, the *Value Line* report highlights the following key points:

- All of PepsiCo's businesses made strong profit progress in 1990.
- Despite investor concerns about the recession's impact, the restaurant business is booming.
- The snack-food division is stressing international expansion.
- Soft-drink earnings are growing briskly despite slowing volume gains.
- This good-quality stock should be a standout performer in the year ahead.

Note also that in terms of the *Value Line* investment rating system, PepsiCo earned a safety rating of 2 (above average) on a scale of 1 to 5.

Because no one knows for certain what a company's future financial results will be, a great deal of emphasis is placed on past and present performance as indicators of the future. In projecting a link between the past and the future, issues falling under the general rubric of the *quality of reported earnings and financial position* become significant considerations. For example, although the amount of reported earnings is important, so too are the rate of earnings generated on available resources, the stability of earnings, the

---

[1]Financial Accounting Standards Board, *Statement of Financial Accounting Concepts No. 1.*, "Objectives of Financial Reporting by Business Enterprises" (Stamford, Conn.: FASB, 1978).

EXHIBIT 14.1

Value Line Investment Services Report for PepsiCo, Inc.

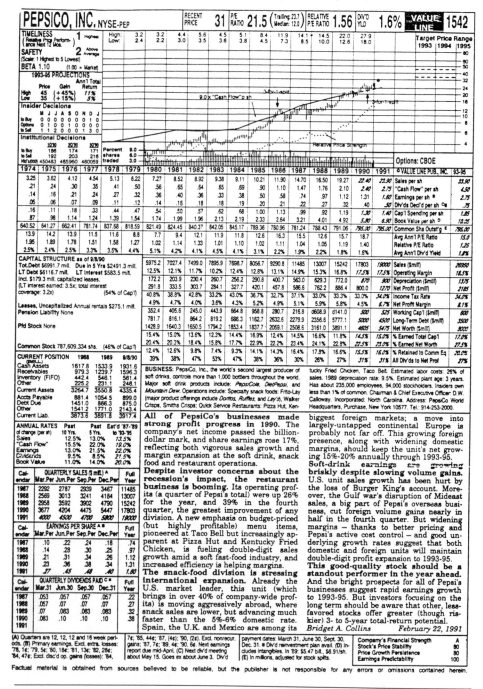

specific sources of earnings, and the accounting methods used to measure the earnings. Similarly, although it is useful to know the size and variety of asset categories, it is also important to determine their liquidity, operating capacity, and flexibility.

In previous chapters, numerous financial ratios were suggested as sources of insight regarding a company's management of the various facets of its operations. For example, in Chapter 4, the accounts receivable turnover ratio was discussed as a means to estimate the rate at which a company's receivables were converted into cash. In Chapter 5, the return on owners' equity ratio was presented as an indication of the return earned by a company on noncreditor funds. Exhibit 14.2 summarizes the various ratios discussed throughout this text and also introduces a new category of indicators, the *return to investors*.

Return to Investors

For publicly held companies, the **return to investors** is one of the most frequently evaluated areas of company performance. Since investors are often the largest group of stakeholders (both in number and in dollars invested) in a company, how well they are rewarded for their investment is of considerable interest and importance. Most indicators of the return to investors are based on current income statement data and, in some cases, on actual stock market price data.

Earnings per share. Perhaps the most often cited measure of shareholder return is a company's **earnings per share,** or EPS. As noted in Chapter 5, EPS represents only those earnings of a company accruing to its voting, or common, shareholders. Thus, in the calculation of EPS, a company's earnings are first reduced for any dividends paid to the preferred shareholders.

The calculation of EPS can be quite complex, depending on whether a company has other securities outstanding that are convertible into, or exchangeable for, additional shares of common stock. In the simplest case in which a company has only common and preferred stock outstanding, the computation of EPS is straightforward:

$$\text{EPS} = \frac{\text{Net income} - \text{Preferred dividends}}{\text{Weighted-average number of common shares outstanding}}.$$

Note that in the calculation of EPS, the divisor is not merely the number of shares outstanding at year-end but rather is an average of the shares outstanding, weighted by the proportion of a given year (or quarter) that the shares were actually in the hands of stockholders.

For a company with securities outstanding that are convertible (e.g., convertible bonds or convertible preferred stock) or exchangeable (e.g., stock options or warrants) for common stock, the calculation of EPS can be surprisingly difficult. Under these conditions, two calculations may be required—one for primary EPS and one for fully diluted EPS.

EXHIBIT 14.2

Summary of Financial Statement Ratios

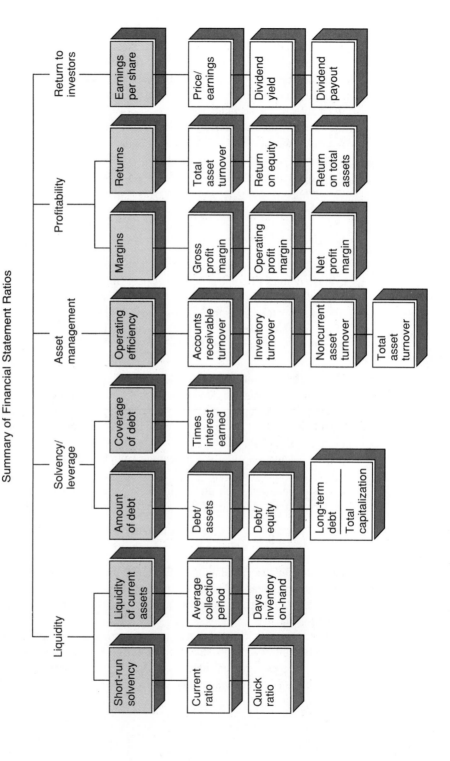

E X H I B I T   1 4 . 2

(continued)

Summary of Financial Statement Ratios
Liquidity:
  Current ratio = Current assets ÷ Current liabilities
  Quick ratio = (Cash + Marketable securities + Receivables) ÷ Current liabilities
  Average receivable collection period = (Average accounts receivable balance ÷ Net sales) × 365 days
  Average number of days' inventory on-hand = (Average inventory balance ÷ Cost of goods sold) × 365 days
Solvency/Leverage:
  Total debt-to-total assets ratio = Total debt ÷ Total assets
  Long-term debt to equity = Long-term debt ÷ Total owners' equity
  Long-term debt to total capitalization ratio = Long-term debt ÷ (Long-term debt + Total owners' equity)
  Times-interest-earned ratio = Net income before interest and income taxes ÷ interest expense
Asset management:
  Accounts receivable turnover = Net credit sales ÷ Average accounts receivable balance
  Inventory turnover = Cost of goods sold ÷ Average inventory balance
  Noncurrent asset turnover = Net sales ÷ Average noncurrent assets
  Total asset turnover = Net sales ÷ Average total assets
Profitability:
  Gross profit margin = (Net sales − Cost of goods sold) ÷ Net sales
  Operating profit margin = Operating income ÷ Net sales
  Net profit margin = Net income ÷ Net sales
  Return on equity = Net income ÷ Average owners' equity
  Return on total assets = Net income ÷ Average total assets
Return to investors:
  Earnings per share (Net income − preferred stock dividends) ÷ Weighted-average common shares outstanding
  Price-earnings ratio = Market price per common share ÷ Primary earnings per share
  Dividend yield = Cash dividend per common share ÷ Market price per common share
  Dividend payout ratio = Cash dividends paid to common stockholders ÷ (Net income − Preferred stock dividends)

Primary EPS is calculated by dividing earnings applicable to common stock by the weighted-average number of common shares outstanding *plus* any common stock equivalents:

$$\text{Primary EPS} = \frac{\text{Earnings applicable to common stock}}{\text{Weighted-average common shares} + \text{Common stock equivalents}}.$$

A **common stock equivalent** is "a security which is not, in form, a common stock but which usually contains provisions to enable its holder to become a common stock-holder. . . ."[2] Stock options and stock warrants are considered to be common stock equivalents at all times; thus, *even if* an option or warrant is not exercised (i.e., exchanged for common stock) by the end of an accounting period, it is treated for EPS calculation purposes *as if* it had been exercised.

---

[2]American Institute of Certified Public Accountants, *APB Opinion No. 15*, "Earnings per Share" (New York: AICPA, 1969).

Determining whether a particular convertible security, such as convertible preferred stock or a convertible bond, is a common stock equivalent is more problematic. Current practice, however, relies on several well-reasoned, albeit arbitrary, rules in making such determinations. If a convertible security's effective yield at the time of issuance is less than 66 2/3 percent of the then current average Aa corporate bond yield, it is considered to be a common stock equivalent. The rationale for this rule is the belief that the only reason an investor would purchase a convertible bond or convertible preferred stock yielding a rate of return substantially below the current market rate is the buyer's intent to convert the security into common stock at some future date. Notice, however, that this rule ignores any difference in investment risk between the convertible security and a corporate Aa bond.

Fully diluted EPS is calculated by including in the divisor *all* potentially dilutive securities in addition to any common stock equivalents:

$$\text{Fully diluted EPS} = \frac{\text{Earnings applicable to common stock}}{\substack{\text{Weighted-average common shares +} \\ \text{Common stock equivalents +} \\ \text{Other potentially dilutive securities}}} .$$

Thus, not only are all the common stock equivalents considered, as is done for primary EPS, but also all convertible securities not qualifying as common stock equivalents are also assumed to have been converted, subject to one caveat: in determining either primary or fully diluted EPS, no security should be included in the calculation of EPS if its inclusion causes the EPS amount to increase (referred to as an antidilutive effect). Only common stock equivalents and convertible securities causing a *dilution* of the EPS are incorporated in the calculations. For example, assume the following EPS:

$$\text{EPS} = \frac{\$12,000,000 \text{ (net income)} - \$5,000,000 \text{ (preferred dividends)}}{\substack{3,500,000 \text{ shares (average shares of} \\ \text{common stock outstanding)}}}$$

$$= \$2.$$

If the outstanding convertible preferred stock is assumed to be converted at the beginning of the year into 1 million common shares, the following would be the new EPS:

$$\text{EPS} = \frac{\$12,000,000}{4,500,000} = \$2.67.$$

Because the convertible preferred stock had an antidilutive effect, it would not be considered in the final EPS calculation.

As this example demonstrates, the earnings applicable to common stockholders for each convertible security included in the EPS denominator requires an adjustment. For example, if the number of common shares attributable to a convertible preferred stock is used to increase the EPS denominator, the numerator should be increased by the amount of preferred dividends that would no longer be required if the conversion took place. The one exception to this involves the exercise of stock options or warrants, which affect only the number of shares outstanding.

Price-earnings (P/E) ratio. One of the most widely used indicators of a company's investment potential is the price-earnings ratio, or P/E multiple:

$$\text{P/E ratio} = \frac{\text{Market price per common share}}{\text{Primary EPS}} .$$

Because the market price of a share of stock is a function of investors' perceptions regarding a company's potential, the same factors that affect those perceptions affect the P/E ratio—factors such as a company's relative investment risk, past earnings record, and growth potential. Many investment houses use the P/E ratio as a criterion to advise their clients as to when to buy or sell stocks. A typical rule of thumb followed by some investment advisers is that a company with a low P/E ratio, assuming it is a sound business enterprise, represents a bargain for potential investors *relative to* a company with a higher P/E ratio. Investing solely, or even principally, on the basis of P/E ratios can be a risky investment strategy. P/E ratios are significantly influenced by the level of reported earnings and, as we will see shortly, it is possible for a company to artificially manage its reported results. Moreover, investing on the basis of P/E ratios ignores the fact that *current* stock prices frequently reflect all publicly available information about a company; thus, it is unlikely that an investor following such a strategy will be able to earn unusual or *abnormal returns*.

At year-end 1990, the P/E ratio for PepsiCo was 20; for Coca-Cola it was 23. If we assume that the two companies represent equivalent investment opportunities and that the P/E ratio is an effective means of identifying underpriced stocks, the year-end P/E ratios suggest that PepsiCo may have been a better investment opportunity in 1990 than Coca-Cola.

Dividend yield. Some investors are principally interested in the actual level of cash distributed by a company to its shareholders. To these investors, the cash dividend yield is an important indicator:

$$\text{Dividend yield} = \frac{\text{Cash dividend per common share}}{\text{Market price per common share}} .$$

This measure informs investors of the current cash rate of return on a given common stock, based on its current selling price. During 1990, PepsiCo's cash dividend yield was 1.4 percent based on the year-end market price; for Coca-Cola, it was 1.7 percent. For an investor interested in current cash income, this measure readily facilitates investment choices.

Dividend payout ratio. A measure of the return actually paid to shareholders is captured in the cash dividend payout ratio:

$$\text{Dividend payout ratio} = \frac{\text{Cash dividends to common shareholders}}{\text{Net income} - \text{Preferred dividends}} .$$

This ratio measures the percentage of a company's earnings that are actually distributed to its shareholders in the form of cash dividends. From an investor's point of view, a higher dividend payout ratio results in immediate increased cash inflows. On the other hand, from management's perspective, a growth-oriented company would want to maintain minimal payout ratios for the purpose of retaining funds to fuel continued growth, whereas a mature company (e.g., a utility company) would desire relatively high payout ratios to compensate for the fact that its potential stock appreciation is probably less than that of a growth-oriented company. In both 1989 and 1990, PepsiCo's cash dividend payout ratio was approximately 27 percent. These percentages are somewhat low when compared, for example, with the 28.0 and 39.0 percent amounts for Coca-Cola for the same periods.

FINANCIAL STATEMENT ANALYSIS: AN ILLUSTRATION

The topic of financial statement analysis has been a common thread linking many of the previous 13 chapters. As Exhibit 14.2 shows, the analysis of financial statements using ratios can be organized into five categories:

1. *Liquidity:* the assessment of a company's ability to meet current short-term obligations as they fall due.
2. *Solvency:* the assessment of a company's long-term debt-payment ability.
3. *Asset management:* the assessment of how effectively a company utilizes its available resources.
4. *Profitability:* the assessment of a company's ability to generate revenues in excess of expenses.
5. *Return to investors:* the assessment of the earnings or cash flows accruing to the owners of a company.

Although each of these categories has been covered in detail elsewhere, it is instructive to review the ratios involved using PepsiCo's 1990 financial statements.

As Exhibit 14.3 reveals, PepsiCo's results for 1990 indicate both positive and negative trends. With respect to liquidity, most of the financial ratios indicate that it is somewhat less liquid than in 1989; however, with respect to solvency, on all measures PepsiCo's long-term debt position has improved. Although profit margins were generally improved, the return on equity and the return on total assets declined when compared to those for 1989. Moreover, the asset management indicators were relatively stable between the two years with the exception of the total asset turnover, which improved by almost 10 percent. Finally, with respect to the return-to-investor indicators, not only were the earnings per share up, but PepsiCo also maintained both its dividend yield and its dividend payout from 1989 to 1990. Overall, investors appeared to be favorably impressed with PepsiCo's 1990 financial results as evidenced by the increasing trend in the company's capital stock price.

Limitations of Ratio Analysis

Ratio analysis is undoubtedly the most widely used analytical technique for interpreting financial statement data. In spite of its widespread use, however, ratio analysis suffers from certain limitations and is subject to certain constraining assumptions.

EXHIBIT 14.3

PEPSICO, INC.
Financial Statement Ratios

	1989	1990
Liquidity		
Current ratio	0.96:1	0.86:1
Quick ratio	0.75:1	0.68:1
Average receivable collection		
period	26.6	27.2
Average number of days' inventory		
on hand	24.1	24.0
Solvency/Leverage		
Total debt-to-total assets ratio	74.2%	71.4%
Long-term debt-to-equity ratio	1.48:1	1.14:1
Long-term debt-to-total capitalization	24%	22%
Times-interest-earned ratio	8.6 times	10.2 times
Asset management		
Accounts receivable turnover	13.7 times	13.4 times
Inventory turnover	15.1 times	15.2 times
Noncurrent asset turnover	3.2 times	3.3 times
Total asset turnover	1.0 times	1.1 times
Profitability		
Gross profit margin	51.0%	51.6%
Operating profit margin	5.9%	6.1%
Net profit margin	5.9%	6.1%
Return on equity	25.6%	24.5%
Return on total assets	6.9%	6.7%
Return to investors		
Earnings per share	$1.13	$1.35
Price/earnings ratio*	16:1	19:1
Dividend yield*	1.5%	1.5%
Dividend payout	28.3%	28.2%

*Price = Fourth-quarter closing price.

For example, since a ratio involves *two* financial statement numbers (e.g., net sales divided by total assets), the reader must be cautious in interpreting its cause when a change in a ratio is observed. Ratio changes may result from a change in either the numerator, the denominator, or both. Thus, when using ratios, the reader must be prepared to look beyond the ratio itself in an effort to understand the economic event(s) causing the change.

Another concern is that, quite often, changes in financial statement data may be more cosmetic than real. For example, the trend analysis of PepsiCo's financial statement data reported in Exhibit 14.3 presupposes stationarity in the basic relationships underlying the financial statement numbers. Consequently, any event—be it a real economic event or a cosmetic one—that disturbs an underlying relation will impact the reported ratios.

Although not an exhaustive listing, the following are examples of cosmetic events that will disturb the underlying financial statement relationships and thus must be taken into consideration by the astute reader:

1. A structural change in the accounting entity (e.g., a merger or an acquisition of another company).
2. A change in an accounting method or principle (e.g., a switch from LIFO to FIFO).
3. A change in accounting estimate (e.g., an increase in the estimated life of a depreciable asset).
4. A change in accounting classification (e.g., segregating the income (or loss) on a division recently sold from the income from operations).

These concerns are particularly relevant when accounting data are investigated for trends over a number of accounting periods. The analysis of financial statement data over multiple periods is frequently called **time-series analysis.**

As noted before, ratio analysis is most effective when the resulting ratios can be compared against some standard. Frequently, that standard is a similar ratio from a prior period, as in a trend analysis of time-series data. Another useful standard, however, is a ratio from a leading competitor or perhaps the industry in general. Unfortunately, the use of **cross-sectional analysis**—that is, the comparison of a given company's ratios with other companies' data or with industry averages—involves certain restrictive assumptions, including these:

1. The individual company is assumed to be structurally similar to the competitor or the average of the industry, which is rarely the case.
2. The industry and the company under review are assumed to use a common set of accounting principles and accounting estimates. As we will see shortly, when a company under review uses one set of GAAP and the industry or comparative company uses another set, large cosmetic ratio differences tend to occur.
3. The company under review and the industry are assumed to experience a common set of external influences. A given company, however, may have undergone an unusual economic event (e.g., a labor strike) having multiple-period implications for its financial data that are not reflected in the industry standard.

Despite these concerns, ratio analysis can be a very powerful analytical tool so long as the analyst recognizes the following important maxim: *Ratios help the financial statement user identify important questions but seldom offer direct answers.* Only by a comprehensive review of the financial statements can answers be obtained.

Horizontal and Vertical Analysis

In addition to ratio analysis, two other types of financial statement analysis are frequently performed—horizontal analysis and vertical analysis. When comparative balance sheets or income statements are presented side by side, the statements can be made more

EXHIBIT 14.4

PEPSICO, INC.
Comparative Income Statements with Horizontal Analysis
For Years Ended December 29, 1990 and 1989
(in millions)

	1990	1989	Amount of Increase (Decrease) during 1990	Percentage Increase (Decrease) during 1990
Net sales	$17,802.7	$15,242.4	$2,560.5	16.8
Costs and expenses				
Cost of sales	8,609.9	7,467.7	1,142.2	15.3
Selling and administrative expense	7,019.0	5,991.8	1,027.2	17.1
Interest expense	688.5	609.6	78.9	12.9
Interest income	(182.1)	(177.2)	4.9	2.8
	16,135.3	13,891.9	2,243.4	16.2
Income from continuing operations before income taxes	1,667.4	1,350.5	316.9	23.5
Provision for income tax	576.8	499.1	77.7	15.6
Net income	$ 1,090.6	$ 901.4	$ 189.2	21.0

meaningful if the dollar amount of increase or decrease and the percentage change is shown. This type of analysis is known as **horizontal analysis** because the data comparisons are made on a horizontal plane from left to right.

Exhibit 14.4 illustrates a horizontal analysis of PepsiCo's income statement. In this two-year comparison, the earlier year (1989) is the base year. The percentage changes are rounded to the nearest tenth of a percent. For PepsiCo, it is noteworthy that although 1990 net sales increased by 16.8 percent over 1989 sales, costs and expenses also increased but at a slower rate (i.e., 16.2 percent). This increase, combined with certain tax benefits that lowered PepsiCo's effective income tax rate, produced a 21 percent growth in net income.

In **vertical analysis,** three financial statement numbers—total assets, total equities, and net sales—are converted to a base of 100 percent. Each item within the assets and equities on the balance sheet, or each item on the income statement, is then expressed as a percentage of the base number. Since for any given set of financial statements the base numbers represent 100 percent, the restated financial statements are called **common-size statements.**

To illustrate vertical analysis, Exhibit 14.5 presents PepsiCo's common-size income statements for 1989 and 1990. An interpretation of vertical statements often parallels the interpretation of horizontal statements. Note that the common-size statements permit both a within-period analysis (e.g., in 1990, costs and expenses were approximately a 90.6 percentage of net sales) and across-period trend analysis (e.g., costs and expenses as a percentage of net sales declined from 91.1 percent in 1989 to 90.6 percent in 1990).

EXHIBIT 14.5

PEPSICO, INC.
Comparative Common-Size Income Statements
For Years Ended December 29, 1990 and 1989
(in millions)

	1990	Common-Size Percentage	1989	Common-Size Percentage
Net sales	$17,802.7	100%	$15,242.4	100%
Cost and expenses				
Cost of sales	8,609.9	48.4	7,467.7	49.0
Selling and administrative expense	7,019.0	39.4	5,991.8	39.3
Interest expense	688.5	3.9	609.6	4.0
Interest income	(182.1)	(1.1)	(177.2)	(1.2)
	16,135.3	90.6	13,891.9	91.1
Income from continuing operations before income taxes	1,667.4	9.4	1,350.5	8.9
Provision for income tax	576.8	3.3	499.1	3.0
Net income	$ 1,090.6	6.1	$ 901.4	5.9

ACCOUNTING INFORMATION
AND STOCK PRICES

As has been repeatedly noted throughout this text, the reporting of earnings and financial position of a company involves considerable latitude in selecting from the array of generally accepted accounting principles, and in the inevitable need for management to make numerous valuation estimates and judgments. Given the flexibility available to corporate management in the presentation of financial results, the very human desire to portray their companies in the best light possible, and their awareness of users' concerns about the quality of reported earnings and financial position, it is important to consider the subtle and not-so-subtle items that external users should look for in financial reports as they perform their evaluations of a company.

Consider, for example, the revenue recognition method decision that managers of construction companies must make. Under GAAP, the revenues of such companies may be presented using either the completed contract method or the percentage of completion method. Under the **completed contract method,** management takes the position that no revenues should be recognized until the work to be provided under a contract is fully completed. Under the **percentage of completion method,** management takes the position that revenue recognition is a function of the amount of work actually completed. Exhibit 14.6 provides a simple illustration contrasting the completed contract and percentage of completion methods for a hypothetical firm. The exhibit reveals that under the completed contract approach, FHAS Corporation would report no earnings in 1990 or 1991, and $1.7 million in earnings in 1992. Under the percentage of completion approach, however, a positive income stream (i.e., $.4 million, $.5 million, and $.8 million, in 1990, 1991, and

EXHIBIT 14.6

Alternative GAAP: Completed
Contract versus Percentage of Completion Methods

In June 1990, FHAS Corporation signed a long-term construction contract to build a shopping center in Houston, Texas. Under the terms of the three-year contract, FHAS would receive a total of $12 million. During 1990, 30 percent of the project was completed at a cost of $3.2 million. In 1991, 40 percent of the project was completed at a cost of $4.3 million; in 1992, the project was completed at a cost of $2.8 million.

Under the **completed contract method,** FHAS would report earnings as follows:

	1990	1991	1992
Revenues	$–0–	$–0–	$12.0 million
Expenses	–0–	–0–	10.3
Net income	$–0–	$–0–	$ 1.7 million
Return on sales	–0–%	–0–%	14.2%

Under the **percentage of completion method,** FHAS would report earnings as follows:

	1990	1991	1992
Revenues	$3.6 million	$4.8 million	$3.6 million
Expenses	3.2	4.3	2.8
Net income	$ .4 million	$ .5 million	$ .8 million
Return on sales	11%	10.4%	22.2%

1992, respectively) is reported in each year. The first method essentially defers all income until 1992, whereas the second spreads the income across the three years as a function of the amount of work actually completed.

It is clear that although the aggregate results, viewed in their entirety over the three-year period, are equivalent, substantially different impressions are created in any individual year as to the relative success of FHAS Corporation in performing under the contract. It is important to recognize that either the completed contract or the percentage of completion method may be adopted for financial reporting purposes. Moreover, the decision to use one method or the other is exclusively a managerial decision, although the percentage of completion method is preferred by most accountants because it more closely reflects the accrual basis of accounting.

As we see from the data in Exhibit 14.6, the method that a company adopts to report its revenues or expenses may have a significant impact on its actual reported results. Not only will the level of revenues and expenses on the income statement be affected, but so too will be the level of reported assets and equities on the balance sheet, along with all the financial ratios calculated using those income statement and balance sheet values. Thus, when analyzing a company's reported performance and financial condition, using either absolute figures or ratios, it is important to know just which accounting methods are being used and how those methods are likely to impact the reported values and calculated ratios. For example, in Exhibit 14.6, note how the trend in the return on sales dramatically differs for the two methods of reporting revenues.

Exhibit 14.7 provides further evidence of this analytical concern. This exhibit presents the income statement and selected financial indicators for two *economically identical* companies that differ *only* in regard to the accounting method used to value the cost of goods sold and ending inventory. A review of these financial data reveals that since inventory costs are rising, FIFO Company appears to be financially better off than LIFO Company—earnings and working capital are higher by $7.8 million and $5.15 million, respectively, and the current ratio (liquidity), the debt-to-equity ratio (solvency), and the return on assets and on sales (profitability) are superior. Only the inventory turnover ratio (asset management) appears to be better for LIFO Company.

But are these financial indicators depicting the true economic reality? Holding the question of taxes aside, the answer is a resounding "No!" The two companies are economically identical in spite of the information revealed by the accounting data and the ratio analysis. If we now add the issue of income taxes and assume that each company uses the same inventory costing method for both IRS purposes and for financial statement purposes, our conclusion is even more startling—the LIFO company is actually superior in economic performance because larger cash flows (due to tax savings) are preserved within the company.

E X H I B I T   1 4 . 7

Alternative GAAP and Financial Statement Analysis: LIFO versus FIFO

Presented below are the income statements and selected financial ratios for two companies that are identical in every respect except with regard to the method of inventory costing and the cost of goods sold:

	FIFO Company	LIFO Company
Net sales	$ 75,000,000	$ 75,000,000
Cost of goods sold	(34,500,000)	(42,300,000)
Gross margin	$ 40,500,000	$ 32,700,000
Other operating expenses	(15,000,000)	(17,000,000)
Net income	$ 25,500,000	$ 17,700,000
Ending inventory	$ 17,250,000	$ 9,450,000
Selected financial ratios:		
Earnings per share	$2.55	$1.77
Current ratio	1.67:1	1.42:1
Working capital	$10.8 m	$5.65 m
Inventory turnover	2:1	4.5:1
Debt-to-equity ratio	1:5.17	1:4.91
Return on assets	10.8%	7.8%
Return on sales	34.0%	23.6%

One thing is clear from these illustrations—the use of different financial accounting methods may produce very different impressions about the financial performance of a company and its management. Of importance, then, is whether these different accounting impressions are also reflected, or even should be reflected, in a company's stock price.

The Efficient Market Hypothesis

Although there is some disagreement over exactly what causes stock prices to move upward and downward, there is little disagreement over the notion that *accounting information* is at least partially responsible for stock price movements. Consider, for example, the news story reported in Exhibit 14.8. This *Wall Street Journal* article reports that PepsiCo's 1990 fourth-quarter earnings were up by 32 percent as compared to the 1989 fourth-quarter results. Not surprisingly, PepsiCo's common stock price responded quite positively to this news release and rose by $1.75, to close at $28.75 per share (or a 6.5 percent increase in share price in one day).

This article and the resulting share price movement depict the role of accounting information for investors and the stock and bond markets in general. Using the latest accounting results, investors form expectations about the future of companies such as PepsiCo and accordingly determine how much they are willing to pay for a share of stock (or a bond) in the company. The positive share price reaction to the PepsiCo news indicates that investors' expectations about the future of PepsiCo were raised by the announcement (and hence their willingness to pay more for the stock). Notice also how quickly investors responded to the news release—the price of PepsiCo's common stock was bid up by $1.75 very shortly after the story appeared on the Associated Press newswire. The story appeared in *The Wall Street Journal* on the day following the press release by PepsiCo, Inc.

The relationship between accounting information and stock prices is largely captured by a theory of the functioning of capital markets called the efficient market hypothesis, or EMH.[3] EMH is a widely accepted theory describing how stock and bond prices respond to information. In fact, the theory is now so well documented that it has been relied on by the U.S. Supreme Court as a description of the behavior of U.S. capital markets.

Under EMH, stock prices are assumed to reflect fully (in terms of price) all publicly available information. When new information (e.g., the PepsiCo earnings announcement) is made public, share prices adjust very quickly to the new information. For example, on July 27, 1990, PepsiCo announced that as a consequence of a doubling of its stock price during the previous 19 months, the company would split its stock on a 3-for-1 basis. Following this news release, PepsiCo's stock jumped $1.375 per share.

Evidence also exists to suggest that the capital markets are not "fooled" by the differences in reported accounting numbers caused by the use of alternative GAAP; that is, sophisticated analysts and investors are apparently able to "see through" the differential accounting effects created by alternative GAAP (e.g., completed contract

---

[3]See T. R. Dyckman and D. Morse, *Efficient Capital Markets and Accounting* (Englewood Cliffs, N.J.: Prentice-Hall, 1986).

E X H I B I T 1 4 . 8

PepsiCo's Net Increased 32 Percent in Fourth Quarter

By DANIEL PEARL, Staff Reporter of THE WALL STREET JOURNAL

PepsiCo Inc., helped by accelerating growth in its restaurant business, said fourth-quarter earnings jumped 32%.

The company reported net income of $265.9 million, or 34 cents a share, compared with $202.1 million, or 25 cents a share, a year earlier. Excluding unusual charges in 1990 and 1989, PepsiCo's earnings gain was 34%. Sales rose 14% to $5.44 billion from $4.79 billion.

In New York Stock Exchange composite trading yesterday, PepsiCo climbed $1.75 a share, closing at $28.75.

The fourth-quarter results, which surpassed many analysts' expectations, included a 39% increase in operating profit for the Purchase, N.Y., company's restaurant group.

Some other large operators in the fast-food industry have reported sluggish earnings gains because of fierce price discounting and slower U.S. consumer spending. McDonald's Corp., for example, last week reported an 8.8% gain in four-quarter net, slightly below most analysts' expectations.

PepsiCo's restaurants, however, are benefiting from some widely publicized marketing moves. Profit was up 65% at its Taco Bell restaurants, for example, primarily in response to a recently introduced "value menu," in which the chain reduced prices on selected items. Same-store sales for company-owned Taco Bell outlets in the U.S. rose 9%.

The Kentucky Fried Chicken unit continued its turnaround, showing an 8% gain in same-store sales, largely because of the popularity of new products and lower prices. Pizza Hut had a 5% gain in same-store sales, and its earnings rose 38%, excluding one-time charges, as more of its business shifted to the fast-growing delivery side of the market, PepsiCo said.

Emanuel Goldman, an analyst with PaineWebber Inc., said PepsiCo's restaurant business was once the greatest source of worry for its investors but now may become the company's strongest business.

"They have become very, very good at the restaurant business—ask McDonald's," he said, noting that price promotions have been highly successful at Pizza Hut and Taco Bell.

Domestic growth for soft drinks, measured in case sales by PepsiCo's bottlers, was less than 1%. The company attributed the sluggish growth largely to its loss of the Burger King Corp. account to Coca-Cola Co. last May. The Diet Pepsi and Mountain Dew brands performed well, PepsiCo said.

The war in the Middle East—an important market for PepsiCo—hurt international sales. Pepsi is well ahead of Coca-Cola in Arab countries, largely because of an Arab boycott of Coke over sales to Israel. The cutoff of concentrate shipments to Iraq and Kuwait held growth in international case sales to 5%, rather than an anticipated 9%.

Still, operating profit in PepsiCo's worldwide soft-drink business rose 25% in the quarter on an 11% increase in sales.

PepsiCo's snack-food division, which contributes 42% of the company's operating profit, had continued volume and margin gains in the U.S., Mexico and Spain and a decline in the United Kingdom, the company said. Frito-Lay's Santitas and Tostitos chips and Rold Gold pretzels led the way to a 7% increase in domestic volume growth in the fourth quarter, while international volume was up 8%.

For the year, PepsiCo's earnings rose 19% to $1.08 billion, or $1.35 a share, from $901.4 million, or $1.13 a share. Sales rose 17% to $17.8 billion from $15.24 billion.

Source: *The Wall Street Journal*, February 7, 1990; reprinted with permission.

versus percentage of completion, LIFO versus FIFO, etc.) and are able to properly adjust share prices (by buying or selling) to reflect the true underlying economic value of a company.

An important implication of this theory is that managers of publicly held companies should be unable to manipulate the value of their companies' stock merely by selecting accounting methods that result in the highest level of reported earnings. Since stock prices reflect only *real* economic changes, they will be relatively unaffected by the cosmetic wealth changes associated with alternative GAAP.

Unfortunately, it is sometimes possible to "fool" the stock market and its many investors by disclosing fraudulent financial data. Since share prices are based on all publicly available information, misleading or fraudulent financial information will often cause share prices to adjust inappropriately. The independent public auditor, however, does investigate a company's records to identify any material misstatements, and although not all fraudulent acts will be identified, most major errors (be they intentional or not) are identified as part of the annual audit investigation.

One approach used by many professional analysts and investors to evaluate a company's performance *independent* of the particular GAAP used to portray that performance is the analysis of cash flows, to which we now turn.

CASH FLOW ANALYSIS REVISITED

Cash flow analysis is probably one of the most important elements of financial statement analysis. Not only are the reported cash flows invariant to the GAAP methods used to portray accrual net income, but cash is also the only asset without which a company cannot operate. As noted in Chapter 6, companies presenting audited financial reports are required to present a statement of cash flows. The focus here is the analysis of those reported cash inflows and outflows.

Exhibit 14.9 presents a partial statement of cash flows for PepsiCo for 1989 and 1990. As the exhibit reveals, PepsiCo's cash and cash equivalents increased by $94.6 million during 1990. Continuing operations provided $2,110 million in cash inflows, financing activities consumed $77.1 million, and investing activities consumed $1,937.3 million in cash.

An important aspect of financial analysis in general, and cash flow analysis in particular, is the development of **pro forma financial statements.** An initial step in developing a pro forma statement of cash flows is to identify those cash inflows and outflows that can reasonably be expected to recur in the future. With this in mind, we labeled the various items in Exhibit 14.9 *R,* for recurring, or left it unlabeled if the item is not expected to be recurring. Admittedly, this decision process is speculative, involving somewhat arbitrary classifications by the financial statement user. But reasonable assertions are possible. For example, the current cash flows from continuing operations *are* likely to be a good estimate of the next period's cash flows from continuing operations, assuming that no material changes in operations occur. Dividends, although discretionary, are considered to be sacrosanct in most firms, and thus are quite likely to be paid in the future. Finally, purchases of property, plant, and equipment are usually considered to be recurring because this type of investment is considered necessary for the continued survival and growth of a company such as PepsiCo.

Using this classification approach and a few assumptions regarding next period's operations, we can generate a rudimentary assessment of PepsiCo's cash flows for 1991.

EXHIBIT 14.9

PEPSICO, INC.
Partial Consolidated Statement of Cash Flow
For Years Ended December 31, 1989 and 1990
(in millions)

	1989	1990	Classification*
Net cash generated by continuing operations	$ 1,885.9	$ 2,110.0	R
Cash flows from investing activities			
Acquisitions and equity investments	(3,296.6)	(630.6)	
Purchases of property, plant, and equipment	943.8	(1,180.1)	R
Proceeds from sale of property and equipment	69.7	45.3	R
Short-term investments, other	(85.6)	(171.9)	
Net cash used for investing activities	(4,256.3)	(1,937.3)	
Cash flow from financing activities			
Proceeds from long-term debt issue	71.7	777.3	R
Payments of long-term debt	(405.4)	(298.0)	R
Short-term borrowings	2,925.5	(86.2)	
Cash dividends paid	(241.9)	(293.9)	R
Other (net)	(28.9)	(176.3)	
Net cash generated by (used for) financing activities	2,321.0	(77.1)	
Effect of exchange rate changes on cash	(17.1)	(1.0)	
Net increase (decrease) in cash and cash equivalents	$ (66.5)	$ 94.6	

*R = Recurring.

For example, if we assume that similar economic conditions will be experienced in 1991 and therefore that the level of operations will remain relatively constant, one estimate of the 1991 cash flows might be as follows:

PEPSICO, INC.
1991 Pro Forma Cash Flows

Net cash flows from continuing operations	$ 2,110.0
Net cash used for investing activities*	$(1,134.8)
Net cash generated by financing activities	$ 185.4
Net increase (decrease) in cash and cash equivalents	$ 1,160.6

*Assumes no new acquisitions or equity investments.

Obviously, this type of analysis depends heavily on the stability of PepsiCo's operations and on the classifications decisions made by the analyst. As a company releases new information to the public, it is useful to incorporate this new data in any pro forma analysis. In so doing, the projected cash flows are likely to be as accurate as possible given the limited access to available corporate data.

SUMMARY

Almost all kinds of information—about a company specifically or about the economy in general—are likely to have some impact on a company's stock price. This is especially true for accounting information, which is frequently used by investors as a basis to predict future company performance and, hence, stock value. Some of the specific indicators that investors use to evaluate current performance and to predict future company performance include earnings per share, the price-earnings ratio, dividend yield, and the payout ratio.

When evaluating a company's performance, investors need to consider the effects of alternative accounting methods (e.g., LIFO versus FIFO, completed contract versus percentage of completion) on the ratios that they use. Failure to consider these accounting method effects may result in a misallocation of investor resources by overpaying when purchasing a company's shares. One way to examine a company's performance independent of the GAAP used to portray its results is to analyze its cash flows. By examining the financial statements in total and by considering the various trends revealed by ratio analysis, horizontal and vertical analysis, and cash flow analysis, the financial statement user should be able to develop a well-informed assessment of a company and its potential.

NEW CONCEPTS AND TERMS

Antidilutive effect (p. 636)

Common-size statements (p. 641)

Common stock equivalent (p. 635)

Completed contract method (p. 642)

Cross-sectional analysis (p. 640)

Dividend payout ratio (p. 637)

Dividend yield (p. 637)

Efficient market hypothesis (p. 645)

Fully diluted EPS (p. 636)

Horizontal analysis (p. 641)

Percentage of completion method (p. 642)

Price-earnings ratio (p. 637)

Primary EPS (p. 635)

Return to investors (p. 633)

Time-series analysis (p. 640)

Vertical analysis (p. 641)

ISSUES FOR DISCUSSION

D14.1 Point: There are too many alternative methods under GAAP—accounting should be more standardized.

Counter-point: Multiple alternative reporting approaches are necessary under GAAP to enable companies to portray the diverse circumstances that they face.

Evaluate the two viewpoints. Which one do you agree with, and why?

D14.2 PepsiCo's annual report reveals that during 1989, it purchased a number of other companies at an aggregate cost of $3.4 billion. Moreover, "goodwill and other intangibles recorded in connection with the 1989 acquisitions totalled $3.0 billion." Thus, the fair market value of the identifiable tangible assets was only $0.4 billion.

Why would PepsiCo pay so much for the other companies if the fair market value was only $.4 billion? Did PepsiCo's management overpay?

D14.3 In early 1990, Lockheed Corporation's common stock was trading on the New York Stock Exchange at approximately $25 per share. NL Industries, a company that already owned about 18 percent of Lockheed's shares, made a tender offer to buy Lockheed's remaining shares at $40 per share, or a premium of $15 per share above Lockheed's current market price per share.

Why would NL Industries offer a premium of 60 percent for the Lockheed shares? If the stock market is efficient, does this indicate that NL overpaid for the Lockheed shares?

D14.4 What are the major limitations of annual reports as a source of information about a company's statement of income?

D14.5 Obtain a copy of any corporation's annual report to stockholders and consider the following questions.:

a. What are the three most significant pieces of information you observe about the company's income statement?
b. What are the three most significant pieces of information you observe about the company's balance sheet?
c. How well did the company do in the most recent year?
d. Was the company better off at the end of the most recent year as compared with the preceding year?
e. How much was the company worth at the end of the most recent year?
f. Compare the company's book value and its market value per share. Why are these values different?
g. How do you explain the difference in the company's profit or loss for the year and its change in cash?
h. How do the five basic concepts listed below affect the financial statements presented in the company's annual report?
  (1). Business entity.
  (2). Historical dollar accounting.
  (3). Use of estimates and exercise of judgment.
  (4). Conservatism.
  (5). Materiality.

D14.6 For what audience are a company's annual reports prepared? Do you think this audience has a good understanding of the information presented in a "typical" annual report?

D14.7 The text suggests that an analyst should learn as much as possible about a company and its environment.

a. Why?
b. To what sources should the analyst go?
c. Can you cite any specific instances in which knowledge of PepsiCo and its environment contributed to your understanding of PepsiCo's 1990 figures?

D14.8 The text states that "the return-on-investment ratio should be used with care and judgment, for the ratio is usually derived from conventional statements that have many limitations."

a. What are some of these limitations?
b. What can the analyst do about these limitations?
c. For purposes of calculating the return on investment, what are the arguments for and against measuring "investment" as

   (1). Total assets including fixed assets at undepreciated cost.
   (2). Reported total assets less idle assets.
   (3). Reported total assets less "nonoperating assets."
   (4). Reported total assets less current liabilities.
   (5). Reported total assets with adjustments for inventories and fixed assets to reflect current replacement costs.
   (6). Which one do you prefer?
d. For purposes of calculating the return on investment, what are the arguments for and against measuring "return" as
   (1). Net income before deduction of interest on debt.
   (2). Net income exclusive of unusual and nonrecurring income.
   (3). Net income exclusive of nonoperating income.
   (4). Net income adjusted to show depreciation on replacement cost of fixed assets.
   (5). Net income before deduction of income taxes.
   (6). Which one do you prefer?

D14.9 In computing inventory turnover, select the best of the following statements and tell why or why not for each:

a. Cost of goods sold stated at LIFO should be divided by average inventory stated at LIFO.
b. Cost of goods sold stated at LIFO should be divided by average inventory stated at FIFO.
c. Cost of goods sold stated at FIFO should be divided by average inventory stated at FIFO.
d. Cost of goods sold stated at FIFO should be divided by average inventory stated at LIFO.

D14.10

a. If the numerator in computing earnings per share is subject to all the limitations of the income statement, how does one account for the concept being so widely quoted?
b. When earnings per share is coupled with market value per share to get the price-earnings ratio, also widely quoted, is the admonition to handle with care appropriate? If so, how so? If not, why not?

PROBLEMS

P14.1 Financial Analysis: The Income Statement. Presented below are the consolidated statements of income for Coca-Cola Enterprises, Inc., for the fiscal years ending 1988, 1989, and 1990. Evaluate Coca-Cola's operations using whatever analyses (e.g., ratio analysis, trend analysis, vertical and horizontal analysis) you believe are appropriate.

COCA-COLA ENTERPRISES, INC.
Consolidated Statements of Income
(in thousands except per share data)

	Fiscal year		
	1990	1989	1988
Net operating revenues	$4,034,043	$3,881,947	$3,874,445
Cost of sales	2,359,267	2,313,032	2,268,038
Gross profit	1,674,776	1,568,915	1,606,407
Selling, general and administrative expenses	1,339,928	1,258,848	1,225,238
Provision for restructuring	9,300	—	27,000
Operating income	325,548	310,067	354,169
Nonoperating income (deductions):			
Interest income	6,566	6,564	8,505
Interest expense	(206,648)	(200,163)	(210,936)
Other income (deductions)—net	(519)	10,463	12,183
Gain on sale of operations	59,300	11,000	103,800
Income before income taxes	184,247	137,931	267,721
Provision for income taxes	90,834	66,207	115,120
Net income	93,413	71,724	152,601
Preferred stock dividend requirements	16,265	18,217	9,882
Net income available to common shareholders	$ 77,148	$ 53,507	$ 142,719
Average common shares outstanding	119,217	129,768	138,755
Net income per common share	$ 0.65	$ 0.41	$ 1.03

P14.2 Financial Analysis: The Balance Sheet. Presented below are the consolidated balance sheets for Coca-Cola Enterprises, Inc., as of fiscal year-end 1989 and 1990. Evaluate Coca-Cola's financial condition using whatever analyses (e.g., ratio analysis, trend analysis, vertical and horizontal analysis) you believe are appropriate. (Use the consolidated statement of income from P14.1 if necessary.)

COCA-COLA ENTERPRISES, INC.
Consolidated Balance Sheets
(In thousands except share data)

	December 28, 1990	December 29, 1989
Assets		
Current		
Cash and cash equivalents, at cost (approximates market)	$ 507	$ 9,674
Trade accounts receivable, less allowances of $18,754 and $13,472, respectively	296,822	297,098
Inventories	128,450	127,880
Prepaid expenses and other assets	69,562	58,735
Total current assets	495,341	493,387
Investments and other long-term assets	105,637	73,286
Property, plant, and equipment		
Land	157,008	129,591
Buildings and improvements	453,100	427,206
Machinery and equipment	1,302,938	1,243,969
Containers	37,238	34,830
	1,950,284	1,835,596
Less allowances for depreciation	723,856	665,999
	1,226,428	1,169,597
Construction in progress	146,319	116,748
	1,372,747	1,286,345
Goodwill and other intangible assets	3,046,871	2,878,928
	$5,020,596	$4,731,946
Liabilities and Shareholders' Equity		
Current		
Accounts payable and accrued expenses	$ 456,765	$ 395,069
Accounts payable to The Coca-Cola Company	21,396	51,657
Loans and notes payable and current maturities of long term-debt	576,630	549,396
Total current liabilities	1,054,791	996,122
Long-term debt	1,960,164	1,755,626
Deferred income taxes	335,008	266,086
Other long-term obligations	44,154	33,975
Shareholders' equity		
Preferred stock, $1 par value Authorized—100,000,000 shares; Issued and outstanding–2,500 shares, at aggregate liquidation preference	250,000	250,000
Common stock, $1 par value Authorized—500,000,000 shares; Issued—140,471,081 shares and 140,363,166 shares, respectively	140,471	140,363
Paid-in capital	1,262,755	1,262,288
Reinvested earnings	382,243	311,198
Common stock in treasury, at cost 25,636,358 shares and 17,317,010 shares, respectively	(408,990)	(283,712)
	1,626,479	1,680,137
	$5,020,596	$4,731,946

P14.3 Financial Analysis: The Statement of Cash Flows. Using the financial statements presented in P14.1 and P14.2, prepare a consolidated statement of cash flows for Coca-Cola Enterprises, Inc., as of fiscal year-end 1990. Using this statement, identify the major sources and uses of cash flows by the company. How would you evaluate the company's overall cash position?

P14.4 Restating Financial Statements: Inventories. Presented below are the condensed financial statements for Scott Furniture as of December 31, 1989, and 1990. In the company's 1990 annual report, the following statement appeared:

> If first-in, first-out had been in use, inventories would have been $1,960 million, $1,654 million, and $1,388 million higher than reported at December 31, 1990, 1989, and 1988, respectively.

Scott had used the LIFO method since 1960 for both tax and financial reporting purposes.

Required:

a. Assume a tax rate of 35 percent and that Scott had adopted the FIFO method (rather than LIFO) in 1960 and used FIFO through 1990. Restate Scott's balance sheets as of year-end 1989 and 1990 to reflect the use of FIFO.

b. By how much would Scott's net income change in 1989 and 1990 if FIFO were used instead of LIFO?

c. Calculate the following ratios for Scott for 1989 and 1990 under both LIFO and FIFO:
   (1). Current ratio.
   (2). Inventory turnover.
   (3). Average number of days' inventory on hand.
   (4). Total debt-to-equity ratio.

d. Under which method do the ratios look best?

Scott Furniture
Condensed Balance Sheets
As of December 31, 1990 and 1989
(in millions)

	December 31 1990	December 31 1989
Assets		
Cash and cash equivalents	104	147
Receivables	912	693
Inventories	1,750	1,670
Land	81	66
Building and equipment (net)	2,928	2,572
Long-term investments	103	85
Other assets and goodwill	220	146
Total	6,098	5,379

	December 31 1990	December 31 1989
Liabilities and Owners' Equity		
Payables and accruals	1067	790
Income tax payable	198	133
Notes payable	430	404
Deferred income tax	23	(24)
Long-term debt (total)	948	1011
Total	2666	2314
Owners' Equity		
Common Stock	180	177
Retained earnings	3252	2888
Total	6098	5379

Scott Furniture
Condensed Statement of Income
For the Years Ending December 31, 1990 and 1989
(in millions)

Sales	8598	7613
Cost of goods sold	6957*	6172
Other expenses (net)	844	715
Income taxes	232	234
Total expenses	8033	7121
Income	565	492
Note:		
Depreciation for year	370	312
Dividends	201	182

*This figure includes depreciation allocable to cost of goods sold.

P14.5 Restating Financial Statements: Depreciation.

Scott Furniture's 1990 annual report included the following statement:

> Depreciation is computed principally using accelerated methods . . . for both income tax and financial reporting purposes. . . . If the straight-line method had always been in use, "Buildings, machinery, and equipment—net" would have been $504 million, $430 million, and $370 million higher than reported at December 31, 1990, 1989, and 1988, respectively, and depreciation expense for 1990, 1989, and 1988 would have been, respectively, $74 million, $60 million, and $48 million less.

Required:

a. Using the condensed financial statements presented in P14.4 and assuming a 35 percent tax rate, restate Scott's balance sheets for 1989 and 1990 to reflect the use of straight-line (rather than accelerated) depreciation. Assume that the straight-line method is used for financial reporting purposes and that accelerated depreciation is used for tax purposes.

b. By how much would Scott's net income change in 1989 and 1990 as a consequence of using the straight-line method?

c. Calculate the following ratios for Scott in 1989 and 1990 under both depreciation approaches:
(1). Return on sales.
(2). Return on total assets.
(3). Noncurrent asset turnover.
(4). Total asset turnover.

d. Under which method do the ratios look best?

P14.6 Restating Financial Statements: Pooling vs. Purchase Accounting. In 1975, Scott Furniture acquired the net assets of Erin Corporation by issuing 1,891,678 shares of Scott Furniture stock to the shareholders of Erin. Scott accounted for this transaction as a pooling-of-interests and, accordingly, included in its balance sheet only $32 million (the book value of Erin's net assets in 1975). The transaction was recorded on Scott's books as follows:

```
Dr.  Net Assets . . . . . . . . . . . . . . . . . . $32.0 million
     Cr.  Capital Stock . . . . . . . . . . . . . . . . . . . . .      $ 3.0 million
     Cr.  Retained Earnings . . . . . . . . . . . . . . . . . .       29.0 million
```

At the time of the acquisition, Scott's capital stock was trading on the over-the-counter market at about $50 per share.

Assume that instead of a stock exchange, Scott had sold its shares for $95 million and had used the proceeds to buy Erin's net assets. Assume that the transaction was accounted for as a purchase and that the fair market value of Erin's identifiable net assets equals $32 million.

Required:

a. Restate Scott's 1989 and 1990 financial statements to reflect the use of purchase accounting rather than pooling-of-interests accounting.

b. By how much would Scott's net income in 1989 and 1990 change?

c. Calculate the following ratios for Scott in 1989 and 1990 under both purchase accounting and pooling-of-interests accounting:
(1). Total debt-to-total assets.
(2). Book value per share. (Assume that 86.5 million shares are outstanding.)
(3). Earnings per share.
(4). Return on equity.

d. Under which method do the ratios look best?

P14.7 Calculating Earnings Per Share. Edna Lake, Inc., reported the following income data for 1990:

Income before extraordinary items	$174,000
Extraordinary loss (net of income taxes*)	(15,000)
Net income	$159,000

*Effective tax rate = 30 percent.

Throughout 1990, the company had 60,000 shares of common stock outstanding. The stock had traded at an average price of $25, and closed on December 31 at $30 per share. The company also had the following securities outstanding during all of 1990:

Common stock options for the purchase of 8,000 shares at a price of $20 per share.

10 percent convertible bonds, with a face value of $190,000. The bonds had been sold for $200,000 and yielded 9.4 percent when the average Aa corporate bond yield was 15 percent. The bonds were convertible into 7,600 shares.

9.2 percent convertible bonds, with a face value of $250,000. The bonds had been sold for $237,500 and yielded 9.7 percent when the average Aa corporate bond yield was 14 percent. The bonds were convertible into 10,000 shares.

Required:

a. Using the above data, calculate the raw EPS, the primary EPS, and the fully diluted EPS for Edna Lake, Inc., for 1990.
b. Which of the three EPS numbers most accurately reflects the company's actual performance during 1990?

P14.8 Financial Analysis by Line-of-Business. Review the business segments data for PepsiCo presented in Chapter 1. Using the financial analysis techniques discussed in Chapter 14, compare PepsiCo's three business segments (i.e., soft drinks, snack foods, and restaurants).

Required:

a. Which segment would you advise PepsiCo to emphasize, and why?
b. Is your recommendation the same for both domestic and international operations?

P14.9 Alternative GAAP: LIFO versus FIFO. The following information was taken from the 1983 financial statements of General Electric Company, a major conglomerate with significant product lines in both industrial and consumer markets:

Inventories are valued on a last-in, first-out basis and carry the following balances (in millions) at December 31:

	1982	1983
Ending inventory	$3,158	$3,029

If FIFO had been used to value the inventories, they would have been $2,152 million higher than reported at December 31, 1983 ($2,266 million higher at year-end 1982). During 1983, net reductions in inventory levels resulted in liquidations of LIFO bases of $114 million, and in 1982, $163 million.

Required:

Presented following are the condensed financial statements of General Electric Company. Using this information, answer the following questions:

a. If GE had used FIFO instead of LIFO in all prior years, how would the company's 1982 and 1983 financial statements differ? (Ignore any effects on income taxes.)
b. Compare the income tax consequences of GE's use of LIFO rather than FIFO in 1983.
c. Estimate the total tax savings that GE has received in all prior years as a consequence of using LIFO rather than FIFO. Assume a tax rate of 33 percent.

d. Calculate the following ratios for 1983 for GE under both FIFO and LIFO:
  (1). Current ratio.
  (2). Quick ratio.
  (3). Inventory turnover.
  (4). Average number of days' inventory on hand.

GENERAL ELECTRIC COMPANY
Statement of Financial Position
For the Year Ending December 31
(in millions)

	1983	1982
Assets:		
Quick assets	$ 7,754	$ 7,327
Inventories	3,158	3,029
Total current assets	$10,912	$10,356
Noncurrent assets	12,376	11,259
Total assets	$23,288	$21,615
Equities:		
Current liabilities	$ 8,688	$ 8,153
Long-term liabilities	3,162	3,099
Total liabilities	$11,850	$11,252
Owners' equity	11,438	10,363
Total equities	$23,288	$21,615

GENERAL ELECTRIC COMPANY
Statement of Earnings
For the Years Ended December 31, 1983, 1982, and 1981
(in millions)

	1983	1982	1981
Sales of products and services rendered	$26,797	$26,500	$27,240
Cost of goods sold	(24,248)	(24,095)	(24,793)
Other income and expenses	450	312	167
Provision for income taxes	(975)	(900)	(962)
Net earnings	$ 2,024	$ 1,817	$ 1,652

P14.10 Alternative GAAP: Leases. MCI is a telecommunications company that leases a substantial quantity of its noncurrent assets. For example, as of March 31, 1982, MCI had leased more than one third of its total noncurrent assets, and the obligations associated with those leases represented nearly 50 percent of the company's total long-term debt.

Presented below are condensed balance sheets for MCI as of March 31, 1982. The company's footnotes revealed the following additional data:

Depreciation of noncurrent assets is calculated using straight-line depreciation, assuming an average useful life of 10 years, unless the lease life is shorter. (No salvage value is assumed.) The value of capitalized leases included in noncurrent assets was as follows (in thousands):

	March 31	
	1982	**1981**
Total capitalized leases	$227,582	$250,451

At March 31, 1982, the aggregate minimum rental commitments under noncancelable leases were as follows:

Years Ending March 31,	**Capital Leases**	**Other Leases**	**Total**
1983	$ 57,876,000	$ 16,610,000	$ 74,486,000
1984	50,753,000	15,443,000	66,196,000
1985	42,721,000	14,441,000	57,162,000
1986	35,620,000	12,669,000	48,289,000
1987	24,410,000	10,580,000	34,990,000
1988 and thereafter	17,213,000	49,220,000	66,433,000
Minimum lease payments	228,593,000	$118,963,000	$347,556,000
Less—Amount representing interest	47,388,000		
Present value of future lease payments (Note 4)	$181,205,000		

Interest rates on capital lease obligations on a weighted-average basis approximate 12%.

Required:

Assuming that all "other leases" should be capitalized on the balance sheet, restate MCI's balance sheet as of March 31, 1982. Calculate the following ratios both before and after restatement:

a. Long-term debt-to-owners' equity.
b. Total debt-to-total assets.

Comment on how the company's bond ratings might be affected following the capitalization of all "other leases."

MCI COMMUNICATIONS CORPORATION
Balance Sheet
As of March 31, 1982 and 1991
(in thousands)

	1982	**1981**
Assets:		
Current assets	$228,428	$ 48,946
Noncurrent assets	631,970	417,946
Total assets	$860,398	$466,892
Equities:		
Current liabilities	$185,540	$ 73,729
Deferred income taxes	34,058	2,409
Long-term debt	400,018	242,707
Owners' equity	240,782	148,047
Total liabilities and owners' equity	$860,398	$466,892

P14.11 Alternative GAAP: LIFO versus FIFO. Presented below are the balance sheets and income statement of Phoenix Imports, Inc., as of December 31, 1991. In the company's annual report, the following statement appeared: "Inventories are valued on a FIFO basis. If LIFO had been used, inventories would have been valued at $889,000 at January 1, 1991, and at $1,270,000 at December 31, 1991."

Required:

Assume a tax rate of 50 percent, and that Phoenix Imports had also been using FIFO for tax purposes. Restate the company's balance sheet and income statement for 1991 to reflect the use of LIFO instead of FIFO. (Would you recommend such a method change for income tax purposes also?) Calculate the following ratios for 1991 under both LIFO and FIFO:

a. Current ratio.
b. Inventory turnover.
c. Average number of days' inventory on hand.
d. Total debt-to-equity ratio.

Which method do you think Phoenix Imports should use, and why?

PHOENIX IMPORTS
Balance Sheet
As of December 31, 1991

Assets		Equities	
Current assets:		Current liabilities:	
Cash	$ 436,000	Accounts payable	$ 820,000
Trade receivables		Accrued expenses payable	80,000
(net of allowance		Total current liabilities	900,000
for uncollectible			
accounts)	828,000		
Inventories	1,720,000		
Prepaid expenses	30,000		
Total current assets	3,014,000		
Noncurrent assets:		Noncurrent liabilities:	
Property, plant, and		Notes payable	2,320,000
equipment	$3,940,000	Deferred federal	
Less: Accumulated		Income taxes	800,000
depreciation	(1,360,000)	Total Liabilities	4,020,000
	2,580,000	Owners' equity:	
Land	560,000	Common stock, $1 par	2,000,000
Deferred research and		Retained earnings	1,284,000
development cost	1,150,000	Total equities	$7,304,000
Total assets	$7,304,000		

PHOENIX IMPORTS
Income Statement
For the Year Ended December 31, 1991

Sales revenue		$4,950,000
Less: Cost of sales		
Beginning inventory	$1,205,000	
Cost of production.......................................	3,665,000	
Goods available for sale	4,870,000	
Less: Ending inventory	1,720,000	
		(3,150,000)
Gross margin		1,800,000
Less: Research and development		
expenses	350,000	
Licensing fees..	100,000	
Selling and administrative expenses	400,000	
		(850,000)
Net income before taxes		950,000
Less: Income taxes...	475,000	
Investment and research tax credits	(60,000)	
		(415,000)
Net income after taxes		$ 535,000

P14.12 Alternative GAAP: Depreciation. Phoenix Imports' 1991 annual report included the following statement: ''Property, plant and equipment is depreciated on a straight-line method. If an accelerated method had been used, the depreciation expense for 1991 would have been $230,000 higher, and the year-end balance in the accumulated depreciation account $450,000 greater.''

Required:

a. Using the financial statements presented in P14.11 and assuming a 50 percent tax rate, restate Phoenix Imports' financial statements for 1991 to reflect the use of accelerated depreciation rather than the straight-line method. Phoenix Imports reports all depreciation as a component of cost of goods sold. (What recommendation would you make for income tax purposes?)

b. Calculate the following ratios for 1991 under both accelerated and straight-line depreciation:

(1). Return on sales.

(2). Return on total assets.

(3). Noncurrent asset turnover.

(4). Total asset turnover.

c. Which method do you think Phoenix Imports should use, and why?

P14.13 Alternative GAAP: Capitalizing versus Expensing R&D. Phoenix Imports' 1991 annual report included the following statement:

The research and development expense for 1991 represented one-half of the actual R&D expenditure for 1991; the remaining balance had been capitalized. The company's policy is to begin amortization of these capitalized costs once a commercially productive asset has been developed. To date, no productive assets have resulted from the research program represented by the currently capitalized R&D costs.

Required:

a. Using the financial statements presented in P14.11 and assuming a 50 percent tax rate, restate Phoenix Imports' financial statements for 1991 to reflect the full current expensing of all R&D costs. (What recommendation would you make for income tax purposes?)
b. Calculate the following ratios for 1991 under the old and new policies regarding expensing R&D expenditures:
   (1). Return on sales.
   (2). Return on total assets.
   (3). Noncurrent asset turnover.
   (4). Total asset turnover.

c. Which method do you think Phoenix Imports should adopt, and why?

P14.14 Alternative GAAP: Completed Contract versus Percentage of Completion.
Thunderbird Construction Company (TCC) was employed to construct a new office facility in downtown Phoenix, Arizona. The three-year project is projected to cost $100 million to complete and is expected to produce gross revenues of $150 million during the three-year period.

In anticipation of the preparation of financial reports covering the project, TCC's controller collected the following financial data (in millions) relating to the project:

	(in millions)		
	1989	**1990**	**1991**
Construction costs incurred	$400	$300	$325
Estimated costs to complete	600	350	—
Progress billings	500	500	500
Collections on billings	—	450	900
Administrative expense	25	25	25

Required:

a. Using the above data, prepare income statements for the company under (1) the completed contract method and (2) the percentage of completion method for each of the three years.
b. Which set of results do you believe most accurately depicts the performance of the company?

P14.15 Calculating Earnings per Share.
Assume that during 1991, FHAS Enterprises has the following securities outstanding:

1. 250,000 shares of common stock with an average market price of $25 per share.
2. Options granted to executives to purchase 4,000 shares of common stock during the next three years at a price of $20 per share.
3. Zero coupon convertible debentures with a maturity value of $10 million, which had been sold at a yield of 12 percent when the Aa corporate bond rate was 14.5 percent. Each $1,000 face value bond is convertible into 15 shares of common stock.
4. Convertible preferred stock, which had been sold at its par value of $100 to yield 9.5 percent. The preferred stock is convertible into 3 shares of common and 3,000 shares are outstanding.

During 1991, FHAS Enterprises earned $3.2 million after taxes. (Assume that taxes are calculated at 33 percent.)

Required:

Calculate the raw, primary, and fully diluted earnings per share for the company.

CASES

C14.1 Ratio Analysis: Ratios Tell a Story Financial results vary among companies for a number of reasons. One reason for the variation can be traced to the characteristics of the industries in which the companies work. Some industries require large investments in property, plant, and equipment; others require very little. In some industries, the product-pricing structure allows companies to earn significant profits per sales dollar; in other industries, the product-pricing structure forces a much lower profit margin. In most low-margin industries, however, companies often experience a relatively high volume of product throughput in their businesses. A number of industries are also characterized by lenient credit terms; others sell for cash only.

A second reason for some of the variation in financial results among companies is the result of management policy. Some companies reduce their manufacturing capacity to match more closely their immediate sales prospects; others carry excess capacity to prepare for future expansion. Another policy-related difference is that some companies finance their assets with borrowed funds, but others avoid that leverage and finance their assets with equity.

Of course, one other reason for some of the variation in reported results among companies is the differing competencies of management. Given the same industry characteristics and the same management policies, different companies report different financial results simply because their managements perform differently.

These differences in industry characteristics, in company policies, and in management performance are reflected in the financial statements and can be highlighted through the use of financial ratios.

Presented following are balance sheets, in percentage form, and selected ratios computed from fiscal 1989 balance sheets and income statements, for 14 companies from the following industries:

1. Vehicle leasing/rental company.
2. Automobile manufacturer.
3. Chemical company.
4. Commercial bank.
5. Computer manufacturer.
6. Discount general merchandise store chain.
7. Electric utility.
8. Fast-food chain.
9. Wholesale food distributor.
10. Railroad company.
11. Supermarket chain.
12. Textile manufacturer.
13. Advertising agency.
14. Software development company.

The ratios below were developed based on the following formulae:

1. Return on sales (ROS) = $\dfrac{\text{Net income}}{\text{Net sales}}$

2. Asset turnover = $\dfrac{\text{Net sales}}{\text{Average total assets}}$

Ratios Tell a Story: 1989

Company Year Ended	1 12/31	2 12/30	3 12/31	4 12/31	5 2/2	6 12/31	7 12/31
Assets							
Cash and equivalents	45.5	1.4	11.3	0.8	5.1	5.7	9.5
Accounts receivable	16.2	9.7	65.5	25.6	2.7	8.7	2.6
Inventory	3.8	29.3	—	30.5	27.2	0.6	2.3
Other current assets	2.3	2.0	—	1.8	2.2	1.7	1.2
Total current assets	67.8	42.4	76.8	58.7	37.2	16.7	15.6
Net plant and equipment	26.0	21.8	2.2	38.6	60.3	76.9	74.4
Other assets	6.2	35.8	21.0	2.7	2.5	6.4	10.0
Financial services assets							
Total assets	100.0%	100.0%	100.0%	100.0%	100.0%	100.0%	100.0%
Liabilities							
Notes payable	0.5	0.7	15.9	0.4	0.7	1.0	2.5
Accounts payable	10.4	25.2	73.5	10.7	23.6	8.0	6.0
Accrued taxes	1.7	—	—	0.4	1.5	1.5	3.1
Other current liabilities	5.5	3.0	.6	9.1	4.9	1.3	4.9
Total current liabilities	18.1	28.9	90.0	20.6	30.7	11.8	16.5
Long-term debt	33.5	36.1	1.9	39.7	11.1	6.8	23.0
Other liabilities	2.3	6.7	1.7	7.1	7.9	31.0	5.5
Financial services liabilities							
Total liabilities	53.9	71.7	93.6	67.4	49.7	49.6	45.0
Equity							
Preferred stock	—	1.9	—	—	—	—	—
Capital stock and surplus	23.2	13.2	1.6	13.9	6.5	6.0	17.4
Retained earnings	55.1	13.2	4.8	18.7	43.8	44.6	38.0
Treasury stock	32.2	—	—			0.2	0.4
Total liabilities and equity	100.0%	100.0%	100.0%	100.0%	100.0%	100.0%	100.0%
ROS (%)	12.22	0.66	11.76	1.72	2.40	13.36	2.86
Asset turnover	1.08	4.59	.10	1.63	4.53	0.45	1.37
ROA (%)	13.20	3.03	1.17	2.80	10.87	6.01	3.89
Financial leverage	2.17	3.53	15.63	3.07	1.99	1.98	1.82
ROE (%)	28.64	10.70	18.38	8.61	21.63	11.89	7.08
Debt to capital	0.42	0.56	0.23	0.55	0.18	0.12	0.29
Current ratio	3.75	1.47	0.85	2.85	1.21	1.42	0.95
Inventory turnover	5.09	14.36	n/a	4.40	14.41	n/a	32.33
Receivables collection-days	63	8	2547	58	2	75	6
Depreciation/sales receivable (%)	6.08	0.65	3.05	2.39	1.6	7.65	5.27

*excluding financial services activity

3. Return on assets (ROA) $=$ $\dfrac{\text{Net income}}{\text{Average total assets}}$

or $=$ ROS $\times$ Asset turnover

4. Financial leverage $=$ $\dfrac{\text{Liabilities} + \text{Owners' equity}}{\text{Owners' equity}}$

or $=$ $\dfrac{\text{Total assets}}{\text{Owners' equity}}$

8 12/31	9 12/31	10 12/31		11 1/31	12 12/31		13 12/31	14 12/31
0.3	0.5	4.3		0.2	2.5		1.7	5.1
6.9	12.4	20.7		2.0	2.9		11.5	66.0
3.1	12.8	12.2		52.7	4.2		8.1	—
3.9	7.4	4.9		2.2	2.3		3.7	7.7
14.2	33.1	42.1		57.1	11.9		25.0	78.8
74.8	34.5	33.7		41.9	11.3		61.5	7.6
11.0	32.4	7.8		1.0	5.3		13.5	13.6
		16.4			71.5			
100.0%	100.0%	100.0%		100.0%	100.0%		100.0%	100.0%
2.9	10.3	3.1		0.6	1.6		9.0	3.1
3.8	10.3	4.1		21.9	6.3		7.0	56.3
0.1	1.2	—		1.9	0.4		0.8	2.6
4.3	7.5	14.7		8.1	4.2		9.2	7.7
11.1	29.3	21.9		32.5	12.5		26.0	69.5
36.6	17.4	7.8		18.8	0.7		36.9	2.1
12.0	7.9	8.6		1.4	5.5		12.0	6.5
		12.2			66.6			
59.7	54.6	50.5		52.7	85.3		74.9	78.1
5.4	—	—		—	0.5		1.7	8.4
24.7	12.6	8.1		3.6	0.7		8.0	17.3
10.2	41.5	41.4		43.7	13.5		15.4	3.8
—	8.7	—						
100.0%	100.0%	100.0%		100.0%	100.0%		100.0%	100.0%
10.49	14.12	5.99	5.86*	4.05	3.99	3.95*	1.17	5.80
0.40	.92	0.83	0.96*	3.60	.63	1.86*	0.66	0.73
4.20	12.99	4.97	5.63*	14.58	2.51	7.35*	0.77	4.22
2.48	2.20	2.02	1.74*	2.11	6.84	2.92*	3.98	4.57
10.41	28.58	10.04	9.79*	30.82	17.17	21.46*	3.06	19.28
0.48	0.25	0.22	0.14*	0.28	0.05	0.07*	0.60	0.09
1.28	1.13	1.65	1.93*	1.76	.95	0.95*	0.96	1.13
4.96	4.03		2.91*	5.35		11.05*	n/a	n/a
63	56	105	92*	2	384	20*	50	51
11.65	6.03	8.65	8.4*	1.03	4.4	4.3	12.3	1.8

This material was prepared by Mark E. Haskins with assistance from Chris Wenger and Robert J. Sack, Darden Graduate School of Business Administration, Charlottesville, Virginia.

5. Return on equity (ROE) = $\dfrac{\text{Net income}}{\text{Average total owner's equity}}$

$or =$ ROA $\times$ Financial leverage

6. Long-term debt to capital = $\dfrac{\text{LT debt}}{\text{LT debt + Owner's equity}}$

7. Current ratio = $\dfrac{\text{Total current assets}}{\text{Total current liabilities}}$

8. Inventory turnover = $\dfrac{\text{Cost of goods sold}}{\text{Average inventory}}$

9. Receivables collection = $\dfrac{\text{Average accounts receivable}}{\text{Net sales/365 days}}$

10. Depreciation as a percentage of sales = $\dfrac{\text{Depreciation}}{\text{Net sales}}$

Required:

a. Study the balance sheet profiles and the financial ratios listed for each of the 14 companies as presented previously. Your first assignment is to match each column in the exhibit with one of the industries listed previously. Be prepared to give the reasons for your pairings and identify those pieces of data that seem to contradict the pairings you have made.

b. Your second assignment is to identify those companies that are in similar industries (there are a number of comparables, although none are exact duplicates) but that report different results because they may have adopted different management policies. Be prepared to identify the different policies and the effect they have had. Also comment on the reason(s) the company may have had for adopting those policies.

C14.2 Accrual versus Cash-Basis Financial Statements: Lone Star Real Estate Corporation.

Lone Star Real Estate Corporation is a land development and sales company located in Dallas, Texas. The company's audited financial statements for the year ended December 31, 1986, and unaudited financial statements for the first six months of 1987 are presented following. A review of the statements reveals that, among other things, the company is profitable and has a substantial net worth and more than $14 million in liquid assets on hand.

In July 1987, however, the company approached its primary lender and requested a renegotiation of the terms of its outstanding notes payable. The president of Lone Star threatened that if the terms of the debt contracts were not suitably restructured, the company would be forced to file for voluntary bankruptcy.

Required:

Analyze the financial statements of Lone Star Real Estate Corporation to determine whether the company has a valid basis for requesting the debt restructuring. Be able to substantiate your position.

LONE STAR REAL ESTATE CORPORATION
Consolidated Balance Sheet
(In thousands)

	June 30, 1987 (Unaudited)	December 31, 1986
Assets		
Cash and investments	$ 14,313	$ 29,877
Accounts receivable (net):		
Other	890	519
Affiliates	1,949	1,693
Notes receivable (net):		
Other	2,545	855
Affiliates (including interest and fees)	44,038	18,592
Inventories of land	519,197	500,115
Rental real estate	13,244	13,438
Other assets	7,233	6,938
Total	$603,411	$572,027
Liabilities and Stockholders' Equity		
Notes payable:		
Other	$418,634	$408,008
Affiliates	1,413	2,447
Accounts payable and accrued liabilities:		
Other	20,902	23,808
Affiliates	6	9
Total liabilities	440,955	434,272
Stockholders' equity:		
Common stock	100	100
Additional paid-in capital	30,475	30,475
Retained earnings	131,881	107,180
Total stockholders' equity	162,456	137,755
Total	$603,411	$572,027

LONE STAR REAL ESTATE CORPORATION
Consolidated Statement of Income (Unaudited)
(In thousands)

	For the Six Months Ended June 30,	
	1987	1986
Revenues		
Sales of land	$13,819	$ 7,194
Management services income	356	215
Development services income	4,080	8,785
Interest and fee income	10,635	8,743
Total	28,890	24,937

	For the Six Months Ended June 30,	
	1987	**1986**
Costs and expenses		
Bad debts expense (reversal)	(9,219)	6,640
Cost of land sold	5,592	3,325
Development services expense	3,712	9,145
Interest expense	22,707	19,569
Interest capitalized	(22,707)	(19,569)
Selling, general, and administrative expenses	4,104	3,216
Total	4,189	22,326
Income (loss) before income taxes	24,701	2,611
Charge equivalent to income taxes	11,362	1,201
Benefit from parent company	(11,362)	(1,201)
Net income (loss)	$24,701	$ 2,611

C14.3 Pro Forma Financial Statements: Hofstedt Oil & Gas Company. The venture capital division of a major U.S. financial institution has elected to fund an investment in an oil and gas exploration and production company that will operate both onshore and offshore in Texas and Louisiana. The initial financing commitment from the bank is for $40 million.

The company's strategic plan calls for an aggressive drilling program to be carried out during 1993. Hofstedt Oil & Gas estimates that it will drill 50 wells at an average cost of $800,000 per well and that 30 of those wells will yield aggregate crude oil reserves of approximately 10 million barrels. The remaining 20 wells are expected to be dry, or commercially unproductive. These forecasts were based on the expert opinion of geologists familiar with the properties and were confirmed by petroleum engineers employed directly by the bank.

The company's production plan calls for a maximum exploitation effort to earn the highest financial return. Tom Hofstedt, president of the company, developed the following production scenario:

Year	Number of Barrels to Be Produced	Estimated Selling Price per Barrel	Estimated Lifting Cost Per Barrel
1993	1,000,000	$30	$5
1994	1,500,000	30	5
1995	1,500,000	35	6
1996	2,500,000	40	7
1997	3,500,000	45	8

Hofstedt Oil & Gas is very concerned about the impact of this operation on its financial statements and on the company's stock price. Consequently, any available accounting policy choices loom as very important in the overall evaluation of the investment. As a result, Hofstedt sent a terse memo to the company's controller, the closing line of which stated: ''Prepare pro forma statements showing the alternative accounting effects on cash flow, income before tax, and financial position if we elect to use the successful efforts method or the full-cost method.''

Required:

For purposes of pro forma statement preparation, assume that the $40 million loan agreement will be repaid as follows: (1) $10 million principal repayment per year to be paid on December 31 beginning on December 31, 1994, and (2) interest payments of 10 percent per year on the balance of the loan outstanding as of the beginning of the year. Ignore income taxes and all other operations. Based on your pro forma cash flows, income statements, and balance sheets for the period 1993 through 1997, what accounting method (successful efforts or full cost) recommendation would you make to Hofstedt, and why?

C14.4 Pro Forma Financial Statements: Brown's Fishing Reel Company.

Mike Brown, a machinist employed at General Gyro, Inc., liked to spend his free time fishing at local lakes. Over the years, he had developed several innovations in fishing equipment. Brown added the new fishing gear to his own equipment and occasionally made copies for friends to use.

As a consequence of the slowdown in defense-related products during the recession of 1991, Brown was among 1,500 employees laid off by General Gyro. He was troubled about the loss of income, as well as the fact that no one could predict when business might increase enough to put the laid-off employees back to work. Brown and his wife discussed the problems caused by the potential cash shortage faced by their family. Her current position as a dental technician would help, but they had become accustomed to spending their combined incomes. Living on just one income would result in many adjustments.

One of Brown's friends suggested the possibility of manufacturing fishing equipment as a full-time occupation. The Browns thought this could be the solution to their long-range income problem, although it would involve risk and sacrifices in the short run. The Browns had savings they had invested for several years. The total they believed they could use to start the new business was $70,000. When Brown's fishing friends heard about his plans, several of them said that they would like to provide part of the equity for the new venture. After talking it over with everyone who was interested in the investment, Brown knew he could count on total start-up equity capital of $170,000.

One of the investors, Tony Bartell, offered to help Brown develop plans for the first year of operations. The two decided to make conservative estimates of figures that would permit Bartell to construct pro forma financial statements. Meanwhile, Brown demonstrated his improved fishing reel to three national sporting goods retailers and two large catalog marketing organizations. With their initial orders and promises of repeat business, he felt confident that first-quarter sales would be $112,000 and that the quarterly growth rate in sales would be 5 percent.

Brown intended to watch operating costs carefully, doing much of the machining himself and hiring other laid-off General Gyro workers on a part-time contract basis. As sales became more predictable, permanent full-time employees would be hired. To reduce risk, Mike wanted costs to be as variable with sales as possible during the first year. He estimated that cost of goods sold could be held to 62 percent of sales.

This case was prepared by Paul D. Cretien, Baylor University.

To provide stable production of machined parts and finished reels, inventories would be maintained so that quarter-ending inventories would equal 95 percent of the next quarter's cost of goods sold. Twenty-five percent of inventory purchases would be paid in cash at the time of purchase; the remaining 75 percent would be paid in the following quarter.

Most sales would be credit sales, with 85 percent of sales dollars received at the end of the quarter following a sale. Small firms would pay cash for the reels shipped, accounting for the remaining 15 percent of collections.

Brown thought that the company should have a cash balance of $5,000 at all times to take care of regular transactions and possible emergency needs. If the projected cash balance fell below the $5,000 target balance at the end of any quarter, the company would use short-term bank credit to cover the deficit. On the other hand, if the pro forma statement indicated a cash surplus, the excess cash would be invested in short-term marketable securities. The company's bank assured Brown and Bartell that excess cash above $5,000 would be placed in money market deposits paying an annual interest rate of 5 percent. The interest on the securities would be received in the quarter following their investment.

Because of lower real estate prices and the numerous properties held by the Resolution Trust Corporation in the local business area, Brown found a building that could be purchased for the bargain price of $120,000. He estimated that $25,000 would be needed for equipment and building improvements to begin production. He decided to estimate total depreciation expense equal to 1.5 percent per month on the combined cost of the building and equipment.

Brown and Bartell approached the banker with a request for a term loan to assist in purchasing the building and equipment. After hearing their plans and viewing the projected figures, the bank officer agreed to provide a $60,000 term loan; principal and interest would be paid in equal quarterly installments over a five-year period. The annual interest rate on the term loan would be 8 percent. The banker suggested that the remaining credit should be in the form of a credit line, with interest paid in the quarter following the borrowing. The amount borrowed on the short-term working capital loan would depend on the financing needed to balance the company's statements at the end of each quarter. The annual rate of interest on short-term borrowing was 6.5 percent. Interest would be paid in the quarter following the one in which the credit was used.

In addition to the cost of goods sold, Brown estimated that the company's administrative and selling costs would be $15,000 per quarter. Start-up expenses, including travel and marketing costs already incurred, would total $6,900 by the time the company started business on January 1, 1992. Other operating expenses were expected to be 5 percent of sales; the company's average tax rate would be 30 percent.

After summarizing their estimated figures, Brown started to work on the statements he wanted to analyze. These included a beginning balance sheet (i.e., the company's financial condition before starting production on December 31, 1991), pro forma quarterly balance sheets and income statements for the first four quarters and for the year ending December 31, 1992, and a pro forma cash flow statement (showing cash from operating activities, investing activities, and financing activities) for each quarter and for the year.

Brown and Bartell realized that the financial projections could determine whether or not Brown's Fishing Reel Company would be a successful venture. The company's investors had agreed that unless the business was expected to return at least 25 percent on stockholders' equity, the risk would be higher than justified by the potential returns.

Brown made several additional assumptions before constructing the pro forma statements: (1) beginning inventory at the end of Quarter 0 will be financed entirely by equity and bank loans; (2) financing with trade credit begins in Quarter 1; (3) income taxes will be calculated and paid at the end of each quarter; (4) any operating losses will be carried forward to offset future taxable income; (5) marketable securities and short-term bank loans are used as "plug" figures to balance the balance sheet, thus one of these accounts should be zero each quarter while the other contains a positive total; and (6) Brown's salary as a manager is included in administrative and selling expense. Otherwise, all stockholder profits are left to accumulate in retained earnings.

Required:

a. Complete the pro forma statements suggested by Brown and Bartell. A summary of the assumptions that will form the basis of the projected results is presented below. Also presented is a loan amortization table showing the payment schedule for the $60,000 term loan.

b. Comment on the expected profitability of the proposed venture. In view of the potential risks, explain why the investors should decide to (1) go ahead with the project or (2) cancel it.

Brown's Fishing Reel Company

Assumptions:

Cost of goods sold as percentage of sales	62.00%
Inventory as percentage of next month's COGS	95.00%
Percentage of merchandise orders paid in cash	25.00%
Percentage of orders paid in following quarter	75.00%
Percentage of sales that are for cash	15.00%
Credit sales as percentage of sales, paid next quarter	85.00%
Selling and administrative expenses per quarter	15,000
Other operating expense as percentage of sales	5.00%
Interest rate on long-term debt	8.00%
Interest rate on short-term debt*	6.50%
Depreciation expense as percentage of building cost	1.50%
Start-up expenses	6,900
Income tax rate	30.00%
Quarterly growth rate in sales	5.00%
Sales expected for first quarter	112,000
Building cost	120,000
Building improvements	25,000
Beginning inventory	87,250
Minimum cash balance	5,000
Owners' equity	170,000
Beginning term loan	60,000
Interest rate on marketable securities*	5.00%

*Interest on balancing accounts is received or paid in the following quarter.

Amortization Schedule: Term Loan

Term loan, initial balance	60,000
Annual interest rate	8.00%
Number of quarters to repay term loan	20
Quarterly payment	3,669

Quarter	Payment	Interest	Principal	Balance
0	—	—	—	60,000
1	3,669	1,200	2,469	57,531
2	3,669	1,151	2,519	55,012
3	3,669	1,100	2,569	52,443
4	3,669	1,049	2,621	49,822
5	3,669	996	2,673	47,149
6	3,669	943	2,726	44,423
7	3,669	888	2,781	41,642
8	3,669	833	2,837	38,805
9	3,669	776	2,893	35,912
10	3,669	718	2,951	32,961
11	3,669	659	3,010	29,951
12	3,669	599	3,070	26,880
13	3,669	538	3,132	23,748
14	3,669	475	3,194	20,554
15	3,669	411	3,258	17,296
16	3,669	346	3,323	13,972
17	3,669	279	3,390	10,582
18	3,669	212	3,458	7,124
19	3,669	142	3,527	3,597
20	3,669	72	3,597	(0)

Financial Reporting in Foreign Countries

With the advent of a global economy, characterized by electronically accessible stock exchanges and multinational enterprises operating in scores of countries, the production, dissemination, and use of financial information is no longer restricted by national borders. The knowledge that one needs to interpret and understand foreign financial statements, however, goes beyond merely acquainting oneself with what accounting methods and practices were used in preparing the documents (though of course this is important). Even if complete standardization of international accounting standards were achieved—which is unlikely to happen for some time to come—one would still need important contextual information to assess the significance of a given piece of financial data. For example, what should we conclude if we find that the equity of a Japanese steel-making firm is only 10 percent of its total capitalization and its current ratio is 0.75? Contextualizing the information from other nations imposes special demands on both managers and investors. The premises on which financial data are constituted in other parts of the world are now a matter of crucial importance.

The focus of this chapter, thus, is the financial reporting by foreign companies. We will examine some of the practices unique to these companies and we will consider the contextual factors that influence those accounting practices.

CONTEXTUAL FACTORS

Legal and Political Environment

One of the fundamental contextual questions that must be asked of any financial reporting system is its relationship to tax law. In the United States and Great Britain, the influence of tax provisions on the calculation of accounting income is minimal. Companies may report one set of figures in their financial statements and a substantially different set on their tax returns. In many other countries, however, taxable income is more closely related to accounting income. In Japan and Germany, for example, expenses must be recorded in the financial statements to qualify as deductible on a company's tax return.

The requirement that accounting and tax income be substantially the same naturally prompts companies to measure income as conservatively as legally possible. Certain expenses, most notably depreciation, are calculated according to legislative requirements and incentives instead of according to business experience. Consequently, accountants and auditors become less concerned with fair presentation than with legal compliance. Because tax law is formulated by national legislative bodies in response to varying political and economic agendas, its influence on financial reporting is one of the most obvious and immediate hindrances to establishing a common set of international reporting standards.

Although corporate tax law and its relationship to financial reporting have a more direct effect on accounting standards, individual tax law also affects them. Tax incentives for individuals are among the tools that governments use to encourage (or discourage) share ownership among small investors, which in turn has an impact on the nature and orientation of corporate financial reporting. Nations eager to develop stronger stock exchanges—Italy is a good example—are not only adjusting governmental regulation to ensure fair and free markets; they are also implementing tax incentives to encourage their citizens to buy and hold stocks. If this trend persists, it is likely to move foreign accounting standards in the direction of Anglo-American reporting practices.

Other legal and political factors impinge on accounting systems as well. For example, the role of government in formulating financial reporting principles and standards, the volatility of the political system (which may affect the frequency of reform), the existence of external pressures (such as membership in the European Economic Community) on governments to revamp systems all affect a country's financial reporting practices.

Business Environment

Because modern financial accountability results from the development of the publicly held corporation with its separation of ownership and management and its limitation of liability, the dominant form of business in an economy can have a material effect on a country's sophistication of financial reporting standards. In Italy, for example, the continuing prominence of small, family-owned companies (and large ones as well) has undoubtedly contributed to the slow development of public-minded financial reporting standards in that country. Although every developed nation recognizes some version of the publicly owned corporation as a primary business entity, the reporting requirements imposed on such companies vary widely. Company law in most countries distinguishes between public and closely held corporations and between "large" and "small" companies (however they may be defined) and adjusts reporting requirements accordingly.

Closely related to the forms of business in a country is the state of its capital markets. The nature of financial reporting standards and the fundamental purpose of the entire reporting system depend on customary sources of capital. In such countries as Germany and Japan, where banks have long played a very powerful role in maintaining economic growth, disclosure tends to be deemphasized because these lenders (who are usually major investors as well) generally have access to internal corporate information. In addition to the banking system, the development of stock exchanges, the distribution of share ownership, the effectiveness of regulation, and the stringency of listing requirements have a powerful effect on financial reporting standards and the extent of disclosure.

A sophisticated and modern system of financial disclosure also requires an accounting profession that is well educated and large enough to ensure its proper functioning. This is readily apparent in countries such as Great Britain and the United States, where the accounting profession has significant responsibility for creating financial reporting standards. But even in nations where financial reporting standards are largely a matter of central legislation, the sophistication and training of the accounting profession (usually because it serves as an adviser to the legislature and is itself charged with developing auditing standards) noticeably affects the quality of financial reporting. Swedish multinationals, for example, under the guidance of a professional elite, consistently publish some of the best annual reports in the world even though Swedish accounting standards are dictated by commercial law.

INTERNATIONALIZING ACCOUNTING STANDARDS

The need to codify and standardize international accounting standards has become a major focal point for multinational companies attempting to communicate with investors and lenders in foreign domains. With no universally accepted set of international financial reporting and disclosure guidelines, multinationals have responded with a variety of strategies ranging from merely translating the text of annual reports into various languages ("convenience translations"), to preparing several sets of statements that report results in different languages and currencies according to different countries' accounting principles ("multiple reporting").

Obviously, reporting strategies that ignore differences in local accounting principles present problems for analysts and investors; those that take them into account require considerably more time and expense on the part of the preparer. Either way, someone must absorb the costs of divergent principles and standards of financial reporting, and generally it has been the multinational company. No wonder, then, that multinationals are supporting **harmonization** of accounting practices because it promises to reduce the differences in reporting requirements and because it promises to make investing more transparent and rational.

International Accounting Standards Committee

Among professional organizations that have greatly contributed to the codification of international accounting practice is the **International Accounting Standards Committee** (IASC). The IASC was founded in 1973 by a group of professional accounting organizations from nine countries and has since grown to include groups from 80 nations. An association of professional accountancy bodies, the IASC is the most widely recognized professional group in charge of developing and issuing international accounting standards. The purpose of the IASC, as stated in its constitution, is as follows:

a. To formulate and publish in the public interest, accounting standards to be observed in the presentation of financial statements and to promote their worldwide acceptance and observance;

b. To work generally for the improvement and harmonization of regulations, accounting standards and procedures relating to the presentation of financial statements.

Given the political and technical barriers that must inevitably slow the harmonization process, the IASC has made considerable headway, issuing over 30 **international accounting standards** (each known as an IAS) since its founding.

Lacking the authority to enforce observance of its standards, the IASC has had to exercise considerable diplomacy and discretion both in formulating standards and in urging their adoption by national standard-setting bodies. It must continually weigh the benefits of greater uniformity in financial reporting practices against the social and economic costs of retooling accounting systems, and it must bear in mind that many financial reporting practices arise from legitimate local needs. Consequently, a typical IAS sets broad principles and leaves details of application to national officials. Often it allows alternative treatments and permits some adaptation to national circumstances.

The IASC has focused principally on obvious targets—financial reporting practices that are clearly arbitrary or unsound—in the belief that filtering out such practices is an important first step toward harmonization. In countries that have not yet issued financial reporting standards or that allow more than one accounting treatment of a given transaction, the IASC has urged local officials to adopt uniform practices consistent with existing international accounting standards. In short, rather than immediately pushing toward complete uniformity, it has instead sought to reduce or prevent needless diversity.

Since early 1987, however, the IASC has been moving toward a new level of international harmonization. At that time, a steering committee on comparability of financial statements was appointed to review existing international accounting standards with the objective of reducing the number of alternative treatments permissible. In January 1989, the IASC released an exposure draft of a standard that would amend 13 previously issued standards, eliminating 23 treatments allowed under these standards and identifying 12 other treatments as preferred in instances in which alternatives would still be allowed. (A final vote on this exposure draft is not scheduled until October 1992.) Preparers who use an alternative treatment in those instances would be required to provide a reconciliation to the preferred treatment. (For example, LIFO would still be allowed if its effects on the balance sheet and income statement were disclosed.) Although the elimination of all alternative treatments will likely prove impracticable, the reconciliation requirement offers a promising solution to the problem of comparability.

Predictably, the IASC has drawn considerable criticism from some quarters. It has been accused of allowing industrialized nations to dominate the standard-setting process, of legislating with little regard for the needs of practitioners and financial analysts, and of serving multinationals and ignoring smaller domestic enterprises. The IASC, however, owes no allegiance to any nation and makes a point of including developing nations on its governing board. It consults with analysts, executives, managerial accountants, and industry groups as standards are developed, and it recognizes that the acceptance of each IAS depends on its usefulness to users and preparers of statements. Small domestic companies as well as giant multinationals are included in its jurisdiction, a fact that the IASC implicitly recognizes by trying to make its standards concise, clear, and simple enough to be useful around the world.

Two other complaints, somewhat broader in scope, are sometimes leveled against the IASC. The first and most common is that the IASC is ineffectual. The lack of an enforcement mechanism has undoubtedly slowed progress toward harmonization, but one can hardly blame the IASC itself for the limitations imposed on it by the politics of national sovereignty. In the endeavor in which the IASC may properly be held accountable—winning acceptance of its standards by dint of negotiation and consultation—the general consensus is that it is making significant progress.

The other charge, made less frequently but more serious, is that the IASC is too concerned with technical conformity and not sensitive enough to the cultural and economic issues underlying national accounting systems. This is a troubling charge, one that ultimately calls into question the feasibility of harmonization. It implicitly asks us to consider what level of reform is necessary for the creation of meaningful international standards. Is it enough to change an accounting system alone, or must legislation, economic habits, even basic cultural attitudes, be altered as well? This is a difficult question to answer because we simply do not yet know enough about the interaction between cultural contexts and financial reporting norms.

FINANCIAL REPORTING IN TWO FOREIGN COUNTRIES

The remaining pages of this chapter provide an introduction to the reporting practices and contextual issues of two countries: Japan and the United Kingdom. Of necessity, the discussion of each will be brief but, we hope, enlightening.

Japan

Although scholars have devised several classifications of international financial reporting systems, Japan's system is difficult to fit into any particular global grouping. Largely because of the cultural differences between Japan and most other developed nations, its system bears no kinship to another system in the way that the American and British systems or the Swiss and German systems, for example, are related. Although Japanese financial reporting practices may share certain technical features in common with foreign systems, it is equally true that a variety of unique cultural factors condition the actual application of its methods in a way that sets Japanese financial reporting apart from its Western analogues.

Cultural environment. Japanese corporations, except for a handful of unusually progressive firms that cultivate an international image, tend to reveal much less in their financial statements than their American counterparts. Beyond providing convenient translations of statements, most Japanese multinationals do little to accommodate foreign readers (or Japanese readers, for that matter). It is still rare to find results restated in accordance with U.S. GAAP (see appendix); nor do the Japanese provide much detailed supplementary information in notes. For example, the financial statements of Nippon Kokan (NKK), a steel-making and shipbuilding concern, include just over three pages of notes, probably half of which provide only general explanations of accounting policies with little or no reference to actual numbers. (NKK's summary of accounting policies appears in Exhibit 15.1.) Needless to say, many foreign investors and financial analysts have complained about such a cautious approach to sharing financial information.

One of Japan's most pervasive and influential cultural features is *dantai iskiki,* or group consciousness, with its related social values of interdependence and harmony. This cultural value profoundly affects the nature of Japanese business relationships and conditions attitudes toward external reporting of financial results. It has become widely known in the West, for example, that Japanese group consciousness creates a level and quality of loyalty within business organizations rarely seen in other cultures, and that it can often cut across lines of loyalty that we would consider "normal." For example, Japanese unions tend to be organized by company and corporate group rather than by trade, suggesting that the members' hierarchy of loyalties is not the same as, say, a U.S. teamster or coal miner. What may be less appreciated by a Westerner is that, as a result, the Japanese expect business relationships to proceed on the basis of implicit and mutual trust rather than on the basis of legally mandated disclosure. "Fairness" in financial reporting—that elusive yet indispensable concept undergirding the attest function in the

United States—in Japan is more apt to be measured by the needs of the immediate corporate community than by appeal to legal abstraction or the judgment of outsiders. Hence, more traditional Japanese managers may not see the desirability of an outside evaluation of internal control systems or of an independent audit of financial statements.

One might argue further that the reluctance of Japanese management to share large amounts of information with investors is related to the strong cultural bias toward uncertainty avoidance (i.e., the desire to control the future). Disclosure, whether by an individual or an organization, by its very nature involves a measure of risk. Thus, it would be logical for a manager who wants to maximize his or her control of circumstances (and what manager does not?) to seek to restrict or at least to manage disclosure to lower potential risks. In a cultural setting that automatically understands and accepts risk avoidance as a value but does not automatically see the importance of legally mandated disclosure, one might expect a bias in the direction of secrecy.

Given the different position of investors in Japanese corporate culture, readers of Japanese statements should be aware of several possible pitfalls. One will not find, for example, supplementary information disclosing assets, sales, and profits by activity or geographic region. Even Sony, a relatively "user-friendly" Japanese multinational that is listed on the New York Stock Exchange and that has adopted limited restatement according to U.S. GAAP, did not include segment information in its 1988 annual report—and, consequently, it received a qualified opinion from Price Waterhouse, its auditor.

Legal and political environment. Many first-time readers of Japanese financial statements are struck by the extremely low net income reported by most Japanese firms. For example, Mitsubishi Electric Corp. reported earnings of 76,796 million yen on sales of 2,976,420 million yen in fiscal 1990—about 2.5 percent. General Electric's net income to sales for 1990 was about 12 percent. Such relatively small earnings, combined with the strong performance of Japanese stocks on the Tokyo stock market, have created dizzying high price-earnings ratios. P-E ratios have ranged up to 60 and beyond in Japan in recent years, compared to an average of 15 or so for most American stocks. Such numbers have led some Western analysts to claim that the Tokyo market is highly overpriced. But before we reach any kind of conclusion, we need to consider several legal and political factors surrounding Japanese reporting that conspire to depress earnings and thereby pump up the P-E ratio.

The most important and obvious reason that Japanese companies report low net income in their financial reports is that Japanese law requires that accounting income equal taxable income. With effective tax rates on undistributed corporate income exceeding 50 percent, companies have a strong incentive to keep reported earnings down, chiefly by taking advantage of favorable depreciation provisions allowed by the Ministry of Finance. Some analysts have accordingly observed that substituting price-net cash flow for the traditional P-E ratio can provide a sounder basis for comparison between Japanese companies and their American counterparts. Linking tax policy to accounting income inevitably distorts the financial statements by encouraging managers to maximize tax benefits rather than to report economic substance.

E X H I B I T   1 5 . 1

NIPPON KOKAN K.K.
Notes to Financial Statements

1. SUMMARY OF SIGNIFICANT ACCOUNTING POLICIES

(a) Basis of Preparation

The accompanying financial statements include only the accounts of NIPPON KOKAN K.K. (the "Company"). The accounts of its subsidiaries are not consolidated.

The accompanying financial statements have been prepared from accounts and records maintained by the Company in accordance with the provisions set forth in the Commercial Code of Japan and in conformity with generally accepted accounting principles and practices in Japan. Certain items presented in the original financial statements have been reclassified for the convenience of readers outside Japan.

As permitted by the Commercial Code of Japan, amounts less than one million yen have been omitted. As a result, the totals shown in the accompanying financial statements do not necessarily agree with the sum of the individual amounts.

(b) Foreign Currency

All assets and liabilities denominated in foreign currencies other than those which were covered by forward exchange contracts are translated into Japanese yen at the historical rates. All revenues and expenses associated with foreign currencies are translated at the rates of exchange prevailing when such transactions are made. Translation gains and losses are credited or charged to income currently. Translation gains and losses arising from long-term forward exchange contracts are deferred and amortized over the remaining lives of those contracts.

(c) Recognition Basis of Sales and Profit on Contracts

The Company has principally adopted the completed contract method for the recognition of sales and gross profit on contracts. Under this method, sales and gross profit applicable to each contract are not recorded until construction is completed and delivery is made to customers

In the case of installment contract sales, profit on such sales is recognized in the period in which installment payments become due. The amounts of such deferred profits are included in other current liabilities in the accompanying balance sheets. Related amounts are charged (or credited) to cost of sales.

(d) Securities

Marketable and investment securities are carried at cost or less. Appropriate write-downs are recorded for

---

Japanese firms also report lower earnings than their U.S. counterparts because their managers are less interested in short-term profitability than in continuous long-term growth. One reflection of this emphasis on the long run is Japanese managers' freedom from the quarterly earnings reports that American companies issue. In this respect, Japanese managers reflect the macroeconomic strategy pursued by the nation's political and financial leaders. Market share, technological progress, and corporate harmony constitute the top priorities of Japanese managers and Japanese political culture. The sacrifice of immediate rewards and comforts for the sake of greater economic power in the future is a central tenet of the national consensus (supported by the cultural ideal of group consciousness) that has made possible the country's remarkable economic progress in recent decades. Such an outlook fits well with the Japanese commitment to lifetime employment, the fulfillment of which would naturally depend on continued economic growth and faith in the future. One could say, then, that the typically low net income

EXHIBIT 15.1

(continued)

securities which incurred substantial losses and are not expected to recover such losses in the near future.

(e) Inventories

Inventories are valued at cost, being determined by the following methods:
Finished goods
    and raw materials ....Moving average method
Work in process ....Specific identification method
Supplies..............................Total average method

(f) Property, Plant and Equipment

Depreciation of machinery at the Keihin Works, other than that of medium diameter seamless pipe mill, which is depreciated under the straight-line method, is computed under the declining balance method: other plant and equipment at the Keihin Works and plant and equipment at the Fukuyama Works under the straight-line method: plant and equipment at other locations under the declining balance method, based on the estimated useful lives of the assets as prescribed by the Japanese income tax regulations.

Maintenance and repairs, including minor renewals and betterments, are charged to income as incurred.

(g) Research and Development Expenses

Research and development expenses are charged to income as incurred.

(h) Income Taxes

Income taxes are calculated on taxable income and charged to income on an accrual basis. Deferred income taxes pertaining to timing differences between financial and tax reporting are not provided.

(i) Estimated Termination Allowances

Employees of the company are generally entitled to receive termination pay when they leave the Company. The payment of termination allowance is determined on the basis of length of service and basic salary at the time of termination.

The Company provides for these termination allowances at 50% of the amount rquired to be paid if all employees retired as of the balance sheet date.

The termination plans are not funded.

(j) Amounts Per 100 Shares of Common Stock

The computation of primary net income per 100 shares is based on the average number of shares of common stock outstanding during each year.

Amounts per 100 shares of common stock assuming full dilution are not significantly different from the per 100 shares data shown in the accompanying statement of income.

Cash dividends per 100 shares of common stock are based on an accrual basis and include, in each year ended March 31, dividends approved by shareholders after such March 31.

---

reported by Japanese firms can be attributed in part to policies adopted by that nation's government and ratified by its managers, its workers, and its people.

Business environment. The dominant form of business organization in Japan is the **kabushiki kaisha** (KK), a type of limited liability company similar to an American corporation. The Japanese Commercial Code requires that a KK elect a statutory auditor to examine the performance of the company's directors and report to shareholders annually. However, there is no requirement that the statutory auditor be independent or qualified to perform the job, and in fact he or she is often a company employee. A large KK—one with stated capital of 500 million yen or liabilities of 20 billion yen—must appoint an independent, professional auditor.

Japanese managers can focus on long-term objectives without having to worry about takeovers because of the pattern of stable shareholding established by corporate families, or **keiretsu,** which dominate the Japanese economy. These giant alliances of *technically* *unaffiliated* companies grew out of the American attempt in the late 1940s to break up the great industrial conglomerations (known as *zaibatsu*) of prewar Japan. When U.S. occupation ended in 1948, companies quietly and informally began to form new ties—generally under the aegis of a major bank and a large trading company—by lending each other money, establishing interlocking directorates, buying each other's stock, and creating helpful patterns of trade within the group. *Keiretsu* tend to be highly diversified, each attempting to form within itself an economic microcosm so as to minimize risk and maximize benefit to individual members.

As Exhibit 15.2 illustrates, group members do not purchase large enough blocks of stock to trigger consolidation requirements. *Keiretsu* (literally, "headless combines") involve no holding company and no controlling board of directors. Although the group as a whole often owns a significant percentage of the voting stock of each of its core members, that ownership is dispersed among a number of companies.

Keiretsu influence the capital structure of Japanese corporations by altering the relationship between debt and risk and, hence, by changing the way in which we should interpret a Japanese balance sheet. Many Japanese firms carry a load of debt that would often prove fatal to an American business. Nippon Kokan's balance sheet, for instance, shows that shareholders' equity accounts for only 11 percent of total assets. Commentators have offered a variety of explanations for this phenomenon: Equity costs more and is scarcer in smaller Asian markets; Japanese workers tend to save rather than invest in stocks; Japanese banks historically have played a central role in the economy because they were the primary sources of capital for reconstruction. Each of these explanations is valid, although some of the national characteristics they describe may be changing. The rise of investment trusts suggests that Japanese workers may be looking for equity investment vehicles, and the liquidity created by success in export markets has made some large trading companies less dependent on banks. But such factors address necessities and

EXHIBIT 15.2

Toyota Motors' Interlocking Shareholdings (1990)

Major Shareholder	Percent Shareholding in Toyota	Toyota Shareholding in Affiliate
Sanwa Bank	4.8%	2.2%
Tokai Bank	4.8	5.2
Mitsui Bank	4.8	4.2
Toyota Auto Loan	4.3	23.4
Nippon Life Insurance Co.	3.6	—
LTCB	3.1	1.0
Taisho Insurance Co.	2.4	2.1
Mitsui Trust	2.3	1.7
	30.1%	

constraints rather than the reasons that debt financing has worked well in Japan for so many years. In fact, many debt-laden Japanese corporations have survived and prospered because of the uniquely cooperative patterns of behavior between members of *keiretsu*.

Much of the debt on a typical Japanese balance sheet has been provided by other members of the *keiretsu*—banks, insurance companies, trading companies—which means that less risk is attached to high levels of debt than would be the case elsewhere. Under normal circumstances, much of a firm's short-term bank debt is automatically rolled over, making it in fact a form of long-term debt. Trade credit, by virtue of extremely favorable terms of payment, also serves as a kind of semipermanent financing provided by major trading companies to their friends. When a group member runs into trouble, its creditors—if it has properly maintained its alliances—rather than abandoning it will in fact extend credit, buy stock, and, if necessary, lend managerial expertise.

Accounting principles. The following are several principles and practices of Japanese accounting of which you should be aware.

Asset valuation. Japanese companies closely adhere to the historical cost principle applied conservatively—a practice that no doubt reflects the relatively low rate of inflation experienced by Japan. Inventories are valued at cost or at market, if market is significantly lower and the value is not expected to recover. In the case of marketable equity securities, lower of cost or market is applied individually but not on a portfolio basis. Fixed assets are stated at cost less accumulated depreciation.

Intercorporate investments. Because Japan's Commercial Code requires neither consolidated statements (in fact, it forbids them) nor comparative data, securities laws have been the primary tool by which the Japanese government has propagated Anglo-American consolidation methods and the inclusion of prior year information. As a result of this approach, however, only those companies whose securities are registered with the Ministry of Finance are subject to consolidation rules, which require firms to publish both consolidated and parent-only financial statements. The ministry essentially accepts the American definition of control, and it requires companies to account for unconsolidated affiliates (20–50 percent owned) under the equity method, but only in their consolidated statements. On unconsolidated (parent-only) financial statements, companies must show investments in other companies at cost or less.

Doubtful accounts. A bad debt allowance is calculated using percentages of receivables predetermined by tax law. It is considered acceptable to charge the allowance up to the legal limit.

Goodwill. When goodwill is acquired through acquisition, it may be capitalized and amortized over a five-year period, usually using the straight-line method.

Leases. Most leases are accounted for as operating leases by both lessor and lessee. However, a 1978 regulation requires some leases to be capitalized, including those that contain a bargain purchase clause, those that involve machinery built specifically for the lessee and cannot be leased to others, and those for which the leased property is land or buildings.

Interest. Interest costs are usually not capitalized, except in the case of real estate development companies.

Appendix A to this chapter presents the financial review section of the annual report of Toyota Motors Corporation, and illustrates many of the above principles and practices.

The United Kingdom

As the first great industrial power of the modern era, the United Kingdom has had a broad and enduring influence on financial reporting practices around the world. Although the historical importance and geographical reach of British practices grows directly out of Great Britain's former role as a world power and pioneer of capitalism, its continuing influence on international accounting standards is more that of an elder partner than a ruler. This shift in the dynamics of power is reflected in the U.K.'s changing trade patterns, which have moved away from its colonies and dependencies of the 19th century to its current membership in the European Economic Community (EEC) and close ties with the United States.

Cultural environment. British attitudes toward business and its social responsibilities are deeply divided and have been since the development of modern capitalism in that country. Even as the landmark companies acts of the 1840s through the 1860s were granting legal existence and limited liability to corporations, social legislation was attempting to provide controls over the new force that had been unleashed. The advent of capitalism, with its unprecedented potential for working both good and ill, had by the end of the 19th century posed one of the central questions of the 20th century: How much and in what way must government involve itself in economic enterprise?

The belief that corporations must look beyond the maximization of profit has become a permanent if oft-debated element in British public opinion. A by-product of this belief is the search for progressive ways to report the results of business operations—new methods to depict the corporation as a locus of cooperation rather than as a unit of competition. One of the most widespread and best-known experiments in this direction is the **value added statement,** which a significant minority of European firms began to include in their corporate reports in the 1970s. (See Exhibit 15.3 for an example of a value added statement taken from the annual report of the BOC Group, a British conglomerate specializing in the liquid gas and health care industries.) Although the popularity of value added statements has declined in recent years as questions have been raised about their usefulness, they continue to be presented along with more traditional documents by a number of prominent British firms.

Devised by a U.S. Treasury official in the 18th century, the concept of **valued added** has since been used by governments as a measure of national income. In the 1970s, it was picked up by corporations, on the recommendation of the British government and the accounting profession, to provide additional information to shareholders, to serve as the basis of employee incentive programs, and to improve public and employee relations by showing what a company does with the wealth it creates.

The basic numerical definition of *value added* is sales less purchases. A refinement on this definition distinguishes gross value added (as just defined) from net value added, which subtracts depreciation as well as purchases from sales. Depending on who is doing the calculating, depreciation may be figured on a historical cost basis or a current cost

EXHIBIT 15.3

BOC GROUP
Consolidated Statement of Value Added
Years Ended 30 September

	1991		1990	
	£ million	%	£ million	%
Value added				
Turnover	2718.5		2643.9	
Bought-in materials, services and depreciation	(1639.3)		(1590.1)	
Value added	1079.2		1053.8	
Application				
To employees as pay or for pensions and welfare schemes	711.8	66.0	658.2	62.5
To banks and other lenders as interest	79.9	7.4	71.9	6.8
To governments as tax on profits	90.1	8.3	89.7	8.5
To partners in partly owned companies	7.3	0.7	5.0	0.5
To group shareholders	96.0	8.9	88.8	8.4
	985.1	91.3	913.6	86.7
Retained within the group	94.1	8.7	140.2	13.3
	1079.2	100.0	1053.8	100.0

basis. Governments typically attempt to calculate depreciation using the latter. The interest in value added has also spawned a variety of ratios (such as value added/payroll costs and operating profit/value added) designed to provide company planners with a new perspective on operations and to express the efficiency of a company in terms that are more easily understandable to the general public.

Legal and political environment. With very few exceptions, such as formation by Royal Charter, British companies are incorporated under the companies act currently in force. (The most recent one at this writing is the Companies Act of 1985.) The act requires all corporations to maintain accounting records that include information sufficient to give a "true and fair view" of the company's financial position and its operations. The phrase "true and fair view" is an important one in British accounting and auditing. Even though its meaning is difficult to ascertain with precision (as is likely to be the case with any standard of "fairness"), it is the key phrase by which auditors express an opinion on a set of financial statements. Companies must present audited financial statements and a directors' report to shareholders at the annual meeting. In addition, they must file these documents with the Registrar of Companies.

The investor orientation that has traditionally dominated British financial reporting is reinforced by U.K. tax law, which gives individuals several important incentives to invest in stocks. Capital gains are taxable, but they are eligible for tax breaks favoring small investors: Net gains less losses carried forward are indexed to eliminate the effects of inflation. An annual exemption, which in 1990 amounted to 5,000 pounds sterling, further decreases the taxable portion of any gain.

The United Kingdom is one of the relatively few nations in the world in which corporate tax law does not serve as the basis for financial reporting. In many countries, firms must keep their books in accordance with the dictates of tax regulations, a procedure that subjects financial reporting practices to the whims of legislators and greatly hinders comparability across national boundaries. In the United Kingdom, however, the process is reversed—income statements are prepared according to British GAAP and then are adjusted to arrive at taxable income.

Business environment. The dominant business entity in Great Britain is the **limited liability company,** also referred to as a *company limited by shares.* A limited liability company may be incorporated as a private or a public concern, the latter having the right to issue securities to the public. Both public and private companies must have at least two stockholders, and public companies must have at least two directors as well. For a limited liability company to be incorporated as a public entity, it must have a minimum share capital of 50,000 pounds and include **public limited company** (or PLC) in its name. A private company is subject to no minimum capital requirement and must include the word *Limited* (or Ltd.) at the end of its name.

Despite governmental efforts, organized labor still exerts a significant if somewhat diminished influence over British society. Whereas membership in U.S. labor unions has never reached 40 percent and currently stands at less than 20 percent, British trade unions represent around 45 to 50 percent of the work force, or about 11 million people. Although labor relations have had little direct impact on accounting methods and conventions, they have undoubtedly affected the disclosure requirements imposed on British corporations. The Companies Act of 1985, for example, requires certain disclosures pertaining to directors' fees and management salaries exceeding 30,000 pounds. Specifically, the company must reveal the amount paid to the chairperson and (if not the same person) to the highest paid director, and it must indicate where remuneration paid to the other directors and to management falls on a pay scale broken into 5,000 pound-sterling increments. The company must also disclose wage and salary expenses, social security costs, and pension costs paid to or on behalf of employees. All of this information may be of interest to union negotiators as well as investors.

British law does not mandate employee representation on company boards (as is the case in Sweden); however, a firm employing 250 or more workers must disclose its policy concerning employee consultation programs. Many individual companies and the Confederation of British Industry (an association of employers) have responded to the legal requirement by publicly supporting voluntary programs for employee participation on the firm level. In addition, many firms encourage share ownership among employees. B.A.T. Industries, the tobacco and retailing conglomerate, touches on these themes in the following summary included in its 1990 directors' report:

Employee involvement in the United Kingdom

B.A.T. Industries actively encourages the development of systems of employee involvement in operating companies. Progress is regularly monitored and reported to the

Board and statements on employee involvement included in the annual reports of UK subsidiaries.

The details of direct involvement processes are appropriately different in each operating company in ways which reflect both individual local needs and the working environment. Typically, however, they include staff committees, briefing groups, in-house newspapers and videos.

The Company believes that financial participation is a fundamental constituent of employee involvement and is an innovator in this area both within the UK and other European community countries in which it operates. The UK Share Participation Scheme is in its fifth year and shares valued at £18.5 million have been appropriated for the benefit of 14,150 employees of the continuing Group. A UK Save-As-You-Earn Share Option Scheme also attracts a great deal of support.

Employment of the disabled in the United Kingdom

The Group's policy on recruitment is based on the ability of a candidate to perform the job. Full and fair consideration is given to applications for employment from the disabled where they have the skills and abilities to perform the job.

If a disabled applicant proves a suitable candidate for employment, modification of facilities and the provision of special equipment is considered favourably. If employees become disabled during the course of their employment and as a result are unable to perform their normal jobs, every effort is made to offer suitable alternative employment, to provide assistance with re-training and to deal with their cases compassionately.

It is Group policy to encourage the training and development of all its employees where this is of benefit to the individual and to the company. This includes the provision of training to meet the special needs of disabled employees.

Although B.A.T. would undoubtedly like to be considered progressive, its policy statement is similar to those of other British multinational firms.

Accounting terminology and practices. Several terms used in British financial statements may confuse or mislead unwary foreign readers. *Fixed assets,* for example, refers to all assets retained for continuous use in the business, not only to property, plant, and equipment (which the British call *tangible fixed assets*). The term *stocks* generally means inventory. Receivables may be lumped under the laconic heading *debtors,* with payables simply listed as *creditors.* On the income statement, called the *profit and loss account,* sales are referred to as *turnover.* Alternatively, *profit and loss account,* and *reserves* or *retained profits* may refer to *retained earnings* or some component thereof. As these examples suggest, one must cultivate a judicious suspicion of familiar terminology; it may be camouflaging a distinctively British usage.

The following illustrate some of the unique British reporting and disclosure practices. (Appendix B to this chapter presents the financial review section of the British Petroleum Company's annual report.)

Format. Although the format of British financial statements varies in a number of ways from that used in American statements, the most noticeable difference is in the arrangement of the balance sheet. British balance sheets following the "horizontal format" resemble American balance sheets but run from *low* liquidity to *high* liquidity; hence, fixed assets appear above current assets, and shareholders' equity above liabilities.

EXHIBIT 15.4

B.A.T. Industries
Balance Sheets

31 December

On behalf of the Board
P. Sheeny, B.P. Garraway *Directors*
21 March 1989

	Group		Company	
	1988	1987	**1988**	1987
	£ millions			
Assets				
Fixed assets				
Tangible fixed assets (note 11)	**2,257**	2,178		
Investments in Group companies (note 13)			**2,371**	2,203
Investments in financial services subsidiaries (note 14)	**3,583**	1,503		
Investments in associated companies (note 15)	**387**	302		
Other investments and long-term loans (note 16)	**173**	186		
	6,400	4,169	**2,371**	2,203
Current assets				
Stocks (note 17)	**1,939**	1,810		
Debtors (note 18)	**960**	1,022	**1,030**	849
Current investments (note 19)	**146**	312		
Short-term deposits	**279**	954		
Cash at bank and in hand	**179**	247	**1**	
	3,503	4,345	**1,031**	849
Total assets	**9,903**	8,514	**3,402**	3,052
Liabilities				
Capital and reserves				
Share capital	**380**	374	**380**	374
Share premium account	**107**	52	**107**	52
Revaluation reserves	**408**	295		
Other reserves		387	**7**	7
Profit and loss account	**2,576**	2,786	**1,187**	1,159
Associated companies	**130**	52		
Interest of B.A.T. Industries' shareholders (note 21)	**3,601**	3,946	**1,681**	1,592
Interest of minority shareholders in subsidiaries	**340**	347		
Shareholders' funds	**3,941**	4,293	**1,681**	1,592
Provisions for liabilities and charges (note 22)	**709**	653		
Creditors				
Borrowings (note 25)	**2,661**	1,471	**500**	518
Creditors (note 26)	**2,592**	2,097	**1,221**	942
Total funds employed	**9,903**	8,514	**3,402**	3,052

Companies that adopt the "vertical format" offset current assets against current liabilities, then offset total assets against current liabilities, balancing this figure against long-term liabilities and stockholders' equity. The balance sheet of B.A.T. Industries (see Exhibit 15.4) provides an example of the horizontal format. The Rolls-Royce PLC balance sheet (see Exhibit 15.5) illustrates the vertical format.

EXHIBIT 15.5

Rolls-Royce PLC
Balance Sheet
At 31 December 1990

	Notes	Group 1990 £m	Group 1989 £m	Company 1990 £m	Company 1989 £m
Fixed assets					
Tangible assets	10	676	658	470	439
Investments—subsidiary undertakings	11	—	—	325	324
—other	12	36	25	37	8
		712	683	832	771
Current assets					
Stocks	13	888	754	701	550
Debtors	14	816	749	887	857
Short-term deposits and cash		431	407	363	293
		2,135	1,910	1,951	1,700
Creditors—amounts falling due within one year					
Borrowings	15	(100)	(52)	(73)	—
Other creditors	16	(1,074)	(939)	(768)	(651)
Net current assets		961	919	1,110	1,049
Total assets less current liabilities		1,673	1,602	1,942	1,820
Creditors—amounts falling due after one year					
Borrowings	17	(161)	(162)	(151)	(151)
Other creditors	18	(127)	(68)	(393)	(342)
Provisions for liabilities and charges	20	(183)	(173)	(137)	(111)
		1,202	1,199	1,261	1,216
Capital and reserves					
Called up share capital	21	192	192	192	192
Share premium account	22	239	238	239	238
Revaluation reserve	22	132	135	127	130
Other reserves	22	22	28	263	265
Profit and loss account	22	579	533	440	391
Shareholders' funds		1,164	1,126	1,261	1,216
Minority interests in subsidiary undertakings	23	38	73	—	—
		1,202	1,199	1.261	1,216

Consolidation. The Companies Act requires companies with subsidiaries to prepare "group accounts." Although theoretically the law would accept group accounts prepared on some basis other than consolidation, they almost always use the consolidation form. (Implementation of the EEC's Seventh Directive, effective in 1990, removes the option of using bases other than consolidation.) Companies must present separate balance sheets for the group and the parent company, but only a group income statement is required. Control is defined as more than a 50 percent share in equity capital (not necessarily voting), or as a smaller shareholding with the power to control the membership of the board of directors.

Valuation of assets. A British company may choose to value its assets according to historical cost principles or alternative valuation rules, or it may choose to use different methods for different assets. According to historical cost rules, current assets should be carried at the lower of cost or net realizable value, and fixed assets at cost less accumulated depreciation (if applicable) and any permanent decline in value. LIFO is not permitted as a basis for inventory valuation for either tax or financial reporting.

The alternative valuation rules allow assets to be written up above cost as follows:

- Inventories, current investments, tangible fixed assets, and intangible fixed assets (except goodwill) may be written up to current cost.
- Long-term investments and tangible fixed assets may be written up to market value as of the date of the last valuation (even if it differs from the balance sheet date).
- Investments in 20 percent or more of an affiliate's stock may be accounted for under the equity method.

It is not uncommon for a firm to revalue its land and buildings periodically, taking the surplus to a revaluation reserve account in the equity section of the balance sheet. This reserve, however, is not available for distribution to shareholders. Companies are required to disclose the bases of valuation for inventories, investments, and fixed assets. In light of the valuation options open to British companies and their possible impact on the balance sheet, a careful reader will surely want to check this information.

Goodwill. Purchased goodwill is defined as the difference between the fair value of consideration given up and the aggregate fair values of the assets received. Normally, neither goodwill nor negative goodwill is carried on the balance sheet; both are written off immediately against retained earnings. Companies may choose, however, to capitalize purchased goodwill (but not negative goodwill) and amortize it over its estimated economic life.

Research and development. Research expenditures are written off immediately, but development costs may be capitalized if they fulfill a number of requirements concerning the technical and commercial feasibility of the project to which they are related. Deferred development expenditures must be reviewed at the end of each period and written off immediately if they no longer meet these feasibility requirements.

Leases. Accepted accounting principles distinguish between operating leases and finance leases, requiring the latter to be capitalized by lessees in financial statements for years beginning on or after July 1, 1987. (Capitalization requirements for lessors had come into effect three years earlier.) Finance leases are deemed to be those that essentially transfer the risks and benefits of ownership to the lessee. Lessees should record an asset to be depreciated over the shorter of the lease term (including likely renewals) or the asset's useful life, to record a liability for future payments to the lessor, and to apportion interest payments between interest expense and repayment of principal. The lessor should record a receivable for the total minimum lease payments plus any residual value, less any provision for bad debts.

Interest costs. The Companies Act allows interest on financing for the construction of assets—both fixed and current—to be capitalized. The generality of the law on this point permits capitalization in cases that would not be acceptable under U.S. GAAP.

Earnings per share. Contrary to U.S. practice, basic earnings per share (called *primary earnings per share* in the United States) is calculated without regard to common stock equivalents. The basis for calculating earnings per share must be disclosed in the notes.

Reconciliation of U.S. and British GAAP. Because British firms are frequently listed on U.S. stock exchanges, some publish a reconciliation of net income and stockholders' equity calculated according to the accounting principles of the two countries. The excerpted schedule and explanatory notes from the Hanson PLC annual report (see Exhibit 15.6) illustrate how the differences listed above may affect these figures. Notice that the differing treatment of goodwill is particularly important in Hanson's case.

SUMMARY

With the passage of time, there has been an increasing blurring of the economic boundaries between countries. Japanese cars, for example, are no longer made only in Japan, but are also manufactured in Tennessee and Ohio, among other locations in the United States. Similarly, British consumer goods are so prevalent in the U.S. marketplace today that consumers rarely view them as "foreign" products.

Just as consumers have come to accept foreign-produced goods, or goods produced in the United States by foreign companies as an everyday occurrence, so have managers and investors come to recognize the opportunities for investing abroad. The ability to identify the best U.K. partner for a European joint venture, for example, and the best Japanese company to invest in depends significantly, however, on a manager's or investor's understanding of the accounting and reporting practices followed by companies of those countries.

In this final chapter, we have examined the accounting principles, practices, and business environment of two countries, Japan and the United Kingdom. Exhibit 15.7 compares and contrasts these accounting practices with those followed in the United States (and discussed in the previous 15 chapters). It is apparent that although many similarities exist, differences can be quite significant. The manager or investor contemplating foreign investment would be wise to develop an understanding of the accounting and business practices prevalent in that country.

NEW CONCEPTS AND TERMS

Harmonization (p. 676)

International accounting standards
   (p. 676)

International Accounting Standards
   Committee (p. 676)

Kabushiki kaisha (p. 681)

Keiretsu (p. 681)

Limited liability company (p. 686)

Public limited company (p. 686)

Value added (p. 684)

Value added statement (p. 684)

EXHIBIT 15.6

HANSON PLC AND SUBSIDIARIES
Reconciliation to U.S. Accounting Principles

The following is a summary of the estimated material adjustments to profit and ordinary shareholders' equity which would be required if US Generally Accepted Accounting Principles (GAAP) had been applied instead of UK GAAP.

Years ended September 30,

	1990 £ million	1989 £ million	1990 $ million	1989 $ million
Profit available for appropriation as reported in the consolidated profit and loss account	1,000	1,101	1,874	2,063
Estimated adjustments:				
Goodwill on disposals	(171)	(92)	(320)	(173)
Items taken to goodwill	107	—	200	—
Goodwill amortisation	(97)	(56)	(182)	(105)
Foreign currency translation	26	(14)	49	(26)
Pensions	78	—	146	—
Taxation	7	(12)	13	(22)
	(50)	(174)	(94)	(326)
Estimated profit available for appropriation (net income) as adjusted to accord with US GAAP	950	927	1,780	1,737
Arising from:				
Continuing operations	962	731	1,802	1,370
Discontinued operations	(12)	196	(22)	367
	950	927	1,780	1,737

	Per Share		Per ADR	
Earnings	p	p	$	$
Undiluted – continuing operations	20.0	18.5	1.87	1.73
– discontinued operations	(0.2)	5.0	(0.02)	0.47
– profit available for appropriation	19.8	23.5	1.85	2.20
Diluted – continuing operations	19.7	16.3	1.85	1.53
– discontinued operations	(0.2)	4.4	(0.02)	0.41
– profit available for appropriation	19.5	20.7	1.83	1.94

Years Ended September 30,

	1990 £ million	1989 £ million	1990 $ million	1989 $ million
Ordinary shareholders' equity as reported in the consolidated balance sheet	2,834	1,046	5,309	1,960
Estimated adjustments:				
Goodwill and other intangibles	3,550	3,724	6,651	6,977
Proposed final dividend	355	237	665	444
Revaluation of land and buildings	(163)	(165)	(305)	(309)
Pensions	78	—	146	—
Taxation	(22)	(17)	(41)	(32)
	3,798	3,779	7,116	7,080
Estimated ordinary shareholders' equity as adjusted to accord with US GAAP	6,632	4,825	12,425	9,040

The exchange rate used to translate the above figures was that ruling at the 1990 balance sheet date ($1.8735 to £).

EXHIBIT 15.6

(continued)

The following are the main US accounting principles which differ from those generally accepted in the United Kingdom as applied by Hanson in its financial statements;

Taxation

Deferred taxation is not provided where, in the opinion of the directors, no liability is likely to arise in the forseeable future. However, under US GAAP, deferred taxation would be provided on a full deferral basis.

UK GAAP permits the reduction of the tax charge by the use of tax losses available at the time of acquisition. However, US GAAP requires that the benefit of such losses is adjusted through goodwill.

Revaluation of land and buildings

Periodically land and buildings are revalued on an existing use basis by professionally qualified external valuers and such assets are written up to the appraised value. Depreciation is, where applicable, calculated on these revalued amounts. When revalued properties are sold, the gain or loss on sale is calculated based on revalued carrying amounts and reflected in income and

any revaluation surplus thus realised is reclassified directly to retained earnings. Under US GAAP such revaluations would not be reflected in financial statements and the gain or loss on sale would be calculated based on original cost and reflected in income. The amount of additional depreciation charged in respect of the revalued properties is not material.

Foreign currencies

Revenues, expenses, assets and liabilities relating to overseas subsidiaries are translated at the year-end rate. Under US GAAP assets and liabilities are

translated as under UK GAAP; however, revenues and expenses are translated at average rates for the year.

Goodwill and other intangibles

Goodwill and other intangible assets arising on the acquisition of a subsidiary are written off in the year in which that subsidiary is acquired. Under US GAAP such

goodwill is capitalised and is amortised through the profit and loss account over its estimated useful life, not exceeding 40 years.

Discontinued operations

When operations, which are regarded as separate business segments, are sold their results and the profit or loss on disposal are reported as arising from discontinued operations with the prior year being

adjusted accordingly. Any remaining goodwill relating to such business is written off in determining the profit or loss on disposal.

Ordinary dividends

Final ordinary dividends are provided in the year in respect of which they are proposed on the basis of the recommendation by the directors which requires

subsequent approval by the shareholders. Under US GAAP dividends are not provided until formally declared.

Pensions

Under UK GAAP, the accounting policy of the group has not been to account for exceptional past pension surpluses. Under US GAAP, such surpluses are

recognised and credited over an appropriate future period.

E X H I B I T   1 5 . 7

Financial Reporting Practices in Three Countries*

UNITED STATES

Accounting Standards

- *Cost basis of financial statement* is entirely on historical cost basis.
- *Consolidated information* is provided by most.
- *Inventory costing method* predominantly used varies with different inventories.
- *Depreciation* is on straight line method.
- *Excess depreciation* is not allowed.
- *Valuation method for long-term investments between 20-50%* of equity is equity method.
- Valuation method for *long-term investments less than 20%* of equity is cost method.
- *Long-term financial leases* are capitalized.
- *Deferred taxes* are recorded when accounting income is not equal to taxable income.
- *Pension expenses* are usually provided.
- *Funding pension liabilities* to outside trustees is common.
- *Accounting method for acquisition* is purchase method by many.
- *Goodwill* is capitalized & amortized.
- *Foreign currency translation* is determined by current rate method.
- *Gains or losses from foreign currency* translation are taken to income statement and/or shareholders' equity.
- *Contingent liabilities* are disclosed by most.
- *Discretionary/non-equity reserves* are not used in general.

Reporting Practices

- *Notes* to the financial accounts are extensively utilized.
- *Income Statement Format* is sales less expenses with more than two years of comparative figures reported by most.
- Foreign exchange gains/losses are reported by many.
- Extraordinary gains/losses are reported by many.
- *Balance Sheet Format* is total assets = liabilities + shareholders' equity in 1 or 2 pages with two years of comparative figures reported by majority.
- Arrangement is by decreasing liquidity order.

- Other intangibles are disclosed by most.
- Preferred stock is reported by many.
- Reserves are reported as statutory/legal reserves by most.
- *Changes in shareholders' equity* are reported by most.
- Appropriation of retained earnings is disclosed by most.
- Changes in working capital or cash flows are reported by most and statement format is net income, investing activities and financing activities on cash basis.
- *Product segmentation* is disclosed by most with sales, operating income and identifiable assets by product line.
- *Geographic segmentation* is disclosed by most with sales, operating income and identifiable assets by area.
  Exports are reported by many.
- *Earnings per share* is reported by most.
  Numerator of EPS is based on the net income after preferred dividend.
  Denominator is the average number of shares outstanding during period.
- *Dividend per share* is reported by most.
- *Shareholders*
  Major shareholding is reported by some and names of the shareholders are disclosed by some.
- *Subsidiary information* is reported with name, domicile and % held by parent.
- *Number of employees* is reported by most on a worldwide basis.
- *Management information*
  Names and titles of principal officers are reported by most.
  List of board members is reported by most.
  Company shares owned by directors/officers are not reported at all.
  Remuneration to directors/officers is reported by some.
- *Research and development expenses* are disclosed by many on worldwide basis.
- *Capital expenditures* are disclosed by most on a worldwide basis.
- *Subsequent events* are disclosed by most.

EXHIBIT 15.7

(continued)

Interim Reports

- *Frequency:* Quarterly.
- *Consolidation* is done.
- *Audit* is not done.

Other Observations

Accounting Standards

- Some consolidation of investments between 20% and 50%, depending on management control.
- Revaluation of accounts is not allowed.

Reporting practices

- *Language of the financial statement* is English.
- Accounts receivable are separated by short term and long term and reported in net.
- Diluted earnings per share are disclosed by most.
- Changes in capital are most frequently achieved through new issues, stock dividends, splits and right issues.
- Multiple classes of common shares are utilized by many.
- Differences in multiple shares are usually in par value.

UNITED KINGDOM

Accounting Standards

- *Cost basis of financial statement* is on historical cost with price level adjusted.
- *Consolidated information* is provided by most.
- *Inventory costing method* predominantly used is first-in-first-out method (FIFO).
- *Depreciation* is on straight line method.
- *Excess depreciation* is not allowed.
- Valuation method for *long-term investments between 20-50%* of equity is equity method.
- Valuation method for *long-term investments less than 20%* of equity is cost method.
- *Long-term financial leases* are capitalized.
- *Deferred taxes* are recorded when accounting income is not equal to taxable income.
- *Pension expenses* are usually provided.
- *Funding pension liabilities* to outside trustees is common.
- *Accounting method for acquisition* is purchase method by most.
- Goodwill is taken to reserves.
- *Foreign currency translation* is determined by current rate method.
- *Gains or losses from foreign currency translation* are taken to income statement and/or shareholders' equity.
- *Contingent liabilities* are disclosed by most.
- *Discretionary/non-equity reserves* are specific reserves.

Reporting Practices

- *Notes* to the financial accounts are extensively utilized.
- *Income Statement Format* is sales less expenses with two years of comparative figures reported by most.
- Foreign exchange gains/losses are reported by many.
- Extraordinary gains/losses are reported by many.
- *Balance Sheet Format* is fixed assets + net working capital − long term debts = shareholders' equity in 1 page with two years of comparative figures reported by majority.
- Arrangement is by increasing liquidity order.
- Other intangibles are disclosed by most.
- Preferred stock is reported by many.
- Reserves are reported as statutory/legal reserves by most.
- *Changes in shareholders' equity* are reported by most.
- Appropriation of retained earnings is disclosed by most.
- Changes in working capital or cash flows are reported by most and statement format is net income, total sources and total uses on modified cash basis.
- *Product segmentation* is disclosed by most with sales and operating income by product line.
- *Geographic segmentation* is disclosed by most with sales only by area.
    Exports are reported by many.

EXHIBIT 15.7

(continued)

- *Earnings per share* is reported by most.
  Numerator of EPS is based on net income before extraordinary items.
  Denominator is the average number of shares outstanding during period.
- *Dividend per share* is reported by most.
- *Shareholders*
  Major shareholding is reported by many and names of the shareholders are frequently disclosed.
- *Subsidiary information* is reported with name, domicile and % held by parent.
- *Number of employees* is reported by most on a worldwide basis.
- *Management information*
  Names and titles of principal officers are reported by most.
  List of board members is reported by most.
  Company shares owned by directors/officers are reported by most.
  Remuneration to directors/officers is reported by most.
- *Research and development expenses* are disclosed by some only.
- *Capital expenditures* are disclosed by most on a worldwide basis.
- *Subsequent events* are reported by some.

Interim Reports

- *Frequency:* Semiannually.
- *Consolidation* is done.
- *Audit* is not done.

Other Observations

Accounting Standards

- Some consolidation of investments between 20% and 50%, depending on management control.

Reporting Practices

- *Language of the financial statement* is English.
- Accounts receivable are separated by short term and long term and reported in net.
- Total assets can be computed indirectly from balance sheet.
- Diluted earnings per share are disclosed by many.
- Changes in capital are most frequently achieved through new issues, stock splits and right issues.
- Multiple classes of common shares are utilized by many.
- Differences in multiple shares are usually in voting rights.

JAPAN

Accounting Standards

- *Cost basis of financial statement* is entirely on historical cost basis.
- *Consolidated information* is provided by many.
- *Inventory costing method* predominantly used varies with different inventories.
- *Depreciation* is on accelerated method.
- *Excess depreciation* is not allowed.
- Valuation method for *long-term investments between 20-50%* of equity is cost and/or equity method.
- Valuation method for *long-term investments less than 20%* of equity is cost method.
- *Long-term financial leases* are capitalized and/or expensed.
- *Deferred taxes* are not recorded when accounting income is not equal to taxable income.
- *Pension expenses* are usually provided.
- *Funding pension liabilities* to outside trustees is partially funded outside.

- *Accounting method for acquisition* is purchase method by many.
- *Goodwill* is capitalized and amortized in 5 to 10 years.
- *Foreign currency translation* is determined by temporal method and/or current rate method.
- *Gains or losses from foreign currency translation* are taken to income statement and/or deferred.
- *Contingent liabilities* are disclosed by many.
- *Discretionary/non-equity reserves* are general-purpose reserves.

Reporting Practices

- *Notes* to the financial accounts are extensively utilized.
- *Income Statement Format* is sales less expenses with two years of comparative figures reported by most.
- Foreign exchange gains/losses are reported by many.
- Extraordinary gains/losses are reported by many.

E X H I B I T   1 5 . 7

(concluded)

- *Balance Sheet Format* is total assets = liabilities + shareholders' equity in 2 pages with two years of comparative figures reported by majority.
- Arrangement is by decreasing liquidity order.
- Other intangibles are disclosed by most.
- Preferred stock is not used at all.
- Reserves are reported as statutory/legal reserves by most.
- *Changes in shareholders' equity* are reported by most.
- Appropriation of retained earnings is disclosed by most.
- Changes in working capital or cash flows are reported by many and statement format is net income, sources/uses or investing/financing activities on cash basis.
- *Product segmentation* is disclosed by most with sales only by product line.
- *Geographic segmentation* is disclosed by some.
   Exports are reported by many.
- *Earnings per share* is reported by most.
   Numerator of EPS is based on the net income after preferred dividend.
   Denominator is the fiscal year-end shares outstanding.
- *Dividend per share* is reported by most.
- *Shareholders*
   Major shareholding is reported by most and names of the shareholders are also disclosed by most.
- *Subsidiary information* is reported with name, domicile and % held by parent.
- *Number of employees* is reported by most on parent company only.
- *Management information*
   Names and titles of principal officers are reported by most.

List of board members is reported by most.
Company shares owned by directors/officers are reported by most.
Remuneration to directors/officers is not reported at all.

- *Research and development expenses* are disclosed by many on parent company basis.
- *Capital expenditures* are disclosed by many on parent company basis.
- *Subsequent events* are reported by many.

Interim Reports

- *Frequency:* Semiannually.
- *Consolidation* is done by a few only.
- *Audit* is not done.

Other Observations

Accounting Standards

- Only domestic majority-owned subsidiaries are consolidated and others at cost method.
- No consolidation of investments between 20% and 50%.
- Revaluation of accounts is not allowed.

Reporting Practices

- *Language of the financial statement* is equally distributed between local language and English.
- Changes in capital are most frequently achieved through new issues, stock dividends and conversions of securities.

Source: V. B. Bavishi, *International Accounting and Auditing Trends,* second edition (Princeton, N.J., center for International Financial Analysis and Research, Inc., 1991).

Toyota Motor Corporation
Annual Report 1990

Review of Operations

An excellent year in our automotive operations again carried sales and earnings to record levels. The 27.4% gain we recorded in net income was due primarily to a 14.9% increase in motor vehicle sales worldwide, though diversified operations in industrial vehicles and in financial services also made notable contributions to the growth in earnings.

Our strong position in the Japanese market remained the central pillar of our sales and earnings performance: business in Japan generated 58.7% of net sales even as our overseas operations continued to expand. And we maintained the integrity of our business and financial performance on a per share basis: net income per share, fully diluted, climbed 26.3% to ¥138, and net assets per share increased 11.9%, to ¥1,384.

Five-Year Sales Breakdown

( ): Overseas Sales

	Billions of Yen	Millions of U.S. Dollars	Billions of Yen			
	1990	1990	1989	1988	1987	1986
Motor vehicles	¥6,645.9	$43,437	¥5,783.9	¥5,218.4	¥4,898.7	¥4,841.5
	(¥3,241.5)	($21,187)	(¥2,649.9)	(¥2,335.7)	(¥2,487.5)	(¥2,615.5)
Parts and components for overseas production	154.1	1,007	123.8	127.4	134.2	140.2
	(154.1)	(1,007)	(123.8)	(127.4)	(134.2)	(140.2)
Parts	739.5	4,834	668.7	605.7	549.9	543.1
	(284.0)	(1,856)	(253.2)	(224.4)	(219.0)	(231.0)
Industrial vehicles	141.2	923	129.7	105.7	87.4	91.7
	(54.6)	(357)	(48.8)	(39.5)	(36.1)	(39.9)
Others	1,512.1	9,883	1,314.9	1,158.6	1,005.2	1,029.7
	(58.5)	(382)	(38.2)	(39.2)	(17.9)	(16.1)
Total	¥9,192.8	$60,084	¥8,021.0	¥7,215.8	¥6,675.4	¥6,646.2
	(¥3,792.7)	($24,789)	(¥3,113.9)	(¥2,766.2)	(¥2,894.7)	(¥3,042.7)

Consolidated Financial Review

Consolidated net income rose 27.4% in the past fiscal year, to ¥441.3 billion ($2,884 million), on a 14.6% increase in net sales, to ¥9,192.8 billion ($60,084 million). *All the figures that appear in the following financial review and elsewhere in this report, except* *where specified otherwise, are consolidated figures based on the results of the Parent Company and its principal subsidiaries and affiliates, as described in note 2(a) of the Notes to Consolidated Financial Statements.*

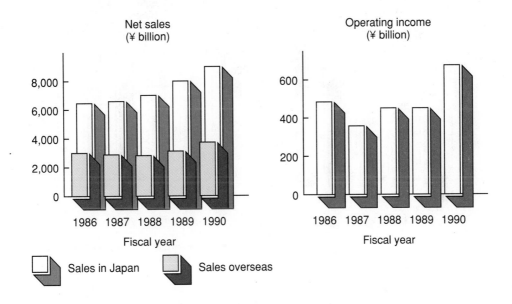

Net sales
(¥ billion)

Operating income
(¥ billion)

Fiscal year

Fiscal year

Sales in Japan   Sales overseas

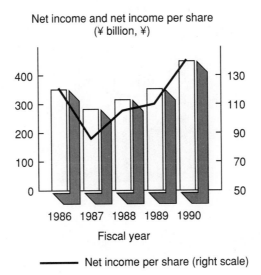

Net income and net income per share
(¥ billion, ¥)

Fiscal year

—— Net income per share (right scale)

Operating Results

The 14.6% growth that we registered in net sales in the past fiscal year resulted principally from unit sales gains in Japan and overseas and a shift toward higher-value models in our automotive product line. Our sales in Japan were up 10.0%, to ¥5,400.1 billion ($35,295 million), and business overseas expanded 21.8%, to

¥3,792.7 billion ($24,789 million). Consequently, sales in Japan accounted for 58.7% of net sales, compared with 61.2% in the previous year.

Our sales of motor vehicles climbed 14.9%, to ¥6,645.9 billion ($43,437 million), and accounted for 72.3% of net sales, compared with 72.1% in the previous year. Sales of parts and components for overseas production rose 24.5% to ¥154.1 billion

Total assets
(¥ billion)

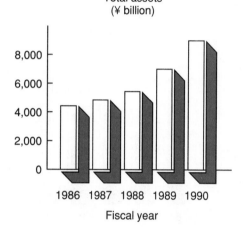

Shareholders' equity and equity ratio
(¥ billion, %)

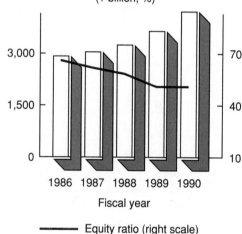

——— Equity ratio (right scale)

Cash flow* and capital investment
(¥ billion)

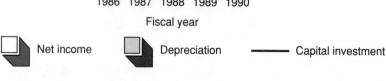

*Cash flow in the narrow sense of net income plus depreciation

($1,007 million), and business in automotive replacement parts expanded 10.6%, to ¥739.5 billion ($4,834 million).

Sales of industrial vehicles were up 8.8%, to ¥141.2 billion ($923 million). Aggregate sales of other products increased 15.0%, to ¥1,512.1 billion ($9,883 million).

Cost of sales rose 11.5%, to ¥7,479.1 billion ($48,883 million), and the gross profit margin was 18.6%, compared with 16.4% in the previous year. Selling, general and administrative expenses increased 26.2%, to ¥1,070.8 billion ($6,999 million). Operating income climbed 37.4%, to ¥643.0 billion ($4,203 million), and the operating profit margin was 7.0%, compared with 5.8% in the previous year.

Net nonoperating income was up 23.5%, to ¥194.8 billion ($1,273 million). This increase is attributable primarily to an increase in the volume of profit-earning assets and to the upturn in market interest rates.

Income before income taxes, at ¥837.8 billion ($5,476 million), was up 33.9% over the previous year. Our equity in earnings of affiliates increased 10.4%, to ¥20.6 billion ($135 million), and net income amounted to ¥441.3 billion ($2,884 million), up 27.4% over the previous year.

Net return on sales was 4.8%, up from 4.3% in the previous year, and fully diluted net income per share increased 26.3%, to ¥138.2 ($0.903). Cash dividends for the full year were ¥19.0 ($0.124) per share, compared with ¥17.7 ($0.116) in the previous year, and shareholders received a 1-for-20 free share distribution in August 1989. That distribution followed a 1-for-20 free share distribution in February 1989, in the previous fiscal period, and, in addition, we made a 1-for-10 free distribution of shares to our shareholders in August 1990, after the close of the fiscal year.

Financial Position

Our financial position remained strong in the past fiscal year. Shareholders' equity increased 14.2%, to ¥4,235.9 billion ($27,685 million) at fiscal year-end, on account of contributions from retained earnings, the conversion of convertible debentures, and the exercise of warrants. Total assets rose 17.9%, to ¥8,431.1 billion ($55,105 million) at fiscal year-end, and the ratio of shareholders' equity to total assets was 50.2% at fiscal year-end, compared with 51.9% the year before. Net assets per share of common stock increased 11.9%, to ¥1,383.7 ($9,04).

Our operations continued to generate a strong cash flow, and net cash provided by operating activities more than doubled, to ¥1,050.4 billion ($6,866 million). The sum of net income and depreciation alone was more than sufficient to fund additions to property, plant and equipment, which totaled ¥526.2 billion ($3,439 million), compared with ¥428.3 billion ($2,799 million) in the previous year. Cash and cash equivalents at fiscal year-end amounted to ¥1,362.3 billion ($8,904 million), up 11.9% over the previous year-end.

Consolidated Financial Statements

Consolidated Balance Sheets
Toyota Motor Corporation and Consolidated Subsidiaries
June 30, 1990 and 1989

	Millions of Yen		Thousands of U.S. Dollars (Note 1)
Assets	1990	1989	1990
Current assets:			
Cash and cash equivalents	¥1,362,309	¥1,217,013	$ 8,903,982
Short-term investments	842,271	718,874	5,505,036
Notes and accounts receivable (Note 5)	1,093,830	964,311	7,149,214
Inventories (Note 3)	337,985	334,226	2,209,051
Other	1,564,993	1,139,879	10,228,714
Less allowance for doubtful receivables	(34,198)	(30,332)	(223,517)
Total current assets	5,167,190	4,343,971	33,772,480

Assets	Millions of Yen		Thousands of U.S. Dollars (Note 1)
	1990	1989	1990
Investments and other assets:			
Investments in securities	**496,684**	419,355	**3,246,300**
Investments in unconsolidated subsidiaries and affiliates	**653,753**	551,208	**4,272,892**
Long-term loans	**204,331**	101,689	**1,335,495**
Other	**358,409**	358,427	**2,342,546**
Less: allowance for doubtful receivables	**(4,763)**	(4,144)	**(31,128)**
Total investments and other assets	**1,708,414**	1,426,535	**11,166,105**
Property, plant, and equipment:			
Land	**366,566**	331,694	**2,395,858**
Buildings and structures	**815,869**	741,161	**5,332,474**
Machinery and equipment	**2,576,287**	2,311,777	**16,838,480**
Construction in progress	**101,677**	52,629	**664,555**
Less: accumulated depreciation	**(2,307,155)**	(2,062,606)	**(15,079,443)**
Net property, plant, and equipment	**1,553,244**	1,374,655	**10,151,924**
Translation adjustments	**2,247**	7,725	**14,687**
Total assets	**¥8,431,095**	¥7,152,886	**$ 55,105,196**

Liabilities and Shareholders' Equity	Millions of yen		Thousands of U.S. dollars (Note 1)
	1990	1989	1990
Current liabilities:			
Short-term debt	**¥ 625,241**	¥ 354,284	**$ 4,086,541**
Notes and accounts payable (Note 5)	**680,528**	585,843	**4,447,897**
Accrued expenses	**555,805**	429,761	**3,632,711**
Accrued income taxes (Note 7)	**318,879**	189,686	**2,084,178**
Deposits received	**171,686**	147,984	**1,122,129**
Other	**339,121**	251,025	**2,216,478**
Total current liabilities	**2,691,260**	1,958,583	**17,589,934**
Long-term liabilities:			
Long-term debt (Note 4)	**1,221,274**	1,219,463	**7,982,182**
Retirement and severance benefits	**255,953**	235,218	**1,672,898**
Other	**9,604**	14,614	**62,771**
Total long-term liabilities	**1,486,831**	1,469,295	**9,717,851**
Minority interest in consolidated subsidiaries	**17,135**	15,431	**111,994**
Contingencies (Note 6)			

Liabilities and Shareholders' Equity	Millions of yen		Thousands of U.S. dollars (Note 1)
	1990	1989	1990
Shareholders' equity (Note 8):			
Common stock, par value ¥50:			
Authorized—6,000,000,000 shares			
Issued—3,061,294,959 shares in 1990	246,783	—	1,612,958
2,857,142,743 shares in 1989	—	187,317	—
Capital surplus	263,177	203,783	1,720,112
Legal reserve	49,561	36,061	323,930
Retained earnings	3,676,352	3,282,420	24,028,447
Less: treasury common stock	(4)	(4)	(30)
Total shareholders' equity	4,235,869	3,709,577	27,685,417
Total liabilities and shareholders' equity	¥8,431,095	¥7,152,886	$55,105,196

Consolidated Statements of Shareholders' Equity
Toyota Motor Corporation and Consolidated Subsidiaries
Years ended June 30, 1990, 1989 and 1988

	Millions of Yen					
	Number of Shares	Common Stock	Capital Surplus	Legal Reserve	Retained Earnings	Treasury Common Stock
Balance, June 30, 1987	2,665,953,287	¥133,298	¥149,810	¥33,324	¥2,728,658	¥(3)
Net income					310,952	
Dividends					(49,321)	
Transfer to legal reserve				38	(38)	
Bonuses to directors and statutory auditors					(597)	
Conversion of convertible debentures (Note 8)	1,284,963	1,240	1,240			
Translation adjustments					(26,641)	
Other					3,303	(3)
Balance, June 30, 1988	2,667,238,250	¥134,538	¥151,050	¥33,362	¥2,966,316	¥(6)
Net income					346,262	
Dividends paid					(52,274)	
Transfer to legal reserve				2,699	(2,699)	
Bonuses to directors and statutory auditors					(679)	
Conversion of convertible debentures (Note 8)	45,133,494	42,806	42,760			
Exercise of warrants (Note 8)	9,946,597	9,973	9,973			
Free distribution of shares	134,824,402					
Translation adjustments					27,318	
Other					(1,824)	2
Balance, June 30, 1989	2,857,142,743	¥187,317	¥203,783	¥36,061	¥3,282,420	¥(4)

	Number of Shares	Millions of Yen				
		Common Stock	Capital Surplus	Legal Reserve	Retained Earnings	Treasury Common Stock
Net income					441,302	
Dividends paid					(55,891)	
Transfer to legal reserve				13,500	(13,500)	
Bonuses to directors and statutory auditors					(683)	
Conversion of convertible debentures (Note 8)	56,214,001	54,837	54,765			
Exercise of warrants (Note 8)	5,081,078	4,629	4,629			
Free distribution of shares	142,857,137					
Translation adjustments					22,704	
Balance, June 30, 1990	3,061,294,959	¥246,783	¥263,177	¥49,561	¥3,676,352	¥(4)

	Thousands of U.S. Dollars (Note 1)				
	Common Stock	Capital Surplus	Legal Reserve	Retained Earnings	Treasury Common Stock
Balance, June 30, 1989	$1,224,297	$1,331,915	$235,694	$21,433,725	$(30)
Net income				2,884,326	
Dividends paid				(365,301)	
Transfer to legal reserve			88,236	(88,236)	
Bonuses to directors and statutory auditors				(4,462)	
Conversion of convertible debentures (Note 8)	358,403	357,939			
Exercise of warrants (Note 8)	20,158	30,258			
Free distribution of shares					
Translation adjustments				148,395	
Balance, June 30, 1990	$1,612,958	$1,720,112	$323,930	$24,028,447	$(30)

See accompanying notes to consolidated financial statements.

Consolidated Statements of Income
Toyota Motor Corporation and Consolidated Subsidiaries
Years ended June 30, 1990, 1989 and 1988

	Millions of Yen			Thousands of U.S. Dollars (Note 1)
	1990	**1989**	**1988**	**1990**
Net sales	**¥9,192,838**	¥8,021,042	¥7,215,798	**$60,083,910**
Cost of sales	**7,479,054**	6,704,924	5,989,300	**48,882,707**
Gross profit	**1,713,784**	1,316,118	1,226,498	**11,201,203**
Selling, general and administrative expenses (Note 7)	**1,070,789**	848,178	758,772	**6,998,622**
Operating income	**642,995**	467,940	467,726	**4,202,581**
Other income (expenses):				
Interest and dividend income	**304,198**	237,111	137,852	**1,988,220**
Interest expense	**(119,162)**	(84,130)	(22,296)	**(778,833)**
Other, net	**9,778**	4,734	26,973	**63,909**
Income before income taxes	**837,809**	625,255	610,255	**5,475,877**
Income taxes (Note 7):				
Current	**410,410**	300,147	320,042	**2,682,418**
Tax effect of timing differences	**4,803**	(2,668)	(5,015)	**31,393**
Minority interests in income of consolidated subsidiaries	**1,461**	979	1,477	**9,551**
Amortization of consolidation difference	**(480)**	359	(457)	**(3,134)**
Equity in earnings of unconsolidated subsidiary and affiliates	**20,647**	18,706	17,658	**134,945**
Net income	**¥ 441,302**	¥ 346,262	¥ 310,952	**$ 2,884,326**

	Yen			U.S. Dollars (Note1)
Amounts per share				
Net income	**¥138.20**	¥109.45	¥102.28	**$0.903**
Dividends	**19.00**	17.69	16.78	**0.124**

See accompanying notes to consolidated financial statements.

Consolidated Statements of Cash Flows
Toyota Motor Corporation and Consolidated Subsidiaries
Years ended June 30, 1990, 1989 and 1988

	Millions of Yen			Thousands of U.S. Dollars (Note 1)
	1990	1989	1988	1990
Cash flows from operating activities:				
Net income	¥ 441,302	¥ 346,262	¥310,952	$ 2,884,326
Adjustments to reconcile net income to net cash provided by operating activities—				
Depreciation and amortization	339,413	295,043	258,378	2,218,386
Allowance for doubtful receivables, net	4,486	11,620	3,084	29,320
Loss on sales of property, plant and equipment	8,198	2,769	29,586	53,582
Provision for retirement and severance benefits, net payment	20,735	9,959	16,870	135,523
Increase (decrease) in minority interests	1,704	2,357	(2,365)	11,137
Changes in current assets				
(Increase) in notes and accounts receivable	(129,519)	(141,291)	(107,670)	(846,529)
(Increase) in inventories	(3,759)	(72,507)	(2,672)	(24,568)
(Increase) in other current assets	(199,148)	(24,343)	(42,997)	(1,301,621)
Changes in current liabilities				
Increase in notes and accounts payable	94,685	69,816	55,307	618,856
Increase in accrued expenses	126,044	121,400	15,684	823,817
Increase (decrease) in accrued income taxes	129,193	(70,620)	114,816	844,399
Increase (decrease) in deposits received	23,702	(85,509)	45	154,915
Increase in other current liabilities	193,400	12,476	6,836	1,264,052
Net cash provided by operating activities	1,050,436	477,432	655,854	6,865,595
Cash flows from investing activities:				
(Increase) decrease in short-term investments	(123,397)	(170,561)	213,464	(806,516)
(Increase) in investments in securities (including investments in unconsolidated subsidiaries and affiliates)	(179,874)	(49,500)	(153,940)	(1,175,647)
(Increase) decrease in long-term loans	(102,642)	(52,745)	48,437	(670,863)
Additions to property, plant and equipment	(526,200)	(428,300)	(359,700)	(3,439,216)
Other	(331,253)	(576,134)	(130,288)	(2,165,052)
Net cash in investing activities	(1,263,366)	(1,277,240)	(382,027)	(8,257,294)
Cash flows from financing activities:				
Increase in short-term debt	270,957	190,289	21,449	1,770,961
Increase in long-term debt	1,811	888,970	109,497	11,837
Proceeds from the exercise of warrants	9,258	19,946	—	60,516
Dividends paid	(55,891)	(52,274)	(49,322)	(365,301)
Other	122,647	120,599	(8,802)	801,608
Net cash provided by financing activities	348,782	1,167,530	72,822	2,279,621
Effect of exchange rate changes on cash and cash equivalents	9,444	9,882	(7,622)	61,725
Net increase in cash and cash equivalents	145,296	377,604	339,027	949,647
Cash and cash equivalents at beginning of period	1,217,013	839,409	500,382	7,954,335
Cash and cash equivalents at end of period	¥1,362,309	¥1,217,013	¥839,409	$ 8,903,982

See accompanying notes to consolidated financial statements.

Notes to Consolidated Financial Statements

1. Basis of Presenting Financial Statements

The accompanying consolidated financial statements have been prepared in accordance with the accounting principles generally accepted in Japan from accounts and records maintained by Toyota Motor Corporation (the "Parent") and its subsidiaries. The Consolidated Statements of Cash Flows have been prepared for the purpose of inclusion in these consolidated financial statements, although such statements are not required in Japan. Relevant notes have been added and certain reclassifications of the accounts in the basic financial statements published in Japan have been made for presentation in a form which is more familiar to readers outside Japan. These reclassifications do not affect values of total assets, shareholders' equity, net sales or net income.

The financial statements presented herein are expressed in yen and, solely for the convenience of the reader, have been translated into U.S. dollars at the rate of ¥153 = US$1, the approximate exchange rate on the Tokyo Foreign Exchange Market on June 29, 1990. These translations should not be construed as representations that the yen amounts have been or could be converted into U.S. dollars.

Certain reclassifications have been made in the 1989 and 1988 financial statements to conform with the presentation for 1990.

2. Summary of Significant Accounting Policies

(a) Consolidation
The consolidated financial statements include the accounts of the Parent and those of its subsidiaries that are significant. Unconsolidated subsidiaries are excluded from the consolidated accounts because they are all small in terms of total assets, net sales, and net income and their inclusion in the consolidated accounts would not, either individually or in the aggregate, affect those accounts significantly in any important respect.

As at June 30, 1990, there were 30 significant subsidiaries out of a total of 173, including five companies that have been included in the Parent's consolidated accounts for the first time in the fiscal year ended on that date. These 30 companies consist of six domestic subsidiaries, seven overseas subsidiaries, and 17 consolidated subsidiaries of overseas subsidiaries. All significant intercompany balances and transactions have been eliminated in consolidation.

Consolidation of the 12 subsidiaries (including three subsidiaries of a subsidiary) whose fiscal years end on the same date as the Parent's fiscal year (June 30) or on the preceding March 31 is based on the accounts of those companies for their regular fiscal years ended on those dates. Consolidation of the 18 subsidiaries (including six subsidiaries of a subsidiary and eight subsidiaries of two of those companies) whose fiscal years end on September 30 or on December 31 is based on the accounts of those companies as calculated for one-year periods ended on the same date as the Parent's fiscal year.

Of the Parent's 143 unconsolidated subsidiaries and its 123 affiliates (companies in which the Parent holds, either directly or indirectly, an equity interest of at least 20% but not more than 50%) at June 30, 1990, investments in nine affiliates, all of them in Japan, are stated at their underlying net equity value. The 143 unconsolidated subsidiaries and the 114 affiliates not accounted for in this way under the equity method have been excluded because they are all small in terms of net income and their inclusion in the consolidated accounts would not, either individually or in the aggregate, affect those accounts significantly in any important respect.

Consolidated net income includes the Parent's equity in the current net earnings of its consolidated subsidiaries and of the affiliates accounted for under the equity method after elimination of unrealized intercompany profits.

The difference between the cost and underlying net equity of investments in consolidated subsidiaries and in the affiliates accounted for under the equity method is deferred and amortized on a straight-line basis over a period of five years, with the exception of minor amounts, which are charged or credited to income in the year of acquisition.

Consolidated subsidiaries:

Domestic consolidated subsidiaries:
   Tokyo Toyota Motor Co., Ltd.
   Tokyo Toyo-pet Motor Sales Co., Ltd.
   Osaka Toyopet Co., Ltd.
   Toyota Tokyo Corolla Co., Ltd.
   Araco Corporation
   Toyota Finance Corporation
Overseas consolidated subsidiaries:
   Toyota Motor Sales, U.S.A., Inc.
   Toyota Deutschland GmbH
   Toyota Motor Sales Australia Ltd.
   Toyota Motor Manufacturing Canada Inc.
   Toyota Motor Thailand Company Limited
   Toyota Motor Finance (Netherlands) B.V.
   Toyota Finance Australia Ltd.

*Consolidated subsidiaries of overseas consolidated subsidiaries:
  Six consolidated subsidiaries of Toyota Motor Sales, U.S.A., Inc., and eight consolidated subsidiaries of two of those companies
  Three consolidated subsidiaries of Toyota Finance Australia Ltd.

Three of the consolidated subsidiaries of Toyota Motor Sales, U.S.A., Inc., and two of the consolidated subsidiaries of Toyota Finance Australia Ltd. have been included in the Parent's consolidated accounts for the first time in the fiscal year ended June 30, 1990.

Affiliates accounted for under the equity method:
  Domestic affiliates:
    Toyoda Automatic Loom Works, Ltd.
    Aichi Steel Works, Limited
    Toyoda Machine Works, Ltd.
    Toyota Auto Body Co., Ltd.
    Toyota Tsusho Corporation
    Aisin Seiki Co., Ltd.
    Nippondenso Co., Ltd.
    Kanto Auto Works, Ltd.
    Toyoda Gosei Co., Ltd.

(b) Securities
Listed securities in Cash and cash equivalents, Short-term investments, and Other investments, including securities managed in *tokkin* (Specified Money Trusts) and *kingai* (Investment Funds in Trust), are stated principally at the lower of cost, as determined by the moving average method, or market value. Other securities are stated principally at cost, as determined by the moving average method, or less.

(c) Inventories

Inventories of the Parent are principally stated at cost, as determined by the periodic average method, Inventories of consolidated subsidiaries are principally stated at cost, as determined by the specific identification method or the LIFO method.

(d) Finance Receivables

A number of consolidated subsidiaries of the Parent engage primarily in financing activities. The finance receivables of these companies account for the largest single element of the amounts listed as "Other" under Current Assets on the Consolidated Balance Sheets and as "Other" under Cash Flows from Investing Activities on the Consolidated Statements of Cash Flows.

(e) Property, plant and equipment and depreciation.

Property, plant and equipment are stated at cost. Depreciation of property, plant and equipment is computed principally by the declining balance method in accordance with provisions of the tax code. Further depreciation of buildings and structures and of machinery and equipment is carried out for assets of the Parent by the declining balance method up to the residual value of the assets.

(f) Foreign currency translation

Accounts of overseas consolidated subsidiaries have been translated into yen at the rate of exchange prevailing at the end of the fiscal year used in consolidating the accounts of each company.

(g) Retirement and severance benefits

The balance of the reserve for employees' retirement and severance benefits of the parent is the amount required if all employees were to terminate their employment involuntarily at the balance sheet date, and that of the consolidated subsidiaries is principally the amount equivalent to the maximum that may be provided under tax laws.

Besides the above, the Parent and three of its domestic consolidated subsidiaries have a contributory pension plan. The assets of the pension fund at March 31, 1990, the most recent available date, totaled ¥273,302 million ($1,786,291 thousand). The remaining domestic consolidated subsidiaries have different types of pension plans, and most of the overseas consolidated subsidiaries have their own pension plans.

(h) Income Taxes

Income taxes are, in principle, accounted for on an accrual basis. Income taxes have been stated to reflect the effect of timing differences arising from additions to and deductions from consolidated income, which are due to transactions such as the elimination of unrealized gains and losses, adjustments of allowances for doubtful receivables and other adjustments for the purpose of consolidation.

(i) Amounts per share

Net income per share is computed based on the average number of common shares and common share equivalents outstanding during the fiscal years and is adjusted retroactively for free distributions of shares.

Dividends per share represent the dividends declared as applicable to the respective years, adjusted retroactively for free distributions of shares.

3. Inventories

Inventories as of June 30, 1990 and 1989, were as follows:

	Millions of Yen		Thousands of U.S. Dollars
	1990	1989	1990
Finished goods	¥235,619	¥258,216	$1,539,989
Raw materials	41,034	34,723	268,197
Work in progress	51,115	32,179	334,087
Supplies	10,217	9,108	66,778
	¥337,985	¥334,226	$2,209,051

4. Long-term Debt

Long-term debt as of June 30, 1990 and 1989, was as follows:

	Millions of Yen		Thousands of U.S. Dollars
	1990	1989	1990
4.0% U.S. dollar bonds due 1993 with warrants	¥ 192,449	¥ 192,449	$1,257,834
1.2% convertible debentures due 1998	251,846	296,796	1,646,052
1¼% U.S. dollar bonds due 1992 with warrants	117,760	117,760	769,673
1.7% convertible debentures due 1996	50,505	115,156	330,098
Straight bonds issued by consolidated subsidiaries (4.5% to 14%, maturing through 1994)	489,629	450,629	3,198,099
Bank loans and other	119,405	46,673	780,426
	¥1,221,274	¥1,219,463	$7,982,182

5. Accounts with Unconsolidated Subsidiaries and Affiliates

The balances at June 30, 1990 and 1989, included the following balances of accounts with unconsolidated subsidiaries and affiliates:

	Millions of Yen		Thousands of U.S. Dollars
	1990	1989	1990
Notes and accounts receivable	¥261,100	¥227,489	$1,706,536
Notes and accounts payable	384,461	337,790	2,512,816

6. Contingencies

At June 30, 1990, export bills discounted amounted to ¥11,650 million ($76,145 thousand). At the same date, consolidated subsidiaries were responsible for ¥4,315 million ($28,204 thousand) in other contingency liabilities, primarily as guarantors for third-party liabilities consisting mainly of bank loans.

7. Income Taxes

Accrued income taxes listed in the Consolidated Balance Sheets include corporation tax, inhabitant tax and enterprise taxes. Income taxes listed in the Consolidated Statements of Income include corporation tax and inhabitant tax. Enterprise taxes are charged to selling, general and administrative expenses.

Enterprise taxes for the fiscal years ended June 30, 1990, 1989 and 1988, were as follows:

	Millions of Yen			Thousands of U.S. Dollars
	1990	1989	1988	1990
Enterprise taxes (including business tax)	¥108,576	¥74,489	¥79,438	$709,645

8. Shareholders' Equity

Under the Japanese Commercial Code, amounts equal to at least 10% of the cash dividends paid by the parent and its domestic subsidiaries must be set aside as a legal reserve until such reserve equals 25% of common stock. The legal reserve may be used to reduce a deficit or may be transferred to common stock by taking appropriate corporate action.

In consolidation, the legal reserves of consolidated subsidiaries are accounted for as retained earnings.

Dividends are approved by the shareholders at a meeting held after the close of the fiscal year to which the dividends are applicable. In addition, a semiannual interim dividend may be paid upon resolution of the Board of Directors, subject to limitations imposed by the Japanese Commercial Code.

Proceeds from the conversion of convertible debentures and the exercise of warrants have been accounted for in approximately equal amounts as common stock and as capital surplus with at least 50% being accounted for as common stock, in accordance with the provisions of the Japanese Commercial Code.

9. Subsequent Event

On August 6, 1990, the Parent made a 1-for-10 free distribution of shares to shareholders of record as of June 30, 1990.

On September 26, 1990, the shareholders of the Parent authorized the payment of a year-end cash dividend to shareholders of record as of June 30, 1990, of ¥10 ($0.07) per share, or a total of ¥30,613 million ($200,085 thousand), and bonuses to directors and statutory auditors of ¥563 million ($3,680 thousand).

Report of Independent Public Accountants

To the Board of Directors of Toyota Motor Corporation

We have examined the consolidated balance sheets of Toyota Motor Corporation and its consolidated subsidiaries as of June 30, 1990 and 1989, and the related consolidated statements of income, shareholders' equity and cash flows for each of the three years in the period ended June 30, 1990, expressed in yen. Our examinations were made in accordance with generally accepted auditing standards in Japan and, accordingly, included such tests of the accounting records and such other auditing procedures as we considered necessary in the circumstances. We did not examine the financial statements of certain consolidated subsidiaries, which statements reflect total assets constituting 24% and 22% of the consolidated totals as of June 30, 1990 and 1989, respectively, and net sales constituting 23%, 21% and 18% of the consolidated totals for the years ended June 30, 1990, 1989 and 1988, respectively. We also did not examine the financial statements of an unconsolidated subsidiary for 1988 and certain affiliates, the investments in which are accounted for under the equity method of accounting for 1990, 1989 and 1988. The equity in net income in these companies represents 3%, 3% and 3% of consolidated net income for the years ended June 30, 1990, 1989 and 1988, respectively. These statements were examined by other auditors whose reports thereon have been furnished to us, and our opinion expressed herein, insofar as it relates to the amounts included for these subsidiaries and affiliates, is based solely on the reports of the other auditors.

In our opinion, based on our examinations and the reports of other auditors, the aforementioned consolidated financial statements, expressed in yen, present fairly the financial position of Toyota Motor Corporation and its consolidated subsidiaries as of June 30, 1990 and 1989, and the results of their operations and their cash flows for each of the three years in the period ended June 30, 1990 and 1989, and the results of their operations and their cash flows for each of the three years in the period ended June 30, 1990, in conformity with generally accepted accounting principles in Japan applied on a consistent basis.

Our examinations also covered the translation of Japanese yen amounts into the United States dollar amounts included in the consolidated financial statements and, in our opinion, such translation has been made in conformity with the basis stated in Note 1 to the consolidated financial statements. Such United States dollar amounts are presented solely for the convenience of readers outside Japan.

Nagoya, Japan
September 26, 1990
Itoh Audit Corporation(s)

Consolidated Financial Summary
Toyota Motor Corporation and Consolidated Subsidiaries
Years ended June 30

Vehicle Units

	1990	1989	1988	1987	1986
Vehicle factory sales:					
Domestic	2,425,809	2,194,327	2,012,447	1,782,194	1,712,054
Overseas	2,003,336	1,919,077	1,859,903	1,907,018	2,004,981
Total	4,429,145	4,113,404	3,872,350	3,689,212	3,717,035

	Millions of Yen	Thousands of U.S. Dollars	Millions of Yen			
Net sales	¥9,192,838	$60,083,910	¥8,021,042	¥7,215,798	¥6,675,411	¥6,646,244
Net income	441,302	2,884,326	346,262	310,952	260,704	345,534
Total assets	8,431,095	55,105,196	7,152,886	5,450,376	4,870,832	4,348,105
Shareholders' equity	4,235,869	27,685,417	3,709,577	3,285,260	3,045,087	2,857,296
Common stock	246,783	1,612,958	187,317	134,538	133,298	133,298
Capital investment	526,200	3,439,216	428,300	359,700	368,800	408,500
Depreciation	339,413	2,218,386	295,043	258,378	245,442	219,083

	Vehicle Units				
	1990		1989	1988	1987	1986
	Yen	U.S. Dollars			Yen		
Amounts per share:						
Net income	¥ 138.20	$0.903	¥ 109.45	¥ 102,28	¥ 86.81	¥117.56
Dividends	19.00	0.124	17.69	16.78	16.78	16.78
Shareholders' equity	1,383.69	9.044	1,236,53	1,117.20	1,036,02	972.13
Equity-to-assets ratio	50.2%		51.9%	60.3%	62.5%	65.7%
Shares outstanding at year-end (thousands)	3,061,295		2,857,143	2,667,238	2,665,953	2,665,953
Employees at year-end	96,849		91,790	86,082	84,207	82,620

Notes: 1. The number of shares used in computing per share amounts has been adjusted to take into account the retroactive effect of free distributions of shares and stock dividends. Net income per share is computed based on the average number of common shares and common share equivalents outstanding during the fiscal years.
2. Dividends include interim cash dividends.
3. U.S. dollar amounts have been translated from yen, solely for the conveniience of the reader, at the rate of ¥153 = US$1, the approximate exchange rate on the Tokyo Foreign Exchange Market on June 29, 1990, the last trading day of the fiscal year.

Unconsolidated Financial Summary
Toyota Motor Corporation
Years ended June 30

	Vehicle Units				
	1990		1989	1988	1987	1986
Vehicle factory sales:						
Domestic	2,432,729		2,215,173	2,034,772	1,789,686	1,720,373
Export	1,608,484		1,807,377	1,796,682	1,800,912	1,965,138
Total	4,041,213		4,022,550	3,831,454	3,590,598	3,685,511
	Millions of Yen	Thousands of U.S. Dollars	Millions of Yen			
Net sales	¥7,998,051	$52,274,840	¥7,190,591	¥6,691,299	¥6,024,910	¥6,304,859
Net income	360,803	2,358,192	305,863	238,007	200,208	255,186
Total assets	5,968,432	39,009,357	5,316,191	4,553,593	4,053,106	3,624,812
Shareholders' equity	3,578,957	23,391,873	3,155,698	2,797,128	2,606,430	2,453,348
Common stock	246,783	1,612,958	187,317	134,538	133,298	133,298
Capital investment	417,600	2,729,412	329,400	224,700	297,000	381,700
Depreciation	276,827	1,809,327	238,869	236,637	230,947	204,507

		Vehicle Units			
	1990		**1989**	**1988**	**1987**	**1986**
	Yen	**U.S. Dollars**		Yen		
Amounts per share:						
Net income	¥ **113.10**	**$0.739**	¥ 96.78	¥ 78.40	¥ 66.67	¥ 86.82
Dividends	**19.00**	**0.124**	17.69	16.78	16.78	16.78
Shareholders' equity	**1,169.10**	**7.641**	1,051.90	951.20	886.78	834.70
Equity to assets ratio	**60.0%**		59.4%	61.4%	64.3%	67.7%
Shares outstanding at year-end (thousands)	**3,061,295**		2,857,143	2,667,238	2,665,953	2,665,953
Employees at year-end	**70,841**		67,814	65,926	64,797	63,890

Note: See notes to consolidated financial summary.

British Petroleum Company Annual Report and Accounts 1990—Excerpts

Shareholding Information

Range of Holdings:	BP Ordinary Shareholders at 31 December 1990		
	Number of Shareholders	Percentage of Total Shareholders	Percentage of Share Capital
1–50	36,392	6.4	—
51–100	27,617	4.9	—
101–150	114,635	20.1	0.3
151–200	6,074	1.1	—
201–250	33,142	5.8	0.1
251–1,000	171,089	30.1	1.7
1,000–10,000	170,267	29.9	8.5
10,001–100,000	8,043	1.4	3.6
100,001–1,000,000	1,424	0.2	9.2
Over 1,000,000	500	0.1	76.6
Total shareholders	569,183	100.0	100.0

Classification of Shareholders:	Number of Shareholders	Percentage of Total Shareholders	Percentage of Share Capital
Individuals	535,519	94.1	11.4
Companies	2,892	0.5	4.2
Trust companies (pension funds, etc.)	3,615	0.6	8.6
Banks and nominees*	25,106	4.4	60.6
Insurance and assurance companies	2,050	0.4	13.3
U.K. government	1	—	1.9
Total shareholders	569,183	100.0	100.0

*Includes the 9.8% holding of the State of Kuwait.

The total number of ordinary shares in issue at 31 December 1990 was 5,364,171 of which approximately 388 million were represented by ADRs.

At 31 December 1990 there were also 3,525 preference shareholders.

Announcement of Dividends and Results

Ordinary shares

Proposed Key Dates for Dividends to Be Declared in 1991 and for The BP Share Dividend Plan:

Announcement	Ex-dividend	Record	Variation*	Payment
14 February 1991	25 February 1991	8 March 1991	11 April 1991	7 May 1991
9 May 1991	20 May 1991	31 May 1991	3 July 1991	7 August 1991
8 August 1991	12 August 1991	23 August 1991	25 September 1991	7 November 1991
7 November 1991	11 November 1991	22 November 1991	3 January 1992	7 February 1992

*This is the date by which participants in the Plan must return forms of variation to the Registrar if they wish to vary the level of their participation in the Plan in time for the following dividend payment. Forms of variation can be obtained from the Registrar at the address given.

First and second preference shares

Dividends are paid on 31 January and 31 July of each year.

Announcement of results

Results are announced in February, May, August and November of each year.

The group's half-year results for 1991 (including notification of the relevant quarterly dividend) will be announced to The International Stock Exchange, London, and will be included in the Half-Year Review which will be sent to shareholders in August.

The first and third quarter results (including notification of the relevant quarterly dividends) will be announced to The International Stock Exchange in the usual way. Shareholders who would like to be placed on the mailing list for these first and third quarterly announcements should write to the Company Secretary. ADR holders in the USA and Canada, and shareholders in Japan, should write to the addresses given.

Taxation

New shares instead of cash dividends

During 1990 the company made available The BP Share Dividend Plan in respect of the quarterly dividends paid in May, August and November 1990 and February 1991.

The amount of the dividend necessary to give an entitlement to one new share was fixed at 336.2p, 322.6p, 362.4p and 330.4p respectively. Each new share received will be treated for income tax purposes, as giving rise to gross income of 448.3p, 430.1p, 483.2p and 440.5p respectively on which basic rate income tax of 112.1p, 107.5p, 120.8p and 110.1p respectively has been paid.

It should be noted that the market value of one new share on the first day of dealing on The International Stock Exchange (the opening value) did not differ by 15% either way from the amount of cash dividend necessary to give an entitlement to one new share. Accordingly, the Inland Revenue will not seek to substitute the opening value for the figures given above of 336.2p, 322.6p, 362.4p, and 330.4p. The relevant opening values for the quarterly dividends paid in May, August and November 1990 and February 1991 were 320.0p, 362.0p, 338.0p and 321.0p respectively.

Capital gains

The market values of BP shares at 6 April 1965 for the purposes of capital gains tax, after adjustment for the conversion, sub-division and capitalisation issue referred to below, were:

  Ordinary shares
  £0.213542 per 25p ordinary share
  First preference shares
  £1.128125 per £1 share
  Second preference shares
  £1.243750 per £1 share

Since 5 April 1965 there have been rights issues of ordinary shares as follows:

One for thirteen at £0.2083: the ex-rights date was 28 February 1966

One for fifteen at £0.4283: the ex-rights date was 14 October 1971

One for seven at £0.9167: the ex-rights date was 23 June 1981

As from the close of business on 5 October 1979 each £1 unit of ordinary stock was converted and sub-divided into four ordinary shares of 25p each, and each existing £1 unit of preference stock was converted into one preference share of £1.

With effect from 1 May 1987 a capitalisation issue was made of two additional ordinary shares of 25p each for each ordinary share held at the close of business on 15 April 1987.

The market values at 31 March 1982 for the purposes of capital gains tax indexation allowance were:

Ordinary shares
£0.95 per 25p ordinary share
First preference shares
£0.565 per £1 share
Second preference shares
£0.645 per £1 share

The company is not a close company within the meaning of the Income and Corporation Taxes Act 1988.

Report of the Auditors

To the Members of The British Petroleum Company p.l.c

We have audited the accounts in accordance with Auditing Standards.

In our opinion the accounts give a true and fair view of the state of affairs of the company and of the group at 31 December 1990 and of the profit and source and

application of funds of the group for the year then ended and have been properly prepared in accordance with the Companies Act 1985.

Ernst & Young
Chartered Accountants
London
14 February 1991

Accounting Policies

Accounting standards

In all material respects, these accounts are prepared in accordance with applicable UK accounting standards.

Accounting convention

The accounts are prepared under the historical cost convention. Historical cost accounts show the profits available to shareholders and are the most appropriate basis for presentation of the group's balance sheet and funds statement. The historical costs results include stock holding gains or losses.

Replacement cost

The results of individual businesses and geographical areas are presented on a replacement cost basis. Replacement cost operating results exclude stock holding gains or losses and reflect the average cost of supplies incurred during the year. Stock holding gains or losses represent the difference between the replacement cost of sales and the historical cost of sales calculated using the first-in- first-out method.

Group consolidation

The group accounts comprise a consolidation of the accounts of the parent company and all its subsidiary undertakings, except for a number of minor undertakings where the amounts involved are insignificant, and include the group proportion of the profits or losses and retained earnings of associated undertakings.

Foreign currencies

On consolidation, assets and liabilities of subsidiary undertakings are translated into sterling at closing rates of exchange. Income and source and application of funds statements are translated at average rates of exchange.

Exchange differences resulting from the translation at closing rates of net investments in subsidiary and associated undertakings, together with differences between income statements translated at average rates and at closing rates, are dealt with in reserves.

Exchange gains and losses arising on long-term foreign currency borrowings used to finance the group's foreign currency investments are also dealt with in reserves.

All other exchange gains or losses on settlement or translation at closing rates of exchange of monetary assets and liabilities are included in the determination of profit for the year.

Stock valuation

Stocks are valued at cost to the group using the first-in first-out method or at net realisable value, whichever is the lower. Stores are stated at or below cost calculated mainly using the average method.

Exploration expenditure

Exploration expenditure is accounted in accordance with the successful efforts method. Exploration expenditure is initially classified as an intangible fixed asset. When proved reserves of oil and gas or commercially exploitable reserves of minerals are determined and development is sanctioned, the relevant expenditure is transferred to tangible production assets. All exploration expenditure determined as unsuccessful is charged against income. Exploration leasehold acquisition costs are amortised over the estimated period of exploration.

Exploration costs incurred under production-sharing contracts are classified as loans within fixed asset investments. Provisions are initially made against these loans in accordance with the successful efforts method. On the determination of proved oil and gas reserves in contract areas provisions against expenditures, which are recoverable under contracts from future production, are written back to income.

Depreciation

Oil and minerals production assets are depreciated using a unit-of-production method based upon estimated proved reserves. Other tangible and intangible assets are depreciated on the straight line method over their estimated useful lives.

Abandonment

Provision is made using a unit-of-production method, based upon estimated proved reserves, for the abandonment of production facilities in accordance with local conditions and requirements on the basis of costs estimated as at balance sheet date. The effect of changes to estimated costs is dealt with on a prospective basis.

Pensions

Most group companies have pension plans the forms and benefits of which vary with conditions and practices in the countries concerned. In most cases plans are funded by contributions to separate funds. Pension costs, including the amortisation of actuarial surpluses and deficiencies, are charged to income over the expected average remaining service lives of employees. The difference between the charge for pensions and total contributions is included within pension provisions or debtors as appropriate.

Leases

Assets held under leases which result in group companies receiving substantially all risks and rewards of ownership (finance leases) are capitalised as tangible fixed assets at the estimated present value of underlying lease payments. The corresponding finance lease obligation is included with borrowings. Rentals under operating leases are charged against income as incurred.

Petroleum revenue tax

The charge for petroleum revenue tax is calculated using a unit-of-production method.

Changes in unit-of-production factors

Changes in factors which affect unit-of-production calculations are dealt with prospectively, not by immediate adjustment of prior years' amounts.

Interest

Interest is capitalised during the period of construction where it relates either to the financing of major projects with long periods of development or to dedicated financing of other projects. All other interest is charged against income.

Research

Expenditure on research is written off in the year in which it is incurred.

Goodwill

Goodwill is the excess of purchase consideration over the fair value of net assets acquired. It is capitalised and amortised over its estimated useful economic life, limited to a maximum period of twenty years.

Deferred taxation

Deferred taxation is calculated, using the liability method, in respect of timing differences arising primarily from the different accounting and tax treatment of depreciation and petroleum revenue tax. Provision is made or recovery anticipated where timing differences are expected to reverse in the foreseeable future.

Comparative figures

Certain previous years' figures have been restated to conform with the 1990 presentation.

Group Income Statement

For the year ended 31 December 1990	Note	£ Million 1990	1989
Turnover	2	**33,039**	29,641
Replacement cost of sales		**24,655**	22,095
Production taxes	3	**1,348**	1,242
Gross profit		**7,036**	6,304
Distribution and administration expenses	4	**4,140**	3,690
Exploration expenditure written off		**460**	480
		2,436	2,134
Other income	6	**526**	803
Replacement cost operating profit		**2,962**	2,937
Stock holding gains		**477**	390
Historical cost operating profit		**3,439**	3,327
Interest expense	7	**671**	794
Profit before taxation		**2,768**	2,533
Taxation	9	**1,042**	744
Profit after taxation		**1,726**	1,789
Minority shareholders' interest		**50**	45
Profit before extraordinary items		**1,676**	1,744
Extraordinary items	10	**12**	390
Profit for the year		**1,688**	2,134
Distribution to shareholders	11	**861**	795
Retained profit for the year		**827**	1,339
Earnings per ordinary share	12	**31.3p**	31.8p

Group Reserves

Group reserves at 1 January		**7,490**	8,297
Exchange adjustments		**(692)**	268
Shares purchased from KIO	27	**—**	(2,423)
Retained profit for the year		**827**	1,339
Other movements		**—**	9
Group reserves at 31 December	28	**7,625**	7,490

Balance Sheets

At 31 December 1990	Note	Group 1990	Group 1989	Parent 1990	Parent 1989
Fixed assets:					
Intangible assets	16	1,447	1,672	—	—
Tangible assets	17	17,481	19,285	—	—
Investments	18	1,413	1,497	2,022	1,755
		20,341	22,454	2,022	1,755
Current assets					
Stocks	19	3,476	3,381	—	—
Debtors	20	6,259	5,361	3,564	3,854
Investments	21	152	151	—	—
Cash at bank and in hand		469	268	1	3
		10,356	9,161	3,565	3,857
Creditors—amounts falling due within one year:					
Finance debt	22	1,713	2,531	—	—
Other creditors	23	7,897	7,037	712	811
Net current assets		746	(407)	2,853	3,046
Total assets less current liabilities		21,087	22,047	4,875	4,801
Creditors—amounts falling due after more than one year:					
Finance debt	22	5,207	5,758	—	—
Other creditors	23	2,144	1,936	5	18
Provisions for liabilities and charges:					
Deferred taxation	9	387	451	—	—
Other provisions	24	2,108	2,461	—	—
Net assets		11,241	11,441	4,870	4,783
Minority shareholders' interest		240	656	—	—
BP shareholders' interest		11,001	10,785	4,870	4,783
Represented by					
Capital and reserves:					
Called up share capital	25	1,353	1,346	1,353	1,346
Share premium account	26	1,826	1,752	1,826	1,752
Capital redemption reserve	27	197	197	197	197
Reserves	28	7,625	7,490	1,494	1,488
		11,001	10,785	4,870	4,783

£ Million

Robert Horton, Director.

Lindsey Alexander, Director.

14 February 1991

Group Source and Application of Funds Statement

| For the Year Ended 31 December 1990 | Note | £ Million | |
		1990	1989
Profit after taxation		1,726	1,789
Extraordinary items		12	390
Items not involving the movement of funds (i)		2,382	2,701
		4,120	4,880
Working capital movement (ii)		(431)	(410)
Other movements (iii)		1,651	303
Funds generated from operations		5,340	4,773
Capital expenditure		(3,751)	(3,433)
Acquisitions	14	(61)	(70)
Net assets of divested coal and minerals interest	15	118	1,694
Dividends paid		(838)	(911)
Funds generated		808	2,053
Financial movements			
Shares issued		(81)	(74)
Shares purchased from KIO	27	—	2,423
Changes in external financing		629	(350)
External funding—decrease		548	1,999
Liquid resources—increase (iv)		260	54
		808	2,053

Notes:

(i) **Items not involving the movement of funds:**

	1990	1989
Depreciation and amounts provided	2,011	2,077
Exploration expenditure written off	460	480
Profit retained by association undertakings	(19)	14
Provisions for liabilities and charges	(70)	130
	2,382	2,701

(ii) **Working capital movement:**

	1990	1989
Stocks	(479)	(729)
Debtors	(1,463)	(808)
Creditors due within one year (excluding finance debt)	1,511	1,127
	(431)	(410)

(iii) **Other movements:**

	1990	1989
Book amount of fixed assets sold	1,270	793
Creditors due after one year (excluding finance debt)	320	154
Minority shareholders' interest	(23)	(36)
Other	84	(608)
	1,651	303

(iv) Liquid resources comprise current asset investments and cash at bank and in hand.

(v) The statement of source and application of funds of overseas subsidiaries are translated into sterling at average rates of exchange in order to reflect more closely the funds flows within those undertakings. Accordingly the figures shown above exclude currency differences arising from the translation of assets and liabilities at closing rates.

Notes on Accounts

	£ Million			
1 Group income statement analysis	Replacement Cost Operating Profit (i)		Turnover (ii)	
By business	**1990**	**1989**	**1990**	**1989**
Exploration and production	**2,086**	1,574	**7,837**	6,855
Refining and marketing	**853**	732	**24,025**	20,598
Chemicals	**129**	548	**3,164**	3,164
Nutrition	**48**	35	**2,682**	2,620
Other businesses and corporate	**(154)**	48	**390**	884
	2,962	2,937	**38,098**	34,121
Less: sales between businesses			**5,059**	4,480
Total	**2,962**	2,937	**33,039**	29,641
By geographical area				
UK (iii)	**406**	787	**12,209**	9,428
Rest of Europe	**571**	525	**10,093**	9,265
USA	**1,470**	1,334	**10,402**	9,938
Rest of world	**515**	291	**3,664**	3,398
	2,962	2,937	**36,368**	32,029
Less: sales between areas			**3,329**	2,388
Total	**2,962**	2,937	**33,039**	29,641

(i) Replacement cost operating profit is before stock holding gains and losses, interest expense and taxation, all of which are attributable to the corporate function.

(ii) Transfers between group companies are made at market prices taking into account the volumes involved.

(iii) UK area includes UK North Sea crude oil activities and the UK-based international activities of BP Oil.

	£ Million	
2 Turnover	**1990**	**1989**
Sales and operating revenue	**41,711**	37,394
Customs duties and sales taxes	**8,672**	7,753
	33,039	29,641
3 Production taxes		
UK petroleum revenue tax	**746**	763
Overseas production taxes	**602**	479
	1,348	1,242

	£ Million	
	1990	**1989**
4 Distribution and administration expenses		
Distribution	**3,838**	3,508
Administration	**302**	182
	4,140	3,690
5 Depreciation and amounts provided		
Included in the income statement under the following headings:		
Depreciation:		
Replacement cost of sales	**1,703**	1,797
Distribution	**257**	233
Administration	**49**	44
	2,009	2,074
Deprecation of capitalised leased assets included above	**56**	32
Amounts provided against fixed asset investments:		
Replacement cost of sales	**2**	3
Exploration expenditure	**56**	57
	58	60
6 Other income		
Share of profits of associated undertakings	**200**	262
Income from other fixed asset investments	**9**	3
Other interest and miscellaneous income	**317**	538
	526	803
Income from listed investments included above	**38**	35
7 Interest expense		
Loans wholly repayable within five years	**399**	506
Other loans	**288**	357
Finance leases	**63**	40
	750	903
Capitalised	**79**	109
Charged against profit	**671**	794
8 Hire, research and audit costs		
Hire charges under operating leases:		
Tanker charters	**228**	225
Plant and machinery	**187**	190
Land and buildings	**153**	128
	568	543
Expenditure on research	**329**	325

Auditors' remuneration—group companies £6.9 million
(£6.7 million) of which the parent company £0.5 million
(£0.5 million).

9 Taxation

United Kingdom corporation tax:

Current at 35%	**792**	1,223
Overseas tax relief	**(452)**	(1,090)
	340	133
Deferred at 35%	**19**	119
	359	252
Advance corporation tax	**(60)**	58
	299	310

Overseas

Current	**686**	428
Deferred	**(2)**	(47)
Associated undertakings	**59**	53
	743	434
	1,042	744

Provisions for deferred taxation	£ Million			
	Provisions		**Gross Potential Liability**	
Analysis of movements during the year:	**1990**	**1989**	**1990**	**1989**
At 1 January	**451**	389	**2,488**	2,202
Exchange adjustments	**(29)**	23	**(264)**	175
Acquisitions	**—**	1	**—**	1
Charge for the year	**17**	72	**118**	242
Extraordinary items	**—**	(34)	**—**	(132)
Deletions	**(52)**	—	**(56)**	—
At 31 December	**387**	451	**2,286**	2,488
of which— United Kingdom	**237**	219	**880**	841
— Overseas	**150**	232	**1,406**	1,647
Analysis by category of timing difference:	**1990**	1989	**1990**	1989
Depreciation	**1,143**	1,140	**2,834**	2,996
Petroleum revenue tax	**(558)**	(458)	**(549)**	(458)
Other items	**(198)**	(231)	**1**	(50)
	387	451	**2,286**	2,488

Advance corporation tax has not been deducted from provisions for deferred taxation.

If provision for deferred taxation had been made on the basis of the gross potential liability the charge for the year would have been increased as follows:

United Kingdom	**20**	26
Overseas	**81**	144
	101	170

10 Extraordinary items

	£ Million	
	1990	**1989**
Profit on sale of Minerals interests	—	267
Profit on sale of Coal interests	**12**	123
	12	390

Total extraordinary profit shown above is
after charging overseas taxation of
£15 million (£363 million).

11 Distribution to shareholders

	Pence per Share		£ Million	
	1990	**1989**	**1990**	**1989**
Preference dividends			**1**	1
Ordinary dividends:				
First quarterly	**39.95**	3.65	**211**	194
Second quarterly	**3.95**	3.65	**212**	194
Third quarterly	**3.95**	3.65	**212**	195
Fourth quarterly	**4.20**	3.95	**225**	211
	16.05	14.90	**861**	795

12 Earnings per ordinary share
The calculation of earnings per
ordinary share is based on
profit before extraordinary
items less preference dividends,
related to the weighted
average of 5,350 million (5,474
million) ordinary shares in
issue during the year.

13 Group balance sheet analysis

	£ Million			
	Capital Expenditure and Acquisitions		Operating Capital Employed (ii)	
By business	**1990**	**1989**	**1990**	**1989**
Exploration and Production	**2,201**	2,037	**10,019**	11,705
Refining and Marketing	**774**	726	**5,717**	5,695
Chemicals	**384**	313	**2,081**	1,941
Nutrition	**152**	172	**949**	1,027
Other businesses and corporate	**301**	255	**380**	298
Total	**3,812**	3,503	**19,146**	20,666
By geographical area				
UK (i)	**1,701**	1,491	**6,135**	5,829
Rest of Europe	**595**	544	**3,137**	2,932
USA	**902**	861	**7,029**	8,552
Rest of World	**614**	607	**2,845**	3,353
Total	**3,812**	3,503	**19,146**	20,666

	£ Million	
Capital Expenditure and Acquisitions	**Operating Capital Employed (ii)**	
	1990	**1989**

(i) UK area includes UK North Sea Crude oil activities and the UK-based international activities of BP Oil

	£ Million	
	1990	**1989**
(ii) Operating capital employed Liabilities for **current deferred taxation**	**19,146**	20,666
	(985)	(936)
Capital employed	**18,161**	19,730
Financed by: Finance debt	**6,920**	8,289
Minority shareholders' interest	**240**	656
BP shareholders' interest	**11,001**	10,785
	18,161	19,730

14 Acquisitions

In 1990 there were minor acquisitions totalling £46 million in the Chemicals and Nutrition businesses. In 1989 acquisitions totalled £65 million, mainly in the Refining and Marketing and Nutrition businesses.

The amounts shown as acquisitions in the group statement of source and application of funds exclude the finance debt of £15 million (£5 million) of acquired companies.

The cost of acquisitions in the group statement of source and application of funds represents the individual asset and liability movements as follows:

	£ Million	
	1990	1989
Intangible assets	22	35
Tangible assets	23	21
Fixed assets— investments	—	11
Working capital	18	4
Provisions	(2)	(1)
	61	70

15 Major disposals

(i) Coal

During 1989 the group sold the majority of its Australian and South African coal interests for a total consideration of £283 million. In 1990 further coal interests were sold for £145 million. Profits after taxation on these sales of £123 million in 1989 and £12 million in 1990 have been accounted as extraordinary items.

(ii) Minerals interests

During 1989, the sale, effective 1 January 1989, of most of BP's minerals interests (excluding the group's 49% interest in the Olympic Dam Joint Venture in Australia) to The RTZ Corporation was completed. Consideration for the sale was £2,384 million. The minerals interests of BP Canada and certain other minor interests were not offered for sale. The profit after taxation on the sale amounting to £267 million was accounted as an extraordinary item.

The amount shown as net assets of coal and minerals interests in the group statement of source and application of funds represents the individual asset and liability movements arising from the disposals as follows:

	£ million	
	1990	1989
Intangible assets	—	84
Tangible assets	101	1,304
Fixed assets— investments	2	160
Working capital	49	199
Other	(34)	(53)
	118	1,694

16 Intangible assets

	Exploration Expenditure			Other Intangibles	Goodwill	Total
	Exploration and Production	Coal	Total			
Cost						
At 1 January 1990	1,626	11	1,637	244	219	2,100
Exchange adjustments	(91)	2	(89)	(36)	(15)	(140)
Acquisitions	—	—	—	4	18	22
Additions	685	6	691	9	7	707
Transfers	(110)	—	(110)	(12)	(1)	(123)
Deletions	(722)	(15)	(737)	(11)	(14)	(762)
At 31 December 1990	**1,388**	**4**	**1,392**	**198**	**214**	**1,804**
Depreciation						
At 1 January 1990	273	6	279	54	95	428
Exchange adjustments	(29)	3	(26)	(8)	(9)	(43)
Charge for the year	401	3	404	16	28	448
Transfers	(10)	(3)	(13)	2	—	(11)
Deletions	(446)	(6)	(452)	—	(13)	(465)
At 31 December 1990	**189**	**3**	**192**	**64**	**101**	**357**
Net book amount						
At 31 December 1990	**1,199**	**1**	**1,200**	**134**	**113**	**1,447**
At 31 December 1989	1,353	5	1,358	190	124	1,672

£ Million

17 Tangible assets—property, plant, and equipment

£ Million

	Exploration and Production	Refining and Marketing	Chemicals	Nutrition	Other	Total	of which: Assets under Construction
Cost							
At 1 January 1990	21,392	7,434	2,361	864	1,679	33,730	2,957
Exchange adjustments	(2,169)	(754)	(148)	(77)	(169)	(3,317)	(123)
Acquisitions	—	—	—	23	—	23	2
Additions	1,444	731	327	106	226	2,834	1,754
Transfers	128	33	8	(4)	(55)	110	(2,137)
Deletions	(2,024)	(431)	(32)	(47)	(397)	(2,931)	(602)
At 31 December 1990	**18,771**	**7,013**	**2,516**	**865**	**1,284**	**30,449**	**1,851**
Depreciation							
At 1 January 1990	8,808	3,563	1,172	311	591	14,445	
Exchange adjustments	(1,023)	(305)	(68)	(24)	(54)	(1,474)	
Charge for the year	1,232	391	153	63	126	1,965	
Transfers	16	33	2	—	(33)	18	
Deletions	(1,361)	(333)	(22)	(29)	(241)	(1,986)	
At 31 December 1990	**7,672**	**3,349**	**1,237**	**321**	**389**	**12,968**	

£ Million

	Exploration and Production	Refining and Marketing	Chemicals	Nutrition	Other	Total	of which: Assets under Construction
Net book amount							
At 31 December 1990	**11,099**	**3,664**	**1,279**	**544**	**895**	**17,481**	**1,851**
At 31 December 1989	12,584	3,871	1,189	553	1,088	19,285	2,957
Principal rates of depreciation	*	2-25%	5-12%	3-25%	5-25%		

*Mainly unit-of production

Assets held under finance leases, capitalised interest and land at net book amount included above:

		Leased Assets			Capitalised Interest	
	Cost	Depreciation	Net	Cost	Depreciation	Net
At 31 December 1990	**1,030**	**245**	**785**	**1,123**	**453**	**670**
At 31 December 1989	692	208	484	1,140	458	682

	Freehold Land	Leasehold Land	
		Over 50 Years Unexpired	Other
At 31 December 1990	**579**	**9**	**26**
At 31 December 1989	607	10	28

18 Fixed assets—investments

£ Million

Group	Associated Undertakings			Other Investments			Loans	Total
	Shares	Loans	Share of Retained Profit	Listed UK	Listed Foreign	Unlisted		
Cost								
At 1 January 1990	504	94	367	1	63	56	570	1,655
Exchange adjustments	(41)	(5)	(21)	—	(10)	(6)	(84)	(167)
Additions	37	60	19	—	—	6	107	229
Transfers	—	22	—	—	—	—	(9)	13
Deletions	(24)	—	—	—	(10)	(18)	(141)	(193)
At 31 December 1990	**476**	**171**	**365**	**1**	**43**	**38**	**443**	**1,537**
Amounts provided								
At 1 January 1990	17	11	—	—	6	—	124	158
Exchange adjustments	(1)	(2)	—	—	(1)	—	(19)	(23)
Provided in the year	5	1	—	—	(4)	—	56	58
Transfers	—	—	—	—	—	—	(7)	(7)
Deletions	(1)	(1)	—	—	—	—	(60)	(62)
At 31 December 1990	**20**	**9**	**—**	**—**	**1**	**—**	**94**	**124**
Net book amount								
At 31 December 1990	**456**	**162**	**365**	**1**	**42**	**38**	**349**	**1,413**
At 31 December 1989	487	83	367	1	57	56	446	1,497
Stock exchange value								
At 31 December 1990				**2**	**49**			
At 31 December 1989				3	63			

Loans include advances under production-sharing contracts of £200 million (£309 million) less amounts provided of £92 million (£109 million).

Parent	Subsidiary Undertakings	Associated Undertakings		Total
	Shares	Shares	Loans	
Cost				
At 1 January 1990	1,756	2	1	1,759
Additions	1,182	—	—	1,182
Deletions	(915)	—	—	(915)
At 31 December 1990	**2,023**	**2**	**1**	**2,026**
Amounts provided				
At 1 January 1990	3	—	1	4
Deletions	—	—	—	—
At 31 December 1990	**3**	**—**	**1**	**4**
Net book amount				
At 31 December 1990	**2,020**	**2**	**—**	**2,022**
At 31 December 1989	1,753	2	—	1,755

The investments in subsidiary and associated undertakings are almost entirely unlisted.

19 Stocks

	£ Million	
	1990	1989
Petroleum	2,463	2,289
Chemicals	353	340
Nutrition	239	251
Other	105	145
	3,160	3,025
Stores	316	356
	3,476	3,381
Replacement cost	3,494	3,449

20 Debtors

£ Million

	Group				Parent			
	1990		1989		1990		1989	
	Within 1 Year	After 1 Year	Within 1 Year	After 1 Year	Within 1 Year	After 1 Year	Within 1 Year	After 1 Year
Trade	3,953	1	3,539	1	—	—	—	—
Group undertakings	—	—	—	—	3,492	53	3,824	—
Associated undertakings	91	21	96	1	—	—	—	—
Prepayments and accrued income	441	135	335	192	—	—	—	—
Taxation recoverable	24	216	50	79	2	—	2	—
Pension prepayment	—	361	—	264	—	—	—	—
Other	911	105	711	93	2	15	11	17
	5,420	839	4,731	630	3,496	68	3,837	17

21 Current assets—investments

	£ Million	
	1990	1989
Listed—UK	57	58
Foreign	60	39
	117	97
Unlisted	35	54
	152	151
Stock exchange value of listed investments	120	102

22 Finance debt

£ Million

	1990		1989	
	Within 1 Year	After 1 Year	Within 1 Year	After 1 Year
Bank loans and overdrafts	789	314	1,343	421
Other loans	860	4,046	1,150	4,802
Obligations under finance leases	64	847	38	535
	1,713	5,207	2,531	5,758

Analysis of bank loans and overdrafts and other loans

£ Million

	1990			1989		
	Bank Loans and Overdrafts	Other Loans	Total	Bank Loans and Overdrafts	Other Loans	Total
Due after 10 years	—	1,153	1,153	1	1,482	1,483
Due within 6 to 10 years	107	1,425	1,532	190	1,485	1,675
5 years	69	275	344	21	304	325
4 years	23	264	287	98	682	780
3 years	73	513	586	39	592	631
2 years	42	416	458	72	257	329
	314	4,046	4,360	421	4,802	5,223
1 year	789	860	1,649	1,343	1,150	2,493
	1,103	4,906	6,009	1,764	5,952	7,716
Secured on assets of group companies	38	7	45	36	8	44

Analysis by currency	Weighted Average Interest Rate %	£ Million	
		1990	1989
Sterling	9	174	569
US dollars	8	4,795	6,163
Australian dollars	13	77	14
Belgian francs	9	11	14
Canadian dollars	11	72	87
Deutschemarks	8	310	373
French francs	10	137	145
Swiss francs	8	122	92
Other currencies	15	311	259
		6,009	7,716

Any borrowing the liability for which is swapped into another currency is accounted as a liability in the swap currency and not in the original currency of denomination.

At 31 December the group had substantial amounts of undrawn borrowing facilities available including approximately £3,742 million (£4,770 million) which was covered by formal commitments.

Information relating to loans wholly or partly repayable more than five years from 31 December is as follows:

	£ Million	
	1990	1989
Wholly repayable after five years	1,879	2,127
Payable by instalments—after five years	806	1,031
—within five years	225	293
	2,910	3,451

Interest rates on these debts range from 7% to 15% with a weighted average of 9%.

	£ Million	
Obligations under finance leases	1990	1989
Minimum future lease payments Payable within:		
1 year	90	67
2 to 5 years	347	254
Thereafter	2,302	965
	2,739	1,286
Less finance charges	1,828	713
Net obligations	911	573

23 Other creditors

£ Million

	Group				Parent			
	1990		1989		1990		1989	
	Within 1 Year	After 1 Year	Within 1 Year	After 1 Year	Within 1 Year	After 1 Year	Within 1 Year	After 1 Year
Trade	2,876	19	2,584	22	—	—	—	—
Group undertakings	—	—	—	—	85	5	145	8
Associated undertakings	162	5	133	5	—	—	—	—
Production taxes	238	1,546	347	1,254	—	—	—	—
Taxation on profits	838	—	614	—	139	—	194	—
Social security	22	—	32	—	17	—	14	—
Accruals and deferred income	1,488	318	1,446	394	20	—	43	—
Dividends	438	—	406	—	438	—	406	—
Other	1,835	256	1,475	261	13	—	9	10
	7,897	2,144	7,037	1,936	712	5	811	18

24 Other provisions

£ Million

	Abandonment	Insurance	Pension	Other	Total
At 1 January 1990	1,540	77	629	215	2,461
Exchange adjustments	(122)	(7)	(40)	(33)	(202)
Charged to income	(76)	(4)	87	14	21
Utilised/deleted	(140)	1	(1)	(32)	(172)
At 31 December 1990	1,202	67	675	164	2,108

Pension provisions comprise amounts provided by
subsidiaries with unfunded plans.

25 Called up share capital

No change was made during 1990 to the parent
company's authorised share capital of £2,000 million.

The allotted share capital at 31 December was as
follows:

	1990		1989	
	Shares	£ Million	Shares	£ Million
8% (now 5.6% + tax credit) cumulative first preference shares of £1 each	7,232,838	7	7,232,838	7
9% (now 6.3% + tax credit) cumulative second preference shares of £1 each	5,473,414	5	5,473,414	5
Ordinary shares of 25p each	5,364,611,171	1,341	5,334,189,096	1,334
		1,353		1,346

During 1990, 3,815,923 ordinary shares were issued
under the share dividend plan at 295.8p; 2,822,319 at
336.2p; 3,022,443 at 322.6p and 2,703,529 at 362.4p
per share. In addition, 18,044,205 ordinary shares were
issued during the year under employee share schemes.
In connection with the purchase of the Standard Oil
minority interest in 1987, the company authorised the
issue of 21,477,228 registered warrants to the former
minority shareholders. Each warrant entitles the
registered holder to subscribe for one American
Depositary Share (ADS), currently representing twelve
ordinary shares, or such number of shares as is

represented by one ADS. Each warrant is exercisable on payment of the exercise price of $80 per warrant at any time up to 31 January 1993. During 1990, 13,656 ordinary shares were issued in respect of warrants

exercised. At 31 December 1990, the total number of ordinary shares represented by the outstanding warrants was 257,708,724 (257,722,380).

26 Share premium account

	£ Million	
	1990	**1989**
At 1 January	**1,752**	1,685
Premium on shares issued:		
Share dividend plan	**37**	48
Employee share schemes and warrants	**37**	19
At 31 December	**1,826**	1,752

27 Purchase of shares from the State of Kuwait (KIO)

On 13 March 1989, the parent company purchased from the KIO 790 million BP ordinary shares at a fully paid price of 247p per share; upon purchase the shares were cancelled. Applying UK tax law to the terms of the purchase, BP was required to account to the Inland Revenue for advance corporation tax (ACT) amounting

to 58p per share. The ACT and the price per fully paid share together with costs were charged against the reserves of the parent company.

The nominal value of the shares cancelled amounting to £197 million was transferred to Capital Redemption Reserve.

28 Reserves

Group reserves include undistributable reserves attributable to:

	£ Million	
	1990	**1989**
Parent company	**10**	10
Subsidiary undertakings	**1,816**	2,019
Associated undertakings	**394**	392
	2,220	2,421

Included in group reserves are amounts retained by overseas subsidiary and associated undertakings which may be liable to taxation if distributed.

Exchange adjustments for the year include unrealised gains of £2 million (£15 million losses) on long-term foreign currency borrowings.

As a consolidated income statement is presented a separate income statement for the parent company is not required to be published. The profit for the year of the group dealt with by the parent company and the reserves of the parent company are as follows:

	£ Million	
	1990	**1989**
At 1 January	**1,488**	2,601
Shares purchased from KIO	**—**	(2,423)
Profit for the year	**867**	2,105
Distribution to shareholders	**(861)**	(795)
At 31 December	**12,494**	1,488

29 Contingent liabilities

There were contingent liabilities at 31 December 1990 in respect of guarantees and indemnities entered into as part of, and claims arising from, the ordinary course of the group's business, upon which no material losses are likely to arise.

Subsidiaries of BP America are engaged in judicial and administrative proceedings in which the State of Alaska is challenging the subsidiaries' valuation of crude oil since 1977 for royalty and 1978 for tax purposes. The

State is also challenging the subsidiaries' determination of taxable income since 1978. BP believes that its subsidiaries have complied with applicable tax legislation and provisions for royalties contained in their Prudhoe Bay and Kuparuk leases, and the subsidiaries are disputing the State's claims. While the amounts claimed and subject to claim are substantial, it is believed that the ultimate resolution will not have a material effect on the financial position of the group.

More than 170 lawsuits have been filed in State and Federal Courts in Alaska, and more US States, seeking compensatory and punitive damages arising out of the Exxon Valdez oil spill in Prince William Sound in March 1989, the ultimate outcome of which cannot yet be determined. Most of those suits name Exxon, Alyeska Pipeline Service Company ('Alyeska'), which operates the oil terminal at Valdez, and the seven oil companies which own Alyeska. Alyeska initially responded to the spill until the response was taken over by Exxon. BP owns a 50% interest in Alyeska through a subsidiary of BP America Inc. The Plaintiffs generally do not specify the amount of damages sought and therefore BP is unable to quantify the amounts at issue. Insofar as this litigation affects Alyeska and its owners, BP intends to defend the suits vigorously.

The parent company has issued guarantees under which amounts outstanding at 31 December 1990 were £5,585 million (£6,871 million) including £5,383 million (£6,419 million) in respect of borrowings by its subsidiary undertakings.

30 Capital commitments

Authorised future capital expenditure by group companies is estimated at £5,500 million (£7,000 million) including approximately £925 million (£980 million) for which contracts have been placed.

31 Lease commitments

£ Million

Annual commitments under operating leases:	1990		1989	
	Land and Buildings	Other	Land and Buildings	Other
Expiring within:				
1 year	18	100	12	87
2 to 5 years	62	86	33	82
Thereafter	154	18	47	12
	234	204	92	181

32 Directors and employees

£ Million

(a) Employee costs:	1990	1989
Wages and salaries	2,240	2,162
Social security costs	251	244
Pension costs	93	79
	2,584	2,485

(b) Average number of employees:	UK	Rest of Europe	USA	Rest of World	Total	UK	Rest of Europe	USA	Rest of World	Total
Exploration and Production	5,400	750	2,900	1,050	10,100	5,700	800	3,000	1,150	10,650
Refining and Marketing	8,050	14,750	22,850	10,450	56,100	7,700	14,200	22,850	11,400	56,150
Chemicals	8,350	4,600	5,350	2,150	20,450	8,200	4,600	5,400	2,200	20,400
Nutrition	3,500	10,750	4,100	1,050	19,400	3,300	10,050	3,650	900	17,900
Other business/corporate	5,550	700	3,250	2,500	12,000	5,800	1,200	4,500	3,250	14,750
	30,850	31,550	38,450	17,200	118,050	30,700	30,850	39,400	18,900	119,850

(c) Emoluments of directors:

Directors received from the parent company £3,139,418 (£3,107,741) made up of fees £247,896 (£151,500) and other emoluments (not including pension

contributions) £2,891,522 (£2,956,241). Pensions, commutations of pensions and other superannuation payments to directors and former directors and their dependants amounted to £3,422,589 (£2,525,828).

Chairmen	1990	1989
Sir Peter Walters to 10 March 1990	**£459,215**	£708,722
R B Horton from 11 March 1990	**£537,302**	

Directors of the company were remunerated as follows:

Gross emoluments £	1990	1989
5,001 – 10,000	**1**	—
15,001 – 20,000	**1**	4
20,001 – 25,000	**4**	4
25,001 – 30,000	**3**	1
30,001 – 35,000	**2**	—
130,001 – 135,000	—	1
240,001 – 245,000	**1**	—
270,001 – 275,000	—	1
305,001 – 310,000	—	1
330,001 – 335,000	**1**	—
365,001 – 370,000	—	2
375,001 – 380,000	—	1
380,001 – 385,000	—	1
385,001 – 390,000	**1**	—
390,001 – 395,000	**1**	—
455,001 – 460,000	**2**	—
595,001 – 600,000	**1**	—
705,001 – 710,000	—	1

33 Pensions

Most group pension plans provide defined benefits that are computed based on an employee's years of service and final pensionable salary. In most cases group companies make contributions to separate funds based on advice from independent actuaries using actuarial methods the objective of which is to provide adequate funds to meet pension obligations as they fall due.

The charge to income for pensions in 1990 of £93 million (£79 million) was assessed in accordance with independent actuarial advice using the projected unit method. Principal assumptions used in calculating the charge were:

	Range
Rate of return on assets/discount rate	7% to 10%
Salary increases	4% to 8%
Pension increases	nil to 6%

At 1 January 1990, the date of the latest actuarial valuations or reviews, the market value of assets of the group's major funded plans was £6,449 million (£5,289 million). The level of funding was 118% (119%) of the benefits accrued to members of those plans, after allowing for expected future increases in earnings.

At 31 December 1990 the deficiency for the principal unfunded schemes on a current funding level basis was £688 million (£676 million). Of this amount £585 million (£541 million) has been provided in the accounts.

34 Employee share schemes

The parent company has a number of share schemes for employees (including executive directors). During the year 7,172,176 (6,404,459) ordinary shares were allotted under UK and overseas participating schemes for nil consideration; 7,006,691 (1,606,610) under UK and overseas SAYE schemes for consideration of £11,363,666 (£2,390,476); 3,069,225 (1,145,500) under the executive and overseas supplemental share option schemes for consideration of £6,183,271 (£2,071,702).

Britoil has employee share option schemes for BP ordinary shares under which 796,113 (258,312) shares were allotted during the year for consideration of £755,396 (£277,702).

BP Canada also has a share option plan for employees.

Options outstanding under employee share schemes

	1990			1989		
	Options	Period	Price	Options	Period	Price
BP—ordinary shares	70,072,372	1991/2000	£0.84/3.38	56,452,544	1990/99	£0.84/2.75
BP Canada—common shares	787,800	1991/2000	Can.$14.25/25.13	649,000	1990/99	Can.$14.25/25.13

Directors' options

The following directors had options for BP ordinary shares granted under the BP group share option schemes	1 January 1990	Granted in 1990	Exercised in 1990	31 December 1990
R B Horton	213,848	89,000	2,310	300,538
B R R Butler	379,500	34,000	60,000	353,500
P J Gillam	416,160	24,388	252,237	188,311
R R Knowland	271,810*	17,000	159,810	129,000
H E Norton	297,500	48,000	70,500	275,000
D A G Simon	404,263	19,000	3,237	420,026

No change in directors' options described above has taken place up to 14 February 1991.

*At 11 March 1990.

35 Subsidiary and associated undertakings and joint ventures

The more important subsidiary and associated undertakings and joint ventures of the group at 31 December 1990 and the group percentage of equity capital or joint venture interest (to nearest whole number) are set out below. The principal country of operation is generally indicated by the company's country of incorporation or by its name. Those held directly by the parent company are marked with an asterisk, the percentage owner being that of the group unless otherwise indicated. A complete list of investments in subsidiary undertakings and joint ventures and of the parent company's investment in associated undertakings will be attached to the parent company's annual return made to the Registrar of Companies.

Subsidiary undertakings	%	Country of incorporation	Principal activities
International			
BP Chemicals (International)	100	England	Chemicals
BP Exploration	100	Scotland	Exploration and production
*BP International	100	England	Integrated oil operations
BP Oil International	100	England	Integrated oil operations
BP Petroleum Development	100	England	Exploration and production
*BP Shipping	100	England	Shipping
Europe			
UK			
BP Capital	100	England	Finance
BP Chemicals	100	England	Chemicals
BP Oil UK	100	England	Refining and marketing
*Britoil (parent 15%)	100	Scotland	Exploration and production
Austria			
*BP Austria	100	Austria	Marketing
Belgium			
BP Belgium (parent 85%)	100	Belgium	Marketing, chemicals and finance
France			
BP France	86	France	Refining and marketing and chemicals
Germany			
Deutsche BP	100	Germany	Refining and marketing
Greece			
BP Greece	100	England	Marketing
Netherlands			
BP Capital	100	Netherlands	Finance
BP Nederland	100	Netherlands	Refining and marketing
Hendrix International	100	Netherlands	Nutrition
Portugal			
BP Portuguesa	100	Portugal	Marketing
Spain			
BP España	100	Spain	Marketing

Subsidiary undertakings	%	Country of incorporation	Principal activities
EUROPE continued			
Sweden			
*Svenska BP	100	Sweden	Marketing
Switzerland			
*BP Switzerland	100	Switzerland	Marketing
Turkey			
*BP Petrolleri	100	Turkey	Marketing
Middle East			
*BP Middle East	100	England	Marketing
Africa			
*BP Africa	100	England	Marketing
*BP Southern Africa	100	South Africa	Marketing
Far East			
Singapore			
*BP Singapore	100	Singapore	Refining and marketing
Australasia			
Australia			
BP Australia	100	Australia	Integrated oil and minerals
BP Finance Australia	100	Australia	Finance
BP Developments Australia	100	USA	Exploration and production
New Zealand			
BP Oil New Zealand	100	New Zealand	Marketing
Western Hemisphere			
Canada			
BP Canada	57	Canada	Oil and minerals exploration and production
USA			
BP America Standard Oil	100	USA	Exploration and production, refining and marketing, pipelines, chemicals, and nutrition

Associated undertakings	%	Country of incorporation	Principal activities	Issued share capital
Abu Dhabi				
Abu Dhabi Gas Liquefaction	16	Abu Dhabi	Natural gas liquefaction	105 million shares of US$1
Abu Dhabi Marine Areas	37	England	Crude oil production	1.65 million shares of £1
Abu Dhabi Petroleum	24	England	Crude oil production	11.21 million ordinary shares of £1
Africa				
Shell and BP South African Petroleum Refineries	50	South Africa	Refining	7.5 million shares of Rand 2
Germany				
Erdölchemie	50	Germany	Chemicals	DM320 million
Ruhrgas	25	Germany	Gas distribution	36 million shares of DM50

Joint ventures	%	Principal place of business	Principal activities
Europe			
Bruce field	37	UK—Offshore	Exploration and production
Forties field	83	UK—Offshore	Exploration and production
Magnus field	85	UK—Offshore	Exploration and production
Miller field	40	UK—Offshore	Exploration and production
Wytch farm	50	UK—Offshore	Exploration and production
Ula field	58	Norway—Offshore	Exploration and production
Australia			
North West Shelf	17	Australia	Natural gas production and shipping
Olympic Dam Project	49	Australia	Minerals
USA			
Prudhoe Bay field	51	Alaska	Exploration and production
Kuparuk field	39	Alaska	Exploration and production
Trans Alaska Pipeline	50	Alaska	Pipelines

36 Oil and gas exploration and production activities (i)

Capitalised costs at 31 December

	£ Million									
	1990					**1989**				
	UK	Rest of Europe	USA	Rest of World	Total	UK	Rest of Europe	USA	Rest of World	Total
Gross capitalised costs:										
proved properties	7,407	868	6,840	1,111	**16,226**	8,282	880	7,878	1,349	18,389
unproved properties	648	9	280	280	**1,217**	787	29	246	462	1,524
	8,055	877	7,120	1,391	**17,443**	9,069	909	8,124	1,811	19,913
Accumulated depreciation	2,108	233	3,473	431	**6,245**	2,845	229	3,661	556	7,291
Net capitalised costs	5,947	644	3,647	960	**11,198**	6,224	680	4,463	1,255	12,622

Costs incurred for the year ended 31 December

	1990					1989				
	UK	Rest of Europe	USA	Rest of World	Total	UK	Rest of Europe	USA	Rest of World	Total
Acquisition of properties:										
proved	—	—	6	—	**6**	—	—	—	—	—
unproved	1	2	58	15	**76**	—	2	48	8	58
	1	2	64	15	**82**	—	2	48	8	58
Exploration and appraisal costs (ii)	341	34	117	173	**665**	280	30	108	175	593
Development costs	839	102	344	106	**1,391**	769	126	326	144	1,365
Total costs	1,181	138	525	294	**2,138**	1,049	158	482	327	2,016

Results of operations for the year ended 31 December

	1990					1989				
	UK	Rest of Europe	USA	Rest of World	Total	UK	Rest of Europe	USA	Rest of World	Total
Turnover: (iii)										
third parties	1,861	64	2,144	197	**4,266**	1,656	201	1,872	237	3,966
sales between businesses	727	229	255	781	**1,992**	806	41	273	532	1,652
	2,588	293	2,399	978	**6,258**	2,462	242	2,145	769	5,618
Exploration expenditure	184	24	100	148	**456**	174	31	115	150	470
Production costs (iv)	1,659	(46)	996	598	**3,207**	1,396	113	833	581	2,923
Depreciation	512	57	477	55	**1,101**	554	48	505	48	1,155
Abandonment (v)	(144)	3	48	2	**(91)**	(138)	2	37	2	(97)
	2,211	38	1,621	803	**4,673**	1,986	194	1,490	781	4,451
Profit before taxation	377	255	778	175	**1,585**	476	48	655	(12)	1,167
Allocable taxes	190	43	338	25	**596**	167	—	158	12	337
Results of operations (vi)	187	212	440	150	**989**	309	48	497	(24)	830

(i) This note relates to the requirements contained within UK Statement of Recommended Practice—Disclosures about oil and gas exploration and production activities. Information given in this note does not relate to the total activities of the group's Exploration and Production segment. Major items excluded are the Alaskan transportation facilities and natural gas gathering and distribution activities.

(ii) All exploration and appraisal costs are initially capitalised within intangible fixed assets in accordance with BP group accounting policy.

(iii) Turnover includes sales of production excluding royalty oil where royalty is payable in kind.

(iv) Includes cost of royalty oil not taken in kind, petroleum revenue tax and other production taxes, and pre-tax gains from divestments.

(v) Abandonment reflects the release of provisions relating to certain North Sea production facilities where amounts provided are in excess of the estimated total costs of abandonment. The net effect, after petroleum revenue tax and allocable taxes, resulted in a credit to results of operations of £29 million (£38 million).

(vi) Income from the group's share of oil and gas produced by associated undertakings is included within results of operations.

Supplementary Information on Oil and Gas Quantities

**Movements in Estimated Net Proved
Reserves of Crude Oil** (i)

	UK	Rest of Europe	USA	Rest of World	Total
			Millions of Barrels		
At 31 December 1988:					
Developed	1,135	156	2,039	177	3,507
Undeveloped	740	135	639	203	1,717 (iii)
	1,875	291	2,678	380	5,224
Changes in 1989 attributable to:					
Revisions of previous estimates	(34)	—	122	(13)	75
Redetermination of interests	(2)	—	(1)	—	(3)
Purchases (sales) of reserves-in-place	(63)	—	4	2	(57)
Extensions, discoveries and other additions	45	53	32	4	134
Improved recovery	—	—	30	1	31
Production	(155)	(20)	(286)	(21)	(482)
	(209)	33	(99)	(27)	(302)
At 31 December 1989:					
Developed	982	179	1,917	173	3,251
Undeveloped	684	145	662	180	1,671 (iii)
	1,666	324	2,579	353	4,922
Changes in 1990 attributable to:					
Revisions of previous estimates	(23)	(2)	150	(5)	120
Redetermination of interests	—	—	(170)	—	(170)
Sales of reserves-in-place	(179)	(19)	—	(90)	(288)
Extensions, discoveries and other additions	183	9	97	69	358
Improved recovery	67	—	86	—	153
Production	(135)	(23)	(269)	(15)	(442)
	(87)	(35)	(106)	(41)	(269)
At 31 December 1990:					
Developed	806	209	1,622	108	2,745
Undeveloped	773	80	851	204	1,908 (iii)
	1,579	289	2,473 (ii)	312	4,653

Associated undertakings
The group also holds proportionate interests, through associated undertakings, in onshore and offshore concessions in Abu Dhabi expiring in 2014 and 2018 respectively. These interests totalled 2,145 million barrels at 31 December 1988, 2,113 million barrels at 31 December 1989 and 2,077 million barrels at 31 December 1990. If recent production levels were to continue, these reserves would not be fully recovered during the period of the concessions.

(i) Crude oil includes natural gas liquids and condensate. Net proved reserves of crude oil exclude production royalties due to others.

(ii) Proved reserves in the Prudhoe Bay field in Alaska include an estimated 119 million barrels upon which a net profit royalty will be payable over the life of the field under the terms of the BP Prudhoe Bay Royalty Trust.

(iii) Includes 271, 275 and 225 million barrels at 31 December 1988, 1989 and 1990 respectively, expected to be produced through the application of improved recovery techniques not yet tested in the relevant reservoirs.

Supplementary Information on Oil and Gas Quantities

**Movements in Estimated Net Proved
Reserves of Natural Gas** (i)

	UK	Rest of Europe	USA	Rest of World	Total
			Billions of Cubic Feet		
At 31 December 1988:					
Developed	2,032	78	1,922	2,028	6,060
Undeveloped	3,914	30	351	1,458	5,753
	5,946	108	2,273	3,486 (iv)	11,813
Changes in 1989 attributable to:					
Revisions of previous estimates	(17)	(5)	(54)	(86)	(162)
Redetermination of interests	12	—	2	(42)	(28)
Sales of reserves-in-place	(25)	—	(54)	(6)	(85)
Extensions, discoveries and other additions	45	74	131	132	382
Improved recovery	—	—	2	—	2
Production	(228)	(13)	(129) (ii)	(108)	(478)
	(213)	56	(102)	(110)	(369)
At 31 December 1989:					
Developed	2,449	77	1,835	1,943	6,304
Undeveloped	3,284	87	336	1,433	5,140
	5,733	164	2,171	3,376 (iv)	11,444
Changes in 1990 attributable to:					
Revisions of previous estimates	(211)	(4)	959	46	790
Redetermination of interests	(36)	—	5	14	(17)
Sales of reserves-in-place	(273)	(78)	(5)	(616)	(972)
Extensions, discoveries and other additions	150	16	75	60	301
Improved recovery	25	—	—	—	25
Production	(242)	(14)	(165) (ii)	(127)	(548)
	(587)	(80)	869	(623)	(421)
At 31 December 1990:					
Developed	2,429	78	2,401	1,629	6,537
Undeveloped	2,717	6	639 (iii)	1,124	4,486
	5,146	84	3,040	2,753 (iv)	11,023

(i) Net proved reserves of natural gas exclude production royalties due to others.

(ii) Includes 40 billion cubic feet in 1989 and 50 billion cubic feet in 1990 of gas consumed in Alaskan operations.

(iii) Excludes 4,285 billion cubic feet of gas in Alaska, the production of which is contingent upon construction of transportation facilities or the development of marketing alternatives.

(iv) Includes reserves located in Australia totalling 1,763, 1,494, and 1,538 billion cubic feet at 31 December 1988, 1989 and 1990 respectively.

Summarised Group Income Statements

	£ Million					$ Million				
	1986	1987	1988	1989	1990	1986	1987	1988	1989	1990
Turnover	27,269	28,328	25,922	29,641	**33,039**	40,085	46,458	46,141	48,611	**59,140**
Operating expenses	25,380	26,301	23,724	27,507	**30,603**	37,308	43,134	42,229	45,111	**54,779**
	1,889	2,027	2,198	2,134	**2,436**	2,777	3,324	3,912	3,500	**4,361**
Other income	786	784	693	803	**526**	1,155	1,286	1,234	1,317	**941**
Replacement cost operating profit	2,675	2,811	2,891	2,937	**2,962**	3,932	4,610	5,146	4,817	**5,302**
Stock holding gains (losses)	(1,173)	133	(232)	390	**477**	(1,724)	218	(413)	639	**854**
Historical cost operating profit	1,502	2,944	2,659	3,327	**3,439**	2,208	4,828	4,733	5,456	**6,156**
Interest expense	544	557	582	794	**671**	800	914	1,036	1,302	**1,201**
Profit before taxation	958	2,387	2,077	2,533	**2,768**	1,408	3,914	3,697	4,154	**4,955**
Taxation	42	785	823	744	**1,042**	62	1,287	1,465	1,220	**1,865**
Profit after taxation	916	1,602	1,254	1,789	**1,726**	1,346	2,627	2,232	2,934	**3,090**
Minority shareholders' interest	99	211	44	45	**50**	145	346	78	74	**90**
Profit before extraordinary items	817	1,391	1,210	1,744	**1,676**	1,201	2,281	2,154	2,860	**3,000**
Extraordinary items	(318)	—	—	390	**12**	(467)	—	—	640	**22**
Profit for the year	499	1,391	1,210	2,134	**1,688**	734	2,281	2,154	3,500	**3,022**
Distribution to shareholders	642	726	823	795	**861**	944	1,190	1,465	1,304	**1,541**
Retained profit (deficit) for the year	(143)	665	387	1,339	**827**	(210)	1,091	689	2,196	**1,481**
Earnings per ordinary share	14.9p	24.9p	20.0p	31.8p	**31.3p**	$0.22	$0.41	$0.36	$0.52	**$0.56**
Dividends per ordinary share	11.67p	12.50p	13.50p	14.90p	**16.05p**					

Per share amounts for 1986 have been adjusted to reflect the two for one capitalisation issue in 1987.

Replacement cost profit										
Historical cost profit before extraordinary items	817	1,391	1,210	1,744	**1,676**	1,201	2,281	2,154	2,860	**3,000**
Stock holding (gains) losses less minority interest	962	(83)	227	(383)	**(472)**	1,414	(136)	404	(628)	**(845)**
Replacement cost profit before extraordinary items	1,779	1,308	1,437	1,361	**1,204**	2,615	2,145	2,558	2,232	**2,155**

Figures given in US dollars have been derived from the sterling amounts as follows:

	£1 = US Dollar				
	1986	1987	1988	1989	1990
Income and source and application of funds statements, capital expenditure and acquisitions—at average exchange rates for the year	1.47	1.64	1.78	1.64	**1.79**
Balance sheets—at year end exchange rates	1.48	1.88	1.81	1.61	**1.93**

Group Source and Application of Funds Statements

	£ Million					$ Million				
	1986	**1987**	**1988**	**1989**	**1990**	**1986**	**1987**	**1988**	**1989**	**1990**
Profit after taxation	916	1,602	1,254	1,789	**1,726**	1,346	2,627	2,232	2,934	**3,090**
Extraordinary items	(318)	—	—	390	**12**	(467)	—	—	640	**22**
Items not involving the movement of funds	3,670	2,322	2,736	2,701	**2,382**	5,395	3,808	4,870	4,429	**4,263**
	4,268	3,924	3,990	4,880	**4,120**	6,274	6,435	7,102	8,003	**7,375**
Working capital movement	591	1,033	(735)	(410)	**(431)**	869	1,694	(1,308)	(672)	**(772)**
Other movements	(338)	360	233	303	**1,651**	(497)	591	415	497	**2,955**
Funds generated from operations	4,521	5,317	3,488	4,773	**5,340**	6,646	8,720	6,209	7,828	**9,558**
Capital expenditure	(3,309)	(2,787)	(3,279)	(3,433)	**(3,751)**	(4,864)	(4,571)	(5,837)	(5,630)	**(6,714)**
Acquisition of Britoil	—	(568)	(2,205)	—	**—**	—	(932)	(3,925)	—	**—**
Standard Oil share purchase	—	(4,672)	—	—	**—**	—	(7,662)	—	—	**—**
Other acquisitions	(500)	(226)	(349)	(70)	**(61)**	(735)	(370)	(621)	(115)	**(109)**
Net assets of divested coal and minerals interests	—	—	—	1,694	**118**	—	—	—	2,778	**211**
Dividends paid										
—BP shareholders	(623)	(670)	(782)	(908)	**(830)**	(916)	(1,099)	(1,392)	(1,489)	**(1,486)**
—Minority shareholders	(202)	(93)	(3)	(3)	**(8)**	(297)	(152)	(5)	(5)	**(14)**
Funds generated (required)	(113)	(3,699)	(3,130)	2,053	**808**	(166)	(6,066)	(5,571)	3,367	**1,446**
Financial movements:										
Shares issued	(15)	(1,481)	(330)	(74)	**(81)**	(22)	(2,429)	(587)	(122)	**(145)**
Shares purchased from KIO	—	—	—	2,423	**—**	—	—	—	3,974	**—**
Changes in external financing	(312)	(1,122)	(1,462)	(350)	**629**	(458)	(1,840)	(2,602)	(574)	**1,126**
External funding —decrease (increase)	(327)	(2,603)	(1,792)	1,999	**548**	(480)	(4,269)	(3,189)	3,278	**981**
Liquid resources —increase (decrease)	214	(1,096)	(1,338)	54	**260**	314	(1,797)	(2,382)	89	**465**
	(113)	(3,699)	(3,130)	2,053	**808**	(166)	(6,066)	(5,571)	3,367	**1,446**

Capital Expenditure and Acquisitions

	£ Million					$ Million				
	1986	1987	1988	1989	1990	1986	1987	1988	1989	1990
By business										
Exploration and Production	1,965	1,976	4,167	2,037	**2,201**	2,889	3,240	7,417	3,341	**3,940**
Refining and Marketing	588	528	771	726	**774**	864	866	1,372	1,191	**1,385**
Chemicals	196	348	256	313	**384**	288	570	456	513	**687**
Nutrition	496	126	157	172	**152**	729	207	279	282	**272**
Other businesses/corporate	564	603	482	255	**301**	829	990	859	418	**539**
Total	3,809	3,581	5,833	3,503	**3,812**	5,599	5,873	10,383	5,745	**6,823**
By geographical area										
UK†	836	1,511	3,424	1,491	**1,701**	1,229	2,478	6,095	2,445	**3,045**
Rest of Europe	535	351	472	544	**595**	787	576	840	892	**1,065**
USA	1,784	1,055	1,210	861	**902**	2,622	1,730	2,154	1,412	**1,614**
Rest of World	654	664	727	607	**614**	961	1,089	1,294	996	**1,099**
Total	3,809	3,581	5,833	3,503	**3,812**	5,599	5,873	10,383	5,745	**6,823**

†UK area includes UK North Sea crude oil activities and the UK-based international activities of BP Oil.

Summarised Group Balance Sheets

	£ Million					$ Million				
	1986	1987	1988	1989	1990	1986	1987	1988	1989	1990
Fixed assets	18,161	18,476	22,237	22,454	**20,341**	26,878	34,735	40,249	36,151	**39,258**
Stocks and debtors	7,965	7,115	6,746	8,742	**9,735**	11,788	13,376	12,210	14,075	**18,789**
Liquid resources	2,529	1,283	340	419	**621**	3,743	2,412	616	674	**1,198**
Total assets	28,655	26,874	29,323	31,615	**30,697**	42,409	50,523	53,075	50,900	**59,245**
Creditors and provisions excluding finance debt	9,875	10,036	10,008	11,885	**12,536**	14,615	18,868	18,115	19,135	**24,194**
Capital employed	18,780	16,838	19,315	19,730	**18,161**	27,794	31,655	34,960	31,765	**35,051**
Financed by:										
Finance debt	5,439	5,569	7,183	8,289	**6,920**	8,050	10,470	13,001	13,345	**13,356**
Minority shareholders' interest	3,424	576	614	656	**240**	5,068	1,083	1,111	1,056	**463**
BP shareholders' interest	9,917	10,693	11,518	10,785	**11,001**	14,676	20,102	20,848	17,364	**21,232**
	18,780	16,838	19,315	19,730	**18,161**	27,794	31,655	34,960	31,765	**35,051**

Ratios

The balance sheet elements shown above in £ million are used in the following ratios:

	1986	1987	1988	1989	1990
Return on average capital employed					
—historical cost	7.8%	12.1%	10.2%	13.2%	**12.7%**
—replacement cost	14.0%	11.4%	11.4%	11.2%	**10.1%**
(Based on profit after taxation before deducting interest expense)					
Return on average BP shareholders' interest	8.3%	13.5%	10.9%	15.6%	**15.4%**
(Based on historical cost profit before extraordinary items)					
Debt to debt-plus-equity ratio	29.0%	33.1%	37.2%	42.0%	**38.1%**
(Finance debt: finance debt plus BP and minority shareholders' interest)					
Adjusted debt to debt-plus-equity ratio	17.9%	27.6%	36.1%	40.8%	**35.9%**
(As above with finance debt reduced by liquid resources)					

Information on Price Changes

The following information is given as an indication to shareholders of the effect of changes in the general level of prices in the UK over the past five years. The figures show the main elements of the financial results and the BP share price, in both money of the year and as adjusted by the average UK retail price index for each year. Per share amounts for 1986 have been adjusted to reflect the two for one capitalisation issue in 1987.

As reported

	£ Million				
	1986	1987	1988	1989	1990
Turnover	27,269	28,328	25,922	29,641	**33,039**
Replacement cost operating profit	2,675	2,811	2,891	2,937	**2,962**
Replacement cost profit before extraordinary items	1,779	1,308	1,437	1,361	**1,204**
Historical cost profit before extraordinary items	817	1,391	1,210	1,744	**1,676**
Earnings per ordinary share	14.9p	24.9p	20.0p	31.8p	**31.3p**
Dividends per ordinary share	11.67p	12.50p	13.50p	14.90p	**16.05p**
Ordinary share price					
High	243p	413p	295p	341p	**376p**
Daily average	202p	313p	257p	293p	**335p**
Low	173p	234p	233p	249p	**304p**

Adjusted for the average UK retail price index of:	97.8	101.9	106.9	115.2	**126.1**

	£ Million				
Turnover	35,160	35,056	30,578	32,446	**33,039**
Replacement cost operating profit	3,449	3,479	3,410	3,215	**2,962**
Replacement cost profit before extraordinary items	2,294	1,619	1,695	1,490	**1,204**
Historical cost profit before extraordinary items	1,053	1,721	1,427	1,909	**1,676**

	£ Million				
	1986	1987	1988	1989	1990
Earnings per ordinary share	19.2p	30.8p	23.6p	34.8p	**31.3p**
Dividends per ordinary share	15.05p	15.47p	15.92p	16.31p	**16.05p**
Ordinary share price					
High	313p	511p	348p	373p	**376p**
Daily average	260p	387p	303p	321p	**335p**
Low	223p	290p	275p	273p	**304p**

Statistics

Group sales	1986	1987	1988	1989	1990
			Thousand Barrels per Day		
Refined petroleum Products					
UK	445	413	457	453	**441**
Rest of Europe	920	990	961	930	**892**
USA	1,003	844	811	898	**925**
Rest of world	372	375	347	382	**385**
	2,740	2,622	2,576	2,663	**2,643**
Crude oil					
UK	630	692	966	731	**938**
Rest of Europe	7	70	64	66	**50**
USA	401	574	490	497	**452**
Rest of world	136	117	70	51	**35**
	1,174	1,453	1,590	1,345	**1,475**
			Million Cubic Feet per Day		
Natural gas					
UK	191	178	386	609	**625**
Rest of Europe	32	44	45	42	**39**
USA	158	234	348	535	**628**
Rest of world	256	271	283	324	**362**
	637	727	1,062	1,510	**1,654**
Chemicals			£ Million		
	2,202	2,443	2,901	3,054	**3,051**
Nutrition					
	1,556	2,070	2,259	2,620	**2,682**

Group crude oil sources (i)	1986	1987	1988	1989	1990
Produced from own reserves: (ii)	Thousand Barrels per Day				
UK	419	402	510	424	370
Rest of Europe	12	46	53	54	63
USA	802	852	857	784	737
Rest of world	118	125	130	150	152
Total production	1,351	1,425	1,550	1,412	1,322
Purchased:					
USA	220	337	226	306	279
Rest of World	1,191	1,290	1,308	1,173	1,320
	1,411	1,627	1,534	1,479	1,599

(i) Crude oil in respect of which royalty is taken in cash is shown as a purchase; royalty oil taken in kind is excluded from both production and purchased oil.

(ii) Oil production includes natural gas liquids and condensate.

Statistics

Group refinery throughputs	1986	1987	1988	1989	1990
	Thousand Barrels per Day				
UK	195	181	199	218	203
Rest of Europe	744	681	746	618	576
USA	622	622	629	717	699
Rest of world	254	254	263	297	301
	1,815	1,738	1,837	1,850	1,779
For BP by others	80	84	87	94	101
Total	1,895	1,822	1,924	1,944	1,880

Estimated net proved reserves of crude oil (i)

Group companies	Millions of Barrels at 31 December				
UK	1,231	1,436	1,875	1,666	1,579
Rest of Europe	196	260	291	324	289
USA (ii)	2,817	2,953	2,678	2,579	2,473
Rest of world	414	356	380	353	312
	4,658	5,005	5,224	4,922	4,653
of which;					
Developed	3,048	3,384	3,507	3,251	2,745
Undeveloped	1,610	1,621	1,717	1,671	1,908
Associated undertakings (BP share)					
Abu Dhabi	1,732	2,126	2,145	2,113	2,077

Estimated net proved reserves of natural gas (i)	1986	1987	1988	1989	1990
Group companies	Billions of Cubic Feet at 31 December				
UK	3,456	3,318	5,946	5,733	5,146
Rest of Europe	110	125	108	164	84
USA	1,832	1,932	2,273	2,171	3,040
Rest of world	3,135	3,200	3,486	3,376	2,753
	8,533	8,575	11,813	11,444	11,023
of which:					
Developed	4,337	4,728	6,060	6,304	6,537
Undeveloped (iii)	4,196	3,847	5,753	5,140	4,486

(i) Net proved reserves of crude oil and natural gas exclude production royalties due to others.

(ii) Proved reserves in the Prudhoe Bay field in Alaska at 31 December 1990 include an estimated 119 million barrels upon which a net profit royalty will be payable over the life of the field under the terms of the BP Prudhoe Bay Royalty Trust.

(iii) At 31 December 1990 total estimated reserves excluded 4,285 billion cubic feet of Alaskan gas the production of which is contingent upon construction of transportation facilities or the development of marketing alternatives.

United States Accounting Principles

The following is a summary of adjustments to profit for the year and to BP shareholders' interest which would be required if generally accepted accounting principles in the United States ('US GAAP') had been applied instead of those generally accepted in the United Kingdom.

	£ Million				
	1986	1987	1988	1989	1990
Profit for the year					
Profit before extraordinary items	817	1,391	1,210	1,744	1,676
Extraordinary items (i)	(318)	—	—	390	12
Profit for the year	499	1,391	1,210	2,134	1,688
Adjustments:					
Deferred taxation (ii)	(126)	(344)	(15)	(42)	(154)
Other	6	3	(15)	5	6
Minority shareholders' interest	44	48	2	(4)	5
Profit for the year as adjusted	423	1,098	1,182	2,093	1,545
Per ordinary share	7.7p	19.7p	19.5p	38.2p	28.9p
Per American depositary receipt*	92.4p	236.4p	234.0p	458.4p	346.8p
	$ Million				
Profit for the year as adjusted	622	1,801	2,104	3,433	2,766
Per ordinary share	$0.11	$0.32	$0.35	$0.63	$0.52
Per American depositary receipt*	$1.36	$3.87	$4.17	$7.56	$6.24

	£ Million				
	1986	**1987**	**1988**	**1989**	**1990**
BP shareholders' interest	9,917	10,693	11,518	10,785	**11,001**
Adjustments:					
Deferred taxation (ii)	(2,525)	(1,853)	(1,894)	(1,669)	**(1,631)**
Other	(137)	(125)	(131)	(155)	**(140)**
Minority shareholders' interest	712	53	56	61	**60**
BP shareholders' interest as adjusted	7,967	8,768	9,549	9,022	**9,290**

	$ Million				
BP shareholders' interest as adjusted	11,791	16,484	17,284	14,525	**17,930**

(i) Under US GAAP the extraordinary items shown above would have been included in the determination of profit before extraordinary items.

(ii) Additional provision for deferred taxation on a full deferral basis.

*(One American depositary receipt its equivalent to twelve 25p ordinary shares.

Information for Overseas Shareholders

United States and Canada

BP shares are traded in the USA and Canada on the New York and Toronto Stock Exchanges in the form of American Depositary Shares (ADSs) and held in the form of American Depositary Receipts (ADRs). Each ADS represents twelve ordinary shares of the company. Details of trading activity are published under the abbreviation "BritPit" in the stock tables of most daily newspapers.

Depositary and Transfer Agent

Morgan Guaranty Trust Company of New York,
ADR Department,
60 Wall Street,
New York, NY 10260
Telephone 212-648-3208

Administration

In the US and Canada the ADR program is administered by BP America. Specific enquiries on administration should be addressed to:
BP America Inc.,
Attention: Stockholder Operations,
200 Public Square
Cleveland, OH 44114-2375.
Telephone: 1-800-648-2357

ADR Market price ranges

(US dollars)	1990		1989	
	High	**Low**	High	Low
1st Quarter	**71**	**61½**	61⅝	53⅝
2nd Quarter	**67⅞**	**59¾**	59⅝	54¼
3rd Quarter	**86¼**	**66⅞**	61⅝	55⅞
4th Quarter	**84½**	**73¾**	65⅞	54⅝

Cash dividends

ADR holders are generally eligible for all dividends or other entitlements attaching to the underlying shares of BP and receive all cash dividends in US dollars (although Canadian resident ADR holders ordinarily receive their dividends in Canadian dollars).

With respect to qualifying US resident ADR holders, the current income tax convention between the UK and the USA includes provisions which entitle them to a refund of the 25/75ths UK tax credit attached to the dividend, less a 15% UK withholding tax charged on the sum of the dividend and the credit. Under the arrangements made by Morgan Guaranty Trust

Company of New York, payment of the tax credit refund, net of the UK withholding tax, is made to a qualifying US resident ADR holder who completes the declaration on the reverse of the dividend check and presents it for payment within three months from its date of issue. Similar arrangements have also been made in respect of qualifying Canadian resident ADR holders.

In 1989, BP introduced quarterly dividend payments with the exchange rate for dividend payments for US and Canadian ADR holders being fixed on the date of declaration rather than on the date of payment.

The following dividends have been declared on ADRs for the under-mentioned years:

	Interim			Final	Total
1986 US$	0.818			1.796	2.614
1987 US$	1.105			2.029	3.134
1988 US$	1.248			1.820	3.068

Quarterly dividends	First	Second	Third	Fourth	Total
1989 US$	0.830	0.802	0.788	0.911	3.331
CAN$	0.983	0.941	0.921	1.099	3.944
1990 US$	0.902	1.002	1.062	1.137	4.103
CAN$	1.052	1.152	1.232	1.314	4.750

BP has been advised by its US counsel that in respect of qualifying US resident ADR holders, subject to certain limitations, the 15% withholding tax will be treated as a foreign income tax that is eligible for credit against the holder's federal income taxes. This credit may be obtained by filing Form 1116 'Computation of Foreign Tax Credit' with the ADR holder's Federal Income Tax return.

Reports to ADR holders

ADR holders receive the annual and interim reports issued to shareholders. If they are a holder of record (i.e. if the ADRs are held by them directly) the annual and interim reports will be sent to them at the record address. If the ADRs are held in a 'Street Name' at a bank or brokerage firm, that institution is responsible for obtaining the materials and forwarding them to the holders.

BP is subject to the requirements for information of the US Securities and Exchange Commission (SEC) as they apply to foreign companies. It files with the SEC the Annual Report on Form 20-F (which corresponds to a 10-K for a US corporation) and other information as required.

BP announces quarterly results in February, May, August and November of each year. Dissemination in the USA and Canada of these and other major items of BP news is made to the news services, including Dow Jones, Reuters, Associated Press and United press International.

Annual general meeting

The 1991 annual general meeting of the company takes place in London on 18 April.

On request, Morgan Guaranty will appoint ADR holders as its proxy; this enables holders to attend the meeting and, on a poll, to vote the underlying ordinary shares.

Japan

BP shares are traded on the Tokyo Stock Exchange. The payment of dividends in Japan is distributed by the shareholders' service agent, Mitsubishi Trust and Banking Corporation. Its address is:
Mitsubishi Trust and Banking Corporation,
4-5 Marunouchi 1-chome,
Chiyoda-ku,
Tokyo 100

Europe

BP shares are traded on stock exchanges in the UK, France, Switzerland, Germany and the Netherlands.

ISSUES FOR DISCUSSION

D15.1 Assume the existence of four underlying financial reporting dimensions[1] as described below:

1. *Professionalism versus statutory control*—a preference for the exercise of individual professional judgment and the maintenance of professional self-regulation as opposed to compliance with prescriptive legal requirements and statutory control.

2. *Uniformity versus flexibility*—a preference for the enforcement of uniform accounting practices between companies and for the consistent use of such practices over time as opposed to flexibility in accordance with the perceived circumstances of individual companies.

3. *Conservatism versus optimism*—a preference for a cautious approach to measurement to cope with the uncertainty of future events as opposed to a more optimistic, laissez-faire, risk-taking approach.

4. *Secrecy versus transparency*—a preference for confidentiality and the restriction of disclosure of information about the business only to those who are closely involved with its management and financing as opposed to a more transparent, open, and publicly accountable approach.

Be prepared to discuss your personal preferences along these dimensions and where you perceive the financial reporting standards in the United States, Japan, and the United Kingdom to be in these regards.

D15.2 Data showing the number of company listings on several international stock exchanges as of 1990 are presented below.*

Exchange	Domestic	Foreign	Foreign Listing as Percentage of Total
Amsterdam	323	240	43
American (US)	789	70	8
Australian	1,162	33	3
Frankfurt	389	354	48
International (London)	2,006	553	22
Madrid	427	2	0
Milan	220	0	0
New York (US)	1,673	96	5
Paris	874	231	21
Stockholm	121	11	8
Tokyo	1,627	125	7
Toronto	1,139	54	5

*Source: International Investor: International Edition (April 1991)

Discuss why such large variations in foreign listings as a percent of total listings might exist.

[1]The source for these four items is S. J. Gray, "Towards a Theory of Cultural Influence on the Development of Accounting Systems Internationally," *Abacus* (24, no. 1 (1988), pp. 1–15.

D15.3 In addition to the data presented in D15.2, consider also the following facts:

1. The largest net investors in international equities in 1988 were Europeans (including U.K. investors), who accounted for 73 percent of the total.

2. The international equity market has grown in value by an average rate of almost 37 percent compounded annually since 1979.

3. In volume (number of shares traded), the international equity market has grown by an average 18 percent compounded annually since 1979.

4. European equity markets (including the United Kingdom) were the major recipients of net (new money) international equity flows in 1988, attracting 82 percent of the total.

In the face of such startling trends, what do you see as the implications for U.S.–based companies and financial institutions?

D15.4 The average 1991 price-earnings ratio for the publicly traded companies in the United States, Japan, and the United Kingdom, monitored in the *Morgan Stanley Capital Investment Perspective,* were 21.1, 35.3, and 15.2, respectively. Discuss the possible causes for the disparity in Japan's P-E ratio when compared to that for the United States and the United Kingdom. What are the resulting implications of this disparity for investors, money managers, and financial analysts?

D15.5 In the spring of 1991, the International Accounting Standards Committee completed its three-year project on the comparability of financial statements. As a result of that project, the IASC is recommending to its member countries, among other things, that LIFO accounting for inventories not be permitted and that the use of the pooling-of-interests treatment for business combinations be limited to situations in which balance sheets are combined and a surviving company is not readily identifiable (see *Institutional Investor,* April 1991, p 185).

Discuss the pros and cons of the IASC's recommendations, keeping in mind the market for international, as opposed to just U.S., financial reporting.

D15.6 It has been argued that a number of factors contribute to the harmonization of worldwide financial reporting practices including the business press, textbooks, multinationals, the Big Six accounting firms, international capital markets, international lenders, the top business schools, the IASC, the United Nations, and the European Economic Community. Among the factors thought to deter harmonization are national pride, different intended audiences, and different legal and tax systems.

a. Discuss the role of each of the factors contributing to harmonizations. Are there others? Are some more important than others? If so, which ones?

b. Discuss the role of each of the deterring factors. Are there others?

c. Discuss the "battle" between the contributing and deterring factors. Can you predict the outcome?

D15.7

a. What are the costs and benefits associated with comparability in financial reporting practices for financial statement preparers in different countries?

b. Should national standards continue in effect with domestic preparers required to reconcile income and owners' equity under two sets of standards (i.e., one domestic and one international)?

D15.8 Compile a list of as many differences as you can identify between the British Petroleum annual report presented in Appendix 15B and what you would expect to find in Exxon's (or any other major U.S. oil company's) annual report for the same period.

a. Discuss the significance of the differences in trying to come to an understanding of the financial profile of British Petroleum.

b. Discuss what the differences might tell you about the business environment and culture in the United Kingdom.

D15.9 Compile a list of as many differences as you can identify between the Toyota annual report presented in Appendix 15A and what you would expect to find in General Motor's (or any other major U.S. auto company's) annual report for the same period.

a. Discuss the significance of the differences in trying to come to an understanding of the financial profile of Toyota.

b. Discuss what the differences might tell you about the business environment and culture in the Japan.

D15.10 As an external user of financial reports, assign a letter grade in each of the following categories for both the Toyota and British Petroleum annual reports. In class compare your grades to those given by your classmates and discuss the differences in terms of:

a. Informativeness.

b. Understandability.

c. Relevance.

PROBLEMS

P15.1 International standard setting. Prepare a one- or two-page brief, to be handed in, spelling out what you believe the _____ role should be in the international standard-setting process. The blank is to be filled in according to the following:

First Letter in Your Last Name	Fill in Blank With
A to D	FASB's
E to K	SEC's
L to N	NYSE's
O to Z	multinationals'

P15.2 France. This chapter does not include information on France. France is clearly an important country in the world economy, especially in the EC. France is home to a number of major multinationals, including Rhone-Poulenc, Lafarge, Peugot, and Renault. Find a recent set of financial statements for one of these French companies. Select a partner in the class and prepare a 10-page (approximate) paper reviewing the financial statement you have chosen and its national context.

The major thrust of the paper should be directed to the company's annual report; you might devote one third of the paper to context and two thirds to your analysis of the company. The paper should provide the following:

1. An overview of the French business climate, its legal structure, its capital tradition, and the resulting accounting and reporting situation.

2. The same analysis of the company's accounting and reporting as was developed in the chapter for Japan and the United Kingdom, namely,
   a. How do these financial statements differ from what you might have expected from a U.S. company in the same industry?
   b. How do these statements illustrate the unique characteristics of the French capital and financial reporting environment?

P15.3 Analyzing the Results of Toyota Motor Corporation. Presented in Appendix A to this chapter are excerpts from the financial statements of Toyota Motor Corporation. Using the analytical techniques discussed in Chapter 14, prepare an analysis of Toyota. Develop specific conclusions regarding the company's liquidity, solvency, asset management, and profitability. Identify those financial ratios that you believe are most likely to be influenced by the business and cultural environment of Japan.

P15.4 Analyzing the Results of British Petroleum Company. Presented in Appendix B to this chapter are excerpts from the financial statements of British Petroleum Company. Using the analytical techniques discussed in Chapter 14, prepare an analysis of BP. Develop specific conclusions regarding the company's liquidity, solvency, asset management, and profitability. Identify those financial ratios that you believe are most likely to be influenced by the business and cultural environment of the United Kingdom.

P15.5 Financial Analysis: U.K. versus U.S. Presented below are the 1990 summary financial results for four chemical companies—three are U.S.–based companies (Dow, duPont, and Monsanto) and the fourth is U.K.–based (ICI):

Dow Chemical Co
  Annual Earning—Consol. Inc. Acct. Yrs. End. Dec. 31:Mil. $

	1990	1989
Net sales	19,773	17,800
Equity in opers. of re- lated cos	cr143	cr138
Fgn. currency transl	cr56	cr58
Net bef. tax, etc	2,563	3,935
Income tax	978	1,436
Minority int.	201	12
Net income	1,384	2,487
*Sh. earns	$5.10	$9.20

(Aft. pfd. divds., avge. shs.: 1990-269,900,000; 1989-270,200,000.

Monsanto Co.
  Annual Earnings—Consol. Inc. Acct. Yrs. End. Dec. 31:Mil. $

	1990	1989
Net sales	8,995	8,681
Net bef. taxes	809	1,015
Inc. taxes	263	336
†Net income	546	679
*Sh earns	$4.23	$5.01
Avge. com. & com. equiv. shs.: 1990-129, 100,000; 1989-135,500,000; adjtd, for May '90 2-for-1 stk. split.		

†Incls, gains of $56,000,000 in 1990 & $44,000,000 in 1989 from divestitures.

du Pont (E.I.) de Nemours & Co.
  Annual Earnings—Consol. Inc. Acct. Yrs. End. Dec. 31:Mil. $

	1990	1989
Net sales	40,047	35,534
Net bef. tax..............................	4,154	4,324
Income tax...............................	1,844	1,844
†Net income.............................	2,310	2,480
*Sh. earns..............................	a$3.40	a$3.53

*Avge. shs.: 1990-675,960,751; 1989-700,505,538.
†Incls, the following: (Mil. $)

	1990	1989
Adjtmt. of pr. yr. tax provs	—	cr89
Sale of portion of int. in a North Sea natural gas prop	cr37	cr38
Amort. of producing props...........	—	dr97
Gain from sale of an instrument systems business	21	—
Settle. of litigation........................	dr15	—
Prov. for restructuring..................	cr7	—
Charge assoc. with the closing of two plants.	33	—

aIncls. benefits of $0.10 in 1990 & $0.04 in 1989 from nonrecurring items.

Imperial Chemical Industries plc (United Kingdom)
  Earnings, years ended Dec. 31 (Consol.—in millions of US $):

	1990	1989
Sales...............................	24,910	25,420
Net before tax................................	1,886	2,947
Inc. bef. extraord. items	1,191	1,795
① Net income	1,293	2,040
Earn., per ADR:		
Bef. extraord. items	$6.79	$10.42
After extraord. items.......	$7.38	$11.95
① After extraordinary items..........		

Note: Results for all periods have been expressed above in US $ at an exchange rate of $1.93 =£1, the rate prevailing on Dec. 31, 1990.

Required:

Compare the financial results of these companies. Using whatever library resources are available, identify the 1990 closing stock price for each of these companies and then calculate a price earnings ratio. What conclusions can you draw about the investment potential of each of the companies.

GLOSSARY

Accelerated Cost Recovery System (ACRS) A method to depreciate tangible assets placed in service between 1981–1986 for U.S. income tax purposes.

Accelerated depreciation A cost allocation method in which depreciation deductions are largest in an asset's earlier years, but decrease over time.

Account (T-account) An accounting information file usually associated with the general ledger, which appears as follows:

Account

Debit side	Credit side

Accounting A language used by businesspeople to communicate the financial status of their enterprise to interested parties.

Accounting cycle The process of analyzing a transaction and then journalizing it, followed by posting it to the ledger accounts, and then preparing a trial balance, any necessary adjusting entries, financial statements, and closing entries.

Accounting equation Assets = Equities; Assets = Liabilities + Owners' equity. An equation depicting the balance sheet or statement of financial position.

Accounting period The time period, usually a quarter or one year, to which accounting reports are related.

Accounting policies The specific accounting principles and practices adopted by a company to report its financial results.

Accounting Principles Board (APB) An organization of the AICPA that established GAAP during the period 1957–1973; some of the APB's opinions remain in force today.

Accounts payable (trade payable) Amounts owed to suppliers for merchandise purchased on

credit but not yet paid for; normally classified as a current liability.

Accounts receivable (trade receivable) Amounts due to a company from customers who purchased goods or services on credit; payment is normally expected in 30, 60, or 90 days.

Accounts receivable turnover ratio A measure of the effectiveness of receivable management calculated as net credit sales for the period divided by the average balance in accounts receivable.

Accrual concept (accrual basis of accounting) An accounting measurement system that records the financial effects of transactions when a business transaction occurs without regard to the timing of the cash effects of the transaction.

Accumulated depreciation (allowance for depreciation) A contra asset account deducted from the acquisition cost of property, plant, and equipment that represents the portion of the original cost of an asset that has been allocated to prior accounting periods.

Active investment An intercorporate investment by an investor-company that allows the investor to exercise influence or control over the operations of the investee-company.

Adjusting entries Journal entries recorded to update or correct the accounts in the general ledger.

Administrative expense A general operating expense, such as depreciation on a company's headquarters building, associated with the overall management of the company; a period expense.

Affiliated company A company in which an investor-company holds an equity investment in excess of 20 percent of the voting capital stock.

Aging of accounts receivables A method of accounting for uncollectible trade receivables in which an estimate of the bad debts expense is determined by classifying the specific receivable balances into age categories and then applying probability estimates of noncollection.

Allocation concept An accounting concept that permits the financial effects of business transactions to be assigned to or spread over multiple accounting periods.

Allowance for Decline in Value of Inventory A contra asset account deducted from the cost basis of ending inventory to reflect the writedown of inventory to its replacement value under the lower-of-cost-or-market method.

Allowance for Decline in Value of Marketable Equity Securities A contra asset account deducted from the cost basis of marketable equity securities; represents the unrealized decline in a portfolio of securities resulting from the application of the lower-of-cost-or-market method.

Allowance for Uncollectible Accounts (allowance for bad debts) A contra asset account deducted from accounts or notes receivable; represents the portion of the outstanding receivables balance whose collection is doubtful.

American Institute of Certified Public Accountants (AICPA) The national professional association of certified public accountants (CPAs) in the United States.

Amortization A cost allocation process that spreads the cost of an intangible asset over the asset's expected useful life.

Annual report The report prepared by a company at year-end for its stockholders and other interested parties. It frequently includes a letter to the shareholders from the chairperson of the board, management's discussion and analysis of financial performance, and a variety of financial highlights in addition to the basic financial statements. It also includes the auditor's report in which the independent accountants express an opinion as to the fairness of the financial data presented in the financial statements.

Annuity A payment, or a receipt, occurring every period for a set number of periods (e.g., interest expense or interest income on a debt instrument).

Antidilutive security A security that, if con-

verted or assumed to be converted into common stock, causes the level of earnings per share to increase.

Asset management The effective utilization of a company's revenue-producing assets; a measure of management's ability to effectively utilize a company's assets to produce income.

Assets Tangible and intangible resources of an enterprise that are expected to provide it future economic benefits.

Audit A process of investigating the adequacy of a company's system of internal controls, the company's consistent use of generally accepted accounting principles, and the presence of material errors or mistakes in the company's accounting data.

Auditor's opinion A report to a company's shareholders and the board of directors issued by an independent auditor summarizing his or her findings with regard to the company's financial statements. The four types of opinions that may be issued are clean or unqualified, qualified, adverse, and disclaimer.

Authorized shares The total number of shares of capital stock that are authorized to be sold under a company's charter of incorporation.

Average cost method An inventory cost-flow method that assigns the average cost of available finished goods to units sold and, thus, to cost of goods sold.

Average days'-inventory-on-hand ratio A measure of the effectiveness of inventory management calculated as 365 days divided by the inventory turnover ratio; a measure of the appropriateness of current inventory levels given current sales volume.

Average receivable collection period A measure of the effectiveness of accounts receivable management calculated by dividing the receivable turnover ratio into 365 days.

Bad debt An account receivable considered to be uncollectible.

Bad debt expense An estimate (under the allowance method) of the dollar amount of accounts receivable that will eventually prove to be uncollectible; the actual bad debts that are written off if the direct write-off method is used.

Balance The difference between the total left-hand (debit) entries and the total right-hand (credit) entries made in an account.

Balance sheet (statement of financial position) An accounting statement describing, as of a specific date, the assets, liabilities, and owners' equity of an enterprise.

Betterment An expenditure that extends the useful life or productive capability of an asset and that is capitalized to the balance sheet as an asset.

Board of directors A group of individuals elected by a company's shareholders to oversee the overall management of the company (i.e., a board of advisers for the company's managers).

Bond (debenture) An interest-bearing obligation issued by a company to various creditors, usually in amounts of $1,000 or $5,000 and payable at some future maturity date.

Bond discount The amount by which the net proceeds of a bond issue are less than the amount of the principal that must be repaid at maturity date. The amount of the bond discount must be amortized over the life of the bond, thereby making the bond's effective rate of interest greater than its coupon rate of interest.

Bond indenture The document in which the details associated with a bond issue are specified.

Bond payable A financial instrument sold in the capital markets, carrying a specified rate of interest (coupon rate) and a specified repayment date (maturity date); usually classified as a long-term liability.

Bond premium The amount by which the net proceeds of a bond issue exceed the amount of the bond principal that must be repaid at maturity date. The amount of the bond premium that must be amortized over the life of the bond, thereby making its effective rate of interest less than its coupon rate of interest.

Book value (per share) The dollar amount of the net assets of a company on a per share of common stock basis; calculated as (total assets minus total liabilities) divided by the number of outstanding shares of class A common stock.

Book value (of an asset) The original cost of an asset less any accumulated depreciation (depletion or amortization) taken to date; also known as *carrying value*.

Business combination When one or more businesses are brought together into one accounting entity but not necessarily into one legal entity.

Callable debt Bonds or other obligations that may be legally retired before maturity at the discretion of the debtor-company.

Capital Another term for owners' equity; also used to mean the total assets of an organization.

Capital budgeting The process of proposing and selecting from among a variety of investment proposals or certain long-lived assets to be acquired. This process frequently considers the net present value of projected cash flows for proposed investments.

Capital expenditure An expenditure for the purchase of a noncurrent asset, usually property, plant, or equipment.

Capitalization The process of assigning value to a balance sheet account, for example a capitalized asset (i.e., a leased asset) or a capitalized liability (e.g., a lease liability).

Capitalization (of a company) The composition of a company's long-term financing, specifically, owners' equity and long-term debt.

Capital lease A noncancellable lease obligation accounted for as a liability on the balance sheet; a lease agreement in which the risks and rewards of asset ownership are passed (either formally or informally) to the lessee.

Capital stock A certificate representing an ownership interest in an enterprise. See also *common stock* and *preferred stock*.

Cash A current asset account representing the amount of money on hand or in the bank.

Cash basis of accounting An accounting measurement system that records the financial effects of business transactions when the underlying event has a cash effect.

Cash discount An amount, usually 2 percent of the gross purchase price, that a buyer may deduct from the final price of an asset if cash is remitted within the discount period, usually 10 days of purchase.

Cash equivalents Bank deposits, usually in the form of certificates of deposit, whose withdrawal may be restricted but whose maturity is expected in the current accounting period.

Cash flow adequacy ratio A cash flow ratio calculated as the cash flow from operations divided by the sum of capital expenditures, dividends paid, and long-term debt repayment; indicates the extent to which cash flows from operations are sufficient to cover asset replacement and capital carrying costs.

Cash flow from operations A measure of the net cash flows from transactions involving sales of goods or services and the acquisition of inputs used to provide the goods or services sold; the excess of cash receipts over cash disbursements relating to the operations of a company for a given period; net income calculated on a cash basis.

Certified public accountant (CPA) An accountant who has passed the Uniform CPA Examination prepared by the American Institute of CPAs and who has met prescribed requirements of the state issuing the CPA certificate.

Charter of incorporation A legal document creating a corporate entity; specifies (among other things) the number and type of shares of capital stock that the corporate entity can sell.

Chart of accounts A list of the general ledger accounts used by an enterprise in its accounting system.

Class B common stock A form of common stock that usually carries a lower voting power and lower dividend return than Class A common stock.

Classified balance sheet A balance sheet that delineates the assets and liabilities as current and noncurrent.

Closing entries Accounting data entries prepared at the end of an accounting period; designed to close or set equal to zero the temporary accounts.

Collateral The value of various assets used as security for various debts, usually bank borrowings, that will be transferred to a creditor if the obligation is not fully paid.

Commitment A type of contingent liability in which the value of the future obligation is known but that is not currently an obligation because various future events or conditions have not transpired or are currently satisfied.

Common-size financial statements Financial statements in which the dollar amounts are expressed as a percentage of some common statement item (e.g., a common-size income statement might express all items as a percentage of sales).

Common stock A form of capital stock that usually carries the right to vote on corporate issues; a senior equity security.

Common stock equivalent A security that is not a common stock but that contains provisions to enable its holder to become a common stockholder.

Compensating balances The percentage of a line of credit or of a loan that a bank requires a borrower to keep on deposit at the bank. Its amount has the effect of increasing the effective interest rate of any amount borrowed.

Completed contract A revenue recognition method in which project or contract revenues are unrecognized until the project or contract is substantially completed.

Compound interest A method of calculating interest by which interest is figured on both the principal of a loan and any interest previously earned but not distributed.

Conservatism concept An accounting concept that stipulates that when there is a choice between two approaches to record an economic event, the one that produces the least favorable yet realistic effect on net income or assets should be adopted.

Consignment Inventory placed with a retailer for sale to a final consumer but not sold to the retailer; title to the inventory is retained by the manufacturer until a final sale occurs.

Consistency concept An accounting concept underlying the preparation of financial statements that stipulates that an enterprise should, when possible, use the same set of GAAP from one accounting period to the next.

Consolidated financial statements Financial statements prepared to reflect the operations and financial condition of a parent company and its wholly or majority-owned subsidiaries.

Consolidated reporting A reporting approach in which the financial statements of the parent and subsidiary companies are combined to form one set of financial statements.

Contingent asset An asset that may arise in the future if certain events occur.

Contingent liability A liability that may arise in the future if certain events occur.

Contra account (contra asset, contra liability, contra owners' equity) An account that is subtracted from a related account; for example, accumulated depreciation is subtracted from the Building or Equipment account; other examples include the Allowance for Uncollectible accounts, the Bond Discount account, and the Treasury Stock account.

Contributed capital The sum of the capital stock accounts and the capital in excess of par (or stated) value accounts. Also called *paid-in capital*.

Conversion The exchange of convertible bonds or convertible preferred stock for a predetermined quantity of common stock.

Conversion ratio The exchange ratio used to determine the number of common shares that will be issued on conversion of a convertible bond or a convertible preferred stock.

Convertible debt (bond) An obligation or debt security exchangeable, or convertible, into the common stock of a company at a prespecified conversion (or exchange) rate.

Convertible preferred stock A preferred stock that is exchangeable or convertible into the com-

mon stock of a company at a prespecified conversion (or exchange) rate.

Corporation A business enterprise owned by one or more owners, called *stockholders,* that has a legal identity separate and distinct from that of its owners.

Cost The total acquisition value of an asset; the value of resources given up to acquire an asset.

Cost of goods manufactured The total cost of goods manufactured in an accounting period; the sum of all product costs (e.g., direct materials, direct labor, and manufacturing overhead).

Cost of goods sold The value assigned to inventory units actually sold in a given accounting period.

Coupon interest rate (face rate) The rate of interest stated on the face of a debt instrument.

Credit An entry on the right side of an account; credits increase liability, owners' equity, and revenue accounts but decrease asset and expense accounts.

Creditor An individual or company that loans cash or other assets to another person or company.

Cumulative preferred stock A preferred stock in which any unpaid prior dividends accumulate year to year (called *dividends in arrears*) and must be paid in full before any current period dividends may be paid to either preferred or common shareholders.

Current asset Those resources of an enterprise, such as cash, inventory, or prepaid expenses, whose consumption or use is expected to occur within the current operating cycle.

Current liability An obligation of an enterprise whose settlement requires the use of current assets or the creation of other current liabilities and occurs within one year.

Current maturity of long-term debt That portion of a long-term obligation that is payable within the next operating cycle or one year.

Current rate method A method of restating foreign financial statements using the current exchange rate.

Current ratio A measure of liquidity and short-term solvency calculated as current assets divided by current liabilities.

Date of declaration The calendar date on which the payment of a cash or stock dividend is officially declared by a company's board of directors.

Date of payment The calendar date on which a cash or stock dividend is actually paid or distributed.

Date of record The calendar date on which a shareholder must own a company's stock to be entitled to receive a declared dividend.

Debenture A general obligation bond of a company.

Debit An entry on the left side of an account; debits increase asset and expense accounts but decrease liability, owners' equity, and revenue accounts.

Debt-to-total assets ratio A measure of solvency or long-term liquidity calculated as total debt divided by total assets.

Declining balance method A method to depreciate the cost of a tangible asset in which the allocated cost is greater in the early periods of the asset's life (i.e., an accelerated method).

Default risk The probability (or risk) that a company will be unable to meet its short-term or long-term obligations.

Defeasance A method of early retirement of debt in which U.S. Treasury notes are purchased and then placed in a trust account to be used to retire the outstanding debt at its maturity.

Deferral A postponement in the recognition of an expense (i.e., Prepaid Insurance) or a revenue (i.e., Unearned Rent) account.

Deferred charge An asset that represents an expenditure whose related expense will not be recognized in the income statement until a future period. Prepaid rent is an example.

Deferred income taxes The portion of a company's income tax expense not currently payable, and that is postponed because of differences in the accounting policies adopted for financial statement purposes versus those policies used for tax reporting purposes.

Deferred revenue Revenue received as cash but not yet earned.

Deficit An accumulated loss in the retained earnings account; a debit balance in retained earnings.

Defined benefit plan A pension plan in which an employer promises to pay certain levels of future benefits to employees on their retirement from the company.

Defined contribution plan A pension plan in which an employer promises to make periodic payments to the plan on behalf of its employees.

Demand deposit A bank account that may be drawn against on demand.

Depletion A cost allocation method for natural resources.

Depreciation A systematic allocation process that allocates the acquisition cost of a long-lived asset over the expected productive life of the asset.

Direct-financing-type lease A capital lease in which the lessor receives income only from financing the ''purchase'' of the leased asset.

Direct write-off method A method of accounting for uncollectible trade receivables in which no bad debt expense is recorded until specific receivables prove to be uncollectible.

Discount A reduction in the price paid for a security or a debt instrument below the security's face value.

Discount rate The rate of interest used to discount a future cash flow stream when calculating its present value.

Discounted cash flows The present value of a future stream of cash flows.

Discounting receivables The process of selling accounts or notes receivables to a bank or other financial company at a discount from the maturity value of the account or note.

Dividend A distribution of the earned income of an enterprise to its owners.

Dividend payout A measure of the percentage

of net income (or cash flows from operations) paid out to shareholders as dividends; calculated as cash dividends divided by net income (or cash dividends divided by the cash flow from operations).

Dividends in arrears The dividends on a cumulative preferred stock that have been neither declared nor paid; not a legal liability of a company until declared.

Dividend yield A measure of the level of cash actually distributed to common stockholders calculated as the cash dividend per common share divided by the market price per common share.

Donated capital The increase in owners' equity resulting from a donation of an asset to a company.

Double-declining-balance depreciation A method of calculating depreciation by which a percentage equal to twice the straight-line percentage is multiplied by the declining book value to determine the depreciation expense for the period. Salvage value is ignored when calculating it.

Double-entry system An accounting record-keeping system that records all financial transactions in the accounting system using (at least) two data entries.

Double taxation The taxation of income at the company-level plus the taxation of dividends declared and paid to investors from the company earnings.

Doubtful account An account receivable thought to be uncollectible.

Early retirement The process of prepaying, or retiring, outstanding debt before its stated maturity.

Earned surplus A term synonymous with retained earnings.

Earnings Income or profit.

Earnings per share A standardized measure of performance calculated as net income divided by the weighted-average number of common shares outstanding during an accounting period.

Economic income The excess or additional resources of an enterprise resulting from its primary business activity and measured relative to the beginning level of resources.

Effective interest method A method to amortize a discount or a premium on a debt instrument based on the time value of money.

Effective interest rate The real rate of interest paid (or earned) on a debt instrument.

Efficient market hypothesis A theory to explain the functioning of capital markets in which stock and bond prices always reflect all publicly available information, and any new information is quickly impounded in security prices.

Emerging Issues Task Force (EITF) An affiliate organization of the FASB whose purpose is to address new accounting and reporting issues before divergent practice can become widely adopted.

Employee Retirement Income and Security Act (ERISA) Legislation passed by the U.S. Congress in 1974 to govern the funding of private pension plans.

Entity concept An accounting convention that views a corporate enterprise as separate and distinct from its owners; thus, the financial statements of the corporation describe only the financial condition of the enterprise itself, not that of its shareholders.

Equity A claim against the assets of a company by creditors or the owners.

Equity in earnings of investee An income statement account representing an investor-company's percentage ownership of an investee's (or subsidiary's) net earnings.

Equity method A method to value intercorporate equity investments by adjusting the investor's cost basis for the percentage ownership in the investee's earnings (or losses) and for any dividends paid by the investee.

Ex-dividend A condition of capital stock if sold (or purchased) after the date of record; that is, the purchaser of an ex-dividend stock is not entitled to receive the most recently declared dividend.

Expenditure An outflow of cash, usually

representing the acquisition of an asset or the incurring of an expense.

Expense An outflow of assets, an increase in liabilities, or both, from transactions involving an enterprise's principal business activity (e.g., sales of products or services).

External reporting Financial reporting to stockholders and others outside an enterprise.

Extraordinary item A loss or gain that is both unusual in nature and infrequent in occurrence.

Face amount (maturity value) The value of a security as stated on the instrument itself.

Factor A financial corporation, bank, or other financial institution that buys accounts and notes receivables from companies; receivables may be purchased with or without recourse.

Factory overhead Another name for manufacturing overhead. For inventory valuation purposes, it is allocated to units of production by some type of rational systematic method.

Federal income tax The tax levied by the federal government on corporate and individual earnings.

Financial accounting The accounting rules and conventions used in preparing external accounting reports.

Financial Accounting Standards Board (FASB) An independent, private sector organization responsible for establishing generally accepted accounting principles.

Financial statements The basic accounting reports issued by a company, including the balance sheet, the income statement, and the statement of cash flows.

Finished goods Inventory having completed the manufacturing process and ready for sale.

Finished goods inventory Fully assembled or manufactured goods available for sale and classified as a current asset on the balance sheet.

First-in, first-out (FIFO) An inventory cost-flow method that assigns the first cost value in finished goods inventory to the first unit sold and thus to cost of goods sold.

Fiscal year Any continuous 12-month period, usually beginning after a natural business peak.

Fixed assets A subcategory of noncurrent assets; usually represented by property, plant, and equipment.

FOB Free-on-board, some location. Examples are FOB shipping point and FOB destination. The location denotes the point at which title passes from the seller to the buyer.

Footnotes Written information by management designed to supplement the numerical data presented in a company's financial statement.

Foreign currency translation adjustment An owners' equity account measuring the change in value of a company's net assets held in a foreign country, attributable to changes in the exchange rate of a foreign currency as compared to the U.S. dollar.

Foreign exchange risk The risk associated with changes in exchange rates between the U.S. dollar and foreign currencies when a company maintains operations in a foreign country.

Form 8-K A special SEC filing required when a material event or transaction occurs between Form 10-Q filing dates. Events that usually necessitate the filing of Form 8-K include a change in control or ownership of an enterprise, the acquisition or disposition of a significant amount of assets, a bankruptcy declaration, the resignation of an executive or director of an enterprise, or a change in the independent external auditor.

Form 10-K The annual financial report filing with the SEC required of all publicly held enterprises.

Form 10-Q The quarterly financial report filing with the SEC required of all publicly held enterprises; it is filed only for the first three quarters of a fiscal year.

Freight-in Freight costs associated with the purchase and receipt of inventory.

Freight-out Freight costs associated with the sale and delivery of inventory.

Fully diluted earnings per share A standardized measure of performance calculated as net income applicable to common stock divided by the weighted-average number of common shares outstanding plus common stock equivalents and any other potentially dilutive securities.

Functional currency The currency of the primary business environment (i.e., country) of a company's operations.

Gain An increase in asset values, usually involving a sale (realized) or revaluation (unrealized), unrelated to the principal revenue-producing activity of a business.

General journal An accounting data file containing a chronological listing of financial transactions affecting an enterprise.

General ledger An accounting data file containing aggregate account information for all accounts listed in an enterprise's chart of accounts.

Generally accepted accounting principles (GAAP) Those methods identified by authoritative bodies (i.e., APB, FASB, SEC) as being acceptable for use in the preparation of external accounting reports.

Generally accepted auditing standards (GAAS) Those auditing practices and procedures established by the AICPA that are used by CPAs to evaluate a company's accounting system and financial results.

Going-concern concept An accounting concept underlying the preparation of financial statements that assumes that the enterprise will continue its operations for the foreseeable future.

Goodwill An intangible asset representing the excess of the purchase price of acquired net assets over their fair market value.

Gross profit (gross margin) A measure of a company's profit on sales calculated as net sales minus the cost of goods or services sold.

Gross profit margin ratio A measure of profitability that assesses the percentage of each sales dollar that is recognized as gross profit (i.e., after deducting the cost of goods sold) and that is available to cover other operating expenses (e.g., selling, administrative, interest, and taxes).

Historical cost concept An accounting concept that stipulates that all economic transactions should be recorded using the dollar value incurred at the time of the transaction.

Holding company (parent company) A company that owns a majority of the voting capital stock of another company.

Income A generic term that may be used to indicate revenue from miscellaneous sources (e.g., interest income or rent income) or the excess of revenue over expenses for product sales or services.

Income and Loss Summary A temporary account used to transfer the net income or loss of an enterprise from the income statement to the retained earnings account on the balance sheet.

Income statement (statement of earnings) An accounting statement describing the revenues earned and expenses incurred by an enterprise for a given period.

Independent auditor A professionally trained individual whose responsibilities include the objective review of a company's financial statements prepared for external distribution.

Inflation A phenomenon of generally rising prices.

Insolvent (bankrupt) A condition in which a company is unable to pay its current obligations as they come due.

Installment basis A method of recognizing revenue that parallels the receipt of cash.

Installment sale A credit sale in which the buyer agrees to make periodic payments, or installments, on the amount owed.

Intangible assets Those resources of an enterprise, such as goodwill, trademarks, or tradenames, that lack an identifiable physical presence.

Intercompany profit The profit resulting when one related company sells to another related company; intercompany profits are removed from the financial statements when consolidated financial statements are prepared.

Intercorporate investments Investments in the stocks and bonds of one company by another.

Interest expense The cost of borrowing funds.

Interim financial statements Financial statements prepared on a monthly or quarterly basis; usually unaudited.

Internal control The policies and procedures implemented by management to safeguard a company's assets and its accounting system against misapplication or misuse.

International Accounting Standards Committee (IASC) An association of professional accounting bodies formed in 1973 to develop and issue international accounting and reporting standards.

Interperiod tax allocation The process of allocating the actual taxes paid by a company over the periods in which the taxes are recognized for accounting purposes.

Inventory The aggregate cost of salable goods and merchandise available to meet customer sales.

Inventory turnover ratio A measure of the effectiveness of inventory management calculated as the cost of goods sold for a period divided by the average inventory held during that period.

Investment ratio A cash flow ratio calculated as capital expenditures divided by the sum of depreciation and proceeds from the sale of assets; indicates the relative change in a company's investment in productive assets.

Investment tax credit A reduction in the current income taxes payable earned through the purchase of various applicable assets.

Investor-company A company that holds an equity investment in another company (the investee-company).

Issued shares The number of authorized shares of capital stock sold to shareholders less any shares repurchased *and* retired.

Journal A chronological record of events and transactions affecting the accounts of a company recorded by means of debits and credits; a financial diary of a company.

Journal entry A data entry into a company's journal system.

Journalize The process of recording data in the journal system of a company by means of debits and credits.

Last-in, first-out (LIFO) An inventory cost-flow method that assigns the last cost value in finished goods inventory to the first unit sold and thus to cost of goods sold.

Lease An agreement to buy or rent an asset.

Leasehold improvement Expenditures made by a lessee to improve or change a leased asset.

Lessee An individual or company who leases an asset.

Lessor The maker of a lease agreement; an individual or company who leases an asset *to* another individual or company.

Leverage The extent to which a company's long-term capital structure includes debt financing; a measure of a company's dependency on debt. A company with large quantities of debt is said to be "highly leveraged."

Liabilities The dollar value of an enterprise's obligations to repay monies loaned to it, to pay for goods or services received by it, or to fulfill commitments made by it.

LIFO liquidation The sale of inventory units acquired or manufactured in a prior period at a lower cost; results when the level of LIFO inventory is reduced below its beginning-of-period level.

Limited liability The concept that shareholders in a corporation are not held personally liable for its losses and debts.

Limited partnership A partnership composed of at least one general partner and at least one limited partner, in which the general partner(s) assumes responsibility for all debts and losses of the partnership.

Line of credit An agreement with a bank by which an organization obtains authorization for short-term borrowings up to a specified amount.

Liquid assets Those current assets, such as cash, cash equivalents, or short-term investments, that either are in cash form or can be readily converted to cash.

Liquidating dividend A cash dividend representing a return of invested capital and, hence, a liquidation of a previous investment.

Liquidation The process of selling off the assets of a business, paying any outstanding debts, and then distributing any remaining cash to the owners.

Liquidity The short-term debt repayment ability of a company; a measure of a company's cash position relative to currently maturing obligations.

Long-term liabilities (noncurrent liabilities) The obligations of a company payable after more than one year.

Loss The excess of expenses over revenues for a single transaction.

Lower of Cost or Market A method to value inventories and marketable securities (both current and long-term); the lower of an asset's cost basis or current market value is used to value the asset account for balance sheet purposes.

Machine-hour method A method to depreciate the cost of a machine or other equipment based on its actual usage.

Maintenance expenditure An expenditure to maintain the original productive capacity of an asset; deducted as an expense.

Managerial accounting The accounting rules and conventions used in the preparation of internal accounting reports.

Manufacturing overhead The factory-related costs indirectly associated with the manufacture or production of a good; for example, the costs of production-line supervision, maintenance of the production equipment, and depreciation of the factory building.

Market price The current fair value of an asset as established by an arms' length transaction between a buyer and a seller.

Marketable securities Short- or long-term investments in the stocks or bonds of other corporations.

Matching concept An accounting concept that stipulates that when revenues are reported, the expenses incurred to generate those revenues should be reported in the same accounting period.

Materiality concept An accounting concept underlying the preparation of financial statements; stipulates that only those transactions that might influence the decisions of a reasonable person should be disclosed in detail in the financial statements; all other information may be presented in summary format.

Maturity date The principal repayment date for a bond or debenture, specified as part of the indenture agreement.

Maturity value (face amount) The amount of cash required to satisfy an obligation at the date of its maturity.

Merger A combination of one or more companies into a single corporate entity.

Minority interest The percentage ownership in the net assets of a subsidiary held by investors other than the parent company.

Modified Accelerated Cost Recovery System (MACRS) A method to depreciate tangible assets placed in service after 1986 for U.S. income tax purposes.

Monetary assets Resources of an enterprise, such as cash and marketable securities, whose principal characteristic is monetary denomination.

Mortgage An agreement in which a lender (the mortgagee) agrees to loan money to a borrower (the mortgagor) to be repaid over a specified period of time and at a specified rate of interest.

Mortgage bond A bond secured or collateralized by a company's noncurrent assets, usually its property, plant, and equipment.

Natural resources Noncurrent, nonrenewable resources such as oil and gas, coal, ore, and uranium.

Negative goodwill The excess of the net book value of an acquired company over the consideration paid for it.

Negotiable instruments Receivables, payables, or securities that can be bought and sold (i.e., negotiated) between companies.

Net assets Total assets minus total liabilities; equal total owners' equity.

Net current assets Current assets minus current liabilities; working capital.

Net income (net earnings) The difference between the aggregate revenues and aggregate expenses of an enterprise for a given accounting period; when aggregate expenses exceed aggregate revenues, the term *net loss* is used.

Net realizable value The amount of funds expected to be received upon the sale or liquidation of an asset.

Net sales Total sales less sales returns and allowances and sales discounts.

Net worth (of an enterprise) Total assets minus total liabilities, or the value of owners' equity; also known as the *book value* of an enterprise.

Nonclassified balance sheet A balance sheet in which the assets and liabilities are not classified as current or noncurrent; in nonclassified balance sheets, assets and liabilities are considered to be noncurrent.

Noncurrent assets The long-lived resources of an enterprise, such as property, plant, and equipment, whose consumption or use is *not* expected to be completed within the current operating cycle.

Noncurrent asset turnover ratio A measure of the effectiveness of noncurrent asset management calculated as net sales for the period divided by the average balance of noncurrent assets.

Noncurrent liability An obligation of an enterprise whose settlement is not expected within one year.

Nonmonetary assets Those resources of an enterprise, such as inventory or equipment, whose principal characteristic is other than its monetary denomination or value.

Notes payable An obligation to repay money or other assets in the future evidenced by a signed contractual agreement or note.

Notes receivable Amounts due a company from customers who purchased goods or services on credit; the obligation is evidenced by a legal document called a *note*.

Operating cycle The average length of time between the investment in inventory and the subsequent collection of cash from the sale of that inventory.

Operating expenses Expenses incurred in carrying out the operations of a business, for example, selling expenses.

Operating funds index A cash flow ratio calculated as net income divided by cash flow from operations that indicates the portion of operating cash flow provided by net income.

Operating lease A lease agreement in which the risks and rewards of asset ownership are retained by the lessor.

Operational risk The probability that unforeseen or unexpected events will occur and consequently reduce or impair the revenue, earnings, and cash flow streams of a company.

Option A contract in which a buyer receives the right to buy inventory or stock in the future at a prespecified price.

Organization costs The expenditures associated with starting a new business venture, including legal fees and incorporation fees; frequently accounted for as an intangible asset of a company.

Outstanding shares The number of authorized shares of capital stock that have been sold to shareholders and are currently in the possession of shareholders; the number of issued shares less the shares held in treasury.

Owners' equity (shareholders' equity) The dollar value of the owners' (or shareholders') investment in an enterprise; may take two forms— the purchase of shares of stock or the retention of earnings in the enterprise for future use.

Paid-In-Capital in Excess of Par Value (Contributed Capital in Excess of Par Value) An owners' equity account reflecting the proceeds from the sale of capital stock in excess of the par value (or stated value) of the capital stock.

Participating preferred stock A preferred stock that entitles shareholders to share in any "excess dividend payments" (i.e., after the common shareholders have received a fair dividend return).

Partnership A business enterprise jointly owned by two or more persons.

Par value A legal value assigned to a share of capital stock that must be considered in recording the proceeds received from the sale of the stock. See also *stated value*.

Passive investment An intercorporate investment in which the investor cannot (or does not) attempt to influence the operations of the investee-company.

Past service cost The cost of committed pension benefits earned by employees for periods of work prior to the adoption of a formal pension plan.

Payback period The period of time required to recover the cash outlay for an asset or other investment.

Pension A retirement plan for employees that will provide income to the employee upon retirement.

Percentage of completion A revenue recognition method in which total project or contract revenues are allocated between several accounting periods on the basis of the actual work completed in those periods.

Percentage of credit sales method A method of accounting for uncollectible trade receivables in which an estimate of the bad debts expense is recorded each period on the basis of the credit sales for the period.

Period cost Costs, such as administrative and selling expenses, associated with the accounting period in which they were incurred.

Periodic inventory system An inventory record-keeping system that determines the quantity of inventory on hand by a physical count.

Permanent accounts Those accounts, principally the balance sheet accounts, that are not closed at the end of an accounting period and that carry accounting information forward from one period to the next.

Permanent difference A difference in reported income or expenses between a company's tax return and its financial statements that will never reverse (i.e., the difference is permanent).

Perpetual inventory system An inventory record-keeping system that continuously (or perpetually) updates the quantity of inventory on hand on the basis of units purchased, manufactured, and sold.

Pledging When assets are used as collateral for a bank loan, the assets are said to have been pledged.

Pooling-of-interests A consolidation method that combines the financial results of a parent-company and its subsidiary on the basis of existing book values.

Posting An accounting process involving the transfer of financial data from the general journal to the general ledger.

Preemptive right The privilege of a shareholder to maintain his or her proportionate ownership in a corporation by being able to purchase an equivalent percentage of all new capital stock offered for sale.

Preferred stock A (usually) nonvoting form of capital stock whose claims to the dividends and assets of a company precede those of common stockholders.

Premium An amount paid in excess of the face value of a security or debt instrument.

Prepaid expenses A current asset that represents prior expenditures and whose consumption is expected to occur in the next accounting period.

Present value The value today of a future stream of cash flows calculated by discounting the cash flows at a given rate of interest.

Price-earnings (P/E) ratio A market-based measure of the investment potential of a security calculated as the market price per share divided by the earnings per share; also known as *P/E multiple*.

Primary earnings per share A standardized measure of performance calculated as net income applicable to common stock (i.e., net income minus preferred stock dividends) divided by the weighted-average number of common shares outstanding plus common stock equivalents.

Price-level-adjusted financial statements Financial statements in which the account balances have been restated to reflect changes in price levels due to inflation.

Prime rate The interest rate charged by banks on borrowings by preferred customers.

Principal The remaining balance of an outstanding obligation to be paid in the future.

Prior period adjustment An accounting event or transaction that does not affect the current period's earnings but instead is reflected as an adjustment to retained earnings.

Product cost A cost directly related to the production of a good or service, for example, the cost of goods sold.

Productivity index A cash flow ratio calculated as the cash flow from operations divided by the capital investment; indicates the relative cash productivity of a company's capital investments.

Profit The excess of revenues over expenses for a single transaction.

Profitability The relative success of a company's operations; a measure of the extent to which accomplishment exceeded effort.

Pro forma (financial statement) A forecasted or projected financial statement for a future accounting period.

Promissory note A written promise to pay a specific sum of money at a specific date; a liability.

Property, plant, and equipment The noncurrent assets of a company, principally used in the revenue-producing operations of the enterprise.

Prospectus A document describing the nature of a business and its recent financial history, usually prepared in conjunction with an offer to sell capital stock or bonds by a company.

Proxy A legal document granting another person or company the right to vote for a shareholder on matters involving a shareholder vote.

Purchase accounting A consolidation method in which the financial results of a parent-company and its subsidiary are combined using the fair market value of the subsidiary's net worth.

Purchase discount A cash discount (usually 2 percent) given to a buyer if the buyer pays for the purchases within the discount period (usually 10 days after purchase).

Purchase Discounts Lost An expense account

representing the finance or interest costs incurred as a consequence of not paying for goods purchased on credit on a timely basis (i.e., 2/10, net 30).

Purchases Goods or inventory acquired for sale or manufacture.

Qualified opinion An opinion issued by an independent auditor indicating that the financial statements of a company are fairly presented on a consistent basis and use generally accepted accounting principles, but for which some concern or exception has been noted.

Quick assets Highly liquid, short-term assets such as cash, cash equivalents, short-term investments, and receivables.

Quick ratio (acid test ratio) A measure of liquidity and short-term solvency calculated as quick assets divided by current liabilities.

Ratio A financial indicator (e.g., the current ratio) formed by comparing two account balances (e.g., current assets and current liabilities).

Raw material inventory Materials and purchased parts awaiting assembly or manufacture; classified as a current asset on the balance sheet.

Realized loss (gain) A loss (gain) that is recognized in the financial statements, usually due to the sale of an asset.

Recognition concept An accounting concept that stipulates that revenues should not be recorded in the accounting records until earned and that expenses should not be recorded until incurred.

Redeemable (callable) preferred stock A preferred stock that may be retired (i.e., redeemed or called) at the discretion of the issuing company, usually after a specified date and usually at a premium above the stated (or par) value of the preferred stock.

Redemption The retirement of preferred stock or bonds before a specified maturity date.

Registrar An independent agent, normally a bank or a trust company, that maintains a record of the number of shares of capital stock of a company that have been issued and to whom.

Relevance concept An accounting concept used

to select which accounting information should be presented in a company's financial statements.

Reliability concept An accounting concept that stipulates that accounting information, and hence accounting reports, must be reliable to be useful to financial statement users.

Reorganization (quasi-reorganization) A process of changing the ownership structure of a company, usually as a direct result of a deficit in retained earnings.

Replacement cost The cost to reproduce or repurchase a given asset (e.g., a unit of inventory).

Retained earnings Those earnings of an enterprise that have been retained in the enterprise (i.e., have not been paid out as dividends) for future corporate use.

Retained earnings—appropriated The amount of total retained earnings that has been allocated for specific corporate objectives, such as the redemption of debt or capital stock.

Retained earnings—restricted The amount of total retained earnings that is legally restricted from being paid out as dividends to shareholders; the restriction usually results from a borrowing agreement with a bank or other financial institution.

Return on owners' equity (ROE) A measure of profitability; a measure of the relative effectiveness of a company in using the assets provided by the owners to generate net income; calculated as net income divided by average owners' equity.

Return on sales ratio (net profit margin ratio) A measure of profitability calculated as the percentage of each sales dollar that is earned as net income; may be either retained in the company or paid out as a dividend.

Return on total assets (ROA) A measure of profitability that assesses the relative effectiveness of a company in using available resources to generate net income; also called the *return on investment,* or ROI; calculated as net income divided by average total assets.

Revenue bond A bond secured or collateralized by a revenue stream from a particular group of assets.

Revenues The inflow of assets, the reduction in liabilities, or both, from transactions involving an enterprise's principal business activity (e.g., sales of products or services).

Sale A legal term suggesting that the title to an asset has passed from a seller to a buyer.

Sale/Leaseback An accounting transaction in which an asset is first sold and then immediately leased back by the selling entity; a financing transaction.

Sales-type lease A capital lease that generates two income streams: (1) from the ''sale'' of the asset and (2) from financing the ''purchase'' of the asset.

Salvage value (residual value). The amount that is expected to be recovered when an asset is retired, removed from active use, and sold.

Securities Act of 1933 A 1933 legislative act of the U.S. Congress that requires certain disclosures by enterprises issuing (or desiring to issue) shares of capital stock.

Securities and Exchange Commission (SEC) A government agency responsible for the oversight of U.S. securities markets; this agency also specifies the form and content of all financial reports by companies issuing securities to the public.

Securities Exchange Act of 1934 A 1934 legislative act of the U.S. Congress that created the Securities and Exchange Commission.

Selling expense Expenses incurred directly as a consequence of selling and delivering a product to customers.

Sinking fund A trust account established in conjunction with the issuance of bonds into which funds are paid periodically to be used to retire the debt at maturity; an asset account.

Sole proprietorship A business enterprise owned by one person.

Solvency The long-term debt repayment ability of a company; a measure of a company's long-term liquidity.

Special journal An accounting data file containing a chronological listing of special financial transactions (e.g., cash purchases or cash receipts) affecting an enterprise.

Specific identification An inventory cost-flow method that assigns the actual cost of producing a specific unit to that unit; the only inventory method that matches exactly the cost flow and physical flow.

Standard product cost An inventory valuation method that uses estimated or projected costs of producing a product rather than actual costs.

Stated value The recorded accounting value of capital stock. See also *par value*.

Statement of cash flows An accounting statement describing the sources and uses of cash flows for an enterprise for a given period.

Statement of owners' equity (statement of shareholders' equity) An accounting statement describing the principal transactions affecting the owners' (or shareholders') interests in an enterprise for a given period.

Statement of retained earnings An accounting statement describing the beginning and ending balances in retained earnings and the major changes to the retained earnings account (e.g., dividends and net income).

Statements of financial accounting standards (SFAS) The official pronouncements of the FASB.

Stewardship The management and supervision of enterprise resources.

Stock certificate A legal document evidencing the purchase of capital stock in a company.

Stock dividend A distribution of additional shares of capital stock to a company's stockholders.

Stockholders' equity The owners' equity of a corporation; comprises paid-in capital and retained earnings.

Stock option A right issued by a company to its employees entitling an employee to buy a set quantity of capital stock in the future at a prespecified price.

Stock split An increase (a forward split) or a decrease (a reverse split) in the number of shares

issued by a company; equivalent to a large stock dividend.

Stock warrant (stock right) A certificate issued by a company that carries the right or privilege to buy a set quantity of capital stock in the future at a prespecified price.

Straight-line method A method to depreciate the cost of a tangible asset or to amortize the cost of an intangible asset in which the allocated cost is constant over the life of the asset.

Subchapter S corporation A small corporation that pays no corporate taxes; all earnings are divided among the owners and are taxed at the individual level.

Subsidiary A company in which an investor-company (the parent) holds an equity investment in excess of 50 percent of the voting stock of the investee-company.

Subsidiary ledger An accounting data file containing detailed account information to supplement or explain the aggregate account balance contained in the general ledger.

Sum-of-the-years'-digits method A method to depreciate the cost of a tangible asset in which the allocated cost is greater in the early periods of the asset's life (i.e., an accelerated method).

Tangible asset Those resources of an enterprise, such as property, plant, and equipment, that possess physical characteristics or have a physical presence.

Temporary accounts Those accounts that are closed at the end of each accounting period, for example, the income statement accounts, dividends, and the income and loss summary.

Temporary difference A difference in reported income or expenses between a company's tax return and its financial statements that will reverse out in some future period.

Times-interest-earned ratio A measure of solvency and leverage calculated as net income plus interest and income taxes divided by interest charges; a measure of the extent to which current interest payments are covered by current earnings.

Time value of money Because money can always be invested at a bank to earn interest for the period it is on deposit, money is said to have a "time value."

Timing differences Differences in the timing of the reporting of certain revenues and expenses for tax purposes and for external financial reporting purposes.

Trade payables See *accounts payable and notes payable*.

Trade receivables See *accounts receivable*.

Transaction concept A concept underlying the preparation of financial statements that requires the source of all accounting information be economic transactions affecting an enterprise and its resources.

Transaction exposure A source of foreign exchange risk resulting from exchange rate fluctuations between the date on which a contract is signed or goods delivered and the date of payment.

Transfer agent An independent agent, usually a bank or a trust company, that maintains a record of, and executes all, capital stock transfers and sales, as well as the payment of dividends on those shares.

Translation exposure A source of foreign exchange risk resulting from the restatement of foreign financial statements denominated in a foreign currency into U.S. dollar-equivalents; also known as *accounting exposure*.

Treasury stock Outstanding capital stock that has been repurchased but not retired and is usually held to be reissued at some future date.

Trend analysis The analysis of ratios or absolute account balances over one or more accounting periods to identify the direction or trend of a company's financial health.

Trial balance A listing of the preadjusted, preclosing account balances from the general ledger designed to verify that the sum of the accounts with debit balances equals the sum of the accounts with credit balances.

Uncollectible account An account receivable that a company expects not to be able to collect.

Underwriter A brokerage house or investment banker hired by a company to help sell a bond or stock offering.

Unearned revenue Revenue that is received as cash but that has not yet been earned.

Unit-of-production method A method to depreciate the cost of a tangible asset or to deplete the cost of a natural resource; the allocated cost is based on the actual production by the asset.

Unrealized Decline in Value of Noncurrent Equity Portfolio A contra owners' equity account representing a write-down in the noncurrent equity portfolio for temporary market fluctuations, as a consequence of the lower-of-cost-or-market method.

Unrealized loss (gain) A loss (gain) that is recognized in the financial statements but is not associated with an asset sale; usually involves a revaluation of an asset value.

Useful life The estimated productive life of a noncurrent asset.

Value-added statement A financial statement prepared by some foreign companies reflecting a measure of the wealth created by the operations of the company and the distribution of that wealth among its major constituents (e.g., employees, investors, and the government).

Vendor A company selling goods or services.

Vested benefits Pension benefits owed to employees at retirement regardless of whether they continue to be employed by the company until they reach retirement age.

Warrant A legal document enabling the holder to buy a set number of shares of capital stock at a prespecified price within a set period of time.

Warranty obligation An obligation for future costs to maintain a product sold in good working condition.

Wasting assets Noncurrent assets, such as natural resources, that decrease in value as a result of depletion or consumption of the asset.

Weighted-average cost method An inventory cost-flow method that assigns the average cost of available finished goods, weighted by the number of units available at each price, to a unit sold and thus cost of goods sold, and to ending inventory.

With (Without) recourse Terms of the sale of an account or note receivable. A sale with recourse obligates the selling company to ''make good'' the receivable in the event that the factor is unable to collect on the receivable; a sale without recourse obligates the factor to assume all liability for noncollectibility.

Work in process inventory Partially completed goods or products; classified as a current asset on the balance sheet.

Working capital A measure of liquidity or short-term solvency calculated as total current assets minus total current liabilities.

INDEX